A MODERN INTRODUCTION
TO *Philosophy*

Readings from Classical and
Contemporary Sources

Third Edition

EDITED BY *Paul Edwards* BROOKLYN COLLEGE

AND *Arthur Pap* LATE OF YALE UNIVERSITY

THE FREE PRESS, *New York*
COLLIER—MACMILLAN LIMITED, *London*

COLLIER–MACMILLAN PUBLISHERS, *London*

Collier-Macmillan Canada, Ltd., Toronto, Ontario

Library of Congress Catalog Card Number: 72-93633

First Printing

Contents

III *Body, Mind and Death*

IV *Moral Judgments*

VII   *A Priori Knowledge*

VIII   *Meaning, Verification and Metaphysics*

Preface to the Third Edition

I N PREPARING THE THIRD EDITION OF this book I have again taken into account the many suggestions that were kindly sent to me by teachers who have been using it. The new edition is considerably larger than its predecessors. Nineteen selections, some of very substantial length, have been added while thirteen of the pieces contained in the second edition have been deleted. By agreement with Mrs. Pap, Arthur Pap's four introductions have not been changed in any way. I have made various changes in my own introductions and one of them—the introduction to the section on the existence of God—has been greatly expanded to take note of the new selections on that subject. The biographical sketches have been brought up to date. The lives of some of the writers who are presented in the new edition for the first time were more colorful than those of most philosophers. For them (especially Kierkegaard and Dostoevsky) I have supplied longer biographies than their purely philosophical importance would warrant.

The annotated bibliographies which appear at the end of each section have been substantially expanded. They have been brought up to date and I have also tried to cover earlier writings more comprehensively. I have taken into account the various new journals that have begun to appear since the second edition went to press. I was also happy · to discover *Sophia,* an excellent little journal published in Melbourne, Australia, which is entirely devoted to the philosophy of religion. I have listed numerous pieces which have appeared in it since its inception in 1962. At the end of each bibliography I have added a paragraph enumerating all related articles in *The Encyclopedia of Philosophy.*

Among the new selections I would like to call special attention to Paul Rée's "Determinism and the Illusion of Moral Responsibility" (Selection 1). Rée was a close associate of Nietzsche during the years when Nietzsche began his onslaught on the ethics and theology of the Christian religion. Rée himself wrote a book on ethics in which he championed a radical form of relativism. Rée was also an atheist and a determinist. In 1885 he published a booklet which contains the clearest, most forceful and most uncompromising defense of hard determinism known to me. Our selection is a translation of some of the highlights of this booklet. For the benefit of readers who wish to know more about this interesting and unjustly forgotten figure I have included a fairly detailed biographical sketch at the end of the book.

The section on the existence of God covers several aspects of the subject not treated in previous editions. The pieces by Trueblood and Fackenheim (Selections 36 and 44) are appeals to religious experience. The former is a systematic presentation of the so-called argument from religious experience which has played an important role in discussions of the existence of God since the early nineteenth century. The latter represents the approach of existentialist believers who deny that they are presenting an *argument* from religious experience. Like other existentialist theologians Fackenheim is a champion of "fideism"—the view that the existence of God and other religious propositions have to be accepted on faith. There is also an elaborate defense of fideism in the extracts from Kierkegaard's *Concluding Unscientific Postscript* which make up Selection 42. Selections from the *Concluding Unscientific Postscript* are commonly confined to certain passages from the chapter on "Subjective Truth," but the full meaning and purpose of Kierkegaard's undertaking cannot be understood without knowing something about his starting-point. This is stated in the Introduction and in Chapter I of *Concluding Unscientific Postscript,* and I have accordingly reprinted several crucial passages from these parts of the book. From the resulting rather long selection the reader will be able to gain an accurate picture of Kierkegaard's position. The discussion between Bernard Williams and Bishop Robinson introduces the topic of "theological reconstruction." Bishop Robinson is in the forefront of a contemporary Protestant movement whose aim it is to make belief in God credible to educated people by purging it of its anthropomorphic elements. Professor Williams explains some of the misgivings that both philosophers and theologians have voiced about reconstructions like those of Bishop Robinson and the late Paul Tillich. In his contribution to the symposium Bishop Robinson tries to show that these misgivings are not justified. He also offers a restatement of the position he had previously advocated in his well-known *Honest to God.*

Symposia or exchanges between philosophers adopting conflicting viewpoints have also been added in two other sections. In "Physics and Perception" (Selection 50), Bertrand Russell offers a number of arguments for rejecting the commonsense view of perception. This selection is now followed by Ernest Nagel's defense of commonsense and Russell's rejoinder to Nagel. The section on "Body, Mind and Death" contains a symposium on the body-mind problem by Viscount Samuel, A. J. Ayer and Gilbert Ryle. In this section I have also restored T. H. Huxley's defense of epiphenomenalism which had been deleted in the second edition. Hume's defense of immortality has been replaced by Clarence Darrow's "The Myth of Immortality." Darrow was not a professional philosopher but he was a powerful thinker and this essay is a hard-hitting statement, in the simplest everyday language, of all the main arguments on the negative side of the question.

Two selections dealing in various ways with the topic of the conditions that must be satisfied if a question is to be "genuine" or intelligible have been added to the final section. Schlick's little-known essay "Unanswerable Questions" is an application of the Verifiability Principle to this issue. My own article "Why?" discusses in some detail the question variously phrased "Why does anything exist?" or "Why is there something and not nothing?" I try to distinguish the various contexts in which this question has been raised and I argue that in the context in which it has seemed to many people overwhelmingly profound the question is really unintelligible.

I should like to thank the following friends and colleagues who have been helpful in various ways: Professors Raziel Abelson of New York University, C. T. R. Adams of Central Florida Junior College, Bruce Aune of the University of Massachusetts at Amherst, Hector-Neri Castaneda of Indiana University, Alburey Castell of the College of Wooster, Wooster, Ohio, Frank B. Dilley of the University of Delaware, William Gerber of the University of Maryland, Adolf Grünbaum of the University of Pittsburgh, Donald Henze of San Fernando Valley State College, Howard Kahane of the Bernard Baruch College of the City University of New York, Donald Levy of Brooklyn College of the City University of New York, John McKenzie of Monash University, Melbourne, Australia, and Carl Wellman of Washington University, St. Louis. I also wish to thank Pauline Pap for the confidence she again reposed in me in connection with the new edition of this work.

P. E.

New York City
June 1972

A MODERN INTRODUCTION TO PHILOSOPHY

THE FREE PRESS TEXTBOOKS
IN PHILOSOPHY

GENERAL EDITOR: *Paul Edwards*

GENERAL INTRODUCTION

As EVERY TEACHER OF INTRODUC-
tory courses in philosophy knows from painful experience in the class
room, it is exceedingly difficult to begin such a course. The word "philosophy" has no clear and unique meaning at all in its everyday usage. The
layman takes it perhaps to refer to a very "deep" subject dealing with highly
"abstract" (or abstruse) matters, but obviously this won't do as a definition.
The wisest procedure may well be to plunge into *medias res,* discuss specific
philosophical problems and then leave it to the student to define philosophy
at the end of the course as the sort of thinking he has been induced to do.
But some people do not want to take the risk of spending mental energy on
the study of a subject before making sure that such exertion is worth while.
They, accordingly, will demand a preliminary definition of philosophy, a
demand which we shall try to satisfy.

To begin with, it must be pointed out that "philosophy" is a highly ambiguous and vague word. Any definition of it, therefore, will be arbitrary in
two respects: first, it will sharply demarcate philosophy from both "science"
and "literature," whereas much of what philosophers have been writing is not
so clearly distinguishable from science (at least theoretical science) or from
literature (at least "philosophical" literature). Secondly, it will usurp the
title "philosophy" for only one of various things that are commonly called
by that name. Further, since this word usually has a laudatory flavor, i.e.,
connotes a respectable and important kind of intellectual activity, the definition will also be *persuasive,* that is, it will express the value judgment that
such and such pursuits are indeed important and worthy of respect, and that
people who do this sort of thing well ought to be commended for it. It is for
this reason that no definition of philosophy can claim to be wholly descriptive and unbiased, no more than this could be claimed for a definition of
such a laudatory term as "democracy."

However, the following definition may well be as unbiased as a defini-

tion of philosophy can be expected to be: critical reflection on the justification of basic human beliefs and analysis of basic concepts in terms of
which such beliefs are expressed. Insofar as this definition is claimed to be
descriptive, the test of its adequacy is, of course, whether the majority of
problems that are commonly called "philosophical" conform to it. Since the
editors believe that the problems discussed in the following eight sections by
classical and contemporary philosophers of reputation constitute a fair
sample of problems ordinarily called "philosophical," the definition can be
tested quite easily by any student of this book.

The question running through the first section is how we can reconcile
certain of our most basic moral beliefs with the teachings or rather the
presuppositions of science. In particular, if all things whatsoever, including
conscious actions, have causes, can man be said to have freedom of action
in any respect? And if not, can we ever hold human beings responsible for
their conduct? These questions are hardly separable from the general
problem of Section IV: how, if at all, moral judgments are rationally
justifiable—a question which invites analysis of the meaning of moral terms.
But then again, what about the general propositions of science themselves?
What is their logical foundation? How can we justify the belief which, according to Hume and many other philosophers, underlies all predictions
made in everyday life and in science, the belief that the future will, or at
least probably will, resemble the past? This is the problem discussed in
Section II. Our everyday conviction that past observations frequently
afford evidence for inferences about the future is an instance of what is
often referred to as a "common-sense belief." The belief in the existence of
a physical world outside of consciousness is another common-sense belief
questioned and discussed by philosophers. How do we know whether a
physical world exists which is independent of human consciousness,
whether the things we perceive exist also when they are not perceived? If
a man were to raise such a question in the midst of the practical business of
everyday life, he would be likely to be laughed at as a lunatic, but this simply
means that ordinary mortals take it for granted that there are physical
objects whether anyone perceives them or not; it does not mean that they
can justify that belief. Section VI is devoted to this time-honored dispute
between "realists" who hold that the common-sense position is justifiable
and "idealists" who think that realism cannot survive philosophical scrutiny.
Another common-sense belief is that every human being has both a mind
and a body which interact in various ways. But here the critical philosopher
steps in and asks: can we consistently believe that the mind acts on the body
and indirectly on the physical environment and also that physical science
teaches the truth, especially in teaching the doctrine of the conservation of
energy and that physical effects must have physical causes? Besides, what
is meant by "mind" anyway? Is there such a thing? If there is, does it
entirely depend on the functioning of the organism, especially the brain, or

may it survive the disintegration of the organism? In other words, is there any rational justification for the belief in immortality? These are the questions dealt with in Section III. Again, is it possible to supply a rational justification of belief in God? Can we establish the existence of God by inductive reasoning as employed by the champions of the so-called argument from design? If not, do the *a priori* arguments in support of theism and deism fare any better? And what about the existence of evil in the world? Is this not incompatible with the traditional claim that the universe is the creation of an all-powerful and all-good deity? These problems are covered in Section V. Questions about the soundness of the *a priori* arguments for the existence of God naturally lead to the question of whether we have any *a priori* knowledge of matters of fact at all. Our knowledge of universal principles like the principles of mathematics and logic has been regarded by most philosophers as *a priori*. But were they right in this? Is our knowledge of these principles not really based on experience? And if it is granted that our knowledge is *a priori* in such cases, does it give us information "about the world" or is it not rather of a purely linguistic kind, telling us what symbols and combinations of symbols are or are not permissible, given certain original linguistic conventions? Section VII is devoted to this very fundamental philosophical problem.

Some of the selections in Sections I-VII of this book are samples of what would generally be considered "metaphysical" speculations. They are attempts to discover truths about the universe by pure thinking rather than by the scientific method of testing theories by observation and controlled experiment. The Platonic theory that over and above the world of visible things there exists a realm of "intelligible" forms, the theory that there is a God who created the universe, the view that human beings possess an indestructible soul, or that consciousness is not restricted to the higher organisms but is present in all matter, are examples of metaphysical speculations. Until fairly recently (say, three or four decades ago) it was the opinion of the majority of philosophers that this sort of theorizing was one of the most important tasks of philosophy. Many contemporary philosophers, however, are in varying degrees sceptical about the fertility of such an enterprise. The most radical attack on metaphysical theorizing is that of the logical positivists, who maintain that all metaphysical statements are really devoid of cognitive meaning, that metaphysics is a kind of conceptual poetry (sometimes written in forbidding prose) that does not convey solid knowledge or even testable conjecture, whatever its literary merits and psychological benefits may be. Whether this critique of metaphysics is justified is one of the most heatedly debated questions at the present time and it forms the subject-matter of the last section of our book.

A number of philosophers, who do not go so far as to condemn metaphysics as cognitively meaningless, nevertheless agree with the logical positivists that the proper, or at any rate the most rewarding, task of philosophy is the clarification of certain basic concepts and propositions which are employed in everyday life and in the various sciences. This conception of philosophy as "analysis" is widespread at the present time, particularly in Great Britain and in the United States. Our book may be regarded as a "modern" introduction to philosophy because analytic philosophy is much more fully represented in it than in most introductory texts. Furthermore, while selections from several of the great classical philosophers are included (Plato, Aquinas, Descartes, Leibniz, Kant, Locke, Berkeley, Hume, Reid, Mill), the majority of our authors are figures on the contemporary philosophical scene. It should be noted, however, that not all contemporary philosophers represented in our book are analytic philosophers. Our only consideration in making selections from contemporary philosophical writing has been the clarity and intelligibility of the writer's language, the importance of his ideas and their relevance to the problems under discussion. In all eight sections we have tried to illustrate conflicting philosophical views and in several instances one selection directly criticizes another selection dealing with the same problem.

We hope that our book will be found useful in college courses introducing students to philosophy by a discussion of sample problems rather than by a purely historical approach (though some essential historical information is also supplied by the introductions to the various sections). Wherever possible, we have chosen fresh, unhackneyed material. The Ayer-Copleston debate on logical positivism is here published for the first time and several of the other selections, although of unquestionable merit, are not widely known and are not easily accessible to most students.

We believe that this book can also be used with profit by the general reader who wishes to find out what philosophy is all about and especially what philosophers are doing today. As already indicated, we have done our best to confine the selections to writings which are free from obscurity and bombast; and for the reader's guidance we have provided each section with an introduction in which the problems and the main rival answers are briefly explained. At the end of each section there is a bibliography for the benefit of those who wish to pursue the subject beyond the elementary level, and biographical information about the authors may be found at the end of the book.

The order in which the sections are arranged is not, of course, binding on either teachers or general readers. We have, in our own teaching, found the order here adopted to possess certain special merits, but like most teachers of introductory courses we frequently vary the sequence. Much no doubt would depend, in any particular case, on the quality of the students and on their background. It may, for example, be wise to introduce the subject of the existence of God relatively early and to postpone discussing the topic of induction, which is not likely to generate the same degree of excitement among beginners. But it is impossible to lay down a general rule as to what sequence of topics is pedagogically best. As every philosopher ought to know, all philosophical problems are organically related, though it is advisable to tackle one at a time. In philosophy one can begin with any problem and be logically led to almost any other problem.

P. E.
A. P.

Key to Abbreviations

The following abbreviations are used throughout the bibliographies in this book:

A	*Analysis*
AJ	*Australasian Journal of Psychology and Philosophy*
APQ	*American Philosophical Quarterly*
Ar. Soc.	*Proceedings of the Aristotelian Society*
Ar. Soc. Sup.	*Proceedings of the Aristotelian Society, Supplementary Volumes*
BJPS	*The British Journal for the Philosophy of Science*
CJP	*Canadian Journal of Philosophy*
D	*Dialogue*
E	*Ethics*
HJ	*Hibbert Journal*
I	*Inquiry*
JP	*Journal of Philosophy*
M	*Mind*
Me	*Metaphilosophy*
N	*Noûs*
P	*Philosophy*
PPR	*Philosophy and Phenomenological Research*
PQ	*Philosophical Quarterly*
PR	*Philosophical Review*
PS	*Philosophy of Science*
PSt	*Philosophical Studies*
Q	*Question*
R	*Ratio*
RM	*Review of Metaphysics*
RS	*Religious Studies*
S	*Sophia*
Sy	*Synthese*
T	*Theoria*

In all references to articles in the *Encyclopedia of Philosophy*, the first numeral designates the volume, the second the page-number. "Agnosticism" (1, 56) means that the article is found in volume 1 and begins on page 56.

p indicates that the book in question is available in paperback.

A MODERN INTRODUCTION TO PHILOSOPHY

1

Determinism, Freedom and Moral Responsibility

INTRODUCTION

Determinism is the theory that everything in the universe is entirely governed by causal laws. It asserts that whatever happens at some specific moment is the outcome of something that happened at a previous moment, i.e., that the present is always "determined" by the past. It may be difficult or impossible to prove that this theory is true. But most people accept it, or something very close to it, in their daily activities. They do so whether they are dealing with inanimate objects or with living organisms, whether they are concerned with involuntary or "voluntary" human behavior.

Let us suppose, for example, that a doctor, after carefully examining a patient, announces that unfortunately he cannot offer any assistance since the patient suffers from a mysterious ailment—one, in fact, which has no cause. The patient would in these circumstances undoubtedly be justified in angrily telling the doctor to keep his jokes for some academic discussion group and in turning to somebody else for help. If the doctor had merely said that he had never come across this kind of illness before and that he knew of no cure for it or that the cause of it had not yet been discovered, we would not necessarily consider his statement absurd. On the contrary, we might even admire him for his candor. We are ready to admit that there are illnesses whose causes are unknown. We are not ready to admit that there are illnesses without a cause.

Let us take another illustration. In Melbourne, Australia, weather forecasts for a period of twenty-four hours are exceedingly reliable. That is to say, the predictions based on the available atmospheric data and the known meteorological laws are almost always correct. In New York City, on the other hand, the official forecasts for a period of twenty-four hours in advance are more often wrong than right. Suppose someone came along and said, "There is an easy explanation for the successes of the Australian and the lack of successes of the New York weather forecasts. In Melbourne the weather is caused —there it is the outcome of preceding conditions; but in New York, more often than not, the weather has no cause. It is 'cut off from,' it is 'disconnected with' what happened before." We would assuredly question the sanity of this man. For we all believe that the failures of the New York meteorologists are to be explained quite differently. We all believe that the weather in New York is just as much the outcome of preceding conditions as the weather in Melbourne. The forecasts are less reliable because of the greater complexities of the factors which have to be taken into account and the greater difficulty of observing them, but certainly not because no causal factors exist.

It is exactly the same with human behavior. We all of us believe, to use Mill's words, that,

> given the motives which are present to an individual's mind, and given like-wise the character and disposition of the individual, the manner in which he will act might be unerringly inferred; that if we knew the person thoroughly, and knew all the inducements which are acting upon him, we could foretell his conduct with as much certainty as we can predict any physical event. . . . No one who believed that he knew thoroughly the circumstances of any case, and the characters of the different persons concerned, would hesitate to foretell how all of them would act. Whatever degree of doubt he may in fact feel, arises from the uncertainty whether he really knows the circumstances, or the character of some one or other of the persons, with the degree of accuracy required; but by no means from thinking that if he did know these things, there could be any uncertainty what the conduct would be.

Or, to quote Kant:

> The actions of men . . . are determined in conformity with the order of nature, by their empirical character and by the other causes which co-operate with that character; and if we could exhaustively investigate all the appear-ances of men's wills, there would not be found a single human action which we could not predict with certainty . . .

We do indeed occasionally say about people that they did or felt certain things without a cause, e.g., "He was in a dreadful mood after an argument with his wife and took out his anger on his secretary, insulting her quite without cause," or "Suddenly he went berserk without cause and in a frightful rampage shot his mother and all his seven children" or "He hates the Jews without cause." However, we do not really in such situations mean literally that the actions or feelings are uncaused. We mean, rather, that they lack adequate justification or that their cause is unknown to us. We do not mean, for instance, that the Jew-baiter's feelings have no cause, but that they have no good ground. We do not mean that the sudden epileptic fury came from nowhere. We mean that we don't know what caused it, and perhaps, also, that on the basis of what we knew about the man's previous record we could not have predicted the attack.

We believe that human actions are caused regardless of whether they are "in" or "out" of character, regardless of whether a person surprises us or acts in accordance with our expectations. Perhaps the following example will help to make this clear. A determinist once engaged in a public debate with an "indeterminist"—i.e., a person who rejects determinism. The debate took place in a college classroom. By the rules of the college everybody had to be out of the building not later than 11 P.M. In the course of his talk the deter-minist predicted that his opponent would not be in the room or in the build-ing at 2 o'clock the following morning. The indeterminist defied this predic-tion. He stayed on, presumably spent a miserable night, had himself discovered in the morning by the cleaning woman, and made sure that he was reported to the dean in charge of such matters for breaking the rules of the college. His action of course falsified the determinist's prediction and greatly surprised all who had been present at the debate. Nevertheless, everyone who heard of the indeterminist's bizarre performance had no doubt that it was just as much due to a cause as any of his other, less unusual actions. Moreover, if it had been known how eager he was to defy the prediction, the outcome could have been predicted. Or, what for our purposes amounts to the same thing: in retrospect we can explain his extraordinary behavior in terms of preceding conditions just as completely as the more customary conduct of other people who in similar circumstances would prefer sleep to defiance.

Although we thus accept determinism at least in our practical activities, the vast majority of people in our culture also indulge in judgments of moral responsibility; and at first sight it seems that these could never be justified, if determinism were true. For we hold people responsible only for those actions which they performed "freely" in the sense that they could have done something other than what they did. But if determinism is true, then everything people do is completely caused; and, given the causal antecedents in any particular case, nothing could happen except what does happen. It seems to follow that nobody can ever act differently from the way he acts, and hence that freedom must be an illusion and that human beings are never properly accountable for their conduct. Alternatively, if freedom is not an illusion, determinism must be false.

The apparent conflict between determinism and freedom has also been formulated in the following way: Let us consider some example of a momentous choice in recent history, e.g., Harry Truman's decision to drop the atomic bomb on Hiroshima. We would normally say that Harry Truman was a free agent in this matter, that there were several alternative courses open to him. Some people have praised him for what he did, while others have cursed him. But all of them, including Harry Truman himself, agree that he carries the responsibility for the decision. Now if determinism is true, it has been argued, it would be absurd to hold Harry Truman responsible, since all he did was predetermined long before he was born. If determinism is true, then the whole future of the universe is in principle predictable. As the result of our imperfect knowledge of the existing conditions at any particular moment and our imperfect knowledge of causal connections, our predictive ability is in practice severely limited. This, however, does not affect the point at issue. Suppose there were a "Superscientist" who knew absolutely everything happening in the universe at one particular moment—say, at 8 A.M. on January 1, 1800. Suppose further that the Superscientist knew absolutely every causal law. If determinism were true, he could predict the entire future of the universe, including Harry Truman's instructions to drop the atomic bomb. But in that case Harry Truman's choice was a bogus affair. If the outcome was known, or rather knowable, in advance, he cannot properly be said to have been choosing. And what is true of Harry Truman's "decision" applies equally to all apparent choices of all other human beings. They are merely apparent and not genuine, if determinism is true. When determinism is stated in this way it appears as a paralyzing doctrine which implies that human efforts are quite pointless. As Eddington put it: "What significance is there to my mental struggle tonight whether I shall or shall not give up smoking, if the laws which govern the matter of the physical universe already preordain for the morrow a configuration of matter consisting of pipe, tobacco and smoke connected to my lips?"

In the light of these and similar considerations, philosophers have asked themselves: Which is true, determinism or freedom? Or can we perhaps believe in both and show that there is no conflict between them? There are three possible answers to these questions, and important writers can be quoted in support of all three. There are, to begin with, philosophers who accept determinism and reject freedom. They usually reason somewhat along the following lines: All the objective, scientific evidence favors determinism. It is true that human beings have a feeling or an "intuition" of freedom. A rational person, however, must be guided by objective evidence and not by intuitions. In our book this position is represented by Paul Rée (Selection 1). Among the great philosophers Spinoza and Schopenhauer may be cited as supporters of a view of this kind, and many celebrated thinkers outside the fold of professional philosophers adopted it. Einstein held it, and so did Freud. Many famous novelists and poets held it, including Melville, Mark Twain, Arthur Schnitzler, A. E. Housman, and Thomas Hardy. The greatest lawyer the United States ever produced, Clarence Darrow, made this view the basis of many of his successful court pleas, as well as of revolutionary suggestions concerning the treatment of criminals. In the famous plea, in which he tried to save the lives of the boy murderers, Loeb and Leopold, Darrow returned to this theme again and again:

> We are all helpless. . . . This weary old world goes on, begetting, with birth and with living and with death; and all of it is blind from the beginning to the end. I do not know what it was that made these boys do this mad act, but I do know there is a reason for it. I know they did not beget themselves. I know that any one of an infinite number of causes reaching back to the beginning might be working out in these boys' minds, whom you are asked to hang in malice and in hatred and injustice. . . .
>
> Nature is strong and she is pitiless. She works in her own mysterious way, and we are her victims. We have not much to do with it ourselves. Nature takes this job in hand, and we play our parts. In the words of old Omar Khayyam, we are:

> > But helpless pieces in the game He plays
> > Upon this checkerboard of nights and days;
> > Hither and thither moves, and checks, and slays,
> > And one by one back in the closet lays.

> What had this boy to do with it? He was not his own father, he was not his own mother; he was not his own grandparents. All of this was handed to him. He did not surround himself with governesses and wealth. He did not make himself. And yet he is to be compelled to pay.

Similar sentiments are expressed by Mark Twain in his highly unorthodox "Reflections on Religion" (written in 1906, but not published until 1963):

> Man is not to blame for what he is. He didn't make himself. He has no control over himself. All the control is vested in his temperament—which he did not create—and in the circumstances which hedge him round from the cradle to the grave and which he did not devise. . . . He is as purely a piece of automatic mechanism as is a watch, and can no more dictate or influence his actions than can the watch. He is a subject for pity, not blame—and not contempt. He is flung head over heels into this world without ever a chance to decline . . .

Secondly, there are philosophers who, agreeing that determinism is not compatible with freedom and moral responsibility, accept freedom and reject determinism. This position has been justified in many different ways, but perhaps the most common defense proceeds along these lines: Nothing can be more certain than what is given in immediate experience. If, for instance,

I see a white patch or feel pleasure, this is more certain than any complicated theory, no matter how eminent the supporters of that theory may be. Now, our experience of freedom is a datum of immediate experience, while determinism is at best a complicated theory. If the two conflict, this indicates that there must be something wrong with determinism. It is true that sometimes we make erroneous judgments of perception. For instance, we might, looking at an object from a distance, judge it to be black, although on closer examination it turns out to be red. But the case of freedom is different. Here further experience only serves to confirm our conviction. On every new occasion when I am confronted with several alternatives, I once again experience my freedom. In the words of Henry Sidgwick:

> It is impossible for me to think at such a moment that my volition is completely determined by my formed character and the motives acting upon it. The opposite conviction is so strong as to be absolutely unshaken by the evidence brought against it; I cannot believe it to be illusory. So far it is unlike the erroneous intuitions which occur in the exercise of the senses: as e.g., the imperfections of sight and hearing. For experience soon teaches me to regard these as appearances whose suggestions are misleading; but no amount of experience of the sway of motives even tends to make me distrust my intuitive consciousness that in resolving after deliberation I exercise free choice as to which of the motives acting on me shall prevail.

Moreover, our moral consciousness must not be denied a hearing, and an adequate philosophy ought to do justice to it. If a scientific theory conflicts with the revelations of our moral consciousness, this, in the last analysis, may be so much the worse for the scientific theory. Among the philosophers represented in the present book William James (Selection 3), H. D. Lewis (Selection 4) and C. A. Campbell (Selection 7) take a view of this kind. It also found in many religious philosophers, especially those with a Catholic background. The same conclusion, though partly for different reasons, was defended by the English physicist Sir Arthur Eddington, who believed that recent discoveries in quantum physics had important bearings on the problem of freedom and determinism. It should be added that, while James and Eddington unhesistatingly identify freedom with chance, Campbell, like his 18th-century predecessor Thomas Reid, refuses to do so. Campbell speaks in this connection of "contra-causal freedom" and he insists that a contra-causally free act is to be carefully distinguished both from actions which are in principle predictable and from chance actions, if such ever occur.

There are, finally, philosophers who maintain that both determinism and our belief in freedom are true, and that any appearance of conflict is deceptive. A reconciling position of this kind was advocated by Kant, in whose work, however, it depends on a highly speculative bifurcation of the universe into the world of "noumena" and the world of "phenomena," which is accepted by very few contemporaries. Hegel and his disciples, notably the British philosophers Green and Bradley, also put forward a theory which attempted to reconcile determinism and freedom. The same theory, incidentally, is found in Engels and other Marxist writers, who followed Hegel completely on this subject. But this attempt at reconciliation, like Kant's, has few adherents today, at least in the English-speaking world. There is, however, a third variety of this general position, which is very widely held. This view goes back at least as far as Hobbes and was given its classic statement by Hume and Mill. It is therefore sometimes called the "Hume-Mill theory." In our book it is represented by the extracts from Mill (Selection 5) and Schlick (Selection 6).

The main idea behind this theory is very simple. If by "free" we meant "uncaused," then of course determinism would imply that nobody is ever a free agent. But when we call an action "free" in ordinary life, we never mean "uncaused"; and this most emphatically includes the kind of conduct about which we pass moral judgments. By calling an action "free" we mean that the agent was not coerced, that he was acting from or in accordance with his own unimpeded desire. Thus if I take a ride in a car because I have been kidnapped, what I do is not free since I act under a threat. Again, if I hand over money to somebody as the result of a post-hypnotic suggestion—something I would not have done but for the hypnotic influence—I am not free since my action springs from somebody else's desire and not my own. But if I take a car ride or give money to a beggar not because I am threatened or because I am under hypnotic suggestion but because I like to do these things and decided to do them, then my actions are free. My actions are free although they are just as much caused as any unfree action. They are free although anybody knowing my general disposition and the state of my body and mind at the preceding moments could have predicted them without difficulty.

Contemporary defenders of this view who are familiar with the facts concerning compulsion neurosis would be inclined to qualify the definition of "free" mentioned in the last paragraph. An action is free, they would say, if it comes from an unimpeded *rational* desire on the part of the agent. While it may not be easy to give a general definition of "rational desire" in this context, there would be up to a point very general agreement as to which desires are rational and which are not. For example, if a rich kleptomaniac steals an article he does not need, he is not a free agent, because the desire from which he is acting is not rational. But if I go into a restaurant and order a steak not because I suffer from a compulsion neurosis (at least not concerning steaks) but simply because I desire to eat a juicy, tender and nourishing steak, my action is free. I am acting in accordance with an unimpeded rational desire.

Philosophers who adopt this position emphatically deny that they are fatalists and that determinism, as they understand it, is a paralyzing doctrine. There is a famous dilemma which may help to illustrate the difference. According to this dilemma, if a person falls off a ship into the sea it is senseless for him to make any attempt to be saved. For he is either fated to drown or else fated to be saved. In the former case efforts are of no avail, in the latter they are unnecessary. This is the position of fatalism. An advocate of the Hume-Mill theory, on the other hand, would maintain that there is a third alternative which has been omitted: the man who fell into the sea may be saved *because of his efforts*—because, for instance, others may hear his cries. The fact that his efforts are themselves caused in no way cancels out the fact that the efforts were, in the case imagined, the cause of his rescue.

Determinism, on the Hume-Mill theory, does indeed claim that all human actions are in principle *predictable*. It does not claim that all actions are *predetermined,* if this means that what human beings do is always independent of their desires, choices, deliberations, and other psychological states and aspirations. The Superscientist, on this view, could have predicted Harry Truman's order to drop the atomic bomb on Hiroshima. But he could have made the prediction only by taking into account Harry Truman's desires and interests and hopes and fears and reflections on the consequences of alternative courses of action. The Superscientist in this picturesque formulation of determinism is not, it should be noted, a superblackmailer or a superhypnotist. He is not influencing or constraining Harry Truman. He is only predicting what will be done.

Most defenders of the Hume-Mill theory trace back the belief that determinism and freedom are incompatible to two factors—to certain confused anthropomorphic notions about causation and also to certain unrecognized ambiguities in ordinary speech. The latter would be said to occur particularly in connection with expressions like "nothing *could* have happened except what actually happened" or "this event *had* to happen." These expressions are commonly used in two very different senses. In one sense, which may be called the "regularity" sense, they merely designate certain invariable sequences. Thus if one billiard ball strikes another with a certain force and the second ball moves, we might easily say that, given the impact of the first ball upon the second, given the application of an unbalanced force, the second ball "had to move"; "it could have done nothing else." But this means no more than that there is an invariable sequence between the application of net forces and the motion or, strictly, the acceleration of the bodies to which the forces are applied. It means that if we know the magnitude and direction of the unbalanced force it is possible to predict that the ball will move in a certain way and not stay at rest or move in any other way. When we say, "the second ball had to move," we do not mean the presence of a constraining or compelling influence such as may occur in a situation involving human beings. We do not mean that the first billiard ball said to the second, "Listen here, you scoundrel, move or I'll knock your brains out!" Nor do we mean that the second ball suffered from a compulsive urge of the kind which makes us say in the case of the kleptomaniac that he had to act the way he did. However, when we say about a human being that he had to act the way he did or that he could have done nothing else, we do as a rule mean to assert the presence of a constraining influence like a threat or a compulsive urge. This may be called the "constraint" sense of the ambiguous expressions we are discussing. Now, a defender of the Hume-Mill theory would argue that determinism properly understood does indeed entail that nothing in the universe, including all human actions, could have been different from what it is. But determinism applies this only in the regularity-sense, which does not at all exclude freedom. Determinism is taken to negate freedom when it is tacitly *mis*understood to claim that no human action could ever have been different in the constraint-sense.

According to these writers the regularity-sense of "nothing else could have happened" or "this had to happen" or "it was necessarily so" and similar expressions must also be carefully distinguished from the sense in which they designate *logical* necessity, as when we say for example that two plus two "has" to equal four or that the sum of the interior angles of a Euclidean triangle "must necessarily" equal 180 degrees. When a defender of the Hume-Mill theory asserts that no event in the universe could have failed to occur he implies: *given* the total set of preceding events. If C is the total set of relevant conditions preceding an event E, the occurrence of E was necessary in the sense, and *only* in the sense, that whenever and wherever conditions like C obtain, an event like E follows. The law connecting C and E is not logically necessary in the sense that it would be self-contradictory to suppose exceptions to it. Nor is the occurrence of any particular event asserted to be logically necessary.

There is something very attractive about all reconciling theories, since they allow us to go on believing both in freedom and in determinism. The Hume-Mill theory in particular, as already noted, has many adherents among contemporary philosophers. It is, however, far from universally accepted and, especially during the last two decades, several philosophers have had second thoughts about it. There are, to begin with, those who simply do not regard determinism as tenable. Some philosophers have recently argued that the very nature of an *action* implies that it cannot be caused in the familiar sense in which the motion of a billiard ball or a reflex is unquestionably caused and in which determinists regard all actions as caused. Writers in the Hume-Mill tradition are frequently criticized in this connection on the ground that they did not adequately distinguish between reasons and causes. This general line of attack is represented in our book by Benn and Peters in Selection 9. It has also been argued that the account offered by the reconcilers of what we mean when we call an action "free" is seriously defective. This line of attack is represented by C. A. Campbell in Selection 7. All these critics are opposed to determinism, but the position of the reconcilers has also been attacked by determinists as being in certain important respects evasive and superficial. It has been argued, for example (see Hospers, "Free Will and Psychoanalysis," Selection 8), that the reconcilers have a very inadequate conception of the springs of human conduct. They are taking account for the most part of conscious motives only, leaving out of account the deeper, unconscious influences. Rephrasing a famous saying of Spinoza's, such a critic might say that the followers of Hume and Mill believe themselves free because they are ignorant of the *true* causes of their actions. The charge that the Hume-Mill theory constitutes an evasion need not, however, rest on an appeal to the role of unconscious motivation. It can and has been advanced by writers who did not question that the real causes of an action are disclosed in introspection. The reconcilers, it has been said, do not pursue the subject far enough. They stop arbitrarily at the desires or volitions which are the causes of some of our actions. We must not stop there. We must go on to ask where our desires come from. If determinism is true there can be no doubt about the answer to this question. Ultimately our desires and our whole character are derived from our inherited equipment and from the environmental influences to which we were subjected at the beginning of our lives. It is clear that we had no hand in shaping either of these and we cannot rationally be held responsible for them. Hence if determinism is true we are ultimately not really free—at least not in the sense required for moral responsibility. Schopenhauer expressed this thought in a telling epigram: "A man can surely do what he wills to do, but he cannot determine what he wills."

P. E.

I Determinism and the Illusion of Moral Responsibility

Paul Rée

(*translated by* STEFAN BAUER-MENGELBERG)

1. Nothing Happens without a Cause

T... O SAY THAT THE WILL IS NOT free means that it is subject to the law of causality. Every act of will is in fact preceded by a sufficient cause. Without such a cause the act of will cannot occur; and, if the sufficient cause is present, the act of will must occur.

To say that the will is free would mean that it is not subject to the law of causality. In that case every act of will would be an absolute beginning [a first cause] and not a link [in a chain of events]: it would not be the effect of preceding causes.

The reflections that follow may serve to clarify what is meant by saying that the will is not free ... Every object—a stone, an animal, a human being —can pass from its present state to another one. The stone that now lies in front of me may, in the next moment, fly through the air, or it may disinte-

[This selection consists of the major portions of Chapters 1 and 2 of Paul Rée's *Die Illusion der Willensfreiheit,* a work published in Berlin in 1885. The third chapter of Rée's booklet, which is omitted here, is a detailed critique of Kant's views on the subject.

The subtitles in this translation were supplied by the editor; the first and fifth take the place of chapter headings in the original text. Cuts have been indicated by the use of dots. The translator has supplied a few minor editorial emendations; these have been put in square brackets.

The rights to the present translation are owned by Stefan Bauer-Mengelberg, Paul Edwards, and Pauline Pap.]

grate into dust or roll along the ground. If, however, one of these *possible* states is to be *realized,* its sufficient cause must first be present. The stone will fly through the air if it is tossed. It will roll if a force acts upon it. It will disintegrate into dust, given that some object hits and crushes it.

It is helpful to use the terms "potential" and "actual" in this connection. At any moment there are innumerably many potential states. At a given time, however, only *one* can become actual, namely, the one that is triggered by its sufficient cause.

The situation is no different in the case of an animal. The donkey that now stands motionless between two piles of hay may, in the next moment, turn to the left or to the right, or he may jump into the air or put his head between his legs. But here, too, the sufficient cause must first be present if of the *possible* modes of behavior one is to be *realized.*

Let us analyze one of these modes of behavior. We shall assume that the donkey has turned toward the bundle on his right. This turning presupposes that certain muscles were contracted. The cause of this muscular contraction is the excitation of the nerves that lead to them. The cause of this excitation of the nerves is a state of the brain. It was in a state of decision. But how did the brain come to be in that condition? Let us trace the states of the donkey back a little farther.

A few moments before he turned, his brain was not yet so constituted as to yield the sufficient cause for the excitation of the nerves in question and for the contraction of the muscles; for otherwise the movement would have occurred. The donkey had not yet "decided" to turn. If he then moved at some subsequent time, his brain must in the meantime have become so constituted as to bring about the excitation of the nerves and the movement of the muscles. Hence the brain underwent some change. To what causes is this change to be attributed? To the effectiveness of an impression that acts as an external stimulus, or to a sensation that arose internally; for example, the sensation of hunger and the idea of the bundle on the right, by jointly affecting the brain, change the way in which it is constituted so that it now yields the sufficient cause for the excitation of the nerves and the contraction of the muscles. The donkey now "wants" to turn to the right; he now turns to the right.

Hence, just as the position and constitution of the stone, on the one hand, and the strength and direction of the force that acts upon it, on the other, necessarily determine the kind and length of its flight, so the movement of the donkey—his turning to the bundle on the right—is no less necessarily the result of the way in which the donkey's brain and the stimulus are constituted at a given moment. That the donkey turned toward this particular bundle was determined by something trivial. If the bundle that the donkey did not choose had been positioned just a bit differently, or if it had smelled different, or if the subjective factor—the donkey's sense of smell or his visual organs—had developed in a somewhat different way, then, so we may assume, the donkey would have turned to the left. But the cause was not complete there, and that is why the effect could not occur, while with respect to the other side, where the cause was complete, the effect could not fail to appear.

For the donkey, consequently, just as for the stone, there are innumerably many *potential* states at any moment; he may walk or run or jump, or move to the left, to the right, or straight ahead. But only the one whose sufficient cause is present can ever become *actual*.

At the same time, there is a difference between the donkey and the stone in that the donkey moves because he wants to move, while the stone moves because it is moved. We do not deny this difference. There are, after all, a good many other differences between the donkey and the stone. We do not by any means intend to prove that this dissimilarity does not exist. We do not assert that the donkey is a stone, but only that the donkey's every movement and act of will has causes just as the motion of the stone does. The donkey moves because he wants to move. But that he wants to move at a given moment, and in this particular direction, is causally determined.

Could it be that there was no sufficient cause for the donkey's wanting to turn around—that he simply wanted to turn around? His act of will would then be an absolute beginning. An assumption of that kind is contradicted by experience and the universal validity of the law of causality. By experience, since observation teaches us that for every act of will some causes were the determining factors. By the universal validity of the law of causality, since, after all, nothing happens anywhere in the world without a sufficient cause. Why, then, of all things should a donkey's act of will come into being without a cause? Besides, the state of willing, the one that immediately precedes the excitation of the motor nerves, is no different in principle from other states—that of indifference, of lassitude, or of weariness. Would anyone believe that all of these states exist without a cause? And if one does not believe that, why should just the state of willing be thought to occur without a sufficient cause?

It is easy to explain why it seems to us that the motion of the stone is necessary while the donkey's act of will is not. The causes that move the stone are, after all, external and visible. But the causes of the donkey's act of will are internal and invisible; between us and the locus of their effectiveness lies the skull of the donkey. Let us consider this difference somewhat more closely. The stone lies before us as it is constituted. We can also see the force acting upon it, and from these two factors, the constitution of the stone and the force, there results, likewise visible, the rolling of the stone. The case of the donkey is different. The state of his brain is hidden from our view. And, while the bundle of hay is visible, its effectiveness is not. It is an internal process. The bundle does not come into visible contact with the brain but acts at a distance. Hence the subjective and the objective factor— the brain and the impact that the bundle has upon it—are invisible.

Let us suppose that we could depict the donkey's soul in high relief, taking account of and making visible all those states, attitudes, and feelings that characterize it before the donkey turns. Suppose further that we could see how an image detaches itself from the bundle of hay and, describing a visible path through the air, intrudes upon the donkey's brain and how it produces a change there in consequence of which certain nerves and muscles move. Suppose, finally, that we could repeat this experiment arbitrarily often, that, if we returned the donkey's soul into the state preceding his turning and let exactly the same impression act upon it, we should always observe the very same result. Then we would regard the donkey's turning to the right as necessary. We would come to realize that the brain, constituted as it was at that moment, had to react to such an impression in precisely that way.

In the absence of this experiment it seems as though the donkey's act of will were not causally determined. We just do not see its being causally determined and consequently believe that no such determination takes place. The act of will, it is said, is the cause of the turning, but it is not itself determined; it is said to be an absolute beginning.

The opinion that the donkey's act of will is not causally determined is held not only by the outsider; the donkey himself, had he the gift of reflection, would share it. The causes of his act of will would elude him, too, since in part they do not become conscious at all and in part pass through consciousness fleetingly, with the speed of lightning. If, for example, what tipped the scales was that he was closer by a hair's breadth to the bundle on the right, or that it smelled a shade better, how should the donkey notice something so trivial, something that so totally fails to force itself upon his consciousness?

In *one* sense, of course, the donkey is right in thinking "I could have turned to the left." His state at the moment, his position relative to the bundle, or its constitution need merely have been somewhat different, and he really would have turned to the left. The statement "I could have acted otherwise" is, accordingly, true in this sense: turning to the left is one of the movements possible for me (in contrast, for example, to the movement of flying); it lies within the realm of my possibilities.

We arrive at the same result if we take the law of inertia as our point of departure. It reads: every object strives to remain in its present state. Expressed negatively this becomes: without a sufficient cause no object can pass from its present state to another one. The stone will lie forever just as it is lying now; it will not undergo the slightest change if no causes—such as the weather or a force—act upon it to bring about a change. The donkey's brain will remain in the same state unchanged for all eternity if no causes— the feeling of hunger or fatigue, say, or external impressions—bring about a change.

If we reflect upon the entire life of the donkey *sub specie necessitatis,* we arrive at the following result. The donkey came into the world with certain properties of mind and body, his genetic inheritance. Since the day of his birth, impressions—of the companions with whom he frolicked or worked, his feed, the climate—have acted upon these properties. These two factors, his inborn constitution and the way in which it was formed through the impressions of later life, are the cause of all of his sensations, ideas, and moods, and of all of his movements, even the most trivial ones. If, for example, he cocks his left ear and not the right one, that is determined by causes whose historical development could be traced back ad infinitum; and likewise when he stands, vacillating, between the two bundles. And when action, the act of feeding, takes the place of vacillation, that, too, is determined: the idea of the one bundle now acts upon the donkey's mind, when it has become receptive to the idea of that particular sheaf, in such a way as to produce actions.

2. Human Beings and the Law of Causality

Let us now leave the realm of animals and proceed to consider man. Everything is the same here. Man's every feeling is a necessary result. Suppose, for example, that I am stirred by a feeling of pity at this moment. To what causes is it to be attributed? Let us go back as far as possible. An infinite amount of time has elapsed up to this moment. Time was never empty; objects have filled it from all eternity. These objects . . . have continually undergone change. All of these changes were governed by the law of causality; not one of them took place without a sufficient cause.

We need not consider what else may have characterized these changes. Only their *formal* aspect, only this *one* point is of concern to us: no change occurred without a cause.

At some time in the course of this development, by virtue of some causes, organic matter was formed, and finally man. Perhaps the organic world developed as Darwin described it. Be that as it may, it was in any case due to causes that I was born on a particular day, with particular properties of body, of spirit, and of heart. Impressions then acted upon this constitution; I had particular governesses, teachers, and playmates. Teaching and example in part had an effect and in part were lost upon me; the former, when my inborn constitution made me receptive to them, when I had an affinity for them. And that is how it has come to be, through the operation of [a chain of] causes, that I am stirred by a feeling of pity at this moment. The course of the world would have had to be somewhat different if my feelings were to be different now.

It is of no consequence for the present investigation whether the inborn capacity for pity, for taking pleasure in another's pain, or for courage remains constant throughout life or whether teaching, example, and activity serve to change it. In any case the pity or pleasure in another's pain, the courage or cowardice, that a certain person feels or exhibits at a given moment is a necessary result, whether these traits are inborn—an inheritance from his ancestors—or were developed in the course of his own life.

Likewise every intention, indeed, every thought that ever passes through the brain, the silliest as well as the most brilliant, the true as well as the false, exists of necessity. In that sense there is no freedom of thought. It is necessary that I sit in this place at this moment, that I hold my pen in my hand in a particular way, and that I write that every thought is necessary; and if the reader should perchance be of the opinion that this is not the case, i.e., if he should believe that thoughts may not be viewed as effects, then he holds this false opinion of necessity also.

Just as sensations and thoughts are necessary, so, too, is action. It is, after all, nothing other than their externalization, their objective embodiment. Action is born of sensations and thoughts. So long as the sensations are not sufficiently strong, action cannot occur, and when the sensations and thoughts are constituted so as to yield the sufficient cause for it, then it must occur; then the appropriate nerves and muscles are set to work. Let us illustrate this by means of an action that is judged differently at different levels of civilization, namely, murder.* Munzinger, for example, says that among the Bogos the murderer, the terror of the neighborhood, who never tires of blood and murder, is a man of respect. Whoever has been raised with such views will not be deterred from murder either by external or by internal obstacles. Neither the police nor his conscience forbids him to commit it. On the contrary, it is his habit to praise murder; his parents and his gods stimulate him to commit it, and his companions encourage him by their example. And so it comes to be that, if there is a favorable opportunity, he does the deed. But is this not terribly trivial? After all, everyone knows that an act of murder is due to *motives!* True, but almost no one (except perhaps a philosopher) knows that an act of murder, and indeed every action, has a *cause.* Motives are a part of the cause. But to admit that there are motives for an action is not yet to recognize that it is causally determined, or to see clearly that the action is determined by thoughts and sensations—which in turn are effects—just as the rolling of a ball is determined by a force. But it is this point, and only this one, to which we must pay heed.

Let us now consider the act of murder from the same point of view in the case of civilized peoples. Someone raised at a higher level of civilization has learned from childhood on to disapprove of murder and to regard it as deserving punishment. God, his parents, and his teachers—in short, all who constitute an authority for him—condemn acts of this kind. It is, moreover, inconsistent with his character, which has been formed in an era of peace. Lastly, too, fear of punishment will deter him. Can murder prosper on such soil? Not easily. Fear, pity, the habit of condemning murder—all these are just so many bulwarks that block the path to such an action. Nevertheless need, passion, or various seductive influences will perhaps remove one after another of these bulwarks. Let us consider the cause of an act of murder

---

* [The German here is *Raubmord,* a compound noun denoting a combination of murder and robbery (with overtones of pillage and rape). In his discussion Rée will focus now on the one aspect, now on the other. To avoid lengthy periphrasis in English, the action in question has been uniformly termed murder. The Bogos to whom Rée refers in the next sentence are a tribe occupying a district in the highlands north of Abyssinia. Werner Munzinger (1832–1875) was a Swiss explorer and linguist who spent many years in Eritrea, Abyssinia, and the Sudan. He described the customs of the Bogos in his book *Über die Sitten und das Recht der Bogos,* published in 1859.]

more closely. First it is necessary to distinguish between two components, the subjective and the objective, in the total cause. The *subjective* part of the cause consists of the state of the murderer at the moment of the deed. To this we must assign all ideas that he had at the time, the conscious as well as the unconscious ones, his sensations, the temperature of his blood, the state of his stomach, of his liver—of each and every one of his bodily organs. The *objective* component consists of the appearance of the victim, the locality in which the deed took place, and the way it was illuminated. The act of murder was necessarily consummated at that moment because these impressions acted upon a human being constituted in that particular way at the time. "Necessarily" means just that the act of murder is an effect; the state of the murderer and the impressions acting upon it are its cause. If the cause had not been complete, the effect could not have occurred. If, for example, the murderer had felt even a trifle more pity at that moment, if his idea of God or of the consequences that his deed would have here on earth had been somewhat more distinct, or if the moon had been a little brighter, so that more light would have fallen upon the victim's face and his pleading eyes—then, perhaps, the cause of the act of murder would not have become complete, and in consequence the act would not have taken place.

Thus for man, as for animal and stone, there are at any moment innumerably many *potential* states. The murderer might, at the moment when he committed the murder, have climbed a tree instead or stood on his head. If, however, instead of the murder one of these actions were to have become *actual,* then its sufficient cause would have had to be present. He would have climbed a tree if he had had the intention of hiding, or of acting as a lookout, that is to say, if at that moment he had had other ideas and sensations. But this could have been the case only if the events that took place in the world had been somewhat different [stretching back in time] ad infinitum.

3. Determinism and Will-Power

But I can, after all, break through the network of thoughts, sensations, and impressions that surrounds me by resolutely saying "I will not commit murder!" No doubt. We must, however, not lose sight of the fact that a resolute "I will" or "I will not" is also, wherever it appears, a necessary result; it does not by any means exist without a cause. Let us return to our examples. Although the Bogo really has reasons only to commit murder, it is nevertheless possible for a resolute "I will not commit murder" to assert itself. But is it conceivable that this "I will not" should occur without a sufficient cause? Fear, pity, or some other feeling, which in turn is an effect, overcomes him and gives rise to this "I will not" before the cause of the murder has yet become complete. Perhaps Christian missionaries have had an influence upon him; hence the idea of a deity that will visit retribution on him for murder comes before his soul, and that is how the "I will not" comes to be. It is easier to detect the causes of the resolute "I will not commit murder" in someone raised at a higher level of civilization; fear, principles, or the thought of God in most cases produce it in time.

A resolute will can be characteristic of a man. No matter how violently jealousy, greed, or some other passion rages within him, he does not want to succumb to it; he does not succumb to it. The analogue of this constitution is a ball that, no matter how violent a force acts upon it, does not budge from its place. A billiard cue will labor in vain to shake the earth. The earth victoriously resists the cue's thrusts with its mass. Likewise man resists the thrusts of greed and jealousy with the mass of his principles. A man of that kind, accordingly, is free—from being dominated by his drives. Does this contradict determinism? By no means. A man free from passion is still subject to the law of causality. He is necessarily free. It is just that the word "free" has different meanings. It may be correctly predicated of man in every sense except a single one: he is not free from the law of causality. Let us trace the causes of his freedom from the tyranny of the passions.

Let us suppose that his steadfastness of will was not inherited, or, if so, merely as a disposition. Teaching, example, and, above all, the force of circumstances developed it in him. From early childhood on he found himself in situations in which he had to control himself if he did not want to perish. Just as someone standing at the edge of an abyss can banish dizziness by thinking "If I become dizzy, then I will plunge," so thinking "If I yield to my excitation—indeed, if I so much as betray it—I will perish" has led him to control of his drives.

It is often thought that those who deny that the will is free want to deny that man has the ability to free himself from being dominated by his drives. However, one can imagine man's power to resist passions to be as great as one wants, even infinitely great; that is to say, a man may possibly resist even the most violent passion: his love of God or his principles have still more power over him than the passion. The question whether even the most resolute act of will is an effect is entirely independent of this.

But is being subject to the law of causality not the weak side of the strong? By no means. Is a lion weak if he can tear a tiger apart? Is a hurricane weak if it can uproot trees? And yet the power by means of which the lion dismembers and the storm uproots is an effect, and not an absolute beginning. By having causes, by being an effect, strength is not diminished.

Just as resolute willing is to be considered an effect, so is irresolute willing. A vacillating man is characterized by the fact that he alternately wants something and then doesn't want it. To say that someone contemplating murder is still vacillating means that at one time the desire for possessions, greed, and jealousy predominate—then he wants to commit murder; at another time fear of the consequences, the thought of God, or pity overcomes him, and then he does not want to commit murder. In the decisive moment, when his victim is before him, everything depends upon which feeling has the upper hand. If at that moment passion predominates, then he wants to commit murder; and then he commits murder.

We see that, from whatever point of view we look at willing, it always appears as a necessary result, as a link [in a chain of events], and never as an absolute beginning.

But can we not prove by means of an experiment that willing is an absolute beginning? I lift my arm because I *want* to lift it . . . Here my *wanting* to lift my arm is the cause of the lifting, but this wanting, we are told, is not itself causally determined; rather, it is an absolute beginning. I simply want to lift my arm, and that is that. We are deceiving ourselves. This act of will, too, has causes; my intention to demonstrate by means of an experiment that my will is free gives rise to my wanting to lift my arm. But how did this intention come to be? Through a conversation, or through reflecting on the freedom of the will. Thus the thought "I want to demonstrate my freedom" has the effect that I want to lift my arm. There is a gap in this chain. Granted that my intention to demonstrate that my will is free stands in some relation to my wanting to lift my arm, why do I not demonstrate my freedom by means of some other movement? Why is it *just my arm* that I want to lift? This specific act of will on my part has not yet been causally explained. Does it perhaps not have causes? Is it an uncaused act of will? Let us note first that someone who wishes to demonstrate that his will is free will usually really extend or lift his arm, and in particular his right arm. He neither tears his hair nor wiggles his belly. This can be explained as follows. Of all of the parts of the body that are subject to our voluntary control, there is none that we move more frequently than the right arm. If, now, we wish to demonstrate our freedom by means of some movement, we will automatically make that one to which we are most accustomed . . . Thus we first have a conversation about or reflection on the freedom of the will; this leads to the intention of demonstrating our freedom; this intention arises in an organism with certain [physiological] habits [such as that of readily lifting the right arm], and as a result we want to lift (and then lift) the right arm.

I remember once discussing the freedom of the will with a left-handed man. He asserted "My will is free; I can do what I want." In order to demonstrate this he extended his *left* arm.

It is easy to see, now, what the situation is with regard to the assertion "I can do what I want." In one sense it is indeed correct; in another, however, it is wrong. The *correct* sense is to regard willing as a cause and action as an effect. For example, I can kill my rival if I want to kill him. I can walk to the left if I want to walk to the left. The causes are *wanting* to kill and *wanting* to walk; the effects are killing and walking. In some way every action must be preceded by the act of willing it, whether we are aware of it or not. According to this view, in fact, I can do *only* what I want to do, and only if I want to do it. The *wrong* sense is to regard willing *merely* as a cause, and not at the same time as the effect of something else. But, like everything else, it is cause *as well as effect*. An absolutely initial act of will does not exist. Willing stands in the middle: it brings about killing and walking to the left; it is the effect of thoughts and sensations (which in turn are effects).

4. Ignorance of the Causation of Our Actions

Hence our volition (with respect to some action) is always causally determined. But it seems to be free (of causes); it seems to be an absolute beginning. To what is this appearance due?

We do not perceive the causes by which our volition is determined, and that is why we believe that it is not causally determined at all.

How often do we do something while "lost in thought"! We pay no attention to what we are doing, let alone to the causes from which it springs. While we are thinking, we support our head with our hand. While we are conversing, we twist a piece of paper in our hand. If we then reflect on our behavior—stimulated perhaps by a conversation about the freedom of the will—and if we are quite incapable of finding a sufficient cause for it, then we believe that there was no sufficient cause for it at all, that, consequently, we could have proceeded differently at that moment, e.g., supporting our head with the left hand instead of the right . . .

To adduce yet another example: suppose that there are two eggs on the table. I take one of them. Why not the other one? Perhaps the one I took was a bit closer to me, or some other trivial matter, which would be very difficult to discover and is of the kind that almost never enters our consciousness, tipped the scales. If I now look back but do not see why I took *that* particular egg, then I come to think that I could just as well have taken the other.

Let us replace "I could have taken the other egg" by other statements containing the expression "I could have." For example, I could, when I took the egg, have chopped off my fingers instead, or I could have jumped at my neighbor's throat. Why do we never adduce such statements . . . but always those contemplating an action close to the one that we really carried out? Because at the moment when I took the egg, chopping off my fingers and murder were far from my mind. From this point of view the two aspects of our subject matter—the fact that acts of will are necessary and that they appear not to be necessary—can be perceived especially clearly. *In fact* taking the other egg was at that moment just as impossible as chopping off a finger. For, whether a nuance of a sensation or a whole army of sensations and thoughts is lacking in the complete cause obviously does not matter; the effect cannot occur so long as the cause is incomplete. But it *seems* as though it would have been possible to take the other egg at that moment; if something almost happened, we think that it could have happened.

While in the case of unimportant matters we perhaps do not notice the causes of our act of will and therefore think that it has no causes, the situation is quite different—it will be objected—in the case of important matters. We did not, after all, marry one girl rather than another while "lost in thought." We did not close the sale of our house while "lost in thought." Rather, everyone sees that motives determined such decisions. In spite of this, however, we think "I could have acted differently." What is the source of this error?

In the case of unimportant matters we do not notice the cause of our action at all; in the case of important ones we perceive it, but not adequately. We do, to be sure, see the separate parts of the cause, but the special relation in which they stood to one another at the moment of the action eludes us.

Let us first consider another example from the realm of animals. A vixen vacillated whether to sneak into the chicken coop, to hunt for mice, or to return to her young in her den. At last she sneaked into the chicken coop. Why? Because she wanted to. But why did she want to? Because this act of will on her part resulted from the relation in which her hunger, her fear of the watchdog, her maternal instinct, and her other thoughts, sensations, and impressions stood to one another at that time. But a vixen with the gift of reflection would, were she to look back upon her action, say "I could have willed differently." For, although she realizes that hunger influenced her act of will, the *degree* of hunger on the one hand, and of fear and maternal instinct on the other, present at the moment of the action elude her. Having become a different animal since the time of the action, perhaps because of it, she thinks—by way of a kind of optical illusion—that she was that other animal already then. It is the same in the case of man. Suppose, for example, that someone has slain his rival out of jealousy. What does he himself, and what do others, perceive with respect to this action? We see that on the one hand jealousy, the desire for possessions, hatred, and rage were present in him, and on the other fear of punishment, pity, and the thought of God. We do not, however, see the particular relation in which hatred and pity, and rage and fear of punishment, stood to one another at the moment of the deed. If we could see this, keep it fixed, and recreate it experimentally, then everyone would regard this action as an effect, as a necessary result.

Let us now, with the aid of our imagination, suppose that the sensations and thoughts of the murderer at the moment of the deed were spread out before us, clearly visible as if on a map. From this reflection we shall learn that *in fact* we are lacking such an overview, and that this lack is the reason why we do not ascribe a cause (or "necessity") to the action.

The kaleidoscopically changing sensations, thoughts, and impressions would, in order for their relation to one another to become apparent, have to be returned to the state in which they were at the moment of the deed, and then made rigid, as if they were being nailed to their place. But beyond that, the thoughts and sensations would have to be spatially extended and endowed with a colored surface; a stronger sensation would have to be represented by a bigger lump. A clearer thought would have to wear, say, a bright red color, a less clear one a gray coloration. Jealousy and rage, as well as pity and the thought of God, would have to be plastically exhibited for us in this way. We would, further, have to see how the sight of the victim acts upon these structures of thoughts and sensations, and how there arises from these two factors first the desire to commit murder and then the act of murder itself.

Moreover, we would have to be able to repeat the process, perhaps as follows: we return the murderer to the state of mind that he had some years before the act of murder; we equip his mind with precisely the same thoughts and sensations, and his body with the same constitution. Then we let the very same impressions act upon them; we bring him into contact with the same people, let him read the same books, nourish him with the same food, and, finally, we will place the murdered person, after having called him back to life, before the murderer with the very same facial expression, in the same illumination and at the same distance. Then, as soon as the parts of the cause have been completely assembled, we would always see that the very same effect occurs, namely, wanting to commit, and then committing, murder.

Finally, too, we would have to vary the experiment, in the manner of the chemists; we would have to be able now to weaken a sensation, now to strengthen it, and to observe the result that this produces.

If these conditions were fulfilled, if we could experimentally recreate the process and also vary it, if we were to see its components and, above all, their relation to one another with plastic clarity before us—on the one hand, the *degree* of jealousy and of rage present at the moment; on the other, the *degree* of fear of punishment and of pity—then we would acknowledge that wanting to commit murder and committing murder are necessary results. But as it is we merely see that, on the one hand, jealousy and related feelings, and, on the other, pity and the idea of God, were present in the murderer. But, since we do not see the particular relation in which the sensations and thoughts stood to one another at the moment of the deed, we simply think that the *one* side could have produced acts of will and actions as well as the *other,* that the murderer could, at the moment when he wanted to commit and did commit murder, just as well have willed and acted differently, say compassionately.

It is the same if we ourselves are the person who acts. We, too, think "I could have willed differently." Let us illustrate this by yet another example. Yesterday afternoon at 6:03 o'clock I sold my house. Why? Because I wished to do so. But why did I wish to do so? Because my intention to change my place of residence, and other circumstances, caused my act of will. But was I compelled to will? Could I not have postponed the sale or forgone it altogether? It seems so to me, because I do not see the particular relation in which my thoughts, sensations, and impressions stood to one another yesterday afternoon at 6:03 o'clock.

Thus: we do not see the sufficient cause (either not at all, in the case of unimportant matters; or inadequately, in the case of important ones); consequently it does not exist for us; consequently we think that our volition and our actions were not causally determined at all, that we could just as well have willed and acted differently. No one would say "I could have willed differently" if he could see his act of will and its causes displayed plastically before him, in an experiment permitting repetition.

But who are the mistaken "we" of whom we are speaking here? Patently the author does not consider himself to be one of them. Does he, then, set himself, along with a few fellow philosophers, apart from the rest of mankind, regarding them as ignorant of the truth? Well, it really is not the case that mankind has always concerned itself with the problem of the freedom of the will and only a small part arrived at the result that the will is not free; rather, in precivilized ages no one, and in civilized ages almost no one, concerned himself with this problem. But of the few who did address themselves to this question, as the history of philosophy teaches us, almost all recognized that there is no freedom of the will. The others became victims of the illusion described above, without ever coming to grips with the problem in its general form (is the will subject to the law of causality or not?) . . .

5. Determinism is Inconsistent with Judgments of Moral Responsibility

We hold ourselves and others responsible without taking into account the problem of the freedom of the will.

Experience shows that, if someone has lied or murdered, he is told that he has acted reprehensibly and deserves punishment. Whether his action is uncaused or whether, like the other processes in nature, it is subject to the law of causality—how would people come to raise such questions in the ordinary course of their lives? Or has anyone ever heard of a case in which people talking about an act of murder, a lie, or an act of self-sacrifice discussed these actions in terms of the freedom of the will? It is the same if we ourselves are the person who acted. We say to ourselves "Oh, if only I had not done this! Oh, if only I had acted differently!" or "I have acted laudably, as one should act." At best a philosopher here or there chances upon the question whether our actions are causally determined or not, certainly not the rest of mankind.

Suppose, however, that someone's attention is directed to the fact that the will is not free. At first it will be very difficult to make this plausible to him. His volition is suspended from threads that are too nearly invisible, and that is why he comes to think that it is not causally determined at all. At last, however—so we shall assume—he does come to recognize that actions are effects, that their causes are thoughts and impressions, that these must likewise be viewed as effects, and so on. How will he then judge these actions? Will he continue to maintain that murder is to be punished by *reprisal* and that benevolent actions are to be considered *meritorious?* By no means. Rather, the first conclusion that he will—validly—draw from his newly acquired insight is that we cannot hold anyone responsible. *"Tout comprendre c'est tout pardonner"*; no one can be made to answer for an *effect*.

In order to illustrate this important truth, that whoever considers intentions to be effects will cease to assign merit or blame for them, let us resume discussion of the examples above. From early childhood on the Bogo (cf. p. 15) has learned to praise murder. The praiseworthiness of such an action already penetrated the consciousness of the child as a secondary meaning of the word "murder," and afterward it was confirmed by every impression: his gods and his fellow men praise murder. In consequence he involuntarily judges acts of murder to be praiseworthy, no matter whether it was he himself or someone else who committed them. Let us assume, now, that a philosopher had succeeded in persuading the Bogos that the act of murder and the intention to practice cruelty are causally determined. Then their judgment would undergo an essential modification.

To conceive of actions and intentions as causally determined, after all, means the following. We go back in the history of the individual, say to his birth, and investigate which of his characteristics are inborn and to what causes they are due.[1] Then, ever guided by the law of causality, we trace the development or transformation of these properties; we see how impressions, teachings, and examples come to him and, if his inborn constitution has an affinity for them, are taken up and transformed by it, otherwise passing by without leaving a trace. Finally we recognize that the keystone, the necessary result of this course of development, is the desire to commit murder and the act of murder.

A Bogo who looks upon murder and the intention to practice cruelty in this way—that is, as an effect—will say that it is impossible to regard them as meritorious.

But will he now look upon these actions with apathy, devoid of all feeling? By no means. He will still consider them to be pleasant or unpleasant, agreeable or disagreeable.

When the action is directed against himself, he will perceive it as pleasant or as unpleasant; the prospect of being murdered is unpleasant for everyone, whether he considers the action to be causally determined or uncaused.

Similarly our liking or dislike for the character of a human being will persist even if we regard it as the result of causes. To say that I find someone agreeable means that I am drawn to him; I like him. Of a landscape, too, one says that it is agreeable, and, just as this liking cannot be diminished even if we consider the trees, meadows, and hills to be the result of causes, so our liking for the character of a human being is not diminished if we regard it *sub specie necessitatis*. Hence to the Bogo who has come to see that murder is causally determined it is still agreeable or disagreeable. Usually he will consider it to be agreeable. He will say that it warms the cockles of his heart to observe such an action; it accords with his wild tem-

---

1. An investigation as detailed as that is, of course, never possible in practice.

perament, as yet untouched by civilization. Therefore he will, in view of the necessity, suspend only the specifically moral practice of regarding it as meritorious. But his liking may become love, and even esteem and reverence. It will be objected, however, that "I revere a mode of behavior" entails "I consider it meritorious for a person to behave in that way," and similarly for esteem. To be sure, the words "reverence" and "esteem" *frequently* have this meaning, and *to the extent that they do* a determinist would cease using them. But all words that denote human feelings have not only one, but several meanings. They have, if I may express it in that way, a harem of meanings, and they couple now with this one, now with that one. So, if I "revere" someone, it means also that I esteem him, that he impresses me, and that I wish to be like him. . . Reverence and esteem in *this* sense can coexist with determinism.

Hence the Bogo who conceives of the intention to practice cruelty and the act of murder as effects can nevertheless consider them to be agreeable or disagreeable, and in a certain sense he can also have esteem and reverence for them, but he will not regard them as meritorious.

Let us now consider the act of murder at high levels of civilization. Civilization, as it progressed, stigmatized murder and threatened penalties for it on earth and in heaven. This censure already penetrates the consciousness of the child as a secondary meaning of the word "murder" and afterward is confirmed through every impression. All the people whom one knows, all the books that one reads, the state with its institutions, pulpit and stage always use "murder" in a censorious sense. That is how it comes to be that we involuntarily declare an act of murder to be blameworthy, be it that others or that we ourselves, driven by passion, committed it. Whether the action was determined by causes or uncaused—that question is raised neither by the person who acted nor by the uninvolved observers. But *if* it is raised, if someone considers the act of murder *sub specie necessitatis,* then he ceases to regard it as blameworthy. He will then no longer want to see punishment in the proper sense—suffering as retribution—meted out for it, but merely punishment as a safety measure.[2] The feelings of liking and dislike, however, will continue to exist even then. On the whole, someone raised at a high level of civilization will have a feeling of dislike for acts of murder; he will not feel drawn to whoever commits it; he will not like him. For such an act does not accord with his temperament, which was formed as he was engaged in non-violent occupations. In spite of the recognition that the action was necessary, this dislike can at times grow to revulsion, and even to contempt—given that the latter notion is stripped of the specifically moral elements that it contains (the attribution of blame). It will then mean something like this: I do not want to be like that person.

The situation is the same in the case of benevolent actions and those performed out of a sense of duty; we cease to regard them as meritorious if we consider them to be effects. Let us look more closely at actions per-

2. Punishments are causes that prevent the repetition of the action punished.

formed out of a sense of duty. To say that someone acts out of a sense of duty means that he performs an action, perhaps contrary to his inclinations, because his conscience commands him to do it. But how does conscience come to issue such commandments? As follows: with some actions (and intentions) there is linked for us from early childhood on a categorical "thou shalt do (or have) them"; for example, "you *should* help everyone as much as possible." If someone then makes this habitual judgment into the guiding principle of his behavior, if he helps a person because his conscience commands "thou *shalt* help thy fellow man," then he is acting "out of a sense of duty" . . . If we want to consider such an action from the point of view of eternity and necessity, we shall have to proceed as follows (cf. p. 23): we investigate (1) the constitution of the child who receives the teaching "thou shalt help," (2) the constitution of those who give it to him. The child absorbing this doctrine has some inborn constitution of nerves, of blood, of imagination, and of reason. The commandment "thou shalt help" is impressed upon this substance with some degree of insistence; the deity, heaven, hell, approval of his fellow men and of his own conscience—these ideas are presented to him, depending upon his teachers, as being more or less majestic and inspiring. And the child transforms them with greater or lesser intensity, depending upon his receptivity. The ultimate constitution of a man, the preponderance within him of the sense of duty over his own desires, is in any case a necessary result, a product of his inborn constitution and the impressions received. To someone who contemplates this, such a temperament may, to be sure, still seem agreeable (perhaps because he himself is or would like to be similarly constituted), but no one can regard as *meritorious* behavior that he conceives to be an *effect*.

But what if we ourselves are the person who acted? Then the circumstances are analogous; then, too, liking and dislike remain, while the attribution of merit or blame (the "pangs of conscience") disappears.

Our own action, too, can remain agreeable or become disagreeable for us after it has occurred. It is agreeable if the disposition from which we acted persists after the action; it will become disagreeable if we change our frame of mind. Suppose, for example, that we have acted vengefully and are still in the same mood; then the act of revenge is still agreeable, whether we conceive it to be an effect or not. If, however, a feeling of pity takes the place of our desire for revenge, then we come to dislike our action; we cannot stand our earlier self—the less so, the more pronounced our feeling of pity is. The reflection that the action is an effect in no way affects this feeling of dislike, perhaps of disgust, or even of revulsion for ourselves. We say to ourselves that the desire for revenge was, to be sure, necessarily stronger than the ideas and impressions that stood in its way, hence the action took place necessarily, too; but now it happens that pity is necessarily present, and, along with it, regrets that we acted as we did. . . .

6. Can We Abandon Judgments of Moral Responsibility?

But is it really possible to shake off feelings of guilt so easily? Do they disappear, like a spook, when the magic word *effect* is pronounced? Is the situation with respect to this feeling not quite like that with regard to dislike? It was, to be sure, necessary that I took revenge, but now I necessarily feel dislike for my own action, along with guilt. I can no more prevent the onset of the one feeling than of the other. But if the feeling of guilt asserts itself in spite of the recognition that actions are effects, should we not suspect that our holding others responsible, too, will persist in spite of this insight? Did we commit an error somewhere? Is it that responsibility and necessity do not exclude each other? The situation is as follows. The reason why we assign moral praise to some actions and moral censure to others has already been mentioned repeatedly. Censure already penetrates the consciousness of the child as a secondary meaning of the words "murder," "theft," "vengefulness," and "pleasure in another's pain," and praise as a secondary meaning of the words "benevolence" and "mercy." That is why censure seems to him to be a constituent part of murder, and praise, of benevolence. At a later point in his life, perhaps in his twentieth year, the insight comes to him from somewhere that all actions are effects and therefore cannot earn merit or blame. What can this poor little insight accomplish against the accumulated habits of a lifetime of judging? The habit of mind of assigning blame for actions like murder makes it very difficult to think of them without this judgment. It is all very well for reason to tell us that we may not assign blame for such actions, since they are effects—our habit of judging, which has become a feeling, will see to it that it is done anyway. But—let habit confront habit! Suppose that, whenever someone involuntarily wants to assign blame or merit for an action, he ascends to the point of view of eternity and necessity. He then regards the action as the necessary result of [a chain of events stretching back into] the infinite past. Through that way of looking at things the *instinctive* association between the action and the judgment will be severed, if not the first time, then perhaps by the thousandth. Such a man will shed the habit of assigning blame or merit for any action whatsoever.

In fact, of course, human beings almost never behave like that; this way of looking at things is completely foreign to them. Furthermore, human beings determine their actions by considering whether they will make them happy or unhappy; but shedding the habit of making judgments [of moral responsibility] would hardly increase their happiness . . .

The situation with respect to a person's character is no different from that with respect to his individual actions. *Customarily* one assigns blame or merit, whether to himself or to others, for a single action: a single act of cheating or of giving offense. But *sometimes* we go back from the action to its source, to a person's character. In reality, of course, character, in its broadest as well as its smallest traits, is just as necessary as an individual action; it is the product of [a chain of events stretching back into] the infinite past, be it that it was inherited in its entirety or that it was formed in part during the individual's lifetime. But with regard to character, too, hardly anyone adopts this point of view. Just as in the case of particular actions, character is regarded neither as free nor as necessary; that is to say, people do not raise the question at all whether the law of causality is applicable also to actions and character. Hence one assigns blame and merit for character as for actions, though they are effects; for one does not see that they are effects. If one sees this, if one regards character *sub specie necessitatis,* then he ceases to assign blame or merit for it. Liking and dislike, on the other hand, nevertheless persist even then: a character closely related to mine will garner my liking, my love, and perhaps even, in the sense mentioned above (p. 24), my esteem and reverence—whether I conceive of it as an effect or not.

Hence we assign blame or merit for character and actions out of the habit of judging, without concerning ourselves with the question whether they are causally determined or not. We cease to assign blame or merit for character and actions as soon as we recognize that they are causally determined (if we ignore the remnants of our habits).

Let us recapitulate: the character, the intentions, and the actions of every human being are effects, and it is impossible to assign blame or merit for effects.

2 The Regularity
of the Moral World

Henry Thomas Buckle

THE BELIEVER IN THE POSSIBILITY OF a science of history is not called upon to hold either the doctrine of pre-destined events, or that of freedom of the will; and the only positions which, in this stage of inquiry, I shall expect him to concede are the following: That when we perform an action, we perform it in consequence of some motive or motives; that those motives are the results of some antecedents; and that, therefore, if we were acquainted with the whole of the antecedents, and with all the laws of their movements, we could with unerring certainty predict the whole of their immediate results. This, unless I am greatly mistaken, is the view which must be held by every man whose mind is unbiased by system, and who forms his opinions according to the evidence actually before him. If, for example, I am intimately acquainted with the character of any person, I can frequently tell how he will act under some given circumstances. Should I fail in this prediction, I must ascribe my error not to the arbitrary and capricious freedom of his will, nor to any supernatural prearrangement, for of neither of these things have we the slightest proof; but I must be content to suppose either that I had been misinformed as to some of the circumstances in which he was placed, or else that I had not sufficiently studied the ordinary operations of his mind. If, however, I were capable of correct reasoning, and if, at the same time, I had a complete knowledge both of his disposition and of all the events by which he was surrounded, I should be able to foresee the line of conduct which, in consequence of those events, he would adopt.

Rejecting, then, the metaphysical dogma of free will, and the theological dogma of predestined events, we are driven to the conclusion that the

[This selection is taken from Chapter II, Volume I, of Buckle's *History of Civilization in England*, a work first published in 1857.]

actions of men being determined solely by their antecedents, must have a character of uniformity, that is to say, must, under precisely the same circumstances, always issue in precisely the same results. And as all antecedents are either in the mind or out of it, we clearly see that all the variations in the results, in other words, all the changes of which history is full, all the vicissitudes of the human race, their progress or their decay, their happiness or their misery, must be the fruit of a double action; an action of external phenomena upon the mind, and another action of the mind upon the phenomena. . . .

The most comprehensive inferences respecting the actions of men, which are admitted by all parties as incontestable truths, are derived from this or from analogous sources: they rest on statistical evidence, and are expressed in mathematical language. And whoever is aware of how much has been discovered by this single method, must not only recognize the uniformity with which mental phenomena succeed each other, but must, I think, feel sanguine that still more important discoveries will be made, so soon as there are brought into play those other powerful resources which even the present state of knowledge will abundantly supply. Without, however, anticipating future inquiries, we are, for the moment, only concerned with those proofs of the existence of a uniformity in human affairs which statisticians have been the first to bring forward. . . .

Of all offenses, it might be supposed that the crime of murder is one of the most arbitrary and irregular. For when we consider that this, though generally the crowning act of a long career of vice, is often the immediate result of what seems a sudden impulse; that when premeditated, its committal, even with the least chance of impunity, requires a rare combination of favorable circumstances for which the criminal will frequently wait; that he has thus to bide his time, and look for opportunities he cannot control; that when the time has come, his heart may fail him; that the question whether or not he shall commit the crime may depend on a balance of conflicting motives, such as fear of the law, a dread of the penalties held out by religion, the prickings of his own conscience, the apprehension of future remorse, the love of gain, jealousy, revenge, desperation;—when we put all these things together, there arises such a complication of causes, that we might reasonably despair of detecting any order or method in the result of those subtle and shifting agencies by which murder is either caused or prevented. But now, how stands the fact? The fact is, that murder is committed with as much regularity, and bears as uniform a relation to certain known circumstances, as do the movements of the tides, and the rotations of the seasons. M. Quetelet,[1] who has spent his life collecting and methodizing the statistics of different countries, states, as the result of his laborious researches, that "in every thing which concerns crime, the same numbers re-occur with a constancy which cannot be mistaken; and that this is the case even with those crimes which seem

---

1. Belgian statistician and astronomer (1796–1874) who pioneered in the statistical analysis of social phenomena. (Ed.)

quite independent of human foresight, such, for instance, as murders, which are generally committed after quarrels arising from circumstances apparently casual. Nevertheless, we know from experience that every year there not only take place nearly the same number of murders, but that even the instruments by which they are committed are employed in the same proportion." This was the language used in 1835 by confessedly the first statistician in Europe, and every subsequent investigation has confirmed his accuracy. For later inquiries have ascertained the extraordinary fact, that the uniform reproduction of crime is more clearly marked, and more capable of being predicted, than are the physical laws connected with the disease and destruction of our bodies. Thus, for instance, the number of persons accused of crime in France between 1826 and 1844 was, by a singular coincidence, about equal to the male deaths which took place in Paris during the same period, the difference being that the fluctuations in the amount of crime were actually smaller than the fluctuations in the mortality; while a similar regularity was observed in each separate offense, all of which obeyed the same law of uniform and periodical repetition.

This, indeed, will appear strange to those who believe that human actions depend more on the peculiarities of each individual than on the general state of society. But another circumstance remains behind still more striking. Among public and registered crimes, there is none which seems so completely dependent on the individual as suicide. Attempts to murder or rob may be, and constantly are, successfully resisted; baffled sometimes by the party attacked, sometimes by the officers of justice. But an attempt to commit suicide is much less liable to interruption. The man who is determined to kill himself, is not prevented at the last moment by the struggles of an enemy; and as he can easily guard against the interference of the civil power, his act becomes as it were isolated; it is cut off from foreign disturbances, and seems more clearly to be the product of his own volition than any other offense could possibly be. We may also add that, unlike crimes in general, it is rarely caused by the instigation of confederates; so that men, not being goaded into it by their companions, are uninfluenced by one great class of external associations which might hamper what is termed the freedom of their will. It may, therefore, very naturally be thought impracticable to refer suicide to general principles, or to detect anything like regularity in an offense which is so eccentric, so solitary, so impossible to control by legislation, and which the most vigilant police can do nothing to diminish. There is also another obstacle that impedes our view: this is, that even the best evidence respecting suicide must always be very imperfect. In cases of drowning, for example, deaths are liable to be returned as suicides which are accidental; while on the other hand, some are called accidental which are voluntary. Thus it is, that self-murder seems to be not only capricious and uncontrollable, but also very obscure in regard to proof; so that on all these grounds it might be reasonable to despair of ever tracing it to those general causes by which it is produced.

This being the peculiarities of this singular crime, it is surely an astonishing fact, that all the evidence we possess respecting it points to one great conclusion, and can leave no doubt on our minds that suicide is merely the product of the general condition of society, and that the individual felon only carries into effect what is a necessary consequence of preceding circumstances. In a given state of society, a certain number of persons must put an end to their own life. This is the general law; and the special question as to who shall commit the crime depends of course upon special laws; which, however, in their total action, must obey the large social law to which they are subordinate. And the power of the larger law is so irresistible, that neither the love of life nor the fear of another world can avail anything towards even checking its operation. The causes of this remarkable regularity I shall hereafter examine; but the existence of the regularity is familiar to whoever is conversant with moral statistics. In the different countries for which we have returns, we find year by year the same proportion of persons putting an end to their own existence; so that, after making allowance for the impossibility of collecting complete evidence, we are able to predict, within a very small limit of error, the number of voluntary deaths for each ensuing period; supposing, of course, that the social circumstances do not undergo any marked change. Even in London, notwithstanding the vicissitudes incidental to the largest and most luxurious capital in the world, we find a regularity greater than could be expected by the most sanguine believer in social laws; since political excitement, mercantile excitement, and the misery produced by the dearness of food, are causes of suicide, and are all constantly varying. Nevertheless, in this vast metropolis, about 240 persons every year make away with themselves; the annual suicides oscillating, from the pressure of temporary causes, between 266, the highest, and 213, the lowest. In 1846, which was the great year of excitement caused by the railway panic, the suicides in London were 266; in 1847 began a slight improvement, and they fell to 256; in 1848 they were 247; in 1849 they were 213; and in 1850 they were 229.

Such is some, and only some, of the evidence we now possess respecting the regularity with which, in the same states of society, the same crimes are necessarily reproduced. To appreciate the full force of this evidence, we must remember that it is not an arbitrary selection of particular facts, but that it is generalized from an exhaustive statement of criminal statistics, consisting of many millions of observations, extending over countries in different grades of civilization, with different laws, different opinions, different morals, different habits. If we add to this, that these statistics have been collected by persons specially employed for that purpose, with every means of arriving at the truth, and with no interest to deceive, it surely must be admitted that the existence of crime according to a fixed and uniform scheme, is a fact more clearly attested than any other in the moral history of man. We have here parallel chains of evidence formed with extreme care, under the most different circumstances, and all pointing in the same direction; all of them forcing us to the conclusion, that the offenses of men are the result not so much of the vices of the individual offender as of that state of society into which that individual is thrown. This is an inference resting on broad and tangible proofs accessible to all the world; and as such cannot be overturned, or even impeached, by any of those hypotheses with which metaphysicians and theologians have hitherto perplexed the study of past events.

Those readers who are acquainted with the manner in which in the physical world the operations of the laws of nature are constantly disturbed, will expect to find in the moral world disturbances equally active. Such aberrations proceed, in both instances, from minor laws, which at particular points meet the larger laws, and thus alter their normal action. Of this, the science of mechanics affords a good example in the instance of that beautiful theory called the parallelogram of forces; according to which the forces are to each other in the same proportion as is the diagonal of their respective parallelograms. This is a law pregnant with great results; it is connected with those important mechanical resources, the composition and resolution of forces; and no one acquainted with the evidence on which it stands, ever thought of questioning its truth. But the moment we avail ourselves of it for practical purposes, we find that in its action it is warped by other laws, such as those concerning the friction of air, and the different density of the bodies on which we operate, arising from their chemical composition, or, as some suppose, from their atomic arrangement. Perturbations being thus let in, the pure and simple action of the mechanical law disappears. Still, and although the results of the law are incessantly disturbed, the law itself remains intact. Just in the same way, the great social law, that the moral actions of men are the product not of their volition, but of their antecedents, is itself liable to disturbances which trouble its operation without affecting its truth. And this is quite sufficient to explain those slight variations which we find from year to year in the total amount of crime produced by the same country. Indeed, looking at the fact that the moral world is far more abundant in materials than the physical world, the only ground for astonishment is, that these variations should not be greater; and from the circumstance that the discrepancies are so trifling, we may form some idea of the prodigious energy of those vast social laws which, though constantly interrupted, seem to triumph over every obstacle, and which, when examined by the aid of large numbers, scarcely undergo any sensible perturbation.

Nor is it merely the crimes of men which are marked by this uniformity of sequence. Even the number of marriages annually contracted is determined, not by the temper and wishes of individuals, but by large general facts, over which individuals can exercise no authority. It is now known that marriages bear a fixed and definite relation to the price of corn; and in England the experience of a century has proved that, instead of having any connection with personal feelings, they are simply regulated by the average earnings of the great mass of people: so that this immense social and religious institution is not only swayed, but is completely controlled by the price of food and the rate of wages. In other cases, uniformity has been detected, though the causes of the uniformity are still unknown. Thus, to give a curious instance, we are now able to prove that even the aberrations of memory are marked by this general character of necessary and invariable order. The post-offices of London nd Paris have latterly published returns of the number of letters which the writers, through fogetfulness, omitted to direct; and, making allowance for the difference of circumstances, the returns are year after yea copies of each other. Year after year the same poportion of letter-writers forget this simple act; so that for each successive period we can actually foretell the number of persons whose memory will fail them in regard to this trifling, and, as it might appear, accidental occurrence.

To those who have a steady conception of the regularity of events, and have firmly seized the great truth that the actions of men, being guided by their antecedents, are in reality never inconsistent, but, however capricious they may appear, only form part of one vast scheme of universal order, of which we in the present state of knowledge can barely see the outline,—to those who understand this, which is at once the key and the basis of history, the facts just adduced, so far from being strange, will be precisely what would have been expected, and ought long since to have been known. Indeed, the progress of inquiry is becoming so rapid and so earnest, that I entertain little doubt that before another century has elapsed, the chain of evidence will be complete, and it will be as rare to find an historian who denies the undeviating regularity of the moral world, as it now is to find a philosopher who denies the regularity of the material world. . . .

3   The Dilemma
of Determinism

William James

Rationality and the Free-Will Controversy

A COMMON OPINION PREVAILS THAT the juice has ages ago been pressed out of the free-will controversy, and that no new champion can do more than warm up stale arguments which everyone has heard. This is a radical mistake. I know of no subject less worn out, or in which inventive genius has a better chance of breaking open new ground—not, perhaps, of forcing a conclusion or of coercing assent, but of deepening our sense of what the issue between the two parties really is, and of what the ideas of fate and of free will imply. At our very side almost, in the past few years, we have seen falling in rapid succession from the press works that present the alternative in entirely novel lights. Not to speak of the English disciples of Hegel, such as Green and Bradley; not to speak of Hinton and Hodgson, nor of Hazard here—we see in the writings of Renouvier, Fouillée, and Delboeuf how completely changed and refreshed is the form of the old disputes. I cannot pretend to vie in originality with any of the masters I have named, and my ambition limits itself to just one little point. If I can make two of the necessarily implied corollaries of determinism clearer to you than they have been made before, I shall have made it possible for you to decide for or against that doctrine with a better understanding of what you are about. And if you prefer not to decide at all, but to remain doubters, you will at least see more plainly what the subject of your hesitation is. I thus disclaim openly on the threshold all pretension to prove to you that the freedom of the will is true. The most I hope is to induce some of you to follow my own example in assum-

[This selection is reprinted, with omissions, from "The Dilemma of Determinsim," an essay which first appeared in 1884.]

ing it true, and acting as if it were true. If it be true, it seems to me that this is involved in the strict logic of the case. Its truth ought not to be forced willy-nilly down our indifferent throats. It ought to be freely espoused by men who can equally well turn their backs upon it. In other words, our first act of freedom, if we are free, ought in all inward propriety to be to affirm that we are free. This should exclude, it seems to me, from the free-will side of the question all hope of a coercive demonstration—a demonstration which I, for one, am perfectly contented to go without.

With thus much understood at the outset, we can advance. But, not without one more point understood as well. The arguments I am about to urge all proceed on two suppositions: first, when we make theories about the world and discuss them with one another, we do so in order to attain a conception of things which shall give us subjective satisfaction; and, second, if there be two conceptions, and the one seems to us, on the whole, more rational than the other, we are entitled to suppose that the more rational one is truer of the two. I hope that you are all willing to make these suppositions with me; for I am afraid that if there be any of you here who are not, they will find little edification in the rest of what I have to say. I cannot stop to argue the point; but I myself believe that all the magnificent achievements of mathematical and physical science—our doctrines of evolution, of uniformity of law, and the rest—proceed from our indomitable desire to cast the world into a more rational shape in our minds than the shape into which it is thrown there by the crude order of our experience. The world has shown itself, to a great extent, plastic to this demand of ours for rationality. How much farther it will show itself plastic no one can say. Our only means of finding out is to try; and I, for one, feel as free to try conceptions of moral as of mechanical or of logical rationality. If a certain formula for expressing the nature of the world violates my moral demand, I shall feel free to throw it overboard, or at least to doubt it, as if it disappointed my demand for uniformity of sequence, for example; the one demand being, so far as I can see, quite as subjective and emotional as the other is. The principle of causality, for example—what is it but a postulate, an empty name covering simply a demand that the sequence of events shall some day manifest a deeper kind of belonging of one thing with another than the mere juxtaposition which now phenomenally appears? It is as much an altar to an unknown god as the one that Saint Paul found at Athens. All our scientific and philosophic ideals are altars to unknown gods. Uniformity is as much so as is free will. If this be admitted, we can debate on even terms. But if any one pretends that while freedom and variety are, in the first instance, subjective demands, necessity and uniformity are something altogether different, I do not see how we can debate at all.

To begin, then, I must suppose you acquainted with all the usual arguments on the subject. I cannot stop to take up the old proofs from causation, from statistics, from the certainty with which we can foretell one another's conduct, from the fixity of character, and all the rest. But there are two *words* which usually encumber these classical arguments, and which we must immediately dispose of if we are to make any progress. One is the eulogistic word *freedom,* and the other is the opprobrious word *chance.* The word "chance" I wish to keep, but I wish to get rid of the word "freedom." Its eulogistic associations have so far overshadowed all the rest of its meaning that both parties claim the sole right to use it, and determinists today insist that they alone are freedom's champions. Old-fashioned determinism was what we may call *hard* determinism. It did not shrink from such words as fatality, bondage of the will, necessitation, and the like. Nowadays, we have a *soft* determinism which abhors harsh words, and, repudiating fatality, necessity, and even predetermination, says that its real name is freedom; for freedom is only necessity understood, and bondage to the highest is identical with true freedom. Even a writer as little used to making capital out of soft words as Mr. Hodgson hesitates not to call himself a "free-will determinist."

Now, all this is a quagmire of evasion under which the real issue of fact has been entirely smothered. Freedom in all these senses presents simply no problem at all. No matter what the soft determinist mean by it— whether he mean the acting without external constraint; whether he mean the acting rightly, or whether he mean the acquiescing in the law of the whole—who cannot answer him that sometimes we are free and sometimes we are not? But there *is* a problem, an issue of fact and not of words, an issue of the most momentous importance, which is often decided without discussion in one sentence—nay, in one clause of a sentence—by those very writers who spin out whole chapters in their efforts to show what "true" freedom is; and that is the question of determinism, about which we are to talk tonight.

Possibilities and Actualities

Fortunately, no ambiguities hang about this word or about its opposite, indeterminism. Both designate an outward way in which things may happen, and their cold and mathematical sound has no sentimental associations that can bribe our partiality either way in advance. Now, evidence of an external kind to decide between determinism and indeterminism is, as I intimated a while back, strictly impossible to find. Let us look at the difference between them and see for ourselves. What does determinism profess?

It professes that those parts of the universe already laid down absolutely appoint and decree what the other parts shall be. The future has no ambiguous possibilities hidden in its womb: the part we call the present is compatible with only one totality. Any other future complement than the one fixed from eternity is impossible. The whole is in each and every part, and welds it with the rest into an absolute unity, an iron block, in which there can be no equivocation or shadow of turning.

> With earth's first clay they did the last man knead,
> And there of the last harvest sowed the seed.
> And the first morning of creation wrote
> What the last dawn of reckoning shall read.

Indeterminism, on the contrary, says that the parts have a certain amount of loose play on one another, so that the laying down of one of them does not necessarily determine what the others shall be. It admits that possibilities may be in excess of actualities, and that things not yet revealed to our knowledge may really in themselves be ambiguous. Of two alternative futures which we conceive, both may now be really possible; and the one become impossible only at the very moment when the other excludes it by becoming real itself. Indeterminism thus denies the world to be one unbending unit of fact. It says there is a certain ultimate pluralism in it; and, so saying, it corroborates our ordinary unsophisticated view of things. To that view, actualities seem to float in a wider sea of possibilities from out of which they are chosen; and, somewhere, indeterminism says, such possibilities exist, and form a part of truth.

Determinism, on the contrary, says they exist *nowhere,* and that necessity on the one hand and impossibility on the other are the sole categories of the real. Possibilities that fail to get realized are, for determinism, pure illusions: they never were possibilities at all. There is nothing inchoate, it says, about this universe of ours, all that was or is or shall be actual in it having been from eternity virtually there. The cloud of alternatives our minds secort this mass of actuality withal is a cloud of sheer deceptions, to which "impossibilities" is the only name which rightfully belongs.

The issue, it will be seen, is a perfectly sharp one, which no eulogistic terminology can smear over or wipe out. The truth *must* lie with one side o rthe other, and its lying with one side makes the other false.

The question relates solely to the existence of possibilities, in the strict sense of the term, as things that may, but need not, be. Both sides admit that a volition, for instance, has occurred. The indeterminists say another volition might have occurred in its place: the determinists swear that nothing could possibly have occurred in its place. Now, can science be called in to tell us which of these two point-blank contradicters of each other is right? Science professes to draw no conclusions but such as are based on matters of facts, things that have actually happened; but how can any amount of assurance that something actually happened give us the least grain of information as to whether another thing might or might not haveh appened in its place? Only facts can be proved by other facts. With things that are possibilities and not facts, facts have no concern. If we have no other evidence than the evidence of existing facts, the possibility-question must remain a mystery never to be cleared up.

And the truth is that facts practically have hardly anything to do with

making us either determinists or indeterminists. Sure enough, we make
a flourish of quoting facts this way or that; and if we are determinists, we
talk about the infallibility with which we can predict one another's conduct;
while if we are indeterminists, we lay great stress on the fact that it is just
because we cannot foretell one another's conduct, either in war or statecraft
or in any of the great and small intrigues and businesses of men, that life
is so intensely anxious and hazardous a game. But who does not see the
wretched insufficiency of this so-called objective testimony on both sides?
What fills up the gaps in our minds is something not objective, not external.
What divides us into *possibility* men and *anti-possibility* men is different
faiths or postulates—postulates of rationality. To this man the world
seems more rational with possibilities in it—to that man more rational with
possibilities excluded; and talk as we will about having to yield to evidence,
what makes us monists or pluralists, determinists or indeterminists, is at
bottom always some sentiment like this.

The Idea of Chance

The stronghold of the deterministic sentiment is the antipathy to the
idea of chance. As soon as we begin to talk indeterminism to our friends,
we find a number of them shaking their heads. This notion of alternative
possibility, they say, this admission that any one of several things may
come to pass, is, after all, only a round-about name for chance; and chance
is something the notion of which no sane mind can for an instant tolerate
in the world. What is it, they ask, but barefaced crazy unreason, the negation of intelligibility and law? And if the slightest particle of it exists
anywhere, what is to prevent the whole fabric from falling together, the
stars from going out, and chaos from recommencing her topsy-turvy reign?
Remarks of this sort about chance will put an end to discussion as
quickly as anything one can find. I have already told you that "chance"
was a word I wished to keep and use. Let us then examine exactly what
it means, and see whether it ought to be such a terrible bugbear to us. I
fancy that squeezing the thistle boldly will rob it of its sting.
The sting of the word "chance" seems to lie in the assumption that it
means something positive, and that if anything happens by chance, it must
needs be something of an intrinsically irrational and preposterous sort.
Now, chance means nothing of the kind. It is a purely negative and relative
term, giving us no information about that of which it is predicated, except
that it happens to be disconnected with something else—not controlled,
secured, or necessitated by other things in advance of its own actual
presence. At this point is the most subtle one of the whole lecture, and at
the same time the point on which all the rest hinges, I beg you to pay
particular attention to it. What I say is that it tells us nothing about what a
thing may be in itself to call it "chance." It may be a bad thing, it may be
a good thing. It may be lucidity, transparency, fitness incarnate, matching

the whole system of other things, when it has once befallen, in an unimaginably perfect way. All you mean by calling it "chance" is that this is not guaranteed, that it may also fall out otherwise. For the system of other things has no positive hold on the chance-thing. Its origin is in a certain fashion negative: it escapes, and says, "Hands off!" coming, when it comes, as a free gift, or not at all.

This negativeness, however, and this opacity of the chance-thing when thus considered *ab extra,* or from the point of view of previous things or distant things, do not preclude its having any amount of positiveness and luminosity from within, and at its own place and moment. All that its chance-character asserts about it is that there is something in it really of its own, something that is not the unconditional property of the whole. If the whole wants this property, the whole must wait till it can get it, if it be a matter of chance. That the universe may actually be a sort of joint-stock society of this sort, in which the sharers have both limited liabilities and limited powers, is of course a simple and conceivable notion.

Nevertheless, many persons talk as if the minutest dose of disconnectedness of one part with another, the smallest modicum of independence, the faintest tremor of ambiguity about the future, for example, would ruin everything, and turn this goodly universe into a sort of insane sand-heap or nulliverse—no universe at all. Since future human volitions are, as a matter of fact, the only ambiguous things we are tempted to believe in, let us stop for a moment to make ourselves sure whether their independent and accidental character need be fraught with such direful consequences to the universe as these.

What is meant by saying that my choice of which way to walk home after the lecture is ambiguous and matter of chance as far as the present moment is concerned? It means that both Divinity Avenue and Oxford Street are called; but that only one, and that one *either* one shall be chosen. Now, I ask you seriously to suppose that this ambiguity of my choice is real; and then to make the impossible hypothesis that the choice is made twice over, and each time falls on a different street. In other words, imagine that I first walk through Divinity Avenue, and then imagine that the powers governing the universe annihilate ten minutes of time with all that it contained, and set me back at the door of this hall just as I was before the choice was made. Imagine then that, everything else being the same, I now make a different choice and traverse Oxford Street. You, as passive spectators, look on and see the two alternative universes—one of them with me walking through Divinity Avenue in it, the other with the same me walking through Oxford Street. Now, if you are determinists you believe one of these universes to have been from eternity impossible: you believe it to have been impossible because of the intrinsic irrationality or accidentality somewhere involved in it. But looking outwardly at these universes, can you say which is the impossible and accidental one, and which the rational and necessary one? I doubt if the most iron-clad determinist among you could have the slightest glimmer of light at this point. In other words, either universe *after the fact* and once there would, to our means of observation and understanding, appear just as rational as the other. There would be absolutely no criterion by which we might judge one necessary and the other matter of chance. Suppose now we relieve the gods of their hypothetical task and assume my choice, once made, to be made forever. I go through Divinity Avenue for good and all. If, as good determinists, you now begin to affirm, what all good determinists punctually do affirm, that in the nature of things I couldn't have gone through Oxford Street—had I done so it would have been chance, irrationality, insanity, a horrid gap in nature—I simply call your attention to this, that your affirmation is what the Germans call a *Machtspruch,* a mere conception fulminated as a dogma and based on no insight into details. Before my choice, either street seemed as natural to you as to me. Had I happened to take Oxford Street, Divinity Avenue would have figured in your philosophy as the gap in nature; and you would have so proclaimed it with the best deterministic conscience in the world.

But what a hollow outcry, then, is this against a chance which, if it were present to us, we could by no character whatever distinguish from a rational necessity! I have taken the most trivial of examples, but no possible example could lead to any different result. For what are the alternatives which, in point of fact, offer themselves to human volition? What are those futures that now seem matters of chance? Are they not one and all like the Divinity Avenue and Oxford Street of our example? Are they not all of them *kinds* of things already here and based in the existing frame of nature? Is any one ever tempted to produce an *absolute* accident, something utterly irrelevant to the rest of the world? Do not all the motives that assail us, all the futures that offer themselves to our choice, spring equally from the soil of the past; and would not either one of them, whether realized through chance or through necessity, the moment it was realized, seem to us to fit that past, and in the completest and most continuous manner to interdigitate with the phenomena already there?

A favorite argument against free will is that if it be true, a man's murderer may as probably be his best friend as his worst enemy, a mother be as likely to strangle as to suckle her first-born, and all of us be as ready to jump from fourth-story windows as to go out of front doors, etc. Users of this argument should probably be excluded from debate till they learn what the real question is. "Free-will" does not say that everything that is physically conceivable is also morally possible. It merely says that of alternatives that really *tempt* our will more than one is really possible. Of course, the alternatives that do thus tempt our will are vastly fewer than the physical possibilities we can coldly fancy. Persons really tempted often do murder their best friends, mothers do strangle their first-born, people do jump out of fourth stories, etc.

The more one thinks of the matter, the more one wonders that so empty and gratuitous a hubbub as this outcry against chance should have found so great an echo in the hearts of men. It is a word which tells us absolutely nothing about what chances, or about the *modus operandi* of the chancing; and the use of it as a war-cry shows only a temper of intellectual absolutism, a demand that the world shall be a solid block, subject to one control—which temper, which demand, the world may not be bound to gratify at all. In every outwardly verifiable and practical respect, a world in which the alternatives that now actually distract *your* choice were decided by pure chance would be by *me* absolutely undistinguished from the world in which I now live. I am, therefore, entirely willing to call it, so far as your choices go, a world of chance for me. To *yourself*, it is true, those very acts of choice, which to me are so blind, opaque, and external, are the opposites of this, for you are within them and effect them. To you they appear as decisions; and decisions, for him who makes them, are altogether peculiar psychic facts. Self-luminous and self-justifying at the living moment in which they occur, they appeal to no outside moment to put its stamp upon them or make them continuous with the rest of nature. Themselves it is rather who seem to make nature continuous; and in their strange and intense function of granting consent to one possibility and withholding it from another, to transform an equivocal and double future into an inalterable and simple past.

But with the psychology of the matter we have no concern this evening. The quarrel which determinism has with chance fortunately has nothing to do with this or that psychological detail. It is a quarrel altogether metaphysical. Determinism denies the ambiguity of future volitions,, because it affirms that nothing future can be ambiguous. But we have said enough to meet the issue. Indeterminate future volitions *do* mean chance. Let us not fear to shout it from the house-tops if need be; for we now know that the idea of chance is, at bottom, exactly the same thing as the idea of gift—the one simply being a disparaging, and the other a eulogistic, name for anything on which we have no effective *claim*. And whether the world be the better or the worse for having either chances or gifts in it will depend altogether on *what* these uncertain and unclaimable things turn out to be.

The Moral Implications of Determinism

And this at last brings us wtihin sight of our subject. We have seen what determinism means: we have seen that indeterminism is rightly described as meaning chance; and we have seen that chance, the very name of which we are urged to shrink from as from a metaphysical pestilence, means only the negative fact that no part of the world, however big, can claim to control absolutely the destinies of the whole. But although, in discussing the word "chance," I may at moments have seemed to be arguing for its real existence, I have not meant to do so yet. We have not yet ascertained whether this be a world of chance or no; at most, we have agreed that it seems so. And I now repeat what I said at the outset, that, from any strict theoretical point of view, the question is insoluble. To deepen our theoretic sense of the *difference* between a world with chances in it and a deterministic world is the most I can hope to do; and this I may now at last begin upon, after all our tedious clearing of the way.

I wish first of all to show you just what the notion that this is a deterministic world implies. The implications I call your attention to are all bound up with the fact that it is a world in which we constantly have to make what I shall, with your permission, call judgments of regret. Hardly an hour passes in which we do not wish that something might be otherwise; and happy indeed are those of us whose hearts have never echoed the wish of Omar Khayyam—

> That we might clasp, ere closed, the book of fate,
>   And make the writer on a fairer leaf
> Inscribe our names, or quite obliterate.
>
> Ah! Love, could you and I with fate conspire
> To mend this sorry scheme of things entire,
>   Would we not shatter it to bits, and then
> Remould it nearer to the heart's desire?

Now, it is undeniable that most of these regrets are foolish, and quite on a par in point of philosophic value with the criticisms on the universe of that friend of our infancy, the hero of the fable, "The Atheist and the Acorn"—

> Fool! had that bough a pumpkin bore,
> Thy whimsies would have worked no more, etc.

Even from the point of view of our own ends, we should probably make a botch of remodelling the universe. How much more then from the point of view of ends we cannot see! Wise men therefore regret as little as they can. But still some regrets are pretty obstinate and hard to stifle—regrets for acts of wanton cruelty or treachery, for example, whether performed by others or by ourselves. Hardly any one can remain *entirely* optimistic after reading the confession of the murderer at Brockton the other day: how, to get rid of the wife whose continued existence bored him, he enveigled her into a deserted spot, shot her four times, and then, as she lay on the ground and said to him, "You didn't do it on purpose, did you dear?" replied, "No, I didn't do it on purpose," as he raised a rock and smashed her skull. Such an occurrence, with the mild sentence and self-satisfaction of the prisoner, is a field for a crop of regrets, which one need not take up in detail. We feel that, although a perfect mechanical fit to the rest of the universe, it is a bad moral fit, and that something else would really have been better in its place.

But for the deterministic philosophy the murder, the sentence, and the prisoner's optimsm were all necessary from eternity; and nothing else for a moment had a ghost of a chance of being put in their place. To admit such a chance, the determinists tell us, would be to make a suicide of reason; so we must steel our hearts against the thought. And here our plot thickens, for we see the first of those difficult implications of determinism and monism which it is my purpose to make you feel. If this Brockton murder was called for by the rest of the universe, if it had come at its preappointed hour, and if nothing else would have been consistent with the sense of the whole, what are we to think of the universe? Are we stubbornly to stick to our judgment of regret, and say, though it *couldn't* be, yet it *would* have been a better universe with something different from this Brockton murder in it? That, of course, seems the natural and spontaneous thing for us to do; and yet it is nothing short of deliberately espousing a kind of pessimism. The judgment of regret calls the murder bad. Calling a thing bad means, if it means anything at all, that the thing ought not be, that something else ought to be in its stead. Determinism, in denying that anything else can be in its stead, virtually defines the universe as a place in which what ought to be is impossible—in other words, as an organism whose constitution is afflicted with an incurable taint, and irremediable flaw. The pessimism of a Schopenhauer says no more than this—that the murder is a symptom; and that it is a vicious symptom because it belongs to a vicious whole, which can express its nature no otherwise than by bringing forth just such a symptom as that at this particular spot. Regret for the murder must transform itself, if we are determinists and wise, into a larger regret. It is absurd to regret the murder alone. Other things being what they are, *it* could not be different. What we should regret is that whole frame of things of which the murder is one member. I see no escape whatever from this pessimistic conclusion if, being determinists, our judgment of regret is to be allowed to stand at all.

The only deterministic escape from pessimism is everywhere to abandon the judgment of regret. That this can be done, history shows to be not impossible. The devil, *quoad existentiam,* may be good. That is, although he be a *principle* of evil, yet the universe, with such a principle in it, may practically be a better universe than it could have been without. On every hand, in a small way, we find that a certain amount of evil is a condition by which a higher form of good is brought. There is nothing to prevent anybody from generalizing this view, and trusting that if we could but see things in the largest of all ways, even such matters as this Brockton murder would appear to be paid for by the uses which follow in their train. An optimism *quand même,* a systematic and infatuated optimism like that ridiculed by Voltaire in his *Candide,* is one of the possible ideal ways in which a man may train himself to look upon life. Bereft of dogmatic hardness and lit up with the expression of a tender and pathetic hope, such an optimism has been the grace of some of the most religious characters that ever lived.

> Throb thine with Nature's throbbing breast,
> And all is clear from east to west.

Even cruelty and treachery may be among the absolutely blessed fruits of time, and to quarrel with any of their details may be blasphemy. The only real blasphemy, in short, may be that pessimistic temper of the soul which lets it give way to such things as regrets, remorse, and grief.

Thus, our deterministic pessimism may become a deterministic optimism at the price of extinguishing our judgments of regret.

But does not this immediately bring us into a curious logical predicament? Our determinism leads us to call our judgments of regret wrong, because they are pessimistic in implying that what is impossible yet ought to be. But how then about the judgments of regret themselves? If they are wrong, other judgments, judgments of approval presumably, ought to be in their place. But as they are necessitated, nothing else *can* be in their place; and the universe is just what it was before—namely, a place in which what ought to be appears impossible. We have got one foot out of the pessimistic bog, but the other one sinks all the deeper. We have rescued our actions from the bonds of evil, but our judgments are now held fast. When murders and treacheries cease to be sins, regrets are theoretic absurdities and errors. The theoretic and the active life thus play a kind of see-saw with each other on the ground of evil. The rise of either sends the other down. Murder and treachery cannot be good without regret being bad: regret cannot be good without treachery and murder being bad. Both, however, are supposed to have been foredoomed; so something must be fatally unreasonable, absurd, and wrong in the world. It must be a place of which either sin or error forms a necessary part. From this dilemma there seems at first sight no escape. Are we then so soon to fall back into the pessimism from which we thought we had emerged? And is there no possible way by which we may, with good intellectual consciences, call the cruelties and the treacheries, the reluctances and the regrets, *all* good together?

Certainly there is such a way, and you are probably most of you ready to formulate it yourselves. But, before doing so, remark how inevitably the question of determinism and indeterminism slides us into the question of optimism and pessimism, or, as our fathers called it, "The question of evil." The theological form of all these disputes is simplest and the deepest, the form from which there is the least escape—not because, as some have sarcastically said, remorse and regret are clung to with a morbid fondness by the theologians as spiritual luxuries, but because they are existing facts in the world, and as such must be taken into account in the deterministic interpretation of all that is fated to be. If they are fated to be error, does not the bat's wing of irrationality cast its shadow over the world? . . .

Morality and Indeterminism

The only consistent way of representing a pluralism and a world whose parts may affect one another through their conduct being either good or bad is the indeterministic way. What interest, zest, or excitement can there be in achieving the right way, unless we are enabled to feel that the wrong way is also a possible and a natural way—nay, more, a menacing and an imminent way? And what sense can there be in condemning ourselves for taking the wrong way, unless we need have done nothing of the sort, unless the right way was open to us as well? I cannot understand the willingness to act, no matter how we feel, without the belief that acts are really good and bad. I cannot understand the belief that an act is bad, without regret at its happening. I cannot understand regret without the admission of real, genuine possibilities in the world. Only then is it other than a mockery to feel, after we have failed to do our best, that an irreparable opportunity is gone from the universe, the loss of which it must forever after mourn.

If you insist that this is all superstition, that possibility is in the eye of science and reason impossibility, and that if I act badly 'tis that the unverse was foredoomed to suffer this defect, you fall right back into the dilemma, the labyrinth, of pessimism and subjectivism, from out of whose toils we have just wound our way.

Now, we are of course free to fall back, if we please. For my own part, though, whatever difficulties may beset the philosophy of objective right and wrong, and the indeterminism it seems to imply, determinism, with its alternative pessimism or romanticism, contains difficulties that are greater still. But you will remember that I expressly repudiated awhile ago the pretension to offer any arguments which could be coercive in a so-called scientific fashion in this matter. And I consequently find myself, at the end of this long talk, obliged to state my conclusions in an altogether personal way. This personal method of appeal seems to be among the very conditions of the problem; and the most any one can do is to confess as candidly as he can the grounds for the faith that is in him, and leave his example to work on others as it may.

Let me, then, without circumlocution say just this. The world is enigmatical enough in all conscience, whatever theory we may take up toward it. The indeterminsm I defend, the free-will theory of popular sense based on the judgment of regret, represents that world as vulnerable, and liable to be injured by certain of its parts if they act wrong. And it represents their acting wrong as a matter of possibility or accident, neither inevitable nor yet to be infallibly warded off. In all this, it is a theory devoid either of transparency or of stability. It gives us a pluralistic, restless universe, in which no single point of view can ever take in the whole scene; and to a mind possessed of the love of unity at any cost, it will, no doubt, remain forever inacceptable. A friend with such a mind once told me that the thought of my universe made him sick, like the sight of the horrible motion of a mass of maggots in their carrion bed.

But while I freely admit that the pluralism and the restlessness are repugnant and irrational in a certain way, I find that every alternative to them is irrational in a deeper way. The indeterminism with its maggots, if you please to speak so about it, offends only the native absolutism of my intellect—an absolutism which, after all, perhaps, deserves to be snubbed and kept in check. But the determinism with its necessary carrion, to continue the figure of speech, and with no possible maggots to eat the latter up, violates my senes of moral reality through and through. When, for example, I imagine such carrion as the Brockton murder, I cannot conceive it as an act by which the universe, as a whole, logically and necessarily expresses its nature without shrinking from complicity with such a whole. And I deliberately refuse to keep on terms of loyalty with the univesre by saying blankly that the murder, since it does flow from the nature of the whole, is not carrion. There are *some* instinctive reactions which I, for one, will not tamper with. The only remaining alternative, the attitude of gnostical romanticism, wrenches my personal instincts in quite as violent a way. It falsifies the simple objectivity of their deliverance. It makes the goose-flesh the murder excites in me a sufficient reason for the perpetration of the crime. It transforms life from a tragic reality into an insincere melodramatic exhibition, as foul or as tawdry as any one's diseased curiosity pleases to carry it out. And with its consecration of the *roman naturaliste* state of mind, and its enthronement of the baser crew of Parisian *littérateurs* among the eternally indispensable organs by which the infinite spirit of things attains to that subjective illumination which is the task of its life, it leaves me in presence of a sort of subjective carrion considerably more noisome than the objective carrion I called it in to take away.

No! better a thousand times, than such systematic corruption of our moral sanity, the plainest pessimism, so it be straightforward; but better far than that, the world of chance. Make as great an uproar about chance as you please, I know that chance means pluralism and nothing more. If some of the members of the pluralism are bad, the philosophy of pluralism, whatever broad views it may deny me, permits me, at least, to turn to the other members with a clean breast of affection and an unsophisticated moral sense. And if I still wish to think of the world as a totality, it lets me feel that a world with a chance in it of being altogether good, even if the chance never come to pass, is better than a world with no such chance at all. That "chance" whose very notion I am exhorted and conjured to banish from my view of the future as the suicide of reason concerning it, that "chance" is—what? Just this—the chance that in moral respects the future may be other and better than the past has been. This is the only chance we have any motive for supposing to exist. Shame, rather, on its repudiation and its denial! For its presence is the vital air which lets the world live, the salt which keeps it sweet. . . .

4   Responsibility and
Absolute Choice

by H. D. Lewis

THE WORD "RESPONSIBILITY" MEANT at first liability to answer, and this carried with it the implication that if the answer was not satisfactory, if we could not give a proper account of our deeds, we were liable to be punished or proceeded against in some way. This is still the meaning of the word in law. To be legally responsible is to be the sort of person who may be punished in certain contingencies.

Law and Morality

But law is one thing, morality another. We can be vicious in many ways without breaking the law, and history and fiction are full of examples of people who have done abominable things, or acted in a mean and detestable spirit, while keeping well within the law. We may likewise be legally guilty and morally innocent. This might happen if we broke the law in genuine ignorance of which it would not be practicable to take account, as the courts would normally do; but we may break the law deliberately and deserve high praise for it. Those who disobeyed Nazi laws in our time preferring to suffer death or brutality in concentration camps, have earned our lasting esteem.

Normally the instrument of reform is persuasion, and where there is proper scope for this, the duty to conform is very high indeed. Law-abiding procedure is usually more important than righting a particular wrong, and no one should forget that to have a right is not the same thing as having a right to insist on that right. If we took the law into our own hands, as officials or private citizens, the moment we thought there was injustice there would be chaos. Appreciation of this, and respect for constitutional pro-

[This article first appeared under the title "Legal and Moral Responsibility" in *The Listener* on October 26, 1961. It is reprinted with the author's permission.]

cedure, is an important feature of British tradition and history, and that presents one of the main ways in which we may contribute to world affairs today. We are perhaps a little unmindful of this heritage at present and too prone to resort to unconstitutional methods, in industrial disputes for example, the moment we think our rights or privileges are endangered. On the other hand it is impressive how much radical change has been brought about (one might almost say a social revolution), in medical service or the nationalization of industries, for example, despite sharp and indeed bitter opposition on the part of a large section of the community—and yet without violence or disorder.

A point may, however, be reached, even in democracies, where the individual must obey his own conscience rather than the law. Each one must finally decide for himself where this point is reached—for the pacifist it comes if he is asked to fight or to support a war. But no one is morally infallible, neither the majority nor the minority; the lone individual may be a crank or an inspired reformer. There *is* a right and wrong to our disputes, the truth is there to seek, but no one has an absolute monopoly of it. We have thus to weigh the issue carefully and with much searching of heart before we try the strong medicine of resistance or disobedience, and if we feel impelled to do so we shall do well to consider the extreme good sense and humility with which Sir Thomas More came reluctantly but bravely to the point of being "the king's good servant, but God's first."

It should be added that moral worth will not turn on the soundness of our judgment, in these or other matters, but on our integrity and firmness. A person may be outwardly wrong to disobey the law, but inwardly or morally justified. In these ways then it becomes plain that law is one thing, morality another. The more the law conforms to ethical standards the better, but there are many moral matters which it would be foolish to try to enforce by law.

Legal responsibility is liability to punishment. Does punishment come into moral responsibility? I should like here to refer to the three main ways in which we usually think of punishment—as retributive, reformative, or deterrent. On the retributive view there is some inherent suitability in punishment, the deed calls for it for its own sake as it were. This must not be confused with vengeance which is for the satisfaction of our own feelings. But even so, and in spite of my regard for the eminent people of today and the past who hold the retributive view, I do not myself see that the situation of wrongdoing is directly improved by the infliction of pain on the offender. I also doubt whether punishment brings about much genuine reform. The more we can combine with punishment other measures for reform the better, but these—being allowed books or taught a trade or having visits from the chaplain—are amenities or ameliorations, not part of the punishment proper. The suffering as such may indeed induce a man "to go straight in the future"—that is the main point of it. But does it make him genuinely sorry, and how often? I leave this fairly open, but for me the whole justification of punishment tends to be deterrence.

We do not, in strictness, have to choose between these theories; they are not exclusive, and many still think that all three elements come into punishment. I incline to allow only the factor of deterrence, to make it, in famous words, "a bad bargain for the offender," including of course would-be offenders; and even if retribution were inherently appropriate I do not see how one could apply it without knowing a good deal more about one another's hearts than is possible for us or necessary for the inevitably rough-and-ready business of enforcing the law.

Punishment and Freedom

Many who share this view are apt to take a further step. They observe that we could make good sense of punishment as deterrence even if our conduct were determined, provided we were physically free and knew what we were doing, and so on. For the fact that I had to do what I did, being the sort of person I was at the time, would not prevent the punishment I receive from affecting my conduct, or that of others, on some future occasion. We house-train puppies on a similar basis. It is then added that moral responsibility is in essentials like legal responsibility, it also consists in liability to punishment of some sort; and since punishment as deterrence is compatible with determinism we seem to have here an easy solvent of the old problem of free will. It was in fact a pseudo-problem all along.

This seems to me gravely mistaken. It implies, as its advocates themselves sometimes stress, that there is no difference between the kleptomaniac and the thief except that the conduct of the thief can be affected by punishment; and this leaves out what matters most about moral accountability. For whether moral guilt calls for punishment or not, that is not the main thing about it; moral responsibility is prior to punishment, and it calls for a sort of freedom which is not disclosed, but rather obscured, by easy assimilation of morality to law. This is best brought out if we consider the sharp distinction we draw between moral and non-moral estimates of worth. Pain is a non-moral evil. You do not think the worse of me if I am in pain, you sympathize with me and help. You rejoice when I am well and happy again. We likewise think it a good thing to be an athlete, or a poet, or a gifted mathematician. We are sorry when people are stupid or inept, but we do not think ill of them or blame them provided they try their best. Few of us understand higher mathematics, but we do not feel guilty on that account.

Moral badness, in short, is entirely different from any other badness; and moral goodness is different from other things also good in themselves. To be a poet, or to enjoy poetry, is a fine thing, but it is not at all the same sort of fine thing as being a good man; and the root difference here turns on the special freedom we have to be good or bad in the moral sense. There is freedom in art or the attainment of knowledge, indeed there are many sorts of freedom, superb in their way. But the freedom which makes us morally good or bad, which gives point to what we say or feel about wickedness, is a freedom of choice, not in the sense of having a certain aptitude, physical or intellectual, but in the sense that we could have done other than we did, although everything else, including our own nature at the time, were the same. It is an ultimate, absolute choice.

The Areas of Absolute Choice

But, you may object, this is absurd. No one has such a choice. We act in character, we rely on one another, and life would be impossible if we did not. I come to the studio to broadcast, expecting the producer, barring accidents, to be here; he expects me and has every reason to assume that, unless I become suddenly delirious, I will give my talk and not break into song or stand on my head in the middle. We do not, in short, expect "any action of any man at any time." There is obvious continuity of character and conduct, and although we miscalculate at times, we also know very largely what to expect of one another. Free will, as absolute choice, seems thus absurd.

It would be absurd if it meant that we could act out of character at *any* time and in *any* regard. That is the absurdity of which the libertarian is often accused. But he is rarely guilty of it, little though his critics today seem to think so. He only holds that there are some respects, and some occasions, when we have "absolute choice," and these are set for us when properly moral matters are involved. If, on the whole, I most want to do one thing, but think it my duty to do something else, then, and then only, it seems to me, I have a choice not determined by character or heredity or environment or anything else. I may do my duty or I may not. The possibilities are genuinely and finally "open." It is not genuinely open to me to burst into song in the broadcasting studio. Physically, I could, but I have not the slightest urge to make a fool of myself in that way. It is plainly not my duty to do so. In the last resort, being the person I am in these circumstances, I am bound to continue my talk to the end. In different conditions, offered a sufficiently large bribe, I might prefer to sing instead, and I might think it a duty to do so if a sufficiently handsome donation were made in return to some important cause.

In the latter case, and perhaps in the first, there would be a real conflict of duty and interest, as there would be, to take a more serious example, if the building were on fire or being bombed and there was reason, as in the war, why the broadcast should continue. I might, in this case, most want to run from danger and have thus to make a moral effort to resist the temptation to escape and to overcome my fear. It is the choice to make or not make, such an effort that is free, and moral worth or disvalue turns on the effort we make, or fail to make, in situations of this sort, not directly on the outward nature of the action.

The conditions in which we exercise choice vary much from one person to another; some would be less frightened than others, for example, if the building were on fire, or more impressed by possibilities of glory or reward. Only the individual himself knows when the supports are inadequate, when character as a whole, and not merely in part, is too weak to induce us by nature to act as we should, and when thus only a moral effort can make us do right. The temptations of one man are not those of another, or of the same man at some other time. The temptations of Tolstoy were not those of Gandhi. For most of us stealing is no temptation; putting it at its lowest the risks to our jobs and reputations are too obvious. But many people are tempted to steal, and we might be tempted too in some situations. Some people are, again, by nature benevolent and patient, others more sensitive, and so on. And the call of duty upon us will vary much in these ways, and according to circumstances. But that we should continue to regard ourselves as responsible beings liable to have to make excruciating moral choices, and not merely be deciding what our preferences are, is of the utmost importance for the worth and dignity of human life as a whole, and for the health of society.

This is not altered if we find that, for certain practical purposes, all we need consider is the reasonableness of a penalty as a deterrent. Let us, by all means, have enlightened or humanitarian views of the treatment of crime. The moral guilt of the criminal, and of all of us in what we do wrong, remains. This may be hard to assess, but it must not be overlooked, even in the courts. It would be absurd for a judge, in sentencing a criminal, to address him as if he were like some unfortunate person who had a highly infectious illness and had to be compulsorily isolated. The criminal has normally brought his punishment on himself by moral as well as legal wrong-doing; he is not just a case to be treated, and it is not for his own good or that of others to think so. The judge is the mouthpiece of the community, and the court, like the pulpit, is a place where the moral quality of conduct is to be upheld and the sense of moral responsibility deepened. But this must be done without smugness or suggesting that crime is the only form of wickedness; nor should it affect the form and degree of the penalty.

There are also difficult pathological cases where it is hard to assign responsibility. Perhaps these are not as common as some writers suggest. Most of us are fully accountable most of the time; and whatever we say of hard cases, we need, most of all in times of stress and confusion, to have the sense of ultimate moral responsibility maintained. To this end we have much to counter in current theology as well as in social science and psychology, and it is for each one to help in his own way by closer heed to that part of our responsibility which consists in considering carefully where our own precise responsibilities lie.

5   Of Liberty and Necessity

John Stuart Mill

Are Human Actions Subject to the Law of Causality?

T HE QUESTION WHETHER THE LAW OF causality applies in the same strict sense to human actions as to other phenomena, is the celebrated controversy concerning the freedom of the will, which, from at least as far back as the time of Pelagious, has divided both the philosophical and the religious world. The affirmative opinion is commonly called the doctrine of Necessity, as asserting human volitions and actions to be necessary and inevitable. The negative maintains that the will is not determined, like other phenomena, by antecedents, but determines itself; that our volitions are not, properly speaking, the effects of causes, or at least have no causes which they uniformly and implicitly obey.

I have already made it sufficiently apparent that the former of these opinions is that which I consider the true one; but the misleading terms in which it is often expressed, and the indistinct manner in which it is usually apprehended, have both obstructed its reception and perverted its influence when received. The metaphysical theory of free-will, as held by philosophers (for the practical feeling of it, common in a greater or less degree to all mankind, is in no way inconsistent with the contrary theory), was invented because the supposed alternative of admitting human actions to be *necessary* was deemed inconsistent with everyone's instinctive consciousness, as well as humiliating to the pride, even degrading to the moral nature of man. Nor do I deny that the doctrine, as sometimes held, is open to these imputations; for the misapprehension in which I shall be able to show that they originate unfortunately is not

[This selection comprises all of Chapter 2, Book VI, of *A System of Logic,* which was published in 1843.]

confined to the opponents of the doctrine, but is participated in by many, perhaps we might say by most, of its supporters.

The Doctrine of Philosophical Necessity

Correctly conceived, the doctrine entitled Philosophical Necessity is simply this: that, given the motives which are present to an individual's mind, and given likewise the character and disposition of the individual, the manner in which he will act might be unerringly inferred; that if we knew the person thoroughly, and knew all the inducements which are acting upon him, we could foretell his conduct with as much certainty as we can predict any physical event. This positions I take to be a mere interpretation of universal experience, a statement in words of what everyone is internally convinced of. No one who believed that he knew thoroughly the circumstances of any case, and the characters of the different persons concerned, would hesitate to foretell how all of them would act. Whatever degree of doubt he may in fact feel arises from the uncertainty whether he really knows the circumstances, or the character of someone or other of the persons, with the degree of accuracy required; but by no means from thinking that if he did know these things, there could be an uncertainty what the conduct should be. Nor does this full assurance conflict in the smallest degree with what is called our feeling of freedom. We do not feel ourselves the less free because those to whom we are intimately known are well assured how we shall will to act in a particular case. We often, on the contrary, regard the doubt of what our conduct will be as a mark of ignorance of our characters, and sometimes even resent it as an imputation. The religious metaphysicians who have asserted the freedom of the will have always maintained it to be consistent with divine foreknowledge of our actions; and if with divine, then with any other foreknowledge. We may bree, and yet another may have reason to be perfectly certain what use we shall make of our freedom. It is not, therefore, the doctrine that our volitions and actions are invariable consequents of our antecedent states of mind, that is either contradicted by our consciousness or felt to be degrading.

But the doctrine of causation, when considered as obtaining between our volitions and their antecedents, is almost universally conceived as involving more than this. Many do not believe, and very few practically feel, that there is nothing in causation but invariable, certain, and unconditional sequence. There are few to whom mere constancy of succession appears a sufficiently stringent bond of union for so peculiar a relation as that of cause and effect. Even if the reason repudiates, the imagination retains, the feeling of some more intimate connection, of some peculiar tie or mysterious constraint exercised by the antecedent over the consequent. Now this it is which, considered as applying to the human will, conflicts with our consciousness and revolts our feelings. We are certain that, in the case of our volitions, there is not this mysterious constraint. We know that we are not compelled, as by a magical spell, to obey any particular motives. We feel that if we wished to prove that we have the power of resisting the motive, we could do so, (that wish being, it needs scarcely be observed, a *new antecedent*); and it would be humiliating to our pride, and (what is of more importance) paralyzing to our desire of excellence, if we thought otherwise. But neither is any such mysterious compulsion now supposed, by the best philosophical authorities, to be exercised by any other cause over its effect. Those who think that causes draw their effects after them by a mystical tie are right in believing that the relation between volitions and their antecedents is of another nature. But they should go farther, and admit that this is also true of all other effects and their antecedents. If such a tie is considered to be involved in the word necessity, the doctrine is not true of human actions; but neither is it then true of inanimate objects. It would be more correct to say that matter is not bound by necessity, than that mind is so.

That the free-will metaphysicians, being mostly of the school which rejects Hume's and Brown's analysis of Cause and Effect, should miss their way for want of the light which that analysis affords, cannot surprise us. The wonder is, that the Necessitarians, who usually admit that philosophical theory, should in practice equally lose sight of it. The very same misconception of the doctrine called Philosophical Necessity which prevents the opposite party from recognising its truth, I believe to exist more or less obscurely in the minds of most Necessitarians, however they may in words disavow it. I am much mistaken if they habitually feel that the necessity which they recognise in actions is but uniformity of order, and capability of being predicted. They have a feeling as if there were at bottom a stronger tie between the volitions and their causes: as if, when they asserted that the will is governed by the balance of motives, they meant something more cogent than if they had only said, that whoever knew the motives, and our habitual susceptibilities to them, could predict how we should will to act. They commit, in opposition to their own scientific system, the very same mistake which their adversaries commit in obedience to theirs; and in consequence do really in some instances suffer those depressing consequences which their opponents erroneously impute to the doctrine itself.

Pernicious Effect of the Term "Necessity"

I am inclined to think that this error is almost wholly an effect of the associations with a word, and that it would be prevented by forebearing to employ, for the expression of the simple fact of causation, so extremely inappropriate a term as Necessity. That word, in its other acceptations, involves much more than mere uniformity of sequence: it implies irresistibleness. Applied to the will, it only means that the given cause will be followed by the effect, subject to all possibilities of counteraction by other causes; but in common use it stands for the operation of those causes exclusively, which are supposed too powerful to be counteracted at all. When we say that all human actions take place of necessity, we only mean that they will certainly happen if nothing prevents:—when we say that dying of want, to those who cannot get food, is a necessity, we mean that it will certainly happen, whatever may be done to prevent it. The application of the same term to the agencies on which human actions depend as is used to express those agencies of nature which are really uncontrollable, cannot fail, when habitual, to create a feeling of uncontrollableness in the former also. This, however, is a mere illusion. There are physical sequences which we call necessary as death for want of food or air; there are others which, though as much cases of causation as the former, are not said to be necessary, as death from poison, which an antidote, or the use of the stomach pump, will sometimes avert. It is apt to be forgotten by people's feelings, even if remembered by their understandings, that human actions are in this last predicament: they are never (except in some cases of mania) ruled by any one motive with such absolute sway that there is no room for the influence of any other. The causes, therefore, on which action depends are never uncontrollable, and any given effect is only necessary provided that the causes tending to produce it are not controlled. That whatever happens could not have happened otherwise unless something had taken place which was capable of preventing it, no one surely needs hesitate to admit. But to call this by the name necessity is to use the term in a sense so different from its primitive and familiar meaning, from that which it bears in the common occasions of life, as to amount almost to a play upon words. The associations derived from the ordinary sense of the term will adhere to it in spite of all we can do; and though the doctrine of Necessity, as stated by most who hold it, is very remote from fatalism, it is probable that most Necessitarians are Fatalists, more or less, in their feelings.

A Fatalist believes, or half believes (for nobody is a consistent Fatalist), not only that whatever is about to happen will be the infallible result of the causes which produce it (which is the true Necessitarian doctrine), but, moreover, that there is no use in struggling against it; that it will happen however we may strive to prevent it. Now, a Necessitarian, believing that our actions follow from our characters, and that our characters follow from our organisation, our education, and our circumstances, is apt to be, with more or less of consciousness on his part, a Fatalist as to his own actions, and to believe that his nature is such, or that his education and circumstances have so moulded his character, that nothing can now prevent him from feeling and acting in a particular way, or at least that no effort of his own can hinder it. In the

words of the sect* which in our own day has most perseveringly incul-
cated and most perversely misunderstood this great doctrine, his character is formed *for* him, and not *by* him; therefore his wishing that it
had been formed differently is of no use; he has no power to alter it. But
this is a grand error. He has, to a certain extent, a power to alter his
character. Its being, in the ultimate resort, formed for him, is not inconsistent with its being, in part, formed *by* him as one of the intermediate
agents. His character is formed by his circumstances (including among
these his particular organisation), but his own desire to mould it in a
particular way is one of these circumstances, and by no means one of
the least influential. We cannot, indeed, directly will to be different from
what we are; but neither did those who are supposed to have formed
our characters directly will that we should be what we are. Their will
had no direct power except over their own actions. They made us what
they did make us by willing, not the end, but the requisite means; and
we, when our habits are not too inveterate, can, by similarly willing the
requisite means, make ourselves different. If they could place us under
the influence of certain circumstances, we in like manner can place
ourselves under the influence of other circumstances. We are exactly as
capable of making our own character, *if we will,* as others are of making
it for us.

Yes (answers the Owenite), but these words, "if we will," surrender
the whole point, since the will to alter our own character is given us,
not by any efforts of ours, but by circumstances which we cannot help;
it comes to us either from external causes or not at all. Most true: if the
Owenite stop here, he is in a position from which nothing can expel
him. Our character is formed by us as well as for us; but the wish which
induces us to attempt to form it is formed for us; and how? Not, in
general, by our organisation, nor wholly by our education, but by our
experience—experience of the painful consequences of the character we
previously had, or by some strong feeling of admiration or aspiration
accidentally aroused. But to think that we have no power of altering our
character, and to think that we shall not use our power unless we desire
to use it, are very different things, and have a very different effect on
the mind. A person who does not wish to alter his character cannot be
the person who is supposed to feel discouraged or paralysed by thinking
himself unable to do it. The depressing effect of the Fatalist doctrine can
only be felt where there *is* a wish to do what that doctrine represents
as impossible. It is of no consequence what we think forms our character, when we have no desire of our own about forming it, but it is of
great consequence that we should not be prevented from forming such
a desire by thinking the attainment impracticable, and that if we have the
desire we should know that the work is not so irrevocably done as to
be incapable of being altered.

* Mill here refers to the social reformer Robert Owen (1771–1858) and his followers.
(Eds.)

And, indeed, if we examine closely, we shall find that this feeling, of our being able to modify our own character *if we wish,* is itself the feeling of moral freedom which we are conscious of. A person feels morally free who feels that his habits or his temptations are not his masters, but he theirs: who even in yielding to them knows that he could resist; that were he desirous of altogether throwing them off, there would not be required for that purpose a stronger desire than he knows himself to be capable of feeling. It is of course necessary, to render our consciouness of freedom complete, that we should have succeeded in making our character all we have hitherto attempted to make it; for if we have wished and not attained, we have, to that extent, not power over our own character—we are not free. Or at least, we must feel that our wish, if not strong enough to alter our character, is strong enough to conquer our character when the two are brought into conflict in any particular case of conduct. And hence it is said with truth, that none but a person of confirmed virtue is completely free.

The application of so improper a term as Necessity to the doctrine of cause and effect in the matter of human character seems to me one of the most signal instances in philosophy of the abuse of terms, and its practical consequences one of the most striking examples of the power of language over our associations. The subject will never be generally understood until that objectionable term is dropped. The free-will doctrine, by keeping in view precisely that portion of the truth which the word Necessity puts out of sight, namely, the power of the mind to co-operate in the formation of its own character, has given to its adherents a practical feeling much nearer to the truth than has generally (I believe) existed in the minds of Necessitarians. The latter may have had a stronger sense of the importance of what human beings can do to shape the characters of one another; but the free-will doctrine has, I believe, fostered in its supporters a much stronger spirit of self-culture.

A Motive Not Always the Anticipation of Pleasure or Pain

There is still one fact which requires to be noticed (in addition to the existence of a power of self-formation) before the doctrine of the causation of human actions can be freed from the confusion and misapprehensions which surround it in many minds. When the will is said to be determined by motives, a motive does not mean always, or solely, the anticipation of a pleasure or of a pain. I shall not here inquire whether it be true that, in the commencements, all our voluntary actions are mere means consciously employed to obtain some pleasure or avoid some pain. It is at least certain that we gradually, through the influence of association, come to desire the means without thinking of the end: the action itself becomes an object of desire, and is performed without reference to any motive beyond itself. Thus far, it may still be objected, that the action having through association become pleasurable, we are, as much as before, moved to act by the anticipation of a pleasure, namely, the pleasure of the action itself. But granting this, the matter does not end here. As we proceed in the formation of habits, and become accustomed to will a particular act or a particular course of conduct because it is pleasurable, we at last continue to will it without any reference to its being pleasurable. Although, from some change in us or in our circumstances, we have ceased to find any pleasure in the action, or perhaps to anticipate any pleasure as the consequence of it, we still continue to desire the action, and consequently to do it. In this manner it is that habits of hurtful excess continue to be practised although they have ceased to be pleasurable; and in this manner also it is that the habit of willing to persevere in the course which he has chosen does not desert the moral hero, even when the reward, however real, which he doubtless receives from the consciousness of well-doing, is anything but an equivalent for the sufferings he undergoes or the wishes which he may have to renounce.

A habit of willing is commonly called a purpose; and among the causes of our volitions, and of the actions which flow from them, must be reckoned not only likings and aversions, but also purposes. It is only when our purposes have become independent of the feelings of pain or pleasure from which they originally took their rise that we are said to have a confirmed character. "A character," says Novalis, "is a completely fashioned will"; and the will, once so fashioned, may be steady and constant, when the passive susceptibilities of pleasure and pain are greatly weakened or materially changed.

With the corrections and explanations now given, the doctrine of the causation of our volitions by motives, and of motives by the desirable objects offered to us, combined without particular susceptibilities of desire, may be considered, I hope, as sufficiently established for the purposes of this treatise.

6   When Is a Man Responsible?

Moritz Schlick

WITH HESITATION AND RELUCTANCE
I prepare to add this chapter to the discussion of ethical problems. For in
it I must speak of a matter which, even at present, is thought to be a fundamental ethical problem, but which got into ethics and has become a much
discussed problem only because of a misunderstanding. This is the so-called
problem of the freedom of the will. Moreover, this pseudo-problem has long
since been settled by the efforts of certain sensible persons; and, above all,
the state of affairs just described has been often disclosed—with exceptional
clarity by Hume. Hence it is really one of the greatest scandals of philosophy that again and again so much paper and printer's ink is devoted to this
matter, to say nothing of the expenditure of thought, which could have
been applied to more important problems (assuming that it would have
sufficed for these). Thus I should truly be ashamed to write a chapter on
"freedom." In the chapter heading, the word "responsible" indicates what
concerns ethics, and designates the point at which misunderstanding arises.
Therefore the concept of responsibility constitutes our theme, and if in
the process of its clarification I must also speak of the concept of freedom
I shall, of course, say only what others have already said better; consoling
myself with the thought that in this way alone can anything be done to put
an end at last to that scandal.

The main task of ethics is to explain moral behavior. To explain means
to refer back to laws: every science, including psychology, is possible only
in so far as there are such laws to which the events can be referred. Since
the assumption that all events are subject to universal laws is called the
principle of causality, one can also say, "Every science presupposes the
principle of causality." Therefore every explanation of human behavior
must also assume the validity of causal laws; in this case the existence of

[This selection consists of Chapter 7 of Schlick's *Problems of Ethics,* with the omission
of one short paragraph. It is here reprinted with the kind permission of Prentice-Hall, Inc.,
New York. The translation is by David Rynin. The English translation of this book appeared
in 1939, the book itself was published in Vienna in 1931.]

psychological laws. All of our experience strengthens us in the belief that this presupposition is realized, at least to the extent required for all purposes of practical life in intercourse with nature and human beings, and also for the most precise demands of technique. Whether, indeed, the principle of causality holds universally, whether, that is, determinism is true, we do not know; no one knows. But we do know that it is impossible to settle the dispute between determinism and indeterminism by mere reflection and speculation, by the consideration of so many reasons for and so many reasons against (which collectively and individually are but pseudo-reasons). Such an attempt becomes especially ridiculous when one considers with what enormous expenditure of experimental and logical skill contemporary physics carefully approaches the question of whether causality can be maintained for the most minute intra-atomic events. . . .

Fortunately, it is not necessary to lay claim to a final solution of the causal problem in order to say what is necessary in ethics concerning responsibility; there is required only an analysis of the concept, the careful determination of the meaning which is in fact joined to the words "responsibility" and "freedom," as these are actually used. If men had made clear to themselves the sense of these propositions, which we use in everyday life, that pseudo-argument which lies at the root of the pseudo-problem, and which recurs thousands of times within and outside philosophical books, would never have arisen.

The argument runs as follows: "If determinism is true, if, that is, all events obey immutable laws, then my will too is always determined, by my innate character and my motives. Hence my decisions are necessary, not free. But if so, then I am not responsible for my acts, for I would be accountable for them only if I could do something about the way my decisions went; but I can do nothing about it, since they proceed with necessity from my character and the motives. And I have made neither, and have no power over them: the motives come from without, and my character is the necessary product of the innate tendencies and the external influences which have been effective during my lifetime. Thus determinism and moral responsibility are incompatible. Moral responsibility presupposes freedom, that is, exemption from causality."

This process of reasoning rests upon a whole series of confusions, just as the links of a chain hang together. We must show these confusions to be such, and thus destroy them.

Two Meanings of the Word "Law"

It all begins with an erroneous interpretation of the meaning of "law." In practice this is understood as a rule by which the state prescribes certain behavior to its citizens. These rules often contradict the natural desires of the citizens (for if they did not do so, there would be no reason for making them), and are in fact not followed by many of them; while others obey, but under compulsion. The state does in fact compel its citizens by imposing certain sanctions (punishment) which serve to bring their desires into harmony with the prescribed laws.

In natural science, on the other hand, the word "law" means something quite different. The natural law is not a prescription as to how something should behave, but a formula, a description of how something does in fact behave. The two forms of "laws" have only this in common: both tend to be expressed in formulae. Otherwise they have absolutely nothing to do with one another, and it is very blameworthy that the same word has been used for two such different things; but even more so that philosophers have allowed themselves to be led into serious errors by this usage. Since natural laws are only descriptions of what happens, there can be in regard to them no talk of "compulsion." The laws of celestial mechanics do not prescribe to the planets how they have to move, as though the planets would actually like to move quite otherwise, and are only forced by these burdensome laws of Kepler to move in orderly paths; no, these laws do not in any way "compel" the planets, but express only what in fact planets actually do.

If we apply this to volition, we are enlightened at once, even before the other confusions are discovered. When we say that a man's will "obeys psychological laws," these are not civic laws, which compel him to make certain decisions, or dictate desires to him, which he would in fact prefer not to have. They are laws of nature, merely expressing which desires he actually has under given conditions; they describe the nature of the will in the same manner as the astronomical laws describe the nature of planets. "Compulsion" occurs where man is prevented from realizing his natural desires. How could the rule according to which these natural desires arise itself be considered as "compulsion"?

Compulsion and Necessity

But this is the second confusion to which the first leads almost inevitably: after conceiving the laws of nature, anthropomorphically, as order imposed *nolens volens* upon the events, one adds to them the concept of "necessity." This word, derived from "need," also comes to us from practice, and is used there in the sense of inescapable compulsion. To apply the word with this meaning to natural laws is of course senseless, for the presupposition of an opposing desire is lacking, and it is then confused with something altogether different, which is actually an attribute of natural laws. That is, universality. It is of the essence of natural laws to be universally valid, for only when we have found a rule which holds of events without exception do we call the rule a law of nature. Thus when we say "a natural law holds necessarily" this has but one legitimate meaning: "It holds in all cases where it is applicable." It is again very deplorable that the word "necessary" has been applied to natural laws (or, what amounts to the same thing, with reference to causality), for it is quite superfluous, since the expression "universally valid" is available. Universal validity is something altogether different from "compulsion"; these concepts belong to spheres so remote from each other that once insight into the error has been gained one can no longer conceive the possibility of a confusion.

The confusion of two concepts always carries with it the confusion of their contradictory opposites. The opposite of the universal validity of a formula, of the existence of a law, is the nonexistence of a law, indeterminism, acausality; while the opposite of compulsion is what in practice everyone calls "freedom." Here emerges the nonsense, trailing through centuries, that freedom means "exemption from the causal principle," or "not subject to the laws of nature." Hence it is believed necessary to vindicate indetermininism in order to save human freedom.

Freedom and Indeterminism

This is quite mistaken. Ethics has, so to speak, no moral interest in the purely theoretical question of "determinism or indeterminism," but only a theoretical interest, namely: in so far as it seeks the laws of conduct, and can find them only to the extent that causality holds. But the question of whether man is morally free (that is, has that freedom which, as we shall show, is the presupposition of moral responsibility) is altogether different from the problem of determinism. Hume was especially clear on this point. He indicated the inadmissible confusion of the concepts of "indeterminism" and "freedom"; but he retained, inappropriately, the word "freedom" for both, calling the one freedom of "the will," the other genuine kind, "freedom of conduct." He showed that morality is interested only in the latter, and that such freedom, in general, is unquestionably to be attributed to mankind. And this is quite correct. Freedom means the opposite of compulsion; a man is free if he does not act under compulsion, and he is compelled or unfree when he is hindered from without in the realization of his natural desires. Hence he is unfree when he is locked up, or chained, or when someone forces him at the point of a gun to do what otherwise he would not do. This is quite clear, and everyone will admit that the everyday or legal notion of the lack of freedom is thus correctly interpreted, and that a man will be considered quite free and responsible if no such external compulsion is exerted upon him. There are certain cases which lie between these clearly described ones, as, say, when someone acts under the influence of alcohol or a narcotic. In such cases we consider the man to be more or less unfree, and hold him less accountable, because we rightly view the influence of the drug as "external," even though it is found within the body; it prevents him from making decisions in the manner peculiar to his nature. If he takes the narcotic of his own will, we make him completely responsible for this act and transfer a part of the responsibility to the consequences, making, as it were, an average or mean condemnation of the whole. In the case of a person who is mentally ill we do not consider him free with respect to those acts in which the disease expresses itself, because we view the illness as a disturbing factor which hinders the normal functioning of his natural tendencies. We make not him but his disease responsible.

The Nature of Responsibility

But what does this really signify? What do we mean by this concept of responsibility which goes along with that of "freedom," and which plays such an important role in morality? It is easy to attain complete clarity in this matter; we need only carefully determine the manner in which the concept is used. What is the case in practice when we impute "responsibility" to a person? What is our aim in doing this? The judge has to discover who is responsible for a given act in order that he may punish him. We are inclined to be less concerned with the inquiry as to who deserves reward for an act, and we have no special officials for this; but of course the principle would be the same. But let us stick to punishment in order to make the idea clear. What is punishment, actually? The view still often expressed, that it is a natural retaliation for past wrong, ought no longer to be defended in cultivated society; for the opinion that an increase in sorrow can be "made good again" by further sorrow is altogether barbarous. Certainly the origin of punishment may lie in an impulse of retaliation or vengeance; but what is such an impulse except the instinctive desire to destroy the cause of the deed to be avenged, by the destruction of or injury to the malefactor? Punishment is concerned only with the institution of causes, of motives of conduct, and this alone is its meaning. Punishment is an educative measure, and as such is a means to the formation of motives, which are in part to prevent the wrongdoer from repeating the act (reformation) and in part to prevent others from committing a similar act (intimidation). Analogously, in the case of reward we are concerned with an incentive.

Hence the question regarding responsibility is the question: Who in a given case, is to be punished? Who is to be considered the true wrongdoer? This problem is not identical with that regarding the original instigator of the act; for the great-grandparents of the man, from whom he inherited his character, might in the end be the cause, or the statesmen who are responsible for his social milieu, and so forth. But the "doer" is the one upon whom the motive must have acted in order, with certainty, to have prevented the act (or called it forth, as the case may be). Consideration of remote causes is of no help here, for in the first place their actual contribution cannot be determined, and in the second place they are generally out of reach. Rather, we must find the person in whom the decisive junction of causes lies. The question of who is responsible is the question concerning the correct point of application of the motive. And the important thing is that in this its meaning is completely exhausted; behind it there lurks no mysterious connection between transgression and requital, which is merely indicated by the described state of affairs. It is a matter only of knowing who is to be punished or rewarded, in order that punishment and reward function as such—be able to achieve their goal.

Thus, all the facts connected with the concepts of responsibility and imputation are at once made intelligible. We do not charge an insane person with responsibility, for the very reason that he offers no unified point for the application of motive. It would be pointless to try to affect him by means of promises or threats, when his confused soul fails to respond to such influence because its normal mechanism is out of order. We do not try to give him motives, but try to heal him (metaphorically, we make his sickness responsible, and try to remove its causes). When a man is forced by threats to commit certain acts we do not blame him, but the one who held the pistol at his breast. The reason is clear: the act would have been prevented had we been able to restrain the person who threatened him; and this person is the one whom we must influence in order to prevent similar acts in the future.

The Consciousness of Responsibility

But much more important than the question of when a man is said to be responsible is that of when he himself feels responsible. Our whole treatment would be untenable if it gave no explanation of this. It is, then, a welcome confirmation of the view here developed that the subjective feeling of responsibility coincides with objective judgment. It is a fact of experience that, in general, the person blamed or condemned is conscious of the fact that he was "rightly" taken to account—of course, under the supposition that no error has been made, that the assumed state of affairs actually occurred. What is this consciousness of having been the true doer of the act, the actual instigator? Evidently not merely that it was he who took the steps required for its performance; but there must be added the awareness that he did it "independently," "of his own initiative," or however it be expressed. This feeling is simply the consciousness of freedom, which is merely the knowledge of having acted on one's own desires. And "one's own desires" are those which have their origin in the regularity of one's character in the given situation, and are not imposed by an external power, as explained above. The absence of the external power expresses itself in the well-known feeling (usually considered characteristic of the consciousness of freedom) that one could also have acted otherwise. How this indubitable experience ever came to be an argument in favor of indeterminism is incomprehensible to me. It is of course obvious that I should have acted differently had I willed something else; but the feeling never says that I could also have willed something else, even though this is true, if, that is, other motives had been present. And it says even less that under exactly the same inner and outer conditions I could also have willed something else. How could such a feeling inform me of anything regarding the purely theoretical question of whether the principle of causality holds or not? Of course, after what has been said on the subject, I do not undertake to demonstrate the principle, but I do deny that from any such fact of consciousness the least follows regarding the principle's validity. This feeling is not the consciousness of the absence of a cause, but of something altogether different, namely, of freedom, which consists in the fact that I can act as I desire.

Thus the feeling of responsibility assumes that I acted freely, that my own desires impelled me; and if because of this feeling I willingly suffer blame for my behavior or reproach myself, and thereby admit that I might have acted otherwise, this means that other behavior was compatible with the laws of volition—of course granted other motives. And I myself desire the existence of such motives and bear the pain (regret and sorrow) caused me by my behavior so that its repetition will be prevented. To blame oneself means just to apply a motive of improvement to oneself, which is usually the task of the educator. But if, for example, one does something under the influence of torture, feelings of guilt and regret are absent, for one knows that according to the laws of volition no other behavior was possible—no matter what ideas, because of their feeling tones, might have functioned as motives. The important thing, always, is that the feeling of responsibility means the realization that one's self, one's own psychic processes constitute the point at which motives must be applied in order to govern the acts of one's body.

Causality as the Presupposition of Responsibility

We can speak of motives only in a causal context; thus it becomes clear how very much of the concept of responsibility rests upon that of causation, that is, upon the regularity of volitional decisions. In fact if we should conceive of a decision as utterly without any cause (this would in all strictness be the indeterministic presupposition) then the act would be entirely a matter of chance, for chance is identical with the absence of a cause; there is no other opposite of causality. Could we under such conditions make the agent responsible? Certainly not. Imagine a man, always calm, peaceful and blameless, who suddenly falls upon and begins to beat a stranger. He is held and questioned regarding the motive of his actions, to which he answers, in his opinion truthfully, as we assume: "There was no motive for my behavior. Try as I may I can discover no reason. My volition was without any cause—I desired to do so, and there is simply nothing else to be said about it." We should shake our heads and call him insane, because we have to believe that there was a cause, and lacking any other we must assume some mental disturbance as the only cause remaining; but certainly no one would hold him to be responsible. If decisions were causeless there would be no sense in trying to influence men; and we see at once that this is the reason why we could not bring such a man to account, but would always have only a shrug of the shoulders in answer to his behavior. One can easily determine that in practice we make an agent the more responsible the more motives we can find for his conduct. If a man guilty of an atrocity was an enemy of his victim, if previously he had shown violent tendencies, if some special circumstance angered him, then we impose severe punishment upon him; while the fewer the reasons to be found for an offense the less do we condemn the agent, but make "unlucky chance," a momentary aberration, or something of the sort, responsible. We do not find the causes of misconduct in his character, and therefore we do not try to influence it for the better: this and only this is the significance of the fact that we do not put the responsibility upon him. And he too feels this to be so, and says, "I cannot understand how such a thing could have happened to me."

In general we know very well how to discover the causes of conduct in the characters of our fellow men; and how to use this knowledge in the prediction of their future behavior, often with as much certainty as that with which we know that a lion and a rabbit will behave quite differently in the same situation. From all this it is evident that in practice no one thinks of questioning the principle of causality, that, thus, the attitude of the practical man offers no excuse to the metaphysician for confusing freedom from compulsion with the absence of a cause. If one makes clear to himself that a causeless happening is identical with a chance happening, and that, consequently, an indetermined will would destroy all responsibility, then every desire will cease that might be father to an indeterministic thought. No one can prove determinism, but it is certain that we assume its validity in all our practical life, and that in particular we can apply the concept of responsibility to human conduct only in as far as the causal principle holds of volitional processes.

For a final clarification I bring together again a list of those concepts which tend, in the traditional treatment of the "problem of freedom," to be confused. In the place of these concepts on the left are put, mistakenly, those of the right, and those in the vertical order form a chain, so that sometimes the previous confusion is the cause of that which follows:

NATURAL LAW	LAW OF STATE
DETERMINISM (CAUSALITY)	COMPULSION
(UNIVERSAL VALIDITY)	(NECESSITY)
INDETERMINISM (CHANCE)	FREEDOM
(NO CAUSE)	(NO COMPULSION)

7   Is "Free Will" a Pseudo-Problem?

C. A. Campbell

Schlick's Account of Moral Responsibility Examined

. . . Let us now examine Schlick's theory. In the first place, it is surely quite unplausible to suggest that the common assumption that moral freedom postulates some breach of causal continuity arises from a confusion of two different types of law. Schlick's distinction between descriptive and prescriptive law is, of course, sound. It was no doubt worth pointing out, too, that descriptive laws cannot be said to "compel" human behaviour in the same way as prescriptive laws do. But it seems to me evident that the usual reason why it is held that moral freedom implies some breach of causal continuity, is not a belief that causal laws "compel" as civil laws "compel," but simply the belief that the admission of unbroken causal continuity entails a *further* admission which is directly incompatible with moral responsibility; *viz.,* the admission that no man could have acted otherwise than he in fact did. Now it may, of course, be an error thus to assume that a man is not morally responsible for an act, a fit subject for moral praise and blame in respect of it, unless he could have acted otherwise than he did. Or, if *this* is not an error, it may still be an error to assume that a man could not have acted otherwise than he did, in the sense of the phrase that is crucial for moral responsibility, without there occurring some breach of causal continuity. Into these matters we shall have to enter very fully at a later stage. But the relevant point at the moment is that these (not *prima facie* absurd) assumptions about the

[This article originally appeared in *Mind*, 1951. It is republished, with some omissions, by the kind permission of the author and editor of *Mind*. The references to Schlick are to the chapter in *Problems of Ethics* which is reprinted in this book as Selection 6, pp. 59 ff. By the "pseudo-problem theory" Campbell means the view of writers like Hume, Mill and Schlick that there is no conflict between determinism and freedom.]

conditions of moral responsibility have very commonly, indeed normally, been made, and that they are entirely adequate to explain why the problem of Free Will finds its usual formulation in terms of partial exemption from causal law. Schlick's distinction between prescriptive and descriptive laws has no bearing at all upon the truth or falsity of these assumptions. Yet if these assumptions are accepted, it is (I suggest) really inevitable that the Free Will problem should be formulated in the way to which Schlick takes exception. Recognition of the distinction upon which Schlick and his followers lay so much stress can make not a jot of difference.

As we have seen, however, Schlick does later proceed to the much more important business of disputing these common assumptions about the conditions of moral responsibility. He offers us an analysis of moral responsibility which flatly contradicts these assumptions; an analysis according to which the only freedom demanded by morality is a freedom which is compatible with Determinism. If this analysis can be sustained, there is certainly no problem of "Free Will" in the traditional sense.

But it seems a simple matter to show that Schlick's analysis is untenable. Let us test it by Schlick's own claim that it gives us what we mean by "moral responsibility" in ordinary linguistic usage.

We do not ordinarily consider the lower animals to be morally responsible. But *ought* we not to do so if Schlick is right about what we mean by moral responsibility? It is quite possible, by punishing the dog who absconds with the succulent chops designed for its master's luncheon, favourably to influence its motives in respect of its future behaviour in like circumstances. If moral responsibility is to be linked with punishment as Schlick links it, and punishment conceived as a form of education, we should surely hold the dog morally responsible? The plain fact, of course, is that we don't. We don't, because we suppose that the dog "couldn't help it": that its action (unlike what we usually believe to be true of human beings) was simply a link in a continuous chain of causes and effects. In other words, we do commonly demand the contra-causal sort of freedom as a condition of moral responsibility.

Again, we do ordinarily consider it proper, in certain circumstances, to speak of a person no longer living as morally responsible for some present situation. But *ought* we to do so if we accept Schlick's essentially "forward-looking" interpretation of punishment and responsibility? Clearly we cannot now favourably affect the dead man's motives. No doubt they could *at one time* have been favourably affected. But that cannot be relevant to our judgment of responsibility if, as Schlick insists, the question of who is responsible "is a matter only of knowing who is to be punished or rewarded." Indeed he expressly tells us, as we saw earlier, that in asking this question we are not concerned with a "great-grand-parent" who may have been the "original instigator," because, for one reason, this "remote cause" is "out of reach." We cannot bring the appropriate educative influence to bear upon it. But the plain fact, of course, is that we do frequently assign moral responsibility for present situations to persons who have long been inaccessible to any punitive action on our part. And Schlick's position is still more paradoxical in respect of our apportionment of responsibility for occurrences in the distant past. Since in these cases there is no agent whatsoever whom we can favorably influence by punishment, the question of moral responsibility here should have no meaning for us. But of course it has. Historical writings are studded with examples.

Possibly the criticism just made may seem to some to result from taking Schlick's analysis too much *au pied de la lettre*. The absurd consequences deduced, it may be said, would not follow if we interpreted Schlick as meaning that a man is morally responsible where his motive is such as can *in principle* be favourably affected by reward or punishment—whether or not we who pass the judgment are in a position to take such action. But with every desire to be fair to Schlick, I cannot see how he could accept this modification and still retain the essence of his theory. For the essence of his theory seems to be that moral responsibility has its whole meaning and importance for us in relation to our potential control of future conduct in the interests of society. (I agree that it is hard to believe that anybody *really* thinks this. But it is perhaps less hard to believe to-day than it has ever been before in the history of modern ethics.)

Again, we ordinarily consider that, in certain circumstances, the *degree* of a man's moral responsibility for an act is affected by considerations of his inherited nature, or of his environment, or of both. It is our normal habit to "make allowances" (as we say) when we have reason to believe that a malefactor had a vicious heredity, or was nurtured in his formative years in a harmful environment. We say in such cases "Poor chap, he is more to be pitied than blamed. We could scarcely expect him to behave like a decent citizen with *his* parentage or upbringing." But this extremely common sort of judgment has no point at all if we mean by moral responsibility what Schlick says that we mean. On *that* meaning the degree of a man's moral responsibility must presumably be dependent upon the degree to which we can favourably affect his future motives, which is quite another matter. Now there is no reason to believe that the motives of a man with a bad heredity or a bad upbringing are either less or more subject to educative influence than those of his more fortunate fellows. Yet it is plain matter of fact that we do commonly consider the degree of a man's moral responsibility to be affected by these two factors.

A final point. The extremity of paradox in Schlick's identification of the question "Who is morally blameworthy?" with the question "Who is to be punished?" is apt to be partially concealed from us just because it is our normal habit to include in the meaning of "punishment" an element of "requital for moral transgression" which Schlick expressly denies to it. On that account we commonly think of "punishment," in its strict sense, as implying moral blameworthiness in the person punished. But if we remember to mean by punishment what Schlick means by it, a purely "educative measure," with no retributive ingredients, his identification of the two questions loses such plausibility as it might otherwise have. For clearly we often think it proper to "punish" a person, in *Schlick's* sense, where we are not at all prepared to say that the person is morally blameworthy. We may even think him morally commendable. A case in point would be the unmistakably sincere but muddle-headed person who at the cost of great suffering to himself steadfastly pursues as his "duty" a course which, in our judgment is fraught with danger to the common weal. We should most of us feel entitled, in the public interest, to bring such action to bear upon the man's motives as might induce him to refrain in future from his socially injurious behaviour: in other words, to inflict upon him what Schlick would call "punishment." But we should most of us feel perfectly clear that in so "punishing" this misguided citizen we are not proclaiming his moral blameworthiness or moral wickedness.

Adopting Schlick's own criterion, then, looking simply "to the manner in which the concept is used,"[1] we seem bound to admit that constantly people do assign moral responsibility where Schlick's theory says they shouldn't, don't assign moral responsibility where Schlick's theory says they should, and assign degrees of moral responsibility where on Schlick's theory there should be no difference in degree. I think we may reasonably conclude that Schlick's account of what we mean by moral responsibility breaks down.

The rebuttal of Schlick's arguments, however, will not suffice of itself to refute the pseudo-problem theory. The indebtedness to Schlick of most later advocates of the theory may be conceded; but certainly it does not comprehend all of significance that they have to say on the problem. There are recent analyses of the conditions of moral responsibility containing sufficient new matter, or sufficient old matter in a more precise and telling form, to require of us now something of a fresh start. In the section which follows I propose to consider some representative samples of these analyses —all of which, of course, are designed to show that the freedom which moral responsibility implies is not in fact a contra-causal type of freedom.

But before reopening the general question of the nature and conditions of moral responsibility there is a *caveat* which it seems to me worth while to enter. The difficulties in the way of a clear answer are not slight; but they are apt to seem a good deal more formidable than they really are because of a common tendency to consider in unduly close association two distinct questions: the question "Is a contra-causal type of freedom implied by moral responsibility?" and the question "Does a contra-causal type of freedom anywhere exist?" It seems to me that many philosophers (and I suspect that Moritz Schlick is among them) begin their inquiry with so firm a conviction that the contra-causal sort of freedom nowhere exists, that they find it hard to take very seriously the possibility that it is *this* sort of freedom that moral responsibility implies. For they are loth to abandon the commonsense belief that moral responsibility itself is something real. The implicit reasoning I take to be this. Moral responsibility is real. If moral responsibility is real, the freedom implied in it must be a fact. But

1. See p. 63 above.

contra-causal freedom is not a fact. Therefore contra-causal freedom is not the freedom implied in moral responsibility. I think we should be on our guard against allowing this or some similar train of reasoning (whose premises, after all, are far from indubitable) to seduce us into distorting what we actually find when we set about a direct analysis of moral responsibility and its conditions.

"Ought" Implies "Can"

The pseudo-problem theorists usually, and naturally, develop their analysis of moral responsibility by way of contrast with a view which, while it has enjoyed a good deal of philosophic support, I can perhaps best describe as the common view. It will be well to remind ourselves, therefore, of the main features of this view.

So far as the *meaning,* as distinct from the *conditions,* of moral responsibility is concerned, the common view is very simple. If we ask ourselves whether a certain person is morally responsible for a given act (or it may be just "in general"), what we are considering, it would be said, is whether or not that person is a fit subject upon whom to pass moral judgment; whether he can fittingly be deemed morally good or bad, morally praiseworthy or blameworthy. This does not take us any great way: but (*pace* Schlick) so far as it goes it does not seem to me seriously disputable. The really interesting and controversial question is about the *conditions* of moral responsibility, and in particular the question whether freedom of a contra-causal kind is among these conditions.

The answer of the common man to the latter question is that it most certainly *is* among the conditions. Why does he feel so sure about this? Not, I argued earlier, because the common man supposes that causal law exercises "compulsion" in the sense that prescriptive laws do, but simply because he does not see how a person can be deemed morally praiseworthy or blameworthy in respect of an act which he could not help performing. From the stand-point of moral praise and blame, he would say—though not necessarily from other stand-points—it is a matter of indifference whether it is by reason of some external constraint or by reason of his own given nature that the man could not help doing what he did. It is quite enough to make moral praise and blame futile that in either case there were no genuine alternatives, no open possibilities, before the man when he acted. He could not have acted otherwise than he did. And the common man might not unreasonably go on to stress the fact that we all, even if we are linguistic philosophers, do in our actual practice of moral judgment appear to accept the common view. He might insist upon the point alluded to earlier in this paper, that we do all, in passing moral censure, "make allowances" for influences in a man's hereditary nature or environmental circumstances which we regard as having made it more than ordinarily difficult for him to act otherwise than he did: the implication being that if we supposed that the man's heredity and environment made it not merely very *difficult* but actually *impossible* for him to act otherwise than he did, we could not properly assign moral blame to him at all.

Let us put the argument implicit in the common view a little more sharply. The moral "ought" implies "can." If we say that A morally ought to have done X, we imply that in our opinion, he could have done X. But we assign moral blame to a man only for failing to do what we think he morally ought to have done. Hence if we morally blame A for not having done X, we imply that he could have done X even though in fact he did not. In other words, we imply that A could have acted otherwise than he did. And that means that we imply, as a necessary condition of a man's being morally blameworthy, that he enjoyed a freedom of a kind not compatible with unbroken causal continuity.

The Reflective and the Unreflective Conception of Moral Responsibility

Now what is it that is supposed to be wrong with this simple piece of argument?—For, of course, it must be rejected by all these philosophers who tell us that the traditional problem of Free Will is a mere pseudo-problem. The argument looks as though it were doing little more than reading off necessary implications of the fundamental categories of our moral thinking. One's inclination is to ask "If one is to think morally at all, how else than this *can* we think?"

In point of fact, there is pretty general agreement among the contemporary critics as to what is wrong with the argument. Their answer in general terms is as follows. No doubt A's moral responsibility does imply that he could have acted otherwise. But this expression "could have acted otherwise" stands in dire need of analysis. When we analyse it, we find that it is not, as is so often supposed, simple and unambiguous, and we find that in *some* at least of its possible meanings it implies *no* breach of causal continuity between character and conduct. Having got this clear, we can further discern that only in one of these *latter* meanings is there any compulsion upon our moral thinking to assert that if A is morally blameworthy for an act, A "could have acted otherwise than he did." It follows that, contrary to common belief, our moral thinking does *not* require us to posit a contra-causal freedom as a condition of moral responsibility.

So much of importance obviously turns upon the validity or otherwise of this line of criticism that we must examine it in some detail and with express regard to the *ipsissima verba* of the critics.

In the course of a recent article in *Mind*[2] entitled "Free Will and Moral Responsibility," Mr. Nowell Smith (having earlier affirmed his belief that "the traditional problem has been solved") explains very concisely the nature of the confusion which, as he thinks, has led to the demand for a

2. January, 1948.

contra-causal freedom. He begins by frankly recognising that "It is evident that one of the necessary conditions of moral action is that the agent 'could have acted otherwise' " and he adds "it is to this fact that the Libertarian is drawing attention."[3] Then, after showing (unexceptionably, I think) how the relationship of "ought" to "can" warrants the proposition which he has accepted as evident, and how it induces the Libertarian to assert the existence of action that is "uncaused," he proceeds to point out, in a crucial passage, the nature of the Libertarian's error:

> The fallacy in the argument (he contends) lies in supposing that when we say "A could have acted otherwise" we mean that A, *being what he was and being placed in the circumstances in which he was placed,* could have done something other than what he did. But in fact we never do mean this.[4]

What then *do* we mean here by "A could have acted otherwise"? Mr. Nowell Smith does not tell us in so many words, but the passage I have quoted leaves little doubt how he would answer. What we really mean by the expression, he implies, is not a *categorical* but a *hypothetical* proposition. We mean "A could have acted otherwise, *if he did not happen to be what he in fact was,* or *if he were placed in circumstances other than those in which he was in fact placed.*" Now, *these* propositions, it is easy to see, are in no way incompatible with acceptance of the causal principle in its full rigour. Accordingly the claim that our fundamental moral thinking obliges us to assert a contra-causal freedom as a condition of moral responsibility is disproved.

Such is the "analytical solution" of our problem offered (with obvious confidence) by one able philosopher of to-day, and entirely representative of the views of many other able philosophers. Yet I make bold to say that its falsity stares one in the face. It seems perfectly plain that the hypothetical propositions which Mr. Nowell Smith proposes to substitute for the categorical proposition cannot express "what we really mean" in this context by "A could have acted otherwise," for the simple reason that these hypothetical propositions have no bearing whatsoever upon the question of the moral responsibility of *A*. And it is *A* whose moral responsibility we are talking about—a definite person *A* with a definitive character and in a definitive set of circumstances. What conceivable significance could it have for our attitude to A's responsibility to know that someone with a *different* character (or *A* with a different character, if that collocation of words has any meaning), or A in a different set of circumstances from those in which A as we are concerned with him was in fact placed, "could have acted otherwise"? No doubt this supposititious being *could* have acted otherwise than the definitive person A acted. But the point is that where we are reflecting, as we are supposed in this context to be reflecting, upon the question of *A*'s moral responsibility, our interest in this supposititious being is precisely *nil*.

3. *Loc. cit.,* p. 49.
4. *Loc. cit.,* p. 49.

The two hypothetical propositions suggested in Mr. Nowell Smith's account of the matter do not, however, exhaust the speculations that have been made along these lines. Another very common suggestion by the analysts is that what we really mean by "A could have acted otherwise" is "A could have acted otherwise *if he had willed, or chosen, otherwise.*" This was among the suggestions offered by G. E. Moore in the well-known chapter on Free Will in his *Ethics.* It is, I think, the suggestion he most strongly favoured: though it is fair to add that neither about this nor about any other of his suggestions is Moore in the least dogmatic. He does claim, for, I think, convincing reasons, that "we *very often* mean by 'could' merely 'would, *if* so-and-so had chosen.' "[5] And he concludes "I must confess that I cannot feel certain that this may not be all that we usually mean and understand by the assertion that we have Free Will."[6]

This third hypothetical proposition appears to enjoy also the support of Mr. C. L. Stevenson. Mr. Stevenson begins the chapter of *Ethics and Language* entitled "Avoidability-Indeterminism" with the now familiar pronouncement of his School that "controversy about freedom and determinism of the will . . . presents no permanent difficulty to ethics, being largely a product of confusions." A major confusion (if I understand him rightly) he takes to lie in the meaning of the term "avoidable," when we say "A's action was avoidable"—or, I presume, "A could have acted otherwise." He himself offers the following definition of "avoidable"—" 'A's action was avoidable' has the meaning of 'If A had made a certain choice, which in fact he did not make, his action would not have occurred.' "[7] This I think we may regard as in substance identical with the suggestion that what we really mean by "A could have acted otherwise" is "A could have acted otherwise *if* he had chosen (or willed) otherwise." For clarity's sake we shall here keep to this earlier formulation. In either formulation the special significance of the third hypothetical proposition, as of the two hypothetical propositions already considered, is that it is compatible with strict determinism. If this be indeed all that we mean by the "freedom" that conditions moral responsibility, then those philosophers are certainly wrong who hold that moral freedom is of the contra-causal type.

Now this third hypothetical proposition does at least possess the merit, not shared by its predecessors, of having a real relevance to the question of moral responsibility. If, *e.g.,* A had promised to meet us at 2 P.M., and he chanced to break his leg at 1 P.M., we should not blame him for his failure to discharge his promise. For we should be satisfied that he *could not* have acted otherwise, even if he had so chosen; or *could not,* at any rate, in a way which would have enabled him to meet us at 2 P.M. The freedom to translate one's choice into action, which we saw earlier is for Schlick the *only* freedom required for moral re-

5. *Ethics,* p. 212.
6. *Loc. cit.,* p. 217.
7. *Ethics and Language,* p. 298.

sponsibility, is without doubt *one* of the conditions of moral responsibility.

But it seems easy to show that this third hypothetical proposition does not exhaust what we mean, and *some*times is not even *part* of what we mean, by the expression "could have acted otherwise" in its moral context. Thus it can hardly be even part of what we mean in the case of that class of wrong actions (and it is a large class) concerning which there is really no question whether the agent could have acted otherwise, *if* he had chosen otherwise. Take lying, for example. Only in some very abnormal situation could it occur to one to doubt whether A, whose power of speech was evinced by his telling a lie, was in a position to tell what he took to be the truth *if* he had so chosen. Of *course* he was. Yet it still makes good sense for one's moral thinking to ask whether A, when lying, "could have acted otherwise": and we still require an affirmative answer to this question if A's moral blameworthiness is to be established. It seems apparent, therefore, that in this class of cases at any rate one does *not* mean by "A could have acted otherwise," "A could have acted otherwise *if* he had so chosen."

What then *does* one mean in this class of cases by "A could have acted otherwise"? I submit that the expression is taken in its simple, categorical meaning, without any suppressed "if" clause to qualify it. Or perhaps, in order to keep before us the important truth that it is only as expressions of *will* or *choice* that acts are of moral import, it might be better to say that a condition of A's moral responsibility is that he could have *chosen* otherwise. We saw that there is no real question whether A who told a lie could have acted otherwise *if* he had chosen otherwise. But there is a very real question, at least for any person who approaches the question of moral responsibility at a tolerably advanced level of reflexion, about whether A could have *chosen* otherwise. Such a person will doubtless be acquainted with the claims advanced in some quarters that causal law operates universally: or/and with the theories of some philosophies that the universe is throughout the expression of a single supreme principle; or/and with the doctrines of some theologians that the world is created, sustained and governed by an Omniscient and Omnipotent Being. Very understandably such world-views awaken in him doubts about the validity of his first, easy, instinctive assumption that there are genuinely open possibilities before a man at the moment of moral choice. It thus becomes for him a real question whether a man could have chosen otherwise than he actually did, and, in consequence, whether man's moral responsibility is really defensible. For how can a man be morally responsible, he asks himself, if his choices, like all other events in the universe, could not have been otherwise than they in fact were? It is precisely against the background of world-views such as these that for reflective people the problem of moral responsibility normally arises.

Furthermore, to the man who has attained this level of reflexion, it will in *no* class of cases be a sufficient condition of moral responsibility for an act that one could have acted otherwise *if* one had chosen otherwise—not even in these cases where there *was* some possibility of the operation of "external constraint." In these cases he will, indeed, expressly recognize freedom from external constraint as a *necessary condition,* but not as a *sufficient* condition. For he will be aware that, even granted *this* freedom, it is still conceivable that the agent had no freedom to choose otherwise than he did, and he will therefore require that the latter sort of freedom be added if moral responsibility for the act is to be established.

I have been contending that, for persons at a *tolerably advanced level of reflexion,* "A could have acted otherwise," as a condition of A's moral responsibility, means "A could have chosen otherwise." The qualification italicised is of some importance. The unreflective or unsophisticated person, the ordinary "man in the street," who does not know or much care what scientists and theologians and philosophers have said about the world, sees well enough that A is morally responsible only if he could have acted otherwise, but in his intellectual innocence he will, very probably, envisage nothing capable of preventing A from having acted otherwise except some material impediment—like the broken leg in the example above. Accordingly, for the unreflective person, "A could have acted otherwise," as a condition of moral responsibility, *is* apt to mean no more than "A could have acted otherwise *if* he had so chosen."

It would appear, then, that the view now favoured by many philosophers, that the freedom required for moral responsibility is merely freedom from external constraint, is a view which they share only with the less reflective type of layman. Yet it should be plain that on a matter of this sort the view of the unreflective person is of little value by comparison with the view of the reflective person. There are some contexts, no doubt, in which lack of sophistication is an asset. But this is not one of them. The question at issue here is as to the kind of impediments which might have prevented a man from acting otherwise than he in fact did: and on this question knowledge and reflexion are surely prerequisites of any answer that is worth listening to. It is simply on account of the limitations of his mental vision that the unreflective man interprets the expression "could have acted otherwise," in its context as a condition of moral responsibility, solely in terms of external constraint. He has failed (as yet) to reach the intellectual level at which one takes into account the implications for moral choices of the world-views of science, religion, and philosophy. If on a matter of this complexity the philosopher finds that his analysis accords with the utterances of the uneducated he has, I suggest, better cause for uneasiness than for self-congratulation.

This concludes the main part of what it seems to me necessary to say in answer to the pseudo-problem theorists. My object so far has been to expose the falsity of those innovations (chiefly Positivist) in the way of argument and analysis which are supposed by many to have made it impossible any longer to formulate the problem of Free Will in the traditional manner. My contention is that, at least so far as these innovations are concerned, the simple time-honoured argument still holds from the nature of the moral ought to the conclusion that moral responsibility implies a contra-causal type of freedom. The attempts to avoid that conclusion by analyzing the proposition "A could have acted otherwise" (acknowledged to be implied in *some* sense in A's moral responsibility) into one or other of certain hypothetical propositions which are compatible with unbroken causal continuity, break down hopelessly when tested against the touchstone of actual moral thinking. It is, I think, not necessary to defend the procedure of testing hypotheses in the ethical field by bringing to bear upon them our actual moral thinking. If there is any other form of test applicable, I should be much interested to learn what it is supposed to be. Certainly "logical analysis" *per se* will not do. That has a function, but a function that can only be ancillary. For what we are seeking to know is the meaning of the expression "could have acted otherwise" not *in the abstract,* but in the context of the question of man's *moral responsibility.* Logical analysis *per se* is impotent to give us this information. It can be of value only in so far as it operates within the orbit of "the moral consciousness." One may admit, with some qualifications, that on a matter of this sort the moral consciousness without logical analysis is blind: but it seems to me to be true without any qualification whatsoever that, on the same problem, logical analysis without the moral consciousness is empty.

Contra-Causal Freedom and Creative Activity

There are times when what seems to a critic the very strength of his case breeds mistrust in the critic's own mind. I confess that in making the criticisms that have preceded I have not been altogether free from uncomfortable feelings of this kind. For the arguments I have criticised, and more particularly the analyses of the conditions of moral responsibility, seem to me to be in many cases quite desperately unplausible. Such a state of affairs ought, I think, to give the critic pause. The thought must at least enter his mind (unless he be a total stranger to modesty) that perhaps, despite his best efforts to be fair, he has after all misrepresented what his opponents are saying. No doubt a similar thought will enter, and perhaps find lodgment in, the minds of many readers.

In this situation there is, however, one course by which the critic may reasonably hope to allay these natural suspicions. He should consider whether there may not be certain predisposing influences at work, extrinsic to the specific arguments, which could have the effect of blinding the proponents of these arguments to their intrinsic demerits. If so, he need not be too much disquieted by the seeming weakness of the case against him. For it is a commonplace that, once in the grip of general prepossessions, even very good philosophers sometimes avail themselves of very bad arguments.

Actually, we can, I think, discern at least two such influences operating powerfully in the case before us. One is sympathy with the general tenets of Positivism. The other is the conviction already alluded to, that man does not in fact possess a contra-causal type of freedom; whence follows a strong presumption that no such freedom is necessary to moral responsibility. . . .

. . . Of far wider and more permanent interest, in my judgment, is the second of the "predisposing influences"—the conviction that there just *is* no contra-causal freedom such as is commonly alleged to be a condition of moral responsibility. A natural desire to "save" moral responsibility issues, logically enough, in attempts to formulate its conditions in a manner compatible with unbroken causal continuity. The consequent analyses may be, as I have urged, very unsatisfactory. But there is no doubt that the conviction that motivates the analysis is supported by reasons of great weight: well-known arguments that are the property of no particular school and which most of us learned in our philosophical cradles. A very brief summary of what I take to be the most influential of these arguments will suffice for the comments I wish to make upon them.

A contra-causal freedom, it is argued, such as is implied in the "categorical" interpretation of the proposition "A could have chosen otherwise than he did," posits a breach of causal continuity between a man's character and his conduct. Now apart from the general presumption in favour of the universality of causal law, there are special reasons for disallowing the breach that is here alleged. It is the common assumption of social intercourse that our acquaintances will act "in character"; that their choices will exhibit the "natural" response of their characters to the given situation. And this assumption seems to be amply substantiated, over a wide range of conduct, by the actual success which attends predictions made on this basis. Where there should be, on the contra-causal hypothesis, chaotic variability, there is found in fact a large measure of intelligible continuity. Moreover, what is the alternative to admitting that a person's choices flow from his character? Surely just that the so-called "choice" is not *that person's* choice at all: that, relatively to the person concerned, it is a mere "accident." Now we cannot really believe this. But if it *were* the case, it would certainly not help to establish *moral* freedom, the freedom required for *moral* responsibility. For clearly a man cannot be morally responsible for an act which does not express his own choice but is, on the contrary, attributable simply to chance.

These are clearly considerations worthy of all respect. It is not surprising if they have played a big part in persuading people to respond sympathetically to the view that "Free Will," in its usual contra-causal formulation, is a pseudo-problem. A full answer to them is obviously not practicable in what is little more than an appendix to the body of this paper; but I am hopeful that something can be said, even in a little space, to show that they are very far from being as conclusive against a contra-causal freedom as they are often supposed to be.

To begin with the less troublesome of the two main objections indicated—the objection that the break in causal continuity which free will involves is inconsistent with the predictability of conduct on the basis of the agent's known character. All that is necessary to meet this objection, I suggest, is the frank recognition, which is perfectly open to the Libertarian, that there is a wide area of human conduct, determinable on clear general principles, within which free will does not effectively operate. The most important of these general principles (I have no space to deal here with the others) has often enough been stated by Libertarians. Free will does not operate in these practical situations in which no conflict arises in the agent's mind between what he conceives to be his "duty" and what he feels to be his "strongest desire." It does not operate here because there just is no occasion for it to operate. There is no reason whatever why the agent should here even contemplate choosing any course other than that prescribed by his strongest desire. In all such situations, therefore, he naturally wills in accordance with strongest desire. But his "strongest desire" is simply the specific *ad hoc* expression of that system of conative and emotive dispositions which we call his "character." In all such situations, therefore, whatever may be the case elsewhere, his will is in effect determined by his character as so far formed. Now when we bear in mind that there are an almost immeasurably greater number of situations in a man's life that conform to *this* pattern than there are situations in which an agent is aware of a conflict between strongest desire and duty, it is apparent that a Libertarianism which accepts the limitation of free will to the *latter* type of situation is not open to the stock objection on the score of "predictability." For there still remains a vast area of human behaviour in which prediction on the basis of known character may be expected to succeed: an area which will accommodate without difficulty, I think, all these empirical facts about successful prediction which the critic is apt to suppose fatal to Free Will.

So far as I can see, such a delimitation of the field of effective free will denies to the Libertarian absolutely nothing which matters to him. For it is precisely that small sector of the field of choices which our principle of delimitation still leaves open to free will—the sector in which strongest desire clashes with duty—that is crucial for moral responsibility. It is, I believe, with respect to such situations, and in the last resort to such situations alone, that the agent himself recognises that moral praise and blame are appropriate. They are appropriate, according as he does or does not "rise to duty" in the face of opposing desires; always granted, that is, that he is free to choose between these courses as genuinely open possibilities. If the reality of freedom be conceded *here,* everything is conceded that the Libertarian has any real interest in securing.

But, of course, the most vital question is, can the reality of freedom be conceded even here? In particular, can the standard objection be met which we stated, that if the person's choice does not, in these situations as elsewhere, flow from his *character,* then it is not *that person's* choice at all.

This is, perhaps, of all the objections to a contra-causal freedom, the one which is generally felt to be the most conclusive. For the assumption upon which it is based, *viz.,* that no intelligible meaning can attach to the claim that an act which is not an expression of the self's *character* may nevertheless be the *self's* act, is apt to be regarded as self-evident. The Libertarian is accordingly charged with being in effect an *In*determinist, whose "free will," in so far as it does not flow from the agent's character, can only be a matter of "chance." Has the Libertarian—who invariably repudiates this charge and claims to be a *Self*-determinist— any way of showing that, contrary to the assumption of his critics, we *can* meaningfully talk of an act as the self's act even though, in an important sense, it is not an expression of the self's "character"?

I think that he has. I want to suggest that what prevents the critics from finding a meaning in this way of talking is that they are looking for it in the wrong way; or better, perhaps, with the wrong orientation. They are looking for it from the stand-point of the *external observer;* the stand-point proper to, because alone possible for, apprehension of the physical world. Now from the external stand-point we may observe processes of change. But one thing which, by common consent, *cannot* be observed from without is *creative activity.* Yet—and here lies the crux of the whole matter—it is precisely creative activity which we are trying to understand when we are trying to understand what is traditionally designated by "free will." For if there should be an act which is genuinely the self's act and is nevertheless not an expression of its character, such an act, in which the self "transcends" its character as so far formed, would seem to be essentially of the nature of creative activity. It follows that to look for a meaning in "free will" from the external stand-point is absurd. It is to look for it in a way that ensures that it will not be found. Granted that a creative activity of any kind is at least *possible* (and I know of no ground for its *a priori* rejection), there is one way, and one way only, in which we can hope to apprehend it, and that is from the *inner* stand-point of direct participation.

It seems to me therefore, that if the Libertarian's claim to find a meaning in a "free" will which is genuinely the self's will, though not an expression of the self's character, is to be subjected to any test that is worth applying, that test must be undertaken from the inner stand-point. We ought to place ourselves imaginatively at the stand-point of the agent engaged in the typical moral situation in which free will is claimed, and ask ourselves whether from *this* stand-point the claim in question does or does not have meaning for us. That the appeal must be to introspection is no doubt unfortunate. But he would be a very doctrinaire critic of introspection who declined to make use of it when in the nature of the case no other means of apprehension is available. Everyone must make the introspective experiment for himself: but I may perhaps venture to report, though at this late stage with extreme brevity, what I at least seem to find when I make the experiment myself.

In the situation of moral conflict, then, I (as agent) have before my mind a course of action X, which I believe to be my duty; and also a course of action Y, incompatible with X, which I feel to be that which I most strongly desire. Y is, as it is sometimes expressed, "in the line of least resistance" for me—the course which I am aware I should take if I let my purely desiring nature operate without hindrance. It is the course towards which I am aware that my *character,* as so far formed, naturally inclines me. Now, as actually engaged in this situation, I find that I cannot help believing that I *can* rise to duty and choose X; the "rising to duty" being effected by what is commonly called "effort of will." And I further find, if I ask myself just what it is I am believing when I believe that I "can" rise to duty, that I cannot help believing that it lies with me here and now, quite absolutely, which of two genuinely open possibilities I adopt; whether, that is, I make the effort of will and choose X, or, on the other hand, let my desiring nature, my char-acter as so far formed, "have its way," and choose Y, the course "in the line of least resistance." These beliefs may, of course, be illusory, but that is not at present in point. For the present argument all that matters is whether beliefs of this sort are in fact discoverable in the moral agent in the situation of "moral temptation." For my own part, I cannot doubt the introspective evidence that they are.

Now here is the vital point. No matter which course, X or Y, I choose in this situation, I cannot doubt, *qua* practical being engaged in it, that my choice is *not* just the expression of my formed character, and yet *is* a choice made by my *self.* For suppose I make the effort and choose X (my "duty"). Since my very purpose in making the "effort" is to enable me to act against the existing "set" of desire, which is the expression of my character as so far formed, I cannot possibly regard the act itself as the expression of my *character.* On the other hand, intro-spection makes it equally clear that I am certain that it is *I* who choose; that the act is not an "accident," but is genuinely *my* act. Or suppose that I choose Y (the end of "strongest desire"). The course chosen here is, it is true, in conformity with my "character." But since I find myself unable to doubt that I *could* have made the effort and chosen X, I cannot possibly regard the choice of Y as *just* the expression of my character. Yet here again I find that I cannot doubt that the choice is *my* choice, a choice for which *I* am justly to be blamed.

What this amounts to is that I *can* and *do* attach meaning, *qua* moral agent, to an act which is not the self's character and yet is genuinely the self's act. And having no good reason to suppose that other persons have a fundamentally different mental constitution, it seems to me probable that anyone else who undertakes a similar experiment will be obliged to submit a similar report. I conclude, therefore, that the argument against "free will" on the score of its "meaninglessness" must be held to fail. "Free Will" does have meaning; though, because it is of the nature of a creative activity, its meaning is discoverable only in an intuition of the practical consciousness of the participating agent. To the agent making a moral choice in the situation where duty clashes with desire, his "self" is known to him as a creatively active self, a self which declines to be identified with his "character" as so formed. Not, of course, that the self's character—let it be added to obviate misunderstanding—either is, or is supposed by the agent to be, devoid of bearing upon his choices, even in the "sector" in which free will is held to operate. On the contrary, such a bearing is manifest in the empirically verifiable fact that we find it "harder" (as we say) to make the effort of will required to "rise to duty" in proportion to the extent that the "dutiful" course conflicts with the course to which our character as so far formed inclines us. It is only in the polemics of the critics that a "free" will is supposed to be incompatible with recognising the bearing of "character" upon choice.

"But what" (it may be asked) "of the all-important question of the *value* of this 'subjective certainty'? Even if what you say is sound as 'phenomenology,' is there any reason to suppose that the conviction on which you lay so much stress is in fact *true*?" I agree that the question is important; far more important, indeed, than is always realised, for it is not always realised that the only direct evidence there *could* be for a creative activity like "free will" is an intuition of the practical consciousness. But this question falls outside the purview of the present paper. The aim of the paper has not been to offer a constructive defence of free will. It has been to show that the problem as traditionally posed is a real, and not a pseudo, problem. A serious threat to that thesis, it was acknowledged, arises from the apparent difficulty of attaching meaning to an act which is not the expression of the self's character and yet *is* the self's own act. The object of my brief phenomenological analysis was to provide evidence that such an act *does* have meaning for us in the one context in which there is any sense in *expecting* it to have meaning.

My general conclusion is, I fear, very unexciting. It is merely that it is an error to suppose that the "Free Will" problem, when correctly formulated, turns out not to be a "problem" at all. Labouring to reinstate an old problem is dull work enough. But I am disposed to think that the philosophic situation to-day calls for a good deal more dull work of a similar sort.

8   Free Will and Psychoanalysis

John Hospers

. . . SCHLICK'S ANALYSIS IS INDEED clarifying and helpful to those who have fallen victim to the confusions he exposes—and this probably includes most persons in their philosophical growing-pains. But *is* this the end of the matter? Is it true that all acts, though caused, are free as long as they are not compelled in the sense which he specifies? May it not be that, while the identification of "free" with "uncompelled" is acceptable, the area of compelled acts is vastly greater than he or most other philosophers have ever suspected? (Moore is more cautious in this respect than Schlick; while for Moore an act is free if it is voluntary in the sense specified above, he thinks there may be another sense in which human beings, and human acts, are not free at all.[1]) We remember statements about human beings being pawns of their early environment, victims of conditions beyond their control, the result of causal influences stemming from their parents, and the like, and we ponder and ask, "Still, are we really free?" Is there not something in what generations of sages have said about man being fettered? Is there not perhaps something too facile, too sleight-of-hand, in Schlick's cutting of the Gordian knot? For example, when a metropolitan newspaper headlines an article with the words "Boy Killer Is Doomed Long before He Is Born,"[2] and then goes on to describe how a twelve-year-old boy has been sentenced to prison for the murder of a girl, and how his parental background includes records of drunkenness, divorce, social maladjustment, and paresis, are we still to say that his act, though voluntary and assuredly not done at the point of a

[This selection is taken from the article bearing the same name which first appeared in *Philosophy and Phenomenological Research*, 1950. It is reprinted with the kind permission of Professor Hospers and the editor. Schlick's discussion of Free Will and Determinism referred to here is reprinted in the present volume, Selection 6, pp. 59 ff. There is a fuller discussion of this topic, more representative of Professor Hospers' present views, in Chapter 10 of *Human Conduct* (New York: Harcourt, Brace & World, 1961).]
    1. *Ethics*, Chapter 6, pp. 217 ff.
    2. *New York Post*, Tuesday, May 18, 1948, p. 4.

gun, is free? The boy has early displayed a tendency toward sadistic activity to hide an underlying masochism and "prove that he's a man"; being coddled by his mother only worsens this tendency, until, spurned by a girl in his attempt on her, he kills her—not simply in a fit of anger, but calculatingly, deliberately. Is he free in respect of his criminal act, or for that matter in most of the acts of his life? Surely to ask this question is to answer it in the negative. Perhaps I have taken an extreme case; but it is only to show the superficiality of the Schlick analysis the more clearly. Though not everyone has criminotic tendencies, everyone has been molded by influences which in large measure at least determine his present behavior; he is literally the product of these influences, stemming from periods prior to his "years of discretion," giving him a host of character traits that he cannot change now even if he would. So obviously does what a man is depend upon how a man comes to be, that it is small wonder that philosophers and sages have considered man far indeed from being the master of his fate. It is not as if man's will were standing high and serene above the flux of events that have molded him; it is itself caught up in this flux, itself carried along on the current. An act is free when it is determined by the man's character, say moralists; but what if the most decisive aspects of his character were already irrevocably acquired before he could do anything to mold them? What if even the degree of will power available to him in shaping his habits and disciplining himself now to overcome the influence of his early environment is a factor over which he has no control? What are we to say of this kind of "freedom"? Is it not rather like the freedom of the machine to stamp labels on cans when it has been devised for just that purpose? Some machines can do so more efficiently than others, but only because they have been better constructed.

It is not my purpose here to establish this thesis in general, but only in one specific respect which has received comparatively little attention, namely, the field referred to by psychiatrists as that of unconscious motivation. In what follows I shall restrict my attention to it because it illustrates as clearly as anything the points I wish to make.

Let me try to summarize very briefly the psychoanalytic doctrine on this point.[3] The conscious life of the human being, including the conscious decisions and volitions, is merely a mouthpiece for the unconscious—not directly for the enactment of unconscious drives, but of the compromise between unconscious drives and unconscious reproaches. There is a Big Three behind the scenes which the automaton called the conscious personality carries out: the id, an "eternal gimme," presents its wish and

3. I am aware that the theory presented below is not accepted by all practicing psychoanalysts. Many non-Freudians would disagree with the conclusions presented. But I do not believe that this fact affects my argument, as long as the concept of unconscious motivation is accepted. I am aware, too, that much of the language employed in the following descriptions is animistic and metaphorical; but as long as I am presenting a view I would prefer to "go the whole hog" and present it in its most dramatic form. The theory can in any case be made clearest by the use of such language, just as atomic theory can often be made clearest to students with the use of models.

demands its immediate satisfaction; the super-ego says no to the wish immediately upon presentation, and the unconscious ego, the mediator between the two, tries to keep peace by means of compromise.

To go into examples of the functioning of these three "bosses" would be endless; psychoanalytic case books supply hundreds of them. The important point for us to see in the present context is that *it is the unconscious that determines what the conscious impulse and the conscious action shall be.* Hamlet, for example, had a strong Oedipus wish, which was violently counteracted by super-ego reproaches; these early wishes were vividly revived in an unusual adult situation in which his uncle usurped the coveted position from Hamlet's father and won his mother besides. This situation evoked strong strictures on the part of Hamlet's super-ego, and it was this that was responsible for his notorious delay in killing his uncle. A dozen times Hamlet could have killed Claudius easily; but every time Hamlet "decided" not to: a free choice, moralists would say—but no, listen to the super-ego: "What you feel such hatred toward your uncle for, what you are plotting to kill him for, is precisely the crime which you yourself desire to commit: to kill your father and replace him in the affections of your mother. Your fate and your uncle's are bound up together." This paralyzes Hamlet into inaction. Consciously all he knows is that he is unable to act; this conscious inability he rationalizes, giving a different excuse each time.[4]

We have always been conscious of the fact that we are not masters of our fate in every respect—that there are many things which we cannot do, that nature is more powerful than we are, that we cannot disobey laws without danger of reprisals, etc. We have become "officially" conscious, too, though in our private lives we must long have been aware of it, that we are not free with respect to the emotions that we feel— whom we love or hate, what types we admire, and the like. More lately still we have been reminded that there are unconscious motivations for our basic attractions and repulsions, our compulsive actions or inabilities to act. But what is not welcome news is that our very acts of volition, and the entire train of deliberations leading up to them, are but façades for the expression of unconscious wishes, or rather, unconscious compromises and defenses.

A man is faced by a choice: shall he kill another person or not? Moralists would say, here is a free choice—the result of deliberation, an action consciously entered into. And yet, though the agent himself does not know it, and has no awareness of the forces that are at work within him, his choice is already determined for him: his conscious will is only an instrument, a slave, in the hands of a deep unconscious motivation which determines his action. If he has a great deal of what the analyst calls "free-floating guilt," he will not; but if the guilt is such

4. See *The Basic Writings of Sigmund Freud,* Modern Library Edition, p. 310. (In *The Interpretation of Dreams.*) Cf. also the essay by Ernest Jones, "A Psycho-analytical Study of Hamlet."

as to demand immediate absorption in the form of self-damaging behavior, this accumulated guilt will have to be discharged in some criminal
action. The man himself does not know what the inner clockwork is;
he is like the hands on the clock, thinking they move freely over the
face of the clock.

A woman has married and divorced several husbands. Now she is
faced with a choice for the next marriage: shall she marry Mr. A, or
Mr. B, or nobody at all? She may take considerable time to "decide"
this question, and her decision may appear as a final triumph of her free
will. Let us assume that A is a normal, well-adjusted, kind, and generous
man, while B is a leech, an impostor, one who will become entangled
constantly in quarrels with her. If she belongs to a certain classifiable psychological type, she will inevitably choose B, and she will do so even if her
previous husbands have resembled B, so that one would think that she "had
learned from experience." Consciously, she will of course "give the matter due consideration," etc., etc. To the psychoanalyst all this is irrelevant chaff in the wind—only a camouflage for the inner workings about
which she knows nothing consciously. If she is of a certain kind of
masochistic strain, as exhibited in her previous set of symptoms, she *must*
choose B: her super-ego, always out to maximize the torment in the
situation, seeing what dazzling possibilities for self-damaging behavior are
promised by the choice of B, compels her to make the choice she does,
and even to conceal the real basis of the choice behind an elaborate
façade of rationalizations.

. . . A man has wash-compulsion. He must be constantly washing
his hands—he uses up perhaps 400 towels a day. Asked why he does
this, he says, "I need to, my hands are dirty"; and if it is pointed out
to him that they are not really dirty, he says, "They feel dirty anyway,
I feel better when I wash them." So once again he washes them. He
"freely decides" every time; he feels that he must wash them, he deliberates for a moment perhaps, but always ends by washing them. What
he does not see, of course, are the invisible wires inside him pulling
him inevitably to do the thing he does: the infantile id-wish concerns
preoccupation with dirt, the super-ego charges him with this, and the
terrified ego must respond, "No, I don't like dirt, see how clean I
like to be, look how I wash my hands!"

Let us see what further "free acts" the same patient engages in
(this is an actual case history): he is taken to a concentration camp,
and given the worst of treatment by the Nazi guards. In the camp he
no longer chooses to be clean, does not even try to be—on the contrary,
his choice is now to wallow in filth as much as he can. All he is aware
of now is a disinclination to be clean, and every time he must choose
he chooses not to be. Behind the scenes, however, another drama is being
enacted: the super-ego, perceiving that enough torment is being adminis-
tered from the outside, can afford to cease pressing its charges in this
quarter—the outside world is doing the torturing now, so the super-ego

is relieved of the responsibility. Thus the ego is relieved of the agony of constantly making terrified replies in the form of washing to prove that the super-ego is wrong. The defense no longer being needed, the person slides back into what is his natural predilection anyway, for filth. This becomes too much even for the Nazi guards: they take hold of him one day, saying, "We'll teach you how to be clean!" drag him into the snow, and pour bucket after bucket of icy water over him until he freezes to death. . . .

Let us take a less colorful, more everyday example. A student at a university, possessing wealth, charm, and all that is usually considered essential to popularity, begins to develop the following personality pattern: although well taught in the graces of social conversation, he always makes a *faux pas* somewhere, and always in the worst possible situation; to his friends he makes cutting remarks which hurt deeply—and always apparently aimed in such a way as to hurt the most: a remark that would not hurt A but would hurt B he invariably makes to B rather than to A, and so on. None of this is conscious. Ordinarily he is considerate of people, but he contrives always (unconsciously) to impose on just those friends who would resent it most, and at just the times when he should know that he should not impose: at 3 o'clock in the morning, without forewarning, he phones a friend in a near-by city demanding to stay at his apartment for the weekend; naturally the friend is offended, but the person himself is not aware that he has provoked the grievance ("common sense" suffers a temporary eclipse when the neurotic pattern sets in, and one's intelligence, far from being of help in such a situation, is used in the interest of the neurosis), and when the friend is cool to him the next time they meet, he wonders why and feels unjustly treated. Aggressive behavior on his part invites resentment and aggression in turn, but all that he consciously sees is others' behavior towards him—and he considers himself the innocent victim of an unjustified "persecution."

Each of these acts is, from the moralist's point of view, free: he chose to phone his friend at 3 A.M.; he chose to make the cutting remark that he did, etc. What he does not know is that an ineradicable masochistic pattern has set in. His unconscious is far more shrewd and clever than is his conscious intellect; it sees with uncanny accuracy just what kind of behavior will damage him most, and unerringly forces him into that behavior. Consciously, the student "doesn't know why he did it"—he gives different "reasons" at different times, but they are all, once again, rationalizations cloaking the unconscious mechanism which propels him willy-nilly into actions that his "common sense" eschews.

The more of this sort of thing one observes, the more he can see what the psychoanalyst means when he talks about *the illusion of freedom*. And the more of a psychiatrist one becomes, the more he is overcome with a sense of what an illusion this free will can be. In some kinds of cases most of us can see it already: it takes no psychiatrist to look at the epileptic and sigh with sadness at the thought that soon this person before you will be as one possessed, not the same thoughtful intelligent person you knew. But people are not aware of this in other contexts, for example when they express surprise at how a person to whom they have been so good could treat them so badly. Let us suppose that you help a person financially or morally or in some other way, so that he is in your debt; suppose further that he is one of the many neurotics who unconsciously identify kindness with weakness and aggression with strength, then he will unconsciously take your kindness to him as weakness and use it as the occasion for enacting some aggression against you. He can't help it, he may regret it himself later; still, he will be driven to do it. If we gain a little knowledge of psychiatry, we can look at him with pity, that a person otherwise so worthy should be so unreliable—but we will exercise realism too, and be aware that there are some types of people that you cannot be good to; in "free" acts of their conscious volition, they will use your own goodness against you.

Sometimes the persons themselves will become dimly aware that "something behind the scenes" is determining their behavior. The divorcee will sometimes view herself with detachment, as if she were some machine (and indeed the psychoanalyst does call her a "repeating-machine"): "I know I'm caught in a net, that I'll fall in love with this guy and marry him and the whole ridiculous merry-go-round will start all over again."

We talk about free will, and we say, for example, the person is free to do so-and-so if he can do so *if* he wants to—and we forget that his wanting to is itself caught up in the stream of determinism, that unconscious forces drive him into the wanting or not wanting to do the thing in question. The analogy of the puppet whose motions are manipulated from behind by invisible wires, or better still, by springs inside, is a telling one at almost every point.

And the glaring fact is that it all started so early, before we knew what was happening. The personality structure is inelastic after the age of five, and comparatively so in most cases after the age of three. Whether one acquires a neurosis or not is determined by that age—and just as involuntarily as if it had been a curse of God . . . only the psychiatrist knows what puppets people really are; and it is no wonder that the protestations of philosophers that "the act which is the result of a volition, a deliberation, a conscious decision, is free" leave these persons, to speak mildly, somewhat cold.

. . . Now, what of the notion of responsibility? What happens to it in our analysis?

Let us begin with an example, not a fictitious one. A woman and her two-year-old baby are riding on a train to Montreal in midwinter. The child is ill. The woman wants badly to get to her destination. She is, unknown to herself, the victim of a neurotic conflict whose nature is irrelevant here except for the fact that it forces her to behave aggressively toward the child, partly to spite her husband whom she despises and who loves the child, but chiefly to ward off super-ego charges of masochistic attachment.

Consciously she loves the child, and when she says this she says it sincerely, but she must behave aggressively toward it nevertheless, just as many children love their mothers but are nasty to them most of the time in neurotic pseudo-aggression. The child becomes more ill as the train approaches Montreal; the heating system of the train is not working, and the conductor pleads with the woman to get off the train at the next town and get the child to a hospital at once. The woman refuses. Soon after, the child's condition worsens, and the mother does all she can to keep it alive, without, however, leaving the train, for she declares that it is absolutely necessary that she reach her destination. But before she gets there the child is dead. After that, of course, the mother grieves, blames herself, weeps hysterically, and joins the church to gain surcease from the guilt that constantly overwhelms her when she thinks of how her aggressive behavior has killed her child.

Was she responsible for her deed? In ordinary life, after making a mistake, we say, "Chalk it up to experience." Here we should say, "Chalk it up to the neurosis." *She* could not help it if her neurosis forced her to act this way—she didn't even know what was going on behind the scenes, her conscious self merely acted out its assigned part. This is far more true than is generally realized: criminal actions in general are not actions for which their agents are responsible; the agents are passive, not active—they are victims of a neurotic conflict. Their very hyperactivity is unconsciously determined.

To say this is, of course, not to say that we should not punish criminals. Clearly, for our own protection, we must remove them from our midst so that they can no longer molest and endanger organized society. And, of course, if we use the word "responsible" in such a way that justly to hold someone responsible for a deed is by definition identical with being justified in punishing him, then we can and do hold people responsible. But this is like the sense of "free" in which free acts are voluntary ones. It does not go deep enough. In a deeper sense we cannot hold the person responsible: we can hold his neurosis responsible, but *he is not responsible for his neurosis,* particularly since the age at which its onset was inevitable was an age before he could even speak.

The neurosis is responsible—but isn't the neurosis a part of *him*? We have been speaking all the time as if the person and his unconscious were two separate beings; but isn't he one personality, including conscious and unconscious departments together?

I do not wish to deny this. But it hardly helps us here; for what people want when they talk about freedom, and what they hold to when they champion it, is the idea that the *conscious* will is the master of their destiny. "I am the master of my fate, I am the captain of my soul"—and they surely mean their conscious selves, the self that they can recognize and search and introspect. Between an unconscious that willy-nilly determines your actions, and an external force which pushes you, there is little if anything to choose. The unconscious is just *as if* it were an outside force; and indeed, psychiatrists will assert that the inner Hitler (your super-ego) can torment you far more than any external Hitler can. Thus the kind of freedom that people want, the only kind they will settle for, is precisely the kind that psychiatry says that they cannot have.

Heretofore it was pretty generally thought that, while we could not rightly blame a person for the color of his eyes or the morality of his parents, or even for what he did at the age of three, or to a large extent what impulses he had and whom he fell in love with, one *could* do so for other of his adult activities, particularly the acts he performed voluntarily and with premeditation. Later this attitude was shaken. Many voluntary acts came to be recognized, at least in some circles, as compelled by the unconscious. Some philosophers recognized this too—Ayer[5] talks about the kleptomaniac being unfree, and about a person being unfree when another person exerts a habitual ascendancy over his personality. But this is as far as he goes. The usual examples, such as the kleptomaniac and the schizophrenic, apparently satisfy most philosophers, and with these exceptions removed, the rest of mankind is permitted to wander in the vast and alluring fields of freedom and responsibility. So far the inroads upon freedom left the vast majority of humanity untouched; they began to hit home when psychiatrists began to realize, though philosophers did not, that the domination of the conscious by the unconscious extended, not merely to a few exceptional individuals, but to all human beings, that the "big three behind the scenes" are not respecters of persons, and dominate us all, even including that *sanctum sanctorum* of freedom, our conscious will. To be sure, the domination by the unconscious in the case of "normal" individuals is somewhat more benevolent than the tyranny and despotism exercised in neurotic cases, and therefore the former have evoked less comment; but the principle remains in all cases the same: the unconscious is the master of every fate and the captain of every soul.

We speak of a machine turning out good products most of the time but every once in a while it turns out a "lemon." We do not, of course, hold the product responsible for this, but the machine, and via the machine, its maker. Is it silly to extend to inanimate objects the idea of responsibility? Of course. But is it any less so to employ the notion in speaking of human creatures? Are not the two kinds of cases analogous in countless important ways? Occasionally a child turns out badly too, even when his environment and training are the same as that of his brothers and sisters who turn out "all right." He is the "bad penny." His acts of rebellion against parental discipline in adult life are traceable to early experiences of real or fancied denial of infantile wishes. Sometimes the denial has been real, though many denials are absolutely necessary if the child is to grow up to observe the common decencies of civilized life; sometimes, if the child has an unusual quantity of narcissism, every event that occurs is interpreted by him as a denial of his wishes, and nothing a parent could do, even granting every

---

5. A. J. Ayer, "Freedom and Necessity," *Polemic* (September–October 1946), pp. 40–43. Reprinted in Ayer, *Philosophical Essays.*

humanly possible wish, would help. In any event, the later neurosis can be attributed to this. Can the person himself be held responsible? Hardly. If he engages in activities which are a menace to society, he must be put into prison, of course, but responsibility is another matter. The time when the events occurred which rendered his neurotic behavior inevitable was a time long before he was capable of thought and decision. As an adult, he is a victim of a world he never made—only this world is inside him.

What about the children who turn out "all right"? All we can say is that "it's just lucky for them" that what happened to their unfortunate brother didn't happen to them; *through no virtue of their own* they are not doomed to the life of unconscious guilt, expiation, conscious depression, terrified ego-gestures for the appeasement of a tyrannical super-ego, that he is. The machine turned them out with a minimum of damage. But if the brother cannot be blamed for his evils, neither can they be praised for their good; unless, of course, we should blame people for what is not their fault, and praise them for lucky accidents.

We all agree that machines turn out "lemons," we all agree that nature turns out misfits in the realm of biology—the blind, the crippled, the diseased; but we hesitate to include the realm of the personality, for here, it seems, is the last retreat of our dignity as human beings. Our ego can endure anything but this; this island at least must remain above the encroaching flood. But may not precisely the same analysis be made here also? Nature turns out psychological "lemons" too, in far greater quantities than any other kind; and indeed all of us are "lemons" in some respect or other, the difference being one of degree. Some of us are lucky enough not to have criminotic tendencies or masochistic mother-attachment or overdimensional repetition-compulsion to make our lives miserable, but most of our actions, those usually considered the most important, are unconsciously dominated just the same. And, if a neurosis may be likened to a curse of God, let those of us, the elect, who are enabled to enjoy a measure of life's happiness without the hell-fire of neurotic guilt, take this, not as our own achievement, but simply for what it is—a gift of God.

Let us, however, quit metaphysics and put the situation schematically in the form of a deductive argument.

1. An occurrence over which we had no control is something we cannot be held responsible for.

2. Events E, occurring during our babyhood, were events over which we had no control.

3. Therefore events E were events which we cannot be held responsible for.

4. But if there is something we cannot be held responsible for, neither can we be held responsible for something that inevitably results from it.

5. Events E have as inevitable consequence Neurosis N, which in turn has as inevitable consequence Behavior B.

6. Since N is the inevitable consequence of E and B is the inevitable consequence of N, B is the inevitable consequence of E.

7. Hence, not being responsible for E, we cannot be responsible for B.

In Samuel Butler's utopian satire *Erewhon* there occurs the following passage, in which a judge is passing sentence on a prisoner:

It is all very well for you to say that you came of unhealthy parents, and had a severe accident in your childhood which permanently undermined your constitution; excuses such as these are the ordinary refuge of the criminal; but they cannot for one moment be listened to by the ear of justice. I am not here to enter upon curious metaphysical questions as to the origin of this or that—questions to which there would be no end were their introduction once tolerated, and which would result in throwing the only guilt on the tissues of the primordial cell, or on the elementary gases. There is no question of how you came to be wicked, but only this—namely, are you wicked or not? This has been decided in the affirmative, neither can I hesitate for a single moment to say that it has been decided justly. You are a bad and dangerous person, and stand branded in the eyes of your fellow countrymen with one of the most heinous known offences.[6]

As moralists read this passage, they may perhaps nod with approval. But the joke is on them. The sting comes when we realize what the crime is for which the prisoner is being sentenced: namely, consumption. The defendant is reminded that during the previous year he was sentenced for aggravated bronchitis, and is warned that he should profit from experience in the future. Butler is employing here his familiar method of presenting some human tendency (in this case, holding people responsible for what isn't their fault) to a ridiculous extreme and thereby reducing it to absurdity.

Assuming the main conclusions of this paper to be true, is there any room left for freedom?

This, of course, all depends on what we mean by "freedom." . . . When "free" means "uncompelled," and only external compulsion is admitted, there are countless free acts. But now we have extended the notion of compulsion to include determination by unconscious forces. With this sense in mind, our question is, "With the concept of compulsion thus extended, and in the light of present psychoanalytic knowledge, is there any freedom left in human behavior?"

If practicing psychoanalysts were asked this question, there is little doubt that their answer would be along the following lines: they would say that they were not accustomed to using the term "free" at all, but that if they had to suggest a criterion for distinguishing the free from the unfree, they would say that a person's freedom is present in *inverse proportion to his neuroticism;* in other words, the more his acts are determined by a *malevolent* unconscious, the less free he is. Thus they would speak of *degrees* of freedom. They would say that as a person is cured of his neurosis, he becomes more free—free to realize capabilities that were blocked by the neurotic affliction. The psychologically well-adjusted indi-

6. Samuel Butler, *Erewhon* (Modern Library edition), p. 107.

vidual is in this sense comparatively the most free. Indeed, those who are cured of mental disorders are sometimes said to have *regained their freedom:* they are freed from the tyranny of a malevolent unconscious which formerly exerted as much of a domination over them as if they had been the abject slaves of a cruel dictator.

But suppose one says that a person is free only to the extent that his acts are *not unconsciously determined at all,* be the unconscious benevolent *or* malevolent? If this is the criterion, psychoanalysts would say, most human behavior cannot be called free at all: our impulses and volitions having to do with our basic attitudes toward life, whether we are optimists or pessimists, tough-minded or tender-minded, whether our tempers are quick or slow, whether we are "naturally self-seeking" or "naturally benevolent" (and *all the acts consequent upon these things*), what things annoy us, whether we take to blondes or brunettes, old or young, whether we become philosophers or artists or businessmen—all this has its basis in the unconscious. If people generally call most acts free, it is not because they believe that compelled acts should be called free, it is rather through not knowing how large a proportion of our acts actually are compelled. Only the comparatively "vanilla-flavored" aspects of our lives—such as our behavior toward people who don't really matter to us—are exempted from this rule.

These, I think, are the two principal criteria for distinguishing freedom from the lack of it which we might set up on the basis of psychoanalytic knowledge. Conceivably we might set up others. In every case, of course, it remains trivially true that "it all depends on how we choose to use the word." The facts are what they are, regardless of what words we choose for labeling them. But if we choose to label them in a way which is not in accord with what human beings, however vaguely, have long had in mind in applying these labels, as we would be doing if we labeled as "free" many acts which we know as much about as we now do through modern psychoanalytic methods, then we shall only be manipulating words to mislead our fellow creatures.

9 Human Action and the Limitations of Causal Explanation

S. I. Benn and R. S. Peters

Determinism to a scientist conveys the general proposition that every event has a cause. Whether this general proposition is true is a very difficult question to decide, but it is certainly assumed to be true by most scientists. To say that an event has a cause is to say that there are universal laws together with statements about initial conditions prevailing at particular times, and that from these two together we can predict an event which we call an "effect." For example, given that under the conditions x,y,z, iron expands when it is heated, and given that the conditions x,y,z, prevail and that this is a case of iron being heated, we can make the prediction that iron will expand. Here we have a typical causal relation. The so-called "cause" is then the event referred to in the statement of initial conditions. And these conditions are regarded as being *sufficient* to explain the effect, if it is a full-blooded causal *explanation*.

Have we such relations in human affairs? The initial difficulty about saying that we have is that it is difficult to maintain that there are any psychological or sociological laws which would enable us to make such definite predictions. There are also difficulties connected with our knowledge of particular situations which constitute the initial conditions; for when we are dealing with stones and bodies falling, their past history is scarcely part of the present situation. But when we are dealing with human beings, their past history is very much part of the present situation, and it

[This selection is from Chapter IX of *Social Principles and the Democratic State* (1959), published in the United States under the title of *Principles of Political Thought*. It is reprinted with the permission of George Allen & Unwin, Ltd.]

is very difficult to know whether a given case is really of the type to which the particular law we have in mind applies. Nevertheless, there are some generalizations in psychology and the social sciences which are reasonably well established. They do not enable us to make detailed predictions; they merely enable us to state the sort of thing that will *tend* to happen under certain typical conditions. In this respect psychology is in no worse plight than other sciences like meteorology. The difficulties arise from the complexity of the subject-matter, and, it might be argued, can be remedied in time.

If, however, we look more closely at these so-called laws in psychology we find, in the main, that they do not give sufficient explanations of human *actions,* of what human beings do deliberately, knowing what they are doing and for which they can give reasons. Freud's brilliant discoveries, for instance, were not of the causes of *actions* like signing contracts or shooting pheasants; rather they were of things that *happen* to a man like dreams, hysteria, and slips of the tongue. These might be called "passions" more appropriately than "actions," and in this respect they are similar to what we call "fits of passion" or "gusts of emotion." Men do not dream or forget a name "on purpose" any more than they are deliberately subject to impulses or gusts of emotion. One class of laws in psychology, then, gives causal explanations which seem sufficient to account for what *happens* to a man, but not for what he does.

There is another class of laws, however, which concern not what happens to men, but what they do—their actions, performances and achievements. But such laws state necessary rather than sufficient conditions. We have in mind here the contributions made by physiological psychologists and those who have studied cognitive skills like learning, remembering, and perceiving. Part of what we mean by such terms is that human beings attain a norm or standard. Remembering is not just a psychological process; for to remember is to be *correct* about what happened in the past. Knowing is not just a mental state; it is to be sure that we are *correct* and to have *good grounds* for our conviction. To perceive something is to be *right* in our claims about what is before our eyes; to learn something is to *improve* at something or to get something *right*. All such concepts have norms written into them. In a similar way, as we have previously argued, a human action is typically something done in order to bring about a result or in accordance with a standard. Such actions can be said to be done more or less intelligently and more or less correctly only because of the norms defining what are ends and what are efficient and correct means to them. It follows that a psychologist who claims that such performances depend on antecedent physiological conditions or mental processes, can at the most be stating necessary conditions. For processes, of themselves, are not appropriately described as correct or incorrect, intelligent or stupid. They only become so in the context of standards laid down by men. As Protagoras taught, nature knows no norms. It may well be true that a man cannot remember without part of his brain being stimulated, or that learning is a function, in part, of antecedent "tension." But the very meaning of "remembering" and "learning" precludes a sufficient explanation in these sorts of naturalistic terms.

Furthermore the problem of the freedom of the will arose mainly in connection with a type of action that is palpably different from a mere movement or process—an action that is preceded by deliberation and choice. For, roughly speaking, a "willed action" was usually taken to mean one in which we think before we act, when we make up our minds in terms of considerations which are relevant to the matter in hand before we act. There are difficulties about developing causal laws for actions of this type which are additional to those already stated about actions in general. Such difficulties are similar to those which the social scientist, as well as the psychologist, has in predicting what human beings will do. This is connected with the fact that into the human being's deliberations about what he is going to do will be introduced considerations about what he is likely to do, which the social scientist may have published. A scientist may discover a causal law connecting the properties of clover with a certain effect upon the digestive organs of sheep. But, when he publishes his findings, the sheep cannot take account of them and modify their behaviour accordingly. But with men it is different. Many causal connections discovered by psychologists may only hold good provided that the people whose actions are predicted in accordance with the law remain ignorant of what it asserts. And it is practically impossible to ensure that this is the case. So, if people know the causes on which a prediction of a certain type of behaviour is based, and if they deliberate before acting they may do something different from what is predicted, just because they recognize these causes. A prediction may thus be valid only on the assumption that the people concerned remain unconscious of the causes on which it is based. Otherwise it may be no more than a warning.

But why cannot causal explanations *also* be given of such informed deliberations which precede actions? We are here confronted with the difficulty of accounting for *logical* thought in causal terms, of giving a causal explanation for rational actions done after deliberation which involves logically relevant considerations. This is an extreme case of the difficulty already cited of giving sufficient explanations in causal terms for actions and performances which involve norms and standards. Yet, as has already been pointed out, such premeditated actions are particularly important in the free-will controversy, as the exercise of "will" has usually been associated with rational deliberation before acting. When a man is solving a geometrical problem and his thoughts are proceeding in accordance with certain logical canons, it is logically absurd to suggest that any causal explanation in terms of movements in his brain, his temperament, his bodily state, and so on, is sufficient *by itself* to explain the movement of his thought. For logical canons are normative and cannot be sufficiently explained in terms of states and processes which are not. Of course there are any number of necessary conditions which must be taken account of. A man cannot think *without* a brain, for instance. But any *sufficient* explanation would have to take account of the *reasons* for his actions. We would have to know the rules of chess, for instance, which gave some *point* to a chess-player's move. Indeed we would only ask for the cause of a chess-player's behaviour if he did something which could not be explained in terms of the rules of chess and the objective at which he was aiming. If, for instance, he refrained from taking his opponent's queen, when this was the obvious and the best move, we might ask "What made him do that?" and we would be asking for a causal explanation, like "he was tired." But this would now be an explanation of what *happened* to him, not of what he did deliberately. We would not ask for such an explanation if there was an obvious reason for his move.*

This example can be generalized and the point made that behaviour is usually explicable not because we know its causes, but because people act in accordance with certain known rules and conventions and adopt appropriate means to objectives which are accepted as legitimate goals. We know why a parson is mounting the pulpit not because we know much about the causes of his behaviour but because we know the conventions governing church services. We would only ask what were the causes of his behaviour if he fainted when he peered out over the congregation or if something similar *happened* to him. Most of our explanations of human behaviour are couched in terms of a purposive, rule-following model, not in causal terms. Moral behaviour, above all other sorts, falls into this purposive, rule-following category. For, as Aristotle put it, it is not a man's passions which are the object of moral appraisal nor his capacity to be subject to such passions; rather we praise or blame a man for what he does about his passions, for the extent to which he controls or fails to control them in various situations. Deliberation and choice may not precede every action, but habits are set up as a result of such deliberation and choice. It is for the exercise of such habits that men are praised and blamed—for the ends which they seek and for the means which they adopt to bring about their ends. Punishment, too, presupposes that men can foresee the consequences of their actions and that they can learn to avoid those to which penalties are attached. Praise and blame, reward and punishment, act as rudders to steer human actions precisely because men deliberate and choose and can be influenced by considerations of consequences. There is a radical difference between actions of this sort and cases where things happen to a man—where he acts "on impulse," has a dream, a vision, or lapse of memory, or where he is afflicted by a feeling of nausea or hysterical paralysis. Questions of the "freedom of the will" do not arise where things happen to a man; only where a man acts and can be praised

* Of course the category of "action" is much wider than that of premeditated action, though it may be co-extensive with that of "rationality." For this covers the sort of things for which a man could have a reason—i.e. which fall under what we call the purposive rule-following model. Premeditated action is a particular case of action where action is *preceded* by rehearsals and deliberation; but often reasons can be given by people for what they do even though they do not deliberate *before* they act.

or blamed, punished or rewarded for what he does. Yet it is precisely in these cases of human actions, as distinct from passions, that causal explanations seem inappropriate as sufficient explanations.

Two sorts of objection might be mounted against this attempt to limit the role of causal explanations of human behaviour. In the first place it might be said that by substituting concepts like rule-following and the pursuit of objectives we were in fact introducing other sorts of causes. Now the word "cause" can be used in this very wide sense. But the terminological question is largely irrelevant; for two sorts of explanations which are logically quite different would then be included under the enlarged concept of "cause." To follow rules, to take steps which are seen to be necessary to reach some sort of objective, to see the point of something, these may be "causes"; but they are causes in quite a different sense of "cause" from things like stomach contractions, brain lesions, acute pains, and so on. The types of explanation must be distinguished whether we use the term "cause" to cover both or not. And certainly seeing the point of something is quite different—even if it is called a "cause"—from the causes prevalent in the physical world. In the early days of the determinist controversy philosophers like Spinoza and Kant used the term "self-determined" to distinguish rational actions from those which could be explained in terms of mechanical causes like movements of the brain and body. Indeed Kant's suggestion that man lives in two worlds, and is subject to two different sorts of causation, is a metaphysical way of bringing out the logical distinction between these two sorts of explanation.

The second objection is the suggestion that all reasons might be rationalizations—a smoke screen for what we are going to do anyway. We are, as it were, pushed by causes in the mechanical, physical sense, whatever we do; but sometimes we throw up an elaborate smokescreen of excuses which make no difference to what we in fact do. If, however, we say that *all* reasons are rationalizations, we make no difference between the behaviour of an obsessive or a compulsive and that of a rational man. If a compulsive believes that his hands are covered in blood and spends his time continually washing them, no relevant considerations will make any difference to his behaviour. All the known tests fail to show blood; yet he still goes on washing his hands. But a civil servant making a complex decision about policy does not proceed like this. He will change his mind and alter policy in the light of relevant considerations. Indeed it is only because people *sometimes* alter their behaviour because of relevant considerations that it makes any *sense* to talk of rationalizations as well as of reasons. A term like "rationalization," which casts aspersions on the reasons given for action, is a verbal parasite. It flourishes because there *are* cases of genuine reasons with which rationalizations can be contrasted. Thus even if all behaviour has causes, in the sense of *necessary* conditions, there are objections to saying that all behaviour—especially rational behaviour —can be *sufficiently* explained by causes of the sort suggested by physical scientists, and by mechanistic philosophers like Hobbes. . . .

Selected Bibliography

(ITEMS PROVIDED WITH ASTERISK ARE MORE ADVANCED)
(FOR KEY TO ABBREVIATIONS SEE PAGE XIX)

Several recent works contain surveys of the various positions which philosophers, scientists, and theologians have adopted on this subject. The fullest treatment is found in M. J. Adler, *The Idea of Freedom* (Garden City: Doubleday, 2 vols., 1958 and 1961), and in H. Ofstad, *An Inquiry into the Freedom of Decision* (London: Allen & Unwin, 1961). Both of these works contain elaborate and very useful bibliographies. Briefer but more readable are D. J. O'Connor, *Free Will* (Garden City: Doubleday, 1971, p) and M. Cranston, *Freedom—A New Analysis* (London: Longmans, Green, 1953). Older works covering the same territory are H. Wildon Carr, *The Free Will Problem* (London: Benn, 1928), and G. H. Palmer, *The Problem of Freedom* (N.Y.: Houghton Mifflin, 1911). There is also a valuable historical survey in Ch. XI, Book IV, of Alexander Bain, *Mental and Moral Science* (London: Longmans, Green, 1872). H. Morris (ed.), *Freedom and Responsibility* (Stanford: Stanford U.P., 1961), S. Morgenbesser and J. Walsh (eds.), *Free Will* (Englewood Cliffs: Prentice-Hall, 1962, p), B. Berofsky (ed.), *Free Will and Determinism* (N.Y.: Harper, 1966, p), W. F. Enteman (ed.), *The Problem of Free Will* (N.Y.: Scribner's, 1967, p), and G. Dworkin (ed.), *Determinism, Free Will, and Moral Responsibility* (Englewood Cliffs: Prentice-Hall, 1970, p) are anthologies devoted entirely to the subject of free will and determinism and its numerous ramifications. S. Hook (ed.), *Determinism and Freedom in the Age of Modern Science* (N.Y.: Collier Books, 1961, p), D. F. Pears (ed.), *Freedom and the Will* (London: Macmillan, 1963), and K. Lehrer (ed.), *Freedom and Determinism* (N.Y.: Random House, 1966, p) are original works containing contributions by philosophers representing diverse viewpoints. The following three anthologies dealing with problems concerning the nature of human action also contain selections bearing on the topics discussed in the present section: N. S. Care and C. Landesman (eds.), *Readings in the Theory of Action* (Bloomington: U. of Indiana P., 1968), A. R. White (ed.), *The Philosophy of Action* (Oxford: O.U.P., 1968, p), and M. Brand (ed.), *The Nature of Human Action* (Glenview, Ill.: Scott Foresman, 1970, p). All these three books contain useful bibliographies. The following general introductions to philosophy discuss in some detail the questions arising in connection with determinism, freedom and moral responsibility: A. Pap, *Elements of Analytic Philosophy* (N.Y.: Macmillan, 1949), A. C. Ewing, *The Fundamental Questions of Philosophy* (London: Routledge, N.Y.: Collier Books, 1962, p), J. Hospers, *An Introduction to Philosophical Analysis* (Englewood Cliffs: Prentice-Hall, second ed., 1967), M. Scriven, *Primary Philosophy* (N.Y.: McGraw-Hill, 1966), J. W. Cornman and K. Lehrer, *Philosophical Problems and Arguments* (N.Y.: Macmillan, 1968), K. Nielsen, *Reason and Practice* (N.Y.: Harper, 1971) and A. Flew, *An Introduction to Western Philosophy* (Indianapolis: Bobbs-Merrill, 1971, p). A number of papers on freedom and responsibility by contemporary theologians are collected in C. P. Ketcham and J. F. Day (eds.), *Faith and Freedom* (N.Y.: Weybright & Talley, 1969, p).

Terminological confusions and discrepancies are rampant in discussions of determinism and free will. For this reason classification of different writers is frequently not easy. It is often, for example, difficult to be sure whether a philosopher adopts what James calls "soft" determinism—the "reconciling" position represented in our selections by Mill and Schlick—or whether he is a "hard determinist" like Rée (Selection 1). In the case of some writers, fortunately there is no doubt. Thus Hobbes, Locke and Hume may be considered as the earliest reconcilers. Hobbes discusses the subject briefly in Ch. XXI of the *Leviathan* and more fully in "Of Liberty and Necessity," which is reprinted in Thomas Hobbes, *Body, Man and Citizen* (ed. R. S. Peters—N.Y.: Collier Books, 1962, p). Locke's treatment is found in Book II, Ch. XXI of the *Essay Concerning Human Understanding*. In more recent times this position has been defended in G. S. Fullerton, *A System of Metaphysics, Ch. 33* (N.Y.: Macmillan, 1904), Bertrand Russell, "Determinism and Morals," *Hibbert Journal*, 1908, reprinted as part of Ch. 1 of Russell's *Philosophical Essays* (London: Allen & Unwin, revised ed., 1966), Ch. VI of G. E. Moore, *Ethics* (London: Oxford U.P., 1912), R. B. Hobart's "Free-Will As Involving Determination and Inconceivable Without It," *M*, 1934, Ch. X of W. D. Ross, *Foundations of Ethics* (Oxford: Clarendon Press, 1939), Ch. XIV of C. L. Stevenson, *Ethics and Language* (New Haven: Yale U.P., 1944), A. J. Ayer, "Freedom and Necessity," *Polemic*, 1946, reprinted in Ayer, *Philosophical Essays* (London: Macmillan, 1954), J. Laird, *On Human Freedom* (London: Allen & Unwin, 1947), P. H. Nowell-Smith, "Free Will and Moral Responsibility," *M*, 1948, reprinted in M. K. Munitz (ed.), *A Modern Introduction to Ethics* (N.Y.: Free Press, 1958), Chs. 19 and 20 of the same author's *Ethics* (London: Penguin Books, 1954, p), Adolf Grünbaum's "Causality and the Science of Human Behavior," reprinted in H. Feigl and M. Brodbeck (eds.), *Readings in the Philosophy of Science* (N.Y.: Appleton-Century-Crofts, 1953), Ch. 20 of R. B. Brandt, *Ethical Theory* (Englewood Cliffs: Prentice-Hall, 1959), A. R. Lacey, "Freewill and Responsibility," *Ar. Soc.*, 1957, G. Williams, "The Natural Causation of Human Freedom," *PPR*, 1959, F. Vivian, *Human Freedom and Responsibility* (London: Chatto & Windus, 1964), Ch. 9 of J. J. C. Smart, *Between Science and Philosophy* (N.Y.: Random House, 1968), J. T. Saunders, "The Temptations of 'Powerlessness'," *APQ*, 1968, and M. Markovic, "Social Determinism and Freedom," in H. E. Kiefer and M. K. Munitz (eds.), *Mind, Science and History* (Albany: State U. of N.Y. P., 1970. C. J. Ducasse is strongly opposed to any Humean analysis of causation, but otherwise he belongs to the same tradition, vigorously defending the view that the acceptance of determinism is perfectly compatible with any intelligible belief in freedom and responsibility. His position is developed in detail in Ch. 11 of *Nature, Mind and Death* (LaSalle, Illinois: Open Court, 1951) and in summary fashion in his contribution to S. Hook (ed.), *op. cit.* The first essay in Gilbert Ryle, *Dilemmas* (Cambridge: Cambridge U.P., 1954), tries to remove one of the "conceptual roadblocks" encountered in reflections on freedom and determinism. There is a very subtle, but regrettably little known, defense of the Hume-Mill position in W. K. C. Clifford, "Right and Wrong: The Scientific Ground of Their Distinction," reprinted in his *Lectures and Essays* (London and N.Y.: Macmillan, 1879). J. Wilson, "Freedom and Compulsion," *M*, 1958, contains a particularly illuminating discussion, showing how some writers who maintain that determinism and freedom are not compatible tend to deprive person-words ("I," "he," etc.) of any meaning. Mill, whose discussion in his *System of Logic* is reprinted as our Selection 5, returned to the subject in Ch. 26 of *An Examination of Sir William Hamilton's Philosophy* (London: Longmans, Green, 1872) from which a selection is reprinted in Morgenbesser and

Walsh, *op. cit.* Mill there argues at some length in defense of the thesis that every human action is the result of the strongest desire. This thesis is exposed to numerous objections in R. B. Edwards, "Is Choice Determined by 'Strongest Motive'?," *APQ,* 1967. It should be pointed out that many contemporary determinists do not endorse the view that every action is the result of the strongest desire—they would regard it as either empirically doubtful or else as a tautology. Like most other soft determinists Mill argued that the predictability of human actions is perfectly consistent with their freedom. This topic is also discussed in A. Lyon, "The Prediction Paradox," *M,* 1959, J. Canfield, "Determinism, Free Will and the Ace Predictor," *M,* 1961, and G. P. Henderson, "Predictability in Human Affairs," in *The Human Agent, Royal Institute of Philosophy Lectures, Volume 1* (London: Macmillan, 1968, p). D. J. O'Connor in "Determinism and Predictability," *BJPS,* 1957, argues that determinism cannot be accurately formulated in terms of the predictability of phenomena. Bertrand Russell's views are vigorously attacked by F. C. S. Schiller in "Choice," *Hibbert Journal,* 1909, which is reprinted as Appendix 2 of Schiller's *The Riddles of the Sphinx* (London: Macmillan, rev. ed., 1910). There is a very careful critical analysis of G. E. Moore's writings on the subject in T. Redpath, "Moore on Free Will," in A. Ambrose and M. Lazerowitz (eds.), *G. E. Moore: Essays in Retrospect* (London: Allen & Unwin, 1970). In his articles, "Action and Agent," *Mo,* 1965, "Responsibility," in M. Brand (ed.), *The Nature of Human Action, op. cit.* and "Responsibility and Freedom," in R. T. De George (ed.), *Ethics and Society* (London: Macmillan, 1968, p), K. Baier supports the position of the reconcilers by a careful analysis of the concept of responsibility. In *Responsibility* (London: Routledge, 1960), J. Glover favors the same general position although he is critical of some earlier attempts to reconcile determinism with our common moral attitudes. In their analyses of responsibility, both Baier and Glover are indebted to the work of the influential legal philosopher, H. A. L. Hart, several of whose papers on the subject are brought together in *Punishment and Responsibility* (London: Oxford U.P., 1968, p). In "Fatalism and Determinism," in K. Lehrer (ed.), *Freedom and Determinism, op. cit.,* and in "Metaphysics and the Concept of a Person," in J. F. Lambert (ed.), *The Logical Way of Doing Things* (New Haven: Yale U.P., 1969), W. Sellars maintains that in view of recent work in the philosophy of mind a position like that of Hume and Mill can be defensibly revised. Sellars is criticized by A. Donagan in "Determinism and Freedom: Sellars and the Reconciliationist Thesis," in H. Castaneda (ed.), *Perception, Action and Reality* (Indianapolis: Indiana U.P., 1972). The same volume contains an abstract of Sellars' reply. One of the most careful recent defenses of soft determinism against all major objections is A. Grünbaum, "Free Will and Laws of Human Behavior," *APQ,* 1971. A subtle and original defense of the reconciling position is contained in H. G. Frankfurt, "Alternate Possibilities and Moral Responsibility," *JP,* 1969. Frankfurt is criticized in D. Blumenfeld, "The Principle of Alternative Possibilities," *JP,* 1971. P. F. Strawson in "Freedom and Resentment," which is available in P. F. Strawson (ed.), *Studies in the Philosophy of Thought and Action* (London: Oxford U.P., 1968, p), also champions a form of reconciliation, but in its detailed working out his attempt differs from the position of most other reconcilers. The Polish Marxist L. Kolakowski (who now teaches in Canada) defends soft determinism in his *Toward a Marxist Humanism* (N.Y.: Grove Press, 1968). He concedes that mechanistic determinism, which regards human action as wholly determined by the reactions of an individual's physical structure to external mechanical stimuli, is inconsistent with freedom. A determinist, however, need not be a mechanist and he has no trouble allowing for freedom if he recognizes that an individual's awareness may be a determinant of behavior.

The idealist variety of reconciliation is stated in the first essay of F. H. Bradley, *Ethical Studies** (Oxford: Clarendon Press, 1927) and in T. H. Green, *Prolegomena to Ethics** (Oxford: Clarendon Press, 1906). It is also supported by Engels in his *Anti-Dühring,* Part I, Ch. XI, and by V. Lenin in *Materialism and Empirio-Criticism,* Ch. III, Section 6. The standard texts of both of these books are printed by the Foreign Languages Publishing House, Moscow. Similar positions are forcefully defended in Ch. V of J. M. E. McTaggart, *Some Dogmas of Religion* (London: Edward Arnold, 1906), A. E. Taylor, *The Elements of Metaphysics* (London: Methuen, N.Y.: Barnes & Noble, 1961, p), and in Ch. III of Book III of Hastings Rashdall, *The Theory of Good and Evil* (Oxford U.P., 1924). The latter book contains also a particularly detailed and fair discussion of the arguments for indeterminism. Kant, who considered himself a kind of reconciler, offers his resolution in the *Critique of Pure Reason** and more fully in *The Groundwork of the Metaphysics of Morals** and the *Critique of Practical Reason.** Useful discussions of this feature of Kant's philosophy may be found in L. W. Beck, *A Commentary on Kant's Critique of Practical Reason* (Chicago: U. of Chicago P., 1960), A. C. Ewing, *Kant's Treatment of Causality* (London: Routledge, 1924), in the same author's *A Short Commentary on Kant's Critique of Pure Reason* (Chicago: U. of Chicago P., 1950), W. T. Jones, *Morality and Freedom in the Philosophy of Kant* (London: Oxford U.P., 1940), and J. Bennett, "The Status of Determinism," *BJPS,* 1963.

One of the leading defenders of hard determinism in the eighteenth century was the Enlightenment philosopher, Baron P. Holbach, who discussed the subject in Chs. 11 and 12 of his monumental *System of Nature,* which was first published in 1770 (an English translation appeared in Boston in 1853), and in his briefer and more popular *Good Sense* (1772). An English translation of the latter is in print under the title *Superstition in All Ages* (N.Y.: The Truthseeker Co., 1920), but it is wrongly ascribed to the Abbé Meslier, whose name appeared on the title page of the first French edition to protect Holbach from persecution. Schopenhauer in his *Essay on the Freedom of the Will* (N.Y.: Liberal Arts Press, 1962, tr. K. Kolenda, p) and in "Free-Will and Fatalism" (*Complete Essays,* Book VI, tr. T. B. Saunders) also approximates to "hard" determinism and so does Spinoza in Part III of the *Ethics.* Shelley, who was strongly influenced both by Holbach and Spinoza, argues in support of hard determinism in a long Note to Canto V of *Queen Mab* ("Necessity! thou mother of the world!"). Among recent writers the most fervent hard determinist was probably Clarence Darrow who stated without any qualifications that no human being is ever morally responsible for any of his actions. Darrow's views are found in his book, *Crime, Its Cause and Treatment* (N.Y.: Crowell, 1922), and in numerous pamphlets published by the Haldeman-Julius Co. of Girard, Kansas. The most moving of these is Darrow's plea in defense of the boy-murderers, Loeb and Leopold, which has been reprinted under the title of "The Crime of Compulsion," in A. Weinberg (ed.), *Attorney for the Damned* (N.Y.: Simon & Schuster, 1957). There are many literary works, including the poems of A. E. Housman and the novels of Melville, Thomas Hardy, and Schnitzler, in which similar views are expressed. Anthony Collins, one of the most important of the English deists, Voltaire, Jonathan Edwards, and Joseph Priestley are usually regarded as determinists who denied freedom, but a careful reading of their works suggests that they are really determinists of the reconciling variety. Collins' *A Philosophical Inquiry Con-*

cerning Human Liberty can be found only in libraries, but the writings of the other three writers just mentioned are easily available. Voltaire's views are stated in several articles of his *Philosophical Dictionary* and also in the little treatise entitled "The Ignorant Philosopher"; Jonathan Edwards' *Freedom of the Will* is available in an edition by P. Ramsey (New Haven: Yale U.P., 1957) which contains an extremely valuable historical introduction; and some of Priestley's writings on the subject were recently reprinted in *Priestley— Selected Writings on Philosophy, Religion and Politics* (ed. J. Passmore, N.Y.: Collier Books, 1965, p). A recent defense of hard determinism is found in P. Edwards, "Hard and Soft Determinism," in S. Hook (ed.), *Determinism and Freedom in the Age of Modern Science, op. cit.* Other defenses of hard determinism are listed below in the paragraph dealing with psychoanalytic writings on the subject. In *The Problem of Freedom and Determinism* (Columbia, Mo.: U. of Missouri P., 1968), E. D'Angelo argues that certain forms of hard determinism are only verbally different from most versions of soft determinism.

A famous defense of indeterminism is contained in Henri Bergson, *Time and Free Will** (N.Y.: Macmillan, 1921). This theory is also supported by Lotze in his books *Microcosmus** (N.Y.: Scribner's, 1894) and *Outlines of the Philosophy of Religion* (Boston: Ginn, 1885), by James Martineau in his *Study of Religion*, Volume II (Oxford: Clarendon Press, 1888), by Charles Peirce in his essay "The Doctrine of Necessity Examined," which is reprinted both in Peirce, *Chance, Love and Logic* (ed. M. R. Cohen, N.Y.: Harcourt, Brace, 1923) and in J. Buchler (ed.), *The Philosophy of Peirce* (N.Y.: Harcourt, Brace, 1940), and Henry Sidgwick, *The Methods of Ethics* (N.Y.: Macmillan, 1907). The last-mentioned book contains a valuable and very balanced discussion of all the main arguments on both sides. Peirce's "tychism" or indeterminism is critically discussed in Ch. 3 of A. J. Ayer, *The Origins of Pragmatism* (San Francisco: Freeman, Cooper, 1968). Two recent full-length defenses of indeterminism are A. M. Munn, *Free Will and Determinism* (London: MacGibbon & Kee, 1960), and K. W. Rankin, *Choice and Chance* (Oxford: Blackwell, 1961). An extreme and somewhat obscure form of indeterminism is defended by Jean-Paul Sartre in *Being and Nothingness** (N.Y.: Philosophical Library, 1956, tr. H. E. Barnes). Selections from this work are reprinted in Morgenbesser and Walsh, *op. cit.*, and in R. Abelson (ed.), *Ethics and Metaethics* (N.Y.: St. Martin's Press, 1963). A briefer and somewhat clearer statement of Sartre's indeterminism is found in his article "Cartesian Freedom" which is available in his *Literary and Philosophical Essays* (N.Y.: Collier Books, 1962, p). Most writings on Sartre are as obscure as Sartre himself. A notable exception is the very lucid critical study, "An Existentialist's Ethics" by A. Plantinga in *RM*, 1958. The American existentialist, Peter Koestenbaum, defends indeterminism in "The Power of Freedom," *Existential Psychiatry*, 1967. Another American existentialist, William Barrett, criticizes determinism in "Determinism and Novelty," in S. Hook, *op. cit.*

A recent development of the position defended by William James in "The Dilemma of Determinism" (see Selection 3) is found in E. A. Sipfle, "A Wager on Freedom," *International Philosophical Quarterly*, 1968. There are interesting discussions of James's defense of "chance" in some of the correspondence between him and diverse philosophers reprinted in R. B. Perry, *The Thought and Character of William James* (Cambridge: Harvard U.P., 1935). Like James, C. Lamont, in *Freedom of Choice Affirmed* (N.Y.: Horizon Press, 1967), argues for the existence of "objective contingency" and tries to make such contingency the foundation of freedom and moral responsibility. Lamont's book is critically discussed in a symposium on "Freedom of Choice" published in 1970 by The Fellowship of Religious Humanists of Yellow Springs, Ohio. This symposium includes contributions by Lamont, van Meter Ames, R. Atkins, J. H. Randall, Jr., W. F. Enteman, J. A. Gould, M. Capek, and S. P. Lamprecht. Indeterminism is also defended in several of the works of the very influential philosopher of science, Sir Karl R. Popper. There are brief discussions of the subject in his *The Logic of Scientific Discovery** (N.Y.: Science Edition, 1961, p) and *Conjectures and Refutation* (N.Y.: Harper, 1968, p) and a much fuller treatment in the extremely interesting lecture, *Of Clouds and Clocks* (St. Louis: Washington U., 1966). Popper's views are criticized in P. E. Meehl's "Psychological Determinism and Human Rationality: A Psychologist's Reactions to Professor Karl Popper's 'of Clouds and Clocks'," and M. Radner, "Popper and Laplace,"—both in M. Radner and S. Winokur (eds.), *Analyses of Theories and Methods of Physics and Psychology* (Minneapolis: U. of Minnesota P., 1970). Another recent defense of indeterminism by a philosopher of science is found in Chs. 6 and 8 of P. Caws, *Science and the Theory of Value* (N.Y.: Random House, 1967, p). The notion of "chance" is discussed in some detail in S. Hook's article "Determinism" in *The Encyclopedia of the Social Sciences* (N.Y.: Macmillan, 1935), in Ch. 10 of Ernest Nagel, *The Structure of Science* (N.Y.: Harcourt Brace, 1961), in D. Bohm, *Causality and Chance in Modern Physics** (London: Routledge, 1957), in M. Bunge, "What Is Chance?" *Science and Society*, 1951 and in L. D. Roberts, "Indeterminism, Chance and Responsibility," *R*, 1971. The concept of chance is also discussed in two recent articles by biologists—T. Dobzhansky, "Scientific Explanation—Chance and Antichance in Organic Evolution," and B. Glass, "The Relation of the Physical Sciences to Biology—Indeterminacy and Causality," both in B. Baumrin (ed.), *Philosophy of Science, The Delaware Seminar* (N.Y.: Interscience Publishers, 1963). A vigorous attack on all forms of determinism is contained in I. Berlin, *Historical Inevitability* (London: Oxford U.P., 1954). A revised version of *Historical Inevitability,* together with replies to his critics, is included in Berlin's *Four Essays on Liberty* (London: Oxford U.P., 1969, p). Berlin's views are criticized in Ch. 15 of Nagel, *op. cit.,* in Ch. III of E. H. Carr, *What Is History?* (London: Macmillan, 1961), in Francis V. Raab, "History, Freedom and Responsibility," *PS*, 1959, and A. Flew's "History and Human Responsibility," *The Rationalist Annual*, 1962. In *The Freedom of the Will* (Oxford: Clarendon Press, 1970), J. R. Lucas argues that Gödel's Theorem implies the falsehood of determinism. Lucas also endorses numerous other arguments against determinism. Indeterminism is also supported in R. L. Franklin, *Freewill and Determinism* (London: Routledge, 1968). Although he favors indeterminism, Franklin regards several of the arguments against determinism as unsound. This work is one of the most comprehensive discussions of the subject published in recent years. A position similar to Franklin's is advocated in R. B. Edwards, *Freedom, Responsibility and Obligation* (The Hague: Nijhoff, 1969).

A number of philosophers who reject determinism do not follow James and Peirce in identifying freedom with chance or contingency. These writers call themselves "libertarians" but they do not wish to be classified as indeterminists. They would not deny that all human actions are caused, but in this statement "cause" does not mean "sufficient condition" and it cannot be analyzed along Humean lines. All these writers would also deny that free human actions are even in principle predictable. One of the earliest supporters of such a position was the Scottish philosopher of "common sense," Thomas Reid, who discussed this subject in great detail in *Essays on the Active Powers of the Human Mind* (this work was reprinted in 1969 in Cambridge by M.I.T.

Press, with an introduction by B. A. Brody). Prominent among contemporary philosophers who belong to this tradition are C. A. Campbell, the author of Selection 7, H. D. Lewis, the author of Selection 4, J. D. Mabbott, and E. F. Carritt. Campbell's libertarianism is developed in *Scepticism and Construction** (London: Allen & Unwin, 1931), in *Of Selfhood and Godhood* (London: Allen & Unwin) and in several papers collected in *In Defence of Free Will* (London: Allen & Unwin, 1967). Campbell's theories were attacked by R. D. Bradley in "Free Will: Problem or Pseudo-Problem?" *AJ*, 1958, and by R. L. Franklin, in "Moral Libertarianism," *PQ*, 1962. There are rejoinders by Campbell in the same volumes of these periodicals. The libertarianism of Reid and Campbell is defended in K. Lehrer, "Can We Know that We Have Free Will by Introspection?" *JP*, 1960. H. D. Lewis works out his position in *Morals and Revelation* (London: Allen & Unwin, 1951) and in his article "Moral Freedom in Recent Ethics," *Ar. Soc.*, 1946–47, reprinted in W. Sellars and J. Hospers (eds.), *Readings in Ethical Theory* (N.Y.: Appleton-Century-Crofts, 2nd ed., 1970). Mabbott's chief discussions are "Free Will and Punishment," in H. D. Lewis (ed.), *Contemporary British Philosophy, Third Series* (London: Allen & Unwin, 1956), and his article on "Free Will" in the *Encyclopaedia Britannica* Vol. 9, pp. 853–857. Carritt defends libertarianism in Ch. 12 of *Ethical and Political Thinking* (Oxford: Clarendon Press, 1947). All these writers emphasize the introspectively given belief in their own freedom which all human beings experience at moments of choice. The question as to just what is given in introspection is very fully discussed in D. Browning, "The Feeling of Freedom," *RM*, 1964, reprinted in W. F. Enteman (ed.), *The Problem of Free Will, op. cit.* R. M. Chisholm and R. Taylor advocate what they call a theory of "agency" which has many affinities with the views of Reid, Campbell, and the other writers mentioned in this paragraph. Chisholm's position is stated in *Human Freedom and the Self* (Lawrence, Kansas: Kansas U.P., 1964, p), in "Freedom and Action" (which includes an adaptation of *Human Freedom and the Self*) in K. Lehrer (ed.), *Freedom and Determinism, op. cit.*, " 'He Could Have Done Otherwise'," *JP*, 1967, reprinted in J. H. Gill (ed.) *Philosophy Today No. 1* (N.Y.: Macmillan, 1968, p), also in Brand (ed.), *The Nature of Human Action, op. cit.*, and in "Some Puzzles about Agency," in K. Lambert (ed.), *The Logical Way of Doing Things, op. cit.* Chisholm is criticized in N. L. Ranken, "The 'Unmoved' Agent and the Ground of Responsibility," *JP*, 1967, K. Baier, "Responsibility and Action," S. McCall, "Ability as a Species of Possibility" (the two last items are contributions to Brand, *The Nature of Human Action, op. cit.*), H. G. Frankfurt, "Freedom of the Will and the Concept of a Person," *JP*, 1971, and J. D. Wallace, "The Influence of Agents," *CJP*, 1971. Taylor's position is developed in his *Metaphysics* (Englewood Cliffs: Prentice-Hall, 1963, p), *Action and Purpose* (Englewood Cliffs: Prentice-Hall, 1966), "Deliberation and Foreknowledge," *APQ*, 1964, "Deliberation and Freedom," *Southern Journal of Philosophy*, 1968, "Causation," *Mo*, 1963 and in his articles on "Determinism" and "Causation" in *The Encyclopedia of Philosophy*. Taylor is criticized in C. Downes, "Can a Determinist Deliberate?" *M*, 1969 and K. W. Rankin, "Can and Might," *CJP*, 1971. A position very similar to that of Chisholm and Taylor is supported in J. Yolton, "Agent Causality," *APQ*, 1966. Other recent writers supporting a theory of agency similar to that of Chisholm and Taylor include A. Danto, S. Hampshire and M. R. Ayers. Danto's views are expressed in "What We Can Do," *JP*, 1963, reprinted in Care and Landesman (eds.), *Readings in the Theory of Action, op. cit.*, and "Freedom and Forebearance," in Lehrer (ed.), *Freedom and Determinism, op. cit.* Danto is more strongly opposed to determinism than Taylor, maintaining that "the concept of action is incompatible with determinism." Hampshire's discussions are found in his *Thought and Action** (London: Chatto & Windus, 1959), *Freedom of the Individual** (N.Y.: Harper, 1965) and *Freedom of Mind and Other Essays** (Princeton: Princeton U.P., 1971). In *The Refutation of Determinism* (London: Methuen, 1968), M. R. Ayers maintains that what he considers to be the basic argument for determinism confuses different kinds of possibility. The bulk of this book is devoted to a discussion of the concept of possibility.

An interesting argument concerning the "self-defeating" character or the "self-stultification" of determinism has been discussed by a number of recent writers. This argument does not attempt to show that determinism is false but rather, that, if it were true, one could not have any good reasons for believing anything, including determinism itself. A typical elaboration of this argument is that of T. Honderich in Ch. 5 of his *Punishment* (Harmondsworth: Penguin Books, 1971, p). Honderich maintains first that one can have rational confidence in a belief only if one could have come to some other belief and then argues that one could *not* have come to any other belief if determinism were true. This argument or variants of it are supported in A. E. Taylor, "Freedom and Personality," *P*, 1939, the same author's "Freedom and Personality Again," *P*, 1942, Ch. 3 of C. S. Lewis, *Miracles* (N.Y.: Macmillan, 1947), Ch. 6 of E. L. Mascall, *Christian Theology and Natural Science* (London: Longmans, Green, 1956), L. Kenner, "Causality, Determinism and Freedom of the Will," *P*, 1964, Ch. 21 of J. R. Lucas, *The Freedom of the Will, op. cit.* and J. N. Jordan, "Determinism's Dilemma," *RM*, 1969. There are replies to C. S. Lewis in G. E. M. Anscombe, "A Reply to Mr. C. S. Lewis' Argument that 'Naturalism' is Self-Refuting," *Socratic Digest* IV (Oxford: Blackwell, 1949), M. Knight, "Consciousness and the Brain," *Science News*, 25 (Harmondsworth: Penguin Books, 1952), and A. Flew, "The Third Maxim," *Rationalist Annual*, 1955. Other critical responses to the self-stultification argument are found in A. J. Ayer's "Fatalism," included in his *Concept of a Person and Other Essays* (London: Macmillan, 1963), A. Flew, "A Rational Animal," in J. R. Smythies (ed.), *Brain and Mind* (London: Routledge, 1965), and D. Wiggins, "Freedom, Knowledge, Belief and Causality," in *Knowledge and Necessity, Royal Institute of Philosophy Lectures Volume 3, op. cit.* There is a reply to Flew's 1955 article in E. Gellner, "Determinism and Validity," *Rationalist Annual*, 1957, and a reply to Gellner by Flew in "Determinism and Validity Again," *Rationalist Annual*, 1958. Further references may be found in Lucas, *op. cit.*, page 116 and Jordan, *op. cit.*, page 48.

The late Sir Arthur Eddington attacked determinism in numerous books and articles, basing his criticisms chiefly on the quantum theory and Heisenberg's so-called "principle of indeterminacy." The main statements of Eddington's position are found in Ch. XIV of his *Nature of the Physical World* (N.Y.: Macmillan, 1928), in Ch. XI of *The Philosophy of Physical Science* (N.Y.: Macmillan, 1939) and in his address, "The Decline of Determinism," published in the *Mathematical Gazette* of May, 1932. Eddington's views are criticized by Lord Samuel in an article, "Cause, Effect, and Professor Eddington," in *The Nineteenth Century and After*, April, 1933, by Bertrand Russell in Ch. VI of *Religion and Science* (London: Oxford U.P., 1935, p) and in a lecture on "Determinism and Physics" (University of Durham Philosophical Society, 1936), and most fully by L. S. Stebbing, *Philosophy and the Physicists* (London: Methuen, 1937). Eddington replied to some of these criticisms in Ch. XIII of *New Pathways in Science* (Cambridge: Cambridge U.P., 1935). Many other distinguished physicists have written on the question of the implications,

:s," and K. Bendall, "LaPlacian Determinism and Omnitemporal
ateness,"—the last three items all in *JP*, 1971. Also unusually stimulat-
e review by G. A. Paul of Stebbing's *Philosophy and the Physicists*
938. The contributions by Bridgman, Nagel, Munitz, and Landé in
. cit., also largely deal with this subject. Nagel, who like Einstein is an
ant determinist, states his own position in considerable detail in Ch.
e Structure of Science, op. cit. Of decisive importance to the question
hilosophical implications of quantum theory is the notion of a deter-
theory or system. This issue is discussed in several of the works just
:d. It is also treated in great detail in R. Montague, "Deterministic
," in D. Wilner (ed.), *Decisions, Values and Groups* (N.Y.: Pergamon
)62) and in B. C. van Fraassen, "A Formal Approach to the Philos-
Science," in R. Colodny (ed.), *Paradigms and Paradoxes* (Pittsburgh:
ttsburgh P., 1972).

ussions from a Catholic point of view and opposed to determinism are
M. Maher, *Psychology* (London: Longmans, Green, 1940) and J. E.
Man and Meaning (N.Y.: McGraw-Hill, 1969). Other discussions of
lem by writers with a religious background are contained in E. W.
*Scientific Theory and Religion** (Cambridge: Cambridge U.P., 1935),
ett, *Religion and Free Will* (Oxford: Clarendon Press, 1913), C. F.
God and Freedom in Human Experience (London: Edward Arnold,
). Von Hildebrand, *Christian Ethics* (N.Y.: McKay, 1935), and D.
ifex, *Providence and Freedom* (London: Burns & Oates, 1960). High-
om the famous exchanges on the subject between Erasmus and Luther
lable in E. F. Winter (ed.), *Erasmus-Luther—Discourse on Free Will*
Ungar, 1961). William of Ockham's treatise on *Predestination, God's*
wledge, and Future Contingents is now available in an English transla-
.Y.: Appleton-Century-Crofts, 1969, p). This volume also contains
ons of other related writings by Ockham. Recent discussions of these
is by analytic philosophers are A. Flew, "Divine Omnipotence and
Freedom" in Flew and MacIntyre (eds.), *New Essays in Philosophical*
y (N.Y.: Macmillan, 1955, p), N. Pike, "Divine Omniscience and
ry Action," *PR*, 1965, reprinted in J. H. Gill (ed.), *Philosophy Today*
(N.Y.: Macmillan, 1969, p) and L. Becker, "Foreknowledge and
nation," *M*, 1972.

ospers, who (in Selection 8) maintains that the conclusions of psycho-
are incompatible with judgments of moral responsibility, offers a re-
nt of his position in his contribution to the volume edited by S. Hook,
Hospers is criticized in some detail in Chs. 8 and 9 of K. Nielsen,
and Practice, op. cit. There is also a critical examination of the thesis
ned by Hospers in P. H. Nowell-Smith, "Psychoanalysis and Moral
ge," *The Rationalist Annual*, 1954. Freud's own views on the subject
found in Ch. XII of *The Psychopathology of Everyday Life* (available
erous editions). Other psychoanalysts who have expressed themselves
subject include Ernest Jones, in his essay, "Free Will and Determinism,"
s reprinted in his *Essays in Applied Psychoanalysis*, Volume II (Lon-
ogarth Press, 1951), Erich Fromm, in *The Heart of Man* (N.Y.:
& Row, 1964), R. Waelder, "The Problem of Freedom in Psychoanalysis,"
tional Journal of Psychoanalysis, 1936, and R. Knight, "Determinism,
m,' and Psychoanalysis," *Psychiatry*, 1946. Recent discussions of these
ated questions by philosophers include H. Fingarette's "Psychoanalytic
tives on Moral Guilt and Responsibility," *PPR*, 1955, a symposium on
roblem of Guilt" in *Ar. Soc. Sup.*, 1947, with H. D. Lewis, J. W.

if any, of recent physical theory on the truth of
deserve special mention in this connection: W
*Theories of the Quantum Theory** (Chicago: U. o
*and Philosophy** (N.Y.: Harper, 1958), and *T.
Nature (N.Y.: Harcourt, Brace, 1958), M. Born,
and Chance (Oxford: Clarendon Pr., 1949), D.
in Modern Physics, op. cit., A. Schrödinger, *Scien
ment (N.Y.: Norton, 1935, p), P. W. Bridgma
(N.Y.: Philosophical Library, 1955), C. F. F. W
Physics (Chicago: U. of Chicago P., 1952), and
discoverer of the quantum theory, Max Planck,
Going? (N.Y.: Norton, 1932) and the *Guthrie L*
Proceedings of the Physical Society, 1932, repri
Thomson (ed.), *Science Today* (London: Eyre &
the majority of contemporary physicists, Einst
determinist. It is possible to get an idea of his vi
in P. A. Schilpp (ed.), *Albert Einstein, Philos*
Press, 1951, p), especially from the essay by Ni
with Einstein on Epistemological Problems in Ato
"A Reply to Criticisms." Bohr's own views are st
*Physics and Human Knowledge** (N.Y.: Wiley, 1
"Causality and Complementarity," *PS,* 1937. Pl
philosopher and a physicist, discussed the subj
Kausalgesetz und seine Grenzen (Vienna: Julius
ism and Indeterminism in Modern Physics," re
and Its Philosophy (N.Y.: Collier Books, 19
Science (Englewood Cliffs: Prentice-Hall, 195
books by physicists strongly favor indeterminism
*ophy of Quantum Mechanics** (N.Y.: Humanitie
Atomic Order: An Introduction to the Philoso
bridge: MIT Press, 1969). The following are
recent articles dealing with this topic: M. Sc
gegenwärtigen Physik,"* *Die Natur-Wissensch*
Rynin as "Causality in Contemporary Physics,
"Indeterminism in Quantum Physics and in Cl
51, A. Grünbaum, "Complementarity in Quant
ical Generalization," *JP,* 1957, Michael Scrive
terminism in Physics," *JP,* 1957, A. Landé, "D
Modern Science," *M,* 1958, R. W. Workman, "
Quantum Theory?" *PS,* 1959, G. F. Dear, "De
BJPS, 1961, F. Waismann, "The Decline and F
(ed.), *Turning Points in Physics* (N.Y.: H
Waismann's *How I See Philosophy* (London: 1
ley, "Determinism or Indeterminism in Micropl
band, "Problems of Microphysics,"* in R. G
Science and Philosophy (U. of Pittsburgh P., 1
The Listener, July, 1964, H. Margenau, "Qua
Determinism," *JP,* 1967, R. G. Swinburne
Knowledge and Necessity, Royal Institute of
op. cit., W. C. Salmon, "Determinism and Ind
in J. Feinberg (ed.), *Reason and Responsibili*
son, 2nd ed., 1971), J. Earman, "LaPlacian D
to Run a Universe?", C. Glymour, "Determ

Harvey, and G. A. Paul as participants, E. H. Madden, "Psychoanalysis and Moral Judgeability," *PPR*, 1957, reprinted in E. H. Madden (ed.), *The Structure of Scientific Thought* (Boston: Houghton Mifflin, 1960), R. Peters, "Freud and Responsibility," *The Nation*, Nov. 16, 1957, the same author's *Authority, Responsibility and Education* (London: Allen & Unwin, 1959), P. Alexander, "Rational Behaviour and Psychoanalytic Explanation," *M*, 1962, reprinted in Care and Landesman, *Readings in the Theory of Action, op. cit.* and A. Flew, "Psychoanalysis and the Philosophical Problem of Free Will" in C. Hanly and M. Lazerowitz (eds.), *Psychoanalysis and Philosophy* (N.Y.: International Universities Press, 1970). Barbara Wootton, the distinguished sociologist, discusses the subject of determinism and moral responsibility in the light of contemporary psychiatric theories in "Humanism and Social Pathology," in J. Huxley (ed.), *The Humanist Frame* (London: Allen & Unwin, 1961), and more fully in her book, *Social Science and Social Pathology* (N.Y.: Macmillan, 1959), which is critically discussed by H. D. Lewis in *Freedom and History, op. cit.* The psychologist, E. G. Boring, discusses the subject of determinism in "When Is Human Behaviour Predetermined?" reprinted in D. E. Dulaney (ed.), *Contributions to Modern Psychology* (Oxford: Oxford U.P., 1958).

It has been maintained by several recent writers that an action, especially a rational action, as opposed to a mere feeling or a mere movement, cannot be causally explained, at any rate in the sense in which the word "cause" has generally been understood by philosophers in the Hume-Mill tradition. In the present work this line of reasoning is adopted in the selection from Benn and Peters (Selection 9). It is developed more fully by Peters in his book, *The Concept of Motivation* (London: Routledge, 1961). A very similar position is worked out in great detail in A. I. Melden, *Free Action* (London: Routledge, 1961). In *Causation in the Law* (Oxford: Clarendon Press, 1959), H. L. A. Hart and A. M. Honoré argue that a Humean account of the cause of an action done for a reason is untenable. Their discussion is not immediately concerned with determinism, but A. C. MacIntyre in "Determinism," *M*, 1957, and P. Herbst in "Freedom and Prediction," *ibid.*, make the distinction between cause and reason the basis for their rejection of determinism. There are answers to MacIntyre by M. C. Bradley and by A. Flew in *M*, 1959, and there are detailed rejoinders to all arguments of this kind in D. Davidson's "Actions, Reasons, and Causes," *JP*, 1963, A. J. Ayer, "Man as a Subject for Science," which is available both in Ayer's *Metaphysics and Common Sense* (London: Macmillan, 1969) and in P. Laslett and W. G. Runciman (eds.), *Philosophy, Politics and Society* (Oxford: Blackwell, 1967) and in B. Berofsky, "Determinism and the Concept of a Person," *JP*, 1964. R. Brandt and J. Kim, in their "Wants as Explanations of Actions," *JP*, 1963, maintain, in opposition to the thesis of writers like Melden and Peters, that human actions can be explained in much the same sense in which it is generally agreed that events are explained in the natural sciences. The articles by MacIntyre, Bradley, and Davidson are reprinted in Berofsky, *op. cit.* The articles by Davidson and Brandt and Kim are reprinted in Care and Landesman, *op. cit.*, Davidson's is also reprinted in White, *op. cit.* Several recent books are entirely devoted to the various problems concerning the nature of action. These include B. Powell, *Knowledge of Actions* (London: Allen & Unwin, 1967), D. G. Brown, *Action* (London: Allen & Unwin, 1968), A. I. Goldman, *A Theory of Human Action* (Englewood Cliffs: Prentice-Hall, 1970), G. Langford, *Human Action* (Garden City: Doubleday, 1971, p), and T. Mischel (ed.), *Human Action: Conceptual and Empirical Issues* (N.Y.: Academic Press, 1969). S. Toulmin, R. S. Peters, and A. I.

Melden are among the contributors to the last-mentioned volume. R. Binkley, R. Bronaugh and A. Marras (eds.), *Agent, Action and Reason* (Oxford: Blackwell, 1971) includes contributions by D. Davidson, J. Cornman, R. Chisholm, B. Aune, R. M. Hare, D. Gauthier, D. F. Pears, and I. Thalberg. It also contains a comprehensive bibliography. The following articles are also concerned with these problems: M. Brodbeck, "Meaning and Action," *PS,* 1963, C. Landesman, "The New Dualism in the Philosophy of Mind," *RM,* 1965, A. Flew, "A Rational Animal," (with comments by C. J. Ducasse, D. M. Mackay, and H. H. Price) in J. R. Smythie's (ed.), *Brain and Mind, op. cit.,* J. Feinberg, "Action and Responsibility," in M. Black, (ed.), *Philosophy in America* (Ithaca: Cornell U.P., 1965), reprinted in White, *op. cit.,* R. Abelson, "Because I Want to," *M,* 1965, A. O. Rorty, "Wants and Justifications," *JP,* 1966 (which is a criticism of Abelson), R. Abelson, "New Stops on the BIWT," *JP,* 1967 (a reply to Rorty), B. Goldberg, "Can a Desire Be a Cause?", *A,* 1965, W. D. Gean, "Reasons and Causes," *RM,* 1966, A. Mac-Intyre, "The Antecedents of Action" in B. Williams and A. Montefiore (eds.), *British Analytical Philosophy* (London: Routledge, 1966), D. Davidson, "The Logical Form of Action Sentences," (with comments by E. J. Lemmon, H. M. Castaneda, and R. M. Chisholm) in N. Rescher (ed.), *The Logic of Decision and Action* (Pittsburgh: U. of Pittsburgh P., 1967), W. P. Alston, "Wants, Actions and Causal Explanation," in H. Castaneda (ed.), *Intentionality, Minds and Perception* (Detroit: Wayne U.P., 1967), I. Thalberg, "Verbs, Deeds and What Happens to Us," *P,* 1967, R. R. Ehman, "Causality and Agency," *R,* 1967, R. Macklin, "Doing and Happening," *RM,* 1968, D. Pears, "Are Reasons for Actions Causes?" in A. Stroll (ed.), *Epistemology* (N.Y.: St. Martin's Press, 1969, p), R. J. Richman, "Responsibility and the Causation of Actions," *APQ,* 1969, the same author's "Reasons and Causes," *AJ,* 1969, A. B. Levison, "Essential and Causal Explanations of Action," *M,* 1969, R. Macklin, "Explanation and Action: Recent Issues and Controversies," *Sy.,* 1969, G. H. Harman, "Knowledge, Reasons, and Causes," *JP,* 1970, K. S. Donnellan, "Causes, Objects, and Producers of Emotions," *ibid.,* P. M. Churchland, "The Logical Character of Action Explanations," *PR,* 1970, B. Berofsky, "Purposive Action," *APQ,* 1970, S. Toulmin, "Reasons and Causes," in R. Borger and F. Cioffi (eds.), *Explanation in the Behavioral Sciences* (Cambridge: Cambridge U.P., 1970), F. Stoutland, "The Logical Connection Argument," in N. Rescher (ed.), *Studies in the Theory of Knowledge* (Oxford: Blackwell, 1970, p), J. E. White, "Avowed Reasons and Causal Explanations," *M,* 1971, R. Audi, "Intentionalistic Explanations of Action," *Me.,* 1971, and J. Rachels, "Reasons for Action," *CJP,* 1971. The Summer 1970 issue of *Inquiry* (Oslo) is devoted to the subject of action, containing articles by A. Stigen, D. S. Shwader, C. Taylor, and others. Ch. 5 of J. A. Shaffer, *Philosophy of Mind* (Englewood Cliffs: Prentice-Hall, 1968, p) is an excellent introductory discussion of all the major questions concerning the nature of action and their relations to the determinism-freewill issue.

S. Hampshire and H. L. A. Hart, in "Decision, Intention and Certainty," *M,* 1958, argue that its logically impossible for a person to know how he is going to decide before he actually makes his decision. In a widely discussed article, "Can the Will Be Caused?" *PR,* 1962, C. Ginet makes this contention the basis of an argument against soft determinism. If human beings ever genuinely decide, then these decisions cannot be caused since, if they were caused, it would be in principle possible for the agent to know in advance the outcome of his decision. Very similar arguments against the possibility of reconciling determinism with the existence of freedom are found in Ch. 4 of

R. Taylor, *Metaphysics, op. cit.* and in the same author's "Deliberation and Foreknowledge," *op. cit.* These and related questions are discussed in the following articles: J. Canfield, "Knowing About Future Decisions," *A*, 1962, P. Swiggart, "Doing and Deciding To Do," *A*, 1962, J. W. Roxbee Cox, "Can I Know Beforehand What I Am Going To Decide?" *PR*, 1963, K. Lehrer, "Decisions and Causes," *PR*, 1963, A. Oldenquist, "Causes, Predictions and Decisions," *A*, 1964, I. Thalberg, "Foreknowledge and Decisions in Advance," *A*, 1964, A. J. Stenner, "On Predicting Our Future," *JP*, 1964, D. P. Gauthier, "How Decisions are Caused," *JP*, 1967, T. O'Connor, "How Decisions are Predicted," *JP*, 1967, D. P. Gauthier, "How Decisions are Caused (But Not Predicted)," *JP*, 1967, A. I. Goldman, "Actions, Predictions, and Books of Life," *APQ*, 1968 (this article is reprinted in a revised version as Ch. 6 of Goldman's *A Theory of Human Action, op. cit.*), D. Pears, "Predicting and Deciding," in P. F. Strawson (ed.), *Studies in the Philosophy of Thought and Action* (London: Oxford U.P., 1968, p), M. Stocker, "How to Prevent Self-Prediction," *JP*, 1968, the same author's "Knowledge, Causation and Decision," *N*, 1968, Q. Boyce Gibson, "The Limits of Social Prediction," *Mo*, 1968, and J. L. Cowan, "Deliberation and Determination," *APQ*, 1969. In "An Essential Unpredictability in Human Behavior," in B. Wolman and E. Nagel (eds.), *Scientific Psychology* (N.Y.: Basic Books, 1965), M. Scriven argues that certain human actions are in principle unpredictable. Scriven is criticized in P. Suppes, "On an Example of Unpredictability in Human Behavior," *PS*, 1964. An argument in some respects similar to Ginet's, attempting to show that it is in principle impossible for an agent to predict his own free acts, is advanced by D. M. Mackay in "Brain and Will," *The Listener*, 1957 and "On the Logical Indeterminacy of a Free Choice," *M*, 1960. There is an answer to Mackay by C. J. F. Williams in *A*, 1960, a rejoinder by Mackay to Williams in *A*, 1961, and a further comment by Williams, *ibid.* Mackay has discussed these questions more recently in "Information and Prediction in Human Sciences," in S. Dockx and P. Bernays (eds.), *Information and Prediction in Science* (N.Y.: Academic Press, 1965) and in his Eddington Lecture, *Freedom of Action in a Mechanistic Universe* (Cambridge: Cambridge U.P., 1967). Mackay's recent pieces are discussed in I. Thalberg, "New Light on Brain Physiology and Free Will," *BJPS*, 1970, I. J. Good, "Free Will and Speed of Computation," *BJPS*, 1971, J. W. N. Watkins, "Freedom and Predictability: An Amendment to Mackay," *ibid.*, and in A. Grünbaum, "Free Will and Laws of Human Behavior," *op. cit.* Mackay replies to some of his critics in "Choice in a Mechanistic Universe," *BJPS*, 1971. In "Free Will in a Mechanistic Universe?", *BJPS*, 1970, P. T. Landsberg and D. A. Evans discuss some of the questions raised by Mackay.

Most of the soft determinists of the Hume-Mill school have offered analyses of "can" statements in terms of hypothetical propositions. According to one fairly widespread view, for example, to say that I could have done something other than what I actually did means simply that I would have done something else if I had wanted to do something else; and if this is all that is meant, it follows that determinism is perfectly compatible with the view that human beings can frequently do something other than what they actually do. This kind of position, in the form in which it is found in the writings of G. E. Moore and Nowell-Smith, was attacked by the very influential Oxford philosopher, John Austin, in his British Academy Lecture, "Ifs and Cans" (1956), which has been reprinted in his *Philosophical Papers* (Oxford: Clarendon Press, 1961), also in H. Morris, *op. cit.*, M. Brand, *op. cit.*, and B. Berofsky, *op. cit.* Austin's lecture has given rise to more discussion than perhaps any other single paper by an Anglo-Saxon philosopher in recent years. It is now generally agreed that the formulations by Moore and Nowell-Smith which Austin attacked are indeed untenable, but it is by no means universally agreed that a hypothetical analysis of some kind is impossible and still less that soft determinism has been put out of court. The following are some recent discussions of the relevant issues: P. H. Nowell-Smith, "Ifs and Cans," *T*, 1960, D. J. O'Connor, "Possibility and Choice," *Ar. Soc. Sup.*, 1960, R. Taylor, "I Can," *PR*, 1960, reprinted in Morgenbesser and Walsh, *op. cit.*, K. Lehrer, "Ifs, Cans, and Causes," *A*, 1960, D. Locke, "Ifs and Cans Revisited," *P*, 1960, J. J. C. Smart, "Free-Will, Praise and Blame," *M*, 1961, R. D. Bradley, " 'Ifs,' 'Cans,' and Determinism" *AJ*, 1962, J. V. Canfield, "The Compatibility of Free Will and Determinism," *PR*, 1962, I. Thalberg, "Abilities and Ifs," *A*, 1962, C. Dore, "On the Meaning of 'Could Have,' " *A*, 1962, K. Baier, "Could and Would," *A Sup.*, 1963, B. Aune, "Abilities, Modalities and Free Will," *PPR*, 1963, C. Dore, "Is Free Will Compatible with Determinism?" *PR*, 1963, J. Canfield, "Free Will and Determinism," *PR*, 1963, D. S. Scarrow, "On an Analysis of 'Could Have,' " *A*, 1963, C. Dore, "More on the Meaning of 'Could Have,' " *ibid.*, A. S. Kaufman, "Ability," *JP*, 1963, A. M. Honoré, "Can and Can't," *M*, 1964, K. Lehrer " 'Could' and Determinism" *A*, 1964, A. C. Ewing, "May Can-Statements Be Analysed Deterministically?" *Ar. Soc.*, 1964, reprinted in his *Nonlinguistic Philosophy* (London: Allen & Unwin, 1968), G. Thomas, "Abilities and Physiology," *JP*, 1964, J. M. Osborn, "Austin's Non-Conditional Ifs," *JP*, 1965, A. R. White, "What Might Have Been," in N. Rescher (ed.), *Studies in the Theory of Knowledge, op. cit.*, A. Ross, "He Could Have Acted Otherwise," in *Festschrift für Hans Kelsen zum 90. Geburtstag* (Vienna: Deuticke, 1971), D. F. Pears, "Ifs and Cans,"—two articles in *CJP*, 1971 and 1972, and M. White, "On What Could Have Happened," in R. Rudner and I. Scheffler (eds.), *Logic and Art: Essays in Honor of Nelson Goodman* (Indianapolis: Bobbs-Merrill, 1972). The following two discussions of the meaning of "can" and "could," prior to the publication of Austin's lecture, are particularly worth mentioning: F. V. Raab's "Free Will and the Ambiguity of 'Could,' " *PR*, 1955, and W. D. Ross, *Foundations of Ethics, op. cit.* (pp. 225–43).

There is a great deal of disagreement about the logical status of the principle, however it is formulated, that every event or phenomenon has a cause. Many of the older determinists regarded the principle as simply an exceedingly general and well-confirmed empirical proposition. Indeterminists also regard it as an empirical proposition, but one which is false. According to one contemporary view, advanced by S. Hampshire in "Multiply General Sentences," *A*, 1950, and even more emphatically by J. G. Warnock in "Every Event Has a Cause,' " in A. Flew (ed.), *Logic and Language,* Second Series (Oxford: Blackwell, 1953), the causal principle is "vacuous," "utterly uninformative," and thus in some important sense "meaningless." In "The Incoherence of Determinism," *P*, 1969, B. Mayo aruges that on analysis determinism is seen to be either a trite pronouncement or else one that cannot claim the support of science. In Section 4 of "Reduction: Ontological and Linguistic Facets," in S. Morgenbesser, *et al.* (eds.), *Philosophy, Science and Method, op. cit.*, C. G. Hempel discusses some of the difficulties of stating determinism in such a way as not to render it trivial. Some contemporary philosophers like Ducasse, *op. cit.*, follow Kant in regarding the causal principle as a logically necessary truth, but probably the most widespread attitude on the part of those favoring determinism is to treat it as a regulative principle or a "heuristic maxim." This view is adopted by E. Nagel, *op. cit.* It is also defended in A. J. Ayer, *Founda-*

tions of Empirical Knowledge (London: Macmillan, 1940), J. Hospers, *An Introduction to Philosophical Analysis, op. cit., an*d by several of the contributors to the volume edited by S. Hook, *op. cit.* There is a very illuminating discussion of this topic in Ch. 17 of A. Pap, *An Introduction to the Philosophy of Science* (N.Y.: Free Press, 1962). According to Pap, the contrast between a "rule of procedure" and a "well-confirmed empirical generalization" is artificial and the principle of causality can with equal propriety be regarded in either way. Nagel is criticized in K. Nielsen, "Is to Abandon Determinism to Withdraw from the Enterprise of Science?" *PPR*, 1967. In *Determinism* (Princeton: Princeton U.P., 1971), B. Berofsky offers a definition of determinism in terms of the notion of law, based on a defense of the regularity-theory of causation. Berofsky maintains that determinism is an intelligible thesis and wavers between the conclusion that it is probably false and the view that we do not possess sufficient knowledge to decide whether it is true.

The concepts of volition and willing, which played an important role in almost all the older discussions, receive some rough handling in Gilbert Ryle, *The Concept of Mind* (London: Hutchinson, N.Y.: Barnes & Noble, 1949, p), and in Ludwig Wittgenstein, *Philosophical Investigations** (Oxford: Blackwell, 1953). Strategic selections from these extremely influential works are found in H. Morris, *op. cit.* Wittgenstein's views are discussed in P. Winch, "Wittgenstein's Treatment of the Will," *R*, 1968. The following are recent articles on the topics of willing and choosing: S. Hampshire, "Self-Knowledge and the Will," *Revue International de Philosophie*, 1953, J. L. Evans, "Choice," *PQ*, 1955, W. D. Glasgow, "On Choosing," *A*, 1957, P. H. Nowell-Smith, "Choosing, Deciding and Doing," *A*, 1958, W. D. Glasgow, "The Concept of Choosing," *A*, 1960, T. F. Daveney, "Choosing," *M*, 1964, and G. N. A. Vesey, "Volition," reprinted in Vesey (ed.), *Body and Mind* (London: Allen & Unwin, 1964), and in D. F. Gustafson (ed.), *Essays in Philosophical Psychology* (Garden City: Doubleday, 1964, p). J. N. Lapsley, (ed.), *The Concept of Willing* (Nashville: Abingdon Press, 1967), contains papers by psychiatrists, theologians and existentialist philosophers. Detailed historical accounts of theories about the nature of volition are found in A. Alexander, *Theories of the Will in the History of Philosophy* (N.Y.: Scribner's, 1898), and V. J. Bourke, *Will in Western Thought* (N.Y.: Sheed & Ward, 1964).

There are numerous interesting articles discussing determinism which cannot easily be fitted into any of the classifications adopted here. These include C. A. Baylis, "Rational Preference, Determinism and Moral Obligation," *JP*, 1950, H. L. A. Hart, "The Ascription of Responsibility and Rights,"* reprinted in A. Flew (ed.), *Essays in Logic and Language.* First Series (Oxford: Blackwell, 1951), F. B. Ebersole, "Free-Choice and the Demand of Morals," *M*, 1952, W. I. Matson, "On the Irrelevance of Free-Will to Moral Responsibility," *M*, 1956, W. F. R. Hardie, "My Own Free Will,"* *P*, 1957, A. Danto and S. Morgenbesser, "Character and Free Will," *JP*, 1957, H. Fain, "Prediction and Constraint," *M*, 1958, B. Mayo, "A Logical Limitation on Determinism," *P*, 1958, P. Foot, "Free Will as Involving Determinism," *PR*, 1959, reprinted in Morgenbesser and Walsh, *op. cit.*, A. Danto, "The Paradigm Case Argument and the Free-Will Problem," *E*, 1959, E. L. Beardsley, "Determinism and Moral Perspectives," *PPR*, 1960, D. Schon, "Rationality in Retrospective and Prospective Deliberation," *ibid.*, V. J. McGill, "Conflicting Theories of Freedom," *ibid.*, R. Handy, "Determinism, Responsibility and the Social Setting," *ibid.*, M. Mandelbaum, "Determinism and Moral Responsibility," *E*, 1960, C. Shute, "The Dilemma of Determinism after 75 Years," *M*, 1961, D. Gallop, "On Being Determined," *M*, 1962, R. C. Skinner, "Freedom of

Choice," *M*, 1963, I. Thalberg, "Freedom of Action and Freedom of Will," *JP*, 1964, J. Hilton, "Indeterminate Determinism," *M*, 1964, a dialogue on "Freewill" by J. Wisdom in his *Paradox and Discovery* (Oxford: Blackwell, 1965), T. Duggan and B. Gert, "Voluntary Abilities," *APQ*, 1967, L. Kenner, "On Blaming," *M*, 1967, M. A. Slote, "Free Will, Determinism and the Theory of Important Criteria," *I*, 1969, and L. C. Holborow, "Blame, Praise and Credit," *Ar. Soc.*, 1971.

Other discussions in books and booklets which are not easy to classify include C. D. Broad's Inaugural Lecture, "Determinism, Indeterminism and Libertarianism,"* reprinted in his book, *Ethics and the History of Philosophy* (N.Y.: Harcourt, Brace, 1952), Ch. VIII of John Wisdom, *Problems of Mind and Matter* (Cambridge: Cambridge U.P., 1934, p), W. B. Gallie, *Free Will and Determinism—Yet Again* (Belfast: Queen's University of Belfast, 1957), A. Farrer, *The Freedom of the Will* (N.Y.: Scribner's, 1958), "On Determinism," by the famous Polish logician, J. Lukasiewicz in his *Selected Works* (N.Y.: Humanities Press, 1971), and the Inaugural Lecture by G. E. M. Anscombe, *Causality and Determination* (Cambridge: Cambridge U.P., 1971). P. Bowes, *Consciousness and Freedom* (London: Methuen, 1971), in addition to dealing with more familiar approaches, contains discussions of the existentialist viewpoint and of Indian theories on the subject of free will. There is a particularly thought-provoking discussion, ending with a confession of bewilderment, in H. L. Mencken's *A Treatise of Right and Wrong* (N.Y.: Knopf, 1934).

The following articles in the *Encyclopedia of Philosophy* deal with various aspects of the problems discussed in the present section: "Can" (B. Aune, 2–18), "Causation" (R. Taylor, 2–56), "Chance" (S. M. Cahn, 2–73), "Choosing, Deciding, and Doing" (A. Oldenquist, 2–96), "Determinism" (R. Taylor, 2–359), "Determinism in History" (W. H. Dray, 2–373), "Guilt" (H. D. Lewis, 3–395), "Must" (B. Aune, 5–414), "Punishment" (S. I. Benn, 7–29), "Reasons and Causes" (K. S. Donnellan, 7–85), "Responsibility, Moral and Legal" (A. S. Kaufman, 7–183), "Self-Prediction" (A. Oldenquist, 7–345) and "Volition" (G. N. A. Vesey, 8–258).

II

Scepticism
and
the Problem
of Induction

INTRODUCTION

WHETHER OR NOT THE LOGICAL POSI-
tivists are right in denying that anything at all can be known *a priori* about the
universe we live in, most philosophers are agreed that we must rely on *induction*
in order to arrive at interesting general conclusions in empirical science—that is,
in all sciences except logic and mathematics. For example, every educated boy
or girl "knows" that water is H_2O. This means that water is composed of
molecules which are themselves composed of two atoms of hydrogen and one
atom of oxygen. Obviously, the chemist did not arrive at this conclusion by
examining water molecules through a microscope. He arrived at it by interpreting by means of the atomic theory of matter the experimentally established
law that in order to produce water by synthetic chemistry one must mix oxygen
and hydrogen in the volume proportion $1:2$. How is this law "established"?
Well, you just experiment and see! But experiment can only tell you that such
and such a result followed such and such conditions at a definite place and
time; when you conclude that the same result will follow the same conditions at
any time and place, you perform an induction, you *generalize* from the observed
facts, you argue from what has actually been observed to cases which have not
been observed. On a less technical level: whenever you bite into an apple, you
generalize from past experience, for you expect that this thing tastes like an
apple on the ground that similar things have always produced that unique taste
sensation in your experience.

Now, Hume, the classical "sceptic" with respect to the foundations of
empirical knowledge, asked the following question: since obviously you can
conceive (imagine) that a thing which looks and feels like an apple should
not taste like an apple, the proposition that all things which look and feel like
apples taste like apples is not *necessary*; no *a priori* proof of it is possible. If
so, do you have any *reason* for believing that the thing which you now hold
in your hand will taste like an apple? "Of course I have a reason," you reply;
"the reason is that similar things have always been found to taste like that."
But then Hume would have pressed you as follows: you presuppose that if
qualities A and B have always been accompanied by quality C in the instances
you have observed, then they will also be accompanied by C in future instances.
You presuppose, in other words, that *nature is uniform*. Clearly, unless you
have a reason for believing this general presupposition, you have no reason for
believing any specific proposition that is, as it were, supported by it. But this

general presupposition is not a necessary proposition either; if it were, then a chaotic world—a world in which what looks like fire sometimes feels hot and sometimes feels cold, in which what looks like milk sometimes tastes like milk, sometimes like orange juice, and sometimes evaporates the moment it is touched by lips, etc.—would be inconceivable, which it is not by any means. What then is our reason for believing that *it* is true? Is it that we infer that nature *will be* uniform from the fact that it *has been* uniform? But to justify this inference and to prove the alleged presupposition of the uniformity of nature is one and the same thing; hence we beg the question if we attempt to prove that nature must be uniform by relying on the inference from what has happened to what will happen (See Hume: Selection 11, pp. 136 f. and Russell: Selection 12, pp. 141 ff.) Conclusion: induction cannot be logically justified at all; it is not even a process of reasoning, but a *habit* of expecting what has happened in such and such circumstances to happen again in similar circumstances. It should be noted that neither Hume nor other sceptics deny the *psychological* fact that we are strongly inclined to believe that the future will be like the past. They and other philosophers discussing this subject are not concerned with questions of psychology but with *logical* problems—with the question of the justification or validity of inductive inferences.

Some modern philosophers have attempted to get around Hume's pessimistic assessment of the power of reason by accusing him of having asked for too much: of course, they say, you can never be *certain* that a prediction will be fulfilled; to that extent Hume was right. But in order to justify an inductive inference—i.e., an inference whose conclusion does not follow with logical necessity from the premises, though the latter are offered as reasons justifying one's acceptance of the conclusion—it is sufficient to show that the conclusion is *probable* relative to the known facts. Hume, however, cannot be accused of having overlooked this answer to his scepticism. What is your basis for saying, he inquired, that given A and B, C is probable? Just that C has been observed to be frequently, though not invariably, present when A and B were present. We predict that probably, though not certainly, this man will get angry if we insult him, because men, or men who in certain relevant respects resemble this man, have in the past been observed to react that way to an insult *in most cases.* Therefore probable reasoning, said Hume, likewise presupposes the uniformity of the course of nature, though a smaller degree of uniformity ("statistical" uniformity, as it is called nowadays), and the problem of justifying predictions remains essentially the same.

John Stuart Mill set himself the task of liberating inductive science from Hume's scepticism without relying, like the Kantians, on *a priori* knowledge of universal propositions about nature. He regarded the experimental methods used by scientists as methods for discovering the true hypothesis by elimination of all but one of the initially possible hypotheses. You wonder whether A is the cause of B (where A and B are repeatable *kinds* of events). You cannot prove that every instance of A will be followed by an instance of B, or every instance of B preceded by an instance of A, by observing all possible instances of these kinds of events. But Mill believed that true generalizations could be discovered *negatively:* a generalization can be *disproved* by a single instance. Nobody could prove that aspirin is an infallible remedy against headache by observing all possible cases of consumption of aspirin, but it is easy to disprove this claim by finding just once that the headache remains after aspirin has been swallowed. Now, suppose you knew that a given kind of effect E must have been caused by either A or B or C, which are circumstances that were present when, or immediately before, an observed instance of E occurred. By applying Mill's experimental methods (which are discussed in most elementary textbooks of logic and scientific method) you might quickly find that neither A nor B is the cause. And then you would have established with certainty that C is the cause, though a conclusive verification of the generalization "every instance of C is followed by an instance of E" or "every instance of E is preceded by an instance of C" by the *direct* method would be impossible.

Mill was acutely aware of a big assumption involved in the use of this indirect method of getting at the true explanation of an effect by elimination of all initially possible alternative explanations: that every event has a cause, called by him "the law of universal causation." If it is indeed presupposed by indirect induction, it would be circular to try to prove it by indirect induction. But can we trust direct induction ("induction by simple enumeration" is the usual name, given to this method by Francis Bacon, the first philosopher of inductive science) in this one instance, though it cannot be trusted in any other instance? Mill tried hard to convince himself and his readers of an affirmative answer to this crucial question. He argued that direct induction is reliable if the sample of instances from which we generalize is very large and diversified, and maintained that this condition of reliability is fulfilled by the generalization that every event has a cause. It may be countered, however, that Mill overlooked that the *instances* which confirm the law of universal causation are themselves specific causal laws, which on his own theory cannot be established by direct induction. And if they are established by indirect induction, which presupposes the law of universal causation, then Mill's attempted empirical proof of the latter is circular after all. But be this as it may, the majority of contemporary philosophers would say that Mill did not succeed in solving Hume's doubt.

As regards their attitude towards this "problem of induction," contemporary philosophers fall roughly into three groups: 1) the enemies of empiricism who commend Hume for having shown brilliantly that a consistent empiricism must shovel its own grave. For, so they argue, according to empiricism synthetic universal propositions, like the propositions we believe to express laws of nature, can be established only by induction from observed instances, not *a priori*. And induction is not a valid method of inference unless we have reason to believe in the validity of some synthetic universal proposition, like Mill's law of universal causation, or some version of a principle of the uniformity of nature. But if so, then we cannot justify our acceptance of any synthetic universal propositions. A consistent empiricism, they maintain, cannot provide a man with reasons for believing any synthetic propositions except those that just describe his present sense-experience, because a belief in what is not perceived here and now is based on inductive inference—as shown by Hume—and inductive inference is not justifiable on empiricist principles. To illustrate: at this moment I believe that there is a bookcase behind the chair in which I am sitting. As I am not perceiving the bookcase now, this belief must rest on inference. I seem to remember to have seen a bookcase at the described place on a number of occasions, and hence infer that I actually did see one there. But it is logically possible, even if this inference from memory be granted, that the bookcase should have been removed, or even should just have vanished, in the meantime. If I exclude this logical possibility without hesitation, it is because I cannot think of any *cause* of the bookcase's disappearance since I last saw it, and refuse to believe that anything happens without cause. Thus belief in a general synthetic proposition emerges once we analyze our grounds for believing the simplest proposition about what is not present to our senses. At this point the paths followed by the critics of empiricism divide: some are content to have pointed up the alternative "either abandon empiricism or remain a Humean sceptic!" without offering a constructive alternative to empiricism; others more or less openly revive Kantianism by claiming *a priori* knowledge of some suitable "principle of induction," i.e., synthetic proposition about nature which must be true if any empirical evidence is to make any inductive conclusion probable. Members of the latter subgroup, though, do not always seem to be clear about what they are doing. They assign to philosophy the task of "justifying" inductive inference and therewith scientific method by making explicit the "presuppositions" on which it rests—as though by showing that p can be true only if q is true one had shown that p *is* true. Group (1) is represented by our selection from Russell's early little book *The Problems of Philosophy*. Students of Russell's later writings are, however, of divided opinion as to whether Russell falls into the first or the second subgroup.

2) Those who seek a solution of Hume's problem within the logic or theory of probability. Nothing less than a painstaking study of the logic of probability is needed for a full understanding of the issues raised by these thinkers from Laplace to Carnap. Expositions of this approach tend to be very technical and for this reason it is not represented in our selections. Very roughly, the problem is this. From the information that all ten marbles in a specified urn are white (and that marbles do not change their color in the process of being drawn) we can deduce the conclusion that, say, the first seven marbles we shall draw are white. The conclusion follows necessarily in the sense that it would be self-contradictory to affirm the premise and at the same time deny the conclusion. Now, the converse inference is not by any means necessary: it does not follow from the fact that the first seven marbles turned out to be white that all the marbles are white. On the other hand, the supposed uniformity of the outcomes of more than half of the possible drawings makes the conclusion that all the marbles are white fairly probable. If the conclusion were false, i.e., if at least one marble in the urn were not white, then it would be fairly improbable that a run of seven white marbles should have occurred. For suppose you compute the number of possible sets of seven marbles that can be formed out of a set of ten marbles, and suppose that all but one of the ten marbles are white, then you would find that the proportion of sets of that size that contain that lone nonwhite marble is much larger than the proportion of those that do not contain it. If we suppose each marble to be as likely to be drawn as any other, and further that the drawn marbles are not replaced before the next drawing, the probability of a run of seven white marbles on the assumption that initially there are nine white and one nonwhite marble, equals $\frac{3}{10}$. Or, suppose that in fact only 800 of 1000 beans in a large bag of beans were good. What would be the probability then that all the beans in a large sample from the bag are good? It would be small, in the sense that among all the possible large samples (say, samples of fifty) only a small proportion would be entirely devoid of bad beans. Therefore, given that nothing but good specimens are found in a large random sample, it is probable that almost all the beans in the bag are good. The idea behind this approach to the problem of induction is that judgments of probability may themselves be *logically certain*, in the same sense in which it is logically certain that if all A are B, then all the members of any given samples of the class A are B. The judgments of probability which are needed to justify our predictions can be established, according to this school of thought, by logic alone; contrary to Hume's claim, no inductive inference is required to establish *them*. It can be proved in the theory of probability, a subject whose theorems are as infallibly certain as any mathematical theorem, that the probability that a sample approximately matches in composition the

class from which it is drawn increases as the sample increases. This theorem does not guarantee that the method of induction *will* lead us to the truth. Even if a generalization has been confirmed a million times and not a single exception to it has been found it does not follow that it is exceptionless. But relative to such extensive confirming evidence it is, according to the mentioned theorem, highly probable that the generalization is true or has very few exceptions. And the validity of this judgment of probability does not depend on any assumptions about the constitution of nature.

3) Those who maintain that the time-honored "problem of induction," whose apparent insolubility has been called by some "the scandal of modern philosophy," is not a genuine problem at all. The discussions by Frederick Will and Max Black in our book represent this point of view. (See Selections 13 and 14.) If a man admits, they say, that things which look and feel like eggs have always (or nearly always) tasted like eggs in past experiences, yet denies that this is a *reason* for believing that the next egg will have the same familiar taste, in other words, that this evidence makes it probable that the next egg will taste similarly, then he just cannot mean by the words "reason" and "probable" what is ordinarily meant by them. He may be using "reason" in the strong sense of "logically conclusive reason," the sense in which the premises of a valid syllogism are a reason for its conclusion. In this sense of "reason" it would be self-contradictory to accept the propositions proffered as reasons and at the same time to question a proposition inferred from them. But then, what more is he denying than that the conclusion of an inductive argument follows *necessarily* from its premises? And isn't this trivial, since the very definition of "induction" implies that the conclusion is not a necessary consequence of the premises that describe the observed facts? The sceptic on this view is simply bemoaning that induction is not deduction. But this seems a senseless complaint. One might as well complain that deduction is not induction.

Furthermore, is it really true that we have to fall back on a principle of the uniformity of nature in order to justify our belief that the fact that dry leaves always burned when lit in the past makes it probable that such matter will burn again if set afire now? What exactly does this alleged principle assert? "Same cause, same effect" is one familiar answer, but it is not clear what this means. If it means "whenever and wherever *exactly* the same conditions are repeated which in the past were attended by effect E, there and then E will occur again," then it is inapplicable for the purpose of justifying a particular inductive inference; for there are always some variations in the conditions. If it means "if the same *relevant* conditions are repeated, then the effect is repeated," the question arises how one is to distinguish relevant from irrelevant conditions. Presumably the recurrence of E is our very criterion for determining whether all relevant conditions were present; that is, if C' is not followed by E whereas C was followed by E, we conclude that some relevant condition must have failed to accompany C'; we do not conclude that in this instance the "same" cause failed to give rise to the "same" effect. But if the principle is thus irrefutable by experience, say the logical positivists, then it is a mere tautology and says nothing about the world at all. And if specific empirical evidence cannot by itself make a specific prediction probable, a tautology will not help either.

Hume raised the problem whether we can ever be justified in accepting the conclusion of an inductive argument. As already pointed out, he questioned not only whether inductive conclusions can ever be certain but even whether they can ever be so much as probable. A position which is less critical of common-sense beliefs about matters of fact is that of the philosophers who maintain that no empirical proposition can ever be absolutely certain. The most we can ever obtain is a high degree of probability. Common sense readily admits that generalizations about nature, like "the planets always revolve around the sun in elliptical orbits," "cats who mate with cats always give birth to cats and never to dogs," "a tooth extraction which is not preceded by some anesthetic always causes pain," cannot be known with absolute certainty. But people who have not been enlightened, or corrupted by philosophical analysis will say that just the same there remain millions of empirical propositions (i.e., propositions whose truth or falsehood must be discovered by experience) of whose truth we can be absolutely certain. To take an extreme example: if I feel and see a table, and my friends assure me that they see and feel the same thing, if further, just to make sure, I sit on what looks and feels like a table and find myself supported, have I not made absolutely certain, then, that there *is* a solid table in the room? Yet, ever since Descartes claimed—at least as critical philosopher, if not as devout Christian—that the only thing which indubitably exists is his own doubt of the existence of anything else, and therewith his own mind ("I think, therefore I exist"), many philosophers have denied that any propositions about the physical world (including the proposition that there is one) are ever certain. Briefly the argument is this: suppose I see what looks like a table but, having recently read Descartes, am in doubt whether what I see is a physical table: perhaps my sense of sight deceives me, perhaps I am dreaming. The natural way to resolve my doubt is to touch the apparent table, put heavy objects on it in order to see whether they are supported, etc. If I still remain in doubt, I may ask other people to come into the room and report whether their sensory experience is the same. But no matter how much corroborating testimony is obtained, a determined sceptic need not concede. For he can always describe possible evidence which, if it became actual, might make one doubtful of the truth of the physical proposition. Thus, what would you say if, after ten carefully selected observers confirmed the verdict of your senses, the next ten observers who had equally proven their visual normality reported that they see nothing at all at the place allegedly occupied by a table, while you and the first group of observers continued to see a table? Perhaps you would then be inclined to doubt their honesty instead of doubting the proposition in question. But what if you then saw them walk through the space seemingly occupied by a solid table? No doubt you would begin to doubt your own perceptual normality: "I must be suffering from an hallucination!" But what if the first group of observers reported that they saw the miraculous event too? You might conclude that there was a table which suddenly vanished without assignable cause, or that you are in the presence here of a kind of table that exists but intermittently, going in and out of existence at intervals for no known reason. But since continuous existence and public observability seem to be part of what one means by a "physical object," it is more likely that in such an event one would doubt the initially confirmed proposition that there was a table in the room.

At any rate, this is the sort of thing philosophers mean when they deny that any physical propositions are verifiable with absolute conclusiveness. They deny it on the ground that any such proposition has an "infinite number of consequences"—such as that the just imagined kinds of events will not occur. Some well-known contemporary representatives of this view are John Dewey, Bertrand Russell, Hans Reichenbach, C. I. Lewis, Rudolf Carnap, and A. J. Ayer. Some go to the extreme of denying that any empirical propositions can be known with complete certainty, others claim that at least propositions which assert nothing beyond what is immediately sensed can be so known: I may be mistaken in saying that there is a white sheet of paper before me, but how could I be mistaken in the cautious assertion that there *seems* to be such a thing before me? (See the selection from Descartes, p. 128.) However, some modern philosophers, who feel that most of the traditional disputes among philosophers are verbal, maintain that the philosophical theory which asserts that no physical proposition can ever be known beyond the shadow of a (theoretical) doubt is nothing but a pointless departure from the ordinary usage of the word "certain." When we say "we have made absolutely certain that there is a table here," we do not mean that we cannot conceive of any future experience that might *then* make us doubtful of the truth of the proposition. Therefore the sceptic is not really refuting a view that is held by common sense. It only looks as though he were refuting the proposition "some physical propositions can be verified with absolute certainty," they say, because in denying this sentence he is using the same *word* "certainty." But since he assigns a new, unusually strong meaning to this word, his disagreement with the common sense view is merely *verbal*. It is like "refuting" the apparently well-confirmed belief that we frequently see the *same* thing at different times by the argument that nothing has exactly the same properties at two different times, that every thing constantly changes in some respect. The proper way of countering this refutation is to point out that in saying, for example, "I have seen the same house before," one just does not *mean* that the house in question has undergone no changes whatever.

Whether nevertheless such a philosophical definition of "certainty" has some point—unlike the definition of a "man" as a biped which is omniscient and 20 feet tall, which entails the surprising consequence that contrary to your previous beliefs there are no men on earth (or does it?)—is a question beyond the scope of an introductory book.

A. P.

The Sphere of the Doubtful

René Descartes

Meditation I

I T IS NOW SOME YEARS SINCE I DE-
tected how many were the false beliefs that I had from my earliest youth
admitted as true, and how doubtful was everything I had since constructed
on this basis; and from that time I was convinced that I must once for all
seriously undertake to rid myself of all the opinions which I had formerly
accepted, and commence to build anew from the foundation, if I wanted
to establish any firm and permanent structure in the sciences. But as this
enterprise appeared to be a very great one, I waited until I had attained an
age so mature that I could not hope that at any later date I should be better
fitted to execute my design. This reason caused me to delay so long that I
should feel that I was doing wrong were I to occupy in deliberation the
time that yet remains to me for action. To-day, then, very opportunely for
the plan I have in view I have delivered my mind from every care [and am
happily agitated by no passions] and since I have procured for myself an
assured leisure in a peaceable retirement, I shall at last seriously and
freely address myself to the general upheaval of all my former opinions.

Now for this object it is not necessary that I should show that all of
these are false—I shall perhaps never arrive at this end. But inasmuch as
reason already persuades me that I ought no less carefully to withhold my
assent from matters which are not entirely certain and indubitable than
from those which appear to me manifestly to be false, if I am able to find
in each one some reason to doubt, this will suffice to justify my rejecting
the whole. And for that end it will not be requisite that I should examine
each in particular, which would be an endless undertaking; for owing to the
fact that the destruction of the foundations of necessity brings with it

[This selection is taken from the first and the second of Descartes' *Meditations,* a work
first published in 1641. The translation is by Elizabeth S. Haldane and G. R. T. Ross and
is reproduced here with the kind permission of the Cambridge University Press.]

the downfall of the rest of the edifice, I shall only in the first place attack those principles upon which all my former opinions rested.

All that up to the present time I have accepted as most true and certain I have learned either from the senses or through the senses; but it is sometimes proved to me that these senses are deceptive, and it is wiser not to trust entirely to any thing by which we have once been deceived.

But it may be that although the senses sometimes deceive us concerning things which are hardly perceptible, or very far away, there are yet many others to be met with as to which we cannot reasonably have any doubt, although we recognise them by their means. For example, there is the fact that I am here, seated by the fire, attired in a dressing gown, having this paper in my hands and other similar matters. And how could I deny that these hands and this body are mine, were it not perhaps that I compare myself to certain persons, devoid of sense, whose cerebella are so troubled and clouded by the violent vapors of black bile, that they constantly assure us that they think they are kings when they are really quite poor, or that they are clothed in purple when they are really without covering, or who imagine that they have an earthenware head or are nothing but pumpkins or are made of glass. But they are mad, and I should not be any the less insane were I to follow examples so extravagant.

At the same time I must remember that I am a man, and that consequently I am in the habit of sleeping, and in my dreams representing to myself the same things or sometimes even less probable things, than do those who are insane in their waking moments. How often has it happened to me that in the night I dreamt that I found myself in this particular place, that I was dressed and seated near the fire, whilst in reality I was lying undressed in bed! At this moment it does indeed seem to me that it is with eyes awake that I am looking at this paper; that this head which I move is not asleep, that it is deliberately and of set purpose that I extend my hand and perceive it; what happens in sleep does not appear so clear nor so distinct as does all this. But in thinking over this I remind myself that on many occasions I have in sleep been deceived by similar illusions, and in dwelling carefully on this reflection I see so manifestly that there are no certain indications by which we may clearly distinguish wakefulness from sleep that I am lost in astonishment. And my astonishment is such that it is almost capable of persuading me that I now dream.

Now let us assume that we are asleep and that all these particulars, e.g. that we open our eyes, shake our head, extend our hands, and so on, are but false delusions; and let us reflect that possibly neither our hands nor our whole body are such as they appear to us to be. At the same time we must at least confess that the things which are represented to us in sleep are like painted representations which can only have been formed as the counterparts of something real and true, and that in this way those general things at least, i.e. eyes, a head, hands, and a whole body, are not imaginary things, but things really existent. For, as a matter of fact, painters, even when they study with the greatest skill to represent sirens and satyrs by forms the most strange and extraordinary, cannot give them natures which are entirely new, but merely make a certain medley of the members of different animals; or if their imagination is extravagant enough to invent something so novel that nothing similar has ever before been seen, and that then their work represents a thing purely fictitious and absolutely false, it is certain all the same that the colors of which this is composed are necessarily real. And for the same reason, although these general things, to wit, [a body], eyes, a head, and such like, may be imaginary, we are bound at the same time to confess that there are at least some other objects yet more simple and more universal, which are real and true; and of these just in the same way as with certain real colours, all these images of things which dwell in our thoughts, whether true and real or false and fantastic, are formed.

To such a class of things pertains corporeal nature in general, and its extension, the figure of extended things, their quantity or magnitude and number, as also the place in which they are, the time which measures their duration, and so on.

That is possibly why our reasoning is not unjust when we conclude from this that Physics, Astronomy, Medicine and all other sciences which have as their end the consideration of composite things, are very dubious and uncertain; but that Arithmetic, Geometry and other sciences of that kind which only treat of things that are very simple and very general, without taking great trouble to ascertain whether they are actually existent or not, contain some measure of certainty and an element of the indubitable. For whether I am awake or asleep, two and three together always form five, and the square can never have more than four sides, and it does not seem possible that truths so clear and apparent can be suspected of any falsity [or uncertainty].

Nevertheless I have long had fixed in my mind the belief that an all-powerful God existed by whom I have been created such as I am. But how do I know that He has not brought it to pass that there is no earth, no heaven, no extended body, no magnitude, no place, and that nevertheless [I possess the perceptions of all these things and that] they seem to me to exist just exactly as I now see them? And, besides, as I sometimes imagine that others deceive themselves in the things which they think they know best, how do I know that I am not deceived every time that I add two and three, or count the sides of a square, or judge of things yet simpler, if anything simpler can be imagined? But possibly God has not desired that I should be thus deceived, for He is said to be supremely good. If, however, it is contrary to His goodness to have made me such that I constantly deceive myself, it would also appear to be contrary to His goodness to permit me to be sometimes deceived, and nevertheless I cannot doubt that He does permit this.

There may indeed be those who would prefer to deny the existence of a God so powerful, rather than believe that all other things are uncertain. But let us not oppose them for the present, and grant that all that is said of a God is a fable; nevertheless in whatever way they suppose that I have arrived at the state of being that I have reached—whether they attribute it to fate or to accident, or make out that it is by a continual succession of antecedents, or by some other method—since to err and deceive oneself is a defect, it is clear that the greater will be the probability of my being so imperfect as to deceive myself ever, as is the Author to whom they assign my origin the less powerful. To these reasons I have certainly nothing to reply, but at the end I feel constrained to confess that there is nothing in all that I formerly believed to be true, of which I cannot in some measure doubt, and that not merely through want of thought or through levity, but for reasons which are very powerful and maturely considered; so that henceforth I ought not the less carefully to refrain from giving credence to these opinions than to that which is manifestly false, if I desire to arrive at any certainty [in the sciences]. . . .

. . . I shall then suppose, not that God who is supremely good and the fountain of truth, but some evil genius not less powerful than deceitful, has employed his whole energies in deceiving me; I shall consider that the heavens, the earth, colors, figures, sound, and all other external things are nought but the illusions and dreams of which this genius has availed himself in order to lay traps for my credulity; I shall consider myself as having no hands, no eyes, no flesh, no blood, nor any senses, yet falsely believing myself to possess all these things; I shall remain obstinately attached to this idea, and if by this means it is not in my power to arrive at the knowledge of any truth, I may at least do what is in my power [i.e. suspend my judgment], and with firm purpose avoid giving credence to any false thing, or being imposed upon by this arch deceiver, however powerful and deceptive he may be. But this task is a laborious one, and insensibly a certain lassitude leads me into the course of my ordinary life. And just as a captive who in sleep enjoys imaginary liberty, when he begins to suspect that his liberty is but a dream, fears to awaken, and conspires with these agreeable illusions that the deception may be prolonged, so insensibly of my own accord I fall back into my former opinions, and I dread awakening from this slumber, lest the laborious wakefulness which would follow the tranquillity of this repose should have to be spent not in daylight, but in the excessive darkness of the difficulties which have just been discussed.

Meditation II

The Meditation of yesterday filled my mind with so many doubts that it is no longer in my power to forget them. And yet I do not see in what manner I can resolve them; and, just as if I had all of a sudden fallen into very deep water, I am so disconcerted that I can neither make certain of setting my feet on the bottom, nor can I swim and so support myself on the surface. I shall nevertheless make an effort and follow anew the same path as that on which I yesterday entered, i.e. I shall proceed by setting aside all that in which the least doubt could be supposed to exist, just as if I had discovered that it was absolutely false; and I shall ever follow in this road until I have met with something which is certain, or at least, if I can do nothing else, until I have learned for certain that there is nothing in the world that is certain. Archimedes, in order that he might draw the terrestrial globe out of its place, and transport it elsewhere, demanded only that one point should be fixed and immoveable; in the same way I shall have the right to conceive high hopes if I am happy enough to discover one thing only which is certain and indubitable.

I suppose, then, that all the things that I see are false; I persuade myself that nothing has ever existed of all that my fallacious memory represents to me. I consider that I possess no senses; I imagine that body, figure, extension, movement and place are but the fictions of my mind. What, then, can be esteemed as true? Perhaps nothing at all, unless that there is nothing in the world that is certain.

But how can I know there is not something different from those things that I have just considered, of which one cannot have the slightest doubt? Is there not some God, or some other being by whatever name we call it, who puts these reflections into my mind? That is not necessary, for is it not possible that I am capable of producing them myself? I myself, am I not at least something? But I have already denied that I had senses and body. Yet I hesitate, for what follows from that? Am I so dependent on body and senses that I cannot exist without these? But I was persuaded that there was nothing in all the world, that there was no heaven, no earth, that there were no minds, nor any bodies: was I not then likewise persuaded that I did not exist? Not at all; of a surety I myself did exist since I persuaded myself of something [or merely because I thought of something]. But there is some deceiver or other, very powerful and very cunning, who ever employs his ingenuity in deceiving me. Then without doubt I exist also if he deceives me, and let him deceive me as much as he will, he can never cause me to be nothing so long as I think that I am something. So that after having reflected well and carefully examined all things, we must come to the definite conclusion that this proposition: I am, I exist, is necessarily true each time that I pronounce it, or that I mentally conceive it.

But I do not yet know clearly enough what I am, I who am certain that I am; and hence I must be careful to see that I do not imprudently take some other object in place of myself, and thus that I do not go astray in respect of this knowledge that I hold to be the most certain and most evident of all that I have formerly learned. That is why I shall now consider anew what I believed myself to be before I embarked upon these last reflections; and of my former opinions I shall withdraw all that might even in a small degree be invalidated by the reasons which I have just brought forward, in order that there may be nothing at all left beyond what is absolutely certain and indubitable. . . .

. . . Certainly it is no small matter if all these things pertain to my nature. But why should they not so pertain? Am I not that being who now doubts nearly everything, who nevertheless understands certain things, who affirms that one only is true, who denies all the others, who desires to know more, is averse from being deceived, who imagines many things, sometimes indeed despite his will, and who perceives many likewise, as by the intervention of the bodily organs? Is there nothing in all this which is as true as it is certain that I exist, even though I should always sleep and though he who has given me being employed all his ingenuity in deceiving me? Is there likewise anyone of these attributes which can be distinguished from my thought, or which might be said to be separated from myself? For it is so evident of itself that it is I who doubts, who understands, and who desires, that there is no reason here to add anything to explain it. And I have certainly the power of imagining likewise; for although it may happen (as I formerly supposed) that none of the things which I imagine are true, nevertheless this power of imagining does not cease to be really in use, and it forms part of my thought. Finally, I am the same who feels, that is to say, who perceives certain things, as by the organs of sense, since in truth I see light, I hear noise, I feel heat. But it will be said that these phenomena are false and that I am dreaming. Let it be so; still it is at least quite certain that it seems to me that I see light, that I hear noise and that I feel heat. That cannot be false; properly speaking it is what is in me called feeling; and used in this precise sense that is no other thing than thinking. . . .

Sceptical Doubts Concerning the Human Understanding

David Hume

Part 1

ALL THE OBJECTS OF HUMAN REASON or inquiry may naturally be divided into two kinds, to wit, "Relations of Ideas," and "Matters of Fact." Of the first kind are the sciences of Geometry, Algebra, and Arithmetic, and, in short, every affirmation which is either intuitively or demonstratively certain. *That the square of the hypothenuse is equal to the square of the two sides* is a proposition which expresses a relation between these figures. *That three times five is equal to the half of thirty* expresses a relation between these numbers. Propositions of this kind are discoverable by the mere operation of thought, without dependence on what is anywhere existent in the universe. Though there never were a circle or triangle in nature, the truths demonstrated by Euclid would forever retain their certainty and evidence.

Matters of fact, which are the second objects of human reason, are not ascertained in the same manner, nor is our evidence of their truth, however great, of a like nature with the foregoing. The contrary of every matter of fact is still possible, because it can never imply a contradiction and is conceived by the mind with the same facility and distinctness as if ever so conformable to reality. *That the sun will not rise tomorrow* is no less intelligible a proposition and implies no more contradiction than the affirmation *that it will rise*. We should in vain, therefore, attempt to demonstrate its falsehood. Were it demonstratively false, it would imply a contradiction and could never be distinctly conceived by the mind.

It may, therefore, be a subject worthy of curiosity to inquire what is

[This selection is Section IV of Hume's *An Inquiry Concerning Human Understanding*, a book first published in 1748.]

the nature of that evidence which assures us of any real existence and matter of fact beyond the present testimony of our senses or the records of our memory. This part of philosophy, it is observable, had been little cultivated either by the ancients or moderns; and, therefore, our doubts and errors in the prosecution of so important an inquiry may be the more excusable while we march through such difficult paths without any guide or direction. They may even prove useful by exciting curiosity and destroying that implicit faith and security which is the bane of all reasoning and free inquiry. The discovery of defects in the common philosophy, if any such there be, will not, I presume, be a discouragement, but rather an incitement, as is usual, to attempt something more full and satisfactory than has yet been proposed to the public.

All reasonings concerning matter of fact seem to be founded on the relation of *cause* and *effect*. By means of that relation alone we can go beyond the evidence of our memory and senses. If you were to ask a man why he believes any matter of fact which is absent, for instance, that his friend is in the country or in France, he would give you a reason, and this reason would be some other fact: as a letter received from him or the knowledge of his former resolutions and promises. A man finding a watch or any other machine in a desert island would conclude that there had once been men in that island. All our reasonings concerning fact are of the same nature. And here it is constantly supposed that there is a connection between the present fact and that which is inferred from it. Were there nothing to bind them together, the inference would be entirely precarious. The hearing of an articulate voice and rational discourse in the dark assures us of the presence of some person. Why? Because these are the effects of the human make and fabric, and closely connected with it. If we anatomize all the other reasonings of this nature, we shall find that they are founded on the relation of cause and effect, and that this relation is either near or remote, direct or collateral. Heat and light are collateral effects of fire, and the one effect may justly be inferred from the other.

If we would satisfy ourselves, therefore, concerning the nature of that evidence which assures us of matters of fact, we must inquire how we arrive at the knowledge of cause and effect.

I shall venture to affirm, as a general proposition which admits of no exception, that the knowledge of this relation is not, in any instance, attained by reasonings a priori, but arises entirely from experience, when we find that any particular objects are constantly conjoined with each other. Let an object be presented to a man of ever so strong natural reason and abilities—if that object be entirely new to him, he will not be able, by the most accurate examination of its sensible qualities, to discover any of its causes or effects. Adam, though his rational faculties be supposed, at the very first, entirely perfect, could not have inferred from the fluidity and transparency of water that it would suffocate him, or from the light and warmth of fire that it would consume him. No object ever discovers, by the qualities which appear to the senses, either the causes which produced it or the effects which will arise from it; nor can our reason, unassisted by experience, ever draw any inference concerning real existence and matter of fact.

This proposition, *that causes and effects are discoverable, not by reason, but by experience,* will readily be admitted with regard to such objects as we remember to have once been altogether unknown to us, since we must be conscious of the utter inability which we then lay under of foretelling what would arise from them. Present two smooth pieces of marble to a man who has no tincture of natural philosophy; he will never discover that they will adhere together in such a manner as to require great force to separate them in a direct line, while they make so small a resistance to a lateral pressure. Such events as bear little analogy to the common course of nature are also readily confessed to be known only by experience, nor does any man imagine that the explosion of gunpowder or the attraction of a loadstone could ever be discovered by arguments *a priori.* In like manner, when an effect is supposed to depend upon an intricate machinery or secret structure of parts, we make no difficulty in attributing all our knowledge of it to experience. Who will assert that he can give the ultimate reason why milk or bread is proper nourishment for a man, not for a lion or tiger?

But the same truth may not appear at first sight to have the same evidence with regard to events which have become familiar to us from our first appearance in the world, which bear a close analogy to the whole course of nature, and which are supposed to depend on the simple qualities of objects without any secret structure of parts. We are apt to imagine that we could discover these effects by the mere operation of our reason without experience. We fancy that, were we brought on a sudden into this world, we could at first have inferred that one billiard ball would communicate motion to another upon impulse, and that we needed not to have waited for the event in order to pronounce with certainty concerning it. Such is the influence of custom that where it is strongest it not only covers our natural ignorance but even conceals itself, and seems not to take place, merely because it is found in the highest degree.

But to convince us that all the laws of nature and all the operations of bodies without exception are known only by experience, the following reflections may perhaps suffice. Were any object presented to us, and were we required to pronounce concerning the effect which will result from it without consulting past observation, after what manner, I beseech you, must the mind proceed in this operation? It must invent or imagine some event which it ascribes to the object as its effect; and it is plain that this invention must be entirely arbitrary. The mind can never possibly find the effect in the supposed cause by the most accurate scrutiny and examination. For the effect is totally different from the cause, and consequently can never be discovered in it. Motion in the second billiard ball is a quite distinct event from motion in the first, nor is there anything in the one to suggest the smallest hint of the other. A stone or piece of metal raised into the air and left without any support immediately falls. But to consider the matter *a priori,* is there anything we discover in this situation which can beget the idea of a downward rather than an upward or any other motion in the stone or metal?

And as the first imagination or invention of a particular effect in all natural operations is arbitrary where we consult not experience, so must we also esteem the supposed tie or connection between the cause and effect which binds them together and renders it impossible that any other effect could result from the operation of that cause. When I see, for instance, a billiard ball moving in a straight line toward another, even suppose motion in the second ball should by accident be suggested to me as the result of their contact or impulse, may I not conceive that a hundred different events might as well follow from that cause? May not both these balls remain at absolute rest? May not the first ball return in a straight line or leap off from the second in any line or direction? All these suppositions are consistent and conceivable. Why, then, should we give the preference to one which is no more consistent or conceivable than the rest? All our reasonings *a priori* will never be able to show us any foundation for this preference.

In a word, then, every effect is a distinct event from its cause. It could not, therefore, be discovered in the cause, and the first invention or conception of it, *a priori,* must be entirely arbitrary. And even after it is suggested, the conjunction of it with the cause must appear equally arbitrary, since there are always many other effects which, to reason, must seem fully as consistent and natural. In vain, therefore, should we pretend to determine any single event or infer any cause or effect without the assistance of observation and experience.

Hence we may discover the reason why no philosopher who is rational and modest has ever pretended to assign the ultimate cause of any natural operation, or to show distinctly the action of that power which produces any single effect in the universe. It is confessed that the utmost effort of human reason is to reduce the principles productive of natural phenomena to a greater simplicity, and to resolve the many particular effects into a few general causes, by means of reasonings from analogy, experience, and observation. But as to the causes of these general causes, we should in vain attempt their discovery, nor shall we ever be able to satisfy ourselves by any particular explication of them. These ultimate springs and principles are totally shut up from human curiosity and inquiry. Elasticity, gravity, cohesion of parts, communication of motion by impulse—these are probably the ultimate causes and principles which we shall ever discover in nature; and we may esteem ourselves sufficiently happy if, by accurate inquiry and reasoning, we can trace up the particular phenomena to, or near to, these general principles. The most perfect philosophy of the natural kind only staves off our ignorance a little longer, as perhaps the most perfect philosophy of the moral or metaphysical kind serves only to discover larger portions of it. Thus the observation of human blindness and weakness is the result of all philosophy, and meets us, at every turn, in spite of our endeavors to elude or avoid it.

Nor is geometry, when taken into the assistance of natural philosophy, ever able to remedy this defect or lead us into the knowledge of ultimate causes by all that accuracy of reasoning for which it is so justly celebrated. Every part of mixed mathematics proceeds upon the supposition that certain laws are established by nature in her operations, and abstract reasonings are employed either to assist experience in the discovery of these laws or to determine their influence in particular instances where it depends upon any precise degree of distance and quantity. Thus it is a law of motion, discovered by experience, that the moment or force of any body in motion is in the compound ratio or proportion of its solid contents and its velocity, and, consequently, that a small force may remove the greatest obstacle or raise the greatest weight if by any contrivance or machinery we can increase the velocity of that force so as to make it an overmatch for its antagonist. Geometry assists us in the application of this law by giving us the just dimensions of all the parts and figures which can enter into any species of machine, but still the discovery of the law itself is owing merely to experience; and all the abstract reasonings in the world could never lead us one step toward the knowledge of it. When we reason *a priori* and consider merely any object or cause as it appears to the mind, independent of all observation, it never could suggest to us the notion of any distinct object, such as its effect, much less show us the inseparable and inviolable connection between them. A man must be very sagacious who could discover by reasoning that crystal is the effect of heat, and ice of cold, without being previously acquainted with the operation of these qualities.

Part II

But we have not yet attained any tolerable satisfaction with regard to the question first proposed. Each solution still gives rise to a new question as difficult as the foregoing and leads us on to further inquiries. When it is asked, *What is the nature of all our reasonings concerning matter of fact?* the proper answer seems to be, that they are founded on the relation of cause and effect. When again it is asked, *What is the foundation of all our reasonings and conclusions concerning that relation?* it may be replied in one word, *experience.* But if we still carry on our sifting humor and ask, *What is the foundation of all conclusions from experience?* this implies a new question which may be of more difficult solution and explication. Philosophers that give themselves airs of superior wisdom and sufficiency have a hard task when they encounter persons of inquisitive dispositions, who push them from every corner to which they retreat, and who are sure at least to bring them to some dangerous dilemma. The best expedient to prevent this confusion is to be modest in our pretensions and even to discover the difficulty ourselves before it is objected to us. By this means we may make a kind of merit of our very ignorance.

I shall content myself in this section with an easy task and shall pretend only to give a negative answer to the question here proposed. I say, then, that even after we have experience of the operations of cause and effect, our conclusions from that experience are *not* founded on reasoning or any process of the understanding. This answer we must endeavor both to explain and to defend.

It must certainly be allowed that nature has kept us at a great distance from all her secrets and has afforded us only the knowledge of a few superficial qualities of objects, while she conceals from us those powers and principles on which the influence of these objects entirely depends. Our senses inform us of the color, weight, and consistency of bread, but neither sense nor reason can ever inform us of those qualities which fit it for the nourishment and support of the human body. Sight or feeling conveys an idea of the actual motion of bodies, but as to that wonderful force or power which would carry on a moving body forever in a continued change of place, and which bodies never lose but by communicating it to others, of this we cannot form the most distant conception. But notwithstanding this ignorance of natural powers and principles, we always presume when we see like sensible qualities that they have like secret powers, and expect that effects similar to those which we have experienced will follow from them. If a body of like color and consistency with that bread which we have formerly eaten be presented to us, we make no scruple of repeating the experiment and foresee with certainty like nourishment and support. Now this is a process of the mind or thought of which I would willingly know the foundation. It is allowed on all hands that there is no known connection between the sensible qualities and the secret powers, and, consequently, that the mind is not led to form such a conclusion concerning their constant and regular conjunction by anything which it knows of their nature. As to past *experience,* it can be allowed to give *direct* and *certain* information of those precise objects only, and that precise period of time which fell under its cognizance: But why this experience should be extended to future times and to other objects which, for aught we know, may be only in appearance similar, this is the main question on which I would insist. The bread which I formerly ate nourished me; that is, a body of such sensible qualities was, at that time, endued with such secret powers. But does it follow that other bread must also nourish me at another time, and that like sensible qualities must always be attended with like secret powers? The consequence seems nowise necessary. At least, it must be acknowledged that there is here a consequence drawn by the mind, that there is a certain step taken, a process of thought, and an inference which wants to be explained. These two propositions are far from being the same: *I have found that such an object has always been attended with such an effect,* and *I foresee that other objects which are in appearance similar will be attended with similar effects.* I shall allow, if you please, that the one proposition may justly be inferred from the other: I know, in fact, that it always is inferred. But if you insist that the inference is made by a chain of reasoning, I desire you to produce that reasoning. The connection between these propositions is not intuitive. There is required a medium which may enable the mind to draw such an inference, if indeed it be drawn by reasoning and argument. What that medium is I must confess passes my comprehension; and it is incumbent on those to produce it who assert that it really exists and is the original of all our conclusions concerning matter of fact.

This negative argument must certainly, in process of time, become altogether convincing if many penetrating and able philosophers shall turn their inquiries this way, and no one be ever able to discover any connecting proposition or intermediate step which supports the understanding in this conclusion. But as the question is yet new, every reader may not trust so far to his own penetration as to conclude, because an argument escapes his inquiry, that therefore it does not really exist. For this reason it may be requisite to venture upon a more difficult task, and, enumerating all the branches of human knowledge, endeavor to show that none of them can afford such an argument.

All reasonings may be divided into two kinds, namely, demonstrative reasoning, or that concerning relations of ideas, and moral or probable reasoning, or that concerning matter of fact and existence. That there are no demonstrative arguments in the case seems evident, since it implies no contradiction that the course of nature may change and that an object, seemingly like those which we have experienced, may be attended with different or contrary effects. May I not clearly and distinctly conceive that a body, falling from the clouds and which in all other respects resembles snow, has yet the taste of salt or feeling of fire? Is there any more intelligible proposition than to affirm that all the trees will flourish in December and January, and will decay in May and June? Now, whatever is intelligible and can be distinctly conceived implies no contradiction and can never be proved false by any demonstrative argument or abstract reasoning *a priori.*

If we be, therefore, engaged by arguments to put trust in past experience and make it the standard of our future judgment, these arguments must be probable only, or such as regard matter of fact and real existence, according to the division above mentioned. But that there is no argument of this kind must appear if our explication of that species of reasoning be admitted as solid and satisfactory. We have said that all arguments concerning existence are founded on the relation of cause and effect, that our knowledge of that relation is derived entirely from experience, and that all our experimental conclusions proceed upon the supposition that the future will be conformable to the past. To endeavor, therefore, the proof of this last supposition by probable arguments, or arguments regarding existence, must be evidently going in a circle and taking that for granted which is the very point in question.

In reality, all arguments from experience are founded on the similarity which we discover among natural objects, and by which we are induced to expect effects similar to those which we have found to follow from such objects. And though none but a fool or madman will ever pretend to dispute the authority of experience or to reject that great guide of human life, it may surely be allowed a philosopher to have so much curiosity at least as to examine the principle of human nature which gives this mighty authority to experience and makes us draw advantage from that similarity which nature has placed among different objects. From causes which appear similar, we expect similar effects. This is the sum of all our experimental conclusions. Now it seems evident that, if this conclusion were formed by reason, it would be as perfect at first, and upon one instance, as after ever so long a course of experience; but the case is far otherwise. Nothing so like as eggs, yet no one, on account of this appearing similarity, expects the same taste and relish in all of them. It is only after a long course of uniform experiments in any kind that we attain a firm reliance and security with regard to a particular event. Now, where is that process of reasoning which, from one instance, draws a conclusion so different from that which it infers from a hundred instances that are nowise different from that single one? This question I propose as much for the sake of information as with an intention of raising difficulties. I cannot find, I cannot imagine any such reasoning. But I keep my mind still open to instruction if anyone will vouchsafe to bestow it on me.

Should it be said that, from a number of uniform experiments, we *infer* a connection between the sensible qualities and the secret powers, this, I must confess, seems the same difficulty, couched in different terms. The question still occurs: On what process of argument is this *inference* founded? Where is the medium, the interposing ideas which join propositions so very wide of each other? It is confessed that the color, consistency, and other sensible qualities of bread appear not of themselves to have any connection with the secret powers of nourishment and support; for otherwise we could infer these secret powers from the first appearance of these sensible qualities without the aid of experience, contrary to the sentiment of all philosophers, and contrary to plain matter of fact. Here, then, is our natural state of ignorance with regard to the powers and influence of all objects. How is this remedied by experience? It only shows us a number of uniform effects resulting from certain objects, and teaches us that those particular objects, at that particular time, were endowed with such powers and forces. When a new object endowed with similar sensible qualities is produced, we expect similar powers and forces, and look for a like effect. From a body of like color and consistency with bread, we expect like nourishment and support. But this surely is a step or progress of the mind which wants to be explained. When a man says, *I have found, in all past instances, such sensible qualities, conjoined with such secret powers,* and when he says, *similar sensible qualities will always be conjoined with similar secret powers,* he is not guilty of a tautology, nor are these propositions in any respect the same. You say that the one proposition is an inference from the other; but you must confess that the inference is not intuitive, neither is it demonstrative. Of what nature is it then? To say it is experimental is begging the question. For all inferences from experience suppose, as their foundation, that the future will resemble the past and that similar powers will be conjoined with similar sensible qualities. If there be any suspicion that the course of nature may change, and that the past may be no rule for the future, all experience becomes useless and can give rise to no inference or conclusion. It is impossible, therefore, that any arguments from experience can prove this resemblance of the past to the future, since all these arguments are founded on the supposition of that resemblance. Let the course of things be allowed hitherto ever so regular, that alone, without some new argument or inference, proves not that for the future it will continue so. In vain do you pretend to have learned the nature of bodies from your past experience. Their secret nature, and consequently all their effects and influence, may change without any change in their sensible qualities. This happens sometimes, and with regard to some objects. Why may it not happen always, and with regard to all objects? What logic, what process of argument secures you against this supposition? My practice, you say, refutes my doubts. But you mistake the purport of my question. As an agent, I am quite satisfied in the point; but as a philosopher who has some share of curiosity, I will not say scepticism, I want to learn the foundation of this inference. No reading, no inquiry has yet been able to remove my difficulty or give me satisfaction in a matter of such importance. Can I do better than propose the difficulty to the public, even though, perhaps, I have small hopes of obtaining a solution? We shall at least, by this means, be sensible of our ignorance, if we do not augment our knowledge.

I must confess that a man is guilty of unpardonable arrogance who concludes, because an argument has escaped his own investigation, that therefore it does not really exist. I must also confess that, though all the learned, for several ages, should have employed themselves in fruitless search upon any subject, it may still, perhaps, be rash to conclude positively that the subject must therefore pass all human comprehension. Even though we examine all the sources of our knowledge and conclude them unfit for such a subject, there may still remain a suspicion that the enumeration is not complete or the examination not accurate. But with regard to the present subject, there are some considerations which seem to remove all this accusation of arrogance or suspicion of mistake.

It is certain that the most ignorant and stupid peasants, nay infants, nay even brute beasts, improve by experience and learn the qualities of natural objects by observing the effects which result from them. When a child has felt the sensation of pain from touching the flame of a candle, he will be careful not to put his hand near any candle, but will expect a similar effect from a cause which is similar in its sensible qualities and appearance. If you assert, therefore, that the understanding of the child is led into this conclusion by any process of argument or ratiocination, I may justly require you to produce that argument, nor have you any pretense to refuse so equitable a demand. You cannot say that the argument is abstruse and may possibly escape your inquiry, since you confess that it is obvious to the capacity of a mere infant. If you hesitate, therefore, a moment or if, after reflection, you produce an intricate or profound argument, you, in a manner, give up the question and confess that it is not reasoning which engages us to suppose the past resembling the future, and to expect similar effects from causes which are to appearance similar. This is the proposition which I intended to enforce in the present section. If I be right, I pretend not to have made any mighty discovery. And if I be wrong, I must acknowledge myself to be indeed a very backward scholar, since I cannot now discover an argument which, it seems, was perfectly familiar to me long before I was out of my cradle.

12   On Induction

Bertrand Russell

IN ALMOST ALL OUR PREVIOUS DISCUS-
sions we have been concerned in the attempt to get clear as to our data in
the way of knowledge of existence. What things are there in the universe
whose existence is known to us owing to our being acquainted with them?
So far, our answer has been that we are acquainted with our sense-data, and,
probably, with ourselves. These we know to exist. And past sense-data
which are remembered are known to have existed in the past. This knowledge supplies our data.

But if we are to be able to draw inferences from these data—if we are
to know of the existence of matter, of other people, of the past before our
individual memory begins, or of the future, we must know general principles
of some kind by means of which such inferences can be drawn. It must be
known to us that the existence of some one sort of thing, A, is a sign of the
existence of some other sort of thing, B, either at the same time as A or at
some earlier or later time, as, for example, thunder is a sign of the earlier
existence of lightning. If this were not known to us, we could never extend
our knowledge beyond the sphere of our private experience; and this sphere,
as we have seen, is exceedingly limited. The question we have now to consider is whether such an extension is possible, and if so, how it is effected.

Let us take as an illustration a matter about which none of us, in fact,
feel the slightest doubt. We are all convinced that the sun will rise tomorrow.
Why? Is this belief a mere blind outcome of past experience, or can it be
justified as a reasonable belief? It is not easy to find a test by which to
judge whether a belief of this kind is reasonable or not, but we can at least
ascertain what sort of general beliefs would suffice, if true, to justify the

[This selection is Chapter VI of Russell's *Problems of Philosophy*, which was first published in 1912. It is here reprinted with the kind permission of Bertrand Russell and the
Oxford University Press. In a letter to the editors Mr. Russell requested that the following
note be printed in conjunction with this selection: "What is said about induction in this
chapter from my *Problems of Philosophy* seems to me now insufficient, though not erroneous.
My present views on the subject are set forth in the last part of *Human Knowledge*."]

judgement that the sun will rise to-morrow, and the many other similar judgements upon which our actions are based.

It is obvious that if we are asked why we believe that the sun will rise to-morrow, we shall naturally answer, "Because it always has risen every day." We have a firm belief that it will rise in the future, because it has risen in the past. If we are challenged as to why we believe that it will continue to rise as heretofore, we may appeal to the laws of motion: the earth, we shall say, is a freely rotating body, and such bodies do not cease to rotate unless something interferes from outside, and there is nothing outside to interfere with the earth between now and to-morrow. Of course it might be doubted whether we are quite certain that there is nothing outside to interfere, but this is not the interesting doubt. The interesting doubt is as to whether the laws of motion will remain in operation until to-morrow. If this doubt is raised, we find ourselves in the same position as when the doubt about the sunrise was first raised.

The *only* reason for believing that the laws of motion will remain in operation is that they have operated hitherto, so far as our knowledge of the past enables us to judge. It is true that we have a greater body of evidence from the past in favour of the laws of motion than we have in favour of the sunrise, because the sunrise is merely a particular case of fulfilment of the laws of motion, and there are countless other particular cases. But the real question is: Do *any* number of cases of a law being fulfilled in the past afford evidence that it will be fulfilled in the future? If not, it becomes plain that we have no ground whatever for expecting the sun to rise to-morrow, or for expecting the bread we shall eat at our next meal not to poison us, or for any of the other scarcely conscious expectations that control our daily lives. It is to be observed that all such expectations are only *probable;* thus we have not to seek for a proof that they *must* be fulfilled, but only for some reason in favour of the view that they are *likely* to be fulfilled.

Now in dealing with this question we must, to begin with, make an important distinction, without which we should soon become involved in hopeless confusions. Experience has shown us that, hitherto, the frequent repetition of some uniform succession or coexistence has been a *cause* of our expecting the same succession or coexistence on the next occasion. Food that has a certain appearance generally has a certain taste, and it is a severe shock to our expectations when the familiar appearance is found to be associated with an unusual taste. Things which we see become associated, by habit, with certain tactile sensations which we expect if we touch them; one of the horrors of a ghost (in many ghost-stories) is that it fails to give us any sensations of touch. Uneducated people who go abroad for the first time are so surprised as to be incredulous when they find their native language not understood.

And this kind of association is not confined to men; in animals also it is very strong. A horse which has been often driven along a certain road resists the attempt to drive him in a different direction. Domestic animals expect food when they see the person who usually feeds them. We know that all these rather crude expectations of uniformity are liable to be misleading. The man who has fed the chicken every day through- out its life at last wrings its neck instead, showing that more refined views as to the uniformity of nature would have been useful to the chicken.

But in spite of the misleadingness of such expectations, they never- theless exist. The mere fact that something has happened a certain number of times causes animals and men to expect that it will happen again. Thus our instincts certainly cause us to believe that the sun will rise to- morrow, but we may be in no better a position than the chicken which unexpectedly has its neck wrung. We have therefore to distinguish the fact that past uniformities *cause* expectations as to the future, from the question whether there is any reasonable ground for giving weight to such expectations after the question of their validity had been raised.

The problem we have to discuss is whether there is any reason for believing in what is called "the uniformity of nature." The belief in the uniformity of nature is the belief that everything that has happened or will happen is an instance of some general law to which there are *no* exceptions. The crude expectations which we have been considering are all subject to exceptions, and therefore liable to disappoint those who entertain them. But science habitually assumes, at least as a working hypothesis, that general rules which have exceptions can be replaced by general rules which have no exceptions. "Unsupported bodies in air fall" is a general rule to which balloons and aeroplanes are exceptions. But the laws of motion and the law of gravitation, which account for the fact that most bodies fall, also account for the fact that balloons and aero- planes can rise; thus the laws of motion and the law of gravitation are not subject to these exceptions.

The belief that the sun will rise to-morrow might be falsified if the earth came suddenly into contact with a large body which destroyed its rotation; but the laws of motion and the law of gravitation would not be infringed by such an event. The business of science is to find uniformities, such as the laws of motion and the law of gravitation, to which, so far as our experience extends, there are no exceptions. In this search science has been remarkably successful, and it may be conceded that such uni- formities have held hitherto. This brings us back to the question: Have we any reason, assuming that they have always held in the past, to suppose that they will hold in the future?

It has been argued that we have reason to know that the future will resemble the past, because what was the future has constantly become the past, and has always been found to resemble the past, so that we really have experience of the future, namely of times which were formerly future, which we may call past futures. But such an argument really begs the very question at issue. We have experience of past futures, but not of future futures, and the question is: Will future futures resemble past futures? This question is not to be answered by an argument which starts from past futures alone. We have therefore still to seek for some principle which shall enable us to know that the future will follow the same laws as the past.

The reference to the future in this question is not essential. The same question arises when we apply the laws that work in our experience to past things of which we have no experience—as, for example, in geology, or in theories as to the origin of the Solar System. The question we really have to ask is: "When two things have been found to be often associated, and no instance is known of the one occurring without the other, does the occurrence of one of the two, in a fresh instance, give any good ground for expecting the other?" On our answer to this question must depend the validity of the whole of our expectations as to the future, the whole of the results obtained by induction, and in fact practically all the beliefs upon which our daily life is based.

It must be conceded, to begin with, that the fact that two things have been found often together and never apart does not, by itself, suffice to *prove* demonstratively that they will be found together in the next case we examine. The most we can hope is that the oftener things are found together, the more probable it becomes that they will be found together another time, and that, if they have been found together often enough, the probability will amount *almost* to certainty. It can never quite reach certainty, because we know that in spite of frequent repetitions there sometimes is a failure at the last, as in the case of the chicken whose neck is wrung. Thus probability is all we ought to seek.

It might be urged, as against the view we are advocating, that we know all natural phenomena to be subject to the reign of law, and that sometimes, on the basis of observation, we can see that only one law can possibly fit the facts of the case. Now to this view there are two answers. The first is that, even if *some* law which has no exceptions applies to our case, we can never, in practice, be sure that we have discovered that law and not one to which there are exceptions. The second is that the reign of law would seem to be itself only probable, and that our belief that it will hold in the future, or in unexamined cases in the past, is itself based upon the very principle we are examining.

The principle we are examining may be called the *principle of induction,* and its two parts may be stated as follows:

(*a*) When a thing of a certain sort A has been found to be associated with a thing of a certain other sort B, and has never been found dissociated from a thing of the sort B, the greater the number of cases in which A and B have been associated, the greater is the probability that they will be associated in a fresh case in which one of them is known to be present;

(*b*) Under the same circumstances, a sufficient number of cases of association will make the probability of a fresh association nearly a certainty, and will make it approach certainty without limit.

As just stated, the principle applies only to the verification of our expectation in a single fresh instance. But we want also to know that there is a probability in favour of the general law that things of the sort A are *always* associated with things of the sort B, provided a sufficient number of cases of association are known, and no cases of failure of association are known. The probability of the general law is obviously less than the probability of the particular case, since if the general law is true, the particular case must also be true, whereas the particular case may be true without the general law being true. Nevertheless the probability of the general law is increased by repetitions, just as the probability of the particular case is. We may therefore repeat the two parts of our principle as regards the general law, thus:

(*a*) The greater the number of cases in which a thing of the sort A has been found associated with a thing of the sort B, the more probable it is (if no cases of failure of association are known) that A is always associated with B;

(*b*) Under the same circumstances, a sufficient number of cases of the association of A with B will make it nearly certain that A is always associated with B, and will make this general law approach certainty without limit.

It should be noted that probability is always relative to certain data. In our case, the data are merely the known cases of coexistence of A and B. There may be other data, which *might* be taken into account, which would gravely alter the probability. For example, a man who had seen a great many white swans might argue, by our principle, that on the data it was *probable* that all swans were white, and this might be a perfectly sound argument. The argument is not disproved by the fact that some swans are black, because a thing may very well happen in spite of the fact that some data render it improbable. In the case of the swans, a man might know that color is a very variable characteristic in many species of animals, and that, therefore, an induction as to color is peculiarly liable to error. But this knowledge would be a fresh datum, by no means proving that the probability relatively to our previous data had been wrongly estimated. The fact, therefore, that things often fail to fulfil our expectations is no evidence that our expectations will not *probably* be fulfilled in a given case or a given class of cases. Thus our inductive principle is at any rate not capable of being *disproved* by an appeal to experience.

The inductive principle, however, is equally incapable of being *proved* by an appeal to experience. Experience might conceivably confirm the inductive principle as regards the cases that have been already examined; but as regards unexamined cases, it is the inductive principle alone that can justify any inference from what has been examined to what has not been examined. All arguments which, on the basis of experience, argue as to the future or the unexperienced parts of the past or present, assume the inductive principle; hence we can never use experience to prove the inductive principle without begging the question. Thus we must either accept the inductive principle on the ground of its intrinsic evidence, or forego all justification of our expectations about the future. If the principle is unsound, we have no reason to expect the sun to rise to-morrow, to expect bread to be more nourishing than a stone, or to expect that if we throw ourselves off the roof we shall fall. When we see what looks like our best friend approaching us, we shall have no reason to suppose that his body is not inhabited by the mind of our worst enemy or of some total stranger. All our conduct is based upon associations which have worked in the past, and which we therefore regard as likely to work in the future; and this likelihood is dependent for its validity upon the inductive principle.

The general principles of science, such as the belief in the reign of law, and the belief that every event must have a cause, are as completely dependent upon the inductive principle as are the beliefs of daily life. All such general principles are believed because mankind have found innumerable instances of their truth and no instances of their falsehood. But this affords no evidence for their truth in the future, unless the inductive principle is assumed.

Thus all knowledge which, on the basis of experience tells us something about what is not experienced, is based upon a belief which experience can neither confirm nor confute, yet which, at least in its more concrete applications, appears to be as firmly rooted in us as many of the facts of experience. The existence and justification of such beliefs—for the inductive principle, as we shall see, is not the only example—raises some of the most difficult and most debated problems of philosophy.

13   Will the Future
Be Like the Past?

F. L. Will

Hume's Scepticism

. . . THE STANDARD ARGUMENT FOR complete inductive scepticism, for the belief that inductive procedures have no rational and no empirical justification whatever, is the one stated in a small variety of ways in the writings of Hume. If one consults these writings in search of an answer to the question of inductive validity one finds the same clear answer argued first in technical detail in the *Treatise,* secondly compressed into a few non-technical paragraphs in the *Abstract of a Treatise of Human Nature,* and thirdly, presented again in a non-technical but somewhat fuller version in a chapter in the *Enquiry Concerning Human Understanding.* There is no basis whatever for any conclusion concerning future matters, according to this argument; there is no way whatever in which such conclusions can be established to be certainly true or even probable. For in the first place no such conclusion can be demonstrated by reasoning alone, since they are all conclusions about matters of fact, and since it is the case that the denial of any assertion of a matter of fact is not self-contradictory. But if one gives up the rationalistic aspiration to demonstrate propositions about matters of fact or existence *a priori,* and turns instead to experience, this road, though apparently more promising at first, likewise ends by leading one exactly nowhere. Clearly no statement about future matters of fact can be established by observation. Future things cannot be observed. Any event or state of affairs which can be observed is by definition not in the future. The only recourse which remains therefore

[This article originally appeared in *Mind,* 1947. It is here reprinted with slight omissions by the kind permission of the author and the editor of *Mind.*]

is the inductive procedure of employing present or past observations and inferring therefrom the nature of the future. But this procedure to which we are all forced, or rather, to which we all should be forced, if we did not, in company with the animals, use it naturally from birth, is in the light of close analysis completely indefensible. For such reasoning assumes, and is quite invalid without the assumption, that the future will be like the past.

> . . . all inferences from experience suppose, as their foundation, that the future will resemble the past, and that similar powers will be conjoined with similar sensible qualities. If there be any suspicion that the course of nature may change, and that the past may be no rule for the future, all experience becomes useless, and can give rise to no inference or conclusion. (*Enquiry,* Section IV.[1])

Will the future "resemble the past"? Or be "comformable to the past"? These are the ways in which in the *Enquiry* Hume expresses the question concerning the uniformity of nature, restricting to its reference toward the future the question which already had been asked in broader terms in the *Treatise.* There, without the temporal restriction, it is argued that the principle of inductive conclusions, the principle upon which reason would proceed if reason determined us in these matters, is *"that instances, of which we have had no experience, must resemble those, of which we have had experience, and that the course of nature continues always uniformly the same."* (Bk. I, Pt. III, Sect. VI.)

However the principle is stated, the argument about it remains the same. It is indispensable, if inductive conclusions are to be justified; but just as it is absolutely indispensable, so, and this is the measure of our logical misfortune, it cannot be established as certain or as probable in any way. It cannot be established by any demonstrative argument. For it is clearly an assertion of a matter of fact, and therefore the kind of assertion whose denial is non-contradictory and conceivable.

> That there are no demonstrative arguments in the case seems evident; since it implies no contradiction that the course of nature may change, and that an object, seemingly like those which we have experienced, may be attended with different or contrary effects. May I not clearly and distinctly conceive that a body, falling from the clouds, and which, in all other respects, resembles snow, has yet the taste of salt or the feeling of fire? Is there any more intelligible proposition than to affirm, that all the trees will flourish in December and January, and decay in May and June? Now whatever is intelligible, and can be distinctly conceived, implies no contradiction and can never be proved false by any demonstrative argument or abstract reasoning *a priori.* (*Enquiry,* Sect. IV.[2] Cf. *Treatise, loc. cit.*)

Any further doubts about the doubtfulness of this principle which is the main-spring of inductive inference are quickly disposed of. No one who understands the principle with its reference to unobserved instances

1. See above, p. 137.
2. See above, p. 135.

will suggest that it can be simply observed to be true. It is still true that one cannot observe the future, or the unobserved generally. And, finally, no one who has a sound logical conscience and appreciates the indispensability of the principle to induction generally will tolerate the suggestion that the principle may be established by inductions from experience. Such a process would be circular.

> It is impossible, therefore, that any arguments from experience can prove this resemblance of the past to the future; since all these arguments are founded on the supposition of that resemblance.

And again:

> . . . all our experimental conclusions proceed upon the supposition that the future will be conformable to the past. To endeavour, therefore, the proof of this last supposition by probable arguments, or arguments regarding existence, must be evidently going in a circle, and taking that for granted, which is the very point in question. (*Enquiry*, Sect. IV.[3])

On this point the *Treatise* (*loc. cit.*) and the *Abstract* speak with one voice. One final quotation from the latter may serve to summarise the conclusion.

> 'Tis evident that *Adam* with all his science, would never have been able to *demonstrate,* that the course of nature must continue uniformly the same, and that the future must be conformable to the past. What is possible can never be demonstrated to be false; and 'tis possible the course of nature may change, since we can conceive such a change. Nay, I will go farther, and assert, that he could not so much as prove by any *probable* arguments, that the future must be conformable to the past. All probable arguments are built on the supposition, that there is this conformity betwixt the future and the past, and therefore can never prove it. This conformity is a *matter of fact,* and if it must be proved, will admit of no proof but from experience. But our experience in the past can be a proof of nothing for the future, but upon a supposition, that there is a resemblance betwixt them. This therefore is a point, which can admit of no proof at all, and which we take for granted without any proof. (*Abstract*, 1938 ed., p. 15.)

Is Inductive Reasoning Really Circular?

. . . It would be more promising in respect to logical neatness and precision for one to consider the alleged circularity of all inductive procedure, which is the central point of the above argument, while using as test case some specific scientific law or principle rather than some affirmation as vague and imprecise as that the future will resemble the past. But, for the purpose of analysing the sceptic's views and meeting the arguments by which these views have been defended, such a procedure would have this deficiency, that no matter what specific scientific general-

3. See above, pp. 135 f.

isation were chosen, one reply which would be sure to be made would consist of an appeal beyond this generalisation to some general beliefs about uniformity, some general Principle of Uniformity which, it would be urged, is assumed somehow in the inductive establishment of this and other scientific generalisations. Since the sceptical argument has been presented in terms of general Principles of Uniformity, and it is in these terms that it is alleged to demonstrate the logical circularity of all inductive reasoning, it seems worth while to attempt to deal with this argument, if one can, in the same terms—in terms of some alleged Principle of Uniformity for which it has been claimed in recent philosophy that it does serve as a wide and basic inductive assumption.

In his *Treatise on Probability*, J. M. Keynes attempts to formulate a set of principles which, if assumed to be true of a given area of subject-matter, would justify, in accordance with the principles of probability, the employment of inductive methods in that area. One of the principles which he discusses, the simplest and at the same time the one for which it seems, at first view, most plausible to contend that it may serve as a broad inductive assumption, is the one to which he gave the name of the "Principle of the Uniformity of Nature." This Principle affirms that nature is uniform in a specific way; and that is in respect to position in space and time. "It involves," writes Keynes, "the assertion of a generalised judgment of irrelevance, namely, of the irrelevance of mere position in time and space to generalisations which have no reference to particular positions in time and space." (P. 226. *Cf.* also pp. 255–256, 263, 276.) It is this principle, he argues, which

> . . . supplies the answer, if it is correct, to the criticism that the instances, on which generalisations are based, are all alike in being past, and that any generalisation, which is applicable to the future, must be based, for this reason, upon imperfect analogy. We judge directly that the resemblance between instances, which consists in their being past, is in itself irrelevant, and does not supply a valid ground for impugning a generalisation. (p. 256)

It is, however, difficult to interpret this so-called Principle in such a way that it makes a statement which is both definite and is not at the same time refuted in some areas of experience. Keynes observes that what this Principle affirms is "that the same total cause always produces the same effect" (p. 248), and this is so; but the difficulty here is that of giving a definite meaning to the important adjective "same" as it applies to causes and effects. Unless there is a specifiable meaning applicable to causes in all fields, the formula "same cause—same effect" is not a univocal principle affirming the presence of a specific kind of uniformity in every area of natural phenomena. Yet, when one sets out to specify just what kind of sameness is meant when this formula is employed, one discovers that there is a great variety of interpretations of this word in different fields of inquiry, and that what determines whether a given set of circumstances is regarded as the same cause, for example, varies from field to field, depending upon the nature of the subject-matter as that is revealed in the various generalisations which are regarded as established for that subject-matter. These generalisations exhibit among themselves great differences in scope and precision, as well as in the degree of confidence with which they are accepted. They include, for example, the generalisations about the coherence and constancy of properties which are involved in our belief in and distinctions among various kinds of material objects. And they include the more precise generalisations, frequently expressed in the form of mathematical equations, which would normally be referred to as "scientific laws," as well as broader generalisations formulated in various accepted Principles and Theories. When this is understood, when one sees that in the employment of the Principle of Uniformity what determines the kind of sameness to which the Principle affirms that differences in mere position in space and time are irrelevant is the specific generalisations, the laws, principles, and so on, which have been established in that field, one is in a better position to understand this so-called Principle and its alleged employment as a general inductive assumption. In any given field the Principle of Uniformity states that mere differences in space and time are irrelevant in just this sense, that there are certain generalisations, true of this field, which describe the conditions under which certain objects exist and events occur, and in which differences in mere position in space and time make little or no detectable difference. That this is so, accordingly, is not an inductive assumption in that field in the sense that it is specified and made before all inductive inquiry in the field. It is an inductive assumption in the more usual sense that conclusions of previous experience and inquiries are available for employment in any field as bases for further investigation in that field.

The primary purpose here is not to elucidate and specify the variations of meaning which such a Principle or formula must undergo if it is to be understood as applying to the great variety of fields in which inductive inquiry is carried on, to the great variety in the kinds of uniformity which the generalisations in these fields describe. The primary purpose is to inquire whether the sceptics are right in insisting that it is impossible to provide a genuine evidence for beliefs about uniformity or whether, on the contrary, it is possible to furnish empirical evidence for these beliefs which, in its employment, does not involve circular reasoning. It is granted that what the Principle of Uniformity affirms in any field, if "Principle" it may be called, is that there is uniformity in that field in this sense and no other; that there are certain specific generalisations which apply to that field and in which mere differences of position in time and space are regarded as irrelevant. In the light of this interpretation of uniformity the question briefly is, how can such a broad affirmation be confirmed or verified by induction without circularity?

For purposes of simplicity, in order to secure the clearest statement of the argument in the fewest words, it will be useful in what follows to abbreviate the statement of this Principle of Uniformity and also to consider it only in reference to time. If it can be shown that what the Principle affirms concerning the irrelevance of time in specific generalisations can be confirmed inductively, it can also be shown in exactly the same way that it is possible to confirm the Principle in its spatial reference also. So abbreviated and restricted, the Principle asserts that, in the specific way just defined, differences in time make no difference. Can this interpretation of the assertion that the future will resemble the past be confirmed? What, if any, is the evidence for it?

It follows directly from the interpretation which has just been given of this principle what the evidence for it must be. If the Principle affirms no more for any given area of fact than the validity in that area of certain generalisations which are uniform with respect to space and time, then the evidence for the Principle must be whatever evidence there is for these particular generalisations. This includes all the observations in the past and present which confirm the presence in that area of the uniformities of which these general statements speak. Belief in the uniformity in a given area is not something which is specifiable apart from the laws, principles, and other generalisations regarded as established in that area, but is itself belief in just the kind of uniformities which these generalisations describe and define. If it is correct, then, to say of any generalisation, *e.g.* of any scientific law, that it is confirmed or verified by empirical evidence, is it not correct to say that, to that extent, there is evidence for belief in the uniformity of nature?

Past and Future

The sceptic's answer to this question repeats that final rejoinder of Hume. Granted that there is empirical evidence which has been used to establish various scientific laws, all that it is evidence for, he insists, is the assertion that *in the past* these laws were true, that in the past differences in time have made no difference. This evidence is absolutely worthless for inferences which speak about the future unless it is possible to assume that the future will be like the past. But stop! That is part of what one is trying to show, that is, that mere differences in temporal position, whether past or future, make no difference in these laws of nature. That the future will be like the past means, among other things, that in the future these laws will hold, that in this specific respect differences in time will make no difference. This cannot be inductively confirmed, the sceptic is saying, because any inductive argument for it assumes it and is therefore, as evidence, completely valueless.

One major source of the plausibility of the sceptic's reasoning lies in the analogies which knowing the future easily suggests and in terms of which one is apt to think and be misled. Is this not, one may ask, like any case of sampling? And must one not take care, when reasoning inductively from samples, that one's samples are fair? If a scientist reasons concerning the behaviour of oxygen, nitrogen, or hydrogen on Mars, if such elements there be on Mars, on the basis of the known behaviour of these elements on the earth, he is assuming that in some respects the samples of the elements on the other planet are like those we have here. Similarly in reasoning about the future behaviour of these elements on the basis of present and past behaviour one must assume that future samples of these elements will be like present and past ones. Now if it is the case that past samples may be regarded as evidence about future ones only upon such an assumption, then no examination of past samples, however extensive, can be regarded as yielding evidence for the assumption itself. Any reasoning which did attempt to employ such samples as evidence for the assumption would be forced to use the assumption as a principle in the reasoning and would therefore beg the whole question at issue.

A physical representation of the kind of analogy presented here might be as follows: Suppose that there was somewhere in the world an enclosure beyond which it was impossible for anyone ever to go or to make any observations. Nothing could be seen, heard, or in any other way perceived beyond the border. The territory beyond the enclosure, forever barred from human perception, is the land of Future. The territory within the enclosure is the land of Present and Past, but since it is overwhelmingly the latter, it all goes under the name of Past. Now suppose that someone within the enclosure is interested in some proposition about the way things behave beyond the enclosure, say, a simple and homely proposition about chickens, to the effect that beyond the enclosure roosters fight more than hens. And he wonders what evidence, if any, there is for this proposition. Of course he cannot observe this to be true. He must base it upon his observation in the land of Past; and if he does base it upon the observed fact that roosters in the land of Past fight more than hens, he must assume that in this respect chickens beyond the enclosure behave like chickens within it, so that, knowing that in the latter area roosters are the more pugnacious, he may employ this knowledge as evidence that things are this way also in the former area. This is an assumption which no empirical evidence, confined as it must be to evidence in Past, can be employed to support. Any attempt to support it with such evidence must itself assume that in respect to the phenomena involved differences between Past and Future are negligible; and since that is exactly what the reasoning is attempting to establish, the process is patently circular.

This is the kind of metaphor which makes friends, and influences people, in this case, to draw the wrong conclusions. There are several faults in the analogy. The chief one is that, as represented, the border between Past and Future is stationary, while in the temporal situation it is not. To duplicate the temporal situation in this respect the analogy should represent the border as constantly moving, revealing as it does constantly, in territory which has hitherto been Future, hens and roosters similar as regards difference in disposition to those already observed in Past. The matter of evidence for the proposition about hens and roosters is then also different. If this proposition is in a position analogous to the beliefs about uniformity which are represented in modern scientific laws, the situation is something like this. Previously inhabitants in Past had drawn more sweeping conclusions concerning the difference between the disposition to fight of male and female chickens. They have discovered recently that in respect to young chicks and pullets this generalisation did not hold. They have therefore revised the proposition to exclude all the known negative instances and speak only and more surely of the behaviour of hens and roosters, meaning by these latter terms just fully grown and developed female and male chickens.

So far as there is any record, chickens in Past have verified this rule; so far as there is any record, every chicken revealed by the ever-receding border has likewise verified it; so far as there is any record there has not been one negative instance. Is it not the case that the inhabitants of Past do have evidence for the proposition that all chickens obey this rule, those already in Past, which they call "Past-chickens," and those also which are not yet in Past but which will be subsequently revealed by the moving border, and which they call not unnaturally "Future-chickens"? They have a vast number of positive instances of the rule, and no negative instances, except those in respect to which the rule has already been revised. In view of the present evidence that in all cases, year after year and century after century, the progressively revealed chickens have verified and do verify this rule, must one not conclude that the inhabitants of past do have evidence for this proposition, and that anyone is wrong who says that they have actually no evidence one way or other?

The sceptic, however, is still prepared to argue his case, and his argument, in terms of the present analogy, has a now familiar ring. That the inhabitants of Past have no evidence whatsoever about the behaviour of Future-chickens, he will insist; and as grounds he will point out that although the border does progressively recede and reveal chickens like those previously observed in Past, these are really not Future-chickens. By the very fact that they have been revealed they are no longer Future-chickens, but are now Past-chickens. Observation of them is not observation of Future-chickens, and any attempt to reason from such observation to conclusions about Future-chickens must therefore assume that Future-chickens are like Past-chickens. For the inhabitants of Past, in these efforts to know the land beyond the border, this is both an inescapable and unknowable presumption.

What should one say of an argument of this kind? Only through some logical slip, one feels strongly, would it be possible to arrive at such a conclusion. One would have thought that the receding border was a matter upon which the inhabitants of Past may legitimately congratulate themselves in the light of their interest in learning what Future-chickens, when they become Past, are going to be like. If the border had not yet begun to recede they would indeed be in an unfortunate position for securing such knowledge. But happily this is not the case. The border is constantly receding. And granting that it will constantly recede, revealing always more of the land of Future, and even granting also that this means that there is an inexhaustible area to be revealed, the inhabitants of Past are in the fortunate position that with the progressive recession they may learn more and more about chickens, Past and Future. They may derive hypotheses from their experience of what has already been revealed and proceed further to test these by the progressive revelations of Future, in the light of which they may be confirmed, refuted, or revised. The sceptic's argument amounts to the assertion that all this apparent good fortune is really illusory and that the sorry Pastians are actually in no better position with respect to knowing about Future-chickens and Future-things generally than they would be if the border never moved at all. For the movement of the border does not reveal Future-chickens, since Future is by definition the land beyond the border. No matter how much or how little is revealed, by the very fact that it is revealed and on this side of the border it is not Future but Past, and therefore, since the land of Future always is beyond observation, no empirical method can produce any evidence that what is in that land is in any way similar to what is not. That this rendering of the sceptic's position, though in the language of the above metaphor, is undistorted and fair may be seen by consulting the words of an illustrious modern sceptic and follower of Hume, Bertrand Russell. In his chapter, "On Induction," in *The Problems of Philosophy*, Russell expressed the matter in this fashion:

It has been argued that we have reason to know that the future will resemble the past, because what was the future has constantly become the past, and has always been found to resemble the past, so that we really have experience of the future, namely of times which were formerly future, which we may call past futures. But such an argument really begs the very question at issue. We have experience of past futures, but not of future futures, and the question is: Will future futures resemble past futures? This question is not to be answered by an argument which starts from past futures alone. We have therefore still to seek for some principle which shall enable us to know that the future will follow the same laws as the past.[4]

This is the central difficulty urged by Hume, Russell, and others in arguing that there can never be any empirical evidence that the future will be like the past. Empirically, in Russell's language, it is possible to have evidence only that this has been true of past and possibly present futures, not that it will be true of future futures. It is the situation in the land of Past all over again. There are generalisations which are constantly being confirmed by experience. But every time a confirming instance occurs it is nullified as evidence by the argument that it is not really a confirming instance at all. For by the fact that it has occurred it is an instance of a past future, and therefore it tells nothing whatever about future futures. In treating of the land of Past it was suggested that there is involved in arguing in this manner a logical slip or error. It remains to investigate how this is the case.

4. See above, pp. 141 f.

Suppose that in 1936, to take but a short span of time, a man says that in the above-defined sense the future will be like the past. In 1936, if he could somehow have shown that 1937 would be like 1936, this would have been evidence for his statement, as even a sceptic would admit. But in 1937, when he does establish that 1937 is like 1936, it has somehow ceased to be evidence. So long as he did not have it, it was evidence; as soon as he gets it it ceases to be. The constant neutralisation of the evidence which is effected in this argument is effected by the same kind of verbal trick which children play upon one another in fun. Child A asks child B what he is going to do to-morrow. B replies that he is going to play ball, go swimming, or what not. Thereupon A says, "You can't do that."

B: Why not?

A: Because to-morrow never comes. When to-morrow comes it won't be to-morrow; it will be to-day. You can never play to-morrow; you can only play to-day.

Again, if a prophet announces that next year will bring a utopia, and if each succeeding year, when the predicted utopia does not come, he defends himself by pointing out that he said "next year" and that obviously this is not next year, no reasonable person would pay much attention to him. Such a person would realise, on a moment's reflection, that the prophet is being deceptive with the word "next." In 1936 "next year" means "1937"; in 1937 it means "1938." Since every year "next year" means a different year, a year yet to come, what the prophet says can never be verified or disproved. If in 1936 he meant by this phrase 1937, as he sensibly should, then this statement can be verified or refuted in 1937. But if, when 1937 comes, he insists that he did not mean 1937, but "next year," and if in 1938 he again insists that he did not mean that year, and so on, then what he seems to be meaning by "next year" is the $n + 1$th year where n is the ever-progressing number of the present year. No one should alter his present activities or his plans for the future on the basis of such a prediction, for, of course, it really is not a prediction. While in the form of a statement about the future it does not say anything about the future, anything which could possibly be true or false in the infinity of time, if infinity it is, which yet remains to transpire. For what the prophet is saying is that utopia will come next year, and by his own interpretation of the words "next year" he is affirming that next year will never come. In other words, at the time which never comes, and hence when nothing occurs, a utopia will occur. This is not even sensible speech; it is a contradiction.

In a similar though less simple way those who employ the sceptical argument about uniformity to show that there is no evidence whatever for any statement about the future are being themselves deceived and are deceiving others by their use of expressions like "next," "future," "future future," and "past future." The man who said in 1936 that the future would be like the past, that mere differences in temporal position make no difference in the behaviour of nature which is described in scientific laws, meant, as he sensibly should, that this was true of the years 1937, 1938, and so on. He said something of the form "all A's are B's" and it has been possible since 1936 to examine the A's of 1937 to 1946 and to see whether what he said is confirmed or disproved by the available evidence. If, however, now that it is 1946, and all this evidence is in, he should remark that since it is 1946 the years 1937–46 are no longer future and therefore have ceased to be evidence for the proposition, then he is guilty of using, or rather abusing the word "future" in the way in which the prophet in the previous example was abusing the word "next." For the only basis for his contention that the observed A's are not confirming evidence, or what is that same thing, that they are confirming instances only if one assumes quite circularly that the future is like the past, is in his illusive use of the word "future." Time does pass, and, because it does, the present is a constantly changing one; and the point of reference for the use of words like "future" and "past" is accordingly different. The correct conclusion to be drawn from the fact that time passes is that the future is constantly being revealed and that, in consequence, we have had and shall have the opportunity to learn more and more accurately what the laws of nature's behaviour are and how therefore the future will be like the past. But this sceptical man has his eyes fixed in fatal fascination upon the movement of time, the constantly changing present. And seeing that, as the present changes, what was once future is not now future, but present, and will shortly be past, he is led to draw the conclusion that after all, for any present whatever, the future is forever hidden behind a veil. . . .

14   The Justification
of Induction

Max Black

The Importance of Induction

IF A DOG BARKS AT ME EACH TIME I PASS
by, I naturally expect him to bark again the next time he sees me. This is an
example of *inductive reasoning* in its most primitive form. From knowledge
about a *sample* of cases, those in which the dog has already barked, I draw
a conclusion about a case not included in that sample—I anticipate what
will happen the next time.

Let us now take a more sophisticated example: On applying a lighted
match to a scrap of cellophane, I find that it catches fire; I conclude that
any similar piece of cellophane would also burn in a similar situation.
Here we have an inference from what happened in *one case* to what would
happen in *any* similar case. One last example: An entomologist finds that
each examined beetle of a certain species has a green spot on its back and
concludes that *all* beetles of that species will have the same marking.

Such familiar examples of inductive reasoning involve a transition
from information about a given set of objects or situations to a conclusion
about some wider, more inclusive, set. We might say that all of them consist of reasoning from *samples*. Let us therefore agree to understand by an

[This selection first appeared in S. Morgenbesser (ed.), *Philosophy of Science Today,* a
volume published in 1967 by Basic Books, Inc., of New York, with whose permission it is
here reprinted.]

inductive argument one in which the conclusion refers to at least one thing that is not referred to by the premises.

The simplest forms of inductive arguments, on whose correctness the more sophisticated ones ultimately depend, can be represented as follows: "Such and such *A*'s are *B;* therefore another *A* is *B*" or, again, "*Some A*'s (selected in such and such a fashion) are *B;* therefore all *A*'s are *B*." We need not consider ways of improving these formulas, since the problem of justifying induction remains essentially the same in all forms of inductive reasoning, whether primitive or sophisticated.

It has been held, very widely though not universally, that the use of inductive reasoning is a distinctive feature of scientific method, integrally connected with the discovery of scientific laws and generalizations. In strict *deductive* reasoning, we are limited to rearranging information about the data referred to in the premises, and never advance to knowledge about the hitherto unobserved; by means of inductive reasoning, however, we make the leap from "some" to "all"; from the known present to the predicted future; from the finite data of observation to laws covering all that will be and could be. The so-called "inductive leap" (from "some" to "any" and "all") seems indispensable in science no less than in ordinary life.

Indeed, the very language we use to refer to persons and material objects implies a belief in the permanence of objects and the continuity of their properties that can be grounded only in inductive reasoning from experience. There can be no serious question of human beings rejecting inductive reasoning as unsound: to do so would be tantamount to destroying the very language we use to talk about the universe and about ourselves and would lead to the kind of last-ditch skepticism that lacks even the words to express itself.

Doubts About Induction

It is altogether reasonable to wonder how the use of this powerful method of reasoning can be justified. Indeed, certain features of inductive argument, as we have defined it, can easily awaken serious disquiet. In logic, we have all been taught that the transition from a "some" in the premises to an "all" in the conclusion is a transparent fallacy: if some men are white-skinned, it by no means follows that *all* men are; how, then, can we be justified in wholesale violation of this plain and simple rule? Again, inductions are notoriously fallible; the gambler who expects a sequence of reds on the roulette wheel to continue indefinitely will soon be undeceived. In our dealings with nature, are we in any stronger position than the gambler who has had a lucky sequence of throws? Are we perhaps about to come to the end of our lucky guesses about nature? How can we possibly *know* that the sun will rise tomorrow?

For the sake of clarity, it is essential to distinguish such sweeping skeptical doubts from practical questions about the reliability of inductive procedures. It is one thing to ask whether a given inductive procedure is sufficiently reliable for a given purpose; different and more basic questions are at issue when we ask how *any* inductive argument can be justified. We have well-tested methods for discriminating random events, such as those that occur on a roulette table, from lawful ones: where practical decision is in question, it would be foolish to consider the contingency that the sun might *not* rise the next day. On the other hand, in cases where inductive conclusions based upon sampling are relatively unreliable, we know in principle how to improve the reliability of the sampling process. There is no difficulty in principle about meeting any practical criticism of a given inductive procedure.

By contrast, the question of justification raised by the philosopher is one of the utmost generality. He is perplexed to understand how *any* inductive reasoning, no matter how satisfactory by the standards of common sense or of good statistical practice, can really count as acceptable. He finds it hard to understand how the "inductive leap," which seems to involve a plain logical fallacy, could *ever* be justified. The problem has no immediate bearing upon scientific practice, but is of the first importance for evaluating the claims of science to be a vehicle of truth about the universe. It seems that unless induction can be justified, our claims to have scientific *knowledge* must be rejected as unfounded and science will have to count as no better than any other unsubstantiated *faith*. However appealing such a skeptical conclusion might be to those who welcome any proof of man's impotence, it is one to be accepted only after the most careful investigation.

Five Attempted Solutions

In the course of the intensive consideration that philosophers of science have given to this problem, almost every conceivable answer has been defended.

1. Perhaps the most drastic solution available consists of a denial that induction plays, or ought to play, any part in scientific method. This view has been most eloquently defended in recent times by Professor Karl Popper, who has argued in numerous writings that the proper business of science is the *deductive testing* of empirical hypotheses. According to him, there is no rational way of arriving at generalizations from the examination of sampled cases—no rational way of making the inductive leap—but once such a generalization has been produced, by whatever means, there *is* a rational way of discovering whether it meets the tests of observation and experiment. Such generalizations or hypotheses can be conclusively *falsified*, but never verified, never shown to be true. The task of empirical science is falsification, putting to the trial of experience bold "conjectures" about the world, and not the impossible task of discovering truth.

For all the ingenuity with which this provocative view has been argued (to which I cannot do justice in this brief essay), the "no induction" view, as it might be called, has not received wide acceptance. It seems too paradoxical a conception of science that it should consist only of the elimination of error, rather than the progressive discovery of approximations to the truth. And induction seems to creep in by the back door in Popper's theory of "corroboration," that is, of the criteria by which we discriminate between the relative strengths of hypotheses, none of which are falsified by the known observational facts.

2. One might think that common sense can provide a simple and satisfactory answer to the problem of induction. If a layman is asked why he trusts an inductive argument from "some" to "all," the chances are he will say that this kind of argument has "always worked in the past." (One might have some doubts about that "always," but no matter.) How foolish it would be, we can imagine the plain man saying, to abandon techniques that have worked so well and have produced such spectacular successes in technology and in pure science. Well, let it be granted that induction *has* "worked" in the past; what grounds does this give us for expecting it to work in the future? If we conclude that induction *will* work because it *has* worked we are arguing—inductively!

As the philosopher David Hume pointed out long ago in a famous discussion of the problem, we seem here to be begging the question. The best method we have for settling specific empirical questions—arguing from the known character of observed instances—leaves us in the lurch when we try to find a *general* justification of induction. To offer an inductive justification to anybody who doubts that induction is *ever* justified is obviously futile. (On the other hand, some modern writers have argued, with some success, that inductive arguments can be applied to themselves, in order to improve their own reliability. It is at any rate not obvious that any objectionable circularity is here involved. The status of such so-called "self-supporting" inductive arguments is still controversial. In any case, self-supporting arguments, even if allowed to be sound, have no direct bearing on the general problem of justification.)

3. A favorite approach to the problem of justification begins by asserting that inductive arguments, in the form considered in this essay, are basically *incomplete*. Transition from "some" to "all," from a premise about a sample to a conclusion about the population from which that sample was drawn, is held to rely upon unstated *assumptions*. Until such assumptions are made explicit, the inductive inference is unsound—the inductive *leap* is never justified by itself: an inductive argument needs an extra premise in order to become valid. There needs to be supplied some principle that "the future will resemble the past" or some more general principle of "the Uniformity of Nature." Once such a principle has been introduced into the argument, and only then, that argument will become logically respectable. (It will be noticed that this line of attack on the problem tacitly assumes that only *deductive* argument is irreproachable.

By implicitly denying the possibility of distinctive inductive arguments, this position resembles the "no induction" view previously mentioned.)

The formulation of general principles that might plausibly play the part of missing premises in inductive arguments is a matter of great difficulty. Since nature obviously exhibits variety as well as uniformity, irregularity as well as order, it is hard to state a principle of uniformity without producing something that is plainly false. For example, the principle that *whenever* some *A*'s are *B,* all *A*'s are *B* is a grotesque overstatement. And even such a sophisticated version as John Maynard Keynes's famous principle of the "Limitation of Independent Variety" has been subjected to damaging criticism. It seems fair to say that nobody has yet produced a suitably qualified candidate for the title of the "Basic Principle of Inductive Inference"—although many have tried.

We need not enter into the technicalities of this attempt to bolster induction by supplying an additional grand premise. There is in my opinion a conclusive objection against this whole line of approach. Imagine the desired general principle produced: then it will be either *a priori* true or contingently true. If the first, it is a necessary truth, holding independently of the facts, like a logical or mathematical principle. But then it cannot support the transition from "some" to "all." It is easy to see that if the conclusion of an inductive argument does not *follow* deductively from the premises, the case is not altered when a necessary truth is added to the premises. But if the proposed principle is contingently true, it would not hold in all possible worlds, but must formulate something true of *our* universe.

How then is *its* truth to be known? Only, it seems, by the familiar methods, the best we know, of observation and inductive reasoning. Indeed, we may go further: our confidence in particular laws of nature, the conclusions of inductive inferences, is *better* grounded than our confidence in the truth of any alleged principle about the general uniformity of nature. Such evidence as we have for the orderliness of the universe is derived from our knowledge of particular regularities and not vice versa. The search for grand principles of induction therefore merely shifts the problem without solving it: the problem of establishing such principles is just the old one of justifying induction—in another and even less tractable form.

4. So far, I have made no reference to probability, in order to avoid complicating what is already a sufficiently complicated subject. Yet problems of induction and of probability are intertwined. It is important to notice, for instance, that the conclusion of a sound inductive argument follows from its premises only with a certain probability. Given a good inductive argument for some conclusion, we can always conceive of *stronger* evidence: inductive inferences can sometimes be compared with respect to their relative strengths in a way that would be quite inappropriate for deductive inferences. Some students of the theory of induction have therefore held that a reference to probability should be part of the conclusion of a properly expressed inductive argument. For instance, the correct con-

clusion from the premise "All examined A's have been B," they say, is not "All A's are B," but perhaps, "It is more probable than not that all A's are B" or something similar. And the suggestion has often been made that neglect of such reference to probability is responsible for the inadequacy of the attempts to justify induction that we have so far considered.

Replacing a conclusion of the form "All A's are B" by a conclusion of the form "It is more probable than not that all A's are B" amounts to weakening the conclusion. (We may recall here that those who hoped to add an extra premise concerning the uniformity of nature were engaged in strengthening the premises. So both lines of attack aim at bringing inductive arguments closer to satisfying the standards of valid deductive argument.)

Our verdict on this attempt to make induction respectable by introducing probability must depend upon the meaning we attach to the relevant probability statement. According to one conception of the meaning of probability, the conclusion "It is more probable than not that all A's are B" follows *strictly* from the premise "All examined A's have been B": it is logically impossible that the premise should be true while the probability conclusion is false. On this interpretation, we would have a valid deductive argument, with no "inductive leap," if we introduced reference to probability into the conclusion. But this reading of inductive arguments is useless: our whole attempt has been to understand how it is possible to end in a conclusion that goes beyond the premises, by referring to things or situations that are not covered by those premises. Replacing the original inductive argument by some deductive substitute, however ingeniously constructed, will not be a solution.

There is another way of understanding probability, according to which the probability conclusion makes a genuinely empirical claim about what would be found true in a large number of similar cases. To say that the conclusion is "It is more probable than not that all A's are B" would be tantamount to saying something like "In most cases in which the examined A's have been B, it will be found subsequently that all A's are B." On this view, the argument, as amended by explicit reference to probability, remains genuinely inductive. But by the same token we are confronted once again with the inductive leap. The new conclusion does not follow strictly from the premises, and we are still faced with the troublesome problem of how it can be rational to go beyond the evidence, in the manner that is characteristic of genuinely inductive arguments.

Those who insist that the conclusions of inductive arguments should be probability statements are faced with the same dilemma that bedevils all previous attempts to justify induction: either the argument is left in its original form, and then it seems to be invalid; or else it is replaced by some valid deductive argument (either by strengthening the premises or by weakening the conclusion), and then it is not an inductive argument at all.

5. I turn, finally, to the so-called "pragmatic" justifications of induction, which have seemed to many modern students of the problem to provide a satisfactory answer to this ancient puzzle. The basic ideas underlying this

approach were independently formulated by Charles Sanders Peirce and by Hans Reichenbach, the latter of whom argued the position with great ingenuity and pertinacity.

Consider the following familiar position in ordinary life. A doctor, who is treating a patient suffering from some serious disease, has reason to believe that the only chance of saving the patient's life is to perform a certain operation; suppose also that there is no guarantee of the operation's proving successful: if the doctor is right in thinking that the patient will die in any case if the operation is not performed, he is justified in operating. To put the matter in another way: If a *necessary condition* for saving the patient's life is performing the operation, then that operation is justified, even though the outcome is unknown and the risks are great. This might be called a case of "nothing to lose by trying"—resort to the dangerous operation may be a "forlorn hope," but it is a justifiable one.

Those who apply this idea to the justification of induction argue as follows: Hume was right when he said that it was impossible to argue from the present to the future, from the known to the unknown. The "inductive leap" cannot be justified in the way that philosophers and scientists have hoped. Nevertheless, we badly need knowledge ranging beyond our observations and nothing can prevent us from trying to obtain it. Suppose it could be shown that the *only way* to reach such knowledge is by following inductive procedures. Then we should be in the position of the doctor or the patient in the original example, with nothing to lose by trying. If following inductive procedures is a *necessary condition* for anticipating the unknown, we shall be practically or—as people say, "pragmatically"—justified in following that procedure.

We may agree that the general line of argument is plausible; its contribution to the problem of justifying induction will depend upon how successful its defenders are in showing that some kind of inductive procedure is a necessary condition for making correct generalizations about the unknown or the unobserved.

The model usually employed has approximately the following character: Suppose we are performing a series of observations and are interested in some property P. If in the first 100 trials we find that P has appeared in 65 cases, we assume provisionally that in the *long run* the proportion of favorable cases will be close to $65/100$. As we continue our trials, we may find, say, 87 favorable cases in the first 150 observations: we therefore correct our estimate and now expect the proportion of favorable cases to be near $85/150$. We proceed in this same way: whenever we find that k out of l trials exhibit the property P, we provisionally assume that the proportion in the long run will be close to k/l.

Since there is no guarantee that the fractions we progressively find in this way will ultimately converge to a limit, our attempt to anticipate the overall character of the entire series of observations may be defeated after all. But *if* there is a limit (which we cannot know) this procedure of successive correction will eventually bring us close to the true value of that limit. We are justified in following the procedure, because we have nothing to lose. If the series of successive fractions is sufficiently irregular, *no* method of forecasting its ultimate character will be possible; while if it has the regularity of a convergent series, our method will bring us close to the desired answer sooner or later.

This idea is too ingenious and too complicated to be criticized in a few words. I have argued at length elsewhere that it fails. Some of the strongest objections that I and other critics have brought to light are technical ones, having to do with the impossibility, according to the pragmatic view, of preferring one method of estimation to another. But the basic objection is that the whole approach concedes too much to the skeptical critics of induction. Those who agree with Hume that *knowledge* of the unobserved is, strictly speaking, impossible, will always find themselves with empty hands at the conclusion of an inductive procedure, no matter how ingeniously they try to wriggle out of their predicament.

The Disappearance of the Problem

We seem now to have arrived at a stalemate. None of the ways of justifying induction that have been explored by a long line of able and acute thinkers seem to offer any prospects of success. Attempts to justify induction by using inductive procedures seem hopelessly circular; attempts to find principles expressing the alleged uniformity of nature simply raise the old questions in a new form; introducing probability statements does not help; and the fashionable "pragmatic" justifications really leave us helpless against skeptical objections to induction. Considering the intensity with which the problem has been studied, there is no hope that we shall do better where so many powerful intellects have labored in vain.

Now when we meet with a situation like this, there is usually reason to suppose that the nature of the problem has been misconceived, and that the apparently insurmountable difficulties arise from misunderstanding. The view is steadily gaining ground that this is the situation with regard to the celebrated problem of justifying induction.

The very notion of justification implies some *standard* of justification: to justify induction must be to show that that kind of reasoning satisfies some relevant criterion of what is regarded as reasonable. Now the long history of the subject shows that nearly everybody who has grappled with the problem has really had before his mind the standards of *deductive* reasoning: however widely the various attempts to justify induction differ, they all assume that the only really reputable mode of reasoning, the only "strict" method, is that in which the conclusion follows by logical necessity from the premises.

But induction, *by definition,* is not deduction: the idea of the so-called "inductive leap" is built into our conception of an inductive argument. To try to convert inductive arguments into deductive ones is as futile an attempt as that of the child who argued that a horse was really a cow—only without horns. The beginning of wisdom in this extremely complicated and controversial domain is therefore the recognition that no *general* justification of induction, of the sort that philosophers of science have hoped to uncover, is either possible or needed. What we *mean* by justifying a specific empirical generalization is an inductive demonstration, using principles that have been found to work in the kind of case in question, that the generalization is true or at least probable. When we try to apply this relatively definite notion of justification to induction itself, the very notion of justification becomes unclear.

It is not so much that we do not know how to justify induction as that we do not know and cannot imagine what we would *accept* as such a justification. Clarity, here—which cannot, of course, be achieved without the hardest intellectual labor—ought to result in the disappearance of the alleged "problem of induction." If this view is correct, as I hold it to be, the problem of induction will eventually be classified with such famous "insoluble" problems as that of squaring the circle or that of inventing perpetual-motion machines. And as in those famous cases, the quest for the impossible does not seem, from the long perspective of history, to have been futile. For the byproducts of serious investigation may be even more important than its ostensible goal. If our knowledge of the character of inductive procedures is as rich and as sophisticated as it is today, no little of the credit must be assigned to those who have labored so long and so unsuccessfully at trying to justify induction.

Selected Bibliography

(ITEMS PROVIDED WITH ASTERISK ARE MORE ADVANCED)
(FOR KEY TO ABBREVIATIONS SEE PAGE XIX)

Lucid and comprehensive discussions of all major philosophical problems concerning probability and induction are found in two articles by M. Black in *The Encyclopedia of Philosophy* ("Induction," 4–169 and "Probability," 6–464). Both of these are reprinted in M. Black, *Margins of Precision* (Ithaca: Cornell U.P., 1970). Important writings on the nature of probability and the problem of the justification of induction are collected in M. Foster and M. Martin, (eds.), *Probability, Confirmation and Simplicity—Readings in the Philosophy of Inductive Logic* (N.Y.: Odyssey Press, 1969).

Expository and critical discussions of Mill's experimental methods are found in M. Cohen and E. Nagel, *Introduction to Logic and Scientific Method* (N.Y.: Harcourt, Brace, 1934), Ch. 13, and S. L. Stebbing, *A Modern Introduction to Logic* (London: Methuen, 1930), Chs. 15 and 17. An introduction to the theory of probability and its application to inductive reasoning may also be found in Chs. 8 and 14 of Cohen and Nagel. Much the same ground is covered in Chs.

14–16 of H. Kahane, *Logic and Philosophy* (Belmont, California: Wadsworth, 1969). The logical foundations of empirical knowledge are dealt with in an elementary way in Chs. 2 and 5 of B. Aune, *Rationalism, Empiricism, and Pragmatism: An Introduction* (N.Y.: Random House, 1970, p), M. Scriven, *Primary Philosophy* (N.Y.: McGraw-Hill, 1966) Ch. 6, J. Hospers, *An Introduction to Philosophical Analysis* (Englewood Cliffs: Prentice-Hall, 2nd ed., 1967), Ch. 4, and A. Pap, *Elements of Analytic Philosophy* (N.Y.: Macmillan, 1949), Chs. 8, 9, and 16. A fuller and more advanced treatment of these and related topics is contained in W. C. Salmon, *The Foundations of Scientific Inference* (Pittsburgh: U. of Pittsburgh P., 1966, p), B. Skyrms, *Choice and Chance* (Belmont, Calif.: Dickenson, 1966, p), and A. Pap, *An Introduction to the Philosophy of Science* (N.Y.: Free Press, 1962).

Bertrand Russell's maturer views on induction may be found, together with a discussion of the theory of probability, in his *Human Knowledge* (London: Allen & Unwin, N.Y.: Simon & Schuster, 1948). J. M. Keynes, *A Treatise on Probability** (London: Macmillan, 1921) is a classic on the problems of induction and probability. W. Kneale, *Probability and Induction** (Oxford: Clarendon Press, 1949), Part II, gives a survey of classical theories of induction from Bacon to Keynes. E. Nagel, *Principles of the Theory of Probability* (Int. Encyclopedia of United Science, Vol. I, No. 6, U. of Chicago P., 1939) is recommended as an introduction to the technical problems of the theory of probability. R. von Mises, *Probability, Statistics and Truth** (N.Y.: Macmillan, 1939) is an introduction to the theory of probability from the point of view of the interpretation of probability as relative frequency. D. Williams, *The Ground of Induction** (Cambridge: Harvard U.P., 1947) is an attempt to solve Hume's problem by pure logic or the mathematical theory of probability. The extremely influential views of Rudolf Carnap are presented most fully in his *Logical Foundations of Probability** (Chicago: U. of Chicago P., 2nd ed., 1962).

In Selection 14 of the present work, M. Black defends the view that the problem of the justification of induction, as it is conceived by Hume and Russell, is a pseudo-problem. Substantially the same approach is adopted in P. Edwards' "Bertrand Russell's Doubts about Induction," *M*, 1949, reprinted in A. Flew (ed.), *Essays in Logic and Language,* First Series (Oxford: Blackwell, 1951), also reprinted, with omissions, in C. L. Reid (ed.), *Basic Philosophical Analysis* (Belmont, Calif.: Dickenson, 1971), in A. Ambrose, "The Problem of Justifying Inductive Inference," *JP*, 1947, reprinted in her *Essays in Analysis* (London: Allen & Unwin, 1966), in Ch. 9 of P. F. Strawson, *Introduction to Logical Theory** (London: Methuen, New York: Wiley, 1952), and in Ch. 4 of A. Flew, *Hume's Philosophy of Belief* (London: Routledge, 1961). There are interesting arguments about the "incoherence" of scepticism concerning induction in A. Campbell's "One Form of Skepticism about Induction," *A*, 1963. In "Scepticism, Rationalism and Language," *Me*, 1971, J. Kees answers the challenge of the sceptic by maintaining that the very existence of language presupposes the falsehood of scepticism. Hume is criticized in D. Stove, "Hume, Probability and Induction," *PR*, 1965, reprinted in J. H. Gill (ed), *Philosophy Today No. 3* (N.Y.: Macmillan, 1970, p), the same author's "Deductivisim," *AJ*, 1970, and in R. Paul, "Appearances and Expectations" *M*, 1969. Two other writers who regard the traditional problem as misconceived are C. A. Fritz in "What is Induction?," *JP*, 1960 and G. Schlesinger in "Induction and Parsimony," *APQ*, 1971. The view that the traditional problem of induction is a pseudo-problem is critically examined in J. O. Urmson's "Some Questions Concerning Validity," which is reprinted in A. Flew (ed.), *Essays in Conceptual*

Analysis (London: Macmillan, 1956). Urmson, though critical, concedes that the writers who regard the problem of induction as a pseudo-problem have greatly advanced the discussion of the whole subject. A similar attitude, both critical and sympathetic, is expressed by R. Harré in Ch. 5 of *An Introduction to the Logic of the Sciences* (London: Macmillan, 1960) and in his earlier article, "Dissolving the 'Problem' of Induction," *P*, 1957. In Ch. 6 of his *The Implications of Induction** (London: Metheun, 1970), L. J. Cohen defends Strawson and Edwards against Urmson's criticisms. Cohen himself, however, offers a different answer to Hume, which he calls the "analogical ratification of induction." The following writers are highly critical of attempts to "dissolve" the problem of induction: J. L. Mackie, *Contemporary Linguistic Philosophy—Its Strength and Its Weakness* (Otago: U. of Otago P., 1956), E. H. Madden, "The Riddle of Induction," *JP*, 1958, reprinted in E. H. Madden (ed.), *The Structure of Scientific Thought* (Boston: Houghton Mifflin, 1960), and E. Harris, "Misleading Analyses," *PQ*, 1953, reprinted in H. D. Lewis (ed.), *Clarity is Not Enough* (London: Allen & Unwin, 1963). Recent critical discussions of the same approach are found in W. C. Salmon, "The Concept of Inductive Evidence," *APQ*, 1965, and Ch. 8 of H. E. Kyburg, Jr., *Probability and Inductive Logic** (New York: Macmillan, 1970). For a critique of F. Will's "Will the Future Be Like the Past?" which is, with minor omissions, reprinted in this section, *see* D. Williams' "Induction and the Future," *M*, 1948. Other articles on the subject by Will include "Is There a Problem of Induction?" *JP*, 1942, "Generalization and Evidence," in M. Black (ed.), *Philosophical Analysis* (Ithaca: Cornell U.P., 1950), and "Justification and Induction," *PR*, 1959. A discussion of the views of D. Williams is contained in D. S. Miller's "Professor Donald Williams versus Hume," *JP*, 1947, and in H. E. Kyburg, Jr., "The Justification of Induction," *JP*, 1956. Hume is criticized from a rationalist point of view in A. C. Ewing, "Causality and Induction," *PPR*, 1952, reprinted in his *Non-Linguistic Philosophy* (London: Allen & Unwin, 1968). In E. H. Madden, "Hume and the Fiery Furnace," *PS*, 1971, and E. H. Madden and P. Hare, "The Powers That Be," *D*, 1971 it is argued that, contrary to Hume and contemporary Humeans, there is a sense in which cause and effect are necessarily connected and that this necessary connection serves as a justification of inductive inferences. In his article "The Problem of Justifying Induction," included in C. Hanly and M. Lazerowitz (eds.), *Psychoanalysis and Philosophy* (N.Y.: International Universities Press, 1970), M. Lazerowitz offers a theory concerning the hidden psychological meaning of doubts about induction. Hume is defended against Stove's criticisms in F. N. Harpley, "Hume's Probabilism," *AJ*, 1971.

Two standpoints adopted by some eminent contemporary philosophers are not represented in any of the selections in the present work. One of these is the attempt to provide a "pragmatic justification" of induction. Suggestions of such a position are already found in Charles Peirce. More recent variants are found in the writings of Hans Reichenbach, W. C. Kneale, R. B. Braithwaite, H. Feigl, and W. Salmon. Kneale's position is stated in Part IV of his *Probability and Induction, op. cit.* Braithwaite's views are expounded in Ch. VIII of his *Scientific Explanation** (N.Y.: Harper, 1960, p). Reichenbach's position is stated in a number of works, including *Experience and Prediction* (Chicago: U. of Chicago P., 1938, p), *Theory of Probability** (Berkeley: U. of California P., 1949), *The Rise of Scientific Philosophy* (Berkeley: U. of California P., 1951, p), and in the article "On the Justification of Induction," *JP*, 1940, reprinted in H. Feigl and W. Sellars (eds.), *Readings in Philosophical Analysis* (N.Y.: Appleton-Century-Crofts, 1949). Reichenbach's position has been defended and further developed in several articles by W. Salmon. The most important of these are "Should We Attempt To Justify Induction?" *PSt*, 1957 (reprinted in part in Canfield and Donnell, *op. cit.*), "Vindication of Induction," in H. Feigl and G. Maxwell (eds.), *Current Issues in the Philosophy of Science* (N.Y.: Holt, Rinehart & Winston, 1961), and "On Vindicating Induction," in H. E. Kyburg, Jr., and E. Nagel (eds.), *Induction: Some Current Issues* (Middletown, Conn.: Wesleyan U.P., 1963). The last of these volumes contains criticisms of Salmon by M. Black and others, as well as Salmon's reply. It also contains many other interesting papers on induction, but most of these are very technical. Feigl's position, which is in some respects akin to that of the philosophers who treat the question as a pseudo-problem, is stated in a number of articles including "De Principiis Non Disputandum . . . ?" in M. Black (ed.), *Philosophical Analysis, op. cit.*, "Scientific Method wtihout Metaphysical Presuppositions," *PSt*, 1954, and "On the Vindication of Induction," *PS*, 1961. The pragmatic position, especially Reichenbach's form of it, has been attacked by J. W. Lenz in "Problems for the Practicalist's Justification of Induction," in Madden, *op. cit.*, and in great detail by M. Black in " 'Pragmatic' Justifications of Induction," reprinted in his *Problems of Analysis* (Ithaca: Cornell U.P., 1954). The first of the two pieces by Salmon mentioned above contains a rejoinder to Black's article, to which Black replied in "Can Induction Be Vindicated?" *PSt*, 1959, reprinted in his *Models and Metaphors* (Ithaca: Cornell U.P., 1962).

The other position not represented in the present work is that of Karl Popper and his followers, who deny that induction has any value or application and who can therefore treat sceptical doubts about the validity of induction as idle. Popper's views are stated in his *The Logic of Scientific Discovery** (London: Hutchinson, 1959) and in a more summary fashion in his articles, "Philosophy of Science: A Personal Report," in C. A. Mace (ed.), *British Philosophy in the Mid-Century* (N.Y.: Macmillan, 1957) and "Conjectural Knowledge: My Solution of the Problem of Induction," *Revue Internationale de Philosophie*, 1971. They are also defended by J. O. Wisdom in *Foundations of Inference in Natural Science* (London: Methuen, 1952), in Agassi's "Empiricism and Inductivism," *PSt*, 1963, J. W. N. Watkins, "Hume, Carnap and Popper," and I. Lakatos, "Changes in the Problem of Inductive Logic," both in I. Lakatos (ed.), *The Problem of Inductive Logic* (Amsterdam: North-Holland Publishing Co., 1968). The same volume contains Popper's "Theories, Experience and Probabilistic Intuitions," in which he replies to his critics, W. C. Salmon, "The Justification of Inductive Rules of Inference," which is critical of Popper, and Carnap's "Inductive Logic and Inductive Intuition." The last-mentioned essay is a very lucid summary of the basic features of Carnap's approach to the subject. A position, very similar to Popper's, is also defended in Ch. 9 of D. Mitchell, *An Introduction to Logic* (Garden City: Doubleday, 1970, p). Criticisms of Popper's views are found in M. Black's *Encyclopedia of Philosophy* article on "Induction," *op. cit.*, the same author's "Induction and Probability" in R. Klibansky (ed.), *Philosophy in the Mid-Century*, Volume I (Florence: La Nuova Italia Editrice, 1958), G. Buchdhal and H. G. Alexander, "Convention, Falsification and Induction," *Ar. Soc. Sup.*, 1960, and in a review by G. J. Warnock of *The Logic of Scientific Discovery* in *M*, 1960. Several of the writers who deny that Hume's problem is genuine, as well as some who champion the pragmatic justification, have argued that in a certain important sense an "inductive justification" of induction is possible without vicious circularity. This idea was propounded in Section IV of the article by P. Edwards, *op. cit.*, by Braithwaite in *Scientific Explanation, op. cit.*, and most fully in M. Black's

"Inductive Support of Inductive Rules," in his *Problems of Analysis, op. cit.* Braithwaite's arguments are criticized in R. C. Coburn's "Braithwaite's Inductive Justification of Induction," *PS,* 1961. Black's paper was attacked by P. Achinstein in *A,* 1962. There is a reply by Black in the same volume of *A,* and a reply to Black's reply by Achinstein in *A,* 1963.

C. I. Lewis, *Mind and the World Order* (N.Y.: Scribner's, 1929), argues, like Reichenbach, that no proposition asserting an objective fact is conclusively verifiable (see esp. Ch. 9). This thesis is elaborated in Lewis' later book, *An Analysis of Knowledge and Valuation** (LaSalle, Illinois: Open Court, 1947), Chs. 7–9. The same view is advocated by A. J. Ayer in *Language, Truth and Logic,* Ch. 5. A comprehensive discussion of the problem of the certainty of empirical propositions was initiated by N. Malcolm's "Certainty and Empirical Statements," *M,* 1942. This is a criticism of the philosopher's denial of certainty based on the analysis of ordinary language. Malcolm's article was answered by M. Black in a note also called "Certainty and Empirical Statements," *M,* 1942. Malcolm continued his criticism in a classic article, "Moore and Ordinary Language," in P. A. Schilpp (ed.), *The Philosophy of G. E. Moore* (Evanston and Chicago: Northwestern U.P., 1942). C. A. Campbell entered the debate with his "Common Sense Propositions and Philosophical Paradoxes," *Ar. Soc.,* 1944–45. A critique of Campbell is advanced by P. Edwards in "Ordinary Language and Absolute Certainty," *PSt,* 1950, which was followed by Campbell's rejoinder, "Mr. Edwards on Absolute Certainty," *ibid.* A revision of Malcolm's views is contained in "On Defending Common Sense," *PR,* 1949. A critique of this article is given in C. Rollins' "Ordinary Language and Procrustean Beds," *M,* 1951, which is answered in Malcolm's "Moore's Use of 'Know'," *M,* 1953. Further exposition of Malcolm's views is found in a symposium in which he participated along with R. M. Chisholm entitled "Philosophy and Ordinary Language," *PR,* 1951. The debate is continued in M. Macdonald's "Sleeping and Waking," *M,* 1953, which is reprinted in D. F. Gustafson (ed.), *Essays in Philosophical Psychology* (Garden City: Doubleday, 1964, p). Malcolm's latest article on this topic is "Dreaming and Skepticism," *PR,* 1956.

A critique of the thesis that no statements asserting existence can be absolutely certain is given in A. Pap's "Indubitable Existential Statements," *M,* 1946. There is a reply to Pap by C. Rollins in "Are There Indubitable Existential Statements?" *M,* 1949, and a rejoinder to Rollins by Pap in "Ostensive Definition and Empirical Certainty," *M,* 1950. The view that empirical statements can be certain is defended in W. T. Stace's "Are All Empirical Statements Merely Hypotheses?" *JP,* 1947. There is a reply to Stace in P. Henle's "On the Certainty of Empirical Statements," *ibid.* A critique of the views of C. I. Lewis is contained in N. Malcolm's "The Verification Argument," in M. Black (ed.), *Philosophical Analysis, op. cit.* Malcolm's arguments are criticized by H. G. Frankfurt in "Philosophical Certainty," *PR,* 1962. Malcolm's "The Verification Argument" is reprinted in his book, *Knowledge and Certainty* (Englewood Cliffs: Prentice-Hall, 1963). In footnotes added in this work, he replies to some of Frankfurt's criticisms. *Knowledge and Certainty* also contains several other papers relevant to the issues covered in this section— "Knowledge and Belief," reprinted from *M,* 1952, "Direct Perception," reprinted from *PQ,* 1953, and "George Edward Moore." Frankfurt is also criticized in M. A. Slote, "Empirical Certainty and the Theory of Important Criteria," *Inquiry,* 1967.

A classical attempt to refute Cartesian scepticism in terms of common sense is G. E. Moore's "Proof of an External World," *Proceedings of the*

British Academy, 1939, reprinted in his *Philosophical Papers* (London: Allen & Unwin, 1959, New York: Collier Books, 1962, p). For a discussion of Moore's arguments see A. Ambrose's "Moore's Proof of an External World," in *The Philosophy of G. E. Moore, op. cit.* Another relevant article in the same volume is M. Lazerowitz' "Moore's Paradox," which is also reprinted in his book, *The Structure of Metaphysics* (London: Routledge, 1955). Moore's last published views on the subject are found in an essay entitled "Certainty," which forms a chapter of *Philosophical Papers, op. cit.* Recent articles discussing Moore's "technique" are J. N. Findlay's "Some Neglected Issues in the Philosophy of G. E. Moore," in his *Language, Mind and Value* (London: Allen & Unwin, N.Y.: Humanities Press, 1963), and J. O. Nelson, "I Know That *Here Is a Hand,*" *A,* 1964. A very important work on the topics discussed by Moore, Malcolm and other of the writers just mentioned is L. Wittgenstein's posthumously published *On Certainty* (Oxford: Blackwell, 1969). Cartesian scepticism is critically examined in H. G. Frankfurt, *Demons, Dreamers and Madmen* (Indianapolis: Bobbs-Merrill, 1970). F. Broadie, *An Approach to Descartes' Meditations* (London: Athlone Press, 1970), A. Kenny, *Descartes: A Study of His Philosophy* (N.Y.: Random House, 1968, p), and in O. K. Bouwsma, "Descartes' Scepticism of the Senses," *M,* 1945.

Sceptical doubts about the senses and induction have led philosophers to discuss the theory of solipsism which, in one of its forms, maintains that human beings cannot know anything beyond the content of their own minds. Recent discussions of this view are found in W. D. Oliver, "A Sober Look at Solipsism," in N. Rescher (ed.), *Studies in the Theory of Knowledge* (Oxford: Blackwell, 1970, p), W. E. Kennick, "On Solipsism," in C. Hanly and M. Lazerowitz (eds.), *Psychoanalysis and Philosophy op. cit.,* and in the article on "Solipsism" by C. D. Rollins in the *Encyclopedia of Philosophy* (7–487). The last-mentioned article contains a bibliography of writings on solipsism.

Extensive bibliographies on various problems concerning induction are contained in Carnap, *Logical Foundations of Probability, op. cit.,* H. E. Kyburg, Jr., *Probability and Inductive Logic, op. cit.,* and the same author's "Recent Work in Inductive Logic," *APQ,* 1964.

III

Body,
Mind
and
Death

INTRODUCTION

S OME PHILOSOPHERS HAVE MAINTAINED
that a human being is simply his body and nothing else besides. Thus Nietzsche
once remarked: "Body am I entirely, and nothing more; and soul is only the
name of something in the body." The same view is also expressed in an epigram
coined by the German philosopher Feuerbach. "A man," he said, "is what he
eats." However, the great majority of philosophers, and especially those with a
religious background, have agreed that human beings are something more than
their bodies; and this something more has variously been referred to as the
mind, the self, or the soul. Is a human being really a mind in addition to his
body? If he is, what exactly is this mind and how is it related to the body?
Finally, are there any good grounds for supposing that his mind survives the
disintegration of his body? These are the main questions discussed in the selections contained in the present section.

At least at first sight, it seems exceedingly plausible to contend that a
human being is something over and above his body. Things like houses and
mountains and also of course human and animal bodies are publicly observable.
All these "physical" objects have extension and occupy positions in space. By
contrast, only a person himself can experience his feelings, sensations, dreams,
or thoughts. A dentist can observe the cavity which causes his patient's pain,
but only the patient himself can feel the pain. If I am angry and shake my
fist, an outsider can see this manifestation of my anger but not the anger itself.
Assuming that a person's dreams or thoughts can be correlated with certain
specific movements of brain molecules, it is theoretically feasible that scientists
might one day perceive these molecular motions. But they would not even then
be experiencing the dreams or thoughts of the person whose brain they were
observing. Feelings, sensations, dreams, and thoughts are the sort of phenomena
which are usually classified as "mental." In calling them mental, philosophers
usually mean that, unlike physical objects, they are "private" or directly
knowable by one person only. Some philosophers also include having no
extension and no spatial location in the meaning of "mental." This, however,
might prove a confusing definition since certain sensations and feelings do
seem to have extension and a location in space.

It is plausible, then, to maintain that a human being possesses a mind as
well as a body. It seems just as reasonable to hold, in the absence of special
considerations to the contrary, that there are causal connections between body
and mind. To give a few simple illustrations: cavities in teeth cause pain, the

impact of light-waves on the retina leads to visual sensations, contact of the tongue with food causes taste sensations, indigestion gives rise to morbid feelings, consumption of large quantities of alcohol produces hallucinations, some drugs make us calm, others more excited. All these are instances of causal influence by the body on the mind, but there seems just as ample evidence of causal relations in the opposite direction: a person who is ill and has nothing to live for is far less likely to recover than one who has many interests and is filled with hope. Expectations of pleasant encounters affect our body in one way, expectations of unpleasant encounters in quite another. Embarrassment causes us to blush, fear to tremble, happiness to smile and sometimes to cry. Perhaps the plainest cases of mind-body causation are "voluntary movements." A man intends to see the tennis matches at Forest Hills and, other things being equal, he really gets there. It would seem very odd indeed to maintain that in this and similar situations the intention or volition was not part of the cause of the person's action.

Philosophers who first make a distinction between the body and the mind and who then proceed to assert that there are causal influences in both directions are known as "dualistic interactionists." They are divided among themselves according to their views about the nature of the body and of the mind respectively. Confining ourselves to the latter topic, we have to distinguish between those who, like the scholastics and Descartes, adopt a "substance" theory and those who, following Hume, adopt a serial or "bundle" conception. The point here at issue may be explained by the following question: is a human being something additional to (a) his body, (b) the various experiences he goes through, (c) the relations between these experiences such as similarity, causation, and memory, and (d) his capacities, habits, temperament, and ideals—that is, his dispositions to act and react in certain ways and have certain experiences if exposed to certain stimuli? According to the substance-theory there is something in human beings over and above these items and something of great importance at that. This extra something is variously referred to as the "subject" or "owner" of the experiences, as the "spiritual substance" which "underlies" them and which gives a human being the unity he possesses.

Among those holding this type of theory there are differences of opinion as to the manner in which the underlying subject is known and also as to how much we can know about it. According to one group, including Sir William Hamilton (1788–1856) and many other philosophers influenced by Kant, no such spiritual substance is given in introspective experience. Its existence has to be *inferred* in order to account for such facts as our personal identity which could not otherwise be explained. Writers who adopt this point of view are usually rather modest in their claims of how much can be known about the attributes of the underlying self. Other philosophers maintain that the substance-self is *given* in experience. In fact it is given in *every* experience. The German philosopher Lotze (1807–1881) was a prominent defender of this position. In a well-known passage he wrote:

> It has been required of any theory which starts without presuppositions and from the basis of experience, that in the beginning it should speak only of sensations and ideas, without mentioning the soul to which, it is said, we hasten without justification to ascribe them. I should maintain, on the contrary, that such a mode of setting out involves a wilful departure from that which is actually given in experience. A mere sensation without a subject is nowhere to be met with as a fact. It is impossible to speak of a bare move-

ment without thinking of the mass whose movement it is; and it is just as impossible to conceive a sensation existing without the accompanying of that which has it—or rather, of that which feels it, for this also is included in the given fact of experience that the relation of the feeling subject to its feeling, whatever its other characteristics may be, is in any case something different from the relation of the moved element to its movement. It is thus and thus only, that the sensation is a given fact; and we have no right to abstract from its relation to its subject because this relation is puzzling, and because we wish to obtain a starting-point which looks more convenient, but is utterly unwarranted by experience.

Many, though not all, of the writers holding this position believe that the self which is thus given in every experience is not only simple and "abiding the same during all the varying modes of consciousness," but is furthermore indestructible and therefore immortal.

According to the bundle-theory a human being is nothing over and above factors (a), (b), (c) and (d) listed above. There are no facts which warrant the inference to a permanent underlying spiritual substance. Nor is such a self ever given in experience. We are apt to mistake as an "owner" of our experiences certain background feelings or sensations which generally accompany them. We are angry against a "background mood" of depression, or we read a letter against a background feeling of delight or disappointment, as the case may be. And practically all our experiences are accompanied by some "marginal" bodily sensations—of our breathing, our eye-ball movements, our stationary or moving limbs, our hunger or satiety, our bodily tensions, and many more. Bertrand Russell has been one of the outstanding champions of the bundle-theory in our own day. "We think and feel and act," he writes in one place,

> but there is not, in addition to thoughts and feelings and actions, a bare entity, the mind or the soul, which does or suffers these occurrences. The mental continuity of a person is a continuity of habit and memory: there was yesterday one person whose feelings I can remember, and that person I regard as myself of yesterday; but in fact, myself of yesterday was only certain mental occurrences which are now remembered, and are regarded as part of the person who now recollects them.

The classical formulation of this view is found in Hume's *Treatise of Human Nature* (See Selection 15, p. 185).

> For my part, when I enter most intimately into what I call myself, I always stumble on some particular perception or other, of heat or cold, light or shade, love or hatred, pain or pleasure. I never catch myself at any time without a perception, and never can observe anything but the perception. When my perceptions are removed for any time, as by sound sleep, so long am I insensible of myself, and may truly be said not to exist. And were all my perceptions removed by death, and I could neither think, nor feel, nor see, nor love, nor hate, after the dissolution of my body, I should be entirely annihilated, nor do I conceive what is further requisite to make me a perfect nonentity. If any one, upon serious and unprejudiced reflection, thinks he has a different notion of himself, I must confess I can reason no longer with him. All I can allow him is, that he may be in the right as well as I, and that we are essentially different in this particular. He may, perhaps, perceive something simple and continued, which he calls himself; though I am certain there is no such principle in me.

But setting aside some metaphysicians of this kind, I may venture to affirm of the rest of mankind, that they are nothing but a bundle or collection of different perceptions, which succeed each other with an inconceivable rapidity, and are in a perpetual flux and movement.

It should be added that some contemporary philosophers go further than Russell and Hume and declare that the substance-theory is *meaningless*. The spiritual substance is not like a mythical animal which we could recognize if we came across it but which as a matter of fact does not exist. We don't even know what it would be like to come across it. "The point is not," in Ayer's words, "that the vast majority of men are unable to perform the difficult feat of experiencing themselves as substances. It is rather that such a feat is not conceivable. There is nothing that would count as stumbling upon oneself, as opposed to some particular perception."

To many philosophers it has seemed that interactionism is open to a number of fatal objections, regardless of whether it conceives the mind as a substance or as a bundle. It is easy enough, the critics have declared, to speak of interaction between body and mind in general terms. As soon, however, as we try to visualize concretely the manner in which the supposed interaction takes place, we are utterly baffled. How exactly, for example, is the last member in the physiological series following the impact of light-rays on the retina transformed into a visual sensation? What exactly does a volition do to the brain-molecules to set in motion the train of events culminating in the person's overt reaction? It is evident that the brain-molecules must somehow be moved for this purpose, but how can something which does not occupy space and which has no extension move a material particle? In the words of W. K. Clifford, a 19th-century mathematician and philosopher:

> ... if anybody says that the will influences matter, the statement is not untrue, but it is nonsense. The will is not a material thing, it is not a mode of material motion. ... The only thing which influences matter is the position of surrounding matter or the motion of surrounding matter.

There is an "enormous gulf," an "impassable chasm," "a gap which cannot be bridged" between phenomena as radically different as brain events on the one hand and psychological events like sensations or volitions on the other. (See John Tyndall, Selection 18, p. 217.)

Moreover, interactionism seems to these philosophers inconsistent with the continuity of physiological processes and also with certain well-established principles of physics. From the point of view of physiology and physics, it is argued, mental events which cause or are caused by bodily events are disturbing and unwanted interlopers for which there is no room. If the causal story were what the interactionist believes it to be, then we should expect a break in the physiological sequences in the body at certain times. The last brain event, for instance, would be followed not by another brain event but by a non-physical event—the sensation; this by another non-physical event—the volition; and this then by the outgoing physiological sequence. In actual fact, however, the critics claim, no such interruption or discontinuity in the physiological processes is ever found.

Even worse, perhaps, interaction appears to be in conflict with the law of the Conservation of Energy. This principle, in one of its most familiar formulations, maintains that the amount of energy in the universe is always constant. This means that energy can be neither created nor destroyed. Yet, if interaction occurs, then energy would be lost when the body affects the mind and energy would be gained when the mind affects the body. We should in all such cases have exceptions to the Conservation of Energy. There is, however, no evidence that such violations of the principle take place. The occurrence of sensations, for example, is not, as far as we know, accompanied by decreases of energy in the body. Nor are volitions followed by increases of energy.

In the light of these and similar considerations numerous philosophers regard interactionism as untenable. They have put forward several alternative theories which would avoid the difficulties we mentioned. Perhaps the simplest of these is the theory known as "monistic" or "reductive" materialism. On this view all psychological terms really refer to some kind of physiological events or processes. It maintains, to use another formulation, that matter alone is real, that a human being is simply his body. This is the position to which we briefly referred at the beginning of this introduction.

Reductive materialism has been held in many different forms. The 18th-century physiologist Cabanis asserted that "thought is a secretion of the brain," a view echoed by the German biologist Vogt, who wrote that "the relation between thought and the brain is roughly of the same order as that between bile and the liver or urine and the bladder." Hobbes and some German materialists of the 19th century believed that thought is nothing more than the movement of particles in the brain and the Danish physiologist Lange claimed that emotions are really nothing but functional disturbances of the body. However, most of these writers also expressed more moderate views not compatible with reductive materialism. Early in the 20th century the German chemist Ostwald and his followers claimed that mental processes are a form of physical energy. In our own day the favorite type of reductive materialism is behaviorism, or at any rate, certain specially radical forms of it. Some behaviorists, it is true, do not maintain that consciousness is identical with any bodily processes. But others, or the same behaviorists on other occasions, maintain that all psychological terms really refer to nothing more than bodily reactions of some kind—to actual bodily responses or to dispositions to respond in certain ways.

Reductive or monistic materialism is in many ways a highly attractive theory. Like other "monistic" theories it would satisfy the widespread intellectual craving to reduce everything to one ultimate reality. It presents the universe as all "of one piece." It also appeals to those who wish to do away with mystery and who fear that once something immaterial is allowed to exist anywhere in the world, the door has been opened to let in such unwelcome guests as the immortal soul or even God. But most important of all, the theory undoubtedly avoids all the supposed difficulties of interactionism. We now no longer have the problem of bridging the "chasm" between body and mind or of visualizing the causal influence of volitions on brain molecules; we no longer need to postulate a gap in the physiological processes of the organism; and of course we no longer have any violations of the Conservation of Energy.

In spite of these attractive features the great majority of philosophers reject reductive materialism. They maintain that it is simply not a true account of our experience. To talk of thought as a "secretion" is absurd. Bile and urine are substances which can be publicly observed, which occupy space, which can be weighed and even bottled. None of this is true of our thoughts. If for example I think of Freud's theory of the death instinct or of the assassination of Abraham Lincoln, my thoughts are not publicly observable; they do not occupy space; they cannot be weighed or bottled. It seems no less absurd to identify thought with movement of brain molecules or emotions with contractions and dilations of blood vessels. It may well be the case that thoughts are always accompanied by certain molecular motions and that emotions always occur along with certain contractions and dilations of blood vessels, but this does not mean that the mental events *are* the bodily processes. To say that thought is really nothing but a certain movement, as the German philosopher Friedrich Paulsen put it in his celebrated critique of reductive materialism, is about as sensible as to say that iron is really made of wood:

> Turn it which way you will, you will never find thought in movement. The common man knows nothing whatever of the motion in the brain or of the vasomotor process, but he knows what anger is, and what thought is, and he means these, when he speaks of them, and not something else of which the physiologist alone knows or thinks he knows.

It is also not the case that sensations are identical with any kind of bodily process or reaction. A person's awareness of red, for example, cannot be the same thing as a molecular movement. It makes sense to ask about the molecular movement such questions as "Is it swift or slow, straight or circular?" But, as Broad has argued, it would make no sense at all to raise these questions about the awareness of red. Conversely, it makes perfectly good sense to ask about the awareness whether it is clear or confused, but such a question could not sensibly be asked about a molecular movement. If a person touches a piece of red-hot iron, to use an illustration given by Ewing, the throb of pain he feels is not at all like the act of withdrawing his hand nor "like anything described in text-books of physiology as happening in the nervous system or the brain." The difference between sensations and bodily events, Ewing insists, is not a question of *a priori* speculative metaphysics, but "as much an empirical matter as that between sight and sound."

Another rival to interactionism is the theory known as "epiphenomenalism." On this view mental events are distinct from any kind of physical substances or movements. They are, however, powerless to interfere with anything in the physical world. Mental states are caused by brain processes, but do not in turn exert any causal influence. They are mere by-products ("epiphenomenon" is the Greek for "by-product"), mere accompanying echoes or shadows of bodily events. Only material structures, including of course human bodies and their parts, are causally active. In the words of Santayana, one of the most famous advocates of this theory:

> There are not two parallel streams, but one stream which, in slipping over certain rocks or dropping into certain pools, begins to babble a wanton music; not thereby losing any part of its substance or changing its course, but un-awares enriching the world with a new beauty.
>   . . . Consciousness is a lyric cry in the midst of business.

In our book epiphenomenalism is defended by T. H. Huxley in "The Automaton Theory" (Selection 19).

Epiphenomenalism is usually considered a form of "materialism" and per-haps a few words of explanation are needed about the meanings of this term in philosophical discussion. We may distinguish a narrower and a broader sense. In the narrower sense materialism asserts that whatever exists is material or physical. In this view "mental" events, in so far as they really exist, are a sub-class of physical occurrences. In the broader sense, materialism merely asserts that matter is in some way the "primary" or "most fundamental" reality. In the latter sense, somebody could be a materialist and at the same time allow that there are mental processes which are not a sub-class of physical occurrences. In this sense, dualism and materialism are not contradictory theories. Epiphenomenalism is not a a form of materialism in the narrower sense, but it clearly is a form of materialism in the broader sense. In the broader sense, even quite a number of dualistic interactionists could be regarded as materialists. There are many interactionists who, after conceding that mind is distinct from body and that there is causal influence both ways, proceed to maintain that matter can exist without mind but that mind cannot exist without matter, or at least that this is highly probable on the basis of a great deal of empirical evidence. Bertrand Russell and Hume adopt such a position in several places. Thus Russell likens the relation between mental events and the brain to that between a river and a river-bed. When the brain is dissolved at death there is no more reason to suppose that mental events will continue than that a river "will persist in its old course after an earthquake has raised a mountain where a valley used to be." Moreover, a river-bed can exist without a river but a river cannot exist without a river-bed; and the same holds for the mind and the body. Writers like Russell may be considered materialists in the broader sense, since they do assert that matter is more "basic" in the way just explained.

Some philosophers, usually classified as materialists, have proposed a theory which is at least fairly similar to epiphenomenalism and which may or may not coincide with it, depending on how the notions of "thing" and "quality" are interpreted. On this view, mental processes are not a species of physical occurrences; and to this extent the theory is dualistic. On the other hand, mental processes cannot be described as "things." Only physical objects are "things." Mental processes are *qualities or attributes of physical organisms*. A human body not only has size and shape and a certain weight and certain colors; it also has certain intellectual and emotional attributes. This view is found, among others, in the writings of the French physician and philosopher Lamettrie (1709–1751) and the English chemist and religious reformer, Joseph Priestley (1733–1804). Both Lamettrie and Priestley strenuously opposed the view that matter is essentially "passive" or "inert" and maintained that feeling and thought could be attributed as "powers" to human and animal bodies on the basis of the same kind of evidence by which we attribute "powers" of attraction and repulsion to matter in general. "Thought is so little incompatible with organized matter," wrote Lamettrie, "that it seems to be one of its properties on a par with electricity, the faculty of motion, impenetrability, and extension."

However, to return to epiphenomenalism. It does not identify mental events with any kind of physiological processes and therefore circumvents the main difficulty of reductive materialism. But in the opinion of many philosophers, it, too, is open to a number of serious objections. In the first place, since it allows causal influence in the direction from body to mind, epiphenomenalism escapes only half of whatever difficulties beset interactionism. Secondly, it has been charged that epiphenomenalism is a "self-stultifying" theory: if it were true we could never be justified in believing that it is true. For if it were true then all our beliefs are entertained not because of any prior awareness of good grounds or adequate evidence, but solely because of physical changes in the brain and nervous system. None of our conclusions, including epiphenomenalism itself, would be based on logic. We would always think, in J. B. Pratt's words, "the way our mechanical brains constrain us to think"; and if in any given case our thought is true, this is so because the brain molecules happened to shake down in a lucky fashion."

Perhaps the most momentous objection to epiphenomenalism consists in the enormous quantity of *prima facie* evidence that the mental processes of human beings do make a difference to their lives and indirectly to inanimate nature as well. It is said that epiphenomenalism implies a truly staggering paradox in this connection. Father Maher, a scholastic critic, has stated this objection very forcefully:

> But reflection discovers consequences still more surprising. The whole past history of the world, the building of cities, the invention of machinery, the commerce of nations, the emigrations of peoples, the rise and fall of civilizations, all that has been done on this planet by human beings, might have happened in precisely the same way if there had never awoke to consciousness a single human mind! All the pain and sorrow, all the joy and gladness, all the love and anger that we suppose have governed the world's history might never have been, and that history *might have run exactly the same course!* The neural groupings, the cerebral movements, which were the true, ultimate, and *only* causes of the various actions of human beings, have never once been interrupted, modified, or interfered with by those "aspects" or "phases" which constitute the "parallel" series of conscious states, since the first man appeared on the earth. Given the original collocation of the material atoms from which the present cosmos has evolved, and every event, down to the least incident of our daily life, was therein rigidly and sufficiently determined, even though no single act of intelligence or volition had ever wakened into life!

Interactionism may have its problems; but according to a number of philosophers they are small when compared with this paradox of epiphenomenalism.

Epiphenomenalists would probably retort that this criticism is based on a misunderstanding of their theory. They would maintain that terms like "willing," "reasoning," "knowing," or "forecasting" really have a double meaning. They do indeed refer to certain conscious states, but they also refer to certain states of the organism. They also refer, that is, to the bodily processes which cause the mental epiphenomena. The reductive materialists are wrong in denying the conscious accompaniments. Critics like Father Maher are guilty of the opposite error—of tacitly equating "ourselves" with our mental states exclusively. To give a simple illustration: A person may quite properly be said to know how to drive a car even if on a given occasion he makes all the appropriate responses without consciously attending to them. The question at issue, an epiphenomenalist would contend, is not whether willing, reasoning, knowing, forecasting and the rest are causally relevant to what happens in the world. For this much is admitted by him no less than by the interactionist. The question is whether we need to bring in something over and above the *body's* knowledge, willing, reasoning or forecasting—whether we have to attribute causal relevance to the conscious side of these phenomena *as well*. If it is maintained that the body alone could never bring about such splendid results as Mozart's operas or the feats of modern engineering, an epiphenomenalist would answer, following Spinoza, that nobody has ever discovered the body's limitations and that this criticism rests therefore on a gratuitous assumption. He would perhaps conclude his answer with the recommendation that we should cease to identify "ourselves" so exclusively with our conscious lives.

Another alternative to interactionism is the view known as "parallelism," which agrees with epiphenomenalism in denying any influence of mental states over our bodies, but which goes further in also denying causal relations in the other direction. The life of a human being on this view consists of two distinct series which never intersect. When light strikes my eye and this is followed by a visual sensation, there is no causal connection between these processes, since the former belongs to the physical and the latter to the mental series of my life. Again, if I eat a chocolate éclair filled with whipped cream, this is usually followed by a feeling of pleasure. But according to parallelism the two events are not causally related. In both of these and in all similar instances there is only a relation of concomitance or of temporal succession.

Most parallelists have not been satisfied to let the matter rest here. They felt obliged to explain the universal correlations between certain kinds of bodily and certain kinds of mental events—e.g., between certain stimulations of the sense organs and the sensations following these, or between volitions and movements of the body. Although these correlations are not causal, parallelists generally conceded that they are not accidental either. Historically, there are three major attempts on the part of parallelists to explain such correlations. The first is that of Malebranche (1638–1715) and the occasionalists who maintain that "corresponding" physical and mental events are "occasions" for God to become active. The physical contact between my tongue and the chocolate éclair is the occasion for God to produce pleasure in me, and my volition to pick up a fork is the occasion for God's production of this motion. Leibniz (1646–1716), who was also a parallelist, did not believe in the *immediate* intervention of God on all these occasions, but believed instead that a "pre-established harmony" exists between the two series. He compared the body and the mind to two clocks which "agree perfectly" and which were from the start made with such "art and accuracy that we can be assured of their future accordance." Similarly, by a "divine prevenient contrivance" body and mind were from the beginning formed "so perfect and regulated with so much accuracy" that although they follow merely their respective laws, they nevertheless always agree with each other "just as if there were mutual influence, or as if God in addition to His general coöperation constantly put His hand thereto."

Not all parallelists, however, have been believers in God or have considered it necessary to bring in God's immediate or remote causal activity to explain the correlations between bodily and mental states. Probably the explanation most popular among them has been some form of "identity" or "double aspect" theory, which goes back to Spinoza and which had many outstanding advocates in later centuries, including Fechner, Wundt, Höffding, Paulsen, and Clifford. On this view bodily and mental processes are really "at bottom" or "ultimately" the same events. They are two "aspects" of the same reality; they are the same thing "viewed" from different angles or known in different ways. Our mental states are the private or "inner" nature or "side" and the corresponding brain processes the publicly observable or "outer" nature of the same phenomena. Numerous illustrations have been adduced to indicate how on this theory the regular concomitance of mental and physical events would be explained. Fechner gave the example of a curved line which is on one side convex and on the other concave. No matter how many turns and twists are found in such a line, a concavity will always correspond to a convexity although there is no causal connection between them. Another illustration, given by the German philosopher Lasswitz, is that of a loan of money: the same sum is an asset for one of the parties and a debit for the other. Feigl compares the body-mind relation to that kind of identity which is discovered by two explorers who "may unwittingly have observed the same mountain from different directions, and only after comparing notes come to realize that it was really identically the same mountain."

Most parallelists would go on to assert that brain processes are not the only phenomena which also have an "inner nature." All things in the universe, including not only human beings and animals, but even plants and what we normally consider inanimate objects, have such an additional inner side. None of them is a purely material structure. All have an aspect which in varying degrees resembles our mental states. "Even in the very lowest organisms, even in the amoeba which swims about in our own blood," writes Clifford, "along with every motion of matter, whether organic or inorganic . . . there is something or other, inconceivably simple to us, which is of the same nature with our own consciousness, although not of the same complexity." Just as our bodies are made up of atoms, so our minds are made up of the rudimentary bits of feeling which are attached to each atom and which are its "inner nature." This theory is usually known as "panpsychism," but some parallelists do not like the term because it suggests that they claim *consciousness* for sticks and stones and stars and atoms, whereas they merely claim some resemblance to consciousness. They do not claim self-awareness or introspection for inanimate phenomena. Only human beings and possibly some animals can *know* their inner nature.

Many writers who have adopted this position prefer the term "universal parallelism." The assumption that some kind of inner process accompanies every physical event enables them, they assert, to give a consistent causal explanation of all mental states without in any way introducing special divine interferences. Supposing I hear a loud noise, of thunder, for example. What is the cause of this sensation? A certain excitation of the auditory nerve and a certain stimulation of the brain, say both the epiphenomenalist and the interactionist. But this answer is not open to the parallelists. Surely the sensation may have a cause. Is it then some state of consciousness? This answer is in most cases ruled out because the sensation may follow no state of consciousness, as when a person awakes from dreamless sleep, or it may follow a state of consciousness which cannot possibly be the cause. For example, my sensation of a loud noise may follow a feeling of pleasure of which it can hardly be the effect. It is at this stage that writers like Paulsen and Fechner appeal to their "hypothesis" of universal parallelism. The causes of the sensation are the inner processes accompanying the excitation of the auditory nerve. The cause of "psychical states" like sensations, writes Paulsen, are other psychical processes "which are unknown to us but whose physical equivalents are physical or chemical processes."

Contemporary philosophers tend to be repelled by wild speculations about God's constant interventions in the universe or a pre-established harmony or a universal "mind-stuff," as Clifford called the "inner side" of physical events. Those philosophers today who are opposed to materialism in all its more radical varieties incline therefore to interactionism in spite of the difficulties with which this theory appears to be confronted. Some of them, like Lord Samuel, may be termed "agnostic interactionists." Their position is roughly that while interaction in both directions is a plain and undeniable fact, the "how" of interaction is still a mystery. The "meeting place" between mind and brain, and exactly "what the mind takes over" at the meeting place, as Lord Samuel puts it, has not yet been discovered (see Samuel's contribution to the symposium, "The Physical Basis of Mind," Selection 20, p. 234). In this belief he is supported by many eminent scientists. Thus Sir Charles Sherrington, who was probably the greatest physiologist of this century, declared that "we have to regard the relation of mind to brain as still not merely unsolved, but still devoid of a basis for the very beginning [of a solution]. . . ." Professor Le Gros Clark, a distinguished Oxford anatomist, writes that physiology and anatomy are unable "even to suggest how the physico-chemical phenomena associated with the passage of nervous impulses from one part of the brain to another can be translated into a mental experience."

Other contemporary interactionists adopt a more confident approach. They claim that most if not all the traditional difficulties of interactionism are altogether spurious. Thus Ducasse rejects as meaningless the question of *how* brain-processes produce mental events or how mental events produce modifications in the brain. He insists that in general the question as to how one event causes another is meaningful "only as regards *remote* causation since what the problem 'how' asks for is an account of the causal steps intermediary between the two events concerned." If, for example, it is asserted that a diet rich in animal fats is one of the causal factors responsible for coronary heart attacks, it makes perfectly good sense to ask how this diet produces such results. The cause and the effect are not here "proximate members" of the same causal series, and the "how" asks for information about intermediate members in the series, such as the exact processes in the circulatory system consequent upon the consumption of animal fats. On the other hand, the sensation and the last member of the physiological series prior to its occurrence are proximate, and the same is true of the volition and the first member of the physiological series following it. Here the nature of the case makes it impossible to obtain intermediate members, and hence the question "how" the cause leads to the effect is meaningless.

Broad and others (see Selection 17, pp. 208 ff.) also maintain that many of the apparent difficulties of interactionism arise from the tendency to approach the body-mind problem with inappropriate and misleading images. We tend to think of the mind as a little man inside the brain, and of introspection as a kind of looking with eyes turned to the inside of our bodies. We then try to "visualize" the "meeting place" of mind and body and the "impact" of one on the other. When such attempts end in failure we feel utterly perplexed. According to Broad, the demand to visualize such an "impact" is illegitimate and shows that its authors, if they are dualists, did not have the courage of their initial conviction to regard mental processes as having no spatial location. The use of words like "gap," "chasm," or "hiatus," furthermore, suggests difficulties which do not really exist. The "gap" of the agnostic interactionists cannot be bridged. Nothing less than a "rope" or a "fluid" consisting first of pure matter, then of 90 percent matter and 10 percent mind, then of 80 percent matter and 20 percent mind . . . and finally of pure mind would satisfy them once the "gap-and-bridge" picture has come to dominate their thinking on this subject. The gap cannot be bridged because there is really no such gap in the first place: the mind is not another physical object, and its relation to the brain cannot be compared to the relation between the banks of a river. Nor does it make sense to speak of "translations" or "transformations" of neural impulses into thought, since thought is not another kind of bodily process or physical energy.

As to the difficulty based on the Conservation of Energy, some writers deny that interaction is in any way incompatible with this principle (see Broad, Selection 17, pp. 205 ff.). Others, like Pratt, concede that interaction is incompatible with the Conservation of Energy and that the influence of the mind on the body can be saved only on the assumption that it is a "genuine creator of energy." Although he is therefore willing to deny the universal application of the Conservation principle, Pratt insists that the breach is only a very minor one:

> If we refuse to admit that the laws which control inorganic matter also absolutely dominate that small portion of the material world in which matter comes into relation with personality, how many of the claims of physical

science will thereby be undermined? In the whole realm of physics and of chemistry, of astronomy and geology, not one. Mechanical science will be forced to give up its claims to absolute sway only in that tiny realm where personality, or perhaps where life, begins to have influence. In this connection it is interesting to note that the demand for the absolute universality of physical laws comes, as a rule, not from the physicists, not from the chemists, but from a small number of biologists, a large number of psychologists, and most of all from the naturalistic school of the philosophers. The mechanistic philosophers are much more royalist than their king, and the demand for the universal sway of the mechanical seems to vary directly with the square of the distance from headquarters.

Quite a number of philosophers are satisfied with answers along one or other of these lines and rest content in interactionism. To many others interaction between the mind and the body remains something incredible. Some of the latter have fallen back on materialist theories. Quite a few are sympathetic to behaviorism (e.g. Gilbert Ryle—see his contribution to the symposium, "The Physical Basis of Mind," Selection 20). John Dewey and some of his disciples appear to favor a theory along the lines of Lamettrie and Priestley, according to which mental processes are attributes of the body. J. J. C. Smart and U. T. Place have revived an identity theory with a materialistic flavor, according to which sensations and other psychological occurrences are "identical with" brain events (see Smart, Selection 21). Smart and Place deny that their position is a form of reductive materialism and regard any such interpretation as the consequence of a misunderstanding of the meaning of "identical" in this context (Smart and Place would presumably maintain that when philosophers like Hobbes spoke of thought as a motion in the brain, they too were not necessarily reductive materialists). Yet other philosophers believe that many of the puzzles on this subject are the result of trying to squeeze the relations between body and mind into some standard pattern. It is a unique relation which one can help to describe by *comparisons* and *contrasts* with other relations. But once it is *identified* with any of these relations we have insoluble problems on our hands, since our customer simply will not fit into the clothes which we have tailored for him.

P. E.

15   Of Personal Identity

David Hume

THERE ARE SOME PHILOSOPHERS WHO imagine we are every moment intimately conscious of what we call our *self*; that we feel its existence and its continuance in existence; and are certain, beyond the evidence of a demonstration, both of its perfect identity and simplicity. The strongest sensation, the most violent passion, say they, instead of distracting us from this view, only fix it the more intensely, and make us consider their influence on *self* either by their pain or pleasure. To attempt a further proof of this were to weaken its evidence; since no proof can be derived from any fact of which we are so intimately conscious; nor is there anything of which we can be certain if we doubt of this.

Unluckily all these positive assertions are contrary to that very experience which is pleaded for them; nor have we any idea of *self,* after the manner it is here explained. For, from what impression could this idea be derived? This question it is impossible to answer without a manifest contradiction and absurdity; and yet it is a question which must necessarily be answered, if we would have the idea of self pass for clear and intelligible. It must be some one impression that gives rise to every real idea. But self or person is not any one impression, but that to which our several impressions and ideas are supposed to have a reference. If any impression gives rise to the idea of self, that impression must continue invariably the same, through the whole course of our lives; since self is supposed to exist after that manner. But there is no impression constant and invariable. Pain and pleasure, grief and joy, passions and sensations succeed each other, and never all exist at the same time. It cannot therefore be from any of these impressions, or from any other, that the idea of self is derived; and consequently there is no such idea.

[This selection consists of section 6, Part IV, Book I, as well as the Appendix (with one small omission) of Hume's *A Treatise of Human Nature,* a work first published in 1739 and 1740.]

But further, what must become of all our particular perceptions upon this hypothesis? All these are different, and distinguishable, and separable from each other, and may be separately considered, and may exist separately, and have no need of anything to support their existence. After what manner therefore do they belong to self, and how are they connected with it? For my part, when I enter most intimately into what I call *myself*, I always stumble on some particular perception or other, of heat or cold, light or shade, love or hatred, pain or pleasure. I never can catch *myself* at any time without a perception, and never can observe anything but the perception. When my perceptions are removed for any time, as by sound sleep, so long am I insensible of *myself*, and may truly be said not to exist. And were all my perceptions removed by death, and could I neither think, nor feel, nor see, nor love, nor hate, after the dissolution of my body, I should be entirely annihilated, nor do I conceive what is further requisite to make me a perfect nonentity. If any one, upon serious and unprejudiced reflection, thinks he has a different notion of *himself*, I must confess I can reason no longer with him. All I can allow him is, that he may be in the right as well as I, and that we are essentially different in this particular. He may, perhaps, perceive something simple and continued, which he calls *himself*; though I am certain there is no such principle in me.

But setting aside some metaphysicians of this kind, I may venture to affirm of the rest of mankind, that they are nothing but a bundle or collection of different perceptions, which succeed each other with an inconceivable rapidity, and are in a perpetual flux and movement. Our eyes cannot turn in their sockets without varying our perceptions. Our thought is still more variable than our sight; and all our other senses and faculties contribute to this change; nor is there any single power of the soul, which remains unalterably the same, perhaps for one moment. The mind is a kind of theater, where several perceptions successively make their appearance; pass, repass, glide away, and mingle in an infinite variety of postures and situations. There is properly no *simplicity* in it at one time, nor *identity* in different, whatever natural propension we may have to imagine that simplicity and identity. The comparison of the theater must not mislead us. They are the successive perceptions only, that constitute the mind; nor have we the most distant notion of the place where these scenes are represented, or of the materials of which it is composed.

What then gives us so great a propension to ascribe an identity to these successive perceptions, and to suppose ourselves possessed of an invariable and uninterrupted existence through the whole course of our lives? In order to answer this question we must distinguish betwixt personal identity, as it regards our thought or imagination, and as it regards our passions or the concern we take in ourselves. The first is our present subject; and to explain it perfectly we must take the matter pretty deep, and account for that identity, which we attribute to plants and animals; there being a great analogy betwixt it and the identity of a self or person.

We have a distinct idea of an object that remains invariable and uninterrupted through a supposed variation of time; and this idea we call that of *identity* or *sameness*. We have also a distinct idea of several different objects existing in succession, and connected together by a close relation; and this to an accurate view affords as perfect a notion of *diversity* as if there was no manner of relation among the objects. But though these two ideas of identity, and a succession of related objects, be in themselves perfectly distinct, and even contrary, yet it is certain that, in our common way of thinking, they are generally confounded with each other. That action of the imagination, by which we consider the uninterrupted and invariable object, and that by which we reflect on the succession of related objects, are almost the same to the feeling, nor is there much more effort of thought required in the latter case than in the former. The relation facilitates the transition of the mind from one object to another, and renders its passage as smooth as if it contemplated one continued object. This resemblance is the cause of the confusion and mistake, and makes us substitute the notion of identity, instead of that of related objects. However at one instant we may consider the related succession as variable or interrupted, we are sure the next to ascribe to it a perfect identity, and regard it as invariable and uninterrupted. Our propensity to this mistake is so great from the resemblance above mentioned, that we fall into it before we are aware; and though we incessantly correct ourselves by reflection, and return to a more accurate method of thinking, yet we cannot long sustain our philosophy, or take off this bias from the imagination. Our last resource is to yield to it, and boldly assert that these different related objects are in effect the same, however interrupted and variable. In order to justify to ourselves this absurdity, we often feign some new and unintelligible principle, that connects the objects together, and prevents their interruption or variation. Thus we feign the continued existence of the perceptions of our senses, to remove the interruption; and run into the notion of a *soul,* and *self,* and *substance,* to disguise the variation. But, we may further observe, that where we do not give rise to such a fiction, our propension to confound identity with relation is so great, that we are apt to imagine something unknown and mysterious, connecting the parts, beside their relation; and this I take to be the case with regard to the identity we ascribe to plants and vegetables. And even when this does not take place, we still feel a propensity to confound these ideas, though we are not able fully to satisfy ourselves in that particular, nor find anything invariable and uninterrupted to justify our notion of identity.

Thus the controversy concerning identity is not merely a dispute of words. For when we attribute identity, in an improper sense, to variable or interrupted objects, our mistake is not confined to the expression, but is commonly attended with a fiction, either of something invariable and uninterrupted, or of something mysterious and inexplicable, or at least with a propensity to such fictions. What will suffice to prove this hypothesis to the satisfaction of every fair inquirer, is to show, from daily experience and observation, that the objects which are variable or interrupted, and yet are supposed to continue the same, are such only as consist of a succession of parts, connected together by resemblance, contiguity, or causation. For as such a succession answers evidently to our notion of diversity, it can only be by mistake we ascribe to it an identity; and as the relation of parts, which leads us into this mistake, is really nothing but a quality, which produces an association of ideas, and an easy transition of the imagination from one to another, it can only be from the resemblance, which this act of the mind bears to that by which we contemplate one continued object, that the error arises. Our chief business, then, must be to prove, that all objects, to which we ascribe identity, without observing their invariableness and uninterruptedness, are such as consist of a succession of related objects.

In order to this, suppose any mass of matter, of which the parts are contiguous and connected, to be placed before us; it is plain we must attribute a perfect identity to this mass, provided all the parts continue uninterruptedly and invariably the same, whatever motion or change of place we may observe either in the whole or in any of the parts. But supposing some very *small* or *inconsiderable* part to be added to the mass, or subtracted from it; though this absolutely destroys the identity of the whole, strictly speaking, yet as we seldom think so accurately, we scruple not to pronounce a mass of matter the same, where we find so trivial an alteration. The passage of the thought from the object before the change to the object after it, is so smooth and easy, that we scarce perceive the transition, and are apt to imagine, that it is nothing but a continued survey of the same object.

There is a very remarkable circumstance that attends this experiment; which is, that though the change of any considerable part in a mass of matter destroys the identity of the whole, yet we must measure the greatness of the part, not absolutely, but by its *proportion* to the whole. The addition or diminution of a mountain would not be sufficient to produce a diversity in a planet; though the change of a very few inches would be able to destroy the identity of some bodies. It will be impossible to account for this, but by reflecting that objects operate upon the mind, and break or interrupt the continuity of its actions, not according to their real greatness, but according to their proportion to each other; and therefore, since this interruption makes an object cease to appear the same, it must be the uninterrupted progress of the thought which constitutes the imperfect identity.

This may be confirmed by another phenomenon. A change in any considerable part of a body destroys its identity; but it is remarkable, that where the change is produced *gradually* and *insensibly,* we are less apt to ascribe to it the same effect. The reason can plainly be no other, than that the mind, in following the successive changes of the body, feels an easy passage from the surveying its condition in one moment, to the viewing of it in another, and in no particular time perceives any interruption in its actions. From which continued perception, it ascribes a continued existence and identity to the object.

But whatever precaution we may use in introducing the changes gradually, and making them proportionable to the whole, it is certain, that where the changes are at last observed to become considerable, we make a scruple of ascribing identity to such different objects. There is, however, another artifice, by which we may induce the imagination to advance a step further; and that is, by producing a reference of the parts to each other, and a combination to some *common end* or purpose. A ship, of which a considerable part has been changed by frequent reparations, is still considered as the same; nor does the difference of the materials hinder us from ascribing an identity to it. The common end, in which the parts conspire, is the same under all their variations, and affords an easy transition of the imagination from one situation of the body to another.

But this is still more remarkable, when we add a *sympathy* of parts to their *common end,* and suppose that they bear to each other the reciprocal relation of cause and effect in all their actions and operations. This is the case with all animals and vegetables; where not only the several parts have a reference to some general purpose, but also a mutual dependence on, and connection with, each other. The effect of so strong a relation is, that though every one must allow, that in a very few years both vegetables and animals endure a *total* change, yet we still attribute identity to them, while their form, size, and substance, are entirely altered. An oak that grows from a small plant to a large tree is still the same oak, though there be not one particle of matter or figure of its parts the same. An infant becomes a man, and is sometimes fat, sometimes lean, without any change in his identity.

We may also consider the two following phenomena, which are remarkable in their kind. The first is, that though we commonly be able to distinguish pretty exactly betwixt numerical and specific identity, yet it sometimes happens that we confound them, and in our thinking and reasoning employ the one for the other. Thus, a man who hears a noise that is frequently interrupted and renewed, says it is still the same noise, though it is evident the sounds have only a specific identity or resemblance, and there is nothing numerically the same but the cause which produced them. In like manner it may be said, without breach of the propriety of language, that such a church, which was formerly of brick, fell to ruin, and that the parish rebuilt the same church of freestone, and according to modern architecture. Here neither the form nor materials are the same, nor is there anything common to the two objects but their relation to the inhabitants of the parish; and yet this alone is sufficient to make us denominate them the same. But we must observe, that in these cases the first object is in a manner annihilated before the second comes into existence; by which means, we are never presented, in any one point of time, with the idea of difference and multiplicity; and for that reason are less scrupulous in calling them the same.

Secondly, we may remark, that though, in a succession of related objects, it be in a manner requisite that the change of parts be not sudden nor entire, in order to preserve the identity, yet where the objects are in their nature changeable and inconstant, we admit of a more sudden transition than would otherwise be consistent with that relation. Thus, as the nature of a river consists in the motion and change of parts, though in less than four-and-twenty hours these be totally altered, this hinders not the river from continuing the same during several ages. What is natural and essential to anything is, in a manner, expected; and what is expected makes less impression, and appears of less moment than what is unusual and extraordinary. A considerable change of the former kind seems really less to the imagination than the most trivial alteration of the latter; and by breaking less the continuity of the thought, has less influence in destroying the identity.

We now proceed to explain the nature of *personal identity,* which has become so great a question in philosophy, especially of late years, in England, where all the abstruser sciences are studied with a peculiar ardor and application. And here it is evident the same method of reasoning must be continued which has so successfully explained the identity of plants, and animals, and ships, and houses, and of all compounded and changeable productions either of art or nature. The identity which we ascribe to the mind of man is only a fictitious one, and of a like kind with that which we ascribe to vegetable and animal bodies. It cannot therefore have a different origin, but must proceed from a like operation of the imagination upon like objects.

But lest this argument should not convince the reader, though in my opinion perfectly decisive, let him weigh the following reasoning, which is still closer and more immediate. It is evident that the identity which we attribute to the human mind, however perfect we may imagine it to be, is not able to run the several different perceptions into one, and make them lose their characters of distinction and difference, which are essential to them. It is still true that every distinct perception which enters into the composition of the mind, is a distinct existence, and is different, and distinguishable, and separable from every other perception, either contemporary or successive. But as, notwithstanding this distinction and separability, we suppose the whole train of perceptions to be united by identity, a question naturally arises concerning this relation of identity, whether it be something that really binds our several perceptions together, or only associates their ideas in the imagination; that is, in other words, whether, in pronouncing concerning the identity of a person, we observe some real bond among his perceptions, or only feel one among the ideas we form of them. This question we might easily decide, if we would recollect what has been already proved at large, that the understanding never observes any real connection among objects, and that even the union of cause and effect, when strictly examined, resolves itself into a customary association of ideas. For from thence it evidently follows, that identity is nothing really belonging to these different perceptions, and uniting them altogether, but is merely a quality which we attribute to them, because of the union of their ideas in the imagination when we reflect upon them. Now, the only qualities which can give ideas a union in the imagination, are these three relations above mentioned. These are the uniting principles in the ideal world, and without them every distinct object is separable by the mind, and may be separately considered, and appears not to have any more connection with any other object than if disjoined by the greatest difference and remoteness. It is therefore on some of these three relations of resemblance, contiguity, and causation, that identity depends; and as the very essence of these relations consists in their producing an easy transition of ideas, it follows that our notions of personal identity proceed entirely from the smooth and uninterrupted progress of the thought along a train of connected ideas, according to the principles above explained.

The only question, therefore, which remains is, by what relations this uninterrupted progress of our thought is produced, when we consider existence of a mind or thinking person. And here it is evident we must confine ourselves to resemblance and causation, and must drop contiguity, which has little or no influence in the present case.

To begin with *resemblance;* suppose we could see clearly into the breast of another, and observe that succession of perceptions which constitutes his mind or thinking principle, and suppose that he always preserves the memory of a considerable part of past perceptions, it is evident that nothing could more contribute to the bestowing a relation on this succession amidst all its variations. For what is the memory but a faculty, by which we raise up the images of past perceptions? And as an image necessarily resembles its object, must not the frequent placing of these resembling perceptions in the chain of thought, convey the imagination more easily from one link to another, and make the whole seem like the continuance of one object? In this particular, then, the memory not only discovers the identity, but also contributes to its production, by producing the relation of resemblance among the perceptions. The case is the same, whether we consider ourselves or others.

As to *causation;* we may observe that the true idea of the human mind, is to consider it as a system of different perceptions or different existences, which are linked together by the relation of cause and effect, and mutually produce, destroy, influence, and modify each other. Our impressions give rise to their correspondent ideas; and these ideas, in their turn, produce other impressions. One thought chases another, and draws after it a third, by which it is expelled in its turn. In this respect, I cannot compare the soul more properly to anything than to a republic or commonwealth, in which the several members are united by the reciprocal ties of government and subordination, and give rise to other persons who propagate the same republic in the incessant changes of its parts. And as the same individual republic may not only change its members, but also its laws and constitutions; in like manner the same person may vary his character and disposition, as well as his impressions and ideas, without losing his identity. Whatever changes he endures, his several parts are still connected by the relation of causation. And in this view our identity with regard to the passions serves to corroborate that with regard to the imagination, by the making our distant perceptions influence each other, and by giving us a present concern for our past or future pains or pleasures.

As memory alone acquaints us with the continuance and extent of this succession of perceptions, it is to be considered, upon that account chiefly, as the source of personal identity. Had we no memory, we never should have any notion of causation, nor consequently of that chain of causes and effects, which constitute our self or person. But having once acquired this notion of causation from the memory, we can extend the same chain of causes, and consequently the identity of our persons beyond our memory, and can comprehend times, and circumstances, and actions, which we have entirely forgot, but suppose in general to have existed. For how few of our past actions are there, of which we have any memory? Who can tell me, for instance, what were his thoughts and actions on the first of January 1715, the eleventh of March 1719, and the third of August 1733? Or will he affirm, because he has entirely forgot the incidents of these days, that the present self is not the same person with the self of that time; and by that means overturn all the most established notions of personal identity? In this view, therefore, memory does not so much *produce* as *discover* personal identity, by showing us the relation of cause and effect among our different perceptions. It will be incumbent on those who affirm that memory produces entirely our personal identity, to give a reason why we can thus extend our identity beyond our memory.

The whole of this doctrine leads us to a conclusion, which is of great importance in the present affair, viz. that all the nice and subtile questions concerning personal identity can never possibly be decided, and are to be regarded rather as grammatical than as philosophical difficulties. Identity depends on the relations of ideas; and these relations produce identity, by means of that easy transition they occasion. But as the relations, and the easiness of the transition may diminish by insensible degrees, we have no just standard by which we can decide any dispute concerning the time when they acquire or lose a title to the name of identity. All the disputes concerning the identity of connected objects are merely verbal, except so far as the relation of parts gives rise to some fiction or imaginary principle of union, as we have already observed.

What I have said concerning the first origin and uncertainty of our notion of identity, as applied to the human mind, may be extended with little or no variation to that of *simplicity*. An object, whose different coexistent parts are bound together by a close relation, operates upon the imagination after much the same manner as one perfectly simple and indivisible, and requires not a much greater stretch of thought in order to its conception. From this similarity of operation we attribute a simplicity to it, and feign a principle of union as the support of this simplicity, and the center of all the different parts and qualities of the object.

... Upon a more strict review of the section concerning *personal identity,* I find myself involved in such a labyrinth that, I must confess, I neither know how to correct my former opinions, nor how to render them consistent. If this be not a good *general* reason for scepticism, it is at least a sufficient one (if I were not already abundantly supplied) for me to entertain a diffidence and modesty in all my decisions. I shall propose the arguments on both sides, beginning with those that induced me to deny the strict and proper identity and simplicity of a self or thinking being.

When we talk of *self* or *subsistence,* we must have an idea annexed to these terms, otherwise they are altogether unintelligible. Every idea is derived from preceding impressions; and we have no impression of self or substance, as something simple and individual. We have, therefore, no idea of them in that sense.

Whatever is distinct is distinguishable, and whatever is distinguishable is separable by the thought or imagination. All perceptions are distinct. They are, therefore, distinguishable, and separable, and may be conceived as separately existent, and may exist separately, without any contradiction or absurdity.

When I view this table and that chimney, nothing is present to me but particular perceptions, which are of a like nature with all the other perceptions. This is the doctrine of philosophers. But this table, which is present to me, and that chimney, may, and do exist separately. This is the doctrine of the vulgar, and implies no contradiction. There is no contradiction, therefore, in extending the same doctrine to all the perceptions.

In general, the following reasoning seems satisfactory. All ideas are borrowed from preceding perceptions. Our ideas of objects, therefore, are derived from that source. Consequently no proposition can be intelligible or consistent with regard to objects, which is not so with regard to perceptions. But it is intelligible and consistent to say that objects exist distinct and independent, without any common *simple* substance or subject of inhesion. This proposition, therefore, can never be absurd with regard to perceptions.

When I turn my reflection on *myself,* I never can perceive this *self* without some one or more perceptions; nor can I ever perceive anything but the perceptions. It is the composition of these, therefore, which forms the self.

We can conceive a thinking being to have either many or few perceptions. Suppose the mind to be reduced even below the life of an oyster. Suppose it to have only one perception, as of thirst or hunger. Consider it in that situation. Do you conceive anything but merely that perception? Have you any notion of *self* or *substance*? If not, the addition of other perceptions can never give you that notion.

The annihilation which some people suppose to follow upon death, and which entirely destroys this self, is nothing but an extinction of all particular perceptions; love and hatred, pain and pleasure, thought and sensation. These, therefore, must be the same with self, since the one cannot survive the other.

Is *self* the same with *substance*? If it be, how can that question have place, concerning the substance of self, under a change of substance? If they be distinct, what is the difference betwixt them? For my part, I have a notion of neither, when conceived distinct from particular perceptions.

Philosophers begin to be reconciled to the principle, *that we have no idea of external substance, distinct from the ideas of particular qualities.* This must pave the way for a like principle with regard to the mind, *that we have no notion of it, distinct from the particular perception.*

So far I seem to be attended with sufficient evidence. But having thus loosened all our particular perceptions, when I proceed to explain the principle of connection, which binds them together, and makes us attribute to them a real simplicity and identity, I am sensible that my account is very defective, and that nothing but the seeming evidence of the precedent reasonings could have induced me to receive it. If perceptions are distinct existences, they form a whole only by being connected together. But no connections among distinct existences are ever discoverable by human understanding. We only *feel* a connection or determination of the thought to pass from one object to another. It follows, therefore, that the thought alone feels personal identity, when reflecting on the train of past perceptions that compose a mind, the ideas of them are felt to be connected together, and naturally introduce each other. However extraordinary this conclusion may seem, it need not surprise us. Most philosophers seem inclined to think, that personal identity *arises* from consciousness, and consciousness is nothing but a reflected thought or perception. The present philosophy, therefore, has so far a promising aspect. But all my hopes vanish when I come to explain the principles that unite our successive perceptions in our thought or consciousness. I cannot discover any theory which gives me satisfaction on this head.

In short, there are two principles which I cannot render consistent, nor is it in my power to renounce either of them, viz. *that all our distinct perceptions are distinct existences,* and *that the mind never perceives any real connection among distinct existences.* Did our perceptions either inhere in something simple and individual, or did the mind perceive some real connection among them, there would be no difficulty in the case. For my part, I must plead the privilege of a sceptic, and confess that this difficulty is too hard for my understanding. I pretend not, however, to pronounce it absolutely insuperable. Others, perhaps, or myself, upon more mature reflections, may discover some hypothesis that will reconcile those contradictions.

16   Of the Nature and Origin of Our Notion of Personal Identity

Thomas Reid

Of Identity in General

THE CONVICTION WHICH EVERY MAN has of his identity, as far back as his memory reaches, needs no aid of philosophy to strengthen it; and no philosophy can weaken it, without first producing some degree of insanity.

The philosopher, however, may very properly consider this conviction as a phenomenon of human nature worthy of his attention. If he can discover its cause, an addition is made to his stock of knowledge; if not, it must be held as a part of our original constitution, or an effect of that constitution produced in a manner unknown to us.

That we may form as distinct a notion as we are able of this phenomenon of the human mind, it is proper to consider what is meant by identity in general, what by our own personal identity, and how we are led into that invincible belief and conviction which every man has of his own personal identity, as far as his memory reaches.

Identity in general I take to be a relation between a thing which is known to exist at one time, and a thing which is known to have existed at another time. If you ask whether they are one and the same, or two different things, every man of common sense understands the meaning of

[This selection is made up of Chapter 4 and parts of Chapter 6 of Essay III as well as a passage from Chapter 5 of Essay VI of Reid's *Essays on the Intellectual Powers of Man,* a work first published in 1785.]

your question perfectly. Whence we may infer with certainty, that every man of common sense has a clear and distinct notion of identity.

If you ask a definition of identity, I confess I can give none; it is too simple a notion to admit of logical definition: I can say it is a relation, but I cannot find words to express the specific difference between this and other relations, though I am in no danger of confounding it with any other. I can say that diversity is a contrary relation, and that similitude and dissimilitude are another couple of contrary relations, which every man easily distinguishes in his conception from identity and diversity.

I see evidently that identity supposes *an uninterrupted continuance of existence*. That which has ceased to exist cannot be the same with that which afterwards begins to exist; for this would be to suppose a being to exist after it ceased to exist, and to have had existence before it was produced, which are manifest contradictions. Continued uninterrupted existence is therefore necessarily implied in identity. Hence we may infer, that identity cannot, in its proper sense, be applied to our pains, our pleasures, our thoughts, or any operation of our minds. The pain felt this day is not the same individual pain which I felt yesterday, though they may be *similar* in kind and degree, and have the same cause. The same may be said of every feeling, and of every operation of mind. They are all successive in their nature, like time itself, no two moments of which can be the same moment. It is otherwise with the parts of absolute space. They always are, and were, and will be the same. So far, I think, we proceed upon clear ground in fixing the notion of identity in general.

Of Our Idea of Personal Identity

It is perhaps more difficult to ascertain with precision the meaning of *personality;* but it is not necessary in the present subject: it is sufficient for our purpose to observe, that all mankind place their personality in something that *cannot be divided, or consist of parts*. A part of a person is a manifest absurdity. When a man loses his estate, his health, his strength, he is still the same person, and has lost nothing of his personality. If he has a leg or an arm cut off, he is the same person he was before. The amputated member is no part of his person, otherwise it would have a right to a part of his estate, and be liable for a part of his engagements. It would be entitled to a share of his merit and demerit, which is manifestly absurd. A person is something indivisible, and is what Leibnitz calls a *monad*.

My personal identity, therefore, implies the continued existence of that indivisible thing which I call *myself*. Whatever this self may be, it is something which thinks, and deliberates, and resolves, and acts, and suffers. I am not thought, I am not action, I am not feeling; I am something that thinks, and acts, and suffers. My thoughts, and actions, and feelings, change every moment; they have no continued, but a successive, existence; but that *self,* or *I,* to which they belong, is permanent, and has the same relation to all the succeeding thoughts, actions, and feelings which I call mine.

Such are the notions that I have of my personal identity. But perhaps it may be said, this may all be fancy without reality. How do you know—what evidence have you—that there is such a permanent self which has a claim to all the thoughts, actions, and feelings which you call yours?

To this I answer, that the proper evidence I have of all this is *remembrance.* I remember that twenty years ago I conversed with such a person; I remember several things that passed in that conversation: my memory testifies, not only that this was done, but that it was done by me who now remembers it. If it was done by me, I must have existed at that time, and continued to exist from that time to the present: if the identical person whom I call myself had not a part in that conversation, my memory is fallacious; it gives a distinct and positive testimony of what is not true. Every man in his senses believes what he distinctly remembers, and everything he remembers convinces him that he existed at the time remembered.

Although memory gives the most irresistible evidence of my being the identical person that did such a thing, at such a time, I may have other good evidence of things which befell me, and which I do not remember: I know who bare me, and suckled me, but I do not remember these events.

It may here be observed (though the observation would have been unnecessary, if some great philosophers had not contradicted it), that it is not my remembering any action of mine that *makes* me to be the person who did it. This remembrance makes me to *know* assuredly that I did it; *but I might have done it, though I did not remember it.* That relation to me, which is expressed by saying that *I did it,* would be the same, though I had not the least remembrance of it. To say that my remembering that I did such a thing, or, as some choose to express it, my being conscious that I did it, makes me to have done it, appears to me as great an absurdity as it would be to say, that my belief that the world was created made it to be created.

When we pass judgment on the identity of other persons than ourselves, we proceed upon other grounds, and determine from a variety of circumstances, which sometimes produce the firmest assurance, and sometimes leave room for doubt. The identity of persons has often furnished matter of serious litigation before tribunals of justice. But no man of a sound mind ever doubted of his own identity, as far as he distinctly remembered.

The identity of a person is a perfect identity: wherever it is real, it admits of no degrees; and it is impossible that a person should be in part the same, and in part different; because a person is a *monad,* and is not divisible into parts. The evidence of identity in other persons than ourselves does indeed admit of all degrees, from what we account certainty, to the least degree of probability. But still it is true, that the same person is perfectly the same, and cannot be so in part or in some degree only.

For this cause, I have first considered personal identity, as that which is perfect in its kind, and the natural measure of that which is imperfect.

We probably at first derive our notion of identity from that natural conviction which every man has from the dawn of reason of *his own* identity and continued existence. The operations of our minds, are all successive, and have no continued existence. But the thinking being has a continued existence, and we have an invincible belief, that it remains the same when all its thoughts and operations change.

Our judgments of the identity of objects of sense seem to be formed much upon the same grounds as our judgments of the identity of *other persons* than ourselves. Wherever we observe great *similarity,* we are apt to presume identity, if no reason appears to the contrary. Two objects ever so like, when they are perceived at the same time, cannot be the same; but if they are presented to our senses at different times, we are apt to think them the same, merely from their similarity.

Whether this be a natural prejudice, or from whatever cause it proceeds, it certainly appears in children from infancy; and when we grow up, it is confirmed in most instances by experience: for we rarely find two individuals of the same species that are not distinguishable by obvious differences. A man challenges a thief whom he finds in possession of his horse or his watch, only on similarity. When the watchmaker swears that he sold this watch to such a person, his testimony is grounded on similarity. The testimony of witnesses to the identity of a person is commonly grounded on no other evidence.

Thus it appears, that the evidence we have of our own identity, as far back as we remember, is totally of a different kind from the evidence we have of the identity of other persons, or of objects of sense. The first is grounded on *memory,* and gives undoubted certainty. The last is grounded on *similarity,* and on other circumstances, which in many cases are not so decisive as to leave no room for doubt. It may likewise be observed, that the identity of *objects of sense* is never perfect. All bodies, as they consist of innumerable parts that may be disjoined from them by a great variety of causes, are subject to continual changes of their own substance, increasing, diminishing, changing insensibly. When such alterations are gradual, because language could not afford a different name for every different state of such a changeable being, it retains the same name, and is considered as the same thing. Thus we say of an old regiment, that it did such a thing a century ago, though there now is not a man alive who then belonged to it. We say a tree is the same in the seed-bed and in the forest. A ship of war, which has successively changed her anchors, her tackle, her sails, her masts, her planks, and her timbers, while she keeps the same name, is the same.

The identity, therefore, which we ascribe to bodies, whether natural or artificial, is not perfect identity; it is rather something which, for the convenience of speech, we call identity. It admits of a great change of the subject, providing the change be *gradual;* sometimes, even of a total change. And the changes which in common language are made consistent with identity differ from those that are thought to destroy it, not in *kind,* but in *number* and *degree.* It has no fixed nature when applied to bodies; and questions about the identity of a body are very often questions about words.

But identity, when applied to persons, has no ambiguity, and admits not of degrees, or of more and less. It is the foundation of all rights and obligations, and of all accountableness; and the notion of it is fixed and precise.

Thought Requires a Thinker

The thoughts of which I am conscious are the thoughts of a being which I call MYSELF, my MIND, my PERSON.

The thoughts and feelings of which we are conscious are continually changing, and the thought of this moment is not the thought of the last; but something which I call *myself* remains under this change of thought. This self has the same relation to all the successive thoughts I am conscious of; they are all *my* thoughts; and every thought which is not my thought must be the thought of some other person.

If any man asks a proof of this, I confess I can give none; there is an evidence in the proposition itself which I am unable to resist. Shall I think, that thought can stand by itself without a thinking being? or that ideas can feel pleasure or pain? My nature dictates to me that it is impossible. And that nature has dictated the same to all men appears from the structure of all languages: for in all languages men have expressed thinking, reasoning, willing, loving, hating, by *personal* verbs, which from their nature require a person who thinks, reasons, wills, loves, or hates. From which it appears, that men have been taught by nature to believe that thought requires a thinker, reason a reasoner, and love a lover.

Here we must leave Mr. Hume, who conceives it to be a vulgar error, that, besides the thoughts we are conscious of, there is a mind which is the subject of those thoughts. If the mind be anything else than impressions and ideas, it must be a word without a meaning. The mind, therefore, according to this philosopher, is a word which signifies a bundle of perceptions; or, when he defines it more accurately, "it is that succession of related ideas and impressions, of which we have an intimate memory and consciousness."

I am, therefore, that succession of related ideas and impressions of which I have the intimate memory and consciousness. But who is the *I* that has this memory and consciousness of a succession of ideas and impressions? Why, it is nothing but that succession itself. Hence I learn, that this succession of ideas and impressions intimately remembers, and is conscious of itself. I would wish to be further instructed, whether the impressions remember and are conscious of the ideas, or the ideas remember and are conscious of the impressions, or if both remember and are conscious of both? and whether the ideas remember those that come after them, as well as those that were before them? These are questions naturally arising from this system, that have not yet been explained.

This, however, is clear, that this succession of ideas and impressions not only remembers and is conscious, but that it judges, reasons, affirms, denies; nay, that it eats and drinks, and is sometimes merry and sometimes sad. If these things can be ascribed to a succession of ideas and impressions, in a consistency with common sense, I should be very glad to know what is nonsense.

The scholastic philosophers have been wittily ridiculed, by representing them as disputing upon this question, *Num chimaera bombinans in vacuo possit comedere secundas intentiones?** And I believe the wit of man cannot invent a more ridiculous question. But, if Mr. Hume's philosophy be admitted, this question deserves to be treated more gravely; for if, as we learn from this philosophy, a succession of ideas and impressions may eat, and drink, and be merry, I see no good reason why a chimera, which, if not the same, is of kin to an idea, may not chew the cud upon that kind of food which the schoolmen call *second intentions*.

Some Strange Consequences of Locke's Account of Personal Identity

Mr. Locke tells us "that personal identity, that is, the sameness of a rational being, *consists in consciousness alone,* and, as far as this consciousness can be extended backwards to any past action or thought, so far reaches the identity of that person. So that whatever has the consciousness of present and past actions is the same person to whom they belong."

This doctrine has some strange consequences, which the author was aware of. (1) . . . that if the same consciousness can be transferred from one intelligent being to another, which he thinks we cannot show to be impossible, *then two or twenty intelligent beings may be the same person.* (2) And if the intelligent being may lose the consciousness of the actions done by him, which surely is possible, then he is not the person that did those actions; so that *one intelligent being may be two or twenty different persons,* if he shall so often lose the consciousness of his former actions.

(3) There is another consequence of this doctrine, which follows no less necessarily, though Mr. Locke probably did not see it. It is, *that a man may be, and at the same time not be, the person that did a particular action.* Suppose a brave officer to have been flogged when a boy at school for robbing an orchard, to have taken a standard from the enemy in his first campaign, and to have been made a general in advanced life; suppose, also, which must be admitted to be possible, that, when he took the

---

* This quotation is part of a passage in *Gargantua and Pantagruel* in which Rabelais is poking fun at the "choice books of the Library of St. Victor," one of which, we are told, is entitled *Quaestio Subtilissima, utrum Chimaera in vacuo bombinans possit comedere secundas intentiones: et fuit debatuata per decem hebdomadas in Consilio Constatiensi.* Father Allan B. Wolter of the Catholic University of America, to whom I am indebted for this information, has suggested the following idiomatic translation: *On the most subtle question: Could a creature of fantasy buzzing in a perfect vacuum feed upon ideas of ideas, debated over a period of ten weeks by the Council of Constance.* [Ed.]

standard, he was conscious of his having been flogged at school, and that, when made a general, he was conscious of his taking the standard, but had absolutely lost the consciousness of his flogging. These things being supposed, it follows, from Mr. Locke's doctrine, that he who was flogged at school is the same person who took the standard, and that he who took the standard is the same person who was made a general. Whence it follows, if there be any truth in logic, that the general is the same person with him who was flogged at school. But the general's consciousness does not reach so far back as his flogging; therefore, according to Mr. Locke's doctrine, he is not the person who was flogged. Therefore the general is, and at the same time is not, the same person with him who was flogged at school. . . .

17

The Traditional Problem
of Body and Mind

C. D. Broad

. . . THERE IS A QUESTION WHICH HAS been argued about for some centuries now under the name of "Interaction"; this is the question whether minds really do act on the organisms which they animate, and whether organisms really do act on the minds which animate them. (I must point out at once that I imply no particular theory of mind or body by the word "to animate." I use it as a perfectly neutral name to express the fact that a certain mind is connected in some peculiarly intimate way with a certain body, and, under normal conditions with no other body. This is a fact even on a purely behaviouristic theory of mind; on such a view to say that the mind M animates the body B would mean that the body B, in so far as it behaves in certain ways, is the Mind M. A body which did not act in these ways would be said not to be animated by a mind. And a different body B′, which acted in the same general way as B, would be said to be animated by a different mind M′.)

The problem of Interaction is generally discussed at the level of en-lightened common-sense; where it is assumed that we know pretty well what we mean by "mind," by "matter" and by "causation." Obviously no solution which is reached at that level can claim to be ultimate. If what we call "matter" should turn out to be a collection of spirits of low intelligence, as Leibniz thought, the argument that mind and body are so unlike that their interaction is impossible would become irrelevant. Again, if causation be nothing but regular sequence and concomitance, as some philosophers have held, it is ridiculous to regard psycho-neural parallelism and interac-tion as mutually exclusive alternatives. For interaction will mean no more than parallelism, and parallelism will mean no less than interaction. Never-theless I am going to discuss the arguments here at the common-sense level,

[This selection consists of extracts from Chapter III of Broad's *The Mind and Its Place in Nature* which was published in 1925. It is here reprinted with the kind permission of Routledge and Kegan Paul, London.]

because they are so incredibly bad and yet have imposed upon so many learned men.

We start then by assuming a developed mind and a developed organism as two distinct things, and by admitting that the two are now intimately connected in some way or other which I express by saying that "this mind animates this organism." We assume that bodies are very much as enlightened common-sense believes them to be; and that, even if we cannot define "causation," we have some means of recognising when it is present and when it is absent. The question then is: "Does a mind ever act on the body which it animates, and does a body ever act on the mind which animates it?" The answer which common-sense would give to both questions is: "Yes, certainly." On the face of it my body acts on my mind whenever a pin is stuck into the former and a painful sensation thereupon arises in the latter. And, on the face of it, my mind acts on my body whenever a desire to move my arms arises in the former and is followed by this movement in the latter. Let us call this common-sense view "Two-sided Interaction." Although it seems so obvious it has been denied by probably a majority of philosophers and a majority of physiologists. So the question is: "Why should so many distinguished men, who have studied the subject, have denied the apparently obvious fact of Two-sided Interaction?"

The arguments against Two-sided Interaction fall into two sets:— Philosophical and Scientific. We will take the philosophical arguments first; for we shall find that the professedly scientific arguments come back in the end to the principles or prejudices which are made explicit in the philosophical arguments.

Philosophical Arguments Against Two-Sided Interaction

No one can deny that there is a close correlation between certain bodily events and certain mental events, and conversely. Therefore anyone who denies that there is action of mind on body and of body on mind must presumably hold (a) that concomitant variation is not an adequate criterion of causal connexion, and (b) that the other feature which is essential for causal connexion is absent in the case of body and mind. Now the common philosophical argument is that minds and mental states are so extremely unlike bodies and bodily states that it is inconceivable that the two should be causally connected. It is certainly true that, if minds and mental events are just what they seem to be to introspection and nothing more, and if bodies and bodily events are just what enlightened common-sense thinks them to be and nothing more, the two are extremely unlike. And this fact is supposed to show that, however closely correlated certain pairs of events in mind and body respectively may be, they cannot be causally connected.

Evidently the assumption at the back of this argument is that concomitant variation, together with a high enough degree of likeness, is an adequate test for causation; but that no amount of concomitant variation can establish causation in the absence of a high enough degree of likeness. Now I am inclined to admit part of this assumption. I think it is practically certain that causation does not simply mean concomitant variation (and, if it did, *cadit quæstio*). Hence the existence of the latter is not *ipso facto,* a proof of the presence of the former. Again, I think it is almost certain that concomitant variation between A and B is not in fact a sufficient sign of the presence of a direct causal relation between the two (I think it may perhaps be a sufficient sign of either a direct causal relation between A and B or of several causal relations which indirectly unite A and B through the medium of other terms C, D, etc.). So far I agree with the assumptions of the argument. But I cannot see the least reason to think that the other characteristic, which must be added to concomitant variation before we can be sure that A and B are causally connected, is a high degree of likeness between the two. One would like to know just how unlike two events may be before it becomes impossible to admit the existence of a causal relation between them. No one hesitates to hold that draughts and colds in the head are causally connected, although the two are extremely unlike each other. If the unlikeness of draughts and colds in the head does not prevent one from admitting a causal connexion between the two, why should the unlikeness of volitions and voluntary movements prevent one from holding that they are causally connected? To sum up: I am willing to admit that an adequate criterion of causal connexion needs some other relation between a pair of events beside concomitant variation; but I do not believe for a moment that this other relation is that of qualitative likeness. . . .

Scientific Arguments Against Two-Sided Interaction

There are, so far as I know, two of these. One is supposed to be based on the physical principle of the Conservation of Energy, and on certain experiments which have been made on human bodies. The other is based on the close analogy which is said to exist between the structures of the physiological mechanism of reflex action and that of voluntary action. I will take them in turn.

(1) *The Argument from Energy.* It will first be needful to state clearly what is asserted by the principle of the Conservation of Energy. It is found that, if we take certain material systems, e.g., a gun, a cartridge, and a bullet, there is a certain magnitude which keeps approximately constant throughout all their changes. This is called "Energy." When the gun has not been fired it and the bullet have no motion, but the explosive in the cartridge has great chemical energy. When it has been fired the bullet is moving very fast and has great energy of movement. The gun, though not moving fast in its recoil, has also great energy of movement because it is very massive. The gases produced by the explosion have some energy of movement and some heat-energy, but much less chemical energy than the unexploded charge had. These various kinds of energy can be measured in

common units according to certain conventions. To an innocent mind there seems to be a good deal of "cooking" at this stage, i.e., the conventions seem to be chosen and various kinds and amounts of concealed energy seem to be postulated in order to make the principle come out right at the end. I do not propose to go into this in detail, for two reasons. In the first place, I think that the conventions adopted and the postulates made, though somewhat suggestive of the fraudulent company-promoter, can be justified by their coherence with certain experimental facts, and that they are not simply made *ad hoc*. Secondly, I shall show that the Conservation of Energy is absolutely irrelevant to the question at issue, so that it would be waste of time to treat it too seriously in the present connexion. Now it is found that the total energy of all kinds in this system, when measured according to these conventions, is approximately the same in amount though very differently distributed after the explosion and before it. If we had confined our attention to a part of this system and its energy this would not have been true. The bullet, e.g., had no energy at all before the explosion and a great deal afterwards. A system like the bullet, the gun, and the charge, is called a "Conservative System"; the bullet alone, or the gun and the charge, would be called "Non-conservative Systems." A conservative system might therefore be defined as one whose total energy is redistributed, but not altered in amount, by changes that happen within it. Of course a given system might be conservative for some kinds of change and not for others.

So far we have merely defined a "Conservative System," and admitted that there are systems which, for some kinds of change at any rate, answer approximately to our definition. We can now state the Principle of the Conservation of Energy in terms of the conceptions just defined. The principle asserts that every material system is either itself conservative, or, if not, is part of a larger material system which is conservative. We may take it that there is good inductive evidence for this proposition.

The next thing to consider is the experiments on the human body. These tend to prove that a living body, with the air that it breathes and the food that it eats, forms a conservative system to a high degree of approximation. We can measure the chemical energy of the food given to a man, and that which enters his body in the form of Oxygen breathed in. We can also, with suitable apparatus, collect, measure and analyse the air breathed out, and thus find its chemical energy. Similarly, we can find the energy given out in bodily movement, in heat, and in excretion. It is alleged that, on the average, whatever the man may do, the energy of his bodily movements is exactly accounted for by the energy given to him in the form of food and of Oxygen. If you take the energy put in food and Oxygen, and subtract the energy given out in waste-products, the balance is almost exactly equal to the energy put out in bodily movements. Such slight differences as are found are as often on one side as on the other, and are therefore probably due to unavoidable experimental errors. I do not propose to criticize the interpretation of these experiments in detail, because, as I shall show soon, they are completely irrelevant to the problem of whether mind and body interact. But there is just one point that I will make before passing on. It is perfectly clear that such experiments can tell us only what happens on the average over a long time. To know whether the balance was accurately kept at every moment we should have to kill the patient at each moment and analyse his body so as to find out the energy present then in the form of stored-up products. Obviously we cannot keep on killing the patient in order to analyse him, and then re-viving him in order to go on with the experiment. Thus it would seem that the results of the experiment are perfectly compatible with the presence of quite large excesses or defects in the total bodily energy at certain moments, provided that these average out over longer periods. However, I do not want to press this criticism; I am quite ready to accept for our present purpose the traditional interpretation which has been put on the experiments.

We now understand the physical principle and the experimental facts. The two together are generally supposed to prove that mind and body cannot interact. What precisely is the argument, and is it valid? I imagine that the argument, when fully stated, would run somewhat as follows: "I will to move my arm, and it moves. If the volition has anything to do with causing the movement we might expect energy to flow from my mind to my body. Thus the energy of my body ought to receive a measurable increase, not accounted for by the food that I eat and the Oxygen that I breathe. But no such physically unaccountable increases of bodily energy are found. Again, I tread on a tin-tack, and a painful sensation arises in my mind. If treading on the tack has anything to do with causing the sensation we might expect energy to flow from my body to my mind. Such energy would cease to be measurable. Thus there ought to be a noticeable decrease in my bodily energy not balanced by increases anywhere in the physical system. But such unbalanced decreases of bodily energy are not found." So it is concluded that the volition has nothing to do with causing my arm to move, and that treading on the tack has nothing to do with causing the painful sensation.

Is this argument valid? In the first place it is important to notice that the conclusion does not follow from the Conservation of Energy and the experimental facts alone. The real premise is a tacitly assumed proposition about causation; viz., that, if a change in A has anything to do with causing a change in B, energy must leave A and flow into B. This is neither asserted nor entailed by the Conservation of Energy. What it says is that, if energy leaves A, it must appear in something else, say B; so that A and B together form a conservative system. Since the Conservation of Energy is not itself the premise for the argument against Interaction, and since it does not entail that premise, the evidence for the Conservation of Energy is not evidence against Interaction. Is there any independent evidence for the premise? We may admit that it is true of many, though not of all, transactions within the physical realm. But there are cases where it is not true even of purely physical transactions; and even if it were always true in the physical realm, it would not follow that it must always be true of trans-physical causation. Take the case of a weight swinging at the end of a string hung from a fixed point. The total energy of the weight is the same at all positions in its course. It is thus a conservative system. But at every moment the direction and velocity of the weight's motion are different, and the proportion between its kinetic and its potential energy is constantly changing. These changes are caused by the pull of the string, which acts in a different direction at each different moment. The string makes no difference to the total energy of the weight; but it makes all the difference in the world to the particular way in which the weight moves and the particular way in which the energy is distributed between the potential and the kinetic forms. This is evident when we remember that the weight would begin to move in an utterly different course if at any moment the string were cut.

Here, then, we have a clear case even in the physical realm where a system is conservative but is continually acted on by something which affects its movement and the distribution of its total energy. Why should not the mind act on the body in this way? If you say that you can see how a string can affect the movement of a weight, but cannot see how a volition could affect the movement of a material particle, you have deserted the scientific argument and have gone back to one of the philosophical arguments. Your real difficulty is either that volitions are so very unlike movements, or that the volition is in your mind whilst the movement belongs to the physical realm. And we have seen how little weight can be attached to these objections.

The fact is that, even in purely physical systems, the Conservation of Energy does not explain what changes will happen or when they will happen. It merely imposes a very general limiting condition on the changes that are possible. The fact that the system composed of bullet, charge, and gun, in our earlier example, is conservative does not tell us that the gun ever will be fired, or when it will be fired, if at all, or what will cause it to go off, or what forms of energy will appear if and when it does go off. The change in this case is determined by pulling the trigger. Likewise the mere fact that the human body and its neighbourhood form a conservative system does not explain any particular bodily movement; it does not explain why I ever move at all, or why I sometimes write, sometimes walk, and sometimes swim. To explain the happening of these particular movements at certain times it seems to be essential to take into account the volitions which happen from time to time in my mind; just as it is essential to take the string into account to explain the particular behaviour of the weight, and to take the trigger into account to explain the going off of the gun at a certain moment. The difference between the gun-system and body-system is that a little energy does flow into the former when the trigger is pulled, whilst it is alleged that none does so when a volition starts a bodily movement. But there is not even this amount of difference between the body-system and the swinging weight.

Thus the argument from energy has no tendency to disprove Two-sided Interaction. It has gained a spurious authority from the august name of the Conservation of Energy. But this impressive principle proves to have nothing to do with the case. And the real premise of the argument is not self-evident, and is not universally true even in purely intra-physical transactions. In the end this scientific argument has to lean on the old philosophic arguments; and we have seen that these are but bruised reeds. Nevertheless, the facts brought forward by the argument from energy do throw some light on the nature of the interaction between mind and body, assuming this to happen. They do suggest that all the energy of our bodily actions comes out of and goes back into the physical world, and that minds neither add energy to nor abstract it from the latter. What they do, if they do anything, is to determine that at a given moment so much energy shall change from the chemical form to the form of bodily movement; and they determine this so far as we can see, without altering the total amount of energy in the physical world.

(2) *The Argument from the Structure of the Nervous System.* There are purely reflex actions, like sneezing and blinking, in which there is no reason to suppose that the mind plays any essential part. Now we know the nervous structure which is used in such acts as these. A stimulus is given to the outer end of an efferent nerve; some change or other runs up this nerve, crosses a synapsis between this and an afferent nerve, travels down the latter to a muscle, causes the muscle to contract, and so produces a bodily movement. There seems no reason to believe that the mind plays any essential part in this process. The process may be irreducibly vital, and not merely physico-chemical; but there seems no need to assume anything more than this. Now it is said that the whole nervous system is simply an immense complication of interconnected nervous arcs. The result is that a change which travels inwards has an immense number of alternative paths by which it may travel outwards. Thus the reaction to a given stimulus is no longer one definite movement, as in the simple reflex. Almost any movement may follow any stimulus according to the path which the afferent disturbance happens to take. This path will depend on the relative resistance of the various synapses at the time. Now a variable response to the same stimulus is characteristic of deliberate as opposed to reflex action.

These are the facts. The argument based on them runs as follows. It is admitted that the mind has nothing to do with the causation of purely reflex actions. But the nervous structure and the nervous processes involved in deliberate action do not differ in kind from those involved in reflex action; they differ only in degree of complexity. The variability which characterises deliberate action is fully explained by the variety of alternative paths and the variable resistances of the synapses. So it is unreasonable to suppose that the mind has any more to do with causing deliberate actions than it has to do with causing reflex actions.

I think that this argument is invalid. In the first place I am pretty sure that the persons who use it have before their imagination a kind of picture of how mind and body must interact if they interact at all. They find that the facts do not answer to this picture, and so they conclude that there is no interaction. The picture is of the following kind. They think of the mind as sitting somewhere in a hole in the brain, surrounded by telephones. And they think of the efferent disturbance as coming to an end at one of these telephones and there affecting the mind. The mind is then supposed to respond by sending an efferent impulse down another of these telephones. As no such hole, with efferent nerves stopping at its walls and afferent nerves starting from them, can be found, they conclude that the mind can play no part in the transaction. But another alternative is that this picture of how the mind must act if it acts at all is wrong. To put it shortly, the mistake is to confuse a gap in an explanation with a spatio-temporal gap, and to argue from the absence of the latter to the absence of the former.

The Interactionist's contention is simply that there is a gap in any purely physiological explanation of deliberate action; i.e., that all such explanations fail to account completely for the facts because they leave out one necessary condition. It does not follow in the least that there must be a spatio-temporal breach of continuity in the physiological conditions, and that the missing condition must fill this gap in the way in which the movement of a wire fills the spatio-temporal interval between the pulling of a bell-handle and the ringing of a distant bell. To assume this is to make the mind a kind of physical object, and to make its action a kind of mechanical action. Really, the mind and its actions are not literally in Space at all, and the time which is occupied by the mental event is no doubt also occupied by some part of the physiological process. Thus I am inclined to think that much of the force which this argument actually exercises on many people is simply due to the presupposition about the modus operandi of interaction, and that it is greatly weakened when this presupposition is shown to be a mere prejudice due to our limited power of envisaging unfamiliar alternative possibilities.

We can, however, make more detailed objections to the argument than this. There is a clear introspective difference between the mental accompaniment of voluntary action and that of reflex action. What goes on in our minds when we decide with difficulty to get out of a hot bath on a cold morning is obviously extremely different from what goes on in our minds when we sniff pepper and sneeze. And the difference is qualitative; it is not a mere difference of complexity. This difference has to be explained somehow; and the theory under discussion gives no plausible explanation of it. The ordinary view that, in the latter case, the mind is not acting on the body at all; whilst, in the former, it is acting on the body in a specific way, does at least make the introspective difference between the two intelligible.

Again, whilst it is true that deliberate action differs from reflex action in its greater variability of response to the same stimulus, this is certainly not the whole or the most important part of the difference between them. The really important difference is that, in deliberate action, the response is varied appropriately to meet the special circumstances which are supposed to exist at the time or are expected to arise later; whilst reflex action is not varied in this way, but is blind and almost mechanical. The complexity of the nervous system explains the possibility of variation; it does not in the least explain why the alternative which actually takes place should as a rule be appropriate and not merely haphazard. And so again it seems as if some factor were in operation in deliberate action which is not present in reflex action; and it is reasonable to suppose that this factor is the volition in the mind.

It seems to me that this second scientific argument has no tendency to disprove interaction; but that the facts which it brings forward do tend to suggest the particular form which interaction probably takes if it happens at all. They suggest that what the mind does to the body in voluntary action, if it does anything, is to lower the resistance of certain synapses and to raise that of others. The result is that the nervous current follows such a course as to produce the particular movement which the mind judges to be appropriate at the time. On such a view the difference between reflex, habitual, and deliberate actions for the present purpose becomes fairly plain. In pure reflexes the mind cannot voluntarily affect the resistance of the synapses concerned, and so the action takes place in spite of it. In habitual action it deliberately refrains from interfering with the resistance of the synapses, and so the action goes on like a complicated reflex. But it can affect these resistances if it wishes, though often only with difficulty; and it is ready to do so if it judges this to be expedient. Finally, it may lose the power altogether. This would be what happens when a person becomes a slave to some habit, such as drug-taking.

I conclude that, at the level of enlightened common-sense at which the ordinary discussion of Interaction moves, no good reason has been produced for doubting that the mind acts on the body in volition, and that the body acts on the mind in sensation. The philosophic arguments are quite inconclusive; and the scientific arguments, when properly understood, are quite compatible with Two-sided Interaction. At most they suggest certain conclusions as to the form which interaction probably takes if it happens at all.

Difficulties in the Denial of Interaction

I propose now to consider some of the difficulties which would attend the denial of Interaction, still keeping the discussion at the same common-sense level. If a man denies the action of body on mind he is at once in trouble over the causation of new sensations. Suppose that I suddenly tread on an unsuspected tin-tack. A new sensation suddenly comes into my mind. This is an event, and it presumably has some cause. Now, however carefully I introspect and retrospect, I can find no other mental event which is adequate to account for the fact that just that sensation has arisen at just that moment. If I reject the common-sense view that treading on the tack is an essential part of the cause of the sensation, I must suppose either that it is uncaused, or that it is caused by other events in my mind which I cannot discover by introspection or retrospection, or that it is caused telepathically by other finite minds or by God. Now enquiry or my neighbors would show that it is not caused telepathically by any event in their minds which they can introspect or remember. Thus anyone who denies the action of body on mind, and admits that sensations have causes, must postulate either (a) immense numbers of unobservable states in his own mind; or (b) as many unobservable states in his neighbors' minds, together with telepathic action; or (c) some non-human spirit together with telepathic action. I must confess that the difficulties which have been alleged against the action of body on mind seem to be mild compared with those of the alternative hypotheses which are involved in the denial of such action.

The difficulties which are involved in the denial of the action of mind on body are at first sight equally great; but I do not think that they turn out to be so serious as those which are involved in denying the action of body on mind. The *prima facie* difficulty is this. The world contains many obviously artificial objects, such as books, bridges, clothes, etc. We know that, if we go far enough back in the history of their production, we always do in fact come on the actions of some human body. And the minds connected with these bodies did design the objects in question, did will to produce them, and did believe that they were initiating and guiding the physical process by means of these designs and volitions. If it be true that the mind does not act on the body, it follows that the designs and volitions in the agents' minds did not in fact play any part in the production of books, bridges, clothes, etc. This appears highly paradoxical. And it is an easy step from it to say that anyone who denies the action of mind on body must admit that books, bridges, and other such objects *could* have been produced even though there had been no minds, no thought of these objects and no desire for them. This consequence seems manifestly absurd to common-sense, and it might be argued that it reflects its absurdity back on the theory which entails it.

The man who denies that mind can act on body might deal with this difficulty in two ways: (1) He might deny that the conclusion *is* intrinsically absurd. He might say that human bodies are extraordinarily complex physical objects, which probably obey irreducible laws of their own, and that we really do not know enough about them to set limits to what their unaided powers could accomplish. This is the line which Spinoza took. The conclusion, it would be argued, *seems* absurd only because the state of affairs which it contemplates is so very unfamiliar. We find it difficult to imagine a body like ours without a mind like ours; but, if we could get over this defect in our powers of imagination, we might have no difficulty in admitting that such a body could do all the things which our bodies do. I think it must be admitted that the difficulty is not so great as that which is involved in denying the action of body on mind. There we had to postulate *ad hoc* utterly unfamiliar entities and modes of action; here it is not certain that we should have to do this.

(2) The other line of argument would be to say that the alleged consequence does not necessarily follow from denying the action of mind on body. I assume that both parties admit that causation is something more than mere *de facto* regularity of sequence and concomitance. If they do not, of course the whole controversy between them becomes futile; for there will certainly be causation between mind and body and between body and mind, in the only sense in which there is causation anywhere. This being presupposed, the following kind of answer is logically possible. When I say that B could not have happened unless A had happened, there are two alternative possibilities. (a) A may itself be an indispensable link in any chain of causes which ends up with B. (b) A may not itself be a link in any chain of causation which ends up in B. But there may be an indispensable link α in any such chain of causation, and A may be a necessary accompaniment or sequent of α. These two possibilities may be illustrated by diagrams. (a) is represented by the figure below:—

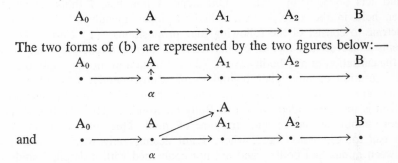

$$A_0 \qquad A \qquad A_1 \qquad A_2 \qquad B$$

The two forms of (b) are represented by the two figures below:—

$$A_0 \qquad A \qquad A_1 \qquad A_2 \qquad B$$

$$\alpha$$

$$A_0 \qquad A \qquad A_1 \qquad A_2 \qquad B$$

and

$$\alpha$$

Evidently, if B cannot happen unless a precedes, and if α cannot happen without A accompanying or immediately following it, B will not be able to happen unless A precedes it. And yet A will have had no part in causing B. It will be noticed that, on this view, α has a complex effect AA_1, of which a certain part, viz., A_1 is sufficient by itself to produce A_2 and ultimately B. Let us apply this abstract possibility to our present problem. Suppose that B is some artificial object, like a book or a bridge. If we admit that this could not have come into existence unless a certain design and volition had existed in a certain mind, we could interpret the facts in two ways. (a) We could hold that the design and volition are themselves an indispensable link in the chain of causation which ends in the production of a bridge or a book. This is the common view, and it requires us to admit the action of mind on body. (b) We might hold that the design and the volition are not themselves a link in the chain of causation which ends in the production of the artificial object; but that they are a necessary accompaniment or sequent of something which is an indispensable link in this chain of causation. On this view the chain consists wholly of physical events; but one of these physical events (viz., some event in the brain) has a complex consequent. One part of this consequent is purely physical, and leads by purely physical causation to the ultimate production of a bridge or a book. The other is purely mental, and consists of a certain design and volition in the mind which animates the human body concerned. If this has any consequences they are purely mental. Each part of this complex consequent follows with equal necessity; this particular brain-state could no more have existed without such and such a mental state accompanying or following it than it could have existed without such and such a bodily movement following it. If we are willing to take some such view as this, we can admit that certain objects could not have existed unless there had been designs of them and desires for them; and yet we could consistently deny that these desires and designs have any effect on the movements of our bodies.

It seems to me then that the doctrine which I will call "One-sided Action of Body on Mind" is logically possible; i.e., a theory which accepts the action of body on mind but denies the action of mind on body. But I do not see the least reason to accept it, since I see no reason to deny that mind acts on body in volition. One-sided Action has, I think, generally been held in the special form called "Epiphenomenalism." I take this doctrine to consist of the following four propositions: (1) Certain bodily events cause certain mental events. (2) No mental event plays any part in the causation of any bodily event. (3) No mental event plays any part in the causation of any other mental event. Consequently, (4) all mental events are caused by bodily events and by them only. Thus Epiphenomenalism is just One-sided Action of Body on Mind, together with a special theory about the nature and structure of mind. This special theory does not call for discussion here, where I am dealing only with the relations between minds and bodies, and am not concerned with a detailed analysis of mind. . . .

Arguments in Favor of Interaction

The only arguments *for* One-sided Action of Body on Mind or for Parallelism are the arguments *against* Two-sided Interaction; and these, as we have seen, are worthless. Are there any arguments in favour of Two-sided Interaction? I have incidentally given two which seem to me to have considerable weight. In favour of the action of mind on body is the fact that we seem to be immediately aware of a causal relation when we voluntarily try to produce a bodily movement, and that the arguments to show that this cannot be true are invalid.* In favour of the action of

* Broad here refers to a discussion on pp. 100–103 of *The Mind and Its Place in Nature* which is not reproduced in our selection. (Eds.)

body on mind are the insuperable difficulties which I have pointed out in accounting for the happening of new sensations on any other hypothesis. There are, however, two other arguments which have often been thought to prove the action of mind on body. These are (1) an evolutionary argument, first used, I believe, by William James; and (2) the famous "telegram argument." They both seem to me to be quite obviously invalid.

(1) The evolutionary argument runs as follows: It is a fact, which is admitted by persons who deny Two-sided Interaction, that minds increase in complexity and power with the growth in complexity of the brain and nervous system. Now, if the mind makes no difference to the actions of the body, this development on the mental side is quite unintelligible from the point of view of natural selection. Let us imagine two animals whose brains and nervous systems were of the same degree of complexity; and suppose, if possible, that one had a mind and the other had none. If the mind makes no difference to the behavior of the body the chance of survival and of leaving descendants will clearly be the same for the two animals. Therefore natural selection will have no tendency to favor the evolution of mind which has actually taken place. I do not think that there is anything in this argument. Natural selection is a purely negative process; it simply tends to eliminate individuals and species which have variations unfavourable to survival. Now, by hypothesis, the possession of a mind is not *unfavourable* to survival; it simply makes no difference. Now it may be that the existence of a mind of such and such a kind is an inevitable consequence of the existence of a brain and nervous system of such and such a degree of complexity. Indeed we have seen that some such view is essential if the opponent of Two-sided Interaction is to answer the common-sense objection that artificial objects could not have existed unless there had been a mind which designed and desired them. On this hypothesis there is no need to invoke natural selection twice over, once to explain the evolution of the brain and nervous system, and once to explain the evolution of the mind. If natural selection will account for the evolution of the brain and nervous system, the evolution of the mind will follow inevitably, even though it adds nothing to the survival-value of the organism. The plain fact is that natural selection does not account for the origin or for the growth in complexity of anything whatever; and therefore it is no objection to any particular theory of the relations of mind and body that, if it were true, natural selection would not explain the origin and development of mind.

(2) The "telegram argument" is as follows: Suppose there were two telegrams, one saying "Our son has been killed," and the other saying: "Your son has been killed." And suppose that one or other of them was delivered to a parent whose son was away from home. As physical stimuli they are obviously extremely alike, since they differ only in the fact that the letter "Y" is present in one and absent in the other. Yet we know that the reaction of the person who received the telegram might be very different according to which one he received. This is supposed to show

that the reactions of the body cannot be wholly accounted for by bodily causes, and that the mind must intervene causally in some cases. Now I have very little doubt that the mind does play a part in determining the action of the recipient of the telegram; but I do not see why this argument should prove it to a person who doubted or denied it. If two very similar stimuli are followed by two very different results, we are no doubt justified in concluding that these stimuli are not the complete causes of the reactions which follow them. But of course it would be admitted by every one that the receipt of the telegram is not the complete cause of the recipient's reaction. We all know that his brain and nervous system play an essential part in any reaction that he may make to the stimulus. The question then is whether the minute structure of his brain and nervous system, including in this the supposed traces left by past stimuli and past reactions, is not enough to account for the great difference in his behaviour on receiving two very similar stimuli. Two keys may be very much alike, but one may fit a certain lock and the other may not. And, if the lock be connected with the trigger of a loaded gun, the results of "stimulating" the system with one or other of the two keys will be extremely different. We know that the brain and nervous system are very complex, and we commonly suppose that they contain more or less permanent traces and linkages due to past stimuli and reactions. If this be granted, it is obvious that two very similar stimuli may produce very different results, simply because one fits in with the internal structure of the brain and nervous system whilst the other does not. And I do not see how we can be sure that anything more is needed to account for the mere difference of reaction adduced by the "telegram argument." . . .

18 The Limitations of Scientific Materialism

John Tyndall

... **Y**OU WILL NOTICE THAT I AM STAT-
ing my truth strongly, as at the beginning we agreed it should be stated.
But I must go still further, and affirm that in the eye of science *the animal
body* is just as much the product of molecular force as the stalk and ear
of corn, or as the crystal of salt or sugar. Many of the parts of the body
are obviously mechanical. Take the human heart, for example, with its
system of valves, or take the exquisite mechanism of the eye or hand.
Animal heat, moreover, is the same in kind as the heat of a fire, being
produced by the same chemical process. Animal motion, too, is as directly
derived from the food of the animal, as the motion of Trevethyck's walking-
engine from the fuel in its furnace. As regards matter, the animal body
creates nothing; as regards force, it creates nothing. Which of you by taking
thought can add one cubit to his stature? All that has been said, then,
regarding the plant may be restated with regard to the animal. Every
particle that enters into the composition of a muscle, a nerve, or a bone, has
been placed in its position by molecular force. And unless the existence of
law in these matters be denied, and the element of caprice introduced, we
must conclude that, given the relation of any molecule of the body to its
environment, its position in the body might be determined mathematically.
Our difficulty is not with the *quality* of the problem, but with its *complexity;*
and this difficulty might be met by the simple expansion of the faculties

[This selection is part of Tyndall's Presidential Address, delivered in 1868, to the Mathematical and Physical Section of the British Association. The full text can be found under
the title of "Scientific Materialism" in Volume II of Tyndall's *Fragments of Science*.]

which we now possess. Given this expansion, with the necessary molecular data, and the chick might be deduced as rigorously and as logically from the egg as the existence of Neptune from the disturbances of Uranus, or as conical refraction from the undulatory theory of light.

You see I am not mincing matters, but avowing nakedly what many scientific thinkers more or less distinctly believe. The formation of a crystal, a plant, or an animal, is in their eyes a purely mechanical problem, which differs from the problems of ordinary mechanics in the smallness of the masses and the complexity of the processes involved. Here you have one half of our dual truth; let us now glance at the other half. Associated with this wonderful mechanism of the animal body we have phenomena no less certain than those of physics, but between which and the mechanism we discern no necessary connection. A man, for example, can say, *I feel, I think, I love;* but how does *consciousness* infuse itself into the problem? The human brain is said to be the organ of thought and feeling; when we are hurt the brain feels it, when we ponder it is the brain that thinks, when our passions or affections are excited it is through the instrumentality of the brain. Let us endeavor to be a little more precise here. I hardly imagine there exists a profound scientific thinker, who has reflected upon the subject, unwilling to admit the extreme probability of the hypothesis that, for every fact of consciousness, whether in the domain of sense, of thought, or of emotion, a definite molecular condition of motion or structure is set up in the brain; or who would be disposed even to deny that if the motion or structure be induced by internal causes instead of external, the effect on consciousness will be the same? Let any nerve, for example, be thrown by morbid action into the precise state of motion which would be communicated to it by the pulses of a heated body, surely that nerve will declare itself hot—the mind will accept the subjective intimation exactly as if it were objective. The retina may be excited by purely mechanical means. A blow on the eye causes a luminous flash, and the mere pressure of the finger on the external ball produces a star of light, which Newton compared to the circles on a peacock's tail. Disease makes people see visions and dream dreams; but, in all such cases, could we examine the organs implicated, we should, on philosophical grounds, expect to find them in that precise molecular condition which the real objects, if present, would superinduce.

The relation of physics to consciousness being thus invariable, it follows that, given the state of the brain, the corresponding thought or feeling, the corresponding state of the brain might be inferred. But how inferred? It would be at bottom not a case of logical inference at all, but of empirical association. You may reply that many of the inferences of science are of this character; the inference, for example, that an electric current of a given direction will deflect a magnetic needle in a definite way; but the cases differ in this, that the passage from the current to the needle, if not demonstrable, is thinkable, and that we entertain no doubt as to the final mechanical solution of the problem. But the passage from the physics of the brain to the corresponding facts of consciousness is unthinkable. Granted that a definite thought, and a definite molecular action in the brain occur simultaneously; we do not possess the intellectual organ, nor apparently any rudiment of the organ, which would enable us to pass, by a process of reasoning, from the one to the other. They appear together, but we do not know why. Were our minds and senses so expanded, strengthened, and illuminated as to enable us to see and feel the very molecules of the brain; were we capable of following all their motions, all their groupings, all their electric discharges, if such there be; and were we intimately acquainted with the corresponding states of thought and feeling, we should be as far as ever from the solution of the problem, "How are these physical processes connected with the facts of consciousness?" The chasm between the two classes of phenomena would still remain intellectually impassable. Let the consciousness of *love,* for example, be associated with a right-handed spiral motion of the molecules of the brain, and the consciousness of *hate* with a left-handed spiral motion. We should then know when we love that the motion is in one direction, and when we hate that the motion is in the other; but the "WHY?" would remain as unanswerable as before.

In affirming that the growth of the body is mechanical, and that thought, as exercised by us, has its correlative in the physics of the brain, I think the position of the "Materialist" is stated, as far as that position is a tenable one. I think the materialist will be able finally to maintain this position against all attacks; but I do not think, in the present condition of the human mind, that he can pass beyond this position. I do not think he is entitled to say that his molecular groupings and his molecular motions *explain* everything. In reality, they explain nothing. The utmost he can affirm is the association of two classes of phenomena, of whose real bond of union he is in absolute ignorance. The problem of the connection of body and soul is as insoluble in its modern form as it was in the prescientific ages. Phosphorus is known to enter into the composition of the human brain, and a trenchant German writer has exclaimed, *"Ohne Phosphor, kein Gedanke."** That may or may not be the case; but even if we knew it to be the case, the knowledge would not lighten our darkness. On both sides of the zone here assigned to the materialist he is equally helpless. If you ask him whence is this "Matter" of which we have been discoursing, who or what divided it into molecules, who or what impressed upon them this necessity of running into organic forms, he has no answer. Science is mute in reply to these questions. But if the materialist is confounded and science rendered dumb, who else is prepared with a solution? To whom has this arm of the Lord been revealed? Let us lower our heads and acknowledge our ignorance, priest and philosopher, one and all.

* "Without phosphorus, no thinking."

19   The Automaton Theory

T. H. Huxley

· · · THERE REMAINS A DOCTRINE TO which Descartes attached great weight, so that full acceptance of it became a sort of note of a thorough-going Cartesian, but which, nevertheless, is so opposed to ordinary prepossessions that it attained more general notoriety, and gave rise to more discussion, than almost any other Cartesian hypothesis. It is the doctrine that brute animals are mere machines or automata, devoid not only of reason, but of any kind of consciousness, which is stated briefly in the *Discourse on Method,* and more fully in the "Replies to the Fourth Objections," and in the correspondence with Henry More.

The process of reasoning by which Descartes arrived at this startling conclusion is well shown in the following passage of the "Réponses:"

> But as regards the souls of beasts, although this is not the place for considering them, and though, without a general exposition of physics, I can say no more on this subject than I have already said in the fifth part of my Treatise on Method; yet, I will further state, here, that it appears to me to be a very remarkable circumstance that no movement can take place, either in the bodies of beasts, or even in our own, if these bodies

[This selection consists of the major parts of Huxley's article, "On the Hypothesis that Animals are Automata and its History," which was first published in 1874. The entire essay can be found in Huxley's volume *Methods and Results,* published by D. Appleton and Co., New York and London.]

have not in themselves all the organs and instruments by means of which the very same movements would be accomplished in a machine. So that, even in us, the spirit, or the soul, does not directly move the limbs, but only determines the course of that very subtle liquid which is called the animal spirits, which, running continually from the heart by the brain into the muscles, is the cause of all the movements of our limbs, and often may cause many different motions, one as easily as the other.

And it does not even always exert this determination; for among the movements which take place in us, there are many which do not depend on the mind at all, such as the beating of the heart, the digestion of food, the nutrition, the respiration of those who sleep; and even in those who are awake, walking, singing, and other similar actions, when they are per-formed without the mind thinking about them. And, when one who falls from a height throws his hands forward to save his head, it is in virtue of no ratiocination that he performs this action; it does not depend upon his mind, but takes place merely because his senses being affected by the present danger, some change arises in his brain which determines the animal spirits to pass thence into the nerves, in such a manner as is re-quired to produce this motion, in the same way as in a machine, and without the mind being able to hinder it. Now since we observe this in ourselves, why should we be so much astonished if the light reflected from the body of a wolf into the eye of a sheep has the same force to excite in it the motion of flight?

After having observed this, if we wish to learn by reasoning, whether certain movements of beasts are comparable to those which are effected in us by the operation of the mind, or, on the contrary, to those which depend only on the animal spirits and the disposition of the organs, it is necessary to consider the difference between the two, which I have ex-plained in the fifth part of the *Discourse on Method* (for I do not think that any others are discoverable), and then it will easily be seen, that all the actions of beasts are similar only to those which we perform with-out the help of our minds. For which reason we shall be forced to con-clude, that we know of the existence in them of no other principle of motion than the disposition of their organs and the continual affluence of animal spirits produced by the heat of the heart, which attenuates and subtilises the blood; and, at the same time, we shall acknowledge that we have had no reason for assuming any other principle, except that, not having distinguished these two principles of motion, and seeing that the one, which depends only on the animal spirits and the organs, exists in beasts as well as in us, we have hastily concluded that the other, which depends on mind and on thought, was also possessed by them.

Reflex Action and Consciously Motivated Behavior

Descartes' line of argument is perfectly clear. He starts from reflex action in man, from the unquestionable fact that, in ourselves, co-ordinate, purposive, actions may take place, without intervention of consciousness or volition, or even contrary to the latter. As actions of a certain degree of complexity are brought about by mere mechanism, why may not actions of still greater complexity be the result of a more refined mechanism? What proof is there that brutes are other than a superior race of marionettes, which eat without pleasure, cry without pain, desire nothing, know nothing, and only simulate intelligence as a bee simulates a mathematician?

The Port Royalists adopted the hypothesis that brutes are machines, and are said to have carried its practical applications so far as to treat domestic animals with neglect, if not with actual cruelty. . . . Modern research has brought to light a great multitude of facts, which not only show that Descartes' view is defensible, but render it far more defensible than it was in his day.

It must be premised, that it is wholly impossible absolutely to prove the presence or absence of consciousness in anything but one's own brain, though, by analogy, we are justified in assuming its existence in other men. Now if, by some accident, a man's spinal cord is divided, his limbs are paralysed, so far as his volition is concerned, below the point of injury; and he is incapable of experiencing all those states of consciousness which, in his uninjured state, would be excited by irritation of those nerves which come off below the injury. If the spinal cord is divided in the middle of the back, for example, the skin of the feet may be cut, or pinched, or burned, or wetted with vitriol, without any sensation of touch, or of pain, arising, in consciousness. So far as the man is concerned, therefore, the part of the central nervous system which lies beyond the injury is cut off from consciousness. It must indeed be admitted, that, if any one think fit to maintain that the spinal cord below the injury is conscious, but that it is cut off from any means of making its consciousness known to the other consciousness in the brain, there is no means of driving him from his position by logic. But assuredly there is no way of proving it, and in the matter of consciousness, if in anything, we may hold by the rule, *De non apparentibus et de non existentibus eadem est ratio.** However near the brain the spinal cord is injured, consciousness remains intact, except that the irritation of parts below the injury is no longer represented by sensation. On the other hand, pressure upon the anterior division of the brain, or extensive injuries to it, abolish consciousness. Hence, it is a highly probable conclusion, that consciousness in man depends upon the integrity of the anterior division of the brain, while the middle and hinder divisions of the brain, and the rest of the nervous centres, have nothing to do with it. And it is further highly probable, that what is true for man is true for other vertebrated animals.

We may assume, then, that in a living vertebrated animal, any segment of the cerebro-spinal axis (or spinal cord and brain) separated from that anterior division of the brain which is the organ of consciousness, is as completely incapable of giving rise to consciousness as we know it to be incapable of carrying out volitions. Nevertheless, this separated segment of the spinal cord is not passive and inert. On the contrary, it is the seat of extremely remarkable powers. In our imaginary case of injury, the man would, as we have seen, be devoid of sensation in his legs, and would have

* "That what is not given in experience may be treated as non-existent." [Eds.]

not the least power of moving them. But, if the soles of his feet were tickled, the legs would be drawn up just as vigorously as they would have been before the injury. We know exactly what happens when the soles of the feet are tickled; a molecular change takes place in the sensory nerves of the skin, and is propagated along them and through the posterior roots of the spinal nerves, which are constituted by them, to the grey matter of the spinal cord. Through that gray matter the molecular motion is reflected into the anterior roots of the same nerves, constituted by the filaments which supply the muscles of the legs, and, travelling along these motor filaments, reaches the muscles, which at once contract, and cause the limbs to be drawn up.

In order to move the legs in this way, a definite co-ordination of muscular contractions is necessary; the muscles must contract in a certain order and with duly proportioned force; and moreover, as the feet are drawn away from the source of irritation, it may be said that the action has a final cause, or is purposive.

Thus it follows, that the grey matter of the segment of the man's spinal cord, though it is devoid of consciousness, nevertheless responds to a simple stimulus by giving rise to a complex set of muscular contractions, co-ordinated towards a definite end, and serving an obvious purpose.

Effect of Brain Damage in a Lower Animal

If the spinal cord of a frog is cut across, so as to provide us with a segment separated from the brain, we shall have a subject parallel to the injured man, on which experiments can be made without remorse; as we have a right to conclude that a frog's spinal cord is not likely to be conscious, when a man's is not.

Now the frog behaves just as the man did. The legs utterly paralysed, so far as voluntary movement is concerned; but they are vigorously drawn up to the body when any irritant is applied to the foot. But let us study our frog a little farther. Touch the skin of the side of the body with a little acetic acid, which gives rise to all the signs of great pain in an uninjured frog. In this case, there can be no pain, because the application is made to a part of the skin supplied with nerves which come off from the cord below the point of section; nevertheless, the frog lifts up the limb of the same side, and applies the foot to rub off the acetic acid; and, what is still more remarkable, if the limb be held so that the frog cannot use it, it will, by and by, move the limb of the other side, turn it across the body, and use it for the same rubbing process. It is impossible that the frog, if it were in its entirety and could reason, should perform actions more purposive than these: and yet we have most complete assurance that, in this case, the frog is not acting from purpose, has no consciousness, and is a mere insensible machine.

But now suppose that, instead of making a section of the cord in the middle of the body, it had been made in such a manner as to separate the hindermost division of the brain from the rest of the organ, and suppose the foremost two-thirds of the brain entirely taken away. The frog is then absolutely devoid of any spontaneity; it sits upright in the attitude which a frog habitually assumes; and it will not stir unless it is touched; but it differs from the frog which I have just described in this, that, if it be thrown into the water, it begins to swim, and swims just as well as the perfect frog does. But swimming requires the combination and successive co-ordination of a great number of muscular actions. And we are forced to conclude, that the impression made upon the sensory nerves of the skin of the frog by the contact with the water into which it is thrown, causes the transmission to the central nervous apparatus of an impulse which sets going a certain machinery by which all the muscles of swimming are brought into play in due co-ordination. If the frog be stimulated by some irritating body, it jumps or walks as well as the complete frog can do. The simple sensory impression, acting through the machinery of the cord, gives rise to these complex combined movements.

It is possible to go a step farther. Suppose that only the anterior division of the brain—so much of it as lies in front of the "optic lobes"—is removed. If that operation is performed quickly and skillfully, the frog may be kept in a state of full bodily vigour for months, or it may be for years; but it will sit unmoved. It sees nothing: it hears nothing. It will starve sooner than feed itself, although food put into its mouth is swallowed. On irritation, it jumps or walks; if thrown into the water it swims. If it be put on the hand, it sits there, crouched, perfectly quiet, and would sit there for ever. If the hand be inclined very gently and slowly, so that the frog would naturally tend to slip off, the creature's fore paws are shifted on to the edge of the hand, until he can just prevent himself from falling. If the turning of the hand be slowly continued, he mounts up with great care and deliberation, putting first one leg forward and then another, until he balances himself with perfect precision upon the edge; and if the turning of the hand is continued, he goes through the needful set of muscular operations, until he comes to be seated in security, upon the back of the hand. The doing of all this requires a delicacy of co-ordination, and a precision of adjustment of the muscular apparatus of the body, which are only comparable to those of a rope-dancer. To the ordinary influences of light, the frog, deprived of its cerebral hemispheres, appears to be blind. Nevertheless, if the animal be put upon a table, with a book at some little distance between it and the light, and the skin of the hinder part of its body is then irritated, it will jump forward, avoiding the book by passing to the right or left of it. Therefore, although the frog appears to have no sensation of light, visible objects act through its brain upon the motor mechanism of its body.

It is obvious, that had Descartes been acquainted with these remarkable results of modern research, they would have furnished him with far more powerful arguments than he possessed in favour of his view of the automatism of brutes. The habits of a frog, leading its natural life, involve such simple adaptations to surrounding conditions, that the machinery which is competent to do so much without the intervention of consciousness, might well do all. And this argument is vastly strengthened by what has been learned in recent times of the marvellously complex operations which are performed mechanically, and to all appearance without consciousness, by men, when, in consequence of injury or disease, they are reduced to a condition more or less comparable to that of a frog, in which the anterior part of the brain has been removed. A case has recently been published by an eminent French physician, Dr. Mesnet, which illustrates this condition so remarkably, that I make no apology for dwelling upon it at considerable length.

The Case of Sergeant F.

A sergeant of the French army, F——, twenty-seven years of age, was wounded during the battle of Bazeilles, by a ball which fractured his left parietal bone. He ran his bayonet through the Prussian soldier who wounded him, but almost immediately his right arm became paralysed; after walking about two hundred yards, his right leg became similarly affected, and he lost his senses. When he recovered them, three weeks afterwards, in a hospital at Mayence, the right half of the body was completely paralysed, and remained in this condition for a year. At present, the only trace of the paralysis which remains is a slight weakness of the right half of the body. Three or four months after the wound was inflicted, periodical disturbances of the functions of the brain made their appearance, and have continued ever since. The disturbances last from fifteen to thirty hours; the intervals at which they occur being from fifteen to thirty days.

For four years, therefore, the life of this man has been divided into alternating phases—short abnormal states intervening between long normal states.

In the periods of normal life, the ex-sergeant's health is perfect; he is intelligent and kindly, and performs, satisfactorily, the duties of a hospital attendant. The commencement of the abnormal state is ushered in by uneasiness and a sense of weight about the forehead, which the patient compares to the constriction of a circle of iron; and, after its termination, he complains, for some hours, of dullness and heaviness of the head. But the transition from the normal to the abnormal state takes place in a few minutes, without convulsions or cries, and without anything to indicate the change to a bystander. His movements remain free and his expression calm, except for a contraction of the brow, an incessant movement of the eyeballs, and a chewing motion of the jaws. The eyes are wide open, and their pupils dilated. If the man happens to be in a place to which he is accustomed, he walks about as usual; but, if he is in a new place, or if obstacles are intentionally placed in his way, he stumbles gently against them, stops, and then, feeling over the objects with his hands, passes on one side of them. He offers no resistance to any change of direction which may be impressed upon him, or to the forcible acceleration or retardation of his movements. He eats, drinks, smokes, walks about, dresses and un-dresses himself, rises and goes to bed at the accustomed hours. Nevertheless, pins may be run into his body, or strong electric shocks may be sent through it, without causing the least indication of pain; no odorous substance, pleasant or unpleasant, makes the least impression; he eats and drinks with avidity whatever is offered, and takes asafoetida, or vinegar, or quinine, as readily as water; no noise affects him; and light influences him only under certain conditions. Dr. Mesnet remarks, that the sense of touch alone seems to persist, and indeed to be more acute and delicate than in the normal state: and it is by means of the nerves of touch, almost exclusively, that his organism is brought into relation with the external world. Here a difficulty arises. It is clear from the facts detailed, that the nervous apparatus by which, in the normal state, sensations of touch are excited, is that by which external influences determine the movements of the body, in the abnormal state. But does the state of consciousness, which we term a tactile sensation, accompany the operation of this nervous apparatus in the abnormal state? Or is consciousness utterly absent, the man being re-duced to an insensible mechanism?

It is impossible to obtain direct evidence in favour of the one conclusion or the other; all that can be said is, that the case of the frog shows that the man may be devoid of any kind of consciousness.

A further difficult problem is this. The man is insensible to sensory impressions made through the ear, the nose, the tongue, and, to a great extent, the eye; nor is he susceptible of pain from causes operating during his abnormal state. Nevertheless, it is possible so to act upon his tactile apparatus, as to give rise to those molecular changes in his sensorium, which are ordinarily the causes of associated trains of ideas. I give a striking example of this process in Dr. Mesnet's words:—

> He was taking a walk in the garden under a bunch of trees. We placed in his hand his walking stick which he had let fall a few minutes before. He feels it, passes his hand over the bent handle a few times, becomes attentive, seems to extend his ear, and suddenly calls out, "Henry," then, "Here they are. There are about twenty to our two! We have reached our end." And then, with his hand behind his back, as if about to leap, he prepares to attack with his weapon. He crouches in the level, green grass, his head concealed by a tree, in the position of a hunter, and follows all the short-distance movements of the enemy which he be-lieves he sees, with accompanying movements of his hands and shoulders.

In a subsequent abnormal period, Dr. Mesnet caused the patient to repeat this scene by placing him in the same conditions. Now, in this case, the question arises whether the series of actions constituting this singular pantomime was accompanied by the ordinary states of consciousness, the appropriate train of ideas, or not? Did the man dream that he was skirmish-ing? Or was he in the condition of one of Vaucauson's automata—a sense-less mechanism worked by molecular changes in his nervous system? The analogy of the frog shows that the latter assumption is perfectly justifiable.

The ex-sergeant has a good voice, and had, at one time, been employed as a singer at a café. In one of his abnormal states he was observed to begin humming a tune. He then went to his room, dressed himself carefully, and took up some parts of a periodical novel, which lay on his bed, as if he were trying to find something. Dr. Mesnet, suspecting that he was seeking his music, made up one of these into a roll and put it into his hand. He appeared satisfied, took his cane and went downstairs to the door. Here Dr. Mesnet turned him round, and he walked quite contentedly, in the opposite direction, towards the room of the concierge. The light of the sun shining through a window now happened to fall upon him, and seemed to suggest the foot-lights of the stage on which he was accustomed to make his appearance. He stopped, opened his roll of imaginary music, put himself into the attitude of a singer, and sang, with perfect execution, three songs, one after the other. After which he wiped his face with his handkerchief and drank, without a grimace, a tumbler of strong vinegar and water which was put into his hand.

Innate and Automatic Behavior Patterns

An experiment which may be performed upon the frog deprived of the fore part of its brain, well known as Goltz's "Quak-versuch," affords a parallel to this performance. If the skin of a certain part of the back of such a frog is gently stroked with the finger, it immediately croaks. It never croaks unless it is so stroked, and the croak always follows the stroke, just as the sound of a repeater follows the touching of the spring. In the frog, this "song" is innate—so to speak *a priori*—and depends upon a mechanism in the brain governing the vocal apparatus, which is set at work by the molecular change set up in the sensory nerves of the skin of the back by the contact of a foreign body.

In man there is also a vocal mechanism, and the cry of an infant is in the same sense innate and *a priori,* inasmuch as it depends on an organic relation between its sensory nerves and the nervous mechanism which governs the vocal apparatus. Learning to speak, and learning to sing, are processes by which the vocal mechanism is set to new tunes. A song which has been learned has its molecular equivalent, which potentially represents it in the brain, just as a musical box, wound up, potentially represents an overture. Touch the stop and the overture begins; send a molecular impulse along the proper afferent nerve and the singer begins his song.

Again, the manner in which the frog, though apparently insensible to light, is yet, under some circumstances, influenced by visual images, finds a singular parallel in the case of the ex-sergeant.

Sitting at a table, in one of his abnormal states, he took up a pen, felt for paper and ink, and began to write a letter to his general, in which he recommended himself for a medal, on account of his good conduct and courage. It occurred to Dr. Mesnet to ascertain experimentally how far vision was concerned in this act of writing. He therefore interposed a screen between the man's eyes and his hands; under these circumstances he went on writing for a short time, but the words became illegible, and he finally stopped, without manifesting any discontent. On the withdrawal of the screen he began to write again where he had left off. The substitution of water for ink in the inkstand had a similar result. He stopped, looked at his pen, wiped it on his coat, dipped it in the water, and began again with the same effect.

On one occasion, he began to write upon the topmost of ten super-imposed sheets of paper. After he had written a line or two, this sheet was suddenly drawn away. There was a slight expression of surprise, but he continued his letter on the second sheet exactly as if it had been the first. This operation was repeated five times, so that the fifth sheet contained nothing but the writer's signature at the bottom of the page. Nevertheless, when the signature was finished, his eyes turned to the top of the blank sheet, and he went through the form of reading over what he had written, a movement of lips accompanying each word; moreover, with his pen, he put in such corrections as were needed, in that part of the blank page which corresponded with the position of the words which required correction, in the sheets which had been taken away. If the five sheets had been transparent, therefore, they would, when superposed, have formed a properly written and corrected letter.

Immediately after he had written his letter, F—— got up, walked down to the garden, made himself a cigarette, lighted and smoked it. He was about to prepare another, but sought in vain for his tobacco-pouch, which had been purposely taken away. The pouch was now thrust before his eyes and put under his nose, but he neither saw nor smelt it; yet, when it was placed in his hand, he at once seized it, made a fresh cigarette, and ignited a match to light the latter. The match was blown out, and another lighted match placed close before his eyes, but he made no attempt to take it; and, if his cigarette was lighted for him, he made no attempt to smoke. All this time the eyes were vacant, and neither winked, nor exhibited any contraction of the pupils. From these and other experiments, Dr. Mesnet draws the conclusion that his patient sees some things and not others; that the sense of sight is accessible to all things which are brought into relation with him by the sense of touch, and, on the contrary, insensible to things which lie outside this relation. He sees the match he holds and does not see any other.

Just so the frog "sees" the book which is in the way of his jump, at the same time that isolated visual impressions take no effect upon him.

As I have pointed out, it is impossible to prove that F—— is absolutely unconscious in his abnormal state, but it is no less impossible to prove the contrary; and the case of the frog goes a long way to justify the assumption that, in the abnormal state, the man is a mere insensible machine.

If such facts as these had come under the knowledge of Descartes, would they not have formed an apt commentary upon that remarkable passage in the *Traité de l'Homme,* which I have quoted elsewhere, but which is worth repetition:

> All the functions which I have attributed to this machine (the body), as the digestion of food, the pulsation of the heart and of the arteries; the nutrition and the growth of the limbs; respiration, wakefulness, and sleep; the reception of light, sounds, odours, flavours, heat, and such like qualities, in the organs of the external senses; the impression of the idea of these in the organ of common sensation and in the imagination; the retention or the impression of these ideas on the memory; the internal movements of the appetites and the passions; and lastly the external movements of all the limbs, which follow so aptly, as well the action of the objects which are presented to the senses, as the impressions which meet in the memory, that they imitate as nearly as possible those of a real man; I desire, I say, that you should consider that these functions in the machine naturally proceed from the mere arrangement of its organs, neither more nor less than do the movements of a clock, or other automaton, from that of its weights and its wheels; so that, so far as these are concerned, it is not necessary to conceive any other vegetative or sensitive soul, nor any other principle of motion or of life, than the blood and the spirits agitated by the fire which burns continually in the heart, and which is no wise essentially different from all the fires which exist in inanimate bodies.

And would Descartes not have been justified in asking why we need deny that animals are machines, when men, in a state of unconsciousness, perform, mechanically, actions as complicated and as seemingly rational as those of any animals?

Animals Are Conscious Automata

But though I do not think that Descartes' hypothesis can be positively refuted, I am not disposed to accept it. The doctrine of continuity is too well established for it to be permissible to me to suppose that any complex natural phenomenon comes into existence suddenly, and without being preceded by simpler modifications; and very strong arguments would be needed to prove that such complex phenomena as those of consciousness, first make their appearance in man. We know, that, in the individual man, consciousness grows from a dim glimmer to its full light, whether we consider the infant advancing in years or the adult emerging from slumber and swoon. We know, further, that the lower animals possess, though less developed, that part of the brain which we have every reason to believe to be the organ of consciousness in man; and as, in other cases, function and organ are proportional, so we have a right to conclude it is with the brain; and that the brutes, though they may not possess our intensity of consciousness, and though from the absence of language, they can have no trains of thoughts, but only trains of feelings, yet have a consciousness which, more or less distinctly, foreshadows our own.

I confess that, in view of the struggle for existence which goes on in the animal world, and of the frightful quantity of pain with which it must be accompanied, I should be glad if the probabilities were in favour of Descartes' hypothesis; but, on the other hand, considering the terrible practical consequences to domestic animals which might ensue from any error on our part, it is as well to err on the right side, if we err at all, and deal with them as weaker brethren, who are bound, like the rest of us, to pay their toll for living, and suffer what is needful for the general good. As Hartley finely says, "We seem to be in the place of God to them"; and we may justly follow the precedents He sets in nature in our dealings with them.

But though we may see reason to disagree with Descartes' hypothesis that brutes are unconscious machines, it does not follow that he was wrong in regarding them as automata. They may be more or less conscious, sensitive, automata; and the view that they are such conscious machines is that which is implicitly, or explicitly adopted by most persons. When we speak of the actions of the lower animals being guided by instinct and not by reason, what we really mean is that, though they feel as we do, yet their actions are the results of their physical organisation. We believe, in short, that they are machines, one part of which (the nervous system) not only sets the rest in motion, and co-ordinates its movements in relation with changes in surrounding bodies, but is provided with special apparatus, the function of which is the calling into existence of those states of consciousness which are termed sensations, emotions, and ideas. I believe that this generally accepted view is the best expression of the facts at present known.

It is experimentally demonstrable—any one who cares to run a pin into himself may perform a sufficient demonstration of the fact—that a mode of motion of the nervous system is the immediate antecedent of a state of consciousness. All but the adherents of "Occasionalism," or of the doctrine of "Pre-established Harmony" (if any such now exist), must admit that we have as much reason for regarding the mode of motion of the nervous system as the cause of the state of consciousness, as we have for regarding any event as the cause of another. How the one phenomenon causes the other we know, as much or as little, as in any other case of causation; but we have as much right to believe that the sensation is an effect of the molecular change, as we have to believe that motion is an effect of impact; and there is as much propriety in saying that the brain evolves sensation, as there is in saying that an iron rod, when hammered, evolves heat.

As I have endeavored to show, we are justified in supposing that something analogous to what happens in ourselves takes place in the brutes, and that the affections of their sensory nerves give rise to molecular changes in the brain, which again give rise to, or evolve, the corresponding states of consciousness. Nor can there be any reasonable doubt that the emotions of brutes, and such ideas as they possess, are similarly dependent upon molecular brain changes. Each sensory impression leaves behind a record in the structure of the brain—an "idea-genous" molecule, so to speak, which is competent, under certain conditions, to reproduce, in a fainter condition, the state of consciousness which corresponds with that sensory impression; and it is these "idea-genous molecules" which are the physical basis of memory.

It may be assumed, then, that molecular changes in the brain are the causes of all the states of consciousness of brutes. Is there any evidence that these states of consciousness may, conversely, cause those molecular changes which give rise to muscular motion? I see no such evidence. The frog walks, hops, swims, and goes through his gymnastic performances quite as well without consciousness, and consequently without volition, as with it; and, if a frog, in his natural state, possesses anything corresponding with what we call volition, there is no reason to think that it is anything but a concomitant of the molecular changes in the brain which form part of the series involved in the production of motion.

The consciousness of brutes would appear to be related to the mechanism of their body simply as a collateral product of its working, and to be as completely without any power of modifying that working as the steam-whistle which accompanies the work of a locomotive engine is without influence upon its machinery. Their volition, if they have any, is an emotion indicative of physical changes, not a cause of such changes.

This conception of the relations of states of consciousness with molecular changes in the brain—of *psychoses* with *neuroses*—does not prevent us from ascribing free will to brutes. For an agent is free when there is nothing to prevent him from doing that which he desires to do. If a greyhound chases a hare, he is a free agent, because his action is in entire accordance with his strong desire to catch the hare; while so long as he is held back by the leash he is not free, being prevented by external force from following his inclination. And the ascription of freedom to the greyhound under the former circumstances is by no means inconsistent with the other aspect of the facts of the case—that he is a machine impelled to the chase, and caused, at the same time, to have the desire to catch the game by the impression which the rays of light proceeding from the hare make upon his eyes, and through them upon his brain.

Much ingenious argument has at various times been bestowed upon the question: How is it possible to imagine that volition, which is a state of consciousness, and, as such, has not the slightest community of nature with matter in motion, can act upon the moving matter of which the body is composed, as it is assumed to do in voluntary acts? But if, as is here suggested, the voluntary acts of brutes—or, in other words, the acts which they desire to perform—are as purely mechanical as the rest of their actions, and are simply accompanied by the state of consciousness called volition, the inquiry, so far as they are concerned, becomes superfluous. Their volitions do not enter into the chain of causation of their actions at all. . . .

The Same Conclusion Applies to Human Beings

It will be said, that I mean that the conclusions deduced from the study of the brutes are applicable to man, and that the logical consequences of such application are fatalism, materialism, and atheism—whereupon the drums will beat the *pas de charge*.

One does not do battle with drummers; but I venture to offer a few remarks for the calm consideration of thoughtful persons, untrammelled by foregone conclusions, unpledged to shore-up tottering dogmas, and anxious only to know the true bearings of the case.

It is quite true that, to the best of my judgment, the argumentation which applies to brutes holds equally good of men; and, therefore, that all states of consciousness in us, as in them, are immediately caused by molecular changes of the brain-substance. It seems to me that in men, as in brutes, there is no proof that any state of consciousness is the cause of change in the motion of the matter of the organism. If these positions are well based, it follows that our mental conditions are simply the symbols in consciousness of the changes which takes place automatically in the organism; and that, to take an extreme illustration, the feeling we call volition is not the cause of a voluntary act, but the symbol of that state of the brain which is the immediate cause of that act. We are conscious automata, endowed with free will in the only intelligible sense of that much-abused term— inasmuch as in many respects we are able to do as we like—but none the less parts of the great series of causes and effects which, in unbroken continuity, composes that which is, and has been, and shall be—the sum of existence.

As to the logical consequences of this conviction of mine, I may be permitted to remark that logical consequences are the scarecrows of fools and the beacons of wise men. The only question which any wise man can ask himself, and which any honest man will ask himself, is whether a doctrine is true or false. Consequences will take care of themselves; at most their importance can only justify us in testing with extra care the reasoning process from which they result.

So that if the view I have taken did really and logically lead to fatalism, materialism, and atheism, I should profess myself a fatalist, materialist, and atheist; and I should look upon those who, while they believed in my honesty of purpose and intellectual competency, should raise a hue and cry against me, as people who by their own admission preferred lying to truth, and whose opinions therefore were unworthy of the smallest attention.

But, as I have endeavored to explain on other occasions, I really have no claim to rank myself among fatalistic, materialistic, or atheistic philosophers. Not among the fatalists, for I take the conception of necessity to have a logical, and not a physical foundation; not among materialists, for I am utterly incapable of conceiving the existence of matter if there is no mind in which to picture that existence; not among atheists, for the problem of the ultimate cause of existence is one which seems to me to be hopelessly out of reach of my poor powers. Of all the senseless babble I have ever had occasion to read the demonstrations of those philosophers who undertake to tell us all about the nature of God would be the worst, if they were not surpassed by the still greater absurdities of the philosophers who try to prove that there is no God. . . .

20   The Physical Basis of Mind:

A Philosophers' Symposium

Viscount Samuel, A. J. Ayer and Gilbert Ryle

Viscount Samuel

I N SO SHORT A BROADCAST, I CAN ONLY
offer baldly my own conclusions on the question debated in this most interesting, and indeed exciting, discussion, without attempting any survey
of the previous contributions.

The discussion has been an approach, from the side of physiology, to
one of the oldest and most fundamental of the problems of philosophy—
the relation between mind and matter. For centuries, philosophers of different schools have made strenuous efforts to resolve one into the other. Some
have sought to show that mind is nothing more than an emanation, in the
course of evolution, from matter; others that matter is nothing more than
a concept of mind, which alone is real. Those efforts have been unsuccessful: neither view has won general assent.

The materialists appear to ignore the obvious lessons of daily experience. We see, every moment, events which cannot be accounted for by
derivations, however subtle, from physical or chemical processes. Watch a
chess-player deliberating for a quarter of an hour whether to move his
queen here or a pawn there. At last he stretches out his hand and does the
one or the other: or he may do neither; using his vocal organs, he may say,

[This symposium was part of a series of broadcasts given over the Third Program of the
British Broadcasting Corporation in 1950 and published by Basil Blackwell, Oxford, as *The
Physical Basis of Mind*. It is here reprinted with the publisher's permission.]

"I resign this game." The physiologist may reveal the nervous and muscular mechanism which operates the hand or the tongue, but not the process which has decided the player's action. Or consider a novelist making up a story, a musician writing a symphony, a scientist engaged in a mathematical calculation; or, indeed, something much simpler, a bird building its nest, and choosing the right materials for each stage; or a cat waiting for a pause in the traffic before crossing the street. All these, and all such, are engaged in some process that is different in kind from electrical attractions and repulsions, or from the processes that unite particles into atoms, atoms into molecules, molecules into objects, and move them about relatively to one another.

The idealists do not account for the fact, which we are bound to accept from astronomy, geology, and anthropology—if we think at all, and if we accept anything at all—that the stars and the planets and this earth existed aeons before man existed; that the universe carried on its activities then— and may properly be assumed to carry them on now—independently of man's perceiving and observing, timing and measuring. The material universe cannot, therefore, be a product of human thought. If it is said that matter may still be an emanation of mind—the mind of God—that is merely an evasion, removing the problem outside the scope of the argument.

The whole effort—to resolve mind into matter or else matter into mind —is the outcome of what T. H. Green called "the philosophic craving for unity." But a craving is something irrational, and we had better beware of becoming addicts. What ground is there for requiring any such unification, either of the one kind or of the other? An essential duality in nature is the alternative that is left.

For those who have proceeded on that assumption, it has been natural and usual to regard the living conscious body as the province of mind and the outside material universe as the province of matter. This series of addresses, which is now concluding, has been most valuable in showing that that is an error; it has put the boundary between the two in the wrong place. The eminent scientists who have taken part in it have clearly established that the acceptance of sense stimuli, the transmission of their effects along the nerve fibres, and their activation of different parts of the brain, are mechanical. Whether the approach is from bio-physics or bio-chemistry, anatomy or pathology, the conclusion is the same—these are material activities, obeying mechanical laws. Dr. Russell Brain who spoke on "Speech and Thought" tells us that "all stimuli reach the brain as electrical patterns"; Professor Le Gros Clark and others describe with great clarity the mechanism of the nervous system as a whole. We must conclude that these processes, although inside the body, are not essentially different from the physical processes that are going on outside; rather they are a continuation. When we feel an electrical shock, the nerve fibres that carry the current are performing a function similar in kind to that of the copper wire between the battery and the hand. When we hear a sound, the mechanism of the auditory organs, including the relevant part of the brain, is specialized, no doubt, but is not fundamentally of a different order from the air-waves which had carried the sound. It follows that the meeting-place between mind and matter in our own experience is not where we had supposed it to be; it is not at the boundary between body and not-body, but is internal.

That, however, does not solve the problem; it merely shifts it. Some meeting-place there must be to account for the brain-mind relation. And we are bound to assume that, although the two are of different orders, they must have something in common, because there is a meeting-place; because the two interconnect and interact; because body (including brain) does in fact condition and influence mind, and mind does in fact condition and influence body.

The painter or sculptor is conditioned and influenced by his materials; the composer by the musical instruments that exist in his time; the architect by the available building materials; the craftsman by his tools; the captain and crew by their ship. But also the artist, composer, architect, craftsman, or navigator chooses the things that he will use and decides the purposes that they shall serve. So with mind and body.

This discussion has helped to clarify the whole problem by establishing the fact that the meeting-place is not at the point where external stimuli impinge upon the nervous system; it is at the points where mind accepts and utilizes the sense-data offered by the brains. But the discussion has not been able to answer the question what it is that takes over at those points; and therefore it could not even begin to consider how the connection may be made.

Here again our scientists are substantially agreed. Professor Le Gros Clark said at the end of his broadcast: "No more than the physiologist is the anatomist able even to suggest how the physico-chemical phenomena associated with the passage of nervous impulses from one part of the brain to another can be translated into a mental experience." Dr. Penfield compares the mechanism of nerve-cell connections to a telephone switchboard. He asks: "What is the real relationship of this mechanism to the mind?" He says that "there is a difference between automatic action and voluntary action: . . . that something else finds its dwelling-place between the sensory complex and the motor mechanism, that there is a switchboard operator as well as a switchboard."* Sir Charles Sherrington has written elsewhere, "That our being should consist of *two* fundamental elements offers, I suppose, no greater inherent improbability than that it should rest on one only." Again, "We have to regard the relation of mind to brain as still not merely unsolved, but still devoid of a basis for its very beginning." And he has ended his stimulating contribution to the present discussion by saying, "Aristotle, 2,000 years ago, was asking how is the mind attached to the body? We are asking that question still."

* W. Russell Brain, LeGros Clark and Wilder Penfield were earlier speakers in the same series. (Ed.)

That, it seems, is where we are now at a standstill. Until science and philosophy can help us to move on from that position we cannot hope that the universe will, for us, be rationalized.

A. J. Ayer

I wonder if Lord Samuel has made it completely clear exactly what the problem is that the philosophers are here called upon to solve? The scientists who have spoken in this series have shown very fully and convincingly how various mental processes—thinking, feeling, perceiving, remembering—are causally dependent upon processes in the brain, but to some of them at least the character of this connection still appears mysterious. Thus, Sir Charles Sherrington remarks that "it is a far cry from an electrical reaction in the brain to suddenly seeing the world around one, with all its distances, colours, and chiaroscuro"; and Professor Adrian confesses to the same "misgivings" when he says that "the part of the picture of the brain which may always be missing is of course the part which deals with the mind, the part which ought to explain how a particular pattern of nerve impulses can produce an idea; or the other way round, how a thought can decide which nerve cells are to come into action."

If this is a genuine problem, it is hard to see why further information about the brain should be expected to solve it. For however much we amplify our picture of the brain, it remains still a picture of something physical, and it is just the question how anything physical can interact with something that is not that is supposed to constitute our difficulty. If what we are seeking is a bridge across a seemingly impassable river, it will not help us merely to elevate one of the banks. It looks, indeed, as if some of the previous speakers were hoping to discover in the brain something describable as the locus of the mind; as if mind and brain could be conceived as meeting at a point in space or as somehow shading into one another: but to me this is not even an intelligible hypothesis. What would it be like to come upon this junction? By what signs would you recognize it if you found it? Descartes had the same problem, and he met it by suggesting that mind and body came together in the pineal gland; but how this conjecture could conceivably be tested he did not explain. The reason he had the problem—the reason why we have it still—is that matter and mind were conceived by him from the outset as distinct orders of being; it is as if there were two separate worlds, such that every event had to belong to one or other of them, but no event could belong to both. But from these premisses it follows necessarily that there can be no bridge or junction; for what would the bridge consist of? Any event that you discovered would have to fall on one or other side of it. So, if there is a difficulty here, it is not because our factual information is scanty, but because our logic is defective. Perhaps this whole manner of conceiving the distinction between mind and matter is at fault. In short, our problem is not scientific but philosophical.

Let us consider, then, what can be meant by saying that a particular pattern of nerve impulses "produces" an idea, or that "a thought decides" which nerve cells are to come into action. What are the facts on which such assertions are based? The facts are that the physiologist makes certain observations, and that these observations fall into different categories. On the one hand there are the observations which lead him to tell his story about nerve cells and electrical impulses. That is to say, the story is an interpretation of the observations in question. On the other hand there are the observations which he interprets by saying that the subject of his experiment is in such and such a "mental" state, that he is thinking, or resolving to perform some action, or feeling some sensation, or whatever it may be. It is then found to be the case that these two sorts of observations can be correlated with one another; that whenever an observation of the first type can be made, there is good reason to suppose that an observation of the second type can be made also. For example, when the scientists make observations which they interpret by saying that such and such nerve cells are undergoing such and such electrical disturbances, they can also make observations which are interpreted by saying that the subject is having sensations of a certain type. Again, when they are able to make such observations as are interpreted by saying that the subject is resolving to perform some action, they can also make further observations which are interpreted by saying that certain impulses are passing through certain of his nerve fibres. It seems to me that when it is asserted that the two events in question—the mental and the physical—are causally connected, that the pattern of nerve impulses "produces" the sensation, or that the thought "decides" which nerve cells are to operate, all that is meant, or at least all that can properly be meant, is that these two sets of observations are correlated in the way that I have described. But if this is so, where is the difficulty? There is nothing especially mysterious about the fact that two different sets of observations are correlated; that, given the appropriate conditions, they habitually accompany one another. You may say that this fact requires an explanation; but such an explanation could only be some theory from which the fact of this correlation could be deduced. And in so far as the theory was not a mere redescription of the facts which it was intended to explain, it would serve only to fit them into a wider context. We should learn from it that not only were these observations correlated, but certain further types of observations were correlated with them. To ask *why* something occurs, if it is not simply equivalent to asking *how* it occurs, is to ask what other things are associated with it. Once the facts are fully described, there is no mystery left.

If there seems to be a mystery in this case, it is because we are misled by our conceptual systems; not by the facts themselves but by the pictures which we use to interpret the facts. The physiologist's story is complete in itself. The characters that figure in it are nerve cells, electrical impulses, and so forth. It has no place for an entirely different cast, of sensations, thoughts, feelings, and the other *personae* of the mental play. And just because it has no place for them they do not intervene in it. The muddle arises from trying to make them intervene, as I am afraid Lord Samuel does. We then get a confused, indeed an unintelligible, story of electrical impulses being transmuted into sensations, or of mental processes interleaved with disturbances of the nervous cells. The picture we are given is that of messengers travelling through the brain, reaching a mysterious entity called the mind, receiving orders from it, and then travelling on. But since the mind has no position in space—it is by definition not the sort of thing that can have a position in space—it does not literally make sense to talk of physical signals reaching it; nor are there such temporal gaps in the procession of nervous impulses as would leave room for the mental characters to intervene. In short, the two stories will not mix. It is like trying to play *Hamlet,* not without the Prince of Denmark, but with Pericles, the Prince of Tyre. But to say that the two stories will not mix is not to say that either of them is superfluous. Each is an interpretation of certain phenomena and they are connected by the fact that, in certain conditions, when one of them is true, the other is true also.

My conclusion is, then, that mind and body are not to be conceived as two disparate entities between which we have to make, or find, some sort of amphibious bridge, but that talking about minds and talking about bodies are different ways of classifying and interpreting our experiences. I do not say that this procedure does not give rise to serious philosophical problems; how, for example, to analyse statements about the thoughts and feelings of others; or how far statements about people's so-called mental processes are equivalent to statements about their observable behaviour. But once we are freed from the Cartesian fallacy of regarding minds as immaterial substances, I do not think that the discovery of causal connections between what we choose to describe respectively as mental and physical occurrences implies anything by which we need to be perplexed.

Gilbert Ryle

The story is told of some peasants who were terrified at the sight of their first railway-train. Their pastor therefore gave them a lecture explaining how a steam-engine works. One of the peasants then said, "Yes, pastor, we quite understand what you say about the steam-engine. But there is really a horse inside, isn't there?" So used were they to horse-drawn carts that they could not take in the idea that some vehicles propel themselves.

We might invent a sequel. The peasants examined the engine and peeped into every crevice of it. They then said, "Certainly we cannot see, feel, or hear a horse there. We are foiled. But we know there is a horse there, so it must be a ghost-horse which, like the fairies, hides from mortal eyes."

The pastor objected, "But, after all, horses themselves are made of moving parts, just as the steam-engine is made of moving parts. You know what their muscles, joints, and blood-vessels do. So why is there a mystery in the self-propulsion of a steam-engine, if there is none in that of a horse? What do you think makes the horse's hooves go to and fro?" After a pause a peasant replied, "What makes the horse's hooves go is four extra little ghost-horses inside."

Poor simple-minded peasants! Yet just such a story has been the official theory of the mind for the last three very scientific centuries. Several, though not all, of the scientists in this series have automatically posed their problem in this very way. I think that Lord Samuel still accepts the whole story, and that Professor Ayer would like to reject it, but does not see how to do so. For the general terms in which the scientists have set their problem of mind and body, we philosophers have been chiefly to blame, though we have been obsessed, not by the rustic idea of horses, but by the newer idea of mechanical contrivances. The legend that we have told and sold runs like this. A person consists of two theatres, one bodily and one non-bodily. In his Theatre A go on the incidents which we can explore by eye and instrument. But a person also incorporates a second theatre, Theatre B. Here there go on incidents which are totally unlike, though synchronized with those that go on in Theatre A. These Theatre B episodes are changes in the states, not of bits of flesh, but of something called "consciousness," which occupies no space. Only the proprietor of Theatre B has first-hand knowledge of what goes on in it. It is a secret theatre. The experimentalist tries to open its doors, but it has no doors. He tries to peep through its windows, but it has no windows. He is foiled.

We tend nowadays to treat it as obvious that a person, unlike a newt, lives the two lives, life "A" and life "B," each completely unlike, though mysteriously geared to the other. Ingrained hypotheses do feel obvious, however redundant they may be. The peasants in my story correctly thought that a steam-engine was hugely different from a cart and automatically but incorrectly explained the difference by postulating a ghost-horse inside. So most of us, correctly thinking that there are huge differences between a clock and a person, automatically but incorrectly explain these differences by postulating an extra set of ghost-works inside. We correctly say that people are not like clocks, since people meditate, calculate, and invent things; they make plans, dream dreams, and shirk their obligations; they get angry, feel depressed, scan the heavens, and have likes and dislikes; they work, play, and idle; they are sane, crazy, or imbecile; they are skilful at some things and bunglers at others. Where we go wrong is in explaining these familiar actions and conditions as the operations of a secondary set of secret works.

Everybody knows quite well when to describe someone as acting absent-mindedly or with heed, as babbling deliriously or reasoning coherently, as feeling angry but not showing it, as wanting one thing but pretending to want another, as being ambitious, patriotic, or miserly. We often get our accounts and estimates of other people and of ourselves wrong; but we more often get them right. We did not need to learn the legend of the two theatres before we were able to talk sense about people and to deal effectively with them. Nor has this fairly new-fangled legend helped us to do it better.

When we read novels, biographies, and reminiscences, we do not find the chapters partitioned into Section "A," covering the hero's "bodily" doings, and Section "B," covering his "mental" doings. We find unpartitioned accounts of what he did and thought and felt, of what he said to others and to himself, of the mountains he tried to climb and the problems he tried to solve. Should an examiner mark the paper written by the candidate's hand but refuse to assess the candidate's wits? Theorists themselves, when actually describing people, sensibly forget Theatre A and Theatre B. Sir Charles Sherrington paid a well-deserved compliment to Professor Adrian, but he did not pay one cool compliment to Professor Adrian "A" and another warmer compliment to Professor Adrian "B."*

In saying that a person is not to be described as a mind coupled with a body I am not saying, with some truculent thinkers, that people are just machines. Nor are engines just wagons or live bodies just corpses. What is wrong with the story of the two theatres is not that it reports differences which are not there but that it misrepresents differences which are there. It is a story with the right characters but the wrong plot. It is an attempt to explain a genuine difference—or rather a galaxy of differences—but its effect, like that of the peasants' theory, is merely to reduplicate the thing to be explained. It says, "The difference between a machine like a human body on the one hand and a human being on the other is that in a human being, besides the organs which we do see, there is a counterpart set of organs which we do not see; besides the causes and effects which we can witness, there is a counterpart series of causes and effects which we cannot witness." So now we ask, "But what explains the differences between what goes on in the Theatre B of a sane man and what goes on in that of a lunatic? A third theatre, Theatre C?"

No, what prevents us from examining Theatre B is not that it has no doors or windows, but that there is no such theatre. What prevented the peasants from finding the horse was not that it was a ghost-horse, but that there was no horse. Nonetheless, the engine *was* different from a wagon and ordinary people *are* different not only from machines, but also from animals, imbeciles, infants, and corpses. They also differ in countless important ways from one another. I have not begun to show how we should grade these differences. I have only shown how we should not grade them.

One last word. In ordinary life (save when we want to sound knowing) we seldom use the noun "Mind" or the adjective "mental" at all. What we do is to talk of people, of people calculating, conjuring, hoping, resolving, tasting, bluffing, fretting, and so on. Nor, in ordinary life, do we talk of "Matter" or of things being "material." What we do is to talk of steel, granite,

* The reference here is to Sir Charles Sherrington and E. D. Adrian who had given earlier talks in the same series. (Ed.)

and water; of wood, moss, and grain; of flesh, bone, and sinew. The umbrella-titles "Mind" and "Matter" obliterate the very differences that ought to interest us. Theorists should drop both these words. "Mind" and "Matter" are echoes from the hustings of philosophy and prejudice the solutions of all problems posed in terms of them.

21   Sensations and

Brain Processes

J. J. C. Smart

THIS PAPER TAKES ITS DEPARTURE
from arguments to be found in U. T. Place's "Is Consciousness a Brain
Process?"[1] I have had the benefit of discussing Place's thesis in a good
many universities in the United States and Australia, and I hope that the
present paper answers objections to his thesis which Place has not considered and that it presents his thesis in a more nearly unobjectionable
form. This paper is meant also to supplement the paper "The 'Mental'
and the 'Physical,' " by H. Feigl,[2] which in part argues for a similar thesis
to Place's.

Suppose that I report that I have at this moment a roundish blurry-
edged after-image which is yellowish towards its edge and is orange towards
its center. What is it that I am reporting? One answer to this question
might be that I am not reporting anything, that when I say that it looks
to me as though there is a roundish yellowy-orange patch of light on the
wall I am expressing some sort of *temptation,* the temptation to say that
there *is* a roundish yellowy-orange patch on the wall (though I may
know that there is not such a patch on the wall). This is perhaps Wittgenstein's view in the *Philosophical Investigations* (see §§ 367, 370). Similarly, when I "report" a pain, I am not really reporting anything (or, if
you like, I am reporting in a queer sense of "reporting"), but am doing
a sophisticated sort of wince. (See § 244: "The verbal expression of pain
replaces crying and does not describe it." Nor does it describe anything

---

[The article from which this selection is taken first appeared in *The Philosophical Review,* 1959. It is reprinted with the kind permission of author and editor.]

1. *British Journal of Psychology,* XLVII (1956), pp. 44–50; reprinted in A. Flew (ed.),
Body, Mind and Death (New York: Macmillan, 1964).

2. *Minnesota Studies in the Philosophy of Science,* Vol. II (Minneapolis: University of
Minnesota Press, 1958), pp. 370–497.

else?)[3] I prefer most of the time to discuss an after-image rather than a pain, because the word "pain" brings in something which is irrelevant to my purpose: the notion of "distress." I think that "he is in pain" entails "he is in distress," that is, that he is in a certain agitation-condition.[4] Similarly, to say "I am in pain" may be to do more than "replace pain behavior": it may be partly to report something, though this something is quite nonmysterious, being an agitation-condition, and so susceptible of behavioristic analysis. The suggestion I wish if possible to avoid is a different one, namely that "I am in pain" is a genuine report, and that what it reports is an irreducibly psychical something. And similarly the suggestion I wish to resist is also that to say "I have a yellowish-orange after-image" is to report something irreducibly psychical.

Why do I wish to resist this suggestion? Mainly because of Occam's razor. It seems to me that science is increasingly giving us a viewpoint whereby organisms are able to be seen as physicochemical mechanisms:[5] it seems that even the behavior of man himself will one day be explicable in mechanistic terms. There does seem to be, so far as science is concerned, nothing in the world but increasingly complex arrangements of physical constituents. All except for one place: in consciousness. That is, for a full description of what is going on in a man you would have to mention not only the physical processes in his tissues, glands, nervous system, and so forth, but also his states of consciousness: his visual, auditory, and tactual sensations, his aches and pains. That these should be *correlated* with brain processes does not help, for to say that they are *correlated* is to say that they are something "over and above." You cannot correlate something with itself. You correlate footprints with burglars, but not Bill Sikes the burglar with Bill Sikes the burglar. So sensations, states of consciousness, do seem to be the one sort of thing left outside the physicalist picture, and for various reasons I just cannot believe that this can be so. That everything should be explicable in terms of physics (together of course with descriptions of the ways in which the parts are put together—roughly, biology is to physics as radio-engineering is to electromagnetism) except the occurrence of sensations seems to me to be frankly unbelievable. Such sensations would be "nomological danglers," to use Feigl's expression.[6] . . . If any philosoph-

3. Some philosophers of my acquaintance, who have the advantage over me in having known Wittgenstein, would say that this interpretation of him is too behavioristic. However, it seems to me a very natural interpretation of his printed words, and whether or not it is Wittgenstein's real view it is certainly an interesting and important one. I wish to consider it here as a possible rival both to the "brain-process" thesis and to straight-out old-fashioned dualism.

4. See Ryle, *The Concept of Mind* (London: Hutchinson's University Library, 1949), p. 93.

5. On this point see Paul Oppenheim and Hilary Putnam, "Unity of Science as a Working Hypothesis," in *Minnesota Studies in the Philosophy of Science*, Vol. II (Minneapolis: University of Minnesota Press, 1958), pp. 3–36.

6. Feigl, *op. cit.*, p. 428. Feigl uses the expression "nomological danglers" for the laws whereby the entities dangle: I have used the expression to refer to the dangling entities themselves.

ical arguments seemed to compel us to believe in such things, I would suspect a catch in the argument. In any case it is the object of this paper to show that there are no philosophical arguments which compel us to be dualists.

The above is largely a confession of faith, but it explains why I find Wittgenstein's position (as I construe it) so congenial. For on this view there are, in a sense, no sensations. A man is a vast arrangement of physical particles, but there are not, over and above this, sensations or states of consciousness. There are just behavioral facts about this vast mechanism, such as that it expresses a temptation (behavior disposition) to say "there is a yellowish-red patch on the wall" or that it goes through a sophisticated sort of wince, that is, says "I am in pain." Admittedly Wittgenstein says that though the sensation "is not a something," it is nevertheless "not a nothing either" (§ 304), but this need only mean that the word "ache" has a use. An ache is a thing, but only in the innocuous sense in which the plain man, in the first paragraph of Frege's *Foundations of Arithmetic,* answers the question "What is the number one?" by "a thing." It should be noted that when I assert that to say "I have a yellowish-orange after-image" is to express a temptation to assert the physical-object statement "There is a yellowish-orange patch on the wall," I mean that saying "I have a yellowish-orange after-image" is (partly) the exercise of the disposition[7] which is the temptation. It is not to *report* that I have the temptation, any more than is "I love you" normally a report that I love someone. Saying "I love you" is just part of the behavior which is the exercise of the disposition of loving someone.

Though for the reasons given above, I am very receptive to the above "expressive" account of sensation statements, I do not feel that it will quite do the trick. Maybe this is because I have not thought it out sufficiently, but it does seem to me as though, when a person says "I have an after-image," he *is* making a genuine report, and that when he says "I have a pain," he *is* doing more than "replace pain-behavior," and that "this more" is not just to say that he is in distress. I am not so sure, however, that to admit this is to admit that there are nonphysical correlates of brain processes. Why should not sensations just be brain processes of a certain sort? There are, of course, well-known (as well as lesser-known) philosophical objections to the view that reports of sensations are reports of brain-processes, but I shall try to argue that these arguments are by no means as cogent as is commonly thought to be the case.

Let me first try to state more accurately the thesis that sensations are

7. Wittgenstein did not like the word "disposition." I am using it to put in a nutshell (and perhaps inaccurately) the view which I am attributing to Wittgenstein. I should like to repeat that I do not wish to claim that my interpretation of Wittgenstein is correct. Some of those who knew him do not interpret him in this way. It is merely a view which I find myself extracting from his printed words and which I think is important and worth discussing for its own sake.

brain-processes. It is not the thesis that, for example, "after-image" or "ache" means the same as "brain process of sort X" (where "X" is replaced by a description of a certain sort of brain process). It is that, in so far as "after-image" or "ache" is a report of a process, it is a report of a process that *happens to be* a brain process. It follows that the thesis does not claim that sensation statements can be *translated* into statements about brain processes. Nor does it claim that the logic of a sensation statement is the same as that of a brain-process statement. All it claims is that in so far as a sensation statement is a report of something, that something is in fact a brain process. Sensations are nothing over and above brain processes. Nations are nothing "over and above" citizens, but this does not prevent the logic of nation statements being very different from the logic of citizen statements, nor does it insure the translatability of nation statements into citizen statements. (I do not, however, wish to assert that the relation of sensation statements to brain-process statements is very like that of nation statements to citizen statements. Nations do not just *happen to be* nothing over and above citizens, for example. I bring in the "nations" example merely to make a negative point: that the fact that the logic of A-statements is different from that of B-statements does not insure that A's are anything over and above B's.)

When I say that a sensation is a brain process or that lightning is an electric discharge, I am using "is" in the sense of strict identity. (Just as in the—in this case necessary—proposition "7 is identical with the smallest prime number greater than 5.") When I say that a sensation is a brain process or that lightning is an electric discharge I do not mean just that the sensation is somehow spatially or temporally continuous with the brain process or that the lightning is just spatially or temporally continuous with the discharge. When on the other hand I say that the successful general is the same person as the small boy who stole the apples I mean only that the successful general I see before me is a time slice[8] of the same four-dimensional object of which the small boy stealing apples is an earlier time slice. However, the four-dimensional object which has the general-I-see-before-me for its late time slice is identical in the strict sense with the four-dimensional object which has the small-boy-stealing-apples for an early time slice. I distinguish these two senses of "is identical with" because I wish to make it clear that the brain-process doctrine asserts identity in the *strict* sense.

I shall now discuss various possible objections to the view that the processes reported in sensation statements are in fact processes in the brain. Most of us have met some of these objections in our first year as

8. See J. H. Woodger, *Theory Construction*, International Encyclopedia of Unified Science, II, No. 5 (Chicago: University of Chicago Press, 1939), p. 38. I here permit myself to speak loosely. For warnings against possible ways of going wrong with this sort of talk, see my note "Spatialising Time," *Mind* (1955), pp. 239–41.

philosophy students. All the more reason to take a good look at them. Others of the objections will be more recondite and subtle.

Objection 1. Any illiterate peasant can talk perfectly well about his after-images, or how things look or feel to him, or about his aches and pains, and yet he may know nothing whatever about neurophysiology. A man may, like Aristotle, believe that the brain is an organ for cooling the body without any impairment of his ability to make true statements about his sensations. Hence the things we are talking about when we describe our sensations cannot be processes in the brain.

Reply. You might as well say that a nation of slugabeds, who never saw the Morning Star or knew of its existence, or who had never thought of the expression "the Morning Star," but who used the expression "the Evening Star" perfectly well, could not use this expression to refer to the same entity as we refer to (and describe as) "the Morning Star."

You may object that the Morning Star is in a sense not the very same thing as the Evening Star, but only something spatiotemporally continuous with it. That is, you may say that the Morning Star is not the Evening Star in the strict sense of "identity" that I distinguished earlier.

There is, however, a more plausible example. Consider lightning. Modern physical science tells us that lightning is a certain kind of electrical discharge due to ionization of clouds of water vapor in the atmosphere. This, it is now believed, is what the true nature of lightning is. Note that there are not two things: a flash of lightning and an electrical discharge. There is one thing, a flash of lightning, which is described scientifically as an electrical discharge to the earth from a cloud of ionized water molecules. The case is not at all like that of explaining a footprint by reference to a burglar. We say that what lightning really is, what its true nature as revealed by science is, is an electrical discharge. (It is not the true nature of a footprint to be a burglar.)

To forestall irrelevant objections, I should like to make it clear that by "lightning" I mean the publicly observable physical object, lightning, not a visual sense-datum of lightning. I say that the publicly observable physical object lightning is in fact the electrical discharge, not just a correlate.of it. The sense-datum, or rather the having of the sense-datum, the "look" of lightning, may well in my view be a correlate of the electrical discharge. For in my view it is a brain state *caused* by the lightning. But we should no more confuse sensations of lightning with lightning than we confuse sensations of a table with the table.

In short, the reply to Objection 1 is that there can be contingent statements of the form "A is identical with B," and a person may well know that something is an A without knowing that it is a B. An illiterate peasant might well be able to talk about his sensations without knowing about his brain processes, just as he can talk about lightning though he knows nothing of electricity.

Objection 2. It is only a contingent fact (if it is a fact) that when we have a certain kind of sensation there is a certain kind of process in our brain. Indeed it is possible, though perhaps in the highest degree unlikely, that our present physiological theories will be as out of date as the ancient theory connecting mental processes with goings on in the heart. It follows that when we report a sensation we are not reporting a brain-process.

Reply. The objection certainly proves that when we say "I have an after-image" we cannot *mean* something of the form "I have such and such a brain-process." But this does not show that what we report (having an after-image) is not *in fact* a brain process. "I see lightning" does not *mean* "I see an electrical discharge." Indeed, it is logically possible (though highly unlikely) that the electrical discharge account of lightning might one day be given up. Again, "I see the Evening Star" does not *mean* the same as "I see the Morning Star," and yet "The Evening Star and the Morning Star are one and the same thing" is a contingent proposition. Possibly Objection 2 derives some of its apparent strength from a "Fido"–Fido theory of meaning. If the meaning of an expression were what the expression named, then of course it *would* follow from the fact that "sensation" and "brain-process" have different meanings that they cannot name one and the same thing.

. . . *Objection 4*. The after-image is not in physical space. The brain-process is. So the after-image is not a brain-process.

Reply. This is an *ignoratio elenchi*. I am not arguing that the after-image is a brain-process, but that the experience of having an after-image is a brain-process. It is the *experience* which is reported in the introspective report. Similarly, if it is objected that the after-image is yellowy-orange, my reply is that it is the experience of seeing yellowy-orange that is being described, and this experience is not a yellowy-orange something. So to say that a brain-process cannot be yellowy-orange is not to say that a brain-process cannot in fact be the experience of having a yellowy-orange after-image. There is, in a sense, no such thing as an after-image or a sense-datum, though there is such a thing as the experience of having an image, and this experience is described indirectly in material object language, not in phenomenal language, for there is no such thing.[9] We describe the experience by saying, in effect, that it is like the experience we have when, for example, we really see a yellowy-orange patch on the wall. Trees and wallpaper can be green, but not the

9. Dr. J. R. Smythies claims that a sense-datum language could be taught independently of the material object language ("A Note on the Fallacy of the 'Phenomenological Fallacy,' " *British Journal of Psychology*, XLVIII [1957], pp. 141–44). I am not so sure of this: there must be some public criteria for a person having got a rule wrong before we can teach him the rule. I suppose someone might *accidentally* learn color words by Dr. Smythies' procedure. I am not, of course, denying that we can learn a sense-datum language in the sense that we can learn to report our experience. Nor would Place deny it.

experience of seeing or imagining a tree or wallpaper. (Or if they are described as green or yellow this can only be in a derived sense.)

Objection 5. It would make sense to say of a molecular movement in the brain that it is swift or slow, straight or circular, but it makes no sense to say this of the experience of seeing something yellow.

Reply. So far we have not given sense to talk of experience as swift or slow, straight or circular. But I am not claiming that "experience" and "brain-process" mean the same or even that they have the same logic. "Somebody" and "the doctor" do not have the same logic, but this does not lead us to suppose that talking about somebody telephoning is talking about someone over and above, say, the doctor. The ordinary man when he reports an experience is reporting that something is going on, but he leaves it open as to what sort of thing is going on, whether in a material solid medium or perhaps in some sort of gaseous medium, or even perhaps in some sort of nonspatial medium (if this makes sense). All that I am saying is that "experience" and "brain-process" may in fact refer to the same thing, and if so we may easily adopt a convention (which is not a change in our present rules for the use of experience words but an addition to them) whereby it would make sense to talk of an experience in terms appropriate to physical processes.

Objection 6. Sensations are private, brain-processes are *public.* If I sincerely say, "I see a yellowish-orange after-image," and I am not making a verbal mistake, then I cannot be wrong. But I can be wrong about a brain-process. The scientist looking into my brain might be having an illusion. Moreover, it makes sense to say that two or more people are observing the same brain-process but not that two or more people are reporting the same inner experience.

Reply. This shows that the language of introspective reports has a different logic from the language of material processes. It is obvious that until the brain-process theory is much improved and widely accepted there will be no *criteria* for saying "Smith has an experience of such-and-such a sort" *except* Smith's introspective reports. So we have adopted a rule of language that (normally) what Smith says goes.

Objection 7. I can imagine myself turned to stone and yet having images, aches, pains, and so on.

Reply. I can imagine that the electrical theory of lightning is false, that lightning is some sort of purely optical phenomenon. I can imagine that lightning is not an electrical discharge. I can imagine that the Evening Star is not the Morning Star. But it is. All the objection shows is that "experience" and "brain-process" do not have the same meaning. It does not show that an experience is not in fact a brain process.

. . . I have now considered a number of objections to the brain-process thesis. I wish to conclude with some remarks on the logical status of the thesis itself. U. T. Place seems to hold that it is a straight-out scientific hypothesis.[10] If so, he is partly right and partly wrong. If the issue is between (say) a brain-process thesis and a heart thesis, or a liver thesis, or a kidney thesis, then the issue is a purely empirical one, and the verdict is overwhelmingly in favor of the brain. The right sorts of things don't go on in the heart, liver, or kidney, nor do these organs possess the right sort of complexity of structure. On the other hand, if the issue is between a brain-or-liver-or-kidney thesis (that is, some form of materialism) on the one hand and epiphenomenalism on the other hand, then the issue is not an empirical one. For there is no conceivable experiment which could decide between materialism and epiphenomenalism. This latter issue is not like the average straight-out empirical issue in science, but like the issue between the nineteenth-century English naturalist Philip Gosse and the orthodox geologists and paleontologists of his day. According to Gosse, the earth was created about 4000 B.C. exactly as described in *Genesis,* with twisted rock strata, "evidence" of erosion, and so forth, and all sorts of fossils, all in their appropriate strata, just as if the usual evolutionist story had been true. Clearly this theory is in a sense irrefutable: no evidence can possibly tell against it. Let us ignore the theological setting in which Philip Gosse's hypothesis had been placed, thus ruling out objections of a theological kind, such as "what a queer God who would go to such elaborate lengths to deceive us." Let us suppose that it is held that the universe just *began* in 4004 B.C. with the initial conditions just everywhere as they were in 4004 B.C., and in particular that our own planet began with sediment in the rivers, eroded cliffs, fossils in the rocks, and so on. No scientist would ever entertain this as a serious hypothesis, consistent though it is with all possible evidence. The hypothesis offends against the principles of parsimony and simplicity. There would be far too many brute and inexplicable facts. Why are pterodactyl bones just as they are? No explanation in terms of the evolution of pterodactyls from earlier forms of life would any longer be possible. We would have millions of facts about the world as it was in 4004 B.C. that just have to be *accepted.*

The issue between the brain-process theory and epiphenomenalism seems to be of the above sort. (Assuming that a behavioristic reduction of introspective reports is not possible.) If it be agreed that there are no cogent philosophical arguments which force us into accepting dualism, and if the brain process theory and dualism are equally consistent with the facts, then the principles of parsimony and simplicity seem to me to

10. *Op. cit.* For a further discussion of this, in reply to the original version of the present paper, see Place's note "Materialism as a Scientific Hypothesis," *Philosophical Review,* LXIX (1960), pp. 101–4.

decide overwhelmingly in favor of the brain-process theory. As I pointed out earlier, dualism involves a large number of irreducible psycho-physical laws (whereby the "nomological danglers" dangle) of a queer sort, that just have to be taken on trust, and are just as difficult to swallow as the irreducible facts about the paleontology of the earth with which we are faced on Philip Gosse's theory.

22 Ten Reasons for
Believing in Immortality

John Haynes Holmes

Nobody can speak on the immortality of the soul at this late date without being acutely conscious of the fact that there is nothing new that can be said. Since the time of Plato, at least, five hundred years before the birth of Jesus, the discussion of immortality has been conducted by the greatest minds upon the highest levels of human thought. Theology, philosophy, psychology and science have all been called upon to make their contributions to the theme. Poetry has offered its voice and religion its faith, with the result that every corner of knowledge has been explored, every depth of truth uncovered and revealed! There is always the possibility, of course, that the veil which hangs over every grave to divide this life from the mystery that lies beyond, may some day be lifted to our gaze. There are those who claim—not without some reason, it seems to me—that they have penetrated this veil, and thus have looked upon the reality of survival after death. But short of some such remarkable discovery as this, there is nothing new to be anticipated in this field. Everything has been said that can be said. The case for immortality is in!

Now it is this case which I want to present to you this morning. Since I cannot hope to say anything that is new, I want to see what I can do in the way of saying something that is old. I cannot say much, to be sure, for no discourse however merciless in length, can compass the range and beauty of the argument for immortality. But since ten is a goodly number, I take ten of the reasons which have brought conviction to the minds of men and offer these as the case for immortality today. I trust that it may be interesting, and also persuasive, especially to the members of our younger

[This essay was first delivered as a sermon at the Community Church in 1929 and published in the *Community Pulpit* for 1929–1930. It is here reprinted with the kind permission of the late Dr. Holmes.]

generation, to be reminded of what has been thought upon this question for many years.

By way of introduction, may I make mention of some two or three reasons for believing in immortality which do not concern me. I speak of these not because they are important, but because some of you may wonder, if I am silent, why they do not appear in my list of ten.

Thus I do not see any reason for believing in immortality because Jesus is reputed to have risen from the dead. In the first place, I do not believe that he rose from the dead. There is no evidence to substantiate this miracle. In the second place, even if he did break the barriers of the tomb, I fail to see what the resurrection of the body has to do with the immortality of the soul. The two things are irrelevant, the one to the other. What we have here is one of the myths of Christianity which, even if it were true, would have nothing seriously to do with our question.

Again, I find no argument for immortality in the succession of the seasons, the revival of nature in the spring, the blossoming of the flowers after the winter's cold. Poets are fond of this idea, as Shelley, for example, when he wrote his famous line,

> If winter comes, can spring be far behind?

I think we may see in it a pretty parable, a rather beautiful poetic concept. But as an argument for immortality, it is what Ruskin called an instance of the "pathetic fallacy." The flowers that blossom in the spring are not the flowers that died the preceding autumn. The tide of life that flows on through nature, season after season, is the same tide that flows on through humanity, generation after generation, and it touches as little in the one case as in the other the survival of the individual. Like most parables, this does not hold when applied rigorously to the issue that is involved.

Again, I must confess that I am not convinced by the argument that men must be immortal because the heart demands it. It is natural that we should cling to those we love. It is inevitable that we should believe that providence, if it be beneficent, must give answer to our plea that we have not permanently separated from our friends and kindred. Whittier was yielding to the deepest impulses of the soul when he suggested in his "Snow Bound" that "Life is ever Lord of Death," because "Love can never lose its own." This is the cry of the human heart, and I personally believe that it is not destined to go unanswered. But a longing is one thing, and a reason is another. I see no evidence, in the scheme of things, that what we want we are therefore going to have. On the contrary, Felix Adler has taught us that frustration is the basic principle of life, that experience is "permeated with the sense of incompleteness," and that this "sense of in-completeness" is a perpetual doom that is laid upon us as "a necessary instrument of spiritual development." Whether this be true or not I do not know, but in either case I still believe that love gives no guarantee of its own survival.

But there are arguments for immortality which seem to suggest that it is true. Surveying all the field, I find myself agreeing with William James that, while we are under no compulsion to believe in immortality, as we are under a compulsion, for example, to believe that "things equal to the same thing are equal to each other," yet we are free to believe, if we so desire, without being guilty of superstition. "You may believe henceforward," said Professor James, "whether you care to profit by the permission or not." There are perfectly good and sufficient reasons, in other words, why an intelligent man may intelligently believe in immortality. Ten of these reasons I propose to submit to you this morning, beginning with those which open up the question, so to speak, and ending with those which close it as a conviction of the soul.

(1) First of all, may I offer the suggestion, not important in itself and yet of real significance to the thinking mind, that we may believe in immortality because there is no reason for *not* believing in it. In discussions of this question we are constantly reminded that immortality has never been proved. To which there is the immediate and inevitable reply that immortality has never been disproved! As there is no positive testimony to prove it true, so is there no negative testimony to prove it untrue. What we have here is an absence of testimony, and such "absence of testimony," says John Fiske, "does not even raise a negative presumption, except in cases where testimony is accessible." In this case, testimony is not accessible. Therefore the question is open "for those general considerations of philosophic analogy and moral probability which are the grounds upon which we can call for help in this arduous inquiry." As the question is open, so must our minds be open. My first reason, therefore, for believing in immortality or for being ready to believe in immortality, is the primarily interesting fact that there is no reason for not believing in immortality. My mind is absolutely at one with that of John Stuart Mill when he said upon his question, "To anyone who feels it conducive either to his satisfaction or to his usefulness to hope for a future state, . . . there is no hindrance to his indulging that hope."

(2) My second reason for believing in immortality is to be found in the universality of the idea. In saying this, I am not seeking to substantiate my position by taking a majority vote upon the question. I am not arguing that a proposition is necessarily true because most persons have believed it. All too many beliefs have clung pertinaciously to the human mind, only in the end to be revealed as superstitions, and it may very well be that this concept of immortality is one of them.

What I have in mind here is the very different consideration that immortality is not merely a belief to be accepted but an idea to be explained. "Here is this wonderful thought," says Emerson, "Wherever man ripens, this audacious belief presently appears. . . . As soon as thought is exercised, this belief is inevitable. . . . Whence came it? Who put it in the mind?" In itself it is remarkable, this idea that the death of the body is not the extinction of personality. Who has ever looked upon a dead body without marvelling that man has ever thought of survival beyond the grave?

Emerson could not explain the fact, as it has appeared in all ages and among all peoples, except upon the supposition that the thought of immortality is "not sentimental" but "elemental"—elemental in the sense that it is "grounded in the necessities and forces we possess."

That this idea is something more than idle speculation is shown by the whole philosophy of evolution, which has given to us that fundamental interpretation of life as "the continuous adjustment of inner relations to outer relations." An organism lives by successfully adjusting itself to the conditions of its environment, by developing itself inwardly in such a way as to meet the conditions of reality. When we find in plant or animal some inner faculty or attitude which is universally present, and which persists from generation to generation, we may be perfectly sure that it represents some correspondence with reality which has made survival possible. Life, in other words, is so definitely a matter of the successful coordination of inner relations with outer relations, that it is altogether impossible to conceive that in any specific relation the subjective term is real and the objective term is non-existent. What exists within is the sign and symbol, and guarantee, of what exists without.

Now man has never existed without the thought of immortality. From the earliest period of his life upon the earth, he has been profoundly concerned with this idea. He has never been able to live without it; even when he has tried to deny it, he has not been able to get rid of it. The immortal life is part of his being, as a line on the surface of a coin is a part of the pattern of its design. And as the line upon the coin could not have been set there except as the impression of the die which stamped its mark upon the metal, so the idea of immortality could not have appeared within the consciousness of man, except as the impression of the reality which made it what it is. Our faculties, our attributes, our ideas, as we have seen, are the reflection of the environment to which we adapt ourselves as the condition of survival. What we feel within is the reaction upon what exists without. As the eye proves the existence of light, and the ear the existence of sound, so the immortal hope may not unfairly be said to prove the existence of the immortal life. It is this that we mean when we say that the universality of the idea is an argument for the acceptance of the idea. In his great essay on "Immortality," Emerson tells us of two men who early in life spent much of their time together in earnest search for some proof of immortality. An accident separated them, and they did not meet again for a quarter of a century. They said nothing, "but shook hands long and cordially. At last his friend said, 'Any light, Albert?' 'None,' replied Albert. 'Any light, Lewis?' 'None,' he replied." And Emerson comments "that the impulse which drew these two minds to this inquiry through so many years was a better affirmative evidence for immortality than their failure to find a confirmation was a negative."

(3) This universal diffusion of the idea of immortality takes on an added significance when I come to my third reason for believing in immortality. I refer to the fact so memorably stated by Cicero. "There is in the

minds of men," he says, "I know not how, a certain presage, as it were, of a future existence; and this takes deepest root in the greatest geniuses and the most exalted souls." The leaders of the race, in other words, have always believed in immortality. They are not separated in this case, as in so many cases, from the masses of ignorant and superstitious men by doctrines of dissent. On the contrary, in this case the ideas of the highest are at one with the hopes of the humblest among mankind.

In referring thus to the great names that are attached to the idea of immortality, I would not have you believe that I am making any blind appeal to the concept of authority. I have never seen any reason for arbitrarily separating our minds from the companionship of other minds. There is such a thing, even for the independent thinker, as a consensus of best opinion which can not be defied without the weightiest of reasons. And in this matter of immortality there is a consensus of best opinion which constitutes, to my mind, one of the most remarkable phenomena in the whole history of human thinking. I have no time this morning to list the names of those who have believed in the immortality of the soul. If I did so, I should have to include the names of scientists from Aristotle to Darwin and Eddington, of philosophers from Plato to Kant and Bergson, of poets from Sophocles to Goethe and Robert Browning, of ethical teachers and public leaders from Socrates to Tolstoi and Mahatma Gandhi. There are dissenters from the doctrine, like Epictetus yesterday and Bernard Shaw today, but the consensus of opinion the other way is remarkable. Even the famous heretics stand in awe before this conception of eternity. Thus, Voltaire declared that "reason agrees with revelation . . . that the soul is immortal." Thomas Paine affirmed that he did not "trouble (himself) about the manner of future existence," so sure he was that "the Power which gave existence is able to continue it in any form." Even Robert G. Ingersoll confessed, as he stood by his brother's grave, that love could "hear the rustle of an angel's wing." In the light of such testimony as this, are we not justified in believing that there is reason for believing in immortality? If not, then we know, with James Martineau, "who are those who are mistaken. Not the mean and grovelling souls who never reached to so great a thought. . . . No, the deceived are the great and holy, whom all men revere; the men who have lived for something better than their happiness and spent themselves on the altar of human good. Whom are we to reverence, and what can we believe, if the inspirations of the highest nature are but cunningly-devised fables?"

(4) This conviction of immortality as rooted in the minds of men, and the greatest men, brings us immediately to the consideration of human nature itself as evidence for its own survival. Thus, my fourth reason this morning for believing in immortality is found in what I would call man's over-endowment as a creature of this earth, his surplus equipment for the adventure of his present life. If we want to know what is needed for successful existence upon this planet, we have only to look at any animal. His equipment of physical attributes and powers seems perfectly adapted to the

necessities of his natural environment. The outfit of man, on the contrary, seems to constitute something like "a vast over-provision" for his necessities. If this life is all, in other words, what need has man for all these mental faculties, moral aspirations, spiritual ideals, which make him to be distinctly a man as contrasted with the animal? If existence upon the earth is his only destiny, why should man not prefer the swiftness of the deer, the strength of the lion, the vision of the eagle, to any endowment of mind and heart, as more adequate provision for the purely physical task of physical survival in a physical world? What we have here is a fundamental discrepancy between the endowment of man and the life he has to live; and this constitutes, if this life be all, an unparalleled violation of the creative economy of the universe. In every other form of life, an organism is equipped to meet the exactions of its immediate environment. Man is equipped for this environment, and also for something more. Why is this not proof that he is destined for something more? As we estimate the length of the voyage of a ship by the character of its equipment, never confusing a little coasting vessel with a transatlantic liner or an arctic exploration steamer, why should we not estimate the length of man's voyage upon the seas of life in exactly the same way? What man bears within himself is evidence that he is destined for some farther port than any upon these shores. What he is in mind and heart and spirit, in the range of his interests and the lift of his soul, can only be explained on the supposition that he is preparing for another and a vaster life. I believe that man is immortal because already the signs of immortality are upon him.

(5) This consideration is basic, and sums up our whole case for immortality as rooted in human nature. But it opens out into other considerations which may well be taken as other reasons for believing in immortality. Thus, I would specify as my fifth reason for believing in immortality the lack of coordination, or proportion, between a man's body and a man's mind. If these two are to be regarded as aspects of a single organism, adapted only to the conditions of this present life, why do they so early begin to pull apart, and the weakness of the one to retard and at last to defeat the other? For a while, to be sure, there seems to be a real co-ordination between soul and body, between the personality, on the one hand, and the physical frame which it inhabits, on the other. Thus the child is in nothing so delightful as in the fact that it is a perfect animal. Then, as maturity approaches, two exactly opposite processes begin to take place within the life of the human being. On the one hand, the body begins to lose its resiliency and harden, to stop its growth and become static, then to decay and at last to dissolve. There is a definite cycle, in other words, in the physical life of the individual. There is a beginning, then a pause, and then an end. It is from first to last a process of completion. But there is no completion in the life of the soul. "Who dares speak the word 'completed,'" says Professor Munsterberg, the great psychologist. "Do not our purposes grow? Does not every newly-created value give us the desire for further achievement? Is our life ever so completely done that no desire has still a

meaning?" The personality of man is an enduring thing. As the body weakens through the years, so the soul only grows the stronger and more wonderful. As the body approaches irrevocably to its end, so the soul only mounts to what seems to be a new beginning. We come to death, in other words, only to discover within ourselves exhaustless possibilities. The aged have testified again and again to this amazing truth that as the body turns to ashes, the spirit mounts as to a flame. Victor Hugo, protesting against the waning of his powers, said, "For half a century I have been writing my thoughts in prose and verse . . . but I feel that I have not said a thousandth part of what is in me." Said James Martineau, on his 80th birthday, "How small a part of my plans have I been able to carry out! Nothing is so plain as that life at its fullest on earth is but a fragment." Robert Browning catches this thought in his poem, "Cleon," where he makes his hero say,

> . . . Every day my sense of joy
> Grows more acute, my soul . . . enlarged, more keen,
> While every day my hairs fall more and more,
> My hand shakes, and the heavy years increase
> The horror quickening still from year to year,
> When I shall know most, and yet least enjoy.

What to do, in such emergency, except what Cleon did,

> . . . imagine to (our) need
> Some future state . . .

(6) But there is a lack of coordination not only between our personalities and our physical bodies, but also between our personalities and the physical world. This is my sixth reason for believing in immortality— that our souls have potentialities and promises which should not, as indeed they cannot, be subject to the chance vicissitudes of earthly fortune. What are we going to say, for example, when we see some life of eminent utility, of great achievement, of character and beauty and noble dedication to mankind, not merely borne down by the body, but cut off sharply before its time by an automobile accident, a disease germ, a bit of poisoned food? What shall we think when we see a Shelley drowned in his thirtieth year by the heedless sea, a Phillips Brooks stricken in the prime of his manhood by a diphtheric sore-throat, a Captain Scott frozen in mid-career by an accident of weather? Is it possible that these lives of ours are dependent upon a fall of snow, a grain of dust, a passing breeze upon the sea? Is it conceivable that our personalities, with all their potencies of spirit, can be destroyed, as our bodies can be broken, by the material forces of the world? Are we to believe that eternal powers can be annihilated by transient accidents? I cannot think so! Rather must I think, as Professor George Herbert Palmer thought, as he looked upon the dead body of his wife, one of the greatest and most beautiful women of her time, stricken ere her years were ripe. "Though no regrets are proper for the manner of her death," said this noble husband, "yet who can contemplate the fact of it and not

call the world irrational if, out of deference to a few particles of disordered matter, it excludes so fair a spirit?"

(7) But this question of the irrationality of a world which would allow death to exercise mastery over a radiant spirit, has application not merely to the individual but also to the race. This brings me to my seventh reason for believing in immortality—a reason drawn from the logic of evolution. There is nothing more familiar, of course, than the fact that this world is the result of a natural process of development which has been going on for unnumbered millions of years. If this process is rational, as man's processes are rational, it must have been working all these eons of time to the achievement of some permanent and worthy end. What is this end? It is not the physical world itself, for the day must come when this earth will be swallowed up by the sun, and all the universe be merged again into the original fire-mist from which it sprang. It is not the works of man, for these perish even as man lives, and must vanish utterly in the last cataclysm of ruin. It is not man himself, for man, like the earth on which he lives, must finally disappear. Is there nothing that will remain as the evidence and vindication of this cosmic process? Or must we believe that, from the beginning, it has been like a child's tower of blocks built up only to be thrown down?

It was the challenge of this contingency, of evolution coming in the end to naught that moved no less a man than Charles Darwin, agnostic though he was, to proclaim the conviction that "it is an intolerable thought that (man) and all other sentient beings are doomed to complete annihilation after such long-continued slow process." Unless the universe is crazy, something must remain. The process must justify itself by producing something that endures. And what can this thing be but the spiritual essence of man's nature—the soul which is immortal? "The more thoroughly we comprehend the process of evolution," says John Fiske, in an unforgettable statement, "the more we are likely to feel that to deny the everlasting persistence of the spiritual element in man is to rob the whole process of its meaning. It goes far toward putting us to permanent intellectual confusion." Which led him to his famous verdict upon all the evidence: "I believe in the immortality of the soul as a supreme act of faith in the reasonableness of God's work."

(8) This leads us deep into the realm of science—to a fundamental principle that provides my eighth reason for believing in immortality. I refer to the principle of persistence or conservation. The gist of this doctrine is that nothing in the universe is ever lost. All energy is conserved. No matter what changes take place in any particular form of energy, that energy persists, if not in the old form then in a new, and the sum total of energy in the universe remains the same. "Whatever is," says Sir Oliver Lodge, speaking of forms of energy in the physical universe, "whatever is, both was and shall be." And he quotes the famous statement of Professor Tait, that "persistence, or conservation, is the test or criterion of real existence."

Now if this principle applies to the "real existence" of the material world, why not to the "real existence" of the spiritual world as well? If it is impossible to think of physical energy as appearing and disappearing, coming into and going out of existence, why is it not equally impossible to think of intellectual or moral or spiritual energy as acting in this same haphazard fashion? We would laugh at a man who contended that the heat in molten metal, which disappears under the cooling action of air or water, had thereby been destroyed. Why should we not similarly laugh at a man who argues that the personality of a human being, which disappears under the chilling influence of death, has thereby been annihilated? What the personality may be, I do not know. Whether it is a form of energy itself, as some scientists assert, or "belongs to a separate order of existence," as Sir Oliver Lodge, for example, argues, I cannot say. But of this thing I am sure—that the soul of man is just as much a force in the world as magnetism or steam, or electricity, and that if the cosmic law of conservation forbids the destruction of the latter, it must as well forbid the destruction of the former. Anything else is inconceivable. The universe cannot be so thrifty of its physical, and so wasteful of its spiritual, resources. It is madness to conceive that the heat of an engine must be preserved, while the love of a heart may be thrown away. What prevails in the great realm of matter can be only an anticipation of what must equally prevail in the greater realm of spirit. For the universe is one. Its laws are everywhere the same. What science has discovered about the conservation of energy is only the physical equivalent of what religion has discovered about the immortality of the soul.

(9) We are coming now to ultimate things—to those first and last questions of origins and meanings. This brings me to my ninth reason for believing in immortality—the fact, namely, that all the values of life exist in man, and in man alone. For the world as we know it and love it is not the world as we receive it, but the world as we make it by the creative genius of the inward spirit. Consider this earthly scene with man eliminated! The sun would be here, and the stars. Mountains would still lift themselves to the skies, and oceans spread afar to vast horizons. Birds would sing, and leaves rustle, and sunsets glow. But what would it all mean without man to see and hear, to interpret? What do the stars mean to the eagle, or the sea to the porpoise, or the mountain to the goat? It is man's ear which has heard the cuckoo as a "wandering voice," his eye which has seen "the floor of heaven thick inlaid with patines of bright gold," his mind which has found "sermons in stone, books in the running brooks, and good in everything." All that is precious in the world—all its beauty, its wonder, its meaning—exists in man, and by man, and for man. The world is what man has done with it in the far reaches of his soul. And we are asked to believe that the being who sees and glorifies shall perish, while the world which he has seen and glorified endures! Such a conclusion is irrational. The being who created the world must himself be greater than the world. The soul which conceives Truth, Goodness and Beauty, must itself be as

eternal as the Truth, Goodness, and Beauty which it conceives. Nothing has any value without man. Man, therefore, is the supreme value. Which is the essence of the Platonic philosophy of eternal life for man!

"Tell me, then," says Socrates in the "Phaedo," "what is that the inherence of which renders the body alive?

"The soul, Cebes replied . . .

"Then whatever the soul possesses, to that she comes bearing life?

"Yes, certainly.

"And is there any opposite to life?

"There is . . . Death.

"And will the soul . . . ever receive the opposite of what she brings?

"Impossible, replied Cebes.

"Then, said Socrates, the soul is immortal!"

(10) These, now, are my main reasons for believing in immortality. I have but one more, the tenth to add. It is the pragmatic argument that faith in an eternal life beyond the grave justifies itself in terms of the life that we are now living upon this side of the grave. For immortality does not concern the future alone; it concerns, also, the present. We are immortal today, if we are ever going to be immortal tomorrow. And this means that we have the chance to put to the test, even now and here, the belief to which we hold. It is the essence of the pragmatic philosophy that what is true will conduce to life, as food conduces to health, and that what is false will destroy life, as poison the body. Whatever is true enlarges and lifts and strengthens the life of man; whatever is false represses and weakens and disintegrates his life. Now what does immortality do when we put its affirmation to this test? What are the consequences which follow if we live as though we were eternal spirits? Can there be any doubt as to the answer?

We see a universe where spiritual values, not material forces, prevail; where personality, whether in ourselves or in others, is precious, and therefore to be conserved; where principles, not possessions, are the supreme concern of life; where man is equal to his task, and labors not in vain for the high causes of humanity; where sacrifice is not foolish but wise, and love "the greatest thing in the world." The man who lives an immortal life takes on immortal qualities. His character assumes the proportions of his faith, and his work the range of his high destiny. "Immortality makes great living," says Dr. Fosdick. Therefore I believe in immortality.

Ten reasons! Are these all? No, they are not all! They are simply ten of the many reasons for the most persistent faith which has ever beset the heart of man. In choosing these ten, I have sought to gather reasons which were reasons, and not mere superstitions—arguments which appeal to intellect rather than emotion, and which are based upon experience rather than credulity. That these reasons prove the idea of immortality to be true, I cannot claim. But there is many an idea which we accept for good reasons, even though it be not proved, as there is many a verdict in court which is returned for good reasons, even though it be not proved, and immortality is one of them. What impresses me, as I follow the course of this great argument through the ages, is what impressed the mind of James Martineau when he said, "We do not believe immortality because we have proved it, but we forever try to prove it because we believe it." Hence the judgment of the poet, Tennyson—

> O, yet we trust that somehow good
>   Will be the final goal of ill,
>   To pangs of nature, sins of will,
> Defects of doubt, and taints of blood.
>
> That nothing walks with aimless feet;
>   That not one life shall be destroyed,
>   Or cast as rubbish to the void,
> When God hath made the pile complete. . . .
>
> I stretch lame hands of faith, and grope
>   And gather dust and chaff, and call
>   To what I feel is Lord of all,
> And faintly trust the larger hope.

23   The Myth of Immortality

Clarence Darrow

THERE IS, PERHAPS, NO MORE STRIKING example of the credulity of man than the widespread belief in immortality. This idea includes not only the belief that death is not the end of what we call life, but that personal identity involving memory persists beyond the grave. So determined is the ordinary individual to hold fast to this belief that, as a rule, he refuses to read or to think upon the subject lest it cast doubt upon his cherished dream. Of those who may chance to look at this contribution, many will do so with the determination not to be convinced, and will refuse even to consider the manifold reasons that might weaken their faith. I know that this is true, for I know the reluctance with which I long approached the subject and my firm determination not to give up my hope. Thus the myth will stand in the way of a sensible adjustment to facts.

Even many of those who claim to believe in immortality still tell themselves and others that neither side of the question is susceptible of proof. Just what can these hopeful ones believe that the word "proof" involves? The evidence against the persistence of personal consciousness is as strong as the evidence of gravitation, and much more obvious. It is as convincing

[This article originally appeared under the title "The Myth of the Soul" in *The Forum*, October, 1928. It is reprinted here with the kind permission of the Clarence Darrow estate.]

and unassailable as the proof of the destruction of wood or coal by fire. If it is not certain that death ends personal identity and memory, then almost nothing that man accepts as true is susceptible of proof . . .

It is customary to speak of a "belief in immortality." First, then, let us see what is meant by the word "belief." If I take a train in Chicago at noon, bound for New York, I believe I will reach that city the next morning. I believe it because I have been to New York. I have read about the city, I have known many other people who have been there, and their stories are not inconsistent with any known facts in my own experience. I have even examined the timetables, and I know just how I will go and how long the trip will take. In other words, when I board the train for New York, I believe I will reach that city because I have *reason* to believe it.

But if I am told that next week I shall start on a trip to Goofville; that I shall not take my body with me; that I shall stay for all eternity: can I find a single fact connected with my journey—the way I shall go, the part of me that is to go, the time of the journey, the country I shall reach, its location in space, the way I shall live there—or anything that would lead to a rational belief that I shall really make the trip? Have I ever known anyone who has made the journey and returned? If I am really to believe, I must try to get some information about all these important facts.

But people hesitate to ask questions about life after death. They do not ask, for they know that only silence comes out of the eternal darkness of endless space. If people really believed in a beautiful, happy, glorious land waiting to receive them when they died; if they believed that their friends would be waiting to meet them; if they believed that all pain and suffering would be left behind: why should they live through weeks, months, and even years of pain and torture while a cancer eats its way to the vital parts of the body? Why should one fight off death? Because he does *not* believe in any real sense: he only hopes. Everyone knows that there is no real evidence of any such state of bliss; so we are told not to search for proof. We are to accept through faith alone. But every thinking person knows that faith can only come through belief. Belief implies a condition of mind that accepts a certain idea. This condition can be brought about only by evidence. True, the evidence may be simply the unsupported statement of your grandmother; it may be wholly insufficient for reasoning men; but, good or bad, it must be enough for the believer or he could not believe.

Upon what evidence, then, are we asked to believe in immortality? There is no evidence. One is told to rely on faith, and no doubt this serves the purpose so long as one can believe blindly whatever he is told. But if there is no evidence upon which to build a positive belief in immortality, let us examine the other side of the question. Perhaps evidence can be found to support a positive conviction that immortality is a delusion.

The Soul

The belief in immortality expresses itself in two different forms. On the one hand, there is a belief in the immortality of the "soul." This is sometimes interpreted to mean simply that the identity, the consciousness, the memory of the individual persists after death. On the other hand, many religious creeds have formulated a belief in "the resurrection of the body" —which is something else again. It will be necessary to examine both forms of this belief in turn.

The idea of continued life after death is very old. It doubtless had its roots back in the childhood of the race. In view of the limited knowledge of primitive man, it was not unreasonable. His dead friends and relatives visited him in dreams and visions and were present in his feeling and imagination until they were forgotten. Therefore the lifeless body did not raise the question of dissolution, but rather of duality. It was thought that man was a dual being possessing a body and a soul as separate entities, and that when a man died, his soul was released from his body to continue its life apart. Consequently, food and drink were placed upon the graves of the dead to be used in the long journey into the unknown. In modified forms, this belief in the duality of man persists to the present day.

But primitive man had no conception of life as having a beginning and an end. In this he was like the rest of the animals. Today, everyone of ordinary intelligence knows how life begins, and to examine the beginnings of life leads to inevitable conclusions about the way life ends. If a man has a soul, it must creep in somewhere during the period of gestation and growth.

All the higher forms of animal life grow from a single cell. Before the individual life can begin its development, it must be fertilized by union with another cell; then the cell divides and multiplies until it takes the form and pattern of its kind. At a certain regular time the being emerges into the world. During its term of life millions of cells in its body are born, die, and are replaced until, through age, disease, or some catastrophe, the cells fall apart and the individual life is ended.

It is obvious that but for the fertilization of the cell under right conditions, the being would not have lived. It is idle to say that the initial cell has a soul. In one sense it has life; but even that is precarious and depends for its continued life upon union with another cell of the proper kind. The human mother is the bearer of probably ten thousand of one kind of cell, and the human father of countless billions of the other kind. Only a very small fraction of these result in human life. If the unfertilized cells of the female and the unused cells of the male are human beings possessed of souls, then the population of the world is infinitely greater than has ever been dreamed. Of course no such idea as belief in the immortality of the germ cells could satisfy the yearnings of the individual for a survival of life after death.

If that which is called a "soul" is a separate entity apart from the body, when, then, and where and how was this soul placed in the human structure? The individual began with the union of two cells, neither of which had a soul. How could these two soulless cells produce a soul? I must leave this search to the metaphysicians. When they have found the answer, I hope they will tell me, for I should really like to know.

We know that a baby may live and fully develop in its mother's womb and then, through some shock at birth, may be born without life. In the past, these babies were promptly buried. But now we know that in many cases, where the bodily structure is complete, the machine may be set to work by artificial respiration or electricity. Then it will run like any other human body through its allotted term of years. We also know that in many cases of drowning, or when some mishap virtually destroys life without hopelessly impairing the body, artificial means may set it in motion once more, so that it will complete its term of existence until the final catastrophe comes. Are we to believe that somewhere around the stillborn child and somewhere in the vicinity of the drowned man there hovers a detached soul waiting to be summoned back into the body by a pulmotor? This, too, must be left to the metaphysicians.

The beginnings of life yield no evidence of the beginnings of a soul. It is idle to say that the something in the human being which we call "life" is the soul itself, for the soul is generally taken to distinguish human beings from other forms of life. There is life in all animals and plants, and at least potential life in inorganic matter. This potential life is simply unreleased force and matter—the great storehouse from which all forms of life emerge and are constantly replenished. It is impossible to draw the line between inorganic matter and the simpler forms of plant life, and equally impossible to draw the line between plant life and animal life, or between other forms of animal life and what we human beings are pleased to call the highest form. If the thing which we call "life" is itself the soul, then cows have souls; and, in the very nature of things, we must allow souls to all forms of life and to inorganic matter as well.

Life itself is something very real, as distinguished from the soul. Every man knows that his life had a beginning. Can one imagine an organism that has a beginning and no end? If I did not exist in the infinite past, why should I, or could I, exist in the infinite future? "But," say some, "your consciousness, your memory may exist even after you are dead. This is what we mean by the soul." Let us examine this point a little.

I have no remembrance of the months that I lay in my mother's womb. I cannot recall the day of my birth nor the time when I first opened my eyes to the light of the sun. I cannot remember when I was an infant, or when I began to creep on the floor, or when I was taught to walk, or anything before I was five or six years old. Still, all of these events were important, wonderful, and strange in a new life. What I call my "consciousness," for lack of a better word and a better understanding, developed with my growth and the crowding experiences I met at every turn. I have a hazy recollection of the burial of a boy soldier who was shot toward the end of the Civil War. He was buried near the schoolhouse when I was seven years old. But I have no remembrance of the assassination of Abraham Lincoln, although I must then have been eight years old. I must have known about it at the time, for my family and my community idolized Lincoln, and all America was in mourning at his death. Why do I remember the dead boy soldier who was buried a year before? Perhaps because I knew him well. Perhaps because his family was close to my childish life. Possibly because it came to me as my first knowledge of death. At all events, it made so deep an impression that I recall it now.

"Ah, yes," say the believers in the soul, "what you say confirms our own belief. You certainly existed when these early experiences took place. You were conscious of them at the time, even though you are not aware of it now. In the same way, may not your consciousness persist after you die, even though you are not aware of the fact?"

On the contrary, my fading memory of the events that filled the early years of my life lead me to the opposite conclusion. So far as these incidents are concerned, the mind and consciousness of the boy are already dead. Even now, am I fully alive? I am seventy-one years old. I often fail to recollect the names of some of those I knew full well. Many events do not make the lasting impression that they once did. I know that it will be only a few years, even if my body still survives decay, when few important matters will even register in my mind. I know how it is with the old. I know that physical life can persist beyond the time when the mind can fully function. I know that if I live to an extreme old age, my mind will fail. I shall eat and drink and go to my bed in an automatic way. Memory— which is all that binds me to the past—will already be dead. All that will remain will be a vegetative existence; I shall sit and doze in the chimney corner, and my body will function in a measure even though the ego will already be practically dead. I am sure that if I die of what is called "old age," my consciousness will gradually slip away with my failing emotions; I shall no more be aware of the near approach of final dissolution than is the dying tree.

In primitive times, before men knew anything about the human body or the universe of which it is a part, it was not unreasonable to believe in spirits, ghosts, and the duality of man. For one thing, celestial geography was much simpler then. Just above the earth was a firmament in which the stars were set, and above the firmament was heaven. The place was easy of access, and in dreams the angels were seen going up and coming down on a ladder. But now we have a slightly more adequate conception of space and the infinite universe of which we are so small a part. Our great telescopes reveal countless worlds and planetary systems which make our own sink into utter insignificance in comparison. We have every reason to think that beyond our sight there is endless space filled with still more planets, so infinite in size and number that no brain has the smallest conception of their extent. Is there any reason to think that in this universe, with its myriads of worlds, there is no other life so important as our own? Is it possible that the inhabitants of the earth have been singled out for special favor and endowed with souls and immortal life? Is it at all reasonable to suppose that any special account is taken of the human atoms that forever come and go upon this planet?

If man has a soul that persists after death, that goes to a heaven of the blessed or to a hell of the damned, where are these places? It is not so easily imagined as it once was. How does the soul make its journey? What does immortal man find when he gets there, and how will he live after he reaches the end of endless space? We know that the atmosphere will be absent; that there will be no light, no heat—only the infinite reaches of darkness and frigidity. In view of modern knowledge, can anyone *really believe* in the persistence of individual life and memory?

The Resurrection of the Body

There are those who base their hope of a future life upon the resurrection of the body. This is a purely religious doctrine. It is safe to say that few intelligent men who are willing to look obvious facts in the face hold any such belief. Yet we are seriously told that Elijah was carried bodily to heaven in a chariot of fire, and that Jesus arose from the dead and ascended into heaven. The New Testament abounds in passages that support this doctrine. St. Paul states the tenet over and over again. In the fifteenth chapter of First Corinthians he says: "If Christ be preached that he arose from the dead, how say some among you that there is no resurrection of the dead? . . . And if Christ be not risen, then is our preaching vain. . . . For if the dead rise not, then is not Christ raised." The Apostles' Creed says: "I believe in the resurrection of the body." This has been carried into substantially all the orthodox creeds; and while it is more or less minimized by neglect and omission, it is still a cardinal doctrine of the orthodox churches.

Two thousand years ago, in Palestine, little was known of man, of the earth, or of the universe. It was then currently believed that the earth was only four thousand years old, that life had begun anew after the deluge about two thousand years before, and that the entire earth was soon to be destroyed. Today it is fairly well established that man has been upon the earth for a million years. During that long stretch of time the world has changed many times; it is changing every moment. At least three or four ice ages have swept across continents, driving death before them, carrying human beings into the sea or burying them deep in the earth. Animals have fed on man and on each other. Every dead body, no matter whether consumed by fire or buried in the earth, has been resolved into its elements, so that the matter and energy that once formed human beings has fed animals and plants and other men. As the great naturalist, Fabre*, has said: "At the banquet of life each is in turn a guest and a dish." Thus the body of every man now living is in part made from the bodies of those who have been dead for ages.

Yet we are still asked to believe in the resurrection of the body. By what alchemy, then, are the individual bodies that have successfully fed the generations of men to be separated and restored to their former identities? And if I am to be resurrected, what particular *I* shall be called from the grave, from the animals and plants and the bodies of other men who shall inherit this body I now call my own? My body has been made over and over, piece by piece, as the days went by, and will continue to be so made until the end. It has changed so slowly that each new cell is fitted into the living part, and will go on changing until the final crisis comes. Is it the child in the mother's womb or the tottering frame of the old man that shall be brought back? The mere thought of such a resurrection beggars reason, ignores facts, and enthrones blind faith, wild dreams, hopeless hopes, and cowardly fears as sovereign of the human mind.

The Indestructability of Matter and Force

Some of those who profess to believe in the immortality of man— whether it be of his soul or of his body—have drawn what comfort they could from the modern scientific doctrine of the indestructibility of matter and force. This doctrine, they say, only confirms in scientific language what they have always believed. This, however, is pure sophistry. It is probably true that no matter or force has even been or ever can be destroyed. But it is likewise true that there is no connection whatever between the notion that personal consciousness and memory persist after death and the scientific theory that matter and force are indestructible. For the scientific theory carries with it a corollary, that the forms of matter and energy are constantly changing through an endless cycle of new combinations. Of what possible use would it be, then, to have a consciousness that was immortal, but which, from the moment of death, was dispersed into new combinations so that no two parts of the original identity could ever be reunited again?

These natural processes of change, which in the human being take the forms of growth, disease, senility, death, and decay, are essentially the same as the processes by which a lump of coal is disintegrated in burning. One may watch the lump of coal burning in the grate until nothing but ashes remains. Part of the coal goes up the chimney in the form of smoke; part of it radiates through the house as heat; the residue lies in the ashes on the hearth. So it is with human life. In all forms of life nature is engaged in combining, breaking down, and recombining her store of energy and

---

* The reference is to Jean H. C. Fabre (1823–1915), a French biologist, renowned for his observations and experiments on insects, spiders, and scorpions. (Ed.)

matter into new forms. The thing we call "life" is nothing other than a state of equilibrium which endures for a short span of years between the two opposing tendencies of nature—the one that builds up, and the one that tears down. In old age, the tearing-down process has already gained the ascendency, and when death intervenes, the equilibrium is finally upset by the complete stoppage of the building-up process, so that nothing remains but complete disintegration. The energy thus released may be converted into grass or trees or animal life; or it may lie dormant until caught up again in the crucible of nature's laboratory. But whatever happens, the man—the *You* and the *I*—like the lump of coal that has been burned, is gone, irrevocably dispersed. All the King's horses and all the King's men cannot restore it to its former unity.

The idea that man is a being set apart, distinct from all the rest of nature, is born of man's emotions, of his loves and hates, of his hopes and fears, and of the primitive conceptions of undeveloped minds. The *You* or the *I* which is known to our friends does not consist of an immaterial something called a "soul" which cannot be conceived. We know perfectly well what we mean when we talk about this *You* and this *Me:* and it is equally plain that the whole fabric that makes up our separate personalities is destroyed, dispersed, disintegrated beyond repair by what we call "death."

The Desire For Another Life

Those who refuse to give up the idea of immortality declare that nature never creates a desire without providing the means for its satisfaction. They likewise insist that all people, from the rudest to the most civilized, yearn for another life. As a matter of fact, nature creates many desires which she does not satisfy; most of the wishes of men meet no fruition. But nature does not create any emotion demanding a future life. The only yearning that the individual has is to keep on living—which is a very different thing. This urge is found in every animal, in every plant. It is simply the momentum of a living structure: or, as Schopenhauer put it, "the will to live." What we long for is a continuation of our present state of existence, not an uncertain reincarnation in a mysterious world of which we know nothing.

The Believer's Last Resort

All men recognize the hopelessness of finding any evidence that the individual will persist beyond the grave. As a last resort, we are told that it is better that the doctrine be believed even if it is not true. We are assured that without this faith, life is only desolation and despair. However that may be, it remains that many of the conclusions of logic are not pleasant to contemplate; still, so long as men think and feel, at least some of them will use their faculties as best they can. For if we are to believe things that are not true, who is to write our creed? Is it safe to leave it to any man or organization to pick out the errors that we must accept? The whole history of the world has answered this question in a way that cannot be mistaken.

And after all, is the belief in immortality necessary or even desirable for man? Millions of men and women have no such faith; they go on with their daily tasks and feel joy and sorrow without the lure of immortal life. The things that really affect the happiness of the individual are the matters of daily living. They are the companionship of friends, the games and contemplations. They are misunderstandings and cruel judgments, false friends and debts, poverty and disease. They are our joys in our living companions and our sorrows over those who die. Whatever our faith, we mainly live in the present—in the here and now. Those who hold the view that man is mortal are never troubled by metaphysical problems. At the end of the day's labor we are glad to lose our consciousness in sleep; and intellectually, at least, we look forward to the long rest from the stresses and storms that are always incidental to existence.

When we fully understand the brevity of life, its fleeting joys and un-avoidable pains; when we accept the fact that all men and women are approaching an inevitable doom: the consciousness of it should make us more kindly and considerate of each other. This feeling should make men and women use their best efforts to help their fellow travellers on the road, to make the path brighter and easier as we journey on. It should bring a closer kinship, a better understanding, and a deeper sympathy for the wayfarers who must live a common life and die a common death.

Selected Bibliography

(ITEMS PROVIDED WITH ASTERISK ARE MORE ADVANCED)
(FOR KEY TO ABBREVIATIONS SEE PAGE XIX)

The following books are devoted entirely to the body-mind problem in its various ramifications: J. Laird, *Our Minds and Their Bodies* (London: Oxford U.P., 1925), C. D. Broad, *The Mind and Its Place in Nature* (London: Routledge, 1925, p), G. F. Stout, *Mind and Matter* (Cambridge: Cambridge U.P., 1931), John Wisdom, *Problems of Mind and Matter* (Cambridge: Cambridge U.P., 1934), J. B. Pratt, *Matter and Spirit* (N.Y.: Macmillan, 1926), D. Drake, *The Mind and Its Place in Nature* (N.Y.: Macmillan, 1925), C. J. Ducasse, *Nature, Mind and Death* (LaSalle, Illinois: Open Court, 1951), G. N. A. Vessey, *The Embodied Mind* (London: Allen & Unwin, 1965), A. R. White, *The Philosophy of Mind* (N.Y.: Random House, 1967, p), J. A. Shaffer, *Philosophy of Mind* (Englewood Cliffs: Prentice-Hall, 1968, p), and K. Campbell, *Body and Mind* (Garden City: Doubleday, 1970, p). The last of these contains a very extensive bibliography. A nineteenth century work covering some of the same ground is Alexander Bain's *Mind and Body* (London: Henry King, 1873). Bain's book contains a valuable historical survey of the different theories on the subject. Introductory discussions of the body-mind problem are found in Ch. 12 of A. Pap, *Elements of Analytic Philosophy* (N.Y.: Macmillan, 1949), Ch. 6 of A. C. Ewing, *The Fundamental Problems of Philosophy* (N.Y.: Collier Books, 1962, p), Ch. 6 of J. Hospers, *An Introduction to Philosophical Analysis* (N.Y.: Prentice-Hall, 2nd ed., 1967), Ch. 4 of J. W. Cornman and K. Lehrer, *Philosophical Problems and Arguments: An Introduction* (N.Y.: Macmillan, 1968) and Chs. 27–30 of K. Nielsen, *Reason and Practice* (N.Y.: Harper, 1971). Each of the following books contains several chapters on the body-mind problem: B. Aune, *Knowledge, Mind and Nature* (N.Y.: Random House, 1967), G. E. Meyers, *Self* (N.Y.: Pegasus, 1969, p) and R. Hoffman, *Language, Mind and Knowledge* (London: Allen & Unwin, 1971). C. A. van Peursen, a continental philosopher belonging to the phenomenological school, discusses the same questions in *Body, Soul, Spirit: A Survey of the Body-Mind Problem* (Oxford: Oxford U.P., 1966). The main competing theories among contemporary Anglo-Saxon philosophers are explained and appraised in J. Shaffer, "Recent Work on the Mind-Body Problem," *APQ*, 1965.

A. Flew, *Body, Mind and Death* (N.Y.: Macmillan, 1964, p), is a historically arranged anthology containing selections from many important philosophers of the past and present who have written on aspects of the body-mind problem. There is special emphasis in it on the topics of personal identity and survival after death. G. N. A. Vesey (ed.), *Body and Mind* (London: Allen & Unwin, 1964), and H. Morick (ed.), *Introduction to the Philosophy of Mind* (Glenview, Ill.: Scott, Foresman, 1970, p) are also chronologically arranged, but the emphasis in them is more on the relation of body and mind than on the topics of personal identity and survival. J. W. Reeves (ed.), *Body and Mind in Western Thought* (Harmondsworth: Penguin Books, 1958, p), has a very long and informative historical introduction and contains some little-known pieces, but its selections do not extend beyond the end of the 19th century. V. C. Chappell (ed.), *The Philosophy of Mind* (Englewood Cliffs: Prentice-Hall, 1962, p), D. F. Gustafson (ed.), *Essays in Philosophical Psychology* (Garden City: Doubleday, 1964, p), and S. Hampshire (ed.), *Philosophy of Mind* (N.Y.: Harper, 1966, p) are useful collections of influential papers by contemporary Anglo-Saxon philosophers. S. Hook (ed.), *Dimensions of Mind* (N.Y.: Collier Books, 1961, p), consists of original contributions by philosophers, psychologists, and mathematicians. Part II is entitled "The Brain and the Machine" and includes papers by Norbert Wiener, M. Scriven, S. Watanabe, and H. Putnam. Scriven and Putnam are also among the writers represented in A. R. Anderson (ed.), *Minds and Machines* (Englewood Cliffs: Prentice-Hall, 1964, p), which reprints the famous piece on "Computing Machinery and Intelligence" by the British mathematician A. M. Turing as well as articles by J. R. Lucas, K. Gunderson, P. Ziff, J. J. C. Smart, and N. Smart. Several papers on the relations between computers and conscious processes are reprinted in K. Sayre and F. J. Crosson (eds.), *The Modelling of Mind* (Notre Dame: Notre Dame U.P., 1963). The philosophical issues raised by cybernetics are explored in F. J. Crosson and K. M. Sayre (eds.), *Philosophy and Cybernetics* (Notre Dame: Notre Dame U.P., 1967) and in K. Gunderson, *Mentality and Machines* (Garden City: Doubleday, 1971, p). The last mentioned volume contains a comprehensive bibliography. Most histories of psychology contain material of interest to the student of the body-mind problem. One of the most readable is

G. S. Brett, *History of Psychology* (London: Allen & Unwin, abridged and annotated ed., 1953). In this connection mention should also be made of W. Dennis (ed.), *Readings in the History of Psychology* (N.Y.: Appleton-Century-Crofts, 1948), which contains a number of selections that should be of interest to philosophers.

Dualistic interactionism is defended in the books by Laird, Pratt, Ducasse, Ewing, Pap and Hospers mentioned in the last paragraph. The classic formulation of this theory is found in Descartes' *Meditations,* his *Passion of the Soul,* and in his correspondence. Many editions of Descartes' works contain also Gassendi's objections to his theory and Descartes' answer. Defenses of interactionism from a Catholic viewpoint are found in M. Maher, *Psychology* (London: Longmans, Green, 1940), in J. E. Royce, *Man and His Nature* (N.Y.: McGraw-Hill, 1961) and the same author's *Man and Meaning* (N.Y.: McGraw-Hill, 1969). In *The Elusive Mind* (London: Allen & Unwin, 1969), H. D. Lewis defends dualistic interactionism against all its major contemporary critics including Wittgenstein, Strawson, Ryle, and Smart. In *The Ghost in the Machine* (N.Y.: Macmillan, 1967) the novelist, Arthur Koestler, defends interactionism against the materialism of various scientists and philosophers. W. McDougall, *Body and Mind* (London: Methuen, 1911), and J. Beloff, *The Existence of Mind* (London: MacGibbon & Kee, 1962), are defenses by psychologists of interactionism, but they are not typical of the views of contemporary psychologists, many of whom are sympathetic to some kind of materialism. Physiologists also frequently show a special interest in the subject. Sir Charles Sherrington in *Man on His Nature* (Cambridge: Cambridge U.P., 1940), p) and J. C. Eccles in *The Neurophysiological Basis of Mind* (Oxford: Clarendon Press, 1953) write in support of dualism, but T. H. Bullock, in his contribution to A. Roe and G. G. Simpson (eds.), *Behavior and Evolution* (New Haven: Yale U.P., 1958), is one of many physiologists favoring materialism. *The Brain and Human Behavior* (Research Publications Association for Research in Nervous and Mental Disease, Vol. 36, 1958) contains a great deal of valuable scientific information. Several of the talks reprinted in P. Laslett (ed.), *The Physical Basis of Mind* (Oxford: Blackwell, 1951), from which our Selection 20 is taken, are summaries of what physiology and anatomy have taught us about the brain. The contributions of the scientists to this volume as well as those of the philosophers are critically discussed in C. A. Mace, "The 'Body-Mind Problem' in Philosophy, Psychology and Medicine," *P,* 1966. Mace is sympathetic to Ryle's viewpoint and highly critical of the Cartesian tradition.

Reductive materialism is defended in Book III of the great philosophical poem *De Rerum Naturae* by the Roman poet Lucretius (the most recent and readable translation by R. Latham is entitled "On the Nature of the Universe" and is available as a Penguin paperback, 1951). It is also defended by Thomas Hobbes in *De Corpore.* All the philosophically interesting parts of this work are available in a new paperback edition of Hobbes' philosophical writings, *Body, Man and Citizen,* edited by R. S. Peters (N.Y.: Collier Books, 1962, p). There are selections from both Lucretius and Hobbes in A. Flew, *op. cit.* The most influential defense of this theory in the 19th century is found in Ludwig Büchner, *Force and Matter* (London: Asher, 1884). The works by Cabanis, Vogt, and Moleschott in which similar views are advocated have not been translated into English. It should be noted that all these writers frequently shift to some milder form of materialism. F. A. Lange's magnificent *History of Materialism* (London: Kegan Paul, 1925, with an introduction to Bertrand Russell) is a mine of information on this subject. Paul Janet, *Materialism of* *the Present Day* (London, 1867) is an informative critical work. The historical development of materialism is sympathetically sketched in the "Belfast Address" by the 19th century physicist John Tyndall, which also contains a fuller statement of the position sketched in Selection 18 of the present work. The "Belfast Address" is available in Volume II of Tyndall's *Fragments of Science*. The great German chemist, Wilhelm Ostwald, propounded a philosophy which he called "energeticism" and which may also be regarded as a form of reductive materialism. An extract from Ostwald's *Lectures on Natural Philosophy* which deals with this subject is available in English in W. Heisenberg, *The Physicist's Conception of Nature* (N.Y.: Harcourt, Brace, 1958). In more recent years, radical varieties of materialism have been defended by J. M. Robertson, the great historian of free-thought, in *Explorations* (London: Watts, 1909), Hugh Elliot, *Modern Science and Materialism* (London: Longmans, Green, 1919), Chapman Cohen, *Materialism Restated* (London: Pioneer Press, 1927), Donald Williams, "Naturalism and the Nature of Things," *PR*, 1944, and T. Kotarbinski, "The Fundamental Ideas of Pansomatism,"* *M*, 1955.

The classic exposition of occasionalism is that of Malebranche in his *Dialogue on Metaphysics and Religion** (London: Allen & Unwin, 1923). A more recent defense of occasionalism is given in Vol. I, Book III, Ch. I of Lotze's *Microcosmus* (Edinburgh: T. R. T. Clark, 1885). The illustration of the two clocks and the parallelism of Leibniz are found in his *Exposition and Defense of the New System* which is reprinted in most popular editions of his works. Parallelism was also defended by the great Danish historian of philosophy, Harold Höffding, in his *The Problems of Philosophy* (N.Y.: Macmillan, 1905). G. T. Fechner, who was the leading parallelist and panpsychist of the 19th century, wrote a number of works which deal with various aspects of the body-mind problem, but very few of these have been translated into English. The most valuable collection of his writings in English is *Religion of a Scientist* (N.Y.: Pantheon, 1946, ed. W. Lowrie). Defenses of both parallelism and panpsychism are also found in W. K. Clifford's articles "Body and Mind" and "Things-in-Themselves," which are reprinted in Volume II of his *Lectures and Essays* (London and New York: Macmillan, 1879), and in Friedrich Paulsen, *Introduction to Philosophy* (N.Y.: Holt, 1906). There are selections from Malebranche, Leibniz, and Clifford in Vesey, *op. cit.* G. S. Fullerton in *A System of Metaphysics* (N.Y.: Macmillan, 1904) and again in *An Introduction to Philosophy* (N.Y.: Macmillan, 1906) champions a form of parallelism, but he admits that his disagreement with interactionists concerns the use of the best language for the body-mind relation rather than the existence of any facts.

Epiphenomenalism is defended, with some reservations and misgivings, by C. D. Broad in *Mind and Its Place in Nature, op. cit.* Earlier defenses are found in Shadworth Hodgson, *The Metaphysics of Experience,** Volume II (London: Longmans, Green, 1898), in G. Santayana, *The Realm of Essence** (Scribner's, 1927), the same author's *Reason and Common Sense* (Scribner's, 1922, Collier, 1962, p), and in H. C. Warren's "The Mechanics of Intelligence," *PR*, 1917. Broad's views are criticized in W. Kneale's contribution to P. A. Schilpp (ed.), *The Philosophy of C. D. Broad* (N.Y.: Tudor Press, 1959), which also contains Broad's reply. The theory is attacked in the books by Pratt and Maher mentioned earlier, also in T. H. Herbert, *Modern Realism Examined* (London: Macmillan, 1879), A. O. Lovejoy, "Pragmatism as Interactionism," *JP*, 1920, and in B. Blanshard, "A Verdict on Epiphenomenalism" in F. C. Dommeyer (ed.), *Current Philosophical Issues* (Springfield: Thomas, 1966). A recent, more sympathetic paper on the subject is J. Lachs, "Epiphenomenalism and the Notion of Cause," *JP*, 1963.

The classical statements of the theory that psychological phenomena are attributes of the body are found in Lamettrie, *Man As a Machine* (LaSalle, Illinois: Open Court, 1912) and in Joseph Priestley, *Disquisitions Relating to Matter and Spirit* (London, 1777). A. Vartanian, *Lamettrie's L'Homme Machine* (Princeton: Princeton U.P., 1960), is a critical edition of Lamettrie's French text containing a great deal of fascinating historical material about the origin of the book and its reception. Holbach in *The System of Nature* (1770) also at times inclines to this view and so does Diderot in several of his works, most of which are unfortunately not available in English. There is some discussion of this topic in "D'Alembert's Dream," which is included in J. Kemp (ed.), *Diderot—Interpreter of Nature* (N.Y.: International Publishers, 1943, p). Parts of this dialogue are also reprinted in L. Crocker (ed.), *Diderot— Selected Writings* (N.Y.: Macmillan, 1966). There are interesting historical accounts of how the mechanistic biology of Descartes led to the mechanistic materialism of certain of the 18th century French philosophers in Ch. IV of A. Vartanian, *Diderot and Descartes* (Princeton: Princeton U.P., 1953), and in L. C. Rosenfield, *From Beast-Machine to Man-Machine* (N.Y.: Oxford U.P., 1941). E. Nagel's "Are Naturalists Materialists?" reprinted in E. Nagel, *Logic without Metaphysics* (Glencoe: Free Press, 1957), is a highly stimulating modern presentation of the same general position as that found in Lamettrie, Diderot, and Priestley. Similar views are also expressed by Y. Krikorian in "A Naturalistic View of Mind," which is included in Y. Krikorian (ed.), *Naturalism and the Human Spirit* (N.Y.: Columbia U.P., 1944). The views of Krikorian and other naturalists are criticized in W. H. Sheldon, "Critique of Naturalism," *JP*, 1945.

There are several varieties of behaviorism. Some psychologists who call themselves behaviorists do not at all deny the existence of "consciousness" but merely exclude it as a proper subject matter of scientific research. Others, and sometimes the same writers in less guarded moments, go further and deny consciousness altogether. Many eminent American psychologists have expressed one or the other of these views. The following are some of their most influential writings: J. B. Watson, *Psychology from the Standpoint of a Behaviorist* (Philadelphia: Lippincott, 1919), the same author's *Behaviorism* (N.Y.: Norton, 1924), K. S. Lashley, "Behaviorism and Consciousness," *Psychological Review,* 1923, A. P. Weiss, *A Theoretical Basis of Human Behavior* (Columbus, Ohio: Adams, 1925), W. S. Hunter, *Human Behavior* (Chicago: U. of Chicago P., 1928), E. C. Tolman, *Purposive Behavior in Animals and Men* (N.Y.: Appleton-Century, 1932), and C. L. Hull, *Principles of Behavior** (N.Y.: Appleton-Century-Crofts, 1943). H. H. Bawden's "The Presuppositions of a Behaviorist Psychology," *Psychological Review,* 1918, is a particularly lucid statement of the more radical form of behaviorism mentioned above. The most important behaviorist among contemporary psychologists is B. F. Skinner. Skinner's position is stated very fully in *Science and Human Behavior* (N.Y.: Macmillan, 1953), and also in a recent paper, "Behaviorism at Fifty," which originally appeared in *Science,* 1963, and is reprinted in T. W. Wann (ed.), *Behaviorism and Phenomenology* (Chicago: U. of Chicago P., 1964). Skinner's views are criticized by N. Malcolm in "Behaviorism as a Philosophy of Psychology," in T. W. Wann, *op. cit.,* and in M. Scriven's "A Study of Radical Behaviorism," in H. Feigl and M. Scriven (eds.), *Minnesota Studies in the Philosophy of Science,* Volume I (Minneapolis: U. of Minnesota P., 1956). A debate between Skinner and B. Blanshard entitled "The Problem of Consciousness," appeared in *PPR,* 1967, and is reprinted in J. H. Gill (ed.), *Philosophy Today No. 2* (N.Y.: Macmillan, 1969, p). In his "Philosophical Behaviorism," which is included in *Knowledge and Necessity, Royal Institute of Philosophy Lectures Volume 3* (London: Macmillan, 1970, p), C. W. K. Mundle criticizes Watson, Skinner, as well as several philosophers (Wittgenstein, Ryle, and Malcolm) whom he regards as behaviorists. An interesting paper in which Hull's work is put into historical perspective is R. S. Peters and H. Tajfel, "Hobbes and Hull— Metaphysicians of Behavior," *BJPS*, 1957.

There is also a theory known as "logical behaviorism" which is not concerned to advocate and justify a program of psychological research but which offers an analysis of the so-called psychological predicates in terms of "behavior" alone. This view is stated in C. G. Hempel's "The Logical Analysis of Psychology," reprinted in H. Feigl and W. Sellars (eds.), *Readings in Philosophical Analysis* (N.Y.: Appleton-Century-Crofts, 1949) and in Rudolf Carnap's "Psychology in Physical Language," which was originally published in 1932 and is now available in an English translation in A. J. Ayer (ed.), *Logical Positivism* (N.Y.: Free Press, 1959, p). Gilbert Ryle's *The Concept of Mind* (London: Hutchinson, N.Y.: Barnes & Noble, 1949, p), which is one of the most influential philosophical works of this century, is also regarded by many reviewers as a defense of logical behaviorism. Ryle further developed some of his ideas in "Feelings," *PQ*, 1951, "Thinking and Language," *Ar. Soc. Sup.*, 1951, "Pleasure," *Ar. Soc. Sup.*, 1954, reprinted in Gustafson, *op. cit.*, and in J. Feinberg (ed.), *Moral Concepts* (London: Oxford U.P., 1970, p), "Sensation," in H. D. Lewis (ed.), *Contemporary British Philosophy*, Third Series (London: Allen & Unwin, N.Y.: Macmillan, 1956), "A Puzzling Element in the Notion of Thinking," *Proceedings of the British Academy*, 1958, reprinted in P. F. Strawson (ed.), *Studies in the Philosophy of Thought and Action* (London: Oxford U.P., 1968, p), "Some Problems About Thinking," in H. E. Kiefer and M. K. Munitz (eds.), *Mind, Science and History* (Albany: State U. of N.Y. P., 1970), and in his contribution to P. Lasslett, *op. cit.*, which is part of our Selection 20. Several of these papers are now available in Ryle's *Collected Papers*, Vol. 2 (London: Hutchinson, 1971). Ryle's most recent explanations of his own position are given in an interview in *The Listener*, January 21, 1971. Ryle there admits that his theory about images in *The Concept of Mind* is seriously defective. The critical literature provoked by Ryle's book and articles is vast but the following seem to be particularly worth mentioning: J. Wisdom, "The Concept of Mind," *Ar. Soc.*, 1949–50, reprinted in his *Other Minds** (Oxford: Blackwell, 1952), J. N. Findlay, "Linguistic Approach to Psychophysics," *Ar. Soc.*, 1949–50, a discussion by A. Hofstadter, D. S. Miller, M. Weitz, and H. King in *JP*, 1951, I. Murdoch, "Thinking and Language," *Ar. Soc. Sup.*, 1951, J. M. Shorter, "Imagination," *M*, 1952, reprinted in Gustafson, *op. cit.*, A. C. Ewing, "Professor Ryle's Attack on Dualism," *Ar. Soc.*, 1952, A. Pap, "Semantic Analysis and Psycho-Physical Dualism," *M*, 1952, A C. Garnett, "Mind as Minding," *ibid.*, Mrs. A. Flew, "Imagining," *P*, 1953, U. T. Place, "The Concept of Heed," *The British Journal of Psychology*, 1954, reprinted in Gustafson, *op. cit.*, A. Flew, "Facts and 'Imagination'," *M*, 1956 (a reply to Shorter's article, *op. cit.*,), T. Penelhum, "The Logic of Pleasure," *PPR*, 1956–57 (reprinted in Gustafson), Bertrand Russell, "What Is Mind?," *JP*, 1958, reprinted in his *My Philosophical Development* (London: Allen & Unwin, N.Y.: Simon & Schuster, 1959), Arthur Danto, "Concerning Mental Pictures," *JP*, 1958, M. Mandelbaum, "Prof. Ryle and Psychology," *PR*, 1958, J. J. C. Smart, "Ryle on Mechanism and Psychology," *PQ*, 1959, J. N. Wright, "Mind and the Concept of Mind," *Ar. Soc. Sup.*, 1959 and D. Bloor, "Is the Official Theory of Mind Absurd?," *BJPS*, 1970. Several of the articles just listed are reproduced in O. P. Wood and G. Pitcher (eds.), *Ryle—A Collection of Critical Essays* (Garden City: Doubleday, 1970, p). This volume also contains a number of original pieces, two of the most detailed reviews of *The Concept of Mind* (by S. Hampshire and J. L. Austin) and a complete bibliography of Ryle's publications. A theory about the nature of thinking closely similar to that of Ryle is advocated by A. J. Ayer in his inaugural lecture, *Thinking and Meaning* (London: H. K. Lewis, 1947). There are criticisms of some or all varieties of behaviorism in the above-mentioned books by Broad, Ducasse, Pratt, and Drake. Other criticisms of behaviorism will be found in Bertrand Russell, *The Outline of Philosophy* (London: Allen & Unwin, N.Y.: Norton, 1927, p), B. Blanshard, *The Nature of Thought*, Volume I (London: Allen & Unwin, 1939), the same writer's "Behaviorism and the Theory of Knowledge," *PR*, 1928, A. O. Lovejoy, "The Paradox of the Thinking Behaviorist," *PR*, 1922, and in W. Köhler, *Gestalt Psychology* (N.Y.: Horace Liveright, 1929, p). More recent criticisms of behaviorism are found in C. I. Lewis, "Some Logical Considerations Concerning the Mental," *JP*, 1941, which is reprinted in Feigl and Sellars, *op. cit.*, and also in Vesey, *op. cit.*, R. S. Peters, "Observationalism in Psychology," *M*, 1951, H. Putnam, "Psychological Concepts, Explication, and Ordinary Language," *JP*, 1957, the same author's "Brains and Behavior," in R. J. Butler (ed.), *Analytical Philosophy, Second Series* (Oxford: Blackwell, 1965), H. H. Price, "Some Objections to Behaviorism," in S. Hook, *op. cit.*, C. H. Whiteley, "Behaviorism," *M*, 1961, and B. Aune, "On Thought and Feeling," *PQ*, 1963. There is a reply to Price by C. D. Rollins in *JP*, 1962, and to Putnam in D. R. Finn, "Putnam and Logical Behaviorism," *M*, 1971. Sympathetic to behaviorism are C. A. Mace in "Physicalism," *Ar. Soc.*, 1936–37 and in "Some Implications of Analytical Behaviorism," *Ar. Soc.*, 1948–49, and P. Ziff in "About Behaviorism," *A*, 1958. Both of the last-mentioned papers are reprinted in Chappell, *op. cit.*

Both Ryle and other recent writers who are sympathetic to logical behaviorism have been strongly influenced by Wittgenstein. It would be inaccurate to regard Wittgenstein as a behaviorist, but his insistence that intelligible discourse requires socially imparted rules for the use of its component words or signs, i.e., the rejection of the possibility of a "private language," is very much in harmony with a behavioristic outlook. Wittgenstein's views on the impossibility of a private language as well as many other provocative remarks on the philosophy of psychology are found in his posthumously published *Philosophical Investigations** (Oxford: Blackwell, 1953). O. R. Jones (ed.), *The Private Language Argument* (London: Macmillan, 1971, p) is an extremely useful anthology on this subject, containing R. Rhees' edition of Wittgenstein's notes for lectures on "Private Experience" and "Sense Data" originally published in *PR*, 1968, as well as discussions of Wittgenstein's views by P. F. Strawson, N. Malcolm, A. J. Ayer, R. Rhees, H. Harvey, N. Garver, C. W. K. Mundle, C. L. Holborow, H. Castaneda, V. C. Chappell, J. F. Thomson, J. J. Thomson, and A. Kenny. The following are articles dealing with the same topics that are not included in the Jones anthology: C. Wellman, "Wittgenstein and the Egocentric Predicament," *M*, 1959, C. L. Hardin, "Wittgenstein on Private Languages," *JP*, 1959, J. D. Carney, "Private Language—The Logic of Wittgenstein's Argument," *M*, 1960, W. Todd, "Private Languages," *PQ*, 1962, K. Stern, "Private Language and Scepticism," *JP*, 1963, C. S. Chihara and J. A. Fodor, "Operationalism and Ordinary Language: A Critique of Wittgenstein," *APQ*, 1965, reprinted in G. Pitcher (ed.), *Wittgenstein: The Philosophical Investigations* (Garden City: Doubleday, 1966, p), J. W. Cornman, "Private Languages and Private Entities," *AJ*, 1968, D. Pole, "The Notion of Logical Privacy: Has Its Incoherence Been Demonstrated?," *Critica* (Mexico), 1968, J. W. Cook, "Human Beings," A.

Manser, "Pain and Private Language" (the two last-mentioned articles are available in P. Winch, ed., *Studies in the Philosophy of Wittgenstein* (London: Routledge, 1969), J. Hintikka, "Wittgenstein on Private Language: Some Sources of Misunderstanding," *M,* 1969, N. Malcolm, "Wittgenstein on the Nature of Mind," in N. Rescher (ed.), *Studies in the Theory of Knowledge* (Oxford: Blackwell, 1970, p), R. Rorty, "Wittgenstein, Privileged Access, and Incommunicability," *APQ,* 1970, B. Goldberg, "The Linguistic Expression of Feeling," *APQ,* 1971, W. G. Lycan, "Noninductive Evidence: Recent Work on Wittgenstein's 'Criteria'," *APQ,* 1971. J. L. Thompson, "About Criteria," *R,* 1971, U. T. Place, "Understanding the Language of Sensations," *AJ,* 1971, J. Wisdom, "Wittgenstein on Private Language," in A. Ambrose and M. Lazerowitz (eds.), *Ludwig Wittgenstein: Philosophy and Language* (London: Allen & Unwin, 1971), and E. R. Winkler, "Skepticism and Private Language," *M,* 1972. Lycan's article contains a very extensive bibliography of recent writings on all aspects of Wittgenstein's views about the mind. J. T. Saunders and D. F. Henze, *The Private Language Argument* (N.Y.: Random House, 1967) is a comprehensive discussion of the same questions in the form of a dialogue. The authors connect the private language problem with arguments presented in P. F. Strawson's *Individuals* to which reference will be made later in this bibliography. N. Malcolm, who is one of the leading expositors and defenders of Wittgenstein's views, has developed his own position in his contribution to the symposium edited by Wann which was previously referred to and in his book, *Dreaming** (London: Routledge & Kegan Paul, 1959), There is an attack on Malcolm's views in A. J. Ayer's "Professor Malcolm on Dreaming," *JP,* 1960, and a reply by Malcolm and rejoinder by Ayer in *JP,* 1961. Malcolm is also criticized by H. Putnam, "Dreaming and 'Depth Grammar'," in R. J. Butler (ed.), *Analytical Philosophy* (Oxford: Blackwell, 1962). The questions raised by Malcolm are also discussed in D. F. Pears, "Professor Norman Malcolm: Dreaming," *M,* 1961, which is reprinted in Gustafson, *op. cit.,* L. Linsky, "Illusions and Dreams," *M,* 1962, and V. C. Chappell, "The Concept of Dreaming," *PQ,* 1963. Malcolm's most recent work is *Problems of Mind—Descartes to Wittgenstein* (N.Y.: Harper, 1971, p).

The problem of "other minds"—how, if at all, we can know what somebody else is thinking or feeling or indeed that there is somebody else who thinks and feels—has been discussed a great deal in recent years. According to the traditional dualistic theory, the ascription of a psychological predicate to another person can never be more than probable and this probability is always based on an analogical argument. Wittgenstein, Ryle, and Wisdom, whatever their differences on questions of detail, would all agree that there was something radically mistaken in this traditional position. There is a clear and straightforward statement of the older viewpoint in Ch. XII of J. S. Mill, *An Examination of Sir Hamilton's Philosophy* (London: Longmans, Green, 1872). Subtler restatements of the same theory are found in Ch. VII of Broad's *The Mind and Its Place in Nature, op. cit.,* and in H. H. Price, "Our Knowledge of Other Minds," *Ar. Soc.,* 1931–32, and "Our Evidence for the Existence of Other Minds," *P,* 1938. A very radical rejection of all views of this kind is advocated by N. Malcolm, "Knowledge of Other Minds," *JP,* 1958, which is reprinted in Chappell, *op. cit.,* Gustafson, *op. cit.,* and Malcolm, *Knowledge and Certainty, op. cit.* Wisdom's discussions are contained in a series of articles in *M,* 1940–42, all of which are reprinted in his book, *Other Minds.** The same volume also reprints Wisdom's contribution to a celebrated symposium on "Other Minds" which originally appeared in *Ar. Soc. Sup.,* 1946. The other symposiast was J. L. Austin, whose contribution is available in A. Flew (ed.), *Logic and Lan-*

guage, Second Series (Oxford: Blackwell, 1953), and in J. L. Austin, *Philosophical Papers* (Oxford: Clarendon Press, 1961). A. J. Ayer, who, in the first edition of *Language, Truth and Logic* (1936), advocated a behavioristic analysis of statements about other people's thoughts and feelings, has defended a more traditional position in recent years, in "One's Knowledge of Other Minds," *T*, 1953, reprinted in his *Philosophical Essays* (London: Macmillan, 1954) and in Gustafson, *op. cit.*, in Ch. V of *The Problem of Knowledge* (Harmondsworth: Penguin Books, 1956, p), in "Privacy," *Proceedings of the British Academy*, 1959, reprinted in his *The Concept of a Person and Other Essays, op. cit.*, and in "Carnap's Treatment of the Problem of Other Minds," in P. A. Schilpp (ed.), *The Philosophy of Rudolf Carnap* (LaSalle, Illinois: Open Court, 1964). The last-mentioned volume contains a reply by Carnap. It should be added that Ayer's later view is in many respects different from traditional dualism. Thus he regards the quest for a general justification of our belief in other minds as misguided. The following recent articles deal with the same questions: M. Shearn's "Other People's Sense-Data,"* *Ar. Soc.*, 1951, P. Alexander's "Other People's Experiences,"* *ibid.*, R. Wollheim's "Privacy," *ibid.*, J. F. Thomson, "The Argument from Analogy and Our Knowledge of Other Minds," *M*, 1951, S. Hampshire, "The Analogy of Feeling," *M*, 1952, A. H. B. Allen, "Other Minds," *ibid.*, R. Wollheim, "Hampshire's Analogy," *ibid.*, J. Watling, "Ayer on Other Minds," *T*, 1954, W. W. Mellor, "Three Problems about Other Minds," *M*, 1956, H. Feigl, "Other Minds and the Egocentric Predicament," *JP*, 1958, R. Hoffman, "The Problem of Other Minds—Genuine or Pseudo?" *PPR*, 1960, S. C. Coval, "Exceptives and Other Minds," *A*, 1959, Bruce Aune, "The Problem of Other Minds," *PR*, 1961, C. Wellman "Our Criteria for Third-Person Psychological Sentences," *JP*, 1961, R. C. Buck, "Non-Other Minds," in R. J. Butler (ed.), *Analytical Philosophy, op. cit.*, H. H. Castaneda, "Criteria, Analogy, and Knowledge of Other Minds," *JP*, 1962, the same author's "Consciousness and Behavior: Their Basic Connections," in a volume he edited, *Intentionality, Minds and Perception* (Detroit: Wayne State U.P., 1967) and his "On the Logic of Attributions of Self-Knowledge to Others," *JP*, 1968, V. C. Chappell, "Myself and Others," *A Sup.*, 1963, D. C. Long, "The Philosophical Concept of a Human Body, *PR*, 1964, P. Ziff, "The Simplicity of Other Minds," *JP*, 1965, A. Plantinga, "Induction and Other Minds," *RM*, 1966, a reply to Plantinga by M. Slote in the same volume and Plantinga's rejoinder in *RM*, 1968, T. Forrest, "*P*-Predicates," I. C. Hungerland, "My Pains and Yours," and N. Malcolm, "The Privacy of Experience," the last three papers appearing in A. Stroll (ed.), *Epistemology* (N.Y.: Harper, 1967, p), L. R. Reinhardt, "Wittgenstein and Strawson on Other Minds," in P. Winch (ed.), *Studies in the Philosophy of Wittgenstein* (London: Routledge, 1969), K. Stern, "Belief in Other Minds," in H. E. Kiefer, M. K. Munitz (eds.), *Mind, Science and History* (Albany: State U. of N.Y. P., 1970), W. Hasker, "Theories, Analogies and Criteria," *APQ*, 1971, and H. Putnam, "Other Minds," in R. Rudner and I. Scheffler (eds.), *Logic and Art: Essays in Honor of Nelson Goodman* (Indianapolis: Bobbs-Merrill, 1972). There are very detailed discussions of the problem in D. Locke, *Myself and Others: A Study in our Knowledge of Minds* (Oxford: O.U.P., 1968) and S. Coval, *Scepticism and the First Person* (London: Methuen, 1966). Several important papers on other minds are reprinted in T. O. Buford (ed.), *Essays on Other Minds* (Urbana: U. of Ill. P., 1970) and in H. Morick (ed.), *Wittgenstein and the Problem of Other Minds* (N.Y.: McGraw-Hill, 1967, p).

The papers by Carnap and Hempel mentioned above are from the early days of logical positivism. Both these writers referred to their views as "physicalism."

Moritz Schlick also called himself a physicalist in his paper, "On the Relation between Psychological and Physical Concepts," reprinted in Feigl and Sellars, *op. cit.* Schlick's position is, however, clearly dualistic and thus not equivalent to logical behaviorism. Hempel and Carnap in later years also abandoned their earlier extreme viewpoint. Carnap's later views are sketched in "Logical Foundations of the Unity of Science," reprinted in Feigl and Sellars, *op. cit.* M. Scriven, "Logical Positivism and the Behavioral Sciences," in P. Achinstein and S. F. Barker (eds.), *The Legacy of Logical Positivism* (Baltimore: Johns Hopkins Press, 1969) is highly critical of logical positivist theories on the subject. C. G. Hempel, "Logical Positivism and the Social Sciences," in the same volume and Herbert Feigl's "The Mind-Body Problem in the Development of Logical Empiricism,"* reprinted in H. Feigl and M. Brodbeck (eds.), *Readings in the Philosophy of Science* (N.Y.: Appleton-Century-Crofts, 1953), are sympathetic discussions of the same theories.

Feigl's own views are stated briefly in "Mind-Body, Not a Pseudo-Problem," in S. Hook, *op. cit.,* and very fully in "The 'Mental' and the 'Physical',"* in H. Feigl and M. Scriven (eds.), *Minnesota Studies in the Philosophy of Science,* Volume II (Minneapolis: U. of Minn. P., 1957). The last-mentioned essay, together with a Postscript was subsequently published as a book bearing the same title (Minneapolis: U. of Minn. P., 1967, p). Feigl's most recent discussions of the subject are "Philosophical Embarrassments of Psychology," in D. P. Schultz (ed.), *The Science of Psychology—Critical Reflections* (N.Y.: Appleton-Century-Crofts, 1970) and "Some Crucial Issues of Mind-Body Monism," *Sy,* 1971. Feigl's position is a modern version of the identity theory. The referents of our introspective reports are, on this view, in some important sense of the word "identical" with those of certain terms of the language that would be used by a neurophysiologist. Feigl emphasizes that, unlike Spinoza's version of the identity theory, his view dispenses with any unknowable underlying Reality of which the mental and the physical are "aspects." P. K. Feyerabend and G. Maxwell (eds.), *Mind, Matter and Method—Essays in Honor of Herbert Feigl* (Minneapolis: U. of Minnesota P., 1966) contains critical discussions of the identity theory by B. Aune, M. Brodbeck, P. E. Meehl, and M. Scriven. The papers by Aune and Meehl are specifically directed at Feigl's version of the identity theory. An identity theory, which is in many respects similar to Feigl's, is also advocated by H. Putnam in his "Minds and Machines" in S. Hook (ed.), *Dimensions of Mind, op. cit.,* and in several other papers including "Robots: Machines or Artificially Created Life?," *JP,* 1964, reprinted in Hampshire, *op. cit.,* "Psychological Predicates," in W. H. Capitain and D. D. Merrill (eds.), *Art, Mind and Religion* (Pittsburgh: U. of Pittsburgh P., 1967—there are critical comments by B. Aune and U. T. Place in this volume), "The Mental Life of Some Machines," in H. Castaneda (ed.), *Intentionality, Minds and Perception, op. cit.* (this volume contains comments by A. Platinga and a reply by Putnam), and "Logical Positivism and the Philosophy of Mind," in P. Achinstein and S. F. Barker (eds.), *The Legacy of Logical Positivism, op. cit.* A. Quinton, in "Mind and Matter," in J. R. Smythies (ed.), *Brain and Mind* (London: Routledge, 1965) supports the identity theory in a very detailed discussion of several of the most difficult questions concerning the body-mind relation. The same volume contains comments on Quinton's paper by C. J. Ducasse, H. H. Price and J. R. Smythies.

The most widely-discussed version of the identity theory in recent years is that of U. T. Place and J. J. C. Smart. The theory was first expounded by Place in "Is Consciousness a Brain Process?" *British Journal of Psychology,* 1956, reprinted both in Flew, *op. cit.,* and in Chappell, *op. cit.* It was subsequently elaborated by Smart in the article parts of which constitute Selection 21 of the present volume. Place and Smart regard their theory as a form of materialism. This was particularly stressed by them in later articles—by Place in "Materialism as a Scientific Hypothesis," *PR*, 1960, and by Smart in "Materialism," *JP*, 1963. The papers by Smart and Place as well as discussions of their theory, several of them highly critical, by J. T. Stevenson, K. Baier, J. Shaffer, J. Cornman, R. Coburn, N. Malcolm, C. Taylor, and J. M. Hinton are reprinted, together with a very clear editorial introduction, in C. V. Borst (ed.), *The Mind-Brain Identity Theory* (London: Macmillan, 1970, p). Another volume entirely devoted to this theory is C. F. Presley (ed.), *The Identity Theory of Mind* (Brisbane, Australia: U. of Queensland P., 1967). It contains papers by D. L. Gunner, C. D. Rollins, P. Herbst, M. Deutscher, B. Medlin, as well as a reply by Smart to his critics. The Smart–Place theory is also discussed in the following articles: G. Pitcher, "Sensations and Brain Processes: A Reply to Professor Smart," *AJ*, 1960, J. Beloff, "The Identity Hypothesis: A Critique" (with comments by W. R. Brain, C. J. Ducasse, A. Flew, and H. H. Price), in J. R. Smythies (ed.), *Brain and Mind, op. cit.*, R. Hoffman, "Malcolm and Smart on Brain-Mind Identity" *P*, 1967, M. O. Hocutt, "In Defense of Materialism," *PPR*, 1967, W. Sellars, "The Identity Approach to the Mind-Body Problem," in his *Philosophical Perspectives* (Springfield, Ill., Thomas, 1967), reprinted in Hampshire, *op. cit.*, R. J. Hirst, "Mind and Brain: the Identity Hypothesis," in *The Human Agent, Royal Institute of Philosophy Lectures Volume I* (London: Macmillan, 1968, p), J. J. Thomson, "The Identity Thesis," in S. Morgenbesser, P. Suppes, M. White (eds.), *Philosophy, Science, and Method* (N.Y.: St. Martin's Press, 1969), M. C. Bradley, "Two Arguments Against the Identity Thesis," in R. Brown and C. D. Rollins (eds.), *Contemporary Philosophy in Australia* (London: Allen & Unwin, 1969), S. Munsat, "Could Sensations Be Processes?", *M*, 1969, D. E. Cooper, "Materialism and Perception," *PQ*, 1970, M. A. Simon, "Materialism, Mental Language and Mind-Body Identity," *PPR*, 1970, S. Candlish, "Mind, Brain and Identity," *M*, 1970, C. H. Whitely, "The Mind-Brain Identity Hypothesis," *PQ*, 1970, R. Pucetti, "A Materialist Fallacy of Mind," *P*, 1970 (there are replies to Pucetti by D. G. Collingridge and L. Stevenson in *P*, 1971), J. Heil, "Sensations, Experiences and Brain Processes," *P*, 1970, S. J. Noren, "Smart's Materialism: The Identity Theory and Translation," *AJ*, 1970, R. Ziedins, "Identification of Characteristics of Mental Events with Characteristics of Brain Events," *APQ*, 1971, F. Stoutland, "Ontological Simplicity and the Identity Hypothesis," *PPR*, 1971, J. D. Carney, "The Compatibility of the Identity Theory with Dualism," *M*, 1971, D. Odegard, "The Sense of 'Mental Events = Corporeal Events'," *Sy.*, 1971, M. Martin, "The Body-Mind Problem and Neurophysiological Reduction," *T*, 1971, J. Kim, "Materialism and the Criterion of the Mental," *Sy.*, 1971, and S. J. Noren, "Smart's Identity Theory, Translation and Incorrigibility," *M*, 1972. There is a reply to Munsat by Place in *M*, 1972. Smart's most recent contribution to the discussion is "Reports of Immediate Experiences," *Sy.*, 1971.

An ingenious way of outflanking scepticism about other minds is advocated in Ch. III of P. F. Strawson, *Individuals* (London: Methuen, 1959), which is a revised and expanded version of Strawson's article by the same name in H. Feigl, M. Scriven, and G. Maxwell (eds.), *Minnesota Studies in the Philosophy of Science*, Volume II, *op. cit.*, reprinted in Chappell, *op. cit.*, Vesey, *op. cit.*, and also in Gustafson, *op. cit.* Strawson's objections to Cartesian dualism are restated in "Self, Mind and Body," available in H. Morick (ed.), *Introduction to the Philosophy of Mind, op. cit.* According to Strawson, the sceptic, in the very act of stating his doubt, tacitly accepts the framework of concepts which his scepticism is calling into question. On Strawson's view, which may be regarded as a version of the identity-theory, the concept of the *person,* must be treated as primitive, and something, x, is a person only if *both* states of consciousness and certain corporeal characteristics are ascribable to it. There have been numerous discussions of Strawson's theory in recent years, including M. C. Bradley, "Mr. Strawson and Skepticism," *A,* 1959, C. D. Rollins, "Personal Predicates," *PQ,* 1960, R. B. Freed and J. A. Fodor, "Pains, Puns, Persons and Pronouns," *A,* 1961, R. Rosthal, "Ascription of Mental Predicates," *PSt.,* 1961, D. Mannison, "On the Alleged Ambiguity of Strawson's P-Predicates," *A,* 1962, H. D. Lewis, "Mind and Body," *Ar. Soc.,* 1962–63. B. Aune, "Feelings, Moods, and Introspection," *M,* 1963, G. Iseminger, "Meaning, Criteria, and P-Predicates," *A,* 1963, S. C. Coval, "Persons and Criteria in Strawson," *PPR,* 1964, V. C. Aldrich, "Behavior, Simulating and Nonsimulating," *JP,* 1966, C. B. Martin, "People," in R. Brown and C. D. Rollins (eds.), *Contemporary Philosophy in Australia, op. cit.* and D. S. Clarke, "A Defense of the No-Ownership Theory," *M,* 1972. There is a very detailed critical discussion in A. J. Ayer's "The Concept of a Person," which is available in his *The Concept of a Person and Other Essays, op. cit.* It is also reprinted in H. Castaneda (ed.), *Intentionality, Minds and Perception, op. cit.,* where it is subjected to critical comments by E. L. Gettier, followed by Ayer's rejoinder. There are critical reviews of Strawson's *Individuals* by J. Urmson in *M,* 1961, by D. Pears, *PQ,* 1961, and by B. A. G. Williams, *P,* 1961.

It was previously mentioned that both Smart and Place developed their version of the mind-brain identity theory along materialistic lines. The kind of materialism which these writers support is, however, significantly different from the reductive materialism of the logical behaviorists. One of the most detailed statements of this view, which he calls "central state materialism" is found in D. M. Armstrong, *A Materialist Theory of Mind* (London: Routledge, 1968) and in his lecture "The Nature of Mind," *Q,* 1968, reprinted in C. B. Borst (ed.), *The Mind-Brain Identity Theory, op. cit.,* which also contains the defenses of materialism by Smart and Place. Other recent writers who advocate radical forms of materialism are P. Feyerabend in "Materialism and the Mind-Body Problem," *RM,* 1963, R. Rorty, "Mind-Body Identity, Privacy and Categories," *RM,* 1965, D. K. Lewis "An Argument for the Identity Theory," *JP,* 1966 and W. V. O. Quine, *Word and Object* (Cambridge: M.I.T. Press, 1960, p, pp. 264–266). Armstrong is criticized in R. H. Kane, "Minds, Causes, and Behavior," *RM,* 1970, Quine is criticized in J. Cornman, "Mental Terms, Theoretical Terms and Materialism," *PS,* 1968, and Rorty is criticized by Cornman in "On the Elimination of 'Sensations' and Sensations," *RM,* 1968. Rorty's "In Defense of Eliminative Materialism," *RM,* 1970, is a reply to Cornman. Several of the articles just mentioned as well as other recent discussions of materialism are collected in J. O'Connor (ed.), *Modern Materialism and Readings on Mind-Body Identity* (N.Y.: Harcourt, Brace, 1969, p), D. M. Rosenthal (ed.), *Materialism and the Mind-Body Problem* (Englewood Cliffs: Prentice-Hall, 1971, p) and in Borst, *op. cit.* Cornman, who maintains that sensations present the toughest problem for materialists, has stated his objections in great detail in *Materialism and Sensations* (New Haven: Yale U.P., 1971). Very sophisticated forms of materialism are advocated by D. C. Dennett in *Content and Consciousness: An Analysis of Mental Phenomena* (London: Routledge, 1969) and in two articles by the English psychologist B. A. Farrell —"Experience," *M,* 1950, reprinted in Chappell, *op. cit.,* and "Some Reflections on the Nature of Consciousness," in B. Rothblatt (ed.), *Changing Perspectives* on Man (Chicago: Chicago U.P., 1968). Mo, April 1972, is devoted to "Materialism Today," including contributions by W. G. Lycan, W. I. Matson, J. W. Cornman, M. Thornton, J. Kim, D. M. Armstrong, and J. J. C. Smart.

A substance-theory similar to the one Reid defends in our Selection 16 was advanced by the 18th century theologian, Bishop Butler, in his "Dissertation of Personal Identity," which is available in Volume I of W. E. Gladstone's edition of Butler's *Works* (Oxford U.P., 1896) and is sometimes printed as an Appendix to Butler's more famous *Analogy of Religion*. Substance-views are defended by Lotze, *Metaphysics* (Oxford: Clarendon Press, 1887), in Ch. 5 of J. McCosh, *An Examination of J. S. Mill's Philosophy* (N.Y.: R. Carter, 1880), in Ch. XXI of Maher, *op. cit.*, in Ch. V of Pratt, *op. cit.*, in Volume I of F. R. Tennant, *Philosophical Theology* (Cambridge: Cambridge U.P., 1930), in Lectures V and VI of C. A. Campbell, *On Selfhood and Godhood* (London: Allen & Unwin, N.Y.: Macmillan, 1957), Ch. 13 of G. P. Klubertanz, *The Philosophy of Human Nature* (N.Y.: Appleton-Century-Crofts, 1953), Ch. 17 of J. E. Royce, *Man and His Nature, op. cit.*, and Ch. 15 of the same author's *Man and Meaning, op. cit.* An unorthodox version of the substance-theory is advocated by J. Laird in *The Problems of the Self* (London: Macmillan, 1917) and *The Idea of the Soul* (London: Hodder & Stoughton, 1924). The Kantian position that acts of perception require a persisting subject is defended by the Kant-scholar, H. J. Paton, in his contribution to Volume 8 of *University of California Publications in Philosophy* (Berkeley: U. of California P., 1926) and in "Self-Identity," *M*, 1929, which is reprinted in his *In Defense of Reason* (London: Hutchinson, 1951). Idealistic views on the subject are also advocated by J. H. Muirhead in his contribution to Volume 9 of the *University of California Publications in Philosophy* (Berkeley: U. of California P., 1927) and by B. Bosanquet and A. S. Pringle-Pattison in the symposium "Do Finite Individuals Possess a Substantive or an Adjectival Mode of Being?" *Ar. Soc.*, 1917–18. "Bundle"—theories substantially similar to Hume's are advocated by J. S. Mill in Ch. XII of *An Examination of Sir William Hamilton's Philosophy, op. cit.*, in various books by Bertrand Russell, most recently in *Portraits from Memory and Other Essays* (London: Allen & Unwin, N.Y.: Simon & Schuster, 1956), and, with some interesting qualifications, in Volume I of W. James, *The Principles of Psychology* (N.Y.: Holt, 1890). T. Penelhum's "Hume on Personal Identity," *PR*, 1955, contains a particularly valuable discussion of the notion of "sameness." Penelhum follows Hume in rejecting the substance-theory, without however endorsing Hume's paradoxical conclusions concerning self-identity. There is an interesting analysis of Hume's position in D. F. Pears, "Hume on Personal Identity," in D. F. Pears (ed.), *David Hume: A Symposium* (London: Macmillan, 1963), and there is a symposium on "Self-Identity," by J. N. Wright and C. A. Mace, taking its point of departure from Hume's position, in *Ar. Soc. Sup.*, 1939. A recent sympathetic discussion of Hume's theory is N. Pike, "Hume's Bundle Theory of the Self: A Limited Defense," *APQ*, 1967. A. J. Ayer discusses Hume's views in his introduction to A. J. Ayer and Raymond Winch (eds.), *The British Empirical Philosophers* (London: Routledge, 1952). He develops his own position more fully in Ch. 5 of *The Problem of Knowledge, op. cit.* and in Book II, Ch. 3 of *The Origins of Pragmatism* (San Francisco: Freeman, Cooper, 1968). Locke, whose views are criticized by Reid in Selection 16, states his position in Ch. 27 of Book II of his *Essay Concerning Human Understanding*. There are useful discussions of Locke in A. Flew, "Locke and the Problem of Personal Identity," *P*, 1951, and A. B. Palma, "Memory and Personal Identity," *AJ*, 1964. There are selections from Locke, Butler, Hume, and James in Flew, *op. cit.*, and from Locke, Hume, and Russell in Vesey, *op.*

cit. Most contemporary philosophers who reject the substance-view as unintelligible or as of no explanatory value do not simply endorse the bundle-theory. Many of them criticize Hume and Mill for having paid no attention to bodily continuity as at least one of the criteria of personal identity. This question and also the question of the relation between memory and personal identity has been widely discussed in recent years. The following items are particularly worth mentioning: I. Gallie, "Is the Self a Substance?", *M,* 1936, H. P. Grice, "Personal Identity," *M,* 1941, B. A. O. Williams, "Personal Identity and Individuation," *Ar. Soc.* 1956–57, C. B. Martin, "Identity and Exact Similarity," *A,* 1958, and Ch. 6 of the same author's *Religious Belief* (Ithaca: Cornell U.P., 1959), G. C. Nerlich, "Sameness, Difference and Continuity," *A,* 1958, S. Shoemaker, "Personal Identity and Memory," *JP,* 1959, T. Penelhum, "Personal Identity, Memory, and Survival," *JP,* 1959, R. Coburn, "Bodily Continuity and Personal Identity," *A,* 1960 (to which there is a reply in the same volume by B. A. O. Williams), J. M. Shorter, "More about Bodily Continuity and Personal Identity," *A,* 1962, A. Quinton," "The Soul," *JP,* 1962, A. Flew, " 'The Soul' of Mr. A. M. Quinton," *JP,* 1963, D. Odegard, "Personal and Bodily Identity," *PQ,* 1969, C. B. Daniels, "Personal Identity," *APQ,* 1969, E. M. Zemach, "Self Identity Without Criteria," *AJ,* 1969, B. Williams, "The Self and the Future," *PR,* 1970, S. Shoemaker, "Persons and their Pasts," *APQ,* 1970, J. M. Shorter, "Personal Identity, Personal Relationships, and Criteria," *Ar. Soc.,* 1970–71, D. Parfit, "Personal Identity," *PR,* 1971, B. Gert, "Personal Identity and the Body," *D,* 1971, A. Sloman, "New Bodies for Sick Persons: Personal Identity without Physical Continuity," *A,* 1971 and three articles on personal identity by T. Penelhum, F. Cowley and D. Parfit in *JP,* 1971. In a number of recent papers, R. M. Chisholm has defended a view concerning personal identity that has many affinities with the views of Reid and Butler. In a paper entitled "The Loose and Popular and the Strict and Philosophical Sense of Identity," which is included in N. S. Care and R. H. Grimm (eds.), *Perception and Personal Identity* (Cleveland: P. of Case Western Reserve U., 1969), he supports the view of Bishop Butler that the identity we ascribe to objects like ships is identity only in the loose and popular sense whereas the identity we ascribe to persons is identity in the strict and philosophical sense. The same volume contains critical comments by S. Shoemaker and a rejoinder by Chisholm. Chisholm also discusses the subject in "Identity Through Possible Worlds," *N,* 1967, and in "Identity Through Time," in H. E. Kiefer and M. K. Munitz (eds.), *Language, Belief and Metaphysics* (Albany: State U. of N.Y. P., 1970). The last-mentioned volume contains critical remarks by P. F. Strawson as well as Chisholm's reply. There is an original, subtle, and very detailed discussion of the entire subject in S. Shoemaker, *Self-Knowledge and Self-Identity* (Ithaca: Cornell U.P., 1963). C. O. Evans, in *The Subject of Consciousness* (London: Allen & Unwin, 1970), argues that the alternatives of substance and bundle theories of the self are not exhaustive and offers a third alternative of his own. Problems concerning the nature of personal identity are closely related to more general puzzles about the nature of identity. These more general questions are explored in P. Geach, "Identity," *RM,* 1967, F. Feldman, "Geach and Relative Identity," *RM,* 1969 (the same issue of *RM* contains a reply by Geach), J. Perry, "The Same F," *PR,* 1970, D. Wiggins, *Identity and Spatio-Temporal Continuity* (Oxford: Blackwell, 1970), D. Odegard, "Identity through Time," *APQ,* 1972, and in M. K. Munitz (ed.), *Identity and Individuation* (N.Y.: N.Y.U.P., 1971). The contributors to the last-mentioned volume include, beside the editor, R. M. Chisholm, R. C. Coburn, S. Shoemaker, M. Cartwright, J. Woods, and W.

Ruddick. There is a detailed critical discussion of Wiggins' book by Shoemaker in *PR*, 1970.

W. R. Alger, *A Critical History of the Doctrine of a Future Life* (N.Y.: Widdleton, 1871), is an enormous book which contains a great deal of information on the history of the belief in immortality. There are selections from Plato, St. Augustine, Aquinas, Butler, and other classical defenders of the belief in immortality in A. Flew (ed.), *Body, Mind and Death, op. cit.* Recent or contemporary presentations of the Catholic position are found in Ch. XXIV of Maher, *op. cit.*, in both of the previously mentioned books by J. E. Royce, Ch. 13 of Klubertanz, *op. cit.*, Ch. V of J. Maritain, *The Range of Reason* (N.Y.: Scribner's, 1952, p), and M. and L. Becqué, *Life After Death* (London: Burns & Oates, 1960). Defenses of the belief in an afterlife, from a Protestant standpoint, are found in John Fiske, *The Destiny of Man* (Boston and N.Y.: Houghton, Mifflin, 1884), the same author's *Life Everlasting* (Boston and N.Y.: Houghton, Mifflin, 1901), Hastings Rashdall, "The Moral Argument for Personal Immortality," in W. R. Matthews (ed.), *King's College Lectures on Immortality* (London: U. of London P., 1920), H. E. Fosdick, *The Assurance of Immortality* (N.Y.: Macmillan, 1926), and A. E. Taylor, *The Christian Hope of Immortality* (London: Unicorn Press, 1938). Sympathetic also is William James, *Human Immortality* (Boston and N.Y.: Houghton, Mifflin, 1898, second edition with an answer to critics, 1917). The unbeliever's position is represented in Hume's essay "On the Immortality of the Soul," which is available in various editions of Hume's writings, e.g., in R. Wollheim (ed.), *David Hume on Religion* (N.Y.: Meridian, 1964, p), in E. S. P. Haynes, *The Belief in Personal Immortality* (London: Watts, 1913), Corliss Lamont, *The Illusion of Immortality* (London: Watts, N.Y.: Putnam, 1935), C. Cohen, *The Other Side of Death* (London: Pioneer Press, 1922), in several chapters of Bertrand Russell, *Why I Am Not a Christian and Other Essays* (London: Allen & Unwin, N.Y.: Simon & Schuster, 1957, p), and in Ch. XI of R. W. Sellars, *The Next Step in Religion* (N.Y.: Macmillan, 1918). The discussions by Maritain and Sellars are reprinted in W. P. Alston (ed.) *Religious Belief and Philosophical Thought* (N.Y.: Harcourt, Brace & World, 1963). A very detailed rebuttal of the so-called moral argument for immortality is contained in Section D of C. D. Broad, *The Mind and Its Place in Nature, op. cit.*

Unbelievers like Hume and Russell did not question the intelligibility of the claim that human beings survive after death. They merely regarded all such statements as very probably false. More recently some philosophers have questioned whether such claims make any sense. There is a tendency to regard all talk about disembodied minds as meaningless and even the belief in reincarnation is criticized as *logically* defective and not merely factually unsupported on the ground that bodily continuity is a necessary condition of personal identity. Such a radically negative position is championed by A. Flew in numerous publications including his introduction to *Body, Mind and Death, op. cit.*, "Can a Man Witness His Own Funeral?", *Hibbert Journal*, 1956, Ch. 4 of his *An Introduction to Western Philosophy* (Indianapolis: Bobbs-Merrill, 1971, p) and "Sense and Survival," *The Humanist* (London), 1960. In *Survival and Disembodied Existence* (London: Routledge, 1970), one of the most detailed discussions of this topic in recent years, T. Penelhum reaches a less completely negative verdict. "The doctrine of disembodied survival," he concludes, "founders because no intelligible account seems possible . . . of the persistence of a disembodied person through time," but Penelhum allows that a doctrine of "astral or ectoplasmic bodies" might escape these difficulties. The questions raised by Flew and Penelhum are also discussed in Ch. 6 of C. B. Martin,

Religious Belief, op. cit., C. Lewy, "Is the Notion of Disembodied Existence Self-Contradictory?" *Ar. Soc.,* 1942–43. A. H. Basson, "The Immortality of the Soul," *M,* 1950 (with answers by Nikan in *M,* 1951, and by C. B. Martin in *M,* 1955), A. C. MacIntyre's "A Note on Immortality," *M,* 1955, J. Knox, Jr., "Can the Self Survive the Death of its Mind?", *RS,* 1969, J. A. Harvie, "The Immortality of the Soul," *RS,* 1969, M. B. Woodhouse, "Selves and Minds: A Reply to Prof. Knox," *RS,* 1970 (followed by Knox's rejoinder), and R. Young, "The Resurrection of the Body," *S,* 1970. Impressed by the contention that it is meaningless to talk about a disembodied consciousness, a number of pro-religious philosophers have come out in favor of the doctrine of the resurrection of the body which has to be taken on faith but which, they maintain, is at least intelligible. Such a position is supported in Ch. 4 of J. Hick, *Philosophy of Religion* (Englewood Cliffs: Prentice-Hall, 1963, p) and in Ch. 2 of P. Geach, *God and the Soul* (London: Routledge, 1969).

Some philosophers have been impressed by the evidence provided for the belief in survival by what is called "psychical research." C. D. Broad has written extensively on this topic. He discussed it in *The Mind and Its Place in Nature, op. cit.,* and more recently in *Human Personality and the Possibility of Its Survival* (Berkeley: U. of California P., 1955) and *Lectures on Psychical Research* (London: Routledge, 1962). C. J. Ducasse reached the conclusion that the material from psychical research makes belief in survival probable. His views are elaborated in Chs. 20 and 21 of *Nature, Mind and Death, op. cit.,* and in *A Critical Examination of the Belief in a Life After Death* (Springfield: Charles C. Thomas, 1961), which contains a very detailed discussion of all aspects of the subject of immortality. The empirical data are surveyed in an article by Gardner Murphy, "An Outline of Survival Evidence," *Journal of the American Society of Psychical Research,* 1945, and in R. H. Thouless, "The Empirical Evidence for Survival," *ibid.,* 1960. D. J. West, *Psychical Research Today* (London: Duckworth, 1954), is a useful survey of all areas of psychical research. After a critical study of this material, E. R. Dodds reaches a negative conclusion in "Why I Do Not Believe in Survival," *Proceedings of the Society for Psychical Research,* 1934. A. Flew, in *A New Approach to Psychical Research* (London: Watts, 1953), questions whether the theory of survival can even in principle be confirmed or disconfirmed by empirical data of any kind. H. H. Price defends the view that belief in survival is intelligible in "What Kind of Next World?", *Tomorrow,* 1956 and in greater detail in "Survival and the Idea of 'Another World'," *Proceedings of the Society for Psychical Research,* 1953. The last-mentioned article was the occasion for an exchange between Price and Flew in *The Journal of the Society of Psychical Research* (London) of the same year. Price's paper was reprinted, together with comments by Flew and Smythies and Price's rejoinders in J. R. Smythies (ed.), *Brain and Mind, op. cit.* Price's latest paper on this subject is "The Problem of Life After Death," *RS,* 1968. J. B. Rhine in his books *The Reach of the Mind* (N.Y.: Sloane, London: Faber & Faber, 1947) and *New World of the Mind* (N.Y.: Sloane, 1953) argues, in effect, as do a number of other writers, that the data of psychical research support dualistic interactionism and are incompatible with any kind of materialism. These claims are questioned in R. Walter, "Parapsychology and Dualism," *Scientific Monthly,* 1954, and also in Flew's *A New Approach to Psychical Research, op. cit.,* and the same author's "Minds and Mystifications," *The Listener,* 1951. There is a lively and illuminating discussion of these and related issues in M. Kneale, R. Robinson, and C. W. K. Mundle, "Is Psychical Research Relevant to Philosophy?", *Ar. Soc. Sup.,* 1950.

The following articles cannot be easily fitted into any of the above categories: A. C. Ewing, "Mental Acts," *M,* 1948, reprinted in Ewing's *Non-Linguistic Philosophy* (London: Allen & Unwin, 1968), two articles by J. N. Findlay—"Recommendations Regarding the Language of Introspection," *PPR,* 1948, and "On Having in Mind," *P,* 1953—J. R. Jones, "The Self in Sensory Cognition," *M,* 1949, W. Kneale, "Experience and Introspection," *Ar. Soc.,* 1949–50, the same author's lecture, *On Having a Mind* (Cambridge: Cambridge U.P., 1962), M. Kneale, "What Is the Mind-Body Problem?", *Ar. Soc.,* 1949–50, R. I. Aaron, "Dispensing with Mind," *Ar. Soc.,* 1951–52, two articles by J. O. Wisdom—"A New Model for the Mind-Body Relationship," *BJPS,* 1952, and "Some Mind-Body Problems," *Ar. Soc.,* 1960–61, D. Mitchell, "Privileged Utterances," *M,* 1953, K. R. Popper, "Language and the Body-Mind Problem," *Proceedings of the XIth International Congress of Philosophy,* Brussels, 1953, the same author's "A Note on the Mind-Body Problem," *A,* 1955, both reprinted in Popper's *Conjectures and Refutations* (N.Y.: Harper, 1963), J. R. Jones and T. R. Miles, "Self-Knowledge," *Ar. Soc. Sup.,* 1956, W. J. Ginnane, "Thoughts," *M,* 1960, H. Hudson, "Why Are Our Feelings of Pain Perceptually Unobservable?", *A,* 1961, M. McCloskey, "Minds," *AJ,* 1962, D. M. Armstrong, "Is Introspective Knowledge Incorrigible?", *PR,* 1963, T. R. Miles, "The 'Mental'–'Physical' Dichotomy," *Ar. Soc.,* 1963–64, T. Duggan, "The Privacy of Experience," *M,* 1963, R. G. Swinburne, "Privacy," *A Sup.,* 1964, D. Locke, "The Privacy of Pains," *A,* 1964, C. Landesman, "Mental Events," *PPR,* 1964, V. Somenzi, "Entropy, Information and Mind-Body Problem," in S. Dockx and P. Bernays (eds.), *Information and Prediction in Science* (N.Y.: Academic Press, 1965), H. H. Price, "The Expressive Theory of the Mind-Body Relation," in F. C. Dommeyer (ed.), *Current Philosophical Issues, op. cit.,* J. Kim, "Psychophysical Laws and Theories of Mind," *T,* 1967, G. N. A. Vesey, "Agent and Spectator: the Double-Aspect Theory," in *The Human Agent, Royal Institute of Philosophy Lectures Volume I, op. cit.,* R. Taylor, "How to Bury the Mind-Body Problem," *APQ,* 1969, N. Brody and P. Oppenheim, "Application of Bohr's Principle of Complementarity to the Mind-Body Problem," *JP,* 1969, T. L. S. Sprigge, "The Privacy of Experience," *M,* 1969, K. Gunderson, "Asymmetries and Mind-Body Perplexities," in M. Radner and S. Winokur (eds.), *Analyses of Theories and Methods of Physics and Psychology* (Minneapolis: U. of Minnesota P., 1970) and W. Alston, "Varieties of Privileged Access," *APQ,* 1971. D. Van de Vate, Jr. (ed.), *Persons, Privacy and Feeling* (Memphis: Memphis State U.P., 1970) contains six essays on various of the questions discussed in the present section. Volume 3 of *The Encyclopedia of the Social Sciences* (N.Y.: Macmillan, 1930) contains an extremely interesting article on "Consciousness" by the Gestalt psychologist, K. Koffka, in which he explains his reasons for opposing the Cartesian tradition. A number of important papers by W. Sellars, including "Empiricism and the Philosophy of Mind," are collected in his book, *Science, Perception and Reality* (London: Routledge, 1964). J. R. Smythies discusses the implications of experiences resulting from drugs like mescaline and LSD in "Some Recent Theories of Mind," in I. T. Ramsey (ed.), *Biology and Personality* (Oxford: Blackwell, 1965). This book also contains comments on Smythies' paper by K. Oldfield, H. H. Price and A. Quinton. In his very provocative and scientifically well-informed *Persons* (London: Macmillan, 1968), R. Puccetti deals with the question as to what would have to exist extraterrestrially to justify the claim that there are persons in the universe over and above human beings.

The following articles in *The Encyclopedia of Philosophy* contain discussions that are relevant to the topics treated in the present section: "Behaviorism" (A. S. Kaufman, 1–268), "Consciousness" (C. Landesman, 2–191), "Images" (A. R. Manser, 4–133), "Imagination" (A. R. Manser, 4–136), "Immortality" (A. Flew, 4–139), "Materialism" (K. Campbell, 5–179), "Mind-Body Problem" (J. Shaffer, 5–336), "Other Minds" (J. M. Shorter, 6–7), "Panpsychism" (P. Edwards, 6–22), "Personal Identity" (T. Penelhum, 6–95), "Private Language Problem" (H. N. Castaneda, 6–458), "Psychological Behaviorism" (C. Taylor, 6–516), "Psychology" (R. S. Peters and C. A. Mace, 7–1), "Ryle, Gilbert" (J. O. Urmson, 7–269), "Thinking" (B. Aune, 8–100), and "Wittgenstein, Ludwig" (N. Malcolm, 8–327).

There is a very comprehensive bibliography covering most aspects of the subject in H. Feigl, *The "Mental" and the "Physical"—The Essay and a Postscript, op. cit.*

IV

Moral
Judgments

Introduction

People constantly use terms like "good" and "evil," "right" and "wrong," "virtuous" and "sinful," "ought," "duty," "obliged," and many others, all of which seem to have a fairly similar function in our discourse. It is customary to refer to them as the "moral" or "ethical" predicates and to say that the sentences in which they occur express "moral" or "ethical" judgments. When people apply opposite moral predicates to the same thing, philosophers say that there is "moral disagreement" between them.

It seems plain at first sight that there is a great deal of difference between moral judgments and straightforward statements of fact. If someone says "Mercy-killing is widely practiced by the medical profession in Connecticut," it is fairly clear what observations, what sort of facts would make his statement true. If, however, he went on to say "and all these mercy-killings are *wrong,* whatever their motives may be," it is not clear, at least not at first sight, what facts would establish the truth or falsehood of his judgment. In fact, it is not obvious that there are *any* facts which could make his claim either true or false. Again, if I say "Several hundred thousand persons from the New York area are at present serving in the armed forces," no one has any doubt about the kind of observations which would prove or disprove what I asserted. But if I said "It is the *duty* of every able-bodied American citizen to serve in the armed forces if called upon to do so," it is far from evident what facts, if any, would prove or disprove my statement.

When philosophers have written on the subject of "ethics" they have, among other things, discussed the question, "What (if any) is the meaning of the moral predicates and the moral judgments in which they occur?" and the related question, "What is the nature of moral disagreement?" They have also discussed a great many other questions, but the two just mentioned are perhaps the most basic. Philosophers have also concerned themselves, for instance, with the question, "What is the greatest good, or the so-called '*summum bonum*'?" And they have given widely conflicting answers to this question. But before this question can be approached in an intelligent fashion, we must have a clear idea as to what the word "good" means. Moreover, if certain theories about the meaning or function of the moral predicates were true, it would be pointless to ask the question about the *summum bonum*—at least, it would be a mistake to suppose that a true answer can be obtained to questions of this kind. Unfortunately, many writers on ethics neglected this very obvious consideration and raised all sorts of questions—about the *summum bonum,* about what we ought and ought not to do, about our unconditional duties, and what have you—without first making any attempt to determine the meaning of the moral predicates.

In this section we are exclusively concerned with the two fundamental questions about the meaning of moral judgments and the nature of moral disagreement. All our selections present various answers to these questions. Theories which attempt to answer these questions are nowadays called "metamoral" or "metaethical" theories. It should be noted that metamoral theories are interpretations of moral judgments but are not themselves moral judgments. This point may be made clear by considering briefly the metamoral theory called "subjectivism," which will be discussed more fully later on. A subjectivist maintains that all moral judgments are really, whatever their linguistic appearance may suggest, statements about the feelings or attitudes of the person who makes the moral judgment. Let us suppose that a certain person, A, has said, "Joseph McCarthy was a good man," and someone else, B, has said that McCarthy was an evil man. Let us next suppose that C is a subjectivist. Now, C's subjectivism does not commit him to endorsing either A's favorable or B's unfavorable moral judgment about McCarthy. It does commit him to a certain *interpretation* of both of their judgments. It commits him to holding that both A and B were merely referring to their own liking or disliking, their own love or hate, approval or disapproval, of Senator McCarthy. The same is true of all other metamoral theories. None of them logically implies a particular moral code or a specific moral judgment. All of them are, in this respect, perfectly neutral.

Before explaining the more important metamoral theories, it will be helpful to introduce some technical terms without which a fruitful discussion of this subject can hardly be carried on. To begin with, it is necessary to define the terms "subjective" and "objective" as applied to statements. A subjective statement, in our present context, is one in which the speaker or writer is referring to his own feeling or attitude or, in general, to a state of his own mind. In an objective statement, on the other hand, the speaker is talking about something other than the state of his own mind. If I say, "I feel angry now," this is a subjective statement in the sense just defined. If I say, "New York has eight million inhabitants," or "Mount Everest is the highest mountain on earth," these are objective statements. If I say, "General MacArthur is full of resentment and bitterness," this is in our sense an objective statement. I am indeed speaking about feelings, but the feelings which are the subject matter of my statement are MacArthur's and not my own. To say that a statement is objective in this sense does not necessarily imply that it is true or that it is supported by strong evidence or that it is made in an unbiased spirit. It merely means that the statement's *subject matter* is something other than the state of the speaker's own mind. The words "subjective" and "objective," are of course commonly used also in other senses. However, it will help to bring out the contrast between the rival metamoral theories if we use these terms here only in the sense just defined.

Next we must distinguish two senses in which people may be said to disagree. Suppose A says, "Nixon will win the election in 1972," and B retorts, "No, he will be defeated by a candidate of the Socialist Workers' Party." It is plain that A and B cannot both be right in this case, though they can both be mistaken. Following C. L. Stevenson, contemporary philosophers label this kind of disagreement "disagreement in belief," meaning by this that the two parties have made mutually incompatible assertions.

Let us consider another illustration. A now says, "I like Nixon," to which B retorts, "I detest him." Here, too, it would be natural to describe the situation as a case of disagreement. But here the two parties are making mutually compatible statements. It may well be the case that A really likes Nixon, while B really detests him. A and B disagree in the sense of entertaining opposite feelings or attitudes towards the same person. Again following Stevenson, philosophers refer to disagreement of this kind as "disagreement in attitude." It is evident that many cases of disagreement in attitude are the consequence of disagreement in belief. Whether this is always so is a much debated question which we do not need to discuss here.

The last distinction which has to be explained concerns two very different senses in which we may talk about the "settlement" or "resolution" of a dispute. Stalin and Trotzky, for example, disagreed as to whether socialism could exist in one country while all the rest of the world remained capitalist. In one sense Stalin very effectively settled this dispute in his favor by having Trotzky assassinated. But although the elimination of Trotzky from the scene settled the dispute in the sense of leaving the field to one of the parties, it did not settle the dispute in another sense—it did not prove that Stalin was right and Trotzky wrong. Again, I may be arguing with somebody whether Beria or Slansky or Zinoviev or Bukharin were "imperialist spies," and by means of forged documents and perjured witnesses I may convince my opponent that the accusations were true. In one sense this would constitute a settlement of our dispute, since we no longer disagree. In another sense, however, it would not mean a resolution of the dispute at all: I would not have proved the charges. These examples are meant to illustrate the distinction between settling or resolving a dispute in the sense of *terminating* it, whether by silencing one of the parties or by achieving agreement, and settling or resolving a dispute in the sense of *proving* one party right and the other party wrong. It will be convenient from now on to refer to the former as the "termination" and to the latter as the "resolution" of a dispute. There can be no doubt that while resolution and termination frequently go together, this is by no means always the case. It certainly happens that people are not convinced although adequate and more than adequate evidence has been presented, and, conversely, that people are convinced when adequate evidence has not been presented.

In surveying the major metamoral theories it is perhaps best to begin with the simplest. This is the theory already mentioned, according to which moral judgments are always nothing more than subjective statements. Moral judgments on this view always assert that the author of the judgment has or tends to have a certain feeling or attitude. This theory is usually known as "subjectivism." Sometimes, to differentiate it from other fairly similar theories, it is called "private subjectivism," sometimes "naive subjectivism." It is found in the writings of Hume and Westermarck and Bertrand Russell, though Russell occasionally inclines more to the emotive theory. It is also a very popular view among people without philosophical training, especially students of psychology and anthropology. It is implicit in such sayings as "Morality is just a matter of taste" or "There is no good, but thinking makes it so." According to subjectivism, moral disagreement is disagreement in attitude and not in belief, and moral disputes can be settled, if at all, only in the sense of being terminated. If I say "Abraham Lincoln was a better man than Joseph McCarthy," and you say "McCarthy was a better man than Lincoln," I can win the argument in the sense of silencing you or by getting you to share my feelings on the subject, but not in the sense of proving that I am right and that you are mistaken.

It is sometimes said that subjectivists are inconsistent in making moral judgments. Bertrand Russell, for instance, has written many books in which he makes all sorts of moral judgments—about marriage and divorce and birth-control, about socialism and communism and capitalism, about envy and cruelty and fear and love. His critics maintain that as a subjectivist he has no right to make these moral judgments, or any others for that matter. It is easy to see that this is not a valid objection. If I first say "There is nothing objectively superior or inferior about the works of different composers—it's all a matter of taste," I am not at all inconsistent in adding "and I happen to like Schubert better than Sibelius, that windy bore." I would be inconsistent only if I added that my preference for Schubert is superior to your preference for Sibelius. Similarly, a subjectivist is not inconsistent in making moral judgments. He would be inconsistent if he claimed a special, non-subjective character for his own moral judgments. He would be inconsistent if he said, "Your moral judgments are merely statements about how you feel, while mine are objective truths."

If this is not a valid objection, there are others, however, which in the opinion of most contemporary philosophers amount to a decisive refutation of subjectivism. Thus, to mention just one standard argument, it is pointed out that whenever two sentences have the same meaning, any facts proving or disproving one of them *ipso facto* prove or disprove the other. For instance, whatever facts are sufficient to prove that Bertrand Russell is an atheist equally prove that Bertrand Russell denies the existence of God. Conversely, if there are facts which prove or disprove one of a pair of sentences without proving or disproving the other, the two sentences cannot mean the same. Thus the facts which prove that Eisenhower is a general do not *ipso facto* prove that he believes in the existence of God; and the sentences "Eisenhower is a general" and "Eisenhower believes in God" do not mean the same. Now, according to subjectivism, moral judgments really mean the same as statements by the speaker about his own feelings. For instance, if A says "Birth-control is an evil practice" it is claimed that he means no more than "I, A, disapprove of birth-control." Let us call the former sentence "p" and the latter sentence "q." It is easy to see that facts which would prove q would certainly not prove p. To prove that he really disapproved of birth-control, A could with perfect relevance point to his record, e.g., his membership in a society opposed to birth control, his enthusiastic support of various moral protection leagues, his speeches and writings in opposition to birth control, and other things of the same kind. But nobody in his senses, neither A himself nor anybody else, would consider these autobiographical facts relevant to the truth of p. Whatever facts would prove p (assuming there are any), they are not the facts which would prove q. Hence p does not mean the same as q; and this holds equally for all moral judgments. It would follow that subjectivism does not give an adequate account of the meaning of moral judgments: whatever we do mean, we don't just mean that we ourselves have a certain feeling or attitude.

This argument and other similar standard arguments (see Ewing, Selection 26, pp. 312 ff.) have convinced most contemporary writers that subjectivism as here defined is an untenable theory. Many contemporary philosophers are nevertheless persuaded that subjectivism was getting at some important truth. They have tried to formulate theories which would escape the difficulties of subjectivism while embodying what is sound in it. Thus, according to Richard Brandt, when a man claims that X is good he means something like "If I had all the facts about X clearly in mind and if I were ethically consistent, I would approve of X." Again, there is the very similar "ideal observer" theory of Adam Smith and others which maintains that "X is good" can be translated into some such statement as "If there were an omniscient, disinterested and dispassionate observer he would approve of X." Another interesting theory has been proposed by the Australian philosopher John Mackie (Selection 30). On his view we constantly "objectify" our feelings of approval and disapproval. When we say about something that it is good we mean that it possesses a certain objective quality and in this respect subjectivists did not offer a correct account of moral judgments. However, although we *mean* more by "X is good" than that we approve it, there exists no such objective quality of goodness as we assert. All we *have a right* to assert is that we approve of X. In so far as subjectivism denies the *existence* of any special qualities of good and bad it is a sound theory. Finally, the emotive theory may be mentioned in this context. It, too, may be regarded as an attempt to restate whatever is worth saving in the contentions of the subjectivists. We shall say more about it a little later.

There are two types of "objectivism" which have been opposed to all the metamoral theories mentioned so far. On all these views moral judgments are objective claims and moral disagreements are essentially disagreements in belief. While they agree up to this point, the two types of objectivism differ very greatly on what they take to be the detailed meaning of moral judgments. The first type of objectivism maintains that the subject matter of moral judgments is always something "natural," that is, something or other which is or can be the object of somebody's experience. On views of this kind there is no such thing as a special moral faculty. The truth or falsehood of moral judgments can always in principle be established by the use of observation and the kind of method used in the natural sciences. Philosophers who adopt this position may be classified as "objective naturalists." Perhaps the most famous form of objective naturalism is the theory known as "utilitarianism." Interpreted as a metamoral theory rather than as a moral judgment, utilitarianism maintains that "X is right" means the same as "X produces the greatest possible happiness for the greatest number of people."

The other type of objectivism asserts that in addition to the senses and to introspection we possess the further faculty of "moral intuition" or "moral insight," and it is by means of this faculty that we recognize the truth, at any rate, of the most basic moral judgments. Philosophers holding this view are referred to as "objective non-naturalists" or "intuitionists." Most, though not all, intuitionists would identify this special moral faculty with the "understanding" or the "*a priori* insight." The moral intuition is not a "hunch" but a rational faculty and the basic moral principles are usually conceived by these writers to have the same status as mathematical and logical principles. They are claimed to be necessary and not merely contingent truths. At the same time they are not definitions but describe real relations in the universe. In the words of Samuel Clarke (1675–1729), an early exponent of this theory:

> These things [the basic moral principles] are so notoriously plain and self-evident, that nothing but the extremest stupidity of Mind, corruption of Manners, or perverseness of Spirit can possibly make any Man entertain the least doubt concerning them. For Man endowed with Reason to deny the Truth of these things, is the very same thing as if . . . a Man that understands Geometry or Arithmetic, should deny the most obvious and known proportions of Lines or Numbers, and perversely contend that the Whole is not equal to all its parts, or that a square is not double to a triangle of equal base and height.

In our own day, views of this general kind have been held, among many others, by Sir David Ross, A. C. Ewing (see Selection 26), and Nicolai Hartmann. It is not clear whether G. E. Moore (see Selection 27), who has probably been the most influential writer on ethics during the last fifty years, is to be included in this group. When writing *Principia Ethica,* Moore certainly believed that "good" and "bad" designated objective qualities of some kind which are not given in ordinary sense-experience, but he nowhere identified our means of coming to know moral principles with the "*a priori* faculty." His view seems closer to the "moral sense" philosophers of the 18th century who believed that human beings came to know moral principles in a special way which was not identical either with introspection or the familiar physical senses. However, they considered themselves empiricists and regarded the special moral faculty as much more like the senses than the *a priori* faculty of the Rationalists.

There is a famous argument against all forms of objective naturalism which has persuaded many philosophers that theories of this kind cannot be true. The argument is already found in some early writers, especially in Richard Price (1723–1792), but it has been stated most forcefully in our own day by G. E. Moore (Selection 27). It is sometimes called the argument of the "open question." Moore himself calls it the "argument against the naturalistic fallacy." The argument is based on a certain technique which Moore devised for testing the correctness of proposed definitions. The technique can be explained most easily by considering a correct and incorrect definition respectively and by constructing a question in each case which contains both the term to be defined and the defining expression. For example, it is undoubtedly correct to say that "atheist" means the same as "person who denies the existence of God," while it would not be correct to say that "atheist" means "wealthy wholesale butcher with a country home in Scarsdale." Supposing now somebody were to ask "I know that Bertrand Russell denies the existence of God, but is he an atheist?" It is clear that this would be a silly or senseless question. We might also very appropriately call it a "closed" question. The question is silly or senseless or closed because the first part of the sentence has already supplied the answer. On the other hand, if somebody said "I know that Ballanti is a wealthy wholesale butcher with a home in Scarsdale, but is he an atheist?" this would not be silly or senseless in the same sense as the earlier question. We could properly call it an "open" question. It is open because in asserting that Ballanti is a wholesale butcher with a home in Scarsdale, the questioner did not assert or imply anything one way or another about Ballanti's views on religion. In general: when we have a correct definition the question we construct must be senseless or closed; when we have an incorrect definition the question must be sensible or open. And the converse must also be true: if a question is closed this can only be so because the two expressions (in our instance "atheist" and "person who denies the existence of God") really have the same meaning; if the question is open this can only be because the two expressions ("atheist" and "wealthy wholesale butcher with a home in Scarsdale") do not mean the same, i.e., because the definition is not correct.

Moore then applied this test to the various definitions of "good" which had been suggested. Thus he examined the utilitarian definition by raising the question "Is producing the greatest happiness a good thing?" This, Moore maintained, is plainly a sensible or open question. Hence "good" and "producing the greatest happiness" do not have the same meaning and the utilitarian definition must be mistaken. Other attempts to define "good" fare no better. The question "Is it a good thing to aid the struggle for survival?" is a sensible question and hence a definition of "good" in terms of "promoting evolution" is incorrect. Again it makes sense to ask "Is obedience to the will of God a good thing?" and hence the corresponding theological definition of "good" is in error.

Moore concludes that "good" is indefinable. This does not mean that it is meaningless. It is indefinable for the same reason that terms like "yellow" or "bitter" or "pleasure" are indefinable. These terms are indefinable because they designate the simplest kind of quality which cannot be analyzed into anything simpler. Other terms can be defined in terms of "yellow" or "bitter" or "pleasure," but these most basic terms can have their meaning explained only by pointing to instances of the qualities they designate. Like them, Moore maintains "good" designates a simple quality which cannot be analyzed into anything simpler. Philosophers who tried to find definitions of "good" had missed this crucial fact. But the quality designated by "good" is not given to the senses, like colors and tastes, or to introspection like love or anger. To mark this difference Moore called it a "non-natural" quality.

When enumerating theories which try to embody whatever is sound in subjectivism, reference was made to the "emotive" theory which is the meta-moral theory favored by most of the "logical positivists." The proponents of this theory accept Moore's open-question argument and agree with him that "good" is indefinable. However, they explain this fact differently. The word "good" is indefinable not because it designates a simple quality disclosed by some special moral faculty, but because it is meaningless—because it designates nothing at all. Or rather: "good" and the other moral predicates have "emotive" but lack "descriptive" or "cognitive" meaning. The defenders of the emotive theory maintain that the function of moral judgments has been radically misconceived by the other theories in the field. Moral judgments are not the sort of thing which can be true or false. They are not statements of fact. Their function is not to give information about anything—not about our own feelings, not about production of the greatest possible happiness and certainly not about some nebulous realm of non-natural qualities. The function of moral judgments is "dynamic": we use them either, like exclamations, to *vent* our emotions, or else, like commands, to *arouse* emotions and *influence* people's actions. If I say "Harry Truman is a good man" this is roughly equivalent to "Harry Truman hurrah!" or "Long live Harry Truman!" If I say "One ought not to cheat in making out one's income tax return" this is like saying "Don't cheat on your income tax return," but in a certain special subtle tone which avoids the directness of a straightforward command.

So far the emotive theory has been stated in its earlier and more radical form. In this form it resembles subjectivism in maintaining that moral disagreement is disagreement in attitude and that moral disputes can be terminated but not resolved. In later years the theory was modified in several ways. Many recent writers would say that moral judgments have both descriptive *and* emotive meaning and that moral disagreement is both disagreement in attitude *and* disagreement in belief. For example if somebody says "Harry Truman is a good man" he is said to express his favorable feelings towards Harry Truman and also to make some such factual assertions as that Harry Truman is courage-ous, sincere, loyal, etc. If I say "One ought not to cheat in making out one's income tax" I am issuing a kind of command, but I am also making or implying some such factual assertion as that cheating on one's income tax return has a tendency to undermine the basis of organized society.

While thus allowing that moral judgments have descriptive meaning, these writers insist that what we here assert is always something "natural"—some-thing whose existence can in principle be ascertained without having to resort to a special moral faculty. To determine for instance whether Harry Truman is courageous or loyal, sense-observations of some kind are all that is required. These later versions of the emotive theory have been aptly referred to as "emotive naturalism."

The emotive theory may be regarded as a species of "prescriptivism." A prescriptivist would be anybody who claims that moral judgments are, like imperatives, prescriptive and not or not merely descriptive. R. M. Hare, one of the most influential contemporary writers on ethics (see Selection 31), who has adopted this terminology, does not deny the affinities between his own position and the emotive theory, but he is also critical of certain of its features, in its earlier as well as in its later versions. Unlike exclamations or ejaculations, moral judgments do not express or evince *emotions* but rather they commit their author "directly or indirectly, to some sort of precept or prescription about actual or conceivable decisions or choices." Or, if they express the speaker's emotion, this is incidental and not essential to their being moral judgments. Insofar as the emotive theory compared moral judgments to imperatives, it was, according to Hare, on the right track, but the aim of imperatives need not be that of arousing *emotions*. They can be used to *guide* conduct, which is something rather different from mere rhetoric or propaganda. Hare shares the view of the later emotivists that moral judgments have descriptive as well as prescriptive meaning, but he goes further than they in insisting that his position allows for the possibility of reasoned argument about moral matters in a way in which theirs does not. On Hare's view, there are certain *logical* relations between moral judgments and it is possible to settle moral disputes not merely in the sense to which we referred above as "termination," but in a stronger sense in which a person may be said to be in the right even though he failed to persuade his opponent.

Different forms of prescriptivism, some of which have not been mentioned in this survey, have won widespread acceptance among the younger philosophers in Britain and the United States. There are also, however, distinguished philosophers who reject all theories of this kind. The selection from Blanshard (Selection 29) contains some arguments against the emotive theory. Other arguments against the emotive theory as well as against Hare's and other versions of prescriptivism can be found in articles and books mentioned in the bibliography at the end of this section.

P. E.

24   The Moral Faculty
and the Principles of Morals

Thomas Reid

The Notion of Duty

A BEING ENDOWED WITH THE ANI-mal principles of action only, may be capable of being trained to certain purposes by discipline, as we see many brute-animals are, but would be altogether incapable of being governed by law.

The subject of law must have the conception of a general rule of conduct, which, without some degree of reason, he cannot have. He must likewise have a sufficient inducement to obey the law, even when his strongest animal desires draw him the contrary way.

This inducement may be a sense of *interest,* or a sense of *duty,* or both concurring.

These are the only principles I am able to conceive, which can reasonably induce a man to regulate all his actions according to a certain general rule or law. They may therefore be justly called the rational principles of action, since they can have no place but in a being endowed with reason, and since it is by them only that man is capable either of political or of moral government.

Without them human life would be like a ship at sea without hands, left to be carried by winds and tides as they happen. It belongs to the rational part of our nature to intend a certain port, as the end of the voyage of life; to take the advantage of winds and tides when they are favourable, and to bear up against them when they are unfavourable.

A sense of interest may induce us to do this, when a suitable reward

[This selection is made up of excerpts from Chapters V, VI and VII of Essay III and Chapter IX of Essay IV of Reid's *Essays on the Active Powers of Man,* a work first published in 1788.]

is set before us. But there is a nobler principle in the constitution of man, which, in many cases, gives a clearer and more certain rule of conduct, than a regard merely to interest would give, and a principle, without which man would not be a moral agent.

A man is prudent when he consults his real interest; but he cannot be virtuous, if he has no regard to duty.

I proceed now to consider this *regard to Duty* as a rational principle of action in man, and as that principle alone by which he is capable either of virtue or vice.

I shall first offer some observations with regard to the *general notion of duty, and its contrary, or of right and wrong in human conduct,* and then consider, *how we come to judge and determine certain things in human conduct to be right, and others to be wrong.*

With regard to the *notion* or *conception* of Duty, I take it to be too simple to admit of a logical definition.

We can define it only by synonymous words or phrases, or by its properties and necessary concomitants, as when we say that it is *what we ought to do—what is fair and honest—what is approvable—what every man professes to be the rule of his conduct—what all men praise—* and, *what is in itself laudable, though no man should praise it.* . . .

If we examine the abstract notion of Duty, or Moral Obligation, it appears to be neither any real quality of the action considered by itself, nor of the agent considered without respect to the action, but a certain relation between the one and the other.

When we say a man ought to do such a thing, the *ought,* which expresses the moral obligation, has a respect, on the one hand, to the person who ought; and, on the other, to the action which he ought to do. Those two correlates are essential to every moral obligation; take away either, and it has no existence. So that, if we seek the place of moral obligation among the categories, it belongs to the category of *relation.*

There are many relations of things, of which we have the most distinct conception, without being able to define them logically. Equality and proportion are relations between quantities, which every man understands, but no man can define. . . .

I observe, in the *next* place, that the notion of duty cannot be resolved into that of interest, or what is most for our happiness.

Every man may be satisfied of this who attends to his own conceptions, and the language of all mankind shows it. When I say, This is my interest, I mean one thing; when I say, It is my duty, I mean another thing. And, though the same course, when rightly understood, may be both my duty and my interest, the conceptions are very different. Both are reasonable motives to action, but quite distinct in their nature.

I presume it will be granted, that, in every man of real worth, there is a principle of honour, a regard to what is honourable or dishonourable, very distinct from a regard to his interest. It is folly in a man to disregard his interest, but to do what is dishonourable, is baseness. The first may move our pity, or in some cases, our contempt; but the last provokes our indignation.

As these two principles are different in their nature, and not resolvable into one, so the principle of honour is evidently superior in dignity to that of interest.

No man would allow him to be a man of honour who should plead his interest to justify what he acknowledged to be dishonourable; but to sacrifice interest to honour never costs a blush.

It likewise will be allowed by every man of honour, that this principle is not to be resolved into a regard to our reputation among men, otherwise the man of honour would not deserve to be trusted in the dark. He would have no aversion to lie, or cheat, or play the coward, when he had no dread of being discovered.

I take it for granted, therefore, that every man of real honour feels an abhorrence of certain actions, because they are in themselves base, and feels an obligation to certain other actions, because they are in themselves what honour requires, and this independently of any consideration of interest or reputation.

This is an immediate moral obligation. This principle of honour, which is acknowledged by all men who pretend to character, is only another name for what we call a regard to duty, to rectitude, to propriety of conduct. It is a moral obligation which obliges a man to do certain things because they are right, and not to do other things because they are wrong.

Ask the man of honour why he thinks himself obliged to pay a debt of honour? The very question shocks him. To suppose that he needs any other inducement to do it but the principle of honour, is to suppose that he has no honour, no worth, and deserves no esteem.

There is, therefore, a principle in man, which, when he acts according to it, gives him a consciousness of worth, and, when he acts contrary to it, a sense of demerit.

From the varieties of education, of fashion, of prejudices, and of habits, men may differ much in opinion with regard to the extent of this principle, and of what it commands and forbids; but the notion of it, as far as it is carried, is the same in all. It is that which gives a man real worth, and is the object of moral approbation.

Men of rank call it *honour,* and too often confine it to certain virtues that are thought most essential to their rank. The vulgar call it *honesty, probity, virtue, conscience.* Philosophers have given it the names of *the moral sense, the moral faculty, rectitude.*

The universality of this principle in men that are grown up to years of understanding and reflection is evident. The words that express it, the names of the virtues which it commands, and of the vices which it forbids, the *ought* and *ought not* which express its dictates, make an essential part of every language. The natural affections of respect to worthy characters, of resentment of injuries, of gratitude for favours, of indignation against the worthless, are parts of the human constitution which suppose a right and a wrong in conduct. Many transactions that are found necessary in the rudest societies go upon the same supposition. In all testimony, in all promises, and in all contracts, there is necessarily implied a moral obligation on one party, and a trust in the other, grounded upon this obligation.

The Clear and Unbiased Dictates of Conscience

We are next to consider, how we learn to judge and determine, that this is right, and that is wrong.

The abstract notion of moral good and ill would be of no use to direct our life, if we had not the power of applying it to particular actions, and determining what is morally good, and what is morally ill.

Some philosophers, with whom I agree, ascribe this to an original power or faculty in man, which they call the *Moral Sense,* the *Moral Faculty, Conscience.* Others think that our moral sentiments may be accounted for without supposing any original sense or faculty appropriated to that purpose, and go into very different systems to account for them.

I am not, at present, to take any notice of those systems, because the opinion first mentioned seems to me to be the truth; to wit, That, by an original power of the mind, when we come to years of understanding and reflection, we not only have the notions of right and wrong in conduct, but perceive certain things to be right, and others wrong. . . .

The truths immediately testified by our moral faculty, are the first principles of all moral reasoning, from which all our knowledge of our duty must be deduced.

By moral reasoning, I understand all reasoning that is brought to prove that such conduct is right, and deserving of moral approbation; or that it is wrong; or that it is indifferent, and, in itself, neither morally good nor ill.

I think, all we can properly call moral judgments, are reducible to one or other of these, as all human actions, considered in a moral view, are either good, or bad, or indifferent.

I know the term *moral reasoning* is often used by good writers in a more extensive sense; but, as the reasoning I now speak of is of a peculiar kind, distinct from all others, and, therefore, ought to have a distinct name, I take the liberty to limit the name of *moral reasoning* to this kind.

Let it be understood, therefore, that in the reasoning I call *moral,* the conclusion always is, That something in the conduct of moral agents is good or bad, in a greater or a less degree, or indifferent.

All reasoning must be grounded on first principles. This holds in moral reasoning, as in all other kinds. There must, therefore, be in morals, as in all other sciences, first or self-evident principles, on which all moral reasoning is grounded, and on which it ultimately rests. From such self-evident principles, conclusions may be drawn synthetically with regard to the moral conduct of life; and particular duties or virtues may be traced back to such principles, analytically. But, without such principles, we can no more establish any conclusion in morals, than we can build a castle in the air, without any foundation.

An example or two will serve to illustrate this.

It is a first principle in morals, That we ought not to do to another what we should think wrong to be done to us in like circumstances. If a man is not capable of perceiving this in his cool moments, when he reflects seriously, he is not a moral agent, nor is he capable of being convinced of it by reasoning.

From what topic can you reason with such a man? You may possibly convince him by reasoning, that it is his interest to observe this rule; but this is not to convince him that it is his duty. To reason about justice with a man who sees nothing to be just or unjust, or about benevolence with a man who sees nothing in benevolence preferable to malice, is like reasoning with a blind man about colour or with a deaf man about sound.

It is a question in morals that admits of reasoning. Whether, by the law of nature, a man ought to have only one wife? We reason upon this question, by balancing the advantages and disadvantages to the family, and to society in general, that are naturally consequent both upon monogamy and polygamy. And, if it can be shown that the advantages are greatly upon the side of monogamy, we think the point is determined. But, if a man does not perceive that he ought to regard the good of society, and the good of his wife and children, the reasoning can have no effect upon him, because he denies the first principle upon which it is grounded.

Suppose, again, that we reason for monogamy from the intention of nature, discovered by the proportion of males and of females that are born —a proportion which corresponds perfectly with monogamy, but by no means with polygamy—this argument can have no weight with a man who does not perceive that he ought to have a regard to the intention of nature.

Thus we shall find that all moral reasonings rest upon one or more first principles of morals, whose truth is immediately perceived without reasoning, by all men come to years of understanding. And this indeed is common to every branch of human knowledge that deserves the name of science. There must be first principles proper to that science, by which the whole superstructure is supported. The first principles of all the sciences, must be the immediate dictates of our natural faculties; nor is it possible that we should have any other evidence of their truth. And in different sciences the faculties which dictate their first principles are very different.

The first principles of morals are the immediate dictates of the moral faculty. They show us, not what man is, but what he ought to be. Whatever is immediately perceived to be just, honest, and honourable, in human conduct, carries moral obligation along with it, and the contrary carries demerit and blame; and, from those moral obligations that are immediately perceived, all other moral obligations must be deduced by reasoning.

He that will judge of the colour of an object, must consult his eyes, in a good light, when there is no medium or contiguous objects that may give it a false tinge. But in vain will he consult every other faculty in this matter. In like manner, he that will judge of the first principles of morals, must consult his conscience, or moral faculty, when he is calm and dispassionate, unbiased by interest, affection, or fashion. As we rely upon the clear and distinct testimony of our eyes, concerning the colours and figures of the bodies about us, we have the same reason to rely with security upon the clear and unbiased testimony of our conscience, with regard to what we ought and ought not to do. In many cases moral worth and demerit are discerned no less clearly by the last of those natural faculties, than figure and colour by the first.

The faculties which nature hath given us, are the only engines we can use to find out the truth. We cannot indeed prove that those faculties are not fallacious, unless God should give us new faculties to sit in judgment upon the old. But we are born under a necessity of trusting them.

Every man in his senses believes his eyes, his ears, and his other senses. He believes his consciousness with respect to his own thoughts and purposes; his memory, with regard to what is past; his understanding, with regard to abstract relations of things; and his taste, with regard to what is elegant and beautiful. And he has the same necessity of believing the clear and unbiased dictates of his conscience, with regard to what is honourable and what is base. . . .

Moral Discernment and the Need of Instruction

The seeds, as it were, of moral discernment are planted in the mind by him that made us. They grow up in their proper season, and are at first tender and delicate, and easily warped. Their progress depends very much upon their being duly cultivated and properly exercised.

It is so with the power of reasoning, which all acknowledge to be one of the most eminent natural faculties of man. It appears not in infancy. It springs up, by insensible degrees, as we grow to maturity. But its strength and vigour depend so much upon its being cultivated and exercised, that we see many individuals, nay, many nations, in which it is hardly to be perceived.

Our intellectual discernment is not so strong and vigorous by nature as to secure us from errors in speculation. On the contrary, we see a great part of mankind, in every age, sunk in gross ignorance of things that are obvious to the more enlightened, and fettered by errors and false notions, which the human understanding, duly improved, easily throws off.

It would be extremely absurd, from the errors and ignorance of mankind, to conclude that there is no such thing as truth; or that man has not a natural faculty of discerning it, and distinguishing it from error. In like manner, our moral discernment of what we ought, and what we ought not to do, is not so strong and vigorous by nature as to secure us from very gross mistakes with regard to our duty.

The variety of opinions among men in points of morality, is not greater, but, as I apprehend, much less than in speculative points; and this variety is as easily accounted for, from the common causes of error, in the one case as in the other; so that it is not more evident, that there is a real distinction between true and false, in matters of speculation than that there is a real distinction between right and wrong in human conduct. . . .

In matters of conduct, as well as in matters of speculation, we are liable to be misled by prejudices of education, or by wrong instruction. But, in matters of conduct, we are also very liable to have our judgment warped by our appetites and passions, by fashion, and by the contagion of evil example.

We must not therefore think, because man has the natural power of discerning what is right and what is wrong, that he has no need of instruction; that this power has no need of cultivation and improvement; that he may safely rely upon the suggestions of his mind, or upon opinions he has got, he knows not how.

What should we think of a man who, because he has by nature the power of moving all his limbs should therefore conclude that he need not be taught to dance, or to fence, to ride, or to swim? All these exercises are performed by that power of moving our limbs which we have by nature; but they will be performed very awkwardly and imperfectly by those who have not been trained to them, and practised in them.

What should we think of a man who, because he has the power by nature of distinguishing what is true from what is false, should conclude that he has no need to be taught mathematics, or natural philosophy, or other sciences? It is by the natural power of human understanding that everything in those sciences has been discovered, and that the truths they contain are discerned. But the understanding, left to itself, without the aid of instruction, training, habit, and exercise, would make very small progress, as every one sees, in persons uninstructed in those matters.

Our natural power of discerning between right and wrong, needs the aid of instruction, education, exercise, and habit, as well as our other natural powers.

. . . .

The Authority of Conscience

Conscience prescribes measures to every appetite, affection, and passion, and says to every other principle of action—So far thou mayest go, but no farther.

We may indeed transgress its dictates, but we cannot transgress them with innocence, nor even with impunity.

We condemn ourselves, or, in the language of scripture, *our heart condemns us,* whenever we go beyond the rules of right and wrong which conscience prescribes.

Other principles of action may have more strength, but this has only authority. Its sentence makes us guilty to ourselves, and guilty in the eyes of our Maker, whatever other principle may be set in opposition to it.

It is evident, therefore, that this principle has, from its nature, an authority to direct and determine with regard to our conduct, to judge, to acquit or to condemn, and even to punish; an authority which belongs to no other principle of the human mind.

It is the candle of the Lord set up within us, to guide our steps. Other principles may urge and impel, but this only authorizes. Other principles ought to be controlled by this; this may be, but never ought to be controlled by any other, and never can be with innocence.

The authority of conscience over the other active principle of the mind, I do not consider as a point that requires proof by argument, but as self-evident. For it implies no more than this—That in all cases a man ought to do his duty. He only who does in all cases what he ought to do, is the perfect man.

. . . .

Moral Judgments and the Moral Attributes of the Supreme Being

If what we call *moral judgment* be no real judgment, but merely a feeling, it follows that the principles of morals which we have been taught to consider as an immutable law to all intelligent beings, have no other foundation but an arbitrary structure and fabric in the constitution of the human mind. So that, by a change in our structure, what is immoral might become moral, virtue might be turned into vice, and vice into a virtue. And beings of a different structure, according to the variety of their feelings, may have different, nay opposite measures of moral good and evil.

It follows that, from our notions of morals, we can conclude nothing concerning a moral character in the Deity, which is the foundation of all religion, and the strongest support of virtue. Nay, this opinion seems to conclude strongly against a moral character in the Deity, since nothing arbitrary or mutable can be conceived to enter into the description of a nature eternal, immutable, and necessarily existent. Mr. Hume seems perfectly consistent with himself, in allowing of no evidence for the moral attributes of the Supreme Being, whatever there may be for his natural attributes.

I cannot help being of a contrary opinion, being persuaded that a man who determined that polite behaviour has great deformity, and that there is great beauty in rudeness and ill-breeding, would judge wrong, whatever his feelings were. In like manner, I cannot help thinking that a man who determined that there is more moral worth in cruelty, perfidy, and injustice, than in generosity, justice, prudence, and temperance, would judge wrong, whatever his constitution was.

On the other hand, if moral judgment be a true and real judgment, the principles of morals stand upon the immutable foundation of truth, and can undergo no change by any difference of fabric, or structure of those who judge of them. There may be, and there are, beings who have not the faculty of conceiving moral truths, or perceiving the excellence of moral worth, as there are beings incapable of perceiving mathematical truths; but no defect, no error of understanding, can make what is true to be false.

. . . The Judge of all the earth, we are sure, will do right. He has given to men the faculty of perceiving the right and the wrong in conduct, as far as is necessary to our present state, and of perceiving the dignity of the one, and the demerit of the other; and surely there can be no real knowledge or real excellence in man, which is not in his Maker.

We may therefore justly conclude, that what we know in part, and see in part, of right and wrong, he sees perfectly; that the moral excellence, which we see and admire in some of our fellow-creatures, is a faint but true copy of that moral excellence which is essential to his nature; and that to tread the path of virtue, is the true dignity of our nature, and imitation of God, and the way to obtain his favour.

25   Science and Ethics

Bertrand Russell

. . . T HE FRAMING OF MORAL RULES,
so long as the ultimate Good is supposed known, is a matter for science. For
example: should capital punishment be inflicted for theft, or only for
murder, or not at all? Jeremy Bentham, who considered pleasure to be the
Good, devoted himself to working out what criminal code would most
promote pleasure, and concluded that it ought to be much less severe than
that prevailing in his day. All this, except the proposition that pleasure is
the Good, comes within the sphere of science.

But when we try to be definite as to what we mean when we say that
this or that is "the Good," we find ourselves involved in very great difficulties. Bentham's creed that pleasure is the Good roused furious opposition,
and was said to be a pig's philosophy. Neither he nor his opponents could
advance any argument. In a scientific question, evidence can be adduced
on both sides, and in the end one side is seen to have the better case—or,
if this does not happen, the question is left undecided. But in a question as
to whether this or that is the ultimate Good, there is no evidence either
way; each disputant can only appeal to his own emotions, and employ such
rhetorical devices as shall rouse similar emotions in others.

Take, for example, a question which has come to be important in
practical politics. Bentham held that one man's pleasure has the same
ethical importance as another man's, provided the quantities are equal; and
on this ground he was led to advocate democracy. Nietzsche, on the
contrary, held that only the great man can be regarded as important on
his own account, and that the bulk of mankind are only means to his well-
being. He viewed ordinary men as many people view animals: he thought
it justifiable to make use of them, not for their own good, but for that of
the superman, and this view has since been adopted to justify the abandon-

[This selection consists of the major parts of Chapter IX of Russell's *Religion and
Science,* which was first published in 1935. It is here reprinted with the kind permission of
Bertrand Russell and Oxford University Press.]

ment of democracy. We have here a sharp disagreement of great practical importance, but we have absolutely no means, of a scientific or intellectual kind, by which to persuade either party that the other is in the right. There are, it is true, ways of altering men's opinions on such subjects, but they are all emotional, not intellectual.

Questions as to "values"—that is to say, as to what is good or bad on its own account, independently of its effects—lie outside the domain of science, as the defenders of religion emphatically assert. I think that in this they are right, but I draw the further conclusion, which they do not draw, that questions as to "values" lie wholly outside the domain of knowledge. That is to say, when we assert that this or that has "value," we are giving expressions to our own emotions, not to a fact which would still be true if our personal feelings were different. To make this clear, we must try to analyze the conception of the Good.

It is obvious, to begin with, that the whole idea of good and bad has some connection with desire. *Prima facie,* anything that we all desire is "good," and anything that we all dread is "bad." If we all agreed in our desires, the matter could be left there, but unfortunately our desires conflict. If I say "what I want is good," my neighbor will say "No, what I want." Ethics is an attempt—though not, I think, a successful one—to escape from this subjectivity. I shall naturally try to show, in my dispute with my neighbor, that my desires have some quality which makes them more worthy of respect than his. If I want to preserve a right of way, I shall appeal to the landless inhabitants of the district; but he, on his side, will appeal to the landowners. I shall say: "What use is the beauty of the countryside if no one sees it?" He will retort: "What beauty will be left if trippers are allowed to spread devastation?" Each tries to enlist allies by showing that his own desires harmonize with those of other people. When this is obviously impossible, as in the case of a burglar, the man is condemned by public opinion, and his ethical status is that of a sinner.

Ethics is thus closely related to politics: it is an attempt to bring the collective desires of a group to bear upon individuals; or, conversely, it is an attempt by an individual to cause his desires to become those of his group. This latter is, of course, only possible if his desires are not obviously opposed to the general interest: the burglar will hardly attempt to persuade people that he is doing them good, though plutocrats make similar attempts, and often succeed. When our desires are for things which all can enjoy in common, it seems not unreasonable to hope that others may concur; thus the philosopher who values Truth, Goodness and Beauty seems, to himself, to be not merely expressing his own desires, but pointing the way to the welfare of all mankind. Unlike the burglar, he is able to believe that his desires are for something that has value in an impersonal sense.

Ethics is an attempt to give universal, and not merely personal, importance to certain of our desires. I say "certain" of our desires, because in regard to some of them this is obviously impossible, as we saw in the case of the burglar. The man who makes money on the Stock Exchange by means of some secret knowledge does not wish others to be equally well informed: Truth (in so far as he values it) is for him a private possession, not the general human good that it is for the philosopher. The philosopher may, it is true, sink to the level of the stock-jobber, as when he claims priority for a discovery. But this is a lapse: in his purely philosophic capacity, he wants only to enjoy the contemplation of Truth in doing which he in no way interferes with others who wish to do likewise. . . .

. . . Every attempt to persuade people that something is good (or bad) in itself, and not merely in its effects, depends upon the art of rousing feelings, not upon an appeal to evidence. In every case the preacher's skill consists in creating in others emotions similar to his own—or dissimilar, if he is a hypocrite. I am not saying this as a criticism of the preacher, but as an analysis of the essential character of his activity.

When a man says "this is good in itself," he seems to be making a statement, just as much as if he said "this is square" or "this is sweet." I believe this to be a mistake. I think that what the man really means is: "I wish everybody to desire this," or rather "Would that everybody desired this." If what he says is interpreted as a statement, it is merely an affirmation of his own personal wish; if, on the other hand, it is interpreted in a general way, it states nothing, but merely desires something. The wish, as an occurrence, is personal, but what it desires is universal. It is, I think, this curious interlocking of the particular and the universal which has caused so much confusion in ethics.

The matter may perhaps become clearer by contrasting an ethical sentence with one which makes a statement. If I say "all Chinese are Buddhists," I can be refuted by the production of a Chinese Christian or Mohammedan. If I say "I believe that all Chinese are Buddhists," I cannot be refuted by any evidence from China, but only by evidence that I do not believe what I say; for what I am asserting is only something about my own state of mind. If, now, a philosopher says "Beauty is Good," I may interpret him as meaning either "Would that everybody loved the beautiful" (which corresponds to "all Chinese are Buddhists") or "I wish that everybody loved the beautiful" (which corresponds to "I believe that all Chinese are Buddhists"). The first of these makes no assertion, but expresses a wish; since it affirms nothing, it is logically impossible that there should be evidence for or against it, or for it to possess either truth or falsehood. The second sentence, instead of being merely optative, does make a statement, but is one about the philosopher's state of mind, and it could only be refuted by evidence that he does not have the wish that he says he has. This second sentence does not belong to ethics, but to psychology or biography. The first sentence, which does belong to ethics, expresses a desire for something, but asserts nothing.

Ethics, if the above analysis is correct, contains no statements, whether true or false, but consists of desires of a certain general kind, namely such as are concerned with the desires of mankind in general—and of gods, angels, and devils, if they exist. Science can discuss the causes of desires, and the means for realizing them, but it cannot contain any genuinely ethical sentences, because it is concerned with what is true or false.

The theory which I have been advocating is a form of the doctrine which is called the "subjectivity" of values. This doctrine consists in maintaining that, if two men differ about values, there is not a disagreement as to any kind of truth, but a difference of taste. If one man says "oysters are good" and another says "I think they are bad," we recognize that there is nothing to argue about. The theory in question holds that all differences as to values are of this sort, although we do not naturally think them so when we are dealing with matters that seem to us more exalted than oysters. The chief ground for adopting this view is the complete impossibility of finding any arguments to prove that this or that has intrinsic value. If we all agreed, we might hold that we know values by intuition. We cannot prove, to a color-blind man, that grass is green and not red. But there are various ways of proving to him that he lacks a power of discrimination which most men possess, whereas in the case of values there are no such ways, and disagreements are much more frequent than in the case of colors. Since no way can be even imagined for deciding a difference as to values, the conclusion is forced upon us that the difference is one of tastes, not one as to any objective truth.

The consequences of this doctrine are considerable. In the first place, there can be no such thing as "sin" in any absolute sense; what one man calls "sin" another may call "virtue," and though they may dislike each other on account of this difference, neither can convict the other of intellectual error. Punishment cannot be justified on the ground that the criminal is "wicked," but only on the ground that he has behaved in a way which others wish to discourage. Hell, as a place of punishment for sinners, becomes quite irrational.

In the second place, it is impossible to uphold the way of speaking about values which is common among those who believe in Cosmic Purpose. Their argument is that certain things which have been evolved are "good," and therefore the world must have had a purpose which was ethically admirable. In the language of subjective values, this argument becomes: "Some things in the world are to our liking, and therefore they must have been created by a Being with our tastes, Whom, therefore, we also like, and Who, consequently, is good." Now it seems fairly evident that, if creatures having likes and dislikes were to exist at all, they were pretty sure to like some things in their environment, since otherwise they would find life intolerable. Our values have been evolved along with the rest of our constitution, and nothing as to any original purpose can be inferred from the fact that they are what they are.

Those who believe in "objective" values often contend that the view which I have been advocating has immoral consequences. This seems to me to be due to faulty reasoning. There are, as has already been said, certain ethical consequences of the doctrine of subjective values, of which the most important is the rejection of vindictive punishment and the notion of "sin." But the more general consequences which are feared, such as the decay of all sense of moral obligation, are not to be logically deduced. Moral obligation, if it is to influence conduct, must consist not merely of a belief, but of a desire. The desire, I may be told, is the desire to be "good" in a sense which I no longer allow. But when we analyze the desire to be "good" it generally resolves itself into a desire to be approved, or, alternatively, to act so as to bring about certain general consequences which we desire. We have wishes which are not purely personal, and, if we had not, no amount of ethical teaching would influence our conduct except through fear of disapproval. The sort of life that most of us admire is one which is guided by large impersonal desires; now such desires can, no doubt, be encouraged by example, education, and knowledge, but they can hardly be created by the mere abstract belief that they are good, nor discouraged by an analysis of what is meant by the word "good."

When we contemplate the human race, we may desire that it should be happy, or healthy, or intelligent, or warlike, and so on. Any one of these desires, if it is strong, will produce its own morality; but if we have no such general desires, our conduct, whatever our ethic may be, will only serve social purposes in so far as self-interest and the interests of society are in harmony. It is the business of wise institutions to create such harmony as far as possible, and for the rest, whatever may be our theoretical definition of value, we must depend upon the existence of impersonal desires. When you meet a man with whom you have a fundamental ethical disagreement—for example, if you think that all men count equally, while he selects a class as alone important—you will find yourself no better able to cope with him if you believe in objective values than if you do not. In either case, you can only influence his conduct through influencing his desires: if you succeed in that, his ethic will change, and if not, not.

Some people feel that if a general desire, say for the happiness of mankind, has not the sanction of absolute good, it is in some way "irrational." This is due to a lingering belief in objective values. A desire cannot, in itself, be either rational or irrational. It may conflict with other desires, and therefore lead to unhappiness; it may rouse opposition in others, and therefore be incapable of gratification. But it cannot be considered "irrational" merely because no reason can be given for feeling it. We may desire A because it is a means to B, but in the end, when we have done with mere means, we must come to something which we desire for no reason, but not on that account "irrationally." All systems of ethics embody the desires of those who advocate them, but this fact is concealed in a mist of words. Our desires are, in fact, more general and less purely selfish than most moralists imagine; if it were not so, no theory of ethics would make moral improvement possible. It is, in fact, not by ethical theory, but by the cultivation of large and generous desires through intelligence, happiness, and freedom from fear, that men can be brought to act more than they do at present in a manner that is consistent with the general happiness of mankind. Whatever our definition of the "Good," and whether we believe it to be subjective or objective, those who do not desire the happiness of mankind will not endeavor to further it, while those who desire it will do what they can to bring it about. . . .

26   The Objectivity of Moral Judgments

A. C. Ewing

O<small>NE CLASS OF ANSWER TO THE QUES-</small>tion how "good" is to be defined is given by the subjectivists. But, before we consider this type of answer, we must try to make clear to ourselves what could be meant by the "objectivity" of ethical judgments or of value judgments in general. It obviously does not mean that they ascribe value properties to physical objects. These clearly do not possess ethical qualities. It might indeed be held that they possessed the property of beauty and therefore the property of intrinsic goodness quite independently of being perceived. This view does not seem to me obviously false, but it is plain that most philosophers who have asserted the objectivity of value judgments did not wish to commit themselves to it, still less to maintain that all value judgments were objective in precisely the same sense as that in which judgments about physical objects are. We can therefore rule out at once the sense of "objective" as referring to what exists independently of being experienced. What then does "objective" mean when used in reference to ethics?

It may mean "claiming to be true." Obviously in this sense judgments about psychological events and dispositions are objective, though they do not refer to what exists independently of experience, and in this sense ethical judgments may be objective. To say they are is indeed to say no more than that they are judgments and not merely something else which we have confused with judgments. But even this much is denied by some

[This selection consists of parts of Chapter I of Ewing's *The Definition of Good*, which appeared in 1947. The American edition was published by the Macmillan Co., the British edition by Routledge and Kegan Paul. The selection is here reprinted with the kind permission of the author and the publishers.]

who maintain that so-called ethical judgments are only exclamations, commands, or wishes.

However, a person who admitted the occurrence of ethical judgments, but denied that they were ever in fact true or that we could ever have any justification for believing them to be true, would not usually be described as holding an objective view of ethics. So "objective" here may be taken as implying that ethical judgments in particular and value judgments in general are sometimes true and can be sometimes known or at least justifiably believed to be true. An objective view involves the rejection of scepticism in ethics.

But this would not by itself be sufficient to satisfy the holders of the view that ethical judgments are objective. Suppose "A is good" simply meant "I have a certain feeling about A." It would then be a judgment and could perfectly well be true and known to be true, yet anybody who maintained such a position would be said to be holding a subjective and not an objective view of ethics. The proposition that ethical judgments are objective, therefore, besides asserting that they are judgments, asserts of them a certain independence of the feelings or attitude of the person judging. They are not merely judgments about his feelings, or for that matter his thoughts. Even if partly based on feeling, they are not about the feeling itself but about something to which the feeling points, and something which cannot adequately be described in terms merely of the man's own psychology.

The view that "ethical judgments are objective" therefore excludes the following views: (a) that they are not really judgments at all, (b) that they are all false or that we are never justified in thinking them true, (c) that they are merely judgments about one's own psychological state or dispositions. Any of these three alternative views may be called "subjective."

The Difficulties of Subjectivism

The simplest form of the subjectivist view is that according to which ethical judgments, though genuine judgments, assert only that the person who makes the judgment has or tends to have certain feelings. "This is good" or "right" on such a view becomes "I have (or tend to have) an emotion of approval on considering this." A number of incredibly paradoxical consequences would follow from the adoption of this view. Firstly, the judgments could not be false unless the person judging had made a mistake about his own psychology. Secondly, two different people would never mean the same thing when they made such a judgment, since each would mean "This is approved by *me*." Indeed the same person would never mean the same by it on two different occasions, because each time he would mean "I *now* feel (or tend to feel) approval of this."

Thirdly, if I judge something to be good and you judge it to be bad, our judgments would never be logically incompatible with each other. It is not a sufficient reply to point out that they can still be incompatible with each other in some different sense, for example in the sense that they express attitudes which are in conflict with each other or lead to incompatible policies. For we do not see merely that A's judgment "This is good" and B's judgment "This is bad" (in the corresponding sense of the word) lead to or express incompatible policies like A's judgment "I desire to further X" and B's judgment "I desire to oppose X." We see that the two judgments logically contradict each other so that it is logically impossible that they could both be true. No doubt, since "good" and "bad" can each be used in different senses, "this is bad" may not always contradict "this is good," because, for example, "good" may mean "instrumentally good" and "bad" may mean "intrinsically bad"; but at any rate they sometimes do so, and on the view under discussion they could, when asserted by different people, never do so. Fourthly, no argument or rational discussion, nor indeed any citation of empirical facts, could be in any degree relevant to supporting or casting doubt on any ethical judgment unless it could be directed to showing that the person who makes the judgment has made a mistake about his own feelings or tendencies to have feelings. It is true that argument or fresh knowledge about the circumstances and likely consequences of an act might lead me to have different feelings about it and so judge it right while I had judged it wrong before, or vice versa; but it would not in any way indicate that my previous judgment was false. The judgments would be different; but since they referred only to my feelings at different times they would not contradict each other any more than "I was ill on January 1" contradicts "I was well on February 1." Yet it is clear that argument can really cast doubt on propositions in ethics.

Fifthly, I could not, while asserting an ethical belief, conceive that I might possibly be wrong in this belief and yet be certain that I now feel (or tend to feel) disapproval. Since it is quite clear that I can conceive this in some cases at least, this argument provides another *reductio ad absurdum* of the theory. To think that an ethical belief now expressed by me may possibly be wrong is not the same as thinking that I may come in the future to have different feelings, for I think that the present judgment may be wrong and not a future one. To put the objection in another way, it would follow from the theory that to say "If I feel approval of A, A is always right (good)" is to utter a tautology. But it is not, it is a piece of gross conceit, if made in any ordinary context. Even if it were true that, if I feel approval of A, I shall always at the time judge A to be right (good), this is quite a different statement. I need not always be certain that my judgments are correct (unless judgment is so defined as to cover only cases of *knowledge*).

Sixthly, it would follow from the theory under discussion that, when I judge that Hitler was bad or acted wrongly, I am not really talking about Hitler at all but about my own psychology.

To me the consequences that I have mentioned are all quite incredible and constitute a fully sufficient *reductio ad absurdum* of the theory from which they are deduced. They hold whether it is applied both to "good" and to "right" or only to one of them. . . .

The Case Against Objectivism

Let us now examine the case against the objectivity of ethical judgments. If it is conclusive we shall have to be subjectivists in the sense that we shall have to admit the impossibility of making any true or at least any justified ethical judgments, even if we do not admit that ethical judgments are of such a nature that they could not conceivably be true at all or true of anything but the mental state or dispositions of the speaker.

One argument is based on the striking differences in ethical views between different people. But the differences between the views of savages and those of modern scientists about eclipses, or between the views of different politicians as to the causes and likely effects of contemporary events, are as great as the differences between the views of savages and of Christians, or the views of democrats and of Nazis, as to ethics. Are we to conclude from this that the scientists are no more right than the savages or that the political events about which the disputes turn have not objectively any causes or effects? If we do not draw this conclusion here, why draw the corresponding conclusion about ethics? There are also various ways of explaining the differences of view that exist without casting doubt on the objectivity of ethics. In the first place, acts which bear the same name may be very different acts in different states of society, because the circumstances and the psychology of the people concerned are very different. So it might be the case that, for example, slavery or polygamy was right, as the course which involved least evil, in certain more primitive societies and wrong in ours. This is quite compatible with the objectivity of ethical judgments. The proposition that slavery was right in ancient Egypt would not contradict the proposition that it was wrong in the United States in 1850 A.D. Both we and the ancient Egyptians may be right in our ethical judgments. Let us, however, take cases where one party is wrong. Now it is important to note that differences in ethical beliefs are often due to differences of opinion as to matters of fact. If A and B differ as to the likely consequences of an action, they may well differ as to whether the action is right or wrong, and this is perhaps the most fertile source of disputes as to what is right. But it is not an ethical difference at all; it is a difference such as arises between rival scientific predictions based on inductive evidence. Differences or apparent differences of opinion of these two kinds obviously constitute no possible argument against the objectivity of ethics.

But there are also genuine ethical differences—that is, differences as to our judgments not of fact but of value. These may sometimes be explained by differences in people's experience of life. If I never experience A, I cannot realize the intrinsic goodness of A and may therefore wrongly subordinate it to something less good. And we must remember that what is intrinsically good is not a physical thing or a physical act, but the experience or state of mind associated with it. Even a long study of philosophical books would not qualify a person to pass a judgment on the intrinsic value of philosophy if he were hopelessly bad at the subject, because then, however many books he read, he would not have a genuinely philosophical experience. Two persons who differ as to the aesthetic value of a picture may really be judging about different things, their several experiences of it. Or at least their judgments will be based on different data. Other differences of view may be due to the misapplication of principles previously accepted, or to genuine intellectual confusions such as the philosopher or even the man of common sense who is not a philosopher could remove. For instance a man may confuse badness and wrongness and conclude or assume, for example, that, because he really sees lying to be always bad (an evil), he sees it to be always wrong, while it may be a case of choosing the lesser evil rather than the greater. Often a man will think that he knows intuitively P to be R when he really only sees it to be Q but confuses Q with R.

Or the judgment that something is good or bad on the whole may have been due to concentrating attention on one side of it while ignoring or underestimating the other sides, as, for instance, militarists concentrate their attention on the unselfish heroism which war brings out in men and forget or underestimate war's evils. Lesser degrees of such onesidedness it is impossible to avoid, and yet they may detrimentally influence ethical judgments. To decide what is right in a particular case is often a difficult matter of balancing the good or evil likely to be produced by one proposed act against that likely to be produced by others. For, even if we do not hold the view that the rightness of an act depends solely on its consequences, we cannot in any case deny that such balancing of the consequences should play the predominant part in at least many ethical decisions. Perhaps, if we foresaw all the consequences clearly as they would be in their factual character and could keep our attention fixed equally on them all, we should always be in agreement as to the degree in which they were good or evil as compared with the consequences of the other possible acts. But, apart from the difficulty of estimating what the consequences of an act will be, it is practically impossible in cases which are at all complex to keep our attention sufficiently fixed at the same time on all the foreseeable consequences likely to be seriously relevant for good or evil, and so we are likely through lack of attention to underestimate the value or disvalue of some as compared to that of others.

The lack of attention I have mentioned is in some degree inevitable, but it is greatly enhanced by the influence of desire and prejudice. It is a commonplace that ethical mistakes are often due to non-intellectual factors. Whether these act only through affecting the attention or whether they can lead to mistaken valuations even in the presence of full attention to the object valued we need not discuss. Their influence is certainly not confined to ethical mistakes; we may note the different conclusions as to the factual consequences of a policy which members of different political parties may draw from the same evidence. There is, in any case, a large class of errors for which some form of "psychoanalysis" (I do not say necessarily the Freudian) is required rather than argument, and another (probably much larger) of which it can be said only that the person in question fell into error because he did not steadfastly will to seek the truth and therefore did not fix his attention on points which displeased him. The convictions of some people as to the objectivity of ethics appear to have been shaken by the fact that enthusiastic Nazis seem to have believed that it was their duty to do things which we are convinced are completely wrong, such as ill-treating the Jews; but is there any reason to think that these Nazis really wanted to arrive at the truth regarding the question whether it was right or wrong to send Jews to concentration camps? If not, we need not be so surprised that they did not attain the truth which they did not seek.

So it may well be the case that all differences in people's judgments whether certain actions are right or wrong or certain things good or bad are due to factors other than an irreducible difference in ethical intuition. But, even if they should not be, we must remember that ethical intuition, like our other capacities, is presumably a developing factor and therefore may be capable of error. But in any case we have said enough to show that great differences of opinion as to ethics are quite compatible with the objectivity of ethical judgments.

Differences between philosophers about the general theory of ethics are remarkably great; but experience shows that very wide philosophical differences are quite compatible with striking agreement as regards the kind of action judged right or wrong, just as radical differences between philosophers in their theory of perception and of physical objects are quite compatible with complete agreement in ordinary life as to what particular physical objects are in a particular place at a particular time. The differences between philosophers are differences not mainly as to their ethical judgments in concrete ethical situations, but as to the general theory explaining these. We may add that the differences between different peoples and different civilizations as to concrete ethical judgments are commonly exaggerated. David Livingstone says that nowhere had he need to teach the African savages at any rate the ethical, as opposed to the religious, portion of the Decalogue. But there is of course a great inconsistency (not only among savages) in confining to a limited group rules which demand universal extension.

The Argument from the Psychological
Origin of Ethical Beliefs

Another argument is that ethical beliefs can be explained psycho-logically as having originated from non-ethical factors such as fear of punishment. Now there must be a psychological history of the origin of any beliefs, and there must have been a time when no ethical ideas or beliefs yet existed, both in the history of the individual and in the history of the race. But this does not prove that ethical beliefs originated solely from the pre-existing ideas through a sort of confusion and were not due to a genuine cognition of properties really present. There was also a time when there were no logical or mathematical ideas, but nobody would entertain a similar argument against logic or mathematics.

Further, to be sceptical about ethics on the strength of a theory as to the origin of ethical ideas would be to give up the more for the far less certain, indeed the extremely uncertain. For such a sceptical theory would rest on the psychology of children if applied to individual development, and the psychology of savages if applied to evolutionary development of the race. But, owing to the impossibility of obtaining reliable introspective evidence, the psychology of children and savages, at least when we consider their higher mental processes or the beginnings of such, is speculative in the extreme. To quote from Broad, "Of all branches of empirical psychology that which is concerned with what goes on in the minds of babies must, from the nature of the case, be one of the most precarious. Babies, whilst they remain such, cannot tell us what their experiences are; and all state-ments made by grown persons about their own infantile experiences on the basis of ostensible memory are certainly inadequate and probably distorted. The whole of this part of psychology therefore is, and will always remain, a mere mass of speculations about infantile mental processes, put forward to explain certain features in the lives of grown persons and incapable in principle of any independent check or verification. Such speculations are of the weakest kind known to science." The psychology of primitive savages is in an equally or almost equally weak position. Some of our ethical judgments, on the other hand, I should insist, are quite or almost as certain as any judgment, and, even if the reader is not prepared to go so far, he must admit that they are at any rate far more certain than could be any theory founded on the psychology of children and savages which explained them away. The same uncertainty must attach to any theory of ethics or analysis of ethical terms based on the way in which children learn the use of the terms. Such a theory is irrelevant unless it is based on a study of what children exactly have in mind and what their mental processes are when they use the words, and how can we possibly have a well founded idea of that when they cannot introspect or adequately report introspections?

Westermarck contends that objectivity is disproved by the fact that ethical judgments are based on emotion; but he does not even try, as far as I can see, to disprove the view that emotions only provide a psychological condition in the absence of which we should not have been in a fit state ever to intuit the characteristic of goodness or the relation of obligation. I certainly should not admit that the emotion was normally or originally prior to at least a confused apprehension of good or evil, rightness or wrongness; but even if I, like some even among the objectivists and non-naturalists, admitted this and made the feeling of the emotion a necessary prior condition of the apprehension, Westermarck's conclusion would not follow. The making of an ethical judgment will in any case presuppose various psychological conditions, but it does not follow that the judgment must be about these conditions. Nobody would argue that ethical judgments must all really be about breathing because breathing is a necessary condition without which we could not have made the judgments. . . .

The Role of Intuition

. . . Probably the principal reason which makes people inclined to deny the objectivity of ethics is the fact that in ethical argument we are very soon brought to a point where we have to fall back on intuition, so that disputants are placed in a situation where there are just two conflicting intuitions between which there seem to be no means of deciding. However, it is not only ethics but all reasoning which presupposes intuition. I cannot argue A, ∴ B, ∴ C without seeing that A entails B and B entails C, and this must either be seen immediately or require a further argument. If it is seen immediately, it is a case of intuition; if it has to be established by a further argument, this means that another term, D, must be interpolated between A and B such that A entails D and D entails B, and similarly with B and C, but then the same question arises about A entailing D, so that sooner or later we must come to something which we see intuitively to be true, as the process of interpolation cannot go on *ad infinitum*. We cannot therefore, whatever we do, get rid of intuition if we are to have any valid inference at all. It may, however, be said that in subjects other than ethics people at any rate agree in their intuitions. But outside mathematics or formal logic this is by no means universally true. There is frequent disagreement about matters of fact as to what has happened or will happen or concerning the causes of something, and when we have exhausted the arguments on a given point in these matters there still remains a difference between the ways in which these arguments are regarded by the disputants. In any science where you cannot prove your conclusions but only make them more or less probable there will be different estimates as to the balance of probability. As in ethics you have to balance different values against each other in order to decide what you ought to do, so here you have to balance different probable arguments, and in order to do this you must rely at some point or other on an estimate of their strength which cannot itself be further justified by mediate reasoning. Yet, when everything has been said in the way of argument, people may not all agree. Some will attribute more weight to one consideration, others to another, as they do in ethical questions about what is the right action in a given case. Our decision as to which of two probable arguments is the stronger may be influenced by other arguments in turn; but in order to deal with the situation rationally we must also estimate the weight of these other arguments, so that in the last resort it is a matter of insight into their nature which cannot be settled by other arguments *ad infinitum*. Just as in a demonstrative argument you must see intuitively how each step follows from the preceding one, so in the case of a probable argument you must rely on estimates of the degree of probability given by the argument as compared to that given by arguments on the other side, and these estimates, unless the degree of probability can be mathematically calculated, must either be themselves intuitive or be deduced from other estimates which are intuitive. I do not wish to maintain that reasoning in these matters is altogether analogous to that which occurs in dealing with ethical questions, but at any rate it is the case here that, as in ethics, we are often confronted with a situation in which we either see or do not see, and cannot logically prove, that what we seem to see is true. Yet we cannot surely therefore conclude that the scientific or historical propositions under discussion are really only propositions about the state of mind of the people who assert them, or that they are neither true nor false, or that we have no justification whatever for believing any of them!

We must therefore have intuition, and in a subject where infallibility is not attainable, intuitions will sometimes disagree. Some philosophers indeed prefer not to call them intuitions when they are wrong, but then the problem will be to distinguish real from ostensible intuitions, since people certainly sometimes think they see intuitively what is not true. Now Lord Russell says: "Since no way can be even imagined for deciding a difference as to values, the conclusion is forced upon us that the difference is one of tastes, not one as to any objective truth";[1] but what I have said shows that we can imagine plenty of ways. I have indicated that errors as to judgments of value may arise (a) from lack of the requisite experience, (b) from intellectual confusions of some sort, (c) from failure to attend adequately to certain aspects of the situation or of the consequences, or (d) from psychological causes such as those with which the psychoanalyst deals. Therefore to remove errors we may (a) supply the lacking experience, or failing this, if possible, describe it in a way which will make its nature clear to the other party; we may (b) dispel intellectual confusions by making adequate distinctions or exposing actual fallacies such as make a person think he has seen that A is C when he has really only seen that A is B and mistakenly identified B with C; we may (c) suggest the direction of attention to the neglected points, or we may (d) use psychological methods. And we shall, if we are wise, also look out to see whether we ourselves

1. See above, Selection 25, p. 308.

have tripped up in any of these ways. Further, even when inference cannot completely prove or disprove, we may use it to confirm or cast doubt on ostensible intuition. The large class of errors which result mainly from an unwillingness really to seek for the truth can hardly be used as an argument against objectivity, since they are due to the moral fault of the persons who are in error and could have been removed if the latter had tried. In these cases the trouble is not that there are no means of deciding but that the means are not used.

The methods I have suggested will not always be successful, but then is there any sphere in which human efforts always do succeed? Even the methodology of physical science cannot lay down rules which will guarantee that any scientist can make discoveries or show him in detail in advance how to prove to others the truth of the discoveries when made. I am not claiming that it is possible in practice to remove all ethical differences, but how do we know that it could not be done if there were a will on each side to listen to what the other had to say and an intelligence to discern the best methods to adopt in order to facilitate a decision? A person cannot be brought into agreement even with the established truths of science if he will not listen to what the scientist says, and there is no reason to think even with ethical intuitions that there are not describable processes by which any cause of error can on principle be removed. I insert the words "on principle" simply because it will still often be the case that none of the disputants thinks of the right way of removing the error or that the person in error will not or cannot take it, as also occurs in disputes about questions of fact outside ethics.

Where the intuitive belief is due to non-intellectual factors of a kind which vitiate it, there seem to be two possibilities of cure. First, the person concerned may lose all tendency to hold the intuitive conviction when its alleged cause is clearly pointed out to him. The alleged cause is then in his case probably at least an essential part of the real cause. If, on the other hand, the intuitive belief remains unimpaired, and the man does not react to the causal explanation in a way which suggests that it has really touched a sore point, this is presumptive evidence that the explanation is mistaken. But, secondly, the cure from a false belief due to non-intellectual factors is more likely to arise because the man has been induced to approach the subject in a new spirit than merely because the true causation of the belief has been suggested to him. After all it is impossible to prove even to an unprejudiced person that such a causal theory as to the origin of a person's belief is really correct. How to induce a person to make such a new approach is a question not of logical argument but of practical psychology.

We must not think of intuition as something quite by itself, uninfluenced by inference; it is helped by inference but sees beyond what could be proved by inference. And, when intuitive ethical views differ, use may be made of inference to support one or other of the clashing views, especially by showing that it fits well into a coherent ethical system. This will not settle the question absolutely conclusively, but it can help toward settlement. Perhaps as the result of the inference one of the parties to the dispute may realize that he does not see by intuition what he claimed to see, but something rather different. It would thus be a great mistake to say that, when two men disagree on an ethical question, there is nothing to be done about it or that there is no scope in ethics for inference. No argument is available which could prove the subjectivity or fallaciousness of all ethics without establishing a similar conclusion about all other branches of study except mathematics and formal logic. . . .

27   The Indefinability of Good

G. E. Moore

"Good" Is a Simple Notion

... **W**HAT, THEN, IS GOOD? HOW IS good to be defined? Now, it may be thought that this is a verbal question. A definition does indeed often mean the expressing of one word's meaning in other words. But this is not the sort of definition I am asking for. Such a definition can never be of ultimate importance in any study except lexicography. If I wanted that kind of definition I should have to consider in the first place how people generally used the word "good," but my business is not with its proper usage, as established by custom. I should, indeed, be foolish, if I tried to use it for something which it did not usually denote: if, for instance, I were to announce that, whenever I used the word "good," I must be understood to be thinking of that object which is usually denoted by the word "table." I shall, therefore, use the word in the sense in which I think it is ordinarily used; but at the same time I am not anxious to discuss whether I am right in thinking that it is so used. My business is solely with that object or idea, which I hold, rightly or wrongly, that the word is generally used to stand for. What I want to discover is the nature of the object or idea, and about this I am extremely anxious to arrive at an agreement.

But, if we understand the question in this sense, my answer to it may seem a very disappointing one. If I am asked "What is good?" my answer is that good is good, and that is the end of the matter. Or if I am asked "How is good to be defined?" my answer is that it cannot be defined, and that is all I have to say about it. But disappointing as these answers may appear, they are of the very last importance. To readers who are familiar with philosophic terminology, I can express their importance by saying that

[This selection is part of Chapter I of Moore's *Principia Ethica,* published by the Cambridge University Press in 1903. It is reproduced here with the kind permission of Professor Moore and the publishers.]

they amount to this: That propositions about the good are all of them synthetic and never analytic; and that is plainly no trivial matter. And the same thing may be expressed more popularly, by saying that, if I am right, then nobody can foist upon us such an axiom as that "Pleasure is the only good" or that "The good is the desired" on the pretence that this is the very meaning of the word.

Let us, then, consider this position. My point is that "good" is a simple notion, just as "yellow" is a simple notion; that, just as you cannot, by any manner of means, explain to any one who does not already know it, what yellow is, so you cannot explain what good is. Definitions of the kind that I was asking for, definitions which describe the real nature of the object or notion denoted by a word, and which do not merely tell us what the word is used to mean, are only possible when the object or notion in question is something complex. You can give a definition of a horse, because a horse has many different properties and qualities, all of which you can enumerate. But when you have enumerated them all, when you have reduced a horse to his simplest terms, then you can no longer define those terms. They are simply something which you think of or perceive, and to any one who cannot think of or perceive them, you can never, by any definition, make their nature known. It may perhaps be objected to this that we are able to describe to others, objects which they have never seen or thought of. We can, for instance, make a man understand what a chimaera is, although he has never heard of one or seen one. You can tell him that it is an animal with a lioness's head and body, with a goat's head growing from the middle of its back, and with a snake in place of a tail. But here the object which you are describing is a complex object; it is entirely composed of parts, with which we are all perfectly familiar—a snake, a goat, a lioness; and we know, too, the manner in which those parts are to be put together, because we know what is meant by the middle of a lioness's back, and where her tail is wont to grow. And so it is with all objects, not previously known, which we are able to define; they are all complex; all composed of parts, which may themselves, in the first instance be capable of similar definition, but which must in the end be reducible to simplest parts, which can no longer be defined. But yellow and good, we say, are not complex: they are notions of that simple kind, out of which definitions are composed and with which the power of further defining ceases.

When we say, as Webster says, "The definition of horse is a 'hoofed quadruped of the genus Equus,' " we may, in fact, mean three different things. (1) We may mean merely: "When I say 'horse,' you are to understand that I am talking about a hoofed quadruped of the genus Equus." This might be called the arbitrary verbal definition: and I do not mean that good is indefinable in that sense. (2) We may mean, as Webster ought to mean: "When most English people say 'horse,' they mean a hoofed quadruped of the genus Equus." This may be called the verbal definition proper, and I do not say that good is indefinable in this sense either; for it is certainly possible to discover how people use a word: otherwise, we could never have known that "good" may be translated by "gut" in German and by "bon" in French. But (3) we may, when we define horse, mean something much more important. We may mean that a certain object, which we all of us know, is composed in a certain manner: that it has four legs, a head, a heart, a liver, etc., etc., all of them arranged in definite relations to one another. It is in this sense that I deny good to be definable. I say that it is not composed of any parts, which we can substitute for it in our minds when we are thinking of it. We might think just as clearly and correctly about a horse, if we thought of all its parts and their arrangement instead of thinking of the whole: we could, I say, think how a horse differed from a donkey just as well, just as truly, in this way, as now we do, only not so easily; but there is nothing whatsoever which we could so substitute for good; and that is what I mean, when I say that good is indefinable.

But I am afraid I have still not removed the chief difficulty which may prevent acceptance of the proposition that good is indefinable. I do not mean to say that *the* good, that which is good, is thus indefinable; if I did think so, I should not be writing on Ethics, for my main object is to help towards discovering that definition. It is just because I think there will be less risk of error in our search for a definition of "the good," that I am now insisting that *good* is indefinable. I must try to explain the difference between these two. I suppose it may be granted that "good" is an adjective. Well "the good," "that which is good," must therefore be the substantive to which the adjective "good" will apply: it must be the whole of that to which the adjective will apply, and the adjective must *always* truly apply to it. But if it is that to which the adjective will apply, it must be something different from that adjective itself; and the whole of that something different, whatever it is, will be our definition of *the* good. Now it may be that this something will have other adjectives, besides "good," that will apply to it. It may be full of pleasure, for example; it may be intelligent: and if these two adjectives are really part of its definition, then it will certainly be true, that pleasure and intelligence are good. And many people appear to think that, if we say "Pleasure and intelligence are good," or if we say "Only pleasure and intelligence are good," we are defining "good." Well, I cannot deny that propositions of this nature may sometimes be called definitions; I do not know well enough how the word is generally used to decide upon this point. I only wish it to be understood that that is not what I mean when I say there is no possible definition of good, and that I shall not mean this if I use the word again. I do most fully believe that some true proposition of the form "Intelligence is good and intelligence alone is good" can be found; if none could be found, our definition of *the* good would be impossible. As it is, I believe *the* good to be definable; and yet I still say that good itself is indefinable.

"Good," then, if we mean by it that quality which we assert to belong to a thing, when we say that the thing is good, is incapable of any definition, in the most important sense of that word. The most important sense of "definition" is that in which a definition states what are the parts which invariably compose a certain whole; and in this sense "good" has no definition because it is simple and has no parts. It is one of those innumerable objects of thought which are themselves incapable of definition, because they are the ultimate terms by reference to which whatever *is* capable of definition must be defined. That there must be an indefinite number of such terms is obvious, on reflection; since we cannot define anything except by analysis, which, when carried as far as it will go, refers us to something, which is simply different from anything else, and which by that ultimate difference explains the peculiarity of the whole which we are defining: for every whole contains some parts which are common to other wholes also. There is, therefore, no intrinsic difficulty in the contention that "good" denotes a simple and indefinable quality. There are many other instances of such qualities.

Consider yellow, for example. We may try to define it, by describing its physical equivalent; we may state what kind of light-vibrations must stimulate the normal eye, in order that we may perceive it. But a moment's reflection is sufficient to show that those light-vibrations are not themselves what we mean by yellow. *They* are not what we perceive. Indeed we should never have been able to discover their existence, unless we had first been struck by the patent difference of quality between the different colours. The most we can be entitled to say of those vibrations is that they are what corresponds in space to the yellow which we actually perceive.

The Naturalistic Fallacy

Yet a mistake of this simple kind has commonly been made about "good." It may be true that all things which are good are *also* something else, just as it is true that all things which are yellow produce a certain kind of vibration in the light. And it is a fact, that Ethics aims at discovering what are those other properties belonging to all things which are good. But far too many philosophers have thought that when they named those other properties they were actually defining good; that these properties, in fact, were simply not "other," but absolutely and entirely the same with goodness. This view I propose to call the "naturalistic fallacy" and of it I shall now endeavor to dispose . . .

Suppose a man says "I am pleased"; and suppose that is not a lie or a mistake but the truth. Well, if it is true, what does that mean? It means that his mind, a certain definite mind, distinguished by certain definite marks from others, has at this moment a certain definite feeling called pleasure. "Pleased" *means* nothing but having pleasure, and though we may be more pleased or less pleased, and even, we may admit for the present, have one or another kind of pleasure; yet in so far as it is pleasure we have, whether there be more or less of it, and whether it be of

one kind or another, what we have is one definite thing, absolutely indefinable, some one thing that is the same in all the various degrees and
in all the various kinds of it that there may be. We may be able to say
how it is related to other things: that, for example, it is in the mind,
that it causes desire, that we are conscious of it, etc., etc. We can, I say,
describe its relations to other things, but define it we can *not*. And if
anybody tried to define pleasure for us as being any other natural object;
if anybody were to say, for instance, that pleasure *means* the sensation
of red, and were to proceed to deduce from that that pleasure is a colour,
we should be entitled to laugh at him and to distrust his future statements about pleasure. Well, that would be the same fallacy which I have
called the naturalistic fallacy. That "pleased" does not mean "having
the sensation of red," or anything else whatever, does not prevent us
from understanding what it does mean. It is enough for us to know that
"pleased" does mean "having the sensation of pleasure," and though
pleasure is absolutely indefinable, though pleasure is pleasure and nothing else whatever, yet we feel no difficulty in saying that we are pleased.
The reason is, of course, that when I say "I am pleased," I do *not* mean
that "I" am the same thing as "having pleasure." And similarly no difficulty need be found in my saying that "pleasure is good" and yet not
meaning that "pleasure" is the same thing as "good," that pleasure *means*
good, and that good *means* pleasure. If I were to imagine that when I
said "I am pleased," I meant that I was exactly the same thing as
"pleased," I should not indeed call that a naturalistic fallacy, although
it would be the same fallacy as I have called naturalistic with reference
to Ethics. The reason for this is obvious enough. When a man confuses
two natural objects with one another, defining the one by the other, if
for instance, he confuses himself, who is one natural object, with "pleased"
or with "pleasure" which are others, then there is no reason to call the
fallacy naturalistic. But if he confuses "good" which is not in the same
sense a natural object, with any natural object whatever, then there is a
reason for calling that a naturalistic fallacy; its being made with regard
to "good" marks it as something quite specific, and this specific mistake
deserves a name because it is so common. As for the reasons why good
is not to be considered a natural object, they may be reserved for discussion in another place. But, for the present, it is sufficient to notice this:
Even if it were a natural object, that would not alter the nature of the
fallacy nor diminish its importance one whit. All that I have said about
it would remain quite equally true: only the name which I have called
it would not be so appropriate as I think it is. And I do not care about
the name; what I do care about is the fallacy. It does not matter what
we call it, provided we recognize it when we meet with it. It is to be
met with in almost every book on Ethics; and yet it is not recognized:
and that is why it is necessary to multiply illustrations of it, and convenient to give it a name. It is a very simple fallacy indeed. When we say
that an orange is yellow, we do not think our statement binds us to hold

that "orange" means nothing else than "yellow," or that nothing can be yellow but an orange. Supposing the orange is also sweet! Does that bind us to say that "sweet" is exactly the same thing as "yellow," that "sweet" must be defined as "yellow"? And supposing it be recognized that "yellow" just means "yellow" and nothing else whatever, does that make it any more difficult to hold that oranges are yellow? Most certainly it does not; on the contrary, it would be absolutely meaningless to say that oranges were yellow, unless yellow did in the end mean just "yellow" and nothing else whatever—unless it was absolutely indefinable. We should not get any very clear notion about things, which are yellow—we should not get very far with our science, if we were bound to hold that everything which was yellow *meant* exactly the same thing as yellow. We should find we had to hold that an orange was exactly the same thing as a stool, a piece of paper, a lemon, anything you like. We could prove any number of absurdities; but should we be the nearer to the truth? Why then, should it be different with "good?" Why, if good is good and indefinable, should we be held to deny that pleasure is good? Is there any difficulty in holding both to be true at once? On the contrary, there is no meaning in saying that pleasure is good, unless good is something different from pleasure. It is absolutely useless, so far as Ethics is concerned, to prove, as Mr. Spencer tries to do, that increase of pleasure coincides with increase of life, unless good *means* something different from either life or pleasure. He might just as well try to prove that an orange is yellow by showing that it always is wrapped up in paper.

In fact, if it is not the case that "good" denotes something simple and indefinable, only two alternatives are possible: either it is a complex, a given whole, about the correct analysis of which there may be disagreement; or else it means nothing at all, and there is no such subject as Ethics. In general, however, ethical philosophers have attempted to define good without recognizing what such an attempt must mean. . . .

It is very natural to make the mistake of supposing that what is universally true is of such a nature that its negation would be self-contradictory: the importance which has been assigned to analytic propositions in the history of philosophy shows how easy such a mistake is. And thus it is very easy to conclude that what seems to be a universal ethical principle is in fact an identical proposition; that, if, for example, whatever is called "good" seems to be pleasant, the proposition "Pleasure is the good" does not assert a connection between two different notions, but involves only one, that of pleasure, which is easily recognized as a distinct entity. But whoever will attentively consider with himself what is actually before his mind when he asks the question "Is pleasure (or whatever it may be) after all good?" can easily satisfy himself that he is not merely wondering whether pleasure is pleasant. And if he will try this experiment with each suggested definition in succession, he may become expert enough to recognize that in every case he has before his mind a unique object, with regard to the connection of which with any other

object, a distinct question may be asked. Every one does in fact understand the question "Is this good?" When he thinks of it, his state of
mind is different from what it would be, were he asked "Is this pleasant,
or desired, or approved?" It has a distinct meaning for him, even though
he may not recognize in what respect it is distinct. Whenever he thinks
of "intrinsic value," or "intrinsic worth," or says that a thing "ought to
exist," he has before his mind the unique object—the unique property of
things—which I mean by "good." Everybody is constantly aware of this
notion, although he may never become aware at all that it is different
from other notions of which he is also aware. But, for correct ethical
reasoning, it is extremely important that he should become aware of this
fact; and as soon as the nature of the problem is clearly understood, there
should be little difficulty in advancing so far in analysis.

"Good," then, is indefinable; and yet, so far as I know, there is only
one ethical writer, Prof. Henry Sidgwick, who has clearly recognized and
stated this fact. . . .

28   Critique of Ethics

A. J. Ayer

The Task of Ethical Philosophy

... It is our business to give an account of "judgments of value" which is both satisfactory in itself and consistent with our general empiricist principles. We shall set ourselves to show that in so far as statements of value are significant, they are ordinary "scientific" statements; and that in so far as they are not scientific, they are not in the literal sense significant, but are simply expressions of emotion which can be neither true nor false. In maintaining this view, we may confine ourselves for the present to the case of ethical statements. What is said about them will be found to apply, *mutatis mutandis,* to the case of aesthetic statements also.

The ordinary system of ethics, as elaborated in the works of ethical philosophers, is very far from being a homogeneous whole. Not only is it apt to contain pieces of metaphysics, and analyses of non-ethical concepts: its actual ethical contents are themselves of very different kinds. We may divide them, indeed, into four main classes. There are, first of all, propositions which express definitions of ethical terms, or judgments about the legitimacy or possibility of certain definitions. Secondly, there are propositions describing the phenomena of moral experience, and their causes. Thirdly, there are exhortations to moral virtue. And, lastly, there are actual ethical judgments. It is unfortunately the case that the distinction between these four classes, plain as it is, is commonly ignored by ethical philosophers; with the result that it is often very difficult to tell from their works what it is that they are seeking to discover or prove.

In fact, it is easy to see that only the first of our four classes, namely

[This selection is taken from Chapter VI of Ayer's *Language, Truth and Logic,* published in Great Britain by Victor Gollancz, Ltd. in 1936, and in the United States by Dover Publications, Inc. It is here reprinted with the kind permission of Professor Ayer and the publishers.]

that which comprises the propositions relating to the definitions of ethical terms, can be said to constitute ethical philosophy. The propositions which describe the phenomena of moral experience, and their causes, must be assigned to the science of psychology, or sociology. The exhortations to moral virtue are not propositions at all, but ejaculations or commands which are designed to provoke the reader to action of a certain sort. Accordingly, they do not belong to any branch of philosophy or science. As for the expressions of ethical judgments, we have not yet determined how they should be classified. But inasmuch as they are certainly neither definitions nor comments upon definitions, nor quotations, we may say decisively that they do not belong to ethical philosophy. A strictly philosophical treatise on ethics should therefore make no ethical pronouncements. But it should, by giving an analysis of ethical terms, show what is the category to which all such pronouncements belong. And this is what we are now about to do.

A question which is often discussed by ethical philosophers is whether it is possible to find definitions which would reduce all ethical terms to one or two fundamental terms. But this question, though it undeniably belongs to ethical philosophy, is not relevant to our present enquiry. We are not now concerned to discover which term, within the sphere of ethical terms, is to be taken as fundamental; whether, for example, "good" can be defined in terms of "right" or "right" in terms of "good," or both in terms of "value." What we are interested in is the possibility of reducing the whole sphere of ethical terms to non-ethical terms. We are enquiring whether statements of ethical value can be translated into statements of empirical fact.

Subjectivism and Utilitarianism

That they can be so translated is the contention of those ethical philosophers who are commonly called subjectivists, and of those who are known as utilitarians. For the utilitarian defines the rightness of actions, and the goodness of ends, in terms of the pleasure, or happiness, or satisfaction, to which they give rise; the subjectivist, in terms of the feelings of approval which a certain person, or group of people, has towards them. Each of these types of definition makes moral judgments into a sub-class of psychological or sociological judgments; and for this reason they are very attractive to us. For, if either was correct, it would follow that ethical assertions were not generically different from the factual assertions which are ordinarily contrasted with them; and the account which we have already given of empirical hypotheses would apply to them also.

Nevertheless we shall not adopt either a subjectivist or a utilitarian analysis of ethical terms. We reject the subjectivist view that to call an action right, or a thing good, is to say that it is generally approved of, because it is not self-contradictory to assert that some actions which are generally approved of are not right, or that some things which are generally approved of are not good. And we reject the alternative subjectivist view that a man who asserts that a certain action is right, or that a certain thing is good, is saying that he himself approves of it, on the ground that a man who confessed that he sometimes approved of what was bad or wrong would not be contradicting himself. And a similar argument is fatal to utilitarianism. We cannot agree that to call an action right is to say that of all the actions possible in the circumstances it would cause, or be likely to cause, the greatest happiness, or the greatest balance of pleasure over pain, or the greatest balance of satisfied over unsatisfied desire, because we find that it is not self-contradictory to say that it is sometimes wrong to perform the action which would actually or probably cause the greatest happiness, or the greatest balance of pleasure over pain, or of satisfied over unsatisfied desire. And since it is not self-contradictory to say that some pleasant things are not good, or that some bad things are desired, it cannot be the case that the sentence "x is good" is equivalent to "x is pleasant," or to "x is desired." And to every other variant of utilitarianism with which I am acquainted the same objection can be made. And therefore we should, I think, conclude that the validity of ethical judgments is not determined by the felicific tendencies of actions, any more than by the nature of people's feelings; but that it must be regarded as "absolute" or "intrinsic," and not empirically calculable.

If we say this, we are not, of course, denying that it is possible to invent a language in which all ethical symbols are definable in non-ethical terms, or even that it is desirable to invent such a language and adopt it in place of our own; what we are denying is that the suggested reduction of ethical to non-ethical statements is consistent with the conventions of our actual language. That is, we reject utilitarianism and subjectivism, not as proposals to replace our existing ethical notions by new ones, but as analyses of our existing ethical notions. Our contention is simply that, in our language, sentences which contain normative ethical symbols are not equivalent to sentences which express psychological propositions, or indeed empirical propositions of any kind.

It is advisable here to make it plain that it is only normative ethical symbols, and not descriptive ethical symbols, that are held by us to be indefinable in factual terms. There is a danger of confusing these two types of symbols, because they are commonly constituted by signs of the same sensible form. Thus a complex sign of the form "x is wrong" may constitute a sentence which expresses a moral judgment concerning a certain type of conduct, or it may constitute a sentence which states that a certain type of conduct is repugnant to the moral sense of a particular society. In the latter case, the symbol "wrong" is a descriptive ethical symbol, and the sentence in which it occurs expresses an ordinary socio-logical proposition; in the former case, the symbol "wrong" is a norma-tive ethical symbol, and the sentence in which it occurs does not, we maintain, express an empirical proposition at all. It is only with norma-tive ethics that we are at present concerned; so that whenever ethical symbols are used in the course of this argument without qualifications, they are always to be interpreted as symbols of the normative type.

Intuitionism

In admitting that normative ethical concepts are irreducible to em-pirical concepts, we seem to be leaving the way clear for the "absolutist" view of ethics—that is, the view that statements of value are not controlled by observation, as ordinary empirical propositions are, but only by a mysterious "intellectual intuition." A feature of this theory, which is seldom recognized by its advocates, is that it makes statements of value unverifi-able. For it is notorious that what seems intuitively certain to one person may seem doubtful, or even false, to another. So that unless it is pos-sible to provide some criterion by which one may decide between con-flicting intuitions, a mere appeal to intuition is worthless as a test of a proposition's validity. But in the case of moral judgments, no such criterion can be given. Some moralists claim to settle the matter by say-ing that they "know" that their own moral judgments are correct. But such an assertion is of purely psychological interest, and has not the slightest tendency to prove the validity of any moral judgment. For dis-sentient moralists may equally well "know" that their ethical views are correct. And, as far as subjective certainty goes, there will be nothing to choose between them. When such differences of opinion arise in connec-tion with an ordinary empirical proposition, one may attempt to resolve them by referring to, or actually carrying out, some relevant empirical test. But with regard to ethical statements, there is, on the "absolutist" or "intuitionist" theory, no relevant empirical test. We are therefore justified in saying that on this theory ethical statements are held to be unverifiable. They are, of course, also held to be genuine synthetic propositions.

Considering the use which we have made of the principle that a synthetic proposition is significant only if it is empirically verifiable, it is clear that the acceptance of an "absolutist" theory of ethics would undermine the whole of our main argument. And as we have already rejected the "naturalistic" theories which are commonly supposed to pro-vide the only alternative to "absolutism" in ethics, we seem to have reached a difficult position. We shall meet the difficulty by showing that the correct treatment of ethical statements is afforded by a third theory, which is wholly compatible with our radical empiricism.

Assertions of Value Are Not Scientific but "Emotive"

We begin by admitting that the fundamental ethical concepts are unanalysable, inasmuch as there is no criterion by which one can test the validity of the judgments in which they occur. So far we are in agreement with the absolutists. But, unlike the absolutists, we are able to give an explanation of this fact about ethical concepts. We say that the reason why they are unanalysable is that they are mere pseudo-concepts. The presence of an ethical symbol in a proposition adds nothing to its factual content. Thus if I say to someone, "You acted wrongly in stealing that money," I am not stating anything more than if I had simply said, "You stole that money." In adding that this action is wrong I am not making any further statement about it. I am simply evincing my moral disapproval of it. It is as if I had said, "You stole that money," in a peculiar tone of horror, or written it with the addition of some special exclamation marks. The tone, or the exclamation marks, adds nothing to the literal meaning of the sentence. It merely serves to show that the expression of it is attended by certain feelings in the speaker.

If now I generalize my previous statement and say, "Stealing money is wrong," I produce a sentence which has no factual meaning—that is, expresses no proposition which can be either true or false. It is as if I had written "Stealing money!!"—where the shape and thickness of the exclamation marks show, by a suitable convention, that a special sort of moral disapproval is the feeling which is being expressed. It is clear that there is nothing said here which can be true or false. Another man may disagree with me about the wrongness of stealing, in the sense that he may not have the same feelings about stealing as I have, and he may quarrel with me on account of my moral sentiments. But he cannot, strictly speaking, contradict me. For in saying that a certain type of action is right or wrong, I am not making any factual statement, not even a statement about my own state of mind. I am merely expressing certain moral sentiments. And the man who is ostensibly contradicting me is merely expressing his moral sentiments. So that there is plainly no sense in asking which of us is in the right. For neither of us is asserting a genuine proposition.

What we have just been saying about the symbol "wrong'" applies to all normative ethical symbols. Sometimes they occur in sentences which record ordinary empirical facts besides expressing ethical feeling about those facts: sometimes they occur in sentences which simply express ethical feeling about a certain type of action, or situation, without making any statement of fact. But in every case in which one would commonly be said to be making an ethical judgment, the function of the relevant ethical word is purely "emotive." It is used to express feeling about certain objects, but not to make any assertion about them.

It is worth mentioning that ethical terms do not serve only to express feeling. They are calculated also to arouse feeling, and so to stimulate action. Indeed some of them are used in such a way as to give the sentences in which they occur the effect of commands. Thus the sentence "It is your duty to tell the truth" may be regarded both as the expression of a certain sort of ethical feeling about truthfulness and as the expression of the command "Tell the truth." The sentence "You ought to tell the truth" also involves the command "Tell the truth," but here the tone of the command is less emphatic. In the sentence "It is good to tell the truth" the command has become little more than a suggestion. And thus the "meaning" of the word "good," in its ethical usage, is differentiated from that of the word "duty" or the word "ought." In fact we may define the meaning of the various ethical words in terms both of the different feelings they are ordinarily taken to express, and also the different responses which they are calculated to provoke.

We can now see why it is impossible to find a criterion for determining the validity of ethical judgments. It is not because they have an "absolute" validity which is mysteriously independent of ordinary sense-experience, but because they have no objective validity whatsoever. If a sentence makes no statement at all, there is obviously no sense in asking whether what it says is true or false. And we have seen that sentences which simply express moral judgments do not say anything. They are pure expressions of feeling and as such do not come under the category of truth and falsehood. They are unverifiable for the same reason as a cry of pain or a word of command is unverifiable—because they do not express genuine propositions.

The Difference Between the Emotive Theory and Orthodox Subjectivism

Thus, although our theory of ethics might fairly be said to be radically subjectivist, it differs in a very important respect from the orthodox subjectivist theory. For the orthodox subjectivist does not deny, as we do, that the sentences of a moralizer express genuine propositions. All he denies is that they express propositions of a unique non-empirical character. His own view is that they express propositions about the speaker's feelings. If this were so, ethical judgments clearly would be capable of being true or false. They would be true if the speaker had the relevant feelings, and false if he had not. And this is a matter which is, in principle, empirically verifiable. Furthermore they could be significantly contradicted. For if I say, "Tolerance is a virtue," and someone answers, "You don't approve of it," he would, on the ordinary subjectivist theory, be contradicting me. On our theory, he would not be contradicting me, because, in saying that tolerance was a virtue, I should not be making any statement about my own feelings or about anything else. I should simply be evincing my feelings, which is not at all the same thing as saying that I have them.

The distinction between the expression of feeling and the assertion of feeling is complicated by the fact that the assertion that one has a certain feeling often accompanies the expression of that feeling, and is then, indeed, a factor in the expression of that feeling. Thus I may simultaneously express boredom and say that I am bored, and in that case my utterance of the words, "I am bored," is one of the circumstances which make it true to say that I am expressing or evincing boredom. But I can express boredom without actually saying that I am bored. I can express it by my tone and gestures, while making a statement about something wholly unconnected with it, or by an ejaculation, or without uttering any words at all. So that even if the assertion that one has a certain feeling always involves the expression of that feeling, the expression of a feeling assuredly does not always involve the assertion that one has it. And this is the important point to grasp in considering the distinction between our theory and the ordinary subjectivist theory. For whereas the subjectivist holds that ethical statements actually assert the existence of certain feelings, we hold that ethical statements are expressions and excitants of feeling which do not necessarily involve any assertions.

We have already remarked that the main objection to the ordinary subjectivist theory is that the validity of ethical judgments is not determined by the nature of their author's feelings. And this is an objection which our theory escapes. For it does not imply that the existence of any feelings is a necessary and sufficient condition of the validity of an ethical judgment. It implies, on the contrary, that ethical judgments have no validity.

Do We Ever Dispute About Questions of Value?

There is, however, a celebrated argument against subjectivist theories which our theory does not escape. It has been pointed out by Moore that if ethical statements were simply statements about the speaker's feelings, it would be impossible to argue about questions of value.[1] To take a typical example: if a man said that thrift was a virtue, and another replied that it was a vice, they would not, on this theory, be disputing with one another. One would be saying that he approved of thrift, and the other that *he* didn't; and there is no reason why both these statements should not be true. Now Moore held it to be obvious that we do dispute about questions of value, and accordingly concluded that the particular form of subjectivism which he was discussing was false.

It is plain that the conclusion that it is impossible to dispute about questions of value follows from our theory also. For as we hold that such sentences as "Thrift is a virtue" and "Thrift is a vice" do not

1. Cf. *Philosophical Studies,* "The Nature of Moral Philosophy."

express propositions at all, we clearly cannot hold that they express incompatible propositions. We must therefore admit that if Moore's argument really refutes the ordinary subjectivist theory, it also refutes ours. But, in fact, we deny that it does refute even the ordinary subjectivist theory. For we hold that one really never does dispute about questions of value.

This may seem, at first sight, to be a very paradoxical assertion. For we certainly do engage in disputes which are ordinarily regarded as disputes about questions of value. But, in all such cases, we find, if we consider the matter closely, that the dispute is not really about a question of value, but about a question of fact. When someone disagrees with us about the moral value of a certain action or type of action, we do admittedly resort to argument in order to win him over to our way of thinking. But we do not attempt to show by our arguments that he has the "wrong" ethical feeling towards a situation whose nature he has correctly apprehended. What we attempt to show is that he is mistaken about the facts of the case. We argue that he has misconceived the agent's motive; or that he has misjudged the effects of the action, or its probable effects in view of the agent's knowledge; or that he has failed to take into account the special circumstances in which the agent was placed. Or else we employ more general arguments about the effects which actions of a certain type tend to produce, or the qualities which are usually manifested in their performance. We do this in the hope that we have only to get our opponent to agree with us about the nature of the empirical facts for him to adopt the same moral attitude towards them as we do. And as the people with whom we argue have generally received the same moral education as ourselves, and live in the same social order, our expectation is usually justified. But if our opponent happens to have undergone a different process of moral "conditioning" from ourselves, so that, even when he acknowledges all the facts, he still disagrees with us about the moral value of the actions under discussion, then we abandon the attempt to convince him by argument. We say that it is impossible to argue with him because he has a distorted or undeveloped moral sense; which signifies merely that he employs a different set of values from our own. We feel that our own system of values is superior, and therefore speak in such derogatory terms of his. But we cannot bring forward any arguments to show that our system is superior. For our judgment that it is so is itself a judgment of value, and accordingly outside the scope of argument. It is because argument fails us when we come to deal with pure questions of value, as distinct from questions of fact, that we finally resort to mere abuse.

In short, we find that argument is possible on moral questions only if some system of values is presupposed. If our opponent concurs with us in expressing moral disapproval of all actions of a given type *t,* then we may get him to condemn a particular action A, by bringing forward arguments to show that A is of type *t.* For the question whether A does or does not belong to that type is a plain question of fact. Given that a man has certain moral principles, we argue that he must, in order to be consistent, react morally to certain things in a certain way. What we do not and cannot argue about is the validity of these moral principles. We merely praise or condemn them in the light of our own feelings.

If anyone doubts the accuracy of this account of moral disputes, let him try to construct even an imaginary argument on a question of value which does not reduce itself to an argument about a question of logic or about an empirical matter of fact. I am confident that he will not succeed in producing a single example. And if that is the case, he must allow that its involving the impossibility of purely ethical arguments is not, as Moore thought, a ground of objection to our theory, but rather a point in favour of it.

Having upheld our theory against the only criticism which appeared to threaten it, we may now use it to define the nature of all ethical enquiries. We find that ethical philosophy consists simply in saying that ethical concepts are pseudo-concepts and therefore unanalysable. The further task of describing the different feelings that the different ethical terms are used to express, and the different reactions that they customarily provoke, is a task for the psychologist. There cannot be such a thing as ethical science, if by ethical science one means the elaboration of a "true" system of morals. For we have seen that, as ethical judgments are mere expressions of feeling, there can be no way of determining the validity of any ethical system, and, indeed no sense in asking whether any such system is true. All that one may legitimately inquire in this connection is, What are the moral habits of a given person or group of people, and what causes them to have precisely those habits and feelings? And this inquiry falls wholly within the scope of the existing social sciences. . . .

29   The New Subjectivism

in Ethics

Brand Blanshard

B Y THE NEW SUBJECTIVISM IN ETHICS
I mean the view that when anyone says "this is right" or "this is good,"
he is only expressing his own feeling; he is not asserting anything true
or false, because he is not asserting or judging at all; he is really making
an exclamation that expresses a favorable feeling.

This view has recently come into much favor. With variations of detail, it is being advocated by Russell, Wittgenstein and Ayer in England,
and by Carnap, Stevenson, Feigl, and others, in this country. Why is it
that the theory has come into so rapid a popularity? Is it because moralists of insight have been making a fresh and searching examination of
moral experience and its expression? No, I think not. A consideration
of the names just mentioned suggests a truer reason. All these names
belong, roughly speaking, to a single school of thought in the theory of
knowledge. If the new view has become popular in ethics, it is because
certain persons who were at work in the theory of knowledge arrived at
a new view *there,* and found, on thinking it out, that it required the
new view in ethics; the view comes less from ethical analysis than from
logical positivism.

As positivists, these writers held that every judgment belongs to one
or other of two types. On the one hand, it may be *a priori* or necessary.
But then it is always analytic, i.e., it unpacks in its predicate part or all
of its subject. Can we safely say that 7+5 make 12? Yes, because 12
is what we mean by "7+5." On the other hand, the judgment may be
empirical, and then, if we are to verify it, we can no longer look to our
meanings only; it refers to sense experience and there we must look for

[This article is reprinted with the kind permission of the author and the editor of
Philosophy and Phenomenological Research, where it first appeared in 1949.]

its warrant. Having arrived at this division of judgments, the positivists raised the question where value judgments fall. The judgment that knowledge is good, for example, did not seem to be analytic; the value that knowledge might have did not seem to be part of our concept of knowledge. But neither was the statement empirical, for goodness was not a quality like red or squeaky that could be seen or heard. What were they to do, then, with these awkward judgments of value? To find a place for them in their theory of knowledge would require them to revise the theory radically, and yet that theory was what they regarded as their most important discovery. It appeared that the theory could be saved in one way only. If it could be shown that judgments of good and bad were not judgments at all, that they asserted nothing true or false, but merely expressed emotions like "Hurrah" or "Fiddlesticks," then these wayward judgments would cease from troubling and weary heads could be at rest. This is the course the positivists took. They explained value judgments by explaining them away.

Now I do not think their view will do. But before discussing it, I should like to record one vote of thanks to them for the clarity with which they have stated their case. It has been said of John Stuart Mill that he wrote so clearly that he could be found out. This theory has been put so clearly and precisely that it deserves criticism of the same kind, and this I will do my best to supply. The theory claims to show by analysis that when we say, "That is good," we do not mean to assert a character of the subject of which we are thinking. I shall argue that we do mean to do just that.

Let us work through an example, and the simpler and commoner the better. There is perhaps no value statement on which people would more universally agree than the statement that intense pain is bad. Let us take a set of circumstances in which I happen to be interested on the legislative side and in which I think every one of us might naturally make such a statement. We come upon a rabbit that has been caught in one of the brutal traps in common use. There are signs that it has struggled for days to escape and that in a frenzy of hunger, pain, and fear, it has all but eaten off its own leg. The attempt failed: the animal is now dead. As we think of the long and excruciating pain it must have suffered, we are very likely to say: "It was a bad thing that the little animal should suffer so." The positivist tells us that when we say this we are only expressing our present emotion. I hold, on the contrary, that we mean to assert something of the pain itself, namely, that it was bad—bad when and as it occurred.

Consider what follows from the positivist view. On that view, nothing good or bad happened in the case until I came on the scene and made my remark. For what I express in my remark is something going on in me at the time, and that of course did not exist until I did come on the scene. The pain of the rabbit was not itself bad; nothing evil was happening when that pain was being endured; badness, in the only sense in which it is involved at all, waited for its appearance till I came and looked and felt. Now that this is at odds with our meaning may be shown as follows. Let us put to ourselves the hypothesis that we had not come on the scene and that the rabbit never was discovered. Are we prepared to say that in that case nothing bad occurred in the sense in which we said it did? Clearly not. Indeed we should say, on the contrary, that the accident of our later discovery made no difference whatever to the badness of the animal's pain, that it would have been every whit as bad whether a chance passer-by happened later to discover the body and feel repugnance or not. If so, then it is clear that in saying the suffering was bad we are not expressing our feelings only. We are saying that the pain was bad when and as it occurred and before anyone took an attitude toward it.

The first argument is thus an ideal experiment in which we use the method of difference. It removes our present expression and shows that the badness we meant would not be affected by this, whereas on positivist grounds it should be. The second argument applies the method in the reverse way. It ideally removes the past event, and shows that this would render false what we mean to say, whereas on positivist grounds it should not. Let us suppose that the animal did not in fact fall into the trap and did not suffer at all, but that we mistakenly believe it did, and say as before that its suffering was an evil thing. On the positivist theory, everything I sought to express by calling it evil in the first case is still present in the second. In the only sense in which badness is involved at all, whatever was bad in the first case is still present in its entirety, since all that is expressed in either case is a state of feeling, and that feeling is still there. And our question is, is such an implication consistent with what we meant? Clearly it is not. If anyone asked us, after we made the remark that the suffering was a bad thing, whether we should think it was relevant to what we said to learn that the incident had never occurred and no pain had been suffered at all, we should say that it made all the difference in the world, that what we were asserting to be bad was precisely the suffering we thought had occurred back there, that if this had not occurred, there was nothing left to be bad, and that our assertion was in that case mistaken. The suggestion that in saying something evil had occurred we were after all making no mistake, because we had never meant anyhow to say anything about the past suffering, seems to me merely frivolous. If we did not mean to say this, why should we be so relieved on finding that the suffering had not occurred? On the theory before us, such relief would be groundless, for in that suffering itself there was nothing bad at all, and hence in its non-occurrence there would be nothing to be relieved about. The positivist theory would here distort our meaning beyond recognition.

So far as I can see, there is only one way out for the positivist. He holds that goodness and badness lie in feelings of approval or disapproval. And there is a way in which he might hold that badness did in this case precede our own feeling of disapproval without belonging to the pain itself. The pain in itself was neutral; but unfortunately the rabbit, on no grounds at all, took up toward this neutral object an attitude of disapproval, and that made it for the first time, and in the only intelligible sense, bad. This way of escape is theoretically possible, but since it has grave difficulties of its own and has not, so far as I know, been urged by positivists, it is perhaps best not to spend time over it.

I come now to a third argument, which again is very simple. When we come upon the rabbit and make our remark about its suffering being a bad thing, we presumably make it with some feeling; the positivists are plainly right in saying that such remarks do usually express feeling. But suppose that a week later we revert to the incident in thought and make our statement again. And suppose that the circumstances have now so changed that the feeling with which we made the remark in the first place has faded. The pathetic evidence is no longer before us; and we are now so fatigued in body and mind that feeling is, as we say, quite dead. In these circumstances, since what was expressed by the remark when first made is, on the theory before us, simply absent, the remark now expresses nothing. It is as empty as the word "Hurrah" would be when there was no enthusiasm behind it. And this seems to me untrue. When we repeat the remark that such suffering was a bad thing, the feeling with which we made it last week may be at or near the vanishing point, but if we were asked whether we meant to say what we did before, we should certainly answer Yes. We should say that we made our point with feeling the first time and little or no feeling the second time, but that it was the same point we were making. And if we can see that what we meant to say remains the same, while the feeling varies from intensity to near zero, it is not the feeling that we primarily meant to express.

I come now to a fourth consideration. We all believe that toward acts or effects of a certain kind one attitude is fitting and another not; but on the theory before us such a belief would not make sense. Broad and Ross have lately contended that this fitness is one of the main facts of ethics, and I suspect they are right. But that is not exactly my point. My point is this: whether there is such fitness or not, we all assume that there is, and if we do, we express in moral judgments more than the subjectivists say we do. Let me illustrate.

In his novel *The House of the Dead,* Dostoevsky tells of his experiences in a Siberian prison camp. Whatever the unhappy inmates of such camps are like today, Dostoevsky's companions were about as grim a lot as can be imagined. "I have heard stories," he writes, "of the most terrible, the most unnatural actions, of the most monstrous murders, told with the most spontaneous, childishly merry laughter." Most of us would say that in this delight at the killing of others or the causing of suffering there is something very unfitting. If we were asked why we thought so, we should say that these things involve great evil and are wrong, and that to take delight in what is evil or wrong is plainly unfitting. Now on the subjectivist view, this answer is ruled out. For before someone takes up an attitude toward death, suffering, or their infliction, they have no moral quality at all. There is therefore nothing about them to which an attitude of approval or condemnation could be fitting. They are in themselves neutral, and, so far as they get a moral quality, they get it only through being invested with it by the attitude of the onlooker. But if that is true, why is any attitude more fitting than any other? Would applause, for example, be fitting if, apart from the applause, there were nothing good to applaud? Would condemnation be fitting if, independently of the condemnation, there were nothing bad to condemn? In such a case, any attitude would be as fitting or unfitting as any other, which means that the notion of fitness has lost all point.

Indeed we are forced to go much farther. If goodness and badness lie in attitudes only and hence are brought into being by them, those men who greeted death and misery with childishly merry laughter are taking the only sensible line. If there is nothing evil in these things, if they get their moral complexion only from our feeling about them, why shouldn't they be greeted with a cheer? To greet them with repulsion would turn what before was neutral into something bad; it would needlessly bring badness into the world; and even on subjectivist assumptions that does not seem very bright. On the other hand, to greet them with delight would convert what before was neutral into something good; it would bring goodness into the world. If I have murdered a man and wish to remove the stain, the way is clear. It is to cry, "Hurrah for murder."

What is the subjectivist to reply? I can only guess. He may point out that the inflicting of death is *not* really neutral before the onlooker takes his attitude, for the man who inflicted the death no doubt himself took an attitude, and thus the act had a moral quality derived from this. But that makes the case more incredible still, for the man who did the act presumably approved it, and if so it was good in the only sense in which anything is good, and then our conviction that the laughter is unfit is more unaccountable still. It may be replied that the victim, too, had his attitude and that since this was unfavorable, the act was not unqualifiedly good. But the answer is plain. Let the killer be expert at his job; let him despatch his victim instantly before he has time to take an attitude, and then gloat about his perfect crime without ever telling anyone. Then, so far as I can see, his act will be good without any qualification. It would become bad only if someone found out about it and disliked it. And that would be a curiously irrational procedure, since the man's approving of his own killing is in itself as neutral as the killing that it approves. Why then should anyone dislike it?

It may be replied that we can defend our dislike on this ground that, if the approval of killing were to go unchecked and spread, most men would have to live in insecurity and fear, and these things are undesirable. But surely this reply is not open; these things are not, on the theory, undesirable, for nothing is; in themselves they are neutral. Why then should I disapprove men's living in this state? The answer may come that if other men live in insecurity and fear, I shall in time be infected myself. But even in my own insecurity and fear there is, on the theory before us, nothing bad whatever, and therefore, if I disapprove them, it is without a shadow of ground and with no more fitness in my attitude than if I cordially cheered them. The theory thus conflicts with our judgments of fitness all along the line.

I come now to a fifth and final difficulty with the theory. It makes mistakes about values impossible. There is a whole nest of inter-connected criticisms here, some of which have been made so often that I shall not develop them again, such as that I can never agree or disagree in opinion with anyone else about an ethical matter, and that in these matters I can never be inconsistent with others or with myself. I am not at all content with the sort of analysis which says that the only contradictions in such cases have regard to facts and that contradictions about value are only differences of feeling. I think that if anyone tells me that having a bicuspid out without an anaesthetic is not a bad experience and I say it is a very nasty experience indeed, I am differing with him in opinion, and differing about the degrees of badness of the experience. But without pressing this further, let me apply the argument in what is perhaps a fresh direction.

There is an old and merciful distinction that moralists have made for many centuries about conduct—the distinction between what is subjectively and what is objectively right. They have said that in any given situation there is some act which, in view of all the circumstances, would be the best act to do; and this is what would be objectively right. The notion of an objectively right act is the ground of our notion of duty: our duty is always to find and do this act if we can. But of course we often don't find it. We often hit upon and do acts that we think are the right ones, but we are mistaken; and then our act is only subjectively right. Between these two acts the disparity may be continual; Professor Prichard suggested that probably few of us in the course of our lives ever succeed in doing *the* right act.

Now so far as I can see, the new subjectivism would abolish this difference at a stroke. Let us take a case. A boy abuses his small brother. We should commonly say, "That is wrong, but perhaps he doesn't know any better. By reason of bad teaching and a feeble imagination, he may see nothing wrong in what he is doing, and may even be proud of it. If so, his act may be subjectively right, though it is miles away from what is objectively right." What concerns me about the new subjectivism is that it prohibits this distinction. If the boy feels this way about his act, then it is right in the only sense in which anything is right. The notion of an objective right lying beyond what he has discovered, and which he ought to seek and do is meaningless. There might, to be sure, be an act that would more generally arouse favorable feelings in others, but that would not make it right for him unless he thought of it and approved it, which he doesn't. Even if he did think of it, it would not be obligatory for him to feel about it in any particular way, since there is nothing in any act, as we have seen, which would make any feeling more suitable than any other.

Now if there is no such thing as an objectively right act, what becomes of the idea of duty? I have suggested that the idea of duty rests on the idea of such an act, since it is always our duty to find that act and do it if we can. But if whatever we feel approval for at the time is right, what is the point of doubting and searching further? Like the little girl in Boston who was asked if she would like to travel, we can answer, "Why should I travel when I'm already there?" If I am reconciled in feeling to my present act, no act I could discover by reflection could be better, and therefore why reflect or seek at all? Such a view seems to me to break the main-spring of duty, to destroy the motive for self-improvement, and to remove the ground for self-criticism. It may be replied that by further reflection I can find an act that would satisfy my feelings more widely than the present one, and that this is the act I should seek. But this reply means either that such general satisfaction is objectively better, which would contradict the theory, or else that, if at the time I don't feel it better, it isn't better, in which case I have no motive for seeking it. When certain self-righteous persons took an inflexible line with Oliver Cromwell, his very Crom-wellian reply was, "Bethink ye, gentlemen, by the bowels of Christ, that ye may be mistaken." It was good advice. I hope nobody will take from me the privilege of finding myself mistaken. I should be sorry to think that the self of thirty years ago was as far along the path as the self of today, merely because he was a smug young jackanapes, or even that the para-gon of today has as little room for improvement as would be allowed by his myopic complacency.

One final remark. The great problems of the day are international problems. Has the new subjectivism any bearing upon these problems? I think it has, and a somewhat sinister bearing. I would not suggest, of course, that those who hold the theory are one whit less public-spirited than others; surely there are few who could call themselves citizens of the world with more right (if "rights" have meaning any longer) than Mr. Russell. But Mr. Russell has confessed himself discontented with his ethical theory, and in view of his breadth of concern, one cannot wonder. For its general acceptance would, so far as one can see, be an interna-tional disaster. The assumption behind the old League and the new United Nations was that there is such a thing as right and wrong in the conduct of a nation, a right and wrong that do not depend on how it happens to feel at the time. It is implied, for example, that when Japan invaded Manchuria in 1931 she might be wrong, and that by discussion and argu-ment she might be shown to be wrong. It was implied that when the Nazis invaded Poland they might be wrong, even though German public senti-ment overwhelmingly approved it. On the theory before us, it would be meaningless to call these nations mistaken; if they felt approval for what they did, then it was right with as complete a justification as could be supplied for the disapproval felt by the rest of the world. In the present dispute between Russia and our own country over southeast Europe, it is nonsense to speak of the right or rational course for either of us to take; if with all the facts before the two parties, each feels approval for its own course, both attitudes are equally justified or unjustified; neither is mistaken; there is no common reason to which they can take an appeal; there are no principles by which an international court could pronounce on the matter; nor would there be any obligation to obey the pronouncement if it were made. This cuts the ground from under any attempt to establish one's case as right or anyone else's case as wrong. So if our friends the subjectivists still hold their theory after I have applied my little ruler to their knuckles, which of course they will, I have but one request to make of them: Do keep it from Mr. Molotov and Mr. Vishinsky.

30   A Refutation of Morals

John Mackie

I N THIS PAPER I DO NOT PRETEND TO BE advancing any particularly new ideas: hardly any of the arguments are original, and indeed most are the stock instruments of all modern discussions of morals. But I think I am justified in offering this re-statement of them, because it is seldom realized how they may be brought together and interrelated, or how radically destructive they are of all common views of morality, when this is done.

We all have moral feelings: all of us find that there are human actions and states of affairs of which we approve and disapprove, and which we therefore try to encourage and develop or to oppose. (This emotion of approval is different from liking, one difference being that its object is more general. If someone stands me a pint, I like it: if someone stands an enemy of mine a pint, I dislike it: but I should approve of a state of society which provided free beer all round. So if I hear of someone whom I have never met and to whom I am personally indifferent being stood a pint, I should not say that I like it, for I am not directly affected, but I may well approve of it, because it is an instance of the sort of thing I want to see everywhere. A thorough distinction of approval from liking and other relations would require further discussion, but perhaps this will serve to indicate a contrast between classes with which we are all in fact acquainted. I shall suggest later a possible source of these generalized emotions.) But most of us do not merely admit that we have such *feelings,* we think we can also *judge* that actions and states are right and good, just as we judge about other matters of fact, that these judgments are either true or false, and that the qualities with which they deal exist objectively. This view, which almost everyone holds, may be crudely called "believing in morals." A few sceptics, however, think that there are only feelings of approval, no ob-

[The article from which this selection is taken originally appeared in *The Australasian Journal of Philosophy,* 1946. It is reprinted here with the kind permission of the author and editor.]

jective moral facts. (Of course the existence of a feeling is an objective fact, but not what is commonly called a moral fact.) One of their main arguments is that moral facts would be "queer," in that unlike other facts they cannot be explained in terms of arrangements of matter, or logical constructions out of sense-data, or whatever the particular theorist takes to be the general form of real things. This argument is not in itself very strong, or even very plausible, for unless we have good *a priori* grounds for whatever is taken as the basic principle of criticism, the criterion of reality, the mere fact that we seem to observe moral qualities and facts would be a reason for modifying that principle. Their other main argument, which is both older and more convincing, though not logically conclusive, is that although at any one time, in a particular social group, there is fairly complete agreement about what is right, in other classes, other countries, and above all in other periods of history and other cultures, the actual moral judgments or feelings are almost completely different, though perhaps there are a few feelings so natural to man that they are found everywhere. Now feelings may well change with changing conditions, but a judgment about objective fact should be everywhere the same: if we have a faculty of moral perception, it must be an extremely faulty one, liable not only to temporary illusions, as sight is, but to great and lasting error. Of course it may be that every society except our own is mistaken, that savages are morally backward because they lack our illuminating experience of the long-term effects of various kinds of action, and so on. But this complacent view (not indeed very popular now) is shaken by the observation that the variations in moral feelings can be explained much more plausibly not as being due to mistakes, but as reflections of social habits. This moral relativity would be less alarming if we could say that the varying judgments were not ultimate, but were applications to different circumstances of a single principle or a small number of principles, which were everywhere recognized—for example, that whatever produces pleasure is good, that whatever society commands is right, or, at the very least, that we should always do what we believe to be right. But these principles are not commonly laid down first, and the particular judgments deduced from them: rather the particular judgments are made by ordinary people, whereas the principles are later invented by philosophers and manipulated in order to explain them. In any case there is just as little agreement about principles as about particular judgments.

We find on further inquiry that most, perhaps all, actual moral judgments are fairly closely correlated with what we may call social demands: any society or social group has regular ways of working, and, in order to maintain these, requires that its members should act in certain ways: the members—from whatever motive, perhaps mainly habit, which has compelled them to adapt their desires to the established customs—obey these requirements themselves and force their fellows to do so, or at least feel obliged to obey and approve of others obeying. They call "right" and "good" whatever accords with these ways of working. Moreover, as the science of social history develops, it is more and more strongly suggested that ways of working and institutions have their own laws of growth, and that the desires or moral views of individuals do not so much control the history of society as arise out of it.

Belief in the objectivity of moral qualities is further undermined when we remark that whenever anyone calls an action or activity or state of affairs right or good (unless he is speaking in an ironical tone or puts these words in inverted commas) he himself either has a feeling of approval, or desires that the action should be done or the activity pursued or the state of affairs come into existence. (Only one of these alternatives is necessary, but they are often found together.)

None of these considerations is conclusive, but each has a certain weight: together they move the moral sceptic (who is often of a scientific and inductive turn of mind, and less devoted than some others to the clear light of intuition or the authority of reason) to conclude that in all probability we do not recognize moral facts, but merely have feelings of approval and disapproval, which arise in general from social demands and therefore vary from one society to another. This view I intend to examine and re-state, and to advance what I regard as decisive arguments for one of its more important aspects.

The simplest formulation of this view is that when someone says "this act is right" he means merely "I approve of this act." The well-known reply simply leaps into the reader's mind: when one person says that an act is right, another that the same act is wrong, they would not on this theory be disagreeing, whereas in fact they think they are. It will not do to say, with Stevenson,[1] that there is a disagreement in attitude, but not in belief: they think, at any rate, that they disagree in belief. Nor does one mean that "society approves of this act," since we frequently meet people who say, "I know society approves of this, but it is wrong all the same." But there is no need for argument: direct introspection shows that when we use the terms "right," "good," and the rest, we never intend merely to state that there are feelings of approval. An improved formulation of the sceptical view is that in saying "this is right," and so on, we are not *stating* any approval, but only *expressing* one, that words like "right" and "wrong," "good" and "bad" are to be compared not with "red" and "square" but with explanations or ejaculations like "ow!" "boo!" and "hurray!" This is certainly nearer the truth, and avoids the previous difficulties, but is, in another way, just as implausible. For we do not think that we are merely ejaculating when we talk in moral terms. If we did, and if someone disagreed with us, we should merely disapprove of his approvals, and either try to coax him into a different emotional attitude, or if he proved obstinate, knock him down. In fact we reason with him. These facts, and the logical tangles that we get into when we try to re-state fairly complex moral situations in the "boo-hurray" language, prove that we think, at least, that we are not merely expressing our emotions but are describing objective facts,

1. *Ethics and Language*, Chapter 1.

and therefore that the meaning of moral terms is not parallel with that of ejaculations. Many refutations of the "boo-hurray" theory have been worked out, but they all depend upon and illustrate the fact that we *think* that we are doing things of quite different sorts when we say "right" and when we say "ow!" Now if philosophy could do no more than elucidate the meaning of the terms of common speech, remove confusions and rationalize the thought of ordinary men, there would be nothing more to be said. Moral terms do mean objective qualities, and everyone who uses them does so because he believes in objective moral facts. But if the very terms of common speech may include errors and confusions within themselves, so that they cannot be used at all without falsity, if, we may add, philosophy may be permitted to inquire into these errors by observing a few facts for itself and founding inductive conclusions on them, the moral sceptic need not be so soon disheartened.

But he must modify his view again, and say that in using moral terms we are as it were objectifying our own feelings, thinking them into qualities existing independently of us. For example, we may see a plant, say a fungus, that fills us with disgust, but instead of stating that we have this feeling, or merely expressing and relieving it by an exclamation, we may ascribe to the fungus a semi-moral quality of foulness, over and above all the qualities that a physical scientist could find in it. Of course, in objectifying our feelings we are also turning them inside out: our feeling about the fungus is one of being disgusted, while the foulness we ascribe to the fungus means that it is disgusting. The supposed objective quality is not simply the feeling itself transferred to an external object, but is something that would inevitably arouse that feeling. (No one would say, "That fungus is foul, but I feel no disgust at it.") The feeling and the supposed quality are related as a seal or stamp and its impression.

This process of objectification is, I think, well known to psychologists and is not new in philosophy. I believe that it resembles what Hume says we do when we manufacture the idea of necessary connection out of our feeling of being compelled, by the association of ideas, to pass from cause to effect, though here the process of turning inside out does not occur.

There are strong influences which might lead us thus to objectify moral feelings. As I have mentioned, our moral judgments seem to arise from approvals borrowed from society, or from some social group, and these are felt by the individual as external to himself. It is for this reason that they are universal in form, applying equally to himself and to others. They are thus formally capable of being objective laws, in contrast to the "selfish" desires of the individual. This generality or universality, which I mentioned as characteristic of the emotion of approval, is reflected in Rousseau's doctrine that the general will and therefore law must be general in their object, and in Kant's criterion of the possibility of universalization of a moral law. Since we inevitably tend to encourage what we approve of, and to impose it upon others, we want everyone to adopt our approvals, and this will most surely come about if they have only to perceive a genuinely existing objective fact, for what we feel is in general private, what we perceive may be common to all. Suppose that we approve of hard work: then if as well as a feeling of approval in our own minds there were an objective fact like "hard work is good," such that everyone could observe the fact and such that the mere observation would arouse in him a like feeling of approval, and even perhaps stimulate him to work, we should eventually get what we want done: people would work hard. And since what we want does not exist in fact, we naturally construct it in imagination: we objectify our feelings so thoroughly that we completely deceive ourselves. I imagine that this is the reason why our belief in moral objectivity is so firm: we much more readily admit that the foulness of a fungus is an objectification than that the depravity of people who break our windows is. If moral predicates were admitted to be what the moral sceptic says they are, we should never be able to extol a state of affairs as good in any sense which would induce people to bring it about, unless they already wanted it, though we might point out that this state had features which in fact they did desire, though they had not realized this: we should never be able to recommend any course of action, except in such terms, as, "if you want to be rich, be economical"; nor could we give commands by any moral authority, though we might again advise "if you don't want a bullet through your brains, come quietly"; and we should never be able to lecture anyone on his wickedness —an alarming prospect. The temptations to objectify feelings of approval, and to retain our belief in morals, are clearly strong ones.

This process of objectifying our feelings is, then, neither impossible nor improbable: there is also abundant evidence that it is just what has occurred. It is commonly believed by moralists that good means desirable in a sense such that the mere recognition that a thing is good makes us desire it, and similarly the conclusion of the practical syllogism is both "this is right" and the performance of the action. This is what we should expect if "right" were the objectification of a tendency to compel or command the kind of act so described, and "good" of desire and approval. This is again indicated by the use of the term "value" which is clearly borrowed from spheres like economics where value is created by demand—in fact a quality manufactured in imagination out of the relation of being demanded by someone, the abstraction being the easier because the demand is not essentially that of a single buyer, but of an indeterminate crowd of potential buyers: the analogy with the objectification of moral feelings, aided by their generality, is very plain. . . .

In attempting to give an account of the origin of moral terms in this process of objectification, I do not, of course, claim that it is complete or precise in all respects. It is still open to discussion and correction on empirical grounds. We might go on to consider this process as a psychological process, investigating its causes, its similarities and contrasts with other mental processes, and the steps of which it is made up. We might ask whether "objectification" or some other name is really the most suitable, and also what are the precise motives objectified: we might consider, for example, Westermarck's argument[2] that "ought" normally expresses a conation, is sometimes but not necessarily or essentially imperative, and has its origin in disapproval rather than approval.

My discussion in this paper is intended to open the way for such discussions, not to settle them once and for all. What I am concerned to establish is simply the logical status of moral terms, not the psychological details of their origin; in effect I am asserting only that there are no facts of the form "this is right," that when we use such words the only fact is the existence of some feelings in ourselves or in others or in both, but that in using these terms we are falsely postulating or asserting something of the simple, objective form "this is right." . . .

· · · ·

2. *The Origin and Development of the Moral Ideas,* Chapter VI.

The Logical Behavior of
the Word "Good"

R. M. Hare

Why Naturalism Is Untenable

Let me illustrate one of the most characteristic features of value-words in terms of a particular example. It is a feature sometimes described by saying that "good" and other such words are the names of "supervenient" or "consequential" properties. Suppose that a picture is hanging upon the wall and we are discussing whether it is a good picture; that is to say, we are debating whether to assent to, or dissent from, the judgment "P is a good picture." It must be understood that the context makes it clear that we mean by "good picture" not "good likeness" but "good work of art"—though both these uses would be value-expressions.

First let us notice a very important peculiarity of the word "good" as used in this sentence. Suppose that there is another picture next to P in the gallery (I will call it Q). Suppose that either P is a replica of Q or Q of P, and we do not know which, but do know that both were painted by the same artist at about the same time. Now there is one thing that we cannot say; we cannot say "P is exactly like Q in all respects save this one, that P is a good picture and Q not." If we were to say this, we should invite the comment, "But how can one be good and the other not, if they are exactly alike? There must be some *further* difference between them to make one good and the other not." Unless we at least admit the relevance of the question "What makes one good and the other not?" we are bound to puzzle our hearers; they will think that something has gone wrong with our use of the word "good." Sometimes we cannot specify just what it is that

[This selection is taken from Part II of *The Language of Morals* (1952). It is reprinted with the kind permission of Mr. Hare and Clarendon Press, Oxford.]

makes one good and the other not; but there always must be something. Suppose that in the attempt to explain our meaning we said: "I didn't say that there *was* any other difference between them; there is just this one difference, that one is good and the other not. Surely you would understand me if I said that one was *signed* and the other not, but that there was otherwise no difference? So why shouldn't I say that one was *good* and the other not, but that there was otherwise no difference?" The answer to this protest is that the word "good" is not like the word "signed"; there is a difference in their logic. . . .

Let us then ask whether there are certain characteristics of pictures which are defining characteristics of a good picture, in the same way as "having all its angles 90 degrees and being a rectilinear plane figure" are defining characteristics of a rectangle. Moore* thought that he could prove that there were no such defining characteristics for the word "good" as used in morals. His argument has been assailed since he propounded it; and it is certainly true that the formulation of it was at fault. But it seems to me that Moore's argument was not merely plausible; it rests, albeit insecurely, upon a secure foundation; there is indeed something about the way in which, and the purposes for which, we use the word "good" which makes it impossible to hold the sort of position which Moore was attacking, although Moore did not see clearly what this something was. Let us, therefore, try to restate Moore's argument in a way which makes it clear why "naturalism" is untenable, not only for the moral use of "good" as he thought, but also for many other uses.

Let us suppose for the sake of argument that there are some "defining characteristics" of a good picture. It does not matter of what sort they are; they can be a single characteristic, or a conjunction of characteristics, or a disjunction of alternative characteristics. Let us call the group of these characteristics C. "P is a good picture" will then mean the same as "P is a picture and P is C." For example, let C mean "Having a tendency to arouse in people who are at that time members of the Royal Academy (or any other definitely specified group of people), a definitely recognizable feeling called 'admiration'. " The words "definitely specified" and "definitely recognizable" have to be inserted, for otherwise we might find that words in the *definiens* were being used evaluatively, and this would make the definition no longer "naturalistic." Now suppose that we wish to say that the members of the Royal Academy have good taste in pictures. To have good taste in pictures means to have this definitely recognizable feeling of admiration for those pictures, and only those pictures, which are good pictures. If therefore we wish to say that the members of the Royal Academy have good taste in pictures, we have, according to the definition, to say something which means the same as saying that they have this feeling of admiration for pictures which have a tendency to arouse in them this feeling.

Now this is not what we wanted to say. We wanted to say that they admired good pictures; we have succeeded only in saying that they admired

* See Selection 27, pp. 322 ff above.

pictures which they admired. Thus if we accept the definition we debar ourselves from saying something that we do sometimes want to say. What this something is will become apparent later; for the moment let us say that what we wanted to do was to *commend* the pictures which the members of the Royal Academy admired. Something about our definition prevented our doing this. We could no longer commend the pictures which they admired, we could only say that they admired those pictures which they admired. Thus our definition has prevented us, in one crucial case, from commending something which we want to commend. That is what is wrong with it.

Let us generalize. If "P is a good picture" is held to mean the same as "P is a picture and P is C," then it will become impossible to commend pictures for being C; it will be possible only to say that they are C. It is important to realize that this difficulty has nothing to do with the particular example that I have chosen. It is not because we have chosen the wrong defining characteristics; it is because, whatever defining characteristics we choose, this objection arises, that we can no longer commend an object for possessing those characteristics.

Let us illustrate this by another example. I am deliberately excluding for the moment moral examples because I want it to be clear that the logical difficulties which we are encountering have nothing to do with morals in particular, but are due to the general characteristics of value-words. Let us consider the sentence "S is a good strawberry." We might naturally suppose that this means nothing more than "S is a strawberry and S is sweet, juicy, firm, red, and large." But it then becomes impossible for us to say certain things which in our ordinary talk we do say. We sometimes want to say that a strawberry is a good strawberry because it is sweet, etc. This—as we can at once see if we think of ourselves saying it—does not mean the same as saying that a strawberry is a sweet, etc., strawberry because it is sweet, etc. But according to the proposed definition this is what it would mean. Thus here again the proposed definition would prevent our saying something that we do succeed in saying meaningfully in our ordinary talk. . . .

Meaning and Criteria

It is a characteristic of "good" that it can be applied to any number of different classes of objects. We have good cricket-bats, good chronometers, good fire-extinguishers, good pictures, good sunsets, good men. The same is true of the word "red"; all the objects I have just listed might be red. We have to ask first whether, in explaining the meaning of the word "good," it would be possible to explain its meaning in all of these expressions at once, or whether it would be necessary to explain "good cricket-bat" first, and then go on to explain "good chronometer" in the second lesson, "good fire-extinguisher" in the third, and so on; and if the latter, whether in each lesson we should be teaching something entirely new—like teaching the meaning of "fast dye" after we had in a previous lesson taught the meaning of "fast motor-car"—or whether it would be just the same lesson over again, with a different example—like teaching "red dye" after we had taught "red motor-car." Or there might be some third possibility.

The view that "good chronometer" would be a completely new lesson, even though the day before we had taught "good cricket-bat," runs at once into difficulties. For it would mean that at any one time our learner could only use the word "good" in speaking of classes of objects which he had learnt so far. He would never be able to go straight up to a new class of objects and use the word "good" of one of them. When he had learnt "good cricket-bat" and "good chronometer," he would not be able to manage "good fire-extinguisher"; and when he had learnt the latter, he would still be unable to manage "good motor-car." But in fact one of the most noticeable things about the way we use "good" is that we are able to use it for entirely new classes of objects that we have never called "good" before. Suppose that someone starts collecting cacti for the first time and puts one on his mantel-piece—the only cactus in the country. Suppose then that a friend sees it, and says "I must have one of those"; so he sends for one from wherever they grow, and puts it on his mantel-piece, and when his friend comes in, he says, "I've got a better cactus than yours." But how does he know how to apply the word in this way? He has never learnt to apply "good" to cacti; he does not even know any *criteria* for telling a good cactus from a bad one (for as yet there are none); but he has learnt to use the word "good," and having learnt that, he can apply it to any class of objects that he requires to place in order of merit. He and his friend may dispute about the criteria of good cacti; they may attempt to set up rival criteria; but they could not even do this unless they were from the start under no difficulty in using the word "good." Since, therefore, it is possible to use the word "good" for a new class of objects without further instruction, learning the use of the word for one class of objects cannot be a different lesson from learning it for another class of objects—though learning the criteria of goodness in a new class of objects may be a new lesson each time. . . .

To teach *what makes* a member of any class a good member of the class is indeed a new lesson for each class of objects; but nevertheless the word "good" has a constant meaning which, once learnt, can be understood no matter what class of objects is being discussed. We have to make a distinction between the meaning of the word "good" and the criteria for its application. . . .

Description and Evaluation

There are two sorts of things that we can say, for example, about strawberries; the first sort is usually called *descriptive,* the second sort *evaluative.* Examples of the first sort of remark are, "This strawberry is sweet" and "This strawberry is large, red, and juicy." Examples of the second sort of remark are "This is a good strawberry" and "This strawberry is just as strawberries ought to be." The first sort of remark is often given as a reason for making the second sort of remark; but the first sort does not by itself entail the second sort, nor vice versa. Yet there seems to be some close logical connexion between them. Our problem is: "What is this connexion?" for no light is shed by saying that there is a connexion, unless we can say what it is.

The problem may also be put in this way: if we knew all the descriptive properties which a particular strawberry had (knew, of every descriptive sentence relating to the strawberry, whether it was true or false), and if we knew also the meaning of the word "good," then what else should we require to know, in order to be able to tell whether a strawberry was a good one? Once the question is put in this way, the answer should be apparent. We should require to know, what are the criteria in virtue of which a strawberry is to be called a good one, or what are the characteristics that make a strawberry a good one, or what is the standard of goodness in strawberries. We should require to be given the major premise. We have already seen that we can know the meaning of "good strawberry" without knowing any of these latter things—though there is also a sense of the sentence "What does it mean to call a strawberry a good one?" in which we should not know the answer to it, unless we also knew the answer to these other questions. It is now time to elucidate and distinguish these two ways in which we can be said to know what it means to call an object a good member of its class. This will help us to see more clearly both the differences and the similarities between "good" and words like "red" and "sweet."

Since we have been dwelling for some time on the differences, it will do no harm now to mention some of the similarities. For this purpose, let us consider the two sentences: "M is a red motor-car" and "M is a good motor-car." . . .

The first similarity between "M is a red motor-car" and "M is a good motor-car" is that both can be, and often are, used for conveying information of a purely factual or descriptive character. If I say to someone "M is a good motor-car," and he himself has not seen, and knows nothing of M, but does on the other hand know what sorts of motor-car we are accustomed to call "good" (knows what is the accepted standard of goodness in motor-cars), he undoubtedly receives information from my remark about what sort of motor-car it is. He will complain that I have misled him, if he subsequently discovers that M will not go over 30 m.p.h., or uses as much oil as petrol, or is covered with rust, or has large holes in the roof. His reason for complaining will be the same as it would have been if I had said that the car was red and he subsequently discovered that it was black. I should have led him to expect the motor-car to be of a certain description when in fact it was of a quite different description.

The second similarity between the two sentences is this. Sometimes we use them, not for actually conveying information, but for putting our hearer into a position subsequently to use the word "good" or "red" for giving or getting information. Suppose, for example, that he is utterly unfamiliar with motor-cars in the same sort of way as most of us are unfamiliar with horses nowadays, and knows no more about motor-cars than is necessary in order to distinguish a motor-car from a hansom cab. In that case, my saying to him "M is a good motor-car" will not give him any information about M, beyond the information that it is a motor-car. But if he is able then or subsequently to examine M, he will have learnt something. He will have learnt that some of the characteristics which M has, are characteristics which make people—or at any rate me—call it a good motor-car. This may not be to learn very much. But suppose that I make judgments of this sort about a great many motor-cars, calling some good and some not good, and he is able to examine all or most of the motor-cars about which I am speaking; he will in the end learn quite a lot, always presuming that I observe a consistent standard in calling them good or not good. He will eventually, if he pays careful attention, get into the position in which he knows, after I have said that a motor-car is a good one, what sort of a motor-car he may expect it to be—for example fast, stable on the road, and so on.

Now if we were dealing, not with "good," but with "red," we should call this process "explaining the meaning of the word"—and we might indeed, in a sense, say that what I have been doing is explaining what one means by "a good motor-car." This is a sense of "mean" about which, as we have seen, we must be on our guard. The processes, however, are very similar. I might explain the meaning of "red" by continually saying of various motor-cars "M is a red motor-car," "N is not a red motor-car," and so on. If he were attentive enough, he would soon get into a position in which he was able to use the word "red" for giving or getting information, at any rate about motor-cars. And so, both with "good" and with "red," there is this process, which in the case of "red" we may call "explaining the meaning," but in the case of "good" may only call it so loosely and in a secondary sense; to be clear we must call it something like "explaining or conveying or setting forth the standard of goodness in motor-cars."

The standard of goodness, like the meaning of "red," is normally something which is public and commonly accepted. When I explain to someone the meaning of "red motor-car," he expects, unless I am known to be very eccentric, that he will find other people using it in the same way. And similarly, at any rate with objects like motor-cars where there is a commonly accepted standard, he will expect, having learnt from me what is the standard of goodness in motor-cars, to be able, by using the expression "good motor-car," to give information to other people, and get it from them, without confusion.

A third respect in which "good motor-car" resembles "red motor-car" is the following: both "good" and "red" can vary as regards the exactitude or vagueness of the information which they do or can convey. We normally use the expression "red motor-car" very loosely. Any motor-car that lies somewhere between the unmistakably purple and the unmistakably orange could without abuse of language be called a red motor-car. And similarly, the standard for calling motor-cars good is commonly very loose. There are certain characteristics, such as inability to exceed 30 m.p.h., which to anyone but an eccentric would be sufficient conditions for refusing to call it a good motor-car; but there is no precise set of accepted criteria such that we can say, "If a motor-car satisfies these conditions, it is a good one; if not, not." And in both cases we could be precise if we wanted to. We could, for certain purposes, agree not to say that a motor-car was "really red" unless the redness of its paint reached a certain measurable degree of purity and saturation; and similarly, we might adopt a very exact standard of goodness in motor-cars. We might refuse the name "good motor-car" to any car that would not go round a certain race-track without mishap in a certain limited time, that did not conform to certain other rigid specifications as regards accommodation, etc. This sort of thing has not been done for the expression "good motor-car"; but, as Mr. Urmson has pointed out, it has been done by the Ministry of Agriculture for the expression "super apple."[1]

It is important to notice that the exactness or looseness of their criteria does absolutely nothing to distinguish words like "good" from words like "red." Words in both classes may be descriptively loose or exact, according to how rigidly the criteria have been laid down by custom or convention. It certainly is not true that value-words are distinguished from descriptive words in that the former are looser, descriptively, than the latter. There are loose and rigid examples of both sorts of word. Words like "red" can be extremely loose, without becoming to the least degree evaluative; and expressions like "good sewage effluent" can be the subject of very rigid criteria, without in the least ceasing to be evaluative. . . .

It is time now to justify my calling the descriptive meaning of "good" secondary to the evaluative meaning. My reasons for doing so are two. First, the evaluative meaning is constant for every class of object for which the word is used. When we call a motor-car or a chronometer or a cricket-bat or a picture good, we are commending all of them. But because we are commending all of them for different reasons, the descriptive meaning is different in all cases. We have knowledge of the evaluative meaning of "good" from our earliest years; but we are constantly learning to use it in new descriptive meanings, as the classes of objects whose virtues we learn to distinguish grow more numerous. Sometimes we learn to use "good" in a new descriptive meaning through being taught it by an expert in a particular field—for example, a horseman might teach me how to recognize a good hunter. Sometimes, on the other hand, we make up a new descriptive meaning for ourselves. This happens when we start having a standard for a class of objects, certain members of which we have started

---

1. *Mind* (1950), p. 152 (also in *Logic and Language*, ii, ed. Flew, p. 166).

needing to place in order of merit, but for which there has hitherto been no standard, as in the "cactus" example.

The second reason for calling the evaluative meaning primary is, that we can use the evaluative force of the word in order to *change* the descriptive meaning for any class of objects. This is what the moral reformer often does in morals; but the same process occurs outside morals. It may happen that motor-cars will in the near future change considerably in design (e.g., by our seeking economy at the expense of size). It may be that then we shall cease giving the name "a good motor-car" to a car that now would rightly and with the concurrence of all be allowed that name. How, linguistically speaking, would this have happened? At present, we are roughly agreed (though only roughly) on the necessary and sufficient criteria for calling a motor-car a good one. If what I have described takes place, we may begin to say "No cars of the nineteen-fifties were really good; there weren't any good ones till 1960." Now here we cannot be using "good" with the same descriptive meaning as it is now generally used with; for some of the cars of 1950 do indubitably have those characteristics which entitle them to the name "good motor-car" in the 1950 descriptive sense of that word. What is happening is that the evaluative meaning of the word is being used in order to shift the descriptive meaning; we are doing what would be called, if "good" were a purely descriptive word, redefining it. But we cannot call it that, for the evaluative meaning remains constant; we are rather altering the standard. This is similar to the process called by Professor Stevenson "persuasive definition";[2] the process is not necessarily, however, highly coloured with emotion. . . .

Commending and Choosing

It is now time to inquire into the reasons for the logical features of "good" that we have been describing, and to ask why it is that it has this peculiar combination of evaluative and descriptive meaning. The reason will be found in the purposes for which it, like other value-words, is used in our discourse. . . .

I have said that the primary function of the word "good" is to commend. We have, therefore, to inquire what commending is. When we commend or condemn anything, it is always in order, at least indirectly, to guide choices, our own or other people's, now or in the future. Suppose that I say "The South Bank Exhibition is very good." In what context should I appropriately say this, and what would be my purpose in so doing? It would be natural for me to say it to someone who was wondering whether to go to London to see the Exhibition, or, if he was in London, whether to pay it a visit. It would, however, be too much to say that the reference to choices is always as direct as this. An American returning from London to New York, and speaking to some people who had no intention of going to London in

2. *Ethics and Language*, ch. ix.

the near future, might still make the same remark. In order, therefore, to show that critical value-judgments are all ultimately related to choices, and would not be made if they were not so related, we require to ask, for what purpose we have standards.

It has been pointed out by Mr. Urmson that we do not speak generally of "good" wireworms. This is because we never have any occasion for choosing between wireworms, and therefore require no guidance in so doing. We therefore need to have no standards for wireworms. But it is easy to imagine circumstances in which this situation might alter. Suppose that wireworms came into use as a special kind of bait for fishermen. Then we might speak of having dug up a very good wireworm (one, for example, that was exceptionally fat and attractive to fish), just as now, no doubt, sea-fishermen might talk of having dug up a very good lug-worm. We only have standards for a class of objects, we only talk of the virtues of one specimen as against another, we only use value-words about them, when occasions are known to exist, or are conceivable, in which we, or someone else, would have to choose between specimens. We should not call pictures good or bad if no one ever had the choice of seeing them or not seeing them (or of studying them or not studying them in the way that art students study pictures, or of buying them or not buying them). Lest, by the way, I should seem to have introduced a certain vagueness by specifying so many alternative kinds of choices, it must be pointed out that the matter can, if desired, be made as precise as we require; for we can specify, when we have called a picture a good one, within what class we have called it good; for example, we can say "I meant a good picture to study, but not to buy."

Some further examples may be given. We should not speak of good sunsets, unless sometimes the decision had to be made, whether to go to the window to look at the sunset; we should not speak of good billiard-cues, unless sometimes we had to choose one billiard-cue in preference to another; we should not speak of good men unless we had the choice, what sort of men to try to become. Leibniz, when he spoke of "the best of all possible worlds," had in mind a creator choosing between the possibilities. The choice that is envisaged need not ever occur, nor even be expected ever to occur; it is enough for it to be envisaged as occurring, in order that we should be able to make a value-judgment with reference to it. It must be admitted, however, that the most useful value-judgments are those which have reference to choices that we might very likely have to make.

It should be pointed out that even judgments about past choices do not refer merely to the past. As we shall see, all value-judgments are covertly universal in character, which is the same as to say that they refer to, and express acceptance of, a standard which has an application to other similar instances. If I censure someone for having done something, I envisage the possibility of him, or someone else, or myself, having to make a similar choice again; otherwise there would be no point in censuring him. Thus, if I say to a man whom I am teaching to drive "You did that manœuvre badly" this is a very typical piece of driving-instruction; and driving-instruction consists in teaching a man to drive not in the past but in the future; to this end we censure or commend past pieces of driving, in order to impart to him the standard which is to guide him in his subsequent conduct.

When we commend an object, our judgment is not solely about that particular object, but is inescapably about objects like it. Thus, if I say that a certain motor-car is a good one, I am not merely saying something about that particular motor-car. To say something about that particular car, merely, would not be to commend. To commend, as we have seen, is to guide choices. Now for guiding a particular choice we have a linguistic instrument which is not that of commendation, namely, the singular imperative. If I wish merely to tell someone to choose a particular car, with no thought of the kind of car to which it belongs, I can say "Take that one." If instead of this I say "That is a good one," I am saying something more. I am implying that if any motor-car were just like that one, it would be a good one too; whereas by saying "Take that one," I do not imply that, if my hearer sees another car just like that one, he is to take it too. But further, the implication of the judgment "That is a good motor-car" does not extend merely to motor-cars *exactly* like that one. If this were so, the implication would be for practical purposes useless; for nothing is exactly like anything else. It extends to every motor-car that is like that one in the *relevant* particulars; and the relevant particulars are its virtues—those of its characteristics for which I was commending it, or which I was calling good about it. Whenever we commend, we have in mind something about the object commended which is the reason for our commendation. It therefore always makes sense, after someone has said "That is a good motor-car," to ask "What is good about it?" or "Why do you call it good?" or "What features of it are you commending?" It may not always be easy to answer this question precisely, but it is always a legitimate question. If we did not understand why it was always a legitimate question, we should not understand the way in which the word "good" functions.

We may illustrate this point by comparing two dialogues (similar to the one on pp. 355 ff. above):

(1) X. Jones' motor-car is a good one.
  Y. What makes you call it good?
  X. Oh, just that it's good.
  Y. But there must be some *reason* for your calling it good, I mean some property that it has in virtue of which you call it good.
  X. No; the property in virtue of which I call it good is just its goodness and nothing else.
  Y. But do you mean that its shape, speed, weight, manœuvrability etc., are irrelevant to whether you call it good or not?
  X. Yes, quite irrelevant; the only relevant property is that of goodness, just as, if I called it yellow, the only relevant property would be that of yellowness.

(2) The same dialogue, only with "yellow" substituted for "good" and "yellowness" for "goodness" throughout, and the last clause ("just as . . . yellowness") omitted.

The reason why X's position in the first dialogue is eccentric is that since, as we have already remarked, "good" is a "supervenient" or "consequential" epithet, one may always legitimately be asked when one has called something a good something, "What is good about it?" Now to answer this question is to give the properties in virtue of which we call it good. Thus, if I have said, "That is a good motor-car" and someone asks "Why? What is good about it?" and I reply "Its high speed combined with its stability on the road," I indicate that I call it good in virtue of its having these properties or virtues. Now to do this is *eo ipso* to say something about other motor-cars which have these properties. If any motor-car whatever had these properties, I should have, if I were not to be inconsistent, to agree that it was, *pro tanto,* a good motor-car; though of course it might, although it had these properties in its favour, have other countervailing disadvantages, and so be, taken all in all, not a good motor-car.

This last difficulty can always be got over by specifying in detail why I called the first motor-car a good one. Suppose that a second motor-car were like the first one in speed and stability, but gave its passengers no protection from the rain, and proved difficult to get into and out of. I should not then call it a good motor-car, although it had those characteristics which led me to call the first one good. This shows that I should not have called the first one good either, if it too had had the bad characteristics of the second one; and so in specifying what was good about the first one, I ought to have added ". . . and the protection it gives to the passengers and the ease with which one can get into and out of it." This process could be repeated indefinitely until I had given a complete list of the characteristics of the first motor-car which were required to make me allow it to be a good one. This, in itself, would not be saying all that there was to be said about my standards for judging motor-cars—for there might be other motor-cars which, although falling short to a certain extent in these characteristics, had other countervailing good characteristics; for example, soft upholstery, large accommodation, or small consumption of petrol. But it would be at any rate some help to my hearer in building up an idea of my standards in motor-cars; and in this lies the importance of such questions and answers, and the importance of recognizing their relevance, whenever a value-judgment has been made. For one of the purposes of making such judgments is to make known the standard.

When I commend a motor-car I am guiding the choices of my hearer not merely in relation to that particular motor-car but in relation to motor-cars in general. What I have said to him will be of assistance to him whenever in the future he has to choose a motor-car or advise anyone else on the choice of a motor-car or even design a motor-car (choose what sort of motor-car to have made) or write a general treatise on the design of motor-cars (which involves choosing what sort of motor-cars to advise other people to have made). The method whereby I give him this assistance is by making known to him a standard for judging motor-cars.

This process has, as we have noticed, certain features in common with the process of defining (making known the meaning or application of) a descriptive word, though there are important differences. We have now to notice a further resemblance between showing the usage of a word and showing how to choose between motor-cars. In neither case can the instruction be done successfully unless the instructor is consistent in his teaching. If I use "red" for objects of a wide variety of colours, my hearer will never learn from me a consistent usage of the word. Similarly, if I commend motor-cars with widely different or even contrary characteristics, what I say to him will not be of assistance to him in choosing motor-cars subsequently, because I am not teaching him any consistent standard —or any standard at all, for a standard is by definition consistent. He will say, "I don't see by what standards you are judging these motor-cars; please explain to me why you call them all good, although they are so different." Of course, I might be able to give a satisfactory explanation. I might say, "There are different sorts of motor-cars, each good in its way; there are sports cars, whose prime requisites are speed and manœuvrability; and family cars, which ought rather to be capacious and economical; and taxis, and so on. So when I say a car is good which is fast and manœuvrable, although it is neither capacious nor economical, you must understand that I am commending it as a sports car, not as a family car." But suppose that I did not recognize the relevance of his question; suppose that I was just doling out the predicate "good" entirely haphazard, as the whim took me. It is clear that in this case I should teach him no standard at all.

We thus have to distinguish two questions that can always be asked in elucidation of a judgment containing the word "good." Suppose that someone says "That is a good one." We can then always ask (1) "Good what— sports car or family car or taxi or example to quote in a logic-book?" Or we can ask (2) "What makes you call it good?" To ask the first question is to ask for the class within which evaluative comparisons are being made. Let us call it the class of comparison. To ask the second question is to ask for the virtues or "good-making characteristics." . . .

Now since it is the purpose of the word "good" and other value-words to be used for teaching standards, their logic is in accord with this purpose. We are therefore in a position at last to explain the feature of the word "good" which I pointed out at the beginning of this investigation. The reason why I cannot apply the word "good" to one picture, if I refuse to apply it to another picture which I agree to be in all other respects exactly similar, is that by doing this I should be defeating the purpose for which the word is designed. I should be commending one object, and so purporting to teach my hearers one standard, while in the same breath refusing to commend a similar object, and so undoing the lesson just imparted. By seeking to impart two inconsistent standards, I should be imparting no standard at all. The effect of such an utterance is similar to that of a contradiction; for in a contradiction, I say two inconsistent things, and so the effect is that the hearer does not know what I am trying to say. . . .

Selected Bibliography

(ITEMS PROVIDED WITH ASTERISK ARE MORE ADVANCED)
(FOR KEY TO ABBREVIATIONS SEE PAGE XIX)

There is an extremely detailed critical review of all major theories about the nature of moral judgments in R. B. Brandt, *Ethical Theory: The Problems of Normative and Critical Ethics* (Englewood Cliffs: Prentice-Hall, 1959). J. Hospers, *Human Conduct* (N.Y.: Harcourt, Brace & World, 1961), is lively and also very comprehensive. Briefer studies, but also clear and reliable, are L. J. Binkley, *Contemporary Ethical Theories* (N.Y.: Citadel Press, 1961), W. K. Frankena, *Ethics* (Englewood Cliffs: Prentice-Hall, 1963, p), J. Wilson, *Reason and Morals* (Cambridge: Cambridge U.P., 1961), and A. Montefiore, *A Modern Introduction to Moral Philosophy* (N.Y.: Praeger, 1959). Informative surveys are contained in T. E. Hill, *Contemporary Ethical Theories* (N.Y.: Macmillan, 1951), and W. H. Werkmeister, *Theories of Ethics* (Lincoln, Nebraska: Johnsen, 1961). M. K. Munitz (ed.), *A Modern Introduction to Ethics* (N.Y.: Free Press, 1958), R. B. Brandt (ed.), *Value and Obligation* (N.Y.: Harcourt, Brace & World, 1961), R. Abelson (ed.), *Ethics and Metaethics* (N.Y.: St. Martin's Press, 1963), P. W. Taylor (ed.), *Problems of Moral Philosophy* (Belmont, Calif.: Dickenson, 1967), K. Pahel and M. Schiller (eds.), *Readings in Contemporary Ethical Theory* (Englewood Cliffs: Prentice-Hall, 1970), and G. Dworkin and J. J. Thomson (eds.), *Ethics* (N.Y.: Harper, 1968), are comprehensive anthologies covering much besides the topics dealt with in the present work. A. Oldenquist (ed.), *Readings in Moral Philosophy* (Boston: Houghton Mifflin, 1964), is an anthology organized along historical lines with a very detailed and helpful introduction by the editor. The selections in W. Sellars and J. Hospers (eds.), *Readings in Ethical Theory* (N.Y.: Appleton-Century-Crofts, 2nd ed., 1970), P. Foot (ed.), *Theories of Ethics* (London: Oxford U.P., 1967, p), and in P. W. Taylor (ed.), *The Moral Judgment: Readings in Contemporary Meta-Ethics* (Englewood Cliffs: Prentice-Hall, 1963, p), concentrate for the most part on the issues discussed in this section. Historical surveys of recent work on the subject are found in W. K. Frankena, "Moral Philosophy at Mid-Century," *PR*, 1951, the same author's contribution to R. M. Chisholm *et al.*, *Philosophy—The Princeton Studies* (Englewood Cliffs: Prentice-Hall, 1964), R. S. Hartman, "General Theory of Value," in R. Klibansky (ed.), *Philosophy in the Mid-Century*, Volume III (Florence: La Nuova Italia Editrice, 1958), and in M. Warnock, *Ethics Since 1900* (London: Oxford U.P., 1960). G. Kerner, *The Revolution in Ethical Theory* (London: Oxford U.P., 1966), G. J. Warnock, *Contemporary Moral Philosophy* (London: Macmillan, 1967, p), R. T. Garner and B. Rosen, *Moral Philosophy* (N.Y.: Macmillan, 1967), W. D. Hudson, *Modern Moral Philosophy* (Garden City: Doubleday, 1970, p), J. Harrison, *Our Knowledge of*

Right and Wrong (London: Allen & Unwin, 1971), and B. Williams, *Morality: An Introduction to Ethics* (N.Y.: Harper, 1972, p) contain detailed critical discussions of several of the major metamoral theories of recent decades. The books by Hudson and Harrison are among the most comprehensive works on the subject published in recent years.

Several English philosophers of the 17th and 18th centuries may be consulted for statements of the rationalist theory concerning the nature of moral judgments. The most important of these are Samuel Clarke, John Balguy, Ralph Cudworth, and Richard Price. Selections from all these writers are contained in Volume II of L. A. Selby-Bigge (ed.), *British Moralists* (Oxford: Clarendon Press, 1897, reprinted as a paperback in 1964 by Bobbs-Merrill of Indianapolis with a new introduction by B. Baumrin). A new edition of Price's *Review of Morals,* with a valuable preface by D. D. Raphael, was brought out by the Clarendon Press in 1948. Contemporary defenses of rationalism are given in Ross, *The Right and the Good** (London: Oxford U.P., 1931), the same author's *Foundations of Ethics* (Oxford: Clarendon Press, 1939), and in D. D. Raphael, *The Moral Sense* (London: Oxford U.P., 1947). Ross and Raphael are criticized in P. F. Strawson's "Ethical Intuitionism," which is reprinted in W. Sellars and J. Hospers, *op. cit.* A. C. Ewing, whose selection in the present work is a defense of rationalism, subsequently modified his position. His latest views are given in his *Second Thoughts in Moral Philosophy* (London: Routledge, 1959). The most recent detailed defense of ethical rationalism is H. J. McCloskey, *Meta-Ethics and Normative Ethics* (The Hague: Martinus Nihjoff, 1969). W. D. Hudson, *Ethical Intuitionism* (London: Macmillan, 1967, p) contains a sympathetic presentation of the views of the 18th century Rationalists as well as the moral sense theorists mentioned in the next paragraph.

The classical formulation of the "moral sense" theory is Hutcheson's *Inquiry Concerning the Original of Our Ideas of Virtue or Moral Good*. Extracts from this and other of Hutcheson's works are given in Volume I of L. A. Selby-Bigge (ed.), *British Moralists, op. cit.* There are helpful commentaries in the above-mentioned book by Raphael and a searching examination in C. D. Broad's "Some Reflections on Moral-Sense Theories in Ethics," which is reprinted in Sellars and Hospers, *op. cit.* G. E. Moore's intuitionism is stated in *Principia Ethica* (Cambridge: Cambridge U.P., 1903), in his smaller book, *Ethics* (London: Oxford U.P., 1912), and in the last two essays of his book, *Philosophical Studies* (London: Kegan Paul, 1922). There are several critical articles in P. A. Schilpp (ed.), *The Philosophy of G. E. Moore* (Evanston & Chicago: Northwestern U.P., 1942), which also contains Moore's reply to his critics. Several of these articles as well as Moore's reply are critically discussed by C. D. Broad in "G. E. Moore's Latest Published Views on Ethics," *M,* 1961. W. K. Frankena's "The Naturalistic Fallacy," *M,* 1939, and G. C. Field's "The Place of Definition in Ethics," *Ar. Soc.,* 1932, are two well-known answers to Moore's open-question argument. Both are reprinted in Sellars and Hospers, *op. cit.* Ch. 5 of C. H. Waddington, *The Ethical Animal* (Chicago: U. of Chicago P., 1967, p) contains a biologist's reply to Moore. In "G. E. Moore on the Naturalistic Fallacy," which is available both in P. F. Strawson (ed.), *Studies in the Philosophy of Thought and Action* (London: Oxford U.P., 1968, p) and in A. Ambrose and M. Lazerowitz (eds.), *G. E. Moore—Essays in Retrospect* (London: Allen & Unwin, 1970), C. Lewy quotes from an unpublished draft which was to be a preface to the second edition of *Principia Ethica* (no second edition was in fact published), in which Moore discusses some ambiguities in his argument against the philosophers who were taken to commit the naturalistic fallacy. Lewy agrees with Moore that, in spite of some confusions in the original formulation, the argument does refute any theory which identifies Good with a concept that is not at least partially ethical. The history of the open-question argument is traced in A. N. Prior, *Logic and the Basis of Ethics* (Oxford: Clarendon Press, 1948). A paper by Moore entitled "Is Goodness a Quality?" which was originally published in 1932, is now available in his *Philosophical Papers* (London: Allen & Unwin, 1958, N.Y.: Collier Books, 1962, p). The following are recent papers criticizing various aspects of Moore's position: A. Duncan-Jones, "Intrinsic Value: Some Comments on the Work of G. E. Moore," P, 1958, B. Cooper, "The Alleged Indefinability of Good," *JP*, 1962, R. F. Holland, "The Autonomy of Ethics," *Ar. Soc. Sup.*, 1958, and B. Baumrin, "Is There a Naturalistic Fallacy?", *APQ*, 1968. Holland's paper was part of a symposium. The other symposiast, H. D. Lewis, defended Moore against certain of Holland's objections. The questions raised by Moore are also discussed in two recent papers by Scandinavian philosophers—M. Blegvad, "Mill, Moore and the Naturalistic Fallacy," and J. Hartnack, "Moral Rules and Tautologies," both published in *Philosophical Essays Dedicated to Gunnar Aspelin* (Lund, Sweden: Gleerup Bokförlag, 1963). There is a sympathetic discussion of intuitionism in J. R. Lucas, "Ethical Intuitionism" *P, 1971*. The view that moral judgments have objective content is defended against some of the arguments commonly employed by subjectivists and emotivists in R. R. Ehman, "Moral Objectivity" *PPR*, 1967, and I. Jenkins, "The Case For Moral Cognitivism," *Tulane Studies in Philosophy*, Vol. XVIII (New Orleans, 1969).

Subjectivism is defended by Hume in Book III of *A Treatise of Human Nature* and also in *An Inquiry Concerning the Principles of Morals*. His position, however, is not always consistent and in places he writes like a utilitarian. Sometimes Hume is also interpreted as a champion of the moral sense theory. More modern defenses of subjectivism are found in E. Westermarck, *The Origin and Development of Moral Ideas* (London: Macmillan, 1912), in the same author's *Ethical Relativity* (N.Y.: Harcourt, Brace, 1932), in Bertrand Russell's essay, "What I Believe," which forms part of *Why I Am Not a Christian and Other Essays* (London: Allen & Unwin, New York: Simon & Schuster, 1957, p), and in his *Human Society in Ethics and Politics* (London: Allen & Unwin, N.Y.: Simon & Schuster, 1955). There are articles by J. Buchler and S. Hook criticizing Russell's subjectivism in P. A. Schilpp (ed.), *The Philosophy of Bertrand Russell* (Evanston and Chicago: Northwestern U.P., 1944). At the end of this volume Russell replies to his critics but concedes that he does not feel altogether satisfied with his own theory. A later discussion of Russell's views on this subject is found in D. H. Monro, "Russell's Moral Theories," *P, 1960*. In an unjustly neglected article, "On the Alleged Objectivity of Moral Judgments," *M, 1962*, W. D. Hudson argues that subjectivism does not have the paradoxical consequences which both Russell and the opponents of subjectivism attribute to it. Ewing's attack on subjectivism, which forms part of Selection 26 of the present book, was answered by H. B. Acton in an article entitled "Moral Subjectivism," in *A, 1948*, which is followed by Ewing's reply in the same volume. A variety of subjectivism is also defended by J. Hartland-Swann, *An Analysis of Morals* (London: Allen & Unwin, 1960). The "ideal observer" theory received its first formulation in Adam Smith, *The Theory of Moral Sentiments*. Parts of this work are reprinted in Volume I of Selby-Bigge (ed.), *British Moralists, op. cit.* In recent years the theory has been discussed by W. Kneale, "Objectivity in Morals," *P, 1950*, reprinted in Sellars and Hospers (eds.), *Readings in Ethical Theory, op. cit.*, J. Rawls, "Outline of a Decision Procedure for Ethics," *PR*, 1951, R. Firth, in "Ethical Absolutism and the Ideal Observer,"* *PPR*, 1952, R. Brandt, in "The Definition of an 'Ideal Observer' in Ethics,"* *ibid.*, 1955, and R. G. Henson, "On Being Ideal," *PR*, 1956. Brandt's own views, which are sympathetic to subjectivism, are worked out in "The Status of Empirical Assertion Theories in Ethics," *M*, 1952, and most fully in Ch. 10 of *Ethical Theory, op. cit.* D. J. Monro, *Empiricism and Ethics* (Cambridge: Cambridge U.P., 1967) contains a detailed restatement and defense of subjectivism.

Westermarck, who was primarily an anthropologist, argued that the data of anthropology provide decisive evidence for subjectivism. Other anthropologists have tended to adopt similar views. If not actually endorsing subjectivism, many of them have concluded that moral judgments cannot be objectively valid in a philosophically significant sense. This entire question of the bearing, if any, of anthropological data on the status of moral principles, has been widely discussed in recent years. Writings by anthropologists include W. G. Sumner, *Folkways* (Boston: Ginn, 1934), M. Herskovits, *Man and His Works* (N.Y.: Knopf, 1948), R. Benedict, *Patterns of Culture* (Boston: Houghton Mifflin, 1934), and "Anthropology and the Abnormal," *Journal of General Psychology*, 1934, R. Linton, "Universal Ethical Principles: An Anthropological View," in R. N. Anshen (ed.), *Moral Principles of Action* (N.Y.: Harper, 1952), and "The Problem of Universal Values," in R. F. Spencer (ed.), *Method and Perspective in Anthropology* (Minneapolis: U. of Minnesota P., 1954), C. Kluckhohn, "Ethical Relativity," *JP*, 1955, and K. Duncker, "Ethical Relativity," *M*, 1939. Selections from Sumner, Benedict, and Linton are reprinted in R. Brandt (ed.), *Value and Obligation, op. cit.* A discussion of this and related questions by philosophers can be found in M. and A. Edel, *Anthropology and Ethics* (Oxford: Blackwell, 1959), J. Ladd, *The Structure of a Moral Code* (Cambridge: Harvard U.P., 1957), R. Brandt, *Hopi Ethics: A Theoretical Analysis* (Chicago: U. of Chicago P., 1954), W. T. Stace, *The Concept of Morals* (N.Y.: Macmillan, 1937, p), and in the following articles: G. Boas, "Cultural Relativism and Standards," in S. Ratner (ed.), *Vision and Action* (New Brunswick: Rutgers U.P., 1953), P. F. Schmidt, "Some Criticisms of Cultural Relativism," *JP*, 1955, D. H. Monro, "Anthropology and Ethics," *AJ*, 1955, two articles by P. Taylor—"Four Types of Ethical Relativism," *PR*, 1954 and "Social Science and Ethical Relativism," *JP*, 1958, and C. Wellman, "Ethical Implications of Cultural Relativity," *JP*, 1963. The two last-mentioned articles are reprinted in P. Taylor (ed.), *Problems of Moral Philosophy, op. cit.* The entire issue of *The Monist* for the Summer of 1963 is devoted to "Ethics and Anthropology." *Ar. Soc. Sup.*, 1946, contains a symposium by L. J. Russell, J. D. Mabbott, and A. Macbeath on the question "Is Anthropology Relevant to Ethics?" There is a very sober and clarifying discussion of all the main issues in Ch. 11 of Brandt, *Ethical Theory, op. cit.*

The earliest formulation of the emotive theory among Anglo-Saxon philosophers is found in C. K. Ogden and I. A. Richards, *The Meaning of Meaning* (London: Kegan Paul, 1923), but it is not developed there in any detail. (There is a formulation of the theory as early as 1911 by the Swedish philosopher Axel Hägerström. Discussion in English of Hägerström's contribution can be found in H. Ofstad, "Objectivity of Norms and Value-Judgments According to Recent Scandinavian Philosophy," *PPR*, 1951). Other early statements are found in a short article by W. F. H. Barnes entitled, "A Suggestion about Value," *A*, 1933, reprinted in Sellars and Hospers, *op. cit.*, and in Rudolf Carnap, *Philosophy and*

Logical Syntax (London: Kegan Paul, 1935), the whole of which is now available in W. P. Alston and G. Nakhnikian (eds.), *Twentieth Century Philosophy* (N.Y.: Free Press, 1963). Probably the most celebrated statement of the theory is C. L. Stevenson's "The Emotive Meaning of Ethical Terms," reprinted in Sellars and Hospers, *op. cit.*, and also in A. J. Ayer (ed.), *Logical Positivism* (N.Y.: Free Press, 1959, p). Stevenson subsequently developed the theory in great detail in *Ethics and Language** (New Haven: Yale U.P., 1943). One of Stevenson's later articles which has received much attention is "The Nature of Ethical Disagreement." It has been reprinted both in Munitz, *op. cit.*, and in Brandt, *Value and Obligation, op. cit.* Ayer replied to some of his critics in his introduction to the second edition of *Language, Truth and Logic*. He restated his position in an article entitled "On the Analysis of Moral Judgments," which is included in his *Philosophical Essays* (London: Macmillan, 1954) and in Munitz, *op. cit.* Ayer's most recent statement is contained in a B.B.C. interview "What Are Philosophers For?" which is reprinted in D. May (ed.), *Good Talk* (London: Gollancz, 1968). Other articles in support of the emotive theory are A. Kaplan, "Are Moral Judgments Assertions?" *PR*, 1942, A. Ross, "On the Method of Ethics," *JP*, 1948, and I. Hedenius, "Values and Duties," *T*, 1949. There is a very careful and detailed defense of the view that moral judgments express approval and disapproval in Series II, Lectures 7 and 8 of H. H. Price, *Belief* (London: Allen & Unwin, 1969). Price imagines an individual who cannot feel pleasure and displeasure, who cannot like or dislike anything, and who also cannot approve or disapprove of anything. Such an individual, he concludes, would not be a moral being. The most careful and elaborate critical discussion of the emotive theory is unquestionably J. O. Urmson's *The Emotive Theory of Ethics* (London: Hutchinson, 1968, p). Earlier criticisms are found in A. Stroll, *The Emotive Theory of Ethics* (Berkeley: U. of California P., 1954), in Ch. II of W. D. Ross, *The Foundations of Ethics, op. cit.*, in C. E. M. Joad, *A Critique of Logical Positivism* (Chicago: U. of Chicago P., 1950), and from a Marxist point of view in B. Dunham, *Man Against Myth* (Boston: Little, Brown, 1947). Among articles in which the emotive theory is attacked, mention may be made of H. Aiken, "Emotive 'Meanings' and Ethical Terms," *JP*, 1944, H. J. Paton, "The Emotive Theory of Ethics," *Ar. Soc. Sup.*, 1948, J. Ladd, "Value Judgments, Emotive Meaning and Attitudes," *JP*, 1949, R. Brandt, "The Emotive Theory of Ethics," *PR*, 1950, V. Tomas, "Ethical Disagreements and the Emotive Theory of Values," *M*, 1951, J. Harrison, "Can Ethics Do without Propositions?" *M*, 1950, and C. A. Campbell, "Ethics without Propositions,"* *M*, 1950, which was an answer to W. F. H. Barnes' "Ethics without Propositions,"* *Ar. Soc. Sup.*, 1948. The following are more recent articles dealing with various aspects of the emotive theory: O. A. Johnson, "On Moral Disagreements," *M*, 1959, A. P. Brogan, "Criticism of Mr. A. J. Ayer's Revised Account of Moral Judgments," *JP*, 1959, R. G. Olson, "Emotivism and Moral Skepticism," *JP*, 1959, J. Wheatley, "A Note on the Emotive Theory," *P*, 1959, D. Rynin, "Non-Cognitive Synonymy and the Definability of 'Good'," in *Logic and Language: Studies Dedicated to Professor Rudolf Carnap on the Occasion of His Seventieth Birthday* (Dordrecht-Holland: D. Reidel, 1962), K. Nielsen, "On Looking Back at the Emotive Theory," *Methodos*, 1962, J. T. Wilcox, "Stevenson and the Referent of an Ethical Statement," *A*, 1963, K. Baier, "Fact, Value and Norm in Stevenson's Ethics," *N*, 1967, H. N. Castaneda, "Ethics and Logic: Stevensonian Emotivism Reconsidered," *JP*, 1967, C. Wellman, "Emotivism and Ethical Objectivity," *APQ*, 1968, reprinted in W. Sellars and J. Hospers (eds.), *Readings in Ethical Theory, op. cit.*, R. W. Newell, "Ethics and Description,"

P, 1968, and L. Foster, "Inductive and Ethical Validity," *APQ,* 1971. Carnap's views are discussed in A. Kaplan, "Logical Empiricism and Value Judgments," in P. A. Schilpp (ed.), *The Philosophy of Rudolf Carnap* (LaSalle, Illinois: Open Court, 1964). The same volume contains an answer by Carnap and a detailed restatement of his position. Several of Stevenson's later articles have been collected in *Facts and Values* (New Haven: Yale U.P., 1963, p). His most recent publication on the subject is "Ethical Fallibility," in R. T. De George (ed.), *Ethics and Society* (London: Macmillan, 1968, p). H. D. Aiken's *Reason and Conduct: New Bearings in Moral Philosophy* (N.Y.: Knopf, 1962) brings together sixteen of Aiken's essays on ethical topics, including several that are critical of the emotive theory.

A number of recent writers, while advocating positions similar to the emotive theory in some important respects, have laid more emphasis on the cognitive or factual content of certain moral judgments, arguing that in a sense, not recognized by Ayer or Stevenson, such judgments can be supported by "good reasons." Views of this kind are found in S. E. Toulmin, *The Place of Reason in Ethics** (Cambridge: Cambridge U.P., 1950), parts of which are reprinted in Oldenquist, *op. cit.,* J. O. Urmson's "On Grading,"* *M,* 1950, which is reprinted in P. Taylor, *The Moral Judgment, op. cit.,* R. M. Hare, *The Language of Morals** (Oxford: Clarendon Press, 1950, p), P H. Nowell-Smith, *Ethics** (London: Penguin Books, 1954), P. Edwards, *The Logic of Moral Discourse* (Glencoe: Free Press, 1955, p), C. Wellman, *The Language of Ethics* (Cambridge: Harvard U.P., 1961), and the same author's *Challenge and Response-Justification in Ethics* (Carbondale, Illinois: Southern Illinois U.P., 1971). Hare, whose work has been particularly influential, elaborated some of his ideas in *Freedom and Reason** (Oxford: Clarendon Press, 1963) and in his articles, "Universalizability," *Ar. Soc.,* 1954, "Geach: Good and Evil," *A,* 1957, "Descriptivism," which is available in W. D. Hudson (ed.), *The Is-Ought Question* (London: Macmillan, 1969, p), "Pain and Evil" *Ar. Soc. Sup.,* 1964, reprinted in J. Feinberg (ed.), *Moral Concepts* (London: Oxford U.P., 1970, p), and "The Promising Game," *Revue Internationale de Philosophie,* 1964. Hare's "Geach: Good and Evil," was written in reply to P. T. Geach's "Good and Evil," *A,* 1956. These two articles are reprinted, with some revisions, in P. Foot (ed.), *Theories of Ethics, op. cit.* Hare's "The Promising Game," was written in reply to J. R. Searle's "How to Derive 'Ought' from 'Is'," *PR,* 1964. These two papers are reprinted both in P. Foot (ed.), *Theories of Ethics, op. cit.,* and in K. Pahel and M. Schiller (eds.), *Readings in Contemporary Ethical Theory, op. cit.* The latter volume also contains Searle's reply to Hare. Hare's most recent publication is *Practical Inferences* (London: Macmillan, 1971), a collection of essays, some of which had not previously been published. Various aspects of Hare's position are discussed in R. B. Brandt, *Ethical Theory, op. cit.,* G. J. Warnock, *Contemporary Moral Philosophy, op. cit.,* G. C. Kerner, *The Revolution in Ethical Theory, op. cit.,* and in the following articles: P. L. Gardiner, "On Assenting to a Moral Principle," *Ar. Soc.,* 1954, J. Harrison, "When Is a Principle a Moral Principle?" *Ar. Soc. Sup.,* 1954, C. Johnson, "Commending and Choosing," *M,* 1957, S. Zink, "Objectivism and Mr. Hare's *Language of Morals,*" *M,* 1957, K. Nielsen, "Good Reasons in Ethics," *T,* 1958, H. J. McCloskey, "Hare's Ethical Subjectivism," *AJ,* 1959, N. Lawrence, "Ethics as a Mandate," *M,* 1961, G. C. Kerner, "Approvals, Reasons, and Moral Argument," *M,* 1962, D. Lewis, " 'Good' and Naturalistic Definitions," *A,* 1964, R. L. Holmes, "Descriptivism, Supervenience, and Universalizability," *JP,* 1966, A. Montefiore, "The Meaning of 'Good' and the Act of Commendation" *PQ*, 1967, L. W. Sumner, "Hare's Arguments against Ethical Naturalism," *JP*, 1967, A. Oldenquist, "Universalizability and the Advantages of Nondescriptivism," *JP*, 1968, J. C. Mackenzie, "Prescriptivism and Rational Behavior," *PQ*, 1968, A. Knox, "The Polemics of 'Descriptive Meaning'," *RM*, 1970, and P. J. Olscamp, "Hare's Failure to Define Good Reasons," *M*, 1970. S. A. Grave, "Too Good a Reason To Be a Reason," *A*, 1959, and H. J. McCloskey, "Nowell-Smith's *Ethics*," *AJ*, 1961, are critical of Nowell-Smith, *op. cit.* Isabelle Hungerland's "Contextual Implication," *Inquiry*, 1960, is a sustained criticism of certain of the ideas found in Nowell-Smith and P. Edwards, *op. cit.* Nowell-Smith himself returned to an elaboration of this notion in "Contextual Implications and Ethical Theory," *Ar. Soc. Sup.*, 1962.

Defenders of the emotive theory and of various more recent forms of non-cognitivism have been concerned to emphasize that in their view moral judgments do not express mere momentary whims but *moral* emotions or attitudes which are something far more settled and organized than whims. This distinction has naturally led to discussions of the question how a moral emotion differs from other emotions and, more generally, what is meant by calling a judgment a "moral" judgment. Many of the books and articles listed in the paragraphs dealing with the emotive theory and with Hare's perscriptivism discuss these questions. They are also discussed in detail in J. Bennett, "Moral Argument," *M*, 1960, W. P. Alston, "Moral Attitudes and Moral Judgments," *N*, 1968, and in various of the papers contained in the following two books: G. Wallace and A. D. M. Walker (eds.), *The Definition of Morality* (London: Methuen, 1970, p) and J. Casey (ed.), *Morality and Moral Reasoning* (London: Methuen, 1971).

Theories which, by our classification, would be considered forms of objective naturalism, are defended by Jeremy Bentham in *The Principles of Morals and Legislation*, John Stuart Mill in his *Utilitarianism*, Herbert Spencer in *The Data of Ethics*, John Dewey in *Human Nature and Conduct* (N.Y.: Holt, 1922) and in *The Theory of Valuation* (Chicago: U. of Chicago P., 1939), R. B. Perry in his *General Theory of Value* (Cambridge: Harvard U.P., 1926), W. T. Stace in *The Concept of Morals, op. cit.*, and the same author's *Man Against Darkness* (Pittsburgh: U. of Pittsburgh P., 1967, p). There are selections from Perry in Taylor, *op. cit.*, and in Sellars and Hospers, *op. cit.*, and from Dewey in several of the anthologies listed in the opening paragraph. Largely because of the influence of G. E. Moore, naturalism of any kind was very much out of fashion in Anglo-Saxon philosophy for the half-century following the publication of *Principia Ethica*. Many of the philosophers who, like Ayer and Hare, for example, did not follow Moore in his own intuitionism, nevertheless agreed that what he called the "naturalistic fallacy" was indeed a fallacy. During the last fifteen years, however, there have been attempts to reinstate naturalism of one kind or another. The anti-naturalist doctrine of the "autonomy of morals"—that "normative" statements are never entailed by factual statements, that there is an unbridgeable gap between the "ought" and the "is"—has been called into question by a number of writers, e.g., by D. Rynin in "The Autonomy of Morals," *M*, 1957, A. N. Prior in "The Autonomy of Ethics," *AJ*, 1960, M. Zimmerman in "The 'Is-Ought': An Unnecessary Dualism," *M*, 1962, J. R. Searle in "How To Derive 'Ought' from 'Is'," *PR*, 1964, which was already mentioned in the preceding paragraph, and M. Black in "The Gap Between 'Is' and 'Should'," *PR*, 1964. There is an answer to Rynin by P. Remnant in *M*, 1959, a criticism of Prior by Shorter in *AJ*, 1961, a reply to Searle by J. and J. Thomson in *PR*, 1964, a rejoinder to Zimmerman by K. Hanley in *M,* 1964 and a reply to Black by M. F. Cohen in *PR,* 1965. The same questions are also explored in a debate-like article, " 'Ought' and 'Is'," *P,* 1958, by R. F. Atkinson and A. Montefiore and in D. R. Kurtzman, " 'Is,' 'Ought,' and the Autonomy of Ethics," *PR,* 1970. The logician, J. Hintikka, discusses the topic in his paper, "Deontic Logic and its Philosophical Morals," which is included in his book, *Models and Modalities* (N.Y.: Humanities Press, 1969). Several of the papers just listed are reprinted in W. D. Hudson (ed.), *The Is-Ought Question, op. cit.* The Cambridge geneticist, C. H. Waddington, who had already defended naturalism in his *The Scientific Attitude* (London: Penguin Books, 1941, p), and in his contribution to a book he edited under the title of *Science and Ethics* (London: Allen & Unwin, 1942), returned to this subject at full length in *The Ethical Animal, op. cit.* Waddington amplified his position in "Naturalism in Ethics and Biology," *P,* 1962. The question of whether the Darwinian theory of evolution has moral implications, after being neglected for many years, is again receiving some attention by philosophers. It is discussed in A. Flew, *Evolutionary Ethics* (London: Macmillan, 1968, p), A. M. Quinton, "Ethics and the Theory of Evolution," in I. T. Ramsey (ed.), *Biology and Personality* (Oxford: Blackwell, 1965), and in Ch. XI of J. Harrison, *Our Knowledge of Right and Wrong, op. cit.* The American logician, C. I. Lewis, devoted a good deal of attention to questions concerning the status of moral judgments, adopting a form of objective naturalism. One of the clearest and most concise statements of his position is his paper, "Value and Facts," which is part of the posthumously published volume, *Values and Imperatives* (Stanford: Stanford U.P., 1969). Naturalistic theories are also defended in P. B. Rice, *Our Knowledge of Good and Evil* (N.Y.: Random House, 1955), R. Osborn, *Humanism and Moral Theory* (London: Allen & Unwin, 1959), P. Glassen, "The Cognitivity of Moral Judgments," *M,* 1959, and W. Todd, "Ethical Analysis," *AJ,* 1962. Brand Blanshard, whose article "The New Subjectivism in Ethics" forms Selection 29 of the present work, argues for an interesting form of naturalism in his wide-ranging book, *Reason and Goodness* (London: Allen & Unwin, N.Y.: Macmillan, 1961), which also contains detailed criticisms of the emotive and other non-cognitivist theories and rejoinders to his critics. The most widely discussed recent attempt to restate naturalism is that of Philippa Foot in her two articles, "Moral Arguments," *M,* 1958, and "Moral Beliefs," *Ar. Soc.,* 1958–59. One or both of these papers are reprinted in several of the anthologies listed in the opening paragraph. There are criticisms of Foot's views by A. Stigen and J. Teichman in *M,* 1960, and by R. Robinson in *M,* 1961. P. Taylor, in " 'Need' Statements," *A,* 1959, criticizes the attempts of certain social scientists and psychologists to establish a "scientific ethics" on the basis of our knowledge of human needs. There are criticisms of this as well as of other types of naturalism in four articles by K. Nielsen—"Ethical Naturalism Once Again," *AJ,* 1962, "Conventionalism in Morals and the Appeal to Human Nature," *PPR,* 1962, "On Taking Human Nature as the Basis for Morality," *Social Research,* 1962, and "On Human Needs and Moral Appraisals," *Inquiry,* 1963. Naturalism in all its main forms is critically examined in E. M. Adams, *Ethical Naturalism and the Modern World-View* (Chapel Hill: U. of North Carolina P., 1960). In "The Objectivity of Value Judgments," *PQ,* 1971, H. Meynell rejects emotivist and prescriptive theories and champions objective naturalism. He maintains that there is entailment of a kind (what he calls "loose entailment") between value-judgments and certain propositions of fact. Naturalism is also defended in G. J. Warnock, *Contemporary Moral Philosophy, op. cit.*

Some important recent articles are not easy to classify. These include S.

Hampshire's "The Fallacies of Moral Philosophy,"* *M,* 1949, J. N. Findlay's "Morality by Convention,"* *M,* 1944, "The Justification of Attitudes," *ibid.,* 1954, and "The Methodology of Normative Ethics"—all three articles reprinted in Findlay, *Language, Mind and Value* (London: Allen & Unwin, N.Y.: Humanities Press, 1963), K. Baier's "Decisions and Descriptions," *M,* 1951, three articles by W. D. Falk—"Morality and Nature," *AJ,* 1950, "Goading and Guiding," *M,* 1953, and "Moral Perplexity," *E,* 1956, K. Britton, "What Does a Moral Judgment Commit Me To?" *Ar. Soc.,* 1953–54, S. A. Grave, "Are the Analyses of Moral Concepts Neutral?" *JP,* 1958, N. Kretzmann, "Desire as a Proof of Desirability," *PQ,* 1958, C. A. Bayliss, "Grading, Values and Choice," *M,* 1958, N. Rescher, "Reasoned Justification," *JP,* 1958, J. Stolnitz, "Notes on Ethical Indeterminacy," *JP,* 1958, W. H. Walsh, "Scepticism about Morals and Scepticism about Knowledge," *P,* 1960, E. L. Pincoffs, "Debatability and Moral Assertions," *PQ,* 1962, W. K. Frankena, "On Saying the Ethical Thing," *Proceedings and Addresses of the American Philosophical Association,* 1966, reprinted in J. H. Gill (ed.), *Philosophy Today, No. 1* (N.Y.: Macmillan, 1968, p), G. P. Henderson, "Moral Nihilism," and K. Nielsen, "On Moral Truth," both in N. Rescher (ed.), *Studies in Moral Philosophy* (Oxford: Blackwell, 1968, p), R. Rhees, "What Are Moral Statements Like?" in his *Without Answers* (London: Routledge, 1969), and R. L. Holmes, "Some Conceptions of Analysis in Recent Ethical Theory," *Me,* 1971. Important recent books which are not easy to classify include E. W. Hall, *What is Value?** (N.Y.: Humanities Press, 1952), the same author's posthumously published *Our Knowledge of Fact and Value* (Chapel Hill: U. of North Carolina P., 1961, ed. E. M. Adams), A. Edel, *Ethical Judgment** (Glencoe: Free Press, 1955), M. Mandelbaum, *The Phenomenology of Moral Experience** (Glencoe: Free Press, 1955), D. D. Raphael, *Moral Judgment* (London: Allen & Unwin, 1955), K. Baier, *The Moral Point of View: A Rational Basis of Ethics* (Ithaca: Cornell U.P., 1958), A. I. Melden (ed.), *Essays in Moral Philosophy* (Seattle: U. of Washington P., 1958), F. E. Sparshott, *An Enquiry into Goodness* (Chicago: U. of Chicago P., 1958), B. Mayo, *Ethics and the Moral Life* (London: Macmillan, 1958), M. G. Singer, *Generalization in Ethics* (New York: Knopf, 1961), P. W. Taylor, *Normative Discourse* (Englewood Cliffs: Prentice-Hall, 1961), S. Zink, *The Concepts of Ethics* (N.Y.: St. Martin's Press, 1962), H. Castaneda and G. Nakhnikian (eds.), *Morality and the Language of Conduct* (Detroit: Wayne State U.P., 1963), G. H. von Wright, *The Varieties of Goodness* (London: Routledge, 1963), D. Gauthier, *Practical Reasoning* (London: Oxford U.P., 1963), G. Kemp, *Reason, Action and Morality* (London: Routledge, 1964), J. Kovesi, *Moral Notions* (London: Routledge, 1967), and J. J. Kupperman, *Ethical Knowledge* (London: Allen & Unwin, 1970).

The following articles in the *Encyclopedia of Philosophy* are relevant to topics discussed in the present section: "Conscience" (C. A. Baylis, 2–189), "Emotive Meaning" (W. P. Alston, 2–486), "Emotive Theory of Ethics" (R. B. Brandt, 2–493), "Epistemology and Ethics" (R. B. Brandt, 3–6), "Ethical Naturalism" (J. Harrison, 3–69), "Ethical Objectivism" (J. Harrison, 3–71), "Ethical Relativism" (R. R. Brandt, 3–75), "Ethical Subjectivism" (J. Harrison, 3–78), "Ethics, History of" (R. Abelson and K. Nielsen, 3–81), "Ethics, Problems of" (K. Nielsen, 3–117), "Good, The" (R. G. Olson, 3–367), "Moral Sense" (E. Sprague, 5–385), and "Ultimate Moral Principles: Their Justification" (A. P. Griffiths, 8–177).

V

The
Existence
of
God

INTRODUCTION

THE WORD "GOD" HAS BEEN USED IN A great many senses. It will be convenient to distinguish between the traditional and revisionary senses of the word. A believer in God in the traditional sense asserts the existence of a supreme personal being who is the creator of the universe or at least the designer of some of its prominent features. Most of the writers whose work is represented in this section, whether they are believers or unbelievers, are concerned with the question of God's existence in this traditional sense of the word. Bishop Robinson in Selection 45 defends belief in God in a revisionary sense. We shall say something about his theological reconstruction at the end of this introduction. For the time being our comments will be exclusively concerned with the views of believers and unbelievers in the traditional God. Most believers in the traditional God claim a great deal more than that the universe was created by a supreme personal being. Christian and Jewish believers also assert that God is eternal, all-powerful, all-knowing, perfectly good and that He possesses many other admirable characteristics. There are, however, philosophers (e.g., J. S. Mill and W. P. Montague) who believe in a finite god and they too can be classified as believers in the traditional God as we have here defined the term.

TYPES OF THEORIES

Believers in the existence of God differ among themselves not only in how much they claim about the divine attributes. There is also disagreement about the relation between God and the universe. Some philosophers merely claim that God created the universe and reject any belief in subsequent divine interferences in the course of nature, such as miracles, answers to prayer, or special revelations of the kind related in the Bible. This view is known as "deism." Voltaire, the most famous deist, argued that the belief in miracles was really blasphemous. For it implies that God bungled, to some extent at least, his original job of creation and had to step in subsequently to make repairs. Opposed to the deists are the more orthodox believers who claim that God originally created the universe and who go on to assert that he does on occasions work miracles, answer prayers, and reveal himself to specific human beings. God is supposed to take an active interest in the good and evil deeds of human beings and divine interventions usually have a moral purpose of some kind. The word "theism" is sometimes used to designate this more orthodox position, but there is no very consistent linguistic usage on this point.

Deism was the first powerful rebellion against traditional theology in Western Europe and the United States; and many of the outstanding philosophers of the 17th and 18th centuries inclined to a view of this kind. During the last hundred years or so, more radical rejections of theology have become fairly common. Probably the most widespread form of unbelief at the present time is "agnosticism." This theory maintains that it is impossible for human beings to know whether there is a God or not. Agnosticism is to be distinguished from atheism which denies the existence of God. It should be noted that, in denying the existence of God, an atheist does not necessarily claim to know the answers to such questions as "What is the origin of life?" or "Where does the universe come from?" He merely rules out as false theological answers to these questions. There has been a great deal of confusion on this subject. Clarence Darrow, for example, based his agnosticism partly on the premise that "whether the universe had an origin—and if it had—what the origin is will never be known by men." An atheist, however, could quite consistently admit that this is an insoluble problem. If somebody asked me "Who killed Carlo Tresca?" I could answer "I don't know and it will probably never be discovered" and I could then quite consistently add "But I know some people who certainly did not kill him—e.g., Julius Caesar or General Eisenhower or Bertrand Russell."

During the last forty years a number of philosophers have gone even further in rejecting the claims of theology. They would say that atheists made an unjustified concession to believers in calling their theory *false*. The theological sentences found in the writings of such philosophers as Aquinas or Leibniz or Descartes, as distinct from the anthropomorphic theology of children and many ordinary believers, are really *meaningless*. This is the position of the "logical positivists" who base their opposition to theology on the so-called "Verifiability Principle." A sentence is meaningful or makes sense, according to this principle, only if we can at least describe what it would be like to test it in experience. It is then maintained that in the case of the theological sentences of Aquinas and many other philosophers such tests cannot even be described and that hence all the sentences in question are senseless. If this were true there would be no need to investigate the arguments which these philosophers offered in support of the existence of God. If the conclusion is meaningless, then the arguments cannot possibly be sound.

At first sight, the view of the logical positivists may seem to be identical with agnosticism. For if theism is a meaningless theory, then so is atheism. If I say, to make up a deliberate piece of nonsense, "There are six pirods under the desk," then a person who counters with a denial, i.e., with the sentence "There are no pirods under the desk," is just as much guilty of nonsense. In thus ruling out theism as well as atheism, the logical positivists do indeed to this extent agree with the agnostics. However, they go further and also declare agnosticism to be a meaningless theory. For if the sentence "There is a God" is nonsensical, then it is meaningless to doubt as well as to deny it. It is just as meaningless to say that we shall never know whether or not there are any pirods under the desk as it is to assert or to deny their existence.

The views of the logical positivists are considered in detail, not in the present but in the final section of this book. It may be worth mentioning here that a number of philosophers, who do not go along with the logical positivists in condemning theological conclusions as meaningless, do agree that some of the *questions* raised in discussions of the existence of God are meaningless. Bertrand Russell, for instance, is not a logical positivist; but he emphatically condemns as senseless such questions as "Why does the universe exist?" or

"Why is there something rather than nothing?" He would say that while it makes sense to ask for the "why" of this or that specific thing, the word loses all meaning when applied to the universe as a whole. It makes sense to demand an explanation of this or that specific phenomenon, but it does not make sense to demand an explanation of the universe. "Every man who exists has a mother," he writes (See Selection 41, p. 479). It does not follow from this that "the human race has a mother—This is a different logical sphere." The question "What is the explanation of the universe?" is in Russell's view as senseless as the question "Who is the mother of the human race?"

Many famous philosophers have advanced arguments which, they hoped, would serve as a rational justification of the belief in God and such arguments form an important chapter in the history of Western philosophy. Since the days of Hume and Kant the majority of these arguments have not been widely accepted among philosophers. They are, however, far from dead and some of them have, to this day, the support of writers whose ability is unquestioned. In any event, even if one concludes that all these arguments are fallacious, a study of them is worth while since in most cases they raise logical issues of much wider application.

The more common arguments may be conveniently divided into six varieties: (1) the ontological argument; (2) the cosmological argument; (3) the teleological argument or the argument from design; (4) the moral argument; (5) the argument from the common consent of mankind and the related argument from a religious instinct; and (6) the appeal to what is called "religious experience." Some writers group the argument from the common consent with the "moral" arguments, but this is merely a question of terminological preference. In the course of these introductory comments nothing will be said about (3), (4) and (5). It is difficult to say anything useful about (4) or (5) in a short space. In the case of the design argument, which is probably the most popular of all, our selections cover it so comprehensively both on the affirmative (Aquinas, p. 409. Copleston, p. 418, and Paley, pp. 419 ff.) and on the negative side (Darrow, pp. 446 ff.) that any comments on it here are quite superfluous. However, our selections dealing with the ontological and the cosmological arguments and with the appeal to religious experience are not as extensive as one might wish and a few further remarks here may be of some help. This is particularly true of the cosmological proof, which is historically the most important next to the design argument. Much of this introduction will therefore be taken up with the cosmological argument and especially the difficulties confronting its advocates.

THE ONTOLOGICAL ARGUMENT

The ontological argument was first put forward by the medieval theologian St. Anselm of Canterbury (See Selection 32) and was subsequently defended by a number of distinguished philosophers including Descartes. It was rejected by Aquinas, by many of Descartes' contemporaries, notably Gassendi, and was exhaustively criticized by Kant. The argument begins by defining "God" as an all-perfect Being, that is, as a Being containing all conceivable perfections. Now, if, in addition to possessing omnipotence, omniscience, and various other admirable qualities, this being did not also possess existence it would be less perfect than if it possessed this additional attribute. If it lacked existence it would not be all-perfect. But by definition God is all-perfect. Hence, among other things, He must exist. The existence of God can thus be established, according to this argument, simply by explicating our concept of God. The definition, or, using scholastic language, the "essence" of God guarantees His existence just as the definition or essence of a "triangle" guarantees that all triangles must have three sides. To say that God exists is *necessarily* true just as it is necessarily true that a triangle has three sides. To say that there is no God is not false but *self-contradictory* the way it would be self-contradictory to say "here is a triangle with four sides."

Kant objected to the ontological argument mainly on the ground that it treats existence as if it were a quality or characteristic or property. To suppose this, however, is to be misled by grammatical similarities. The word "exists" is not indeed meaningless, but it has quite a different function from "property-words" like "green" or "pleased" or "all-powerful" or "having three sides." The following illustration will perhaps serve to bring out the difference. Suppose I am an explorer and claim to have discovered a new species of animal which I call "gangle." I have been asked to explain what I mean by calling an animal a "gangle" and I have given this answer: "By a gangle I mean a mammal with eleven noses, seven blue eyes, bristly hair, sharp teeth and wheels in the place of feet." Let us now contrast two supplementary remarks I might make. The first time I add "furthermore a gangle has three long tails." The second time I add "furthermore, let me insist that gangles exist." It is evident that these are two radically different additions. In the first case I was adding to the definition of "gangle"; I was enlarging the concept; I was mentioning a further property which a thing must possess before I would call it a "gangle." The second time I was doing something quite different. I was not enlarging the concept of gangle. I was saying that there is something to which the concept applies, that the combination of characteristics or qualities *previously* mentioned belong to something.

Only characteristics or qualities can enlarge a concept. Since existence is not a characteristic or quality it follows that it cannot be part of any concept. It cannot be part of the concept of God any more than of the concept of cat or gangle. It may well be true that God exists, but this conclusion cannot be derived from the concept of the all-perfect Being any more than the existence of centaurs or hippogriffs or leprechauns could be deduced from an analysis of the corresponding concepts. It has also been pointed out that if the ontological argument were sound we could, with equal justice, prove the existence of a perfect scientist, a perfect singer, and any other number of perfect beings. This alone is sufficient to indicate that there is something drastically wrong with it.

THE COSMOLOGICAL ARGUMENT

We next turn to the cosmological proof. This has taken a number of forms, the most important of which are known as the "causal argument" and "the argument from contingency," respectively. In some writers, like Samuel Clarke, they are combined, but it is best to keep them apart as far as possible. The causal argument is the second of the "five ways" of Aquinas (Selection 33, p. 408. See also Copleston, Selection 34, pp. 415 ff. and the Russell-Copleston debate, Selection 41, pp. 478 ff.) and roughly proceeds as follows: we find that the things around us come into being as the result of the activity of other things. These causes are themselves the result of the activity of yet other things. But such a causal series cannot "go back to infinity." Hence there must be a first member, a member which is not itself caused by any preceding member—an uncaused or "first" cause.

It has frequently been pointed out that even if this argument were sound it would not establish the existence of *God*. It would not show that the first cause is all-powerful or all-good or that it is in any sense personal. Somebody believing in the eternity of atoms or of matter generally could quite consistently accept the conclusion. Defenders of the causal argument usually concede this and insist that the argument is not in itself meant to prove the existence of God. Supplementary arguments are required to show that the first cause must have the attributes assigned to the deity. They claim, however, that the argument, if valid, would at least be an important step towards a complete proof of the existence of God.

Does the argument succeed in proving so much as a first cause? This will depend mainly on the soundness of the premise that an infinite series of causes is impossible. Aquinas supports this premise by maintaining that the opposite belief involves a plain absurdity. To suppose that there is an infinite series of causes logically implies that nothing exists now; but we know that plenty of things do exist now; and hence any theory which implies that nothing exists now must be wrong. Let us take some causal series and refer to its members by the letters of the alphabet:

$$A \longrightarrow B \qquad . \quad . \quad . \quad . \quad . \quad . \quad W \longrightarrow X \longrightarrow Y \longrightarrow Z$$

Z stands here for something presently existing, e.g., Margaret Truman. Y represents the cause or part of the cause of Z, say Harry Truman. X designates the cause or part of the cause of Y, say Harry Truman's father, etc. Now, Aquinas reasons, whenever we take away the cause, we also take away the effect: if Harry Truman had never lived, Margaret Truman would never have been born. If Harry Truman's father had never lived, Harry Truman and Margaret Truman would never have been born. If A had never existed none of the subsequent members of the series would have come into existence. But it is precisely A that the believer in the infinite series is "taking away." For in maintaining that the series is infinite he is denying that it has a first member; he is denying that there is such a thing as a first cause; he is, in other words, denying the existence of A. Since without A, Z could not have existed, his position implies that Z does not exist now; and this is plainly false.

Critics of the argument would object that it does not do justice to the supporter of the infinite series of causes. They would say that Aquinas had failed to distinguish between the two statements

(1) A did not exist, and
(2) A is not uncaused.

To say that the series is infinite implies (2), but it does not imply (1). The following parallel may be helpful here: Suppose Captain Spaulding had said "I am the greatest explorer who ever lived" and somebody replied "No, you are not." This answer would be denying that the Captain possessed the exalted attribute he had claimed for himself, but it would not be denying his existence. It would not be "taking him away." Similarly, the believer in the infinite series is not "taking A away." He is taking away the privileged status of A; he is taking away its "first causiness," if you like. He does not deny the existence of A or of any particular member of the series. He denies that A or anything else is the first member of the series. Since he is not taking A away, he is not taking B away and thus he is also not taking X, Y, or Z away.

His view, then, does not commit him to the absurdity that nothing exists now or, more specifically, that Margaret Truman does not exist now. It may be noted in this connection that a believer in the infinite series is not necessarily denying the existence of supernatural beings. He is merely committed to denying that such a being, if it exists, is uncaused. He is committed to holding that whatever other impressive attributes a supernatural being might possess, the attribute of being a first cause is not among them.

It is perhaps worth adding that the fallacy just pointed out recurs in slightly different shapes in many later defenders of the cosmological argument. Thus Locke, in trying to establish the existence of at least one eternal being, an "eternal source," claims that anybody who denies this conclusion is committed to the absurdity that there was a time when nothing existed and the consequent absurdity that things which subsequenly came into existence were produced by this "pure nothing." In Locke's own words:

> Man knows by an intuitive certainty, that bare nothing can no more produce any real being, than it can be equal to two right angles. If a man knows not that non-entity, or the absence of all being, cannot be equal to two right angles, it is impossible he should know any demonstration in Euclid. If therefore we know there is some real being, and that non-entity cannot produce any real being, it is an evident demonstration, that from eternity there has been something; since what was not from eternity had a beginning; and what had a beginning must be produced by something else. . . .
>
> There is no truth more evident, than that something must be from eternity. I never yet heard of any one so unreasonable, or that could suppose so manifest a contradiction, as a time wherein there was perfectly nothing: this being of all absurdities the greatest, to imagine that pure nothing, the perfect negation and absence of all beings, should ever produce any real existence.

The answer to this is quite simple; If there were an infinite series of causes, then something would always exist even if every member of the series had a beginning. Locke fails to distinguish the following two propositions:

(1) There was a time at which nothing existed, and
(2) There is nothing which did not have a beginning.

A person who denies the existence of an "eternal source" is committed to (2) but not to (1). He is committed to holding that, no matter how far back one may go in a causal series, one will never find a thing without a beginning. He is not committed to the view that at some stage one will cease to find anything. A member of a series is not "nothing" just because it had a beginning or, more generally, because its duration is finite. To admit that something (i.e., some thing or other) has always existed is not tantamount to admitting that any one thing is eternal. Since a person who denies the existence of an eternal being is not committed to (1), he is also not committed to the claim that something came from nothing.

The causal argument has also been criticized on many counts. Thus it has been asserted that, even if otherwise valid, the argument would not prove a *single* first cause. For there does not seem to be any good ground for supposing that all the various causal series in the universe ultimately merge. Hence even if it is granted that no series of causes can be infinite, the possibility of a plurality of first members has not been ruled out. Nor does the argument, according to some critics, establish the *present* existence of the first cause. It does not prove this since experience clearly shows that an effect may exist long after its cause has been destroyed. There are also other objections and some of these will be discussed further on in this introduction.

Many defenders of the causal argument would contend that at least some of these criticisms rest on a misunderstanding. They would probably go further and contend that the argument was not quite fairly stated in the first place— or at any rate that if it was fair to some of its adherents, it was not fair to others. They would in this connection distinguish between two types of causes —what they call "causes *in fieri*" and what they call "causes *in esse*." A cause *in fieri* is a factor which brought or helped to bring an effect into existence. A cause *in esse* is a factor which "sustains" or helps to sustain the effect "in being." The parents of a human being would be an example of a cause *in fieri*. If somebody puts a book in my hand and I keep holding it up, his putting it there would be the cause *in fieri,* and my holding it would be the cause *in esse* of the book's position. The builder of a house is its cause *in fieri;* the materials which, in virtue of their rigidity, keep it in existence are its cause *in esse*. Sometimes the cause *in fieri* and the cause *in esse* are identical. In this connection Father Joyce gives the example of a candle which produces light in a room in the first place and whose continued presence is required if the illumination is to continue.

Using this distinction, a defender of the argument now reasons in the following way. To say that there is an infinite series of causes *in fieri* does not lead to any absurd conclusion. But Aquinas is concerned only with causes *in esse* and an infinite series of *such* causes is impossible. In the words of the contemporary American Thomist, R. P. Phillips:

> . . . Each member of the series of causes possesses being solely by virtue of the actual present operation of a superior cause. . . . Life is dependent, *inter alia,* on a certain atmospheric pressure, this again on the continual operation of physical forces, whose being and operation depends on the position of the earth in the solar system, which itself must endure relatively unchanged, a state of being which can only be continuously produced by a definite—if unknown—constitution of the material universe. This constitution, however, cannot be its own cause. That a thing should cause itself is impossible: for in order that it may cause it is necessary for it to exist, which it cannot do, on the hypothesis, until it has been caused. So it must *be* in order to cause itself, and it cannot *be* until it has caused itself. Thus, not being uncaused nor yet its own cause, it must be caused by another, which produces and preserves it. It is plain, then, that as no member of this series possesses being except in virtue of the actual present operation of a superior cause, if there be no first cause actually operating none of the dependent causes could operate either. We are thus irresistibly led to posit a first efficient cause which, while itself uncaused, shall impart causality to a whole series. . . .
>
> The series of causes which we are considering is not one which stretches back into the past; so that we are not demanding a beginning of the world at some definite moment reckoning back from the present, but an actual cause now operating, to account for the present being of things.

The supporter of the infinite series of causes, in the words of Father Joyce,

> . . . is asking us to believe that although each link in a suspended chain is prevented from falling simply because it is attached to the one above it, yet if only the chain be long enough, it will, taken as a whole, need no support, but will hang loose in the air suspended from nothing.

This formulation of the causal argument unquestionably circumvents one of the objections mentioned previously. If Y is the cause *in esse* of an effect, Z, then it must exist as long as Z exists. If the argument were valid in this form it would therefore prove the present and not merely the past experience of a first cause. In this form the argument is, however, less convincing in another respect. To maintain that all "natural" or "phenomenal" objects— things like tables and mountains and human beings—require a cause *in fieri* is not implausible, though even here Mill and others have argued that strictly speaking only *changes* require a causal explanation. It is far from plausible on the other hand to claim that all natural objects require a cause *in esse*. It may be granted that the air around us is a cause *in esse* of human life and further that certain gravitational forces among the causes *in esse* of the air being where it is. But when we come to gravitational forces or at any rate to material particles like atoms or electrons, it is difficult to see what cause *in esse* they require. To those not already convinced of the need for a super-natural First Cause some of the remarks by the supporters of the argument in this connection appear merely dogmatic and question-begging. Most people would grant that particles like atoms did not cause themselves, since they would in that event have had to exist before they began existing. It is not at all evident, however, that these particles cannot be uncaused. Professor Phillips and all other supporters of the causal argument immediately proceed to claim that there *is* something else which needs no cause *in esse*. They themselves admit thus, a critic would say, that there is nothing self-evident about the proposition that everything must have a cause *in esse*. Their entire procedure here, incidentally, seems to lend substance to Schopenhauer's gibe that supporters of the cosmological argument treat the law of universal causation like "a hired cab which we dismiss when we have reached our destination."

But waiving this and all similar objections, an opponent would maintain that the restatement of the argument in terms of causes *in esse* in no way avoids the main difficulty which was previously mentioned. A believer in the infinite series would insist that his position was just as much misrepresented now as before. He is no more removing the member of the series which is supposed to be the first cause *in esse* than he was removing the member which had been declared to be the first cause *in fieri*. He is again merely denying a privileged status to it. He is not denying the reality of the cause *in esse* labelled "A." He is not even necessarily denying that it possesses supernatural attributes. He is again merely taking away its "first causiness."

To many critics it appears that the advocates of the causal argument in either form frequently confuse in their own minds an infinite series with one which is long but finite. If a book, Z, is to remain in its position, say 100 miles up in the air, there must be another object, say another book, Y, underneath it, to serve as its support. If Y is to remain where it is, it will need another support, X, beneath it. Suppose that this series of supports, one below the other, continues for a long time but, eventually, say after 100,000 members, comes to a first book which is not resting on any other book or indeed on any other support. In that event the whole collection would come crashing down. What we seem to need is a first member of the series, a first support (like the earth) which does not need another member as *its* support, which in other words is "self-supporting."

This is evidently the sort of picture that supporters of the First Cause argument have before their minds when they rule out the possibility of an infinite series. A critic of the argument would counter that such a picture is not a fair representation of the theory of the infinite series. A *finite* series of books would indeed come crashing down since the first or lowest member would not have a predecessor on which it could be supported. If the series were infinite, however, this would not be the case. In that event every member *would* have a predecessor to support itself on and there would be no crash. That is to say: a crash can be avoided either by a finite series with a first self-supporting member or by an infinite series. Similarly, the present existence of motion is equally compatible with the theory of a first unmoved mover and with the theory of an infinite series of moving objects; and the present existence of causal activity is compatible with the theory of a first cause *in esse* as much as with the theory of an infinite series of such causes.

No staunch defender of the cosmological argument would give up at this stage. Even if there were an infinite series of causes *in fieri* or *in esse*, he would contend, this still would not do away with the need for an ultimate, a first cause. As Father Copleston put it in his debate with Bertrand Russell (Selection 41, p. 478):

> Every object has a phenomenal cause, if you insist on the infinity of the series. But the series of phenomenal causes is an insufficient explanation of the series. Therefore, the series has not a phenomenal cause, but a transcendent cause. . . . An infinite series of contingent beings will be, to my way of thinking, as unable to cause itself as one contingent being.

A critic would retort that the demand to find the cause of the series as a whole rests on the erroneous assumption that the series is something over and above the members of which it is composed. It is tempting to suppose this, at least by implication, because the word "series" is a noun like "dog" or "man." Like the expression "this dog" or "this man" the phrase "this series" is easily taken to designate an individual object. But reflection shows this to be an error. If we have explained the individual members there is nothing additional left to be explained. Supposing I see a group of five Eskimos standing on the corner of Sixth Avenue and 50th Street and I wish to explain why the group came to New York. Investigation reveals the following stories:

> Eskimo No. 1 did not enjoy the extreme cold in the polar region and decided to move to a warmer climate;
> No. 2 is the husband of Eskimo No. 1. He loves her dearly and did not wish to live without her;
> No. 3 is the son of Eskimos 1 and 2. He is too small and too weak to oppose his parents;
> No. 4 saw an advertisement in the *New York Times* for an Eskimo to appear on television;
> No. 5 is a private detective engaged by the Pinkerton Agency to keep an eye on Eskimo No. 4.

Let us assume that we have now explained in the case of each of the five Eskimos why he or she is in New York. Somebody then asks: "All right, but what about the group as a whole, why is *it* in New York?" This would plainly be an absurd question. There is no group over and above the five members and if we have explained why each of the five members is in New York, we have *ipso facto* explained why the group is there. A critic of the cosmological argument would claim that it is just as absurd to ask for the cause of the series as a whole, as distinct from asking for the causes of individual members.

It is most unlikely that a determined defender of the cosmological line of reasoning would surrender even here. He would probably admit that the series is not a thing over and above its members and that it does not make sense to ask for the cause of the series if the cause of each member has already been found. He would insist, however, that when he asked for the explanation of the entire series, he was not asking for its cause. He was really saying that a series, finite or infinite, is not "intelligible" or "explained" if it consists of nothing but "contingent" members. To quote Father Copleston once more (Selection 41, p. 478):

> What we call the world is intrinsically unintelligible apart from the existence of God. The infinity of the series of events, if such an infinity could be proved, would not be in the slightest degree relevant to the situation. If you add up chocolates, you get chocolates after all, and not a sheep. If you add up chocolates to infinity, you presumably get an infinite number of chocolates. So, if you add up contingent beings to infinity, you still get contingent beings, not a necessary being.

This last quotation is really a summary of the "contingent argument," the other main form of the cosmological proof. It may be stated more fully in these words: All around us we perceive contingent beings. This includes all physical objects and also all human minds. In calling them "contingent" we mean that they might not have existed. We mean that the universe can be *conceived* without this or that physical object, without this or that human being, however certain their actual existence may be. These contingent beings we can trace back to other contingent beings—e.g., a human being to his parents. However, since these other beings are also contingent, they do not provide a real or full explanation. The contingent beings we originally wanted explained have not yet become intelligible, Since the beings to which they have been traced back are no more necessary than they were. It is just as true of our parents, for example, as it is of ourselves, that they might not have existed. We can, then, properly explain the contingent beings around us only by tracing them back ultimately to some necessary being, to something which exists necessarily, which has "the reason for its existence within itself." The existence of contingent beings, in other words, implies the existence of a necessary being. (It is unnecessary to enter here into the controversy whether this statement of the contingency argument may be regarded as an explication of the third of the five ways of Aquinas. There is some dispute as to what Aquinas meant by "necessary being" and consequently about the proper interpretation of the third way. However, the formulation here presented is unquestionably an accurate summary of an argument adduced by several distinguished philosophers and one which is eminently worth discussing, whether Aquinas would endorse it or not.)

This contingency argument seems to be even more beset with difficulties than the causal form of the cosmological proof. In the first place, Kant and many other writers contend that it really commits the same error as the ontological argument in tacitly regarding existence as an attribute or characteristic. To say that there is a necessary being is to say that it would be a self-contradiction to deny its existence. This would mean that at least one existential statement is a necessary truth; and this in turn presupposes that in at least one case existence is contained in a concept. But, for reasons outlined in connection with the ontological argument, it seems plain to very many philosophers that existence is not a characteristic, that it can hence never be contained in a concept and that no existential statement can ever be a necessary truth. To talk about anything "existing necessarily" is in their view about as sensible as to talk about round squares. They conclude that the contingency argument is quite absurd. Scholastic philosophers like Father Copleston would reply that existence *is* a characteristic and would thus also reject the Kantian criticism of the ontological argument. They do reject the ontological argument but not as radically as Kant and for different reasons.

Let us assume that this difficulty can somehow be surmounted and that the expression "necessary being," as it is intended by the champions of the contingency argument, might conceivably apply to something. There remain other objections which are of great weight in the opinion of many writers. One of these may perhaps be best explained by first quoting again from the debate between Bertrand Russell and Father Copleston:

> RUSSELL: . . . It all turns on this question of sufficient reason, and I must say you haven't defined "sufficient reason" in a way that I can understand—what do you mean by sufficient reason? You don't mean cause?
>
> COPLESTON: Not necessarily. Cause is a kind of sufficient reason. Only contingent being can have a cause. God is his own sufficient reason; and he is not cause of himself. By sufficient reason in the full sense I mean an explanation adequate for the existence of some particular being.
>
> RUSSELL: But when is an explanation adequate? Suppose I am about to make a flame with a match. You may say that the adequate explanation of that is that I rub it on the box.
>
> COPLESTON: Well for practical purposes—but theoretically, that is only a partial explanation. An adequate explanation must ultimately be a total explanation, to which nothing further can be added.
>
> RUSSELL: Then I can only say that you're looking for something which can't be got, and which one ought not to expect to get.
>
> COPLESTON: To say that one has not found it is one thing; to say that one should not look for it seems to me rather dogmatic.
>
> RUSSELL: Well, I don't know. I mean, the explanation of one thing is another thing which makes the other thing dependent on yet another, and you have to grasp this sorry scheme of things entire to do what you want, and that we can't do.

Russell's criticism may be expanded in the following way. The contingency argument rests on a misconception of what an explanation is and does, and similarly on what it is that makes phenomena "intelligible." Or else it involves an obscure and arbitrary redefinition of "explanation," "intelligible," and related terms. Normally, we are satisfied that we have explained a phenomenon if we have found its cause or if we have exhibited some other uniform connection between it and something else. Confining ourselves to the former case, which is probably the most common, we might say that a phenomenon, Z, has been explained if it has been traced back to a group of factors, a, b, c, d, etc., which are its cause. These factors are the full and real explanation of Z quite regardless of whether they are pleasing or displeasing, admirable or contemptible, necessary or contingent. The explanation would not be adequate only if the factors listed are not really the cause of Z. If they are the cause of Z, the explanation would be adequate even though each of the factors is merely a "contingent being."

Let us suppose that we have been asked to explain why General Eisenhower won the election of 1952. "He was an extremely popular general," we might answer, "while Stevenson was relatively little known; moreover there was a great deal of resentment over the scandals in the Truman Administration." If somebody complained that this was only a partial explanation we might mention additional antecedents such as the widespread belief that the Democrats had allowed Communist agents to infiltrate the State Department, that Eisenhower was a man with a winning smile, and that unlike Stevenson he had shown the good sense to say one thing on race relations in the North and quite another in the South. Theoretically, we might go further and list the motives of all American voters during the weeks or months preceding the elections. If we could do this we would have explained Eisenhower's victory. We would have made it intelligible. We would "understand" why he won and why Stevenson lost. Perhaps there is a sense in which we might make Eisenhower's victory even more intelligible if we went further back and discussed such matters as the origin of American views on Communism or of racial attitudes in the North and South. However, to explain the outcome of the election in any ordinary sense, loose or strict, it would not be necessary to go back to pre-historic days or to the amoeba or to a first cause, if such a first cause exists. Nor would our explanation be considered in any way defective because each of the factors mentioned was a "contingent" and not a necessary being. The only thing that matters is whether the factors were really the cause of Eisenhower's election. If they were, then it has been explained, although they are contingent beings. If they were not the cause of Eisenhower's victory, we would have failed to explain it, even if each of the factors were a necessary being.

If it is granted that in order to explain a phenomenon or to make it intelligible we need not bring in a necessary being, the contingency argument breaks down. For a series, as was already pointed out, is not something over and above its members; and every contingent member of it could in that case be explained by reference to other contingent beings. It is evident from Russell's remarks that he would go further in his criticisms. Even if it were granted, he would argue, both that the phrase "necessary being" is meaningful and that all explanations are defective unless the phenomena to be explained are traced back to a necessary being, the conclusion would not have been established. The conclusion that a necessary being actually exists does not follow from the premise that phenomena have not been really or fully explained without the introduction of a necessary being. The conclusion follows from this premise together with the additional premise that *there are* explanations of phenomena in this special sense of the word. It is this further premise which Russell and many other philosophers would question. They do not merely question whether human beings can ever obtain explanations in this sense, but whether they exist. To assume without further ado that phenomena have explanations or an explanation in *this* sense is to beg the very point at issue. The use of the same word "explanation" in two crucially different ways, a critic would argue, lends the second premise a plausibility it does not really possess. It may indeed be highly plausible to assert that phenomena have explanations, whether we have found them or not, in the ordinary sense in which this usually means that they have causes. It is then tempting to suppose, because of the use of the same word, that they also have explanations in a sense in which this implies dependence on a necessary being. But this does not follow in the least.

THE ARGUMENT FROM RELIGIOUS EXPERIENCE

Kant, who rejected the ontological, the cosmological and also the teleological argument, produced an argument of his own which belongs to the species known as moral arguments for the existence of God. Moral arguments enjoyed much popularity in the 19th century both among writers who followed Kant in the rejection of the other arguments and also among Catholic philosophers who remained unmoved by Kant's criticisms. In recent years, however, the popularity of moral arguments appears to have greatly declined and today, among philosophers with a Protestant background, the argument for religious experience is more widely employed than any of the other arguments for the existence of God.

The main point at issue in this argument may be stated as follows: There are human beings who claim to have experiences in the course of which they have immediate knowledge of God. In these "religious" experiences they claim to have as direct a "contact" with the "Creator and Sustainer of the universe" as we ordinarily have with physical objects when we see or touch them. Of course God is not physical and He is not known by means of the physical senses; but the contact is just as real, perhaps even more so. Cardinal Newman, for instance, referring to his conversion through a religious experience many years after it had taken place, wrote that he was still more certain of its veracity than that he had "hands and feet."

That experiences take place in which people *believe* to have contact with God can hardly be questioned. It has, however, been debated whether any of these experiences are "veridical," whether any of those who have religious experiences *really make contact* with the deity. There are roughly three points of view on this topic. There is, first, the affirmative position which maintains that while no doubt some religious experiences have to be classified as "delusive," in others human beings are really in touch with the ultimate spiritual Cause of the universe. There is, secondly, the negative position which, in its more radical form, maintains that all religious experiences are of the same nature as either illusions or hallucinations. Bertrand Russell and Freud are among those who endorse this view. "From a scientific point of view," Russell remarks, "we can make no distinction between the man who eats little and sees heaven and the man who drinks much and sees snakes." There is also the more modest version of the negative position which contends merely that the veridical character of religious experiences cannot be established. Finally, there is a middle-of-the-road position according to which human beings do, in some of these religious experiences, come into contact with "an aspect of reality" not given in more ordinary types of experience. But it is held that this aspect is probably misdescribed by the use of theological language. Broad and Stace are perhaps the most eminent exponents of views of this kind.

In the case of sense-experiences we possess certain fairly precise criteria which enable us to discriminate between those which are veridical and those which are deceptive. Suppose one day I come home at nine in the evening and see, or think I see, the tenor Jussi Bjoerling in my living room, although he has been announced to sing Manrico in *Trovatore* at that very moment. I could determine whether my visual experience is veridical by looking more closely and by making use of senses other than sight. I could for instance try to start a conversation with what I take to be Jussi Bjoerling and I could try to put my hands in the place where he would be if my visual experience were veridical. I could also call in other observers, preferably such as are sane and sober and not dominated by conscious or unconscious wishes for the presence of distinguished Swedish tenors. Again I could test certain statements which are logical consequences of the assumption that it is really Jussi Bjoerling who is in my apartment. Thus I could call up Mr. Bing at the Metropolitan Opera and check if Jussi Bjoerling is performing in *Trovatore* as scheduled.

If I am told that he is, this would indicate that I am the victim of an hallucination. If on the other hand I am told that Jussi Bjoerling had to be suddenly replaced, that he has lately gone in for skillful burglaries on the upper West Side in Manhattan and that he was last seen heading in the direction of my apartment, this would tend to confirm the veridical nature of my visual experience.

Are there any such tests in the case of religious experiences? The defenders of this argument maintain that there are at least analogous criteria. In the first place they point to the large quantity of reports and the relative agreement in their contents. This would correspond to calling in other observers in the case of sense-experiences. They next point to the high moral and intellectual caliber of at least some of those reporting religious experiences. This would correspond to the sanity and soberness of the observers. Finally, attention is drawn to the vast beneficial differences which religious experiences make to the lives of many who have them. This is compared by the defenders of the argument to affirmative tests of statements which logically follow from the assumption that a certain sense-experience is veridical. To do justice to the argument it is necessary to state each of these points at greater length.

It is argued that among people who have had religious experiences we must include not only mystics and saints who have perhaps had these experiences more intensely than others. We must also include countless modest and humble believers who experienced the presence of God in the course of prayers and meditations, and in moments of stress and crisis. These experiences furthermore are not confined to Christians and Jews but are equally or even more common in Eastern religions. "By the most conservative estimate," writes Professor Trueblood (Selection 36, p. 441),

. . . the number of persons who have reported religious experience, not in the sense of ecstatic trance, and not in the sense of mere inference from the order of nature, but with a deep assurance of the divine undergirding, is many millions . . .

It is true that religious experiences are not universal in the human race. But this proves nothing. No experience, not even sight, is universal. To have an experience, certain receptive powers are required. From the fact that there are blind people it does not follow that our visual experiences are generally deceptive. Moreover, the testimony of those who fail to have an experience has no logical weight if they did not fulfill the conditions required for having the experience. "The religious opinions of the unreligious," to quote Trueblood, "are no more valuable than are the scientific opinions of the unscientific."

The mere quantity of reports of religious experiences would not provide much evidence if there were very great differences in their content. While they do vary greatly concerning details, depending on the age in which the person lived and the particular religious background from which he came, these reports are remarkably similar as regards their essential features. All or nearly all speak of contact with a Being immeasurably greater than the person himself which is in some sense the ultimate Reality and which provides love and assurance. "We could seldom guess," according to Dean Inge (1860–1954), one of the foremost authorities on the history of mysticism, "whether a paragraph describing the highest spiritual experiences was written in the Middle Ages or in modern times, in the north or south of Europe, by a Catholic or by a Protestant." It is an "impressive fact," in the words of James Bisset Pratt, an American philosopher of the first half of the twentieth century, that religious experiences with a similar content "spring up spontaneously and independently in remotely separated lands, among peoples of unrelated races, in nearly all the ages and in all the religions with which we are acquainted."

The "qualitative fitness" of the reporters is also important. The defenders of this argument would usually admit that those claiming religious experiences have included cranks, lunatics and plain frauds. A substantial number of them were, however, sincere beyond any question. It would be fantastic to suppose that men like Pascal, Newman, Fox, Gandhi, or Tolstoy were "engaged in a grand hoax." Nor can it be reasonably maintained that all these men were lacking in critical powers. There is, then, in Trueblood's words:

> . . . a substantial body of evidence coming from sensitive men, who are in command of their faculties, and properly qualified, on both moral and intellectual grounds, so that they inspire trust in that to which they bear testimony.

Finally, it is claimed that the beneficial consequences of religious experiences provide an indirect confirmation of their veridical character.

> In religion we cannot reasonably look for a mark on photographic plates, but we can reasonably look for a mark on human lives. If the experience of God is what men claim it is, we should expect to see a general change in their character; we should expect them to walk with a new step.

And that is precisely, according to Professor Trueblood and other defenders of the arguments, what we find in abundance. Religious experience "suffuses entire lives with joy." It gives people "a new strength and a new tenderness." It "sensitizes their consciences to social wrong, such as that of slavery and poverty." It "makes weak men bold and proud men humble." It enables them to endure extreme sorrows and hardships and persecutions.

So much for the defense of this argument. Let us now look at the answers offered by those who reject it. Taking the last point first, many of them have questioned whether religious experiences really have such powerful effects for the good. It is true, they would argue, that some famous mystics, like St. Francis or William Blake, were persons of exceptional kindness and compassion; but it is very doubtful if this was due to their religious visions. There have after all been quite a few kindly unbelievers and perhaps St. Francis and Blake would have been kind and compassionate in the absence of religious experiences or even in the absence of any religious belief. Furthermore, if it is granted that religious experiences have sometimes had beneficial effects there seems equal evidence that some of the most dreadful persecutions were instigated by men who claimed to be fulfilling divine orders. Who has not heard of fanatics committing murders, arson, and all kinds of violent deeds in the conviction that they were thus carrying out the commands of the deity? If "marks on human lives" count, a critic would assert, it is not easy to see why these "negative marks" are to be ruled out. For there is no reason to suppose that the persecutors and the cranks were any less sincere in their reports than the gentle believers. If a defender of the argument condemns the experiences of fanatics as delusions on the ground that God is good (in his sense) and cannot therefore have given such hideous instructions, he would be assuming the very thing he should prove.

In any case, however, a critic would maintain that beneficial results are no evidence that belief is sound or an experience veridical. A heroic attitude has frequently been induced by beliefs which were illusory. Nazi spies and saboteurs willingly gave their lives in the service of the Führer whom they took to be noble, sane, and selfless. It is an understatement to say that he was none of these. Julius and Ethel Rosenberg showed great courage in going to their death, but their opinions about the nature of the Soviet system under Stalin were altogether mistaken, as even Communists admit today. Nor is there any reason to suppose that hallucinations cannot have powerful effects on a person's life. In the case of paranoid individuals they do and the effects are not by any means always harmful. When the individual believes himself to be Christ or "the Ruler of the Universe" his delusions usually lead to kindly rather than to cruel deeds. The beneficial effects of religious experiences are hence not incompatible with the view that they are deceptive. They cannot properly be compared to the positive outcome of tests which prove a sense-experience to be veridical.

As for the "quality" of the reporters, a critic might well admit that quite a number of them were men of high moral and intellectual standing. But this, he would go on, can be considered evidence only for the claim that they were not lying when they reported their experiences. It cannot be considered evidence for the further claim that God was actually present on these occasions. It is certainly not impossible for a person of high moral and intellectual standing to become the victim of a delusion. There would be very general agreement that just this has happened in not a few cases. In earlier days, when the belief in demons was widespread, countless sincere and intelligent men reported struggles with the devil and his agents who were tempting them to commit immoral deeds. There is little doubt that these experiences were hallucinations. Again, William Blake had visions not only of the deity but also of Moses, David, Julius Caesar, Shakespeare, Dante, Voltaire, and King Edward III. He was a man of great gifts and matchless sincerity but it seems clear that these experiences were not veridical. William Gladstone, the great Liberal Prime Minister of the Victorian era, habitually "consulted God" before making any major decisions and God apparently always advised a course which was to the political and personal advantage of Mr. Gladstone. Even most devoutly religious people of that period, especially those favoring the Conservative Party, considered it very unlikely that God had really appeared to Mr. Gladstone in these "consultations." Men of intelligence and good moral reputation do not, in other words, seem to be immune from hallucinations. If the conditions which generally lead to delusions are present in such men, they are likely to produce the same result as in anybody else.

A critic would similarly contend that the quantity of the reports as well as their relative unanimity is not at all incompatible with the view that God is never actually present in any of these experiences. If religious experiences are due to certain ungratified needs in people who have been reared in a religious environment and if these unfulfilled needs are widespread, then we would expect religious experiences to occur quite frequently even on the assumption that they are delusions. If the needs in question are similar and the religious backgrounds somewhat different, we would expect the content of the experiences to be fairly similar as regards their basic features and to be rather different in peripheral details. And this, a critic would add, is precisely what we find.

All of this, even if sound, would not show that religious experiences are always delusive. It would merely show that their veridical nature had not been established. Some opponents of the argument would go a great deal further. They would offer a theory of the origin of religious experiences

which in their opinion makes it extremely probable that all the alleged contacts with God are complete delusions. Since the days of the German philosopher Feuerbach (1804–1872) and more especially since the publication
of the theories of Freud and certain of his disciples, many unbelievers have
reasoned on this topic roughly along the following lines. People whose lives
are devoid of certain forms of earthly love and warmth tend to escape into
a world of dreams and make-believe. Not finding satisfaction for some of
their deepest and most powerful longings in their physical and human environment, they seek consolation and substitute-gratification in a world of their
own making which can be managed more easily than the hard and cold universe
around them. People who have religious experiences and mystical longings,
the critics would proceed, must be put into this class. Experience shows that
every one of them has not found fulfillment of some very basic mundane
yearning. It is only reasonable to infer that religious experiences are part and
parcel of one of the systems of fantasy in which the person finds some semblance of the love and warmth that is denied to him in his earthly contacts.
As confirmation of this theory the unbelievers would point to the fact or the
alleged fact that those who have religious experiences most vividly and most
frequently show a great many overt similarities to the insane, if they are not
indeed generally so classified. The critics would also point to the observation
of some eminent psychologists that a person's proneness to religious experiences and mystical feelings diminishes in almost exact proportion as he
reestablishes contact with the terrestrial world and finds satisfaction for his
biological and social needs.

In the opinion of some writers it would not follow that religious experiences
are always delusions even if a theory such as that outlined in the last paragraph were correct. Professor Broad offers the following rebuttal to the
unbeliever's argument:

> Suppose, for the sake of argument, that there is an aspect of the world
> which remains altogether outside the ken of ordinary persons in their
> daily life. Then it seems very likely that some degree of mental and physi-
> cal abnormality would be a necessary condition for getting sufficiently
> loosened from the objects of ordinary sense-perception to come into
> cognitive contact with this aspect of reality. Therefore the fact that those
> persons who claim to have this peculiar kind of cognition generally ex-
> hibit certain mental and physical abnormalities is rather what might be
> anticipated if their claims were true. One might need to be slightly "cracked"
> in order to have some peep-holes into the super-sensible world.

If this is a valid retort then Freudian theories of the genesis of religious
experiences would not show them to be delusions. Perhaps such theories do
nonetheless constitute a powerful challenge to the defenders of the appeal to
religious experience. For it might be said that if we have a perfectly good
explanation of a certain phenomenon in terms of natural causes it becomes
superfluous to explain it in terms of some supernatural reality. There was a
time when hysterical and other neurotic symptoms were explained as due to
"possession" by evil spirts. It would not be accurate to say that the "possession" theory has been shown to be false, if only because one hardly knows
what it would be like to falsify such a theory. Nevertheless, it has generally
been abandoned, since we now have reasonably well-confirmed explanations
of hysterical symptoms in terms of such natural causes as repressed emotions
and nervous lesions. Similarly, if the Freudian theory about the causation of

religious experience were true, this would not show that the theological explanation is false, but it would make the latter redundant.

FIDEISM

We have not so far considered a viewpoint which has become increasingly influential among pro-religious philosophers in recent years. This is the position known as "fideism"—belief in God (or other religious propositions) on the basis of faith alone. We will from now on contrast fideists with "rationalistic" believers, including among the latter any believer who justifies his position by reference to one or more of the arguments which are claimed to show that the existence of God (or some other religious theory) is either certain or probable. In this sense of the word believers like Paley and Mill who offered what they took to be empirical arguments will count as rationalistic believers no less than philosophers like Anselm and Descartes who advanced *a priori* proofs. Fideistic believers are ready to concede that the arguments for the existence of God are not valid, but they commonly add that this is not necesarily a cause for concern. Faith, in the words of John Hick, "stands ultimately upon the ground of religious experience and is not a product of philosophical reasoning." A person either has faith in which case he does not need any logical arguments or else he does not in which case no amount of arguments will give it to him. If somebody were convinced by one of the arguments for the existence of God and if he accepted the conclusion of the argument in a purely intellectual way, he would not thereby have become a religious person. If he continued to live just as he had before becoming convinced by the argument, he would, to most intents and purposes, have remained an unbeliever. His assent to the existence of God, to use Cardinal Newman's terminology, would be merely "notional." Kierkegaard, a leading figure in the fideist tradition, went so far as to maintain that those who tried to prove the existence of God are enemies of true faith. Faith, on Kierkegaard's view, involves risk, but there would be no risk if the existence of God or immortality were as solidly established as mathematical theorems and scientific laws (see Selection 42, pp. 482–502). Similar sentiments have been expressed by many other philosophers who do not go along with all the details of Kierkegaard's fideism. If the existence of God were unquestionably certain like a physical fact, writes John Hick, it "would leave no ground for a free human response of trust, self-commitment and obedience." If we could produce logically coercive arguments, in the words of Alasdair MacIntyre, "we should be as bereft of the possibility of making a free decision to love God as we should be if every utterance of doubt and unbelief was answered by thunder-bolts from heaven." On such a view Kant and Hume were really preparing the way for faith with their demolition of the arguments for the existence of God.

In one respect, of course, fideistic believers are better off than their rationalistic counterparts. Since they offer no arguments to show that belief in God is either certain or probable, the fideists need not worry about the shortcomings and difficulties that beset the various proofs advanced by rationalistic believers. Fideists have sometimes inferred from this that their position, unlike that of the rationalists, is immune from *any* criticisms. Some noted unbelievers have reluctantly agreed with this contention. "The new theology," writes Bertrand Russell, referring to fideism, "cannot be refuted since it does not profess to prove its points." Similarly, Ernest Nagel concedes that fideism is "impregnable to rational criticism." It should be pointed out that there is something very confused and misleading in all such comments, whether they come from fideists or from unbelievers. Like the rationalistic believers, the fideist is making a claim about the universe and not merely about his own state of mind or the state of mind of other believers. He is claiming that the world was created and is governed by an all-powerful and all-good God and not merely that he and others believe this. Insofar as the fideist presents no evidence for his postiion, the critic has indeed nothing to argue against; but this does not prevent him from attacking *the conclusion itself*. To make this clear let us briefly consider the case of somebody who maintains, admitting from the outset that he has no evidence for this proposition and that it is based on faith alone, that Shakespeare was a German. Since he offers no evidence, there is no evidence that can be attacked; but this would not prevent us from disproving his assertion by reference to Shakespeare's birth-certificate and various other incontrovertible facts about his life. Any plea by this person that he gave no evidence will not have the slightest bearing on the soundness of the refutation. Returning to the fideist in theology, it should be remembered that his assertion has the same publicly testable consequences about the world as that of the rationalistic believer (e.g., that there is no evil or at any rate no pointless or ultimately meaningless evil) and if the argument from evil, or any other argument, refutes the assertion of the rationalistic believer, it equally refutes that of the fideist.

Hick is a fideist who is acutely aware of this feature of the situation. He agrees that the fideist's case would become untenable if it could be shown that the statement "God exists" is meaningless or self-contradictory or false or if, though it may not be known to be false, the state of the evidence clearly favored the negative side. Accordingly, Hick has devoted much effort to rebut the challenges of philosophers who maintain that belief in God is one or other of these things—meaningless, self-contradictory, false or improbable. Thus he has argued that belief in God is not meaningless. Accepting the Verifiability Principle, Hick insists that statements asserting the existence of God are in principle verifiable—not indeed by any observations in this life, but by "eschatological" observations, i.e., observations carried out in a life after death. Again Hick believes in a God who is both omnipotent and perfectly good and he concedes that fideism would be fatally undermined if such a belief were incompatible with the evil that is found in the world. It can be shown, Hick believes, that belief in God is not incompatible with the evil in the world (see Selections 39 and 40). We will leave it to the reader to decide whether Hick offers a satisfactory answer to the problem of evil. Whether he does or not, he is clearly right in seeing the necessity on the fideist's part to answer this challenge and the other challenges listed above.

Let us suppose that belief in God is not meaningless or self-contradictory and that it cannot be shown to be false. Let us furthermore assume either that there is no evidence for or against the existence of God or else that the evidence is evenly balanced. Would we then be free to believe or would it be our duty to suspend judgment? More generally, are we ever entitled to believe in a proposition which is not supported by the preponderance of the available evidence? Many distinguished scientists and philosophers have answered this question with a resounding "No." The nineteenth-century mathematician W. K. Clifford (1845–1879), in a famous essay entitled "The Ethics of Belief," reached the conclusion that it was intellectually immoral and a shameful betrayal of our duties as thinking rational beings to believe anything simply on the basis of faith. Clifford's view was shared, among others, by Bertrand Russell who formulated the following "precept of veracity": "Give to any hypothesis which it is worth your while to consider that degree of credence which the evidence warrants." The appeal to faith, on Russell's view, is not only unjustified but potentially very harmful. The appeal to faith, he writes, "allows us to indulge in pleasant dreams." It is opposed to intellectual honesty and courage. "Where traditional beliefs about the universe are concerned, craven fears . . . are considered praiseworthy, while intellectual courage, unlike courage in battle, is regarded as unfeeling and materialistic." Moreover, fideism is liable to lead to persecution and intolerance. If a person bases his belief on reason he will support it by argument rather than by persecution and will abandon his position if the argument goes against him. If, however, his belief is based on faith, he will conclude that argument is useless and will "therefore resort to force either in the form of persecution or by stunting and distorting the minds of the young whenever he has the power to control their education."

In opposition to writers like Clifford and Russell, William James argued in "The Will to Believe" that in certain circumstances it *is* justifiable to accept a proposition even if it is not favored by the preponderance of the available evidence. It is widely agreed that James' own presentation of this position is marred by serious confusions, but a number of philosophers believe that he was fundamentally right. The late Professor C. J. Ducasse (1881–1969) offered a much more careful defense of James' main thesis than is found in "The Will to Believe" and it may be of interest to consider Ducasse's reformulation. He begins by inviting us to consider the following situation: somebody is driving down a steep hill when the brakes of his car suddenly fail. As he tries to shift into low gear, the gears strip. The person is now faced with the alternatives of jumping out or staying in the car. He is faced, in the sense in which James uses this word, with a "forced option." The option is forced in that there are only two alternatives. He does not have a third alternative of suspending judgment since refusal to decide is tantamount to deciding in favor of staying in the car. The driver, we will further assume, has no evidence that staying in the car is more likely to avoid serious injury than jumping out. In such a situation, Ducasse observes, "decision is and has to be non-rational in the sense of being instinctive, impulsive and temperamental." The decision is not indeed irrational, but it is also not favored by the available evidence. Ducasse next asks us to consider the case of a person who has been brought up as a believer in God. After careful study he reaches the conclusion that belief in God is neither meaningless or self-contradictory and that there is no evidence either for or against the existence of God. Belief in God is to him a source of strength and courage and beneficence to other people, and so far as he can see it does not lead to any undesirable results (he is, for example, not at all intolerant of those who do not share his belief). He also knows that by adopting certain courses of action, for example by associating with certain people and attending certain meetings, it is possible to strengthen his belief, while it is possible to weaken and even undermine it by associating with other people and attending different kinds of gatherings. Ought such a person to try to strengthen or to weaken his belief? Ducasse concludes that for this person it would be perfectly rational to try to strengthen his belief in God:

> It would be rational, not in the sense that there is a preponderance of evidence for the truth of the proposition he believes and that his belief of it is determined by this, but in the sense that although he has no evidence for or against the truth of that proposition, belief itself of that proposition has the effect of making him a happier, more courageous, more beneficent person than would disbelief of it.

It should be noted that the believer whose case Ducasse discusses would be rational only if belief in God is not meaningless or self-contradictory and if the evidence against belief is not stronger than the evidence in its favor. Hick, as we saw, is substantially in accord with this proviso and the majority of fideists who have reflected on the subject would probably endorse such an approach. Kierkegaard and those who follow him all the way, however, would dissent most emphatically. Kierkegaard had no time for theologians who tried to explain away difficulties and thus "shirk something of the pain and crisis of decision." Kierkegaard did not indeed think that the evidence against the existence of God was stronger than the favorable evidence, but he did regard belief in the "absolute paradox" (the incarnation of God in the person of Jesus) as "absurd." While it is not entirely clear what he meant by this, it is certain that Kierkegaard regarded belief in the reincarnation as highly objectionable from a logical or rational point of view. He nevertheless taught that faith in the absolute paradox was both possible and highly desirable. The person who has this faith achieves the highest kind of life attainable for human beings. Moreover it is only by attaining such faith that one can become a Christian and only a Christian can gain eternal happiness. To be told that one ought to believe something although or perhaps even because it is "logically repellent" sounds like strange advice, but it is an essential part of Kierkegaard's defense of Christianity and it is intimately connected with his doctrine, celebrated by contemporary existentialists as a major contribution to human thought, that "truth is subjectivity." Selection 42 contains many of the most important passages in which Kierkegaard expounds his position. Selection 43 provides a critical assessment.

BUBER, FACKENHEIM AND THE APPEAL TO BIBLICAL FAITH

A form of fideism, somewhat similar to Kierkegaard's but also differing in various details, is advanced by Emil Fackenheim in Selection 44. Fackenheim's views are largely derived from certain of the ideas of the highly influential Jewish philosopher Martin Buber (1878–1965). The approach of Buber and Fackenheim is not by any means confined to Jewish theologians. Substantially identical views are found in several Christian writers, for example, in the work of the English theologian John Baillie (1886–1960) and the contemporary Welsh philosopher, D. Z. Phillips. Before taking up Fackenheim's main contentions it may be helpful to say something about Buber's doctrine of the "eclipse of God" to which Fackenheim alludes in several places but which he does not explain in any detail. This doctrine, which Fackenheim has elsewhere described as "perhaps the greatest achievement of Buber's career," was put forward in response to the sufferings of the Jewish people during the Nazi period. This is of course one particularly striking illustration of the problem of evil which we mentioned a little earlier. If there is an all-powerful God he surely could have prevented extermination camps like Auschwitz and if the all-powerful God were perfectly good he would have prevented them; but in fact these camps did exist and six million Jews, many of them women and children, were wiped out within a period of less than five years. Buber himself has vividly stated the problem:

One asks again and again: how is a Jewish life still possible after Auschwitz? I would like to frame this question more correctly: how is a life with God still possible in a time in which there is an Auschwitz? The estrangement

has become too cruel, the hiddenness too deep . . . Dare we recommend
to the survivors of Auschwitz, the Job of the gas chambers: "Give thanks
unto the Lord, for He is good; for His mercy endureth forever"?

Phenomena like Auschwitz, according to Buber, do not show that there is no
God but rather that there are periods when God is in eclipse. It is not just that
modern men, because of their absorption in technology and material progress,
have become incapable of hearing God's voice. God himself is silent in our
age and this is the real reason why his voice has not been heard. "Let us ask,"
writes Buber

> whether it may not be literally true that God formerly spoke to us and is
> now silent, and whether this is not to be understood as the Hebrew Bible
> understands it, namely that the living God is not only a self-revealing but
> also a self-concealing God. Let us realize what it means to live in the age of
> such a concealment, such a divine silence.

Buber, for one, remained convinced that the eclipse of God will not last forever. We have to "endure the divine silence," confident in the expectation that
before too long "the word between heaven and earth will again be heard."
    Let us now turn to the main contentions of Fackenheim's "On the Eclipse
of God." The first of these is the claim that if only we see how "Biblical faith"
differs from the attitude of a scientist toward his hypotheses we will realize that
the believer's position is impregnable. Science is "forever" hypothetical. If a
scientist's hypothesis is disconfirmed he will modify or abandon it. The Biblical
believer will do nothing of the sort. "What could one make of a religious faith
which was forever hypothetical, wavering between belief in good times and
unbelief in bad?" Once the nature of Biblical faith is understood it is easy to
see why the evil that unquestionably exists in the world does not disprove it.
If there is good fortune, it "reveals the hand of God." If fortune is bad and if
this cannot be explained as just punishment, the conclusion is that "God's ways
are unintelligible, not that there are no ways of God." Neither times of external nor of internal darkness are regarded by "adherents of Biblical faith
. . . as evidence against God, but rather—to use Martin Buber's expression—
as evidence of an 'eclipse of God.' " Tragedy does not destroy Biblical faith—
it merely tests it. What is true of evil equally applies to the empty heart within.
"A full heart within indicates the Divine Presence; an empty heart bespeaks
not the non-existence or unconcern of God, but merely His temporary absence."
It is thus apparent that "religious faith can be, and is, empirically verifiable;
but nothing empirical can possibly refute it." (Fackenheim's italics.) The considerations which show that neither the evil without nor the empty heart within
can disprove belief in God equally apply to any and all scientific discoveries.
Biblical belief is empirically irrefutable and hence "scientific evidence can no
more affect it than the evidence of historical tragedy or the evidence of an
empty heart." If the Bible contains a statement that is contradicted by scientific evidence, this does not show either that God was in error or that he was
not the author of the statement. We must keep in mind that although the Biblical God has always revealed Himself he has also always concealed Himself.
"At most, therefore, modern science should have had no greater effect on
Biblical belief than to show that its God was even more inscrutable than had
hitherto been thought, and His revelations even more ambiguous and intermittent."
    Fackenheim's second main contention concerns the place assigned to re-
ligious experience by the Biblical believer. Both he and Buber claim that some

human beings have "meetings" with God and that ultimately all religions are based on such "supreme meetings." God appears to the believer who is "primordially open" to receive Him. Buber and Fackenheim insist on the directness of God's presence. God, writes Buber, is "the Being that is directly, most nearly, and lastingly, over against us." Again, "the immediacy and, as it were, bodily nearness" that man experiences in his meetings with the divine, overwhelm him," whether they "fill him with awe, transport him with rapture, or merely give him guidance." A person who has "glanced" at God does not require any arguments for His existence:

> That this glance of the Being exists, wholly unillusory, yielding no images, no other court in the world attests than that of faith. It is not to be proved; it is only to be experienced; man has experienced it.

In thus appealing to meetings with God, Buber and Fackenheim are not, in their opinion, putting forward an argument from religious experience. Such an argument amounts to inferring the existence of God and in this way it misses out on the fact that, as Fackenheim puts it in one place, "the Divinity is immediately present to the believer." "Man does not have private feelings from which he infers the Divine." No, the reverse is true. If a person is related to God at all, then "he is primordially open to Him; and his subjective feelings . . . are mere by-products of this primordial openness." An argument from religious experience, furthermore, is unable to support the Biblical believer's "*certainty* of standing in relation to . . . God." The Biblical believer does not treat his belief in God as the best available theory to account for a certain range of observed facts. Anyone adopting such a position does not merely abandon the certainty of Biblical faith, but, since in all likelihood the theological explanation is not the most plausible one available, he in effect. in Fackenheim's words, "executes, so far as his core-commitment is concerned, immediate and total surrender" to the unbeliever.

Let us now briefly examine these contentions. First, what about Fackenheim's contention, that although Biblical faith is empirically verifiable nothing can possibly refute it? This may not unjustly be called the "heads I win, tails you lose" strategy. It clearly involves a confusion between psychological (and philosophically quite irrelevant) considerations and the real logical issues at stake between the believer and his critics. The question at stake is whether, in the light of the evil in the world and various other considerations, the assertions, the claims of the believer have not been shown to be false or highly improbable or in some other way absurd or untenable. This question is in no way even approached if we are told that a truly Biblical believer will not abandon his faith, no matter what he finds in the world. From the *unbudgability,* the immovability, the unconvertability of the Biblical believer, nothing whatever follows about the *undisprovability* of his position. Fackenheim is here simply misled by the ambiguity of certain expressions he employs like "destroy" and "test." The horrors of the world may not in fact destroy a given religious person's faith in the sense of *causing him to abandon it,* but this in no way shows that they do not destroy it in the sense of *disproving* the assertions which are the content of his faith.

There is of course no doubt that human beings are frequently so attached to their beliefs that they will not give them up, come what may. Bigots believe all sorts of things about Jews, Negroes, Catholics and other groups which are not in accordance with the facts. What they believe usually fulfils some deep emotional need and no amount of evidence to the contrary can shake them out of their prejudices. During the Hitler period Nazi sympathizers throughout the world persistently denied that there were any such places as concentration camps were reputed to be. When the British troops liberated Bergen-Belsen and other concentration camps in Western Germany they took pictures of what they found and these were subsequently shown in theaters in the United States among other countries. The pro-Nazis refused to see these movies on the ground that they were the usual Jewish propaganda. Examples could be multiplied indefinitely. It is not precisely news that human beings behave in this way. What is remarkable is that a philosopher should admire conduct of this kind and advocate it as an intellectual policy of great virtue. Richard Robinson, a contemporary Oxford philosopher, has described the kind of faith defended by Fackenheim as "a great vice, an example of obstinately refusing to listen to reason . . . , a form of self-hypnosis."

It is worth pointing out that "God exists" and "God is good," as they are intended by Fackenheim's Biblical believer, are perfect examples of statements which fall under the ban of the "falsifiability principle" defended by Antony Flew in Selection 46. According to Flew—and this is a view shared by quite a few other contemporary philosophers—a statement is not really intelligible, it has no factual content if it is compatible with any conceivable state of affairs. If I say about X that he is my trusted friend I make a genuine factual assertion provided that I exclude certain kinds of behavior on X's part. As the expression "trusted friend" is normally used, I would presumably exclude such things as delight on X's part when hearing of a misfortune that has befallen me, spiteful remarks by him about me behind my back or malicious letters to my employers. Let us suppose, however, that I do not retract the statement "X is my trusted friend" in any of these circumstances, not even when I find out that he has hired a thug to assassinate me. Let me suppose that I will not regard the statement as false under any conceivable circumstances. In that event I have really emptied the expression "trusted friend" of any content and my statement that X is my trusted friend has become quite vacuous. Is this not precisely what Fackenheim's Biblical believer is doing? We are told that he will retain his faith *no matter what may happen* and it is for this reason that his faith is declared to be "irrefutable." Let us suppose that Hitler had been victorious and conquered the world and that Auschwitz was succeeded by super-Auschwitzes for the entire life span of the human species. Let us go still further and assume that there is another life and that it is not one in which good and just people enjoy eternal bliss but on the contrary a place of such monstrous horrors that Auschwitz appears pale by comparison. The Biblical believer, as depicted by Fackenheim, would even then maintain that the universe is ruled by a good God. In that case, however, what he maintains is surely compatible with any conceivable state of affairs and hence, if Flew's point is well-taken, it is devoid of factual content.

What about Buber's doctrine of the eclipse of God, the view that there are periods when God is concealing himself from the world? The obvious retort to it is that God's self-concealment is inconsistent with his perfect goodness or indeed with any kind of goodness on his part. If a child is in terrible trouble and his father knows about it and could come to the child's help but refuses to do so, i.e., begins to "conceal" himself, this would not, surely, be the mark of a perfectly good father. On the contrary, we would regard him as a monster. It is difficult to see what other response could be justified toward a deity behaving in this fashion. If a Jew in Auschwitz desperately needs God's assistance, if God knows about the Jew's need (and he must know it since he is omniscient), if God furthermore is capable of coming to the Jew's assistance (since he is omnipotent he can do this) and if he nevertheless refuses to do so but instead "conceals himself," then this is not simply a deity falling short of complete goodness but a monstrous deity in comparison with whom, as Bertrand Russell once put it, Nero would have to be regarded as a saint.

Buber and Fackenheim, as we saw, insist that they are not offering an argument from religious experience and that their position is hence immune from the objections that are commonly advanced against philosophers like Trueblood (see pp. 435–445 above). A critic would counter that in fact they *are* presenting us with an argument from religious experience, but one that is *incompletely stated*. It must be emphasized that unillusory glances and self-authenticating encounters have been claimed by a great many people who would be dismissed by Buber and Fackenheim as clearly the victims of delusion. Michael Rohan, the Australian farm-worker who in 1969 set fire to the Al Aksa Mosque (and who was acquitted on the grounds of insanity) did so on orders of God who had chosen him to be King of Jerusalem and Judea. Charles Guiteau, the man who assassinated President Garfield, also acted on instructions from God. Nor are encounters by people who are clearly insane the only ones that Buberites would dismiss as delusions. John Baillie, the English theologian mentioned above, who was an admirer of Buber and a man whose sanity was beyond question, had encounters that no Jew could regard as veridical. After presenting a general position that is strikingly similar to Buber's, in which rationalistic arguments for the existence of God are rejected, Baillie tells us that "our knowledge of God rests rather on the revelation of His personal Presence as Father, Son, and Holy Spirit." It "comes through our direct personal encounter with Him in the Person of Jesus Christ his Son our Lord." If, however, some encounters are merely apparent and not real, if some "glances" are illusory, we need criteria to distinguish the merely apparent and illusory encounters from the real ones; and this is one of the things that arguments from religious experience have attempted to do. The difference between the Buberite position and the more traditional one is that the Buberites have not even attempted to specify such criteria. It is not unfair to comment that they have given us a broken-backed argument from religious experience. Without questioning his sincerity, we cannot simply take it on Buber's word that certain of his glances are "wholly unillusory" and that he and his followers have had "real encounters" with the divine. Presumably the same claim would be made by those who, by Buber's own acknowledgments, have had illusory glances and merely apparent encounters.

BISHOP ROBINSON'S THEOLOGICAL RECONSTRUCTION

Bishop Robinson is a leading figure in a movement within contemporary Protestantism which attempts to make the Christian religion acceptable to educated people in the modern world. For a full understanding of the issues discussed by Professor Williams and Bishop Robinson in Selection 45 is is necessary to know something about this development. Paul Tillich (1886–1965), one of the most influential Protestant theologians of recent times who was in many ways the founder of this movement, waged a lifelong battle against what he called "monarchic monotheism." Most ordinary religious believers as well as many theistic philosophers, according to Tillich, tend to think of God as a magnified man—a king residing somewhere in space or a cosmic policeman who observes human transgressions while the earthly policemen are not looking. Traditional theism, Tillich writes, treats God as an "individual substance," a "cause alongside other causes," as a "heavenly, completely perfect person who resides above the world and mankind." There is no such perfect person residing above the world and intelligent educated men should not be asked to believe such nonsense. Against this kind of theology, "the protest of atheism is correct." The defenders of such a position "are more dangerous for religion than the so-called atheistic scientists." Monarchic monotheism is not only incredible. It is also a degrading doctrine. For the omnipotent, completely perfect person tends to be conceived of as "an invisible tyrant, the being in contrast with whom all other beings are without freedom and subjectivity." We must oppose views of this kind not only in the interest of truth and genuine religion but also in the interest of human freedom.

Bishop Robinson is in complete agreement with these sentiments and in his *Honest to God,* a booklet which caused a tremendous stir when it was published in 1963, he set out to continue Tillich's demolition of monarchic monotheism and to sketch a new conception of God which would be free from the anthropomorphism of the older creeds. There was a time, Bishop Robinson notes, when people believed quite literally in a three-decker universe. Much of the terminology of the Bible is, "crudely spatial." It speaks of a God "up there" and of Jesus "going up" to and "coming down" from Heaven. Over the centuries educated believers abandoned this literal belief in the three-decker universe and replaced it by belief in a God who is vaguely "out there," in some way perhaps beyond outer space. Most contemporary believers are inclined to think of God as a kind of "visitor from outer space." Such a conception of God "underlies every popular presentation of the Christian drama of salvation, whether from the pulpit or the presses." The time has come to purge ourselves of such a belief. However, the abandonment of a God "out there" is a much more radical break than the rejection of a God "up above" and it is likely to meet far more violent opposition. Most people would be seriously disturbed by the thought that belief in a God "out there" should need to die at all:

> For it *is* their God, and they have nothing to put in its place. And for the words "they" and "their" it would be more honest to substitute "we" and "our." For it is the God of our own upbringing and conversation, the God of our fathers and of our religion, who is under attack. Every one of us lives with some mental picture of a God "out there," a God "to" whom we pray and to whom we "go" when we die.

The change from belief in a God "up above" to a God "out there" liberated Christianity from a flat-earth cosmology, but it was no more than a transposition of spatial metaphors. To be asked to stop believing in the God "out there" is bound to appear as an "outright denial of God" since, to the ordinary way of thinking, believing in God is the same thing as believing in the existence of "such a supreme and separate Being." Nevertheless, difficult as it is going to be, we must now destroy belief in such an "idol." This is the only way of "making Christianity meaningful" for future generations.

Many critics of *Honest to God* complained that while Bishop Robinson made it quite clear what he was opposed to, he did not succeed in presenting anything like an intelligible and consistent alternative. Some critics pointed to a tendency on his as well as on Tillich's part to identify God with the deeper aspirations of human beings. God is not "out there" at all, but inside of us insofar as we have deep emotions and commitments. In *Honest to God* Bishop Robinson had quoted, with enthusiastic approval, a passage from Tillich's *The Shaking of the Foundations* (reproduced by Professor Williams on p. 538) in

which Tillich identified belief in God with the conviction that "life has depth."
According to Robinson, Tillich in this passage spoke "with a new and indestructible relevance and made the traditional language of a God that came in from
outside both remote and artificial." Professor Williams points out that, in one
fairly straight-forward reading, Tillich's remarks amount to atheism. If God is
identified with the deepest aspirations of human beings, then there would be
no God if there were no human beings. If this is what one's position comes
to, Williams observes, it is highly misleading and a kind of verbal deception
to say that one still believes in God. Bishop Robinson, in his contribution to
the symposium, insists that he does believe in a God who transcends the
existence of human attitudes. As he uses the word "God," it does not stand
for any of the commitments or concerns of human beings but for the reality
to which certain kinds of commitment are a response:

> "God" refers not to the commitment but to something that hits you, sur-
> rounds you, with a grace and a claim from which you cannot finally get
> away.

If all human beings were eliminated from the universe, God would still be real:

> God's reality doesn't depend on us and our aspirations—rather, our being is
> grounded in his.

What is this God, who is not "out there," who is not a magnified man, a
super-person, but who nevertheless transcends human beings and in whom our
being is "grounded"? The clue to the answer, we are told, is the nature of
personal relations. From the moment of birth, Robinson reminds us, we find
ourselves in relationships to other persons. In these we are "drawn out not
merely to reaction and response" but also to "freedom and responsibility."
This enables us to see what the non-anthropomorphic believer means by God:

> What the believer is saying is that such a relationship, such a love, is the
> element in which all things live and move and have their being. It is what
> draws the whole process of evolution onwards and upwards to its fulfilment
> in mind and spirit.

The Taoist sees a certain norm at the center of everything. The Christian, on
the other hand, sees at the center of everything "a grace that meets and claims
him in love":

> The question of God is the question whether persons and personal relation-
> ships are simply on their own, up against it, in a fundamentally alien
> universe. For to believe in God is to affirm that at the heart of things, as the
> most real thing in the world, is a love and purpose to which persons and
> personal relationships are, so far, the highest *response*. This is the way the
> grain of the universe runs.

The Bible tells us both that God is a rock and that God is a father. God is
not a person and hence we cannot literally say that God is a father, but He is
more like a father than he is like a rock:

> What the Christian is affirming by using the word "God" is something about
> the *relationship* in which he finds himself to be held. In human terms, it is
> less misleading to describe it in personal language than in impersonal.

The Christian finds "a kind of security" in God and this is more like that of
a parent's love "than that of an immovable lump of stone." Belief in such a

God is no idle speculation. On the contrary, it makes the greatest difference to a person's life: "Affirming . . . that 'God is love' is staking one's whole being on the fact that this is the final truth about the nature of things." The new teaching, it appears, even helps us to overcome death. It tells us that

> In everything, however loveless, there is a purpose and a love to be met and responded to from which *nothing,* not even death can separate us.

The statement that love, grace and purpose are at the heart of things, Robinson maintains, is not meaningless, but he does not profess to be able to prove it. It is an "affirmation" which has to be accepted as "an act of trust."

Has Bishop Robinson succeeded in offering a coherent alternative to the anthropomorphic theology he rejects? To some readers it will seem that he has given us little more than meaningless verbiage. We are told that there is no God in the sense of there being another person over and above the ordinary persons we know; but at the same time we are assured that "at the heart of things," at the "still center of everything" there is a love and purpose and grace, that "*all* things live and move and have their being" in love. All the three key-words here—"love," "purpose," and "grace"—are originally introduced to refer to emotions, attitudes and actions of human beings, i.e., persons. Our language provides no sense for these expressions when they are not applied to persons or at least to animate beings. It does make sense to speak of God's love when God is regarded as a person, but, in denying that there is such a God, Robinson has deprived himself of the kind of subject to whom purposes and love and grace can be intelligibly ascribed. It should be remembered that when Robinson claims that all things have their being in love or that love is at the heart of things, this is *not* meant to be a statement about human attitudes or responses but about *that* to which human beings respond. Robinson uses the words "love" and "grace" and "purpose" in contexts in which ordinary language has assigned no sense to them, but he has not explained any new sense in which these words are to be understood. The Bishop emphatically rejects the view of believers who see a hidden purpose in "why particular things happen or do not happen to particular people." Such a view, he tells us, is not only untenable but also immoral. Referring to the mining disaster in Aberfan, he remarks that there is no purpose or intention in the slipping of a coal tip, "unless it be human negligence." The very next moment, however, he assures us that "in everything, however loveless, there is a purpose and love to be met and responded to" and earlier he told us that God, i.e., the love and grace and purpose of everything, "hits, meets and surrounds" us. What, to use William James' expression, is the cash-value of such talk? If the Aberfan disaster or the more recent and much more enormous tragedy of the hurricanes that devastated large areas of Pakistan do not have a hidden purpose, what is their unhidden purpose? Hitler's persecution of the Jews and of his political opponents, the Bishop would surely agree, was not inspired by hidden love. What and where in such a case was the unhidden love? When a man is struck down by leukemia in the prime of life or when, like Bishop Robinson's American disciple, Bishop Pike, he dies an agonizing death in the desert, where is the grace that "hits" and "surrounds" us? When a lion devours a deer, where does the Bishop find the love that is supposedly at the heart of everything? Unless Robinson can answer these questions one is tempted to conclude that what he has given us is empty rhetoric and not a coherent theory.

The emptiness of the new love-theology can also be seen by considering the gamble in which the believer is supposed to be engaged. "Affirming that 'God is love'," Robinson writes, "is staking one's whole being on the fact that this is the final truth about the nature of things." The risk involved seems well worth taking since "this is the way the grain of the universe runs." In staking one's life on the love-theology, one is, it appears, backing the favorite horse or the favorite candidate. A little reflection will show that this talk of the risks which the believer is supposed to be running is utterly spurious. Let us recall what is involved when a person is really taking a risk. Let us suppose that a man is suffering from a painful and chronic ailment which does not, however, endanger his life. A surgeon tells him that there is an operation which, if successful, results in a complete cure, but that it is a very dangerous operation. The man decides to take the chance. Here it would be quite appropriate to say that the patient is staking his life on the surgical skill of his physician. This statement makes sense because two conditions are fulfilled— we can specify what the staking consists in and also what the staking is for. Pascal's famous wager also fulfills these conditions: the staking, as Pascal is commonly understood, consists in the person's leading a "Christian" life in which he subordinates pleasures to religious duties and the prize (if the wager is successful) is eternal bliss. Neither of these two conditions are satisfied in the case of the Bishop's gamble, or at any rate nothing he has said gives any indication as to how they would be fulfilled. What, corresponding to the money invested by a gambler, the self-denials of the Pascalian believer, the dangerous operation undertaken by the man who suffers from a chronic ailment, is a person doing who is staking "his whole being" on the belief that love is at the center of all things? And what is the prize for the sake of which he is supposed to be staking his whole being? What will he obtain if the gamble is successful and what is he losing or going to lose if it is unsuccessful? Bishop Robinson does not appear to believe in an after-life in which human beings obtain rewards and punishments for their deeds on earth. In any event his view that love and grace and purpose are in all things is independent of any eschatological assumptions. A traditional believer in an all-mighty Judge who distributes eschatological rewards and punishments has an answer to the question concerning the nature of the prize involved in the believer's gamble. Robinson, who does not believe in such an all-mighty Judge, has no answer.

If these critical comments are justified we must conclude that Bishop Robinson has not succeeded in offering a viable theological reconstruction. This does not of course mean that none is possible. Any other attempt would have to be examined on its merits.

P.E.

32 There Exists Something Than Which a Greater Cannot Be Thought

St. Anselm

Preface

Some time ago, at the urgent request of some of my brethren, I published a brief work,[1] as an example of meditation on the grounds of faith. I wrote it in the role of one who seeks, by silent reasoning with himself, to learn what he does not know. But when I reflected on this little book, and saw that it was put together as a long chain of arguments, I began to ask myself whether *one* argument might possibly be found, resting on no other argument for its proof, but sufficient in itself to prove that God truly exists, and that he is the supreme good, needing nothing outside himself, but needful for the being and well-being of all things. I often turned my earnest attention to this problem, and at times I believed that I could put my finger on what I was looking for, but at other times it completely escaped my mind's eye, until finally, in despair, I decided to give up searching for something that seemed impossible to find. But when I tried to put the whole question out of my mind, so as to avoid crowding out other matters, with which I might make some progress, by this useless preoccupation, then, despite my unwillingness and

[This selection comprises the Preface, Chapters II, III, and IV of the *Proslogion* (1077–1078) and excerpts from Anselm's reply to the criticisms by Gaunilo. It is reprinted from *A Scholastic Miscellany*, Vol. X, LCC, ed. and tr. by E. R. Fairweather, published in 1956. It is used by permission of the Westminster Press, Philadelphia, and the Student Christian Movement Press, London.]

1. The *Monologion*, probably Anselm's first work, was written at Bec in the second half of 1076. (Translator's note.)

resistance, it began to force itself on me more persistently than ever. Then, one day, when I was worn out by my vigorous resistance to the obsession, the solution I had ceased to hope for presented itself to me, in the very turmoil of my thoughts, so that I enthusiastically embraced the idea which, in my disquiet, I had spurned.

I thought that the proof I was so glad to find would please some readers if it were written down. Consequently, I have written the little work that follows, dealing with this and one or two other matters, in the role of one who strives to raise his mind to the contemplation of God and seeks to understand what he believes. Neither this essay nor the other one I have already mentioned really seemed to me to deserve to be called a book or to bear an author's name; at the same time, I felt that they could not be published without some title that might encourage anyone into whose hands they fell to read them, and so I gave each of them a title. The first I called *An Example of Meditation on the Grounds of Faith,* and the second *Faith Seeking Understanding.*

But when both of them had been copied under these titles by a number of people, I was urged by many people—and especially by Hugh, the reverend archbishop of Lyons, apostolic legate in Gaul, who ordered this with apostolic authority—to attach my name to them. In order to do this more fittingly, I have named the first *Monologion* (or *Soliloquy*), and the second *Proslogion* (or *Address*).

God Truly Is

And so, O Lord, since thou givest understanding to faith, give me to understand—as far as thou knowest it to be good for me—that thou dost exist, as we believe, and that thou art what we believe thee to be. Now we believe that thou art a being than which none greater can be thought. Or can it be that there is no such being, since "the fool hath said in his heart, 'There is no God' "? But when this same fool hears what I am saying—"A being than which none greater can be thought"—he understands what he hears, and what he understands is in his understanding, even if he does not understand that it exists. For it is one thing for an object to be in the understanding, and another thing to understand that it exists. When a painter considers beforehand what he is going to paint, he has it in his understanding, but he does not suppose that what he has not yet painted already exists. But when he has painted it, he both has it in his understanding and understands that what he has now produced exists. Even the fool, then, must be convinced that a being than which none greater can be thought exists at least in his understanding, since when he hears this he understands it, and whatever is understood is in the understanding. But clearly that than which a greater cannot be thought cannot exist in the understanding alone. For if it is actually in the understanding alone, it can be thought of as existing also in reality, and this is greater.

Therefore, if that than which a greater cannot be thought is in the understanding alone, this same thing than which a greater cannot be thought is that than which a greater can be thought. But obviously this is impossible. Without doubt, therefore, there exists, both in the understanding and in reality, something than which a greater cannot be thought.

God Cannot Be Thought of as Nonexistent

And certainly it exists so truly that it cannot be thought of as nonexistent. For something can be thought of as existing, which cannot be thought of as not existing, and this is greater than that which *can* be thought of as not existing. Thus, if that than which a greater cannot be thought can be thought of as not existing, this very thing than which a greater cannot be thought is *not* that than which a greater cannot be thought. But this is contradictory. So, then, there truly is a being than which a greater cannot be thought—so truly that it cannot even be thought of as not existing.

And *thou* art this being, O Lord our God. Thou so truly art, then, O Lord my God, that thou canst not even be thought of as not existing. And this is right. For if some mind could think of something better than thou, the creature would rise above the Creator and judge its Creator; but this is altogether absurd. And indeed, whatever is, except thyself alone, can be thought of as not existing. Thou alone, therefore, of all beings, hast being in the truest and highest sense, since no other being so truly exists, and thus every other being has less being. Why, then, has "the fool said in his heart, 'There is no God,'" when it is so obvious to the rational mind that, of all beings, thou dost exist supremely? Why indeed, unless it is that he is a stupid fool?

How the Fool Has Said in His Heart
What Cannot Be Thought

But how did he manage to say in his heart what he could not think? Or how is it that he was unable to think what he said in his heart? After all, to say in one's heart and to think are the same thing. Now if it is true —or, rather, since it is true—that he thought it, because he said it in his heart, but did not say it in his heart, since he could not think it, it is clear that something can be said in one's heart or thought in more than one way. For we think of a thing, in one sense, when we think of the word that signifies it, and in another sense, when we understand the very thing itself. Thus, in the first sense God can be thought of as nonexistent, but in the second sense this is quite impossible. For no one who understands what God is can think that God does not exist, even though he says these words in his heart—perhaps without any meaning, perhaps with some quite extraneous meaning. For God is that than which a greater cannot be thought, and whoever understands this rightly must understand that he exists in such a way that he cannot be nonexistent even in thought. He, therefore, who understands that God thus exists cannot think of him as nonexistent.

Thanks be to thee, good Lord, thanks be to thee, because I now understand by thy light what I formerly believed by thy gift, so that even if I were to refuse to believe in thy existence, I could not fail to understand its truth.

Reply to the Criticisms of Gaunilo

. . . But, you say, suppose that someone imagined an island in the ocean, surpassing all lands in its fertility. Because of the difficulty, or rather the impossibility, of finding something that does not exist, it might well be called "Lost Island." By reasoning like yours, he might then say that we cannot doubt that it truly exists in reality, because anyone can easily conceive it from a verbal description.[2] I state confidently that if anyone discovers something for me, other than that "than which a greater cannot be thought," existing either in reality or in thought alone, to which the logic of my argument can be applied, I shall find his lost island and give it to him, never to be lost again. But it now seems obvious that this being than which a greater cannot be thought cannot be thought of as nonexistent, because it exists by such a sure reason of truth. For otherwise it would not exist at all. In short, if anyone says that he thinks it does not exist, I say that when he thinks this, he either thinks of something than which a greater cannot be thought or he does not think. If he does not think, he does not think of what he is not thinking of as nonexistent. But if he does think, then he thinks of something which cannot be thought of as nonexistent. For if it could be thought of as nonexistent, it could be thought of as having a beginning and an end. But this is impossible. Therefore, if anyone thinks of it, he thinks of something that cannot even be thought of as nonexistent. But he who thinks of this does not think that it does not exist; if he did, he would think what cannot be thought. Therefore, that than which a greater cannot be thought cannot be thought of as nonexistent.

You say, moreover, that when it is said that the highest reality cannot be *thought of* as nonexistent, it would perhaps be better to say that it cannot be *understood* as nonexistent, or even as possibly nonexistent. But it is more correct to say, as I said, that it cannot be thought. For if I had said that the reality itself cannot be understood not to exist, perhaps you yourself, who say that according to the very definition of the term what is false cannot be understood, would object that nothing that is can be

2. Cf. Gaunilo, *Pro insipiente*, 6.

understood as nonexistent. For it is false to say that what exists does not exist. Therefore it would not be peculiar to God to be unable to be understood as nonexistent. But if some one of the things that most certainly are can be understood as nonexistent, other certain things can similarly be understood as nonexistent. But this objection cannot be applied to "thinking," if it is rightly considered. For although none of the things that exist can be understood not to exist, still they can all be thought of as nonexistent, except that which most fully is. For all those things—and only those—which have a beginning or end or are composed of parts can be thought of as nonexistent, along with anything that does not exist as a whole anywhere or at any time (as I have already said). But the only being that cannot be thought of as nonexistent is that in which no thought finds beginning or end or composition of parts, but which any thought finds as a whole, always and everywhere.

You must realize, then, that you can think of yourself as nonexistent, even while you know most certainly that you exist. I am surprised that you said you did not know this. For we think of many things as nonexistent when we know that they exist, and of many things as existent when we know that they do not exist—all this not by a real judgment, but by imagining that what we think is so. And indeed, we can think of something as nonexistent, even while we know that it exists, because we are able at the same time to think the one and know the other. And yet we cannot think of it as nonexistent, while we know that it exists, because we cannot think of something as at once existent and nonexistent. Therefore, if anyone distinguishes these two senses of the statement in this way, he will understand that nothing, as long as it is known to exist, can be thought of as nonexistent, and that whatever exists, except that than which a greater cannot be thought, can be thought of as nonexistent, even when it is known to exist. So, then, it is peculiar to God to be unable to be thought of as nonexistent, and nevertheless many things, as long as they exist, cannot be thought of as nonexistent. I think that the way in which it can still be said that God is thought of as nonexistent is stated adequately in the little book itself.[3]

3. Cf. *Proslogion,* Chapter IV. (See p. 405 above.)

33   The Five Ways

Thomas Aquinas

THE EXISTENCE OF GOD CAN BE PROVED in five ways.

The first and more manifest way is the argument from motion. It is certain, and evident to our senses, that in the world some things are in motion. Now whatever is in motion is put in motion by another, for nothing can be in motion except it is in potentiality to that towards which it is in motion; whereas a thing moves inasmuch as it is in act. For motion is nothing else than the reduction of something from potentiality to actuality. But nothing can be reduced from potentiality to actuality, except by something in a state of actuality. Thus that which is actually hot, as fire, makes wood, which is potentially hot, to be actually hot, and thereby moves and changes it. Now it is not possible that the same thing should be at once in actuality and potentiality in the same respect, but only in different respects. For what is actually hot cannot simultaneously be potentially hot; but it is simultaneously potentially cold. It is therefore impossible that in the same respect and in the same way a thing should be both mover and moved, i.e., that it should move itself. Therefore, whatever is in motion must be put in motion by another. If that by which it is put in motion be itself put in motion, then this also must needs be put in motion by another, and that by another again. But this cannot go on to infinity, because then there would be no first mover, and, consequently, no other mover; seeing that subsequent movers move only inasmuch as they are put in motion by the first mover; as the staff moves only because it is put in motion by the hand. Therefore it is necessary to arrive at a first mover, put in motion by no other; and this everyone understands to be God.

The second way is from the nature of the efficient cause. In the world of sense we find there is an order of efficient causes. There is no case

[This selection is taken from the *Summa Theologica*, Part I, translated by the English Dominican Fathers. It is here reproduced with the kind permission of Benziger Brothers, New York, and Burns Oates Washbourne, Ltd., London.]

known (neither is it, indeed, possible) in which a thing is found to be the efficient cause of itself; for so it would be prior to itself, which is impossible. Now in efficient causes it is not possible to go on to infinity, because in all efficient causes following in order, the first is the cause of the intermediate cause, and the intermediate is the cause of the ultimate cause, whether the intermediate cause be several or one only. Now to take away the cause is to take away the effect. Therefore, if there be no first cause among efficient causes, there will be no ultimate, nor any intermediate cause. But if in efficient causes it is possible to go on to infinity, there will be no first efficient cause, neither will there be an ultimate effect, nor any intermediate efficient causes; all of which is plainly false. Therefore it is necessary to admit a first efficient cause, to which everyone gives the name of God.

The third way is taken from possibility and necessity and runs thus. We find in nature things that are possible to be and not to be, since they are found to be generated, and to corrupt, and consequently, they are possible to be and not to be. But it is impossible for these always to exist, for that which is possible not to be at some time is not. Therefore, if everything is possible not to be, then at one time there could have been nothing in existence. Now if this were true, even now there would be nothing in existence, because that which does not exist only begins to exist by something already existing. Therefore, if at one time nothing was in existence, it would have been impossible for anything to have begun to exist; and thus even now nothing would be in existence—which is absurd. Therefore, not all beings are merely possible, but there must exist something the existence of which is necessary. But every necessary thing either has its necessity caused by another, or not. Now it is impossible to go on to infinity in necessary things which have their necessity caused by another, as has been already proved in regard to efficient causes. Therefore we cannot but postulate the existence of some being having of itself its own necessity, and not receiving it from another, but rather causing in others their necessity. This all men speak of as God.

The fourth way is taken from the gradation to be found in things. Among beings there are some more and some less good, true, noble, and the like. But "more" and "less" are predicated of different things, according as they resemble in their different ways something which is the maximum, as a thing is said to be hotter according as it more nearly resembles that which is hottest; so that there is something which is truest, something best, something noblest, and, consequently, something which is uttermost being; for those things that are greatest in truth are greatest in being, as it is written in *Metaph.* ii. Now the maximum in any genus is the cause of all in that genus; as fire, which is the maximum of heat, is the cause of all hot things. Therefore there must also be something which is to all beings the cause of their being, goodness, and every other perfection; and this we call God.

The fifth way is taken from the governance of the world. We see that things which lack intelligence, such as natural bodies, act for an end, and this is evident from their acting always, or nearly always, in the same way, so as to obtain the best result. Hence it is plain that not fortuitously, but designedly, do they achieve their end. Now whatever lacks intelligence cannot move towards an end, unless it be directed by some being endowed with knowledge and intelligence; as the arrow is shot to its mark by the archer. Therefore some intelligent being exists by whom all natural things are directed to their end; and this being we call God.

34 Commentary on

"The Five Ways" of Aquinas

F. C. Copleston

. . . A<small>QUINAS DID NOT, OF COURSE,</small> deny that people can come to know that God exists by other ways than by philosophic reflection. Nor did he ever assert that the belief of most people who accept the proposition that God exists is the result of their having elaborated metaphysical arguments for themselves or of their having thought through the metaphysical arguments developed by others. Nor did he confuse a purely intellectual assent to the conclusion of such a metaphysical argument with a living Christian faith in and love of God. But he did think that reflection on quite familiar features of the world affords ample evidence of God's existence. The reflection itself, sustained and developed at the metaphysical level, is difficult, and he explicitly recognized and acknowledged its difficulty: he certainly did not consider that everyone is capable of sustained metaphysical reflection. At the same time the empirical facts on which this reflection is based were for him quite familiar facts. In order to see the relation of finite things to the being on which they depend we are not required to pursue scientific research, discovering hitherto unknown empirical facts. Nor does the metaphysician discover God in a manner analogous to the explorer who suddenly comes upon a hitherto unknown island or flower. It is attention and reflection which are required rather than research or exploration.

What, then, are the familiar facts which for Aquinas imply the existence of God? Mention of them can be found in the famous "five ways" of proving God's existence, which are outlined in the *Summa theologica* (Ia, 2, 3). In the first way Aquinas begins by saying that "it is certain, and it

[This selection is part of Chapter 3 of F. C. Copleston's *Aquinas*, published in the Pelican Philosophy Series in 1955. It is here reprinted with the kind permission of Father Copleston and Penguin Books, Ltd.]

is clear from sense-experience, that some things in this world are moved."
It must be remembered that he, like Aristotle, understands the term
"motion" in the broad sense of change, reduction from a state of potentiality
to one of act; he does not refer exclusively to local motion. In the second
way he starts with the remark that "we find in material things an order of
efficient causes." In other words, in our experience of things and of their
relations to one another we are aware of efficient causality. Thus while in
the first way he begins with the fact that some things are acted upon and
changed by other things, the second way is based upon the fact that some
things act upon other things, as efficient causes. In the third way he starts
by stating that "we find among things some which are capable of existing
or not existing, since we find that some things come into being and pass
away." In other words, we perceive that some things are corruptible or
perishable. In the fourth proof he observes that "we find in things that
some are more or less good and true and noble and so on (than others)."
Finally in the fifth way he says: "we see that some things which lack
knowledge, namely natural bodies, act for an end, which is clear from the
fact that they always or in most cases act in the same way, in order to
attain what is best."

There is, I think, little difficulty in accepting as empirical facts the
starting-points of the first three ways. For nobody really doubts that
some things are acted upon and changed or "moved," that some things act
on others, and that some things are perishable. Each of us is aware, for
example, that he is acted upon and changed, that he sometimes acts as an
efficient cause, and that he is perishable. Even if anyone were to cavil at
the assertion that he is aware that he himself was born and will die, he
knows very well that some other people were born and have died. But
the starting-points of the two final arguments may cause some difficulty.
The proposition that there are different grades of perfections in things
stands in need of a much more thorough analysis than Aquinas accords it
in his brief outline of the fourth way. For the schematic outlining of the
five proofs was designed, not to satisfy the critical minds of mature philosophers, but as introductory material for "novices" in the study of theology.
And in any case Aquinas could naturally take for granted in the thirteenth
century ideas which were familiar to his contemporaries and which had
not yet been subjected to the radical criticism to which they were later
subjected. At the same time there is not very much difficulty in understanding the sort of thing which was meant. We are all accustomed to think
and speak as though, for example, there were different degrees of intelligence and intellectual capacity. In order to estimate the different degrees
we need, it is true, standards or fixed points of reference; but, given these
points of reference, we are all accustomed to make statements which imply
different grades of perfections. And though these statements stand in need
of close analysis, they refer to something which falls within ordinary experience and finds expression in ordinary language. As for the fifth way, the
modern reader may find great difficulty in seeing what is meant if he con-

fines his attention to the relevant passage in the *Summa theologica*. But if he looks at the *Summa contra Gentiles* (1, 13) he will find Aquinas saying that we see things of different natures co-operating in the production and maintenance of a relatively stable order or system. When Aquinas says that we see purely material things acting for an end, he does not mean to say that they act in a manner analogous to that in which human beings consciously act for definite purposes. Indeed, the point of the argument is that they do not do so. He means that different kinds of things, like fire and water, the behaviour of which is determined by their several "forms," co-operate, not consciously but as a matter of fact, in such a way that there is a relatively stable order or system. And here again, though much more would need to be said in a full discussion of the matter, the basic idea is nothing particularly extraordinary nor is it contrary to our ordinary experience and expectations.

It is to be noted also that Aquinas speaks with considerable restraint: he avoids sweeping generalizations. Thus in the first argument he does not say that all material things are "moved" but that we see that some things in this world are moved or changed. In the third argument he does not state that all finite things are contingent but that we are aware that some things come into being and pass away. And in the fifth argument he does not say that there is an invariable world-order or system but that we see natural bodies acting always or in most cases in the same ways. The difficulty, therefore, which may be experienced in regard to Aquinas' proofs of God's existence concerns not so much the empirical facts or alleged empirical facts with which he starts as in seeing that these facts imply God's existence.

Perhaps a word should be said at once about this idea of "implication." As a matter of fact Aquinas does not use the word when talking about the five ways: he speaks of "proof" and of "demonstration." And by "demonstration" he means in this context what he calls *demonstratio quia* (*S.T., Ia, 2, 2*), namely a causal proof of God's existence, proceeding from the affirmation of some empirical fact, for example that there are things which change, to the affirmation of a transcendent cause. It is, indeed, his second proof which is strictly the causal argument, in the sense that it deals explicitly with the order of efficient causality; but in every proof the idea of ontological dependence on a transcendent cause appears in some form or other. Aquinas' conviction was that a full understanding of the empirical facts which are selected for consideration in the five ways involves seeing the dependence of these facts on a transcendent cause. The existence of things which change, for instance, is, in his opinion, not self-explanatory: it can be rendered intelligible only if seen as dependent on a transcendent cause, a cause, that is to say, which does not itself belong to the order of changing things.

This may suggest to the modern reader that Aquinas was concerned with causal explanation in the sense that he was concerned with framing an empirical hypothesis to explain certain facts. But he did not regard the proposition affirming God's existence as a causal hypothesis in the sense of being in principle revisable, as a hypothesis, that is to say, which might conceivably have to be revised in the light of fresh empirical data or which might be supplanted by a more economical hypothesis. This point can perhaps be seen most clearly in the case of his third argument, which is based on the fact that there are things which come into being and pass away. In Aquinas' opinion no fresh scientific knowledge about the physical constitution of such things could affect the validity of the argument. He did not look on a "demonstration" of God's existence as an empirical hypothesis in the sense in which the electronic theory, for example, is said to be an empirical hypothesis. It is, of course, open to anyone to say that in his own opinion cosmological arguments in favour of God's existence are in fact analogous to the empirical hypotheses of the sciences and that they have a predictive function; but it does not follow that this interpretation can legitimately be ascribed to Aquinas. We should not be misled by the illustrations which he sometimes offers from contemporary scientific theory. For these are mere illustrations to elucidate a point in terms easily understandable by his readers: they are not meant to indicate that the proofs of God's existence were for him empirical hypotheses in the modern sense of the term.

Does this mean, therefore, that Aquinas regarded the existence of God as being logically entailed by facts such as change or coming into being and passing away? He did not, of course, regard the proposition "there are things which come into being and pass away" as logically entailing the proposition "there is an absolutely necessary or independent being" in the sense that affirmation of the one proposition and denial of the other involves one in a verbal or formal linguistic contradiction. But he thought that metaphysical analysis of what it objectively means to be a thing which comes into being and passes away shows that such a thing must depend existentially on an absolutely necessary being. And he thought that metaphysical analysis of what it objectively means to be a changing thing shows that such a thing depends on a supreme unmoved mover. It follows that for Aquinas one is involved in a contradiction if one affirms the propositions "there are things which come into being and pass away" and "there are things which change" and at the same time denies the propositions "there is an absolutely necessary being" and "there is a supreme unmoved mover." But the contradiction can be made apparent only by means of metaphysical analysis. And the entailment in question is fundamentally an ontological or causal entailment. . . .

. . . After these general remarks I turn to Aquinas' five proofs of the existence of God. In the first proof he argues that "motion" or change means the reduction of a thing from a state of potentiality to one of act, and that a thing cannot be reduced from potentiality to act except under the influence of an agent already in act. In this sense "everything which is moved must be moved by another." He argues finally that in order to avoid an infinite regress in the chain of movers, the existence of a first unmoved mover must be admitted. "And all understand that this is God."

A statement like "all understand that this is God" or "all call this (being) God" occurs at the end of each proof, and I postpone consideration of it for the moment. As for the ruling out of an infinite regress, I shall explain what Aquinas means to reject after outlining the second proof, which is similar in structure to the first.

Whereas in the first proof Aquinas considers things as being acted upon, as being changed or "moved," in the second he considers them as active agents, as efficient causes. He argues that there is a hierarchy of efficient causes, a subordinate cause being dependent on the cause above it in the hierarchy. He then proceeds, after excluding the hypothesis of an infinite regress, to draw the conclusion that there must be a first efficient cause, "which all call God."

Now, it is obviously impossible to discuss these arguments profitably unless they are first understood. And misunderstanding of them is only too easy, since the terms and phrases used are either unfamiliar or liable to be taken in a sense other than the sense intended. In the first place it is essential to understand that in the first argument Aquinas supposes that movement or change is dependent on a "mover" acting here and now, and that in the second argument he supposes that there are efficient causes in the world which even in their causal activity are here and now dependent on the causal activity of other causes. That is why I have spoken of a "hierarchy" rather than of a "series." What he is thinking of can be illustrated in this way. A son is dependent on his father, in the sense that he would not have existed except for the causal activity of his father. But when the son acts for himself, he is not dependent here and now on his father. But he is dependent here and now on other factors. Without the activity of the air, for instance, he could not himself act, and the life-preserving activity of the air is itself dependent here and now on other factors, and they in turn on other factors. I do not say that this illustration is in all respects adequate for the purpose; but it at least illustrates the fact that when Aquinas talks about an "order" of efficient causes he is not thinking of a series stretching back into the past, but of a hierarchy of causes, in which a subordinate member is here and now dependent on the causal activity of a higher member. If I wind up my watch at night, it then proceeds to work without further interference on my part. But the activity of the pen tracing these words on the page is here and now dependent on the activity of my hand, which in turn is here and now dependent on other factors.

The meaning of the rejection of an infinite regress should now be clear. Aquinas is not rejecting the possibility of an infinite series as such. We have already seen that he did not think that anyone had ever succeeded in showing the impossibility of an infinite series of events stretching back into the past. Therefore he does not mean to rule out the possibility of an infinite series of causes and effects, in which a given member depended on the preceding member, say X on Y, but does not, once it

exists, depend here and now on the present causal activity of the preceding member. We have to imagine, not a lineal or horizontal series, so
to speak, but a vertical hierarchy, in which a lower member depends
here and now on the present causal activity of the member above it. It
is the latter type of series, if prolonged to infinity, which Aquinas rejects.
And he rejects it on the ground that unless there is a "first" member, a
mover which is not itself moved or a cause which does not itself depend
on the causal activity of a higher cause, it is not possible to explain the
'motion' or the causal activity of the lowest member. His point of view
is this. Suppress the first unmoved mover and there is no motion or
change here and now. Suppress the first efficient cause and there is no
causal activity here and now. If therefore we find that some things in the
world are changed, there must be a first unmoved mover. And if there
are efficient causes in the world, there must be a first efficient, and completely non-dependent, cause. The word "first" does not mean first in the
temporal order, but supreme or first in the ontological order.

A remark on the word "cause" is here in place. What precisely Aquinas
would have said to the David Humes either of the fourteenth century or
of the modern era it is obviously impossible to say. But it is clear that
he believed in real causal efficacy and real causal relations. He was aware,
of course, that causal efficacy is not the object of vision in the sense in
which patches of colours are objects of vision; but the human being, he
considered, is aware of real causal relations and if we understand "perception" as involving the co-operation of sense and intellect, we can be
said to "perceive" causality. And presumably he would have said that the
sufficiency of a phenomenalistic interpretation of causality for purposes
of physical science proves nothing against the validity of a metaphysical
notion of causality. It is obviously possible to dispute whether his analyses
of change or 'motion' and of efficient causality are valid or invalid and
whether there is such a thing as a hierarchy of causes. And our opinion
about the validity or invalidity of his arguments for the existence of God
will depend very largely on our answers to these questions. But mention
of the mathematical infinite series is irrelevant to a discussion of his
arguments. And it is this point which I have been trying to make clear.

In the third proof Aquinas starts from the fact that some things come
into being and perish, and he concludes from this that it possible for
them to exist or not to exist: they do not exist "necessarily." He then
argues that it is impossible for things which are of this kind to exist always; for "that which is capable of not existing, at some time does not
exist." If all things were of this kind, at some time there would be nothing. Aquinas is clearly supposing for the sake of argument the hypothesis
of infinite time, and his proof is designed to cover this hypothesis. He
does not say that infinite time is impossible: what he says is that if time
is infinite and if all things are capable of not existing, this potentiality
would inevitably be fulfilled in infinite time. There would then be nothing. And if there had ever been nothing, nothing would now exist. For

no thing can bring itself into existence. But it is clear as a matter of fact that there are things. Therefore it can never have been true to say that there was literally no thing. Therefore it is impossible that all things should be capable of existing or not existing. There must, then, be some necessary being. But perhaps it is necessary in the sense that it must exist if something else exists; that is to say, its necessity may be hypothetical. We cannot, however, proceed to infinity in the series or hierarchy of necessary beings. If we do so, we do not explain the presence here and now of beings capable of existing or not existing. Therefore we must affirm the existence of a being which is absolutely necessary (*per se necessarium*) and completely independent. "And all call this being *God*."

This argument may appear to be quite unnecessarily complicated and obscure. But it has to be seen in its historical context. As already mentioned, Aquinas designed his argument in such a way as to be independent of the question whether or not the world existed from eternity. He wanted to show that on either hypothesis there must be a necessary being. As for the introduction of hypothetical necessary beings, he wanted to show that even if there are such beings, perhaps within the universe, which are not corruptible in the sense in which a flower is corruptible, there must still be an absolutely independent being. Finally, in regard to terminology, Aquinas uses the common medieval expression "necessary being." He does not actually use the term "contingent being" in the argument and talks instead about "possible" beings; but it comes to the same thing. And though the words "contingent" and "necessary" are now applied to propositions rather than to beings, I have retained Aquinas' mode of speaking. Whether one accepts the argument or not, I do not think that there is any insuperable difficulty in understanding the line of thought.

The fourth argument is admittedly difficult to grasp. Aquinas argues that there are degrees of perfections in things. Different kinds of finite things possess different perfections in diverse limited degrees. He then argues not only that if there are different degrees of a perfection like goodness there is a supreme good to which other good things approximate but also that all limited degrees of goodness are caused by the supreme good. And since goodness is a convertible term with being, a thing being good in so far as it has being, the supreme good is the supreme being and the cause of being in all other things. "Therefore there is something which is the cause of the being and goodness and of every perfection in all other things; and this we call *God*."

Aquinas refers to some remarks of Aristotle in the *Metaphysics;* but this argument puts one in mind at once of Plato's *Symposium* and *Republic*. And the Platonic doctrine of participation seems to be involved. Aquinas was not immediately acquainted with either work, but the Platonic line of thought was familiar to him from other writers. And it has not disappeared from philosophy. Indeed, some of those theists who reject or doubt the validity of the "cosmological" arguments seem to feel a marked attraction for some variety of the fourth way, arguing that in the recognition of objective values we implicitly recognize God as the supreme value. But if the line of thought represented by the fourth way is to mean anything to the average modern reader, it has to be presented in a rather different manner from that in which it is expressed by Aquinas, who was able to assume in his readers ideas and points of view which can no longer be presupposed.

Finally, the fifth proof, if we take its statement in the *Summa theologica* together with that in the *Summa contra Gentiles,* can be expressed more or less as follows. The activity and behaviour of each thing is determined by its form. But we observe material things of very different types co-operating in such a way as to produce and maintain a relatively stable world-order or system. They achieve an "end," the production and maintenance of a cosmic order. But non-intelligent material things certainly do not co-operate consciously in view of a purpose. If it is said that they co-operate in the realization of an end or purpose, this does not mean that they intend the realization of this order in a manner analogous to that in which a man can act consciously with a view to the achievement of a purpose. Nor, when Aquinas talks about operating "for an end" in this connexion, is he thinking of the utility of certain things to the human race. He is not saying, for example, that grass grows to feed the sheep and that sheep exist in order that human beings should have food and clothing. It is of the unconscious co-operation of different kinds of material things in the production and maintenance of a relatively stable cosmic system that he is thinking, not of the benefits accruing to us from our use of certain objects. And his argument is that this co-operation on the part of heterogeneous material things clearly points to the existence of an extrinsic intelligent author of this co-operation, who operates with an end in view. If Aquinas had lived in the days of the evolutionary hypothesis, he would doubtless have argued that this hypothesis supports rather than invalidates the conclusion of the argument.

35 The Watch
and the Human Eye

William Paley

A Watch Implies a Watchmaker

IN CROSSING A HEATH, SUPPOSE I pitched my foot against a *stone,* and were asked how the stone came to be there; I might possibly answer, that, for anything I knew to the contrary, it had lain there forever: nor would it perhaps be very easy to show the absurdity of this answer. But suppose I had found a *watch* upon the ground, and it should be inquired how the watch happened to be in that place: I should hardly think of the answer which I had before given, that, for anything I knew, the watch might have always been there. Yet why should not this answer serve for the watch as well as for the stone? Why is it not as admissible in the second case, as in the first? For this reason, and for no other, viz. that, when we come to inspect the watch, we perceive (what we could not discover in the stone) that its several parts are framed and put together for a purpose, e.g., that they are so formed and adjusted as to produce motion, and that motion so regulated as to point out the hour of the day; that if the different parts had been differently shaped from what they are, of a different size from what they are, or placed after any other manner, or in any other order, than that in which they are placed, either no motion at all would have been carried on in the machine, or none which would have answered the use that is now served by it. . . . This mechanism being observed (it requires indeed an examination of the instrument, and perhaps some previous knowledge of the subject, to perceive and understand it; but being once, as we have said, observed and understood), the inference, we

[This selection comprises part of Chapters I–VI of Paley's *Evidences of the Existence and Attributes of the Deity,* a book first published in 1802.]

think, is inevitable; that the watch must have had a maker; that there must have existed, at sometime, and at some place or other, an artificer or artificers, who formed it for the purpose which we find it actually to answer; who comprehended its construction, and designed its use.

Nor would it, I apprehend, weaken the conclusion, that we had never seen a watch made, that we had never known an artist capable of making one; that we were altogether incapable of executing such a piece of workmanship ourselves, or of understanding in what manner it was performed; all this being no more than what is true of some exquisite remains of ancient art, of some lost arts, and, to the generality of mankind, of the more curious productions of modern manufacture. Does one man in a million know how oval frames are turned? Ignorance of this kind exalts our opinion of the artist's skill, if he be unseen and unknown, but raises no doubt in our minds of the existence and agency of such an artist, at some former time, and in some place or other. Nor can I perceive that it varies at all the inference, whether the question arise concerning a human agent, or concerning an agent of a different species, or an agent possessing, in some respects, a different nature.

Neither, secondly, would it invalidate our conclusion, that the watch sometimes went wrong, or that it seldom went exactly right. The purpose of the machinery, the design and the designer, might be evident, and in the case supposed would be evident, in whatever way we accounted for the irregularity of the movement, or whether we could account for it or not. It is not necessary that a machine be perfect, in order to show with what design it was made: still less necessary, where the only question is, whether it were made with any design at all.

Nor, thirdly, would it bring any uncertainty into the argument, if there were a few parts of the watch, concerning which we could not discover, or had not yet discovered, in what manner they conduced to the general effect; or even some parts, concerning which we could not ascertain whether they conduced to that effect in any manner whatever. For, as to the first branch of the case; if by the loss, or disorder, or decay of the parts in question, the movement of the watch were found in fact to be stopped, or disturbed, or retarded, no doubt would remain in our minds as to the utility or intention of these parts, although we should be unable to investigate the manner according to which, or the connexion by which, the ultimate effect depended upon their action or assistance; and the more complex is the machine, the more likely is this obscurity to arise. Then, as to the second thing supposed, namely, that there were parts which might be spared, without prejudice to the movement of the watch, and that we had proved this by experiment—these superfluous parts, even if we were completely assured that they were such, would not vacate the reasoning which we had instituted concerning other parts. The indication of contrivance remained, with respect to them, nearly as it was before.

Nor, fourthly, would any man in his senses think the existence of the watch, with its various machinery, accounted for, by being told that it was one out of possible combinations of material forms; that whatever he had found in the place where he found the watch, must have contained some internal configuration or other; and that this configuration might be the structure now exhibited, viz. of the works of a watch, as well as a different structure.

Nor, fifthly, would it yield to his inquiry more satisfaction to be answered, that there existed in things a principle of order, which had disposed the parts of the watch into their present form and situation. He never knew a watch made by the principle of order; nor can he even form to himself an idea of what is meant by a principle of order distinct from the intelligence of the watchmaker.

Sixthly, he would be surprised to hear that the mechanism of the watch was no proof of contrivance, only a motive to induce the mind to think so. . . .

Neither, lastly, would our observer be driven out of his conclusion, or from his confidence in its truth, by being told that he knew nothing at all about the matter. He knows enough for his argument. He knows the utility of the end: he knows the subserviency and adaptation of the means to the end. These points being known, his ignorance of other points, affect not the certainty of his reasoning. The consciousness of knowing little need not beget a distrust of that which he does know.

Even a "Self-Reproducing" Watch Implies a Watchmaker

Suppose, in the next place, that the person who found the watch, should, after sometime, discover, that, in addition to all the properties which he had hitherto observed in it, it possessed the unexpected property of producing, in the course of its movement, another watch like itself (the thing is conceivable), that it contained within it a mechanism, a system of parts, a mould for instance, or a complex adjustment of lathes, files, and other tools, evidently and separately calculated for this purpose; let us inquire, what effect ought such a discovery to have upon his former conclusion.

The first effect would be to increase his admiration of the contrivance, and his conviction of the consummate skill of the contriver. Whether he regarded the object of the contrivance, the distinct apparatus, the intricate, yet in many parts intelligible mechanism, by which it was carried on, he would perceive in this new observation, nothing but an additional reason for doing what he had already done,—for referring the construction of the watch to design, and to supreme art. If that construction *without* this property, or which is the same thing, before this property had been noticed, proved intention and art to have been employed about it, still more strong would the proof appear, when he came to the knowledge of this farther property, the crown and perfection of all the rest.

He would reflect, that though the watch before him were, *in some sense,* the maker of the watch which was fabricated in the course of its movements, yet it was in a very different sense from that in which a carpenter, for instance, is the maker of a chair; the author of its contrivance, the cause of the relation of its parts to their use. With respect to these, the first watch was no cause at all to the second: in no such sense as this was it the author of the constitution and order, either of the parts which the new watch contained, or of the parts by the aid and instrumentality of which it was produced. We might possibly say, but with great latitude of expression, that a stream of water ground corn; but no latitude of expression would allow us to say, no stretch of conjecture could lead us to think, that the stream of water built the mill, though it were too ancient for us to know who the builder was. What the stream of water does in the affair, is neither more nor less than this; by the application of an unintelligent impulse to a mechanism previously arranged, arranged independently of it, and arranged by intelligence, an effect is produced, viz. the corn is ground. But the effect results from the arrangement. The force of the stream cannot be said to be the cause or author of the effect, still less of the arrangement. Understanding and plan in the formation of the mill were not the less necessary, for any share which the water has in grinding the corn; yet is this share the same as that which the watch would have contributed to the production of the new watch, upon the supposition assumed in the last section. Therefore:

Though it be now no longer probable, that the individual watch which our observer had found was made immediately by the hand of an artificer, yet doth not this alteration in anywise affect the inference, that an artificer had been originally employed and concerned in the production. The argument from design remains as it was. Marks of design and contrivance are no more accounted for now than they were before. In the same thing, we may ask for the cause of different properties. We may ask for the cause of the color of a body, of its hardness, of its heat; and these causes may be all different. We are now asking for the cause of that subserviency to a case, that relation to an end, which we have remarked in the watch before us. No answer is given to this question by telling us that a preceding watch produced it. There cannot be design without a designer; contrivance, without a contriver; order, without choice; arrangement, without anything capable of arranging; subserviency and relation to a purpose, without that which could intend a purpose; means suitable to an end, and executing their office in accomplishing that end, without the end ever having been contemplated, or the means accommodated to it. Arrangement, disposition of parts, subserviency of means to an end, relation of instruments to a use, imply the presence of intelligence and mind. No one, therefore, can rationally believe, that the insensible, inanimate watch, from which the watch before us issued, was the proper cause of the mechanism we so much admire in it;—could be truly said to have constructed the instrument, disposed its parts, assigned their office, determined their order, action, and mutual dependency, combined their several motions into one result, and that also a result connected with the utilities of other beings. All these properties, therefore, are as much unaccounted for as they were before.

Impossibility of an Infinite Regress

Nor is anything gained by running the difficulty farther back, i.e., by supposing the watch before us to have been produced from another watch, that from a former, and so on indefinitely. Our going back ever so far brings us no nearer to the last degree of satisfaction upon the subject. Contrivance is still unaccounted for. We still want a contriver. A designing mind is neither supplied by this supposition, nor dispensed with. If the difficulty were diminished the farther we went back, by going back indefinitely we might exhaust it. And this is the only case to which this sort of reasoning applies. Where there is a tendency, or, as we increase the number of terms, a continual approach towards a limit, *there,* by supposing the number of terms to be what is called infinite, we may conceive the limit to be attained: but where there is no such tendency, or approach, nothing is effected by lengthening the series. There is no difference, as to the point in question (whatever there may be as to many points), between one series and another; between a series which is finite, and a series which is infinite. A chain, composed of an infinite number of links, can no more support itself, than a chain composed of a finite number of links. And of this we are assured (though we never *can* have tried the experiment), because, by increasing the number of links, from ten, for instance, to a hundred, from a hundred to a thousand, etc., we make not the smallest approach, we observe not the smallest tendency, towards self-support. There is no difference in this respect (yet there may be a great difference in several respects) between a chain of a greater or less length, between one chain and another, between one that is finite and one that is infinite. This very much resembles the case before us. The machine which we are inspecting demonstrates, by its construction, contrivance and design. Contrivance must have had a contriver; design, a designer; whether the machine immediately proceeded from another machine or not. That circumstance alters not the case. That other machine may, in like manner, have proceeded from a former machine: nor does that alter the case; contrivance must have had a contriver. That former one from one preceding it: no alteration still; a contriver is still necessary. No tendency is perceived, no approach towards a diminution of this necessity. It is the same with any and every succession of these machines; a succession of ten, of a hundred, of a thousand; with one series as with another; a series which is finite, as with a series which is infinite. In whatever other respects they may differ, in this they do not. In all, equally, contrivance and design are unaccounted for.

The question is not simply, How came the first watch into existence? which question, it may be pretended, is done away by supposing the series of watches thus produced from one another to have been infinite, and consequently to have had no such *first,* for which it was necessary to provide a cause. This, perhaps, would have been nearly the state of the question, if nothing had been before us but an unorganized, un-mechanized substance, without mark or indication of contrivance. It might be difficult to show that such substance could not have existed from eternity, either in succession (if it were possible, which I think it is not, for unorganized bodies to spring from one another) or by individual per-petuity. But that is not the question now. To suppose it to be so, is to suppose that it made no difference whether we had found a watch or a stone. As it is, the metaphysics of that question have no place; for, in the watch which we are examining, are seen contrivance, design; an end, a purpose; means for the end, adaptation to the purpose. And the question which irresistibly presses upon our thoughts, is, whence this contrivance and design? The thing required is the intending mind, the adapting hand, the intelligence by which the hand was directed. This question, this de-mand, is not shaken off, by increasing a number or succession of substances, destitute of these properties; nor the more, by increasing that number to infinity. If it be said, that upon the supposition of one watch being produced from another in the course of that other's movements, and by means of the mechanism within it, we have a cause for the watch in my hand, viz. the watch from which it proceeded: I deny, that for the design, the contrivance, the suitableness of means to an end, the adaptation of instruments to a use (all means which we discover in a watch), we have any cause whatever. It is in vain, therefore, to assign a series of such causes, or to allege that a series may be carried back to infinity; for I do not admit that we have yet any cause at all of the phenomena, still less any series of causes either finite or infinite. Here is contrivance, but no contriver: proofs of design, but no designer.

Our observer would farther also reflect, that the maker of the watch before him, was, in truth and reality, the maker of every watch produced from it; there being no difference (except that the latter manifests a more exquisite skill) between the making of another watch with his own hands, by the mediation of files, lathes, chisels, etc., and the disposing, fixing, and inserting of these instruments, or of others equivalent to them, in the body of the watch already made, in such a manner as to form a new watch in the course of the movements which he had given to the old one. It is only working by one set of tools instead of another.

The conclusion which the *first* examination of the watch, of its works, construction, and movement, suggested, was, that it must have had, for the cause and author of that construction, an artificer, who understood its mechanism, and designed its use. This conclusion is invincible. A *second* examination presents us with a new discovery. The watch is found, in the course of its movement, to produce another watch, similar to itself: and not only so, but we perceive in it a system or organization, separately calculated for that purpose. What effect would this discovery have or ought it to have, upon our former inference? What, as hath already been said, but to increase, beyond measure, our admiration of the skill which had been employed in the formation of such a machine! Or shall it, instead of this, all at once turn us round to an opposite conclusion, viz. that no art or skill whatever has been concerned in the business, although all other evidences of art and skill remain as they were, and this last and supreme piece of art be now added to the rest? Can this be maintained without absurdity? Yet this is atheism.

This is atheism: for every indication of contrivance, every manifestation of design, which existed in the watch, exists in the works of nature; with the difference, on the side of nature, of being greater and more, and that in a degree which exceeds all computation. I mean, that the contrivances of nature surpass the contrivances of art, in the complexity, subtlety, and curiosity of the mechanism; and still more, if possible, do they go beyond them in number and variety: yet, in a multitude of cases, are not less evidently mechanical, not less evidently contrivances, not less evidently accommodated to their end, or suited to their office, than are the most perfect productions of human ingenuity.

The Eye and the Telescope

I know no better method of introducing so large a subject, than that of comparing a single thing with a single thing; an eye, for example, with a telescope. As far as the examination of the instrument goes, there is precisely the same proof that the eye was made for vision, as there is that the telescope was made for assisting it. They are made upon the same principles; both being adjusted to the laws by which the transmission and reflection of rays of light are regulated. I speak not of the origin of the laws themselves; but such laws being fixed, the construction in both cases, is adapted to them. For instance; these laws require, in order to produce the same effect, that the rays of light, in passing from water into the eye, should be refracted by a more convex surface than when it passes out of air into the eye. Accordingly we find, that the eye of a fish, in that part of it called the crystalline lens, is much rounder than the eye of terrestrial animals. What plainer manifestation of design can there be than this difference? What could a mathematical instrument-maker have done more, to show his knowledge of his principle, his application of that knowledge, his suiting of his means to his end; I will not say to display the compass or excellence of his skill and art, for in these all comparison is indecorous, but to testify counsel, choice, consideration, purpose?

To some it may appear a difference sufficient to destroy all similitude between the eye and the telescope, that the one is a perceiving organ, the other an unperceiving instrument. The fact is, that they are both instruments. And as to the mechanism, at least as to mechanism being employed, and even as to the kind of it, this circumstance varies not the analogy at all. . . . The lenses of the telescope, and the humours of the eye, bear a complete resemblance to one another, in their figure, their position, and in their power over the rays of light, viz. in bringing each pencil to a point at the right distance from the lens; namely in the eye, at the exact place where the membrane is spread to receive it. How is it possible, under circumstances of such close affinity, and under the operation of equal evidence, to exclude contrivance from the one, yet to acknowledge the proof of contrivance having been employed, as the plainest and clearest of all propositions, in the other?

The resemblance between the two cases is still more accurate, and obtains in more points than we have yet represented, or than we are, on the first view of the subject, aware of. In dioptric telescopes there is an imperfection of this nature. Pencils of light, in passing through glass lenses, are separated into different colors, thereby tinging the object, especially the edges of it, as if it were viewed through a prism. To correct this inconvenience had been long a desideratum in the art. At last it came into the mind of a sagacious optician, to inquire how this matter was managed in the eye; in which there was exactly the same difficulty to contend with as in the telescope. His observation taught him, that, in the eye, the evil was cured by combining lenses composed of different substances, i.e. of substances which possessed different refracting powers. Our artist borrowed thence his hint; and produced a correction of the defect by imitating, in glasses made from different materials, the effects of the different humours through which the rays of light pass before they reach the bottom of the eye. Could this be in the eye without purpose, which suggested to the optician the only effectual means of attaining that purpose?

But farther; there are other points, not so much perhaps of strict resemblance between the two, as of superiority of the eye over the telescope, which being found in the laws that regulate both, may furnish topics of fair and just comparison. . . .

Further Evidence of Design in the Eye

In considering vision as achieved by the means of an image formed at the bottom of the eye, we can never reflect without wonder upon the smallness, yet correctness, of the picture, the subtility of the touch, the fineness of the lines. A landscape of five or six square leagues is brought into a space of half an inch diameter; yet the multitude of objects which it contains, are all preserved; are all discriminated in their magnitudes, positions, figures, colors. The prospect from Hampstead-hill is compressed into the compass of a sixpence, yet circumstantially represented. A stage-coach, travelling at its ordinary speed for half an hour, passes, in the eye, only over one-twelfth of an inch, yet is this change of place in the image distinctly perceived throughout its whole progress; for it is only by means of that perception that the motion of the coach itself is made sensible to the eye. If anything can abate our admiration of the smallness of the visual tablet compared with the extent of vision, it is a reflection, which the view of nature leads us, every hour, to make, viz. that in the hands of the Creator, great and little are nothing.

Sturmius held, that the examination of the eye was a cure for atheism. Besides that conformity to optical principles which its internal constitution displays, and which alone amounts to a manifestation of intelligence having been exerted in the structure; besides this, which forms no doubt, the leading character of the organ, there is to be seen, in everything belonging to it and about it, an extraordinary degree of care, and anxiety for its preservation, due, if we may so speak, to its value and its tenderness. It is lodged in a strong, deep, bony socket, composed by the junction of seven different bones, hollowed out at their edges. In some few species, as that of the coatimondi, the orbit is not bony throughout; but whenever this is the case, the upper, which is the deficient part, is supplied by a cartilaginous ligament; a substitution which shows the same care. Within this socket it is embedded in fat, of all animal substances the best adapted both to its repose and motion. It is sheltered by the eyebrows; an arch of hair, which like a thatched penthouse, prevents the sweat and moisture of the forehead from running down into it.

But it is still better protected by its lid. Of the superficial parts of the animal frame, I know none which, in its office and structure, is more deserving of attention than the eyelid. It defends the eye; it wipes it; it closes it in sleep. Are there, in any work of art whatever, purposes more evident than those which this organ fulfills? or an apparatus for executing those purposes more intelligible, more appropriate, or more mechanical? If it be overlooked by the observer of nature, it can only be because it is obvious and familiar. This is a tendency to be guarded against. We pass by the plainest instances, whilst we are exploring those which are rare and curious; by which conduct of the understanding, we sometimes neglect the strongest observations, being taken up with others, which though more recondite and scientific, are, as solid arguments, entitled to much less consideration.

In order to keep the eye moist and clean (which qualities are necessary to its brightness and its use), a wash is constantly supplied by a secretion for the purpose; and the superfluous brine is conveyed to the nose through a perforation in the bone as large as a goose-quill. When once the fluid has entered the nose, it spreads itself upon the inside of the nostril, and is evaporated by the current of warm air, which, in the course of respiration, is continually passing over it. Can any pipe or outlet for carrying off the waste liquor from a dye-house or a distillery, be more mechanical than this is? It is easily perceived, that the eye must want moisture: but could the want of the eye generate the gland which produces the tear, or bore the hole by which it is discharged,—a hole through a bone? . . .

Some Objections Answered

Every observation which was made concerning the watch, may be repeated with strict propriety concerning the eye; concerning animals; concerning plants; concerning, indeed, all the organized parts of the works of nature:

1. Imperfections in the Mechanism

When we are inquiring simply after the existence of an intelligent Creator, imperfection, inaccuracy, liability to disorder, occasional irregularities, may subsist in a considerable degree, without inducing any doubt into the question; just as a watch may frequently go wrong, seldom perhaps exactly right, may be faulty in some parts, defective in some, without the smallest ground of suspicion from thence arising that it was not a watch; not made; or not made for the purpose ascribed to it. When faults are pointed out, and when a question is started concerning the skill of the artist, or the dexterity with which the work is executed, then, indeed, in order to defend these qualities from accusation, we must be able, either to expose some intractableness and imperfection in the materials, or point out some invincible difficulty in the execution, into which imperfection and difficulty the matter of complaint may be resolved; or if we cannot do this, we must adduce such specimens of consummate art and contrivance, proceeding from the same hand, as may convince the inquirer of the existence, in the case before him, of impediments like those which we have mentioned, although, what from the nature of the case is very likely to happen, they be unknown and unperceived by him. This we must do in order to vindicate the artist's skill, or, at least, the perfection of it; as we must also judge of his intention, and of the provision employed in fulfilling that intention, not from an instance in which they fail, but from the great plurality of instances in which they succeed. But, after all, these are different questions from the question of the artist's existence; or, which is the same, whether the thing before us be a work of art or not: and the question ought always to be kept separate in the mind. So likewise it is in the works of nature. Irregularities and imperfections are of little or no weight in the consideration, when that consideration relates simply to the existence of a Creator. When the argument respects his attributes, they are of weight; but are then to be taken in conjunction (the attention is not to rest upon them, but they are to be taken in conjunction) with the unexceptionable evidences which we possess, of skill, power, and benevolence, displayed in other instances; which evidences may, in strength, number, and variety, be such, and may so overpower apparent blemishes, as to induce us, upon the most reasonable ground, to believe, that these last ought to be referred to some cause, though we be ignorant of it, other than defect of knowledge or of benevolence in the author.

2. Apparently Useless Parts

There may be also parts of plants and animals, as there were supposed to be of the watch, of which, in some instances, the operation, in others, the use, is unknown. These form different causes; for the operation may be unknown, yet the use be certain. Thus it is with the lungs of animals. It does not, I think, appear, that we are acquainted with the action of the air upon the blood, or in what manner that action is communicated by the lungs; yet we find that a very short suspension of their office destroys the life of the animal. In this case, therefore, we may be said to know the use, nay we experience the necessity, of the organ, though we are ignorant of its operation. Nearly the same thing may be observed of what is called the lymphatic system. We suffer grievous inconveniences from its disorder, without being informed of the office which it sustains in the economy of our bodies. There may possibly also be some few examples of the second class, in which not only the operation is unknown, but in which experiments may seem to prove that the part is not necessary; or may leave a doubt, how far it is even useful to the plant or animal in which it is found. This is said to be the case with the spleen; which has been extracted from dogs, without any sensible injury to their vital function. Instances of the former kind, namely, in which we cannot explain the operation, may be numerous; for they will be so in proportion to our ignorance. They will be more or fewer to different persons, and in different stages of science. Every improvement of knowledge diminishes their number. There is hardly, perhaps, a year passes that does not, in the works of nature, bring some operation, or some mode of operation, to light, which was before undiscovered,—probably unsuspected. Instances of the second kind, namely, where the part appears to be totally useless, I believe to be extremely rare; compared with the number of those of which the use is evident, they are beneath any assignable proportion; and, perhaps, have never been submitted to a trial and examination sufficiently accurate, long enough continued, or often enough repeated. No accounts which I have seen are satisfactory. The mutilated animal may live and grow fat, (as was the case of the dog deprived of its spleen,) yet may be defective in some other of its functions; which, whether they can all, or in what degree of vigor and perfection, be performed, or how long preserved, without the extirpated organ, does not seem to be ascertained by experiment. But to this case, even were it fully made out, may be applied the consideration which we suggested concerning the watch, viz. that these superfluous parts do not negative the reasoning which we instituted concerning those parts which are useful, and of which we know the use. The indication of contrivance, with respect to them, remains as it was before.

3. The Possible Role of Chance

One atheistic way of replying to our observations upon the works of nature, and to the proofs of a Deity which we think that we perceive in them, is to tell us, that all which we see must necessarily have had some form, and that it might as well be its present form as any other. Let us now apply this answer to the eye, as we did before to the watch. Something or other must have occupied that place in the animal's head; must have filled up, we will say, that socket: we will say also, that it must have been of that sort of substance which we call animal substance, as flesh, bone, membrane, cartilage, etc. But that it should have been an eye, knowing as we do, what an eye comprehends—viz. that it should have consisted, first, of a series of transparent lenses (very different, by the by, even in their substance, from the opaque materials of which the rest of the body is, in general at least, composed; and with which the whole of its surface, this single portion of it excepted, is covered); secondly, of a black cloth or canvas (the only membrane of the body which is black) spread out behind these lenses, so as to receive the image formed by pencils of light transmitted through them; and placed at the precise geometrical distance at which, and at which alone, a distinct image could be formed, namely, at the concourse of the refracted rays; thirdly, of a large nerve communicating between this membrane and the brain; without which, the action of light upon the membrane; however modified by the organ, would be lost to the purposes of sensation: that this fortunate conformation of parts should have been the lot, not of one individual out of many thousand individuals, like the great prize in a lottery, or like some singularity in nature, but the happy chance of a whole species; nor of one species out of many thousand species, with which we are acquainted, but of by far the greatest number of all that exist; and that under varieties, not casual or capricious, but bearing marks of being suited to their respective exigencies—that all this should have taken place, merely because something must have occupied those points in every animal's forehead—or, that all this should be thought to be accounted for, by the short answer, "that whatever was there, must have

had some form or other," is too absurd to be made more so by any aug-
mentation. We are not contented with this answer; we find no satisfaction
in it, by way of accounting for appearances of organization far short of
those of the eye, such as we observe in fossil shells, petrified bones, or
other substances which bear the vestiges of animal or vegetable recre-
ments, but which, either in respect of utility, or of the situation in which
they are discovered, may seem accidental enough. It is no way of accounting even for these things, to say that the stone, for instance, which is
shown to us, (supposing the question to be concerning a petrification,)
must have contained some internal conformation or other. Nor does it
mend the answer to add, with respect to the singularity of the conformation, that, after the event, it is no longer to be computed what the chances
were against it. This is always to be computed, when the question is,
whether a useful or imitative conformation be the produce of chance,
or not: I desire no greater certainty in reasoning, than that by which
chance is excluded from the present disposition of the natural world.
Universal experience is against it. What does chance ever do for us? In
the human body, for instance, chance, i.e., the operation of causes without design, may produce a wen, a wart, a mole, a pimple, but never an
eye. Amongst inanimate substances, a clod, a pebble, a liquid drop might
be; but never was a watch, a telescope, an organized body of any kind;
answering a valuable purpose by a complicated mechanism, the effect
of chance. In no assignable instance hath such a thing existed without
intention somewhere.

4. The Theory of the Elimination of the Unfit

There is another answer, which has the same effect as the resolving
of things into chance; which answer would persuade us to believe, that
the eye, the animal to which it belongs, every other animal, every plant,
indeed every organized body which we see, are only so many out of the
possible varieties and combinations of being which the lapse of infinite
ages has brought into existence: that the present world is the relic of that
variety; millions of other bodily forms and other species having perished,
being by the defect of their constitutions incapable of preservation, or of
continuance by generation. Now there is no foundation whatever for this
conjecture in anything which we observe in the works of nature; no such
experiments are going on at present; no such energy operates, as that
which is here supposed, and which should be constantly pushing into
existence new varieties of beings: Nor are there any appearances to support
an opinion, that every possible combination of vegetable or animal structure
has formerly been tried. Multitudes of conformations, both of vegetables and
animals, may be conceived capable of existence and succession, which yet
do not exist. Perhaps almost as many forms of plants might have been

found in the fields, as figures of plants can be delineated upon paper. A countless variety of animals might have existed, which do not exist. Upon the supposition here stated, we should see unicorns and mermaids, sylphs and centaurs, the fancies of painters, and the fables of poets, realized by examples. Or, if it be alleged that these may transgress the limits of possible life and propagation, we might, at least, have nations of human beings without nails upon their fingers, with more or fewer fingers and toes than ten; some with one eye, others with one ear, with one nostril, or without the sense of smelling at all. All these, and a thousand other imaginable varieties, might live and propagate. We may modify any one species many different ways, all consistent with life, and with the actions necessary to preservation, although affording different degrees of conveniency and enjoyment to the animal. And if we carry these modifications through the different species which are known to subsist, their number would be incalculable. No reason can be given why, if these deperdits ever existed, they have now disappeared. Yet, if all possible existences have been tried, they must have formed part of the catalogues.

But, moreover, the division of organized substances into animals and vegetables, and the distribution and sub-distribution of each into genera and species, which distribution is not an arbitrary act of the mind, but founded in the order which prevails in external nature, appear to me to contradict the supposition of the present world being the remains of an indefinite variety of existences; of a variety which rejects all plan. The hypothesis teaches, that every possible variety of being hath, at one time or other, found its way into existence (by what cause or in what manner is not said), and that those which were badly formed, perished; but how or why those which survived should be cast, as we see that plants and animals are cast, into regular classes, the hypothesis does not explain; or rather, the hypothesis is inconsistent with this phenomenon.

The hypothesis, indeed, is hardly deserving of the consideration which we have given to it. What should we think of a man who, because we had never ourselves seen watches, telescopes, stocking mills, steam engines, etc., made, knew not how they were made, or by whom,—would have us believe that these machines, instead of deriving their curious structures from the thought and design of their inventors and contrivers, in truth derive them from no other origin than this, viz. that a mass of metals and other materials having run when melted into all possible figures, and combined themselves in all possible forms and shapes, and proportions, these things which we see, are what were left from the accident, as best worth preserving: and, as such, are become the remaining stock of a magazine, which, at one time or other, has by this means, contained every mechanism, useful and useless, convenient and inconvenient, into which such like materials could be thrown? I cannot distinguish the hypothesis as applied to the works of nature, from this solution, which no one would accept as applied to a collection of machines. . . .

Our Ignorance of Many Points Need Not
Suspend Our Assurance of a Few

The confidence which we place in our observations upon the works of nature, in the marks which we discover of contrivance, choice, and design, and in our reasoning upon the proofs afforded us, ought not to be shaken, as it is sometimes attempted to be done, by bringing forward to our view our own ignorance, or rather the general imperfection of our knowledge of nature. Nor, in many cases, ought this consideration to affect us, even when it respects some parts of the subject immediately under our notice. True fortitude of understanding consists in not suffering what we know to be disturbed by what we do not know. If we perceive a useful end, and means adapted to that end, we perceive enough for our conclusion. If these things be clear, no matter what is obscure. The argument is finished. For instance; if the utility of vision to the animal which enjoys it, and the adaptation of the eye to this office, be evident and certain (and I can mention nothing which is more so), ought it to prejudice the inference which we draw from these premises, that we cannot explain the use of the spleen? Nay, more; if there be parts of the eye, viz. the cornea, the crystalline, the retina, in their substance, figure, and position, manifestly suited to the formation of an image by the refraction of rays of light, at least, as manifestly as the glasses and tubes of a dioptric telescope are suited to that purpose; it concerns not the proof which these afford of design, and of a designer, that there may perhaps be other parts, certain muscles, for instance, or nerves in the same eye, of the agency or effect of which we can give no account; any more than we should be inclined to doubt, or ought to doubt, about the construction of a telescope, viz. for what purpose it was constructed, or whether it were constructed at all, because there belonged to it certain screws and pins, the use or action of which we did not comprehend. I take it to be a general way of infusing doubts and scruples into the mind to recur to its own ignorance, its own imbecility; to tell us that upon these subjects we know little; that little imperfectly; or rather, that we know nothing properly about the matter. These suggestions so fall in with our consciousness, as sometimes to produce a general distrust of our faculties and our conclusions. But this is an unfounded jealousy. The uncertainty of one thing, does not necessarily affect the certainty of another thing. Our ignorance of many points need not suspend our assurance of a few. Before we yield, in any particular instance, to the skepticism which this sort of insinuation would induce, we ought accurately to ascertain, whether our ignorance or doubt concern those precise points upon which our conclusion rests. Other points are nothing. Our ignorance of other points may be of no consequence to these, though they be points, in various respects, of great importance. A just reasoner removes from his consideration, not only what he knows, but what he does not know, touching matters not strictly connected with his argument, i.e., not forming the very steps of his deduction; beyond these, his knowledge and his ignorance are alike relative.

Were there no example in the world of contrivance except that of the eye, it would be alone sufficient to suppose the conclusion which we draw from it, as to the necessity of an intelligent Creator. It could never be got rid of because it could not be accounted for by any other supposition, which did not contradict all the principles we possess of knowledge: the principles, according to which things do, as often as they can be brought to the test of experience, turn out to be true or false. . . . If other parts of nature were inaccessible to our inquiries, or even if other parts of nature presented nothing to our examination but disorder and confusion, the validity of this example would remain the same. If there were but one watch in the world, it would not be less certain that it had a maker. If we had never in our lives seen any but one single kind of hydraulic machine, yet, if of that one kind we understood the mechanism and use, we should be as perfectly assured that it proceeded from the hand, and thought, and skill of a workman, as if we visited a museum of the arts, and saw collected there twenty different kinds of machines for drawing water, or a thousand different kinds for other purposes. Of this point, each machine is a proof, independently of all the rest. So it is with the evidences of a divine agency. The proof is not a conclusion which lies at the end of a chain of reasoning, of which chain each instance of contrivance is only a link, and of which, if one link fail, the whole fails; but is an argument separately supplied by every separate example. An error in stating an example affects only that example. The argument is cumulative, in the fullest sense of that term. The eye proves it without the ear; the ear without the eye. The proof in each example is complete; for when the design of the part, and the conduciveness of its structure to that design is shown, the mind may set itself at rest; no future consideration can detract anything from the force of the example.

36   The Evidential Value of

Religious Experience

D. E. Trueblood

The Primary Datum of Religion

O NE OF THE MOST AMAZING FAILURES of historic theology has been the failure to employ, in the substantiation of religious belief, the same kind of empirical evidence which has long been used in support of scientific belief. The failure to make use of empirical evidence in religion is the more amazing when we begin to realize how abundant the evidence is, and how truly it has been the real basis of belief in actual practice. "I had heard of thee by the hearing of the ear, but now mine eye seeth thee," is echoed in every generation.

That fact that religious experience occurs is a fact with which every philosophy must eventually deal. The claim which such experience makes, the claim to actual contact, not merely with persons and things, but with the Creator and Sustainer of the universe, is so stupendous and so insistent that it cannot be neglected. Our philosophy must either explain it away or construct a world view consistent with it.

The reasonable procedure is to look at religious experience as we look at any other datum. It is the primary datum of religion, and it awaits analysis. If we are scientifically minded we approach experience without prejudice and with humility. The scientific temper demands that we neither *accept* the data of experience uncritically nor *reject* it uncritically. We do

[This selection consists of the major portions of Chapter XII of D. E. Trueblood's *The Logic of Belief*, a book published in 1942. It is here reprinted with the permission of Harper & Row.]

not know what any experience is worth in the verification of belief until we analyze it, subjecting it to all the appropriate tests available. The mere fact that millions have reported that they have known God directly is not absolute proof that they have really done so, but, on the other hand, to assume, prior to critical testing, that they have not really done so would be unscientific in the extreme.

It must be made clear that we are not referring to *belief* in this connection, but to reported experience. The two are different. Belief may arise from many sources, some of them intellectually respectable and some of them not respectable. There can be belief *because* of direct experience and there can be belief *apart from* direct experience. The point we are making is not that millions of men have believed in God, something almost too obvious to bother to mention, but rather that millions of men have reported and continue to report that they have known God with the directness and intimacy with which they know other persons or physical objects.

Not all religious experience is the same, but there are characteristic features which appear with astonishing regularity and which are not especially difficult to describe. Normally it is not some experience wholly separated from other experiences, but a particular way in which all reality is apprehended. It comes about most naturally in the mood of prayer or worship, but is by no means limited to stated times for these, either individually or collectively. Ordinarily religious experience has nothing to do with visions, ecstasies, raptures or other phenomena which are usually considered abnormal. It is true that some mystics have experienced these exalted states of consciousness or unconsciousness, but they are no part of *normative* religious experience.[1] It, on the contrary, is as unspectacular as breathing or sleeping. For most men and women religious experience has been a calm assurance of the reality of a relationship which gives meaning to existence.

The chief reason why the opinion has become current that religious experience is rare, and therefore of little evidential value, is that there has been a misunderstanding concerning what is denoted by the term "religious experience." This misunderstanding has been created in large measure by certain writers, of whom Professor Leuba* is characteristic, who have claimed to study the empirical phenomena of religion, but in doing so have limited their study to the *bizarre*. The result is that they have made the discipline known as the psychology of religion sound like a branch of abnormal psychology.

---

1. Unusual mental states, such as "speaking with tongues," have frequently been minimized, even by those reporting them personally.

* James Henry Leuba (1868–1946), American psychologist who specialized in the study of various aspects of religious belief in such works as *The Psychological Origin and Nature of Religion* (1909), *The Belief in God and Immortality* (1916), and *The Psychology of Religious Mysticism* (1925). Leuba was highly critical of traditional religion. (Ed.)

The Characteristics of Religious Experience

Interesting as may be the study of peculiar mental phenomena, that is no part of our present purpose. We are concerned with the logical structure of belief, and, for this purpose, we are interested in the unspectacular. This normative experience may be described by making certain definite propositions about it which are related to one another as steps in the progressive narrowing of the field.

(1) *Religious experience is perceptual.* By this we mean that experience, as reported, is not a matter of either speculation or imagination, but of something independent of the observer with which the observer has established contact. God might be either imagined or perceived, just as a tree might be imagined or perceived. We say the tree is perceived when the tree is experienced as external to the mind of the perceiver. Imagination is free to indulge in wishful thinking; perception is limited by the nature of the real as known. The point is that religious experience reports itself as so limited.

Perhaps it is necessary to remind the reader that perceptual and sensory are not identical concepts. Perception refers to a relation to an *object* and is thus distinct from *conception,* as well as from imagination. Sensation, on the other hand, refers to the kind of experience which comes through the instrumentality of end organs, of which ears and eyes are conspicuous examples. There can be nonperceptual sensation, as a blow on the head may easily demonstrate, and, unless normative religion is a delusion, there is a vast amount of non-sensory perception, i.e., real contact with a perceived object, *without* the instrumentality of the sensory end organs. If God is really known, as so many have claimed to know Him, it is clear that He is not known by means of our auditory, optic or tactual nerves. Sometimes the language of sense has been used in the reports of vivid religious experience, but nearly always such language is consciously figurative. This is well illustrated by the Psalmist's appeal, "O taste and see that the Lord is good." The very fact that men speak so often of an *inward* sense is evidence that they are not talking about the actual sensory apparatus. What they mean is that their awareness of God is *as vivid, as incontestable,* as any sensory experience ever is. One of the great seventeenth century interpreters of such experience attempted, in the following words, to tell his Dutch friend Heer Paets, what he meant by an "inward sense."

> An example of an inward, supernatural sense is when the heart or soul of a pious man feels in itself divine motions, influences and operations, which sometimes are as the voice or speech of God, sometimes as a most pleasant and glorious illustration or visible object to the inward eye, sometimes as a most sweet savour or taste, sometimes as a heavenly and divine warmness or (so to speak) melting of the soul in the love of God.[2]

2. Robert Barclay, *Truth Triumphant,* p. 897.

It would be stupid to minimize the value of expressions like those of Barclay on the ground that they are figures of speech. The more important any disclosure is, the more necessary figures of speech become. The necessity for figures of speech arises from the fact that intelligible language is used for the purpose of making known what was formerly unknown, and this can only be done by establishing some similarity with what is already known. Thus we seek to make the experience of color understandable to the congenitally blind by comparing color with musical tone, though we are well aware that the two are not the same. Similarly, those who have tried to make religious experience understandable to others not conscious of it, have used the language of sense, while recognizing that it is not really sensory. They mean that it has the vividness, the certitude, the striking quality of that which impinges on ears, eyes, and other organs. An impressive testimony to this effect is that of Newman, when, speaking of his *inward conversion,* he affirmed years later that he was still more certain of it "than that I have hands and feet."[3]

It was, apparently, in an effort to emphasize the perceptual character of his own religious experience that the celebrated French mathematician, Blaise Pascal, used the word "Fire" in capital letters, as the central feature of the record of his life-shaking experience. This record, which Pascal's servant found sewed into the scholar's coat, at the time of his death, was made up largely of interjections, the normal language of assured contact. The word "Fire" was most emphasized, probably in the effort to show that what he perceived had about it the same indubitable quality that we find in the flame, which warms, lights, and even burns.

Perhaps there is no need to remark in passing that when we speak of perception as *contact with an object,* we are not necessarily referring to a *physical* object. The object is that which is perceived, whatever it is. It would be both unphilosophical and unscientific to assert dogmatically that the only objects of perception are physical bodies. The kinds of objects in which we must believe depend wholly on the kind of evidence which is available. The correct method is not to decide in advance whether or not there are nonphysical objects of perception, but rather to begin with the data of experience and wait to see to what conclusions we are led by the analysis of this experience.

(2) *Religious experience is cognitive,* in that it claims to be the kind of perception which gives the perceiver actual knowledge of God. In short it is possible, in religious experience, to go beyond Pascal's memorable hour, when there was certainty of contact, but little more. The prophets, in all generations, claim that their experience of God is such that they learn something about His nature, and His will for men. We are not discussing now the correctness of this knowledge, since such discussion should come later in this chapter; we are saying merely that the primary datum of religion includes a "knowledge claim."

Naturally it is not easy for men to tell others *what* they know, since

---

3. John Henry Newman, *Apologia pro Vita Sua,* Everyman edition, p. 31.

language here becomes more inadequate than it ordinarily is, and poetry becomes inevitable, but this is not the important point. The point is that knowledge is claimed, though never perfect knowledge. The devout man in all generations says with St. Paul, "I know in part." It has long been recognized that men, in their knowledge of God, can touch no more than the hem of His garment. But to know in part, is to know something.

(3) *Religious experience is personal,* not in the sense that every devout man has consciously believed that God is a "Person," but that the experience characteristically recorded is of the kind which we normally associate with persons. The experience has about it, as aesthetic experience has, the augustness which we cannot expect contact with a mere "thing" to inspire. In many cases, and most strikingly in the experience of Jesus, the relationship is consciously personal. God is addressed in prayer as "O Father," and the second person is used when a pronoun is employed . . .

Religion is not so much the thrill of discovery, as the awareness of being assaulted. The witness to this comes from testimonies as far apart as Francis Thompson's *Hound of Heaven* and Karl Barth's theology of crisis. Religion is not so much finding God, as reaction to the Reality which has found us. It is not so much man's bargain with God, as it is man's response to God's grace. But the point of all this, to which there is abundant testimony covering the greater part of three thousand years, is that this is the way we react to the tremendous soul-stirring experience of *being loved. It is persons who do the loving. . . .*

Assuming that the foregoing brief description of religious experience is sufficient for our present purposes, we can proceed to show the main structure of the argument based upon it. All that we know arises in experience. Our reason for believing that there is a physical order is the fact that millions of men report an experience of such an order. In a similar manner millions of men in all times and places have experienced God as the Sustainer of their lives. Therefore, God is.

The only reason for not accepting this forthright empirical evidence is the fact that experience can be delusory. Not everything that men experience exists. Two experiences given at a court trial and referring to the same event are sometimes contradictory. Though we cannot dispense with the ultimate appeal to experience we cannot take experience at its face value. But this applies to sensory experience just as truly as it applies to religious experience. Why, then, are there so many who deny the evidential value of religious experience while they accept the evidential value of sensory experience? The fact that men may make mistakes about the interpretation of their sense perceptions does not lead the ordinary intelligent person to the conclusion that sense perception is a purely subjective affair, but the fact that some men have had religious experiences which we must regard as illusory has led a number of otherwise critical persons to the conclusion that religious experience is a purely subjective affair and no revelation of the real. It is indeed a curious leap to conclude from the fact that men make mistakes, that there is no reality which they are making mistakes *about.*

This curious logic arises from an epistemological confusion, which in turn arises from an unrecognized metaphysical prejudice in favor of naturalism. Many theological writers have made the confusion easier by constantly referring to religion as an affair of the *inner* life. The consequence is that, for many, the serious question of the validity of religious experience is supposedly answered by pointing out that all religious experiences are mental—they are merely *in the mind*. How, then, can they have evidential value? But all experiences are in the mind in this sense of the word. My perception of the bird in the tree is as much in my mind as my perception of God. Strictly speaking, every man is like Karl Pearson's imagined telephone operator,* locked forever in his windowless exchange, but supplied with wires connecting him with what he takes to be an outside world. He cannot know for sure that there is an outside world at all. Even if he checks his messages by reference to the experience of another operator in another room, he has not escaped his "egocentric predicament" because this added evidence comes in what is merely another wire. Why should he trust his ideas about what purports to be a second operator any more than his ideas about the twentieth subscriber?

There are some persons who object to an empirical analysis which brackets sensory experience and religious experience, referring to the relation between them as an *analogy*. The facts to which we are now pointing show that this objection misses the mark. There is not an analogy between the two types of experience in regard to the subjective predicament; there is an *identity*. The notion that sensory experience has some advantage in certainty of objective reference turns out to be a mere superstition.

Many people appear to suppose that there is some *absolute* test of veracity in ordinary sense experience, but reflection shows that none exists. I see a flaw in the windowpane and the question arises whether this is just a figment of my imagination or really there. Accordingly, I go over and touch the glass. But does this prove my original contention? All I have is another experience which, indeed, increases the presumptive value of my first observation, but I can never escape the circle of subjectivity.

When this particular confusion is dispelled the greatest barrier to a fair estimate of the situation is removed. To list an experience as inner or subjective is not sufficient to deny its objectivity, for on that ground there would be no objective world at all. Though all experiences are subjectively known, they may be *occasioned* by objective stimuli. Thus the assertion of subjectivity is no denial of objectivity. The chief question is the question of reference. Ideas *in the mind* may refer to what is *outside the mind,* in that it exists independently, so far as the individual mind is concerned. The concept of objectivity, one of the most advanced of which the human mind is capable, involves not only the ability to distinguish between the self which

---

* Professor Trueblood's reference is to Karl Pearson (1857–1936), a distinguished statistician, scientist and philosopher of science who, in his widely read *Grammar of Science* (first published in 1892), developed a representative theory of perception similar to that defended by Bertrand Russell in Selection 50 below. The analogy of the telephone operator occurs in § 11 of the *Grammar of Science*. (Ed.)

experiences and the world which is experienced, but also the ability to distinguish between what the experient wishes were the case, and what he is forced to believe is the case.

The Tests of Veracity

To know precisely what belongs to the objective order is a problem of the greatest difficulty, and one never fully solved in any extended area. We solve the problem, insofar as we solve it at all, not by the application of some special *means,* but rather by the humble process of noting converging lines of agreement with experience as known. If Karl Pearson's lonely telephone operator finds that fire alarms are coming in simultaneously on many of his wires and if the alarms refer to the same place, he is justified in believing that there really is a fire. When people who differ in many ways have substantial agreement about one item, we consider it more reasonable to posit objective status than to accept a miracle of coincidence. In this we may be wrong, but we have no suitable alternative.

The agreement, of course, must be of a particular kind to have any value. In testing the veracity of religious experience four tests are of especial importance.

(1) *Number of reporters.* Other things being equal an experience has more veracity if it is widely shared. One reason for doubting the objective status of the animals seen in *delirium tremens* is that those who see them are so badly outnumbered.

The number of persons who have reported religious experience, not in the sense of ecstatic trance, and not in the sense of mere inference from the order of nature, but with a deep assurance of the divine undergirding, is many millions and, indeed, it is difficult to think of any similar data that are so numerous. The abundance of such reports in the Old and New Testament is enough to give us pause, but this is by no means the end of the story. When we think of the humble souls who have made their testimony in Christian lands in the intervening years, as well as many more quite outside the Christian tradition, we begin to see that we are dealing with one of the best attested experiences in the world. "The simple fact is," as Canon Raven has said, "that those who would explain away religion are hardly aware of the greatness of the task or of the qualifications necessary for it."[4]

The evidence upon which we can depend comes to us chiefly in three ways. (a) In the first place there is the vocal testimony, especially that which has appeared in gatherings similar to the Methodist "class meeting." Some of this can be discounted, especially when it follows the fashionable religious pattern of the day, but, taken as a whole, the vocal testimonies are so numerous and so sincere that it is impossible for a reasonable person to dismiss them as unworthy of attention.

4. Charles E. Raven, *Jesus and the Gospel of Love,* London, 1931, p. 73.

(b) A second source of evidence is found in literary records, especially those of spiritual autobiography. This material, as is well known, is an important part of our literature, from Augustine's *Confessions* to Newman's *Apologia* and beyond.[5] Even the Quaker journals alone make an impressive showing *and all of them were written in order to provide the very data with which we are here concerned.*

(c) If these two sources were the only ones the evidence would be impressive, but they do not exhaust the data. The experiences of most people cannot be known by their own direct report, since they are too modest or are lacking in facility of expression. Accordingly we must learn what their experience is from the worship in which they share, the readings which they prize, and the prayers to which they turn for the expression of their own devotional life. Thus the Hebrew Psalms tell us something, not merely about the experience of the few persons who originally composed them, but chiefly about the experience of the millions, of all creeds, who have found in the Psalms the best expression of what they would like to say and cannot. The satisfaction found in the use of hymns, many of which are forthright testimonies to divine acquaintance, gives us similar evidence. The testimony implicit in prayer is similarly great. We cannot know how many pray, but all will agree that the number is enormous. Anyone who believes in prayer is bearing witness thereby to direct contact between the human and the divine, inasmuch as God is supposed to hear our prayers . . .

Any thorough study of the number of the reports must include some reference to the fact that the report is not universal in the human race. There is not space here for an exhaustive treatment of this matter, but two relevant points can be made briefly. One is that *no* human experience, not even sight, is strictly universal, for experience depends in part on receptive powers. The higher we go, as in music for example, the less universal experience is. The other point is that failure to report experience has no evidential value, *unless* the individual concerned has met the appropriate conditions. The testimony of those who have not met the requirements has no logical weight and need not be seriously considered, whatever their qualifications in other ways. *The religious opinions of the unreligious are no more valuable than are the scientific opinions of the unscientific.*

(2) *The quality of the reporters* is more important than the numbers. Great numbers are not sufficient unless they include those who have qualitative fitness. The majority has frequently been wrong. Is there a substantial body of evidence coming from sensitive men, who are in command of their faculties, and properly qualified, on both moral and intellectual grounds, so that they inspire trust in that to which they bear testimony? We want to be sure of a substantial body of men and women of sufficiently good character not to engage in deliberate deceit and of sufficiently critical intelligence not to be self-deceived.

That answer is that there is a substantial body of evidence which meets

5. Reliable modern studies of this rich deposit are available in Gaius Glenn Atkins' *Pilgrims of the Lonely Road,* and Willard L. Sperry's Lowell Lectures, *Strangers and Pilgrims.*

these qualifications. That the great majority of reporters have been honest needs little support. It is not credible that the increase in personal effectiveness and power would come if men were consciously deceiving others in what they say on the deepest questions. This personal effectiveness is recognized even by those who reject the evidential value of the testimony. Furthermore, no serious reader can look at the written testimony of men like Pascal, Newman, and Fox and suppose that these men were engaged in a grand hoax.

The more important question concerns the sanity of the reporters and their capacity to resist delusion. Even if men are *honest,* their testimony is valueless if they are easily deluded. But the fact is that the reports come from a number of the most critical and sane persons the world has known, providing we use any standard test of sanity and critical power . . .

The only way to avoid the weight of such testimony is to make religious experience an *evidence* of an unbalanced mind, but that is to beg the question in a flagrant manner. It is obviously true that some of those who have reported vivid religious experience have been mentally unbalanced, but this situation is by no means peculiar to religion. There are unbalanced people in every field. If some necessary connection between mental aberrations and religious experience could be demonstrated, the credibility of witnesses would be undermined, but no such demonstration is forthcoming. Undoubtedly there are some truths revealed to eccentrics which are hidden from the normal and prudent, but the overwhelming majority of those who participate in prayer are so sane as to be almost uninteresting. That is why their testimony so seldom finds its way into psychology books.

(3) *The agreement of the reports* is our third test of veracity. Even if the reports are numerous and the reporters persons of proven integrity as well as critical judgment, the evidence is not good unless there is fundamental agreement in what is said. Part of the reason for doubting the objective reference to the animals "seen" by patients suffering from *delirium tremens* is that two or more patients do not "see" the same snakes.

Upon a superficial view, it is easy to conclude that the reports of the religious consciousness are more remarkable for their diversity than for their convergence. This conclusion is strengthened by the development of many sects. As we consider the matter carefully, however, we discover that the obvious differences, so easily recognized by the populace, refer chiefly to matters of organization and liturgical details, on the one hand, and to differences of creed on the other. It is when we concentrate on the actual record of experience that we are struck with the great degree of convergence in the testimony. There is, indeed, the most distressing divergency on all questions *about* religion, but not in the experience *of* religion. To use William James' familiar distinction, that on which men have argued is "knowledge about," and that on which they have agreed is "acquaintance with." . . .

Such conclusions are enforced by a simple experiment. Take a number of records of direct religious experience, read them to listeners, putting all into the same tongue, and see what success the listeners have in separating and locating them. In many cases there is no way to identify the reports at all, and an ancient Hindu testimony is sometimes mistaken for a modern Christian testimony. "We need not trouble ourselves to ask," writes Dr. Inge, "and we could seldom guess without asking, whether a paragraph describing the highest spiritual experiences was written in the Middle Ages or in modern times, in the north or south of Europe, by a Catholic or by a Protestant."[6] . . .

(4) *The fourth and final test of the veracity of religious experience is the difference it makes.* It is not necessary to be a pragmatist in order to recognize that the pragmatic test is one among others. That there has been a new quality of life in countless persons as a result of religious experience is beyond serious doubt.

In religion we cannot reasonably look for a mark on photographic plates, but we can reasonably look for a mark on human lives. If the experience of God is what men claim it is, we should expect to see a general change in their character; we should expect them to walk with a new step. It is this that we can check abundantly in a way that should be convincing to the open-minded. The evidence of altered lives, including both new strength and new tenderness, is so great that only a small portion of it has ever been committed to print. Not all of those who have reported religious experience have demonstrated "the fruits of the spirit," but, in considering evidence of this kind, we are concerned not so much with what is universal as with what is typical. We can show the typical verification through moral strength, by pointing to characteristic experiences in different settings.

The sense of God's presence has been sufficient to make men courageous in the face of persecution, to sensitize their conscience to social wrong, such as that as slavery and poverty, and, above all, has suffused entire lives with joy. . . .

The pragmatic test of the veracity of religious experience has seldom been more vividly illustrated than in the letters of German pastors, which have been written in concentration camps during the last few dreadful years. The following expressions are characteristic:

"I cannot tell you how thankful I am for the inner experience I have been permitted to have in these days. Though I walk through the valley of the shadow, I fear no evil, for Thou art with me. This presence of God in such a situation becomes even now a precious reality. And how good it is that our faith may now manifest itself really as faith, not merely in words, but in deeds and in the attitude in which we stand ready to take upon ourselves unpleasantness for the sake of the faith, if God thus permits it that men oppress us for our faith's sake. No one will be able to say any more what formerly in foolishness was sometimes said: He merely talks that way because he is paid for it. . . .

"God's ways are wonderful. And where He leads through dark ways, there one experiences his glory most. And again and again the experience

6. W. R. Inge, *Studies of English Mystics,* p. 35.

is repeated: 'You thought to bring evil upon me, but God thought to turn it to good.' . . .

"God has thrown us Christian people in our church to-day out of all safe nests, out of all the nests of earthly security and human calculations and plans, cast us out as it were into emptiness, into nothingness. In sudden shock and terror we may have felt sometimes in these years as if we were plunging into a bottomless abyss, sinking away into nothingness. What are we now to do? Now we must fly if we do not want to be borne away by the storms of oppression into the yawning chasms of despair. But if we only really learn to believe, yes, learn really to believe in God, and in firm belief and trusting prayer spread our wings, then we shall experience— and how many times in these years we have already experienced it with amazement and awe—that we do not sink away; there is a power there which holds us, we are borne by God's eternal father-arms, we are sustained in the storms."[7]

What can we say in the face of testimonies so tremendous, testimonies repeated in so many generations? Drugs and delusions may sustain men for a time, but here is something which wears out all opposition. It makes weak men bold and proud men humble. Words seem impertinent and silence the only adequate response. If that which sustains men and makes them praise God in both bright and dark hours be not reality, where is reality to be found?

Conclusion

Thus we see that the empirical evidence for the hypothesis of God as real is the strongest evidence of all. It is the most difficult to escape, especially in a scientific age when experience is respected. We need, however, to integrate this evidence with the other evidence which comes from our knowledge of nature and of our own being. The full strength of each line of evidence appears, not in isolation, but in conjunction.

The conclusion to which we are driven is that in religion we have a situation in which the evidence of objectivity is even better than it is in natural science because the corroboration comes from such a long time and from such widely separated areas. The miracle of coincidence is so great that it is bound to be unacceptable to thoughtful persons. Yet what other alternative is there unless belief in God as objectively real is accepted? Herein lies part of the deep significance of the ancient saying that it is hard to believe, but harder still to disbelieve.

7. From *Und Lobten Gott,* private translation of my colleague, Helena Nye. The Student Christian Movement has brought out a translation, *I Was in Prison.*

37   The Delusion of
Design and Purpose

Clarence Darrow

Seldom do the believers in mysti-
cism fail to talk about the evidence of purpose and design shown in the
universe itself. This idea runs back at least one hundred and five years, to
Paley's "Natural Theology." There was a time when this book was a part
of the regular course in all schools of higher learning, which then included
theology; but the book is now more likely to be found in museums.

Paley points out that if a man travelling over the heath should find a
watch and commence examining it he would soon discover in the watch
itself abundant evidence of purpose and design. He would observe the
wheels that fit into each other and turn the hour hand and the minute
hand, the crystal made to fit over the face, etc., etc.

What the hypothetical man would observe and conclude would depend on the man. Most men that we know would think that the watch
showed a design to accomplish a certain purpose, and therefore must
have had a maker. They would reach that conclusion because they are
familiar with tools and their use by man. But, suppose the watch had
been picked up by a bushman or some other savage or an ape? None of
them would draw an inference, for the article would be new to them.
Supposing, instead of a man, a coyote or wolf came upon the watch,
turned it over and examined it, would the animal read or sense any design? Most assuredly not. Suppose the civilized man should pick up an
unfamiliar object, a stone, or a piece of quartz; he might view it and examine it, but it would never enter his head that it was designed, and yet on

[This selection is the whole of Chapter 44 of Darrow's book, *The Story of My Life*,
published in 1932. It is reproduced with the kind permission of Charles Scribner's Sons,
New York and London.]

close inspection and careful study the stone or quartz is just as marvellous as the watch.

Paley passes from the watch to the human structure and shows how the mouth and teeth are adjusted to prepare the food for man's digestion, and how his stomach is formed to digest it; how the eye and ear were made to carry sensations to the brain, etc. Many of the clergy say the same thing to-day, in spite of the fact that the organs of man were never made for any such purpose. In fact, man never was made. He was evolved from the lowest form of life. His ancestor in the sea slowly threw its jellylike structure around something that nourished it and absorbed it. Slowly through ages of continued development and change and mutations the present man was evolved, and with him the more perfect and adaptable and specialized structure, with which he sees and hears and takes his food, and digests it and assimilates it to his structure. The stomach was not made first, and then food created for its use. The food came first, and certain forms of life slowly developed an organ that would absorb food to be utilized in the process of growth. By degrees, through the survival of the construction most fitted for life, the stomach and digestive apparatus for men and other animals gradually grew and unfolded in endless time.

To discover that certain forms and formations are adjusted for certain action has nothing to do with design. None of these developments are perfect, or anywhere near so. All of them, including the eye, are botchwork that any good mechanic would be ashamed to make. All of them need constant readjustment, are always out of order, and are entirely too complicated for dependable work. They are not made for any purpose; they simply grew out of needs and adaptations; in other words, they happened. Just as God must have happened, if he exists at all.

Turning from Paley and his wornout watch to the universe and the physical world in general, is there any more evidence here? First, the "design and order" sharks ought to tell what they mean by their terms, and how they find out what they think they understand. To say that a certain scheme or process shows order or system, one must have some norm or pattern, and that is the universe itself, from which we fashion our ideas. We have observed this universe and its operation and we call it order. To say that the universe is patterned on order is to say that the universe is patterned on the universe. It can mean nothing else.

The earth revolves around the sun in a long curve not far from a circle. Does that show order? Let us suppose that instead of going in a circle it formed a rectangle. Would this not have been accepted as order? Suppose it were a triangle, or any other figure. Suppose it took a toothlike course, would that, then be considered order? As a matter of fact, the earth does not go regularly in the same path around the sun; it is drawn out into the universe with the whole solar system, and never travels the same course twice. The solar system really has an isolated place in space. The sun furnishes light and heat to nine different planets, of which the earth is one of the smallest and most insignificant. The earth has one satellite, the moon. Saturn and Jupiter have eight moons each, and, besides that, Saturn has a ring that looks very beautiful from here, running all around the planet. We do know that all the planets of the solar system, and the sun as well, are made of the same stuff. It is most likely that every moving thing in the universe has the same constituents as the earth. What is the plan that gave Jupiter eight moons, while only one was lavished upon the earth, supposed to be the special masterpiece of the Almighty, and for whose benefit all the hosts of the heavens were made? Jupiter is three hundred and seventeen times the weight of the earth, and it takes four years for it to go around the sun. Perhaps the universe was made for inhabitants that will one day live on Jupiter.

It is senseless to talk about order and system and design in the universe. Sir James Jeans' book, published in 1931, *The Stars in Their Courses,* tells us his theory of the origin of our solar system, which is of more interest to us than the Milky Way. The theory of Jeans, and most of the other astronomers, is that there was a time when all the planets of the solar system were a part of the sun, and that some wandering star in its course across the heavens entered the sphere of the sun and dragged after it the planets and the moons that make up the solar system by the power of gravitation. This is the planetismal theory, postulated by Professors Chamberlain and Moulton, of the University of Chicago. These mighty chunks of matter were drawn from the sun rushed on through space at a terrific speed, and each was caught by gravitation and revolved around the sun. Their distance from the sun depended largely upon their size before gravitation held them in its grasp.

There is nothing in the solar system that could be called design and order. It came from a catastrophe of whose immensity no one could even dream. Religionists have pointed to the ability of an astronomer to fix the time of an eclipse as evidence of system. There are only a few heavenly bodies involved in an eclipse of the sun or moon, from the standpoint of the earth. The motions and positions of all these bodies are well known, and from this the passage of another heavenly planet or the moon between the earth and the sun can be easily determined. It matters not whether the date of an eclipse is far-off or near-by, the method is the same. To an astronomer the computation is as simple as the question propounded to the first grade pupil: "If John had three apples and James gave him two more, how many apples would John then have?"

We know that gravitation caught the various planets at a certain point as they sped across space, and that these accidents of colliding bodies are very rare; the reason is that regardless of what seems to be the distance between the stars, they are so far apart that it is almost impossible for them ever to meet. To quote from Jeans: "For the most part, each voyage is in splendid isolation, like a ship on the ocean. In a scale model on which the stars are ships, the average ship will be well over a million miles from its neighbor."

Still, catastrophes have occurred and do occur. Our solar system was probably born from one. The moon was thrown from the earth by some pull of gravitation. The heavens are replete with dark planets, and parts of planets, and meteors hurrying through space. Now and then one drops onto the earth, and is preserved in some park or museum; so that in various parts of the world numerous specimens exist. If there was any purpose in the creation of the universe, or any part of it, what was it? Would any mortal dare to guess?

Our solar system is one of the smallest of the endless systems of which we have any knowledge. Our earth is eight thousand miles in diameter. The star, Betelgeuse, is so large that it would fill all space occupied in the heavens in the whole orbit made by the earth going around the sun. There are many stars known to be much larger than Betelgeuse. The diameter of this sun is thirty-seven thousand times that of our little earth, for which all the universe is supposed to have been made, and whose inhabitants are endowed with everlasting life.

When the telescope is turned toward the heavens we learn another story. Leaving the sparsely settled section of eternity in which we live forever, and going out into the real main universe, we find worlds on worlds, systems upon systems, and nebula after nebula. No one can possibly imagine the dimensions of endless space. The great Nebula M.31 in Andromeda is so far away from the earth that it takes light nine hundred thousand millions of years to reach our planet. The nebula itself is so vast that it takes fifty thousand years for light to cross it. To make it still more simple I have taken the pains to figure the distance of this nebula from our important planet, called the earth, which boasts of a diameter of eight thousand miles. This nebula is 5,279,126,400,000,-000,000 miles away from us, if my computations are right. I would not positively guarantee the correctness of the answer, but I think it is all right, although I did it by hand. I have gone over the figures three times, and got a different result each time, so I think the answer can be pretty well depended upon. I cannot help feeling sorry for the residents of Nebula M.31 in Andromeda, when I think what a great deprivation they must suffer through living so far away from our glorious planet, which Mark Twain named "the wart," but which theology has placed at the centre of the universe and as the sole concern of gods and men.

What lies beyond Andromeda? No one can answer that question. And still there is every reason to believe that other worlds and systems and nebulae reach out into stellar space, without end. It is obvious that no one can form a conception of the extent of space or the infinite number of suns and planets with which the limitless sky is strewn. No one can vision a beginning or an end. If it were possible for any fertile mind to imagine a conception of the end of space, then we should wonder what lies beyond that limit. We cannot attain the slightest comprehension of the extent of our pigmy solar system, much less any of the greater ones. The planet which is the farthest from our sun is Pluto, one of the smallest in our system. The diameter of Pluto's orbit around the sun is only about 7,360,000,000 miles. This may be taken as the extent of our solar system. This can be compared with the distance to the nebula in Andromeda, which I hesitate to record again, showing the trifling importance of our whole solar system in so much of the universe as we can scan.

When the new telescope is completed and mounted on the top of Mount Wilson, it is hoped that we can produce figures of distance that are real figures.

Among the endless number of stars that whirl in the fastnesses of illimitable space, how many millions of billions of planets are likely to be in existence? How many of these may possibly have as much special and historical importance as the tiny globe to which we so frantically cling? To find that number, go and count the grains of sand on all the coasts of all the waters of the earth, and then think of the catastrophe that would result to the coasts if one grain were shattered or lost.

In spite of the countless numbers of bodies moving about in limitless space, and the distances between them so great that they seldom clash, still they do sometimes clash. What is our solar system in comparison with the great nebula out there in the beginning, or end, or middle stretch of real space? Compared with that part of the heavens the density of the stellar population of our solar system is like the prairies of Kansas compared with the city of New York. Can anything be inferred about the origin or arrangement of all this, so far as man can tell, except that it is the outcome of the merest, wildest chance?

But let us try to clear the cobwebs from our brains, and the dizziness from our stomachs, and come back to earth, as it were. Let us talk of something where we can deal with what at least approaches facts. Does the earth show design, and order, and system, and purpose? Again, it would be well for the designers to tell what the scheme really is. If the plan is so clear as to justify the belief in a master designer, then it must be plain that the believers should be able to give the world some idea of the purpose of it all. Knowing winks and Delphic utterances and cryptic insinuations are not enough. Was the earth ever designed for the home of man? Sir James Jeans, in his admirable book on astronomy, shows us in no uncertain way that it evidently was not; that the human race has made the most of a bad environment and a most unfortunate habitation. Strange that the high-priests of superstition should so convulsively clutch Jeans and Eddington; neither one believes in the God of the theologians; neither believes in a special revelation, although Jeans does manage to say that Venus is the planet that the religionists thought was the star that led the camels over the desert to the stable where Jesus was born. Is this science or religion?—this bit of hearsay.

Even had this planet been meant for life, it plainly was not meant for human life. Three-fourths of the surface is covered with water, which would show that if it was ever designed for life it was designed for fishes and not for men. But what about the dry land? Two-thirds of this is not fitted for human beings. Both the polar zones are too cold for the abode of man. The equatorial regions are too hot. Vast deserts are spread out in various sections, and impassable and invincible mountain ranges make human habitation and the production of food impossible over immense areas. The earth is small enough, to begin with; the great seas, the wide useless stretches of land and the hostile climates have shrunk the livable portion almost to the vanishing point, and it is continually shrinking day by day. The human race is here because it is here, and it clings to the soil because there is nowhere else to go.

Even a human being of very limited capacity could think of countless ways in which the earth could be improved as the home of man, and from the earliest time the race has been using all sorts of efforts and resources to make it more suitable for its abode. Admitting that the earth is a fit place for life, and certainly every place in the universe where life exists is fitted for life, then what sort of life was this planet designed to support? There are some millions of different species of animals on this earth, and one-half of these are insects. In numbers, and perhaps in other ways, man is in a great minority. If the land of the earth was made for life, it seems as if it was intended for insect life, which can exist almost anywhere. If no other available place can be found they can live by the million on man, and inside of him. They generally succeed in destroying his life, and, if they have a chance, wind up by eating his body.

Aside from the insects, all sorts of life infest the earth and sea and air. In large portions of the earth man can make no headway against the rank growths of jungles and the teeming millions of animals that are seeking his death. He may escape the larger and most important of these only to be imperilled and probably eaten by the microbes, which seem instinctively to have their own idea of the worth and purpose of man's existence. If it were of any importance, we might view man from the standpoint of the microbe and consider his utility as the microbe's "meal-ticket." Can any one find any reason for claiming that the earth was meant for man, any more than for any other form of life that is spawned from land and sea and air?

But, how well is the earth itself adapted to human life? Even in the best parts of this world, speaking from the standpoint of man, one-fourth of the time it is too cold and another fourth of the seasons it is too hot, leaving little time for the comfort and pleasure of the worthiest product of the universe, or, that small fraction of it that we have some limited knowledge about.

Passing up the manifold difficulties that confront man and his brief life and career upon this mundane sphere, let us look at the world itself. It is a very wobbly place. Every year, upon the surface of this globe, and in the seas that cover such a major part of it, there are ten thousand earthquakes, ranging from light shocks to the total destruction of large areas of territory and annihilation of great numbers of human lives. Were these, too, designed? Then, there is no such meaning as is usually applied to the word "design." What "design" was there in the earthquake that destroyed Lisbon in 1755? The entire city was blotted out, together with the destruction of thirty thousand to forty thousand human beings. This earthquake occurred on a Sunday which was also a saint's day, and a large number were killed in a cathedral, which was also destroyed. And yet people talk about design and purpose and order and system as though they knew the meaning of the words.

Let us look at the earth as it exists to-day. It is not the same earth that came into some sort of separate existence millions of years ago. It has not only experienced vast and comparatively sudden changes, like the throwing up of mountain ranges in the cooling and contracting processes, but other changes not so sudden and acute have worked their way through ages of time, and changes are still going on all the time all over the earth. New lands keep rising, others sinking away. Volcanoes are sending out millions of tons of matter each year, new islands are rising above the surface of the sea, while other islands are lowered beneath the waves. Continents are divided by internal forces and the ruthless powers of the sea.

Great Britain was cut off from the mainland not so very long ago, according to geological time. The shores of America and Africa were once connected, as seems evident from looking at the maps, and countless other geological shiftings have happened all over the surface and inside the earth, so that the world was no more made as it is now than was man created as we find him to-day. The destruction of the island of Martinique, and the Mont Pelée disaster, the earthquake of San Francisco, are all within the memory of many now living. Active volcanoes are continuously pouring solid matter into the waters and slowly or rapidly building up new land where once was only sea.

The various archipelagoes are instances of this formation of fairly recent times. The Allegheny Mountains were once thirty thousand feet high. The crevices of their rocks have been penetrated by rain, split by frost and ice, pulverized by friction, and every minute are moving off toward the Gulf of Mexico. This range of mountains, which once reached an altitude of thirty thousand feet at the highest point, now has its highest peak but six thousand feet above the sea. These mountains have been worn down day after day, and the Ohio and Tennessee and Mississippi Rivers, carrying off the sediment, are building up the delta on the Louisiana coast. The earth and its seas were never made; they are in constant flux, moved by cold and heat and rain, and with no design or purpose that can be fathomed by the wit of man.

The delta of the Nile has through the long ages been carried down in mud and sand and silt from two thousand miles away and deposited in the open sea; and this is also called design by those who look for things they wish to find.

Nature brings hordes of insects that settle over the land and destroy the farmers' crops. Who are the objects of the glorious design: the farmers who so patiently and laboriously raise the crops or the grasshoppers that devour them? It must be the insects, because the farmers hold prayer meetings and implore their God to kill the bugs, but the pests go on with their deadly work unmolested. Man prates glibly about design, but Nature furnishes not a single example or fact as proof. Perhaps the microbe who bores a hole into the vitals of man and brings him down to his death may believe in a Providence and a design. How else could he live so royally on the vitals of one of the lords of creation?

All that we know is that we were born on this little grain of sand we call the earth. We know that it is one of the smallest bits of matter that floats in the great shoreless sea of space, and we have every reason to believe that it is as inconsequential in every other respect. On board the same craft, sailing the same seas, are all sorts of living things, fighting each other, and us, that each may survive. Most of these specimens are living on the carcasses of the dead. The strongest instinct of most of our crew is to stay here and live. The strongest in intellect and prowess live the longest. Nature, in all her manifestations, is at war with life, and sooner or later will doubtless have her way. No one can give a reason for any or all of the manifestations which we call life. We are like a body of shipwrecked sailors clutching to a raft and desperately engaged in holding on.

Men have built faith from hopes. They have struggled and fought in despair. They have frantically clung to life because of the will to live. The best that we can do is to be kindly and helpful toward our friends and fellow passengers who are clinging to the same speck of dirt while we are drifting side by side to our common doom.

38 The Sufferings of Little Children

Fyodor Dostoevsky

"I MUST MAKE YOU ONE CONFESSION," Ivan began. "I could never understand how one can love one's neighbours. It's just one's neighbours, to my mind, that one can't love, though one might love those at a distance. I once read somewhere of John the Merciful, a saint, that when a hungry, frozen beggar came to him, he took him into his bed, held him in his arms, and began breathing into his mouth, which was putrid and loathsome from some awful disease. I am convinced that he did that from 'self-laceration,' from the self-laceration of falsity, for the sake of the charity imposed by duty, as a penance laid on him. For any one to love a man, he must be hidden, for as soon as he shows his face, love is gone."

"Father Zossima has talked of that more than once," observed Alyosha; "he, too, said that the face of a man often hinders many people not practised in love, from loving him. But yet there's a great deal of love in mankind, and almost Christ-like love. I know that myself, Ivan."

"Well, I know nothing of it so far, and can't understand it, and the innumerable mass of mankind are with me there. The question is, whether that's due to men's bad qualities or whether it's inherent in their nature. To my thinking, Christ-like love for men is a miracle impossible on earth. He

[This selection consists of all except the last three paragraphs of Chapter IV of Book V of Dostoevsky's *The Brothers Karamazov*. The translation is by Constance Garnett, published by Random House of New York.]

was God. But we are not gods. Suppose I, for instance, suffer intensely. Another can never know how much I suffer, because he is another and not I. And what's more, a man is rarely ready to admit another's suffering (as though it were a distinction). Why won't he admit it, do you think? Because I smell unpleasant, because I have a stupid face, because I once trod on his foot. Besides there is suffering and suffering; degrading, humiliating suffering such as humbles me—hunger, for instance—my benefactor will perhaps allow me; but when you come to higher suffering—for an idea, for instance—he will very rarely admit that, perhaps because my face strikes him as not at all what he fancies a man should have who suffers for an idea. And so he deprives me instantly of his favour, and not at all from badness of heart. Beggers, especially genteel beggers, ought never to show themselves, but to ask for charity through the newspapers. One can love one's neighbours in the abstract, or even at a distance, but at close quarters it's almost impossible. If it were as on the stage, in the ballet, where if beggars come in, they wear silken rags and tattered lace and beg for alms dancing gracefully, then one might like looking at them. But even then we should not love them. But enough of that. I simply wanted to show you my point of view. I meant to speak of the suffering of mankind generally, but we had better confine ourselves to the sufferings of the children. That reduces the scope of my argument to a tenth of what it would be. Still we'd better keep to the children, though it does weaken my case. But, in the first place, children can be loved even at close quarters, even when they are dirty, even when they are ugly (I fancy, though, children never are ugly). The second reason why I won't speak of grown-up people is that, besides being disgusting and unworthy of love, they have a compensation—they've eaten the apple and know good and evil, and they have become 'like god.' They go on eating it still. But the children haven't eaten anything, and are so far innocent. Are you fond of children, Alyosha? I know you are, and you will understand why I prefer to speak of them. If they, too, suffer horribly on earth, they must suffer for their fathers' sins, they must be punished for their fathers, who have eaten the apple; but that reasoning is of the other world and is incomprehensible for the heart of man here on earth. The innocent must not suffer for another's sins, and especially such innocents! You may be surprised at me, Alyosha, but I am awfully fond of children, too. And observe, cruel people, the violent, the rapacious, the Karamazovs are sometimes very fond of children. Children while they are quite little—up to seven, for instance—are so remote from grown-up people; they are different creatures, as it were, of a different species. I knew a criminal in prison who had, in the course of his career as a burglar, murdered whole families, including several children. But when he was in prison, he had a strange affection for them. He spent all his time at his window, watching the children playing in the prison yard. He trained one little boy to come up to his window and made great friends with him. . . . You don't know why I am telling you all this, Alyosha? My head aches and I am sad."

"You speak with a strange air," observed Alyosha uneasily, "as though you were not quite yourself."

"By the way, a Bulgarian I met lately in Moscow," Ivan went on, seeming not to hear his brother's words, "told me about the crimes committed by Turks and Circassians in all parts of Bulgaria through fear of a general rising of the Slavs. They burn villages, murder, outrage women and children, they nail their prisoners by the ears to the fences, leave them so till morning, and in the morning they hang them—all sorts of things you can't imagine. People talk sometimes of bestial cruelty, but that's a great injustice and insult to the beasts; a beast can never be so cruel as a man, so artistically cruel. The tiger only tears and gnaws, that's all he can do. He would never think of nailing people by the ears, even if he were able to do it. These Turks took a pleasure in torturing children, too; cutting the unborn child from the mother's womb, and tossing babies up in the air and catching them on the points of their bayonets before their mother's eyes. Doing it before the mother's eyes was what gave zest to the amusement. Here is another scene that I thought very interesting. Imagine a trembling mother with her baby in her arms, a circle of invading Turks around her. They've planned a diversion; they pet the baby, laugh to make it laugh. They succeed, the baby laughs. At that moment a Turk points a pistol four inches from the baby's face. The baby laughs with glee, holds out its little hands to the pistol, and he pulls the trigger in the baby's face and blows out its brains. Artistic, wasn't it? By the way, Turks are particularly fond of sweet things, they say."

"Brother, what are you driving at?" asked Alyosha.

"I think if the devil doesn't exist, but man has created him, he has created him in his own image and likeness."

"Just as he did God, then?" observed Alyosha.

" 'It's wonderful how you can turn words,' as Polonius says in *Hamlet*," laughed Ivan. "You can turn my words against me. Well, I am glad. Yours must be a fine God, if man created Him in His image and likeness. You asked just now what I was driving at. You see, I am fond of collecting certain facts, and, would you believe, I even copy anecdotes of a certain sort from newspapers and books, and I've already got a fine collection. The Turks, of course, have gone into it, but they are foreigners. I have specimens from home that are even better than the Turks. You know we prefer beating—rods and scourges—that's our national institution. Nailing ears is unthinkable for us, for we are, after all, Europeans. But the rod and the scourge we have always with us and they cannot be taken from us. Abroad now they scarcely do any beating. Manners are more humane, or laws have been passed, so that they don't dare to flog men now. But they make up for it in another way just as national as ours. And so national that it would be practically impossible among us, though I believe we are being inoculated with it, since the religious movement began in our aristocracy. I have a charming pamphlet, translated from the French, describing how, quite recently, five years ago, a murderer, Richard, was executed—a young man,

I believe, of three and twenty, who repented and was converted to the Christian faith at the very scaffold. This Richard was an illegitimate child who was given as a child of six by his parents to some shepherds on the Swiss mountains. They brought him up to work for them. He grew up like a little wild beast among them. The shepherds taught him nothing, and scarcely fed or clothed him, but sent him out at seven to herd the flock in cold and wet, and no one hesitated or scrupled to treat him so. Quite the contrary, they thought they had every right, for Richard had been given to them as a chattel, and they did not even see the necessity of feeding him. Richard himself describes how in those years, like the Prodigal Son in the Gospel, he longed to eat of the mash given to the pigs, which were fattened for sale. But they wouldn't even give him that, and beat him when he stole from the pigs. And that was how he spent all his childhood and his youth, till he grew up and was strong enough to go away and be a thief. The savage began to earn his living as a day labourer in Geneva. He drank what he earned, he lived like a brute, and finished by killing and robbing an old man. He was caught, tried, and condemned to death. They are not sentimentalists there. And in prison he was immediately surrounded by pastors, members of Christian brotherhoods, philanthropic ladies, and the like. They taught him to read and write in prison, and expounded the Gospel to him. They exhorted him, worked upon him, drummed at him incessantly, till at last he solemnly confessed his crime. He was converted. He wrote to the court himself that he was a monster, but that in the end God had vouchsafed him light and shown grace. All Geneva was in excitement about him—all philanthropic and religious Geneva. All the aristocratic and well-bred society of the town rushed to the prison, kissed Richard and embraced him; 'You are our brother, you have found grace.' And Richard does nothing but weep with emotion, 'Yes, I've found grace! All my youth and childhood I was glad of pigs' food, but now even I have found grace. I am dying in the Lord.' 'Yes, Richard, die in the Lord; you have shed blood and must die. Though it's not your fault that you knew not the Lord, when you coveted the pig's food and were beaten for stealing it (which was very wrong of you, for stealing is forbidden); but you've shed blood and you must die.' And on the last day, Richard, perfectly limp, did nothing but cry and repeat every minute: 'This is my happiest day. I am going to the Lord.' 'Yes,' cry the pastors and the judges and philanthropic ladies. 'This is the happiest day of your life, for you are going to the Lord!' They all walk or drive to the scaffold in procession behind the prison van. At the scaffold they call to Richard: 'Die, brother, die in the Lord, for even thou hast found grace!' And so, covered with his brothers' kisses, Richard is dragged on to the scaffold, and led to the guillotine. And they chopped off his head in brotherly fashion, because he had found grace. Yes, that's characteristic. That pamphlet is translated into Russian by some Russian philanthropists of aristocratic rank and evangelical aspirations, and has been distributed gratis for the enlightenment of the people. The case of Richard is interesting because it's national. Though to us it's absurd to cut off a man's head, because he has become our brother and has found grace, yet we have our own specialty, which is all but worse. Our historical pastime is the direct satisfaction of inflicting pain. There are lines in Nekrassov describing how a peasant lashes a horse on the eyes, 'on its meek eyes,' every one must have seen it. It's peculiarly Russian. He describes how a feeble little nag had foundered under too heavy a load and cannot move. The peasant beats it, beats it savagely, beats it at last not knowing what he is doing in the intoxication of cruelty, thrashes it mercilessly over and over again. 'However weak you are, you must pull, if you die for it.' The nag strains, and then he begins lashing the poor defenceless creature on its weeping, on its 'meek eyes.' The frantic beast tugs and draws the load, trembling all over, gasping for breath, moving sideways, with a sort of unnatural spasmodic action—it's awful in Nekrassov. But that's only a horse, and God has given horses to be beaten. So the Tatars have taught us, and they left us the knout as a remembrance of it. But men, too, can be beaten. A well-educated, cultured gentleman and his wife beat their own child with a birch-rod; a girl of seven. I have an exact account of it. The papa was glad that the birch was covered with twigs. 'It stings more,' said he, and so he began stinging his daughter. I know for a fact there are people who at every blow are worked up to sensuality, to literal sensuality, which increases progressively at every blow they inflict. They beat for a minute, for five minutes, for ten minutes, more often and more savagely. The child screams. At last the child cannot scream, it gasps, 'Daddy! daddy!' By some diabolical unseemly chance the case was brought into court. A counsel is engaged. The Russian people have long called a barrister 'a conscience for hire.' The counsel protests in his client's defence. 'It's such a simple thing,' he says, 'an everyday domestic event. A father corrects his child. To our shame be it said, it is brought into court.' The jury, convinced by him, give a favourable verdict. The public roars with delight that the torturer is acquitted. Ah, pity I wasn't there! I would have proposed to raise a subscription in his honour! . . . Charming pictures.

"But I've still better things about children. I've collected a great, great deal about Russian children, Alyosha. There was a little girl of five who was hated by her father and mother, 'most worthy and respectable people, of good education and breeding.' You see, I must repeat again, it is a peculiar characteristic of many people, this love of torturing children, and children only. To all other types of humanity these torturers behave mildly and benevolently, like cultivated and humane Europeans; but they are very fond of tormenting children, even fond of children themselves in that sense. It's just their defenselessness that tempts the tormentor, just the angelic confidence of the child who has no refuge and no appeal, that sets his vile blood on fire. In every man, of course, a demon lies hidden—the demon of rage, the demon of lustful heat at the screams of the tortured victim, the demon of lawlessness let off the chain, the demon of diseases that follow on vice, gout, kidney disease, and so on.

"This poor child of five was subjected to every possible torture by those cultivated parents. They beat her, thrashed her, kicked her for no reason till her body was one bruise. Then, they went to greater refinements of cruelty—shut her up all night in the cold and frost in a privy, and because she didn't ask to be taken up at night (as though a child of five sleeping its angelic, sound sleep could be trained to wake and ask), they smeared her face and filled her mouth with excrement, and it was her mother, her mother did this. And that mother could sleep, hearing the poor child's groans! Can you understand why a little creature, who can't even understand what's done to her, should beat her little aching heart with her tiny fist in the dark and the cold, and weep her meek unresentful tears to dear, kind God to protect her? Do you understand that, friend and brother, you pious and humble novice? Do you understand why this infamy must be and is permitted? Without it, I am told, man could not have existed on earth, for he could not have known good and evil. Why should he know that diabolical good and evil when it costs so much? Why, the whole world of knowledge is not worth that child's prayer to 'dear, kind God'! I say nothing of the sufferings of grown-up people, they have eaten the apple, damn them, and the devil take them all! But these little ones! I am making you suffer, Aloysha, you are not yourself. I'll leave off if you like."

"Never mind. I want to suffer too," muttered Alyosha.

"One picture, only one more, because it's so curious, so characteristic, and I have only just read it in some collection of Russian antiquities. I've forgotten the name. I must look it up. It was in the darkest days of serfdom at the beginning of the century, and long live the Liberator of the People! There was in those days a general of aristocratic connections, the owner of great estates, one of those men—somewhat exceptional, I believe, even then—who, retiring from the service into a life of leisure, are convinced that they've earned absolute power over the lives of their subjects. There were such men then. So our general, settled on his property of two thousand souls, lives in pomp, and domineers over his poor neighbours as though they were dependents and buffoons. He has kennels of hundreds of hounds and nearly a hundred dog-boys—all mounted, and in uniform. One day a serf boy, a little child of eight, threw a stone in play and hurt the paw of the general's favourite hound. 'Why is my favourite dog lame?' He is told that the boy threw a stone that hurt the dog's paw. 'So you did it.' The general looked the child up and down. 'Take him.' He was taken— taken from his mother and kept shut up all night. Early that morning the general comes out on horseback, with the hounds, his dependents, dog-boys, and huntsmen, all mounted around him in full hunting parade. The servants are summoned for their edification, and in front of them all stands the mother of the child. The child is brought from the lock-up. It's a gloomy cold, foggy autumn day, a capital day for hunting. The general orders the child to be undressed; the child is stripped naked. He shivers, numb with terror, not daring to cry. . . . 'Make him run,' commands the general. 'Run! run!' shout the dog-boys. The boy runs. . . . 'At him!' yells the general, and he sets the whole pack of hounds on the child. The hounds

catch him, and tear him to pieces before his mother's eyes! . . . I believe
the general was afterwards declared incapable of administering his estates.
Well—what did he deserve? To be shot? To be shot for the satisfaction of
our moral feelings? Speak, Alyosha!"

"To be shot," murmured Alyosha, lifting his eyes to Ivan with a pale,
twisted smile.

"Bravo!" cried Ivan delighted. "If even you say so . . . You're a pretty
monk! So there is a little devil sitting in your heart, Alyosha Karamazov!"

"What I said was absurd, but——"

"That's just the point that 'but'!" cried Ivan. "Let me tell you, novice,
that the absurd is only too necessary on earth. The world stands on absurdities, and perhaps nothing would have come to pass in it without them. We
know what we know!"

"What do you know?"

"I understand nothing," Ivan went on, as though in delirium. "I don't
want to understand anything now. I want to stick to the fact. I made up
my mind long ago not to understand. If I try to understand anything, I
shall be false to the fact and I have determined to stick to the fact."

"Why are you trying me?" Alyosha cried, with sudden distress. "Will
you say what you mean at last?"

"Of course, I will; that's what I've been leading up to. You are dear to
me, I don't want to let you go, and I won't give you up to your Zossima."*

Ivan for a minute was silent, his face became all at once very sad.

"Listen! I took the case of children only to make my case clearer. Of
the other tears of humanity with which the earth is soaked from its crust
to its centre, I will say nothing. I have narrowed my subject on purpose. I
am a bug, and I recognise in all humility that I cannot understand why the
world is arranged as it is. Men are themselves to blame, I suppose; they
were given paradise, they wanted freedom, and stole fire from heaven,
though they knew they would become unhappy, so there is no need to pity
them. With my pitiful, earthly, Euclidian understanding, all I know is that
there is suffering and that there are none guilty; that cause follows effect,
simply and directly; that everything flows and finds its level—but that's only
Euclidian nonsense, I know that, and I can't consent to live by it! What
comfort is it to me that there are none guilty and that cause follows effect
simply and directly, and that I know it—I must have justice, or I will
destroy myself. And not justice in some remote infinite time and space,
but here on earth, and that I could see myself. I have believed in it. I want
to see it, and if I am dead by then, let me rise again, for if it all happens
without me, it will be too unfair. Surely I haven't suffered, simply that I,
my crimes and my sufferings, may manure the soil of the future harmony
for somebody else. I want to see with my own eyes the hind lie down with
the lion and the victim rise up and embrace his murderer. I want to be
there when every one suddenly understands what it has all been for. All
the religions of the world are built on this longing, and I am a believer. But

* Alyosha is studying for the priesthood and Zossima is the name of his superior (Ed.).

then there are the children, and what am I to do about them? That's a question I can't answer. For the hundredth time I repeat, there are numbers of
questions, but I've only taken the children, because in their case what I
mean is so unanswerably clear. Listen! If all must suffer to pay for the
eternal harmony, what have children to do with it, tell me, please? It's
beyond all comprehension why they should suffer, and why they should pay
for the harmony. Why should they, too, furnish material to enrich the soil
for the harmony of the future? I understand solidarity in sin among men.
I understand solidarity in retribution, too; but there can be no such solidarity with children. And if it is really true that they must share responsibility
for all their fathers' crimes, such a truth is not of this world and is beyond
my comprehension. Some jester will say, perhaps, that the child would have
grown up and have sinned, but you see he didn't grow up, he was torn to
pieces by the dogs, at eight years old. Oh, Alyosha, I am not blaspheming!
I understand, of course, what an upheaval of the universe it will be, when
everything in heaven and earth blends in one hymn of praise and everything that lives and has lived cries aloud: 'Thou art just, O Lord, for Thy
ways are revealed.' When the mother embraces the fiend who threw her
child to the dogs, and all three cry aloud with tears, 'Thou art just, O
Lord!' then, of course, the crown of knowledge will be reached and all
will be made clear. But what pulls me up here is that I can't accept that
harmony. And while I am on earth, I make haste to take my own measures.
You see, Alyosha, perhaps it really may happen that if I live to that
moment, or rise again to see it, I, too, perhaps, may cry aloud with the rest,
looking at the mother embracing the child's torturer, 'Thou art just, O
Lord!' but I don't want to cry aloud then. While there is still time, I
hasten to protect myself and so I renounce the higher harmony altogether.
It's not worth the tears of that one tortured child who beat itself on the
breast with its little fist and prayed in its stinking outhouse, with its unexpiated tears to 'dear, kind God'! It's not worth it, because those tears
are unatoned for. They must be atoned for, or there can be no harmony.
But how? How are you going to atone for them? Is it possible? By their
being avenged? But what do I care for avenging them? What do I care for
a hell for oppressors? What good can hell do, since those children have
already been tortured? And what becomes of harmony, if there is hell? I
want to forgive. I want to embrace. I don't want more suffering. And if the
sufferings of children go to swell the sum of sufferings which was necessary
to pay for truth, then I protest that the truth is not worth such a price. I
don't want the mother to embrace the oppressor who threw her son to the
dogs! She dare not forgive him! Let her forgive him for herself, if she will,
let her forgive the torturer for the immeasurable suffering of her mother's
heart. But the sufferings of her tortured child she has no right to forgive;
she dare not forgive the torturer, even if the child were to forgive him!
And if that is so, if they dare not forgive, what becomes of harmony? Is
there in the whole world a being who would have the right to forgive and
could forgive? I don't want harmony. From love for humanity I don't want

it. I would rather be left with the unavenged suffering. I would rather
remain with my unavenged suffering and unsatisfied indignation, *even if I
were wrong.* Besides, too high a price is asked for harmony; it's beyond
our means to pay so much to enter on it. And so I hasten to give back my
entrance ticket, and if I am an honest man I am bound to give it back as
soon as possible. And that I am doing. It's not God that I don't accept,
Alyosha, only I most respectfully return Him the ticket."

"That's rebellion," murmured Alyosha, looking down.

"Rebellion? I am sorry you call it that," said Ivan earnestly. "One can
hardly live in rebellion, and I want to live. Tell me yourself, I challenge
you—answer. Imagine that you are creating a fabric of human destiny
with the object of making men happy in the end, giving them peace and
rest at last, but that it was essential and inevitable to torture to death only
one tiny creature—that baby beating its breast with its fist, for instance—
and to found that edifice on its unavenged tears, would you consent to be
the architect on those conditions? Tell me, and tell the truth."

"No, I wouldn't consent," said Alyosha softly.

"And you can admit the idea that men for whom you are building it
would agree to accept their happiness on the foundation of the unexpiated
blood of a little victim? And accepting it would remain happy for ever?"

"No, I can't admit it. Brother," said Aloysha suddenly, with flashing
eyes, "you said just now, is there a being in the whole world who would
have the right to forgive and could forgive? But there is a Being and He
can forgive everything, all and for all, because He gave His innocent blood
for all and everything. You have forgotten Him, and on Him is built the
edifice, and it is to Him they cry aloud, 'Thou art just, O Lord, for Thy
ways are revealed!' " . . .

39   The Problem of Evil

John Hick

To MANY, THE MOST POWERFUL positive objection to belief in God is the fact of evil. Probably for most agnostics it is the appalling depth and extent of human suffering, more than anything else, that makes the idea of a loving Creator seem so implausible and disposes them toward one or another of the various naturalistic theories of religion.

As a challenge to theism, the problem of evil has traditionally been posed in the form of a dilemma: if God is perfectly loving, he must wish to abolish evil; and if he is all-powerful, he must be able to abolish evil. But evil exists; therefore God cannot be both omnipotent and perfectly loving.

Certain solutions, which at once suggest themselves, have to be ruled out so far as the Judaic-Christian faith is concerned.

To say, for example (with contemporary Christian Science), that evil is an illusion of the human mind, is impossible within a religion based upon the stark realism of the Bible. Its pages faithfully reflect the characteristic mixture of good and evil in human experience. They record every kind of sorrow and suffering, every mode of man's inhumanity to man and of his painfully insecure existence in the world. There is no attempt to regard evil as anything but dark, menacingly ugly, heart-rending, and crushing. In the Christian scriptures, the climax of this history of evil is the crucifixion of Jesus, which is presented not only as a case of utterly unjust suffering, but as the violent and murderous rejection of God's Messiah. There can be no doubt, then, that for biblical faith, evil is unambiguously evil, and stands in direct opposition to God's will.

Again, to solve the problem of evil by means of the theory (sponsored, for example, by the Boston "Personalist" School)[1] of a finite deity who

[This selection is part of Chapter III of *Philosophy of Religion* (1963). It is reprinted with the kind permission of the author and of Prentice-Hall, Inc., Englewood Cliffs.]
1. Edgar Brightman's *A Philosophy of Religion* (Englewood Cliffs, N.J.: Prentice-Hall, Inc., 1940), Chaps. 8–10, is a classic exposition of one form of this view.

does the best he can with a material, intractable and co-eternal with himself, is to have abandoned the basic premise of Hebrew-Christian monotheism; for the theory amounts to rejecting belief in the infinity and sovereignty of God.

Indeed, any theory which would avoid the problem of the origin of evil by depicting it as an ultimate constituent of the universe, coordinate with good, has been repudiated in advance by the classic Christian teaching, first developed by Augustine, that evil represents the going wrong of something which in itself is good.[2] Augustine holds firmly to the Hebrew-Christian conviction that the universe is *good*—that is to say, it is the creation of a good God for a good purpose. He completely rejects the ancient prejudice, widespread in his day, that matter is evil. There are, according to Augustine, higher and lower, greater and lesser goods in immense abundance and variety; but everything which has being is good in its own way and degree, except in so far as it may have become spoiled or corrupted. Evil—whether it be an evil will, an instance of pain, or some disorder or decay in nature—has not been set there by God, but represents the distortion of something that is inherently valuable. Whatever exists is, as such, and in its proper place, good; evil is essentially parasitic upon good, being disorder and perversion in a fundamentally good creation. This understanding of evil as something negative means that it is not willed and created by God; but it does not mean (as some have supposed) that evil is unreal and can be disregarded. Clearly, the first effect of this doctrine is to accentuate even more the question of the origin of evil.

Theodicy,[3] as many modern Christian thinkers see it, is a modest enterprise, negative rather than positive in its conclusions. It does not claim to explain, nor to explain away, every instance of evil in human experience, but only to point to certain considerations which prevent the fact of evil (largely incomprehensible though it remains) from constituting a final and insuperable bar to rational belief in God.

In indicating these considerations it will be useful to follow the traditional division of the subject. There is the problem of *moral evil* or wickedness: why does an all-good and all-powerful God permit this? And there is the problem of the *non-moral evil* of suffering or pain, both physical and mental: why has an all-good and all-powerful God created a world in which this occurs?

Christian thought has always considered moral evil in its relation to human freedom and responsibility. To be a person is to be a finite center of freedom, a (relatively) free and self-directing agent responsible for one's own decisions. This involves being free to act wrongly as well as to act rightly. The idea of a person who can be infallibly guaranteed

2. See Augustine's *Confessions*, Book VII, Chap. 12; *City of God*, Book XII, Chap. 3; *Enchiridion*, Chap. 4.
3. The word "theodicy" from the Greek *theos* (God) and *dike* (righteous) means the justification of God's goodness in face of the fact of evil.

always to act rightly is self-contradictory. There can be no guarantee in advance that a genuinely free moral agent will never choose amiss. Consequently, the possibility of wrongdoing or sin is logically inseparable from the creation of finite persons, and to say that God should not have created beings who might sin amounts to saying that he should not have created people.

This thesis has been challenged in some recent philosophical discussions of the problem of evil, in which it is claimed that no contradiction is involved in saying that God might have made people who would be genuinely free and who could yet be guaranteed always to act rightly. A quotation from one of these discussions follows:

> If there is no logical impossibility in a man's freely choosing the good on one, or on several occasions, there cannot be a logical impossibility in his freely choosing the good on every occasion. God was not, then, faced with a choice between making innocent automata and making beings who, in acting freely, would sometimes go wrong: there was open to him the obviously better possibility of making beings who would act freely but always go right. Clearly, his failure to avail himself of this possibility is inconsistent with his being both omnipotent and wholly good.[4]

A reply to this argument is suggested in another recent contribution to the discussion.[5] If by a free action we mean an action which is not externally compelled but which flows from the nature of the agent as he reacts to the circumstances in which he finds himself, there is, indeed, no contradiction between our being free and our actions being "caused" (by our own nature) and therefore being in principle predictable. There is a contradiction, however, in saying that God is the cause of our acting as we do but that we are free beings in relation to God. There is, in other words, a contradiction in saying that God has made us so that we shall of necessity act in a certain way, and that we are genuinely independent persons in relation to him. If all our thoughts and actions are divinely predestined, however free and morally responsible we may seem to be to ourselves, we cannot be free and morally responsible in the sight of God, but must instead be his helpless puppets. Such "freedom" is like that of a patient acting out a series of posthypnotic suggestions: he appears, even to himself, to be free, but his volitions have actually been predetermined by another will, that of the hypnotist, in relation to whom the patient is not a free agent.

A different objector might raise the question of whether or not we deny God's omnipotence if we admit that he is unable to create persons who are free from the risks inherent in personal freedom. The answer that has always been given is that to create such beings is logically im-

4. J. L. Mackie, "Evil and Omnipotence," *Mind* (April, 1955), p. 209. A similar point is made by Antony Flew in "Divine Omnipotence and Human Freedom," *New Essays in Philosophical Theology*. An important critical comment on these arguments is offered by Ninian Smart in "Omnipotence, Evil and Supermen," *Philosophy* (April, 1961), with replies by Flew (January, 1962) and Mackie (April, 1962).
5. Flew, in *New Essays in Philosophical Theology*.

possible. It is no limitation upon God's power that he cannot accomplish the logically impossible, since there is nothing here to accomplish, but only a meaningless conjunction of words[6]—in this case "person who is not a person." God is able to create beings of any and every conceivable kind; but creatures who lack moral freedom, however superior they might be to human beings in other respects, would not be what we mean by persons. They would constitute a different form of life which God might have brought into existence instead of persons. When we ask why God did not create such beings in place of persons, the traditional answer is that only persons could, in any meaningful sense, become "children of God," capable of entering into a personal relationship with their Creator by a free and uncompelled response to his love.

When we turn from the possibility of moral evil as a correlate of man's personal freedom to its actuality, we face something which must remain inexplicable even when it can be seen to be possible. For we can never provide a complete causal explanation of a free act; if we could, it would not be a free act. The origin of moral evil lies forever concealed within the mystery of human freedom.

The necessary connection between moral freedom and the possibility, now actualized, of sin throws light upon a great deal of the suffering which afflicts mankind. For an enormous amount of human pain arises either from the inhumanity or the culpable incompetence of mankind. This includes such major scourges as poverty, oppression and persecution, war, and all the injustice, indignity, and inequity which occur even in the most advanced societies. These evils are manifestations of human sin. Even disease is fostered to an extent, the limits of which have not yet been determined by psychosomatic medicine, by moral and emotional factors seated both in the individual and in his social environment. To the extent that all of these evils stem from human failures and wrong decisions, their possibility is inherent in the creation of free persons inhabiting a world which presents them with real choices which are followed by real consequences.

We may now turn more directly to the problem of suffering. Even though the major bulk of actual human pain is traceable to man's misused freedom as a sole or part cause, there remain other sources of pain which are entirely independent of the human will, for example, earthquake, hurricane, storm, flood, drought, and blight. In practice, it is often impossible to trace a boundary between the suffering which results from human wickedness and folly and that which falls upon mankind from without. Both kinds of suffering are inextricably mingled together in human experience. For our present purpose, however, it is important to note that the latter category does exist and that it seems to be built into the very structure of our world. In response to it, theodicy, if it is wisely conducted, follows a negative path. It is not possible to show positively

6. As Aquinas said, ". . . nothing that implies a contradiction falls under the scope of God's omnipotence." *Summa Theologica*, Part I, Question 25, article 4.

that each item of human pain serves the divine purpose of good; but, on the other hand, it does seem possible to show that the divine purpose as it is understood in Judaism and Christianity could not be forwarded in a world which was designed as a permanent hedonistic paradise.

An essential premise of this argument concerns the nature of the divine purpose in creating the world. The skeptic's assumption is that man is to be viewed as a completed creation and that God's purpose in making the world was to provide a suitable dwelling-place for this fully-formed creature. Since God is good and loving, the environment which he has created for human life to inhabit is naturally as pleasant and comfortable as possible. The problem is essentially similar to that of a man who builds a cage for some pet animal. Since our world, in fact, contains sources of hardship, inconvenience, and danger of innumerable kinds, the conclusion follows that this world cannot have been created by a perfectly benevolent and all-powerful deity.[7]

Christianity, however, has never supposed that God's purpose in the creation of the world was to construct a paradise whose inhabitants would experience a maximum of pleasure and a minimum of pain. The world is seen, instead, as a place of "soul-making" in which free beings grappling with the tasks and challenges of their existence in a common environment, may become "children of God" and "heirs of eternal life." A way of thinking theologically of God's continuing creative purpose for man was suggested by some of the early Hellenistic Fathers of the Christian Church, especially Irenaeus. Following hints from St. Paul, Irenaeus taught that man has been made as a person in the image of God but has not yet been brought as a free and responsible agent into the finite likeness of God, which is revealed in Christ.[8] Our world, with all its rough edges, is the sphere in which this second and harder stage of the creative process is taking place.

This conception of the world (whether or not set in Irenaeus' theological framework) can be supported by the method of negative theodicy. Suppose, contrary to fact, that this world were a paradise from which all possibility of pain and suffering were excluded. The consequences would be very far-reaching. For example, no one could ever injure anyone else: the murderer's knife would turn to paper or his bullets to thin air; the bank safe, robbed of a million dollars, would miraculously become filled with another million dollars (without this device, on however large a scale, proving inflationary); fraud, deceit, conspiracy, and treason would somehow always leave the fabric of society undamaged. Again, no one would ever be injured by accident: the mountain-climber, steeplejack, or playing child falling from a height would float unharmed to the ground; the reckless driver would never meet with disaster. There would be no

7. This is the nature of David Hume's argument in his discussion of the problem of evil in his *Dialogues*, Part XI.
8. See Irenaeus' *Against Heresies*, Book IV, Chaps. 37 and 38.

need to work, since no harm could result from avoiding work; there would be no call to be concerned for others in time of need or danger, for in such a world there could be no real needs or dangers.

To make possible this continual series of individual adjustments, nature would have to work by "special providences" instead of running according to general laws which men must learn to respect on penalty of pain or death. The laws of nature would have to be extremely flexible: sometimes gravity would operate, sometimes not; sometimes an object would be hard and solid, sometimes soft. There could be no sciences, for there would be no enduring world structure to investigate. In eliminating the problems and hardships of an objective environment, with its own laws, life would become like a dream in which, delightfully but aimlessly, we would float and drift at ease.

One can at least begin to imagine such a world. It is evident that our present ethical concepts would have no meaning in it. If, for example, the notion of harming someone is an essential element in the concept of a wrong action, in our hedonistic paradise there could be no wrong actions— nor any right actions in distinction from wrong. Courage and fortitude would have no point in an environment in which there is, by definition, no danger or difficulty. Generosity, kindness, the *agape* aspect of love, prudence, unselfishness, and all other ethical notions which presuppose life in a stable environment, could not even be formed. Consequently, such a world, however well it might promote pleasure, would be very ill adapted for the development of the moral qualities of human personality. In relation to this purpose it would be the worst of all possible worlds.

It would seem, then, that an environment intended to make possible the growth in free beings of the finest characteristics of personal life, must have a good deal in common with our present world. It must operate according to general and dependable laws; and it must involve real dangers, difficulties, problems, obstacles, and possibilities of pain, failure, sorrow, frustration, and defeat. If it did not contain the particular trials and perils which—subtracting man's own very considerable contribution— our world contains, it would have to contain others instead.

To realize this is not, by any means, to be in possession of a detailed theodicy. It is to understand that this world, with all its "heartaches and the thousand natural shocks that flesh is heir to," an environment so manifestly not designed for the maximization of human pleasure and the minimization of human pain, may be rather well adapted to the quite different purpose of "soul-making."[9]

These considerations are related to theism as such. Specifically, Christian theism goes further in the light of the death of Christ, which is seen paradoxically both (as the murder of the divine Son) as the worst thing

9. This brief discussion has been confined to the problem of human suffering. The large and intractable problem of animal pain is not taken up here. For a discussion of it, see, for example, Nels Ferré, *Evil and the Christian Faith* (New York: Harper & Row, Publishers, Inc., 1947), Chap. 7; and Austin Farrer, *Love Almighty and Ills Unlimited* (New York: Doubleday & Company, Inc., 1961), Chap. 5.

that has ever happened and (as the occasion of man's salvation) as the best thing that has ever happened. As the supreme evil turned to supreme good, it provides the paradigm for the distinctively Christian reaction to evil. Viewed from the standpoint of Christian faith, evils do not cease to be evils; and certainly, in view of Christ's healing work, they cannot be said to have been sent by God. Yet, it has been the persistent claim of those seriously and wholeheartedly committed to Christian discipleship that tragedy, though truly tragic, may nevertheless be turned, through a man's reaction to it, from a cause of despair and alienation from God to a stage in the fulfillment of God's loving purpose for that individual. As the greatest of all evils, the crucifixion of Christ, was made the occasion of man's redemption, so good can be won from other evils. As Jesus saw his execution by the Romans as an experience which God desired him to accept, an experience which was to be brought within the sphere of the divine purpose and made to serve the divine ends, so the Christian response to calamity is to accept the adversities, pains, and afflictions which life brings, in order that they can be turned to a positive spiritual use.[10]

At this point, theodicy points forward in two ways to the subject of life after death.

First, although there are many striking instances of good being triumphantly brought out of evil through a man's or a woman's reaction to it, there are many other cases in which the opposite has happened. Sometimes obstacles breed strength of character, dangers evoke courage and unselfishness, and calamities produce patience and moral steadfastness. But sometimes they lead, instead, to resentment, fear, grasping selfishness, and disintegration of character. Therefore, it would seem that any divine purpose of soul-making which is at work in earthly history must continue beyond this life if it is ever to achieve more than a very partial and fragmentary success.

Second, if we ask whether the business of soul-making is worth all the toil and sorrow of human life, the Christian answer must be in terms of a future good which is great enough to justify all that has happened on the way to it.*

10. This conception of providence is stated more fully in John Hick, *Faith and Knowledge* (Ithaca: Cornell University Press, 1957), Chap. 7, from which some sentences are incorporated in this paragraph.

* In his later book, *Evil and the God of Love,* Professor Hick discusses in detail how the appeal to a life after death completes his theodicy. The next selection, Selection 40, contains some extracts from this work. (Ed.)

40   Evil and the Infinite
Future Good

John Hick

. . . W<small>E CANNOT HOPE TO STATE</small> a Christian theodicy without taking seriously the doctrine of a life beyond the grave. This doctrine is not, of course, based upon any theory of natural immortality, but upon the hope that beyond death God will resurrect or re-create or reconstitute the human personality in both its inner and its outer aspects. The Christian claim is that the ultimate life of man—after what further scenes of "soul-making" we do not know—lies in that Kingdom of God which is depicted in the teaching of Jesus as a state of exultant and blissful happiness, symbolized as a joyous banquet in which all and sundry, having accepted God's gracious invitation, rejoice together. And Christian theodicy must point forward to that final blessedness, and claim that this infinite future good will render worth while all the pain and travail and wickedness that has occurred on the way to it. Theodicy cannot be content to look to the past, seeking an explanation of evil in its origins, but must look towards the future, expecting a triumphant resolution in the eventual perfect fulfilment of God's good purpose. We cannot, of course, concretely picture to ourselves the nature of this fulfilment; we can only say that it represents the best gift of God's infinite love for His children.

[This selection is taken from Chapter XVII of John Hick, *Evil and the God of Love*, published by Harper & Row in 1966. It is reprinted with Professor Hick's permission.]

But no other acceptable possibility of Christian theodicy offers itself than that in the human creature's joyous participation in the completed creation his sufferings, struggles, and failures will be seen to be justified by their outcome.[1] We must thus affirm in faith that there will in the final accounting be no personal life that is unperfected and no suffering that has not eventually become a phase in the fulfilment of God's good purpose. Only so, I suggest, is it possible to believe both in the perfect goodness of God and in His unlimited capacity to perform His will. For if there are finally wasted lives and finally unredeemed sufferings, either God is not perfect in love or He is not sovereign in rule over His creation.

It is perhaps worth pointing out here the difference between this position and another to which it is in some ways similar, namely the view that the promised joys of heaven are to be related to man's earthly travails as a compensation or reward. This suggests a divine arrangement equitably proportioning compensation to injury, so that the more an individual has suffered beyond his desert the more intense or the more prolonged will be the heavenly bliss that he experiences. Thus those who have suffered most will subsequently have cause to rejoice most; and presumably, if the just proportion is to be preserved, none will enjoy an endless or infinite bliss, since none will have suffered an unending or unlimited injury. As distinct from such a book-keeping view, what is being suggested here, so far as men's sufferings are concerned, is that these sufferings—which for some people are immense and for others relatively slight—will in the end lead to the enjoyment of a common good which will be unending and therefore unlimited, and which will be seen by its participants as justifying all that has been endured on the way to it. The "good eschaton" will not be a reward or a compensation proportioned to each individual's trials, but an infinite good that would render worth while any finite suffering endured in the course of attaining to it. . . .

Christian theodicy claims, then, that the end to which God is leading us is a good so great as to justify all the failures and suffering and sorrow that will have been endured on the way to it. The life of the Kingdom of God will be an infinite, because eternal, good, outweighing all temporal and therefore finite evils. We cannot visualize the life of the redeemed and perfected creation, for all our imagery is necessarily drawn from our present "fallen" world. We can think only in very general terms of the opening up before us of new dimensions of reality "which eye hath not seen nor ear heard nor the heart of man conceived";[2] a new intensity and vividness of experience; of expanded capacities for fulfilment in personal relationships, artistic and other forms of creativity, knowledge, wonder, the enjoyment of beauty, and yet other goods and kinds of goods at present beyond our ken.

But, having said this, questions and difficulties at once arise. Could

1. Cf. Emil Brunner, *Man in Revolt,* trans. Olive Wyon (London: Lutterworth Press, 1939), p. 454.
2. I Corinthians ii. 9.

even an endless heavenly joy ever heal the scars of deep human suffering? It has been said (by Leon Bloy) that *"Souffrir passe; avoir souffert ne passe jamais."** Physical pain is quickly forgotten; but the memory and the effects of mental and emotional anguish can remain with us throughout our lives and presumably beyond this life so long as there is continuity of personal identity. Would not, then, the recollection of past miseries, shames, crimes, injustices, hatreds, and agonies—including the recollection of witnessing the sufferings of others—destroy the happiness of heaven?[3]

It is very difficult to resolve such a question; for we do not know what is possible, let alone what is probable, in realms of being so far beyond our present experence. We can think only in terms of what Plato called "likely tales." It may be that the personal scars and memories of evil remain forever, but are transfigured in the light of the universal mutual forgiveness and reconciliation on which the life of heaven is based. Or it may be that the journey to the heavenly Kingdom is so long, and traverses such varied spheres of existence, involving so many new and transforming experiences, that in the end memory of our earthly life is dimmed to the point of extinction. There is no evident ground or need to decide between such possibilities, and I mention them only to suggest that the puzzle that was raised, although not at present soluble, is also not such as to overthrow the theodicy that we have been developing.

---

* "Suffering passes, but the fact that one has suffered remains forever."
3. For a powerful underlining of this question, see Dostoevsky's *The Brothers Karamazov,* pt. II, bk. v, chap. 4. (See Selection 38 above)

41 The Existence of God

—A Debate

Bertrand Russell and F. C. Copleston

COPLESTON: AS WE ARE GOING TO discuss the existence of God, it might perhaps be as well to come to some provisional agreement as to what we understand by the term "God." I presume that we mean a supreme personal being—distinct from the world and creator of the world. Would you agree—provisionally at least—to accept this statement as the meaning of the term "God"?

RUSSELL: Yes, I accept this definition.

COPLESTON: Well, my position is the affirmative position that such a being actually exists, and that His existence can be proved philosophically. Perhaps you would tell me if your position is that of agnosticism or of atheism. I mean, would you say that the non-existence of God can be proved?

RUSSELL: No, I should not say that: my position is agnostic.

COPLESTON: Would you agree with me that the problem of God is a problem of great importance? For example, would you agree that if God does not exist, human beings and human history can have no other purpose than the purpose they choose to give themselves, which—in practice—is likely to mean the purpose which those impose who have the power to impose it?

RUSSELL: Roughly speaking, yes, though I should have to place some limitation on your last clause.

COPLESTON: Would you agree that if there is no God—no absolute Being—there can be no absolute values? I mean, would you agree that if there is no absolute good that the relativity of values results?

[This debate was broadcast in 1948 on the Third Program of the British Broadcasting Corporation. It was published in *Humanitas* (Manchester) and is reprinted here with the kind permission of Bertrand Russell and Father Copleston.]

RUSSELL: No, I think these questions are logically distinct. Take, for instance, G. E. Moore's *Principia Ethica,* where he maintains that there is a distinction of good and evil, that both of these are definite concepts. But he does not bring in the idea of God to support that contention.

COPLESTON: Well, suppose we leave the question of good till later, till we come to the moral argument, and I give first a metaphysical argument. I'd like to put the main weight on the metaphysical argument based on Leibniz's argument from "Contingency" and then later we might discuss the moral argument. Suppose I give a brief statement on the metaphysical argument and that then we go on to discuss it?

RUSSELL: That seems to me to be a very good plan.

The Argument from Contingency

COPLESTON: Well, for clarity's sake, I'll divide the argument into distinct stages. First of all, I should say, we know that there are at least some beings in the world which do not contain in themselves the reason for their existence. For example, I depend on my parents, and now on the air, and on food, and so on. Now, secondly, the world is simply the real or imagined totality or aggregate of individual objects, none of which contain in themselves alone the reason for their existence. There isn't any world distinct from the objects which form it, any more than the human race is something apart from the members. Therefore, I should say, since objects or events exist, and since no object of experience contains within itself the reason of its existence, this reason, the totality of objects, must have a reason external to itself. That reason must be an existent being. Well, this being is either itself the reason for its own existence, or it is not. If it is, well and good. If it is not, then we must proceed farther. But if we proceed to infinity in that sense, then there's no explanation of existence at all. So, I should say, in order to explain existence, we must come to a being which contains within itself the reason for its own existence, that is to say, which cannot not exist.

RUSSELL: This raises a great many points and it is not altogether easy to know where to begin, but I think that, perhaps, in answering your argument, the best point at which to begin is the question of necessary being. The word "necessary," I should maintain, can only be applied significantly to propositions. And, in fact, only to such as are analytic—that is to say—such as it is self-contradictory to deny. I could only admit a necessary being if there were a being whose existence it is self-contradictory to deny. I should like to know whether you would accept Leibniz's division of propositions into truths of reason and truths of fact. The former—the truths of reason—being necessary.

COPLESTON: Well, I certainly should not subscribe to what seems to be Leibniz's idea of truths of reason and truths of fact, since it would appear that, for him, there are in the long run only analytic propositions. It would seem that for Leibniz truths of fact are ultimately reducible to truths of reason. That is to say, to analytic propositions, at least for an omniscient mind. Well, I couldn't agree with that. For one thing, it would fail to meet the requirements of the experience of freedom. I don't want to uphold the whole philosophy of Leibniz. I have made use of his argument from contingent to necessary being, basing the argument on the principle of sufficient reason, simply because it seems to me a brief and clear formulation of what is, in my opinion, the fundamental metaphysical argument for God's existence.

RUSSELL: But, to my mind, "a necessary proposition" has got to be analytic. I don't see what else it can mean. And analytic propositions are always complex and logically somewhat late. "Irrational animals are animals" is an analytic proposition; but a proposition such as "This is an animal" can never be analytic. In fact, all the propositions that can be analytic are somewhat late in the build-up of propositions.

COPLESTON: Take the proposition "If there is a contingent being then there is a necessary being." I consider that that proposition hypothetically expressed is a necessary proposition. If you are going to call every necessary proposition an analytic proposition, then—in order to avoid a dispute in terminology—I would agree to call it analytic, though I don't consider it a tautological proposition. But the proposition is a necessary proposition only on the supposition that there is a contingent being. That there is a contingent being actually existing has to be discovered by experience, and the proposition that there is a contingent being is certainly not an analytic proposition, though once you know, I should maintain, that there is a contingent being, it follows of necessity that there is a necessary being.

RUSSELL: The difficulty of this argument is that I don't admit the idea of a necessary being and I don't admit that there is any particular meaning in calling other beings "contingent." These phrases don't for me have a significance except within a logic that I reject.

COPLESTON: Do you mean that you reject these terms because they won't fit in with what is called "modern logic"?

RUSSELL: Well, I can't find anything that they could mean. The word "necessary," it seems to me, is a useless word, except as applied to analytic propositions, not to things.

COPLESTON: In the first place, what do you mean by "modern logic"? As far as I know, there are somewhat differing systems. In the second place, not all modern logicians surely would admit the meaninglessness of metaphysics. We both know, at any rate, one very eminent modern thinker whose knowledge of modern logic was profound, but who certainly did not think that metaphysics are meaningless or, in particular, that the problem of God is meaningless. Again, even if all modern logicians held that metaphysical terms are meaningless, it would not follow that they were right. The proposition that metaphysical terms are meaningless seems to me to be a proposition based on an assumed philosophy. The dogmatic position behind it seems to be this: What will not go into my machine is non-existent, or it is meaningless; it is the expression of emotion. I am simply trying to point out that anybody who says that a particular system of modern logic is the sole criterion of meaning is saying something that is over-dogmatic; he is dogmatically insisting that a part of philosophy is the whole of philosophy. After all, a "contingent" being is a being which has not in itself the complete reason for its existence, that's what I mean by a contingent being. You know, as well as I do, that the existence of neither of us can be explained without reference to something or somebody outside us, our parents, for example. A "necessary" being, on the other hand, means a being that must and cannot not exist. You may say that there is no such being, but you will find it hard to convince me that you do not understand the terms I am using. If you do not understand them, then how can you be entitled to say that such a being does not exist, if that is what you do say?

RUSSELL: Well, there are points here that I don't propose to go into at length. I don't maintain the meaninglessness of metaphysics in general at all. I maintain the meaninglessness of certain particular terms—not on any general ground, but simply because I've not been able to see an interpretation of those particular terms. It's not a general dogma—it's a particular thing. But those points I will leave out for the moment. And I will say that what you have been saying brings us back, it seems to me, to the ontological argument that there is a being whose essence involves existence, so that his existence is analytic. That seems to me to be impossible, and it raises, of course, the question what one means by existence, and as to this, I think a subject named can never be significantly said to exist but only a subject described. And that existence, in fact, quite definitely is not a predicate.

COPLESTON: Well, you say, I believe, that it is bad grammar, or rather bad syntax to say for example "T. S. Eliot exists"; one ought to say, for example, "He, the author of *Murder in the Cathedral,* exists." Are you going to say that the proposition, "The cause of the world exists," is without meaning? You may say that the world has no cause; but I fail to see how you can say that the proposition that "the cause of the world exists" is meaningless. Put it in the form of a question: "Has the world a cause?" or "Does a cause of the world exist?" Most people surely would understand the question, even if they don't agree about the answer.

RUSSELL: Well, certainly the question "Does the cause of the world exist?" is a question that has meaning. But if you say "Yes, God is the cause of the world" you're using God as a proper name; then "God exists" will not be a statement that has meaning; that is the position that I'm maintaining. Because, therefore, it will follow that it cannot be an analytic proposition ever to say that this or that exists. For example, suppose you take as your subject "the existent round-square," it would look like an analytic proposition that "the existent round-square exists," but it doesn't exist.

COPLESTON: No, it doesn't, then surely you can't say it doesn't exist unless you have a conception of what existence is. As to the phrase "existent round-square," I should say that it has no meaning at all.

RUSSELL: I quite agree. Then I should say the same thing in another context in reference to a "necessary being."

COPLESTON: Well, we seem to have arrived at an impasse. To say that a necessary being is a being that must exist and cannot not exist has for me a definite meaning. For you it has no meaning.

RUSSELL: Well, we can press the point a little, I think. A being that must exist and cannot not exist, would surely, according to you, be a being whose essence involves existence.

COPLESTON: Yes, a being the essence of which is to exist. But I should not be willing to argue the existence of God simply from the idea of His essence because I don't think we have any clear intuition of God's essence as yet. I think we have to argue from the world of experience to God.

RUSSELL: Yes, I quite see the distinction. But, at the same time, for a being with sufficient knowledge it would be true to say "Here is this being whose essence involves existence!"

COPLESTON: Yes, certainly if anybody saw God, he would see that God must exist.

RUSSELL: So that I mean there is a being whose essence involves existence although we don't know that essence. We only know there is such a being.

COPLESTON: Yes, I should add we don't know the essence *a priori*. It is only *a posteriori* through our experience of the world that we come to a knowledge of the existence of that being. And then one argues, the essence and existence must be identical. Because if God's essence and God's existence was not identical, then some sufficient reason for this existence would have to be found beyond God.

RUSSELL: So it all turns on this question of sufficient reason, and I must say you haven't defined "sufficient reason" in a way that I can understand—what do you mean by sufficient reason? You don't mean cause?

COPLESTON: Not necessarily. Cause is a kind of sufficient reason. Only contingent being can have a cause. God is His own sufficient reason; and He is not cause of Himself. By sufficient reason in the full sense I mean an explanation adequate for the existence of some particular being.

RUSSELL: But when is an explanation adequate? Suppose I am about to make a flame with a match. You may say that the adequate explanation of that is that I rub it on the box.

COPLESTON: Well, for practical purposes—but theoretically, that is only a partial explanation. An adequate explanation must ultimately be a total explanation, to which nothing further can be added.

RUSSELL: Then I can only say that you're looking for something which can't be got, and which one ought not to expect to get.

COPLESTON: To say that one has not found it is one thing; to say that one should not look for it seems to me rather dogmatic.

RUSSELL: Well, I don't know. I mean, the explanation of one thing is another thing which makes the other thing dependent on yet another, and you have to grasp this sorry scheme of things entire to do what you want, and that we can't do.

COPLESTON: But are you going to say that we can't, or we shouldn't even raise the question of the existence of the whole of this sorry scheme of things—of the whole universe?

RUSSELL: Yes. I don't think there's any meaning in it at all. I think the word "universe" is a handy word in some connections, but I don't think it stands for anything that has a meaning.

COPLESTON: If the word is meaningless, it can't be so very handy. In any case, I don't say that the universe is something different from the objects which compose it (I indicated that in my brief summary of the proof), what I'm doing is to look for the reason, in this case the cause of the objects—the real or imagined totality of which constitute what we call the universe. You say, I think that the universe—or my existence if you prefer, or any other existence—is unintelligible?

RUSSELL: First may I take up the point that if a word is meaningless it can't be handy. That sounds well but isn't in fact correct. Take, say, such a word as "the" or "than." You can't point to any object that those words mean, but they are very useful words; I should say the same of "universe." But leaving that point, you ask whether I consider that the universe is unintelligible. I shouldn't say unintelligible—I think it is without explanation. Intelligible, to my mind, is a different thing. Intelligible has to do with the thing itself intrinsically and not with its relations.

COPLESTON: Well, my point is that what we call the world is intrinsically unintelligible, apart from the existence of God. You see, I don't believe that the infinity of the series of events—I mean a horizontal series, so to speak—if such an infinity could be proved, would be in the slightest degree relevant to the situation. If you add up chocolates you get chocolates after all and not a sheep. If you add up chocolates to infinity, you presumably get an infinite number of chocolates. So if you add up contingent beings to infinity, you still get contingent beings, not a necessary being. An infinite series of contingent beings will be, to my way of thinking, as unable to cause itself as one contingent being. However, you say, I think, that it is illegitimate to raise the question of what will explain the existence of any particular object?

RUSSELL: It's quite all right if you mean by explaining it, simply finding a cause for it.

COPLESTON: Well, why stop at one particular object? Why shouldn't one raise the question of the cause of the existence of all particular objects?

RUSSELL: Because I see no reason to think there is any. The whole concept of cause is one we derive from our observation of particular things; I see no reason whatsoever to suppose that the total has any cause whatsoever.

COPLESTON: Well, to say that there isn't any cause is not the same thing as saying that we shouldn't look for a cause. The statement that there isn't any cause should come, if it comes at all, at the end of the inquiry, not the beginning. In any case, if the total has no cause, then to my way of thinking it must be its own cause, which seems to me impossible. Moreover, the statement that the world is simply there if in answer to a question, presupposes that the question has meaning.

RUSSELL: No, it doesn't need to be its own cause, what I'm saying is that the concept of cause is not applicable to the total.

COPLESTON: Then you would agree with Sartre that the universe is what he calls "gratuitous"?

RUSSELL: Well, the word "gratuitous" suggests that it might be something else; I should say that the universe is just there, and that's all.

COPLESTON: Well, I can't see how you can rule out the legitimacy of asking the question how the total, or anything at all comes to be there. Why something rather than nothing, that is the question? The fact that we gain our knowledge of causality empirically, from particular causes, does not rule out the possibility of asking what the cause of the series is. If the word "cause" were meaningless or if it could be shown that Kant's view of the matter were correct, the question would be illegitimate I agree; but you don't seem to hold that the word "cause" is meaningless, and I do not suppose you are a Kantian.

RUSSELL: I can illustrate what seems to me your fallacy. Every man who exists has a mother, and it seems to me your argument is that therefore the human race must have a mother, but obviously the human race hasn't a mother—that's a different logical sphere.

COPLESTON: Well, I can't really see any parity. If I were saying "every object has a phenomenal cause, therefore, the whole series has a phenomenal cause," there would be a parity; but I'm not saying that; I'm saying, every object has a phenomenal cause if you insist on the infinity of the series—but the series of phenomenal causes is an insufficient explanation of the series. Therefore, the series has not a phenomenal cause but a transcendent cause.

RUSSELL: That's always assuming that not only every particular thing in the world, but the world as a whole must have a cause. For that assumption I see no ground whatever. If you'll give me a ground I'll listen to it.

COPLESTON: Well, the series of events is either caused or it's not caused. If it is caused, there must obviously be a cause outside the series. If it's not caused then it's sufficient to itself, and if it's sufficient to itself it is what I call necessary. But it can't be necessary since each member is contingent, and we've agreed that the total has no reality apart from its members, therefore, it can't be necessary. Therefore, it can't be (caused) —uncaused—therefore it must have a cause. And I should like to observe in passing that the statement "the world is simply there and is inexplicable" can't be got out of logical analysis.

RUSSELL: I don't want to seem arrogant, but it does seem to me that I can conceive things that you say the human mind can't conceive. As for things not having a cause, the physicists assure us that individual quantum transitions in atoms have no cause.

COPLESTON: Well, I wonder now whether that isn't simply a temporary inference.

RUSSELL: It may be, but it does show that physicists' minds can conceive it.

COPLESTON: Yes, I agree, some scientists—physicists—are willing to allow for indetermination within a restricted field. But very many scientists are not so willing. I think that Professor Dingle, of London University, maintains that the Heisenberg uncertainty principle tells us something about the success (or the lack of it) of the present atomic theory in correlating observations, but not about nature in itself, and many physicists would accept this view. In any case, I don't see how physicists can fail to accept the theory in practice, even if they don't do so in theory. I cannot see how science could be conducted on any other assumption than that of order and intelligibility in nature. The physicist presupposes, at least tacitly, that there is some sense in investigating nature and looking for the causes of events, just as the detective presupposes that there is some sense in looking for the cause of a murder. The metaphysician assumes that there is sense in looking for the reason or cause of phenomena, and, not being a Kantian, I consider that the metaphysician is as justified in his assumption as the physicist. When Sartre, for example, says that the world is gratuitous, I think that he has not sufficiently considered what is implied by "gratuitous."

RUSSELL: I think—there seems to me a certain unwarrantable extension here; a physicist looks for causes; that does not necessarily imply that there are causes everywhere. A man may look for gold without assuming that there is gold everywhere; if he finds gold, well and good, if he doesn't he's had bad luck. The same is true when the physicists look for causes. As for Sartre, I don't profess to know what he means, and I shouldn't like to be thought to interpret him, but for my part, I do think the notion of the world having an explanation is a mistake. I don't see why one should expect it to have, and I think what you say about what the scientist assumes is an over-statement.

COPLESTON: Well, it seems to me that the scientist does make some such assumption. When he experiments to find out some particular truth, behind that experiment lies the assumption that the universe is not simply discontinuous. There is the possibility of finding out a truth by experiment. The experiment may be a bad one, it may lead to no result, or not to the result that he wants, but that at any rate there is the possibility, through experiment, of finding out the truth that he assumes. And that seems to me to assume an ordered and intelligible universe.

RUSSELL: I think you're generalizing more than is necessary. Undoubtedly the scientist assumes that this sort of thing is likely to be found and will often be found. He does not assume that it will be found, and that's a very important matter in modern physics.

COPLESTON: Well, I think he does assume or is bound to assume it tacitly in practice. It may be that, to quote Professor Haldane, "when I light the gas under the kettle, some of the water molecules will fly off as vapor, and there is no way of finding out which will do so," but it doesn't follow necessarily that the idea of chance must be introduced except in relation to our knowledge.

RUSSELL: No it doesn't—at least if I may believe what he says. He's finding out quite a lot of things—the scientist is finding out quite a lot of things that are happening in the world, which are, at first, beginnings of causal chains—first causes which haven't in themselves got causes. He does not assume that everything has a cause.

COPLESTON: Surely that's a first cause within a certain selected field. It's a relatively first cause.

RUSSELL: I don't think he'd say so. If there's a world in which most events, but not all, have causes, he will then be able to depict the probabilities and uncertainties by assuming that this particular event you're interested in probably has a cause. And since in any case you won't get more than probability that's good enough.

COPLESTON: It may be that the scientist doesn't hope to obtain more than probability, but in raising the question he assumes that the question of explanation has a meaning. But your general point then, Lord Russell, is that it's illegitimate even to ask the question of the cause of the world?

RUSSELL: Yes, that's my position.

COPLESTON: If it's a question that for you has no meaning, it's of course very difficult to discuss it, isn't it?

RUSSELL: Yes, it is very difficult. What do you say—shall we pass on to some other issue?

Religious Experience

COPLESTON: Let's. Well, perhaps I might say a word about religious experience, and then we can go on to moral experience. I don't regard religious experience as a strict proof of the existence of God, so the character of the discussion changes somewhat, but I think it's true to say that the best explanation of it is the existence of God. By religious experience I don't mean simply feeling good. I mean a loving, but unclear, awareness of some object which irresistibly seems to the experiencer as something transcending the self, something transcending all the normal objects of experience, something which cannot be pictured or conceptualized, but of the reality of which doubt is impossible—at least during the experience. I should claim that cannot be explained adequately and without residue, simply subjectively. The actual basic experience at any rate is most easily explained on the hypothesis that there is actually some objective cause of that experience.

RUSSELL: I should reply to that line of argument that the whole argument from our own mental states to something outside us, is a very tricky affair. Even where we all admit its validity, we only feel justified in doing so, I think, because of the consensus of mankind. If there's a crowd in a room and there's a clock in a room, they can all see the clock. The fact that they can all see it tends to make them think that it's not an hallucination: whereas these religious experiences do tend to be very private.

COPLESTON: Yes, they do. I'm speaking strictly of mystical experience proper, and I certainly don't include, by the way, what are called visions. I mean simply the experience, and I quite admit it's indefinable, of the transcendent object or of what seems to be a transcendent object. I remember Julian Huxley in some lecture saying that religious experience, or mystical experience, is as much a real experience as falling in love or appreciating poetry and art. Well, I believe that when we appreciate poetry and art we appreciate definite poems or a definite work of art. If we fall in love, well, we fall in love with somebody and not with nobody.

RUSSELL: May I interrupt for a moment here. That is by no means always the case. Japanese novelists never consider that they have achieved a success unless large numbers of real people commit suicide for love of the imaginary heroine.

COPLESTON: Well, I must take your word for these goings on in Japan. I haven't committed suicide, I'm glad to say, but I have been strongly influenced in the taking of two important steps in my life by two biographies. However, I must say I see little resemblance between the real influence of those books on me and the mystic experience proper, so far, that is, as an outsider can obtain an idea of that experience.

RUSSELL: Well, I mean we wouldn't regard God as being on the same level as the characters in a work of fiction. You'll admit there's a distinction here?

COPLESTON: I certainly should. But what I'd say is that the best explanation seems to be the not purely subjectivist explanation. Of course, a subjectivist explanation is possible in the case of certain people in whom there is little relation between the experience and life, in the case of deluded people and hallucinated people, and so on. But when you get what one might call the pure type, say St. Francis of Assisi, when you get an experience that results in an overflow of dynamic and creative love, the best explanation of that it seems to me is the actual existence of an objective cause of the experience.

RUSSELL: Well, I'm not contending in a dogmatic way that there is not a God. What I'm contending is that we don't know that there is. I can only take what is recorded as I should take other records and I do find that a very great many things are reported, and I am sure you would not accept things about demons and devils and what not—and they're reported in exactly the same tone of voice and with exactly the same conviction. And the mystic, if his vision is veridical, may be said to know that there are devils. But I don't know that there are.

COPLESTON: But surely in the case of the devils there have been people speaking mainly of visions, appearances, angels or demons and so on. I should rule out the visual appearances, because I think they can be explained apart from the existence of the object which is supposed to be seen.

RUSSELL: But don't you think there are abundant recorded cases of people who believe that they've heard Satan speaking to them in their hearts, in just the same way as the mystics assert God—and I'm not talking now of an external vision, I'm talking of a purely mental experience. That seems to be an experience of the same sort as mystics' experience of God, and I don't see that from what mystics tell us you can get any argument for God which is not equally an argument for Satan.

COPLESTON: I quite agree, of course, that people have imagined or thought they have heard or seen Satan. And I have no wish in passing to deny the existence of Satan. But I do not think that people have claimed to have experienced Satan in the precise way in which mystics claim to have experienced God. Take the case of a non-Christian, Plotinus. He admits the experience is something inexpressible, the object is an object of love, and therefore, not an object that causes horror and disgust. And the effect of that experience is, I should say, borne out, or I mean the validity of the experience is borne out in the records of the life of Plotinus. At any rate it is more reasonable to suppose that he had that experience if we're willing to accept Porphyry's account of Plotinus's general kindness and benevolence.

RUSSELL: The fact that a belief has a good moral effect upon a man is no evidence whatsoever in favor of its truth.

COPLESTON: No, but if it could actually be proved that the belief was actually responsible for a good effect on a man's life, I should consider it a presumption in favor of some truth, at any rate of the positive part of the belief if not of its entire validity. But in any case I am using the character of the life as evidence in favor of the mystic's veracity and sanity rather than as a proof of the truth of his beliefs.

RUSSELL: But even that I don't think is any evidence. I've had experiences myself that have altered my character profoundly. And I thought at the time at any rate that it was altered for the good. Those experiences were important, but they did not involve the existence of something outside me, and I don't think that if I'd thought they did, the fact that they had a wholesome effect would have been any evidence that I was right.

COPLESTON: No, but I think that the good effect would attest your veracity in describing your experience. Please remember that I'm not saying that a mystic's mediation or interpretation of his experience should be immune from discussion or criticism.

RUSSELL: Obviously the character of a young man may be—and often is—immensely affected for good by reading about some great man in history, and it may happen that the great man is a myth and doesn't exist, but the boy is just as much affected for good as if he did. There have been such people. Plutarch's *Lives* take Lycurgus as an example, who certainly did not exist, but you might be very much influenced by reading Lycurgus under the impression that he had previously existed. You would then be influenced by an object that you'd loved, but it wouldn't be an existing object.

COPLESTON: I agree with you on that, of course, that a man may be influenced by a character in fiction. Without going into the question of what it is precisely that influences him (I should say a real value) I think that the situation of that man and of the mystic are different. After all the man who is influenced by Lycurgus hasn't got the irresistible impression that he's experienced in some way the ultimate reality.

RUSSELL: I don't think you've quite got my point about these historical characters—these unhistorical characters in history. I'm not assuming what you call an effect on the reason. I'm assuming that the young man reading about this person and believing him to be real loves him—which is quite easy to happen, and yet he's loving a phantom.

COPLESTON: In one sense he's loving a phantom, that's perfectly true, in the sense, I mean, that he's loving X or Y who doesn't exist. But at the same time, it is not, I think, the phantom as such that the young man loves; he perceives a real value, an idea which he recognizes as objectively valid, and that's what excites his love.

RUSSELL: Well, in the same sense we had before about the characters in fiction.

COPLESTON: Yes, in one sense the man's loving a phantom—perfectly true. But in another sense he's loving what he perceives to be a value.

The Moral Argument

RUSSELL: But aren't you now saying in effect, I mean by God whatever is good or the sum total of what is good—the system of what is good, and, therefore, when a young man loves anything that is good he is loving God. Is that what you're saying, because if so, it wants a bit of arguing.

COPLESTON: I don't say, of course, that God is the sum total or system of what is good in the pantheistic sense; I'm not a pantheist, but I do think that all goodness reflects God in some way and proceeds from Him, so that in a sense the man who loves what is truly good, loves God even if he doesn't advert to God. But still I agree that the validity of such an interpretation of a man's conduct depends on the recognition of God's existence, obviously.

RUSSELL: Yes, but that's a point to be proved.

COPLESTON: Quite so, but I regard the metaphysical argument as probative, but there we differ.

RUSSELL: You see, I feel that some things are good and that other things are bad. I love the things that are good, that I think are good, and I hate the things that I think are bad. I don't say that these things are good because they participate in the Divine goodness.

COPLESTON: Yes, but what's your justification for distinguishing between good and bad or how do you view the distinction between them?

RUSSELL: I don't have any justification any more than I have when I distinguish between blue and yellow. What is my justification for distinguishing between blue and yellow? I can see they are different.

COPLESTON: Well, that is an excellent justification, I agree. You distinguish blue and yellow by seeing them, so you distinguish good and bad by what faculty?

RUSSELL: By my feelings.

COPLESTON: By your feelings. Well, that's what I was asking. You think that good and evil have reference simply to feeling?

RUSSELL: Well, why does one type of object look yellow and another look blue? I can more or less give an answer to that thanks to the physicists, and as to why I think one sort of thing good and another evil, probably there is an answer of the same sort, but it hasn't been gone into in the same way and I couldn't give it you.

COPLESTON: Well, let's take the behavior of the Commandant of Belsen. That appears to you as undesirable and evil and to me too. To Adolf Hitler we suppose it appeared as something good and desirable. I suppose you'd have to admit that for Hitler it was good and for you it is evil.

RUSSELL: No, I shouldn't quite go so far as that. I mean, I think people can make mistakes in that as they can in other things. If you have jaundice you see things yellow that are not yellow. You're making a mistake.

COPLESTON: Yes, one can make mistakes, but can you make a mistake if it's simply a question of reference to a feeling or emotion? Surely Hitler would be the only possible judge of what appealed to his emotions.

RUSSELL: It would be quite right to say that it appealed to his emotions, but you can say various things about that; among others, that if that sort of thing makes that sort of appeal to Hitler's emotions, then Hitler makes quite a different appeal to my emotions.

COPLESTON: Granted. But there's no objective criterion outside feeling then for condemning the conduct of the Commandant of Belsen, in your view?

RUSSELL: No more than there is for the color-blind person who's in exactly the same state. Why do we intellectually condemn the color-blind man? Isn't it because he's in the minority?

COPLESTON: I would say because he is lacking in a thing which normally belongs to human nature.

RUSSELL: Yes, but if he were in the majority, we shouldn't say that.

COPLESTON: Then you'd say that there's no criterion outside feeling that will enable one to distinguish between the behavior of the Commandant of Belsen and the behavior, say, of Sir Stafford Cripps or the Archbishop of Canterbury.

RUSSELL: The feeling is a little too simplified. You've got to take account of the effects of actions and your feelings towards those effects. You see, you can have an argument about it if you say that certain sorts of occurrences are the sort you like and certain others the sort you don't like. Then you have to take account of the effects of actions. You can very well say that the effects of the actions of the Commandant of Belsen were painful and unpleasant.

COPLESTON: They certainly were, I agree, very painful and unpleasant to all the people in the camp.

RUSSELL: Yes, but not only to the people in the camp, but to outsiders contemplating them also.

COPLESTON: Yes, quite true in imagination. But that's my point. I don't approve of them, and I know you don't approve of them, but I don't see what ground you have for not approving of them, because after all, to the Commandant of Belsen himself, they're pleasant, those actions.

RUSSELL: Yes, but you see I don't need any more ground in that case than I do in the case of color perception. There are some people who think everything is yellow, there are people suffering from jaundice, and I don't agree with these people. I can't prove that the things are not yellow, there isn't any proof, but most people agree with me that they're not yellow, and most people agree with me that the Commandant of Belsen was making mistakes.

COPLESTON: Well, do you accept any moral obligation?

RUSSELL: Well, I should have to answer at considerable length to answer that. Practically speaking—yes. Theoretically speaking I should have to define moral obligation rather carefully.

COPLESTON: Well, do you think that the word "ought" simply has an emotional connotation?

RUSSELL: No, I don't think that, because you see, as I was saying a moment ago, one has to take account of the effects, and I think right conduct is that which would probably produce the greatest possible balance in intrinsic value of all the acts possible in the circumstances, and you've got to take account of the probable effects of your action in considering what is right.

COPLESTON: Well, I brought in moral obligation because I think that one can approach the question of God's existence in that way. The vast majority of the human race will make, and always have made, some distinction between right and wrong. The vast majority I think has some consciousness of an obligation in the moral sphere. It's my opinion that the perception of values and the consciousness of moral law and obligation are best explained through the hypothesis of a transcendent ground of value and of an author of the moral law. I do mean by "author of the moral law" an arbitrary author of the moral law. I think, in fact, that those modern atheists who have argued in the converse way "there is no God; therefore, there are no absolute values and no absolute law," are quite logical.

RUSSELL: I don't like the word "absolute." I don't think there is anything absolute whatever. The moral law, for example, is always changing. At one period in the development of the human race, almost everybody thought cannibalism was a duty.

COPLESTON: Well, I don't see that differences in particular moral judgments are any conclusive argument against the universality of the moral law. Let's assume for the moment that there are absolute moral values, even on that hypothesis it's only to be expected that different individuals and different groups should enjoy varying degrees of insight into those values.

RUSSELL: I'm inclined to think that "ought," the feeling that one has about "ought," is an echo of what has been told one by one's parents or one's nurses.

COPLESTON: Well, I wonder if you can explain away the idea of the "ought" merely in terms of nurses and parents. I really don't see how it can be conveyed to anybody in other terms than itself. It seems to me that if there is a moral order bearing upon the human conscience, that that moral order is unintelligible apart from the existence of God.

RUSSELL: Then you have to say one or other of two things. Either God only speaks to a very small percentage of mankind—which happens to include yourself—or He deliberately says things that are not true in talking to the consciences of savages.

COPLESTON: Well, you see, I'm not suggesting that God actually dictates moral precepts to the conscience. The human being's idea of the content of the moral law depends certainly to a large extent on education and environment, and a man has to use his reason in assessing the validity of the actual moral ideas of his social group. But the possibility of criticizing the accepted moral code presupposes that there is an objective standard, that there is an ideal moral order, which imposes itself (I mean the obligatory character of which can be recognized). I think that the recognition of this ideal moral order is part of the recognition of contingency. It implies the existence of a real foundation of God.

RUSSELL: But the law-giver has always been, it seems to me, one's parents or someone like. There are plenty of terrestrial law-givers to account for it, and that would explain why people's consciences are so amazingly different in different times and places.

COPLESTON: It helps to explain differences in the perception of particular moral values, which otherwise are inexplicable. It will help to explain changes in the matter of the moral law in the content of the precepts as accepted by this or that nation, or this or that individual. But the form of it, what Kant calls the categorical imperative, the "ought," I really don't see how that can possibly be conveyed to anybody by nurse or parent because there aren't any possible terms, so far as I can see, with which it can be explained. It can't be defined in other terms than itself, because once you've defined it in other terms than itself you've explained it away. It's no longer a moral "ought." It's something else.

RUSSELL: Well, I think the sense of "ought" is the effect of somebody's imagined disapproval, it may be God's imagined disapproval, but it's somebody's imagined disapproval. And I think that is what is meant by "ought."

COPLESTON: It seems to me to be external customs and taboos and things of that sort which can most easily be explained simply through environment and education, but all that seems to me to belong to what I call the matter of the law, the content. The idea of the "ought" as such can never be conveyed to a man by the tribal chief or by anybody else, because there are no other terms in which it could be conveyed. It seems to me entirely——[Russell breaks in].

RUSSELL: But I don't see any reason to say that—I mean we all know about conditioned reflexes. We know that an animal, if punished habitually for a certain sort of act, after a time will refrain. I don't think the animal refrains from arguing within himself, "Master will be angry if I do this." He has a feeling that that's not the thing to do. That's what we can do with ourselves and nothing more.

COPLESTON: I see no reason to suppose that an animal has a consciousness of moral obligation; and we certainly don't regard an animal as morally responsible for his acts of disobedience. But a man has a consciousness of obligation and of moral values. I see no reason to suppose that one could condition all men as one can "condition" an animal, and I don't suppose you'd really want to do so even if one could. If "behaviorism" were true, there would be no objective moral distinction between the emperor Nero and St. Francis of Assisi. I can't help feeling, Lord Russell, you know, that you regard the conduct of the Commandant at Belsen as morally reprehensible, and that you yourself would never under any circumstances act in that way, even if you thought, or had reason to think, that possibly the balance of the happiness of the human race might be increased through some people being treated in that abominable manner.

RUSSELL: No. I wouldn't imitate the conduct of a mad dog. The fact that I wouldn't do it doesn't really bear on this question we're discussing.

COPLESTON: No, but if you were making a utilitarian explanation of right and wrong in terms of consequences, it might be held, and I suppose some of the Nazis of the better type would have held that although it's lamentable to have to act in this way, yet the balance in the long run leads to greater happiness. I don't think you'd say that, would you? I think you'd say that that sort of action is wrong—and in itself, quite apart from whether the general balance of happiness is increased or not. Then, if you're prepared to say that, then I think you must have some criterion of right and wrong, that is outside the criterion of feeling, at any rate. To me, that admission would ultimately result in the admission of an ultimate ground of value in God.

RUSSELL: I think we are perhaps getting into confusion. It is not direct feeling about the act by which I should judge, but rather a feeling as to the effects. And I can't admit any circumstances in which certain kinds of behavior, such as you have been discussing, would do good. I can't imagine circumstances in which they would have a beneficial effect.

I think the persons who think they do are deceiving themselves. But if there were circumstances in which they would have a beneficial effect, then I might be obliged, however reluctantly, to say—"Well, I don't like these things, but I will acquiesce in them," just as I acquiesce in the Criminal Law, although I profoundly dislike punishment.

COPLESTON: Well, perhaps it's time I summed up my position. I've argued two things. First, that the existence of God can be philosophically proved by a metaphysical argument; secondly, that it is only the existence of God that will make sense of man's moral experience and of religious experience. Personally, I think that your way of accounting for man's moral judgments leads inevitably to a contradiction between what your theory demands and your own spontaneous judgments. Moreover, your theory explains moral obligation away, and explaining away is not explanation. As regards the metaphysical argument, we are apparently in agreement that what we call the world consists simply of contingent beings. That is, of beings no one of which can account for its own existence. You say that the series of events needs no explanation: I say that if there were no necessary being, no being which must exist and cannot not exist, nothing would exist. The infinity of the series of contingent beings, even if proved, would be irrelevant. Something does exist; therefore, there must be something which accounts for this fact, a being which is outside the series of contingent beings. If you had admitted this, we could then have discussed whether that being is personal, good, and so on. On the actual point discussed, whether there is or is not a necessary being, I find myself, I think, in agreement with the great majority of classical philosophers.

You maintain, I think, that existing beings are simply there, and that I have no justification for raising the question of the explanation of their existence. But I would like to point out that this position cannot be substantiated by logical analysis; it expresses a philosophy which itself stands in need of proof. I think we have reached an impasse because our ideas of philosophy are radically different; it seems to me that what I call a part of philosophy, that you call the whole, insofar at least as philosophy is rational. It seems to me, if you will pardon my saying so, that besides your own logical system—which you call "modern" in opposition to antiquated logic (a tendentious adjective)—you maintain a philosophy which cannot be substantiated by logical analysis. After all, the problem of God's existence is an existential problem whereas logical analysis does not deal directly with problems of existence. So it seems to me, to declare that the terms involved in one set of problems are meaningless because they are not required in dealing with another set of problems, is to settle from the beginning the nature and extent of philosophy, and that is itself a philosophical act which stands in need of justification.

RUSSELL: Well, I should like to say just a few words by way of summary on my side. First, as to the metaphysical argument: I don't admit the connotations of such a term as "contingent" or the possibility of explanation in Father Copleston's sense. I think the word "contingent" inevitably suggests the possibility of something that wouldn't have this what you might call accidental character of just being there, and I don't think this is true except in the purely causal sense. You can sometimes give a causal explanation of one thing as being the effect of something else, but that is merely referring one thing to another thing and there's no—to my mind—explanation in Father Copleston's sense of anything at all, nor is there any meaning in calling things "contingent" because there isn't anything else they could be. That's what I should say about that, but I should like to say a few words about Father Copleston's accusation that I regard logic as all philosophy—that is by no means the case. I don't by any means regard logic as all philosophy. I think logic is an essential part of philosophy and logic has to be used in philosophy, and in that I think he and I are at one. When the logic that he uses was new—namely, in the time of Aristotle, there had to be a great deal of fuss made about it; Aristotle made a lot of fuss about that logic. Nowadays it's become old and respectable, and you don't have to make so much fuss about it. The logic that I believe in is comparatively new, and therefore I have to imitate Aristotle in making a fuss about it; but it's not that I think it's all philosophy by any means—I don't think so. I think it's an important part of philosophy, and when I say that, I don't find a meaning for this or that word, that is a position of detail based upon what I've found out about that particular word, from thinking about it. It's not a general position that all words that are used in metaphysics are nonsense, or anything like that which I don't really hold.

As regards the moral argument, I do find that when one studies anthropology or history, there are people who think it their duty to perform acts which I think abominable, and I certainly can't, therefore, attribute Divine origin to the matter of moral obligation, which Father Copleston doesn't ask me to; but I think even the form of moral obligation, when it takes the form of enjoining you to eat your father or what not, doesn't seem to me to be such a very beautiful and noble thing; and, therefore, I cannot attribute a Divine origin to this sense of moral obligation, which I think is quite easily accounted for in quite other ways.

42   Eternal Happiness,

Subjectivity and Truth

Soren Kierkegaard

The Eternal Happiness
Promised by Christianity

OUR TREATMENT OF THE PROBLEM merely deals with the question of the individual's relationship to Christianity. It has nothing whatever to do with the systematic zeal of the personally indifferent individual to arrange the truths of Christianity in paragraphs; it deals with the concern of the infinitely interested individual for his own relationship to such a doctrine. To put it as simply as possible, using myself by way of illustration: I, Johannes Climacus,* born in this city and now thirty years old, a common ordinary human being like most people, assume that there awaits me a highest good, an eternal happiness, in the same sense that such a good awaits a servant-girl or a professor. I have heard that Christianity proposes itself as a condition for the acquirement of this good, and now I ask how I may establish a proper relationship to this doctrine. "What extraordinary presumption," I seem to hear a thinker say, "what egotistical vanity to dare lay so much stress upon one's own petty self in

[This selection consists of extracts from the Introduction, Book I, Chapter I, and Book II, Part II, Chapters I and II of Kierkegaard's *Concluding Unscientific Postscript,* a book first published in Copenhagen in 1846. The English translation by David F. Swenson first appeared in 1941. The selection is reprinted with the permission of Princeton University Press.]

* *Concluding Unscientific Postscript,* like several of Kierkegaard's other books, was published under the pseudonym of Johannes Climacus. The title page lists Johannes Climacus as author and S. Kierkegaard as "responsible for publication." (Ed.)

this theocentric age, in the speculatively significant nineteenth century, which is entirely immersed in the great problems of universal history." I shudder at the reproof; and if I had not already hardened myself against a number of fearful things, I would no doubt slink quietly away, like a dog with his tail between his legs. But my conscience is quite clear in this matter; it is not I who have become so presumptuous of my own accord, but it is Christianity itself which compels me to ask the question in this manner. It puts quite an extraordinary emphasis upon my own petty self, and upon every other self however petty, in that it proposes to endow each self with an eternal happiness, provided a proper relationship is established.

Without having understood Christianity, since I merely present the problem, I have still understood enough to apprehend that it proposes to bestow an eternal happiness upon the individual man, thus presuming an infinite interest in his eternal happiness as *conditio sine qua non;* an interest by virtue of which the individual hates father and mother, and thus doubtless also snaps his fingers at speculative systems and outlines of universal history. Although I am only an outsider, I have at least understood so much, that the only unpardonable offense against the majesty of Christianity is for the individual to take his relationship to it for granted, treating it as a matter of course. However unassuming it may seem to permit oneself this kind of a relationship to Christianity, Christianity judges it as insolence. I must therefore respectfully decline the assistance of all the theocentric helpers and helpers' helpers, in so far as they propose to help me into Christianity on such a basis. Then I rather prefer to remain where I am, with my infinite interest, with the problem, with the possibility.

It is not entirely impossible that one who is infinitely interested in his eternal happiness may sometime come into possession of it. But it is surely quite impossible for one who has lost a sensibility for it (and this can scarcely be anything else than the infinite interest), ever to enjoy an eternal happiness. If the sense for it is once lost, it may perhaps be impossible to recover it. . . .

The objective problem consists of an inquiry into the truth of Christianity. The subjective problem concerns the relationship of the individual to Christianity. To put it quite simply: How may I, Johannes Climacus, participate in the happiness promised by Christianity? . . .

Faith and Historical Documentation

When Christianity is viewed from the standpoint of its historical documentation, it becomes necessary to secure an entirely trustworthy account of what the Christian doctrine really is. If the inquirer were infinitely interested in behalf of his relationship to the doctrine he would at once despair; for nothing is more readily evident than that the greatest attainable certainty with respect to anything historical is merely an *approximation*. And an approximation, when viewed as a basis for an eternal happiness, is wholly inadequate, since the incommensurability makes a result impossible. But the interest of the inquiring subject being merely historical (whether he also has an infinite interest in Christianity in his capacity as believer, in which case the whole enterprise might readily come to involve him in several contradictions; or whether he stands aloof, yet without any passionate negative decision *qua* unbeliever), he begins upon the tremendous task of research, adding new contributions of his own, and continuing thus until his seventieth year. Just two weeks before his death he looks forward to the publication of a new work, which it is hoped will throw light upon one entire side of the inquiry. Such an objective temper is an epigram, unless its antithesis be an epigram over it, over the restless concern of the infinitely interested subject, who surely needs to have such a question answered, related as it is to his eternal happiness. And in any case he will not upon any consideration dare to relinquish his interest until the last moment.

When one raises the historical question of the truth of Christianity, or of what is and is not Christian truth, the Scriptures at once present themselves as documents of decisive significance. The historical inquiry therefore first concentrates upon the Bible.

Here it is necessary for the scholar to secure the maximum of dependability; for me, on the contrary, it is of importance not to make a display of learning, or to betray the fact that I have none. In the interest of my problem it is more important to have it understood and remembered that even with the most stupendous learning and persistence in research, and even if all the brains of all the critics were concentrated in one, it would still be impossible to obtain anything more than an approximation; and that an approximation is essentially incommensurable with an infinite personal interest in an eternal happiness.

When the Scriptures are viewed as a court of last resort for determining what is and is not Christian doctrine, it becomes necessary to make sure of the Scriptures historically and critically.

In this connection there are a number of topics that come up for consideration: the canonicity of the individual books, their authenticity, their integrity, the trustworthiness of their authors; and a dogmatic guaranty is posited: Inspiration. When one thinks of the labors which the English have devoted to digging the tunnel under the Thames,[1] the tremendous expenditure of energy involved, and then how a little accident may for a long time obstruct the entire enterprise, one will be able to form a fitting conception of this critical undertaking as a whole. How much time, what great industry, what splendid talents, what distinguished scholarship have been requisitioned from generation to generation in order to bring this miracle to pass. And yet a little dialectical doubt touching the presuppositions may suddenly arise, sufficient for a long time to unsettle the whole, closing the subterranean way to Christianity which one has attempted to construct objectively and scientifically, instead of letting the problem remain subjective, as it is.

---

1. A work begun in 1825 but owing to many disasters not finished until 1845 (note supplied by Walter Lowrie).

One sometimes hears uneducated or half educated people, or conceited geniuses, speak with contempt of the labor of criticism devoted to ancient writings; one hears them foolishly deride the learned scholar's careful scrutiny of the most insignificant detail, which is precisely the glory of the scholar, namely, that he considers nothing insignificant that bears upon his science. No, philological scholarship is absolutely within its rights, and the present author yields to none in profound respect for that which science consecrates. But the scholarly critical theology makes no such clear and definite impression upon the mind; its entire procedure suffers from a certain conscious or unconscious ambiguity. It constantly seems as if this labor of criticism were suddenly about to yield a result for faith, issue in something relevant to faith. Here lies the difficulty. When a philologist prepares an edition of one of Cicero's writings, for example, and performs his task with great acumen, the scholarly apparatus held in beautiful sub-servience to the control of the spirit; when his ingenuity and his familiarity with the period, gained through formidable industry, combine with his in-stinct for discovery to overcome obstacles, preparing a clear way for the meaning through the obscure maze of the readings, and so forth—then it is quite safe to yield oneself in whole-hearted admiration. For when he has finished, nothing follows except the wholly admirable result that an ancient writing has now through his skill and competence received its most accurate possible form. But by no means that I should now base my eternal happi-ness on this work; for in relation to my eternal happiness, his astonishing acumen seems, I must admit, inadequate. Aye, I confess that my admira-tion for him would be not glad but despondent, if I thought he had any such thing in mind. But this is precisely how the learned theologian goes to work; when he has completed his task (and until then he keeps us in sus-pense, but holds this prospect before us) he draws the conclusion: *ergo,* now you can base your eternal happiness on these writings.

Anyone who posits inspiration, as a believer does, must consistently consider every critical deliberation, whether for or against, as a misdirec-tion, a temptation for the spirit. And anyone who plunges into these critical inquiries without being a believer, cannot possibly intend to have inspira-tion emerge as a result. Who then really has any interest in the whole in-quiry?

But the contradiction remains unnoticed because the mode of approach is purely objective; and then indeed the contradiction is no longer there. The inquirer forgets what he has up his sleeve, except in so far as he occasionally stimulates and encourages himself lyrically by referring to it; or indulges in lyrical polemics with the aid of eloquence. But let an indi-vidual approach this enterprise, let him propose in infinite personal passion to attach his eternal happiness to the result: he will readily perceive that there is no result, and that none is to be expected; and the contradiction will bring him to despair. Luther's rejection of the Epistle of James will alone suffice. In relation to an eternal happiness, and an infinite passionate interest in its behalf (in which latter alone the former can exist), an iota is of importance, of infinite importance; or rather, despair over the contradiction involved will teach him that there is no possibility of getting through along this road. . . .

I assume that the critics have succeeded in proving about the Bible everything that any learned theologian in his happiest moment has ever wished to prove about the Bible. These books and no others belong to the canon; they are authentic; they are integral; their authors are trustworthy—one may well say, that it is as if every letter were inspired. . . .

Well then, everything being assumed in order with respect to the Scriptures—what follows? Has anyone who previously did not have faith been brought a single step nearer to its acquisition? No, not a single step. Faith does not result simply from a scientific inquiry; it does not come directly at all. On the contrary, in this objectivity one tends to lose that infinite personal interestedness in passion which is the condition of faith, the *ubique et nusquam* in which faith can come into being. Has anyone who previously had faith gained anything with respect to its strength and power? No, not in the least. Rather is it the case that in this voluminous knowledge, this certainty that lurks at the door of faith and threatens to devour it, he is in so dangerous a situation that he will need to put forth much effort in great fear and trembling, lest he fall a victim to the temptation to confuse knowledge with faith. While faith has hitherto had a profitable schoolmaster in the existing uncertainty, it would have in the new certainty its most dangerous enemy. For if passion is eliminated, faith no longer exists, and certainty and passion do not go together. Whoever believes that there is a God and an over-ruling providence finds it easier to preserve his faith, easier to acquire something that definitely is faith and not an illusion, in an imperfect world where passion is kept alive, than in an absolutely perfect world. In such a world faith is in fact unthinkable. Hence also the teaching that faith is abolished in eternity.

How fortunate then that this wishful hypothesis, this beautiful dream of critical theology, is an impossibility, because even the most perfect realization would still remain an approximation. And again how fortunate for the critics that the fault is by no means in them! If all the angels in heaven were to put their heads together, they could still bring to pass only an approximation, because an approximation is the only certainty attainable for historical knowledge—but also an inadequate basis for an eternal happiness.

I assume now the opposite, that the opponents have succeeded in proving what they desire about the Scriptures, with a certainty transcending the most ardent wish of the most passionate hostility—what then? Have the opponents thereby abolished Christianity? By no means. Has the believer been harmed? By no means, not in the least. Has the opponent made good a right to be relieved of responsibility for not being a believer? By no means. Because these books are not written by these authors, are not authentic, are not in an integral condition, are not inspired (though this cannot be disproved, since it is an object of faith), it does not follow that these authors have not existed; and above all, it does not follow that Christ has not existed. In so far, the believer is equally free to assume it; equally free, let us note this well, for if he had assumed it by virtue of any proof, he would have been on the verge of giving up his faith. If matters ever come to this pass, the believer will have some share of guilt, in so far as he has himself invited this procedure, and begun to play into the hands of unbelief by proposing to demonstrate.

Here is the crux of the matter, and I come back to the case of the learned theology. For whose sake is it that the proof is sought? Faith does not need it; aye, it must even regard the proof as its enemy. But when faith begins to feel embarrassed and ashamed, like a young woman for whom her love is no longer sufficient, but who secretly feels ashamed of her lover and must therefore have it established that there is something remarkable about him—when faith thus begins to lose its passion, when faith begins to cease to be faith, then a proof becomes necessary so as to command respect from the side of unbelief. . . .

The Task of Becoming Subjective

Objectively we consider only the matter at issue, subjectively we have regard to the subject and his subjectivity; and behold, precisely this subjectivity is the matter at issue. This must constantly be borne in mind, namely, that the subjective problem is not something about an objective issue, but is the subjectivity itself. For since the problem in question poses a decision, and since all decisiveness, as shown above, inheres in subjectivity, it is essential that every trace of an objective issue should be eliminated. If any such trace remains, it is at once a sign that the subject seeks to shirk something of the pain and crisis of the decision; that is, he seeks to make the problem to some degree objective . . . Hence we do not here raise the question of the truth of Christianity in the sense that when this has been determined, the subject is assumed ready and willing to accept it. No, the question is as to the mode of the subject's acceptance; and it must be regarded as an illusion rooted in the demoralization which remains ignorant of the subjective nature of the decision, or as an evasion springing from the disingenuousness which seeks to shirk the decision by an objective mode of approach, wherein there can in all eternity be no decision, to assume that the transition from something objective to the subjective acceptance is a direct transition, following upon the objective deliberation as a matter of course. On the contrary, the subjective acceptance is precisely the decisive factor; and an objective acceptance of Christianity is paganism or thoughtlessness.

Christianity proposes to endow the individual with an eternal happiness, a good which is not distributed wholesale, but only to one individual at a time. Though Christianity assumes that there inheres in the subjectivity of the individual, as being the potentiality of the appropriation of this good, the possibility for its acceptance, it does not assume that the subjectivity is immediately ready for such acceptance, or even has, without further ado, a real conception of the significance of such a good. The development or transformation of the individual's subjectivity, its infinite concentration in itself over against the conception of an eternal happiness, that highest good of the infinite—this constitutes the developed potentiality of the primary potentiality which subjectivity as such presents. In this way Christianity protests every form of objectivity; it desires that the subject should be infinitely concerned about himself. It is subjectivity that Christianity is concerned with, and it is only in subjectivity that its truth exists, if it exists at all; objectively, Christianity has absolutely no existence. If its truth happens to be in only a single subject, it exists in him alone; and there is greater Christian joy in heaven over this one individual than over universal history and the System,* which as objective entities are incommensurable for that which is Christian.

It is commonly assumed that no art or skill is required in order to be subjective. To be sure, every human being is a bit of a subject, in a sense. But now to strive to become what one already is: who would take the pains to waste his time on such a task, involving the greatest imaginable degree of resignation? Quite so. But for this very reason alone it is a very difficult task, the most difficult of all tasks in fact, precisely because every human being has a strong natural bent and passion to become something more and different. And so it is with all such apparently insignificant tasks, precisely their seeming insignificance makes them infinitely difficult. In such cases the task itself is not directly alluring, so as to support the aspiring individual; instead, it works against him, and it needs an infinite effort on his part merely to discover that his task lies here, that this is his task—an effort from which he is otherwise relieved. To think about the simple things of life, about what the plain man also knows about a fashion, is extremely forbidding; for the differential distinction attainable even through the utmost possible exertion is by no means obvious to the sensual man. No indeed, thinking about the high-falutin is very much more attractive and glorious.

When one overlooks this little distinction, humoristic from the Socratic standpoint and infinitely anxious from the Christian, between being something like a subject so called, and being a subject, or becoming one, or being what one is through having become what one is: then it becomes wisdom, the admired wisdom of our own age, that it is the task of the subject increasingly to divest himself of his subjectivity in order to become more and more objective. It is easy to see what this guidance understands by being a subject of a sort. It understands by it quite rightly the accidental, the angular, the selfish, the eccentric, and so forth, all of which every human being can have enough of. Nor does Christianity deny that such things should be gotten rid of; it has never been a friend of loutishness. But the difference is, that philosophy teaches that the way is to become objective, while Christianity teaches that the way is to become subjective, i.e., to be-

* When Kierkegaard speaks of "universal history" and "the System" he refers to Hegel's philosophy which was one of the chief targets of his polemic. (Ed.)

come a subject in truth. Lest this should seem a mere dispute about words, let me say that Christianity wishes to intensify passion to its highest pitch; but passion is subjectivity, and does not exist objectively. . . .

The task of becoming subjective, then, may be presumed to be the highest task, and one that is proposed to every human being; just as, correspondingly, the highest reward, an eternal happiness, exists only for those who are subjective; or rather, comes into being for the individual who becomes subjective. . . .

Truth Is Subjectivity

When the question of truth is raised in an objective manner, reflection is directed objectively to the truth, as an object to which the knower is related. Reflection is not focused upon the relationship, however, but upon the question of whether it is the truth to which the knower is related. If only the object to which he is related is the truth, the subject is accounted to be in the truth. When the question of the truth is raised subjectively, reflection is directed subjectively to the nature of the individual's relationship; if only the mode of this relationship is in the truth, the individual is in the truth even if he should happen to be thus related to what is not true. Let us take as an example the knowledge of God. Objectively, reflection is directed to the problem of whether this object is the true God; subjectively, reflection is directed to the question whether the individual is related to a something *in such a manner* that his relationship is in truth a God-relationship. . . .

The existing individual who chooses to pursue the objective way enters upon the entire approximation-process by which it is proposed to bring God to light objectively. But this is in all eternity impossible, because God is a subject, and therefore exists only for subjectivity in inwardness. The existing individual who chooses the subjective way apprehends instantly the entire dialectical difficulty involved in having to use some time, perhaps a long time, in finding God objectively; and he feels this dialectical difficulty in all its painfulness, because every moment is wasted in which he does not have God. That very instant he has God, not by virtue of any objective deliberation, but by virtue of the infinite passion of inwardness. The objective inquirer, on the other hand, is not embarrassed by such dialectical difficulties as are involved in devoting an entire period of investigation to finding God—since it is possible that the inquirer may die tomorrow; and if he lives he can scarcely regard God as something to be taken along if convenient, since God is precisely that which one takes *a tout prix,* which in the understanding of passion constitutes the true inward relationship to God.

It is at this point, so difficult dialectically, that the way swings off for everyone who knows what it means to think, and to think existentially; which is something very different from sitting at a desk and writing about what one has never done, something very different from writing *de omnibus dubitandum* and at the same time being as credulous existentially as the most sensuous of men. Here is where the way swings off, and the change is marked by the fact that while objective knowledge rambles comfortably on by way of the long road of approximation without being impelled by the urge of passion, subjective knowledge counts every delay a deadly peril, and the decision so infinitely important and so instantly pressing that it is as if the opportunity had already passed.

Now when the problem is to reckon up on which side there is most truth, whether on the side of one who seeks the true God objectively, and pursues the approximate truth of the God-idea; or on the side of one who, driven by the infinite passion of his need of God, feels an infinite concern for his own relationship to God in truth (and to be at one and the same time on both sides equally, is as we have noted not possible for an existing individual, but is merely the happy delusion of an imaginary I-am-I): the answer cannot be in doubt for anyone who has not been demoralized with the aid of science. If one who lives in the midst of Christendom goes up to the house of God, the house of the true God, with the true conception of God in his knowledge, and prays, but prays in a false spirit; and one who lives in an idolatrous community prays with the entire passion of the infinite, although his eyes rest upon the image of an idol: where is there most truth? The one prays in truth to God though he worships an idol; the other prays falsely to the true God, and hence worships in fact an idol.

When one man investigates objectively the problem of immortality, and another embraces an uncertainty with the passion of the infinite: where is there most truth, and who has the greater certainty? The one has entered upon a never-ending approximation, for the certainty of immortality lies precisely in the subjectivity of the individual; the other is immortal, and fights for his immortality by struggling with the uncertainty. Let us consider Socrates. Nowadays everyone dabbles in a few proofs; some have several such proofs, others fewer. But Socrates! He puts the question objectively in a problematic manner: *if* there is an immortality. He must therefore be accounted a doubter in comparison with one of our modern thinkers with the three proofs? By no means. On this "if" he risks his entire life, he has the courage to meet death, and he has with the passion of the infinite so determined the pattern of his life that it must be found acceptable—*if* there is an immortality. Is any better proof capable of being given for the immortality of the soul? But those who have the three proofs do not at all determine their lives in conformity therewith; if there is an immortality it must feel disgust over their manner of life: can any better refutation be given of the three proofs? The bit of uncertainty that Socrates had, helped him because he himself contributed the passion of the infinite; the three proofs that the others have do not profit them at all, because they are dead to spirit and enthusiasm, and their three proofs, in lieu of proving anything else, prove just this. A young girl may enjoy all the sweetness of love on the basis of what is merely a weak hope that she is beloved, because she rests everything on this weak hope; but many a wedded matron more than once subjected to the strongest expressions of love, has in so far indeed had proofs, but strangely enough has not enjoyed *quod erat demonstrandum*. The Socratic ignorance, which Socrates held fast with the entire passion of his inwardness, was thus an expression for the principle that the eternal truth is related to an existing individual, and that this truth must therefore be a paradox for him as long as he exists; and yet it is possible that there was more truth in the Socratic ignorance as it was in him, than in the entire objective truth of the System, which flirts with what the times demand and accommodates itself to *Privatdocents*.

The objective accent falls on WHAT is said, the subjective accent on HOW it is said. This distinction holds even in the aesthetic realm, and receives definite expression in the principle that what is in itself true may in the mouth of such and such a person become untrue. In these times this distinction is particularly worthy of notice, for if we wish to express in a single sentence the difference between ancient times and our own, we should doubtless have to say: "In ancient times only an individual here and there knew the truth; now all know it, except that the inwardness of its appropriation stands in an inverse relationship to the extent of its dissemination. Aesthetically the contradiction that truth becomes untruth in this or that person's mouth, is best construed comically: In the ethico-religious sphere, accent is again on the "how." But this is not to be understood as referring to demeanor, expression, or the like; rather it refers to the relationship sustained by the existing individual, in his own existence, to the content of his utterance. Objectively the interest is focussed merely on the thought-content, subjectively on the inwardness. At its maximum this inward "how" is the passion of the infinite, and the passion of the infinite is the truth. But the passion of the infinite is precisely subjectivity, and thus subjectivity becomes the truth . . . Only in subjectivity is there decisiveness, to seek objectivity is to be in error. It is the passion of the infinite that is the decisive factor and not its content, for its content is precisely itself. In this manner subjectivity and the subjective "how" constitute the truth.

But the "how" which is thus subjectively accentuated precisely because the subject is an existing individual, is also subject to a dialectic with respect to time. In the passionate moment of decision, where the road swings away from objective knowledge, it seems as if the infinite decision were thereby realized. But in the same moment the existing individual finds himself in the temporal order, and the subject "how" is transformed into a striving, a striving which receives indeed its impulse and a repeated renewal from the decisive passion of the infinite, but is nevertheless a striving.

When subjectivity is the truth, the conceptual determination of the truth must include an expression for the antithesis to objectivity, a memento of the fork in the road where the way swings off; this expression will at the same time serve as an indication of the tension of the subjective inwardness. Here is such a definition of truth: *An objective uncertainty held fast in an appropriation-process of the most passionate inwardness is the truth,* the highest truth attainable for an *existing* individual. At the point where the way swings off (and where this is cannot be specified objectively, since it is a matter of subjectivity), there objective knowledge is placed in abeyance. Thus the subject merely has, objectively, the uncertainty; but it is this which precisely increases the tension of that infinite passion which constitutes his inwardness. The truth is precisely the venture which chooses an objective uncertainty with the passion of the infinite. I contemplate the order of nature in the hope of finding God, and I see omnipotence and wisdom; but I also see much else that disturbs my mind and excites anxiety. The sum of all this is an objective uncertainty. But it is for this very reason that the inwardness becomes as intense as it is, for it embraces this objective uncertainty with the entire passion of the infinite. In the case of a mathematical proposition the objectivity is given, but for this reason the truth of such a proposition is also an indifferent truth.

But the above definition of truth is an equivalent expression for faith. Without risk there is no faith. Faith is precisely the contradiction between the infinite passion of the individual's inwardness and the objective uncertainty. If I am capable of grasping God objectively, I do not believe, but precisely because I cannot do this I must believe. If I wish to preserve myself in faith I must constantly be intent upon holding fast the objective uncertainty, so as to remain out upon the deep, over seventy thousand fathoms of water, still preserving my faith.

Faith and the Absurd

. . . The Socratic ignorance gives expression to the objective uncertainty attaching to the truth, while his inwardness in existing is the truth. To anticipate here what will be developed later, let me make the following remark. The Socratic ignorance is an analogue to the category of the absurd, only that there is still less of objective certainty in the absurd, and in the repellent effect that the absurd exercises. It is certain only that it is absurd, and precisely on that account it incites to an infinitely greater tension in the corresponding inwardness. The Socratic inwardess in existing is an analogue to faith; only that the inwardness of faith, corresponding as it does, not to the repulsion of the Socratic ignorance, but to the repulsion exerted by the absurd, is infinitely more profound.

. . . Without risk there is no faith, and the greater the risk the greater the faith; the more objective security the less inwardness (for inwardness is precisely subjectivity), and the less objective security the more profound the possible inwardness. When the paradox is paradoxical in itself, it repels the individual by virtue of its absurdity, and the corresponding passion of inwardness is faith. . . .

When Socrates believed that there was a God, he held fast to the objective uncertainty with the whole passion of his inwardness, and it is precisely in this contradiction and in this risk, that faith is rooted. Now it is otherwise. Instead of the objective uncertainty, there is here a certainty, namely, that objectively it is absurd; and this absurdity, held fast in the passion of inwardness, is faith. The Socratic ignorance is as a witty jest in comparison with the earnestness of facing the absurd; and the Socratic existential inwardness is as Greek light-mindedness in comparison with the grave strenuosity of faith.

. . . The absurd is precisely by its objective repulsion the measure of the intensity of faith in inwardness. Suppose a man who wishes to acquire faith; let the comedy begin. He wishes to have faith, but he wishes also to safe-guard himself by means of an objective inquiry and its approximation-process. What happens? With the help of the approximation-process the absurd becomes something different; it becomes probable, it becomes in-creasingly probable, it becomes extremely and emphatically probable. Now he is ready to believe it, and he ventures to claim for himself that he does not believe as shoemakers and tailors and simple folk believe, but only after long deliberation. Now he is ready to believe it; and lo, now it has become precisely impossible to believe it. Anything that is almost probable, or probable, or extremely and emphatically probable, is something he can almost know, or as good as know, or extremely and emphatically almost *know*—but it is impossible to *believe*. For the absurd is the object of faith, and the only object that can be believed. . . .

There has been said much that is strange, much that is deplorable, much that is revolting about Christianity; but the most stupid thing ever said about it is, that it is to a certain degree true. There has been said much that is strange, much that is deplorable, much that is revolting about en-thusiasm; but the most stupid thing ever said about it is, that it is to a certain degree. There has been said much that is strange, much that is de-plorable, much that is revolting about love, but the most stupid thing ever said about it is, that it is to a certain degree. And when a man has prosti-tuted himself by speaking in this manner about enthusiasm and love, he has betrayed his stupidity, which in this case is not in the direction of intelli-gence, however, since it has its ground rather in the fact that the under-standing has become too large, in the same sense as when a disease of the liver is caused by an enlargement of the liver, and hence, as another author has remarked, "is the flatness that salt takes on when it loses its savor": then there is still one phenomenon left, Christianity. If the sight of en-thusiasm has not sufficed to help him break with the understanding, if love has not been able to emancipate him from his slavery: then let him consider Christianity. Let him be offended, he is still human; let him despair of ever himself becoming a Christian, he is yet perhaps nearer than he believes; let him fight to the last drop of blood for the extermination of Christianity, he is still human—but if he is able here to say: it is true to a certain degree, then he is stupid.

Perhaps someone will think that I tremble to say this, that I must be prepared for a terrible castigation at the hands of speculative philosophy. By no means. The speculative philosopher will here again be quite consistent with himself, and say: "There is a certain degree of truth in what the man says, only we cannot stop there, but must advance beyond it." It would also be strange if my insignificance should succeed where even Christianity had failed, namely, in bringing the speculative philosopher to the point of passion; if so, then my little fragment of philosophy would suddenly take on a significance I had least of all dreamed of.

But whoever is neither cold nor hot is nauseating; and just as the hunter is ill-served by a weapon that misses fire at the crucial moment, so God is ill-served by misfiring individuals. Had not Pilate asked objectively what truth is, he would never have condemned Christ to be crucified. Had he asked subjectively, the passion of his inwardness respecting what in the decision facing him he had *in truth to do,* would have prevented him from doing wrong. It would then not have been merely his wife who was made anxious by the dreadful dream, but Pilate himself would have become sleepless. But when a man has something so infinitely great before his eyes as the objective truth, he can afford to set at naught his little bit of subjectivity, and what he as subject has to do. And the approximation-process of the objective truth is figuratively expressed in washing the hands, for objectively there is no decision, and the subjective decision shows that one was in error nevertheless, through not understanding that the decision inheres precisely in subjectivity.

Suppose, on the other hand, that subjectivity is the truth, and that subjectivity is an existing subjectivity, then, if I may so express myself, Christianity fits perfectly into the picture. Subjectivity culminates in passion, Christianity is the paradox, paradox and passion are a mutual fit, and the paradox is altogether suited to one whose situation is, to be in the extremity of existence. Aye, never in all the world could there be found two lovers so wholly suited to one another as paradox and passion, and the strife between them is like the strife between lovers, when the dispute is about whether he first aroused her passion, or she his. And so it is here; the existing individual has by means of the paradox itself come to be placed in the extremity of existence. And what can be more splendid for lovers than that they are permitted a long time together without any alteration in the relationship between them, except that it becomes more intensive in inwardness? And this is indeed granted to the highly unspeculative understanding between passion and the paradox, since the whole of life in time is vouchsafed, and the change comes first in eternity. . . .

Faith has in fact two tasks: to take care in every moment to discover the improbable, the paradox; and then to hold it fast with the passion of inwardness. The common conception is that the improbable, the paradoxical, is something to which faith is related only passively; it must provisionally be content with this relationship, but little by little things will become better, as indeed seems probable. O miraculous creation of confusions in speaking about faith! One is to begin believing, in reliance upon the probability that things will soon become better. In this way probability is after all smuggled in, and one is prevented from believing; so that it is easy to understand that the fruit of having been for a long time a believer is, that one no longer believes, instead of, as one might think, that the fruit is a more intensive inwardness in faith. No, faith is self-active in its relation to the improbable and the paradoxical, self-active in the discovery, and self-active in every moment holding it fast—in order to believe. Merely to lay hold of the improbable requires all the passion of the infinite and its concentration in itself; for the improbable and the paradoxical are not to be reached by the understanding's quantitative calculation of the more and more difficult. Where the understanding despairs, faith is already present in order to make the despair properly decisive, in order that the movement of faith may not become a mere exchange within the bargaining sphere of the understanding. But to believe against the understanding is martyrdom; to begin to get the understanding a little in one's favor, is temptation and retrogression. This martyrdom is something that the speculative philosopher is free from. That he must pursue his studies, and especially that he must read many modern books, I admit is burdensome; but the martyrdom of faith is not the same thing. What I therefore fear and shrink from, more than I fear to die and to lose my sweetheart, is to say about Christianity that it is to a certain degree true. If I lived to be seventy years old, if I shortened the night's sleep and increased the day's work from year to year, inquiring into Christianity—how insignificant such a little period of study, viewed as entitling me to judge in so lofty a fashion about Christianity! For to be so embittered against Christianity after a casual acquaintance with it, that I declared it to be false: that would be far more pardonable, far more human. But this lordly superiority seems to me the true corruption, making every saving relationship impossible—and it may possibly be the case, that Christianity is the truth. . . .

43   Kierkegaard and the "Truth" of Christianity

Paul Edwards

The Alleged Turning Point in European Philosophy

Existentialists, especially those who follow either Heidegger or Jaspers, find a great deal objectionable in what they variously call "scientism," "scientific rationalism," and "positivism." In this article I shall discuss one of the alleged defects of scientific rationalism, that it recognizes only one kind of truth—the kind that existentialists call "objective truth." "One great achievement of existential philosophy," writes William Barrett, "has been a new interpretation of the idea of truth in order to point out that there are different kinds of truth, where a rigid scientific rationalism had postulated but one kind: objective scientific truth." (W. Barrett and H. Aiken, eds., *Philosophy in the Twentieth Century*, from here on abbreviated as PTC, Vol. 2, p. 149.) Not only scientific rationalists but traditional metaphysicians from Plato to Aquinas and Hegel are judged to be equally at fault here: they too have failed to recognize any truth other than the objective variety. It was Kierkegaard who for the first time effectively challenged the assumptions shared by scientific rationalists and traditional metaphysicians. Kierkegaard, in Barrett's words, "had to re-open the whole question of the meaning of truth . . . his stand on the question may well have marked a turning point in European philosophy." (*Irrational Man,* from now on abbreviated as IM, p. 152.)

[This selection is a slightly condensed version of an article that first appeared in *Philosophy*, 1971. It is reprinted with the permission of the editor of *Philosophy*.]

The doctrine that "may well have marked a turning point in European philosophy" is Kierkegaard's theory identifying truth with "subjectivity." We are given to understand that, in addition to being a major contribution to epistemology, this doctrine supplies us with a new way of justifying religious belief. Kierkegaard did indeed concede that theological claims cannot be justified by the kind of proof that is found in Aquinas and Descartes, but he denied that "reflection inevitably destroys Christianity and is its natural enemy." There is such a thing as "a god-fearing reflection" which, so far from destroying Christianity, "once more brings the springs of Christianity into play." (*The Journals of Kierkegaard,* p. 261, Entry 813.) Once our god-fearing reflection shows us that objective truth is not the only kind of truth and, more specifically, once we realize that a person may be in the truth although what he believes is absurd from a purely rational point of view, we shall see that the Kantian critique and the various anti-theological considerations urged by unbelievers cannot affect religion properly understood. What "seemed so catastrophic to Kant," to quote William Barrett, namely that "the existence of God cannot be proved rationally," will then be seen to be "perfectly acceptable" to the believer. (PTC, Vol. 2, p. 150.) Kierkegaard's doctrine that truth is subjectivity has thus been hailed as a turning point in European theology no less than in philosophy, and Kierkegaard's influence on theologians. has been immense. "Present day Protestant theology," Barrett remarks, "practically lives off Kierkegaard's capital." (IM, p. 156.) In view of the rather precarious hold on life that Protestantism has displayed in recent decades a skeptic might wonder just how substantial the capital could be that it lives off. And this is precisely what I wish to investigate in the present article: is Kierkegaard's theory that truth is subjectivity really an important discovery? Does it embody *any* significant insights? Has Kierkegaard provided Christians or other believers with anything that can be regarded as a justification? And if Kierkegaard has not provided believers with a justification, has he at least supplied a new method of warding off the objections of unbelievers?

Reason and Eternal Happiness

Kierkegaard has frequently been described as an irrationalist but he evidently was not opposed to the use of reason and science in the treatment of factual questions about the ordinary or secular world. He would not have denied that by the use of scientific techniques human beings have accumulated a great deal of knowledge. However, when it comes to religious questions Kierkegaard denied that reason and science are of any use. He himself was primarily concerned with his own eternal happiness and with his relation to Christianity as a means of securing this happiness. In the introduction to *Concluding Unscientific Postscript* he wrote:

I, Johannes Climacus, born in this city and now thirty years old, a common ordinary human being like most people, assume that there awaits me a highest good, an eternal happiness, in the same sense that such a good awaits a servant-girl or a professor. I have heard that Christianity proposes itself as a condition for the acquirement of this good, and now I ask how I may establish a proper relationship to this doctrine. . . .

Christianity . . . puts quite an extraordinary emphasis upon my own petty self, and upon every other self however petty, in that it proposes to endow each self with an eternal happiness, provided a proper relationship is established.[1]

This naturally leads to the question:

How may I, Johannes Climacus, participate in the happiness promised by Christianity? (*Concluding Unscientific Postscript,* from now on abbreviated as CUP, pp. 19–20.)

The question of whether I shall live forever and what I must do to reach this goal, to obtain "that thing one would more than gladly do everything to earn" (CUP, p. 156) is of "infinite personal interest" and requires decisive action here and now. Where my infinite interest is concerned I must have certainty. Nothing less will do. Science and reason, however, cannot give me this certainty and hence they must be banished from religious discussion. Kierkegaard discusses three inadequacies of reason as an instrument in justifying religious beliefs: (1) reason can give us probability, but probability is not enough; (2) there is no evidence for or against religious doctrines and hence reason will give us even less than probability; and (3) in fact religious doctrines are "absurd," "impossible," "inconceivable"—i.e. if we followed reason we would have to reject them and not merely suspend judgment or arrive at a tentative endorsement. As I understand Kierkegaard, there is no inconsistency here since these different defects are asserted of different religious doctrines.

In the case of these religious claims where reason may give us grounds for belief the most it can provide is probability or what Kierkegaard calls "approximation":

Even with the most stupendous learning and persistence in research and even if all the brains of all the critics were concentrated in one, it would still be impossible to obtain anything more than an approximation; and that approximation is essentially incommensurable with an infinite personal interest in eternal happiness. (CUP, p. 26.)

1. Like Barrett and other existentialists I am assuming throughout this article that Kierkegaard may be identified with Johannes Climacus, the pseudonymous author of *Concluding Unscientific Postscript* and *Fear and Trembling.* Such an identification has been questioned by several writers, most recently by Professor Alastair McKinnon in "Kierkegaard's Irrationalism Revisited," *International Philosophical Quarterly,* June 1969. I do not feel qualified to take sides on this question of Kierkegaard-scholarship. If Professor McKinnon is right, some sentences in the present essay would have to be reworded, but nothing essential would be affected. I am concerned with the soundness or otherwise of the doctrine that truth is subjectivity as it has been interpreted by contemporary existentialists who regard it as a momentous contribution. Whether or how far Kierkegaard himself really believed it or any of the other theories proposed in the pseudonymous writings is quite another matter.

Probability or approximation may be all that we need in questions of lesser importance like the buying of a car or the choice of a profession or even the selection of a marriage partner, but we cannot possibly be satisfied with it when the question is how to secure eternal life:

> While objective knowledge rambles comfortably on by way of the long road of approximation without being impelled by the urge of passion, subjective knowledge counts every delay a deadly peril, and the decision so infinitely important and so instantly pressing that it is as if the opportunity has already passed. (CUP, p. 179.)

These remarks appear to apply to the various historical assertions found in the Bible. When it comes to the question of the existence of God, reason by itself cannot even give probability:

> I contemplate the order of nature in the hope of finding God, and I see omnipotence and wisdom; but I also see much else that disturbs my mind and excites anxiety. (CUP, p. 182.)[2]

Reason cannot, as Aquinas and Descartes taught, establish the existence of God; but at least it does not, on Kierkegaard's view, condemn belief in the existence of God as absurd. However, this is precisely the verdict that reason must pronounce on the peculiarly Christian doctrine (what Kierkegaard habitually calls the "supreme" or "absolute paradox") that in the person of Christ God became man—that here the eternal became temporal. "This historical datum," (that God "fused with an individual man")

> is compounded in a way contradictory to all thinking. . . . That that which in accordance with its nature is eternal comes into existence in time, is born, grows up, and dies—this is a breach with all thinking. (CUP, p. 513.)

The "contradiction that God has existed in human form" (CUP, p. 38) is from a rational point of view quite absurd, but it is precisely such an absurdity that the true Christian must believe:

> The absurd is the object of faith, and the only object that can be believed. (CUP, p. 189.)

When Socrates believed that there was a God, he "held fast to the objective uncertainty with the whole passion of his inwardness," but from a rational point of view the Christian is in a worse predicament.

> Instead of the objective uncertainty, there is here a certainty, namely, that objectively it is absurd. (CUP, p. 188.)

The pagan who "ventures everything" on a belief in immortality does not have any evidence to back his belief, but the venture of the believer in the incarnation is "far more difficult" since he is required to "believe *against*

---

2. There is not a similarly clear pronouncement on the state of the objective evidence for immortality, but it seems fairly plain that Kierkegaard did not think of the traditional proofs for immortality any more favorably than of those in support of God's existence. He does remark in one place (CUP, p. 155) that "systematically, immortality cannot be proved at all."

the understanding." (CUP, p. 384, my italics.) Christianity requires of its adherents faith in something that is

> an offense to the Jews and a folly to the Greeks—and an absurdity to the understanding. (CUP, p. 191.)

If I am to be a Christian

> I have to learn precisely to give up my finite understanding and therewith the custom of discrimination which is natural to me. (CUP, p. 159.)

In this way we can see that it is more and not less difficult for a learned and intelligent man to be or to become a Christian than it is for one who is simple and ignorant.

> Becoming a Christian really is the most difficult of all human tasks, since although it is the same for all men it is nevertheless proportioned to the capacity of each individual. . . . When faith requires a man to give up his reason, it becomes equally difficult for the cleverest and the most stupid person to believe, or it becomes in a sense more difficult for the clever. (CUP, p. 337.)

> The greater a man's equipment of knowledge and culture, the more difficult it is for him to become a Christian. (CUP, p. 342.)

> Religious suffering . . . is precisely the consciousness of the contradiction, which is pathetically and tragically incorporated in the consciousness of the religious individual. (CUP, p. 432.)

It is unnecessary for our purposes to inquire into the sense or senses in which Kierkegaard uses "absurd," "breach with all thinking," and similar expressions in the statements just quoted. Whatever their exact meaning, there is no doubt that Kierkegaard regarded the doctrine of the incarnation as highly objectionable from the point of view of reason so that it would have to be rejected if it were simply a matter of rational considerations.[3]

Truth Is Subjectivity

Since reason cannot give us the required certainty, we have to turn elsewhere. Instead of trying to defend religious doctrines by an appeal to evidence, we must become "passionate" and "subjective." "The conclusions of the passion," Kierkegaard writes in one place, "are the only reliable ones."[4] In any event, only by becoming passionate and subjective can we achieve the truth and the certainty that reason is unable to supply:

3. There is no agreement among commentators as to what Kierkegaard meant by "absurd." References to the literature on this topic may be found in the Bibliography to the present section, page 565 below.

4. *Fear and Trembling,* p. 109. Kierkegaard adds "that is, the only convincing conclusions" which is not at all the same thing. However, here and elsewhere Kierkegaard appears to assert that the conclusions of the passions are *both* reliable and convincing.

> It is subjectivity that Christianity is concerned with, and it is only in sub-
> jectivity that its truth exists, if it exists at all; objective Christianity has
> absolutely no existence. (CUP, p. 116.)

This is a dark saying, but Kierkegaard makes a fairly elaborate attempt to
explain himself. To begin with, he observes that in the case of any particular
belief it is possible to distinguish between what is believed or what one
might call its "objective content" and how it is believed, or the subjective
attitude of the individual who holds the belief in question. Not only can
such a distinction always be made, but Kierkegaard seems to be saying that
it is frequently very important to make it and that this is particularly so
when it comes to religious beliefs:

> The objective accent falls on *WHAT* is said, the subjective accent on *HOW*
> it is said. This distinction holds even in the aesthetic realm, and receives
> definite expression in the principle that what is in itself true may in the mouth
> of such and such a person become untrue. (CUP, p. 181.)

Kierkegaard here evidently thinks of the kind of situation in which we might
agree with what a particular person is saying and yet find it odd and even
distasteful that *he,* of all people, should be saying it. Sometimes we might
even refer to such people as "living lies" although what they say is quite
true or the sort of thing that we ourselves approve of. For example, there
are numerous contemporary theologians who talk a great deal about the
virtues of love, about the desirability of leading an "agapistic" life, but
who are themselves totally incapable of any love for anybody, who are cold
and pretentious and whose most characteristic emotions are pettiness and
vanity. Another example would be a person who is filled with (poorly concealed) anti-semitic impulses but who nevertheless holds forth at length
about the great contributions of the Jews to civilization, the injustice of
racial and religious discrimination, and so on. We might, in such a case, use
words not too different from those used by Kierkegaard in the above
passage and say that "what is in itself true becomes in the mouth of this
person untrue." We might talk in this way, but as we shall see later on, it is
an unhelpful and potentially confusing way of talking.

　　Kierkegaard probably also has in mind somewhat different situations
in which an individual is not so much insincere as inadequately involved
in what he is asserting or believing. Somebody may, for example, defend a
certain solution to the problem of induction which is in fact plausible and
which he supports very intelligently; and yet he may not have thought
the problem through as deeply as another person who arrived at the identical solution after a long period of puzzlement and anxiety. That this is at
least one of the things which Kierkegaard has in mind becomes evident in
the passage following the one just quoted.

> In these times this distinction is particularly worthy of notice, for if we wish to
> express in a single sentence the difference between ancient times and our own,
> we should doubtless have to say: "In ancient times only an individual here
> and there knew the truth; now all know it, except that the inwardness of its

appropriation stands in an inverse relationship to the extent of its dissemination." (CUP, *ibid.*)

The distinction between the *how* and the *what* of a belief is one essential ingredient of Kierkegaard's doctrine that truth is subjectivity. Another is his conception of faith which differs significantly from that of many other writers in the Christian tradition. In Kierkegaard's view there can be no such thing as faith without risk. It is risk which gives faith the kind of tension that Kierkegaard regards as extremely desirable. A feeling of security is neither admirable nor any indication that the person has attained the right God-relationship. Quite the reverse: such a sense of security is "the one certain sign that the individual does not stand in a relationship to God." (CUP, p. 407.) Real faith involves "the tremendous risk of objective insecurity" (CUP, p. 188) and this means that the believer is fully aware of the objective uncertainty of what he believes:

> Faith is precisely the contradiction between the infinite passion of the individual's inwardness and the objective uncertainty. If I am capable of grasping God objectively, I do not believe, but precisely because I cannot do this I must believe. If I wish to preserve myself in faith I must constantly be intent upon holding fast the objective uncertainty, so as to remain out upon the deep, over seventy thousand fathoms of water, still preserving my faith. (CUP, p. 182.)

One cannot have this kind of faith in a mathematical proposition whose "objectivity is given," i.e., which can be rationally established—such a proposition will never be anything more than an "indifferent truth." However, in the case of such topics as God or immortality, we do have the required objective uncertainty. It is this objective uncertainty that

> increases the tension of that infinite passion which constitutes [a person's] inwardness. The truth is precisely the venture which chooses an objective uncertainty with the passion of the infinite. I contemplate the order of nature in the hope of finding God, and I see omnipotence and wisdom: but I also see much else that disturbs my mind and excites anxiety. The sum of all this is an objective uncertainty. But it is for this very reason that the inwardness becomes as intense as it is, for it embraces this objective uncertainty with the entire passion of the infinite. (*ibid.*)

Faith involves decision or, as Kierkegaard often calls it, "a leap." There is, however, no room for decision where the proposition at stake is not inherently dubious. The person who adopts "the objective mode of approach" and attempts to explain away difficulties seeks in effect "to shirk something of the pain and crisis of decision." (CUP, p. 115.) The rationalistic theologian prides himself on not believing "as shoemakers and tailors and simple folk believe." For him the Christian assertions have become "extremely and emphatically probable," but "anything that is almost probable, or probable, or extremely and emphatically probable is something . . . that it is impossible to *believe*." (CUP, p. 189, Kierkegaard's italics.)

We now come to Kierkegaard's final point. There are two senses in which a person may be said to be "in the truth." He may be in the truth in the objective sense in that what he believes or asserts is in accordance with the facts or he may be in the truth in the subjective sense in that his way of believing is of the right kind, displaying "the entire passion of the infinite." Less rhetorically expressed, Kierkegaard evidently means that a person is in the truth in the subjective sense if he believes whatever he believes sincerely and without reservations, i.e., that he is totally and not just partially committed to the belief in question. Kierkegaard explains this distinction in one of the most famous passages in his works:

> *When the question of truth is raised in an objective manner, reflection is directed objectively to the truth, as an object to which the knower is related. Reflection is not focussed upon the relationship, however, but upon the question of whether it is the truth to which the knower is related. If only the object to which he is related is the truth, the subject is accounted to be in the truth. When the question of the truth is raised subjectively, reflection is directed subjectively to the nature of the individual's relationship; if only the mode of this relationship is in the truth, the individual is in the truth, even if he should happen to be thus related to what is not true.* (CUP, p. 178, Kierkegaard's italics.)

Kierkegaard not only insists that we should carefully observe the distinction between the two senses of being in the truth just explained, but he goes further and urges that there is "more truth" in being subjectively in the truth than in being objectively in the truth:

> Only in subjectivity is there decisiveness, to seek objectivity is to be in error. It is the passion of the infinite that is the decisive factor and not its content. (CUP, p. 181.)

> When the problem is to reckon up on which side there is most truth, whether on the side of one who seeks the true God objectively, and pursues the approximate truth of the God-idea; or on the side of one who, driven by the infinite passion of his need of God, feels an infinite concern for his own relationship to God in truth . . . the answer cannot be in doubt for anyone who has not been demoralized with the aid of science. (CUP, p. 179.]

Those whom science has not "demoralized" will declare without the least hesitation that there is more truth on the side of the passionately involved God-seeker than on the side of the believer who treats the problem as a purely intellectual question on a par with scientific and mathematical problems. A primitive but sincere and passionate idol-worshipper has more truth in spite of his defective theology than a learned theologian who lacks the appropriate inwardness:

> If one who lives in the midst of Christendom goes up to the house of God, the house of the true God, with the true conception of God in his knowledge, and prays, but prays in a false spirit; and one who lives in an idolatrous community prays with the entire passion of the infinite, although his eyes rest upon the image of an idol: where is there most truth? The one prays in truth to God though he worships an idol; the other prays falsely to the true God, and hence worships in fact an idol. (CUP, p. 180.)

Kierkegaard brings these three points together in his new "definition" of truth:

> Objectively the interest is focussed merely on the thought-content, subjectively on the inwardness. At its maximum this inward "how" is the passion of the infinite, and the passion of the infinite is the truth. But the passion of the infinite is precisely subjectivity, and thus subjectivity becomes the truth. . . . In this manner subjectivity and the subjective "how" constitute the truth. (CUP, p. 181.)

> When subjectivity is the truth, the conceptual determination of the truth must include an expression for the antithesis to objectivity. . . . Here is such a definition of truth: *An objective uncertainty held fast in an appropriation-process of the most passionate inwardness is the truth,* the highest truth attainable for an existing individual. (CUP, p. 182, Kierkegaard's italics.)

It should be clear now why Kierkegaard's strategy so strongly appeals to theologians who have been impressed by the soundness of Kant's criticisms of the traditional arguments for the existence of God and immortality. If one is concerned to be objectively in the truth in religious matters one's position will no doubt be adversely affected by the soundness of the Kantian attack, but no such adverse implications are in store for the believer whose aim is to be subjectively in the truth. To quote William Barrett once more:

> The truth with which religion is ultimately concerned, said Kierkegaard, has nothing to do with questions of rational proof. We do not exclaim, "There is a genuinely religious person!" when we happen to encounter a man who is an expert in all the subtle dialectic of theology. If we have ever encountered a genuinely spiritual person, we know that the heart of the matter lies elsewhere; in the being of the total person, not in the cerebrations of reason. Religious truth is realized actively and inwardly in the life of the individual man; it is not something embodied in a system of concepts like science. Hence the fact that seemed so catastrophic to Kant—that the existence of God could not be proved rationally—is perfectly acceptable. For God is never real in our lives when He is considered a mere object of scientific proof or disproof. (PTC, Vol 2, pp. 149–150.)

Kierkegaard's Two Positions

A proper evaluation of Kierkegaard's doctrine that truth is subjectivity and his use of it as a means of defending Christianity is impossible unless it is realized that what he offers us is not a single theory but an amalgamation of two quite distinct positions. As a consequence, it is not easy to criticize. Whenever one of the two positions which make up the total theory is justly attacked, Kierkegaard's defenders are liable to claim that he has been misunderstood and to point to the other position against which the objections are indeed without any force.

Perhaps we should begin by pointing out that although much of the time

Kierkegaard appears to tell us that we should forget about the objective questions except as a means of heightening the tension of inwardness, he does revert to these issues and as a Christian he must do so. Putting it in different words, Kierkegaard reverts and must revert, from the new sense of "true" in which to say that a belief is true means no more than that it is held sincerely and without reservations, to the old sense in which it means that it is in accordance with the facts or with reality. A person is not a Christian in any traditional sense, and certainly not in Kierkegaard's sense, if he has ceased to believe that certain propositions are true in the old sense of "true": he has ceased to be a Christian if he does not believe that *as a matter of fact* there is a God, that God manifested himself in the person of Christ, and that human beings are immortal. It is not enough to believe that believing any or all of these things with infinite passion is something admirable. One should recall here what led Kierkegaard to his defense of inwardness in the first place and what made him disparage reason as a tool in religious apologetics. Reason cannot give us certainty, but in a matter so all-important as our eternal salvation nothing less than certainty will do. Kierkegaard is here concerned to assure his eternal salvation. He is not or not merely concerned to defend the view that believing in eternal salvation with appropriate inwardness is something admirable.

In one place Kierkegaard explains that he is not much worried about the opinions of his fellow-men. What, he asks, "is the hour and a half I have to live with men, what but a brief instant compared with eternity?" It is God's opinion and God's judgment that is all-important:

> But woe unto me if the Deity were to condemn me in my most inward man for the fact that I wanted mendaciously to be systematic and world-historical, and to forget what it is to be a man, and therewith forget what it means that He is the Deity. Woe unto me. Woe unto me in time, and still more dreadfully when He gets hold of me in eternity! (CUP, p. 163.)

Let us suppose that Kierkegaard was mistaken about the nature of God and that what God prizes is intellectual rectitude and not the feverish inwardness that Kierkegaard valued so highly. Let us suppose that when Kierkegaard comes up for judgment God addresses him with these words: "You led a miserable and contemptible life. The last man I judged was a Scottish philosopher by the name of David Hume and I rewarded him with eternal bliss. He did not believe in immortality, he did not believe in my existence, and he most emphatically rejected the doctrine of the incarnation. He was right on the last point—for your information Jesus was just a man, in many ways an admirable man, but he was not my son. Hume's unbelief in immortality and my existence were errors but they were most creditable errors since he followed the best available evidence, which is all that a human being can do. He followed the available evidence although it took great courage to do so since the conclusions were anything but pleasant. You on the other hand were a coward. You refused to follow the evidence and concocted all sorts of crudely fallacious theories to make yourself believe the pleasant conclusion that you would live happily forever. I detest such cowardice. Because of my merciful constitution I will not sentence you to eternal damnation but will extinguish you anon. Before I do so I will let you make a final statement. What do you have to say for yourself, you wretch?" I very much doubt that Kierkegaard would reply, "I stand vindicated. The fact that you are about to annihilate me and that, unlike David Hume, I shall miss out on eternal happiness is of no importance. I believed what I did without reservations. Hence I was in the truth. Hence I achieved the highest kind of life. The rest is of no consequence." On the contrary, Kierkegaard would regard himself as defeated and refuted—defeated and refuted because although "in the truth" in the subjective sense, it would now become apparent that he was not also in the truth in the objective sense. In spite of his numerous declarations to the effect that "every trace of an objective issue should be eliminated." (CUP, p. 115). Kierkegaard just as often realized that as a Christian he could not do this. When Kierkegaard reverts to the objective issues he has a tendency to bring up passionate involvement as some kind of evidence for the objective truth of the religious assertions. Thus, in one place, when he tells us that there is no "systematic proof" for immortality and admonishes us to have "a most passionate interest" in our eternal existence, he adds "and precisely in the interest lies the *proof*." (CUP, p. 155, my italics.) Earlier we found him remarking that only the conclusions of the passion are reliable and in the *Journals* he observes that "there is a 'how' which has this quality, that if *it* is truly given, the 'what' is also given; and that is the 'how of faith' "; and we are furthermore assured that "inwardness at its maximum proves to be objectivity." (*The Journals of Kierkegaard,* p. 355, Entry 1021.) It should be noted that the conclusions of the passion are not just passionate —they are also reliable and "reliable" is obviously not a synonym for "passionate." The interest in immortality is not merely a subjective state but it also provides us with "proof." Inwardness at its maximum is not only inwardness but also objectivity and the *what* of faith, though not the what of other mental states, is "given" when its how is truly given, which evidently means that if the believer is really subjectively in the truth, he is also objectively right.

Now, whatever may be true of other contentions that are also found in Kierkegaard and may be regarded as part of his defense of Christianity, the position just sketched is a glaring and horrendous non-sequitur. Once we revert to the objective questions, references to pitches of inwardness, to genuineness and unreserved commitment are totally irrelevant, as Kierkegaard himself indeed recognized in several places: our interest is not any kind of proof that we are immortal; the fact that a proposition was suggested by the "passion" does not make it reliable; and no *how,* regardless of how truly it is given, guarantees that its what is also given, i.e., that what is asserted is true.

So much for the first of Kierkegaard's positions. The other amounts to praise of inwardness, of genuineness and lack of reservations in one's belief as the highest kind of life accompanied by a recommendation to avoid all questions of objective evidence in religious matters.[5] It is difficult to suppose that Kierkegaard, as a believing Christian, could seriously adopt this position, but many of his remarks do seem to imply it. In any event this position does not embody any fallacies. Now, however, we do not have a position that has any resemblance to theology or supernaturalism or to the Christianity that Kierkegaard evidently wanted to justify in the first place. What we now have is a value judgment—a piece of moral or perhaps psychotherapeutic advice—which is consistent with the most thorough-going atheism. We no longer have the claim that there is a God or that any of us will enjoy eternal bliss if we behaved in a certain way. Instead we have the claim that if we believed these things or perhaps, like the idol-worshipper, certain other things in the right frame of mind, we would have achieved the highest kind of existence.

To say that only a believer can attain the highest form of existence is not at all the same thing as to say that what the believer believes is true in the ordinary, familiar sense of "true." The following analogy may help to make this clear. Let us imagine a psychiatrist who holds the view that the best safeguard against neurotic symptoms is intense and unqualified faith of some kind. If, for example, he has a patient who is a Stalinist but whose faith is wavering, he will do his utmost to restore his patient's attachment. He will counsel him, among other things, to read books like the study of the Soviet Union by Sidney and Beatrice Webb or the former Dean of Canterbury's notorious whitewash, *The Socialist Sixth of the World*, and to avoid certain other books like the writings of Koestler and Bertrand Russell; he will urge him to associate with certain people and definitely not to associate with certain others, to attend certain meetings and definitely not to attend certain other meetings, and so on. If he has a patient who is a follower of Ayn Rand but who has begun to have doubts about this lady's wisdom, the psychiatrist will take measures to allay the doubts and restore the original allegiance and he will proceed in a similar fashion with restive Protestants, Catholics, Jews, Trotzkyites, Scientologists, Maoists, and whatever other waverers he should encounter. It is obvious that this psychiatrist is not himself committed to any of the faiths which he tries to strengthen in his patients.

It may be objected that this analogy is not fair to Kierkegaard since what he praises is not blind and ignorant belief, the retention of faith by means of deliberately shutting one's eyes to unpleasant facts, but rather belief in spite of a full awareness of difficulties and objections. It is only through an awareness of such difficulties that the maximum tension can be achieved. There is justice in this observation, but it does not affect the only point at issue right now. If I preach that the greatest thing in life is the state of "infinite tension" that comes to a believer (be he a Christian, Jew or whatnot) who has retained his faith even after he has been made aware

---

5. What matters is passion: "The scribbling modern philosophy holds passion in contempt; and yet passion is the culmination of existence for an existing individual—and we are all of us existing individuals." (CUP, p. 176.)

of the full power of the most powerful objections that the ablest critics have put forward and if I admire those who have achieved such a state, I am not thereby committed to accepting any of these faiths. It would be perfectly consistent for me to dismiss them all as illusions or nonsense, though they would be illusion and nonsense that happened to be means of achieving the greatest things in life. Moreover, the original analogy was not wholly unfair. Although Kierkegaard does indeed maintain that the believer who is in the truth achieves the required tension as the result of knowing the logical defects of his position, both he and his admirers *also* again and again praise the simple sincere believer, "the simple-minded . . . whom God wishes to preserve in their lovable simplicity (CUP, p. 152n.), the "illiterate peasant" (Barrett, IM p. 152), the man who worships an idol but in the right spirit; and these simple sincere believers are presumably not familiar with the "learned" objections to their religions.

The upshot of our discussion so far is that Kierkegaard has not offered anything that can be called a justification of Christianity, that he has not offered us any grounds for regarding Christian belief as true in any sense in which this has been questioned by its opponents. The first of the two positions detectable in his writings is indeed an attempt to show that the doctrines of Christianity are true, but it is a huge and obvious non-sequitur. The second position, which is in effect a commendation of inwardness or subjectivity as the highest thing a person can achieve, does not embody any fallacies, but it is no longer a defense of Christianity. These difficulties are not apparent only if one has failed to see that we have two positions and not merely one. This fact in turn is obscured by the use of "true" in a new sense while evidently retaining many of the associations of its old sense. We shall say more about this technique in the next section.

The "New Interpretation" of Truth

William Barrett maintains that Kierkegaard has provided us with a "new interpretation of the idea of truth"; and this, as we saw, is claimed to have been a major turning point in European philosophy. The clear suggestion is that Kierkegaard has made a great discovery of some kind. In actual fact Kierkegaard's "new interpretation" of truth is not a discovery of anything whatever but an exceedingly misleading redefinition of a familiar word which is then made, by some of Kierkegaard's admirers rather than by Kierkegaard himself, the basis of a fallacious reply to the critics of religious belief.

Redefinitions, to be sure, *need* not be misleading and sometimes they are very amply justified. In mechanics the word "work" does not mean quite the same as it does in everyday life. The physicist's redefinition of "work" is justified because for the purposes of mechanics *some* word is needed to refer to the product of a force acting on a body and the displacement of the body in the direction of the force consequent upon this action; and the ordinary meaning of "work" is not too far removed from this. Again, whether he realized it or not, Freud in effect redefined the words "desire" and "motive" in such a way that it became possible to talk of unconscious as well as conscious desires and motives; and it is at least arguable that it is only by means of his broader concepts that certain human actions and feelings can be adequately explained. However, it should be noted that in the case of these defensible redefinitions the new sense of the word is continuous with the old one and furthermore it is possible to specify the gains that are involved in the new ways of talking.

There are other redefinitions which involve no such gains and which moreover are bound to produce confusion. Let us suppose, for example, that I decide to use the word "shoe" in a new way, making it equivalent to "footwear." In my new sense of "shoe" I will apply the word not only to what are presently called shoes but also, among other things, to socks. If, for example, I wear what are normally called "gray socks" under black shoes, I will now say "I am wearing two pairs of shoes—gray cotton shoes inside my black leather shoes." One may, if one so desires, call the redefinition a "new interpretation of the idea of a shoe" but it clearly embodies no discovery of any kind and no insight into anything whatever. Redefinition or reinterpretation, it is a pointless and confusing verbal practice—pointless because we already have the word "sock" to refer to socks and confusing because unless we are constantly reminded that the word "shoe" is used in a new way we are bound to reintroduce some or all of its old associations. As far as I can see, exactly the same verdict must be pronounced on Kierkegaard's handling of the word "true." We have certain expressions at our disposal for referring to what he calls being in the truth in the subjective sense—"believing sincerely," "believing genuinely," "believing without reservations," and others, whereas we reserve the word "true" for what Kierkegaard calls being in the truth in the objective sense. We frequently say and we easily understand such things as "He really deeply and genuinely believed such and such, but it turned out to be false." If we started using the word "true" to mean also what we now mean by "believing genuinely" or "believing without reservations" nothing but confusion could result. Since people have a tendency to revert to accepted or ordinary senses, such confusion is very likely to occur and in fact, as pointed out in the previous section, it is precisely this that has occurred in the present instance. You do not make a false or doubtful proposition true by calling it true any more than you make socks into shoes by calling them shoes.

As soon as we cut through the verbal fog and do not allow any of the associations of the old sense of "true" to mislead us, we shall see that Kierkegaard's "new interpretation" of truth does absolutely nothing to ward off the Kantian critique or any of the other well-known objections to theistic belief. Kant's critique was disturbing presumably because it made it doubtful whether theism was true. More radical critics of religious belief gave reasons for supposing that theism is false. It is evident that "true" and "false" are here used in the objective sense. The believers were disturbed because they wanted to be right in the objective sense, because they wished to be assured that *what* they believed was true—that there is a God and an afterlife and whatever else made up their religions. If it could be shown that the theistic arguments attacked by Kant can withstand his criticism and that the atheistic critics used arguments of dubious validity, this would certainly be to the point and it would rightly reduce grounds for concern. To be told, however, that they need not worry so long as their belief is genuine (which is all that being in the truth in the subjective sense comes to) is totally beside the point. It does not give the believers what they needed or wanted. Nor, assuming they are genuine believers, does it give them anything of whose possession they were not already assured. It would be difficult to find a more perfect illustration of the fallacy of *ignoratio elenchi*.

William Barrett tells us that "strictly speaking, subjective truth is not a truth that I *have,* but a truth that I *am. . . .* This kind of truth is not a truth of the intellect but of the whole man." (IM, p. 153, Barrett's italics.) Calvin O. Schrag, another prominent American existentialist, remarks that "truth is not something which I *possess* or *have,* but rather something which I *am* and *live.*" (*Existence and Freedom,* p. 7, Schrag's italics.) These weird ways of talking do not in any way improve matters either for Kierkegaard or for the believers whom he is supposed to protect. For ultimately all that is ever meant by these locutions is that the believer's belief is genuine, that his religion is not merely a verbal profession but something that deeply affects his life; and this is no answer to those who tried to show that *what* the believer believes is false or baseless or otherwise objectionable.

We can easily see the futility of appealing to sincerity as a ground for belief if we imagine a defense of "atheistic truth" along the same lines. A "Kierkegaardian" defender of atheism would observe that the genuineness of a given individual's atheism has nothing to do with his skill in the subtleties of logical argument. "If we have ever encountered a genuine atheist," he might go on, "we know that the heart of the matter lies elsewhere; in the being of the total person, not in the cerebrations of reason. We don't say 'here is a real atheist' when we meet a person who brilliantly defends atheism in a philosophical discussion but about whom we also know that he prays to God when he is in trouble, that he thanks God when things go well, that he secretly goes to confession once a month and that he obeys the various moral prohibitions of the church in which he was raised although he admits that there is no rational basis for them. We do say about a man 'here is a true atheist' if we know that fears of God's wrath and hopes of Divine rewards play no role whatsoever in his life; that when in trouble he does not pray to God for help and when things go well he does not thank God for his good fortune; that when searching for the explanation of a phenomenon he does not consider Divine intervention as a serious candidate; and that he does not follow moral rules unless they can be justified independently of alleged Divine commands. Atheistic truth is realized actively and inwardly in the life of the individual man." Believers in God would be the first to object, and rightly so, to such talk about "atheistic truth" when what is meant is the genuineness of this or that person's atheism. They would point out that the sincerity of the atheist is no answer to logical arguments against his position and that it is no ground whatever for supposing that the atheist is right, i.e., that atheism is true. If this rejection of a Kierkegaardian defense of atheism is justified, as it surely is, it is difficult to see why a similar rejection of a Kierkegaardian defense of theism or any other religious doctrine is not equally justified. That there are sincere and committed Christians as well as sincere and committed atheists is not something that is seriously disputed and is in itself of no philosophical interest. The philosophically interesting question is: Who is right—the Christian or the atheist or neither? Kierkegaard's "revolutionary" contribution leaves this question exactly where it was.

Chaotic Implications

I have so far omitted one important feature of Kierkegaard's position. In the famous passage quoted on page 512 Kierkegaard implies that he can tell who is worshipping the true God and who is merely worshipping an idol. The question that immediately arises in one's mind is whether such a discrimination is possible on Kierkegaard's principles. More generally, it appears that if a person is "in the truth" simply because he believes something sincerely and without reservations then the adherents of the most diverse and contradictory philosophies, religions, and ideologies would all be equally in the truth so long as the *how* of their beliefs was of the appropriate kind. Christians (whether Protestant or Catholic), Jews, Mohammedans, Hegelians, Platonists, Stalinists, Hitlerites, Trotzkyites, the followers of Ayn Rand, Scientologists, and many more would all be in the truth provided only that they displayed the right inwardness. Even the sincere and committed atheist could not be excluded from the list.

There is little doubt that Kierkegaard had some awareness of this difficulty and that he attempted to meet it. Thus he notes in one place that we must distinguish the inwardness of the religious believer from the "aberrant inwardness" of the fanatic and the type of "subjective madness" illustrated by Don Quixote. "It is a self-contradiction and therefore comical to be infinitely interested in that which in its maximum still always remains an approximation" (CUP, p. 32), by which Kierkegaard here means something finite and limited. Don Quixote does indeed display a passion of inwardness no less intense than that of religious believers, but instead of concerning himself with such all-important subjects as eternal salvation his passion is focused on "particular finite fixed ideas," on "little finitudes" that "do not really concern anybody." (CUP, pp. 174–175.) The "unfortunate individual"[6] whose infinite concern is inappropriately directed to something

6. In a moving passage Kierkegaard distinguishes between the "subjective" madness of the person who is infinitely concerned but not about the right object and "the much more

finite and unimportant is not in the truth, but this does not mean that the religious believer, whose concern is appropriately directed to the infinite, fails to be in the truth.

If we accept this distinction between genuine and "aberrant" inwardness some of the chaotic implications of Kierkegaard's doctrine would be avoided. It now becomes possible for Kierkegaard to maintain that the worshippers of human deities like Hitler, Stalin, Trotzky, or Ayn Rand are not in the truth even when their pitch of inwardness is "infinite." They are not in the truth because the object of their infinite concern is not the infinite God but somebody finite and imperfect. The distinction between genuine and aberrant inwardness does not, however, allow Kierkegaard to dispose of the believers in various non-Christian religions or in philosophies like those of Plato, Spinoza, and Hegel, whose adherents, provided of course that their pitch is sufficiently intense, are directing their inwardness toward the infinite and not toward a finite and imperfect individual in the world. It is doubtful whether Kierkegaard ever faced this last-mentioned difficulty but there are some interesting remarks in various places which may be regarded as an attempt to deal with the problem. The point seems to be that because of the paradoxical nature of what is affirmed, Christianity and Christianity alone intensifies the believer's passion to its "highest pitch." (CUP, p. 117.) One of the fullest statements occurs near the very end of the *Postscript:*

> Faith is the objective uncertainty due to the repulsion of the absurd held fast by the passion of inwardness, which in this instance is intensified to the utmost degree. This formula fits only the believer, no one else, not a lover, not an enthusiast, not a thinker, but simply and solely the believer who is related to the absolute paradox. (p. 540)

Earlier Kierkegaard had been quite explicit on the same question:

> Without risk there is no faith, and the greater the risk the greater the faith; the more objective security the less inwardness . . . and the less objective security the more profound the possible inwardness. (CUP, p. 188.)

Kierkegaard regarded the doctrine of the incarnation as presenting very special intellectual obstacles which are not presented by the mere assertion of the existence of God or the other infinites and absolutes that are found in the systems of non-Christian metaphysicians; and the tension that is an essential part of the infinite passion of genuine inwardness can be attained only by somebody who has to face the special "repulsion" presented by the incarnation doctrine.

There are many reasons for questioning this last claim. Is it really the case that the highest pitch of inwardness can be generated only by doctrines

---

inhuman madness" of those who are totally devoid of inwardness. "One shrinks from looking into the eyes of a madman of the former type lest one be compelled to plumb there the depths of his delirium; but one dares not look at a madman of the latter type at all, for fear of discovering that he has eyes of glass and hair made from carpet-rags; that he is, in short, an artificial product." (p. 175) which the believer finds so repellent? And, more basically, can a human being really believe something that he acknowledges to be absurd?[7] Even if we disregard these difficulties, it is quite clear that Kierkegaard has failed to offer a criterion that would achieve the desired result of excluding *all* non-Christians from the class of those who are in the truth. The appeal to the absolute paradox may indeed dispose of non-theistic believers in a metaphysical absolute, of deists and perhaps even of Jews since the creed of none of these groups involves the doctrine of an incarnation. It does not, however, rule out believers in the numerous religions which contain savior-stories closely analogous to the story of Jesus. A believer in these other religions would be faced with obstacles of the same kind (with the same "repulsion of the absurd") and hence he *could* achieve the tension that is required for the highest pitch of inwardness. Kierkegaard would be proceeding in an entirely arbitrary fashion if he maintained that Christians are in the truth but believers in these other savior-religions are not.

There is, however, a much more basic objection to the first of Kierkegaard's efforts to answer the charge that his doctrine involves chaotic consequences. The point here is exceedingly simple. We are told that the infinite concern felt by fanatics and by those who are subjectively mad does not put them "in the truth" because their infinite concern is inappropriate to the objects to which it is directed. Their infinite concern is inappropriate because the objects are finite and unimportant. Such remarks make good sense, but they clearly imply that the passion of the fanatics and the madmen are inappropriate because *in fact* the objects of their concern do not possess certain characteristics. By the same token, if there were no God or no God of the kind the Christian believes in or if Jesus never lived or if he lived but was in fact just another human being, the passion of the Christian believer would also be misdirected or "aberrant." That the objects of the fanatic's and the madman's passion are not what they take them to be (e.g., that Stalin was not as wise and beneficent as his worshippers believed) is something we know from observation, i.e., by appeal to objective evidence. But if the door is once opened to objective evidence then any evidence that atheists and other unbelievers might be able to bring up against what the Christian believes in can no longer be ruled out as irrelevant. We can now regard a person as in the truth only if, in addition to feeling infinite concern, it is also the case that the object or objects appropriate to this infinite concern do in fact exist. The distinction between genuine and aberrant inwardness, in other words, destroys the believer's immunity from rational criticism that Kierkegaard's doctrine was supposed to secure.

7. This will no doubt depend on what is meant by "absurd." If Kierkegaard means something weaker than self-contradictory there may be no problem here. In one place he speaks of the paradox as "the improbable" (CUP, p. 209) and this is something that human beings are quite capable of believing. However, if the paradox consists of statements which the believer knows to be self-contradictory, "believing the absurd" becomes an unintelligible expression.

[I wish to thank my friend, Donald Levy, for offering valuable criticisms and suggestions. I also greatly profited from reading in manuscript the chapter on Kierkegaard that is to appear in the third series of Professor Brand Blanshard's Gifford Lectures, *Reason and Religion*.]

44   On the Eclipse of God

Emil L. Fackenheim

$\mathbf{I}$N ONE OF HIS WRITINGS MARTIN Heidegger quotes with approval, as applying to the present, these words of the early 19th-century German poet Hoelderlin: "Alas, our generation walks in night, dwells as in Hades, without the Divine." When Hoelderlin wrote those words, there cannot have been many people who agreed with him, for it was an age which thought of itself as about to reach the very summit of religious enlightenment. In our own age, by contrast—an age which is acquainted with catastrophe and stands in fear of even greater catastrophes to come—hardly anyone can think of himself as walking in anything but night. And while it is not immediately clear whether this means that we must dwell "without the Divine"—indeed, that is the question to which these reflections are addressed—it is at any rate perfectly clear that we are undergoing an unprecedented crisis of religious faith.

[This article first appeared in *Commentary*, June 1964, and was subsequently reprinted in a collection of the author's essays, *In Quest for Past and Future* (Indiana University Press, 1968). It is reprinted with the publisher's permission. Professor Fackenheim has requested that the following note be printed in conjunction with this selection: "Since writing 'On the Eclipse of God' I have advanced doctrines which may seem to be partial retractions but are in fact only additional necessary distinctions. These may be found in 'Jewish Faith and the Holocaust' (*Commentary*, August 1968), 'Elijah and the Empiricists' (*The Religious Situation*, Beacon Press, 1969), and *God's Presence in History* (New York University Press, 1970)."]

The Indestructability of Biblical Faith

According to a widespread view, it is the very catastrophes of the 20th century which have brought the crisis about. The ancient belief that the Divine is with us—that God lives and cares—cannot, it is said, be sustained in the face of these catastrophes, for to sustain it requires smugness and blindness to tragedy. Yet the fact is that this view reflects a complete lack of understanding of the nature of religious faith in general and Biblical faith in particular. Biblical faith—and I mean both Jewish and Christian— is never destroyed by tragedy but only tested by it; and in the test it both clarifies its own meaning and conquers tragedy. Here, precisely, lies the secret of its strength.

Consider a few representative examples. The prophet Jeremiah lives to see the destruction of the Temple, of Jerusalem, of the whole national existence of Judah. He does not deny the tragedy or seek to explain it away. But neither does it occur to him that God's existence has now been refuted, or that He can no longer be conceived as just, or as loving His people, Israel. To Jeremiah the destruction of the Temple *is* a manifestation of divine justice. And it does not mark the end of divine love: "There is hope for the future."

The case of Job is still more extreme because Job is struck by tragedies which are explicitly said to be beyond the bounds of any conceivable divine justice. Yet Job never denies the existence of God; nor does he follow his wife's suggestion that he curse God and die. His faith is reduced to utter unintelligibility, yet he persists in it.

Let me give a final example which, at least in one respect, is still more extreme—the example of the Psalmist. Even in the midst of unintelligible tragedy, Job never wholly loses his sense of the presence of God. The Psalmist *in extremis,* however, does, when he complains that God has "hidden His face." God is not—at least not now—present. Unlike Job, the Psalmist does not ask that God's ways be made intelligible to him. He does not ask that the valley of the shadows or the netherworld be made to vanish; he asks only that God be present while he walks through them, as God was present to him before. Yet even in this most extreme of all crisis situations—God having "hidden His face"—the Psalmist never loses his faith. He never says that God does not, after all, exist; nor that, though existing, He has finally ceased to care. (In practice the two assertions would amount to the same thing.) What he does say is that, unaccountably, God has hidden His face; that He has hidden it for only a while; and that He will turn His face back to man again.

Put radically, this means that there is no experience, either without or within, that can possibly destroy religious faith. Good fortune without reveals the hand of God; bad fortune, if it is not a matter of just punishment, teaches that God's ways are unintelligible, not that there *are* no ways of God. A full heart within indicates the Divine Presence; an empty heart bespeaks not the non-existence or unconcern of God, but merely His temporary absence. *Religious faith can be, and is, empirically verifiable; but nothing empirical can possibly refute it.*

Philosophers of science rightly assert that such an attitude toward the empirical is in principle illegitimate in the sciences. It is, however, hardly surprising that it should be of the essence of religious faith. Science is forever hypothetical. But what could one make of a religious faith which was forever hypothetical, wavering between belief in good times and unbelief in bad? Since, as we have seen, the characteristic of genuine faith is not only to survive in tragic times but to survive in them most triumphant, it is no accident that adherents of Biblical faith should always have regarded times of external or internal darkness not as evidence against God, but rather— to use Martin Buber's expression—as evidence of an "eclipse of God." To follow Buber's metaphor, an eclipse of the sun is something that occurs, not to or in the sun, but between the sun and the eye; moreover, this occurrence is temporary. Hence the catastrophes of our time, however great, cannot by themselves account for the contemporary crisis of religious belief; or rather, they can be regarded as having produced this crisis only on the assumption that religious belief was already undermined. What, then, undermined it?

Biblical Faith and Modern Science

Most people would say: modern science. The story begins with Copernicus, who shows that the earth is but one of many stars; it is carried forward by Darwin, who shows that man is but a higher animal; and it culminates with Freud, who shows that the one indubitably distinctive human characteristic—rationality—is neither very significant nor even very distinctive. Once at the center of the universe, man has been moved to the periphery. Once the crown of creation, man has become a fleck of dust.

Another and related aspect is perhaps still more important. The pre-modern universe was shot through with value: there was a hierarchy of purposes into which man with his human purposes could fit and feel at home. By contrast, the universe of modern science is a universe of fact without purpose; and because man cannot live without purpose, there arises a dichotomy between "fact" and "value." Values are now human *only:* man finds that he and his values have no counterpart in the world of sheer fact around him—he is radically alone. When Aristotle gazed at the stars, he could regard them as manifesting purposes somehow akin to human purposes. When the Stranger of Albert Camus's novel gazes at the stars, he must regard them as neutral. Thus it seems that man is not only a marginal being within the universe of modern science, but also that his purposes and values, inextricably bound up with any conceivable religion lack the kind of "objective" warrant which could be given them by some Archimedean point outside himself. How, then, can he still look upon himself as being under the special care of a cosmic God?

But this whole argument, however plausible on the surface, is utterly invalid. Since Biblical belief is empirically irrefutable, scientific evidence can no more affect it than the evidence of historical tragedy or the evidence of an empty heart. The Biblical God, to be sure, has always revealed Himself. But He has always concealed Himself as well. At most, therefore, modern science should have had no greater effect on Biblical belief than to show that its God was even more inscrutable than had hitherto been thought, and His revelations even more ambiguous and intermittent.

Perhaps, however, it would be rash to dismiss the threat of modern science to Biblical faith on such general grounds alone. Conceivably there is a special affinity between that faith and the *Weltanschauung* of the premodern world, and conceivably the very different *Weltanschauung* that goes with modern science is radically in conflict with Biblical faith. Science may be unable to refute faith, yet it may be that one cannot really live by both.

But is it true that pre-modern science and Biblical faith are temperamentally compatible, while modern science and Biblical faith are mutually hostile? A. N. Whitehead argues, and argues plausibly, that the opposite is the case. According to Whitehead, pre-modern and modern science differ not only in their conclusions about nature but also in their approach to nature. Pre-modern science did not experiment with—"torture"—nature: who would wish to torture something divine, or shot through with divinity? It was because they regarded nature as divine that the Greeks thought only of contemplating it and not of putting it to human use. Thus, though they developed so much else, they never systematically developed experimentation. To the Protestant mind, schooled in the Bible, nature is not divine, but the *work* of God; and God created it for human use. It was this belief—still according to Whitehead—that made modern experimental science possible. Hence one might well conclude that in some ways modern science is closer in spirit to Biblical faith than its pre-modern predecessor. Is there not rivalry between a science which finds gods in nature and a faith whose God is beyond nature? And is not a science for which nature is at any rate un-divine free from conflict with a faith which, however different in all other respects, agrees at least on this one point?

Nevertheless, it might still remain true that this un-divine nature of modern science threatens, if it does not rule out, any religious recourse to a Divinity beyond nature. If man is a mere fleck of dust in a blind universe, can he plausibly resort to such a God—a God, furthermore, essentially concerned with *him*? But closer inspection reveals that this is, and has been since the rise of modern science, only half the story. As the *object* of scientific investigation, man may be infinitely small. As the *subject* undertaking the investigation, however, he is infinitely large, if only because he knows that he is infinitely small. Man, growing ever smaller in stature as modern science progressed, at the same time grew ever larger as well; for whereas all else in the universe was only part of a whole, it was man who *knew* the whole and his own position within it. And so far as we can tell

even today, man is unique in this respect. What makes him unique, moreover, is not a mere capacity for abstract theory which is relevant to a few
thinkers alone; it is the power this capacity gives him to transform nature,
as well as to transform the whole human condition. Because of technology
man can be more fully controlled than ever before; he becomes the object
of physical and social engineering. But the engineer is himself human.

I hope it is clear that my purpose is not to exalt human greatness in an
attempt—like those of earlier times—to struggle by means of faith in man
toward faith in God. Rather what I want to stress is man's dialectical condition: that he is at once small and large, part of the universe and yet not
reducible to a mere part—in short, and for better or worse, a terror, wonder, and mystery to himself. Now in this regard, modern man is not really
so far from the Psalmiṣt who writes: "What is man that Thou art mindful
of him, and the son of man that Thou shouldst think of him? Yet hast Thou
made him but little lower than the angels, and crowned him with honor and
glory." It is, to be sure, a decisive difference that the Psalmist feels at once
small and large *before God*. His feeling and ours, however, have much in
common.

If, then, the historical catastrophes of our time cannot explain the
crisis of contemporary religious belief, neither can modern science and all
its works. Indeed, one might go so far as to say that the whole battle
between science and religion rests on nothing but gigantic misunderstandings on both sides. It was because faith had *already* been undermined by
the time this battle was joined in the 19th century, that religion had to
resort either to a fundamentalism hostile to all science, or else to a modern-
ism seeking props for its own weakness in a science which would not and
could not provide them.

Biblical Faith versus Subjective Reductionism

Our question concerning the cause of the modern crisis of faith thus
remains unanswered. In seeking the answer, we do well to keep a firm grasp
on the essence of Biblical faith, which is the *believer's certainty of standing
in relation to an unprovable and irrefutable God*. What could have undermined such a certainty? The process was extremely complex, but let us for
the sake of better understanding try to describe it as though it took place in
three clearly distinct stages.

First came what may be called the discovery of the circle of authority
and faith. A pre-modern man, if asked about the grounds of his religious
certainty, would presumably have pointed to an authority—a prophet, a
sacred scripture, a church, even the voice of his own heart. This, however,
involves a circle. If Moses beheld the Presence of God in the burning bush,
it was because he was already open to that Presence; a modern agnostic,
beholding the same bush, would perceive only a chemical phenomenon. No
conceivable datum—neither a natural fact, nor an inner experience, nor an

existing scripture—can serve as an authority authenticating a religious truth except for those already prepared to accept that truth on faith. Faith may base itself on authority; but the authority *is* an authority only where faith can be presupposed.

The discovery of this circle is not by itself fatal to faith, as can be seen from the fact that pre-modern thinkers were by no means wholly unaware of it. (Saint Thomas Aquinas knew, for example, that he could not argue with a nonbeliever on the basis of the revealed Scriptures, since the issue between them was precisely whether the Scriptures *were* revealed.) Nevertheless, the discovery, by focusing attention on faith instead of on authority, leads the modern critic to a second and more decisive step. To the believer, faith is the *immediate relation* between himself and God. To the critic, faith is merely the *feeling* of standing in such a relation, plus an *inference* from that feeling to an actual God.

The step just described may seem a matter of mere philosophical subtlety; yet everything centers around it. For once this second step is taken, the third—and it is the *coup de grâce*—quickly follows; the elimination, with the help of Ockham's razor, of the inferred God. Ockham asserted the rational necessity of eliminating unnecessary assumptions, as one shaves off an unwanted beard. And it is all too clear that God, as an assumption made to account for the feeling of His Presence, is indeed both unwanted and unnecessary.

In the first place, a God inferred to explain religious feelings would at most be a probable inference, capable of refutation and never really certain. And in the second place, anyone in agreement with Kant (and with a good many other philosophers as well) would regard such an inference—moving from a natural effect to a supernatural cause—as in principle illegitimate.

Thus modern criticism, operating through three stages, explains faith as an inference from religious feeling, and eliminates the inference as a redundancy. To complete the destruction of faith, it remains only to explain how the inference should ever have been mistaken for an immediate relationship. *That* is achieved by defining God as in fact an unconscious projection, and faith as in fact a solitary disport with religious feelings (however these, in turn, are to be explained).

The reason we can consider this whole process—which may be termed subjectivist reductionism—as *the* cause of the modern religious crisis, is that it is not a mere intellectual argument carried on by abstract thinkers. Subjectivist reductionism has become a modern—perhaps *the* modern— way of life. Which came first—the argument or the way of life—we need not here inquire.

Much that passes for an independent assault on religion is actually a version, or an application, of the three-stage argument just presented. Consider, first, Biblical criticism, which, it is sometimes supposed, constitutes a refutation of the claim that the Scriptures are the revealed word of God. But in fact Biblical criticism either presupposes what it imagines itself to be proving, or else it leaves the issue open. For if the critic declares that what the Bible itself regards as the reflection of human dialogues with God is nothing more than an expression of the evolution of religious feelings and ideas, it is he who has brought such categories to the Bible, not the Bible which has yielded them to him. His criticism, in other words, already assumes a position of subjectivist reductionism.

Consider, next, humanism. Feuerbach, possibly the greatest of modern humanists, speaks for all: "What man is not, but wills to be or wishes to be, just that and only that, nothing else, is God." But to the religious believer, God is not what *he* wills to be; He is the other-than-human with Whom the believer stands in relation. How, then, does the humanist refute the believer? Only by a form of subjectivist reductionism. And what is true of Feuerbach is true of Marx and Freud as well. To unmask *some* gods as pseudo-gods, they can rely on specific empirical evidence in specific spheres. But to unmask all gods as pseudo-gods is in the end to rest one's case not on specific empirical evidence but on an *a priori* philosophical argument; and the argument is a form of subjectivist reductionism.

So pervasive is subjectivist reductionism in the modern world that it has enlisted friends of religion as well as foes in its ranks—although it must be said that this friendship is of the most dubious kind. Its nature may be illustrated by two examples, the one widespread and popular, the other more or less confined to academics. Pragmatism—and a good deal of popular psychology as well—is apt to assert that while religious beliefs are mere wish- or need-projections, they are useful, or even necessary, for comfortable survival in an uncomfortable world. The question thus arises as to how they can be preserved, and the answer would appear to be: by keeping their illusory character concealed. For who can live by a belief which he knows to be illusory? Yet such concealment is not only practically impossible in the modern world; the particular friends of religion presently under consideration do not even seem to desire it. Hence in many circles religion has become a collective make-believe: something which is good for most, accepted as true by others, rejected as false by oneself. Religion of this sort is not a bulwark against religious crisis; it is one of its gravest manifestations.

Much the same can be said of the other, more academic forms of friendship for religion displayed by some of the linguistic philosophers who have now taken over from the logical positivists. Logical positivism was a clear foe of religious faith. It declared religious language to be emotive only, referring to no objective reality. Thus "God" really meant "three cheers for the world"; and a revivalist preacher, urging his congregation to give three cheers for God, was really saying "Let's give three cheers for three cheers for the world." Here was subjectivist reductionism accompanied by forthright hostility. The heirs of logical positivism, the linguistic philosophers, on the whole feel no such hostility. Science tells us about the world, they say, while religion reflects attitudes toward the world—and why should we not have attitudes? Indeed, how can we live without them? But if religion is acknowledged to be an attitude *only,* and the God toward whom religion is an attitude is excluded, then subjectivist reductionism has won the day. Defending the attitude *as* attitude does not protect religious faith: it helps bring about its doom.

Buber's Restatement of Biblical Faith

Has subjectivist reductionism, then, won the day? It has not. For the Biblical faith has been restated in our time, both by Jews and Christians, with a purity perhaps unmatched in centuries; and this restatement has fully risen to the challenge posed by subjectivist reductionism.

Here are two quotations, one taken from Bertrand Russell's *My Philosophical Development,* the other from Buber's *Eclipse of God.* Russell writes:

> If A loves B the relation . . . consists in certain states of mind of A. Even an atheist must admit that a man can love God. It follows that love of God is a state of the man who feels it, and not properly a relational fact.

Contrast this with Buber:

> Great images of God fashioned by mankind are born, not of imagination, but of real encounters with Divine power and glory.

Russell here admirably states the subjectivist-reductionist view. Although he expressly speaks only of the love of God, what he says would apply equally well to faith. Just as an atheist can "admit that a man can love God," he can admit faith in another man. Faith would be a subjective state and God would become an inference made by the believer which the atheist would declare invalid.

Buber's statement, once contrasted with Russell's, is seen in its full significance and polemical power. Man does not have private feelings from which he infers the Divine. *If related to God at all, he is primordially open to Him; and his subjective feelings and the images of God he fashions are mere by-products of this primordial openness.* No doubt man can be imprisoned by images and feelings, and no doubt he can seek to escape from the prison of these images and feelings by inferring from them to a God beyond them. But such imprisonment is pseudo-religion, and the attempt to escape from it is futile. Or rather, the true escape is not to infer God from images and feelings, but to turn away from these to God Himself.

On Buber's thesis, an atheist can certainly "admit that a man can love God." But it is questionable whether an atheist can do something far more important—understand what the love of God *means.* For how can he distinguish between the pseudo-love which, being feeling *only,* is a disguised love of self, and the real love which obtains between God and man? And what holds of the distinction between love and pseudo-love also holds of the distinction between "great" images of God and trivial or superficial ones. Perhaps the atheist does not wholly lack the power to make these distinctions; but then, not everyone protesting atheism is a simple and unequivocal atheist.

Here we have, then, two assertions. How are we to judge between them? I will approach this decisive question through a perennial problem, though it can carry us only to the threshhold of an answer. Philosophers often ask how one can know other minds. I can immediately know my own feelings; and I can immediately observe other people's behavior. But how can I know the feelings of others? Well, I can infer them from their behavior. But this inference would seem to presuppose that their behavior is like mine—that, for example, they behave when they feel pain as I do when I feel pain. This assumption may be perfectly plausible. But it *is* an assumption. Hence I can never know, and certainly never know *immediately,* that I am not radically alone.

I am persuaded that, while this line of reasoning has some value in bringing to light certain specific philosophical issues, it is altogether misguided. A self is primordially open to other selves; and unless it were thus open it would never become a self at all. A child *becomes* an "I" in a relation of openness to a "Thou"; indeed, he knows the meaning of "Thou" before he knows the meaning of "I." There is, to be sure, a problem involved in knowing other selves. But the problem is not whether they exist; it is who they are. And it arises, not because the self is to begin with in a subjectivist prison from which it must subsequently try to escape; it arises because, born free of prisons of this kind, the self is subsequently cast into them by the breakdown of communication. And when the breakdown is complete there is mental disease.

This much, at least, would seem arguable or even demonstrable: genuine love between humans does not consist of subjectivist solitudes externally related; it is *one* relation, although always impaired in its unity, often threatened by temporary eclipse and sometimes by total destruction. A demonstration of this proposition, however, would—as has already been said—take us only to the threshold of the question we have been struggling with. For it might well be the case that, whereas genuine love between humans consists of an immediate relation, the love of God consists of feeling *only*. Indeed, this is bound to be true if the faith which knows this God is itself nothing more than subjective feeling. What, in the light of the foregoing, are we to make of this possibility?

The first thing to say is that if it is true, there can be no genuine love of God at all, since there can be no openness to the other which even love between humans requires. The second thing is that pseudo-love of God is the legitimate object of destructive criticism, and that from a perspective like Buber's, one cheerfully supports the criticism. And the third and most important thing to say is that genuine love of God—if there be such love—escapes the grasp of the subjectivist critic. For genuine love of God, which is openness to the Divine, can be known only in actual openness, and this is precisely what the critic cannot or will not have. Hence he is left only with the images and feelings which are its byproduct. How then can he judge them *as* byproducts? How, indeed, can he safely distinguish between the pseudo-faith and pseudo-love which are merely feelings projected onto a pseudo-god, and the genuine faith and love which constitute a relation to God? It would seem, therefore, that the critic's reduction even of pseudo-faith must always remain ambiguous, and can never be final.

This does not prevent him, however, from *deciding* that religious images and feelings are *never* "born of real encounters," that they are *always* mere "imagination." Only in making this decision, he does not give a *demonstration*. Buber's response to the challenge of subjectivist reductionism has disclosed that it does not refute Biblical faith, but rather that it opposes one faith to another. Biblical faith stakes all on man's primordial openness to the Divine—an openness, to be sure, which is interrupted by eclipses of God. The reductionist "faith" stakes all on the thesis that man is primordially shut off from God, and that all supposed openness is mere self-delusion. But in the perspective of Buber's modern reaffirmation of the Biblical faith, reductionism itself appears as a self-delusion: it mistakes withdrawal from God for the natural and inevitable human condition.

In such manner does faith refute the refutation proposed by subjectivist reductionism. But this is not to say that faith can prove its own case against subjectivist reductionism. It cannot refute but only reject it; and it can testify against it. For the argument cuts both ways. The reductionist cannot use observable data—religious images and feelings—to demonstrate the subjectivity of faith. But neither can the believer use these same data to demonstrate the objectivity of faith. For not only is it the case that the reductionist critic cannot or will not enter into the actual relation of openness to God; it is also the case that for the believer himself the "knowledge" obtained is shot through with the gravest of risks. After all, does not disguised self-love, being disguised, mistake itself for love of God? Are not god-projections, being unconscious, mistaken for real gods by those who are prey to them?

Some part of this risk has always been understood by believers in the Biblical tradition, who realized that false prophets, no less than true, can be sincere. The full extent of the risk, however, has become obvious only to the modern believer. His ancestor rarely doubted that man was in principle open to the Divine; hence the risk of which he was aware extended for the most part only to deciding when and how such openness was truly manifest. The modern believer, by contrast, has glimpsed the possibility that all openness to the Divine may be pseudo-openness only—that man may be radically alone. He does not stand in immediate openness to the Divine. He seeks, in Kierkegaard's expression, an immediacy after reflection. The Psalmist *in extremis* experienced an eclipse of God. The extremity of faith in the modern age is uncertainty as to whether what is experienced *is* an eclipse of God, or the final exposure of an illusion.

Hence if the modern believer works and waits for an end to this eclipse, he must carry in his working and waiting a uniquely modern burden. The Psalmist *in extremis* could rest in the irrefutability of faith. The modern believer *in extremis* must endure the full impact of its being undemonstrable as well; he must suffer the knowledge that to the world around him the absent God is a non-existent God, and that he himself can do no more than testify to the contrary.

Under these circumstances, it is natural that there should be those who wish to be told whether the present crisis of religious faith will lead to a renewal. But anyone who asks for a prediction does not understand what has been said. Pronouncements upon the future that is at stake here could not take the form of scientific or historical prediction, but only of indulgence in prophecy. And a rabbinic sage wisely observed that when Biblical times came to an end, prophecy was taken away from prophets and given over to fools and children.

45   Has "God" a Meaning?
—A Discussion

Bernard Williams and John A. T. Robinson

Bernard Williams

People are often tempted to think
of questions about meaning as though they were all on the level of
the most trivial disagreements about the use of a particular word, the sort
of disagreements that are rightly called "merely verbal": exemplified, for
instance, in the fact that Americans use the word "suspenders" to refer
to what we call "braces." Obviously, no sane person would waste time
arguing about which was the right word to use, or what the word "suspenders" *really* meant. But most questions about meaning are not nearly
as superficial as this, and in issues of metaphysics or religion we cannot
proceed in this way.

Philosophers have become extremely conscious of the fact that it is
possible to use language in an impressive and profound-seeming way,
without what one says having any meaning at all, or at least—and this is
an important point—without its having the sort of meaning that the
speaker would like it to have.

Some speaker may think that he is making an important statement
about the nature of the universe, or of history, or something, and it may
turn out, when he is pressed, that no meaning has been given to his sayings
which is determinate enough for him to be making any recognizable claim

[This discussion first appeared in *Question* No. 1 (1968). It is reprinted here with the
permission of Professor Williams, Bishop Robinson and the editor of *Question.*]

at all. In particular, this will be so if there is nothing definite to distinguish what is involved in this man's claim from what would be involved in denying that claim. There has to be a difference between what things are like if it is true and what things are like if it isn't. If there is really no difference between what things are like if a certain claim is true, and what they are like if it is not true, we can say that that claim has no content at all.

One very simple example, from the field of religious belief: and I should say at once that I don't think that to criticize the sort of view I am going to mention is, in itself, to criticize any serious form of religious belief, since few serious religious believers would believe anything as simple as this. But there have been people who have thought that God's purposes were positively manifested in natural disasters such as eruptions and earthquakes; for instance, by the punishment of wicked persons overwhelmed by these catastrophes. It is pointed out that the same catastrophes tend rather indiscriminately to involve also innocent persons, such as small children; or presumably virtuous persons, such as members of religious orders. The simple believer then replies that this manifests God's purpose in another way, since it is good that the innocent and virtuous should go to Heaven.

He is then asked, presumably, why other innocent and virtuous persons are not given this benefit to go to Heaven quickly, but left to suffer on earth to a hearty old age; and many of the wicked, indeed, seem to do quite well and are not despatched. Something is then said to the effect that it is also good that the virtuous should have life on earth, and that the punishment of the wicked be delayed for a while, and so on. And after all this we see that absolutely anything that happened to the virtuous, the wicked, or the in-between will count equally well; natural calamities directed by God turn out to be utterly indistinguishable in principle from natural calamities not directed by anyone; and the content of the claim that the happening of such incidents reveals any sort of Divine purpose dissolves in thin air.

As I said before, I don't think the very naïve view I've just mentioned would be held by serious religious believers; in fact, I believe it would be condemned by them, as superstitious. The fact that this superstitious view turned out to be vacuous and have no content would be held by many sceptical philosophers to be the case, in a more sophisticated way, as regards the central tenets of a religion such as Christianity. One form of this more general sort of philosophical criticism was advanced by the "logical positivists."

Logical positivism started in the early years of this century, and was developed principally in Vienna in the 'twenties. It became known in this country through a very remarkable book by Professor A. J. Ayer, called *Language, Truth and Logic,* which was published in 1936. The positivists held that there were only two sorts of statements that genuinely have meaning. One sort were statements which were true merely because of the definitions of the terms used in them: a boring example is "all bachelors are unmarried." These need not bother us. The other sort of meaningful statement consisted of those that could be shown to be true or shown to be false by some possible sense-experience: for instance, by some possible scientific experiment or observation. All other remarks not of these two types were considered by the positivists to be meaningless. This doctrine obviously dealt pretty hard with statements of religion, which certainly don't seem to be typically verifiable by science.*

Many philosophers now would agree that a principal criticism of logical positivism was the very narrow view it took of something's being meaningful. It is obviously wrong just to lump together as meaningless everything that fails the positivist test; pieces of poetry, commands, expressions of wishes, and lots of other pieces of ordinary meaningful language fail the test and yet have meaning. The positivist challenge has helped to make philosophers more conscious of different sorts of meaning. While this is so, I do not think that the positivist position, in an essential respect, is just to be dismissed. For even if it overlooked a lot of kinds of meaning, it seems to me at least roughly right about one central sort of meaning: the sort of meaning which belongs to statements which one can claim to be true or false. This point can be made in terms of belief: that to believe is to believe *something,* and if there is anything that one believes, one ought to be able to say in some way—if not in the very narrow terms of sense-experience— what the difference is between what one believes being true and what one believes not being true. In the case of religious statements, in particular statements about God, the important question, to my mind, is not whether they have a meaning, or no meaning: the important question is, what sort of meaning they have.

And this is a question which affects whether one wants to go on making such statements or not.

There is no doubt that some people at some times have given a meaning to the statement that God exists, and to other statements about God, which came very near to making those statements into a sort of supplement to science: God came in where science left off. This is the God which the Bishop of Woolwich called in his book *Honest to God* "the God of the gaps"—the gaps, that is to say, in science. Taken in this way, statements about God were certainly not empty or vacuous in the sort of way I have been talking about before. They made a fairly definite claim: that certain phenomena, such as the adaptation of animals to their environment, or, again, the existence of living things, did not admit of a scientific explanation. These negative claims that certain sorts of scientific explanation were impossible were certainly not empty; the trouble was that they have turned out to be false, since such scientific explanations are forthcoming and there is every sign that they will go on being forthcoming. So if that was the sort of thing meant by religious statements, if that was the sort of meaning they had, they would have to be written off as a hopeful bet against science, which science won.

At this point, some modern theologian may come along, and say some-

* One of Ayer's statements of the Verifiability Principle and its destructive implications is contained in Selection 63 of the present book. (Ed.)

thing like this: "I agree that the attempts to make God fill in holes in science is hopeless: the existence of God is not a hypothesis, supplementary to science, and never should have been regarded as such." I also think the theologian may justly add that these sorts of arguments do a disservice to religion by making God into an abstract or scientific object, instead of something of living concern to people. "Christianity is about people caring; it essentially involves taking a serious attitude to the world, to personal relationships, to society. When someone says he is a Christian, and that he believes in God, it is such an attitude that he declares. His statements of his religion are not meaningless: they have just this meaning, that the speaker declares such an attitude to life."

This modern theologian I have made up is at best a composite figure; he is probably a caricature. But the tone is familiar. And my reply to him is this. "If that is what Christian remarks mean, and only that, then people should stop making them. The Christian vocabulary is unnecessary; if you want to say 'I care about personal relationships,' we have a very good English sentence for saying that, which does not mention God—namely the sentence, 'I care about personal relationships.' What is worse, the Christian vocabulary is, for the purpose you give it, actively misleading. For it is quite obvious that historically the claims of Christianity have not just been ways of expressing certain attitudes to the world and to other people: they have been taken to be, if true, very important truths which *give reasons* for having those attitudes towards personal relationships and so on. To represent the words of Christianity as merely expressing these essentially secular attitudes is in fact to have given the thing up, while retaining the vocabulary."

It may be objected that I am engaged in the old sceptics' game of insisting that Christianity be represented in the most conservative and implausible forms so that I go on disbelieving it. I hope that that is not what I am doing. What I am rather trying to do is to insist that if Christianity is to be Christianity at all there has to be something to be believed or disbelieved, and that this has to be something over and above a mere belief about the secular order.

Christianity is a religion which is very historically articulate; one knows a good deal about what has been believed at different stages of its development. It is also a religion which is tied to certain texts, in particular, of course, the Bible and of course to a particular figure, Christ, about whom one is told something in those texts. Given this, it seems to me possible to identify certain beliefs which must be held if it is Christianity that is being believed at all. I will suggest just one—very unambitiously and, one would hope, platitudinously. This is that God is transcendent to human affairs and to human attitudes in a sense which has the following consequence (though it is supposed to mean more as well): that God would exist whether human beings and their attitudes existed or not—even if there were no human beings or human aspirations, there would still be a God.

To believe this is certainly not enough to constitute one's being a

Christian, as I understand it. A Christian has, for instance, to go on to say something very special about Christ (and not just that Christ was a better moral teacher than Socrates). But I shall leave the rest, and concentrate on this one point: that to believe what I just very roughly spelled out is at least *necessary* to having Christian beliefs. And I think it is worth asking oneself very carefully when confronted with some reinterpretation of Christian doctrine whether it passes this test: that it represents God as a being who would be there even if no human beings, or indeed other finite conscious beings, were there. If it does not, then I suspect you no longer have any form of Christianity, but probably some form of religious Humanism.

All this is still about meaning. I said the problem was about *what* Christian and other religious statements are said to mean. There is a limit to what they can be made to mean; when their meaning has changed too much, in particular when it is identified too closely with a meaning which refers *only* to human life, there is no point in going on making them in the religious form. Sometimes of course—perhaps one must say, very often—it is not at all easy to discover whether this has happened or not: clouds of ambiguity stand in the way. In this connection I think we should look extremely closely at a famous passage from Paul Tillich's *The Shaking of the Foundations* (pp. 63 f) quoted in *Honest to God,* which seems to suggest that to deny that God exists is to deny that life has depth. Tillich wrote:

> The Name of this infinite and inexhaustible depth and ground of all being is *God*. That depth is what the word *God* means. And if that word has not much meaning for you, translate it, and speak of the depths of your life, of the source of your being, of your ultimate concern, of what you take seriously without any reservation. Perhaps, in order to do so, you must forget everything traditional that you have learned about God, perhaps even the word itself. For if you know that God means depth, you know much about him. You cannot then call yourself an atheist or unbeliever, for you cannot think or say: Life has no depth. Life is shallow. Being itself is surface only. If you could say this in complete seriousness, you would be an atheist; but otherwise you are not. He who knows about depth knows about God.

This raises many questions. In the sense in which "life has depth" is a statement which only superficial people are going to reject—can it really be enough to represent what "God exists" is supposed to mean? When people said that God exists, were they really saying just that life has depth?

Is Tillich really saying that believing in God is just the *same* as not being superficial? If not, what more? What sort of thing does his pervasive phrase, the "ground of our being," mean? Is the "ground of our being" something that would be there even if we were not? Or is the "ground of our being" something more like our deepest aspirations, which presumably would not be there if we were not?

I do not think that "God," or statements containing that word, have no meaning. I think they can have all sorts of meanings. On some, they are very difficult to interpret indeed. On others, they seem to me to make claims which can be at least well enough identified to be seen to be substantial; in those meanings, which are various, the claims seem to me personally, I must say, to be false. But at least there is something to be false, and something to be disbelieved. In yet other meanings that are given to them, they say nothing, or too little, or something of the wrong sort—representing, for instance, merely some human aspiration. Then there is nothing to be false, nothing to disbelieve. But when that is so, there is nothing to be true, nothing to believe, either.

John A. T. Robinson

I would like to begin by saying outright that the word God does not have *a* meaning, in the usual sense in which we use that phrase. For instance, if we ask what is the meaning of the word "dog" (which is simply the same three letters the other way round), what we mean is: "How does the dictionary define it?" or "What other word would you put in its place?" In fact, if you look up the word "dog" in the *Concise Oxford Dictionary* you will realize how difficult it is to define even a dog. "Quadruped of many breeds, wild and domesticated" would be just as good a definition of "cat." If you can't put a dog into words you are hardly likely to put God into words.

The reality "God," if it is really to be *God* and not just an idol we can get our hands or our minds round, is by definition indefinable. What the *word* does is not to define God but to *point* to a mystery at the heart of our experience. It is saying that there is something which cannot be expressed, and yet which cannot be eliminated. The function of the word "God" is primarily to draw attention to this element, this dimension, if you like, in experience, which cannot be reduced to anything else.

In one sense, any word will do for this; and it may help to begin with a tradition that doesn't use the word "God," which has for us become so loaded. In the sixth century B.C. (about the time of the prophet Jeremiah) there lived one of the greatest Chinese philosophers, Lao Tzu. He was the founder of what we now call Taoism, so called because for him the word "*Tao*" stood for this mystery at the centre of reality. It is certainly not the same as the Christian "God," but in many ways it performs the same function. It means, literally, "the Way," and perhaps its nearest equivalent in Biblical terms is "Wisdom" or "the Word." Thus he says, "All things originate from *Tao,* conform to *Tao,* and to *Tao* they at last return." And the point from which he starts is this: "The *Tao* that can be talked about is not the Eternal *Tao.* The name that can be named is not the Eternal Name." If you think you can put your finger on it or get it wrapped up in words, you haven't got it: "He who speaks does not know. He who knows does not speak." And he uses the famous metaphor of the wheel. The usefulness of a wheel entirely depends on the hole in the middle. What the word *"Tao"* does, or the word "God," is not to fill in that hole, so that you can now say what is in the middle, but precisely to keep guard over it—to insist that no amount of talk about the rim or the spokes tells you everything.

I don't think that's *all* there is to be said about God—otherwise he would simply be a meaningless blank. I shall come back to the content, to the colour, which the Christian and other traditions give to this word. But I would insist that it's a word that doesn't have *a* meaning which you can define. It's a way of witnessing to the belief that at the heart of our experienced relationships there is a mystery that can't be translated without remainder simply into language about man and the world (or, in other words, the spokes of the wheel).

But the trouble is precisely that the word "God" *has* come for most of us to have *a* meaning, a definition, which we can't dissociate from it. In fact, ironically, the *Concise Oxford Dictionary* is much more precise in its definition of "god" than it is of "dog"! "God," it says, with a small "g," is a "superhuman being worshipped as having power over nature and human fortunes," and with a big "G," "Supreme Being, Creator and Ruler of the universe." Do you see what's happened? God has become a substantial, supernatural Being, and talk about "God" is description of this Being. "Do you believe in God?" comes to mean "Do you believe that such a Being exists?", and whether the word "God" has meaning is made to turn on whether it is possible to make meaningful statements, not about our experience, but about an entity quite "out of this world."

Something very definite has been put in the hole. According to this interpretation, God-language must refer to this superhuman Being: it can have no other reference. And this is the point at which a good many modern theologians, myself included, would want to put in an objection. They would argue something like this.

The description of God as a supernatural Being or heavenly Person is one way of trying to make real and vivid to the human imagination the mysterious reality in experience over which the word stands guard. But it is not by any means a necessary way, and it is not what the word "God" *means.*

Let us stand back again for a moment and look at a tradition other than our own. The ancient Greeks, everyone would agree, had many profound religious insights, which are given classic expression in their tragedies. Many of these we can still enter into and make our own. What we cannot do is to take seriously the way in which they found it helpful to represent these religious realities, namely, by projecting them as gods and goddesses living on top of Mount Olympus or anywhere else. For them it made the realities more vivid, more "human," more related to everyday life. For us it simply makes them remote and ridiculous.

In the same way, Christians in the past have found that it made evil and the shadow-side of life more real by picturing it as personified in a Devil. But today, so far from bringing the reality of evil closer to human experience, as it did for medieval man, this merely makes it remote and ridiculous. The last way now to get people to take the depth of evil seriously would be to press them to believe in the existence of a supernatural figure called the Devil.

So with God. I believe strongly in the reality for which the word stands. But I do not think that the seriousness with which I take this reality depends *at all* on whether a Being exists up there, out there, or anywhere else. For this is no longer a way of representing it that is natural to most men and women today. The pity is that the word "God" has become so completely identified with this particular image or projection that both those who want to preserve the image (and there is absolutely nothing wrong with it if it serves) *and* those who want to deny the reality it stands for join in saying that the word "God" means this Being *or means nothing*. If you don't accept this identification, then you are accused of being disloyal, dishonest, or merely confused. But I want to protest vigorously against being put in this position by conservative Christians and by Humanists alike.

For me the word "God" refers to something very meaningful, though I would be the first to recognize that the *word* may now be burdened with so many associations as to be more trouble than it's worth. I should be content to cut loose from it. It was St. Thomas Aquinas, perhaps the greatest theologian ever, who said, "Wise people do not worry about names." And if we could get by without the word "God" I shouldn't shed any tears. But I doubt if we can. We need something to guard that hole, and I see no other single word to replace it. However, it's the reality that I'm concerned with, not the word. What is that reality?

Traditionally, language about God has described, as I have said, an invisible spiritual Being existing in himself quite outside of and apart from our experience. If this is the reference of the language, then I would agree with those modern philosophers who question whether we can ever make any meaningful statements about God. For is there any way of verifying them, anything in our experience that could count for or against their truth? We might just as well be making statements about celestial mermaids.

In reaction, some present-day theologians have swung to the opposite extreme and said that God-language is essentially a way of indicating what *we* hold to be of ultimate significance. It doesn't tell us about anything outside us, but it tells us a great deal about us. It describes, as it were, what we should be prepared to go to the stake for, our life's commitment. To say, for instance, that Jesus is God is to say that for us he is of final or decisive significance.

Now, I would agree that this is an important part of what is involved in using God-language. It *is* a way of expressing ultimate concern. If it didn't include this, if it didn't engage our whole being, then it wouldn't be about what is most real at all. This is a valid protest, because so much talk about "God" is in fact about something or someone who only comes in, as it were, as a sort of long-stop. It's not really talk about *God* at all.

On the other hand, I would agree with Professor Williams that if God-statements are *only* statements about man, only ways of saying, for instance, with whatever accent of finality, "I care about personal relationships," then there's no reason why you should have to use the word "God." And those who argue like this would mostly draw the conclusion that you *don't* have to. You can; but, if you prefer, you can express the same thing in other language. If this just means that you needn't be tied to the word "God," fair enough. But if it means that language about God can be translated into language about man without remainder, then I would agree that you've really given up talking about the reality for which the word "God" has traditionally stood.

For this reality has always been seen as that to which any human commitment and concern is simply *response*. "God" refers not to the commitment but to something that hits you, meets you, surrounds you, with a grace and a claim from which you cannot finally get away. Consider these typical religious statements:

> *Thus saith the Lord*
> *Abba, Father*
> *Herein is love not that we loved God, but that he first loved us*
> *Thou mastering me God! Giver of breath and bread. . . . Over again I feel*
> *thy finger and find thee.*

These are not simply statements about human attitudes; they are responses to *how things are seen to be,* to that in which human life is grounded—viewed not simply as an impersonal regularity but as claiming one in freedom and responsibility, not simply as an "It" but as a "Thou." It is *this,* as the ultimate truth about reality, that God-language is affirming. Or, rather, to be accurate, it is this that God-language is affirming as it is used in the Judaeo-Christian tradition. For while the Bible certainly agrees that God cannot be defined, and shows great reluctance even in using his name, it is equally clear that God is no blank. He makes himself known; and, above all, the grace and the claim of the "Thou" "come through" supremely in Jesus the Christ.

To sum up, as I see it, language about God describes not a Being outside our experience, nor simply human attitudes, but what we respond to as ultimately and unconditionally real. Affirming, for instance, that "God is love" is staking one's whole being on the fact that this is the final truth about the nature of things. Of course, believing in God doesn't just mean supposing that life has depth (though I agree that the quotation from Tillich to which Professor Williams referred is open to that interpretation). Of course, to take another point he raised, God's reality doesn't depend on us and our aspirations—rather, our being is grounded in his. Let me try to make this clear by using an analogy—which is always dangerous.

What makes us *persons* doesn't depend simply on our genes and the rest of our biological inheritance. It depends on the fact that from the moment of birth we find ourselves in a relationship to other persons, beginning with mother-love, in which we are drawn out, not merely to reaction and response, but to freedom and responsibility. What the believer is saying is that such a relationship, such a love, is the element in which all things live and move and have their being. It is what draws the whole process of evolution onwards and upwards to its fulfilment in mind and spirit. This is the reality to which he can but stumblingly point by using this (in itself) meaningless monosyllable "God."

Finally, I should like to come back to the *difference* between what the Christian is affirming by the personal name "God" and what the Taoist means by *Tao*. In many ways, as I said, the two words perform a similar function. But what the Taoist sees at the still centre of everything is a Way, a certain norm or law of life. What the Christian responds to is a grace that meets and claims him in love. It is this difference that is indicated by speaking of God as "personal."

But we should be careful here. This does *not* mean that the Christian necessarily thinks of God, as I said before, as *a* supernatural Person. He *may* picture or project the reality in this way in order to make it easier to imagine—as men have personified the Devil. But though in the past it has helped to personify God as a sort of super-Man, I am very doubtful whether it helps today. It just makes him incredible. What the Christian is affirming by using the word "God" is something about the *relationship* in which he finds himself to be held. In human terms, it is less misleading to describe it in personal language than in impersonal. For instance, the kind of security which he finds in God is more like that of a parent's love than that of an immovable lump of stone. In fact, the Bible uses both images: God is a Rock, and God is a Father. But the point is that *both* are equally metaphors. He *is* not either. There is not a super-Person out there any more than a super-Rock.

But the idea of a Person behind phenomena, an invisible Man who manipulates everything, "allowing" this and "sending" that, dies very hard. Hence the idea left in so many minds to which Professor Bernard Williams referred, and which he admitted would be condemned by serious believers, namely, that to speak of "God" means claiming to trace a hidden purpose in why particular things happen or do not happen to particular people. By sufficiently ingenious reckoning, as he said, you can make absolutely anything, good, bad, or indifferent, demonstrate the hand of God: "natural calamities directed by God turn out to be utterly indistinguishable . . . from such calamities not directed by anyone." Statements about "God" being "at work" in this or that event become utterly vacuous and meaningless.

But because vast numbers of people *do* think that this is what believers mean by a personal God at work, let me say as strongly as I can that I reject it totally. Not only is it meaningless. It is immoral. If God were a planner, manipulating, or at least privy to, the Aberfan disaster, why didn't he evacuate the children first, as any human planner would?

But this is not what I mean or I hope any mature Christian means by providence. He doesn't see an invisible Hand deliberately pulling strings. What he does say is that in everything, however purposeless (and there is no purpose or intention in the slipping of a coal tip, unless it be human negligence), that in everything, however loveless, there is a purpose and a love to be met and responded to from which *nothing*, not even death, can separate us. There is a reality deeper than tragedy which can *give* meaning even to that which in itself is meaningless.

Someone has said that the question of God is the question of whether man is alone in the universe or not. This is misleading, I think, if it implies that everything turns on whether there is some other invisible Person, like man, somewhere around. But it is right if by that is meant that the question of God is the question whether persons and personal relationships are simply on their own, up against it, in a fundamentally alien universe. For to believe in God is to affirm that at the heart of things, as the most real thing in the world, is a love and a purpose to which persons and personal relationships are, so far, the highest *response*. This is the way the grain of the universe runs.

This I do not believe to be a meaningless statement—though it is, of course, an act of trust. It is not just a statement of my commitment—"the promise to pay" is not on my side alone. It is an affirmation about how things are, defined and vindicated, for me, in what I see in Christ, including all that has led up to him and all that has flowed from him.

46   Theology and Falsification

Antony Flew

L ET US BEGIN WITH A PARABLE. IT IS A parable developed from a tale told by John Wisdom in his haunting and revelatory article "Gods."[1] Once upon a time two explorers came upon a clearing in the jungle. In the clearing were growing many flowers and many weeds. One explorer says, "Some gardener must tend this plot." The other disagrees, "There is no gardener." So they pitch their tents and set a watch. No gardener is ever seen. "But perhaps he is an invisible gardener." So they set up a barbed-wire fence. They electrify it. They patrol with bloodhounds. (For they remember how H. G. Wells's "invisible man" could be both smelt and touched though he could not be seen.) But no shrieks ever suggest that some intruder has received a shock. No movements of the wire ever betray an invisible climber. The bloodhounds never give cry. Yet still the Believer is not convinced. "But there is a gardener, invisible, intangible, insensible to electric shocks, a gardener who has no scent and makes no sound, a gardener who comes secretly to look after the garden which he loves." At last the Sceptic despairs, "But what remains of your

[This paper first appeared in *New Essays in Philosophical Theology,* edited by Antony Flew and Aladair MacIntyre and published in 1955. It is reprinted with the permission of the SCM Press of London and the Macmillan Company of New York.]
    1. *Proceedings of the Aristotelian Society,* 1944–5.

original assertion? Just how does what you call an invisible, intangible, eternally elusive gardener differ from an imaginary gardener or even from no gardener at all?"

In this parable we can see how what starts as an assertion, that something exists or that there is some analogy between certain complexes of phenomena, may be reduced step by step to an altogether different status, to an expression perhaps of a "picture preference."[2] The Sceptic says there is no gardener. The Believer says there is a gardener (but invisible, etc.). One man talks about sexual behavior. Another man prefers to talk of Aphrodite (but knows that there is not really a superhuman person additional to, and somehow responsible for, all sexual phenomena). The process of qualification may be checked at any point before the original assertion is completely withdrawn and something of that first assertion will remain (Tautology). Mr. Wells's invisible man could not, admittedly, be seen, but in all other respects he was a man like the rest of us. But though the process of qualification may be, and of course usually is, checked in time, it is not always judiciously so halted. Someone may dissipate his assertion completely without noticing that he has done so. A fine brash hypothesis may thus be killed by inches, the death by a thousand qualifications.

And in this, it seems to me, lies the peculiar danger, the endemic evil, of theological utterance. Take such utterances as "God has a plan," "God created the world," "God loves us as a father loves his children." They look at first sight very much like assertions, vast cosmological assertions. Of course, this is no sure sign that they either are, or are intended to be, assertions. But let us confine ourselves to the cases where those who utter such sentences intend them to express assertions. (Merely remarking parenthetically that those who intend or interpret such utterances as cryptocommands, expressions of wishes, disguised ejaculations, concealed ethics, or as anything else but assertions, are unlikely to succeed in making them either properly orthodox or practically effective.)

Now to assert that such and such is the case is necessarily equivalent to denying that such and such is not the case.[3] Suppose then that we are in doubt as to what someone who gives vent to an utterance is asserting, or suppose that, more radically, we are sceptical as to whether he is really asserting anything at all, one way of trying to understand (or perhaps it will be to expose) his utterance is to attempt to find what he would regard as counting against, or as being incompatible with, its truth. For if the utterance is indeed an assertion, it will necessarily be equivalent to a denial of the negation of that assertion. And anything which would count against the assertion, or which would induce the speaker to withdraw it and to admit that it had been mistaken, must be part of (or the whole of) the meaning of the negation of that assertion. And to know the meaning of the negation of an assertion is, as near as makes no matter, to know the meaning of that

---

2. Cf. J. Wisdom, "Other Minds," *Mind*, 1940; reprinted in his *Other Minds* (Blackwell, 1952).

3. For those who prefer symbolism: $p \equiv \sim \sim p$.

assertion.[4] And if there is nothing which a putative assertion denies then there is nothing which it asserts either: and so it is not really an assertion. When the Sceptic in the parable asked the Believer, "Just how does what you call an invisible, intangible, eternally elusive gardener differ from an imaginary gardener or even from no gardener at all?" he was suggesting that the Believer's earlier statement had been so eroded by qualification that it was no longer an assertion at all.

Now it often seems to people who are not religious as if there was no conceivable event or series of events the occurrence of which would be admitted by sophisticated religious people to be a sufficient reason for conceding "There wasn't a God after all" or "God does not really love us then." Someone tells us that God loves us as a father loves his children. We are reassured. But then we see a child dying of inoperable cancer of the throat. His earthly father is driven frantic in his efforts to help, but his Heavenly Father reveals no obvious sign of concern. Some qualification is made—God's love is "not a merely human love" or it is "an inscrutable love," perhaps—and we realize that such sufferings are quite compatible with the truth of the assertion that "God loves us as a father (but, of course . . .)." We are reassured again. But then perhaps we ask: what is this assurance of God's (appropriately qualified) love worth, what is this apparent guarantee really a guarantee against? Just what would have to happen not merely (morally and wrongly) to tempt but also (logically and rightly) to entitle us to say "God does not love us" or even "God does not exist"? I therefore put to the succeeding symposiasts* the simple central questions: "What would have to occur or to have occurred to constitute for you a disproof of the love of, or of the existence of, God?"

4. For by simply negating $\sim p$ we get $p: \sim \sim p \equiv p$.
* *New Essays in Philosophical Theology* contains replies to Flew by R. M. Hare and Basil Mitchell, a rejoinder by Flew, and comments by I. M. Crombie. (Ed.)

Selected Bibliography

(ITEMS PROVIDED WITH ASTERISK ARE MORE ADVANCED)
(FOR KEY TO ABBREVIATIONS SEE PAGE XIX)

There are several works by Catholic philosophers in which the traditional arguments for the existence of God (other than the ontological argument) are defended in elaborate detail. Clear and authoritative works are G. H. Joyce, *The Principles of Natural Theology* (London and N.Y.: Longmans, Green, 1951), R. P. Phillips, *Modern Thomistic Philosophy,* Volume II (Westminster, Maryland: The Newman Bookshop, 1935), and R. Garrigou-Lagrange, *God, His Existence and His Nature** (English translation in 2 volumes, St. Louis: Herter, 1934 and 1936). Discussions by Protestant writers are contained in G. Dawes

Hicks, *The Philosophical Bases of Theism** (London: Allen & Unwin, 1937) and in D. E. Trueblood, *The Logic of Belief* (N.Y.: Harper, 1942), from which our Selection 36 has been extracted. An unorthodox pro-theological position is also advocated by William James in his *The Will To Believe* (N.Y.: Longmans, Green, 1897) and *The Varieties of Religious Experience* (N.Y.: Longmans, Green, 1902). The following are anthologies representing most of the conflicting viewpoints: W. P. Alston (ed.), *Religious Belief and Philosophical Thought* (N.Y.: Harcourt, Brace & World, 1963), J. Hick (ed.), *The Existence of God* (N.Y.: Macmillan, 1964, p), the same editor's *Classical and Contemporary Readings in the Philosophy of Religion* (Englewood Cliffs: Prentice-Hall, 1964), N. Smart (ed.), *Historical Selections in the Philosophy of Religion* (N.Y.: Harper & Row, 1962), C. Hartshorne and W. L. Reese (eds.), *Philosophers Speak of God* (Chicago: U. of Chicago P., 1953), G. I. Mavrodes and S. C. Hackett (eds.), *Problems and Perspectives in the Philosophy of Religion* (N.Y.: Harper, 1970), R. E. Santoni (ed.), *Religious Language and the Problem of Religious Knowledge* (Bloomington: Indiana U.P., 1968, p), D. Mitchell (ed.), *The Philosophy of Religion* (London: Oxford U.P., 1971, p), and J. Donnelly (ed.), *Logical Analysis and Contemporary Theism* (N.Y.: Fordham U.P., 1972). The following introductions to the philosophy of religion contain detailed discussions of various arguments for the existence of God: J. Hick, *The Philosophy of Religion* (Englewood Cliffs: Prentice-Hall, 1963, p), T. McPherson, *The Philosophy of Religion* (London: Van Nostrand, 1965, p), H. D. Lewis, *Philosophy of Religion* (London: English U.P., 1965), J. F. Ross, *Introduction to the Philosophy of Religion* (N.Y.: Macmillan, 1969, p), and N. Smart, *The Philosophy of Religion* (N.Y.: Random House, 1970, p). The most comprehensive recent work on all the questions treated in the present section is T. Penelhum, *Religion and Rationality* (N.Y.: Random House, 1971). The following general introductions to philosophy also contain critical appraisals of the arguments for and against the existence of God: A. C. Ewing, *The Fundamental Questions of Philosophy* (London: Routledge, N.Y.: Collier Books, 1962, p), J. Hospers, *An Introduction to Philosophical Analysis* (Englewod Cliffs: Prentice-Hall, 2nd ed., 1967), M. Scriven, *Primary Philosophy* (N.Y.: McGraw-Hill, 1966), J. W. Cornman and K. Lehrer, *Philosophical Problems and Arguments* (N.Y.: Macmillan, 1968), K. Nielsen, *Reason and Practice* (N.Y.: Harper & Row, 1971) and A. Flew, *An Introduction to Western Philosophy* (Indianapolis: Bobbs-Merrill, 1971, p). J. Collins, *God in Modern Philosophy* (Chicago: Regnery, 1959), is a critical survey, from a Catholic point of view, of different philosophical positions on the subject from the 15th century to the present. J. Macquarrie, *Twentieth-Century Religious Thought: The Frontiers of Philosophy and Theology, 1900–1960* (N.Y.: Harper & Row, 1963), contains discussions of all major philosophies of religion of the present century with special emphasis on the existentialist theologians. A. E. Taylor's article, "Theism," in *Hastings Encyclopedia of Religion and Ethics* (N.Y.: Scribner's, 1928), is a particularly useful historical survey of the entire subject of rational arguments concerning the existence of God. Readers should be warned, however, that some of Taylor's historical intepretations, especially his reading of Hume, are not shared by most other scholars.

Paley was undoubtedly one of the most persuasive defenders of the design argument and several chapters of the work from which our selection has been taken are now available as a paperback: *Natural Theology: Or, Evidences of the Existence and Attributes of the Deity, Collected from the Appearances of*

Nature (ed. F. Ferré, Indianapolis: Bobbs-Merrill, 1963, p). Paley was, however, by no means the first exponent of what one might call "theological biology." This tradition goes back at least as far as the 17th century naturalist, John Ray, who published his *The Wisdom of God in Creation* in 1691. The last major work of this kind was a multivolume cooperative effort of several scientists and theologians, *The Bridgewater Treatises* (1833–36), in which it was argued in great detail that the environment of organisms was intelligently designed for their preservation and especially for the benefit of man. All the writers mentioned so far were believing Christians, but the design argument has also been advocated by thinkers who were either hostile or indifferent to Christianity. It was the favorite argument of most of the 17th and 18th century deists, including Voltaire and Thomas Paine, and it was advocated, with some reservations, in the second half of the 19th century by John Stuart Mill, in his *Three Essays on Religion* (N.Y.: Holt, 1874). The most important of Mill's three essays, entitled "Theism," is now available in a new paperback edition, with an introduction by R. Taylor (Indianapolis: Bobbs-Merrill, 1957). In our own day, very few philosophers have been impressed by the logical force of the argument in any of its shapes. F. R. Tennant, *Philosophical Theology*, Volume II, Ch. IV (N.Y. and London: Cambridge U.P., 1930), A. E. Taylor, *Does God Exist?* (N.Y.: Macmillan, 1947), and P. Bertocci, *Introduction to the Philosophy of Religion*, Chs. 13–15 (N.Y.: Prentice-Hall, 1951) are among the few defenses of the argument by professional philosophers in recent years. However, it remains a favorite with all kinds of popular writers, including religiously-minded scientists. A. C. Morrison, who was the president of the New York Academy of Sciences, defended a new version of the argument in his *Man Does Not Stand Alone* (N.Y.: F. H. Revell, 1944). Highlights from Morrison's book were twice reprinted in *Reader's Digest*, but no statement of the opposite viewpoint has ever appeared in this publication. The French biologist, Lecomte du Noüy, in his best-selling book, *Human Destiny* (N.Y.: Longmans, Green, 1947), argued that certain facts of biology cannot be explained by "chance" but must be attributed to divine planning. Morrison's argument is criticized by the English mathematician, H. Levy, in "God and Mathematics," *The Humanist* (London), March, 1961, in H. Jack, "A Recent Attempt to Prove God's Existence," *PPR*, 1965, and in G. C. Nerlich's article, "Popular Arguments for the Existence of God," in the *Encyclopedia of Philosophy* (6–407). Du Noüy's book is criticized in Ch. 19 of E. Nagel, *Logic Without Metaphysics* (Glencoe: Free Press, 1957). The general topic of "chance" and "design" is briefly discussed in A. J. Ayer's "Chance," which is available in his *Metaphysics and Common Sense* (London: Macmillan, 1969) and in greater detail in Ch. 9 of Arthur Pap, *Elements of Analytic Philosophy* (N.Y.: Macmillan, 1949) and in Ch. VIII of Phillip Frank, *Das Kausalgesetz und seine Grenzen* (Vienna: Springer, 1932). Frank's book, which is one of the classics of logical positivism, is unfortunately not available in English. In "God and Probability," *RS*, 1969, D. H. Mellor, after a careful analysis of different kinds of probability statements, concludes that it is highly misleading to speak of the "probability" of the hypothesis which the theist is trying to defend. Tennant's views are sympathetically discussed in N. Smart, *Philosophers and Religious Truth* (London: SCM Press, 1964).

The most famous critique of the design argument is found in Hume's *Dialogues Concerning Natural Religion,* and in Section XI of his *Inquiry Concerning Human Understanding.* There is a splendid edition of Hume's *Dialogues* edited by N. Kemp Smith (Edinburgh and N.Y.: Nelson, 2nd ed., 1947). In addition to providing a detailed analysis of Hume's discussions and a full account of the development of Hume's views on religious topics, Kemp Smith reprints some little-known documents, including an extract from Bayle's *Continuation des Pensées Diverses*, from which Hume derived one of his chief objections to the design argument. Another volume containing a great deal of fascinating historical material is R. H. Hurlbutt III, *Hume, Newton and the Design Argument* (Lincoln: U. of Nebraska P., 1965). There are valuable commentaries on Hume's views in A. Flew, *Hume's Philosophy of Belief* (London: Routledge, N.Y.: Humanities Press, 1961), and in B. A. O. Williams, "Hume on Religion," in D. F. Pears (ed.), *David Hume: A Symposium* (London: Macmillan, 1963). Hume's objections to the design argument are criticized in R. G. Swinburne, "The Argument from Design," *P*, 1968 and L. Pearl, "Hume's Criticism of the Argument from Design," *Mo*, 1970. Theological biology, as found in the writings of Paley and other members of this tradition, was given its death-blow by the success of the Darwinian theory. Darwin's own strongly anti-theological views are found in his *Autobiography*, but readers should be warned that early editions of this work were heavily censored. The complete text was made available for the first time by Darwin's granddaughter, Nora Barlow, in *The Autobiography of Charles Darwin* (London: Collins, 1958). The impact of Darwin's ideas on theological debates is traced in G. Himmelfarb, *Darwin and the Darwinian Revolution* (London: Chatto and Windus, 1959), and in W. Irvine, *Apes, Angels and Victorians* (N.Y.: Meridian Books, 1959, p). One of Darwin's contemporaries, the leading American botanist, Asa Gray, wrote extensively on the relations between the Darwinian theory and natural theology, arguing that there was no conflict between them. There is a new edition of Gray's papers on the subject by A. H. Dupree under the title, *Darwiniana* (Cambridge: Harvard U.P., 1963). Most of the critical works mentioned in the next paragraph (Laird, Ducasse, Broad, Russell, Flew, and Matson) contain criticisms of the design argument. Recent critical articles are John Anderson's "Design," *AJ*, 1936, reprinted in his *Studies in Empirical Philosophy* (Sydney: Angus & Robertson, 1962), G. G. Simpson, "Plan and Purpose in Nature," in his *This View of Life* (N.Y.: Harcourt, Brace, 1960, p) and T. McPherson, "The Argument from Design," *P*, 1957. R. G. Swinburne in "The Argument from Design," *P*, 1968, defends the argument. There is a reply to Swinburne by A. Olding in *RS*, 1971. M. H. Carré's "The Divine Watchmaker," *Rationalist Annual*, 1965, is an amusing account of the history of the design argument up to the time of Darwin. A new version of the design argument is defended in Ch. 7 of R. Taylor, *Metaphysics* (Englewood Cliffs: Prentice-Hall, 1963, p). Taylor's argument is criticized in J. Narveson, "On a New Argument from Design," *JP*, 1965, W. H. O'Briant, "A New Argument from Design," *S*, 1967, and in E. D. Klemke, "The Argument from Design," *R*, 1969. An unusual indirect defense of the design argument is offered by A. Plantinga in his widely-discussed *God and Other Minds* (Ithaca: Cornell U.P., 1967). Plantinga begins by maintaining that the best reason we have for belief in other minds is the so-called analogical argument and that the best reason for belief in God is the teleological argument. He then argues that the teleological and the analogical arguments suffer from the same defect. It follows that belief in other minds is justified only if belief in God is justified. Surely, however, belief in other minds is justified. Hence, belief in God is also justified. Plantinga's argument is critically discussed in W. L. Rowe, "God and Other Minds," *N*, 1969, A. E. Tomberlin, "Is Belief in God Justified?" *JP*, 1970, G. E. Hughes, "Plantinga on the Rationality of God's Existence," *PR*, 1970, and in W. N. Christensen and J. King-Farlow, "Gambling on Other Minds—Human and Divine," *S*, 1971. An argument, in some respects quite similar to Plantinga's, is found in Berkeley's *Alciphron* IV and *Principles of Human Knowledge*, §§ 145–49.

Perhaps the most influential critic—even more so than Hume—of the traditional arguments for the existence of God was Kant, whose fullest discussion of this topic occurs toward the end of the *Critique of Pure Reason*, in the chapter entitled "The Ideal of Pure Reason." Contemporary works in which arguments for the existence of God are critically examined are J. Laird, *Theism and Cosmology** (London: Allen & Unwin, 1940), the same author's *Mind and Deity** (London: Allen & Unwin, 1941), C. J. Ducasse, *A Philosophical Scrutiny of Religion* (N.Y.: Ronald Press, 1953), C. D. Broad, *Religion, Philosophy and Psychical Research* (N.Y.: Harcourt, Brace, 1953), W. I. Matson, *The Existence of God* (Ithaca, Cornell U.P., 1965) and A. Flew, *God and Philosophy* (London: Hutchinson, 1966). Bertrand Russell's objections to the different defenses of theology may be found in his *A Critical Exposition of the Philosophy of Leibniz** (London: Allen & Unwin, 2nd ed., 1937), in *Religion and Science* (London: Oxford U.P., 1935, p), and in *Why I Am Not a Christian and Other Essays* (London: Allen & Unwin, N.Y.: Simon & Schuster, 1957, p). A. J. Ayer's objections to the design and first-cause arguments are formulated in "The Fallacies of Deism," *Polemic*, No. 1. Careful critical discussions of different ways of justifying theological conclusions are found in R. W. Hepburn, *Christianity and Paradox* (London: Watts, 1958), and C. B. Martin, *Religious Belief** (Ithaca: Cornell U.P., 1959). In *Difficulties in Christian Belief* (London: SCM Press, 1959), A. C. MacIntyre uncompromisingly rejects all the traditional arguments, but tries to justify belief by means of a distinction between "proof" and "trust." In his essay, "The Existence of God," in A. Flew and A. C. MacIntyre (eds.), *New Essays in Philosophical Theology* (N.Y.: Macmillan, 1955, p), which is also reprinted in W. P. Alston, *op. cit.*, J. J. C. Smart attacks the traditional arguments, but, like MacIntyre, ends on a pro-religious note. It should be added that since writing these pieces, both MacIntyre and Smart have abandoned their belief in God.

The cosmological argument is defended by Aquinas in the first three of his *Five Ways* (*see* Selection 33) and it also figures prominently in the debate between Bertrand Russell and Father Copleston (Selection 34). There is a highly sympathetic exposition of Aquinas' arguments by P. T. Geach in G. E. M. Anscombe and P. T. Geach, *Three Philosophers* (Oxford: Blackwell, 1961). In some of its forms, the cosmological argument goes back to Plato (*The Laws*, Book X), and to Aristotle (*Metaphysics*, xii). It was also advocated by many of the great 17th and 18th century philosophers, including Descartes in *Meditations* (III), Locke in the *Essay Concerning Human Understanding* (Book IV, Ch. 10), and Leibniz in various places, including the essay "On the Ultimate Origination of Things," which is reprinted in many popular editions of his writings. In addition to Kant, critics of the argument among great philosophers include Hume (in Part IX of the *Dialogues Concerning Natural Religion*), Mill in the same essay in which he defended the design argument, *op. cit.*, and Bertrand Russell. Selections on the cosmological argument from Plato, Aristotle, Aquinas, Hume, Kant, and a number of contemporary philosophers are collected in D. R. Burrill (ed.), *The Cosmological Arguments* (N.Y.: Doubleday, 1967, p). Most of the works listed in the preceding paragraph contain critical discussions of the cosmological argument. Other recent attacks include W. Kaufmann, *Critique of Religion and Philosophy*, Ch. V (N.Y.: Harper,

1958, p), P. Edwards, "The Cosmological Argument," *Rationalist Annual*, 1959, C. J. F. Williams, *"Hic autem non est procedere in infinitum"* (St. Thomas Aquinas), *M*, 1960, and R. W. Hepburn, "From World to God," *M*, 1963, reprinted in B. Mitchell, *op. cit.* Edwards and Williams are criticized by P. Brown in "Infinite Causal Regression," *PR*, 1966, reprinted in A. Kenny (ed.), *Aquinas: A Collection of Critical Essays* (N.Y.: Doubleday, 1969, p). Aquinas is defended by J. Owens in "Aquinas on Infinite Regress," *M*, 1962. There is an answer to Owens by J. F. M. Hunter in *M*, 1964. In "Flew on Aquinas," *P*, 1968, L. C. Belecky defends Aquinas against criticisms put forward by Flew in *God and Philosophy, op. cit.* J. F. Ross, in "God and Logical Necessity," *PQ*, 1961, opposes some of J. J. C. Smart's criticisms of the argument, but offers other objections of his own. The cosmological argument is also defended against J. Smart by H. B. Veach in "A Case for Transempirical and Supernaturalistic Knowledge Claims," in P. K. Feyerabend and G. Maxwell (eds.), *Mind, Matter and Method* (Minneapolis: U. of Minnesota P., 1966). P. Brown, in "St. Thomas' Doctrine of Necessary Being," *PR*, 1964, claims that Hepburn, Smart, Martin, Edwards, and Father Copleston all misunderstood Aquinas and that hence their criticisms are invalid, at least insofar as they are directed at his versions of the argument. Kant's criticisms of the cosmological argument are vigorously attacked in T. A. Johnston, S.J., "A Note on Kant's Criticism of the Arguments for the Existence of God," *AJ*, 1943, to which there is a reply, defending Kant, by P. Remnant, "Kant and the Cosmological Argument," *AJ*, 1959. Several neo-Thomist writers have tried to reformulate the cosmological argument so as to circumvent the classical objections. Such reformulations are found in two boks by E. L. Mascall—*He Who Is* (London: Longmans, 1943) and *Existence and Analogy* (London: Longmans, 1949)—and in A. Farrer, *Finite and Infinite* (London: Dacre Press, 1943). There is a critical examination of such reformulations in W. E. Kennick, "A New Way with the Five Ways," *AJ*, 1960. Kant's criticisms of the cosmological argument are defended against recent objections in W. H. Baumer, "Kant on Cosmological Arguments," *Mo*, 1967. Aquinas' third argument is criticized in B. Medlin, "The Contingency Argument," *S*, 1966, and T. Mautner, "Aquinas' Third Way," *APQ*, 1969. There is a reply to Medlin by M. Miller in *S*, 1967. The question of whether the Third Way of Aquinas commits the fallacy of composition is discussed in R. B. Edwards, "Composition and the Cosmological Argument," *M*, 1968 and R. N. Mabey, Jr., "Confusion and the Cosmological Argument," *M*, 1971. *The Monist*, 1970, contains the following five articles on the cosmological argument: W. Norris Clarke, "A Curious Blind Spot in the Anglo-American Tradition of Antitheistic Arguments," B. R. Reichenbach, "Divine Necessity and the Cosmological Argument," M. Tooley, "Does the Cosmological Argument Entail the Ontological Argument?" F. B. Dilley, "Descartes' Cosmological Argument," and W. L. Rowe, "Two Criticisms of the Cosmological Argument." The last-mentioned author also discusses the argument in "The Cosmological Argument," *N*, 1971. Descartes' version of the cosmological argument is also discussed in H. B. Stainsby, "Descartes' Argument for God," *S*, 1967. In Ch. 3 of his *Philosophical Theology* (Indianapolis: Bobbs-Merrill, 1969), J. F. Ross develops a "modal" argument for the existence of God which has some similarities to traditional versions of the cosmological argument. He further develops this argument in "On Proofs for the Existence of God," *Mo.*, 1970. The argument from motion, as it is found in Aquinas, is discussed by J. Salamucha in "The Proof *Ex Motu* for the Existence of God," *New Scholasticism, 1958*, reprinted in A. Kenny (ed.), *Aquinas, op. cit.* and, as it is found in various other classical figures, by M. J. Buckley in *Motion and Motion's God* (Princeton: Princeton U.P., 1971). There is a very comprehensive critical discussion of all of Aquinas' arguments in A. Kenny, *The Five Ways* (London: Routledge, 1969). A detailed critical appraisal of Aquinas' arguments is also found in Ch. 3 of V. Preller, *Divine Science and the Science of God—A Reformulation of Thomas Aquinas* (Princeton: Princeton U.P., 1967). Some popular writers have made the claim that certain of the cosmological theories of contemporary physicists allow them to restate the cosmological argument as a kind of "scientific" proof of the existence of God. There are critical discussions of such metaphysical interpretations of physical theories in S. Toulmin's contribution to S. Toulmin, R. W. Hepburn, and A. MacIntyre, *Metaphysical Beliefs* (London: SCM Press, 1957) and in S. Hook's "Modern Knowledge and the Concept of God," which is found in his book, *The Quest for Being* (N.Y.: St. Martin's Press, 1961). The relevant scientific theories are lucidly presented and analyzed in M. K. Munitz, "Creation and the 'New' Cosmology," *BJPS*, 1954–55, in the same author's *Space, Time and Creation* (Glencoe: Free Press, 1957, p), and in J. D. North, *The Measure of the Universe—A History of Modern Cosmology* (Oxford: Clarendon Press, 1965). There are valuable discussions of the concept of explanation which plays a crucial role in some forms of the cosmological argument in K. Baier, *The Meaning of Life* (Canberra: Commonwealth Government Printer, 1957), reprinted in M. Weitz (ed.), *Twentieth Century Philosophy: The Analytic Tradition* (N.Y.: Free Press, 1966, p), in Ch. I of E. Nagel, *Sovereign Reason* (Glencoe: Free Press, 1954), and in J. Hospers, "What Is Explanation?" *JP*, 1946, which is reprinted in A. Flew (ed.), *Essays in Conceptual Analysis* (London: Macmillan, 1956).

St. Anselm's *Proslogium*, from which our Selection 32 is taken, is available in several editions. The definitive translation by M. J. Charlesworth was published in 1965 in Oxford by Clarendon Press. This volume contains a valuable introduction and philosophical commentary by the translator. Another useful edition is that of S. Deane (LaSalle, Illinois: Open Court, 1938), which, in addition to Anselm's text, contains early criticisms as well as discussions by later philosophers. Descartes' defense of the ontological argument in his *Meditations*, was criticized by a number of his contemporaries. These, as well as Descartes' reply, are available in A. Plantinga (ed.), *The Ontological Argument* (Garden City: Doubleday, 1965, p). This volume also contains selections from other philosophers of the past and present who discussed the ontological argument as well as an introduction by R. Taylor. There is a comprehensive critical discussion of Descartes' argument in A. Kenny, *Descartes: A Study of his Philosophy* (N.Y.: Random House, 1968). The major portions of Kenny's discussion are reprinted, together with comments by N. Malcolm, T. Penelhum, B. Williams, and E. Sosa, as well as Kenny's reply in J. Margolis (ed.), *Fact and Existence* (Oxford: Blackwell, 1969). The ontological argument was also discussed by Leibniz (sympathetically) in his *New Essays,* Appendix I, and by Aquinas (critically) in *Summa Theologica,* Pt. I, Q. 2, art. 1. The most famous criticism is that of Kant in the *Critique of Pure Reason,* but some of Kant's points had been anticipated by earlier writers, especially Gassendi and Hume. The discussions by Anselm, his early critic, Gaunilo, Aquinas, Descartes, Leibniz, and Kant are reprinted in J. Hick (ed.), *The Existence of God, op. cit.* Selections from Anselm, various commentators on Anselm (including the theologian Karl Barth) as well as contemporary discussions of the ontological argument are reprinted in J. Hick and A. McGill (eds.), *The Many-Faced Argument* (N.Y.: Macmillan, 1967). To beginners in philosophy, the ontological argument seems little more than a pun and quite obviously invalid. While the great majority of professional philosophers would endorse the view that the argument is unsound, it has nevertheless exercised a special fascination for many of them. There is far from universal agreement among those who reject the argument as to just where it fails; and from time to time philosophers of stature have made attempts to restate the argument so that it would not be open to any of the usual objections. One such attempt was made by the Oxford philosopher, R. G. Collingwood, in his book, *An Essay on Philosophical Method* (Oxford: Clarendon Press, 1933). There is a reply to this revival of the ontological argument in Gilbert Ryle, "Mr. Collingwood and the Ontological Argument," *M*, 1935, a reply to Ryle by E. E. Harris in *M*, 1936, and a reply by Ryle to Harris in *M*, 1937. The two articles by Ryle are reprinted in Volume 2 of his *Collected Papers* (London: Hutchinson, 1971). The two articles as well as the piece by Harris are reprinted in Hick and McGill, *op. cit.* Another attempt to revive the argument, although without a flat endorsement, is found in N. Rescher's "The Ontological Proof Revisited," *AJ*, 1959. There is a reply to Rescher by K. Gunderson and R. Routley in "Mr. Rescher's Reformulation of the Ontological Proof," *AJ*, 1960. Undoubtedly the most widely discussed defense of a form of the ontological argument in recent years is that by Norman Malcolm in "Anselm's Ontological Arguments," *PR*, 1960, reprinted in his *Knowledge and Certainty* (Englewood Cliffs: Prentice-Hall, 1963), also in Hick and McGill, *op. cit.*, Plantinga, *op. cit.*, and Hick, *The Existence of God, op. cit.* There were replies to Malcolm by R. E. Allen, R. Abelson, T. Penelhum, A. Plantinga, P. Henle, and G. B. Matthews in *PR*, 1961. Other articles containing comments on Malcolm's argument are J. Yolton's "Prof. Malcolm on St. Anselm, Belief, and Existence," *P*, 1961, P. T. Brown, "Prof. Malcolm on Anselm's Ontological Arguments," *A*, 1961, F. Zabeeh, "The Ontological Argument and How and Why Some Speak of God," *PPR*, 1961–62, W. J. Huggett, "The Non-Existence of Ontological Arguments," *PR*, 1962, W. Baumer, "Anselm, Truth, and Necessary Being," *P*, 1962, R. C. Coburn, "Professor Malcolm on God," *AJ*, 1963, F. Scott, "Scotus, Malcolm and Anselm," *Mo*, 1965, and A. C. Ewing, "Further Thoughts on the Ontological Argument," *RS*, 1969. W. P. Alston in "The Ontological Argument Revisited," *PR*, 1960, C. L. Hardin, "An Empirical Refutation of the Ontological Argument," *A*, 1961, and J. Shaffer in "Existence, Predication, and the Ontological Argument," *M*, 1962, reject the argument, but express dissatisfaction with the usual Kantian criticisms. Alston's article is reprinted in Plantinga, *op. cit.*, and also in W. Doney (ed.), *Descartes —A Collection of Critical Essays* (Garden City: Doubleday, 1967, p). The last-mentioned volume also contains a criticism of Alston by Plantinga. There are very detailed attacks on Kant's criticism of the ontological argument in S. M. Engel, "Kant's 'Refutation' of the Ontological Argument," *PPR*, 1963, and A. Plantinga, "Kant's Objection to the Ontological Argument," *JP*, 1966. Kant is defended in W. H. Baumer, "Ontological Arguments Still Fail," *Mo*, 1966 and in R. C. Coburn, "Animadversions on Plantinga's Kant," *R*, 1971. Another contemporary philosopher favoring the ontological argument is Charles Hartshorne in his books, *Man's Vision of God* (Chicago: Willett, Clark, 1941), *The Logic of Perfection* (LaSalle, Illinois: Open Court, 1963) and *Anselm's Discovery* (LaSalle, Illinois: Open Court, 1966, p) and in several articles including "What Did Anselm Discover?" which is available in Hick and McGill, *op. cit.* Hartshorne's views are criticized by J. O. Nelson in "Modal Logic and the Ontological Proof of God's Existence," *RM*, 1963. There is an answer to Nelson by Hartshorne in *RM*, 1964. Both Malcolm and Hartshorne are criticized by

Hick in his "A Critique of the 'Second Argument'," which is included in Hick and McGill. *op. cit.* The German logician Heinrich Scholz also saw much merit in the ontological argument. His paper, unfortunately not available in an English translation, is reprinted in his *Mathesis Universalis* (Basel: Benno Schwabe, 1961). The following recent papers also deal with various aspects of the ontological argument: M. J. Charlesworth, "St. Anselm's Argument," *S,* 1962, D. P. Dryer, "The Concept of Existence in Kant," G. E. Scott, "Quine, God and Modality," P. Crawford, "Existence, Predication and Anselm," (the last three articles all in *Mo,* 1966), D. M. Lochhead, "Is Existence a Predicate in Anselm's Argument?" *RS,* 1966, L. T. Howe, "Conceivability and the Ontological Argument," *S,* 1966, the same author's "Existence as a Perfection: a Reconsideration of the Ontological Argument," *RS,* 1968, C. Crittenden, "The Argument from Perfection to Existence," *RS,* 1968, J. Hintikka, "On the Logic of the Ontological Argument," in K. Lambert (ed.), *The Logical Way of Doing Things* (New Haven: Yale U.P., 1969), D. Lewis, "Anselm and Actuality," *N,* 1970, J. B. Stearns, "Anselm and the Two-Argument Hypothesis," *Mo,* 1970, M. Roth, "A Note on Anselm's Ontological Argument," *M,* 1970, and R. M. Adams, "The Logical Structure of Anselm's Arguments," *PR,* 1971. J. Berg, "An Examination of the Ontological Proof," *T,* 1961 and W. E. Mann, "Definite Descriptions and the Ontological Argument," *T,* 1967, make heavy use of symbolic logic in their discussions of the argument. Occasionally attempts are made by unbelievers to offer what is in effect an ontological argument for the non-existence of God. J. N. Findlay offered such a "negative proof" in his "Can God's Existence Be Disproved?" *M,* 1948, which, together with criticisms and Findlay's reply, is reprinted in A. Flew and A. C. MacIntyre (eds.), *op. cit.,* also in Findlay's book, *Language, Mind and Value* (London: Allen & Unwin, N.Y.: Humanities Press, 1963). Other recent atheistic arguments of this kind are advanced in R. Puccetti, "The Concept of God," *PQ,* 1964, and in J. L. Pollock, "Proving the Non-Existence of God," *I,* 1966. There is a reply to Pollock by D. Föllesdal in the same volume of *I.* D. and M. Haight in "An Ontological Argument for the Devil," *Mo,* 1970, and C. K. Grant in a note in *A,* 1957, argue that if the ontological argument proves the existence of God, it equally proves the existence of the devil—a consequence which would not be welcomed by all believers. There are discussions of Grant's contention by R. J. Rickman and T. Waldman in *PSt,* 1958–60. L. S. Feuer in "God, Guilt and Logic: The Psychological Basis of the Ontological Argument," *I,* 1968, offers a theory about the motives of those who accept the ontological argument. Feuer is severely criticized in *I,* 1969, by E. D. Watt and W. L. Sessions. There is a very comprehensive bibliography, covering all aspects of the ontological argument, in Hick and McGill, *op. cit.*

Most of the discussions of the ontological argument sooner or later deal with the question, "Is existence a characteristic?" and this question is of great philosophical interest, quite aside from any implications the answers to it might have upon the validity of the ontological or any other argument for the existence of God. Some of the most influential treatments of this topic during the present century occur in the writings of Bertrand Russell. In this connection, reference should be made to Russell's series of articles, "The Philosophy of Logical Atomism" which are now reprinted in his *Logic and Knowledge** (London: Allen & Unwin, 1956) and to Chs. XV and XVI of the *Introduction to Mathematical Philosophy** (London: Allen & Unwin, 1919). There is an important symposium by W. Kneale and G. E. Moore entitled "Is Experience a Predicate?"* *Ar. Soc. Sup.,* 1936. Kneale's contribution is reprinted in H. Feigl and W.

Sellars (eds.), *Readings in Philosophical Analysis* (N.Y.: Appleton-Century-Crofts, 1949), Moore's article is reprinted in his *Philosophical Papers* (London: Allen & Unwin, 1958, N.Y.: Collier Books, 1962, p). The following articles also discuss this question: H. S. Leonard, "The Logic of Existence," *PSt,* 1956, G. Nakhnikian and W. C. Salmon, " 'Exists' As a Predicate," *PR,* 1957, M. Kitely, "Existence and the Ontological Argument," *PPR,* 1958, R. Cartwright, "Negative Existentials," *JP,* 1960, reprinted in C. E. Caton (ed.), *Philosophy and Ordinary Language* (Urbana: U. of Illinois P., 1963), K. Baier, "Existence," *Ar. Soc.,* 1960–61, F. Ebersole, "Whether Existence is a Predicate," *JP,* 1963, M. Kiteley, "Is Existence a Predicate?" *M,* 1964, P. F. Strawson, "Is Existence Never a Predicate?" *Critica* (Mexico) 1967, D. F. Pears and J. Thomson, "Is Existence a Predicate?" in P. F. Strawson (ed.), *Philosophical Logic* (London: Oxford U.P., 1967, p), C. J. F. Williams, "Baier on the Equivocal Character of 'Exists'," *M,* 1969, D. Welker, "Existential Statements," *JP,* 1970, and W. E. Kennick, "More on Existence and Predication," in A. Ambrose and M. Lazerowitz (eds.), *G. E. Moore: Essays in Retrospect* (London: Allen & Unwin, 1970). Russell's views about the proper analysis of existence-statements were anticipated by the great German logician Gottlob Frege. There are strategic quotations from Frege's very technical writings, together with explanatory comments and criticism, in J. W. Forgie, "Frege's Objection to the Ontological Argument," *N,* 1972.

The notion of a "necessary being," which figures prominently in the ontological as well as in one of the versions of the cosmological argument, is discussed in A. N. Prior, "Is Necessary Existence Possible?," *PPR,* 1955, R. L. Franklin, "Necessary Being," *A,* 1957, P. A. E. Hutchins, "Necessary Being," *AJ,* 1957, T. Penelhum, "Divine Necessity," *M,* 1960, reprinted in B. Mitchell, *op. cit.,* J. Hick, "God as Necessary Being," *JP,* 1960, C. J. F. Williams, "God and 'Logical Necessity'," *PQ,* 1961, A. Kenny, "Necessary Being," *S,* 1962, the same author's "God and Necessity," in B. Williams and A. Montefiore (eds.), *British Analytical Philosophy* (London: Routledge, 1966), A. Plantinga, "Necessary Being," in A. Plantinga (ed.), *Faith and Philosophy* (Grand Rapids, Mich.: W. B. Erdman's, 1964), C. Hartshorne, "Is the Denial of Existence Ever Contradictory?" *JP,* 1966 (which is a reply to Plantinga), R. L Franklin, "Some Sorts of Necessity," *S,* 1964, A. Daher, "God and Factual Necessity," *RS,* 1970, and R. M. Adams, "Has It Been Proved That All Real Existence Is Contingent?", *APQ,* 1971.

Many Protestant philosophers, who have abandoned the cosmological and teleological arguments, have championed the so-called argument from religious experience which is defended by D. E. Trueblood in our Selection 36. The characteristics of what are called religious experiences are very fully explored in R. Otto, *The Idea of the Holy* (London: H. Milford, 1923). Detailed recent presentations of the actual argument are found in H. D. Lewis, *Our Experience of God* (London: Allen & Unwin, 1959), J. Baillie, *The Sense of the Presence of God* (N.Y.: Scribner's, 1962) and H. P. Owen, *The Christian Knowledge of God* (London: Athlone Press, 1969). The major parts of Trueblood's *The Knowledge of God* (N.Y.: Harper, 1939) are devoted to the argument from religious experience. It is also championed by the British psychologist, R. H. Thouless, in *An Introduction to the Psychology of Religion* (Cambridge: Cambridge U.P., 1961, p). Thouless defends the argument against various psychologists in his article "Has Psychology Explained Religion Away?" *Hibbert Journal,* *1951.* The argument is also defended by A. C. Ewing in "Awareness of God," *P,* 1965, reprinted in his *Nonlinguistic Philosophy* (London: Allen & Unwin,

1968). In Ch. 6 of *The Politics of Experience* (N.Y.: Pantheon Books, 1967), the Scottish psychiatrist R. D. Laing, whose work has received a great deal of attention in recent years, defends a highly unorthodox version of the argument, maintaining that the religious experiences of schizophrenics are veridical. The argument is criticized in Chs. 3 and 4 of R. Hepburn, *op. cit.,* in Ch. 5 of C. B. Martin, *op. cit.,* in Ch. 7 of A. C. MacIntyre, *op. cit.,* in Ch. IX of H. J. Paton, *The Modern Predicament* (N.Y.: Collier Books, 1962, p), in Part 3 of Matson, *Existence of God, op. cit.,* and Ch. 6 of Flew, *God and Philosophy, op. cit.* The argument continues to be discussed widely by philosophers. The following are some recent contributions to the periodical literature: N. Kemp Smith, "Is Divine Existence Credible?" *Proceedings of the British Academy,* 1931, Axel Hägerström, "Lectures on So-Called Spiritual Religion," *T,* 1948, H. D. Lewis and C. H. Whiteley, "The Cognitive Factor in Religious Experience," *Ar. Soc. Sup.,* 1955, reprinted in R. E. Santoni (ed.), *Religious Language and the Problem of Religious Knowledge, op. cit.,* B. A. Farrell, "Psychological Theory and the Belief in God," *The International Journal of Psychoanalysis, 1955,* F. C. Copleston, "The Philosophical Relevance of Religious Experience," *P,* 1956, H. J. N. Horsburgh, "The Claims of Religious Experience," *AJ,* 1957, F. E. Sparshott, "The Central Problem of Philosophy," *University of Toronto Quarterly,* 1961, J. Burnheim, "The Concept of Religious Experience," *S,* 1967, and L. C. Becker, "A Note on Religious Experience Arguments," *RS,* 1971. A discussion of the evidential value of religious experience is also found in G. I. Mavrodes, *Belief in God* (N.Y.: Random House, 1970, p). It should be added that C. D. Broad, who was critical of all other arguments, showed some sympathy for the appeal to religious experience.

The moral argument for the existence of God is defended in the three Catholic works mentioned above, and also, less systematically but more movingly, in Cardinal Newman's *A Grammar of Assent* (N.Y.: McKay, 1947, ed. C. F. Harrold). Kant, who completely rejected the ontological, cosmological, and teleological arguments, justified his own belief in God by reference to a form of the moral argument. His exposition of it is found in the *Critique of Practical Reason.** Numerous Protestant philosophers of the 19th and early 20th centuries, often influenced by Kant, advocated versions of the moral argument. Such defenses are found in Ch. III of Hastings Rashdall, *Philosophy and Religion* (London: Duckworth, 1909), Ch. 13 of W. R. Sorley, *Moral Values and the Idea of God* (N.Y.: Cambridge U.P., 1919), A. E. Taylor, *The Faith of a Moralist* (London: Macmillan, 1930), the same author's *Does God Exist? op. cit.,* and J. Baillie, *The Interpretation of Religion* (Edinburgh: T. and T. Clark, 1929). More recently the argument has been defended in H. P. Owen, *The Moral Argument for Christian Theism* (London: Allen & Unwin, 1965) and I. Trethowan, *Absolute Value: A Study in Christian Ethics* (London: Allen & Unwin, 1970). There is a sympathetic discussion, though nothing like an endorsement, in Ch. 21 of H. J. Paton, *The Modern Predicament, op. cit.*

The argument from evil against the belief in a deity that is claimed to be both all-good and all-powerful is strikingly presented in several of the writings of the 17th century philosopher, Pierre Bayle. Some of Bayle's discussions of this topic are contained in a new volume edited by R. Popkin: *Bayle's Historical and Critical Dictionary—Selections* (Indianapolis: Bobbs Merrill, 1965, p). It was Bayle who stimulated Leibniz to his famous and much-ridiculed defense of the traditional position in his *Theodicy* (London: Routledge, 1951, tr. E. M. Huggard). One of the most famous and powerful presentations of the argument from evil is contained in Parts X and XI of Hume's *Dialogues concerning*

Natural Religion. Perhaps the most powerful statements of the argument in the 19th century are contained in Mill's essay, "Nature," which forms part of his *Three Essays on Religion, op. cit.* (it is now separately available as a Liberal Arts Press paperback with an introduction by G. Nakhnikian) and Ch. 7 of Mill's *An Examination of Sir William Hamilton's Philosophy* (London: Longmans, Green, 1872). The latter is reprinted in N. Pike (ed.), *God and Evil* (Englewood Cliffs: Prentice-Hall, 1964, p). Other forceful statements of the arguments are found in J. M. E. McTaggart, *Some Dogmas of Religion* (London: Edward Arnold, 1906), C. H. Whiteley, *An Introduction to Metaphysics* (London: Methuen, 1950), and, in a more technical form, by John Wisdom in "God and Evil,"* *M,* 1935, John Mackie in "Evil and Omnipotence,"* *M,* 1955, and H. J. McCloskey, "God and Evil," *PQ,* 1960. (There is a reply to Mackie by S. A. Grave in *M,* 1956.) The articles by Mackie and McCloskey are reprinted in Pike, *God and Evil, op. cit.;* Mackie's article is also reprinted in B. Mitchell, *op. cit.* The fullest statement of the argument in recent years is found in E. H. Madden and P. H. Hare, *Evil and the Concept of God* (Springfield, Illinois: Thomas, 1968). Replies to the argument on the part of believers may be found in D. J. B. Hawkins, *The Essentials of Theism* (London and N.Y.: Sheed & Ward, 1949), Josiah Royce, *The Religious Aspect of Philosophy* (N.Y.: Houghton Mifflin, 1887), F. R. Tennant, *Philosophical Theology,* Volume II (Cambridge U.P., 1930), N. Ferré, *Evil and the Christian Faith* (N.Y.: Harper, 1947), F. Petit, *The Problem of Evil* (London: Burns & Oates, 1959), J. Ross, *Philosophical Theology, op. cit.,* M. B. Ahern, *The Problem of Evil* (London: Routledge, 1971), and J. Hick, *Evil and the God of Love* (N.Y.: Harper, 1966) from which our Selection 40 is taken. Paul Siwek, *The Philosophy of Evil** (N.Y.: Ronald Press, 1956), is a full-length treatment of this problem by a well-known Catholic philosopher. A popular reply by a distinguished literary critic is C. S. Lewis, *The Problem of Pain* (N.Y.: Macmillan, 1962). Hick is criticized in R. Puccetti, "The Loving God—Some Observations on John Hick's *Evil and the God of Love,*" *RS,* 1967. Hick replied to Puccetti in "God, Evil and Mystery," *RS,* 1968. There is an answer to Mackie's article in *M,* 1958, by P. M. Farrell and a defense of Mackie against Farrell by M. Zimmerman in *M,* 1961. Plantinga offers his reply in *God and Other Minds, op. cit.,* and in "The Free Will Defense," in M. Black (ed.), *Philosophy in America* (London: Allen & Unwin, 1965), reprinted in B. Mitchell (ed.), *op. cit.* There is a critical discussion of Plantinga's solution in C. Dore, "Plantinga on the Free Will Defense," *RM,* 1971. Madden and Hare, whose book was mentioned earlier, discuss the problem of evil also in "Evil and Unlimited Power," *RM,* 1966 and "On the Difficulty of Evading the Problem of Evil," *PPR,* 1967. Madden, on his own, discusses the problem in "The Riddle of God and Evil," in F. C. Dommeyer (ed.), *Current Philosophical Issues* (Springfield, Illinois: Thomas, 1966) and "Evil and the Concept of a Limited God," *PSt,* 1967. Madden and Hare are criticized in J. King-Farlow, "Must the Gods Madden Madden?" *PPR,* 1968. There is a reply to King-Farlow in Madden and Hare, "Why Hare Must Hound the Gods," *PPR,* 1969. Hume's treatment of the problem is criticized in N. Pike, "Hume on Evil," *PR,* 1963, reprinted in Pike, *God and Evil, op. cit.* There is a defense of Hume against Pike in D. F. Henze, "On Some Alleged Humean Insights and Oversights," *RS,* 1970. Hume is also defended in W. H. Capitan, "Part X of Hume's Dialogues," *APQ,* 1966, reprinted in V. C. Chappell (ed.), *Hume: A Collection of Critical Essays* (Garden City: Doubleday, 1966, p). In order to circumvent the problem of evil, some philosophers have abandoned traditional theism and have instead advocated belief in a finite god. In this connection mention should be made of E. S. Brightman, *The Problem of God* (N.Y.: Abingdon Press, 1930), and P. Bertocci, *Introduction to the Philosophy of Religion, op. cit.* Recent articles on the problem of evil include H. D. Aiken, "God and Evil," *E,* 1958, reprinted in his *Reason and Conduct* (N.Y.: Knopf, 1962), N. Smart, "Omnipotence, Evil and Supermen," *P,* 1961, reprinted in Pike, *op. cit.,* replies to Smart by Flew and Mackie in *P,* 1962, G. Schlesinger, "The Problem of Evil and the Problem of Suffering," *APQ,* 1964, N. La Para, "Suffering, Happiness and Evil," *S,* 1965, H. Khatchadourian, "God, Happiness and Evil," *RS,* 1966, H. J. McCloskey, "Evil and the Problem of Evil," *S,* 1966, T. Penelhum, "Divine Goodness and the Problem of Evil," *RS,* 1966, D. J. Hoitenga, "Logic and the Problem of Evil," *APQ,* 1967, J. King-Farlow, "Evil and Other Worlds," *S,* 1967, F. G. Downing, "God and the Problems of Evil," *S,* 1968, K. E. Yandell, "Ethics, Evils and Theism," *S,* 1969, G. S. Kane, "Theism and Evil," *S,* 1970, and C. Dore, "An Examination of the 'Soul-Making' Theodicy," *APQ,* 1970.

There has been much controversy as to whether recent findings in physics and other sciences lend support to the belief in God. Sir James Jeans in *The Mysterious Universe* (N.Y.: Macmillan, 1930) took the affirmative side in this dispute. Sir Arthur Eddington endorsed similar conclusions, though with some reservations. His views are expressed in *The Nature of the Physical World* (N.Y.: Macmillan, 1928) and in *Science and the Unseen World* (N.Y.: Macmillan, 1929). The American physicist, W. G. Pollard, has tried to derive theological conclusions from certain features of quantum theory in his *Chance and Providence* (N.Y.: Scribner's, 1958). The view that science and religion are perfectly compatible is defended by the mathematician Warren Weaver in "Can a Scientist Believe in God?" which is reprinted in L. Rosen (ed.), *A Guide to the Religions of America* (N.Y.: Simon & Schuster, 1955, p). J. A. O'Brien in *God and Evolution* (Notre Dame: U. of Notre Dame P., 1961) argues that traditional theism is compatible with the facts of evolutionary biology. The views of Jeans and Eddington are critically examined in Bertrand Russell, *The Scientific Outlook* (N.Y.: Free Press, 1948, p), L. S. Stebbing, *Philosophy and the Physicists* (London: Methuen, 1937), C. Cohen, *God and the Universe* (London: Pioneer Press, 1946), and W. R. Inge, *God and the Astronomers* (London: Longmans, Green, 1933). Einstein's views on this subject are found in *The World As I See It* (London: Watts, 1935) and *Out of My Later Years* (N.Y.: Philosophical Library, 1950).

Mysticism is explained and defended in Evelyn Underhill, *Mysticism* (London: Macmillan, 1930), W. R. Inge, *Christian Mysticism* (London: Methuen, 1932), the same author's *Mysticism in Religion* (Chicago: U. of Chicago P., 1948), R. M. Jones, *Pathways to the Reality of God* (N.Y.: Macmillan, 1931), and R. C. Zaehner, *Mysticism, Sacred and Profane* (N.Y.: Oxford U.P., 1961, p). Much more sophisticated and philosophically of great interest are W. T. Stace, *Time and Eternity* (Princeton: Princeton U.P., 1952) and the same author's *Mysticism and Philosophy* (London: Macmillan, 1961). Stace is also the editor of *The Teachings of the Mystics* (N.Y.: New American Library, 1960, p), an anthology of writings by mystics. Other recent anthologies of this kind are F. C. Happold, *Mysticism* (Baltimore: Penguin Books, 1963, p) and A. Fremantle (ed.), *The Protestant Mystics* (Boston: Little, Brown, 1964). Critical of mysticism are J. H. Leuba, *The Psychology of Religious Mysticism* (N.Y.: Harcourt, Brace, 1925) and Bertrand Russell in Ch. VII of *Religion and Science* (London: Oxford U.P., 1935, p). G. Godwin, *The Great Mystics* (London: Watts, 1945), contains interesting material about many of the great mystics, presented from a skeptical point of view. The following articles deal with various claims made on behalf of mystical experiences: P. Henle, "Mysticism and Semantics," *PPR*, 1949, W. P. Alston, "Ineffability," *PR*, 1956, R. M. Gale, "Mysticism and Philosophy," *JP*, 1960, R. Hoffman, "Logic, Meaning and Mystical Intuition," *PSt*, 1960, M. Kohl, "The Unanimity Argument and the Mystics," *HJ*, 1960, N. Smart, "Mystical Experience," *S*, 1962, another article by N. Smart bearing the same title in W. H. Capitan and D. D. Merrill (eds.), *Art, Mind and Religion* (Pittsburgh: U. of Pittsburgh P., 1967), the same author's "Interpretation and Mystical Experience," *RS*, 1965, and J. Findlay, "The Logic of Mysticism," *RS*, 1966, reprinted in his *Ascent to the Absolute* (London: Allen & Unwin, 1970). There are critical comments on Smart's paper by N. Pike and P. F. Schmidt in *Art, Mind and Religion*. The articles by Alston and Gale are reprinted in S. M. Cahn (ed.), *Philosophy of Religion, op. cit.*

The classical formulations of agnosticism are Ch. I of Sir Leslie Stephen, *An Agnostic's Apology* (N.Y.: Putnam, 1903) and T. H. Huxley's essay "Agnosticism," reprinted in his book, *Science and the Christian Tradition* (N.Y.: Appleton, 1894). More recently, agnosticism has been defended by Clarence Darrow in "Why I Am an Agnostic," reprinted in A. and L. Weinberg (eds.), *Clarence Darrow—Verdicts Out of Court* (Chicago: Quadrangle Books, 1963). The atheist's position is given in Charles Bradlaugh's lecture, "A Plea for Atheism," which is reprinted in the Centenary Volume, *Charles Bradlaugh— Champion of Liberty* (London: Watts, 1933). Atheism is also defended in Volume II of Holbach's *System of Nature* (English translation, Boston, 1853). There is a selection from Holbach in W. P. Alston, *op. cit. The System of Nature* can nowadays be found in libraries only, but the English translation of a briefer work in which Holbach champions atheism is in print. The real title is *Good Sense*, but it is available as *Superstition in All Ages* (N.Y.: The Truthseeker Co., 1920). It is wrongly ascribed in this edition to the Abbé Meslier, whose name Holbach used on the title page of the original edition to hide his authorship. Holbach strongly influenced Shelley, who defended atheism on numerous occasions, for example in the very early and short "The Necessity of Atheism" and in the more substantial pieces, "A Refutation of Deism" and "There Is No God." The last of these is one of the Notes to Canto VII of *Queen Mab*. All three discussions are included in D. L. Clark (ed.), *Shelley's Prose* (Albuquerque: U. of New Mexico P., 1954). A famous 19th century work defending atheism is Ludwig Feuerbach's *The Essence of Christianity* (1841, English translation by George Eliot, N.Y.: Harper, 1953, p). A selection from Feuerbach is reprinted in J. Hick, *The Existence of God, op. cit.* Schopenhauer rarely used the term "atheism," but he is usually and quite properly classified as an atheist. His fullest discussion of the objections to traditional theology are found in an essay entitled, "The Christian System," and in his "Religion: A Dialogue." Both of these are available in a translation by T. B. Saunders in *Complete Essays of Schopenhauer* (N.Y.: Wiley, 1942). Robert Ingersoll called himself an "agnostic," but most of his arguments are really arguments for atheism. His main arguments are found in Volume IV, pp. 497 ff. of his *Works* (N.Y.: Dresden Publishing Co., 1902). Although he retains the word "God," John Dewey can also be regarded as an atheist in the most customary sense of the term. His views are expressed in "A God or the God?" *The Christian Century*, 1933, and in the book, *A Common Faith* (New Haven: Yale U.P., 1934). There is a full-length defense of atheism in C. Cohen, *Theism or Atheism?* (London: Pioneer Press, 1921). Recent defenses of atheism are found in E. Nagel, "Atheism," in J. E. Fairchild (ed.), *Basic Beliefs* (N.Y.: Sheridan House, 1959), M. Scriven, *Primary Philosophy, op. cit.,* H. J. McCloskey, "On Being an Atheist," *Q,* 1968, P. Edwards, "Difficulties in the Idea of God," in E. H. Madden, R. Handy and M. Farber (eds.), *The Idea of God* (Springfield, Illinois: Thomas, 1968—this volume also contains commentaries by D. Evans and P. Kurtz and a reply by Edwards), and K. Nielsen, "In Defense of Atheism," with comments by J. Macquarrie, in H. E. Kiefer and M. K. Munitz (eds.), *Contemporary Philosophical Thought, Volume III* (Albany: State U. of N.Y. P., 1970). W. T. Stace defends atheism in the title essay of his *Man Against Darkness* (Pittsburgh: U. of Pittsburgh P., 1967, p). It should be added however, that Stace subsequently abandoned his atheism. Atheism is also defended by the famous French biologist Jacques Monod in *Chance and Necessity* (N.Y.: Knopf, 1971). Atheism is criticized by the distinguished historian of philosophy, E. Gilson, in "The Idea of God and Difficulties of Atheism," in R. M. Hutchins and M. J. Adler (eds.), *The Great Ideas Today—1969* (Chicago: Encyclopaedia Britannica Inc., 1969). A completely naturalistic and secular world-view is advocated by Bertrand Russell in *Why I Am Not a Christian, op. cit.* Russell wavers between calling himself an "agnostic" and an "atheist."

A number of contemporary Anglo-Saxon philosophers would reject the believer's position on the ground that it is meaningless or unintelligible rather than on the ground that it is false. This is the position advocated in Ch. VI of A. J. Ayer, *Language, Truth, and Logic* (London: Gollancz, N.Y.: Dover Publications, 2nd ed., 1946, p), and by Rudolf Carnap in his famous article, "The Elimination of Metaphysics through Logical Analysis of Language," first published in 1932, and now available in English translation in A. J. Ayer (ed.), *Logical Positivism* (N.Y.: Free Press, 1959, p). Carnap, however, makes a distinction between what he calls "mythology" and what he calls "metaphysical" theology. He regards the former as false and treats only the latter, which he takes to be philosophically more interesting, as meaningless. Some of the philosophers associated with the so-called "linguistic movement" are also hostile to belief in God but they are less ready than Ayer or Carnap to condemn theological utterances as meaningless. John Wisdom's essay, "God," which is reprinted in his *Philosophy and Psychoanalysis* (Oxford: Blackwell, 1953) and in A. Flew (ed.), *Logic and Language,* First Series (Oxford: Blackwell, 1951), discusses the curious logical status of theological claims, and A. Flew, in his contribution to the symposium on "Theology and Falsification" in A. Flew and A. C. MacIntyre, *op. cit.* (reprinted in our book as Selection 46) challenges believers to tell him with what conceivable state of affairs a sentence like "God is love" is incompatible, implying that there is none and that this reflects adversely on the cognitive status of such utterances. There are replies to Flew in the same volume by R. M. Hare, B. Mitchell, and I. M. Crombie, as well as a further comment by Flew. Flew is also criticized by G. B. Matthews, "Theology and Natural Theology," *JP,* 1964. There are additional contributions to this discussion in D. R. Duff-Forbes, "Theology and Falsification Again," *AJ,* 1961, A. Flew, "Falsification and Hypothesis in Theology," *AJ,* 1962, J. Kellenberger, "We No Longer Have Need of that Hypothesis," *S,* 1969, A. M. Wheeler, "Are Theological Utterances Assertions?" *S,* 1969, H. E. Allison, "Faith and Falsifiability," *RM,* 1969, J. Kellenberger, "The Falsification Challenge," *RS,* 1969 (with a reply by Flew, critical comments by T. McPherson and a rejoinder by Kellenberger in the same volume), and E. F. Mooney, "Assertion and Commitment in Religious Belief," *S,* 1971. Hare is criticized in H. J. M. Horsburgh, "Mr. Hare on Theology and Falsification," *PQ,* 1956. Hare, Crombie, and

Mitchell are also among the contributors to B. Mitchell (ed.), *Faith and Logic* (London: Allen & Unwin, 1957), a volume exploring several of the issues discussed in *New Essays in Philosophical Theology*. The questions raised by Flew and other empiricistic critics of religion are discussed in some detail in A. McKinnon, *Falsification and Belief* (The Hague: Mouton, 1970). A recent volume dealing with these questions and consisting of recorded dialogues between the two authors is K. Bendall and F. Ferré, *Exploring the Logic of Faith* (N.Y.: Association Press, 1962, p). John Wisdom's most recent discussion of this subject, "The Modes of Thought and the Logic of God," is available in J. Hick (ed.), *The Existence of God, op. cit.*

The challenge of the logical positivists and some of the other philosophers just referred to has led to various attempts to re-interpret theological sentences in such a way that they are not ruled out by the verifiability principle or by other empiricistic meaning-criteria. R. B. Braithwaite, in *An Empiricist's View of the Nature of Religious Belief* (Cambridge: Cambridge U.P., 1955), which is reprinted in J. Hick, *The Existence of God, op. cit.*, advocates a "conative" reconstruction according to which religious utterances should be regarded as moral assertions which are psychologically reinforced by "stories." A position in many respects similar to Braithwaite's, but independently arrived at, is advocated in P. Schmidt, *Religious Knowledge* (N.Y.: Free Press, 1961). Other reconstructions are found in T. R. Miles, *Religion and the Scientific Outlook* (London: Allen & Unwin, 1959), J. Wilson, *Language and Christian Belief* (London: Macmillan, 1958), in several of the writings of John Hick, including *Faith and Knowledge* (Ithaca: Cornell U.P., 2nd ed., 1966) and "Theology and Verification," *Theology Today*, 1960, and in a number of the contributions to *New Essays in Philosophical Theology*. Useful surveys, as well as criticism, of these attempts at reconstruction are found in W. T. Blackstone, *The Problem of Religious Knowledge* (Englewood Cliffs: Prentice-Hall, 1963, p), and F. Ferré, *Language, Logic and God* (N.Y.: Harper, 1961). There is a sardonic attack on several of these "positivistic" versions of theology in J. Passmore's "Christianity and Positivism," *AJ*, 1957. Braithwaite's reconstruction is attacked by H. J. N. Horsburgh in "Professor Braithwaite and Billy Brown," *AJ*, 1958, and in the Appendix to Ch. 1 of A. Boyce Gibson, *Theism and Empiricism* (London: SCM Press, 1970). Braithwaite's views are also discussed in K. Yandell, "Empiricism and Theism," *S*, 1968 (the same volume contains comments by K. Nielsen and a reply by Yandell). Hick's version is criticized in K. Nielsen, "Eschatological Verification," *Canadian Journal of Theology*, 1963, A. Olding, "Resurrection Bodies and Resurrection Worlds," *M*, 1970, and J. J. Clarke, "John Hick's Resurrection," *S*, 1971. Hick's "Theology and Verification" is reprinted in Hick, *The Existence of God, op. cit.*, Mitchell, *The Philosophy of Religion, op. cit.*, and Cahn, *Philosophy of Religion, op. cit.* The last-mentioned volume also reprints Nielsen's "Eschatological Verification." Wilson is criticized in K. Nielsen, " 'Christian Positivism' and the Appeal to Religious Experience," *Journal of Religion*, 1962. Nielsen's criticism of Hick is answered in G. I. Mavrodes, "God and Verification," *Canadian Journal of Theology*, 1964, to which there is a rejoinder by Nielsen in the same volume. Other recent articles discussing these questions are W. E. P. Kennick, "The Language of Religion," *PR*, 1956, T. Penelhum, "Logic and Theology," *Canadian Journal of Theology*, 1958, E. D. Klemke, "Are Religious Statements Meaningful?" *The Journal of Religion*, 1960, R. Binkley, "What Characterizes Religious Language?" *Journal for the Scientific Study of Religion*, 1962, K. Nielsen, "On Speaking of God," *T*, 1962, and W. Norris Clarke, "How the Philosopher Can Give Meaning To

Language About God," with comments by W. T. Parry and T. Langan in E. H. Madden, R. Handy and M. Farber (eds.), *The Idea of God, op. cit.* In "Religious Assertions in the Light of Contemporary Philosophy," *P*, 1957, which is included in his *Non-Linguistic Philosophy* (London: Allen & Unwin, 1968), A. C. Ewing argues, in opposition to all positivistic tendencies, that theological assertions do have objective meaning, however difficult it may be to justify their truth. H. D. Lewis in "Contemporary Empiricism and the Philosophy of Religion," *ibid.*, evaluates the various contributions to *New Essays in Philosophical Theology*. The same questions about the cognitive content, if any, and possible non-cognitive interpretations of theological claims are discussed by several of the contributors to S. Hook (ed.), *Religious Experience and Truth* (N.Y.: New York University P., 1961) and in J. Hick (ed.), *Philosophers and Faith* (London: Macmillan, 1964). In his contribution to the former of these volumes, which is also reprinted in his *Philosophic Turnings* (Ithaca: Cornell U.P., 1966), P. Ziff argues for the intelligibility of statements asserting the existence of God. Ziff is criticized in K. Nielsen, "The Intelligibility of God-Talk," *RS*, 1970. The entire Spring 1963 issue of *The Monist* is devoted to the topic of "Religious Language and Philosophy." Contributors include H. D. Lewis, B. L. Clarke, T. Organ, G. B. Matthews and R. R. Ehman. W. Christian, *Meaning and Truth in Religion* (Princeton: Princeton U.P., 1964), and R. S. Heimbeck, *Theology and Meaning* (London: Allen & Unwin, 1969) are recent full-length studies of these questions. An attempt to interpret theism as a theory which is, in principle, open to verification or falsification in human experience is found in the last chapter of H. H. Price, *Belief* (London: Allen & Unwin, 1969). In "Differences Between Scientific and Religious Assertions," which is included in I. G. Barbour (ed.), *Science and Religion: New Perspectives on the Dialogue* (N.Y.: Harper, 1968), D. D. Evans argues that religious assertions do have content since they refer to the "depth-experiences" of human beings.

Wittgenstein, whose influence on philosophers in the Anglo-Saxon world has been immense, was not a religious believer, but certain of his ideas have been made the foundation of a novel defense of religious belief. This position is sometimes referred to as "Wittgensteinian fideism." Prominent among those who support this viewpoint are P. Winch, W. D. Hudson, and D. Z. Phillips. Winch's views are given in *The Idea of a Social Science* (London: Routledge, 1958) and "Understanding a Primitive Society," *APQ*, 1964. Hudson has stated his position in *Ludwig Wittgenstein—The Bearing of His Philosophy Upon Religious Belief* (London: Lutterworth, Richmond: John Knox P., 1968, p) and "Some Remarks on Wittgenstein's Account of Religious Belief," in *Talk of God—Royal Institute of Philosophy Lectures Volume 2* (London: Macmillan, 1969, p). Phillips' main publications are *The Concept of Prayer* (London: Routledge, 1965) and a series of essays collected in *Faith and Philosophical Enquiry* (London: Routledge, 1970). D. Z. Phillips (ed.), *Religion and Understanding* (Oxford: Blackwell, 1967) and D. M. High (ed.), *New Essays on Religious Language* (N.Y.: Oxford U.P., 1969, p) are anthologies containing (among other things) papers by Wittgensteinian believers. The former of these reprints Winch's "Understanding a Primitive Society." A very detailed critique of the leading ideas of these writers is found in K. Nielsen, "Wittgensteinian Fideism," *P*, 1967, to which there is a reply by Hudson in *P*, 1968, with a rejoinder by Nielsen in *P*, 1969 (Nielsen's original article contains numerous further references to writings by Wittgensteinian fideists). Hudson's version of Wittgensteinian fideism is criticized in M. Durrant, "The Use of 'Pictures' in Religious Belief," *S*, 1971. Phillips is criticized in K. Nielsen, "Language and the Concept of God," *Q*, 1969, in A. J. Watt, "Religious Beliefs and Pictures," *S*, 1970, and in P. Edwards, "A Critical Examination of 'Subjective Christianity'," *Q*, 1971. *Q*, 1972, contains an exchange between H. Meynell and Nielsen on the issues raised by Nielsen's previous criticisms of Phillips. N. Malcolm, whose article on the ontological argument is regarded as a basic text by some Wittgensteinian fideists, is criticized in D. F. Henze, "Language-Games and the Ontological Argument," *RS*, 1968. Wittgenstein's only substantial discussion of religious belief is found in his *Lectures and Conversations on Aesthetics, Psychology and Religious Belief* (Oxford: Blackwell, 1966, p). D. M. High, *Language, Persons, and Belief* (N.Y.: Oxford U.P., 1967) is a very detailed discussion of the bearing of Wittgenstein's later work on religious questions. It was, however, written before the publication of the *Lectures and Conversations*. R. H. Bell, "Wittgenstein and Descriptive Theology," *RS*, 1969 and T. Sherry, "Is Religion a 'Form of Life'?", *APQ*, 1972 are more recent attempts to assess the relevance of Wittgenstein's philosophy to religious questions.

Some of the problems concerning the meaningfulness of theological utterances were not unknown to Thomas Aquinas and other medieval philosophers. To meet the difficulty, as he perceived it, Aquinas formulated his doctrine of "analogical predication." When we speak of God as "good" or as "powerful," we do not, Aquinas concedes, use these words in their literal senses. On the other hand, we are not using them equivocally either: we are using them analogically. There has been a good deal of interest in recent years in this Thomistic doctrine of analogy and in the question as to whether it, or any amended version of it, can be used to answer the challenge of the logical positivists and other recent critics of traditional theology. Contemporary defenses of the theory are found in Ch. VIII of G. H. Joyce, *Principles of Natural Theology, op. cit.*, in Ch. VII of F. Copleston, *Contemporary Philosophy* (London: Burns and Oates, 1956), and in E. L. Mascall, *Existence and Analogy, op. cit., passim*. In Aquinas, the doctrine is stated in the *Summa Theologica*, Part I, Question 13, article 5. The 16th century commentary by Thomas Cajetan is now available in English under the title of *The Analogy of Names* (Pittsburgh: Duquesne U.P., 1959). It is criticized in Ch. 6 of F. Ferré *Language, Logic, and God, op. cit.*, and in Chs. 5 and 7 of W. T. Blackstone, *The Problem of Religious Knowledge, op. cit.* Among recent articles dealing with these questions, the following are particularly worth mentioning: P. Hayner, "Analogical Predication," *JP*, 1958, I. R. Simon, "On Order in Analogical Sets," *The New Scholasticism*, 1960, T. McPherson, "Assertion and Analogy," *Ar. Soc.*, 1959–60, J. F. Ross, "Analogy as a Rule of Meaning for Religious Language," *International Philosophical Quarterly*, 1961, the same author's "Analogy and the Resolution of Some Cognitivity Problems," *JP*, 1970 (with comments by G. I. Mavrodes in the same volume), and G. Weiler, "Beliefs and Attributes," *P*, 1961. R. McInerny, *The Logic of Analogy* (The Hague: Martinus Nijhoff, 1961), is a scholarly, sympathetic, and somewhat unorthodox study of the Thomistic theory.

William James' defense of fideism to which reference is made in the editorial introduction to the present section is found in the title essay of *The Will to Believe, op. cit.* James is criticized by Bertrand Russell in Ch. 29 of *A History of Western Philosophy* (London: Allen & Unwin, N.Y.: Simon & Schuster, 1946, p) and in two articles by the unjustly forgotten American philosopher Dickinson Miller—" 'The Will to Believe' and the Duty to Doubt," *International Journal of Ethics*, 1898–99 and "James' Doctrine of 'The Right to Believe'," *PR*, 1942. Ducasse's attempt to defend a suitably qualified version of

James' approach is given in Ch. 9 of his *A Philosophical Scrutiny of Religion, op. cit.* and in his correspondence with Dickinson Miller. The relevant portions of this correspondence are reproduced in P. H. Hare and E. H. Madden, "William James, Dickinson Miller and C. J. Ducasse on the Ethics of Belief," *Transactions of the Charles S. Peirce Society, 1968.*

The literature on Kierkegaard is immense, but there are relatively few critical discussions of his theory that truth is subjectivity. W. Kaufmann, in Ch. 10 of *From Shakespeare to Existentialism* (Boston: Beacon Press, 1959, p) is severely critical of this theory and of various of Kierkegaard's other views. A. E. Murphy, "On Kierkegaard's Claim that Truth is Subjectivity," in his *Reason and the Common Good* (Englewood Cliffs: Prentice-Hall, 1963) is also highly critical. The criticisms in Ch. 5 of A. Boyce Gibson, *Theism and Empiricism, op. cit.,* are much milder. The question of what Kierkegaard meant when he said that the Christian, in believing in the "absolute paradox," believes something that is "absurd," has been much debated among Kierkegaard commentators. H. M. Garelick, in his *The Anti-Christianity of Kierkegaard* (The Hague: Martinus Nijhoff, 1965, p) argues that the Christian, on Kierkegaard's view, must believe self-contradictory statements. The view that Kierkegaard did not regard the assertion that God "fused with an individual man" as a self-contradiction and that it is mistaken to think of him as an irrationalist is defended in M. H. Søe, "Kierkegaard's Doctrine of the Paradox," in H. A. Johnson and N. Thulstrup (eds.), *A Kierkegaard Critique* (Chicago: Regnery, 1962, p), and in A. Mc-Kinnon's articles "Kierkegaard: 'Paradoks' and Irrationalism," *Journal of Existentialism,* 1967, "Believing the Paradox: a Contradiction in Kierkegaard?" *Harvard Theological Review,* 1968 and "Kierkegaard's Irrationalism Revisited," *IPQ,* 1969. There is also a full discussion of this question in H. E. Allison, "Christianity and Nonsense," *RM,* 1967, reprinted in J. H. Gill (ed.), *Philosophy Today No. 1* (N.Y.: Macmillan, 1968, p). In "Kierkegaard's Irrationalism Revisited," *op. cit.,* McKinnon argues forcefully that the views expressed under the pseudonym Johannes Climacus in *Concluding Unscientific Postscript* (from which our Selection 42 is taken) are not identical with Kierkegaard's own position. It should be pointed out that if this is so it in no way lessens the importance of evaluating the soundness of the theory that truth is subjectivity. It is this doctrine that a number of contemporary existentialists and pro-religious writers regard as a momentous contribution and whether Kierkegaard himself accepted the theory is a question of purely biographical interest.

Bishop Robinson, whose contribution to the discussion, "Has 'God' a Meaning?" is part of our Selection 45, explains his revisions of traditional theology more fully in *Honest to God* (London: SCM Press, 1963, p), *Exploration Into God* (Stanford U.P., 1967, p) and *The New Reformation?* (London: SCM Press, 1965, p). Special attention should be called to Appendix I of the last-mentioned book which addresses itself to the question "Can a Truly Contemporary Person *Not* Be An Atheist?" A report of an extended interview with Bishop Robinson (along with much other material on theologians holding similar views) is contained in V. Mehta, *The New Theologian* (London: Weidenfeld and Nicolson, 1965). D. L. Edwards (ed.), *The Honest to God Debate* (Philadelphia: Westminster Press, 1963, p) reprints numerous reactions to *Honest to God* on the part of traditional believers as well as some unbelievers. It also contains Robinson's replies.

E. Fackenheim, the author of Selection 44, develops his ideas more fully in *God's Presence in History* (N.Y.: New York University P., 1970) and in various of the essays in *In Quest For Past and Future* (Bloomington: Indiana U.P.,

1968). Martin Buber, whose philosophy forms the foundation of Fackenheim's discussion, was not a systematic writer. *The Eclipse of God* (N.Y.: Harper, 1952, p) and *Between Man and Man* (N. Y.: Macmillan, 1965, p) contain what are perhaps the clearest statements of Buber's leading ideas. The more famous *I and Thou* (N.Y.: Scribner's, 2nd ed., 1958, p) is more difficult, but its "Postscript" helps to clear up Buber's views on several topics. P. A. Schilpp and M. Friedman (eds.), *The Philosophy of Martin Buber* (LaSalle, Illinois: Open Court, 1967) contains an autobiographical sketch by Buber and a number of discussions of Buber's philosophy as well as Buber's replies. R. E. Wood, *Martin Buber's Ontology* (Evanston: Northwestern U.P., 1969) is a detailed commentary on Buber's philosophy. A sympathetic and unusually clear account is found in M. Wyschogrod's article on Buber in the *Encyclopedia of Philosophy* (1–409). P. Edwards, *Buber and Buberism—A Critical Evaluation* (Lawrence: U. of Kansas P., 1970, p) is a detailed and highly critical examination of Buber's theories as well as those of his disciples. It includes a full discussion of Fackenheim's defense of religious belief.

The following articles in the *Encyclopedia of Philosophy* contain discussions that are relevant to topics treated in the present section: "Agnosticism" (R. W. Hepburn, 1–56), "Analogy in Theology" (F. Ferré, 1–94), "Anselm, St." (R. E. Allen and E. R. Fairweather, 1–28), "Atheism" (P. Edwards, 1–174), "Common Consent Arguments for the Existence of God" (P. Edwards, 2–147), "Cosmological Arguments for the Existence of God" (R. W. Hepburn, 2–232), "Cosmology" (M. K. Munitz, 2–237), "Creation, Religious Doctrine of" (R. W. Hepburn, 2–252), "Degrees of Perfection Argument for the Existence of God" (D. Sanford, 2–324), "Deism" (E. C. Mossner, 2–326), "Demiurge" (R. Bambrough, 2–337), "Evil, Problem of" (J. Hick, 3–16), "Faith" (J. Hick, 3–165), "Fideism" (R. H. Popkin, 3–201), "Gaunilo" (R. E. Allen, 3–273), "God, Concepts of" (H. P. Owen, 3–344), "Infinity in Theology and Metaphysics" (H. P. Owen, 4–190), "Moral Arguments for the Existence of God" (R. W. Hepburn, 5–381), "Mysticism, History of" (N. Smart, 5–419), "Mysticism, Nature and Assessment of" (R. W. Hepburn, 5–429), "Ontological Argument for the Existence of God" (J. Hick, 5–538), "Pantheism" (A. MacIntyre, 6–31), "Perfection" (H. P. Owen, 6–87), "Philosophy of Religion, History of" (H. D. Lewis, 6–276), "Philosophy of Religion, Problems of" (W. Alston, 6–285), "Physicotheology" (M. H. Carré, 6–300), "Religion, Psychological Explanations of" (W. P. Alston, 7–148), "Religion and Morality" (P. H. Nowell-Smith, 7–150), "Religion and Science" (J. J. C. Smart, 7–158), "Religious Experience, Argument for the Existence of God" (R. W. Hepburn, 7–163), "Religious Language" (W. P. Alston, 7–168), "Teleological Argument for the Existence of God" (W. P. Alston, 8–84), "Theism" (H. P. Owen, 8–97), and "Thomas Aquinas, St." (B. J. Bourke, 8–105).

VI

Perception
and the
Physical
World

INTRODUCTION

Unreflective primitive men assume that the things they see and touch exist also at times when they are not seen or touched or perceived in any other way; they further take it for granted that things have just those qualities which they appear to have. Let us dignify this unsophisticated creed with the name "naive realism." Its second part has seemed to various philosophers to involve a patent contradiction. Does not the same penny which appears circular when viewed from directly above, appear elliptical when viewed sideways? Does not the same stick which looks straight in air look crooked when halfway immersed in transparent water? Does not the same volume of water feel warm to one hand and cold to the other hand under certain well-known conditions? But if we assumed that everything really has every quality it appears to have, these facts would force us into the contradictory conclusion that the penny is both circular and elliptical, that the stick is both straight and crooked, that the water is both hot and cold, and so on; thus argue the philosophical critics of naive realism. And up to this point they would probably be joined by educated common sense. But some of them continue to press common sense as follows: If the physical penny is circular, and what we see from certain perspectives is not circular, then it cannot be the physical penny itself which is seen from those perspectives. If the physical stick is straight, and the stick which we see is not, then it cannot be the physical stick that is seen. Further, how can color be a quality "in" the things that appear to be colored in different ways, considering that the apparent color of a thing varies with conditions of illumination as well as organic conditions (think of "jaundice," for example)? Indeed, if whatever we see has some color or other and whatever we touch has some temperature or other, and if color and temperature are not qualities of physical objects at all, then it follows that we never perceive physical objects at all. Nobody would maintain, said Locke, that the pain he feels when in contact with fire is in the fire; why then maintain that the warmth and the color are in the fire? And if you admit that the coldness which we ascribe to snow is only a sensation produced by snow when in contact with a sentient organism, why should you suppose that the snow's whiteness is something "objective," independent of sensation? Conclusion: since physical objects in themselves, i.e., as they are when they are not perceived, have neither color nor temperature, what we directly perceive are *ideas* (modern writers speak of "sense-data" or "sensa" or "percepts"), not physical objects. Whether or not the sense-data resemble the physical objects to which they are believed to "correspond" in some sense, they are at any rate distinct from them. This philosophical theory is commonly called (epistemological) dualism. According to Locke, who held a special form of this theory, we are mistaken in supposing that to all the qualities of our sense-data there correspond similar qualities in the objects. Colors, for example, correspond to certain arrangements of the molecules at the surfaces of physical objects by virtue of which the latter reflect light of a particular wave length into the eyes of sentient organisms, but such structures do not resemble sensations of color. The apparently brown penny "as it is in itself" does not have a color nor a degree of temperature at all, any more than the fire has a quality resembling the pain it produces. On the other hand, said Locke, ideas of shape and size and motion and weight do correspond to similar properties of physical objects. The penny may not have that particular shape which it appears to have under certain conditions, but it does have a shape; and it may not have the particular size it appears to have from such and such a distance (it certainly could not have all the apparent sizes, for that would contradict the assumption of constancy of size), but it does have a size. Those qualities which are in the objects themselves, he called "primary," and those which only characterize our sense-data he called "secondary."

Strangely, Locke seems to have forgotten an elementary distinction in the course of his critique of naive realism, a distinction he himself had made explicitly: that between a quality of a thing and the corresponding idea (sense-datum). "Whatsoever the mind perceives in itself, or is the immediate object of perception, thought, or understanding, that I call 'idea'; and the power to produce any idea in our mind, I call 'quality' of the subject wherein that power is." Does not the snowball have the power to produce a sensation of whiteness, in the sense that an organism endowed with eyesight will see white if it looks at a snowball by daylight? But if this is what we mean by saying that the snowball is white or has the quality we call "white," then the snowball is white just as much as it is round. What could be meant by saying, with Locke, that the whiteness is not "in" the snowball? That the snowball does not experience a sensation of whiteness? True enough, but neither does it experience a sensation of roundness. Does it mean that the invisible particles of which the snowball is composed are not themselves white? Evidently Locke had this in mind, for he emphasized that the secondary qualities, unlike the primary qualities, are not possessed by the atoms (the "insensible particles") of which bodies are composed. But if the atoms have no color, no temperature and no smell, does it follow that visible, tangible and smellable aggregates of atoms do not have such qualities either?

The classical critique of Locke's dualism, however, represented in our readings by the selection from Berkeley, took a completely different line: it amounted to an abandonment of the first part of the naive realist creed along with its second part. Berkeley accepted the thesis that the qualities Locke called "secondary" exist "nowhere but in the mind." But he accused Locke of inconsistency in crediting the primary qualities with existence "outside the mind." Locke had argued that it is inconsistent to say that the warmth which is felt at a certain distance from a fire is in the fire but that the pain which is felt as one comes closer to the fire is only in the mind. He had thus called attention to the variation of perceived qualities with variations of the conditions of perception. But Berkeley pointed out that in just the same way the apparent size, shape, weight, velocity of objects varies with conditions of perception. If, for example, the penny appears round from one perspective and elliptical from another perspective, what right do we have to say that the roundness is in the penny or "real" and the ellipticalness only in our mind or "apparent"? Further, he held it to be meaningless to suppose that there exist bodies which have primary qualities but no secondary qualities, on the ground that this is unimaginable: we cannot imagine something that has size and shape without being colored any more than we can imagine something that is colored without having any size or shape. It should be noted that in so arguing Berkeley presupposed the principle that what is intelligible must be imaginable. This principle is the basis of his famous polemic against "abstract general ideas," like triangularity, humanity, materiality, etc. (See the discussion of universals, in the introduction to Section VII.) It is impossible to imagine a triangle which is not a specific kind of triangle, equilateral or isosceles or scalene, large or small; therefore, said Berkeley, an abstract noun like "triangularity" does not stand for an idea at all. General words, like "man," "triangle," "house," are significant not by virtue of standing for an abstract idea, like an idea of a triangle that is not any specific sort of triangle, but by virtue of representing indifferently *any* particular of a certain sort.

Once a philosopher has gone so far, i.e., has deprived physical objects "as they are in themselves" of all specific qualities human beings are acquainted with through sense-perception, two alternatives remain open to him: he may postulate the existence of physical objects while confessing that their nature is completely unknown, that we do not know anything about them. This was the position of Kant who, considerably influenced by Locke, Berkeley and Hume, came to the conclusion that we know nothing about "things in themselves," that empirical knowledge is confined to "phenomena" (his term for Locke's "ideas," meaning literally "appearances"). The second alternative is the thoroughgoing *idealism* of Berkeley, i.e., the doctrine that nothing exists "outside the mind" at all—with the notable exception of minds other than Berkeley's. In order to understand what reasons led Berkeley to such a paradoxical theory, we must take into account his critique of the notion of "substance." Locke had pointed out quite rightly that ordinary men suppose a certain "I know not what" in which the observed qualities inhere, or which "supports" them somehow. We speak of the qualities which a thing "has," implying by our language that the thing is distinct from its qualities. But, said Berkeley, to speak of something, call it "matter," which supports the qualities we sense and is not itself observable, is just to talk nonsense:

It is said *extension* is a *mode* or accident *of matter,* and that matter is the *substratum* that supports it. Now I desire that you would explain what is meant by matter's *supporting* extension . . . It is evident *support* cannot here be taken in its usual or literal sense, as when we say that pillars support a building: in what sense therefore must it be taken? . . . If we inquire into what the most accurate philosophers declare themselves to mean by *material substance,* we shall find them acknowledge, they have no other meaning annexed to those sounds, but the idea of *being in general,* together *with the relative notion of its supporting accidents.* The general idea of being appeareth to me the most abstract and incomprehensible of all other; and as for its supporting accidents, this, as we have just now observed, cannot be understood in the common sense of those words; it must therefore be taken in some other sense, but what that is they do not explain. So that when I consider the *two parts* or branches which make the signification of the words *material substance,* I am convinced there is no distinct meaning annexed to them.

If we talk sense, then we cannot mean by a physical object anything else than the very sum-total of qualities which are misleadingly called the qualities of the object. Note how grammatical similarities may mislead: we speak of the possessions, or of the wives, of Mr. Soandso, and here Mr. Soandso is obviously distinct from his possessions and from his wives but it does not follow that a thing is distinct from its qualities though we use the same particle "of." Mr. Soandso can be seen, touched, and in other ways experienced apart from his possessions. But what about the material substance? We cannot perceive it apart from the sense-qualities. In fact, we do not even know what it would be like to experience *it*. The basis of Berkeley's criticism of this theory is a striking anticipation of the later attacks by the logical positivists on metaphysical theories in general. (Cf. the introduction to Section VIII, pp. 750 ff.)

It is thus that Berkeley arrived at his famous thesis *esse est percipi,* to exist is to be perceived. What he meant is that it is just as meaningless, or self-contradictory, to suppose that something which is not a mind exists without being perceived, as to suppose the existence of a husband without a wife. Of course, it does not at all seem self-contradictory to suppose that the earth and the whole solar system existed long before any perceptions, any form of consciousness, emerged in connection with animal life. Indeed, said Berkeley, I can admit all this, for the entire material universe has always existed in the divine consciousness. Berkeley's theology enabled him to reconcile his philosophy with common-sense realism.

G. E. Moore, one of the early and influential critics of idealism in England, undertook to refute Berkeleyan idealism. What he set out to prove, however, was not that "esse est percipi" is a *false* proposition, but that it is an *unfounded* proposition. Perhaps, said Moore in his challenging essay "The Refutation of Idealism," consciousness is present everywhere in the universe, as asserted by idealists; but is there any reason for supposing this? Now, Berkeley had maintained that green, the quality, is as indistinguishable from a *sensation of* green as a pain is indistinguishable from a sensation of pain. He might have said that a logically correct language, a language which is not philosophically misleading, would speak of green and round and loud sensations just as ordinary English speaks of painful sensations, not of "sensations of pain." But Moore tried to show that Berkeley confused two demonstrably distinct things: the awareness (the sensation) and the object of awareness (the sense-datum). "Esse is held to be percipi," in Moore's words, "because *what is experienced* is held to be identical with *the experience of it*." In any sensation, Moore maintains, we must distinguish between two elements—the awareness or consciousness and that of which we are aware, the object of awareness. A sensation of blue and a sensation of red have the common element, awareness, but they differ as regards the object. It certainly would be a self-contradiction to maintain that an *awareness* of blue could exist without a perceiver. From this, however, it does not follow that the *blue* could not exist without a perceiver. It may not be possible to prove that sense-data which no mind is aware of exist but the supposition is not self-contradictory like the supposition that there are husbands that have no wives.

But some modern philosophers, including perhaps Professor Moore himself at the present time, do not find this refutation of idealism convincing. For it rests on an artificial analysis of sensation into an *act* and an *object,* and there is no evidence, they would say, that there are such "acts" that are distinguishable from their "objects." As has been suggested by Professor C. J. Ducasse in the course of a refutation of Moore's refutation of idealism, seeing green may be like dancing a waltz rather than like eating bread: in saying that a couple is dancing a waltz we are *characterizing* the activity of dancing itself (we might say "they are dancing waltzily"), and analogously we are characterizing our sensation when we say we see green, we are not asserting, according to this analysis, a relation of awareness between our mind and an entity that conceivably might exist apart from that relationship. As against Moore, Stace defends idealism, in a rejoinder ironically entitled "The Refutation of Realism," in a diplomatic way: perhaps Berkeley was right in saying that "unsensed sense-datum" (like a patch of blue which is not part of anybody's visual field) is a contradiction in terms, perhaps Moore was right in denying this. But be this as it may, at least nobody could disprove idealism by proving that the things we perceive exist also when they are not perceived. If the realist chooses to believe in the existence of a physical world outside of consciousness, nobody can prevent him, but it should be understood that this belief is faith, not a belief based on reasons.

Is there any reason for believing that physical objects, i.e., such things as stones, chairs, monkeys, mountains, etc., exist at times when they are not perceived? Philosophers who think there is fall into two groups; those who hold that the belief is justifiable by a *causal argument,* and those who attempt to justify it by means of a *phenomenalist* analysis of what is meant by a "physical object" and by the statement that physical objects exist independently of being perceived. The causal argument starts from Locke's dualistic assumption that what we directly perceive are sense-data (or "percepts" in Russell's terminology) which are numerically and qualitatively distinct from physical objects; for example, visual sense-data are colored, whereas physical objects are alleged to be colorless. It then alleges that physical objects must be postulated in order to account for the remarkable regularity in the succession of sense-data and also for the remarkable similarity between the sense-data perceived by different observers. If you come into a room and seem to see a cat there contrary to expectation, you may at first suspect that you are hallucinating. You look again and touch, you look again and touch again, finding that similar visual sense-data recur and are followed by similar tactual sense-data. You ask other observers to look and touch and find that they report similar sense-data. Of course, you cannot perceive sense-data that are not your own. But you infer from the verbal sense-data you perceive ("yes, John, there *is* a cat there") that the mind you are communicating with—however the belief that there *is* another mind with which you are communicating may be justifiable—perceived feline sense-data similar to those that would cause you under similar circumstances to produce similar sounds. Is it not highly probable, then, that all these similar sense-data are caused by processes originating from a physical cat? In particular, scientists who share the plain man's belief in the existence of a physical world outside the mind tell us that light waves are reflected from the cat's fur into the retina of the observer's eyes and initiate in the optic nerve a process terminating in the visual area of the brain. The cat may not exactly resemble the feline sense-data which it helps produce, but according to this argument it is highly probable that there is a cat at the place and time in question because the occurrence of the sense-data would be highly improbable if there were not. Again, we must assume that the reddish-yellowish and warm sense-data we perceive when gazing at a certain spot in the sky are produced by processes originating from the sun the physicist talks about, though the latter is not at all similar to the perceived sun, being neither yellow nor hot. Such is the view held by many physicists and philosophers, among them Sir Arthur Eddington and Bertrand Russell, who in this respect are unmistakably descendants of

Locke. Russell even goes to the extreme of affirming that whatever a man *perceives,* in contradistinction to what he *infers* as the external cause of his perceptions, is in his own brain; for it is a percept (sense-datum), not a physical object, and the locus of a man's percepts, says Russell, is his brain. If the reader should, legitimately, be puzzled by this statement, it is advisable that he ponder the semantic question in what sense of "in" perceptions can be said to be in a brain.

The phenomenalist challenges, in the first place, the dualism which under-lies the causal argument, the dualism between sense-data and physical objects. Chiefly two arguments have been used to support Locke's claim that we never directly perceive a physical object: a) the argument from illusions, b) the physical argument. A) says that the identification of the perceived object with the physical object in the case of illusions, like those of the bent stick and the elliptical penny, would lead to contradiction, and that it would be arbi-trary to distinguish perceived and physical object in the case of illusory perception and to identify them in the case of real perception. But surely this is wrong. It would of course be contradictory to say that the stick we perceive is both straight and bent, but why not say, as is customary, that we see a real stick which *appears* crooked? According to phenomenalism, to ascribe a par-ticular quality to an object is to predict how it would appear under specified conditions of perception. Thus, when we say that the stick is straight though it now appears (to the eye) to be crooked, we are saying that it would feel straight if it were touched, and/or that it would look straight in a relatively non-refracting medium like air. There is no contradiction in saying that a thing appears to have one quality if observed in one way, and appears to have another quality if observed in a different way. b) Physicists have reason to believe that when we see something, light waves that travel at enormous yet finite speed have just reached our eyes after having been reflected or emitted from the thing we see. And physiologists have reason to believe that between the moment when light stimulates the optic nerve and the actual sensation neural energy travels up to the visual area of the brain. Since there is, then, a tiny time-interval separating the sensation from the moment when the described physical process, the external stimulation of the organism, gets started, it is concluded that the sense-datum cannot be identical with the physical object. Now, if by the "sense-datum" is meant *that which* one directly perceives, the conclusion of the physical argument certainly does not follow. For though a visual sensation is an event that is perfectly distinct from any physical events, including reflections of light-waves and stimulations of optic nerves, nobody claims that a visual sensation is ever an *object* of perception: one *has* a visual sensation when one sees something, but it would not even make sense to speak of *seeing* one's visual sensation (or for that matter anyone else's). In other words: sensations are undoubtedly different from physical objects, but since it would be absurd to say that we *perceive* sensations, the distinctness of sensations from physical objects does not justify the contention that we don't perceive physical objects. Furthermore, to deny on the authority of scientific theories that we ever see physical objects or processes would seem to be putting the cart before the horse, since it is hard to see how theories which make assertions about physical objects and processes could be verified if physical objects and processes were never seen at all. How, so a critic of the physical argument for dualism might ask, could physiologists verify their theory about the physiological causation of sensations if they could not at least perceive nervous systems and what goes on in them, but first had to infer their existence from their own "percepts"? Wouldn't this very inference *presuppose* the theory to be verified? If, on the other hand, the physical argument merely purports to establish that the sensation is distinct from the sensed physical object, that is so obvious that no argument is needed to support it. Surely it does not follow that the objects which we sense are not physical. If there were good reasons for denying that the physical sun is red and hot and that the physical table is brown and solid, then, indeed, we could not consistently hold that we see the physical sun and physical tables. But a phenomenalist would deny that there are good reasons for such a denial. He would reject Locke's dualism between secondary and primary qualities. "The sun is red" *means* "the sun appears red under such and such conditions," "the table is solid" *means* "the table feels solid and there are no visible holes in it" (though there may be invisible holes between invisible electrons), which propositions are undeniably true and perfectly compatible with physical theory.

The phenomenalist justification of the common sense belief in the existence of unperceived physical objects is inseparable from the phenomenalist analysis of propositions about physical objects. Berkeley had argued against Locke that when a plain man says "there is a tree in front of me" he does not mean "my present tree-like sense-data are caused by a physical object which cannot be perceived but only inferred, and which is in most respects dissimilar to the sense-data," but just "my present visual field contains tree-like sense-data" (at least Berkeley defended the latter analysis when he was oblivious of God). The phenomenalist agrees with the negative part and disagrees with the positive part of Berkeley's claim. Like Berkeley, he rejects the dualistic conception of physical objects on the ground that it makes propositions about physical objects wholly unverifiable whereas plain men mean something verifiable by such propositions as "there is a tree at this place": for how could one ever find out whether the inference from the sense-data to the physical object is valid? If I see a shadow and infer that there is a man behind me who casts the shadow, the inference can be verified by turning around and seeing the man directly. But according to the dualist no physical object could conceivably be directly perceived; when I turn my head in order to verify my interpretation of the shadow, I still only perceive my sense-data, there is nothing else for me to perceive, according to the dualist. However, the phenomenalist offers an analysis of such propositions which is compatible with the belief that physical objects exist when they are not perceived (not even by God!): "there is a table in room 210" does not entail that table-like sensations actually occur in conjunction with room-210-like sensations; it only entails (and is entailed by) the proposition that table-like sensations *would* occur *if* room-210-like sensations were to occur. When you say "the vase is fragile" you do not mean that it actually breaks at the moment, nor do you even predict that it ever will break; you only make the *conditional* prediction that it would break if it were dropped. Similarly, says the phenomenalist, to assert the existence of a physical object of kind K is not to assert that K-like sensations occur nor that they will ever occur; but it is to assert that K-like sensations would occur if certain conditions, such as sensations of looking in a certain direction at a certain time, were fulfilled.

To be quite accurate, we ought to distinguish two forms of phenomenalism. According to one form, statements about physical objects are to be analyzed in terms of *sensations* that occur under specified conditions; according to the other form they are to be analyzed in terms of *sense-data* that are perceived under specified conditions. Sensations are commonly regarded as mental events whose occurrence can be known with absolute certainty by one and only one mind; thus many philosophers would characterize my seeing a blue, round patch against a white background as a sensation, and they hold that a proposition asserting its occurrence ("I see a blue, round patch") can be directly known to be true by myself but can only be inferred with probability by other people. Other phenomenalists, however, speak of *perception of sense-data,* where sense-data are not "parts" of any mind though perceptions of sense-data are mental events. The latter form of phenomenalism is obviously bound up with the analysis of sensations into an awareness and a (possibly non-physical) object of awareness in terms of which Moore criticized Berkeley and which some contemporary philosophers of perception reject. It should be noted, however, that the use of the terminology of "sense-data" and "perceptions of sense-data" does not necessarily commit a phenomenalist to such a controversial theory. Sometimes the use of the word "sense-datum" is just a convenient device for indicating that no claim about the physical world is being made, that one is merely describing one's sense-experience. For example, if one says in ordinary language "I see a red apple," one thereby implies that *there is* a red apple in the environment; if it turns out that there is not, one will retract the statement as false, saying "I thought I saw a red apple but since, as it turned out, there is no such thing here, I could not really have seen one." The technical statement "I see a sense-datum of a red apple (a red-apple-like sense-datum)" may simply serve the purpose of annulling, as it were, the implication that the perception is veridical, that there is a physical apple at the place and time in question. In other words, it focuses attention on the character of the sense-experience, and is easily translatable into ordinary, non-technical language: "I seem to see a red apple." Whiteley, for example, uses the terminology of sense-data in formulating and discussing phenomenalism, but it is unlikely that he thereby intends to impute to phenomenalists the awareness-object analysis of sensations which was central in Moore's "Refutation of Idealism."

Phenomenalists are painfully aware of the difficulty to express the "conditions" under which certain kinds of sense-data regularly occur if a certain kind of physical object exists in a language that mentions only sensations, not physical objects and events. For example, a phenomenalist analysis of "a boy will enter the room at exactly 4 P.M. July 17, 1956" would run somewhat as follows: "if sensations of looking at the door occur at 4 P.M. July 17, 1956, then simultaneously sensations of a boy entering will occur." But this analysis is not purely phenomenalistic, because a state of a physical clock is referred to; the phenomenalist would therefore have to go on to translate "it is 4 P.M. July 17, 1956" into the language of sensations. The phenomenalist analysis of physical propositions also runs into the following difficulty. A conditional statement like "if a visually normal observer were to look at the door, he would see a boy entering" contains words that refer to physical objects like "observer," "door," "boy." It therefore does not express an analysis in terms of sense-data exclusively. In order to satisfy this requirement we must, in the first place, refrain from mentioning any sentient organisms with eyes and ears, and secondly replace "looking at the door" by "having a sensation of looking at the door" or "seeming to look at the door," so meant that the statement "a sensation of looking at the door occurs" only characterizes the sensation without entailing that there is a physical door which is involved in a physical stimulation of an organism. Similarly, "there occurs a sensation of a boy entering the door" must be so meant that it could be true even if no boys or doors existed (in the sense in which it could be true that, in a state of delirium, one seems to see a dragon although there are no dragons). But now, if "a boy enters the door at time t" were synonymous with "if a sensation of looking at the door occurred at t, then a sensation of a boy entering would occur at t," then it would be a contradiction to suppose that a boy enters the door at t, a sensation of looking at the door occurs at t, yet no sensation of a boy entering the door occurs at t. And this sort of thing clearly might happen, since "a sensation of looking at the door occurs" is not allowed to entail "somebody actually looks at the door." For example, someone might look at a picture of the door which resembles the door so closely that he mistakenly believes that he is looking at the door itself. Clearly he will not see a boy entering the picture of the door and yet a boy may really enter the real door. It seems, then, that a phenomenalist is caught in a dilemma: either he mentions physical objects and physical conditions in his translation or else his translation is demonstrably inadequate. But be this as it may, if such translations into the language of sense-data are feasible, then the phenomenalist can show that common-sense realism is justifiable by ordinary inductive reasoning: each time I had sensations of entering room 210, there followed table-like sensations; this is my basis for believing that even now, while I am far from room 210, there is a table there. What is the content of this belief? Just, says the phenomenalist, that if sensations of entering room 210 recurred now, they would again be followed by table-like sensations: same cause, same effect!

Some philosophers, however, feel that this is not the sort of thing plain men (including themselves in their non-academic life) mean when they assert the existence of an unperceived physical object. When they are pressed by the phenomenalist to explain what else is meant by such assertions, they usually cannot do it. But they might counter that there is no more reason to suppose that the physical language must, if it is meaningful, be reducible to the language of sensations than there is for supposing that the language of sensations must, if it is meaningful, be reducible to the physical language. It does not seem possible to express the meanings of such statements describing subjective states as "I see red," "John feels pain in his left hand" in physical language, i. e., language describing publicly observable events like movements of an organism, or physiological processes. Perhaps the converse sort of reduction favored by phenomenalists, a reduction of statements about physical objects and processes to statements about actual and possible sensations, is equally unfeasible.

A. P.

47   Sense Qualities and
Material Substances

John Locke

The Idea of Material Substance

I... IDEAS OF SUBSTANCES, HOW MADE. —The mind being, as I have declared, furnished with a great number of the simple ideas, conveyed in by the senses, as they are found in exterior things, or by reflection on its own operations, takes notice also, that a certain number of these simple ideas go constantly together; which being presumed to belong to one thing, and words being suited to common apprehensions, and made use of for quick dispatch, are called, so united in one subject, by one name: which, by inadvertency, we are apt afterward to talk of, and consider as one simple idea, which indeed is a complication of many ideas together; because, as I have said, not imagining how these simple ideas can subsist by themselves, we accustom ourselves to suppose some substratum wherein they do subsist, and from which they do result; which therefore we call substance.

Our idea of substance in general.—So that if any one will examine himself concerning his notion of pure substance in general, he will find he has no other idea of it at all, but only a supposition of he knows not what support of such qualities, which are capable of producing simple ideas in us; which qualities are commonly called accidents. If any one should be asked, what is the subject wherein colour or weight inheres, he would have nothing to say, but the solid extended parts: and if he were demanded, what is it that solidity and extension adhere in, he would not be in a much better case than the Indian, who, saying that the world

[This selection consists of sections 1–4 of Chapter XXIII, Book II, and sections 7–19, 23, and 26 of Chapter VIII, Book II, of Locke's *Essay Concerning Human Understanding,* a book first published in 1690.]

was supported by a great elephant, was asked what the elephant rested on; to which his answer was, a great tortoise. But being again pressed to know what gave support to the broad-backed tortoise, replied, something he knew not what. And thus here, as in all other cases where we use words without having clear and distinct ideas, we talk like children; who being questioned what such a thing is, which they know not, readily give this satisfactory answer, that it is something; which in truth signifies no more, when so used either by children or men, but that they know not what; and that the thing they pretend to know and talk of, is what they have no distinct idea of at all, and so are perfectly ignorant of it, and in the dark. The idea then we have, to which we give the general name substance, being nothing but the supposed, but unknown support of those qualities we find existing, which we imagine cannot subsist, *sine re substante,* without something to support them, we call that support *substantia;* which, according to the true import of the word, is in plain English, standing or upholding.

Of the sorts of substances.—An obscure and relative idea of substance in general being thus made, we come to have the ideas of particular sorts of substances, by collecting such combinations of simple ideas, as are by experience and observation of men's senses taken notice of to exist together, and are therefore supposed to flow from the particular internal constitution, or unknown essence of that substance. Thus we come to have the ideas of a man, horse, gold, water, etc., of which substances, whether any one has any other clear idea, farther than of certain simple ideas co-existent together, I appeal to every man's own experience. It is the ordinary qualities observable in iron, or a diamond, put together, that make the true complex idea of those substances, which a smith or a jeweller commonly knows better than a philosopher; who, whatever substantial forms he may talk of, has no other idea of those substances, than what is framed by a collection of those simple ideas which are to be found in them; only we must take notice, that our complex ideas of substances, besides all those simple ideas they are made up of, have always the confused idea of something to which they belong, and in which they subsist. And therefore, when we speak of any sort of substances, we say it is a thing having such or such qualities: as body is a thing that is extended, figured, and capable of motion; spirit, a thing capable of thinking; and so hardness, friability, and power to draw iron, we say, are qualities to be found in a loadstone. These, and the like fashions of speaking, intimate that the substance is supposed always something besides the extension, figure, solidity, motion, thinking, or other observable ideas, though we know not what it is.

No less idea of substance in general.—Hence, when we talk or think of any particular sort of corporeal substances, as horse, stone, etc., though the idea we have of either of them be but the complication or collection of those several simple ideas of sensible qualities, which we used to find united in the thing called horse or stone; yet because we cannot conceive how they should subsist alone, or one in another, we suppose them existing in and supported by some common subject; which support we denote by the name substance, though it be certain we have no clear or distinct idea of that thing we suppose a support. . . .

Primary and Secondary Qualities

Ideas in the mind, qualities in bodies. To discover the nature of our ideas the better, and to discourse of them intelligibly, it will be convenient to distinguish them, as they are ideas or perceptions in our minds, and as they are modifications of matter in the bodies that cause such perceptions in us; that so we may not think (as perhaps usually is done) that they are exactly the images and resemblances of something inherent in the subject; most of those of sensation being in the mind no more the likeness of something existing without us than the names that stand for them are the likeness of our ideas, which yet upon hearing they are apt to excite in us.

Whatsoever the mind perceives in itself, or is the immediate object of perception, thought, or understanding, that I call "idea;" and the power to produce any idea in our mind, I call "quality" of the subject wherein that power is. Thus a snowball having the power to produce in us the ideas of white, cold, and round, the powers to produce those ideas in us as they are in the snowball, I call "qualities;" and as they are sensations or perceptions in our understandings, I call them "ideas;" which ideas, if I speak of them sometimes as in the things themselves, I would be understood to mean those qualities in the objects which produce them in us.

Primary qualities. Qualities thus considered in bodies are, First, such as are utterly inseparable from the body, in what estate soever it be; such as, in all the alterations and changes it suffers, all the force can be used upon it, it constantly keeps; and such as sense constantly finds in every particle of matter which has bulk enough to be perceived, and the mind finds inseparable from every particle of matter, though less than to make itself singly be perceived by our senses: *v.g.,* take a grain of wheat, divide it into two parts, each part has still solidity, extension, figure, and mobility; divide it again, and it retains still the same qualities: and so divide it on till the parts become insensible, they must retain still each of them all those qualities. For, division (which is all that a mill or pestle or any other body does upon another, in reducing it to insensible parts) can never take away either solidity, extension, figure, or mobility from any body, but only makes two or more distinct separate masses of matter of that which was but one before; all which distinct masses, reckoned as so many distinct bodies, after division, make a certain number. These I call *original* or *primary* qualities of body, which I think we may observe to produce simple ideas in us, viz., solidity, extension, figure, motion or rest, and number.

Secondary qualities. Secondly, such qualities, which in truth are nothing in the objects themselves, but powers to produce various sensations in us by their primary qualities, *i.e.,* by the bulk, figure, texture, and motion of their insensible parts, as colours, sounds, tastes, etc., these I call *secondary* qualities. To these might be added a third sort, which are allowed to be barely powers, though they are as much real qualities in the subject as those which I, to comply with the common way of speaking, call qualities, but, for distinction, *secondary* qualities. For, the power in fire to produce a new colour or consistence in wax or clay by its primary qualities, is as much a quality in fire as the power it has to produce in me a new idea or sensation of warmth or burning, which I felt not before, by the same primary qualities, viz., the bulk, texture, and motion of its insensible parts.

How primary qualities produce their ideas. The next thing to be considered is, how bodies produce ideas in us; and that is manifestly by impulse, the only way which we can conceive bodies operate in.

If, then, external objects be not united to our minds when they produce ideas in it, and yet we perceive these original qualities in such of them as singly fall under our senses, it is evident that some motion must be thence continued by our nerves or animal spirits, by some parts of our bodies, to the brain or the seat of sensation, there to produce in our minds the particular ideas we have of them. And since the extension, figure, number, and motion of bodies of an observable bigness, may be perceived at a distance by the sight, it is evident some singly imperceptible bodies must come from them to the eyes, and thereby convey to the brain some motion which produces these ideas which we have of them in us.

How secondary. After the same manner that the ideas of these original qualities are produced in us, we may conceive that the ideas of secondary qualities are also produced, viz., by the operation of insensible particles on our senses. For it being manifest that there are bodies, and good store of bodies, each whereof are so small that we cannot by any of our senses discover either their bulk, figure, or motion (as is evident in the particles of the air and water, and others extremely smaller than those, perhaps as much smaller than the particles of air or water as the particles of air or water are smaller than pease or hailstones): let us suppose at present that the different motions and figures, bulk and number, of such particles, affecting the several organs of our senses, produce in us those different sensations which we have from the colours and smells of bodies, *v.g.,* that a violet, by the impulse of such insensible particles of matter of peculiar figures and bulks, and in different degrees and modifications of their motions, causes the ideas of the blue colour and sweet scent of that flower to be produced in our minds; it being no more impossible to conceive that God should annex such ideas to such motions with which they have no similitude, than that he should annex the idea of pain to the motion of a piece of steel dividing our flesh, with which that idea hath no resemblance.

What I have said concerning colours and smells may be understood also of tastes and sounds, and other like sensible qualities; which, whatever reality we by mistake attribute to them, are in truth nothing in the objects themselves, but powers to produce various sensations in us, and depend on those primary qualities, viz., bulk, figure, texture, and motion of parts, as I have said.

Ideas of primary qualities are resemblances; of secondary, not. From whence I think it is easy to draw this observation, that the ideas of primary qualities of bodies are resemblances of them, and their patterns do really exist in the bodies themselves; but the ideas produced in us by these secondary qualities have no resemblance of them at all. There is nothing like our ideas existing in the bodies themselves. They are, in the bodies we denominate from them, only a power to produce those sensations in us; and what is sweet, blue, or warm in idea, is but the certain bulk figure, and motion of the insensible parts in the bodies themselves, which we call so.

Flame is denominated *hot* and *light;* snow, *white* and *cold;* and manna, *white* and *sweet,* from the ideas they produce in us which qualities are commonly thought to be the same in those bodies that those ideas are in us, the one the perfect resemblance of the other, as they are in a mirror; and it would by most men be judged very extravagant, if one should say otherwise. And yet he that will consider that the same fire that at one distance produces in us the sensation of warmth, does at a nearer approach produce in us the far different sensation of pain, ought to bethink himself what reason he has to say, that his idea of warmth which was produced in him by the fire, is actually in the fire, and his idea of pain which the same fire produced in him the same way is not in the fire. Why is whiteness and coldness in snow and pain not, when it produces the one and the other idea in us, and can do neither by the bulk, figure, number and motion of its solid parts?

The particular bulk, number, figure, and motion of the parts of fire or snow are really in them, whether any one's senses perceive them or no; and therefore they may be called *real* qualities, because they really exist in those bodies. But light, heat, whiteness, or coldness, are no more really in them than sickness or pain is in manna. Take away the sensation of them; let not the eyes see light or colours, nor the ears hear sounds; let the palate not taste, nor the nose smell; and all colours, tastes, odours, and sounds, as they are such particular ideas, vanish and cease, and are reduced to their causes, *i.e.,* bulk, figure, and motion of parts.

A piece of manna of a sensible bulk is able to produce in us the idea of a round or square figure; and, by being removed from one place to another, the idea of motion. This idea of motion represents it as it really is in the manna moving; a circle or square are the same, whether in idea or existence, in the mind or in the manna; and this both motion and figure are really in the manna, whether we take notice of them or no: this every body is ready to agree to. Besides, manna, by the bulk, figure, texture, and motion of its parts, has a power to produce the sensations of sickness, and sometimes of acute pains or grippings, in us. That these ideas of sickness and pain are not in the manna, but effects of its operations on us, and are nowhere when we feel them not; this also every one readily agrees to. And yet men are hardly to be brought to think that sweetness and whiteness are not really in manna, which are but the effects of the operations of manna by the motion, size, and figure of its particles on the eyes and palate; as the pain and sickness caused by manna, are confessedly nothing but the effects of its operations on the stomach and guts by the size, motion, and figure of its insensible parts (for by nothing else can a body operate, as has been proved): as if it could not operate on the eyes and palate, and thereby produce in the mind particular distinct ideas which in itself it has not, as well as we allow it can operate on the guts and stomach, and thereby produce distinct ideas which in itself it has not. These ideas being all effects of the operations of manna on several parts of our bodies, by the size, figure, number, and motion of its parts, why those produced by the eyes and palate should rather be thought to be really in the manna than those produced by the stomach and guts: or why the pain and sickness, ideas that are the effects of manna, should be thought to be nowhere when they are not felt: and yet the sweetness and whiteness, effects of the same manna on other parts of the body, by ways equally as unknown, should be thought to exist in the manna, when they are not seen nor tasted; would need some reason to explain.

Ideas of primary qualities are resemblances; of secondary, not. Let us consider the red and white colours in porphyry: hinder light but from striking on it, and its colours vanish; it no longer produces any such ideas in us. Upon the return of light, it produces these appearances on us again. Can any one think any real alterations are made in the porphyry by the presence or absence of light, and that those ideas of whiteness and redness are really in porphyry in the light, when it is plain it has no colour in the dark? It has indeed such a configuration of particles, both night and day, as are apt, by the rays of light rebounding from some parts of the hard stone, to produce in us the idea of redness, and from others the idea of whiteness. But whiteness or redness are not in it at any time, but such a texture that hath the power to produce such a sensation in us. . . .

. . . *Three sorts of qualities in bodies.* The qualities then that are in bodies, rightly considered, are of three sorts:

First. The bulk, figure, number, situation, and motion or rest of their solid parts; those are in them, whether we perceive them or no; and when they are of that size that we can discover them, we have by these an idea of the thing as it is in itself, as is plain in artificial things. These I call *primary* qualities.

Secondly. The power that is in any body, by reason of its insensible primary qualities, to operate after a peculiar manner on any of our senses, and thereby produce in us the different ideas of several colours, sounds, smells, tastes, &c. These are usually called *sensible* qualities.

Thirdly. The power that is in any body, by reason of the particular constitution of its primary qualities, to make such a change in the bulk, figure, texture, and motion of another body, as to make it operate on our senses differently from what it did before. Thus the sun has a power to make wax white, and fire, to make lead fluid. These are usually called "powers."

The first of these, as has been said, I think may be properly called real, original, or primary qualities, because they are in the things themselves, whether they are perceived or no; and upon their different modifications it is that the secondary qualities depend.

The other two are only powers to act differently upon other things, which powers result from the different modifications of these primary qualities. . . .

. . . *Secondary qualities twofold: first, immediately perceivable; secondly, mediately perceivable.* To conclude: Besides those before-mentioned primary qualities in bodies, viz., bulk, figure, extension, number, and motion of their solid parts, all the rest whereby we take notice of bodies, and distinguish them one from another, are nothing else but several powers in them depending on those primary qualities, whereby they are fitted, either by immediately operating on our bodies, to produce several different ideas in us; or else by operating on other bodies, so to change their primary qualities as to render them capable of producing ideas in us different from what before they did. The former of these, I think, may be called secondary qualities immediately perceivable; the latter, secondary qualities mediately perceivable.

48 The First Dialogue Between Hylas and Philonous

George Berkeley

Philonous. GOOD MORROW, HYLAS: I DID not expect to find you abroad so early.

HYLAS. It is indeed something unusual; but my thoughts were so taken up with a subject I was discoursing of last night, that finding I could not sleep, I resolved to rise and take a turn in the garden.

PHIL. It happened well, to let you see what innocent and agreeable pleasures you lose every morning. Can there be a pleasanter time of the day, or a more delightful season of the year? That purple sky, those wild but sweet notes of birds, the fragrant bloom upon the trees and flowers, the gentle influence of the rising sun, these and a thousand nameless beauties of nature inspire the soul with secret transports; its faculties too being at this time fresh and lively, are fit for those meditations, which the solitude of a garden and tranquillity of the morning naturally dispose us to. But I am afraid I interrupt your thoughts: for you seemed very intent on something.

HYL. It is true, I was, and shall be obliged to you if you will permit me to go on in the same vein; not that I would by any means deprive myself of your company, for my thoughts always flow more easily in conversation with a friend, than when I am alone: but my request is, that you would suffer me to impart my reflexions to you.

PHIL. With all my heart, it is what I should have requested myself if you had not prevented me.

HYL. I was considering the odd fate of those men who have in all ages, through an affectation of being distinguished from the vulgar, or some unaccountable turn of thought, pretended either to believe nothing

[This selection comprises the entire first of the *Three Dialogues Between Hylas and Philonous*, a work first published in 1713.]

at all, or to believe the most extravagant things in the world. This how-ever might be borne, if their paradoxes and scepticism did not draw after them some consequences of general disadvantage to mankind. But the mischief lieth here; that when men of less leisure see them who are sup-posed to have spent their whole time in the pursuits of knowledge pro-fessing an entire ignorance of all things, or advancing such notions as are repugnant to plain and commonly received principles, they will be tempted to entertain suspicions concerning the most important truths, which they had hitherto held sacred and unquestionable.

PHIL. I entirely agree with you, as to the ill tendency of the affected doubts of some philosophers, and fantastical conceits of others. I am even so far gone of late in this way of thinking, that I have quitted several of the sublime notions I had got in their schools for vulgar opinions. And I give it you on my word; since this revolt from metaphysical notions to the plain dictates of nature and common sense, I find my understanding strangely enlightened, so that I can now easily comprehend a great many things which before were all mystery and riddle.

HYL. I am glad to find there was nothing in the accounts I heard of you.

PHIL. Pray, what were those?

The Notion of Material Substance

HYL. You were represented, in last night's conversation, as one who maintained the most extravagant opinion that ever entered into the mind of man, to wit, that there is no such thing as *material substance* in the world.

PHIL. That there is no such thing as what *philosophers* call *material substance,* I am seriously persuaded: but, if I were made to see anything absurd or sceptical in this, I should then have the same reason to re-nounce this that I imagine I have now to reject the contrary opinion.

HYL. What! can anything be more fantastical, more repugnant to Common Sense, or a more manifest piece of Scepticism, than to believe there is no such thing as *matter?*

PHIL. Softly, good Hylas. What if it should prove that you, who hold there is, are, by virtue of that opinion, a greater sceptic, and main-tain more paradoxes and repugnances to Common Sense, than I who believe no such thing?

HYL. You may as soon persuade me, the part is greater than the whole, as that, in order to avoid absurdity and Scepticism, I should ever be obliged to give up my opinion in this point.

PHIL. Well then, are you content to admit that opinion for true, which upon examination shall appear most agreeable to Common Sense, and re-mote from Scepticism?

HYL. With all my heart. Since you are for raising disputes about the plainest things in nature, I am content for once to hear what you have to say.

PHIL. Pray, Hylas, what do you mean by a *sceptic?*

HYL. I mean what all men mean—one that doubts of everything.

PHIL. He then who entertains no doubt concerning some particular point, with regard to that point cannot be thought a sceptic.

HYL. I agree with you.

PHIL. Whether doth doubting consist in embracing the affirmative or negative side of a question?

HYL. In neither; for whoever understands English cannot but know that *doubting* signifies a suspense between both.

PHIL. He then that denies any point, can no more be said to doubt of it, than he who affirmeth it with the same degree of assurance.

HYL. True.

PHIL. And, consequently, for such his denial is no more to be esteemed a sceptic than the other.

HYL. I acknowledge it.

PHIL. How cometh it to pass then, Hylas, that you pronounce me a *sceptic,* because I deny what you affirm, to wit, the existence of Matter? Since, for aught you can tell, I am as peremptory in my denial, as you in your affirmation.

HYL. Hold, Philonous, I have been a little out in my definition; but every false step a man makes in discourse is not to be insisted on. I said indeed that a *sceptic* was one who doubted of everything; but I should have added, or who denies the reality and truth of things.

PHIL. What things? Do you mean the principles and theorems of sciences? But these you know are universal intellectual notions, and consequently independent of Matter. The denial therefore of this doth not imply the denying them.

HYL. I grant it. But are there no other things? What think you of distrusting the senses, of denying the real existence of sensible things, or pretending to know nothing of them. Is not this sufficient to denominate a man a *sceptic?*

PHIL. Shall we therefore examine which of us it is that denies the reality of sensible things, or professes the greatest ignorance of them; since, if I take you rightly, he is to be esteemed the greatest *sceptic?*

HYL. That is what I desire.

The Nature of Sensible Things

PHIL. What mean you by Sensible Things?

HYL. Those things which are perceived by the senses. Can you imagine that I mean anything else?

PHIL. Pardon me, Hylas, if I am desirous clearly to apprehend your notions, since this may much shorten our inquiry. Suffer me then to ask you this farther question. Are those things only perceived by the senses which are perceived immediately? Or, may those things properly be said to be *sensible* which are perceived mediately, or not without the intervention of others?

HYL. I do not sufficiently understand you.

PHIL. In reading a book, what I immediately perceive are the letters; but mediately, or by means of these, are suggested to my mind the notions of God, virtue, truth, &c. Now, that the letters are truly sensible things, or perceived by sense, there is no doubt: but I would know whether you take the things suggested by them to be so too.

HYL. No, certainly: it were absurd to think *God* or *virtue* sensible things; though they may be signified and suggested to the mind by sensible marks, with which they have an arbitrary connexion.

PHIL. It seems then, that by *sensible things* you mean those only which can be perceived *immediately* by sense?

HYL. Right.

PHIL. Doth it not follow from this, that though I see one part of the sky red, and another blue, and that my reason doth thence evidently conclude there must be some cause of that diversity of colours, yet that cause cannot be said to be a sensible thing, or perceived by the sense of seeing?

HYL. It doth.

PHIL. In like manner, though I hear variety of sounds, yet I cannot be said to hear the causes of those sounds?

HYL. You cannot.

PHIL. And when by my touch I perceive a thing to be hot and heavy, I cannot say, with any truth or propriety, that I feel the cause of its heat or weight?

HYL. To prevent any more questions of this kind, I tell you once for all, that by *sensible things* I mean those only which are perceived by sense; and that in truth the senses perceive nothing which they do not perceive *immediately:* for they make no inferences. The deducing therefore of causes or occasions from effects and appearances, which alone are perceived by sense, entirely relates to reason.

PHIL. This point then is agreed between us—That *sensible things are those only which are immediately perceived by sense.* You will farther inform me, whether we immediately perceive by sight anything beside light, and colours, and figures; or by hearing, anything but sounds; by the palate, anything beside taste; by the smell, beside odours; or by the touch, more than tangible qualities.

HYL. We do not.

PHIL. It seems, therefore, that if you take away all sensible qualities, there remains nothing sensible?

HYL. I grant it.

PHIL. Sensible things therefore are nothing else but so many sensible qualities, or combinations of sensible qualities?

HYL. Nothing else.

PHIL. *Heat* then is a sensible thing?

HYL. Certainly.

PHIL. Doth the *reality* of sensible things consist in being perceived? or, is it something distinct from their being perceived, and that bears no relation to the mind?

HYL. To *exist* is one thing, and to be *perceived* is another.

PHIL. I speak with regard to sensible things only. And of these I ask, whether by their real existence you mean a subsistence exterior to the mind, and distinct from their being perceived?

HYL. I mean a real absolute being, distinct from, and without any relation to, their being perceived.

PHIL. Heat therefore, if it be allowed a real being, must exist without the mind?

HYL. It must.

PHIL. Tell me, Hylas, is this real existence equally compatible to all degrees of heat, which we perceive; or is there any reason why we should attribute it to some, and deny it to others? And if there be, pray let me know that reason.

HYL. Whatever degree of heat we perceive by sense, we may be sure the same exists in the object that occasions it.

PHIL. What! the greatest as well as the least?

HYL. I tell you, the reason is plainly the same in respect of both. They are both perceived by sense; nay, the greater degree of heat is more sensibly perceived; and consequently, if there is any difference, we are more certain of its real existence than we can be of the reality of a lesser degree.

PHIL. But is not the most vehement and intense degree of heat a very great pain?

HYL. No one can deny it.

PHIL. And is any unperceiving thing capable of pain or pleasure?

HYL. No, certainly.

PHIL. Is your material substance a senseless being, or a being endowed with sense and perception?

HYL. It is senseless without doubt.

PHIL. It cannot therefore be the subject of pain?

HYL. By no means.

PHIL. Nor consequently of the greatest heat perceived by sense, since you acknowledge this to be no small pain?

HYL. I grant it.

PHIL. What shall we say then of your external object; is it a material substance, or no?

HYL. It is a material substance with the sensible qualities inhering in it.

Sensible Things Exist Only in the Mind

PHIL. How then can a great heat exist in it, since you own it cannot in a material substance? I desire you would clear this point.

HYL. Hold, Philonous, I fear I was out in yielding intense heat to be a pain. It should seem rather, that pain is something distinct from heat, and the consequence or effect of it.

PHIL. Upon putting your hand near the fire, do you perceive one simple uniform sensation, or two distinct sensations?

HYL. But one simple sensation.

PHIL. Is not the heat immediately perceived?

HYL. It is.

PHIL. And the pain?

HYL. True.

PHIL. Seeing therefore they are both immediately perceived at the same time, and the fire affects you only with one simple or uncompounded idea, it follows that this same simple idea is both the intense heat immediately perceived, and the pain; and, consequently, that the intense heat immediately perceived is nothing distinct from a particular sort of pain.

HYL. It seems so.

PHIL. Again, try in your thoughts, Hylas, if you can conceive a vehement sensation to be without pain or pleasure.

HYL. I cannot.

PHIL. Or can you frame to yourself an idea of sensible pain or pleasure in general, abstracted from every particular idea of heat, cold, tastes, smells, etc.?

HYL. I do not find that I can.

PHIL. Doth it not therefore follow, that sensible pain is nothing distinct from those sensations or ideas, in an intense degree?

HYL. It is undeniable; and, to speak the truth, I begin to suspect a very great heat cannot exist but in a mind perceiving it.

PHIL. What! are you then in that sceptical state of suspense between affirming and denying?

HYL. I think I may be positive in the point. A very violent and painful heat cannot exist without the mind.

PHIL. It hath not therefore, according to you, any *real* being?

HYL. I own it.

PHIL. Is it therefore certain, that there is no body in nature really hot?

HYL. I have not denied there is any real heat in bodies. I only say, there is no such thing as an intense real heat.

PHIL. But, did you not say before that all degrees of heat were equally real; or, if there was any difference, that the greater were more undoubtedly real than the lesser?

HYL. True: but it was because I did not then consider the ground there is for distinguishing between them, which I now plainly see. And it is this:

because intense heat is nothing else but a particular kind of painful sensation; and pain cannot exist but in a perceiving being; it follows that no intense heat can really exist in an unperceiving corporeal substance. But this is no reason why we should deny heat in an inferior degree to exist in such a substance.

PHIL. But how shall we be able to discern those degrees of heat which exist only in the mind from those which exist without it?

HYL. That is no difficult matter. You know the least pain cannot exist unperceived; whatever, therefore, degree of heat is a pain exists only in the mind. But, as for all other degrees of heat, nothing obliges us to think the same of them.

PHIL. I think you granted before that no unperceiving being was capable of pleasure, any more than of pain.

HYL. I did.

PHIL. And is not warmth, or a more gentle degree of heat than what causes uneasiness, a pleasure?

HYL. What then?

PHIL. Consequently, it cannot exist without the mind in an unperceiving substance, or body.

HYL. So it seems.

PHIL. Since, therefore, as well those degrees of heat that are not painful, as those that are, can exist only in a thinking substance; may we not conclude that external bodies are absolutely incapable of any degree of heat whatsoever?

HYL. On second thoughts, I do not think it so evident that warmth is a pleasure as that a great degree of heat is a pain.

PHIL. I do not pretend that warmth is as great a pleasure as heat is a pain. But, if you grant it to be even a small pleasure, it serves to make good my conclusion.

HYL. I could rather call it an *indolence*. It seems to be nothing more than a privation of both pain and pleasure. And that such a quality or state as this may agree to an unthinking substance, I hope you will not deny.

PHIL. If you are resolved to maintain that warmth, or a gentle degree of heat, is no pleasure, I know not how to convince you otherwise than by appealing to your own sense. But what think you of cold?

HYL. The same that I do of heat. An intense degree of cold is a pain; for to feel a very great cold, is to perceive a great uneasiness: it cannot therefore exist without the mind; but a lesser degree of cold may, as well as a lesser degree of heat.

PHIL. Those bodies, therefore, upon whose application to our own, we perceive a moderate degree of heat, must be concluded to have a moderate degree of heat or warmth in them; and those, upon whose application we feel a like degree of cold, must be thought to have cold in them.

HYL. They must.

PHIL. Can any doctrine be true that necessarily leads a man into an absurdity?

HYL. Without doubt it cannot.

PHIL. Is it not an absurdity to think that the same thing should be at the same time both cold and warm?

HYL. It is.

PHIL. Suppose now one of your hands hot, and the other cold, and that they are both at once put into the same vessel of water, in an intermediate state; will not the water seem cold to one hand, and warm to the other?

HYL. It will.

PHIL. Ought we not therefore, by your principles, to conclude it is really both cold and warm at the same time, that is, according to your own concession, to believe an absurdity?

HYL. I confess it seems so.

PHIL. Consequently, the principles themselves are false, since you have granted that no true principle leads to an absurdity.

HYL. But, after all, can anything be more absurd than to say, *there is not heat in the fire?*

PHIL. To make the point still clearer; tell me whether, in two cases exactly alike, we ought not to make the same judgment?

HYL. We ought.

PHIL. When a pin pricks your finger, doth it not rend and divide the fibres of your flesh?

HYL. It doth.

PHIL. And when a coal burns your finger, doth it any more?

HYL. It doth not.

PHIL. Since, therefore, you neither judge the sensation itself occasioned by the pin, nor anything like it to be in the pin; you should not, conformably to what you have now granted, judge the sensation occasioned by the fire, or anything like it, to be in the fire.

HYL. Well, since it must be so, I am content to yield this point, and acknowledge that heat and cold are only sensations existing in our minds. But there still remain qualities enough to secure the reality of external things.

PHIL. But what will you say, Hylas, if it shall appear that the case is the same with regard to all other sensible qualities, and that they can no more be supposed to exist without the mind, than heat and cold?

HYL. Then indeed you will have done something to the purpose; but that is what I despair of seeing proved.

Tastes

PHIL. Let us examine them in order. What think you of *tastes*—do they exist without the mind, or no?

HYL. Can any man in his senses doubt whether sugar is sweet, or wormwood bitter?

PHIL. Inform me, Hylas. Is a sweet taste a particular kind of pleasure or pleasant sensation, or is it not?

HYL. It is.

PHIL. And is not bitterness some kind of uneasiness or pain?

HYL. I grant it.

PHIL. If therefore sugar and wormwood are unthinking corporeal substances existing without the mind, how can sweetness and bitterness, that is, pleasure and pain, agree to them?

HYL. Hold, Philonous, I now see what it was deluded me all this time. You asked whether heat or cold, sweetness and bitterness, were not particular sorts of pleasure and pain; to which I answered simply, that they were. Whereas I should have thus distinguished:—those qualities, as perceived by us, are pleasures or pains; but not as existing in the external objects. We must not therefore conclude absolutely, that there is no heat in the fire, or sweetness in the sugar, but only that heat or sweetness, as perceived by us, are not in the fire or sugar. What say you to this?

PHIL. I say it is nothing to the purpose. Our discourse proceeded altogether concerning sensible things, which you defined to be, *the things we immediately perceive by our senses*. Whatever other qualities, therefore, you speak of, as distinct from these, I know nothing of them, neither do they at all belong to the point in dispute. You may, indeed, pretend to have discovered certain qualities which you do not perceive, and assert those insensible qualities exist in fire and sugar. But what use can be made of this to your present purpose, I am at a loss to conceive. Tell me then once more, do you acknowledge that heat and cold, sweetness and bitterness (meaning those qualities which are perceived by the senses), do not exist without the mind?

HYL. I see it is to no purpose to hold out, so I give up the cause as to those mentioned qualities. Though I profess it sounds oddly, to say that sugar is not sweet.

PHIL. But, for your farther satisfaction, take this along with you: that which at other times seems sweet, shall, to a distempered palate, appear bitter. And, nothing can be plainer than that divers persons perceive different tastes in the same food; since that which one man delights in, another abhors. And how could this be, if the taste was something really inherent in the food?

HYL. I acknowledge I know not how.

Odours

PHIL. In the next place, *odours* are to be considered. And, with regard to these, I would fain know whether what hath been said of tastes doth not exactly agree to them? Are they not so many pleasing or displeasing sensations?

HYL. They are.

PHIL. Can you then conceive it possible that they should exist in an unperceiving thing?

HYL. I cannot.

PHIL. Or, can you imagine that filth and ordure affect those brute animals that feed on them out of choice, with the same smells which we perceive in them?

HYL. By no means.

PHIL. May we not therefore conclude of smells, as of the other forementioned qualities, that they cannot exist in any but a perceiving substance or mind?

HYL. I think so.

Sounds

PHIL. Then as to *sounds,* what must we think of them: are they accidents really inherent in external bodies, or not?

HYL. That they inhere not in the sonorous bodies is plain from hence: because a bell struck in the exhausted receiver of an air-pump sends forth no sound. The air, therefore, must be thought the subject of sound.

PHIL. What reason is there for that, Hylas?

HYL. Because, when any motion is raised in the air, we perceive a sound greater or lesser, according to the air's motion; but without some motion in the air, we never hear any sound at all.

PHIL. And granting that we never hear a sound but when some motion is produced in the air, yet I do not see how you can infer from thence, that the sound itself is in the air.

HYL. It is this very motion in the external air that produces in the mind the sensation of *sound.* For, striking on the drum of the ear, it causeth a vibration, which by the auditory nerves being communicated to the brain, the soul is thereupon affected with the sensation called *sound.*

PHIL. What! is sound then a sensation?

HYL. I tell you, as perceived by us, it is a particular sensation in the mind.

PHIL. And can any sensation exist without the mind?

HYL. No, certainly.

PHIL. How then can sound, being a sensation, exist in the air, if by the *air* you mean a senseless substance existing without the mind?

HYL. You must distinguish, Philonous, between sound as it is perceived by us, and as it is in itself; or (which is the same thing) between the sound we immediately perceive, and that which exists without us. The former, indeed, is a particular kind of sensation, but the latter is merely a vibrative or undulatory motion in the air.

PHIL. I thought I had already obviated that distinction, by the answer I gave when you were applying it in a like case before. But, to say no more of that, are you sure then that sound is really nothing but motion?

HYL. I am.

PHIL. Whatever therefore agrees to real sound, may with truth be attributed to motion?

HYL. It may.

PHIL. It is then good sense to speak of *motion* as of a thing that is *loud, sweet, acute, or grave.*

HYL. I see you are resolved not to understand me. Is it not evident those accidents or modes belong only to sensible sound, or *sound* in the common acceptation of the word, but not to *sound* in the real and philosophic sense; which, as I just now told you, is nothing but a certain motion of the air?

PHIL. It seems then there are two sorts of sound—the one vulgar, or that which is heard, the other philosophical and real?

HYL. Even so.

PHIL. And the latter consists in motion?

HYL. I told you so before.

PHIL. Tell me, Hylas, to which of the senses, think you, the idea of motion belongs? to the hearing?

HYL. No, certainly; but to the sight and touch.

PHIL. It should follow then, that, according to you, real sounds may possibly be *seen* or *felt,* but never *heard.*

HYL. Look you, Philonous, you may, if you please, make a jest of my opinion, but that will not alter the truth of things. I own, indeed, the inferences you draw me into sound something oddly; but common language, you know, is framed by, and for the use of the vulgar: we must not therefore wonder if expressions adapted to exact philosophic notions seem uncouth and out of the way.

PHIL. Is it come to that? I assure you, I imagine myself to have gained no small point, since you make so light of departing from common phrases and opinions; it being a main part of our inquiry, to examine whose notions are wildest of the common road, and most repugnant to the general sense of the world. But, can you think it no more than a philosophical paradox, to say that *real sounds are never heard,* and that the idea of them is obtained by some other sense? And is there nothing in this contrary to nature and the truth of things?

HYL. To deal ingenuously, I do not like it. And, after the concessions already made, I had as well grant that sounds too have no real being without the mind.

Colours

PHIL. And I hope you will make no difficulty to acknowledge the same of *colours.*

HYL. Pardon me: the case of colours is very different. Can anything be plainer than that we see them on the objects?

PHIL. The objects you speak of are, I suppose, corporeal Substances existing without the mind?

HYL. They are.

PHIL. And have true and real colours inhering in them?

HYL. Each visible object hath that colour which we see in it.

PHIL. How! is there anything visible but what we perceive by sight?

HYL. There is not.

PHIL. And, do we perceive anything by sense which we do not perceive immediately?

HYL. How often must I be obliged to repeat the same thing? I tell you, we do not.

PHIL. Have patience, good Hylas; and tell me once more, whether there is anything immediately perceived by the senses, except sensible qualities. I know you asserted there was not; but I would now be informed, whether you still persist in the same opinion.

HYL. I do.

PHIL. Pray, is your corporeal substance either a sensible quality, or made up of sensible qualities?

HYL. What a question that is! who ever thought it was?

PHIL. My reason for asking was, because in saying, *each visible object hath that colour which we see in it,* you make visible objects to be corporeal substances; which implies either that corporeal substances are sensible qualities, or else that there is something beside sensible qualities perceived by sight: but, as this point was formerly agreed between us, and is still maintained by you, it is a clear consequence, that your *corporeal substance* is nothing distinct from *sensible qualities.*

HYL. You may draw as many absurd consequences as you please, and endeavour to perplex the plainest things; but you shall never persuade me out of my senses. I clearly understand my own meaning.

PHIL. I wish you would make me understand it too. But, since you are unwilling to have your notion of corporeal substance examined, I shall urge that point no farther. Only be pleased to let me know, whether the same colours which we see exist in external bodies, or some other.

HYL. The very same.

PHIL. What! are then the beautiful red and purple we see on yonder clouds really in them? Or do you imagine they have in themselves any other form than that of a dark mist or vapour?

HYL. I must own, Philonous, those colours are not really in the clouds as they seem to be at this distance. They are only apparent colours.

PHIL. Apparent call you them? how shall we distinguish these apparent colours from real?

HYL. Very easily. Those are to be thought apparent which, appearing only at a distance, vanish upon a nearer approach.

PHIL. And those, I suppose, are to be thought real which are discovered by the most near and exact survey.

HYL. Right.

PHIL. Is the nearest and exactest survey made by the help of a microscope, or by the naked eye?

HYL. By a microscope, doubtless.

PHIL. But a microscope often discovers colours in an object different from those perceived by the unassisted sight. And, in case we had microscopes magnifying to any assigned degree, it is certain that no object whatsoever, viewed through them, would appear in the same colour which it exhibits to the naked eye.

HYL. And what will you conclude from all this? You cannot argue that there are really and naturally no colours on objects: because by artificial managements they may be altered, or made to vanish.

PHIL. I think it may evidently be concluded from your own concessions, that all the colours we see with our naked eyes are only apparent as those on the clouds, since they vanish upon a more close and accurate inspection which is afforded us by a microscope. Then, as to what you say by way of prevention: I ask you whether the real and natural state of an object is better discovered by a very sharp and piercing sight, or by one which is less sharp?

HYL. By the former without doubt.

PHIL. Is it not plain from *Dioptrics* that microscopes make the sight more penetrating, and represent objects as they would appear to the eye in case it were naturally endowed with a most exquisite sharpness?

HYL. It is.

PHIL. Consequently the microscopical representation is to be thought that which best sets forth the real nature of the thing, or what it is in itself. The colours, therefore, by it perceived are more genuine and real than those perceived otherwise.

HYL. I confess there is something in what you say.

PHIL. Besides, it is not only possible but manifest, that there actually are animals whose eyes are by nature framed to perceive those things which by reason of their minuteness escape our sight. What think you of those inconceivably small animals perceived by glasses? must we suppose they are all stark blind? Or, in case they see, can it be imagined their sight hath not the same use in preserving their bodies from injuries, which appears in that of all other animals? And if it hath, is it not evident they must see particles less than their own bodies; which will present them with a far different view in each object from that which strikes our senses? Even our own eyes do not always represent objects to us after the same manner. In the jaundice every one knows that all things seem yellow. Is it not therefore highly probable those animals in whose eyes we discern a very different texture from that of ours, and whose bodies abound with different humours, do not see the same colours in every object that we do? From all which, should it not seem to follow that all colours are equally apparent, and that none of those which we perceive are really inherent in any outward object?

HYL. It should.

PHIL. The point will be past all doubt, if you consider that, in case colours were real properties or affections inherent in external bodies, they could admit of no alteration without some change wrought in the very bodies themselves: but, is it not evident from what hath been said that, upon the use of microscopes, upon a change happening in the humours of the eye, or a variation of distance, without any manner of real alteration in the thing itself, the colours of any object are either changed, or totally disappear? Nay, all other circumstances remaining the same, change but the situation of some objects, and they shall present different colours to the eye. The same thing happens upon viewing an object in various degrees of light. And what is more known than that the same bodies appear differently coloured by candlelight from what they do in the open day? Add to these the experiment of a prism which, separating the heterogeneous rays of light, alters the colour of any object, and will cause the whitest to appear of a deep blue or red to the naked eye. And now tell me whether you are still of opinion that every body hath its true real colour inhering in it; and, if you think it hath, I would fain know farther from you, what certain distance and position of the object, what peculiar texture and forma-tion of the eye, what degree or kind of light is necessary for ascertaining that true colour, and distinguishing it from apparent ones.

HYL. I own myself entirely satisfied, that they are all equally apparent, and that there is no such thing as colour really inhering in external bodies, but that it is altogether in the light. And what confirms me in this opinion is, that in proportion to the light colours are still more or less vivid; and if there be no light, then are there no colours perceived. Besides, allowing there are colours on external objects, yet, how is it possible for us to perceive them? For no external body affects the mind, unless it acts first on our organs of sense. But the only action of bodies is motion; and motion cannot be communicated otherwise than by impulse. A distant object therefore cannot act on the eye; nor consequently make itself or its properties perceivable to the soul. Whence it plainly follows that it is immediately some contiguous substance, which, operating on the eye, occasions a perception of colours: and such is light.

PHIL. How! is light then a substance?

HYL. I tell you, Philonous, external light is nothing but a thin fluid substance, whose minute particles being agitated with a brisk motion, and in various manners reflected from the different surfaces of outward objects to the eyes, communicate different motions to the optic nerves; which, being propagated to the brain, cause therein various impressions; and these are attended with the sensations of red, blue, yellow, etc.

PHIL. It seems then the light doth no more than shake the optic nerves.

HYL. Nothing else.

PHIL. And consequent to each particular motion of the nerves, the mind is affected with a sensation, which is some particular colour.

HYL. Right.

PHIL. And these sensations have no existence without the mind.

HYL. They have not.

PHIL. How then do you affirm that colours are in the light; since by *light* you understand a corporeal substance external to the mind?

HYL. Light and colours, as immediately perceived by us, I grant cannot exist without the mind. But in themselves they are only the motions and configurations of certain insensible particles of matter.

PHIL. Colours then, in the vulgar sense, or taken for the immediate objects of sight, cannot agree to any but a perceiving substance.

HYL. That is what I say.

PHIL. Well then, since you give up the point as to those sensible qualities which are alone thought colours by all mankind beside, you may hold what you please with regard to those invisible ones of the philosophers. It is not my business to dispute about *them;* only I would advise you to bethink yourself, whether, considering the inquiry we are upon, it be prudent for you to affirm—*the red and blue which we see are not real colours, but certain unknown motions and figures which no man ever did or can see are truly so.* Are not these shocking notions, and are not they subject to as many ridiculous inferences, as those you were obliged to renounce before in the case of sounds?

Are the Primary Qualities Really in Bodies?

HYL. I frankly own, Philonous, that it is in vain to stand out any longer. Colours, sounds, tastes, in a word all those termed *secondary qualities,* have certainly no existence without the mind. But by this acknowledgment I must not be supposed to derogate anything from the reality of Matter, or external objects; seeing it is no more than several philosophers maintain, who nevertheless are the farthest imaginable from denying Matter. For the clearer understanding of this, you must know sensible qualities are by philosophers divided into *Primary* and *Secondary.* The former are Extension, Figure, Solidity, Gravity, Motion, and Rest; and these they hold exist really in bodies. The latter are those above enumerated; or, briefly, *all sensible qualities beside the Primary;* which they assert are only so many sensations or ideas existing nowhere but in the mind. But all this, I doubt not, you are apprised of. For my part, I have been a long time sensible there was such an opinion current among philosophers, but was never thoroughly convinced of its truth until now.

Extension and Figures

PHIL. You are still then of opinion that *extension* and *figures* are inherent in external unthinking substances?

HYL. I am.

PHIL. But what if the same arguments which are brought against Secondary Qualities will hold good against these also?

HYL. Why then I shall be obliged to think, they too exist only in the mind.

PHIL. Is it your opinion the very figure and extension which you perceive by sense exist in the outward object or material substance?

HYL. It is.

PHIL. Have all other animals as good grounds to think the same of the figure and extension which they see and feel?

HYL. Without doubt, if they have any thought at all.

PHIL. Answer me, Hylas. Think you the senses were bestowed upon all animals for their preservation and well-being in life? or were they given to men alone for this end?

HYL. I make no question but they have the same use in all other animals.

PHIL. If so, is it not necessary they should be enabled by them to perceive their own limbs, and those bodies which are capable of harming them?

HYL. Certainly.

PHIL. A mite therefore must be supposed to see his own foot, and things equal or even less than it, as bodies of some considerable dimension; though at the same time they appear to you scarce discernible, or at best as so many visible points?

HYL. I cannot deny it.

PHIL. And to creatures less than the mite they will seem yet larger?

HYL. They will.

PHIL. Insomuch that what you can hardly discern will to another extremely minute animal appear as some huge mountain?

HYL. All this I grant.

PHIL. Can one and the same thing be at the same time in itself of different dimensions?

HYL. That were absurd to imagine.

PHIL. But, from what you have laid down it follows that both the extension by you perceived, and that perceived by the mite itself, as likewise all those perceived by lesser animals, are each of them the true extension of the mite's foot; that is to say, by your own principles you are led into an absurdity.

HYL. There seems to be some difficulty in the point.

PHIL. Again, have you not acknowledged that no real inherent property of any object can be changed without some change in the thing itself?

HYL. I have.

PHIL. But, as we approach to or recede from an object, the visible extension varies, being at one distance ten or a hundred times greater than at another. Doth it not therefore follow from hence likewise that it is not really inherent in the object?

HYL. I own I am at a loss what to think.

PHIL. Your judgment will soon be determined, if you will venture to think as freely concerning this quality as you have done concerning the rest. Was it not admitted as a good argument, that neither heat nor cold was in the water, because it seemed warm to one hand and cold to the other?

HYL. It was.

PHIL. Is it not the very same reasoning to conclude, there is no extension or figure in an object, because to one eye it shall seem little, smooth, and round, when at the same time it appears to the other, great, uneven, and angular?

HYL. The very same. But does this latter fact ever happen?

PHIL. You may at any time make the experiment, by looking with one eye bare, and with the other through a microscope.

HYL. I know not how to maintain it; and yet I am loath to give up *extension,* I see so many odd consequences following upon such a concession.

PHIL. Odd, say you? After the concessions already made, I hope you will stick at nothing for its oddness. But, on the other hand, should it not seem very odd, if the general reasoning which includes all other sensible qualities did not also include extension? If it be allowed that no idea, nor anything like an idea, can exist in an unperceiving substance, then surely it follows that no figure, or mode of extension, which we can either perceive, or imagine, or have any idea of, can be really inherent in Matter; not to mention the peculiar difficulty there must be in conceiving a material substance, prior to and distinct from extension, to be the *substratum* of extension. Be the sensible quality what it will—figure, or sound, or colour, it seems alike impossible it should subsist in that which doth not perceive it.

Motion

HYL. I give up the point for the present, reserving still a right to retract my opinion, in case I shall hereafter discover any false step in my progress to it.

PHIL. That is a right you cannot be denied. Figures and extension being despatched, we proceed next to *motion.* Can a real motion in any external body be at the same time both very swift and very slow?

HYL. It cannot.

PHIL. Is not the motion of a body swift in a reciprocal proportion to the time it takes up in describing any given space? Thus a body that describes a mile in an hour moves three times faster than it would in case it described only a mile in three hours.

HYL. I agree with you.

PHIL. And is not time measured by the succession of ideas in our minds?

HYL. It is.

PHIL. And is it not possible ideas should succeed one another twice as fast in your mind as they do in mine, or in that of some spirit of another kind?

HYL. I own it.

PHIL. Consequently the same body may to another seem to perform its motion over any space in half the time that it doth to you. And the same reasoning will hold as to any other proportion: that is to say, according to your principles (since the motions perceived are both really in the object) it is possible one and the same body shall be really moved the same way at once, both very swift and very slow. How is this consistent either with common sense, or with what you just now granted?

HYL. I have nothing to say to it.

Solidity

PHIL. Then as for *solidity;* either you do not mean any sensible quality by that word, and so it is beside our inquiry: or if you do, it must be either hardness or resistance. But both the one and the other are plainly relative to our senses: it being evident that what seems hard to one animal may appear soft to another, who hath greater force and firmness of limbs. Nor is it less plain that the resistance I feel is not in the body.

HYL. I own the very *sensation* of resistance, which is all you immediately perceive, is not in the body; but the *cause* of that sensation is.

PHIL. But the causes of our sensations are not things immediately perceived, and therefore are not sensible. This point I thought had been already determined.

HYL. I own it was; but you will pardon me if I seem a little embarrassed: I know not how to quit my old notions.

PHIL. To help you out, do but consider that if *extension* be once acknowledged to have no existence without the mind, the same must necessarily be granted of motion, solidity, and gravity; since they all evidently suppose extension. It is therefore superfluous to inquire particularly concerning each of them. In denying extension, you have denied them all to have any real existence.

HYL. I wonder, Philonous, if what you say be true, why those philosophers who deny the Secondary Qualities any real existence should yet attribute it to the Primary. If there is no difference between them, how can this be accounted for?

PHIL. It is not my business to account for every opinion of the philosophers. But, among other reasons which may be assigned for this, it seems probable that pleasure and pain being rather annexed to the former than the latter may be one. Heat and cold, tastes and smells, have something more vividly pleasing or disagreeable than the ideas of extension, figure, and motion affect us with. And, it being too visibly absurd to hold that pain or pleasure can be in an unperceiving Substance, men are more easily weaned from believing the external existence of the Secondary than the

Primary Qualities. You will be satisfied there is something in this, if you recollect the difference you made between an intense and more moderate degree of heat; allowing the one a real existence, while you denied it to the other. But, after all, there is no rational ground for that distinction; for, surely an indifferent sensation is as truly *a sensation* as one more pleasing or painful; and consequently should not any more than they be supposed to exist in an unthinking subject.

Absolute and Sensible Extension and Motion

HYL. It is just come into my head, Philonous, that I have somewhere heard of a distinction between absolute and sensible extension. Now, though it be acknowledged that *great* and *small,* consisting merely in the relation which other extended beings have to the parts of our own bodies, do not really inhere in the substances themselves; yet nothing obliges us to hold the same with regard to *absolute extension,* which is something abstracted from *great* and *small,* from this or that particular magnitude or figure. So likewise as to motion; *swift* and *slow* are altogether relative to the succession of ideas in our own minds. But, it doth not follow, because those modifications of motion exist not without the mind, that therefore absolute motion abstracted from them doth not.

PHIL. Pray what is it that distinguishes one motion, or one part of extension, from another? Is it not something sensible, as some degree of swiftness or slowness, some certain magnitude or figure peculiar to each?

HYL. I think so.

PHIL. These qualities, therefore, stripped of all sensible properties, are without all specific and numerical differences, as the schools call them.

HYL. They are.

PHIL. That is to say, they are extension in general, and motion in general.

HYL. Let it be so.

Abstract Ideas

PHIL. But it is a universally received maxim that *Everything which exists is particular.* How then can motion in general, or extension in general, exist in any corporeal substance?

HYL. I will take time to solve your difficulty.

PHIL. But I think the point may be speedily decided. Without doubt you can tell whether you are able to frame this or that idea. Now I am content to put our dispute on this issue. If you can frame in your thoughts a distinct *abstract idea* of motion or extension, divested of all those sensible modes, as swift and slow, great and small, round and square, and the like, which are acknowledged to exist only in the mind, I will then yield the point you contend for. But if you cannot, it will be unreasonable on your side to insist any longer upon what you have no notion of.

HYL. To confess ingenuously, I cannot.

PHIL. Can you even separate the ideas of extension and motion from the ideas of all those qualities which they who make the distinction term *secondary?*

HYL. What! is it not an easy matter to consider extension and motion by themselves, abstracted from all other sensible qualities? Pray how do the mathematicians treat of them?

PHIL. I acknowledge, Hylas, it is not difficult to form general propositions and reasonings about those qualities, without mentioning any other; and, in this sense, to consider or treat of them abstractedly. But, how doth it follow that, because I can pronounce the word *motion* by itself, I can form the idea of it in my mind exclusive of body? or, because theorems may be great of extension and figures, without any mention of *great* or *small,* or any other sensible mode of quality, that therefore it is possible such an abstract idea of extension, without any particular size or figure, or sensible quality, should be distinctly formed, and apprehended by the mind? Mathematicians treat of quantity, without regarding what other sensible qualities it is attended with, as being altogether indifferent to their demonstrations. But, when laying aside the words, they contemplate the bare ideas, I believe you will find, they are not the pure abstracted ideas of extension.

HYL. But what say you to *pure intellect?* May not abstracted ideas be framed by that faculty?

PHIL. Since I cannot frame abstract ideas at all, it is plain I cannot frame them by the help of *pure intellect,* whatsoever faculty you understand by those words. Besides, not to inquire into the nature of pure intellect and its spiritual objects, as *virtue, reason, God,* or the like, thus much seems manifest—that sensible things are only to be perceived by sense, or represented by the imagination. Figures, therefore, and extension, being originally perceived by sense, do not belong to pure intellect: but, for your farther satisfaction, try if you can frame the idea of any figure, abstracted from all particularities of size, or even from other sensible qualities.

HYL. Let me think a little— I do not find that I can.

PHIL. And can you think it possible that should really exist in nature which implies a repugnancy in its conception?

HYL. By no means.

PHIL. Since therefore it is impossible even for the mind to disunite the ideas of extension and motion from all other sensible qualities, doth it not follow, that where the one exist there necessarily the other exist likewise?

HYL. It should seem so.

PHIL. Consequently, the very same arguments which you admitted as conclusive against the Secondary Qualities are, without any farther application of force, against the Primary too. Besides, if you will trust your senses, is it not plain all sensible qualities coexist, or to them appear as being in the same place? Do they ever represent a motion, or figure, as being divested of all other visible and tangible qualities?

HYL. You need say no more on this head. I am free to own, if there be no secret error or oversight in our proceedings hitherto, that *all* sensible qualities are alike to be denied existence without the mind. But, my fear is that I have been too liberal in my former concessions, or overlooked some fallacy or other. In short, I did not take time to think.

PHIL. For that matter, Hylas, you may take what time you please in reviewing the progress of our inquiry. You are at liberty to recover any slips you might have made, or offer whatever you have omitted which makes for your first opinion.

Sensation and Objects

HYL. One great oversight I take to be this—that I did not sufficiently distinguish the *object* from the *sensation*. Now, though this latter may not exist without the mind, yet it will not thence follow that the former cannot.

PHIL. What object do you mean? the object of the senses?

HYL. The same.

PHIL. It is then immediately perceived?

HYL. Right.

PHIL. Make me to understand the difference between what is immediately perceived and a sensation.

HYL. The sensation I take to be an act of the mind perceiving; besides which, there is something perceived; and this I call the *object*. For example, there is red and yellow on that tulip. But then the act of perceiving those colours is in me only, and not in the tulip.

PHIL. What tulip do you speak of? Is it that which you see?

HYL. The same.

PHIL. And what do you see beside colour, figure, and extension?

HYL. Nothing.

PHIL. What you would say then is that the red and yellow are coexistent with the extension; is it not?

HYL. That is not all; I would say they have a real existence without the mind, in some unthinking substance.

PHIL. That the colours are really in the tulip which I see is manifest. Neither can it be denied that this tulip may exist independent of your mind or mine; but, that any immediate object of the senses—that is, any idea, or combination of ideas—should exist in an unthinking substance, or exterior to *all* minds, is in itself an evident contradiction. Nor can I imagine how this follows from what you said just now, to wit, that the red and yellow were on the tulip *you saw,* since you do not pretend to *see* that unthinking substance.

HYL. You have an artful way, Philonous, of diverting our inquiry from the subject.

PHIL. I see you have no mind to be pressed that way. To return then to your distinction between *sensation* and *object;* if I take you right, you distinguish in every perception two things, the one an action of the mind, the other not.

HYL. True.

PHIL. And this action cannot exist in, or belong to, any unthinking thing; but, whatever beside is implied in a perception may?

HYL. That is my meaning.

PHIL. So that if there was a perception without any act of the mind, it were possible such a perception should exist in an unthinking substance?

HYL. I grant it. But it is impossible there should be such a perception.

PHIL. When is the mind said to be active?

HYL. When it produces, puts an end to, or changes, anything.

PHIL. Can the mind produce, discontinue, or change anything, but by an act of the will?

HYL. It cannot.

PHIL. The mind therefore is to be accounted *active* in its perceptions so far forth as *volition* is included in them?

HYL. It is.

PHIL. In plucking this flower I am active; because I do it by the motion of my hand, which was consequent upon my volition; so likewise in applying it to my nose. But is either of these smelling?

HYL. No.

PHIL. I act too in drawing the air through my nose; because my breathing so rather than otherwise is the effect of my volition. But neither can this be called *smelling:* for, if it were, I should smell every time I breathed in that manner?

HYL. True.

PHIL. Smelling then is somewhat consequent to all this?

HYL. It is.

PHIL. But I do not find my will concerned any farther. Whatever more there is—as that I perceive such a particular smell, or any smell at all— this is independent of my will, and therein I am altogether passive. Do you find it otherwise with you, Hylas?

HYL. No, the very same.

PHIL. Then, as to seeing, is it not in your power to open your eyes, or keep them shut; to turn them this or that way?

HYL. Without doubt.

PHIL. But, doth it in like manner depend on *your* will that in looking on this flower you perceive *white* rather than any other colour? Or, directing your open eyes towards yonder part of the heaven, can you avoid seeing the sun? Or is light or darkness the effect of your volition?

HYL. No, certainly.

PHIL. You are then in these respects altogether passive?

HYL. I am.

PHIL. Tell me now, whether *seeing* consists in perceiving light and colours, or in opening and turning the eyes?

HYL. Without doubt, in the former.

PHIL. Since therefore you are in the very perception of light and colours altogether passive, what is become of that action you were speaking of as an ingredient in every sensation? And doth it now follow from your own concessions, that the perception of light and colours, including no action in it, may exist in an unperceiving substance? And is not this a plain contradiction?

HYL. I know not what to think of it.

PHIL. Besides, since you distinguish the *active* and *passive* in every perception, you must do it in that of pain. But how is it possible that pain, be it as little active as you please, should exist in an unperceiving substance? In short, do but consider the point, and then confess ingenuously, whether light and colours, tastes, sounds, etc., are not all equally passions or sensations in the soul. You may indeed call them *external objects,* and give them in words what subsistence you please. But, examine your own thoughts, and then tell me whether it be not as I say?

HYL. I acknowledge, Philonous, that upon a fair observation of what passes in my mind, I can discover nothing else but that I am a thinking being, affected with variety of sensations; neither is it possible to conceive how a sensation should exist in an unperceiving substance.—But then, on the other hand, when I look on sensible things in a different view, considering them as so many modes and qualities, I find it necessary to suppose a *material substratum,* without which they cannot be conceived to exist.

The Material Substratum

PHIL. *Material substratum* call you it? Pray, by which of your senses came you acquainted with that being?

HYL. It is not itself sensible; its modes and qualities only being perceived by the senses.

PHIL. I presume then it was by reflexion and reason you obtained the idea of it?

HYL. I do not pretend to any proper positive *idea* of it. However, I conclude it exists, because qualities cannot be conceived to exist without a support.

PHIL. It seems then you have only a relative *notion* of it, or that you conceive it not otherwise than by conceiving the relation it bears to sensible qualities?

HYL. Right.

PHIL. Be pleased therefore to let me know wherein that relation consists.

HYL. Is it not sufficiently expressed in the term *substratum,* or *substance?*

PHIL. If so, the word *substratum* should import that it is spread under the sensible qualities or accidents?

HYL. True.

PHIL. And consequently under extension?

HYL. I own it.

PHIL. It is therefore somewhat in its own nature entirely distinct from extension?

HYL. I tell you, extension is only a mode, and Matter is something that supports modes. And is it not evident the thing supported is different from the thing supporting?

PHIL. So that something distinct from, and exclusive of, extension is supposed to be the *substratum* of extension?

HYL. Just so.

PHIL. Answer me, Hylas. Can a thing be spread without extension? or is not the idea of extension necessarily included in *spreading?*

HYL. It is.

PHIL. Whatsoever therefore you suppose spread under anything must have in itself an extension distinct from the extension of that thing under which it is spread?

HYL. It must.

PHIL. Consequently, every corporeal substance, being the *substratum* of extension, must have in itself another extension, by which it is qualified to be a *substratum:* and so on to infinity? And I ask whether this be not absurd in itself, and repugnant to what you granted just now, to wit, that the *substratum* was something distinct from and exclusive of extension?

HYL. Aye but, Philonous, you take me wrong. I do not mean that Matter is *spread* in a gross literal sense under extension. The word *substratum* is used only to express in general the same thing with *substance.*

PHIL. Well then, let us examine the relation implied in the term *substance.* Is it not that it stands under accidents?

HYL. The very same.

PHIL. But, that one thing may stand under or support another, must it not be extended?

HYL. It must.

PHIL. Is not therefore this supposition liable to the same absurdity with the former?

HYL. You still take things in a strict literal sense. That is not fair, Philonous.

PHIL. I am not for imposing any sense on your words: you are at liberty to explain them as you please. Only, I beseech you, make me understand something by them. You tell me Matter supports or stands under accidents. How! is it as your legs support your body?

HYL. No; that is the literal sense.

PHIL. Pray let me know any sense, literal or not literal, that you understand it in.—How long must I wait for an answer, Hylas?

HYL. I declare I know not what to say. I once thought I understood well enough what was meant by Matter's supporting accidents. But now, the more I think on it the less can I comprehend it: in short I find that I know nothing of it.

PHIL. It seems then you have no idea at all, neither relative nor positive, of Matter; you know neither what it is in itself, nor what relation it bears to accidents?

HYL. I acknowledge it.

PHIL. And yet you asserted that you could not conceive how qualities or accidents should really exist, without conceiving at the same time a material support of them?

HYL. I did.

PHIL. That is to say, when you conceive the *real* existence of qualities, you do withal conceive Something which you cannot conceive?

HYL. It was wrong, I own. But still I fear there is some fallacy or other. Pray what think you of this? It is just come into my head that the ground of all our mistake lies in your treating of each quality by itself. Now, I grant that each quality cannot singly subsist without the mind. Colour cannot without extension, neither can figure without some other sensible quality. But, as the several qualities united or blended together form entire sensible things, nothing hinders why such things may not be supposed to exist without the mind.

PHIL. Either, Hylas, you are jesting, or have a very bad memory. Though indeed we went through all the qualities by name one after another, yet my arguments, or rather your concessions, nowhere tend to prove that the Secondary Qualities did not subsist each alone by itself; but, that they were not *at all* without the mind. Indeed, in treating of figure and motion we concluded they could not exist without the mind, because it was impossible even in thought to separate them from all secondary qualities, so as to conceive them existing by themselves. But then this was not the only argument made use of upon that occasion. But (to pass by all that hath been hitherto said, and reckon it for nothing, if you will have it so) I am content to put the whole upon this issue. If you can conceive it possible for any mixture or combination of qualities, or any sensible object whatever, to exist without the mind, then I will grant it actually to be so.

Is the Existence of Unperceived Objects Conceivable?

HYL. If it comes to that the point will soon be decided. What more easy than to conceive a tree or house existing by itself, independent of, and unperceived by, any mind whatsoever? I do at this present time conceive them existing after that manner.

PHIL. How say you, Hylas, can you see a thing which is at the same time unseen?

HYL. No, that were a contradiction.

PHIL. Is it not as great a contradiction to talk of *conceiving* a thing which is *unconceived?*

HYL. It is.

PHIL. The tree or house therefore which you think of is conceived by you?

HYL. How should it be otherwise?

PHIL. And what is conceived is surely in the mind?

HYL. Without question, that which is conceived is in the mind.

PHIL. How then came you to say, you conceived a house or tree existing independent and out of all minds whatsoever?

HYL. That was I own an oversight; but stay, let me consider what led me into it.—It is a pleasant mistake enough. As I was thinking of a tree in a solitary place, where no one was present to see it, methought that was to conceive a tree as existing unperceived or unthought of; not considering that I myself conceived it all the while. But now I plainly see that all I can do is to frame ideas in my own mind. I may indeed conceive in my own thoughts the idea of a tree, or a house, or a mountain, but that is all. And this is far from proving that I can conceive them *existing out of the minds of all Spirits.*

PHIL. You acknowledge then that you cannot possibly conceive how any one corporeal sensible thing should exist otherwise than in a mind?

HYL. I do.

PHIL. And yet you will earnestly contend for the truth of that which you cannot so much as conceive?

HYL. I profess I know not what to think; but still there are some scruples remain with me. Is it not certain I *see things at a distance?* Do we not perceive the stars and moon, for example, to be a great way off? Is not this, I say, manifest to the senses?

PHIL. Do you not in a dream too perceive those or the like objects?

HYL. I do.

PHIL. And have they not then the same appearance of being distant?

HYL. They have.

PHIL. But you do not thence conclude the apparitions in a dream to be without the mind?

HYL. By no means.

PHIL. You ought not therefore to conclude that sensible objects are without the mind, from their appearance, or manner wherein they are perceived.

HYL. I acknowledge it. But doth not my sense deceive me in those cases?

The Idea of Distance

PHIL. By no means. The idea or thing which you immediately perceive, neither sense nor reason informs you that *it* actually exists without the mind. By sense you only know that you are affected with such certain sensations of light and colours, etc. And these you will not say are without the mind.

HYL. True: but, beside all that, do you not think the sight suggests something of *outness* or *distance?*

PHIL. Upon approaching a distant object, do the visible size and figure change perpetually, or do they appear the same at all distances?

HYL. They are in a continual change.

PHIL. Sight therefore doth not suggest, or any way inform you, that the visible object you immediately perceive exists at a distance,[1] or will be perceived when you advance farther onward; there being a continued series of visible objects succeeding each other during the whole time of your approach.

HYL. It doth not; but still I know, upon seeing an object, what object I shall perceive after having passed over a certain distance: no matter whether it be exactly the same or no: there is still something of distance suggested in the case.

PHIL. Good Hylas, do but reflect a little on the point, and then tell me whether there be any more in it than this: From the ideas you actually perceive by sight, you have by experience learned to collect what other ideas you will (according to the standing order of nature) be affected with, after such a certain succession of time and motion.

HYL. Upon the whole, I take it to be nothing else.

PHIL. Now, is it not plain that if we suppose a man born blind was on a sudden made to see, he could at first have no experience of what may be *suggested* by sight?

HYL. It is.

PHIL. He would not then, according to you, have any notion of distance annexed to the things he saw; but would take them for a new set of sensations, existing only in his mind?

HYL. It is undeniable.

PHIL. But, to make it still more plain: is not *distance* a line turned endwise to the eye?

HYL. It is.

PHIL. And can a line so situated be perceived by sight?

HYL. It cannot.

PHIL. Doth it not therefore follow that distance is not properly and immediately perceived by sight?

HYL. It should seem so.

1. [See the *Essay towards a New Theory of Vision,* and its *Vindication.*] Note added by Berkeley in the 1734 edition.

PHIL. Again, is it your opinion that colours are at a distance?

HYL. It must be acknowledged they are only in the mind.

PHIL. But do not colours appear to the eye as coexisting in the same place with extension and figures?

HYL. They do.

PHIL. How can you then conclude from sight that figures exist without, when you acknowledge colours do not; the sensible appearance being the very same with regard to both?

HYL. I know not what to answer.

PHIL. But, allowing that distance was truly and immediately perceived by the mind, yet it would not thence follow it existed out of the mind. For, whatever is immediately perceived is an idea: and can any idea exist out of the mind?

HYL. To suppose that were absurd: but, inform me, Philonous, can we perceive or know nothing beside our ideas?

PHIL. As for the rational deducing of causes from effects, that is beside our inquiry. And, by the senses you can best tell whether you perceive anything which is not immediately perceived. And I ask you, whether the things immediately perceived are other than your own sensations or ideas? You have indeed more than once, in the course of this conversation, declared yourself on those points; but you seem, by this last question, to have departed from what you then thought.

Do Ideas Represent External Objects?

HYL. To speak the truth, Philonous, I think there are two kinds of objects:—the one perceived immediately, which are likewise called *ideas;* the other are real things or external objects, perceived by the mediation of ideas, which are their images and representations. Now, I own ideas do not exist without the mind; but the latter sort of objects do. I am sorry I did not think of this distinction sooner; it would probably have cut short your discourse.

PHIL. Are those external objects perceived by sense, or by some other faculty?

HYL. They are perceived by sense.

PHIL. How! Is there anything perceived by sense which is not immediately perceived?

HYL. Yes, Philonous, in some sort there is. For example, when I look on a picture or statue of Julius Cæsar, I may be said after a manner to perceive him (though not immediately) by my senses.

PHIL. It seems then you will have our ideas, which alone are immediately perceived, to be pictures of external things: and that these also are perceived by sense, inasmuch as they have a conformity or resemblance to our ideas?

HYL. That is my meaning.

PHIL. And, in the same way that Julius Cæsar, in himself invisible, is nevertheless perceived by sight; real things, in themselves imperceptible, are perceived by sense.

HYL. In the very same.

PHIL. Tell me, Hylas, when you behold the picture of Julius Cæsar, do you see with your eyes any more than some colours and figures, with a certain symmetry and composition of the whole?

HYL. Nothing else.

PHIL. And would not a man who had never known anything of Julius Cæsar see as much?

HYL. He would.

PHIL. Consequently he hath his sight, and the use of it, in as perfect a degree as you?

HYL. I agree with you.

PHIL. Whence comes it then that your thoughts are directed to the Roman emperor, and his are not? This cannot proceed from the sensations or ideas of sense by you then perceived; since you acknowledge you have no advantage over him in that respect. It should seem therefore to proceed from reason and memory: should it not?

HYL. It should.

PHIL. Consequently, it will not follow from that instance that anything is perceived by sense which is not immediately perceived. Though I grant we may, in one acceptation, be said to perceive sensible things mediately by sense: that is, when, from a frequently perceived connexion, the immediate perception of ideas by one sense *suggests* to the mind others, perhaps belonging to another sense, which are wont to be connected with them. For instance, when I hear a coach drive along the streets, immediately I perceive only the sound; but, from the experience I have had that such a sound is connected with a coach, I am said to hear the coach. It is nevertheless evident that, in truth and strictness, nothing can be *heard* but *sound;* and the coach is not then properly perceived by sense, but suggested from experience. So likewise when we are said to see a red-hot bar of iron; the solidity and heat of the iron are not the objects of sight, but suggested to the imagination by the colour and figure which are properly perceived by that sense. In short, those things alone are actually and strictly perceived by any sense, which would have been perceived in case that same sense had then been first conferred on us. As for other things, it is plain they are only suggested to the mind by experience, grounded on former conceptions. But, to return to your comparison of Cæsar's picture, it is plain, if you keep to that, you must hold the real things, or archetypes of our ideas, are not perceived by sense, but by some internal faculty of the soul, as reason or memory. I would therefore fain know what arguments you can draw from reason for the existence of what you call *real things* or *material objects.* Or, whether you remember to have seen them formerly as they are in themselves; or, if you have heard or read of any one that did.

HYL. I see, Philonous, you are disposed to raillery; but that will never convince me.

PHIL. My aim is only to learn from you the way to come at the knowledge of *material beings.* Whatever we perceive is perceived immediately or mediately: by sense, or by reason or reflexion. But, as you have excluded sense, pray shew me what reason you have to believe their existence; or what *medium* you can possibly make use of to prove it, either to mine or your own understanding.

HYL. To deal ingenuously, Philonous, now I consider the point, I do not find I can give you any good reason for it. But, thus much seems pretty plain, that it is at least possible such things may really exist. And, as long as there is no absurdity in supposing them, I am resolved to believe as I did, till you bring good reasons to the contrary.

PHIL. What! Is it come to this, that you only *believe* the existence of material objects, and that your belief is founded barely on the possibility of its being true? Then you will have me bring reasons against it: though another would think it reasonable the proof should lie on him who holds the affirmative. And, after all, this very point which you are now resolved to maintain, without any reason, is in effect what you have more than once during this discourse seen good reason to give up. But, to pass over all this; if I understand you rightly, you say our ideas do not exist without the mind, but that they are copies, images, or representations, of certain originals that do?

HYL. You take me right.

PHIL. They are then like external things?

HYL. They are.

PHIL. Have those things a stable and permanent nature, independent of our senses; or are they in a perpetual change, upon our producing any motions in our bodies—suspending, exerting, or altering, our faculties or organs of sense?

HYL. Real things, it is plain, have a fixed and real nature, which remains the same notwithstanding any change in our senses, or in the posture and motion of our bodies; which indeed may affect the ideas in our minds; but it were absurd to think they had the same effect on things existing without the mind.

PHIL. How then is it possible that things perpetually fleeting and variable as our ideas should be copies or images of anything fixed and constant? Or, in other words, since all sensible qualities, as size, figure, colour, &c., that is, our ideas, are continually changing, upon every alteration in the distance, medium, or instruments of sensation; how can any determinate material objects be properly represented or painted forth by several distinct things, each of which is so different from and unlike the rest? Or, if you say it resembles some one only of our ideas, how shall we be able to distinguish the true copy from all the false ones?

HYL. I profess, Philonous, I am at a loss. I know not what to say to this.

PHIL. But neither is this all. Which are material objects in themselves—perceptible or imperceptible?

HYL. Properly and immediately nothing can be perceived but ideas. All material things, therefore, are in themselves insensible, and to be perceived only by our ideas.

PHIL. Ideas then are sensible, and their archetypes or originals insensible?

HYL. Right.

PHIL. But how can that which is sensible be *like* that which is insensible? Can a real thing, in itself *invisible,* be like a *colour;* or a real thing, which is not *audible,* be like a *sound?* In a word, can anything be like a sensation or idea, but another sensation or idea?

HYL. I must own, I think not.

PHIL. Is it possible there should be any doubt on the point? Do you not perfectly know your own ideas?

HYL. I know them perfectly; since what I do not perceive or know can be no part of my idea.

PHIL. Consider, therefore, and examine them, and then tell me if there be anything in them which can exist without the mind: or if you can conceive anything like them existing without the mind.

HYL. Upon inquiry, I find it is impossible for me to conceive or understand how anything but an idea can be like an idea. And it is most evident that *no idea can exist without the mind.*

PHIL. You are therefore, by your principles, forced to deny the *reality* of sensible things; since you made it to consist in an absolute existence exterior to the mind. That is to say, you are a downright sceptic. So I have gained my point, which was to shew your principles led to Scepticism.

HYL. For the present I am, if not entirely convinced, at least silenced.

PHIL. I would fain know what more you would require in order to a perfect conviction. Have you not had the liberty of explaining yourself all manner of ways? Were any little slips in discourse laid hold and insisted on? Or were you not allowed to retract or reinforce anything you had offered, as best served your purpose? Hath not everything you could say been heard and examined with all the fairness imaginable? In a word, have you not in every point been convinced out of your own mouth? And, if you can at present discover any flaw in any of your former concessions, or think of any remaining subterfuge, any new distinction, colour, or comment whatsoever, why do you not produce it?

HYL. A little patience, Philonous. I am at present so amazed to see myself ensnared, and as it were imprisoned in the labyrinths you have drawn me into, that on the sudden it cannot be expected I should find my way out. You must give me time to look about me and recollect myself.

PHIL. Hark; is not this the college bell?

HYL. It rings for prayers.

PHIL. We will go in then, if you please, and meet here again tomorrow morning. In the meantime, you may employ your thoughts on this morning's discourse, and try if you can find any fallacy in it, or invent any new means to extricate yourself.

HYL. Agreed.

49   Stars, Atoms and Sensations

W. T. Stace

So far as I know scientists still talk about electrons, protons, neutrons, and so on. We never directly perceive these, hence if we ask how we know of their existence the only possible answer seems to be that they are an inference from what we do directly perceive. What sort of an inference? Apparently a causal inference. The atomic entities in some way impinge upon the sense of the animal organism and cause that organism to perceive the familiar world of tables, chairs, and the rest.

But is it not clear that such a concept of causation, however interpreted, is invalid? The only reason we have for believing in the law of causation is that we *observe* certain regularities or sequences. We observe that, in certain conditions, *A* is always followed by *B*. We call *A* the cause, *B* the effect. And the sequence *A-B* becomes a causal law. It follows that all *observed* causal sequences are between sensed objects in the familiar world of perception, and that all known causal laws apply solely to the world of sense and not to anything beyond or behind it. And this in turn means that we have not got, and never could have, one jot of evidence for believing that the law of causation can be applied *outside* the realm of perception, or that

[This selection is a slight abbreviation of Stace's article "Science and the Physical World" which was published in 1967 in his *Man against Darkness and other Essays*. It is reprinted with the permission of the University of Pittsburgh Press.]

that realm can have any causes (such as the supposed physical objects) which are not themselves perceived.

Put the same thing in another way. Suppose there is an observed sequence *A-B-C*, represented by the vertical lines in the diagram below.

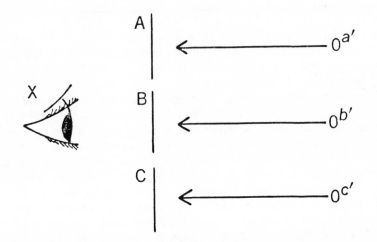

The observer X sees, and can see, nothing except things in the familiar world of perception. What *right* has he, and what *reason* has he, to assert cause of *A, B,* and *C*, such as *a', b', c',* which he can never observe, behind the perceived world? He has no *right*, because the law of causation on which he is relying has never been observed to operate outside the series of perceptions, and he can have, therefore, no evidence that it does so. And he has no *reason* because the phenomenon *C* is *sufficiently* accounted for by the cause *B*, *B* by *A*, and so on. It is unnecessary and superfluous to introduce a *second* cause *b'* for *B*, *c'* for *C*, and so forth. To give two causes for each phenomenon, one in one world and one in another, is unnecessary, and perhaps even self-contradictory.

Is it denied, then, it will be asked, that the star causes light waves, that the waves cause retinal changes, that these cause changes in the optic nerve, which in turn causes movements in the brain cells, and so on? No, it is not denied. But the observed causes and effects are all in the world of perception. And no sequences of sense-data can possibly justify going outside that world. If you admit that we never observe anything except sensed objects and their relations, regularities, and sequences, then it is obvious that we are completely shut in by our sensations and can never get outside them. Not only causal relations, but all other observed relations, upon which *any* kind of inferences might be founded, will lead only to further sensible objects and their relations. No inference, therefore, can pass from what is sensible to what is not sensible.

The fact is that atoms are *not* inferences from sensations. No one denies, of course, that a vast amount of perfectly valid inferential reasoning takes place in the physical theory of the atom. But it will not be found to be in any strict logical sense inference *from sense-data to atoms*. An *hypothesis* is set up, and the inferential processes are concerned with the application of the hypothesis, that is, with the prediction by its aid of further possible sensations and with its own internal consistency.

That atoms are not inferences from sensations means, of course, that from the existence of sensations we cannot validly infer the existence of atoms. And this means that we cannot have any reason at all to believe that they exist. And that is why I propose to argue that they do not exist— or at any rate that no one could know it if they did, and that we have absolutely no evidence of their existence.

What status have they, then? Is it meant that they are false and worthless, merely untrue? Certainly not. No one supposes that the entries in the Nautical Almanac "exist" anywhere except on the pages of that book and in the brains of its compilers and readers. Yet they are "true," inasmuch as they enable us to predict certain sensations, namely, the positions and times of certain perceived objects which we call the stars. And so the formulae of the atomic theory are true in the same sense, and perform a similar function.

I suggest that they are nothing but shorthand formulae, ingeniously worked out by the human mind, to enable it to predict its experience, i.e. to predict what sensations will be given to it. By "predict" here I do not mean to refer solely to the future. To calculate that there was an eclipse of the sun visible in Asia Minor in the year 585 B.C. is, in the sense in which I am using the term, to predict.

In order to see more clearly what is meant, let us apply the same idea to another case, that of gravitation. Newton formulated a law of gravitation in terms of "forces." It was supposed that this law—which was nothing but a mathematical formula—governed the operation of these existent forces. Nowadays it is no longer believed that these forces exist at all. And yet the law can be applied just as well without them to the prediction of astronomical phenomena. It is a matter of no importance to the scientific man whether the forces exist or not. That may be said to be a purely philosophical question. And I think the philosopher should pronounce them fictions. But that would not make the law useless or untrue. If it could still be used to predict phenomena, it would be just as true as it was.

It is true that fault is now found with Newton's law, and that another law, that of Einstein, has been substituted for it. And it is sometimes supposed that the reason for this is that forces are no longer believed in. But this is not the case. Whether forces exist or not simply does not matter. What matters is the discovery that Newton's law does *not* enable us accurately to predict certain astronomical facts such as the exact position of the planet Mercury. Therefore another formula, that of Einstein, has been substituted for it which permits correct predictions. This new law, as it happens, is a formula in terms of geometry. It is pure mathematics and nothing else. It does not contain anything about forces. In its pure form it does not even contain, so I am informed, anything about "humps and hills in space-time." And it does not matter whether any such humps and hills exist. It is truer than Newton's law, not because it substitutes humps and hills for forces, but solely because it is a more accurate formula of prediction.

Not only may it be said that forces do not exist. It may with equal truth be said that "gravitation" does not exist. Gravitation is not a "thing," but a mathematical formula, which exists only in the heads of mathematicians. And as a mathematical formula cannot cause a body to fall, so gravitation cannot cause a body to fall. Ordinary language misleads us here. We speak of the law "of" gravitation, and suppose that this law "applies to" the heavenly bodies. We are thereby misled into supposing that there are *two* things, namely, the gravitation and the heavenly bodies, and that one of these things, the gravitation, causes changes in the other. In reality nothing exists except the moving bodies. And neither Newton's law nor Einstein's law is, strictly speaking, a law of gravitation. They are both laws of moving bodies, that is to say, formulae which tell us how these bodies will move.

Now, just as in the past "forces" were foisted into Newton's law (by himself, be it said), so now certain popularizers of relativity foisted "humps and hills in space-time" into Einstein's law. We hear that the reason why the planets move in curved courses is that they cannot go through these humps and hills, but have to go round them! The planets just get "shoved about," not by forces, but by the humps and hills! But these humps and hills are pure metaphors. And anyone who takes them for "existences" gets asked awkward questions as to what "curved space" is curved "in."

It is not irrelevant to our topic to consider *why* human beings invent these metaphysical monsters of forces and bumps in space-time. The reason is that they have never emancipated themselves from the absurd idea that science "explains" things. They were not content to have laws which merely told them *that* the planets will, as a matter of fact, move in such and such ways. They wanted to know "why" the planets move in those ways. So Newton replied, "Forces." "Oh," said humanity, "that explains it. We understand forces. We feel them every time someone pushes or pulls us." Thus the movements were supposed to be "explained" by entities familiar because analogous to the muscular sensations which human beings feel. The humps and hills were introduced for exactly the same reason. They seem so familiar. If there is a bump in the billiard table, the rolling billiard ball is diverted from a straight to a curved course. Just the same with the planets. "Oh, I see!" says humanity, "that's quite simple. That *explains* everything."

But scientific laws, properly formulated, never "explain" anything. They simply state, in an abbreviated and generalized form, *what happens*. No scientist, and in my opinion no philosopher, knows *why* anything happens, or can "explain" anything. Scientific laws do nothing except state the brute fact that "when *A* happens, *B* always happens too." And laws of this kind obviously enable us to predict. If certain scientists substituted humps and hills for forces, then they have just substituted one superstition for another. For my part I do not believe that *science* has done this, though some *scientists* may have. For scientists, after all, are human beings with the same craving for "explanations" as other people.

I think that atoms are in exactly the same position as forces and the bumps and hills of space-time. In reality the mathematical formulae which are the scientific ways of stating the atomic theory are simply formulae for calculating what sensations will appear in given conditions. But just as the weakness of the human mind demanded that there should correspond to the formula of gravitation a real "thing" which could be called "gravitation itself" or "force," so the same weakness demands that there should be a real thing corresponding to the atomic formulae, and this real thing is called the atom. In reality the atoms no more cause sensations than gravitation causes apples to fall. The only causes of sensations are other sensations. And the relation of atoms to sensations to be felt is not the relation of cause to effect, but the relation of a mathematical formula to the facts and happenings which it enables the mathematician to calculate. . . .

It will not be out of place to give one more example to show how common fictitious existences are in science, and how little it matters whether they really exist or not. This example has no strange and annoying talk of "bent spaces" about it. One of the foundations of physics is, or used to be, the law of the conservation of energy. I do not know how far, if at all, this has been affected by the theory that matter sometimes turns into energy. But that does not affect the lesson it has for us. The law states, or used to state, that the amount of energy in the universe is always constant, that energy is never either created or destroyed. This was highly convenient, but it seemed to have obvious exceptions. If you throw a stone up into the air, you are told that it exerts in its fall the same amount of energy which it took to throw it up. But suppose it does not fall. Suppose it lodges on the roof of your house and stays there. What has happened to the energy which you can nowhere perceive as being exerted? It seems to have disappeared out of the universe. No, says the scientist, it still exists as *potential* energy. Now what does this blessed word "potential"—which is thus brought in to save the situation—mean as applied to energy? It means, of course, that the energy does not exist in any of its regular "forms," heat, light, electricity, etc. But this is merely negative. What positive meaning has the term? Strictly speaking, none whatever. Either the energy exists or it does not exist. There is no realm of the "potential" half-way between existence and non-existence. And this existence of energy can only consist in its being exerted. If the energy is not being exerted, then it is not energy and does not exist. Energy can no more exist without energizing than heat can exist without being hot. The "potential" existence of the energy is, then, a fiction. The actual empirically verifiable facts are that if a certain quantity of energy *e* exists in the universe and then disappears out of the universe (as happens when the stone lodges on the roof), the same amount of energy *e* will always reappear, begin to exist again, in certain known conditions. That is the fact which the law of the conservation of energy actually expresses. And the fiction of potential energy is introduced simply because it is convenient and makes the equations easier to work. They could be worked quite well without it, but would be slightly more complicated. In either case the function of the law is the same. Its object is to apprise us that if in certain conditions we have certain perceptions (throwing up the stone), then in certain other conditions we shall get certain other perceptions (heat, light, stone hitting skull, or other such). But there will always be a temptation to hypostatize the potential energy as an "existence," and to believe that it is a "cause" which "explains" the phenomena.

If the views which I have been expressing are followed out, they will lead to the conclusion that, strictly speaking, *nothing exists except sensations* (and the minds which perceive them). The rest is mental construction or fiction. But this does not mean that the conception of a star or the conception of an electron are worthless or untrue. Their truth and value consist in their capacity for helping us to organize our experience and predict our sensations.

50   Physics and Perception

Bertrand Russell

W<small>HEN WE CONSIDER PERCEPTION—</small>
visual or auditory—of an external event, there are three different matters
to be examined. There is first the process in the outside world, from
the event to the percipient's body; there is next the process in his body,
in so far as this can be known by an outside observer; lastly, there is
the question, which must be faced sooner or later, whether the percipient
can perceive something of the process in his body which no other observer could perceive. We will take these points in order.

If it is to be possible to "perceive" an event not in the percipient's
body, there must be a physical process in the outer world such that,
when a certain event occurs, it produces a stimulus of a certain kind at
the surface of the percipient's body. Suppose, for example, that pictures
of different animals are exhibited on a magic lantern to a class of children, and all the children are asked to say the name of each animal in
turn. We may assume that the children are sufficiently familiar with animals to say "cat," "dog," "giraffe," "hippopotamus," etc., at the right
moments. We must then suppose—taking the physical world for granted
—that some process travels from each picture to the eyes of the various
children, retaining throughout these journeys such peculiarities that, when
the process reaches their eyes, it can in one case stimulate the word
"cat" and in another the word "dog." All this the physical theory of light
provides for. But there is one interesting point about language that should
be noticed in this connection. If the usual physical theory of light is correct, the various children will receive stimuli which differ greatly according
to their distance and direction from the picture, and according to the way
the light falls. There are also differences in their reactions, for, though

[This selection consists of parts of Chapters XII and XIII of *The Outline of Philosophy*
published by George Allen and Unwin in 1927. The book was published in the United
States by W. W. Norton and Co., under the title *Philosophy*. The extracts are reproduced
with the kind permission of Bertrand Russell and the publishers.]

they all utter the word "cat," some say it loud, others soft, some in a soprano voice, some in a contralto. But the differences in their reactions are much less than the differences in the stimuli. . .

The fact that it is possible for a number of people to perceive the same noise or the same colored pattern obviously depends upon the fact that a physical process can travel outward from a center and retain certain of its characteristics unchanged, or very little changed. The most notable of such characteristics is frequency in a wave-motion. That, no doubt, affords a biological reason for the fact that our most delicate senses, sight and hearing, are sensitive to frequencies, which determine color in what we see and pitch in what we hear. If there were not, in the physical world, processes spreading out from centers and retaining certain characters practically unchanged, it would be impossible for different percipients to perceive the same object from different points of view, and we should not have been able to discover that we all live in a common world.

We come now to the process in the percipient's body, in so far as this can be perceived by an outside observer. This raises no new philosophical problems, because we are still concerned, as before, with the perception of events outside the observer's body. The observer, now, is supposed to be a physiologist, observing, say, what goes on in the eye when light falls upon it. His means of knowing are, in principle, exactly the same as in the observation of dead matter. An event in an eye upon which light is falling causes light-waves to travel in a certain manner until they reach the eye of the physiologist. They there cause a process in the physiologist's eye and optic nerve and brain, which ends in what he calls "seeing what happens in the eye he is observing." But this event, which happens in the physiologist, is not what happened in the eye he was observing; it is only connected with this by a complicated causal chain. Thus our knowledge of physiology is no more direct or intimate than our knowledge of processes in dead matter; we do not know any more about our eyes than about the trees and fields and clouds that we see by means of them. The event which happens when a physiologist observes an eye is an event in him, not on the eye that he is observing.

. . . It may be said that we do not in fact proceed to *infer* the physical world from our perceptions, but that we begin at once with a rough-and-ready knowledge of the physical world, and only at a late stage of sophistication compel ourselves to regard our knowledge of the physical world as an inference. What is valid in this statement is the fact that our knowledge of the physical world is not at first inferential, but that is only because we take our percepts to *be* the physical world. Sophistication and philosophy come in at the stage at which we realize that the physical world cannot be identified with our percepts. When my boy was three years old, I showed him Jupiter, and told him that Jupiter was larger than earth. He insisted that I must be speaking of some other Jupiter, because, as he patiently explained, the one he was seeing was obviously quite small.

After some efforts, I had to give it up and leave him unconvinced. In the case of the heavenly bodies, adults have got used to the idea that what is really there can only be *inferred* from what they see; but where rats in mazes are concerned, they still tend to think that they are seeing what is happening in the physical world. The difference, however, is only one of degree, and naive realism is as untenable in the one case as in the other. There are differences in the perceptions of two persons observing the same process; there are sometimes no discoverable differences between two perceptions of the same persons observing different processes, e.g., pure water and water full of bacilli. The subjectivity of our perceptions is thus of practical as well as theoretical importance.

    . . . A lamp at the top of a tall building might produce the same visual stimulus as Jupiter, or at any rate one practically indistinguishable from that produced by Jupiter. A blow on the nose might make us "see stars." Theoretically, it should be possible to apply a stimulus direct to the optic nerve, which should give us a visual sensation. Thus when we think we see Jupiter, we may be mistaken. We are less likely to be mistaken if we say that the surface of the eye is being stimulated in a certain way, and still less likely to be mistaken if we say that the optic nerve is being stimulated in a certain way. We do not eliminate the risk of error completely unless we confine ourselves to saying that an event of a certain sort is happening in the brain; this statement may still be true if we see Jupiter in a dream.

    But, I shall be asked, what do you know about what is happening in the brain? Surely nothing. Not so, I reply. I know what is happening in the brain exactly what naive realism thinks it knows about what is happening in the outside world. But this needs explaining, and there are other matters that must be explained first.

    When the light from a fixed star reaches me, I see the star if it is night and I am looking in the right direction. The light started years ago, probably many years ago, but my reaction is primarily something that is happening *now*. When my eyes are open, I see the star; when they are shut, I do not. Children discover at a fairly early age that they see nothing when their eyes are shut. They are aware of the difference between seeing and not seeing, and also of the difference between eyes open and eyes shut; gradually they discover that these two differences are correlated —I mean that they have expectations of which this is the intellectualist transcription. Again, children learn to name the colors, and to state correctly whether a thing is blue or red or yellow or whatnot. They ought not to be sure that light of the appropriate wave-length started from the object. The sun looks red in a London fog, grass looks blue through blue spectacles, everything looks yellow to a person suffering from jaundice. But suppose you ask: What color are you seeing? The person who answers, in these cases, red for the sun, blue for the grass, and yellow for the sickroom of the jaundiced patient, is answering quite truly. And in each of these cases he is stating something that he *knows*. What he knows in such cases is what I call a "percept." I shall contend later that, from the standpoint of physics, a percept is in the brain; for the present, I am only concerned to say that a percept is what is most indubitable in our knowledge of the world.

I do not in fact entertain any doubts that physics is true in its main lines. The interpretation of physical formulae is a matter as to which a considerable degree of uncertainty is possible; but we cannot well doubt that there is an interpretation which is true roughly and in the main. I shall come to the question of interpretation later; for the present, I shall assume that we may accept physics in its broad outlines, without troubling to consider how it is to be interpreted. On this basis, the above remarks on perception seem undeniable. We are often misled as to what is happening, either by peculiarities of the medium between the object and our bodies, or by unusual states of our bodies, or by a temporary or permanent abnormality in the brain. But in all these cases *something* is really happening, as to which, if we turn our attention to it, we can obtain knowledge that is not misleading. At one time when, owing to illness, I had been taking a great deal of quinine, I became hypersensitive to noise, so that when the nurse rustled the newspaper I thought she was spilling a scuttle of coals on the floor. The interpretation was mistaken, but it was quite true that I heard a loud noise. It is commonplace that a man whose leg has been amputated can still feel pains in it; here again, he does really feel the pains, and is only mistaken in his belief that they come from his leg. A percept is an observable event, but its interpretation as knowledge of this or that event in the physical world is liable to be mistaken, for reasons which physics and physiology can make fairly clear.

Perhaps there is nothing so difficult for the imagination as to teach it to feel about space as modern science compels us to think. This is the task which must now be attempted. . . . The gist of the matter is that percepts . . . are in our heads; that percepts are what we can know with most certainty; and that percepts contain what naive realism thinks it knows about the world.

But when I say that my percepts are in my head, I am saying something which is ambiguous until the different kinds of space have been explained, for the statement is only true in connection with *physical* space. There is also a space in our percepts, and of this space the statement would not be true. When I say that there is space in our percepts, I mean nothing at all difficult to understand. I mean—to take the sense of sight, which is the most important in this connection—that in what we see at one time there is up and down, right and left, inside and outside. If we see, say, a circle on a blackboard, all these relations exist within what we see. The circle has a top half and a bottom half, a right-hand half and a left-hand half, an inside and an outside. Those relations alone are enough to make up a space of sorts. But the space of every-day life is filled out with what we derive from touch and movement—how a thing feels when we touch it, and what movements are necessary in order to grasp it. Other elements also come into the genesis of the space in which everybody believes who has not been troubled by philosophy; but it is unnecessary for our purposes to go into this question any more deeply. The point that concerns us is that a man's percepts are private to himself: what I see, no one else sees; what I hear, no one else hears; what I touch, no one else touches; and so on. True, others hear and see something very like what I hear and see, if they are suitably placed; but there are always differences. Sounds are less loud at a distance; objects change their visual appearance according to the laws of perspective. Therefore it is impossible for two persons at the same time to have exactly identical percepts. It follows that the space of percepts, like the percepts, must be private; there are as many perceptual spaces as there are percipients. My percept of a table is outside my percept of my head, in my perceptual space; but it does not follow that it is outside my head as a physical object in physical space. Physical space is neutral and public: in this space, all my percepts are in my head, even the most distant star *as I see it*. Physical and perceptual space have relations, but they are not identical, and failure to grasp the difference between them is a potent source of confusion.

To say that you see a star when you see the light that has come from it is no more correct than to say that you see New Zealand when you see a New Zealander in London. Your perception when (as we say) you see a star is causally connected, in the first instance, with what happens in the brain, the optic nerve, and the eye, then with a light-wave which, according to physics, can be traced back to the star as its source. Your sensations will be closely similar if the light comes from a lamp at the top of a mast. The physical space in which you believe the "real" star to be is an elaborate inference; what is given is the private space in which the speck of light you see is situated. It is still an open question whether the space of sight has depth, or is merely a surface, as Berkeley contended. This does not matter for our purposes. Even if we admit that sight alone shows a difference between an object a few inches from the eyes and an object several feet distant, yet you certainly cannot, by sight alone, see that a cloud is less distant than a fixed star, though you may *infer* that it is, because it can hide the star. The world of astronomy, from the point of view of sight, is a surface. If you were put in a dark room with little holes cut in the ceiling in the pattern of the stars letting light come through, there would be nothing in your immediate visual data to show that you were not "seeing the stars." This illustrates what I mean by saying that what you see is *not* "out there" in the sense of physics.

We learn in infancy that we can sometimes touch objects we see, and sometimes not. When we cannot touch them at once, we can sometimes do so by walking to them. That is to say, we learn to correlate sensations of sight with sensations of touch, and sometimes with sensations of movement followed by sensations of touch. In this way we locate our sensations in a three-dimensional world. Those which involve sight alone we think of as "external," but there is no justification for this view. What you see when you see a star is just as internal as what you feel when you feel a headache. That is to say, it is internal from the stand-point of *physical* space. It is distant in your private space, because it is not associated with sensations of touch, and cannot be associated with them by means of any journey you can perform.

To make the matter definite, let us suppose that a physiologist is observing a living brain—no longer an impossible supposition, as it would have been formerly. It is natural to suppose that what the physiologist sees is in the brain he is observing. But if we are speaking of physical space, what the physiologist sees is in his own brain. It is in no sense in the brain that he is observing, though it is in the percept of that brain, which occupies part of the physiologist's perceptual space. Causal continuity makes the matter perfectly evident: light-waves travel from the brain that is being observed to the eye of the physiologist, at which they only arrive after an interval of time, which is finite though short. The physiologist sees what he is observing only after the light-waves have reached his eye; therefore the event which constitutes his seeing comes at the end of a series of events which travel from the observed brain into the brain of the physiologist. We cannot, without a preposterous kind of discontinuity, suppose that the physiologist's percept, which comes at the end of this series, is anywhere else but in the physiologist's head.

It is extraordinarily difficult to divest ourselves of the belief that the physical world is the world we perceive by sight and touch; even if, in our philosophic moments, we are aware that this is an error, we never-theless fall into it again as soon as we are off our guard. The notion that what we see is "out there" in physical space is one which cannot survive while we are grasping the difference between what physics supposes to be really happening, and what our senses show us as happening; but it is sure to return and plague us when we begin to forget the argument. Only long reflection can make a radically new point of view familiar and easy.

Our illustrations hitherto have been taken from the sense of sight; let us now take one from the sense of touch. Suppose that, with your eyes shut, you let your finger-tip press against a hard table. What is really happening? The physicist says that your finger-tip and the table consist, roughly speaking, of vast numbers of electrons and protons; more cor-rectly, each electron and proton is to be thought of as a collection of processes of radiation, but we can ignore this for our present purposes. Although you think you are touching the table, no electron or proton in your finger ever really touches an electron or proton in the table, because this would develop an infinite force. When you press, repulsions are set up between parts of your finger and parts of the table. If you try to press upon a liquid or a gas, there is room in it for the parts that are repelled to get away. But if you press a hard solid, the electrons and protons that try to get away, because electrical forces from your finger repel them, are unable to do so, because they are crowded close to others which elbow them back to more or less their original position, like people in a dense crowd. Therefore the more you press the more they repel your finger. The repulsion consists of electrical forces, which set up in the nerves a current whose nature is not very definitely known. This current runs into the brain, and there has effects which, so far as the physiologist is concerned, are almost wholly conjectural. But there is one effect which is not conjectural, and that is the sensation of touch. This effect, owing to physiological inference or perhaps to a reflex, is associated by us with the finger-tip. But the sensation is the same if, by artificial means, the parts of the nerve nearer the brain are suitably stimulated—e.g., if your hand has been amputated and the right nerves are skilfully manipulated. Thus our confidence that touch affords evidence of the existence of bodies at the place which we think is being touched is quite misplaced. As a rule we are right, but we can be wrong; there is nothing of the nature of an infallible revelation about the matter. And even in the most favorable case, the perception of touch is something very different from the mad dance of electrons and protons trying to jazz out of each other's way, which is what physics maintains is really taking place at your finger-tip. . . .

51 Bertrand Russell's
Theory of Perception

Ernest Nagel

R USSELL'S CONCERN WITH THE POSI-
tive sciences is dominated almost exclusively by "the problem of the relation between the crude data of sense and the space, time, and matter of
mathematical physics."[1] Like many of his contemporaries, he has been impressed by the highly abstract character of physical theory, and by the
prima facie ·difference between the manifest traits of the world which are
exhibited in our daily experience with it and its constitution as reported by
the theoretical sciences. The theories of classical physics already provided
ample materials for embroidering this difference; those theories employed
such notions as that of instantaneous velocities, point-particles, mathematically continuous motions, and perfectly rigid and elastic bodies, although
there appears to be nothing in our common experience to which these notions are applicable. But it was the advent of relativity theory and quantum
mechanics, with their novel geometries and chronometries and their revolutionary conceptions of matter and causality, which supplied the chief
stimulus to Russell's preoccupation with the problem. . . .

[This and the next selection are extracted from *The Philosophy of Bertrand Russell,*
Vol. V of *The Library of Living Philosophers,* published by Northwestern University in
1944 and hereafter published by Open Court Co., La Salle, Illinois. They are reprinted with
the permission of Professor Paul A. Schilpp, the editor of *The Library of Living Philosophers.*]
  1. *Our Knowledge of the External World* (from now on abbreviated as *OKEW*), p. viii.

Like most philosophers, Russell believes that any discussion of the relation between theoretical physics and experience starts with admitting the familiar facts of common knowledge. But he maintains that on the one hand this knowledge is vague, complex, and inexact, and that on the other hand some types of its "data" are more certain and more "indubitable" than others. In order to obtain a secure foundation for knowledge we must therefore separate out those beliefs which are "inferred" from or "caused" by other beliefs, from the beliefs which are both logically and psychologically prior to all others. The "hardest" or "most certain" of all data (that is, data which "resist the solvent influence of critical reflection") are the truths of logic and the particular facts of sense.[2] The logical starting point of a philosophical inquiry into physics must therefore be with our immediate, direct perceptions. The problem of the relation of theoretical physics to the facts of experience can therefore be amplified as follows:

> The laws of physics are believed to be at least approximately true, though they are not logically necessary; the evidence for them is empirical. All empirical evidence consists, in the last analysis, of perceptions; thus the world of physics must be, in some sense, continuous with the world of perceptions, since it is the latter which supplies the evidence for the laws of physics. . . .
>
> The evidence for the truth of physics is that our perceptions occur as the laws of physics would lead us to expect—e.g., we see an eclipse when the astronomers say there will be an eclipse. But physics never says anything about perceptions; it does not say that we shall see an eclipse, but something about the sun and the moon. The passage from what physics asserts to the expected perception is left vague and casual; it has none of the mathematical precision belonging to physics itself. We must therefore find an interpretation of physics which gives a due place to perceptions; if not, we have no right to appeal to the empirical world.[3]

Russell's problem has therefore a two-fold aspect. One phase of it consists in finding an "interpretation" for physics which will make its propositions relevant to the crude materials of sense; and, as will appear, this concern leads Russell to adopt the view that all the objects of common-sense and developed science are logical constructions out of *events*—our perceptions being a proper sub-class of the class of events. The other phase of the problem consists in justifying the truth-claims of physics; and this concern leads Russell to examine what data may serve as the most indubitable foundation for our knowledge, and to a discussion of the causal theory of perception as the ground for assuming the existence of events that are not perceptions. The two aspects of the problem are not independent, since the resolution of the second depends in part on the answer to the first, whereas the first requires that the "indubitable entities" (which it is the business of the second to specify) are already available. . . .

I shall comment briefly on the following views central to Russell's epistemology: that our percepts are located in our brains; that the causal theory of perception is the ground for inferring the existence of unperceived

2. *OKEW*, 75.
3. *Analysis of Matter* (from here on abbreviated as *AM*), 6–7.

events; and that our knoweldge of physical objects is "inferred" from percepts in our brain.

Russell maintains that, although it may be natural to suppose that what a physiologist sees when he is observing a living brain is in the brain he is observing, in fact "if we are speaking of physical space, what the physiologist sees is in his own brain."[4] This seems to me incredibly wrong if the word "see" is being used in the ordinary sense in which we talk about seeing a physical object; and it is this ordinary sense of the word which Russell is employing when he supposes a physiologist to be observing a brain. There might indeed be a sense of "see" in which I see my own brain, though I have not the slightest inkling as to what that sense is. I do know, however, that I have never seen any portion of my own brain, and that I have seen many physical objects—where the statement that I have not seen one but seen the other is to be understood in the customary sense of "see." To deny the facts expressed by the statement seems to be absurd; and such a denial can be understood only if we suppose that the person making the denial is misusing language. Moreover, such facts seem to me basic for every sound epistemology and every sound interpretation of science; and, however difficult it may be to do so, the findings of physics and physiology must be interpreted so as to square with them.

The evidence Russell offers for the causal theory of perception derives whatever plausibility it has from the tacit assumptions of common-sense knowledge; accordingly, it is not this theory which can justify such common-sense assumptions as that our perceptions may have unperceived causes. Russell's chief argument for that theory consists in showing that if we accept the theory we can formulate the course of events in "simple causal laws." For example, he declares that if many people see and hear a gun fired, the further they are situated from it the longer is the interval between the seeing and the hearing. He thinks it is therefore "natural to suppose that the sound travels over the intervening space, in which case something must be happening even in places where there is no one with ears to hear."[5] But why does it seem "natural" to suppose this? Does not the "naturalness" receive its support from the experimental confirmations which are found for such assumptions in the context of our manipulating physical objects? Russell also thinks that, although the phenomenalist view (that there are no unperceived events) is not logically impossible, it is an unplausible view, because it is incompatible with physical determinism.[6] But why is the assumption unplausible that "imaginary" or "fictitious" entities are causally efficacious? If the unplausibility does not rest upon the findings of disciplined experience, embodied in common-sense knowledge, upon what can it rest? . . .

It is a common error of Russell's critics to interpret his view that the physical world is a logical construction, as if he intended to deny that there

4. *Philosophy* (from here on abbreviated as *P*), 140 (See Selection 50 above, p. 627).
5. *AM*, 209.
6. *AM*, 214.

are physical objects in the ordinary sense of this phrase. For this misunderstanding he is at least partly to blame. Thus he declares: "Common sense imagines that when it sees a table it sees a table. This is gross delusion."[7] Again, commenting on Dr. Johnson's refutation of Berkeley, he maintains that "If he had known that his foot never touched the stone, and that both were only complicated systems of wave-motions, he might have been less satisfied with his refutation."[8] And elsewhere he says that on the view he is recommending, "the 'pushiness' of matter disappears altogether. . . . 'Matter' is a convenient formula for describing what happens where it isn't."[9] . . .

. . . Is it a delusion when, under appropriate circumstances, we claim to see a table? . . . In the sense in which we ordinarily use the word "see" and "table," it may be quite true that we do see a table: this mode of expressing what is happening is the appropriate way of putting the matter. Again, if when Dr. Johnson kicked a stone his foot never touched the stone, what *did* his foot do? To say that his foot never touched the stone, because both his foot and the stone were systems of radiation, is to *misuse* language; for in the specified context the words "foot," "stone," "kicked," and "touched" are being so used that it is correct to say Dr. Johnson kicked a stone and therefore his foot touched it. To be sure, under some other circumstances, and for the sake of certain ends, it might be advisable to use a different language in describing what had happened. But it obviously cannot be wrong to employ ordinary language in accordance with ordinary usage. And finally, it seems to me grotesque to say that the "pushiness" of matter can disappear as a consequence of a new analysis or redefinition of matter. We have learned to apply the word "pushy" to certain identifiable characteristics of material objects; and such a use of the word is correct, simply because that is the usage that had been established for it. Whatever may be the outcome of analyzing material objects, their identifiable properties will remain their identifiable properties, and it will be correct to apply the standardized expressions to them. It will certainly not be correct to designate a physical body as a formula. . . .

7. *The ABC of Relativity*, 213.
8. *P*, 279. Russell's reference is to the following passage in James Boswell's *Life of Dr. Samuel Johnson:* "After we came out of church, we stood talking for some time together of Bishop Berkeley's ingenious sophistry to prove the nonexistence of matter, and that everything in the universe is merely ideal. I observed, that though we are satisfied his doctrine is not true, it is impossible to refute it. I never shall forget the alacrity with which Johnson answered, striking his foot with mighty force against a large stone, till he rebounded from it, 'I refute it thus!' " (Ed.)
9. *P*, 159.

52   A Reply to Ernest Nagel

Bertrand Russell

THERE ARE CERTAIN OCCURRENCES which are commonly called "perceptions," such as seeing the sun, hearing a clap of thunder, or smelling a rotten egg. What sort of relation can these occurrences have to the sun, the thunder, and the rotten egg respectively?

I have been surprised to find the causal theory of perception treated as something that could be questioned. I can well understand Hume's questioning of causality in general, but if causality in general is admitted, I do not see on what grounds perception should be excepted from its scope. Take the question of time: a gun is fired, let us say, and people are ranged at various points 100 metres, 200 metres, 300 metres, and so on, distant from it. They hear the noise successively. This evidence would be considered amply sufficient, but for philosophic prejudice, for the establishment of a causal law making the hearing of the noise an effect of a disturbance travelling outward from the gun. Or take seeing the sun: if I take suitable measures, I see it at certain times and not at others, and the times when the suitable measures will succeed do not depend on me. The event which I call "seeing the sun" occurs only—if science is right—when electromagnetic waves of suitable frequency have spent about eight minutes travelling across the intervening space, and have then produced various physiological effects. The waves can be stopped by a screen, the physiological effects by destroying the optic nerve or excising the visual centres in the brain. If this is not to be accepted as evidence of the causal ancestry of "seeing the sun," all scientific reasoning will have to be remodelled.

We can now state the epistemological problem: Accepting the truth of physics, and knowing, otherwise than through the study of physics, certain experiences which are commonly called "seeing the sun," what is the relation between these experiences and the sun? There is in the first place a causal connection: as a rule, the sun is part of a causal chain leading to "seeing the sun," and this causal chain is such that the light-waves which start from the sun are not much impeded in their course until they reach the eye. (Otherwise seeing a plant which has grown by the help of sun-light would be a case of seeing the sun; so, in fact, would seeing anything by daylight.) It is obviously possible to produce, by artificial means, an occurrence which will seem to the percipient to be a case of "seeing the sun" though in fact it is not so. Unless a special kind of causal connection with the sun exists, we are not "seeing the sun," even though our experience may be indistinguishable from one in which we *are* "seeing the sun." All this may be awkward, but it cannot be denied except by those who deny physics.

This brings me to Mr. Nagel's essay. He seems to be engaged in a vehement defence of common sense, and he points out, quite truly, that all science starts from common sense. How, then, does science differ from common sense? It differs mainly by the fact that its percentage of mistakes is smaller. By "mistakes" I mean, to begin with, beliefs which are proved wrong by leading to surprise, as, for instance, that the things one sees in a mirror are "real." If I do not know about radio, I shall think there is a strange man in the house when it is only the news. If you give a savage a box containing a gyrostat, he will think it is bewitched because he cannot turn it round. *Most* of our common-sense beliefs must be right from a practical point of view, or else science could never get started; but some turn out wrong. Science diminishes their number; in this sense it corrects common sense in spite of starting from it. The procedure is exactly like that of correcting testimony by other testimony, where it is assumed throughout that testimony is *usually* trustworthy.

Mr. Nagel asserts with passion that he has seen tables, but he adds that he means this in the sense in which we ordinarily use the words "see" and "table." I might agree if he would take the phrase "see a table" as a whole. Like Mr. Nagel, I have often had the experience called "seeing a table." My objection is that the phrase, as commonly understood, involves false metaphysics. I see, let us say, something continuous, rectangular, shiny, and brown. My seeing is certainly an event in me, though Mr. Nagel is deeply shocked when I say that what I see is in me. American realists induced me to abandon the distinction between a sensation and sense-datum, but the very men who repudiate this distinction object to the inference that the sense-datum is in me. (I shall return to this point shortly.) But in any case what I see when I "see a table" is simultaneous with my seeing, whereas the table as the physical object connected with my seeing is slightly earlier. (The sun is eight minutes earlier, some nebulae hundreds of thousands of years earlier.) What I see has secondary properties recognized, since Locke, as not belonging to the physical object, and primary qualities concerning which the same has been recognized since Berkeley—or since Kant, by those who dislike Berkeley. In what sense, then, can we be said to see the physical object which *is* the table according to physics?

When once the causal process leading from the table to my percept is recognized in all its complexity, it becomes obvious that only by a miracle could my percept resemble the table at all closely. What is more, if this miracle does take place, only a divine revelation can assure us that it does. No such revelation has been vouchsafed to me, and I am therefore left in doubt as to whether the table resembles my visual percept in any respects except those in which physics says it does.

Mr. Nagel is indignant with me because I use the word "see" in an unusual sense. I admit this. The usual sense implies naïve realism, and whoever is not a naïve realist must either eschew the word "see" or use it in a new sense. Common sense says: "I see a brown table." It will agree to both the statements: "I see a table" and "I see something brown." Since, according to physics, tables have no colour, we must either (a) deny physics, or (b) deny that I see a table, or (c) deny that I see something brown. It is a painful choice; I have chosen (b), but (a) or (c) would lead to at least equal paradoxes.

I come finally to a statement of mine which profoundly shocks Mr. Nagel, as it has shocked various other philosophers; I mean the statement that, when a physiologist looks at another man's brain, what he sees is in his own brain and not in the other man's. I have not so far found any philosopher who knew what I meant by this statement. My defence of it must consist of explaining it, since the arguments brought against it are against some view totally different from mine.

Mr. Nagel says: "I know that I have never seen any portion of my own brain, and that I have seen many physical objects." He goes on to explain that he is using "see" in its customary sense.

It may be that my theory of matter is quite absurd, but at any rate it is not the theory that Mr. Nagel is refuting. I do not think that my visual percepts are a "portion" of my brain; "portion" is a material concept. Briefly, omitting niceties and qualifications, my view is this: A piece of matter is a system of events; if the piece of matter is to be as small as possible, these events must all overlap, or be "compresent." Every event occupies a finite amount of space-time, i.e., overlaps with events which do not overlap with each other. Certain collections of events are "points" or perhaps minimum volumes, since the existence of collections generating points is uncertain. Causal laws enable us to arrange points (or minimum volumes) in a four-dimensional order. Therefore when the causal relations of an event are known, its position in space-time follows tautologically. The causal and temporal connections of percepts with events in afferent and efferent nerves gives percepts a position in the brain of the perceiver. Observe that a "portion" of a brain is a set of points (or minimum volumes); an event may be a member of certain points (or minimum volumes) that are members of the brain, and is then said to be "in" the brain, but it is not "part" of the brain. It is a member of a member of the brain.

The inferences by which physicists pass from percepts to physical objects (which we are assuming valid) only enable us to know certain facts about the structure of the physical world as ordered by means of causal relations, compresence, and contiguity. Beyond certain very abstract mathematical properties, physics can tell us nothing about the character of the physical world. But there is one part of the physical world which we know otherwise than through physics, namely that part in which our thoughts and feelings are situated. These thoughts and feelings, therefore, are members of the atoms (or minimum material constituents) of our brains. This theory may seem fantastic, but in any case it is not the theory that Mr. Nagel refutes.

I have only one more point to make against Mr. Nagel. He says that if, as I maintain, "things" are those series that obey the laws of physics, then these laws are definitions. Not so; it is "things" that are being defined, and it is an empirical fact (if it is a fact) that there are series obeying the laws of physics and having some of the properties we expect of "things." Quantum theory has made it impossible to use the notion of "thing" (or "matter") in dealing with microscopic phenomena, but in dealing with macroscopic phenomena the notion still has an approximate validity.

Before leaving Mr. Nagel's essay I should like to say that, although I do not agree with him, I am grateful to his criticism for compelling me to clarify the expression of my opinions on various important points. I think it is reasonable to hope that our controversy may be helpful to readers, and that towards this end each of us will have done his part.

53   Phenomenalism

C. H. Whiteley

The Meaning of Words

. . . WHEN I AM TEACHING A CHILD
the meaning of the word "table," I point to the table, so that he sees it; I
put his hand to it, so that he feels it; that is, I cause him to sense certain
sense-data. Surely it is with these sense-data that he thereupon associates
the sound "table"; when he sees and feels similar sense-data, he repeats
"table." It is by the differences in what they look like and feel like that he
distinguishes tables from chairs and apples and half-crowns. It is natural to
conclude that when he uses the word "table" or "apple," he is using it to
describe what he sees, feels, tastes, etc., rather than to propound some
theory about an invisible and intangible material substance.

The word "table" *means* a certain visible squareness and brownness,
a certain tangible hardness; i.e., it means a certain type of sense-experience.
When I say "There is a table in this room" I am describing the sense-data
which I am now sensing, and if I do not sense such sense-data, then, being
a truthful person, I do not say that there is a table in the room. If someone
else says that there is, I test his statement by looking and feeling, i.e., by
finding out whether the appropriate sense-data are available; if they are not,
I dismiss his statement as false. If I say "Socrates drank his companions
under the table," I am not describing any sense-experiences which I have
now, but I am describing sense-experiences which I suppose Socrates and
his companions to have had at another time and place.

We cannot, of course, identify "the table" with any one single sense-
datum; an experience which was entirely unique and did not recur would
not be worth naming. The function of words is not to name everything
we see or hear, but to pick out the recurrent patterns in our experience.

[This selection consists of portions of Chapters VI and VII of C. H. Whiteley's *An
Introduction to Metaphysics,* a book published in 1949 by Methuen and Co., Ltd., London.
It is reproduced here with the kind permission of Professor Whiteley and the publisher.]

They identify our present sense-data as being of the same group or type as others which we have sensed before. A word, then, describes, not a single experience, but a group or type of experiences; the word "table" describes all the various sense-data which we normally refer to as appearances or sensations "of" the table. So a material thing is not indeed identical with any sense-datum; but neither is it something different in kind from sense-data. It is a group, or class, or system of sense-data; and nothing but sense-data goes to constitute it. So this doctrine may be expressed by saying that every statement we make about a material thing is equivalent to another statement about sense-data.

The Advantages of Phenomenalism

This analysis of the notion of a material thing is called Phenomenalism, since it makes of a material thing a group of phenomena, appearances, instead of a transcendent reality distinct from appearances. It is a widespread view, and has been accepted by many philosophers who do not call themselves Idealists and are far from accepting Berkeley's view that the fundamental reality is Mind. The term "idealism" itself, however, though it has shifted in meaning since, does properly denote just this part of Berkeley's theory, that the material world—"the whole choir of heaven and furniture of the earth" says Berkeley—consists of what he calls "ideas" and I have been calling "sense-data." The word in this sense has nothing to do with ideals, and the theory would have been called "ideaism" but for considerations of pronunciation.

Phenomenalism, then, is the doctrine that all statements about material objects can be completely analyzed into statements about sense-data. The analysis of any such statement must be very complex; and the value of the "material-object language" is that it enables us to refer in one word, such as "table," to a vast number of sense-data differing very much among themselves. The group of sense-data constituting the table includes all the different views I can obtain at different distances, from different angles, in different lights, no two of them exactly alike, but all of them variations on one central pattern; it includes sense-data of touch, and those of sound (though these last seem somewhat more loosely connected with the main visuo-tactual group); and with other kinds of material things, such as apples, sense-data of taste and smell form important constituents of the thing.

This type of theory has certain clear advantages. On the representative theory, the very existence of a material world or of any given material object must always be in principle doubtful. I am directly aware of my sense-data, and so can be certain of their existence and character: but "material objects" are quite different—their existence and character can be known only by an inference, which cannot give the complete certainty which comes from observation. Descartes, for example, accepts this consequence of the theory, and will not allow himself to believe that there is a material world at all, until he has convinced himself that there exists an omnipotent and benevolent God who would never have led him to believe in the material world if it had not been real. But if Descartes really succeeded in keeping up this attitude of doubt for more than a moment, few men have been able to imitate him. We *cannot* believe that the existence of the table is in any way subject to doubt.

The phenomenalist theory, by making the existence of the table *the same thing* as the occurrence of certain sense-data, removes that doubt; for the system of sense-data constituting the table has beyond doubt come under my observation.

The theory not only removes the doubt, but makes it clear why we cannot seriously entertain it. The Plain Man was right after all: material things are seen and touched, are objects of direct awareness, and it is by seeing and touching that we know that they exist, though no material thing is straightforwardly identical with what I am seeing and touching *at this particular moment.*

So, by accepting the phenomenalist analysis, we escape being involved in any reference to an unobservable Matter. We can preserve our empiricism inviolate, and talk about the things we see and hear and smell and touch, and not about other hypothetical things beyond the reach of our observation. Science, the knowledge of nature, on this view becomes the recording, ordering and forecasting of human experiences. Therein lies its interest for us. If the physical world lay outside our experience, why should we be concerned with it?

Criticisms of Phenomenalism

But these advantages of phenomenalism are purchased at a cost. Along several different lines the phenomenalist interpretation of our statements about material things seems to conflict with our usual beliefs, and produces paradoxes not very easy to accept.

(1) In ordinary speech we are accustomed to draw a distinction between "appearance" and "reality," and to allow that a thing may appear to be what it is not, as Descartes' stick half under water may appear bent although it is really straight. Hence we reckon some of our perceptions as "real" or "true" or "genuine," and others as "illusions." The representative theory of perception is in accordance with this way of thinking; for on that theory our sense-data are in some respects copies of material things; some are accurate copies, and so are genuine and true, others are inaccurate copies, and so false and illusory. The representative theory differs from common sense mainly in holding that the discrepancies between the sense-datum and the material object which it represents are greater than we realize.

But what is the phenomenalist to make of this distinction? He can admit no essential difference between appearance and reality; for on his view the appearances *are* the reality. Material things consist of appearances—sense-data—and of nothing else. And these sense-data all actually occur and so are equally real. Moreover, they are what they appear to be; their reality consists in appearing, and the suggestion that they might "really" have qualities which they do not appear to have is without meaning. Thus the phenomenalist has no justification for classifying them into "real" and "unreal," or "genuine" and "counterfeit." The various sense-data which go to constitute a material object, such as my table, are of many different shapes and colors. All of them are equally real, and none of them can be *the* "real shape" or "real color" of the table. Evidently tables are more versatile objects than we thought, and may have as many different shapes and colors as there are occasions of observing them. Why then should we come by the idea that there is only one "real shape," and the rest are mere appearances?

The phenomenalist solution of this difficulty is to allow that in a strict philosophical sense of the word "real," the distinction between reality and appearance cannot be drawn. But the purpose of the common-sense distinction between appearance and reality is not to pry into the ultimacies of metaphysics, but to enable us to deal with the experiences we encounter. What causes us to condemn an experience as an "illusion" is that it leads us astray. A mirage is an illusion because it causes us to make a mistake. But what kind of mistake? Surely, not the mistake of thinking that we now see trees and water, but the mistake of expecting that we shall soon be able to have a drink and sit in the shade. The mistake consists in the false expectation of certain other sense-data. Thus the illusoriness is not in the sense-datum itself, but in the expectation which we form when we sense it.

Error of this sort is possible because sense-data are not chaotic, but in the main are arranged in orderly series. Normally, when the visual sense-data belonging to water are obtainable, so are the gustatory sense-data of drinking water and relieving one's thirst. The mirage deceives us because, abnormally, we get the visual sense-data without the gustatory ones. Mirror-images may deceive us because the things seen in a mirror cannot be observed from the back and cannot be touched. Thus a "real" table consists of a complete set of sense-data of different senses related to one another in certain systematic ways (e.g., visual sense-data become continuously smaller and auditory ones continuously fainter as we move away from a certain region of space). When, as in the case of a table seen in a mirror, you have some members of the set but not others, you say that what is seen in the mirror is not a "real" table, or is not "really" there.

Again, the stick in water may lead us into error because sticks that "look bent" usually "feel bent" as well; and so we are surprised to find that it "feels straight," and say that though it "looks bent" it is not "really" bent.

The precise interpretation of the word "real" is different in different contexts. But in general, say phenomenalists, it will be found that what we call the "real world" is not a world different from that of appearances; it is a selection from the world of appearances, a collection of appearances which are normal, systematic, and so reliable. The "unreal" consists of eccentric appearances which in one way or another fail to fit in with the normal type of sets of sense-data, and therefore cause us to form false expectations.

(2) Sensations come and go. Few of them last for very long, and none of them lasts for ever. If we add up all the occasions in my life on which I have been looking at this table, we get a very short period indeed. And, like the rest of my species, I frequently go to sleep, and cease to perceive any material object whatsoever. That is to say, if a material thing consists of sense-data, its existence must be intermittent. Sense-data belonging to the thing exist only now and again, and most of the time they do not exist at all. But material objects such as tables are normally supposed to be permanent things, which endure uninterruptedly for very long periods. How can a permanent object be made out of momentary sense-data?

If I am alone in the room and close my eyes, there are then no sense-data belonging to the table; are we to suppose that I can annihilate so substantial a material object simply by shutting my eyes? It seems as though the phenomenalist must deny that any such statement as "There is a table in the room" can be true unless there is someone there seeing or touching it; and he must also deny that any such statement as "The table has been here for twenty years" can be true, unless (what seems most improbable) gangs of watchers have been observing it in relays for the whole of that time.

The phenomenalist answer to these difficulties involves a radical reinterpretation of the whole notion of a permanent material thing. That the existence of the table should be permanent in the way in which my waking experience is uninterrupted, that the table should last for twenty years in the way that my hearing a performance of a symphony can last for three-quarters of an hour, is of course impossible on a phenomenalist view. Whatever kind of permanence is attributed to the table must be understood in another sense.

Clearly, when I say that there is a table in the now uninhabited attic, I am not describing the sense-data of anyone. But, though the statement cannot be a description of *actual* sense-data, it can be a description of *possible* sense-data; and this is what it is according to phenomenalists. To say that there is a table there now is to say that *if* there were anyone in the room he *would* be having the kind of experience which we call seeing a table. "There is a table" means "Go and look and you will see a table." And to say that it has been there twenty years means that if at any time during those years anyone had been in the room, he could have seen or touched a table.

So we must modify our original account of the nature of a material thing. It consists not merely of actual sense-data, but also of possible sense-data; or, more precisely, of the fact that under certain conditions sense-data are obtainable. What is permanent is then not any sense-datum or group of sense-data, but the possibility of obtaining sense-data of a certain kind. Hence J. S. Mill defined matter as "the permanent possibility of sensation."

I think this much at least must be admitted: if it is true that there is a table in the attic, it is also true that if anyone with the use of normal eyes in a good light were to be in the attic now, he would have the experience of seeing the table; if it is true that the table has been there for twenty years, it is also true that if anyone had been there under those conditions at any time during those twenty years, he would have had the experience of seeing the table. That is to say, the statement about sense-data is involved in or implied by the statement about the table. According to the phenomenalist, such statements about possible sense-data constitute the whole of what the statement about the table means. All statements about material objects are equivalent to statements about what people have experienced, or would have experienced if circumstances had been different.

He points out that if we try to imagine the presence of the table in the attic, what we do is to imagine what it would look like and feel like. If we want to test the statement that it is there, we go and look. Statements which are not, in the final analysis, about actual or possible experiences, cannot be tested at all, and are therefore without meaning for us.

Berkeley himself gives another explanation of the permanence of material things. According to his theory, God is eternally perceiving everything, and therefore, at times when neither I nor any other human being or animal is perceiving the table, God is still perceiving it. But whether or not this is really the case, it is obviously not a correct interpretation of what we mean when we attribute continuous existence in time to the table. For if it were, we should not believe in permanent material things at all unless we believed, not only in God, but in an omnisentient God such as Berkeley believed in.

(3) According to our ordinary notions of them, material objects are causally active: they do things. The table supports the tablecloth, the fire warms the room. Material objects exercise force, have influences on one another and incidentally on ourselves, causing, among other things, our sensations of them. This continually active causal interplay makes up the system of nature, which it is the business of science to study and reduce to laws. Does not science explain what happens by referring events to their causes, which in the material realm at least are material things, exercising physical force? Surely, the room cannot be warmed by my visual sense-datum of a fire! Still less can it be warmed by the possibility of a visual sense-datum of a fire during my absence, when I am not looking at the fire but the room gets warmed all the same. When we all sit round the table and sense sense-data very similar in shape, size and color, what is the explanation of this fact, if not that there is an independent table which is the common cause of all our similar sense-data? Berkeley himself admits, or rather insists, that an "idea" is "inert," and can *do* nothing.

Phenomenalist Analysis of Causation

To deal with this problem, we need a fresh analysis and re-interpretation of the notion of cause, parallel to the phenomenalist re-interpretation of the notion of "substance" or "thing." Such an analysis was given in David Hume's *Treatise of Human Nature* (1739), and modern phenomenalists in the main follow his line of thought. Hume's aim is to interpret statements about cause and effect in such a way that the relation between a cause and its effect shall be an observable fact, and shall contain nothing mysterious or occult. For unless the words "cause and effect" described something we could observe, they would not, according to Hume, be intelligible to us.

What, then, do I observe in cases in which I should naturally use causal language? I am watching a game of billiards. I observe the event which I might naturally describe by saying that one ball A moved across the table and made or caused another ball B to roll into a pocket. What do I actually *see*? I see a certain sequence of events: first the movement of A, then the touching of A and B, then the movement of B. This temporal sequence of movements, the one which I call the effect following on the one I call the cause, seems to be all the visible relation there is between them.

But obviously, mere temporal sequence is not the same thing as causation; *post hoc* is not the same as *propter hoc;* plenty of other things preceded the movement of my billiard-ball in time which were not causes of it. Yet nothing seems to be observable but temporal sequence—first one event, then the other. Whence do I get this notion of the ball being made or caused or forced to move?

If I were pushing the ball myself, I should be aware of myself making a certain muscular effort, *trying* to make it move; and, when I observe the collision of the two balls and the ensuing movement of B, I may perhaps have a vague image of a similar kind of pushing going on between the balls. But if I do, it is clear that this feeling of muscular effort is not observed in the situation presented to my senses, but is a "projection" of my own past feelings in similar situations. For billiard-balls do not have muscles, or make efforts, and even if they did, I could not observe what efforts they were making, I could only observe their movements.

Certainly when I see the collision, I expect that the second ball will move—there is a "felt tendency of the mind" to pass from the "cause" to the "effect," but this is a psychological fact about me, not a physical fact about the balls. There seems nothing in the observed situation corresponding to the words "cause," "power," "force," which I am inclined to apply to it; only the observed sequence of one event on the other. But how, then, do I distinguish between those temporal antecedents of an event which are its causes, and those which are not? How do I establish the difference between *post hoc* and *propter hoc*?

The answer is plain enough; I repeat the experiment, and if the same sequence of events recurs, I conclude that it was a causal and not an accidental sequence. The reason I believe that the movement of the ball was caused by the impact of the other ball, and not by somebody lighting a cigarette at the same time, is that I know by long experience that balls always move when they are struck by other balls moving fairly quickly, whereas they do not usually move when men light cigarettes in their neighborhood. When medical men inquire into the cause of cancer, what they are looking for is something which always happens to a man before he becomes ill with cancer, just as, when they say that malaria is caused by the bite of a mosquito, they mean that a man has always been bitten by a mosquito before developing malaria. The observable fact which leads us to say that C is the cause of E is the fact that events of the kind C are followed by events of the kind E, not once or sometimes, but whenever they occur.

Causality, as a fact about the world, is then, according to Hume, a relation of invariable sequence. What is required to convert *post hoc* into *propter hoc* is regular repetition. To say that every event has a cause is to say that for any event E there is another event (or complex of "conditions") C such that whenever an event of the kind C occurs, an event of the kind E follows. It is to say that the sequence of phenomena is patterned, systematic; that there are in nature discoverable regularities.

But these regularities are discoverable among the observed phenomena themselves, and not between phenomena and something transcending phenomena. Causation, thus interpreted, is a relation between sense-data. The causes, that is to say, the invariable antecedents, of sense-experiences, are other sense-experiences.

Of course, not all causes are actually observed phenomena. In the analysis of cause, as in the analysis of substance, we must sometimes refer to possible sense-data which are not actual. But to say, for example, that a burst pipe was caused by the formation of a lump of ice which I have not seen, is not to desert the realm of sense-data; it is only to refer to sense-data which were not actually observed, but which might, in principle, have been observed; if I had been in a position to look at the interior of the pipe, I should have seen a lump of ice there.

Thus Hume and his followers do not deny that the relation of cause and effect is a real feature of the world; but they interpret it as a relation between sense-data, actual or possible. So the principle of causality does not carry us beyond the sphere of the observed and the observable, or compel us to admit the existence of "material substance" over and above systems of sense-data.

Thus, on this theory, the material world consists of sets of sense-experiences, together with the fact that an indefinitely large number of other similar sense-experiences might be had under certain specified conditions. Its "substances" are orderly groups of sense-data; and its causal relations are relations of regular sequence between sense-data of specified kinds. The main business of science is to discover causal laws, i.e., to reveal the patterns in that complex of experiences we call Nature. Science tells us what experiences to expect as the sequel to the experiences we are now having, and so renders our knowledge of the world systematic. . . .

The Paradoxes of Phenomenalism

. . . If we adopt phenomenalism, let us not do so without being clearly and fully aware of what it involves. (1) It involves the denial that physical objects are permanent, or exist unperceived. It must be granted to the phenomenalists that when I say "There is a table upstairs," I am at least implying that if you were to go upstairs and look (given normal eyesight, normal lighting, etc.) you would have certain visual sense-data. But it seems quite clear to me that this is not the whole nor the essential part of what I am asserting. For when I say that the table is there, I am stating something about what exists or happens *in fact, now;* my statement is about the actual present, and not, as the phenomenalists make it, about the possible future. And if the phenomenalist account is to be accepted, we must say that this statement is a mistake. There is nothing at all in the attic now; there is no attic now at all; for there is nobody perceiving it.

(2) We must very seriously revise our opinions about the nature of causality. As a rule, we are in the habit of believing that a cause is something which actually exists or occurs, and that something which does not actually exist or occur can have no effects. This opinion must be given up if we accept the phenomenalist view. For on that view, to say that the bursting of pipes is caused by the formation of ice in them is to say that whenever one observes or could observe sense-data of the set constituting a burst pipe, one either has or could have previously observed sense-data of the set constituting a lump of ice inside that pipe. But quite clearly, in practically every instance of this rule, nobody does actually observe the ice; the sense-data of the ice are possible, not actual. That is to say, causality in such a case is a relation between something and nothing, between an actually observed burst, and a hypothetical proposition to the effect that if something had happened which did not happen and in practice could not have happened, then something else would have happened which also did not happen. This interpretation flouts our usual assumption that what might have happened but did not happen can have no effects. The actual material agents of physics and common sense must be replaced by a set of hypothetical facts relating to unfulfilled conditions. If this is so, it is difficult to see why we should suppose that these hypothetical propositions are true. If I leave a fire in my room, I expect it to be warm on my return; but is this not because I believe that the fire is still now burning, a real present fire exercising an influence on a real present atmosphere? I cannot see what reason can be given for expecting the room to be warmed, independently of my

reasons for supposing that the fire *is* burning *now* (and not that, *if* I went and looked, I should see flame). I can see reason for believing in regularities in nature holding between one event and another; but no reason at all for believing in regularities holding between one event which happened and another which might have happened but did not.

(3) A similar paradox arises with regard to other persons. According to the phenomenalist theory, all the statements I make about the consciousnesses of other people must be interpreted in terms of actual or possible observations of my own. A statement like "Jones is bored but he is not giving any sign of it" is a contradiction in terms, for on this theory the boredom *is* the sign. The only experiences I can intelligibly talk about or think about are my own, and whatever is not expressible in terms of actual or possible observations of mine is not intelligible to me. That is, there is no good argument for phenomenalism which is not an equally good argument for solipsism—the doctrine that the only experience in the world is my experience, and the only person existing in the universe is myself.

These paradoxical conclusions have been accepted by able philosophers, and one cannot therefore say that they are beyond belief. But they are markedly at variance with the ordinary assumptions, not only of common sense, but also of scientific investigation (for, whatever some scientists may manage to persuade themselves, they are not concerned only with the cataloguing and ordering of phenomena, but believe themselves to be dealing with permanent and independent objects). Hence we must demand very strong reasons indeed for accepting them. . . .

54   The Real World Is
Astonishingly Rich
and Complex

W. A. Sinclair

IF I NOW TRY TO OUTLINE TO YOU
some alternative theory of knowledge, I shall of course have to do so
in terms of that new alternative theory itself, because what I write will
not make sense in any other way. At first you will interpret what I
write in terms of the old familiar representative view. The consequence
is that if I were now to begin a systematic exposition, you would find
yourself at once regarding it as either incomprehensible or wrong, for the
very good reason that, on the representative theory whose lingering influence still affects you, the new alternative view would not make sense.
This constitutes a special disability which makes the study of the theory
of knowledge peculiarly difficult. We all suffer from it.

The best and indeed the only way that I can think of to circumvent
this very real difficulty is to begin not by a systematic and definitive
exposition, but by a discussion intended to do no more than give the
reader some first hint of the alternative theory that I have in mind. There-
after, as we advance, the theory will I hope become by stages progressively
clearer.

For this purpose, and in this manner, let us turn our attention once
more to our sense-organs. When we consider how they detect things in
our environment, the point that at once impresses us is how little they
do in fact detect. Consider our eyes. The retinas of the eyes detect light-
waves as do the sensitized films in cameras. As the scientists would put

[This selection comprises Chapter VII of *An Introduction to Philosophy* (1944). It is
reprinted here with the permission of Oxford University Press.]

it, they react to light-waves, i.e., to electro-magnetic vibrations of a certain range of wave-length. They do not react to other electro-magnetic vibrations which are either longer or shorter in wave-length than light-waves, though otherwise similar; and there are innumerable other such electro-magnetic vibrations all around us at all times.

This is a somewhat surprising fact of which comparatively few people seem to be aware. Take an analogy to make it clearer. Suppose that you are on board ship, and that you lean over the side and look down at the waves. There is not only one sort of wave on the surface of the water, but many sorts. Some of them are very large and very long, the distance from the crest of one wave to the crest of the next being about the length of the ship. If you are in mid-ocean there may even be still longer waves, the deep sea swell, which are so long that you cannot easily pick out the crests by the eye, though you can feel their presence by the slow rise and fall of the whole ship. In addition to those very long waves there are all sorts of smaller waves also, the distance from the crest of one to the crest of the next being a matter of yards or feet. There are also still smaller wavelets chasing each other over the surface of the water hither and thither, some of them so small that the distance from the crest of one to the crest of the next may be only a fraction of an inch. All those different waves, of such widely differing wave-lengths, are passing hither and thither over the surface of the water all the time.

Something very similar to this is happening in the room in which you are now sitting, the waves in this case being electro-magnetic waves such as light-waves and wireless waves. Passing through the room hither and thither at enormous velocities, and passing through your body also, are electro-magnetic waves of innumerable different lengths. Some are very long indeed, so long that the crest of one wave is miles away from the crest of the next. Others are so short that the crest of one is only a most minute fraction of a millimeter away from the next. There are all sorts of others whose lengths fall in between these extremes. They are all there. They are all in the room, i.e., passing through the room, at the instant at which you are reading this.

Some of them, but only a very few of them, are of such a length that they affect your eyes. If an electro-magnetic wave is shorter than about 1/30,000 of an inch, and longer than about 1/60,000 of an inch, then it affects the retina. When waves between these upper and lower limits are reflected by objects and fall on the eye, they cause changes in the retina, and this in turn causes changes in the nerves behind the eye, which in turn cause changes in the brain; after which, in some way we do not understand, we have the experience we call "seeing." For that reason, waves between those upper and lower limits of length are called "visible," or "light-waves."

There are also other electro-magnetic waves passing through the room which are exactly like these, only somewhat longer. They do not affect the retina, but they do affect certain nerve-endings in the skin. They cause nerve-currents to pass along nerves from the skin to the brain, and after these reach the brain we have the experience we call "feeling heat." If somebody thoughtfully provides a hot drink for you at bedtime, then the glass will not be visible if you switch out your bedside light, but you will be able to feel the heat of it on your hand when you bring your hand close to it. This is because the heated liquid is emitting waves of the lengths that affect the heat-sensitive organs in your skin, but is not emitting the very slightly shorter waves which would affect the retinas of your eyes. There are yet other electro-magnetic waves also, which are exactly the same except that they are longer still. They do not affect the body at all. Then there are others even longer, which do not affect the body, but do affect wireless receiving sets. These are called "radio-frequencies" or "wireless waves." We are familiar with the lengths of such waves from reading the dials on any wireless set. All these different waves are round about us at all times, even though our sense-organs fail to detect them. If you had a wireless set beside you at this moment, and were slowly to turn the tuning knob, you would hear one station after the other. All those stations are sending their waves through the room, and through your body, at this moment, but none of them caused any reaction in your body, and you would not have known they were there at all, unless you had used the wireless set to detect them. Your sense-organs themselves do not detect them.

Not only are there in the room around you those waves which you cannot detect because they are longer than those to which your sense-organs react; there are also innumerable other waves which you do not detect because they are shorter than those to which your sense-organs react, such as ultra-violet rays, gamma-rays, and others.

The point of this long string of examples is to emphasize how very small is the range of electro-magnetic waves which are detected by our sense-organs. If the range of wave-lengths known to the scientists were represented by a line from the top to the bottom of this page, then the part of that range that our sense-organs detect—namely light-waves and heat-waves—would be represented by a section of the line too small to see except with a magnifying glass.

So, speaking picturesquely and loosely, our eyes are blind to very nearly all that surrounds us. We can console ourselves for this deficiency by the consideration that it is well that things are so, because otherwise we should no doubt be hopelessly confused. It appears to be only because our eyes are blind to very nearly everything, because they neglect very nearly everything, that we are able to see things around us as we do. If our eyes detected more, we should then no doubt experience only confusion, something analogous to the confusion we experience at present if we listen to an unsatisfactory wireless set which reacts at the same time not only to one wave-length but to neighboring wave-lengths also. This produces a jumble of sounds, with one program on top of another. If our eyes were not blind to all but a very limited range of wave-lengths, we might well have a similar sort of confusion in our visual experience. (The reader will at this point probably inquire what is meant by calling our normal daily experience "orderly" as distinguished from that possible state of confusion. Is there, he may ask, any independent standard of what constitutes confusion, or is what we call "order" only that kind of confusion with which we have grown familiar and with which we are consequently able to cope? This is the kind of question that will or will not appear significant to the reader according to the amount of questioning thought that he has given to the matter. We shall return to this opinion later in a context that will make the point more clear.)

The same considerations apply to hearing, except of course that the waves are waves in air, and not electro-magnetic waves. At the present moment there are air waves of all sorts of wave-lengths passing to and fro in the air of the room you are in. They are falling on the drums of your ears. If these air-waves are longer than about thirty-five feet you cannot hear them. If they are shorter than about seven-eighths of an inch you cannot hear them. Dogs, as you probably know, can hear sounds that human beings cannot hear, because dog's ears react to sound-waves shorter than those to which human ears react. Poachers become applied scientists in this connection, for they make whistles which produce air-waves just long enough to make a dog's ears react, but not long enough to make the gamekeeper's ears react.

So, again speaking picturesquely and loosely, our ears are deaf to very nearly everything, just as our eyes are blind to very nearly everything. The same applies to all our other sense-organs. They react to only minute sections of all that surrounds them, and do not react to the vast remainder. In this way they may be said to select for our attention only very minute sections of our environment, very minute sections indeed.

If you have already read some modern writings on the theory of knowledge you may at this point find yourself saying "But the sensa or sensibilia are not selected. They are somehow created," and if you have not read any such writings you may find yourself raising the same objection by saying that our sensations are not selected but created. This is an instance of that slipping back into a representationist way of thinking, or "three-term" theory of knowledge, of which I spoke as a perpetual plague at the beginning of the chapter. The objection is one which can quite logically be made if we hold a representationist view, but not otherwise. Whether we do hold a representationist view or not is another question. I believe that we can not, while others may think differently, but the point here is that if we make the above objection, we have thereby tacitly assumed the representationist view. The reason for emphasizing this at length is that many writers tend to make the above objection while at the same time maintaining and believing themselves to have abandoned the representationist way of thinking.

Now, in the light of all this, let us take stock. As a result of thinking along with Berkeley, and as a result of the change in our thinking which he brought about, and as a result of our further cogitation on the points in this chapter, we now find ourselves taking a view which is the opposite of that held by philosophers like Descartes and Locke.

They held that the real world was somewhat dull and uninteresting, and that the secondary qualities, the warmth and color of our daily experience, had no real counterparts, but were merely something added to our own private mental pictures. They thought, indeed, that the richness of our experience was an illusion, and that there existed nothing real corresponding to it.

We now have come to a view which is precisely the opposite, namely that the real world is almost unbelievably rich and complicated, so complicated that we should be confused and bewildered if we experienced anything more than minute and much simplified selections from it. What we experience (that is to say the world as we know it in ordinary day-to-day experience) is only a fragmentary selection of the real world; and we experience such minute selections as we do experience because our sense-organs react to them only, and are blind and deaf and unfeeling to all the vast remainder.

Let us now consider more fully what is involved in the preceding. Suppose—to make a fanciful but not necessarily misleading analogy, though still speaking somewhat loosely—that there is a large aerial fixed up outside your house, with the lead-in coming through the window and the end of the wire lying loose on a table. Let us have some friends in to see you, and let us fall to discussing what program is, as people say, "coming down" the lead-in. Suppose that I have with me a very simple little wireless set of my own. It has no adjustable tuning device, but has fixed tuning, and is so made that it will react to the B.B.C. Home Service wave-length and to no other. It has no loud-speaker, but only earphones, so that I can hear it, while none of the others can. When I pick up the lead-in, and touch the wire against the proper terminal on my little set, I say: "It's the B.B.C. Home Service that is coming down the lead-in," for that is what I hear. In the room there is another friend of yours who also has his own little set. It is exactly like mine, only it is tuned to the B.B.C. Forces Program. He pick up the lead-in, touches it to his set and says: "No, it's the Forces Program." Let us also have an American visitor in the room, with a set tuned to the Boston short-wave station in his own country. He puts the lead-in on to his set, and he says: "No, you are both wrong. The program coming down this lead-in is the program of the Boston short-wave station."

If we three then asked you to explain to us this apparently incomprehensible situation, you could do so quite easily. You would explain to us that these different programs were all of them coming down the lead-in, and that each of us could hear only the one to which he was himself tuned. You would explain that what was coming down the lead-in was in reality extremely complicated, and that the wireless set that each of us was using served to pick out for each of us from that complicated congestion only one particular range of electro-magnetic vibrations. You would explain that each of us was unaware of the other ranges of wave-lengths, because each of us had only his own wireless set, permanently tuned to just one range of wave-lengths. You would add that there were innumerable other ranges of wave-lengths also, such as those radiated by the various Continental stations, by ships and aircraft, and so forth, all of which were coming down the lead-in as well, though nobody in the room detected any of them, because nobody in the room had a set tuned to any of them.

This is a somewhat grotesque situation to imagine, but it makes quite a good analogy to explain the situation in which you and I and all men are, in our daily experience. There are surrounding us at this moment what can be described as innumerable electro-magnetic vibrations, of innumerably different wave-lengths, to nearly all of which we are blind, and similarly there are innumerable air-waves of innumerably different wave-lengths, to nearly all of which we are deaf.

Only the most minute sections of them are of the lengths to which our eyes and ears and other sense-organs are tuned, and the experience we call "seeing and hearing and feeling the things around us," is simply the experience that arises from the reaction of our sense-organs to that very minute section, while the vast remainder is neglected. That remainder is all there too, even though our sense-organs do not react to it, much as in our analogy all the programs were, as we say, coming down that lead-in, though we each reacted to and were aware of only one of them, while not reacting to and not being aware of the others.

This analogy is admittedly an over-statement of the differences between the experiences that different men have. It is an over-statement of the differences between what the sense-organs of one man detect and what the sense-organs of another man detect. These differences are in fact *comparatively* small. It is, however, by no means an over-statement of the differences between what the sense-organs of men react to and what the sense-organs of animals and insects react to. Insects and butterflies and bees, for instance, have eyes that react to electro-magnetic vibrations whose lengths are fairly near the lengths that human eyes react to, but the range of lengths to which they react is not by any means the same. In some cases they react to longer waves, in some cases to shorter. Bees in particular are very remarkable, for the retinas of their eyes change with the seasons, and in late autumn they react to a range of electro-magnetic vibrations which is measurably different from the range to which they react in spring. Moreover, at one period of the year, there is, in the middle of the range of vibrations to which they do react, a gap to which they do not react.

This line of thought leads to an explanation of that puzzle which we used as a means of starting our inquiry, namely that the men we call color-blind see only one uniform color in two lights, while you and I see two different colors. The fact that a color-blind man sees no difference in two lights which to us look conspicuously different makes us think at first that his eyes must be very unlike ours. Yet, though his eyes are not quite the same as ours, they are not by any means as different from ours as are, say, the eyes of a bee. The color-blind man's difference from people of normal color vision is comparatively small. The explanation of his different experience appears to be as follows.

The waves, or what can be described as the waves, which cause you and me to see what we call red, are longer than the waves that cause us to see what we call green, but only very slightly longer, only by about 1/120,000 of an inch. Our retinas react to the longer waves in a way which is different from the way in which they react to waves 1/120,000 inch shorter, and hence we have different experiences, i.e., we see different colors. The color-blind man's retina is not so discriminating. It reacts in the same way to both sets of waves. Hence he sees only one color, no matter whether it be the longer or the shorter waves that are falling upon his retina. Probably he sees the world around him much as normal people see an etching or a drawing, rather than as they see a colored painting.

To sum up the outcome of this state of our inquiry, it is beginning to appear that we do experience reality directly, yet that different people can have different experiences because, owing to the nature of our sense-organs, we do not experience anything like the whole of reality, but only some astonishingly small scraps of it, there being in some cases different scraps for different people.

We have therefore passed far beyond the theory of Descartes and Locke that the real world is simple, bare and colorless, and that we each add the richness of color and warmth and all the other secondary qualities to the private and largely illusory picture that each of us has in his own mind. Instead, we have now come to the opposite, and incidentally much pleasanter, conclusion that the real world is astonishingly rich and complex, containing genuinely in itself all those interesting qualities which Descartes and Locke believed were illusions. The real world is what I experience it to be. It is also what you experience it to be, and what the next man experiences it to be; and what the color-blind man experiences it to be; and what animals and insects experience it to be; and a very great deal more also. The reason why we have different experiences is not that each of us has a private and subjective picture, but that each of us picks out and attends to only a part of the immensely rich and complex world in which we find ourselves, and one man's part may not be the same as another man's part.

By this time an alternative theory has begun to emerge, or in other words an alternative way of looking upon the question of the nature of knowledge is becoming possible. It must, however, be specifically noted that this alternative theory is no more than suggested; and, further, that the argument by which it has been suggested cannot be used as a proof, because the means I have used to suggest it is observation of the working of our sense-organs, and our sense-organs are themselves observed by us in precisely the same way as are tables and chairs, and are subject to the same qualifications. Whatsoever the conclusions that we come to about tables and chairs and how we know them, we must hold the same conclusions about our sense-organs themselves and about the way we know them. We must not fall into the capacious trap, into which so many amateur philosophers fall, of thinking that we can produce a theory of knowledge by arguing from the working of the sense-organs, and forgetting that in so doing they may have contradicted the suppositions underlying the view they take of our knowledge of those quite material objects, namely our own sense-organs, on which the new alleged theory is based.

Selected Bibliography

(ITEMS PROVIDED WITH ASTERISK ARE MORE ADVANCED)
(FOR KEY TO ABBREVIATIONS SEE PAGE XIX)

Plato's dialogue *Theaetetus* contains the first evaluation, in the history of philosophy, of perception as a means to knowledge. Berkeley's *The Principles of Human Knowledge,* which covers similar ground as the *Three Dialogues between Hylas and Philonous,* is a classic of British empiricism which every student of philosophy ought to know. The same holds for Hume's *Treatise of Human Nature,* Book I, Part IV, esp. Section 2. This is a classical formulation of phenomenalism, though it is controversial whether Hume was consistently a phenomenalist. G. J. Warnock, *Berkeley* (Harmondsworth: Penguin Books, 1953, p), is not only a most illuminating commentary on Berkeley's theories on the subject, but contains also original reflections which have been widely discussed in recent years. A close commentary on Hume's theory of perception and physical reality may be found in H. H. Price, *Hume's Theory of the External World** (Oxford: Clarendon Press, 1940). Bertrand Russell, *The Problems of Philosophy* (London: Oxford U.P.: 1912, p), Chs. 1–4, provides a beautifully lucid and simple introduction to the problems of Locke and Berkeley, including a critique of Berkeleyan idealism. Elementary expositions and critiques of the theories of Berkeley and Locke may also be found in C. H. Whiteley, *An Introduction to Metaphysics* (London: Methuen, 1950), Ch. 5, A. C. Ewing, *The Fundamental Questions of Philosophy* (London: Routledge, N.Y.: Collier Books, 1962, p), Ch. 4, A. Pap, *Elements of Analytic Philosophy* (N.Y.: Macmillan, 1949), Ch. 7, J. Hospers, *Introduction to Philosophical Analysis* (Englewood Cliffs: Prentice-Hall, 2nd ed., 1967), Ch. 6, and Ch. 10 of A. Flew, *An Introduction to Western Philosophy* (Indianapolis: Bobbs-Merrill, 1971, p). Numerous recent articles on Locke and Berkeley are reprinted in C. B. Martin and D. M. Armstrong (eds.), *Locke and Berkeley* (Garden City: Doubleday, 1968, p). G. Engle and G. Taylor (eds.), *Berkeley's Principles of Human Knowledge: Critical Studies* (Belmont, Calif.: Wadsworth, 1968, p) is an anthology entirely devoted to Berkeley. The following are recent articles on Locke and Berkeley not included in either of these anthologies: R. Woolhouse, "Berkeley, the Sun That I See by Day, and that Which I Imagine By Night," *P*, 1968, G. Pitcher, "Minds and Ideas in Berkeley," *APQ*, 1969, J. A. Brunton, "The Absolute Existence of Unthinking Things," *P*, 1970, and M. Mandelbaum "Locke's Realism" in his *Philosophy, Science and Sense Perception* (Baltimore: Johns Hopkins Press, 1964). One of the earliest critics of Berkeley's idealism and Hume's phenomenalism was Thomas Reid, the founder of the Scottish school of Common Sense. Two of Reid's books dealing with this subject have recently been reprinted—*Essays on the Intellectual Powers of Man* (Cambridge: M.I.T. Press, 1969) and *An Inquiry Into the Human Mind* (Chicago: U. of Chicago P., 1970). The latter volume contains a very detailed and illuminating introduction by T. Duggan concerning Reid's own views on sensation and perception.

R. J. Hirst (ed.), *Perception and the External World* (N.Y.: Macmillan, 1965, p), is a very useful anthology which contains selections from important philosophers of the past and present, as well as from physiologists and psychologists who have made contributions to the subject of perception. Under the title *Perceiving, Sensing, and Knowing*, R. J. Swartz has brought together a number of outstanding contributions to the subject of perception by 20th century Anglo-Saxon philosophers (Garden City: Doubleday, 1965, p). G. J. Warnock (ed.), *The Philosophy of Perception* (London: Oxford U.P., 1967, p) contains several recent articles on the subject. R. M. Chisholm (ed.), *Realism and the Background of Phenomenology* (N.Y.: Free Press of Glencoe, 1960), contains selections from Prichard, the American "New Realists," Samuel Alexander, Russell, Lovejoy, G. E. Moore, and the influential Continental realists, Brentano and Meinong. The volume edited by Hirst has a detailed annotated bibliography, the anthology edited by Chisholm has a very full bibliography of writings by realists of all shades, and there is an extensive listing of works published in the 20th century in the book edited by Swartz. A useful historical account of the entire topic is found in D. W. Hamlyn, *Sensation and Perception* (N.Y.: Humanities Press, 1961). Ch. 6 of the same author's *The Theory of Knowledge* (Garden City: Doubleday, 1970, p) is an excellent introductory discussion of the main problems of perception. Chs. 9–12 of J. Passmore, *A Hundred Years of Philosophy* (Harmondsworth: Penguin Books, 2nd ed., 1968, p) give a detailed account of recent developments in Anglo-Saxon philosophy. A survey of recent and contemporary theories of perception is also contained in T. E. Hill, *Contemporary Theories of Knowledge* (N.Y.: Ronald Press, 1961). G. M. Wyburn (ed.), *Human Senses and Perception* (Edinburgh and London: Oliver & Boyd, 1964), is a particularly useful cooperative volume consisting of contributions by the editor, a physiologist, R. W. Pickford, a psychologist, and R. J. Hirst, a philosopher, each presenting highlights of the contributions of their respective fields to the subject of perception. C. W. K. Mundle, *Perception: Facts and Theories* (London: Oxford U.P., 1971, p) contains a detailed critical survey of rival philosophical theories of perception. It includes a great deal of interesting material drawn from psychology and physiology. Like Mundle, B. A. Farrell in "A Psychological Look at Some Problems of Perception," in *Knowledge and Necessity, Royal Institute of Philosophy Lectures Vol. 3* (London: Macmillan, 1970, p) maintains that philosophers have not sufficiently taken into account the experimental work of psychologists. An elementary psychological account is M. D. Vernon, *The Psychology of Perception* (Baltimore: Penguin Books, 1962, p). D. C. Beardsley and M. Wertheimer (eds.), *Readings in Perception* (Princeton: Van Nostrand, 1958) is a source-book mainly intended for psychologists, but contains much of interest to philosophers as well. There are selections from K. Koffka, the Gestalt psychologist, Lord Brain, the physiologist, and the great 19th century scientist Helmholtz in Hirst, *op. cit.* The following works are entirely devoted to the subject of perception: J. R. Smythies, *Analysis of Perception** (London: Routledge, 1956), R. M. Chisholm, *Perceiving—A Philosophical Study** (Ithaca: Cornell U.P., 1957), R. J. Hirst, *The Problems of Perception* (London: Allen & Unwin, 1959), and D. M. Armstrong, *Perception and the Physical World* (London: Routledge, 1961). All four authors are critical of phenomenalism; Chisholm and Armstrong favor a theory of direct perception, while Hirst and Smythies defend representative accounts. Other recent works on perception which have been widely noted in the literature are D. Locke, *Perception and Our Knowledge of the External* (London: Allen & Unwin, 1968), W. D. Joske, *Material Objects* (London: Macmillan, 1967), F. I. Dretske, *Seeing and Knowing* (Chicago: U. of Chicago P., 1969) and J. E. Soltis, *Seeing, Knowing and Believing* (London: Allen & Unwin, 1966). G. Vesey, *Perception* (Garden City: Doubleday, 1971, p) is a recent introductory treatment of the subject. A more difficult recent work is F. N. Sibley (ed.), *Perception—A Philosophical Symposium* (London: Methuen, 1971). The participants in this symposium include G. J. Warnock, W. Kneale, G. Vesey, B. O'Shaughnessy, and B. Williams. Several chapters of B. Aune, *Knowledge, Mind and Nature* (N.Y.: Random House, 1967) are devoted to problems of perception.

Classical writings in the idealist tradition, including selections from Berkeley, G. E. Moore's celebrated "The Refutation of Idealism,"* and H. Rashdall's *Philosophy and Religion,* Ch. 1 (which is an attempt to strengthen Berkeley's arguments for epistemological idealism), are collected in A. C. Ewing (ed.), *The Idealist Tradition from Berkeley to Blanshard* (N.Y.: Free Press, 1957). This work also contains a very extensive bibliography. A defense of idealism is given in J. E. Creighton's "Two Types of Idealism," *PR,* 1917. W. T. Stace, whose "Stars, Atoms, and Sensations" is Selection 49 of the present work, has stated his own position on the subject more fully in *The Theory of Knowledge and Existence* (Oxford: Clarendon Press, 1932) and *The Nature of the World* (Princeton: Princeton U.P., 1940). Stace's paper "The Refutation of Realism," *M,* 1934, is available in several anthologies, including the Ewing anthology mentioned in this paragraph. For statements of the position of the American realists who reacted against the idealist tradition in Britain and the United States, *see* R. B. Perry, E. B. Holt, *et al., The New Realism* (N.Y.: Macmillan, 1912), D. Drake, A. O. Lovejoy, J. B. Pratt, *et al., Essays in Critical Realism** (N.Y.: Macmillan, 1920), R. W. Sellars, *The Philosophy of Physical Realism* (N.Y.: Macmillan, 1932), W. P. Montague, *The Ways of Knowing* (N.Y.: Macmillan, 1925), Part II and Postscript, A. O. Lovejoy, *The Revolt Against Dualism* (Chicago: Open Court, 1930), and D. Drake, *An Invitation to Philosophy* (Boston: Houghton, Mifflin, 1933). An influential critique of idealism is R. B. Perry's "The Egocentric Predicament," *JP,* 1910. In three articles in *The Monist,* 1933 and 1934, entitled respectively "The *A Priori* Argument for Subjectivism," "The Inductive Argument for Subjectivism," and "The Inductive Argument for Realism," Donald Williams dissects in great detail the various arguments put forward by the idealists and defends realism as the best-supported of all scientific hypotheses. In England, the most important rebels against idealism were Bertrand Russell and G. E. Moore, whose "Refutation of Idealism," originally published in 1903, has already been mentioned.

This was perhaps the single most influential writing of the entire movement and it is available in several other collections, including Moore's own *Philosophical Studies* (London: Kegan Paul, 1922). For a critique of Moore *see* C. J. Ducasse's "Moore's Refutation of Idealism"* in P. Schilpp (ed.), *The Philosophy of G. E. Moore* (Evanston and Chicago: Northwestern U.P., 1942). In the same volume there is Moore's reply to Ducasse, to which Ducasse in turn replied in his book, *Nature, Mind and Death* (LaSalle, Illinois: Open Court, 1951), Ch. 13. This is perhaps also the best place to mention Moore's later essay, "A Defense of Common Sense,"* in J. H. Muirhead (ed.), *Contemporary British Philosophy*, Second Series (London: Allen & Unwin, 1925), which is also reprinted in Moore's *Philosophical Papers* (London: Allen & Unwin, 1959, N.Y.: Collier Books, 1962, p) and in R. M. Chisholm (ed.), *Realism and the Background of Phenomenology, op. cit.* This paper contains a critique of philosophical paradoxes in general of which idealism, at least in some of its forms, is a prominent example. Of the other writings by British realists, mention should be made of Samuel Alexander's British Academy Lecture of 1914, "The Basis of Realism," which is reprinted in Chisholm, *op. cit.*, John Laird, *A Study in Realism* (Cambridge: Cambridge U.P., 1920), and G. Dawes Hicks, *Critical Realism** (London: Macmillan, 1938). An extreme form of realism was advocated by the Scotch philosopher John Anderson, who was greatly influenced by Samuel Alexander, and whose work has come to be more widely known in recent years. Two of his papers are particularly relevant here: "The Knower and the Known,"* *Ar. Soc.*, 1926–27, and "Realism and Some of Its Critics," *AP*, 1930, both reprinted in his book, *Studies in Empirical Philosophy* (Sydney: Angus & Robertson, 1962). Broad's important works on the subject are listed below in the paragraph dealing with the writings for and against the sense-datum theory.

Representative theories of perception, more or less similar to those advocated by the American critical realists, are still widely favored by physiologists and other scientists who are interested in the subject of perception. They are defended, for example, in J. C. Eccles, *The Neurophysiological Basis of Mind* (Oxford: Clarendon Press, 1953), W. R. Brain, *Mind, Perception and Science* (Oxford: Blackwell, 1951), J. R. Smythies, *op. cit.*, and the same author's "The Representative Theory of Perception," in J. R. Smythies (ed.), *Brain and Mind* (London: Routledge, 1965). This volume contains comments on Smythies' paper by W. R. Brain and H. H. Price and a rejoinder by Smythies. A representative theory is also advocated by R. J. Hirst, *The Problems of Perception, op. cit.*, whose views are criticized by C. W. K. Mundle in "Common Sense versus Mr. Hirst's Theory of Perception," *Ar. Soc. Sup.*, 1959. There is a reply by Hirst in the same volume. Very recent defenses of critical realism are found in M. Mandelbaum, *Philosophy, Science, and Sense Perception, op. cit.*, and in a paper on "Physical Realism" by W. Sellars in his *Philosophical Perspectives* (Springfield, Illinois: Thomas, 1967). One of the most determined opponents of all kinds of "epistemological dualism" was John Dewey whose critical discussions of such theories may be found in Ch. XXV of *Logic: The Theory of Inquiry** (N.Y.: Holt, 1939) and in "Conduct and Experience," in C. Murchison (ed.), *Psychologies of 1930* (Worcester: Clark U.P., 1930). Dewey's views on perception are also stated in his essays, "Naive Realism versus Representative Realism," "Epistemological Realism: The Alleged Ubiquity of the Knowledge Relation," and "The Existence of the World as a Logical Problem," all of which are contained in his *Essays in Experimental Logic* (Chicago: U. of Chicago P., 1916). A highly stimulating article presenting views akin to those of Dewey is E. B. McGilvary's "Perceptual and Memory Perspectives,"* *JP,* 1933.

Bertrand Russell's *The Problems of Philosophy* has already been mentioned. Other statements of his views on perception may be found in his books, *Our Knowledge of the External World* (London: Allen & Unwin, 2nd ed., 1926, p), *Mysticism and Logic* (London: Allen & Unwin, 1917, p), *Human Knowledge* (London: Allen & Unwin, N.Y.: Simon & Schuster, 1948), *The Analysis of Matter** (London: Allen & Unwin, 1927, N.Y.: Dover Publications, 1954 p), and *The Outline of Philosophy* (London: Allen & Unwin, 1927) from which our Selection 47 has been extracted. L. S. Stebbing, *Philosophy and the Physicists* (London: Methuen, 1937, p), Part II, is a critique of Lockean dualism and the contention of such thinkers as Eddington and Russell that it is supported by physics. Views similar to those of Stebbing are expressed in Ch. V of Gilbert Ryle, *Dilemmas* (Cambridge: Cambridge U.P., 1954, p). Russell's later views are also subjected to detailed criticism in Norman Malcolm's "Russell's *Human Knowledge,*" *PR,* 1949. A very detailed appraisal of Russell's views on the subject is C. A. Fritz, *Bertrand Russell's Construction of the External World* (London: Routledge, 1952). Earlier articles, critical of Russell's position, are H. A. Newman, "Mr. Russell's Causal Theory of Perception." *M,* 1928, H. A. Prichard, "Mr. Bertrand Russell's *Outline of Philosophy,*" *ibid.,* and J. H. Woodger, "Mr. Russell's Theory of Perception," *Mo,* 1930. In a very interesting paper entitled "Russell's Neutral Monism," in P. A. Schilpp (ed.), *The Philosophy of Bertrand Russell* (Evanston and Chicago: Northwestern U.P., 1944), W. T. Stace brings out clearly how there is a phenomenalistic tendency in Russell's work on perception which competes with a tendency to champion some form of "scientific realism." Russell's favorite argument that we cannot ever see the physical object itself since it takes time for light to travel from the object to the perceiver and since at the time at which the perceiving takes place the object may have ceased to exist, is discussed in G. E. Myers, "Perception and the 'Time-Lag' Argument," *A,* 1957, F. Ebersole, "How Philosophers See Stars," *M,* 1965, R. G. Henson, "Ordinary Language, Common Sense and the Time-Lag Argument," *M,* 1967, W. A. Suchting, "Perception and the Timegap Argument," *PQ,* 1969, L. S. Carrier, "The Time-Gap Argument," *AJ,* 1969, and T. D. Perry, "Language Reform in the Time-Gap Problem," *Me,* 1971. The articles by Ebersole and Henson are reprinted in J. H. Gill (ed.), *Philosophy Today No. 2* (N.Y.: Macmillan, 1969, p). This argument is placed in its historical perspective in Ch. I of Lovejoy's *The Revolt Against Dualism, op. cit.* The main issues discussed by Russell, Eddington, and their critics also figure prominently in two symposia—"Realism and Modern Physics"* (J. Laird, C. E. M. Joad, L. S. Stebbing), *Ar. Soc. Sup.,* 1929, and "The Causal Theory of Perception"* (H. P. Grice and A. R White), *Ar. Soc. Sup.,* 1961. The latter of these is reprinted in Warnock, *op cit.* Grice's part of this symposium is also reprinted in Swartz, *op. cit.* Grice is criticized in J. Teichmann, "Perception and Causation," *Ar. Soc.,* 1970–71.

Russell and Eddington, like most of the American critical realists, advocate a Lockean position concerning the so-called secondary qualities. T. P. Nunn in "Are Secondary Qualities Independent of Perception?" *Ar. Soc.,* 1909–10, like some of the American "new" realists, took up an extreme "objectivistic" view on the subject somewhat similar to that advocated by W. A. Sinclair in Selection 54 in the present volume. This topic continues to be widely discussed in the literature. There is an illuminating article, containing much interesting historical material, by R. Jackson, "Locke's Distinction Between Primary and Secondary

Qualities," in *M*, 1929, reprinted in C. B. Martin and D. M. Armstrong (eds.), *Locke and Berkeley, op. cit.* The topic is discussed in Ch. 9 of Chisholm, *op. cit.*, in Ch. 6 of Hirst, *op. cit.*, Ch. 14 of Armstrong, *op. cit.*, C. J. F. Williams, "Are Primary Qualities Qualities?" *PQ*, 1969, and G. G. Brittan, Jr., "Measurability, Commonsensibility, and Primary Qualities," *AJ*, 1969. Basing himself on recent scientific work, J. J. C. Smart defends a Lockean position concerning colors in his article "Colors," *P*, 1961, and more fully and applying the same position to other secondary qualities, in Ch. IV of *Philosophy and Scientific Realism* (London: Routledge, 1963). A similar position regarding heat is defended by C. Strang in "The Perception of Heat," *Ar. Soc.*, 1960–61. The views of Smart and Strang are criticized in J. W. R. Cox, "Are Perceptible Qualities 'In' Things?" *A*, 1963. Berkeley's views on heat are carefully examined in G. N. A. Vesey, "Berkeley and Sensations of Heat," *PR*, 1960, and D. Armstrong, "Berkeley's Puzzle About the Water That Seems Both Hot and Cold," *A*, 1955. Questions concerning the status of colors are also discussed in B. Harrison, "On Describing Color," *Inquiry*, 1967, F. N. Sibley, "Colors," *Ar. Soc.*, 1967–68, Ch. 7 of B. Aune, *Knowledge, Mind and Nature, op. cit.*, in W. Sellars, "Phenomenalism," included in H. Castaneda (ed.), *Intentionality, Minds, and Perception* (Detroit: Wayne State U.P., 1967) which also contains comments by B. Aune and Sellars' rejoinder, A. Olding, "Armstrong, Smart and the Ontological Status of Secondary Qualities," *AJ*, 1968, K. Campbell, "Colors," and D. M. Armstrong, "Color-Realism and the Argument From Microscopes," both of the last-mentioned items appearing in R. Brown and C. R. Rollins (eds.), *Contemporary Philosophy in Australia* (London: Allen & Unwin, 1969), and in G. Pitcher, *A Theory of Perception* (Princeton: Princeton U.P., 1971). Returning to older literature, there is an extremely interesting criticism of the Lockean position in Ch. I of F. H. Bradley, *Appearance and Reality* (1893). One of the very first philosophers who maintained, explicitly in opposition to the Galileo-Locke viewpoint, that it is quite illogical to regard primary qualities as having objective reality while denying this status to secondary qualities, was the 17th-century skeptic, Pierre Bayle. Bayle's discussion of this topic is now available in English in R. Popkin (ed.), *Bayle's Historical and Critical Dictionary—Selections* (Indianapolis: Bobbs-Merrill, 1965, p). Another question which was already discussed by Locke and Berkeley has received some discussion in recent works. This is the question of whether we can give a coherent account of the external world and our knowledge of it without introducing some such entity as Locke's "substance" or Kant's "thing-in-itself." The foremost opponent of any kind of substance-theory is undoubtedly Bertrand Russell, especially in his later works. His view that a "thing" should be regarded as a "bundle of qualities" and not as an unknowable substratum is expounded in Ch. 6 of *An Inquiry into Meaning and Truth* (London: Allen & Unwin, N.Y.: Norton, 1940) and in Ch. XXIII of *The Analysis of Matter, op. cit.* Other recent discussions of this topic include L. S. Stebbing, "Concerning Substance," *Ar. Soc.*, 1929–30, W. Kneale, "The Notion of a Substance," *Ar. Soc.*, 1939–40, C. D. Broad, "Berkeley's Denial of Material Substance," *PR*, 1954, reprinted in C. B. Martin and D. M. Armstrong (eds.), *Locke and Berkeley, op. cit.*, A. H. Basson (Cavendish), "The Problem of Substance," *Ar. Soc.*, 1948–49, M. Lazerowitz, "Substratum," in M. Black (ed.), *Philosophical Analysis* (Ithaca: Cornell U.P., 1950). J. Bennett, "Substance, Reality and Primary Qualities," *APQ*, 1965, and D. Odegard, "Locke and Substance," *D*, 1969. There are several interesting essays on this subject in volume 9 of the *University of California Publications in Philosophy*

(Berkeley: U. of California P., 1927), which is entitled "The Problem of Substance."

The following are three influential 19th century works containing defenses of phenomenalism and modifications of the earlier versions found in Berkeley and Hume: John Stuart Mill, *An Examination of Sir William Hamilton's Philosophy* (London: Longmans, Green, 1872), Karl Pearson, *The Grammar of Science* (first published 1891, Everyman edition, 1937), Chs. 2–5, and Ernst Mach, *Contributions towards the Analysis of Sensations* (Chicago: Open Court, 1897). The latter is criticized by Lenin in *Materialism and Empirio-Criticism* (Moscow: Foreign Languages Publishing House, 1952). Lenin is answered in G. A. Paul's "Lenin's Theory of Perception," *A,* 1938, reprinted in M. Mac-Donald (ed.), *Philosophy and Analysis* (Oxford: Blackwell, 1954), and by H. B. Acton, *The Illusion of the Epoch* (London: Cohen & West, 1955). Mill's theory of perception is critically discussed in H. H. Price, "Mill's View of the External World," *Ar. Soc.,* 1926–27 and in J. P. Day "Mill on Matter," *P,* 1963, which is reprinted in J. B. Schneewind (ed.), *Mill* (Garden City: Double-day, 1968, p).

Of more recent origin is the defense of phenomenalism found in Ch. V of A. J. Ayer, *The Foundations of Empirical Knowledge* (London: Macmillan, 1940), and the same writer's "Phenomenalism," *Ar. Soc.,* 1946–47, which is reprinted in A. J. Ayer, *Philosophical Essays* (London: Macmillan, 1953). Ayer returned to the subject of perception in Ch. 3 of *The Problem of Knowledge* (Harmondsworth: Pelican Books, 1956, p) in which there is a partial retraction of his phenomenalism and, more recently, in Book II, Ch. 3 of *The Origins of Pragmatism* (London: Macmillan, San Francisco: Freeman, Cooper, and Co., 1968), and Chs. 5, 7 and 9 of *Russell and Moore: The Analytical Heritage* (London: Macmillan, 1971). Ayer's later views are criticized in A. P. Griffiths, "Ayer on Perception," *M,* 1960. Moritz Schlick, the founder of the Vienna Circle, who began as a kind of critical realist, advocated a form of phenomenalism in his later work. His article, "Positivism and Realism," which was first published in 1932, is now available in English translation in A. J. Ayer (ed.), *Logical Positivism* (N.Y.: Free Press, 1959, p). Discussions of the issues raised by Schlick can be found in W. Barrett's "On the Existence of an External World," *JP,* 1939, and F. Will's "Verifiability and the External World," *PS,* 1940. Perhaps the most sophisticated and detailed defense of phenomenalism is C. I. Lewis, *An Analysis of Knowledge and Valuation** (LaSalle, Illinois: Open Court, 1947), Chs. 7–9. A critique of Lewis' phenomenalism is given in R. M. Chisholm's "The Problem of Empiricism,"* *JP,* 1948. In the same volume is Lewis' reply, "Professor Chisholm and Empiricism."* R. Firth refers to the Lewis-Chisholm debate and sides with phenomenalism in his "Radical Empiricism and Perceptual Relativity," *PR,* 1950. There are criticisms of phenomenalism in several of the books previously mentioned, e.g., in Hirst, *op. cit.,* Chisholm, *op. cit.,* Armstrong, *op. cit.,* and Smart, *op. cit.,* and also in Ch. VII of A. C. Ewing, *Idealism, A Critical Survey* (London: Methuen, 1934), where the rejection of phenomenalism is combined with a causal argument for the existence of physical objects. Ewing was also one of the participants in a symposium, together with H. H. Price and D. G. C. MacNabb, on "The Causal Argument for Physical Objects," *Ar. Soc. Sup.,* 1945, which contains a very full discussion of phenomenalism. An argument against phenomenalism which has also been employed by several later critics is advanced by G. F. Stout in "Phenomenalism," *Ar. Soc.,* 1938–39, to which D. C. G. MacNabb replied in a paper with the same title in *Ar. Soc.,* 1940–41. There is a defense of Stout's criticism against MacNabb in W. F. Hardie's "The Paradox of Phenomenalism,"

Ar. Soc., 1945–46. All of the following articles are also in varying degrees critical of phenomenalism: C. D. Broad, "Phenomenalism," *Ar. Soc.*, 1914–15, P. Marhenke, "Phenomenalism," in M. Black (ed.), *Philosophical Analysis, op. cit.*, I. Berlin, "Empirical Propositions and Hypothetical Statements," *M,* 1950 (reprinted in R. J. Swartz, *op. cit.*), R. J. Spilsbury, "Dispositions and Phenomenalism," *M,* 1950, M. Black, "The Language of Sense-Data," in his *Problems of Analysis* (Ithaca: Cornell U.P., 1954), E. M. Adams, "The Inadequacy of Phenomenalism," *PR,* 1959, and J. W. Yolton, "Seeming and Being," *PQ,* 1961. There is a critical discussion of phenomenalism in Ch. 3 of B. Aune, *Rationalism, Empiricism, and Pragmatism* (N.Y.: Random House, 1970, p). A paper dealing especially with the question of phenomenalist versus realist interpretations of scientific theory is H. Feigl's "Existential Hypotheses,"* *PS,* 1950.

The main pioneers of the sense-datum theory were Bertrand Russell, G. E. Moore, and C. D. Broad. Russell's first version of a theory of this kind was advanced in the *The Problems of Philosophy, op. cit.;* later versions containing significant changes in position are found in *Our Knowledge of the External World, op. cit.,* and *Mysticism and Logic, op. cit.* In the Preface to *The Problems of Philosophy,* Russell referred to "unpublished writings" by G. E. Moore to which he was indebted in developing his own theory of perception. These were lectures given by Moore in 1910–11 and eventually published as *Some Main Probems of Philosophy* (London: Allen & Unwin, 1953, N.Y.: Collier Books, 1962, p). Moore's sense-datum theory is expounded in the opening chapters of this book as well as in several papers reprinted in his *Philosophical Studies, op. cit.* Moore's views are criticized in O. K. Bouwsma's "Moore's Theory of Sense-Data," in P. A. Schilpp (ed.), *The Philosophy of G. E. Moore, op. cit.,* and in P. Marhenke's "Moore's Analysis of Sense-Perception,"* *ibid.* Replies by Moore are contained in the same volume. Moore's last discussion of this topic was a short paper entitled "Visual Sense-Data," in C. A. Mace (ed.), *British Philosophy in the Mid-Century* (London: Allen & Unwin, N.Y.: Macmillan, 1957), which is reprinted in R. J. Swartz, *op. cit.* Selections from lectures given by Moore in 1928–29 dealing with the same topics were posthumously published as *Lectures on Philosophy* (London: Allen & Unwin, 1966).

A theory of sense-data or "sensa," as non-mental and non-physical entities that are directly perceived, is worked out by C. D. Broad in his books, *Perception, Physics and Reality** (Cambridge U.P., 1914), *Scientific Thought** (London: Routledge, 1923) and *The Mind and Its Place in Nature** (London: Routledge, 1925, p), Ch. 4. The latter chapter aims to demonstrate that no consistent theory of perception can be reconciled with all common sense beliefs about perception. A more recent discussion of this subject by Broad is a series of articles entitled "Professor Marc-Wogau's *Theorie der Sinnesdaten,*" *M,* 1947. Broad's views on perception are the subject of a minute critique in terms of the analysis of ordinary language by M. Lean, *Sense-Perception and Matter* (London: Routledge, 1953). P. A. Schilpp (ed.), *The Philosophy of C. D. Broad* (N.Y.: Tudor Press, 1959), contains critical articles dealing with Broad's views on perception by H. H. Price, K. Marc-Wogau, and J. W. Yolton as well as Broad's reply. A sense-datum theory is also defended in H. H. Price, *Perception* (London: Methuen, 1932), which is one of the most elaborate and carefully argued treatises on the entire subject of perception published in recent decades. G. E. Moore and G. F. Stout were the participants in an Aristotelian Society symposium entitled "The Status of Sense-Data,"* (*Ar. Soc.,* 1913–14). A later Aristotelian Society symposium entitled "The Nature of Sensible Appearances"* (*Ar. Soc.,* 1926) had as its participants G. E. Moore, G. Dawes

Hicks, H. H. Price, and L. S. Stebbing. Moore's contribution to the former of these is available in his *Philosophical Studies, op. cit.* Recent restatements and defenses of sense-data theories are found in N. Brown, "Sense-Data and Material Objects," *M,* 1957, and *The Nature of Experience* (London: Oxford U.P., 1959) by the distinguished physiologist, W. R. Brain. Sense-data theories are criticized, from an idealist point of view, in R. G. Collingwood, "Sensation and Thought," *Ar. Soc.,* 1923–24, and C. A. Campbell, "Sense-Data and Judgment in Sensory Cognition," *M,* 1947, in a rather different context in Ch. 7 of G. Ryle, *The Concept of Mind* (London: Hutchinson, N.Y.: Barnes & Noble, 1949, p) and in Ch. 14 of C. J. Ducasse, *Nature, Mind and Death, op. cit.* The following are recent articles especially worth mentioning, some of them highly critical of the sense-datum theory: G. A. Paul's "Is There a Problem about Sense-Data" *Ar. Soc. Sup.,* 1936, reprinted in A. Flew (ed.), *Essays in Logic and Language,* First Series (Oxford: Blackwell, 1951), W. H. F. Barnes, "The Myth of Sense-Data," *Ar. Soc.,* 1944–45, A. J. Ayer, "The Terminology of Sense-Data," *M,* 1945, reprinted in his *Philosophical Essays, op. cit.,* R. R. Firth, "Sense-Data and the Percept Theory," *M,* 1949–50, reprinted in Swartz, *op. cit.,* A. M. Quinton, "The Problem of Perception," *M,* 1955, which is reprinted both in Swartz, *op. cit.,* and in Warnock, *op. cit.,* C. H. Whiteley, "Sense Data," *P,* 1969, and J. Hintikka, "On the Logic of Perception," which is included in Hintikka's *Models and Modalities* (N.Y.: Humanities Press, 1969). Some of the writers here listed as "critics" of the sense-datum theory do not maintain that it is false, but rather that it is a proposal to use a certain language and as such neither true nor false and hence that the authors of the theory, who regarded it as in some sense a discovery, misconceived its nature. A critic who does regard the sense-datum theory as "untenable," is C. F. Wallraff in "Sense-Datum Theory and Observational Fact," *JP,* 1958. His rejection of the theory is based on the data of experimental psychology. There is a particularly sustained attack on the doctrine that we never perceive material objects but only sense-data in J. L. Austin, *Sense and Sensibilia* (Oxford: Clarendon Press, 1962, reconstructed from manuscript notes by G. J. Warnock). This book, which calls into question a number of assumptions made by philosophers of very different schools, has given rise to a great deal of discussion in philosophical periodicals. The fullest critical reviews which have so far appeared are by R. J. Hirst in *PQ,* 1963, R. Harrod in *P,* 1963, and R. Firth in *PR,* 1964. One of Austin's prime targets was Ayer who replied to Austin in "Has Austin Refuted the Sense-Datum Theory?" which is included in Ayer's *Metaphysics and Common Sense* (London: Macmillan, 1969).

The following articles cannot be easily fitted into any of the classifications adopted above: R. B. Braithwaite, "Propositions about Material Objects," *Ar. Soc.,* 1937–38, A. M. Quinton and K. Britton, "Seeming," *Ar. Soc. Sup.,* 1952, M. MacDonald, "Linguistic Philosophy and Perception," *P,* 1953, G. N. A. Vesey, "Unthinking Assumptions and Their Justification," *M,* 1954, G. J. Warnock, "Seeing," *Ar. Soc.,* 1954–55, W. F. R. Hardie, "Ordinary Language and Perception," *PQ,* 1955, G. N. A. Vesey, "Seeing and Seeing-As," *Ar. Soc.,* 1955–56, C. A. Fritz, "Sense Perception and Matter," *PPR,* 1956, D. W. Hamlyn, "The Visual Field and Perception," *Ar. Soc.,* 1957, R. Aaron, "The Common Sense View of Sense Perception," *Ar. Soc.,* 1957, E. M. Adams, "Perception and the Language of Appearing," *JP,* 1958, J. Hartnack, "Remarks on the Concept of Sensation," *JP,* 1959, C. M. Myers, "Phenomenal Organization and Perceptual Mode," *P,* 1959, D. S. Shwayder, "The Varieties and the Objects of Visual Phenomena," *M,* 1961, E. H. Wolgast, "Qualities and Illusions," *M*, 1962, P. Unger, "Our Knowledge of the Material World," in N. Rescher (ed.), *Studies in the Theory of Knowledge* (Oxford: Blackwell, 1970, p), J. L. Pollock, "Perceptual Knowledge," *PR*, 1971, P. L. McKee, "Perception and Physiology," *M*, 1971, and two articles both entitled "Perception from an Evolutionary Point of View," by A. Shimony and F. I. Dretske, *JP*, 1971.

The following articles in the *Encyclopedia of Philosophy* contain material relevant to the topics discussed in the present section: "Berkeley, George" (H. B. Acton, 1–295), "Broad, Charlie Dunbar" (R. Brown, 1–396), "Common Sense" (S. A. Grave, 2–155), "Critical Realism" (A. G. Ramsberger, 2–261), "Heat, Sensations of" (G. N. A. Vesey, 3–429), "Locke, John" (J. G. Clapp, 4–487), "Moore, George Edward" (J. O. Nelson, 5–372), "New Realism" (T. Robischon, 5–485), "Perception" (R. J. Hirst, 6–79), "Phenomenalism" (R. J. Hirst, 6–130), "Primary and Secondary Qualities" (R. J. Hirst, 6–455), "Realism" (R. J. Hirst, 7–77), "Russell, Bertrand," Section on his Epistemology and Metaphysics (W. P. Alston, 7–239), "Sensa" (R. J. Hirst, 7–407), "Sound" (G. N. A. Vesey, 7–500), "Touch" (G. N. A. Vesey, 8–150), and "Vision" (G. N. A. Vesey, 8–252).

P. K. Machamer, "Recent Work on Perception," *APQ*, 1970, contains a very comprehensive bibliography.

VII

A Priori
Knowledge

INTRODUCTION

EVER SINCE PLATO PHILOSOPHERS HAVE been impressed by the fact that there are universal propositions which we can apparently know to be true with absolute certainty, though we could not possibly observe all, or even a large proportion of the instances to which they apply. Such propositions, called "necessary propositions" by philosophers, are especially to be found in mathematics, the science which establishes its theorems with such infallible certainty that the expression "mathematical certainty" has become part of the everyday idiom. In Plato's dialogue *Meno* (Selection 55), a slave boy is led by Socrates to "see" that a square whose side is a diagonal of a given square has exactly twice the area of the latter (the proposition in question is a special case of the "Pythagorean theorem"). How can we know that it is so in every possible case of a square with inscribed diagonals? How can we know that not only the triangles we have drawn on the blackboard in order to "verify" by measurement that the internal angles add up to 180° have an angle sum of 180° but that all conceivable triangles have it? Philosophers who hold that experience is the only source of human knowledge ("empiricism") may, like John Stuart Mill, say that our conviction is nothing but a habit of association, built up by repeated observation that one property is conjoined with another, but a philosopher who holds such geometrical knowledge to be independent of experience, *a priori* ("rationalism"), retorts: If such were the case, why are we not convinced to an equal degree that all crows are black, or that all bodies have weight, or that the ground gets wet whenever it rains? It seems that we can conceive of exceptions to the latter propositions (even if we find it hard to believe that there ever will be any), in a way in which we cannot conceive of exceptions to the former propositions. If we found a square whose side is the diagonal of another foursided figure, yet whose area was not double that of the latter, we would conclude that the latter figure is not exactly square; indeed, we would abandon any previously entertained beliefs that were relevant *except* the belief in the absolute validity of the theorem.

At any rate, this is the way Plato, Kant, Leibniz, Locke and many other philosophers felt and feel about mathematical knowledge. In describing it as *a priori* knowledge (following Kant's terminology), philosophers refer to its apparent independence of experience: we claim to know that two pebbles and two pebbles make four pebbles even on Mars, before having verified this by actual counting after a strenuous trip in a rocketship. Perhaps we also believe that if there are crows on Mars they are black, yet we would admit that this is only *probable* on the basis of past experience; it is conceivable that on Mars or on some other planet there should be animals which are exactly like the animals we usually call "crows" except that their feathers are, say, red. In this sense our knowledge of the proposition that all crows are black is said to be *empirical,* and traditionally empirical knowledge has been said to lack that *certainty* which attaches to *a priori* knowledge.

It is important to understand in exactly what sense *a priori* knowledge is "independent of experience." No philosopher has ever denied that a child has to learn that two and two make four by learning to count, and that the latter process involves contact with concrete objects. But this only means that without sense-experience one cannot acquire the *concepts* of number, in this case the concepts "two" and "four," that is, a child who has never learned to count, to associate different numerals with distinguishable objects, will not even understand what "two and two makes four" *means.* What the philosophers who believe in *a priori* knowledge assert is only that once the concepts have been acquired, the proposition can be "seen" to be true by just thinking about it (by "the mere operation of thought," in Hume's phrase). Consider the statement "for any objects A, B, C: if A is bigger than B and B is bigger than C, then A is bigger than C." Obviously, a being without sense of sight and sense of touch would have no concept of the relation designated by the word "bigger," hence such a being would not even understand that statement. But in saying that its truth is independent of experience, philosophers only mean that anyone who *understands* it will see that it is necessarily true, that it could not possibly be refuted by any observations at any time or place.

Therefore a philosopher who believes in *a priori* knowledge is not thereby committed to a belief in "innate ideas." It is true that some philosophers have maintained that there are concepts which in some sense are "in" our minds before all sense-experience. Thus Descartes believed that the concept of "substance," i.e., of a *thing* which is said to *have* various sensible qualities, was innate: we only perceive qualities, changing and stable, like colors, shapes, sizes, degrees of hardness and temperature, but not the identical thing which undergoes such observable changes; how, then, could we have acquired the idea of substance through sense-experience? And Kant added a famous battery of "categories," among them the concept of causal connection: experience tells us that one kind of event is regularly followed by another kind of event but it does not reveal necessary connections between events. We observe, said Kant (like Hume before him), that a stone gets warmer when the sun shines on it, but not that it *must* get warmer when exposed to sunshine; hence the concept of such necessary connections, said Kant, must have been in the mind before sense-experience. Nevertheless, the question of the origin of concepts is logically independent of the question of *a priori* knowledge of propositions. This is even historically indicated by the fact that both Locke and Hume, who insisted on the origin in experience of all ideas (concepts) whatsoever (see Selection 62), at the same time wrote at length about the shortcomings of empirical knowledge by comparison with the certainty of *a priori* knowledge. That nothing can be both red and blue all over at the same time, we know *a priori,* but unless our eyes had been appropriately stimulated we would have no ideas of these qualities.

The philosopher not only makes the distinction between *a priori* knowledge and empirical knowledge by reflecting on the appropriate methods of justifying our beliefs; he goes on to ask how *a priori* knowledge is possible. Plato apparently was so perplexed by the fact that we can know universal propositions independently of experience that he had to invent a myth in order to account for it: the soul remembers visions it has enjoyed in a former disembodied life. Other philosophers, less poetical than Plato, tried to account for it in terms of a distinction between two kinds of entities, a distinction that played a vital role in Plato's philosophy: universals (Plato called them "forms," Locke "ideas"), and particulars. When we look at the blackboard, we see particular triangles, but when we prove the Euclidean theorem about triangles we think of the universal *triangularity,* i.e., that which all the particular triangles have in common and by virtue of which they are all triangles. Every particular triangle has a particular size, for example, but when we classify it as a triangle we abstract from this particular feature and focus attention on a property which it shares with similar figures; it is this *common* property which philosophers call a *universal.* Again, we can see particular cubical objects at different places at the same time, or at the same place at different times, but when we think about the nature of a cube (as when we say to ourselves "every cube *must* have twelve edges") we think, in the terminology of those philosophers, about a universal that is identically present in all visible and tangible cubes. Whenever we classify a particular thing or event—in short, a "particular"—as being of such and such a kind, we consider it as an instance of some universal, or set of universals tied together by a single name, like "cow," "man," "table," "rain," "thunder." According to Locke's doctrine in the *Essay Concerning Human Understanding* and Russell's in *The Problems of Philosophy,* we can be certain that every particular which is an instance of universal A is also an instance of universal B, though we can never survey all past, present and future instances of these universals, if we "see" with our intellectual eye a certain relation between A and B, a relation which is sometimes called "necessary connection," sometimes "entailment." If we can see that squareness entails equilateralness, and that being a cube entails having twelve edges, then we can be sure in advance of sense-experience (think of the original meaning of *"a priori"* in Latin: before!) that there are no squares that are not equilateral, nor cubes that do not have twelve edges.

Kant complicated the question of how *a priori* knowledge is possible. He noticed, like Locke before him, that it is not in the least surprising that we should be absolutely certain that all squares are equilateral and that all bachelors are unmarried; after all, the predicates here are contained in the subjects, i.e., part of what we mean by "square" is an equilateral figure, and part of what we mean by "bachelor" is an unmarried individual; hence we are merely certain that nothing is both equilateral and not equilateral, and that nothing is both unmarried and married (at the same time, of course!). In Kant's terminology, these propositions are *analytic;* they can be proved by sole appeal to the "law of contradiction" according to which no proposition can be both true and false, nothing can both have and not have the same property at the same time. (Kant's distinction between analytic and synthetic propositions was anticipated by Locke, though Locke did not use these terms.) Yet, Kant was left with a difficult problem because he was convinced that *a priori* knowledge is not restricted to analytic propositions which, as he said, "do not really enlarge our knowledge." He believed that all arithmetical and geometrical propositions are *synthetic,* i.e., such that, unlike analytic propositions, they can be denied without self-contradiction, and at the same time are known *a priori;* hence his famous question, "How are synthetic judgments *a priori* possible?" For example, we are absolutely certain that the shortest distance between any two points, anywhere in space, is the straight line; yet the subject "straight line" does not seem to contain the predicate "shortest distance between two points" as a part or the whole of its very meaning, the way this must be said of the relation between "square" and "equilateral." Therefore the denial of this axiom, viz. "there is a line connecting two points which is shorter than the straight line connecting them," is not self-contradictory though it is intuitively inconceivable. Kant's problem was this: if the property B is not part or all of what we mean by "A," how can we be certain that absolutely everything to which "A" applies has B? Experience cannot be the basis of our certainty, for experience only tells us that all instances of A that have so far been observed are also instances of B. Kant's answer is best elucidated by means of an analogy. Consider the proposition "every visible object is blue." It is undoubtedly synthetic, and experience even refutes it. But suppose that our eyes were so constituted that only blue light affecting the retinae gave rise to color sensations, so that objects emitting or reflecting light of different wave lengths remained invisible. In that case our universal synthetic proposition would be constantly confirmed by experience, and if we knew that our eyes were so constituted, we could even be certain that no object of different color would ever be seen. In somewhat the same sense, the space we experience must necessarily conform to the propositions of Euclidean geometry, according to Kant, because these propositions express the mind's ways of ordering what is "given" in sense-experience. In other words, they describe the mind's "forms of spatial intuition" which must be imposed on the material affecting our senses before it can become an object of scientific knowledge.

Whatever one may think of this rather obscure answer to the question "How are synthetic *a priori* judgments about space possible?" it must be admitted that Kant formulated distinctions and by means of them a problem that played a great role in subsequent inquiries into the nature of human knowledge. One who is not familiar with the distinctions between analytic propositions, self-contradictory propositions (i.e., propositions which violate the law of contradiction, like "some unmarried men are married," "some equilateral figures are not equilateral"), synthetic propositions that can be known by experience only and synthetic propositions that can be known *a priori*, will be unable to understand much of the technical discussions in modern philosophy. Furthermore, Kant for the first time raised the critical question of central concern to contemporary logical positivism, whether *metaphysical* knowledge, i.e., *a priori* knowledge of synthetic propositions about the world that are outside the province of mathematics, is at all possible. Metaphysicians and theologians before Kant were busy offering *a priori* proofs for such dogmas of Christianity as the existence of a personal God, the immortality of the soul, and the freedom of man. But Kant, noting that these propositions are synthetic and that the methods of mathematics were unavailable for their proof, urged philosophers to suspend controversy pro or con such propositions until they had investigated the "critical" problem whether a science of metaphysics in this sense is at all possible. To be sure, Kant's way of defining the distinction between analytic and synthetic in terms of the relation between "subject" and "predicate" is not satisfactory in the light of modern logic. A great many propositions do not have subject-predicate form at all; still we may ask whether they are analytic in the sense that the attempt to deny them would end in such plain self-contradiction as the attempt to deny that all white swans are white. For example, consider the two formally similar propositions: a) for any tennis players A, B, C: if A can beat B and B can beat C, then A can beat C (in tennis, of course!); b) for any events A, B, C: if A precedes B, and B precedes C, then A precedes C. Clearly a) is empirical; even if it were true, this could be known only by watching tennis matches, and at any rate we can *conceive* of an exception to this generalization. Just as clearly b) is known to be true *a priori*. In the above sense of "analytic," which is not restricted to propositions of the form "all A are B," we can then go on to ask whether b) is analytic or synthetic. If it were analytic, then a statement of the form "A precedes B and B precedes C but A does not precede C" should be reducible to a self-contradiction of the same kind as "A both precedes and does not precede B," "there are white swans that are not white," etc. That is the question.

According to Kant, such propositions of Euclidean geometry as "two straight lines cannot enclose a space (i.e., are either parallel or else intersect just once)" are not only self-evident, such that no mind can conceive of exceptions to them; they also hold necessarily for any part of physical space that might ever be experienced. This influential doctrine came to be challenged in the 19th century in two quite different ways. John Stuart Mill cited precedents in the history of science where propositions that seemed absolutely self-evident were later shown to be false. He argued that self-evidence is nothing more sacred than a habit of associating qualities which have always gone together in experience. Mill even maintained that the laws of arithmetic, like "2 + 2 = 4," are generalizations from experience, not *a priori* truths, a view which most philosophers of science find unacceptable. (See Russell, Selection 59, and Ayer, Selection 60.) The other challenge originated from the mathematicians. Since no mathematician had ever succeeded in deducing Euclid's "parallel axiom" (given a point outside a straight line S, there is exactly one straight line containing that point and parallel to S) from the other axioms of Euclidean geometry, it was suspected that it could be denied without resulting inconsistency in the geometrical system. Indeed, such "non-Euclidean" systems were constructed and found to be internally just as consistent as Euclidean geometry (if the latter *is* consistent). So far Kant's theory of geometry had not been dealt a fatal blow: for Kant might have replied that non-Euclidean geometry merely proves that the parallel axiom is not a necessary *consequence* of the other axioms of Euclidean geometry, which is perfectly compatible with their all being necessarily true. Yet, the situation became truly ticklish for the Kantians (who were academically so strong in Germany at that time that the great mathematician Gauss was afraid to publish his researches in non-Euclidean geometry!), when Riemannian geometry, which is a brand of non-Euclidean geometry, even proved to be applicable to physical space in the context of the general theory of relativity. For had not Kant maintained that physicists could rest assured—on the authority of his theory of knowledge—that no measurements would ever disconfirm the Euclidean axioms and theorems?

There remains to be mentioned still a third attack on Kant, launched by the modern logicians, and the historical stage will be set for a new, much more sophisticated kind of "empiricism," as philosophers call the doctrine that experience is the only source of knowledge about the universe we live in: *logical empiricism*, or *logical positivism*. Kant had maintained that some kind of "temporal intuition" is required to see the truth of an arithmetical equation, not just analysis of the meanings of symbols. The equation "7 + 5 = 12," he argued, does not just explicate the meaning of "the sum of five and seven," the way "all triangles have three interior angles" just explicates the meaning of "triangle." Indeed, it could not be maintained that "7 + 5" is synonymous with "12" the way "triangle" is synonymous with "closed rectilinear figure with three angles"; nor would it be plausible to hold that anybody who understands the expression "the sum of seven and five" as well as the meaning of "12" thereby already knows the equation to be true, for undoubtedly we first had to learn by counting that 7 and 5 add up to twelve. On this ground, roughly speaking, Kant held that such propositions are synthetic, though our knowledge of them is *a priori*. But Bertrand Russell pointed out that the psychological process of counting, of learning numbers, had nothing to do with the logical analysis of arithmetical concepts and propositions. Using the techniques of symbolic logic, a discipline of which he is a founding father, he undertook to define the concepts of mathematics, from such simple ones as "one" to such complicated ones as "integral," on the sole basis of logical concepts: "not," "all," "there is," "or," "and," etc. (He was anticipated by the German logician Gottlob Frege, who had been thinking about the logical foundations of arithmetic along surprisingly similar lines. But Frege was ignored by his countrymen.) As a result, it was shown in *Principia Mathematica,* a monumental work which is for modern logic what Newton's *Principia mathematica philosophiae naturalis* was for modern physics, that mathematics (geometry excepted) is really a branch of logic. If so, argued the logicians, then Kant was wrong in supposing that mathematical knowledge involved a faculty of "intuition" which is not involved in logical reasoning. In order to deduce, for example, from the premise that two collections A and B which have no elements in common each contain two elements, the conclusion that the sum of A and B contains four elements, only an appeal to laws of logic is required, such laws as "if every A is B and some A are C, then some B are C" or "if something is either A or B but is not A, then it is B."

Partly under the influence of Russell's work in logic and philosophy of mathematics, a group of Viennese thinkers (the "Vienna Circle") who were in close touch with developments in mathematics and physics and who were disgusted with the vague kind of speculative metaphysics that dominated the German universities, went further and inquired into the source of the infallibility of logic. If mathematics is not different from logic, then an understanding of the origin of logical necessity ought to lift the mystery with which the traditional philosophers, especially Kant, surround *a priori* knowledge. Stimulated by the ideas of Wittgenstein (1889–1951), they declared that all logically necessary propositions, indeed all propositions that can be known *a priori*, are *tautologies*. The concept of tautology is similar to Kant's concept of analytic judgment, but more exactly a tautology is the following sort of statement: it is composed of simpler statements in such a way that it is true no matter whether the statements of which it is composed are true or false. The simplest example of tautology is a statement of the form "p or not p," e.g., "either it will rain tomorrow, or—it will not rain tomorrow." Clearly we do not need to wait and see in order to assent to this "prediction"; for that very reason it is not really a prediction at all, it tells us precisely nothing. A tautology is, in positivist terminology, devoid of factual content, it says nothing about the world. Most tautologies are far more complicated, and it may require subtle techniques of logical analysis to size them up as tautologies, but the principle remains the same: since a tautology is true no matter what may be the case, in other words, excludes no possibilities, it tells us nothing about the world. Such was the logical positivists' deflation of *a priori* knowledge: if we can be certain *a priori* of the truth of a proposition, then that proposition really says no more than "either it will rain or it won't." It should be noted that an attempted denial of a tautology would result in self-contradiction: I deny that it will rain, and I also deny that it will not rain; but if I deny that it will not rain, then I affirm that it will rain, which I have already denied.

Therefore the positivist thesis that we can have *a priori* knowledge of tautologies only, is equivalent to a flat rejection of Kant's doctrine that some synthetic propositions can be known *a priori*.

What is the nature of geometrical propositions according to logical positivism? Is it not plain that the proposition "two nonparallel straight lines have only one point in common" is not a tautology like "a straight line is a straight line"? And is it not undeniable that exceptions to it are inconceivable, so that our knowledge of it is *a priori?* The logical positivist replies: what do you mean by "straight"? Would you call two lines straight if after diverging from a point of intersection they were found to meet again? If not, then you are implicitly *defining* straight lines as lines that satisfy the axiom in question, and the latter accordingly is analytic. If, on the other hand, you have an independent criterion of straightness, then the axiom is synthetic. But such an independent criterion must be formulated in physical terms, e.g., a straight line is the path of a light ray. In that case the axiom becomes a physical hypothesis subject to test but thereby loses its *a priori* certainty. As Einstein once put it: insofar as the propositions of geometry are certain, they say nothing about reality, and insofar as they say something about reality they are not certain.

What is the purpose of arithmetic and algebra if these models of exact science consist exclusively of tautologies, as asserted by logical positivism? In connection with this question it is important to understand that a tautology, as logical positivists use the term, is not necessarily a trivial, self-evident statement like "a house is a house" or "it will either rain or it won't." It may not at all be self-evident that a given proposition is a tautology but this may have to be revealed by a lengthy process of symbolic transformation. In particular, the equations of higher algebra and the calculus are transformable, step by step, into identities, but it may require great mathematical skill to perform the transformation, which is what their "proof" consists in. Once their tautological validity has been established, they are used as tools of deduction in empirical inquiries. Suppose, for example, you want to know how many cubic inches are contained in a certain cubical box. If you have ascertained by measurement that its side has a length of 12 inches, you will use your arithmetical knowledge that $12 \times 12 \times 12 = 1728$, thereby saving yourself the trouble of trying to determine by a lengthy process of counting how many cubic inches can be fitted into the box. This shows that tautologies perform a useful function in empirical science as instruments of deduction.

The positivistic theory of *a priori* knowledge, however, provokes two questions: 1) if *a priori* knowledge is not knowledge about the world, what sort of knowledge is it then? It it knowledge at all? 2) We know that such and such propositions are tautologies, like the weatherman's foolproof "prediction"; and this means that we know that such propositions are true *in all possible cases*. Right. But how do we know that? It is not easy to get a clear-cut answer to these questions, but roughly speaking the answer to both of them that is offered is: it all amounts to knowing *how* to use words, how to stick to linguistic conventions consistently. Thus, consider again "all squares are equilateral." We are absolutely certain of this because we are determined to apply the word "square" only to equilateral figures. We can be sure that we shall never discover a square that is not equilateral, simply because we have decided, or rather have been conditioned, not to *call* a figure "square" unless we believe it to have equal sides. Now consider a law of logic like the following: whatever proposition is implied by true propositions is itself true. How can we be absolutely sure of this? It would surely be naive to say that we believe it because we have just never come across a false proposition that was implied by true propositions. For what would it be like to encounter such an exceptional case? Suppose you met a man who agreed with your prediction that if X were the Democratic candidate for the presidency, X would be elected president, and who like yourself is subsequently informed by the newspapers that X indeed was nominated by the Democratic Party. You then wait till the election comes around, and discover that the Democratic candidate is defeated in the election. You turn to your friend and say "our prediction has not come true." What would you say if he replied "well, it is true that X has not been elected although he was the selected candidate, but this does not refute my prediction that he would be elected if he were the chosen candidate; it rather refutes the principle that whatever proposition is implied by a true proposition must itself be true"? If you were properly trained in logic, you would retort as follows: If we have a true proposition p and another proposition q which is implied by p, then if somebody maintains that nevertheless q may be false, he is simply not using "imply" in its ordinary sense. In saying that p implies q one has already denied that p could be true if q were false. In saying "if p, then q" one has already denied that p could be true if q is false, hence "if p, then q; but p and not q" adds up to a flat contradiction.

Logical positivists conclude from this sort of consideration that a law of logic, like "if p implies q, and p is true, then q is true," is an implicit definition, in this instance of "implies" or "if, then." If one were to deny it, one would either change the conventional meanings of these expressions or else one would contradict oneself. The necessity of the laws of logic consists in the fact that, given the conventional definition, or rules of usage of the relevant expressions, they cannot be denied without self-contradiction. Does this theory, however, lend support to the view that the logical necessity of a proposition results from arbitrary linguistic conventions? If this view were correct, then it should be possible to destroy the logical necessity of a proposition by a mere change of definition. It may seem that this is indeed possible. Decide, for example, to mean by "father" what is ordinarily meant by "man" and it will be quite easy to find exceptions to the allegedly necessary proposition that all fathers are parents. Yet, a moment's reflection should reveal the confusion underlying this argument: of course, whether the *sentence* "all fathers are parents" expresses a necessary truth depends on the meanings of the words "father" and "parent," and that these words are used the way they are at present used in English is a matter of convention; we could, if we so desired, use them otherwise. But this does not mean that the necessary truth of the *proposition* expressed by this sentence could be destroyed by altering linguistic conventions, for if the meanings of the words are changed then the same sentence will express a different proposition. Similarly, if we decided to mean by "12" what is now meant by "11" then we would no longer be asserting something true by the sentence "7 + 5 = 12." This, however, would in no way affect the necessary truth of what we are *now* asserting by means of this sentence. A proposition is something one intends to affirm by means of a given sentence, not the sentence itself. *That which* a Frenchman asserts by means of the sentence "le chat est dans la cuisine" is the same as *that which* an American would assert by means of the different sentence "the cat is in the kitchen." It is what is here technically called "proposition" (though it is but fair to warn the reader that some philosophers—e.g., Ayer in Selection 63, pp. 760 ff., use the word "proposition" to refer to declarative *sentences*). And obviously the truth of what a man intends to say, of the proposition he asserts, cannot be destroyed by putting a different interpretation on the words he uses.

It is not easy to say in what precise sense the necessity of a proposition is, according to logical positivists like Ayer, "based" on linguistic rules. As we have seen, it would be completely indefensible to say it is based on linguistic rules in the sense that the *same proposition* which is necessarily true might not have been necessarily true if words had been used differently and would cease to be necessarily true if words should be used differently in the future. And most logical positivists would probably concede this point. But the reader will have to decide for himself whether there remains, after this concession has been made, a significant issue between logical positivists and their critics in regard to the nature of *a priori* knowledge. A close comparative study of Ayer's "The *A Priori*" (Selection 60) and Ewing's "The '*A Priori*' and the Empirical" (Selection 61) is recommended for that purpose.

A. P.

55   Knowledge as Recollection

Plato

. . . MEN. AND HOW WILL YOU inquire, Socrates, into that which you do not know? What will you put forth as the subject of inquiry? And if you find what you want, how will you ever know that this is the thing which you did not know?

SOC. I know, Meno, what you mean; but just see what a tiresome dispute you are introducing. You argue that a man cannot inquire either about that which he knows, or about that which he does not know; for if he knows, he has no need to inquire; and if not, he cannot; for he does not know the very subject about which he is to inquire.

MEN. Well, Socrates, and is not the argument sound?

SOC. I think not.

MEN. Why not?

SOC. I will tell you why: I have heard from certain wise men and women who spoke of things divine that—

MEN. What did they say?

SOC. They spoke of a glorious truth, as I conceive.

MEN. What was it and who were they?

SOC. Some of them were priests and priestesses who had studied how they might be able to give a reason of their profession; there have been poets also who spoke of these things by inspiration, like Pindar and many others who were inspired. And they say—mark now and see whether their words are true—they say that the soul of man is immortal, and at one time has an end, which is termed dying, and at another time is born again, but is never destroyed. And the moral is that a man ought to live always in perfect holiness. *"For in the ninth year Persephone sends the souls of those from whom she has received the penalty of an-*

[This extract is taken from Plato's dialogue *Meno,* and is reproduced in Benjamin Jowett's translation. Whenever in this dialogue the word "feet" is used in connection with areas, it means "square feet." (Eds.)]

cient crime back again from beneath into the light of the sun above, and these are they who become noble kings and mighty men and great in wisdom and are called saintly heroes in after ages." The soul, then, as being immortal, and having been born again many times, and having seen all things that exist, whether in this world or in the world below, has knowledge of them all; and it is no wonder that she should be able to call to remembrance all that she ever knew about virtue and about everything; for as all nature is akin, and the soul has learned all things, there is no difficulty in her eliciting, or as men say learning, out of a single recollection, all the rest, if a man is strenuous and does not faint; for all inquiry and all learning is but recollection. And therefore we ought not to listen to this sophistical argument about the impossibility of inquiry; for it will make us idle, and is sweet only to the sluggard; but the other saying will make us active and inquisitive. In that confiding, I will gladly inquire with you into the nature of virtue.

MEN. Yes, Socrates; but what do you mean by saying that we do not learn, and that what we call learning is only a process of recollection? Can you teach me how this is?

SOC. I told you, Meno, just now that you are a rogue, and now you ask whether I can teach you, when I am saying that there is no teaching, but only recollection; and thus you imagine that you will involve me in a contradiction.

MEN. Indeed, Socrates, I protest that I had no such intention. I only asked the question from habit; but if you can prove to me that what you say is true, I wish that you would.

SOC. It will be no easy matter, but I will try to please you to the utmost of my power. Suppose that you call one of your numerous attendants, that I may demonstrate on him.

MEN. Certainly. Come hither, boy.

SOC. He is Greek, and speaks Greek, does he not?

MEN. Yes, indeed; he was born in the house.

SOC. Attend now to the questions which I ask him, and observe whether he learns of me or only remembers.

MEN. I will.

SOC. Tell me, boy, do you know that a figure like this is a square?

BOY. I do.

SOC. And you know that a square figure has these four lines equal?

BOY. Certainly.

SOC. And these lines which I have drawn through the middle of the square are also equal?

BOY. Yes.

SOC. A square may be any size?

BOY. Certainly.

SOC. And if one side of the figure be of two feet, and the other side be of two feet, how much will the whole be? Let me explain: if in one direction the space was of two feet, and in the other direction of one foot, the whole would be of two feet taken once?

BOY. Yes.

SOC. But since this side is also of two feet, there are twice two feet?

BOY. There are.

SOC. Then the square is of twice two feet?

BOY. Yes.

SOC. And how many are twice two feet? Count and tell me.

BOY. Four, Socrates.

SOC. And might there not be another square twice as large as this, and having like this the lines equal?

BOY. Yes.

SOC. And of how many feet will that be?

BOY. Of eight feet.

SOC. And now try and tell the length of the line which forms the side of that double square: this is two feet—what will that be?

BOY. Clearly, Socrates, it will be double.

SOC. Do you observe, Meno, that I am not teaching the boy anything, but only asking him questions; and now he fancies that he knows how long a line is necessary in order to produce a figure of eight square feet; does he not?

MEN. Yes.

SOC. And does he really know?

MEN. Certainly not.

SOC. He only guesses that because the square is double, the line is double.

MEN. True.

SOC. Observe him when he recalls the steps in regular order. (*To the Boy.*) Tell me, boy, do you assert that a double space comes from a double line? Remember that I am not speaking of an oblong, but of a figure equal every way, and twice the size of this—that is to say of eight feet; and I want to know whether you still say that a double square comes from a double line?

BOY. Yes.

SOC. But does not this line become doubled if we add another such line here?

BOY. Certainly.

SOC. And four such lines will make a space containing eight feet?

BOY. Yes.

SOC. Let us describe such a figure: Would you not say that this is the figure of eight feet?

BOY. Yes.

SOC. And are there not these four divisions in the figure, each of which is equal to the figure of four feet?

BOY. True.

Soc. And is not that four times four?

Boy. Certainly.

Soc. And four times is not double?

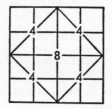

Boy. No, indeed.

Soc. But how much?

Boy. Four times as much.

Soc. Therefore the double line, boy, has given a space, not twice, but four times as much.

Boy. True.

Soc. Four times four are sixteen—are they not?

Boy. Yes.

Soc. What line would give you a space of eight feet, as this gives one of sixteen feet—do you see?

Boy. Yes.

Soc. And the space of four feet is made from this half line?

Boy. Yes.

Soc. Good; and is not a space of eight feet twice the size of this, and half the size of the other?

Boy. Certainly.

Soc. Such a space, then, will be made out of a line greater than this one, and less than that one?

Boy. Yes, I think so.

Soc. Very good; I like to hear you say what you think. And now tell me, is not this a line of two feet and that of four?

Boy. Yes.

Soc. Then the line which forms the side of eight feet ought to be more than this line of two feet, and less than the other of four feet?

Boy. It ought.

Soc. Try and see if you can tell me how much it will be.

Boy. Three feet.

Soc. Then if we add a half to this line of two, that will be the line of three. Here are two and there is one; and on the other side, here are two also and there is one: and that makes the figure of which you speak?

Boy. Yes.

Soc. But if there are three feet this way and three feet that way, the whole space will be three times three feet?

Boy. That is evident.

Soc. And how much are three times three feet?

Boy. Nine.

Soc. And how much is the double of four?

Boy. Eight.

Soc. Then the figure of eight is not made out of a line of three?

Boy. No.

Soc. But from what line?—tell me exactly; and if you would rather not reckon, try and show me the line.

Boy. Indeed, Socrates, I do not know.

Soc. Do you see, Meno, what advances he has made in his power of recollection? He did not know at first, and he does not know now, what is the side of a figure of eight feet; but then he thought that he knew, and answered confidently as if he knew, and had no difficulty; now he has a difficulty, and neither knows nor fancies that he knows.

Men. True.

Soc. Is he not better off in knowing his ignorance?

Men. I think that he is.

Soc. If we have made him doubt, and given him the "torpedo's shock," have we done him any harm?

Men. I think not.

Soc. We have certainly, as would seem, assisted him in some degree to the discovery of the truth; and now he will wish to remedy his ignorance, but then he would have been ready to tell all the world again and again that the double space should have a double side.

Men. True.

Soc. But do you suppose that he would ever have inquired into or learned what he fancied that he knew, though he was really ignorant of it, until he had fallen into perplexity under the idea that he did not know, and had desired to know?

Men. I think not, Socrates.

Soc. Then he was the better for the torpedo's touch?

Men. I think so.

Soc. Mark now the further development. I shall only ask him, and not teach him, and he shall share the inquiry with me; and do you watch and see if you find me telling or explaining anything to him, instead of eliciting his opinion. Tell me, boy, is not this a square of four feet which I have drawn?

Boy. Yes.

Soc. And now I add another square equal to the former one?

Boy. Yes.

Soc. And a third, which is equal to either of them?

Boy. Yes.

Soc. Suppose that we fill up the vacant corner?

Boy. Very good.

Soc. Here, then, there are four equal spaces?

Boy. Yes.

Soc. And how many times larger is this space than this other?

Boy. Four times.

Soc. But it ought to have been twice only, as you will remember.

Boy. True.

Soc. And does not this line, reaching from corner to corner, bisect each of these spaces?

Boy. Yes.

Soc. And are there not here four equal lines which contain this space?

Boy. There are.

Soc. Look and see how much this space is.

Boy. I do not understand.

Soc. Has not each interior line cut off half of the four spaces?

Boy. Yes.

Soc. And how many spaces are there in this section?

Boy. Four.

Soc. And how many in this?

Boy. Two.

Soc. And four is how many times two?

Boy. Twice.

Soc. And this space is of how many feet?

Boy. Of eight feet.

Soc. And from what line do you get this figure?

Boy. From this.

Soc. That is, from the line which extends from corner to corner of the figure of four feet?

Boy. Yes.

Soc. And that is the line which the learned call the diagonal. And if this is the proper name, then you, Meno's slave, are prepared to affirm that the double space is the square of the diagonal?

Boy. Certainly, Socrates.

Soc. What do you say of him, Meno? Were not all these answers given out of his own head?

Men. Yes, they were all his own.

Soc. And yet, as we were just now saying, he did not know?

Men. True.

Soc. But still he had in him those notions of his—had he not?

Men. Yes.

Soc. Then he who does not know may still have true notions of that which he does not know?

Men. He has.

Soc. And at present these notions have just been stirred up in him, as in a dream; but if he were frequently asked the same questions, in different forms, he would know as well as any one at last?

Men. I dare say.

Soc. Without any one teaching him he will recover his knowledge for himself, if he is only asked questions?

MEN. Yes.

Soc. And this spontaneous recovery of knowledge in him is recollection?

MEN. True.

Soc. And this knowledge which he now has must he not either have acquired or always possessed?

MEN. Yes.

Soc. But if he always possessed this knowledge he would always have known; or if he has acquired the knowledge he could not have acquired it in this life unless he has been taught geometry; for he may be made to do the same with all geometry and every other branch of knowledge. Now, has any one ever taught him all this? You must know about him if, as you say, he was born and bred in your house.

MEN. And I am certain that no one ever did teach him.

Soc. And yet he has the knowledge?

MEN. The fact, Socrates, is undeniable.

Soc. But if he did not acquire the knowledge in this life, then he must have had and learned it some other time?

MEN. Clearly he must.

Soc. Which must have been the time when he was not a man?

MEN. Yes.

Soc. And if there have been always true thoughts in him, both at the time when he was and was not a man, which only need to be awakened into knowledge by putting questions to him, his soul must have always possessed this knowledge, for he always either was or was not a man?

MEN. Obviously.

Soc. And if the truth of all things always existed in the soul, then the soul is immortal. Wherefore be of good cheer and try to recollect what you do not know, or rather what you do not remember.

MEN. I feel, somehow, that I like what you are saying.

Soc. And I, Meno, like what I am saying. Some things I have said of which I am not altogether confident. But that we shall be better and braver and less helpless if we think that we ought to inquire, than we should have been if we indulged in the idle fancy that there was no knowing and no use in seeking to know what we do not know—that is a theme upon which I am ready to fight, in word and deed, to the utmost of my power. . . .

56   Necessary Truths and the Natural Light Within Us

G. W. Leibniz

. . . B<small>EING ITSELF AND TRUTH ARE NOT</small> known wholly through the senses; for it would not be impossible for a creature to have long and orderly dreams, resembling our *life,* of a sort that everything which it thought it perceived through the senses would be but mere *appearances.* There must therefore be something beyond the senses, which distinguishes the true from the apparent. But the truth of the demonstrative sciences is exempt from these doubts, and must even serve for judging of the truth of sensible things. For as able philosophers, ancient and modern, have already well remarked:—if all that I should think that I see should be but a dream, it would always be true that I who think while dreaming, would be something, and would actually think in many ways, for which there must always be some reason.

Thus what the ancient Platonists have observed is very true, and is very worthy of being considered, that the existence of intelligible things and particularly of the *Ego* which thinks and which is called spirit or soul, is incomparably more sure than the existence of sensible things; and that thus it would not be impossible, speaking with metaphysical rigor, that there should be at bottom only these intelligible substances, and that sensible things should be but appearances. While on the other hand our lack of attention makes us take sensible things for the only true things. It is well also to observe that if I should discover any demonstrative truth, mathematical or other, while dreaming (as might in fact be), it would be just as certain as if I had been awake. This shows us how intelligible truth is independent of the truth or of the existence outside of us of sensible and material things.

[This selection is taken from a letter by Leibniz to Queen Sophie Charlotte of Prussia, written in 1702. The translation is by Professor Philip P. Wiener. Reprinted with the permission of Charles Scribner's Sons from L<small>EIBNIZ</small> selections, pp. 359–362, 363–364, edited by Philip P. Wiener. Copyright 1951 Charles Scribner's Sons.]

This conception of *being* and of *truth* is found therefore in the Ego and in the understanding, rather than in the external senses and in the perception of external objects.

There we find also what it is to affirm, to deny, to doubt, to will, to act. But above all we find there the *force of the consequences* of reasoning, which are a part of what is called the *natural light*. For example, from this premise, that *no wise man is wicked,* we may, by reversing the terms, draw this conclusion, that *no wicked man is wise.* Whereas from this sentence, that *every wise man is praiseworthy,* we cannot conclude by converting it, that *every one praiseworthy is wise* but only that *some praiseworthy ones are wise.* Although we may always convert particular affirmative propositions, for example, if *some wise man is rich* it must also be that *some rich men are wise,* this cannot be done in particular negatives. For example, we may say that *there are charitable persons who are not just,* which happens when charity is not sufficiently regulated; but we cannot infer from this that *there are just persons who are not charitable;* for in justice are included at the same time charity and the rule of reason.

It is also by *this natural light* that the *axioms* of mathematics are recognized; for example, that *if from two equal things the same quantity be taken away the things which remain are equal;* likewise that *if in a balance everything is equal on the one side and on the other, neither will incline,* a thing which we foresee without ever having experienced it. It is upon such foundations that we construct arithmetic, geometry, mechanics and the other demonstrative sciences; in which, in truth, the senses are very necessary, in order to have certain ideas of sensible things, and experiments are necessary to establish certain facts, and even useful to verify reasonings as by a kind of proof. But the force of the demonstrations depends upon intelligible notions and truths, which alone are capable of making us discern what is necessary, and which, in the conjectural sciences, are even capable of determining demonstratively the degree of probability upon certain given suppositions, in order that we may choose rationally among opposite appearances, the one which is greatest. Nevertheless this part of the art of reasoning has not yet been cultivated as much as it ought to be.

But to return to *necessary truths,* it is generally true that we know them only by this natural light, and not at all by the experiences of the senses. For the senses can very well make known, in some sort, what is, but they cannot make known what *ought to be* or could not be otherwise.

For example, although we may have experienced numberless times that every massive body tends toward the centre of the earth and is not sustained in the air, we are not sure that this is necessary as long as we do not understand the reason of it. Thus we could not be sure that the same thing would occur in air at a higher altitude, at a hundred or more leagues above us; and there are philosophers who imagine that the earth is a magnet, and as the ordinary magnet does not attract the needle when a little removed from it, they think that the attractive force of the earth does not extend very far either. I do not say that they are right, but I do say that one cannot go very certainly beyond the experiences one has had, when one is not aided by reason.

This is why the geometricians have always considered that what is only proved by *induction* or by examples, in geometry or in arithmetic, is never perfectly proved. For example, experience teaches us that odd numbers continuously added together produce the square numbers, that is to say, those which come from multiplying a number by itself. Thus 1 and 3 make 4, that is to say 2 times 2. And 1 and 3 and 5 make 9, that is to say 3 times 3. And 1 and 3 and 5 and 7 make 16, that is 4 times 4. And 1 and 3 and 5 and 7 and 9 make 25, that is 5 times 5. And so on.

$$
\begin{array}{cccc}
1 & 1 & 1 & 1 \\
3 & 3 & 3 & 3 \\
- & 5 & 5 & 5 \\
4 & - & 7 & 7 \\
  & 9 & - & 9 \\
  &   & 16 & - \\
  &   &   & 25 \\
2 & 3 & 4 & 5 \\
\times & \times & \times & \times \\
2 & 3 & 4 & 5 \\
\hline
4 & 9 & 16 & 25
\end{array}
$$

However, if one should experience it a hundred thousand times, continuing the calculation very far, he may reasonably think that this will always follow; but he does not therefore have absolute certainty of it, unless he learns the demonstrative reason which the mathematicians found out long ago. . . .

. . . In truth there are *experiments* which succeed numberless times and ordinarily, and yet it is found in some extraordinary cases that there are *instances* where the experiment does not succeed. For example, if we should have found a hundred thousand times that iron put all alone on the surface of water goes to the bottom, we are not sure that this must always happen. And without recurring to the miracle of the prophet Elisha, who made iron float, we know that an iron pot may be made so hollow that it floats, and that it can even carry besides a considerable weight, as do boats of copper or of tin. And even the abstract sciences like geometry furnish cases in which what ordinarily occurs occurs no longer. For example, we ordinarily find that two lines which continually approach each other finally meet, and many people will almost swear that this could never be otherwise. And nevertheless geometry furnishes us with extraordinary lines, which are for this reason called *asymptotes,* which prolonged *ad infinitum* continually approach each other, and nevertheless never meet.

This consideration shows also that there is a *light born within us.* For since the senses and inductions could never teach us truths which are thoroughly universal, nor that which is absolutely necessary, but only that which is, and that which is found in particular examples; and since we nevertheless know necessary and universal truths of the sciences, a privilege which we have above the brutes; it follows that we have derived these truths in part from what is within us. Thus we may lead a child to these by simple interrogations, after the manner of Socrates, without telling him anything, and without making him experiment at all upon the truth of what is asked him. And this could very easily be practiced in numbers and other similar matters.

I agree, nevertheless, that in the present state the external senses are necessary to us for thinking, and that, if we had none, we could not think. But that which is necessary for something does not for all that constitute its essence. Air is necessary for life, but our life is something else than air. The senses furnish us the matter for reasoning, and we never have thoughts so abstract that something from the senses is not mingled therewith; but reasoning requires something else in addition to what is perceivable by the senses. . . .

57 Introduction to the "Critique of Pure Reason"

Immanuel Kant

1. The Distinction Between Pure and Empirical Knowledge

THERE CAN BE NO DOUBT THAT ALL our knowledge begins with experience. For how should our faculty of knowledge be awakened into action did not objects affecting our senses partly of themselves produce representations, partly arouse the activity of our understanding to compare these representations, and, by combining or separating them, work up the raw material of the sensible impressions into that knowledge of objects which is entitled experience? In the order of time, therefore, we have no knowledge antecedent to experience, and with experience all our knowledge begins.

But though all our knowledge begins with experience, it does not follow that it all arises out of experience. For it may well be that even our empirical knowledge is made up of what we receive through impressions and of what our own faculty of knowledge (sensible impressions serving merely as the occasion) supplies from itself. If our faculty of knowledge makes any such addition, it may be that we are not in a position to distinguish it from the raw material, until with long practice of attention we have become skilled in separating it.

This, then, is a question which at least calls for closer examination, and does not allow of any off-hand answer:—whether there is any knowledge

[This selection consists of the first six sections of the introduction to the second edition of Kant's *Critique of Pure Reason*. The first edition of this work was published in 1781, the second in 1787. The translation here used is that of Norman Kemp Smith and is reprinted with the kind permission of the translator, of Macmillan and Company, Ltd., London, and St. Martin's Press, New York.]

that is thus independent of experience and even of all impressions of the senses. Such knowledge is entitled *a priori,* and distinguished from the *empirical,* which has its sources *a posteriori,* that is, in experience.

The expression "*a priori*" does not, however, indicate with sufficient precision the full meaning of our question. For it has been customary to say, even of much knowledge that is derived from empirical sources, that we have it or are capable of having it *a priori,* meaning thereby that we do not derive it immediately from experience, but from a universal rule—a rule which is itself, however, borrowed by us from experience. Thus we would say of a man who undermined the foundations of his house, that he might have known *a priori* that it would fall, that is, that he need not have waited for the experience of its actual falling. But still he could not know this completely *a priori.* For he had first to learn through experience that bodies are heavy, and therefore fall when their supports are withdrawn.

In what follows, therefore, we shall understand by *a priori* knowledge, not knowledge independent of this or that experience, but knowledge absolutely independent of all experience. Opposed to it is empirical knowledge, which is knowledge possible only *a posteriori,* that is, through experience. *A priori* modes of knowledge are entitled pure when there is no admixture of anything empirical. Thus, for instance, the proposition, "every alteration has its cause," while an *a priori* proposition, is not a pure proposition, because alteration is a concept which can be derived only from experience.

II. We Are in Possession of Certain Modes of A Priori Knowledge, and Even the Common Understanding Is Never Without Them

What we here require is a criterion by which to distinguish with certainty between pure and empirical knowledge. Experience teaches us that a thing is so and so, but not that it cannot be otherwise. First, then, if we have a proposition which in being thought is thought as *necessary,* it is an *a priori* judgment; and if, besides, it is not derived from any proposition except one which also has the validity of a necessary judgment, it is an absolutely *a priori* judgment. Secondly, experience never confers on its judgments true or strict, but only assumed and comparative *universality,* through induction. We can properly only say, therefore, that, so far as we have hitherto observed, there is no exception to this or that rule. If, then, a judgment is thought with strict universality, that is, in such manner that no exception is allowed as possible, it is not derived from experience, but is valid absolutely *a priori.* Empirical universality is only an arbitrary extension of a validity holding in most cases to one which holds in all, for instance, in the proposition, "all bodies are heavy."

When, on the other hand, strict universality is essential to a judgment, this indicates a special source of knowledge, namely, a faculty of *a priori* knowledge. Necessity and strict universality are thus sure criteria of *a priori* knowledge, and are inseparable from one another. But since in the employment of these criteria the contingency of judgments is sometimes more easily shown than their empirical limitation, or, as sometimes also happens, their unlimited universality can be more convincingly proved than their necessity, it is advisable to use the two criteria separately, each by itself being infallible.

Now it is easy to show that there actually are in human knowledge judgments which are necessary and in the strictest sense universal, and which are therefore pure *a priori* judgments. If an example from the sciences be desired, we have only to look to any of the propositions of mathematics; if we seek an example from the understanding in its quite ordinary employment, the proposition, "every alteration must have a cause," will serve our purpose. In the latter case, indeed, the very concept of a cause so manifestly contains the concept of a necessity of connection with an effect and of the strict universality of the rule, that the concept would be altogether lost if we attempted to derive it, as Hume* has done, from a repeated association of that which happens with that which precedes, and from a custom of connecting representations, a custom originating in this repeated association, and constituting therefore a merely subjective necessity. Even without appealing to such examples, it is possible to show that pure *a priori* principles are indispensable for the possibility of experience, and so to prove their existence *a priori*. For whence could experience derive its certainty, if all the rules, according to which it proceeds, were always themselves empirical, and therefore contingent? Such rules could hardly be regarded as first principles. At present, however, we may be content to have established the fact that our faculty of knowledge does have a pure employment, and to have shown what are the criteria of such an employment.

Such *a priori* origin is manifest in certain concepts, no less than in judgments. If we remove our empirical concept of a body, one by one, every feature in it which is [merely] empirical, the color, the hardness or softness, the weight, even the impenetrability, there still remains the space which the body (now entirely vanished) occupied, and this cannot be removed. Again, if we remove from our empirical concept of any object, corporeal or incorporeal, all properties which experience has taught us, we yet cannot take away that property through which the object is thought as substance or as inhering in a substance (although this concept of substance is more determinate than that of an object in general). Owing, therefore, to the necessity with which this concept of

* Kant here disputes Hume's denial of "necessary connections" between causes and their effects; see Selection 11. Hume's analysis of causation as "constant conjunction" between events whose conjunction is not logically necessary, is also discussed in Selection 53. (Eds.)

substance forces itself upon us, we have no option save to admit that it has its seat in our faculty of *a priori* knowledge.

III. Philosophy Stands in Need of a Science
Which Shall Determine the Possibility,
the Principles, and the Extent of All
A Priori *Knowledge*

But what is still more extraordinary than all the preceding is this, that certain modes of knowledge leave the field of all possible experiences and have the appearance of extending the scope of our judgments beyond all limits of experience, and this by means of concepts to which no corresponding object can ever be given in experience.

It is precisely by means of the latter modes of knowledge, in a realm beyond the world of the senses, where experience can yield neither guidance nor correction, that our reason carries on those enquiries which owing to their importance we consider to be far more excellent, and in their purpose far more lofty, than all the understanding can learn in the field of appearances. Indeed we prefer to run every risk of error rather than desist from such urgent enquiries, on the ground of their dubious character, or from disdain and indifference. These unavoidable problems set by pure reason itself are *God, freedom,* and *immortality.* The science which, with all its preparations, is in its final intention directed solely to their solution is metaphysics; and its procedure is at first dogmatic, that is, it confidently sets itself to this task without any previous examination of the capacity or incapacity of reason for so great an undertaking.

Now it does indeed seem natural that, as soon as we have left the ground of experience, we should, through careful enquiries, assure ourselves as to the foundations of any building that we propose to erect, not making use of any knowledge that we possess without first determining whence it has come, and not trusting to principles without knowing their origin. It is natural, that is to say, that the question should first be considered, how the understanding can arrive at all this knowledge *a priori,* and what extent, validity, and worth it may have. Nothing, indeed, could be more natural, if by the term "natural" we signify what fittingly and reasonably ought to happen. But if we mean by "natural" what ordinarily happens, then on the contrary nothing is more natural and more intelligible than the fact that this enquiry has been so long neglected. For one part of this knowledge, the mathematical, has long been of established reliability, and so gives rise to a favourable presumption as regards the other part, which may yet be of quite different nature. Besides, once we are outside the circle of experience, we can be sure of not being *contradicted* by experience. The charm of extending our knowledge is so great that nothing short of encountering a direct contradiction can suffice to arrest us in our course; and this can be avoided, if we are careful in our fabrications—which none the less will still remain fabrications. Mathematics gives us a shining example of how far, independently of experience, we can progress in *a priori* knowledge. It does, indeed, occupy itself with objects and with knowledge solely in so far as they allow of being exhibited in intuition.* But this circumstance is easily overlooked, since this intuition can itself be given *a priori*, and is therefore hardly to be distinguished from a bare and pure concept. Misled by such a proof of the power of reason, the demand for the extension of knowledge recognises no limits. The light dove, cleaving the air in her free flight, and feeling its resistance, might imagine that its flight would be still easier in empty space. It was thus that Plato left the world of the senses, as setting too narrow limits to the understanding, and ventured out beyond it on the wings of the ideas, in the empty space of the pure understanding. He did not observe that with all his efforts he made no advance—meeting no resistance that might, as it were, serve as a support upon which he could take a stand, to which he could apply his powers, and so set his understanding in motion. It is, indeed, the common fate of human reason to complete its speculative structures as speedily as may be, and only afterwards to enquire whether the foundations are reliable. All sorts of excuses will then be appealed to, in order to reassure us of their solidity, or rather indeed to enable us to dispense altogether with so late and so dangerous an enquiry. But what keeps us, during the actual building, free from all apprehension and suspicion, and flatters us with a seeming thoroughness, is this other circumstance, namely, that a great, perhaps the greatest, part of the business of our reason consists in analysis of the concepts which we already have of objects. This analysis supplies us with a considerable body of knowledge, which, while nothing but explanation or elucidation of what has already been thought in our concepts, though in a confused manner, is yet prized as being, at least as regards its form, new insight. But so far as the matter or content is concerned, there has been no extension of our previously possessed concepts, but only an analysis of them. Since this procedure yields real knowledge *a priori*, which progresses in an assured and useful fashion, reason is so far misled as surreptitiously to introduce, without itself being aware of so doing, assertions of an entirely different order, in which it attaches to given concepts others completely foreign to them, and moreover attaches them *a priori*. And yet it is not known how reason can be in a position to do this. Such a question is never so much as thought of. I shall therefore at once proceed to deal with the difference between these two kinds of knowledge.

* Kant means that geometrical concepts can be represented by diagrams. In proving, e. g., the Euclidean theorem that the sum of the interior angles of a triangle equals 180° one usually draws a triangle and then draws a straight line through one vertex parallel to the opposite side. He also refers to the possibility of representing numbers by points. (Eds.)

IV. The Distinction between Analytic
and Synthetic Judgments

In all judgments in which the relation of a subject to the predicate is thought (I take into consideration affirmative judgments only, the subsequent application to negative judgments being easily made), this relation is possible in two different ways. Either the predicate B belongs to the subject A, as something which is (covertly) contained in this concept A; or B lies outside the concept A, although it does indeed stand in connection with it. In the one case I entitle the judgment analytic, in the other synthetic. Analytic judgments (affirmative) are therefore those in which the connection of the predicate with the subject is thought through identity; those in which this connection is thought without identity should be entitled synthetic. The former, as adding nothing through the predicate to the concept of the subject, but merely breaking it up into those constituent concepts that have all along been thought in it, although confusedly, can also be entitled explicative. The latter, on the other hand, add to the concept of the subject a predicate which has not been in any wise thought in it, and which no analysis could possibly extract from it; and they may therefore be entitled ampliative. If I say, for instance, "All bodies are extended," this is an analytic judgment. For I do not require to go beyond the concept which I connect with "body" in order to find extension as bound up with it. To meet with this predicate, I have merely to analyse the concept, that is, to become conscious to myself of the manifold which I always think in that concept. The judgment is therefore analytic. But when I say, "All bodies are heavy," the predicate is something quite different from anything that I think in the mere concept of body in general; and the addition of such a predicate therefore yields a synthetic judgment.

Judgments of experience, as such, are one and all synthetic. For it would be absurd to found an analytic judgment on experience. Since, in framing the judgment, I must not go outside my concept, there is no need to appeal to the testimony of experience in its support. That a body is extended is a proposition that holds *a priori* and is not empirical. For, before appealing to experience, I have already in the concept of body all the conditions required for my judgment. I have only to extract from it, in accordance with the principle of contradiction, the required predicate, and in so doing can at the same time become conscious of the necessity of the judgment—and that is what experience could never have taught me. On the other hand, though I do not include in the concept of a body in general the predicate "weight," none the less this concept indicates an object of experience through one of its parts, and I can add to that part other parts of this same experience, as in this way belonging together with the concept. From the start I can apprehend the concept of body and analytically through the characters of extension, impenetrability, figure, etc., all of which are thought in the concept. Now, however, looking back on the experience from which I have derived this concept of body, and finding weight to be invariably connected with the above characters, I attach it as a predicate to the concept; and in doing so I attach it synthetically, and am therefore extending my knowledge. The possibility of the synthesis of the predicate "weight" with the concept of "body" thus rests upon experience. While the one concept is not contained in the other, they yet belong to one another, though only contingently, as parts of a whole, namely, of an experience which is itself a synthetic combination of intuitions.

But in *a priori* synthetic judgments this help is entirely lacking. [I do not here have the advantage of looking around in the field of experience.] Upon what, then, am I to rely, when I seek to go beyond the concept A, and to know that another concept B is connected with it? Through what is the synthesis made possible? Let us take the proposition, "Everything which happens has its cause." In the concept of "something which happens," I do indeed think an existence which is preceded by a time, etc., and from this concept analytic judgments may be obtained. But the concept of a "cause" lies entirely outside the other concept, and signifies something different from "that which happens," and is not therefore in any way contained in this latter representation. How come I then to predicate of that which happens something quite different, and to apprehend that the concept of cause, though not contained in it, yet belongs, and indeed necessarily belongs, to it? What is here the unknown = X which gives support to the understanding when it believes that it can discover outside the concept A a predicate B foreign to this concept, which it yet at the same time considers to be connected with it? It cannot be experience, because the suggested principle has connected the second representation with the first, not only with greater universality, but also with the character of necessity, and therefore completely *a priori* and on the basis of mere concepts. Upon such synthetic, that is, ampliative principles, all our *a priori* speculative knowledge must ultimately rest; analytic judgments are very important, and indeed necessary, but only for obtaining that clearness in the concepts which is requisite for such a sure and wide synthesis as will lead to a genuinely new addition to all previous knowledge.

V. In All Theoretical Sciences of Reason Synthetic A Priori Judgments Are Contained as Principles

1. *All mathematical judgments, without exception, are synthetic.* This fact, though incontestably certain and in its consequences very important, has hitherto escaped the notice of those who are engaged in the analysis of human reason, and is, indeed, directly opposed to all their conjectures. For as it was found that all mathematical inferences proceed

in accordance with the principle of contradiction (which the nature of all apodeictic certainty requires), it was supposed that the fundamental propositions of the science can themselves be known to be true through that principle. This is an erroneous view. For though a synthetic proposition can indeed be discerned in accordance with the principle of contradiction, this can only be if another synthetic proposition is presupposed, and if it can then be apprehended as following from this other proposition; it can never be so discerned in and by itself.

First of all, it has to be noted that mathematical propositions, strictly so called, are always judgments *a priori,* not empirical; because they carry with them necessity, which cannot be derived from experience. If this be demurred to, I am willing to limit my statement to *pure* mathematics, the very concept of which implies that it does not contain empirical, but only pure *a priori* knowledge.

We might, indeed, at first suppose that the proposition $7 + 5 = 12$ is a merely analytic proposition, and follows by the principle of contradiction from the concept of a sum of 7 and 5. But if we look more closely we find that the concept of the sum of 7 and 5 contains nothing save the union of the two numbers into one, and in this no thought is being taken as to what that single number may be which combines both. The concept of 12 is by no means already thought in merely thinking this union of 7 and 5; and I may analyse my concept of such a possible sum as long as I please, still I shall never find the 12 in it. We have to go outside these concepts, and call in the aid of the intuition which corresponds to one of them, our five fingers, for instance, or, as Segner does in his *Arithmetic,* five points, adding to the concept of 7, unit by unit, the five given in intuition. For starting with the number 7, and for the concept of 5 calling in the aid of the fingers of my hand as intuition, I now add one by one to the number 7 the units which I previously took together to form the number 5, and with the aid of that figure [the hand] see the number 12 coming into being. That 5 should be added to 7, I have indeed already thought in the concept of a sum $= 7 + 5$, but not that this sum is equivalent to the number 12. Arithmetical propositions are therefore always synthetic. This is still more evident if we take larger numbers. For it is then obvious that, however we might turn and twist our concepts, we could never, by the mere analysis of them, and without the aid of intuition, discover what [the number is that] is the sum.

Just as little is any fundamental proposition of pure geometry analytic. That the straight line between two points is the shortest, is a synthetic proposition. For my concept of *straight* contains nothing of quantity, but only of quality. The concept of the shortest is wholly an addition, and cannot be derived, through any process of analysis, from the concept of the straight line. Intuition, therefore, must here be called in; only by its aid is the synthesis possible. What here causes us commonly to believe that the predicate of such apodeictic judgments is already contained in our concept, and that the judgment is therefore analytic, is merely the ambiguous character of the terms used. We are required to join in thought a certain predicate to a given concept, and this necessity is inherent in the concepts themselves. But the question is not what we *ought* to join in thought to the given concept, but what we *actually* think in it, even if only obscurely; and it is then manifest that, while the predicate is indeed attached necessarily to the concept, it is so in virtue of an intuition which must be added to the concept, not as thought in the concept itself.

Some few fundamental propositions, presupposed by the geometrician, are, indeed, really analytic, and rest on the principle of contradiction. But, as identical propositions, they serve only as links in the chain of method and not as principles; for instance, $a = a$; the whole is equal to itself; or $(a + b) > a$, that is, the whole is greater than its part. And even these propositions, though they are valid according to pure concepts, are only admitted in mathematics because they can be exhibited in intuition.

2. *Natural science (physics) contains* a priori *synthetic judgments as principles.* I need cite only two such judgments: that in all changes of the material world the quantity of matter remains unchanged; and that in all communication of motion, action and reaction must always be equal. Both propositions, it is evident, are not only necessary, and therefore in their origin *a priori,* but also synthetic. For in the concept of matter I do not think its permanence, but only its presence in the space which it occupies. I go outside and beyond the concept of matter, joining to it *a priori* in thought something which I have not thought *in* it. The proposition is not, therefore, analytic, but synthetic, and yet is thought *a priori;* and so likewise are the other propositions of the pure part of natural science.

3. *Metaphysics,* even if we look upon it has having hitherto failed in all its endeavours, is yet, owing to the nature of human reason, a quite indispensable science, and *ought to contain* a priori *synthetic knowledge.* For its business is not merely to analyse concepts which we make for ourselves *a priori* of things, and thereby to clarify them analytically, but to extend our *a priori* knowledge. And for this purpose we must employ principles which add to the given concept something that was not contained in it, and through *a priori* synthetic judgments venture out so far that experience is quite unable to follow us, as, for instance, in the proposition, that the world must have a first beginning, and such like. Thus metaphysics consists, at least *in intention,* entirely of *a priori* synthetic propositions.

VI. The General Problem of Pure Reason

Much is already gained if we can bring a number of investigations under the formula of a single problem. For we not only lighten our own task, by defining it accurately, but make it easier for others, who would test our results, to judge whether or not we have succeeded in what we set out to do. Now the proper problem of pure reason is contained in the question: How are *a priori* synthetic judgments possible?

That metaphysics has hitherto remained in so vacillating a state of uncertainty and contradiction, is entirely due to the fact that this problem, and perhaps even the distinction between analytic and synthetic judgments, has never previously been considered. Upon the solution of this problem, or upon a sufficient proof that the possibility which it desires to have explained does in fact not exist at all, depends the success or failure of metaphysics. Among philosophers, David Hume* came nearest to envisaging this problem, but still was very far from conceiving it with sufficient definiteness and universality. He occupied himself exclusively with the synthetic proposition regarding the connection of an effect with its cause (*principium causalitatis*), and he believed himself to have shown that such an *a priori* proposition is entirely impossible. If we accept his conclusions, then all that we call metaphysics is a mere delusion whereby we fancy ourselves to have rational insight into what, in actual fact, is borrowed solely from experience, and under the influence of custom has taken the illusory semblance of necessity. If he had envisaged our problem in all its universality, he would never have been guilty of this statement, so destructive of all pure philosophy. For he would then have recognised that, according to his own argument, pure mathematics, as certainly containing *a priori* synthetic propositions, would also not be possible; and from such an assertion his good sense would have saved him.

In the solution of the above problem, we are at the same time deciding as to the possibility of the employment of pure reason in establishing and developing all those sciences which contain a theoretical *a priori* knowledge of objects, and have therefore to answer the questions:

> How is pure mathematics possible?
> How is pure science of nature possible?

Since these sciences actually exist, it is quite proper to ask *how* they are possible; for that they must be possible is proved by the fact that they exist.[1] But the poor progress which has hitherto been made in metaphysics, and the fact that no system yet propounded can, in view of the essential purpose of metaphysics, be said really to exist, leaves everyone sufficient ground for doubting as to its possibility.

Yet, in a certain sense, this *kind of knowledge* is to be looked upon as given; that is to say, metaphysics actually exists, if not as a science, yet still as natural disposition (*metaphysica naturalis*). For human reason, without being moved merely by the idle desire for extent and variety of knowledge, proceeds impetuously, driven on by an inward need, to questions such as cannot be answered by any empirical employment of reason, or by principles thence derived. Thus in all men, as soon as their reason

---

* See Selection 11. (Eds.)

1. Many may still have doubts as regards pure natural science. We have only, however, to consider the various propositions that are to be found at the beginning of (empirical) physics, properly so called, those, for instance, relating to the permanence in the quantity of matter, to inertia, to the equality of action and reaction, etc., in order to be soon convinced that they constitute a *physica pura,* or *rationalis,* which well deserves, as an independent science, to be separately dealt with in its whole extent, be that narrow or wide.

has become ripe for speculation, there has always existed and will always continue to exist some kind of metaphysics. And so we have the question:

How is metaphysics, as natural disposition, possible?

that is, how from the nature of universal human reason do those questions arise which pure reason propounds to itself, and which it is impelled by its own need to answer as best it can?

But since all attempts which have hitherto been made to answer these natural questions—for instance, whether the world has a beginning or is from eternity—have always met with unavoidable contradictions, we cannot rest satisfied with the mere natural disposition to metaphysics, that is, with the pure faculty of reason itself, from which, indeed, some sort of metaphysics (be it what it may) always arises. It must be possible for reason to attain to certainty whether we know or do not know the objects of metaphysics, that is, to come to a decision either in regard to the objects of its enquiries or in regard to the capacity or incapacity of reason to pass any judgment upon them, so that we may either with confidence extend our pure reason or set to it sure and determinate limits. This last question, which arises out of the previous general problem, may, rightly stated, take the form:

How is metaphysics, as science, possible?

Thus the critique of reason, in the end, necessarily leads to scientific knowledge; while its dogmatic employment, on the other hand, lands us in dogmatic assertions to which other assertions, equally specious, can always be opposed—that is, in *scepticism.*

This science cannot be of any very formidable prolixity, since it has to deal not with the objects of reason, the variety of which is inexhaustible, but only with itself and the problems which arise entirely from within itself, and which are imposed upon it by its own nature, not by the nature of things which are distinct from it. When once reason has learnt completely to understand its own power in respect of objects which can be presented to it in experience, it should easily be able to determine, with completeness and certainty, the extent and the limits of its attempted employment beyond the bounds of all experience.

We may, then, and indeed we must, regard as abortive all attempts, hitherto made, to establish a metaphysic *dogmatically.* For the analytic part in any such attempted system, namely, the mere analysis of the concepts that inhere in our reason *a priori,* is by no means the aim of, but only a preparation for, metaphysics proper, that is, the extension of its *a priori* synthetic knowledge. For such a purpose, the analysis of concepts is useless, since it merely shows what is contained in these concepts, not how we arrive at them *a priori.* A solution of this latter problem is required, that we may be able to determine the valid employment of such concepts in regard to the objects of all knowledge in general. Nor is much self-denial needed to give up these claims, seeing that the undeniable, and in the dogmatic procedure of reason also unavoidable, contradictions of reason with itself have long since undermined the authority of every metaphysical system yet propounded. Greater firmness will be required if we are not to be deterred by inward difficulties and outward opposition from endeavouring, through application of a method entirely different from any hitherto employed, at last to bring to a prosperous and fruitful growth a science indispensable to human reason—a science whose every branch may be cut away but whose root cannot be destroyed.

John Stuart Mill

ＩF, AS LAID DOWN IN THE TWO PRECEDING chapters, the foundation of all sciences, even deductive or demonstrative sciences, is induction, if every step in the ratiocinations even of geometry is an act of induction, and if a train of reasoning is but bringing many inductions to bear upon the same subject of inquiry and drawing a case within one induction by means of another, wherein lies the peculiar certainty always ascribed to the sciences which are entirely, or almost entirely, deductive? Why are they called the exact sciences? Why are mathematical certainty and the evidence of demonstration common phrases to express the very highest degree of assurance attainable by reason? Why are mathematics by almost all philosophers, and (by some) even those branches of natural philosophy which, through the medium of mathematics, have been converted into deductive sciences, considered to be independent of the evidence of experience and observation and characterized as systems of necessary truth?

The Alleged Necessity of the Propositions of Geometry Is Illusory

The answer I conceive to be that this character of necessity ascribed to the truths of mathematics and (even with some reservations to be hereafter made) the peculiar certainty attributed to them is an illusion, in order to sustain which, it is necessary to suppose that those truths relate to, and express the properties of, purely imaginary objects. It is acknowledged that the conclusions of geometry are deduced, partly at least, from the so-called definitions, and that those definitions are assumed to be correct representations, as far as they go, of the objects with which geometry is conversant.

[This selection is taken from Chapters V and VI of Book II of *A System of Logic,* a book first published in 1843.]

Now we have pointed out that from a definition as such no proposition, unless it be one concerning the meaning of a word, can ever follow, and that what apparently follows from a definition follows in reality from an implied assumption that there exists a real thing conformable thereto. This assumption, in the case of the definitions of geometry, is not strictly true; there exist no real things exactly conformable to the definitions. There exist no points without magnitude; no lines without breadth, nor perfectly straight; no circles with all their radii exactly equal, nor squares with all their angles perfectly right. It will perhaps be said that the assumption does not extend to the actual, but only to the possible, existence of such things. I answer that, according to any test we have of possibility, they are not even possible. Their existence, so far as we can form any judgment, would seem to be inconsistent with the physical constitution of our planet at least, if not of the universe. To get rid of this difficulty and at the same time to save the credit of the supposed system of necessary truth, it is customary to say that the points, lines, circles, and squares which are the subject of geometry exist in our conceptions merely and are part of our minds, which minds, by working on their own materials, construct an *a priori* science, the evidence of which is purely mental and has nothing whatever to do with outward experience. By howsoever high authorities this doctrine may have been sanctioned, it appears to me psychologically incorrect. The points, lines, circles, and squares which anyone has in his mind are (I apprehend) simply copies of the points, lines, circles, and squares which he has known in his experience. Our idea of a point I apprehend to be simply our idea of the *minimum visibile,* the smallest portion of surface which we can see. A line, as defined by geometers, is wholly inconceivable. We can reason about a line as if it had no breadth, because we have a power, which is the foundation of all the control we can exercise over the operations of our minds, the power, when a perception is present to our senses or a conception to our intellects, of *attending* to a part only of that perception or conception instead of the whole. But we cannot *conceive* a line without breadth; we can form no mental picture of such a line; all the lines which we have in our minds are lines possessing breadth. If anyone doubts this, we may refer him to his own experience. I much question if anyone who fancies that he can conceive what is called a mathematical line thinks so from the evidence of his consciousness; I suspect it is rather because he supposes that, unless such a conception were possible, mathematics could not exist as a science, a supposition which there will be no difficulty in showing to be entirely groundless.

Since, then, neither in nature nor in the human mind do there exist any objects exactly corresponding to the definitions of geometry, while yet that science cannot be supposed to be conversant about nonentities, nothing remains but to consider geometry as conversant with such lines, angles, and figures as really exist, and the definitions, as they are called, must be regarded as some of our first and most obvious generalizations concerning those natural objects. The correctness of those generalizations, *as* generalizations, is without a flaw; the equality of all the radii of a circle is true of all circles; so far as it is true of any one, but it is not exactly true of any circle; it is only nearly true, so nearly that no error of any importance in practice will be incurred by feigning it to be exactly true. When we have occasion to extend these inductions or their consequences to cases in which the error would be appreciable—to lines of perceptible breadth or thickness, parallels which deviate sensibly from equidistance, and the like—we correct our conclusions by combining with them a fresh set of propositions relating to the aberration, just as we also take in propositions relating to the physical or chemical properties of the material if those properties happen to introduce any modification into the result, which they easily may, even with respect to figure and magnitude, as in the case, for instance, of expansion by heat. So long, however, as there exists no practical necessity for attending to any of the properties of the object except its geometrical properties or to any of the natural irregularities in those, it is convenient to neglect the consideration of the other properties and of the irregularities and to reason as if these did not exist; accordingly, we formally announce in the definitions that we intend to proceed on this plan. But it is an error to suppose, because we resolve to confine our attention to a certain number of the properties of an object, that we therefore conceive, or have an idea of, the object denuded of its other properties. We are thinking, all the time, of precisely such objects as we have seen and touched and with all the properties which naturally belong to them, but, for scientific convenience, we feign them to be divested of all properties except those which are material to our purpose and in regard to which we deign to consider them.

The peculiar accuracy supposed to be characteristic of the first principles of geometry thus appears to be fictitious. The assertions on which the reasonings of the science are founded do not, any more than in other sciences, exactly correspond with the fact, but we suppose that they do so, for the sake of tracing the consequences which follow from the supposition. The opinion of Dugald Stewart respecting the foundations of geometry is, I conceive, substantially correct: that it is built on hypotheses; that it owes to this alone the peculiar certainty supposed to distinguish it; and that in any science whatever, by reasoning from a set of hypotheses, we may obtain a body of conclusions as certain as those of geometry, that is, as strictly in accordance with the hypotheses and as irresistibly compelling assent, *on condition* that those hypotheses are true.

When, therefore, it is affirmed that the conclusions of geometry are necessary truths, the necessity consists in reality only in this, that they correctly follow from the suppositions from which they are deduced. Those suppositions are so far from being necessary that they are not even true; they purposely depart, more or less widely, from the truth. The only sense in which necessity can be ascribed to the conclusions of any scientific investigation is that of legitimately following from some assumption which, by the conditions of the inquiry, is not to be questioned. In this relation, of course, the derivative truths of every deductive science must stand to the inductions or assumptions on which the science is founded, and which, whether true or untrue, certain or doubtful in themselves, are always supposed certain for the purposes of the particular science. . . .

The Axioms Are Experimental Truths

. . . What is the ground of our belief in axioms—what is the evidence on which they rest? I answer, they are experimental truths, generalizations from observation. The proposition, "Two straight lines cannot inclose a space"—or, in other words, "Two straight lines which have once met, do not meet again, but continue to diverge"—is an induction from the evidence of our senses.

This opinion runs counter to a scientific prejudice of long standing and great strength, and there is probably no proposition enunciated in this work for which a more unfavorable reception is to be expected. It is, however, no new opinion, and, even if it were so, would be entitled to be judged not by its novelty, but by the strength of the arguments by which it can be supported. I consider it very fortunate that so eminent a champion of the contrary opinion as Dr. Whewell has found occasion for a most elaborate treatment of the whole theory of axioms in attempting to construct the philosophy of the mathematical and physical sciences on the basis of the doctrine against which I now contend. Whoever is anxious that a discussion should go to the bottom of the subject must rejoice to see the opposite side of the question worthily represented. If what is said by Dr. Whewell, in support of an opinion which he has made the foundation of a systematic work, can be shown not to be conclusive, enough will have been done, without going elsewhere in quest of stronger arguments and a more powerful adversary.

It is not necessary to show that the truths which we call axioms are originally *suggested* by observation and that we should never have known that two straight lines cannot inclose a space if we had never seen a straight line, thus much being admitted by Dr. Whewell and by all, in recent times, who have taken his view of the subject. But they contend that it is not experience which *proves* the axiom, but that its truth is perceived *a priori,* by the constitution of the mind itself, from the first moment when the meaning of the proposition is apprehended, and without any necessity for verifying it by repeated trials, as is requisite in the case of truths really ascertained by observation.

They cannot, however, but allow that the truth of the axiom, "Two straight lines cannot inclose a space," even if evident independently of experience, is also evident from experience. Whether the axiom needs confirmation or not, it receives confirmation in almost every instant of our lives, since we cannot look at any two straight lines which intersect one another without seeing that from that point they continue to diverge more and more. Experimental proof crowds in upon us in such endless profusion, and without one instance in which there can be even a suspicion of an exception to the rule, that we should soon have stronger ground for believing the axiom, even as an experimental truth, than we have for almost any of the general truths which we confessedly learn from the evidence of our senses. Independently of *a priori* evidence, we should certainly believe it with an intensity of conviction far greater than we accord to any ordinary physical truth, and this, too, at a time of life much earlier than that from which we date almost any part of our acquired knowledge, and much too early to admit of our retaining any recollection of the history of our intellectual operations of that period. Where, then, is the necessity for assuming that our recognition of these truths has a different origin from the rest of our knowledge when its existence is perfectly accounted for by supposing its origin to be the same? when the causes which produce belief in all other instances exist in this instance, and in a degree of strength as much superior to what exists in other cases as the intensity of the belief itself is superior? The burden of proof lies on the advocates of the contrary opinion; it is for them to point out some fact inconsistent with the supposition that this part of our knowledge of nature is derived from the same sources as every other part.

This, for instance, they would be able to do, if they could prove chronologically that we had the conviction (at least practically) so early in infancy as to be anterior to those impressions on the senses upon which, on the other theory, the conviction is founded. This, however, cannot be proved, the point being too far back to be within the reach of memory and too obscure for external observation. The advocates of the *a priori* theory are obliged to have recourse to other arguments. These are reducible to two, which I shall endeavor to state as clearly and as forcibly as possible.

In the first place it is said that if our assent to the proposition that two straight lines cannot inclose a space were derived from the senses, we could only be convinced of its truth by actual trial, that is, by seeing or feeling the straight lines, whereas, in fact, it is seen to be true by merely thinking of them. That a stone thrown into water goes to the bottom may be perceived by our senses, but mere thinking of a stone thrown into the water would never have led us to that conclusion; not so, however, with the axioms relating to straight lines: if I could be made to conceive what a straight line is, without having seen one, I should at once recognize that two such lines cannot inclose a space. Intuition is "imaginary looking,"[1] but experience must be real looking; if we see a property of straight lines to be true by merely fancying ourselves to be looking at them, the ground of our belief cannot be the senses, or experience; it must be something mental.

To this argument it might be added in the case of this particular axiom (for the assertion would not be true of all axioms) that the evidence of it from actual ocular inspection is not only unnecessary but unattainable. What says the axiom? That two straight lines *cannot* inclose a space; that,

1. Whewell's *History of Scientific Ideas*, I, p. 140.

after having once intersected, if they are prolonged to infinity they do not meet, but continue to diverge from one another. How can this, in any single case, be proved by actual observation? We may follow the lines to any distance we please, but we cannot follow them to infinity; for aught our senses can testify, they may, immediately beyond the farthest point to which we have traced them, begin to approach, and at last meet. Unless, therefore, we had some other proof of the impossibility than observation affords us, we should have no ground for believing the axiom at all.

To these arguments, which I trust I cannot be accused of understanding, a satisfactory answer will, I conceive, be found, if we advert to one of the characteristic properties of geometrical forms—their capacity of being painted in the imagination with a distinctness equal to reality; in other words, the exact resemblance of our ideas of form to the sensations which suggest them. This, in the first place, enables us to make (at least with a little practice) mental pictures of all possible combinations of lines and angles which resemble the realities quite as well as any which we could make on paper; and, in the next place, make those pictures just as fit subjects of geometrical experimentation as the realities themselves, inasmuch as pictures, if sufficiently accurate, exhibit, of course, all the properties which would be manifested by the realities at one given instant and on simple inspection; and in geometry we are concerned only with such properties, and not with that which pictures could not exhibit, the mutual action of bodies one upon another. The foundations of geometry would, therefore, be laid in direct experience, even if the experiments (which in this case consist merely in attentive contemplation) were practiced solely upon what we call our ideas, that is, upon the diagrams in our minds, and not upon outward objects. For in all systems of experimentation we take some objects to serve as representatives of all which resemble them, and in the present case the conditions which qualify a real object to be the representative of its class are completely fulfilled by an object existing only in our fancy. Without denying, therefore, the possibility of satisfying ourselves that two straight lines cannot inclose a space by merely thinking of straight lines without actually looking at them, I contend that we do not believe this truth on the ground of the imaginary intuition simply, but because we know that the imaginary lines exactly resemble real ones and that we may conclude from them to real ones with quite as much certainty as we could conclude from one real line to another. The conclusion, therefore, is still an induction from observation. And we should not be authorized to substitute observation of the image in our mind for observation of the reality, if we had not learned by long continued experience that the properties of the reality are faithfully represented in the image, just as we should be scientifically warranted in describing an animal which we have never seen from a picture made of it with a daguerreotype, but not until we had learned by ample experience that observation of such a picture is precisely equivalent to observation of the original. . . .

What We Cannot Conceive Is Not Therefore Impossible

. . . The first of the two arguments in support of the theory that axioms are *a priori* truths having, I think, been sufficiently answered, I proceed to the second, which is usually the most relied on. Axioms (it is asserted) are conceived by us not only as true, but as universally and necessarily true. Now, experience cannot possibly give to any proposition this character. I may have seen snow a hundred times and may have seen that it was white, but this cannot give me entire assurance even that all snow is white, much less that snow *must* be white. "However many instances we may have observed of the truth of a proposition, there is nothing to assure us that the next case shall not be an exception to the rule. If it be strictly true that every ruminant animal yet known has cloven hoofs, we still cannot be sure that some creature will not hereafter be discovered which has the first of these attributes, without having the other. . . . Experience must always consist of a limited number of observations; and, however numerous these may be, they can show nothing with regard to the infinite number of cases in which the experiment has not been made." Besides, axioms are not only universal, they are also necessary. Now, "experience cannot offer the smallest ground for the necessity of a proposition. She can observe and record what has happened; but she cannot find, in any case, or in any accumulation of cases, any reason for what *must* happen. She may see objects side by side; but she cannot see a reason why they must ever be side by side. She finds certain events to occur in succession; but the succession supplies, in its occurrence, no reason for its recurrence. She contemplates external objects; but she cannot detect any internal bond, which indissolubly connects the future with the past, the possible with the real. To learn a proposition by experience, and to see it to be necessarily true, are two altogether different processes of thought."[2] And Dr. Whewell adds, "If anyone does not clearly comprehend this distinction of necessary and contingent truths, he will not be able to go along with us in our researches into the foundations of human knowledge; nor, indeed, to pursue with success any speculation on the subject."[3] . . .

Although Dr. Whewell has naturally and properly employed a variety of phrases to bring his meaning more forcibly home, he would, I presume, allow that they are all equivalent, and that what he means by a necessary truth would be sufficiently defined, a proposition the negation of which is not only false but inconceivable. I am unable to find in any of his expressions, turn them what way you will, a meaning beyond this, and I do not believe he would contend that they mean anything more.

This, therefore, is the principle asserted: that propositions, the negation of which is inconceivable, or, in other words, which we cannot figure to

2. *History of Scientific Ideas,* I, pp. 65–67.
3. *Ibid.,* I, p. 60.

ourselves as being false, must rest on evidence of a higher and more cogent description than any which experience can afford.

Now I cannot but wonder that so much stress should be laid on the circumstance of inconceivableness when there is such ample experience to show that our capacity or incapacity of conceiving a thing has very little to do with the possibility of the thing in itself, but is, in truth, very much an affair of accident, and depends on the past history and habits of our own minds. There is no more generally acknowledged fact in human nature than the extreme difficulty at first felt in conceiving anything as possible, which is in contradiction to long established and familiar experience, or even to old familiar habits of thought. And this difficulty is a necessary result of the fundamental laws of the human mind. When we have often seen and thought of two things together and have never in any one instance either seen or thought of them separately, there is by the primary law of association an increasing difficulty, which may in the end become insuperable, of conceiving the two things apart. This is most of all conspicuous in uneducated persons who are, in general, utterly unable to separate any two ideas which have once become firmly associated in their minds; and if persons of cultivated intellect have any advantage on the point, it is only because, having seen and heard and read more, and being more accustomed to exercise their imagination, they have experienced their sensations and thoughts in more varied combinations and have been prevented from forming many of these inseparable associations. But this advantage has necessarily its limits. The most practiced intellect is not exempt from the universal laws of our conceptive faculty. If daily habit presents to anyone for a long period two facts in combination, and if he is not led during that period either by accident or by his voluntary mental operations to think of them apart, he will probably in time become incapable of doing so even by the strongest effort, and the supposition that the two facts can be separated in nature will at last present itself to his mind with all the characters of an inconceivable phenomenon. There are remarkable instances of this in the history of science, instances in which the most instructed men rejected as impossible, because inconceivable, things which their posterity, by earlier practice and longer perseverance in the attempt, found it quite easy to conceive, and which everybody now knows to be true. There was a time when men of the most cultivated intellects and the most emancipated from the dominion of early prejudice could not credit the existence of antipodes, were unable to conceive, in opposition to old association, the force of gravity acting upward instead of downward. The Cartesians long rejected the Newtonian doctrine of the gravitation of all bodies toward one another, on the faith of a general proposition, the reverse of which seemed to them to be inconceivable—the proposition that a body cannot act where it is not. All the cumbrous machinery of imaginary vortices, assumed without the smallest particle of evidence, appeared to these philosophers a more rational mode of explaining the heavenly motions than one which involved what seemed to them so great an absurdity. And they no doubt found it as impossible to conceive that a body should act upon the earth from the distance of the sun or moon as we find it to conceive an end to space or time, or two straight lines inclosing a space. Newton himself had not been able to realize the conception or we should not have had his hypothesis of a subtle ether, the occult cause of gravitation, and his writings prove that though he deemed the particular nature of the intermediate agency a matter of conjecture, the necessity of *some* such agency appeared to him indubitable.

If, then, it be so natural to the human mind, even in a high state of culture, to be incapable of conceiving and on that ground to believe impossible what is afterward not only found to be conceivable but proved to be true, what wonder if in cases where the association is still older, more confirmed, and more familiar, and in which nothing ever occurs to shake our conviction or even suggest to us any conception at variance with the association, the acquired incapacity should continue and be mistaken for a natural incapacity? It is true, our experience of the varieties in nature enables us, within certain limits, to conceive other varieties analogous to them. We can conceive the sun or moon falling, for though we never saw them fall, nor ever, perhaps, imagined them falling, we have seen so many other things fall, that we have innumerable familiar analogies to assist the conception, which, after all, we should probably have some difficulty in framing, were we not well accustomed to see the sun and moon move (or appear to move) so that we are only called upon to conceive a slight change in the direction of motion, a circumstance familiar to our experience. But when experience affords no model on which to shape the new conception, how is it possible for us to form it? How, for example, can we imagine an end to space or time? We never saw any object without something beyond it, nor experienced any feeling without something following it. When, therefore, we attempt to conceive the last point of space, we have the idea irresistibly raised of other points beyond it. When we try to imagine the last instant of time, we cannot help conceiving another instant after it. Nor is there any necessity to assume, as is done by a modern school of metaphysicians, a peculiar fundamental law of the mind to account for the feeling of infinity inherent in our conceptions of space and time; that apparent infinity is sufficiently accounted for by simpler and universally acknowledged laws.

Now, in the case of a geometrical axiom, such, for example, as that two straight lines cannot inclose a space—a truth which is testified to us by our very earliest impressions of the external world—how is it possible (whether those external impressions be or be not the ground of our belief) that the reverse of the proposition *could* be otherwise than inconceivable to us? What analogy have we, what similar order of facts in any other branch of our experience, to facilitate to us the conception of two straight lines inclosing a space? Nor is even this all. I have already called attention to the peculiar property of our impressions of form, that the ideas or mental images exactly resemble their prototypes and adequately represent them for the purposes of scientific observation. From this and from the intuitive character of the observation, which in this case reduces itself to simple inspection, we cannot so much as call up in our imagination two straight lines, in order to attempt to conceive them inclosing a space, without by that very act repeating the scientific experiment which establishes the contrary. Will it really be contended that the inconceivableness of the thing, in such circumstances, proves anything against the experimental origin of the conviction? Is it not clear that in whichever mode our belief in the proposition may have originated, the impossibility of our conceiving the negative of it must, on either hypothesis, be the same? As, then, Dr. Whewell exhorts those who have any difficulty in recognizing the distinction held by him between necessary and contingent truths to study geometry—a condition which I can assure him I have conscientiously fulfilled—I, in return, with equal confidence, exhort those who agree with him to study the general laws of association, being convinced that nothing more is requisite than a moderate familiarity with those laws to dispel the illusion which ascribes a peculiar necessity to our earliest inductions from experience and measures the possibility of things in themselves by the human capacity of conceiving them. . . .

The Science of Numbers Is Inductive

. . . What we have now asserted, however, cannot be received as universally true of deductive or demonstrative sciences until verified by being applied to the most remarkable of all those sciences, that of Numbers, the theory of the Calculus, Arithmetic and Algebra. It is harder to believe of the doctrines of this science than of any other, either that they are not truths *a priori* but experimental truths, or that their peculiar certainty is owing to their being not absolute but only conditional truths. This, therefore, is a case which merits examination apart, and the more so because on this subject we have a double set of doctrines to contend with: that of the *a priori* philosophers on one side; and, on the other, a theory the most opposite to theirs which was at one time very generally received and is still far from being altogether exploded among metaphysicians.

This theory attempts to solve the difficulty apparently inherent in the case by representing the propositions of the science of numbers as merely verbal and its processes as simple transformations of language, substitutions of one expression for another. The proposition, "Two and one is equal to three," according to these writers, is not a truth, is not the assertion of a really existing fact, but a definition of the word three, a statement that mankind have agreed to use the name three as a sign exactly equivalent to two and one, to call by the former name whatever is called by the other more clumsy phrase. According to this doctrine, the longest process in algebra is but a succession of changes in terminology by which equivalent

expressions are substituted one for another, a series of translations of the
same fact from one into another language; though how, after such a series
of translations, the fact itself comes out changed (as when we demonstrate
a new geometrical theorem by algebra) they have not explained, and it is a
difficuly which is fatal to their theory.

It must be acknowledged that there are peculiarities in the processes
of arithmetic and algebra which render the theory in question very
plausible, and have not unnaturally made those sciences the stronghold of
Nominalism. The doctrine that we can discover facts, detect the hidden
processes of nature, by an artful manipulation of language is so contrary
to common sense that a person must have made some advances in philosophy to believe it: men fly to so paradoxical a belief to avoid, as they
think, some even greater difficulty which the vulgar do not see. What has
led many to believe that reasoning is a mere verbal process is that no
other theory seemed reconcilable with the nature of the science of numbers.
For we do not carry any ideas along with us when we use the symbols of
arithmetic or of algebra. In a geometrical demonstration we have a mental
diagram, if not one on paper; AB, AC, are present to our imagination as
lines, intersecting other lines, forming an angle with one another, and
the like; but not so a and b. These may represent lines or any other
magnitudes, but those magnitudes are never thought of; nothing is realized
in our imagination but a and b. The ideas which, on the particular occasion, they happen to represent are banished from the mind during every
intermediate part of the process between the beginning, when the premises
are translated from things into signs, and the end, when the conclusion is
translated back from signs into things. Nothing, then, being in the
reasoner's mind but the symbols, what can seem more inadmissible than to
contend that the reasoning process has to do with anything more? We
seem to have come to one of Bacon's prerogative instances, an *experi-
mentum crucis* on the nature of reasoning itself.

Nevertheless, it will appear on consideration that this apparently so
decisive instance is no instance at all; that there is in every step of an
arithmetical or algebraical calculation a real induction, a real inference of
facts from facts; and that what disguises the induction is simply its comprehensive nature and the consequent extreme generality of the language. All
numbers must be numbers of something; there are no such things as numbers in the abstract. *Ten* must mean ten bodies, or ten sounds, or ten
beatings of the pulse. But though numbers must be numbers of something,
they may be numbers of anything. Propositions, therefore, concerning
numbers have the remarkable peculiarity that they are propositions concerning all things whatever, all objects, all existences of every kind known
to our experience. All things possess quantity, consist of parts which can
be numbered, and in that character possess all the properties which are
called properties of numbers. That half of four is two must be true whatever
the word four represents, whether four hours, four miles, or four pounds
weight. We need only conceive a thing divided into four equal parts (and

all things may be conceived as so divided) to be able to predicate of it every property of the number four, that is, every arithmetical proposition in which the number four stands on one side of the equation. Algebra extends the generalization still farther; every number represents that particular number of all things without distinction, but every algebraical symbol does more; it represents all numbers without distinction. As soon as we conceive a thing divided into equal parts, without knowing into what number of parts, we may call it *a* or *x,* and apply to it, without danger of error, every algebraical formula in the books. The proposition, $2(a + b) = 2a + 2b,$ is a truth coextensive with all nature. Since, then, algebraical truths are true of all things whatever, and not, like those of geometry, true of lines only or of angles only, it is no wonder that the symbols should not excite in our minds ideas of any things in particular. When we demonstrate the forty-seventh proposition of Euclid, it is not necessary that the words should raise in us an image of all right-angled triangles, but only of some one right-angled triangle; so in algebra we need not, under the symbol *a,* picture to ourselves all things whatever, but only some one thing; why not, then, the letter itself? The mere written characters, *a, b, x, y, z,* serve as well for representatives of things in general as any more complex and apparently more concrete conception. That we are conscious of them, however, in their character of things and not of mere signs is evident from the fact that our whole process of reasoning is carried on by predicating of them the properties of things. In resolving an algebraic equation, by what rules do we proceed? By applying at each step to *a, b,* and *x* the proposition that equals added to equals make equals, that equals taken from equals leave equals, and other propositions founded on these two. These are not properties of language or of signs as such, but of magnitudes, which is as much as to say of all things. The inferences, therefore, which are successively drawn are inferences concerning things, not symbols; though as any things whatever will serve the turn, there is no necessity for keeping the idea of the thing at all distinct, and consequently the process of thought may, in this case, be allowed without danger to do what all processes of thought, when they have been performed often, will do if permitted, namely, to become entirely mechanical. Hence the general language of algebra comes to be used familiarly without exciting ideas, as all other general language is prone to do from mere habit, though in no other case than this can it be done with complete safety. But when we look back to see from whence the probative force of the process is derived, we find that at every single step, unless we suppose ourselves to be thinking and talking of the things and not the mere symbols, the evidence fails.

There is another circumstance which, still more than that which we have now mentioned, gives plausibility to the notion that the propositions of arithmetic and algebra are merely verbal. That is that when considered as propositions respecting things, they all have the appearance of being identical propositions. The assertion, "two and one is equal to three," considered as an assertion respecting objects, as for instance, "two pebbles and one pebble are equal to three pebbles," does not affirm equality between two collections of pebbles, but absolute identity. It affirms that if we put one pebble to two pebbles, those very pebbles are three. The objects, therefore, being the very same, and the mere assertion that "objects are themselves" being insignificant, it seems but natural to consider the proposition, "two and one is equal to three," as asserting mere identity of signification between the two names.

This, however, though it looks so plausible, will not bear examination. The expression "two pebbles and one pebble" and the expression "three pebbles" stand, indeed, for the same aggregation of objects, but they by no means stand for the same physical fact. They are names of the same objects, but of those objects in two different states; though they *de*note the same things, their *con*notation is different. Three pebbles in two separate parcels, and three pebbles in one parcel, do not make the same impression on our senses; and the assertion that the very same pebbles may by an alteration of place and arrangement be made to produce either the one set of sensations or the other, though a very familiar proposition, is not an identical one. It is a truth known to us by early and constant experience, an inductive truth, and such truths are the foundation of the science of numbers. The fundamental truths of that science all rest on the evidence of sense; they are proved by showing to our eyes and our fingers that any given number of objects—ten balls, for example—may by separation and rearrangement exhibit to our senses all the different sets of numbers the sums of which is equal to ten. All the improved methods of teaching arithmetic to children proceed on a knowledge of this fact. All who wish to carry the child's *mind* along with them in learning arithmetic, all who wish to teach numbers, and not mere ciphers—now teach it through the evidence of the senses, in the manner we have described. . . .

. . . The inductions of arithmetic are of two sorts: first, those which we have just expounded, such as "one and one are two," "two and one are three," etc., which may be called the definitions of the various numbers, in the improper or geometrical sense of the word *definition;* and secondly, the two following axioms: "The sums of equals are equal," "The differences of equals are equal." These two are sufficient, for the corresponding propositions respecting unequals may be proved from these by a *reductio ad absurdum.*

These axioms, and likewise the so-called definitions, are, as has already been said, results of induction, true of all objects whatever and, as it may seem, exactly true without the hypothetical assumption of unqualified truth where an approximation to it is all that exists. The conclusions, therefore, it will naturally be inferred, are exactly true, and the science of numbers is an exception to other demonstrative sciences in this, that the categorical certainty which is predicable of its demonstrations is independent of all hypothesis.

On more accurate investigation, however, it will be found that, even in this case, there is one hypothetical element in the ratiocination. In all propositions concerning numbers, a condition is implied without which none of them would be true, and that condition is an assumption which may be false. The condition is that $1 = 1$, that all the numbers are numbers of the same or of equal units. Let this be doubtful, and not one of the propositions of arithmetic will hold true. How can we know that one pound and one pound make two pounds, if one of the pounds may be troy and the other avoirdupois? They may not make two pounds of either, or of any weight. How can we know that a forty horse power is always equal to itself, unless we assume that all horses are of equal strength? It is certain that 1 is always equal in *number* to 1, and, where the mere number of objects, or of the parts of an object, without supposing them to be equivalent in any other respect, is all that is material, the conclusions of arithmetic, so far as they go to that alone, are true without mixture of hypothesis. There are such cases in statistics, as, for instance, an inquiry into the amount of the population of any country. It is indifferent to that inquiry whether they are grown people or children, strong or weak, tall or short; the only thing we want to ascertain is their number. But whenever, from equality or inequality of number, equality or inequality in any other respect is to be inferred, arithmetic carried into such inquiries becomes as hypothetical a science as geometry. All units must be assumed to be equal in that other respect, and this is never accurately true, for one actual pound weight is not exactly equal to another, nor one measured mile's length to another; a nicer balance or more accurate measuring instruments would always detect some difference.

What is commonly called mathematical certainty, therefore, which comprises the twofold conception of unconditional truth and perfect accuracy, is not an attribute of all mathematical truths, but of those only which relate to pure number, as distinguished from quantity in the more enlarged sense, and only so long as we abstain from supposing that the numbers are a precise index to actual quantities. The certainty usually ascribed to the conclusions of geometry and even to those of mechanics is nothing whatever but certainty of inference. We can have full assurance of particular results under particular suppositions, but we cannot have the same assurance that these suppositions are accurately true, nor that they include all the data which may exercise an influence over the result in any given instance. . . .

59   On Our Knowledge of General Principles

Bertrand Russell

I<small>N ALL OUR KNOWLEDGE OF GENERAL</small> principles, what actually happens is that first of all we realize some particular application of the principle, and then we realize that the particularity is irrelevant, and that there is a generality which may equally truly be affirmed. This is of course familiar in such matters as teaching arithmetic: "two and two are four" is first learned in the case of some particular pair of couples, and then in some other particular case, and so on, until at last it becomes possible to see that it is true of *any* pair of couples. The same thing happens with logical principles. Suppose two men are discussing what day of the month it is. One of them says, "At least you will admit that *if* yesterday was the 15th to-day must be the 16th." "Yes," says the other, "I admit that." "And you know," the first continues, "that yesterday was the 15th, because you dined with Jones, and your diary will tell you that was on the 15th." "Yes," says the second; "therefore today *is* the 16th."

Now such an argument is not hard to follow; and if it is granted that its premises are true in fact, no one will deny that the conclusion must also be true. But it depends for its truth upon an instance of a general logical principle. The logical principle is as follows: "Suppose it known that *if* this is true, then that is true. Suppose it also known that this *is* true, then it follows that that is true." When it is the case that if this is true, that is true, we shall say that this "implies" that, and that that "follows from" this. Thus our principle states that if this implies that, and this is true, then that is true. In other words, "anything implied by a true proposition is true," or "whatever follows from a true proposition is true."

[This selection consists of most of Chapter VII and parts of Chapter VIII of Russell's *Problems of Philosophy*, which was first published in 1912. It is here reprinted with the kind permission of Oxford University Press.]

This principle is really involved—at least, concrete instances of it are involved—in all demonstrations. Whenever one thing which we believe is used to prove something else, which we consequently believe, this principle is relevant. If any one asks: "Why should I accept the results of valid arguments based on true premises?" we can only answer by appealing to our principle. In fact, the truth of the principle is impossible to doubt, and its obviousness is so great that at first sight it seems almost trivial. Such principles, however, are not trivial to the philosopher, for they show that we may have indubitable knowledge which is in no way derived from objects of sense.

The above principle is merely one of a certain number of self-evident logical principles. Some at least of these principles must be granted before any argument or proof becomes possible. When some of them have been granted, others can be proved, though these others, so long as they are simple, are just as obvious as the principles taken for granted. For no very good reason, three of these principles have been singled out by tradition under the name of "Laws of Thought."

They are as follows:

(1) *The law of identity:* "Whatever is, is."

(2) *The law of contradiction:* "Nothing can both be and not be."

(3) *The law of excluded middle:* "Everything must either be or not be."

These three laws are samples of self-evident logical principles, but are not really more fundamental or more self-evident than various other similar principles: for instance, the one we considered just now, which states that what follows from a true premise is true. The name "laws of thought" is also misleading, for what is important is not the fact that we think in accordance with these laws, but the fact that things behave in accordance with them; in other words, the fact that when we think in accordance with them we think *truly*. But this is a large question, to which we must return at a later stage.

In addition to the logical principles which enable us to prove from a given premise that something is *certainly* true, there are other logical principles which enable us to prove, from a given premise, that there is a greater or less probability that something is true. An example of such principles—perhaps the most important example—is the inductive principle.

One of the great historic controversies in philosophy is the controversy between the two schools called respectively "empiricists" and "rationalists." The empiricists—who are best represented by the British philosophers, Locke, Berkeley, and Hume—maintained that all our knowledge is derived from experience; the rationalists—who are represented by the Continental philosophers of the seventeenth century, especially Descartes and Leibniz —maintained that, in addition to what we know by experience, there are certain "innate ideas" and "innate principles," which we know independently of experience. It has now become possible to decide with some confidence as to the truth or falsehood of these opposing schools. It must be admitted, for the reasons already stated, that logical principles are known to us, and cannot be themselves proved by experience, since all proof presupposes them. In this, therefore, which was the most important point of the controversy, the rationalists were in the right.

On the other hand, even that part of our knowledge which is *logically* independent of experience (in the sense that experience cannot prove it) is yet elicited and caused by experience. It is on occasion of particular experiences that we become aware of the general laws which their connections exemplify. It would certainly be absurd to suppose that there are innate principles in the sense that babies are born with a knowledge of everything which men know and which cannot be deduced from what is experienced. For this reason, the word "innate" would not now be employed to describe our knowledge of logical principles. The phrase "*a priori*" is less objectionable, and is more usual in modern writers. Thus, while admitting that all knowledge is elicited and caused by experience, we shall nevertheless hold that some knowledge is *a priori,* in the sense that the experience which makes us think of it does not suffice to prove it, but merely so directs our attention that we see its truth without requiring any proof from experience.

There is another point of great importance, in which the empiricists were in the right as against the rationalists. Nothing can be known to *exist* except by the help of experience. That is to say, if we wish to prove that something of which we have no direct experience exists, we must have among our premises the existence of one or more things of which we have direct experience. Our belief that the Emperor of China exists, for example, rests upon testimony, and testimony consists, in the last analysis, of sense-data seen or heard in reading or being spoken to. Rationalists believed that, from general consideration as to what *must* be, they could deduce the existence of this or that in the actual world. In this belief they seem to have been mistaken. All the knowledge that we can acquire *a priori* concerning existence seems to be hypothetical: it tells us that *if* one thing exists, another must exist, or, more generally, that *if* one proposition is true, another must be true. This is exemplified by the principles we have already dealt with, such as "*if* this is true, and this implies that, then that is true," or "*if* this and that have been repeatedly found connected, they will probably be connected in the next instance in which one of them is found." Thus the scope and power of *a priori* principles is strictly limited. All knowledge that something exists must be in part dependent on experience. When anything is known immediately, its existence is known by experience alone; when anything is proved to exist, without being known immediately, both experience and *a priori* principles must be required in the proof. Knowledge is called *empirical* when it rests wholly or partly upon experience. Thus all knowledge which asserts existence is empirical, and the only *a priori* knowledge concerning existence is hypothetical, giving connections among things that exist or may exist, but not giving actual existence. . . .

All pure mathematics is *a priori,* like logic. This was strenuously denied by the empirical philosophers, who maintained that experience was as much the source of our knowledge of arithmetic as of our knowledge of geography. They maintained that by the repeated experience of seeing two things and two other things, and finding that altogether they made four things, we were led by induction to the conclusion that two things and two other things would *always* make four things altogether. If, however, this were the source of our knowledge that two and two are four, we should proceed differently, in persuading ourselves of its truth, from the way in which we do actually proceed. In fact, a certain number of instances are needed to make us think of two abstractly, rather than of two coins or two books or two people, or two of any other specified kind. But as soon as we are able to divest our thoughts of irrelevant particularity, we become able to *see* the general principle that two and two are four; any one instance is seen to be *typical,* and the examination of other instances becomes unnecessary.[1]

The same thing is exemplified in geometry. If we want to prove some property of *all* triangles, we draw some one triangle and reason about it; but we can avoid making use of any property which it does not share with all other triangles, and thus, from our particular case, we obtain a general result. We do not, in fact, feel our certainty that two and two are four increased by fresh instances, because, as soon as we have seen the truth of this proposition, our certainty becomes so great as to be incapable of growing greater. Moreover, we feel some quality of *necessity* about the proposition "two and two are four," which is absent from even the best attested empirical generalizations. Such generalizations always remain mere facts: we feel that there might be a world in which they were false, though in the actual world they happen to be true. In any possible world, on the contrary, we feel that two and two would be four: this is not a mere fact, but a necessity to which everything actual and possible must conform.

The case may be made clearer by considering a genuinely empirical generalization, such as "All men are mortal." It is plain that we believe this proposition, in the first place, because there is no known instance of men living beyond a certain age, and in the second place because there seem to be physiological grounds for thinking that an organism such as a man's body must sooner or later wear out. Neglecting the second ground, and considering merely our experience of men's mortality, it is plain that we should not be content with one quite clearly understood instance of a man dying, whereas, in the case of "two and two are four," one instance does suffice, when carefully considered, to persuade us that the same must happen in any other instance. Also we can be forced to admit, on reflection, that there may be some doubt, however slight, as to whether *all* men are mortal. This may be made plain by the attempt to imagine two different worlds, in one of which there are men who are not mortal, while in the other two and two make five. When Swift invites us to consider

1. Cf. A. N. Whitehead, *Introduction to Mathematics* (Home University Library).

the race of Struldbugs who never die, we are able to acquiesce in imagination. But a world where two and two make five seems quite on a different level. We feel that such a world, if there were one, would upset the whole fabric of our knowledge and reduce us to utter doubt.

The fact is that, in simple mathematical judgments such as "two and two are four," and also in many judgments of logic, we can know the general proposition without inferring it from instances, although some instance is usually necessary to make clear to us what the general proposition means. This is why there is real utility in the process of *deduction,* which goes from the general to the general, or from the general to the particular, as well as in the process of *induction,* which goes from the particular to the particular, or from the particular to the general. It is an old debate among philosophers whether deduction ever gives *new* knowledge. We can now see that in certain cases, at least, it does do so. If we already know that two and two always make four, and we know that Brown and Jones are two, and so are Robinson and Smith, we can deduce that Brown and Jones and Robinson and Smith are four. This is new knowledge, not contained in our premises, because the general proposition, "two and two are four," never told us there were such people as Brown and Jones and Robinson and Smith, and the particular premises do not tell us that there were four of them, whereas the particular proposition deduced does tell us both these things.

But the newness of the knowledge is much less certain if we take the stock instance of deduction that is always given in books on logic, namely, "All men are mortal; Socrates is a man, therefore Socrates is mortal." In this case, what we really know beyond reasonable doubt is that certain men, A, B, C, were mortal, since, in fact, they have died. If Socrates is one of these men, it is foolish to go the roundabout way through "all men are mortal" to arrive at the conclusion that *probably* Socrates is mortal. If Socrates is not one of the men on whom our induction is based, we shall still do better to argue straight from our A, B, C, to Socrates, than to go round by the general proposition, "all men are mortal." For the probability that Socrates is mortal is greater, on our data, than the probability that all men are mortal. (This is obvious, because if all men are mortal, so is Socrates; but if Socrates is mortal, it does not follow that all men are mortal.) Hence we shall reach the conclusion that Socrates is mortal with a greater approach to certainty if we make our argument purely inductive than if we go by way of "all men are mortal" and then use deduction.

This illustrates the difference between general propositions known *a priori,* such as "two and two are four," and empirical generalizations such as "all men are mortal." In regard to the former, deduction is the right mode of argument, whereas in regard to the latter, induction is always theoretically preferable, and warrants a greater confidence in the truth of our conclusion, because all empirical generalizations are more uncertain than the instances of them.

We have now seen that there are propositions known *a priori,* and that among them are the propositions of logic and pure mathematics. . . The question which must next occupy us is this: How is it possible that there should be such knowledge? And more particularly, how can there be knowledge of general propositions in cases where we have not examined all the instances, and indeed never can examine them all, because their number is infinite? These questions, which were first brought prominently forward by the German philosopher Kant, are very difficult, and historically very important. . . .

Kant's stock instance was the proposition $7 + 5 = 12$. He pointed out, quite truly, that 7 and 5 have to be put together to give 12: the idea of 12 is not *contained* in them, nor even in the idea of adding them together. Thus he was led to the conclusion that all pure mathematics, though *a priori,* is synthetic; and this conclusion raised a new problem of which he endeavored to find the solution.

The question which Kant put at the beginning of his philosophy, namely "How is pure mathematics possible?" is an interesting and difficult one, to which every philosophy which is not purely sceptical must find some answer. The answer of the pure empiricists, that our mathematical knowledge is derived by induction from particular instances, we have already seen to be inadequate, for two reasons: first, that the validity of the inductive principle itself cannot be proved by induction;[2] secondly, that the general propositions of mathematics, such as "two and two always make four," can obviously be known with certainty by consideration of a single instance, and gain nothing by enumeration of other cases in which they have been found to be true. Thus our knowledge of the general propositions of mathematics (and the same applies to logic) must be accounted for otherwise than our (merely probable) knowledge of empirical generalizations such as "all men are mortal."

The problem arises through the fact that such knowledge is general, whereas all experience is particular. It seems strange that we should apparently be able to know some truths in advance about particular things of which we have as yet no experience; but it cannot easily be doubted that logic and arithmetic will apply to such things. We do not know who will be the inhabitants of London a hundred years hence; but we know that any two of them and any other two of them will make four of them. This apparent power of anticipating facts about things of which we have no experience is certainly surprising. Kant's solution of the problem, though not valid in my opinion, is interesting. It is, however, very difficult, and is differently understood by different philosophers. We can, therefore, only give the merest outline of it, and even that will be thought misleading by many exponents of Kant's system.

What Kant maintained was that in all our experience there are two elements to be distinguished, the one due to the object (i.e., to what we have called the "physical object"), the other due to our own nature. . . .

2. See Selection 12, pp. 143–144.

He considers that the crude material given in sensation—the color, hardness, etc.—is due to the object, and that what we supply is the arrangement in space and time, and all the relations between sense-data which result from comparison or from considering one as the cause of the other or in any other way. His chief reason in favor of this view is that we seem to have *a priori* knowledge as to space and time and causality and comparison, but not as to the actual crude material of sensation. We can be sure, he says, that anything we shall ever experience must show the characteristics affirmed of it in our *a priori* knowledge, because these characteristics are due to our own nature, and therefore nothing can ever come into our experience without acquiring these characteristics.

The physical object, which he calls the "thing in itself," he regards as essentially unknowable; what can be known is the object as we have it in experience, which he calls the "phenomenon." The phenomenon, being a joint product of us and the thing in itself, is sure to have those characteristics which are due to us, and is therefore sure to conform to our *a priori* knowledge. Hence this knowledge, though true of all actual and possible experience, must not be supposed to apply outside experience. Thus in spite of the existence of *a priori* knowledge, we cannot know anything about the thing itself or about what is not an actual or possible object of experience. In this way he tries to reconcile and harmonize the contentions of the rationalists with the arguments of the empiricists.

Apart from minor grounds on which Kant's philosophy may be criticized, there is one main objection which seems fatal to any attempt to deal with the problem of *a priori* knowledge by his method. The thing to be accounted for is our certainty that the facts must always conform to logic and arithmetic. To say that logic and arithmetic are contributed by us does not account for this. Our nature is as much a fact of the existing world as anything, and there can be no certainty that it will remain constant. It might happen, if Kant is right, that to-morrow our nature would so change as to make two and two become five. This possibility seems never to have occurred to him, yet it is one which utterly destroys the certainty and universality which he is anxious to vindicate for arithmetical propositions. . . .

Reflection, moreover, seems to make it clear that, if there is any truth in our arithmetical beliefs, they must apply to things equally whether we think of them or not. Two physical objects and two other physical objects must make four physical objects, even if physical objects cannot be experienced. To assert this is certainly within the scope of what we mean when we state that two and two are four. Its truth is just as indubitable as the truth of the assertion that two phenomena and two other phenomena make four phenomena. Thus Kant's solution unduly limits the scope of *a priori* propositions, in addition to failing in the attempt at explaining their certainty.

Apart from the special doctrines advocated by Kant, it is very common among philosophers to regard what is *a priori* as in some sense mental, as concerned rather with the way we must think than with any fact of the outer world. We noted in the preceding chapter the three principles commonly called "laws of thought." The view which led to their being so named is a natural one, but there are strong reasons for thinking that it is erroneous. Let us take as an illustration the law of contradiction. This is commonly stated in the form "Nothing can both be and not be," which is intended to express the fact that nothing can at once have and not have a given quality. Thus, for example, if a tree is a beech it cannot also be not a beech; if my table is rectangular it cannot also be not rectangular, and so on.

Now what makes it natural to call this principle a law of *thought* is that it is by thought rather than by outward observation that we persuade ourselves of its necessary truth. When we have seen that a tree is a beech, we do not need to look again in order to ascertain whether it is also not a beech; thought alone makes us know that this is impossible. But the conclusion that the law of contradiction is a law of *thought* is nevertheless erroneous. What we believe, when we believe the law of contradiction, is not that the mind is so made that it must believe the law of contradiction. *This* belief is a subsequent result of psychological reflection, which presupposes the belief in the law of contradiction. The belief in the law of contradiction is a belief about things, not only about thoughts. It is not, e.g., the belief that if we *think* a certain tree is a beech, we cannot at the same time *think* that it is not a beech; it is the belief that if the tree *is* a beech, it cannot at the same time *be* not a beech. Thus the law of contradiction is about things, and not merely about thoughts; and although belief in the law of contradiction is a thought, the law of contradiction itself is not a thought, but a fact concerning the things in the world. If this, which we believe when we believe the law of contradiction, were not true of the things in the world, the fact that we were compelled to *think* it true would not save the law of contradiction from being false; and this shows that the law is not a law of *thought*.

A similar argument applies to any other *a priori* judgment. When we judge that two and two are four, we are not making a judgment about our thoughts, but about all actual or possible couples. The fact that our minds are so constituted as to believe that two and two are four, though it is true, is emphatically not what we assert when we assert that two and two are four. And no fact about the constitution of our minds could make it *true* that two and two are four. Thus our *a priori* knowledge, if it is not erroneous, is not merely knowledge about the constitution of our minds, but is applicable to whatever the world may contain, both what is mental and what is non-mental.*

---

* Under the influence of Ludwig Wittgenstein, Russell, some years after writing *The Problems of Philosophy,* changed his views about the nature of mathematical and logical principles. His later position is akin to that expressed by A. J. Ayer in the next selection. Russell's own statement can be found in Chapter XVII of *The Analysis of Matter* (London: Routledge & Kegan Paul, 1927). (Ed.)

60   The *A Priori*

A. J. Ayer

Empiricism and Rationalism

... Having admitted that we are empiricists, we must now deal with the objection that is commonly brought against all forms of empiricism; the objection, namely, that it is impossible on empiricist principles to account for our knowledge of necessary truths. For, as Hume conclusively showed, no general proposition whose validity is subject to the test of actual experience can ever be logically certain. No matter how often it is verified in practice, there still remains the possibility that it will be confuted on some future occasion. The fact that a law has been substantiated in $n - 1$ cases affords no logical guarantee that it will be substantiated in the nth case also, no matter how large we take n to be. And this means that no general proposition referring to a matter of fact can ever be shown to be necessarily and universally true. It can at best be a probable hypothesis. And this, we shall find, applies not only to general propositions, but to all propositions which have a factual content. They can none of them ever become logically certain. This conclusion, which we shall elaborate later on, is one which must be accepted by every consistent empiricist. It is often thought to involve him in complete scepticism; but this is not the case. For the fact that the validity of a proposition cannot be logically guaranteed in no way entails that it is irrational for us to believe it. On the contrary, what is irrational is to look for a guarantee where none can be forthcoming; to demand certainty where probability is all that is obtainable. We have already remarked upon this, in referring to the work of Hume. And we shall make the point clearer when we come to treat of probability, in explaining the

[This selection is Chapter IV, except for small omissions, of Ayer's *Language, Truth and Logic*, published in Great Britain by Victor Gollancz, Ltd., in 1936, and in the United States by Dover Publications, Inc. It is here reprinted with the kind permission of Professor Ayer and the publishers.]

use which we make of empirical propositions. We shall discover that there is nothing perverse or paradoxical about the view that all the "truths" of science and common sense are hypotheses; and consequently that the fact that it involves this view constitutes no objection to the empiricist thesis.

Where the empiricist does encounter difficulty is in connection with the truths of formal logic and mathematics. For whereas a scientific generalization is readily admitted to be fallible, the truths of mathematics and logic appear to everyone to be necessary and certain. But if empiricism is correct no proposition which has a factual content can be necessary or certain. Accordingly the empiricist must deal with the truths of logic and mathematics in one of the two following ways: he must say either that they are not necessary truths, in which case he must account for the universal conviction that they are; or he must say that they have no factual content, and then he must explain how a proposition which is empty of all factual content can be true and useful and surprising.

If neither of these courses proves satisfactory, we shall be obliged to give way to rationalism. We shall be obliged to admit that there are some truths about the world which we can know independently of experience; that there are some properties which we can ascribe to all objects, even though we cannot conceivably observe that all objects have them. And we shall have to accept it as a mysterious inexplicable fact that our thought has this power to reveal to us authoritatively the nature of objects which we have never observed. Or else we must accept the Kantian explanation which, apart from the epistemological difficulties which we have already touched on, only pushes the mystery a stage further back.

It is clear that any such concession to rationalism would upset the main argument of this book. For the admission that there were some facts about the world which could be known independently of experience would be incompatible with our fundamental contention that a sentence says nothing unless it is empirically verifiable. And thus the whole force of our attack on metaphysics would be destroyed. It is vital, therefore, for us to be able to show that one or other of the empiricist accounts of the propositions of logic and mathematics is correct. If we are successful in this, we shall have destroyed the foundations of rationalism. For the fundamental tenet of rationalism is that thought is an independent source of knowledge, and is moreover a more trustworthy source of knowledge than experience; indeed some rationalists have gone so far as to say that thought is the only source of knowledge. And the ground for this view is simply that the only necessary truths about the world which are known to us are known through thought and not through experience. So that if we can show either that the truths in question are not necessary or that they are not "truths about the world," we shall be taking away the support on which rationalism rests. We shall be making good the empiricist contention that there are no "truths of reason" which refer to matters of fact.

The course of maintaining that the truths of logic and mathematics are not necessary or certain was adopted by Mill. He maintained that these propositions were inductive generalizations based on an extremely large number of instances. The fact that the number of supporting instances was so very large accounted, in his view, for our believing these generalizations to be necessarily and universally true. The evidence in their favor was so strong that it seemed incredible to us that a contrary instance should ever arise. Nevertheless it was in principle possible for such generalizations to be confuted. They were highly probable, but, being inductive generalizations, they were not certain. The difference between them and the hypotheses of natural science was a difference in degree and not in kind. Experience gave us very good reason to suppose that a "truth" of mathematics or logic was true universally; but we were not possessed of a guarantee. For these "truths" were only empirical hypotheses which had worked particularly well in the past; and, like all empirical hypotheses, they were theoretically fallible.

I do not think that this solution of the empiricist's difficulty with regard to the propositions of logic and mathematics is acceptable. In discussing it, it is necessary to make a distinction which is perhaps already enshrined in Kant's famous dictum that, although there can be no doubt that all our knowledge begins with experience, it does not follow that it all arises out of experience.[1] When we say that the truths of logic are known independently of experience, we are not of course saying that they are innate, in the sense that we are born knowing them. It is obvious that mathematics and logic have to be learned in the same way as chemistry and history have to be learned. Nor are we denying that the first person to discover a given logical or mathematical truth was led to it by an inductive procedure. It is very probable, for example, that the principle of the syllogism was formulated not before but after the validity of syllogistic reasoning had been observed in a number of particular cases. What we are discussing, however, when we say that the logical and mathematical truths are known independently of experience, is not a historical question concerning the way in which these truths were originally discovered, nor a psychological question concerning the way in which each of us comes to learn them, but an epistemological question. The contention of Mill's which we reject is that the propositions of logic and mathematics have the same status as empirical hypotheses; that their validity is determined in the same way. We maintain that they are independent of experience in the sense that they do not owe their validity to empirical verification. We may come to discover them through an inductive process; but once we have apprehended them we see that they are necessarily true, that they hold good for every conceivable instance. And this serves to distinguish them from empirical generalizations. For we know that a proposition whose validity depends upon experience cannot be seen to be necessarily and universally true.

1. *Critique of Pure Reason*, 2nd ed. Introduction, section i. (See p. 686 above.)

In rejecting Mill's theory, we are obliged to be somewhat dogmatic. We can do no more than state the issue clearly and then trust that his contention will be seen to be discrepant with the relevant logical facts. The following considerations may serve to show that of the two ways of dealing with logic and mathematics which are open to the empiricist, the one which Mill adopted is not the one which is correct.

The Irrefutability of the Propositions of Mathematics and Logic

The best way to substantiate our assertion that the truths of formal logic and pure mathematics are necessarily true is to examine cases in which they might seem to be confuted. It might easily happen, for example, that when I came to count what I had taken to be five pairs of objects, I found that they amounted only to nine. And if I wished to mislead people I might say that on this occasion twice five was not ten. But in that case I should not be using the complex sign "$2 \times 5 = 10$" in the way in which it is ordinarily used. I should be taking it not as the expression of a purely mathematical proposition, but as the expression of an empirical generalization, to the effect that whenever I counted what appeared to me to be five pairs of objects I discovered that they were ten in number. This generalization may very well be false. But if it proved false in a given case, one would not say that the mathematical proposition "$2 \times 5 = 10$" had been confuted. One would say that I was wrong in supposing that there were five pairs of objects to start with, or that one of the objects had been taken away while I was counting, or that two of them had coalesced, or that I had counted wrongly. One would adopt as an explanation whatever empirical hypothesis fitted in best with the accredited facts. The one explanation which would in no circumstances be adopted is that ten is not always the product of two and five.

To take another example: if what appears to be a Euclidean triangle is found by measurement not to have angles totalling 180 degrees, we do not say that we have met with an instance which invalidates the mathematical proposition that the sum of the three angles of a Euclidean triangle is 180 degrees. We say that we have measured wrongly, or, more probably, that the triangle we have been measuring is not Euclidean. And this is our procedure in every case in which a mathematical truth might appear to be confuted. We always preserve its validity by adopting some other explanation of the occurrence.

The same thing applies to the principles of formal logic. We may take an example relating to the so-called law of excluded middle, which states that a proposition must be either true or false, or, in other words, that it is impossible that a proposition and its contradictory should neither of them be true. One might suppose that a proposition of the form "x has stopped doing y" would in certain cases constitute an exception to this law. For instance, if my friend has never yet written to me, it seems fair to say that it is neither true nor false that he has stopped writing to me. But in fact one would refuse to accept such an instance as an invalidation of the law of excluded middle. One would point out that the proposition "My friend has stopped writing to me" is not a simple proposition, but the conjunction of the two propositions "My friend wrote to me in the past" and "My friend does not write to me now": and, furthermore, that the proposition "My friend has not stopped writing to me" is not, as it appears to be, contradictory to "My friend has stopped writing to me," but only contrary to it. For it means "My friend wrote to me in the past, and he still writes to me." When, therefore, we say that such a proposition as "My friend has stopped writing to me" is sometimes neither true nor false, we are speaking inaccurately. For we seem to be saying that neither it nor its contradictory is true. Whereas what we mean, or anyhow should mean, is that neither it nor its apparent contradictory is true. And its apparent contradictory is really only its contrary. Thus we preserve the law of excluded middle by showing that the negating of a sentence does not always yield the contradictory of the proposition originally expressed.

There is no need to give further examples. Whatever instance we care to take, we shall always find that the situations in which a logical or mathematical principle might appear to be confuted are accounted for in such a way as to leave the principle unassailed. And this indicates that Mill was wrong in supposing that a situation could arise which would overthrow a mathematical truth. The principles of logic and mathematics are true universally simply because we never allow them to be anything else. And the reason for this is that we cannot abandon them without contradicting ourselves, without sinning against the rules which govern the use of language, and so making our utterances self-stultifying. In other words, the truths of logic and mathematics are analytic propositions or tautologies. In saying this we are making what will be held to be an extremely controversial statement, and we must now proceed to make its implications clear.

The Nature of Analytic Propositions

The most familiar definition of an analytic proposition, or judgment, as he called it, is that given by Kant. He said[2] that an analytic judgment was one in which the predicate B belonged to the subject A as something which was covertly contained in the concept of A. He contrasted analytic with synthetic judgments, in which the predicate B lay outside the subject A, although it did stand in connection with it. Analytic judgments,

2. *Critique of Pure Reason*, 2nd ed., Introduction, sections iv and v. (See pp. 691 ff., above.)

he explains, "add nothing through the predicate to the concept of the subject, but merely break it up into those constituent concepts that have all along been thought in it, although confusedly." Synthetic judgments, on the other hand, "add to the concept of the subject a predicate which has not been in any wise thought in it, and which no analysis could possibly extract from it." Kant gives "all bodies are extended" as an example of an analytic judgment, on the ground that the required predicate can be extracted from the concept of "body," "in accordance with the principle of contradiction"; as an example of a synthetic judgment, he gives "all bodies are heavy." He refers also to "$7 + 5 = 12$" as a synthetic judgment, on the ground that the concept of twelve is by no means already thought in merely thinking the union of seven and five. And he appears to regard this as tantamount to saying that the judgment does not rest on the principle of contradiction alone. He holds, also, that through analytic judgments our knowledge is not extended as it is through synthetic judgments. For in analytic judgments "the concept which I already have is merely set forth and made intelligible to me."

I think that this is a fair summary of Kant's account of the distinction between analytic and synthetic propositions, but I do not think that it succeeds in making the distinction clear. For even if we pass over the difficulties which arise out of the use of the vague term "concept," and the unwarranted assumption that every judgment, as well as every German or English sentence, can be said to have a subject and a predicate, there remains still this crucial defect. Kant does not give one straightforward criterion for distinguishing between analytic and synthetic propositions; he gives two distinct criteria, which are by no means equivalent. Thus his ground for holding that the proposition "$7 + 5 = 12$" is synthetic is, as we have seen, that the subjective intension of "$7 + 5$" does not comprise the subjective intension of "12"; whereas his ground for holding that "all bodies are extended" is an analytic proposition is that it rests on the principle of contradiction alone. That is, he employs a psychological criterion in the first of these examples, and a logical criterion in the second, and takes their equivalence for granted. But, in fact, a proposition which is synthetic according to the former criterion may very well be analytic according to the latter. For, as we have already pointed out, it is possible for symbols to be synonymous without having the same intensional meaning for anyone: and accordingly from the fact that one can think of the sum of seven and five without necessarily thinking of twelve, it by no means follows that the proposition "$7 + 5 = 12$" can be denied without self-contradiction. From the rest of his argument, it is clear that it is this logical proposition, and not any psychological proposition, that Kant is really anxious to establish. His use of the psychological criterion leads him to think that he has established it, when he has not.

I think that we can preserve the logical import of Kant's distinction between analytic and synthetic propositions, while avoiding the confusions which mar his actual account of it, if we say that a proposition is analytic when its validity depends solely on the definitions of the symbols it contains, and synthetic when its validity is determined by the facts of experience. Thus, the proposition "There are ants which have established a system of slavery" is a synthetic proposition. For we cannot tell whether it is true or false merely by considering the definitions of the symbols which constitute it. We have to resort to actual observation of the behavior of ants. On the other hand, the proposition "Either some ants are parasitic or none are" is an analytic proposition. For one need not resort to observation to discover that there either are or are not ants which are parasitic. If one knows what is the function of the words "either," "or," and "not," then one can see that any proposition of the form "Either p is true or p is not true" is valid, independently of experience. Accordingly, all such propositions are analytic.

It is to be noticed that the proposition "Either some ants are parasitic or none are" provides no information whatsoever about the behavior of ants, or, indeed, about any matter of fact. And this applies to all analytic propositions. They none of them provide any information about any matter of fact. In other words, they are entirely devoid of factual content. And it is for this reason that no experience can confute them.

When we say that analytic propositions are devoid of factual content, and consequently that they say nothing, we are not suggesting that they are senseless in the way that metaphysical utterances are senseless. For, although they give us no information about any empirical situation, they do enlighten us by illustrating the way in which we use certain symbols. Thus if I say, "Nothing can be colored in different ways at the same time with respect to the same part of itself," I am not saying anything about the properties of any actual thing; but I am not talking nonsense. I am expressing an analytic proposition, which records our determination to call a color expanse which differs in quality from a neighboring color expanse a different part of a given thing. In other words, I am simply calling attention to the implications of a certain linguistic usage. Similarly, in saying that if all Bretons are Frenchmen, and all Frenchmen Europeans, then all Bretons are Europeans, I am not describing any matter of fact. But I am showing that in the statement that all Bretons are Frenchmen, and all Frenchmen Europeans, the further statement that all Bretons are Europeans is implicity contained. And I am thereby indicating the convention which governs our usage of the words "if" and "all."

We see, then, that there is a sense in which analytic propositions do give us new knowledge. They call attention to linguistic usages, of which we might otherwise not be conscious, and they reveal unsuspected implications in our assertions and beliefs. But we can see also that there is a sense in which they may be said to add nothing to our knowledge. For they tell us only what we may be said to know already. Thus, if I know that the existence of May Queens is a relic of tree-worship, and I discover that May Queens still exist in England, I can employ the tautology "If p implies q, and p is true, q is true" to show that there still exists a relic of tree-worship in England. But in saying that there are still May Queens in England, and that the existence of May Queens is a relic of tree-worship, I have already asserted the existence in England of a relic of tree-worship. The use of the tautology does, indeed, enable me to make this concealed assertion explicit. But it does not provide me with any new knowledge, in the sense in which empirical evidence that the election of May Queens had been forbidden by law would provide me with new knowledge. If one had to set forth all the information one possessed, with regard to matters of fact, one would not write down any analytic propositions. But one would make use of analytic propositions in compiling one's encyclopedia, and would thus come to include propositions which one would otherwise have overlooked. And, besides enabling one to make one's list of information complete, the formulation of analytic propositions would enable one to make sure that the synthetic propositions of which the list was composed formed a self-consistent system. By showing which ways of combining propositions resulted in contradictions, they would prevent one from including incompatible propositions and so making the list self-stultifying. But in so far as we had actually used such words as "all" and "or" and "not" without falling into self-contradiction, we might be said already to know what was revealed in the formulation of analytic propositions illustrating the rules which govern our usage of these logical particles. So that here again we are justified in saying that analytic propositions do not increase our knowledge. . . .

The Propositions of Geometry

The mathematical propositions which one might most pardonably suppose to be synthetic are the propositions of geometry. For it is natural for us to think, as Kant thought, that geometry is the study of the properties of physical space, and consequently that its propositions have factual content. And if we believe this, and also recognize that the truths of geometry are necessary and certain, then we may be inclined to accept Kant's hypothesis that space is the form of intuition of our outer sense, a form imposed by us on the matter of sensation, as the only possible explanation of our *a priori* knowledge of these synthetic propositions. But while the view that pure geometry is concerned with physical space was plausible enough in Kant's day, when the geometry of Euclid was the only geometry known, the subsequent invention of non-Euclidean geometries has shown it to be mistaken. We see now that the axioms of a geometry are simply definitions, and that the theorems of a geometry are simply the logical consequences of these definitions.[3] A geometry is not in itself about physical space; in itself it cannot be said to be "about" anything. But we can use a geometry to reason about physical space. That

3. Cf. H. Poincaré, *La Science et l'Hypothèse*, Part II, Chapter iii.

is to say, once we have given the axioms a physical interpretation, we can proceed to apply the theorems to the objects which satisfy the axioms. Whether a geometry can be applied to the actual physical world or not, is an empirical question which falls outside the scope of the geometry itself. There is no sense, therefore, in asking which of the various geometries known to us are false and which are true. In so far as they are all free from contradiction, they are all true. What one can ask is which of them is the most useful on any given occasion, which of them can be applied most easily and most fruitfully to an actual empirical situation. But the proposition which states that a certain application of a geometry is possible is not itself a proposition of that geometry. All that the geometry itself tells us is that if anything can be brought under the definitions, it will also satisfy the theorems. It is therefore a purely logical system, and its propositions are purely analytic propositions.

It might be objected that the use made of diagrams in geometrical treatises shows that geometrical reasoning is not purely abstract and logical, but depends on our intuition of the properties of figures. In fact, however, the use of diagrams is not essential to completely rigorous geometry. The diagrams are introduced as an aid to our reason. They provide us with a particular application of the geometry, and so assist us to perceive the more general truth that the axioms of the geometry involve certain consequences. But the fact that most of us need the help of an example to make us aware of those consequences does not show that the relation between them and the axioms is not a purely logical relation. It shows merely that our intellects are unequal to the task of carrying out very abstract processes of reasoning without the assistance of intuition. In other words, it has no bearing on the nature of geometrical propositions, but is simply an empirical fact about ourselves. Moreover, the appeal to intuition, though generally of psychological value, is also a source of danger to the geometer. He is tempted to make assumptions which are accidentally true of the particular figure he is taking as an illustration, but do not follow from his axioms. It has, indeed, been shown that Euclid himself was guilty of this, and consequently that the presence of the figure is essential to some of his proofs.[4] This shows that his system is not, as he presents it, completely rigorous, although of course it can be made so. It does not show that the presence of the figure is essential to a truly rigorous geometrical proof. To suppose that it did would be to take as a necessary feature of all geometries what is really only an incidental defect in one particular geometrical system.

We conclude, then, that the propositions of pure geometry are analytic. And this leads us to reject Kant's hypothesis that geometry deals with the form of intuition of our outer sense. For the ground for this hypothesis was that it alone explained how the propositions of geometry could be both true *a priori* and synthetic: and we have seen that they are not synthetic. Similarly our view that the propositions of arithmetic

4. Cf. M. Black, *The Nature of Mathematics*, p. 154.

are not synthetic but analytic leads us to reject the Kantian hypothesis[5] that arithmetic is concerned with our pure intuition of time, the form of our inner sense. And thus we are able to dismiss Kant's transcendental æsthetic without having to bring forward the epistemological difficulties which it is commonly said to involve. For the only argument which can be brought in favor of Kant's theory is that it alone explains certain "facts." And now we have found that the "facts" which it purports to explain are not facts at all. For while it is true that we have *a priori* knowledge of necessary propositions, it is not true, as Kant supposed, that any of these necessary propositions are synthetic. They are without exception analytic propositions, or, in other words, tautologies.

We have already explained how it is that these analytic propositions are necessary and certain. We saw that the reason why they cannot be confuted in experience is that they do not make any assertion about the empirical world. They simply record our determination to use words in a certain fashion. We cannot deny them without infringing the conventions which are presupposed by our very denial, and so falling into self-contradiction. And this is the sole ground of their necessity. As Wittgenstein puts it, our justification for holding that the world could not conceivably disobey the laws of logic is simply that we could not say of an unlogical world how it would look.[6] And just as the validity of an analytic proposition is independent of the nature of the external world, so is it independent of the nature of our minds. It is perfectly conceivable that we should have employed different linguistic conventions from those which we actually do employ. But whatever these conventions might be, the tautologies in which we recorded them would always be necessary. For any denial of them would be self-stultifying.

We see, then, that there is nothing mysterious about the apodeictic certainty of logic and mathematics. Our knowledge that no observation can ever confute the proposition "$7 + 5 = 12$" depends simply on the fact that the symbolic expression "$7 + 5$" is synonymous with "12," just as our knowledge that every oculist is an eye-doctor depends on the fact that the symbol "eye-doctor" is synonymous with "oculist." And the same explanation holds good for every other *a priori* truth.

How Can Tautologies Be Surprising?

What is mysterious at first sight is that these tautologies should on occasion be so surprising, that there should be in mathematics and logic the possibility of invention and discovery. As Poincaré says: "If all the assertions which mathematics puts forward can be derived from one another by formal logic, mathematics cannot amount to anything more

5. This hypothesis is not mentioned in the *Critique of Pure Reason*, but was maintained by Kant at an earlier date.
6. *Tractatus Logico-Philosophicus*, 3.031.

than an immense tautology. Logical inference can teach us nothing essentially new, and if everything is to proceed from the principle of identity, everything must be reducible to it. But can we really allow that these theorems which fill so many books serve no other purpose than to say in a round-about fashion 'A = A'?"[7] Poincaré finds this incredible. His own theory is that the sense of invention and discovery in mathematics belongs to it in virtue of mathematical induction, the principle that what is true for the number 1, and true for $n + 1$ when it is true for n,[8] is true for all numbers. And he claims that this is a synthetic *a priori* principle. It is, in fact, *a priori,* but it is not synthetic. It is a defining principle of the natural numbers, serving to distinguish them from such numbers as the infinite cardinal numbers, to which it cannot be applied.[9] Moreover, we must remember that discoveries can be made, not only in arithmetic, but also in geometry and formal logic, where no use is made of mathematical induction. So that even if Poincaré were right about mathematical induction, he would not have provided a satisfactory explanation of the paradox that a mere body of tautologies can be so interesting and so surprising.

The true explanation is very simple. The power of logic and mathematics to surprise us depends, like their usefulness, on the limitations of our reason. A being whose intellect was infinitely powerful would take no interest in logic and mathematics.[10] For he would be able to see at a glance everything that his definitions implied, and, accordingly, could never learn anything from logical inference which he was not fully conscious of already. But our intellects are not of this order. It is only a minute proportion of the consequences of our definitions that we are able to detect at a glance. Even so simple a tautology as "$91 \times 79 = 7189$" is beyond the scope of our immediate apprehension. To assure ourselves that "7189" is synonymous with "91×79" we have to resort to calculation, which is simply a process of tautological transformation—that is, a process by which we change the form of expressions without altering their significance. The multiplication tables are rules for carrying out this process in arithmetic, just as the laws of logic are rules for the tautological transformation of sentences expressed in logical symbolism or in ordinary language. As the process of calculation is carried out more or less mechanically, it is easy for us to make a slip and so unwittingly contradict ourselves. And this accounts for the existence of logical and mathematical "falsehoods," which otherwise might appear paradoxical. Clearly the risk of error in logical reasoning is proportionate to the length and the complexity

7. *La Science et l'Hypothèse,* Part I, Chapter i.
8. This was wrongly stated in previous editions as "true for n when it is true for $n + 1$."
9. Cf. B. Russell's *Introduction to Mathematical Philosophy,* Chapter iii, p. 27.
10. Cf. Hans Hahn, "Logik, Mathematik und Naturerkennen," *Einheitswissenschaft,* Heft II, p. 18. "Ein allwissendes Wesen braucht keine Logik und Mathematik." [An English translation of this pamphlet is now available in *Logical Positivism,* an anthology edited by Professor Ayer and published by The Free Press. (Eds.)]

of the process of calculation. And in the same way, the more complex an analytic proposition is, the more chance it has of interesting and surprising us.

It is easy to see that the danger of error in logical reasoning can be minimized by the introduction of symbolic devices, which enable us to express highly complex tautologies in a conveniently simple form. And this gives us an opportunity for the exercise of invention in the pursuit of logical enquiries. For a well-chosen definition will call our attention to analytic truths, which would otherwise have escaped us. And the framing of definitions which are useful and fruitful may well be regarded as a creative act.

Having thus shown that there is no inexplicable paradox involved in the view that the truths of logic and mathematics are all of them analytic, we may safely adopt it as the only satisfactory explanation of their *a priori* necessity. And in adopting it we vindicate the empiricist claim that there can be no *a priori* knowledge of reality. For we show that the truths of pure reason, the propositions which we know to be valid independently of all experience, are so only in virtue of their lack of factual content. To say that a proposition is true *a priori* is to say that it is a tautology. And tautologies, though they may serve to guide us in our empirical search for knowledge, do not in themselves contain any information about any matter of fact.

61   The "A Priori" and

the Empirical

A. C. Ewing

Meaning of the Distinction;
"A Priori" Character of Mathematics

IN THE THEORY OF KNOWLEDGE, THE
first point that confronts us is the sharp distinction between two kinds of
knowledge which have been called respectively *a priori* and empirical.
Most of our knowledge we obtain by observation of the external world
(sense-perception) and of ourselves (introspection). This is called empirical knowledge. But some knowledge we can obtain by simply thinking. That
kind of knowledge is called *a priori*. Its chief exemplifications are to be
found in logic and mathematics. In order to see that $5 + 7 = 12$ we do not
need to take five things and seven things, put them together, and then
count the total number. We can know what the total number will be
simply by thinking.

Another important difference between *a priori* and empirical knowledge is that in the case of the former we do not see merely that something,
S, is in fact P, but that it must be P and why it is P. I can discover that a
flower is yellow (or at least produces sensations of yellow) by looking at
it, but I cannot thereby see why it is yellow or that it must be yellow. For
anything I can tell it might equally well have been a red flower. But with
a truth such as that $5 + 7 = 12$ I do not see merely that it is a fact but
that it must be a fact. It would be quite absurd to suppose that $5 + 7$ might
have been equal to 11 and just happened to be equal to 12, and I can see
that the nature of 5 and 7 constitutes a fully adequate and intelligible

[This selection is part of Chapter II of *The Fundamental Problems of Philosophy*
(1951). It is reprinted here with the permission of Routledge and Kegan Paul, London,
and the Macmillan Company, New York.]

reason why their sum should be 12 and not some other number. It is indeed conceivable that some of the things which make the two groups of 5 and 7 might, when they were put together, fuse like drops of water, or even vanish, so that there were no longer 12 things; but what is inconceivable is that there could *at the same time* be 5 + 7 things of a certain kind at once in a certain place and yet less than 12 things of that kind in that place. Before some of the things fused or vanished they would be 5 + 7 in number and also 12 in number, and after the fusion or disappearance they would be neither 5 + 7 nor 12. When I say in this connection that something is inconceivable, I do not mean merely or primarily that we cannot conceive it—this is not a case of a mere psychological inability like the inability to understand higher mathematics. It is a positive insight: we definitely see it to be impossible that certain things could happen. This we do not see in the case of empirical propositions which are false: they are not true but might for anything we know have been true. It is even conceivable, so far as we can see, that the fundamental laws of motion might have been quite different from what they are, but we can see that there could not have been a world which contradicted the laws of arithmetic. This is expressed by saying that empirical propositions are *contingent,* but true *a priori* propositions *necessary.* What we see to be necessary is not indeed that arithmetic should apply to the universe. It is conceivable that the universe might have been constituted entirely of a homogeneous fluid, and then, since there would have been no distinction between different things, it is difficult to see how arithmetic could have applied to it. What we do see is that arithmetic must be true of whatever can be numbered at all.

We must not be misled here by the fact that in order to come to understand arithmetic we originally required examples. Once we have learned the beginnings of arithmetic in the kindergarten with the help of examples, we do not need examples any more to grasp it, and we can see the truth of many arithmetic propositions, e.g., that $3112 + 2467 = 5579$, of which we have never had examples. We have probably never taken 3112 things and 2467 things, put them together and counted the resulting set, but we still know that this is what the result of the counting would be. If it were empirical knowledge, we could not know it without counting. The examples are needed, not to prove anything, but only in order to enable us to come to understand in the first instance what is meant by number.

In geometry we indeed stand more in need of examples than in arithmetic, though I think this is only a psychological matter. In arithmetic we only need examples at the most elementary stage, but in geometry most people need a drawn figure, or at least an image of one in their minds, to see the validity of most proofs. But we must distinguish between an illustration and the basis of a proof. If the particular figure were not merely an illustration but the basis of the theorem, the latter would have to be proved by measuring it, but a measurement with a ruler or protractor never figures in Euclid's proofs. That the proof is not really based on the figure drawn is shown by the fact that we can still follow a proof concerning the properties of right-angled triangles even if the figure used to illustrate it is so badly drawn that it is obviously not a right-angled triangle at all. Again, if geometry were empirical, it would be a very hazardous speculation from the single example before us on the blackboard to conclude that all triangles had a property. It might be an individual idiosyncracy of some triangles and not others. These considerations should be conclusive of themselves, but we might add that recent developments in geometry have had the effect of much loosening the connection between geometrical proofs and the empirical figure. It is possible to work out non-Euclidean geometries where we cannot depend on figures.

The "A Priori" in Logic

Another important field for *a priori* knowledge is logic. The laws of logic must be known *a priori* or not at all. They certainly are not a matter for empirical observation, and the function of logical argument is just to give us conclusions which we have not discovered by observation. The argument would be superfluous if we had observed them already. We are able to make inferences because there is sometimes a logical connection between one or more propositions (the premise or premises) and another proposition, the conclusion, such that the latter must be true if the former is. Then, if we know the former, we can assert the latter on the strength of it, thus anticipating any experience. To take an example, there is a story that Mr. X., a man of high reputation and great social standing, had been asked to preside at a big social function. He was late in coming, and so a Roman Catholic priest was asked to make a speech to pass the time till his arrival. The priest told various anecdotes, including one which recorded his embarrassment when as confessor he had to deal with his first penitent and the latter confessed to a particularly atrocious murder. Shortly afterwards Mr. X. arrived, and in his own speech he said: "I see Father———— is here. Now, though he may not recognize me, he is an old friend of mine, in fact I was his first penitent." It is plain that such an episode would enable one to infer that Mr. X. had committed a murder without having observed the crime. The form of inference involved: The first penitent was a murderer, Mr. X. was the first penitent, therefore Mr. X. was a murderer—is of the famous kind to which logicians have given the name of *syllogism*. The importance of syllogisms has often been exaggerated, but they are as important as any kind of inference, and we cannot deny that in many cases a syllogism has given people information of which they were not in any ordinary sense aware before they used the syllogism and which they did not acquire by observation. Inference is only possible because there are special connections between the propositions involved such that one necessarily follows from others. It is a chief function of logic to study these connections, of which that expressed in the syllogism is by no means the only one.

(A *syllogism* consists of three propositions, two forming the *premises* and the other the *conclusion*. Each proposition can be expressed by a subject and predicate connected by the verb to be, the *copula,* and if we call everything which stands as either subject or predicate a *term,* there must be three and only three terms in the syllogism. The one common to the two premises is called the *middle term,* and it is on this common element that the inference depends. The other two, having been connected by means of it, occur without it in the conclusion. Thus in the usual example of the syllogism—All men are mortal, Socrates is a man, ∴ Socrates is mortal— man is the middle term connecting Socrates with mortality so that we could, even if he had not already died, know that he was mortal.)

Other Cases of the "A Priori"

A priori knowledge, while most prominent in mathematics and logic, is not limited to these subjects. For instance, we can see *a priori* that the same surface cannot have two different colors all over at the same time, or that a thought cannot have a shape. Philosophers have been divided into *rationalists* and *empiricists* according to whether they stressed the *a priori* or the empirical element more. The possibility of metaphysics depends on *a priori* knowledge, for our experience is quite inadequate to enable us to make on merely empirical grounds any sweeping generalizations of the kind the metaphysician desires. The term *a priori* covers both self-evident propositions, i.e. those which are seen to be true in their own right, and those which are derived by inference from propositions themselves self-evident.

The Linguistic Theory of the "A Priori" and the Denial that "A Priori" Propositions or Inferences Can Give New Knowledge

At the present time even empiricist philosophers recognize the impossibility of explaining away *a priori* propositions as merely empirical generalizations, but they are inclined to the view that *a priori* propositions and *a priori* reasoning are merely concerned with language, and so cannot tell us anything new about the real world. Thus it is said that, when we make an inference, the conclusion is just part of the premises expressed in different language.[1] If so, inference would be of use merely for clarifying our language and would involve no real advance in knowledge. Some inferences are of this type, e.g. A is a father, therefore A is male. But are they all? That would be hard indeed to square with the *prima facie* novelty of many conclusions. Take, for instance, the proposition that the square on the hypotenuse of a right-angled triangle is equal to the sum of the squares

---

1. This theory is not applied to *inductive* inference.

on the other two sides. Such a proposition can be inferred from the axioms and postulates of Euclid, but it certainly does not seem to be included in their meaning. Otherwise we should know it as soon as we understood the axioms and postulates. The example I gave of the murder discovered by a logical argument seems to be another case of a fact not known at all beforehand by the reasoner which is discovered by his reasoning. Extreme empiricist philosophers contend that this appearance of novelty is really illusory, and that in some sense we knew the conclusion all along; but they have never succeeded in making clear in what sense we did so. It is not enough to say that the conclusion is implicit in the premises. "Implicit" means "implied by," and of course a conclusion is implied by its premises, if the inference is correct at all. But this admission leaves quite open the question whether or not a proposition can follow from a different one which does not contain it as part of itself; and since we obviously can by deductive inference come to know things which we did not know before in any ordinary sense of "know," we must treat the empiricist's claim as unjustified till he has produced a clearly defined sense of "implicit in" or "contained in" which leaves room for that novelty in inference which we all cannot help really admitting. In any ordinary sense of "know" the conclusion is not in the cases I have mentioned known prior to the inference, and since the premises are and indeed must be known before we know the conclusion, it is therefore in no ordinary sense of "part" part of the premises.

It is indeed sometimes said that the premises include the conclusion in a confused form, but it is obvious that the beginner in geometry cannot be said to be aware of Pythagoras's theorem even in a confused form though he may know all the premises from which it can be deduced. Nor does awareness of the propositions that A was B's first penitent and that B's first penitent was a murderer include even confusedly the awareness that A was a murderer as long as the premises are not combined. When they are combined therefore something new appears that was not present to consciousness before in any way; there is a new discovery. We can also show by definite logical argument that the interpretation we are discussing does not enable one to avoid the admission of novelty in inference. For, what is it to know something in a confused form? It is surely to know some general attributes present in a whole but not others. To be aware of p even confusedly must involve discriminating some general attributes in p, and those are given in the premises, which are admittedly understood in some degree. If we do not discriminate any attributes, the confusion is too great for argument to be possible at all. Now it is admitted that, when we reach the conclusion, we do discriminate attributes which we did not discriminate before, even if they are alleged to have been contained in the confused whole which was present to our minds before we started inferring. It is further admitted that the conclusion follows necessarily from the premises. Therefore the general attributes which we discriminated at the time when we knew only the premises and not the conclusion must be linked with the attributes we discriminate afterwards in such a way that the latter follow necessarily from the former. So we still have to admit that sheer *a priori* inference can enable us to discover new attributes. In some cases it may take a good while to draw the inference, in other cases it may be practically instantaneous as soon as the premises are known and combined, but whether it takes a long or a short time to draw the inference cannot be relevant to the principle.

Nevertheless, the view that inference cannot yield new conclusions dies hard, and so it will not be superfluous to bring further arguments. (1) "This has shape" admittedly follows logically from "this has size" and vice versa. If the view I am criticizing were true, "this has size" would, therefore, have to include in its meaning "this has shape," and "this has shape" would also have to include in its meaning "this has size." But this would only be possible if the two sentences meant exactly the same thing, which they obviously do not. (2) Take an argument such as—Montreal is to the north of New York, New York is to the north of Washington, therefore Montreal is to the north of Washington. If the view I am discussing is true, the conclusion is part of the premises. But it is not part of either premise by itself, otherwise both premises would not be needed. So the only way in which it could be part of both together would be if it were divisible into two propositions one of which was part of the first and the other part of the second. I defy anybody to divide it in this way. (3) The proposition "Socrates was a philosopher" certainly entails the proposition "if Socrates had measles some philosophers have had measles," but it cannot be that the second proposition is included in the first. For the first proposition certainly does not include the notion of measles.

What is really the same view is often expressed by saying that all *a priori* propositions are "analytic." A distinction has commonly been drawn between *analytic* propositions, in which the predicate is in the notion of the subject already formed before the proposition is asserted, so that the proposition gives no new information, and *synthetic* propositions in which the predicate is not so contained and which are thus capable of giving new information.[2] Analytic propositions are essentially verbal, being all true by definition, e.g. all fathers are male. As an example of a synthetic proposition we could take any proposition established by experience such as "I am cold" or "It is snowing," but empiricists often assert that there are no synthetic *a priori* propositions. That this view cannot be justified may be shown at once. The proposition that there are no synthetic *a priori* propositions, since it cannot be established by empirical observations, would be, if justified, itself a synthetic *a priori* proposition, and we cannot affirm it as a synthetic *a priori* proposition that there are no synthetic *a priori* propositions. We may therefore dismiss off-hand any arguments for

2. This definition would have to be amended slightly to suit modern logicians who (I think, rightly) deny that all propositions are of the subject-predicate form, but this would not alter the principle though importing a complication of detail with which we need not deal here.

the theory. Such arguments, whatever they were, would have to involve synthetic *a priori* propositions. Further, the view must be false if it is ever true that the conclusion of an inference is not part of its premises. For, if the proposition—S is Q—ever follows validly from—S is P, the proposition —all that is SP is SQ, must be true *a priori*. But, unless the concept Q is part of the concept SP, the proposition—all that is SP is SQ—cannot be analytic. Therefore our arguments against the view that in all valid inferences the conclusion is part of the premises expressed in different language are also arguments against the view that all *a priori* propositions are analytic.

The analytic view seems plausible when we are concerned with the simplest propositions of logic and arithmetic, but we must not assume that a proposition is analytic because it is obvious. Though it may be very difficult to determine precisely where analytic propositions end and synthetic propositions begin, we cannot use this as a ground for denying the latter. It is very difficult to say precisely where blue ends and green begins, since the different shades run into each other imperceptibly, but we cannot therefore argue that all blue is really green. Taking arithmetic, even if there is a good deal of plausibility in saying that $2 + 2$ is included in the meaning of "4," there is none in saying $95 - 91$ or $\dfrac{216}{2} - \dfrac{287 + 25}{3}$ are so included. Yet, if the analytic view were true, all the infinite numerical combinations which could be seen *a priori* to be equal to 4 would have to be included in the meaning of "4."

Some empiricists, without committing themselves to the view that all *a priori* propositions are analytic, still say these are a matter of arbitrary choice or verbal convention. They are influenced here by a modern development in the view of geometry. It used to be held that the axioms of Euclid expressed a direct insight into the nature of physical space, but this is denied by modern scientists, and the view is taken that they are arbitrary postulates which geometricians make because they are interested in what would follow *if* they were true. Whether they are true or not is then a matter of empirical fact to be decided by science. But, even if this suggests that the premises of our *a priori* arguments may be arbitrary postulates, this does not make the subsequent steps arbitrary. From the postulates of Euclid it follows that the three angles of a triangle are equal to two right angles. If the original postulates are arbitrary, it is not certain that the conclusion is true of the real world; but it is still not an arbitrary matter that it follows from the postulates. The postulates may well be false, but there can be no doubt that *if* they were true the conclusions must be so, and it is in this hypothetical working out of the consequences of postulates which may not be true that pure geometry consists. The *a priori* necessity of pure geometry is not therefore in the least invalidated by modern developments. What is *a priori* is that the conclusions follow from the axioms and postulates, and this is not at all affected by the (empirical) discovery that not all the axioms and postulates exactly apply to the physical world. (Applied Euclidean geometry is possible in practice because it is an empirical fact that they approximately apply. The divergencies only show themselves when we consider unusually great velocities or distances.)

If not only the postulates but the successive stages in the inference were themselves arbitrary, we might just as well infer from the same premises that the angles of a triangle were equal to a million right angles or to none at all. All point in inference would be lost. Dictators may do a great deal, but they cannot alter the laws of logic and mathematics; these laws would not change even if by a system of intensive totalitarian education every human being were persuaded to fall in with a world dictator's whim in the matter and believe they were different from what they are. Nor can they change with alterations in language, though they may be expressed differently. That the truth of *a priori* propositions does not just depend on the nature of language can be easily seen when we consider that, even if we do not know any Fijian or Hottentot, we can know that also in these languages and not only in the languages we know the proposition $5 + 7 = 12$ must be true. It is of course true that by altering the meaning of the words we could make the proposition we expressed by "$5 + 7 = 12$" false, e.g. if I used "12" in a new sense to mean what other people mean by "11," but then it would be a different proposition. I could play the same trick with empirical propositions and say truly, e.g., that "fire does not burn" or "there is an elephant in this room" if I used "burn" to mean "drown" or "elephant" to mean "table." This does not in the least impair the obviousness of the contrary propositions established by experience. Finally, as we argued above that the proposition that there can be no synthetic *a priori* propositions would itself, if justified, have to be a synthetic *a priori* proposition, so we may argue that the proposition that all *a priori* propositions are a matter of arbitrary linguistic convention would, if true, have to be itself a matter of arbitrary linguistic convention. It therefore could not be vindicated by any argument and would be merely a matter of a new usage of words arbitrarily established by the persons who assert it, since it certainly does not express the usual meaning of "*a priori* propositions." So we must reject any attempt to explain away the *a priori* as a genuine source of new knowledge. If the attempt had succeeded, we should have had to admit that philosophy in anything like its old sense was impossible, for philosophy clearly cannot be based merely on observation.

The views we have been criticizing contain the following elements of truth. (1) *A priori* propositions can be seen to be true and the conclusions of an inference seen to follow from their premises without any further observation, provided we understand the meaning of the words used. But to say that q follows from p once we understand the meaning of the words is not to say that q is part of the meaning of the words used to express p. "Follow from" and "be part of" are not synonyms. (2) If q follows from p you cannot assert p and deny q without contradicting yourself, but this is only to say that in that case the denial of q implies the denial of p. It is not to say that q is part of what you assert when you assert p, unless we already assume that what is implied is always part of what implies it, i.e. beg the question at issue. (3) An *a priori* proposition cannot be fully understood without being seen to be true. It may be impossible to understand something fully without understanding something else not included in it at all, so it may still be synthetic.

People have been inclined to deny synthetic *a priori* propositions because they could not see how one characteristic could necessarily involve another, but that this could not happen would be itself a synthetic *a priori* metaphysical proposition. People have also thought that it was necessary to give some sort of explanation of *a priori* knowledge, and could not see how this could be done except in terms of language. To this I should reply that there is no reason to suppose that *a priori* knowledge requires some special explanation any more than does our ability to attain knowledge empirically by observation. Why not take it as an ultimate fact? Human beings certainly cannot explain everything, whether there is ultimately an explanation for it or not. . . .

Selected Bibliography

(ITEMS PROVIDED WITH ASTERISK ARE MORE ADVANCED)
(FOR KEY TO ABBREVIATIONS SEE PAGE XIX)

Locke's *Essay Concerning Human Understanding* is a classic on the problem of *a priori* knowledge. Book I criticizes the Cartesian theory of innate ideas. Book IV deals with the extent and certainty of knowledge. It contains the theory that universal propositions which are not merely verbal ("trifling") can be known with certainty only if one sees, intuitively, or with the help of deduction, a necessary connection between distinct ideas. This work is the first comprehensive treatise on the nature and origin of human knowledge in the history of philosophy. Leibniz' *New Essays Concerning Human Understanding* is a critical commentary, from the point of view of rationalism, on Locke's *Essay*. Book I, containing a defense of "innate ideas" against Locke's attack, is especially recommended. The theory of innate ideas has recently been revived by the linguist, N. Chomsky, in a number of widely discussed publications. *Cartesian Linguistics: A Chapter in the History of Rationalist Thought* (N.Y.: Harper, 1966) and *Language and Mind* (N.Y.: Harcourt Brace, 1968, p) are two of Chomsky's books in which this theory is explained in some detail. Chomsky has also stated his position in "Linguistics and Philosophy," in S. Hook (ed.), *Language and Philosophy* (N.Y.: New York University P., 1969). This volume contains critical discussions of Chomsky's views by a number of contemporary philosophers including W. V. Quine, R. Wells, N. Goodman, P. Kurtz, T. Nagel, K. Stern, M. Zimmerman, R. Abelson, and G. Harman, as well as Chomsky's reply to Harman. A symposium on Chomsky's theory, consisting of a short statement by Chomsky himself and critical responses by H. Putnam and N. Goodman, is contained in J. R. Searle (ed.), *The Philosophy of Language* (London: Oxford U.P., 1971, p). Another critical essay on Chomsky's theory is R. Edgley, "Innate Ideas," in *Knowledge and Necessity, Royal Institute of Philosophy Lectures Volume 3* (London: Macmillan, 1970, p). The most recent extended discussions of Chomsky's position are found in S. Toulmin, "Brain and Language: A Commentary," *Sy*, 1971, J. Searle, "Chomsky's Revolution in Linguistics," *The New York Review of Books*, June 29, 1972 and in the Appendix of W. Stegmüller, *Main Currents in Contemporary German, British and American Philosophy* (Bloomington: Indiana U.P., 1971). The following anthologies contain selections on the disputes between rationalists and empiricists: E. Nagel and R. B. Brandt (eds.), *Meaning and Knowledge* (N.Y.: Harcourt, Brace, 1965), C. Landesman (ed.), *The Foundations of Knowledge* (Englewood Cliffs: Prentice-Hall, 1970, p), L. W. Sumner and J. Woods (eds.), *Necessary Truths* (N.Y.: Random House, 1969, p) and R. Sleigh (ed.), *Necessary Truth* (Englewood Cliffs: Prentice-Hall, 1972, p). An elaborate defense of rationalism, together with very full critical discussions of rival theories, can be found in B. Blanshard, *The Nature of Thought*, Volume II (London: Allen & Unwin, 1939).

Elementary introductions to the problem of *a priori* knowledge may be found in Ch. 9 of D. W. Hamlyn, *Theory of Knowledge* (Garden City: Doubleday, 1970, p), Chs. 6 and 16 of A. Pap, *Elements of Analytic Philosophy* (N.Y.: Macmillan, 1949), Ch. 3 of J. Hospers, *An Introduction to Philosophical Analysis* (Englewood Cliffs: Prentice-Hall, 2nd ed., 1967), Chs. 2 and 4 of B. Aune, *Rationalism, Empiricism and Pragmatism: An Introduction* (N.Y.: Random House, 1970, p), and Ch. 11 of A. Flew, *An Introduction to Western Philosophy* (Indianapolis: Bobbs-Merrill, 1971, p). Two recent logic textbooks contain detailed discussions of the status of logical and mathematical principles: D. Mitchell, *An Introduction to Logic* (Garden City: Doubleday, 1970, p) and H. Kahane, *Logic and Philosophy* (Belmont, Calif.: Wadsworth, 1969). The fullest treatment of the entire subject in recent years, containing much useful historical material, is A. Pap, *Semantics and Necessary Truth* (New Haven: Yale U.P., 1958). While influenced by logical positivism, Pap concludes that there are synthetic *a priori* propositions. There is a very clarifying discussion of contemporary theories about *a priori* knowledge in Section 3 of R. M. Chisholm's contribution to R. M. Chisholm *et al., Philosophy —The Princeton Studies* (Englewood Cliffs: Prentice-Hall, 1964). I. M. Copi and J. A. Gould (eds.), *Readings on Logic* (N.Y.: Macmillan, 1964, p), contains selections from various great philosophers on the status of the so-called "Laws of Thought."

A critical treatment of Kant from the point of view of American pragmatism may be found in C. I. Lewis, *Mind and the World Order* (N.Y.: Scribner's, 1929). Lewis emphasizes, against Kant, the analytic nature of all *a priori* truth and discusses the function of *a priori* propositions in empirical inquiry. A more sophisticated and technical elaboration of his theory is contained in his later book, *An Analysis of Knowledge and Valuation** (La Salle, Illinois: Open Court, 1947), especially Chs. 3–6. Hans Reichenbach, *The Rise of Scientific Philosophy* (Berkeley and Los Angeles: U. of California P., 1951, p), contains a critique of Kantian rationalism by a leading logical empiricist. Helpful critical discussions of Kant's views on the subject are also contained in C. D. Broad, "Kant's Theory of Mathematical and Philosophical Reasoning," *Ar. Soc.*, 1941– 42, C. Parsons, "Kant's Philosophy of Arithmetic" in S. Morgenbesser, P. Suppes, M. White (eds.), *Philosophy, Science and Method* (N.Y.: St. Martin's Press, 1969), and N. Garver, "The Variability of the Analytic" *PPR*, 1971.

The theory that mathematical propositions are empirical generalizations, which is defended by J. S. Mill in Selection 58, is developed more fully by Mill in his *An Examination of Sir William Hamilton's Philosophy* (London: Longmans, Green, 1872), and in Alexander Bain, *Deductive Logic* (London: Longmans, Green, 1879). Mill's theory was criticized at length by James McCosh in *An Examination of J. S. Mill's Philosophy* (N.Y.: R. Carter, 1880). A briefer, but famous and important, criticism of Mill is found in G. Frege, *The Foundations of Arithmetic* (Oxford: Blackwell, 1953, tr. J. L. Austin). More recent discussions of Mill's theory concerning the nature of mathematics are R. Jackson, "Mill's Treatment of Geometry," *M*, 1941, reprinted in J. B. Schneewind (ed.), *Mill* (Garden City: Doubleday, 1968, p) and K. Britton, "The Nature of Arithmetic—A Reconsideration of Mill's Views," *Ar. Soc.*, 1947. A novel version of the view that the propositions of arithmetic are in some important sense empirical is defended by J. Mackie in his "Proof," *Ar. Soc. Sup.*, 1966. Mackie is criticized in R. D. Bradley and M. K. Rennie, "Must the Propositions of Arithmetic be Empirical?", *N*, 1971.

Much debated among contemporary philosophers is the thesis that mathematics is reducible to logic. Recommended to laymen as an introduction to this point of view is Bertrand Russell, *Introduction to Mathematical Philosophy* (London: Allen & Unwin, 1919), especially Chs. 1, 2, 13, 14, and 18. The nature of mathematics and logic is discussed also in R. Carnap's "The Old and the New Logic," translated from the German in A. J. Ayer (ed.), *Logical Positivism* (N.Y.: Free Press, 1959, p), in the same author's "Formal and Factual Science,"* in H. Feigl and M. Brodbeck (eds.), *Readings in the Philosophy of Science* (N.Y.: Appleton-Century-Crofts, 1949), C. G. Hempel, "The Nature of Mathematical Truth," reprinted in H. Feigl and W. Sellars, *Readings in Philosophical Analysis* (N.Y.: Appleton-Century-Crofts, 1949), G. Ryle, K. Popper, C. Lewy, "Why Are the Calculuses of Logic and Mathematics Applicable to Reality?"* *Ar. Soc. Sup.*, 1946, R. Von Mises, *Positivism: A Study in Human Understanding* (Cambridge: Harvard U.P., 1951), the relevant portions of which are reprinted in J. Newman (ed.), *The World of Mathematics*, Volume 3 (N.Y.: Simon & Schuster, 1956, p), K. Menger's "The New Logic," *PS*, 1937, and W. Kneale's "Truths of Logic," *Ar. Soc.*, 1946. P. Benacerraf and H. Putnam (eds.), *Philosophy of Mathematics* (Englewood Cliffs: Prentice-Hall, 1964) is an extremely useful anthology containing extracts from the writings of outstanding philosophers and mathematicians on the problems discussed in the present section. It also contains a very clear and helpful introduction by the editors. S. Körner, *The Philosophy of Mathematics* (London: Hutchinson, 1960), and S. F. Barker, *Philosophy of Mathematics* (Englewood Cliffs: Prentice-Hall, 1964, p) are useful introductory works dealing with philosophical problems concerning the nature of mathematics. An interesting recent discussion of some of the questions about the nature of mathematics which are puzzling to philosophers and to mathematicians is C. S. Chihara, "Mathematical Discovery and Concept Formulation," *PR*, 1963.

The status of geometrical propositions has been very widely discussed in recent years by philosophers, mathematicians, and physicists. Among the most important discussions by philosophers are Chapter 8 of E. Nagel's *The Structure of Science* (N.Y.: Harcourt, Brace & World, 1961), C. G. Hempel's "Geometry and Empirical Science," available in H. Feigl and W. Sellars (eds.), *Readings in Philosophical Analysis, op. cit.*, M. Black's "Conventionalism in Geometry and the Interpretation of Necessary Statements," *PS*, 1942, Ch. 8 of Reichenbach, *op. cit.* and the same author's *Philosophy of Space and Time* (N.Y.: Dover, 1957, p). R. D. Bradley in "Geometry and Necessary Truth," *PR*, 1964, is critical of both Nagel and Reichenbach. Einstein's views are stated in an essay, "Geometry and Experience," which is reprinted in his book, *Sidelights of Relativity* (London: Methuen, 1922). Poincaré's very influential discussion is found in Chs. III–V of *Science and Hypothesis* (N.Y.: Dover Publications, 1955, p). Extracts from Einstein as well as Poincaré are reprinted in H. Feigl and M. Brodbeck (eds.), *Readings in the Philosophy of Science, op. cit.* More difficult are A. Grünbaum, *Geometry and Chronometry in Philosophical Perspective* (Minneapolis: U. of Minnesota P., 1968), E. W. Adams, "The Empirical Foundations of Elementary Geometry,"* in H. Feigl and G. Maxwell (eds.), *Current Issues in the Philosophy of Science* (N.Y.: Holt, Rinehart & Winston, 1961), and H. P. Robertson, "Geometry as a Branch of Physics,"* in P. A. Schilpp (ed.), *Albert Einstein—Philosopher Scientist* (N.Y.: Tudor Press, 1951). There is a very clear discussion of the main issues in Ch. 7 of A. Pap, *An Introduction to the Philosophy of Science* (N.Y.: Free Press, 1962).

The theory that all necessary propositions are tautologies was clearly stated for the first time by Ludwig Wittgenstein in his *Tractatus Logico-Philosophicus** (London: Kegan Paul, N.Y.: Harcourt, Brace, 1922, new English translation by D. F. Pears and B. F. McGuinness, 1962). Under the influence of Wittgenstein, Bertrand Russell abandoned his rationalism and came to adopt a conventionalistic position on the nature of mathematics. There are brief discussions in several of his later books, the most extended being Ch. XVII of *The Analysis of Matter* (London: Kegan Paul, 1927, N.Y.: Dover Publications, 1954, p). A simple and unsophisticated exposition of the linguistic or conventionalistic theory of *a priori* propositions, one of the first formulations of such a theory, is given by a member of the "Vienna Circle," H. Hahn, in "Logic, Mathematics and Knowledge of Nature," English translation in A. J. Ayer (ed.), *Logical Positivism, op. cit.* Carnap's "The Old and the New Logic," which is contained in the same volume and to which reference was made above, defends the same position. Moritz Schlick, another of the founders of logical positivism, defends the linguistic theory against Kantians and phenomenologists in "Is There a Material *A Priori?*" which is available in English translation in Feigl and Sellars, *op. cit.* F. Waismann defends the linguistic theory against the kind of objection found in rationalistic critics like Blanshard and Ewing in Ch. 3 of his posthumously published *The Principles of Linguistic Philosophy* (London: Macmillan, 1965). There are sympathetic discussions of the linguistic theory in the following works by philosophers who would not usually be classified as logical positivists: Ch. VII of K. Britton, *Communication—A Philosophical Study of Language* (London: Kegan Paul, 1939), the same author's "Are Necessary Truths True by Convention?" *Ar. Soc. Sup.*, 1947, C. D. Hardie, "The Necessity of *A Priori* Propositions," *Ar. Soc.*, 1937–38, N. Malcolm's two articles, "Are Necessary Propositions Really Verbal?" and "The Nature of Entailment," both in *M*, 1940, D. A. Gasking's "Mathematics and the World," *AJ*, 1940, reprinted in A. Flew (ed.), *Logic and Language*, Second Series (Oxford: Blackwell, 1953), and in Benacerraf and Putnam, *op. cit.*, P. Edwards, "Do Necessary Propositions 'Mean Nothing'?" *JP*, 1949, B. Lake, "Necessary and Contingent Statements," *A*, 1952, M. Black, "Necessary Statements and Rules," *PR*, 1958, reprinted in his *Models and Metaphors* (Ithaca: Cornell U.P., 1962), the same author's "The Justification for Logical Axioms," in his *Margins of Precision* (Ithaca: Cornell U.P., 1970), A. Quinton, "The *A Priori* and the Analytic," *Ar. Soc.*, 1963, which is reprinted in P. F. Strawson (ed.), *Philosophical Logic* (London: Oxford U.P., 1967 p), and M. Lazerowitz, "Necessity and Language," in A. Ambrose and M. Lazerowitz (eds.), *Ludwig Wittgenstein: Philosophy and Language* (London: Allen & Unwin, 1971). There is a symposium on the linguistic theory and its difficulties in *A*, 1936, with M. Black, A. J. Ayer, and C. H. Whiteley as participants.

The following articles are in varying degrees critical of the linguistic theory: C. D. Broad, "Are There Synthetic *A Priori* Truths?" *Ar. Soc. Sup.*, 1936, W. V. Quine, "Truth by Convention,"* originally published in 1936 and reprinted both in Feigl and Sellars, *op. cit.*, and in Benacerraf and Putnam, *op. cit.*, C. H. Whiteley, "Truths by Convention," *A*, 1937, D. Williams, "The Nature and Variety of the *A Priori*," *A*, 1938, M. MacDonald, "Necessary Propositions," *A*, 1940, J. Bennett, "A Myth about Logical Necessity," *A*, 1961, and S. F. Barker, "Logical Positivism and the Philosophy of Mathematics," in P. Achinstein and S. F. Barker (eds.), *The Legacy of Logical Positivism* (Baltimore: Johns Hopkins Press, 1969). A. C. Ewing, some of whose criticisms of the linguistic theory are contained in our Selection 61 develops his objections in great detail in his article, "The Linguistic Theory of *A Priori* Propositions,"* *Ar. Soc.*, 1940. W. Kneale criticizes the theory in "Are Necessary Truths True by Convention?" *Ar. Soc. Sup.*, 1947, and more recently in Ch. X of his great historical work, *The Development of Logic* (London: Oxford U.P., 1962). There is a reply by Gasking to D. Williams in *A*, 1939, and there are critical discussions of Gasking's own article, "Mathematics and the World," in H. Castaneda's "Arithmetic and Reality," *AJ*, 1959, reprinted in Benacerraf and Putnam, *op. cit.*, and in D. Locke's "Mathematical Statements," *AJ*, 1963. A. Pap criticized the linguistic theory in a number of articles, including "Necessary Propositions and Linguistic Rules,"* in *Semantica* (issued by *Archivio di Filosofia*, Rome), 1955, and "Are All Necessary Propositions Analytic?" *PPR*, 1950. Pap's chief objections are restated in *Semantics and Necessary Truth*, *op. cit.* B. Blanshard, whose *Nature of Thought*, *op. cit.*, had already contained numerous objections to the linguistic theory, returned to the attack with full force in his *Reason and Analysis* (London: Allen & Unwin, LaSalle, Illinois: Open Court, 1962). E. Nagel in his very influential article "Logic Without Ontology," first published in 1944 and now available in his *Logic Without Metaphysics* (N.Y.: Free Press, 1957) and reprinted also in Feigl and Sellars, *op. cit.*, and in Benacerraf and Putnam, *op. cit.*, combines the linguistic approach with the contextualistic logic of John Dewey. Similarly influenced both by logical positivists and by John Dewey is A. Pasch, *Experience and the Analytic: A Reconsideration of Empiricism* (Chicago: U. of Chicago P., 1958). Ayer's version of the linguistic theory is criticized by C. A. Campbell in "Contradiction: 'Law' or 'Convention'?" There are exchanges between D. F. Henze and Campbell on the subject in *A*, 1961 and 1962.

The possibility of making a reasonably precise distinction between synthetic and analytic statements as well as the view that such a distinction is of philosophical importance was pretty universally taken for granted until fairly recently. Within the last 20 years or so, however, the possibility of making such a distinction and also the philosophical importance of it, if it can be made, have been seriously questioned. In this connection, mention should be made of a series of articles by F. Waismann entitled "Analytic-Synthetic," *A*, 1949–52, which is reprinted in Waismann's *How I See Philosophy* (London: Macmillan, 1968), W. H. Walsh, "Analytic-Synthetic," *Ar. Soc.*, 1953–54 (which discusses points raised by Waismann), M. G. White, "Analytic-Synthetic: An Untenable Dualism," reprinted in L. Linsky (ed.), *Semantics and the Philosophy of Language* (Urbana: U. of Illinois P., 1952), and especially W. V. Quine's important paper, "Two Dogmas of Empiricism,"* reprinted in W. V. Quine, *From a Logical Point of View* (Cambridge: Harvard U.P., 1953), and also in Benacerraf and Putnam, *op. cit.* There are criticisms of Quine in B. Mates,

"Analytic Sentences," *PR,* 1951, R. M. Martin, "On 'Analytic'," *PSt,* 1952, A. Hofstadter, "The Myth of the Whole," *JP,* 1954, M. Weitz, "Analytic Statements," *M,* 1954, H. P. Grice and P. F. Strawson, "In Defense of a Dogma," *PR,* 1956, J. Bennett, "Analytic-Synthetic," *Ar. Soc.,* 1959, G. H. Bird, "Analytic and Synthetic," *PQ,* 1961, F. Sommers, "Meaning Relations and the Analytic," *JP,* 1963, H. Putnam, "The Analytic and the Synthetic," and G. Maxwell, "The Necessary and the Contingent"—both in H. Feigl and G. Maxwell (eds.), *Minnesota Studies in the Philosophy of Science,* Volume III, *op. cit.* It should be added that several of these articles are by no means wholly opposed to Quine and concede that some of his objections to traditional views are well taken. More recent discussions of this subject by Quine are in his article "Carnap and Logical Truth,"* in P. A. Schilpp (ed.), *The Philosophy of Rudolf Carnap* (LaSalle, Illinois: Open Court, 1964), in his popular paper "Necessary Truth" which is included in Quine's *The Ways of Paradox* (N.Y.: Random House, 1966), and in his book, *Word and Object** (Cambridge: M.I.T. Press, 1960, p), which contains replies to several of his critics. There is a very thorough critical discussion of *Word and Object* by C. F. Presley in *AJ,* 1961. Carnap's rejoinder to Quine is found in his "Reply to Criticisms," in *The Philosophy of Rudolf Carnap, op. cit.* Carnap's later views on these questions are also contained in the two articles "Meaning Postulates"* and "Meaning and Synonymy in Natural Languages," which are reprinted as Supplements to the second edition of *Meaning and Necessity* (Chicago: U. of Chicago P., 1956, p). There is an extremely interesting and suggestive paper on the subject, in harmony with Carnap's approach, by the mathematician J. G. Kemeny, entitled "Analyticity versus Fuzziness," in *Synthese,* 1963. In "Degrees of Analyticity,"* *Philosophia* (Jerusalem), 1971, Y. Bar-Hillel argues that the apparent conflict on this subject between Carnap and Quine can be reconciled. In *Logic, Physics and Metaphysics* (Auckland, New Zealand: U. of Auckland P., 1967), R. D. Bradley criticizes Quine's claim that the propositions of mathematics and logic, just like those of the sciences, are open to revision and he also defends the propriety of distinguishing between synthetic and analytic statements. Quine's "Two Dogmas of Empiricism," and several of the papers criticizing him are reprinted in Sumner and Woods (eds.), *Necessary Truths, op. cit.* and in R. C. Sleigh (ed.), *Necessary Truth, op. cit.* Several papers in D. Davidson and J. Hintikka (eds.), *Words and Objections: Essays on the Work of Quine* (Dordrecht, Holland: Reidel, 1969) contain critical discussions of Quine's approach. The same volume contains replies by Quine. A novel attempt to provide an account of the analytic-synthetic distinction (for natural languages) is found in J. Katz, *The Philosophy of Language* (New York: Harper, 1966). There is a criticism of Katz by L. Linsky in "Analytic/Synthetic and Semantic Theory," *Sy,* 1970.

Philosophers who accept the analytic-synthetic distinction continue to debate whether there are or indeed whether there could be any synthetic *a priori* statements. H. G. Alexander, in "Necessary Truth," *M,* 1957, is critical of both Kneale's view that there are objective "natural necessitations" and Quine's view that there are no statements whose truth is established by purely verbal considerations, but he concludes that there are good grounds for abandoning the classification of meaningful statements as either analytic *a priori* or synthetic *a posteriori.* H. Langford, in "A Proof That Synthetic *A Priori* Propositions Exist," *JP,* 1949, and S. Toulmin in "A Defense of Synthetic Necessary Truth," *M,* 1949, argue, as the titles of their papers indicate, that there are synthetic *a priori* propositions, although traditional rationalists would not derive much comfort from their conclusions. Toulmin's paper is criticized by D. Pears,

"Synthetic Necessary Truth,"* M, 1950. Pears' views are also expressed in "Incompatibilities of Colors,"* in A. Flew (ed.), Logic and Language, Second Series (Oxford: Blackwell, 1953). The topic discussed in the last of these papers has figured prominently in many recent articles. A number of philosophers believe that the linguistic theory breaks down when it comes to statements like "Nothing can be both red and green all over," which are claimed to be both synthetic and necessary. The following are recent articles dealing with this question: V. C. Aldrich, "The Last Word on Being Red and Blue All Over," PSt, 1954, D. S. Shwayder, "Mr. Aldrich's 'Last Word'," PSt, 1955, H. Putnam, "Reds, Greens and Logical Analysis,"* PR, 1956, A. Pap, "Once More: Colors and the Synthetic A Priori,"* PR, 1957 (reply to Putnam), H. Putnam, "Reds and Greens Again: A Rejoinder to Arthur Pap,"* ibid., P. Glassen, "Reds, Greens, and the Synthetic A Priori," PSt, 1958, J. J. C. Smart, "Incompatible Colors," PSt, 1959, two articles in A, 1961, by P. Remnant and J. Hilton, both entitled "Red and Green All Over Again," F. Ferré, "Color Incompatibility and Language-Games," M, 1961, and replies to Ferré by R. Arbini and P. Swiggart in M, 1963, C. Radford, "The Insolubility of the Red-Green Problem," A, 1963, and A. Sloman, "Color Incompatibilities and Analyticity," A Sup., 1964. In "Denial of the Synthetic A Priori," P, 1960, O. A. Johnson argues that the proposition, "There are no synthetic a priori propositions," is itself both synthetic and a priori, and he concludes that empiricism must hence be untenable.

The following articles contain interesting material but are not easy to classify: F. Waismann, "Are There Alternative Logics?" Ar. Soc., 1945–46, reprinted in his How I See Philosophy, op. cit., W. Sellars, "Is There a Synthetic A Priori?" PS, 1946, reprinted in S. Hook (ed.), American Philosophers at Work (N.Y.: Criterion Books, 1956), R. J. Butler, "Language Strata and Alternative Logics," AJ, 1955, A. Hofstadter, "Six Necessities," JP, 1957, L. W. Beck, "On the Meta-Semantics of the Problem of the Synthetic A Priori," M, 1957, D. W. Hamlyn, "Analytic Truths," M, 1956, the same author's "On Necessary Truth," M, 1961, R. Robinson, "Necessary Propositions," M, 1958, M. Bunge, "Analyticity Redefined," M, 1961, L. S. Donnellan, "Necessity and Criteria," and H. Putnam, "It Ain't Necessarily So," both in JP, 1962, C. D. McGee, "Pre-Ceremonial Relations," PQ, 1963, B. Aune, "Is There an Analytic A Priori?" JP, 1963, J. Hintikka, "Are Mathematical Truths Synthetic A Priori?"* JP, 1968, D. B. Locke, "The Necessity of Analytic Truths," P, 1969, and R. Cole and H. Kahane, "Hard and Soft Intensionalism," RM, 1970.

Wittgenstein's later views concerning the nature of mathematical necessity are contained in his posthumously published Remarks on the Foundations of Mathematics* (Oxford: Blackwell, N.Y.: Macmillan, 1956). Some commentators interpret his remarks as a form of conventionalism, but it is not clear that Wittgenstein ever reached a position that really satisfied him. Selections from Wittgenstein as well as commentaries by A. R. Anderson, M. Dummett, and P. Bernays are reprinted in Benacerraf and Putnam, op. cit. An account of Wittgenstein's views on mathematics over the years is given in Alice Ambrose's "Wittgenstein on Some Questions in the Foundations of Mathematics," JP, 1955, which is reprinted in her Essays in Analysis (London: Allen & Unwin, 1966). Some of Wittgenstein's remarks about logical necessity are criticized by E. J. Nell in "The Hardness of the Logical 'Must'," A, 1961, to which there is a reply in the same volume by C. S. Chihara. These issues are also discussed in J. F. Bennett and O. P. Wood, "On Being Forced to a Conclusion," Ar. Soc. Sup., 1961, A. B. Levison, "Wittgenstein and Logical Laws," PQ, 1964, A. Sloman, "Explaining Logical Necessity," Ar. Soc., 1968–69, D. S. Shwayder, "Wittgenstein on Mathematics" in P. Winch (ed.), Studies in the *Philosophy of Wittgenstein* (London: Routledge, 1969), and Ch. 7 of D. Pears, *Wittgenstein* (London: Collins, 1971, p).

The following articles in the *Encyclopedia of Philosophy* deal with topics treated in the present section: "Analytic and Synthetic Statements" (D. W. Hamlyn, 1–105), "*A Priori* and *A Posteriori*" (D. W. Hamlyn, 1–140), "Contingent and Necessary Statements" (D. W. Hamlyn, 2–198), "Empiricism" (D. W. Hamlyn, 2–199), "Epistemology, History of" (D. W. Hamlyn, 3–8), "Geometry" (S. F. Barker, 3–285), "Innate Ideas" (J. O. Nelson, 4–196), "Kant, Immanuel" (W. H. Walsh, 4–305), "Laws of Thought" (S. Körner, 4–414), "Linguistic Theory of the *A Priori*" (R. W. Ashby, 4–479), "Mathematics, Foundations of" (C. Parsons, 5–188), "Rationalism" (B. Williams, 6–224), and "Synonymity" (L. Linsky, 8–54).

VIII

Meaning,
Verification
and
Metaphysics

INTRODUCTION

THERE HAS BEEN REPEATED REFERENCE, both in the editorial introductions and in selected readings, to *logical positivism*. The rise of logical positivism after the first world war is undoubtedly one of the most significant revolutions in the history of philosophy. We have already seen that in its radical rejection of all claims to *a priori* knowledge of synthetic propositions, logical positivism denies the very possibility of metaphysics in the Kantian sense; for as Kant defined "metaphysics," metaphysics is a discipline that pretends to offer *a priori* proofs of important synthetic propositions, like "there is a God," "the soul is immortal," "the material universe has a beginning in time." This attack on metaphysics from the platform "all necessary propositions (i.e., propositions that can be known *a priori*) are analytic" must, however, be distinguished from the attitude of the agnostic, who says: "Perhaps such metaphysical propositions are true, perhaps they are false, but we shall never know whether they are true or whether they are false—at least not during this life. For they cannot be empirically verified, by sense-perception and inference from perceived facts, nor is human reason strong enough to discover *a priori* whether they are true or false. Therefore the metaphysician is just wasting his, and his audience's, time." The logical positivists also maintain that the metaphysician is wasting his time, but for the very different reason that his statements are devoid of cognitive meaning. For the logical positivists maintain that all cognitively significant statements are either analytic—in which case they elucidate the meanings of words but convey no information about the world—or else empirical—in which case they make assertions about the world, but can be determined as true or false only by experience, not *a priori;* hence it follows that sentences which allegedly express metaphysical propositions in the above sense of "metaphysical" do not express propositions at all.

We are thus led to the positivist theory of meaning, the so-called *verifiability theory of meaning*. It is the most trenchant weapon with which metaphysics, in the sense in which Kant used the word when he inquired into the possibility of metaphysics as a science, has ever been fought. If a sentence by which a speaker purports to state a fact, to make an assertion, is not empirically verifiable, says our theory, then nothing is asserted by it at all; it is neither true nor false, just the way "he eats quadratic equations for breakfast" or "time walks faster than space" would ordinarily be said to be neither true nor false but just meaningless. If, for example, the statement "there is an infinite spirit which is omniscient, omnipotent, and good, and this spirit is the creator of the universe" is not empirically verifiable in the sense that observations can be described that would, if they were made, confirm or disconfirm it, then nothing that is either true or false is asserted by it. There is only a cognitively meaningless sentence which seems to many people to be meaningful because it is grammatically similar to unquestionably meaningful sentences, and because *emotions* of a religious kind, as well as mental pictures, are associated with it. The sentence is cognitively meaningless, according to the positivist, in the sense that no conceivable state of affairs is described by it, just the way the sentence "he eats quadratic equations for breakfast" and "time walks faster than space" do not describe conceivable states of affairs if the constituent words are used in their customary senses.

The logical positivists' attack on metaphysics might be succinctly stated by the following syllogism: all metaphysical statements are empirically unverifiable; all empirically unverifiable statements are (cognitively) meaningless; therefore all metaphysical statements are (cognitively) meaningless. The second premise of the argument is the verifiability theory of meaning, in negative form; the equivalent positive form is, of course, "all (cognitively) meaningful statements are empirically verifiable." We shall presently examine the relevant concept of empirical verifiability, but let us first focus attention on the minor premise. Obviously even a philosopher who accepts the verifiability theory of meaning need not accept the conclusion of the syllogism, for he may hold that some metaphysical statements are empirically verifiable. Clearly, whether such a position is tenable depends on the meaning of "metaphysical." Now a logical positivist would contend that empirical unverifiability is a common characteristic of many statements that have been subjects of perennial controversy in the history of philosophy and that have been called "metaphysical" by philosophers. For example, he maintains that no conceivable observations could settle the dispute as to whether the essence of reality is spiritual or material; that no conceivable observations could settle the dispute between Platonists and Aristotelians as to whether there exist universals apart from particulars (see Introduction to Section VII, p. 668, or between Aristotelians and Nominalists as to whether there are universals identically present in many particulars at the same time or whether, as the Nominalists contend, there exist only particulars that resemble each other in varying degrees. We shall consider further examples of such metaphysical disputes later on, but in the meantime it should be conceded that not all statements that have been called "metaphysical" by various philosophers confirm the positivists' minor premise. Some philosophers, for example, would say that the law of universal causation, or the law of the uniformity of nature, are metaphysical propositions even if, as maintained by Mill, they should themselves be generalizations from experience which are confirmed, though not conclusively verified, by experience. It is, however, far more likely that a philosopher who refers to these propositions as metaphysical thereby means to say that their validity is to be discovered *a priori*. Again, the assertion by materialists that all consciousness is causally conditioned by material processes, or that consciousness has a merely "epiphenomenal" existence (see Introduction to Section III), may be called "metaphysical" by some philosophers though they would not deny that empirical evidence is relevant to the question of the truth of materialism, or of epiphenomenalism. Very likely, "metaphysical proposition" in this usage means "a very general, fundamental proposition about reality."

If, then, we interpret the positivists' minor premise as a generalization about all statements that have ever been called "metaphysical" in the history of philosophy, it is probably false. If, on the other hand, it is intended by the positivist as analytic, as a *definition* of "metaphysical statement," then we must keep in mind that even if the major premise is granted, the argument does not prove that metaphysical statements in some other sense of "metaphysical," e.g., the vague sense specified and illustrated above, are (cognitively) meaningless. But from the question whether the verifiability theory of meaning entails the (cognitive) meaninglessness of all metaphysics in every conventional sense of the word "metaphysics," we must distinguish the question whether that theory itself is valid. And the latter question obviously cannot be decided until the *meaning* of that very theory of meaning is clarified. To this task we must now turn.

An important ancestor of the positivist view that statements which are claimed to express profound insight into the nature of the universe, though they are neither analytic (and thus subject to the judgment of logic and mathematics) nor empirical (and thus subject to the judgment of the empirical sciences), are cognitively meaningless, is the empiricism of Locke, Berkeley, and Hume. Locke attempted to show in detail, in the second book of his great *Essay Concerning Human Understanding,* how all simple ideas come into the mind through the channels of sensation or reflection (by "reflection" he meant what is nowadays called "introspection"; thus the ideas of pain and pleasure are acquired by introspective awareness of felt pain and pleasure). Hume formulated the principle "no (simple) idea without corresponding, antecedent impression," using the term "impression" to cover both perceptions and introspectable feelings. This principle implies that if an alleged idea does not correspond to any impression nor is resolvable into simpler ideas that do correspond to impressions, then it is not a genuine idea at all. To illustrate the principle: it led Hume to the conclusion that the allegedly innate idea of "substance" is no idea at all, that "substance" is just a meaningless word. He was more consistent than Berkeley on this point, for he rejected the alleged idea of mental substance ("soul," "self," "mind") just as decidedly as Berkeley had rejected the alleged idea of material substance: when I introspect, said Hume, I come upon a succession of perceptions and feelings, but I do not discover an alleged "self." In modern semantical terminology, Hume's principle reads as follows: if a term allegedly refers to something which is in principle unobservable then it does not refer to anything, i.e., it has no *descriptive meaning*. Of course, a term may have a perfectly clear descriptive meaning although nothing *exists* to which it applies; we know what we are talking about when we talk about dragons, mermaids, giants, golden mountains, etc. But in that case we understand the term because it is defined by means of terms that do apply to items of experience: fire, breathing, serpent, fish, woman, higher than ten feet, gold, mountain.

Now, says the positivist, take an expression like "infinite spirit." I am not rejecting it as meaningless on the ground that an infinite spirit is not directly observable: after all, if I rejected metaphysics because it talks about things that are not directly observable, I would have to reject theoretical physics too, for surely electrons and fields of force are not directly observable either. However, there is this difference between the sentences of theoretical physics and the sentences of metaphysics: the former are indirectly testable in experience, i.e., the physicists are prepared to tell me what sort of observations would confirm (though not perhaps verify conclusively) and what sort of observations would disconfirm their hypotheses. If two physicists offer conflicting hypotheses in order to explain the observed facts, empirical tests can be described for deciding which hypothesis is true, or probably true. For example, the wave theory and the particle theory of light imply incompatible consequences as regards the ratio of the velocity of light in water to the velocity of light in air. But suppose that one metaphysician, to pick a random example, asserts that the observable qualities of an apple inhere in a substance, call it "the apple-in-itself," and another metaphysician denies this, maintaining that qualities can exist without being supported by a substance. Are there any conceivable observations that are relevant for deciding the question who is right? No. It follows, says the positivist, that neither metaphysician has asserted anything at all; though he may think that he has made an assertion because he fails to distinguish metaphorical meaning from literal meaning. The statement that there exists an infinite spirit is in this respect just like the statement that all observable qualities are attached to unobservable substances ("substrata"): no conceivable observations can be described that have a clear bearing on the truth or falsehood of the theistic hypothesis, the way the outcome of measurements of the velocity of light in water had a bearing on the question whether the wave theory of light is true. There is no agreement among theologians, for example, what amount of suffering in the world is compatible with the assertion that the world is the creation of a spirit which is both omnipotent and good. It follows that the theologian is not saying anything about the world when he utters the sentence "the world was created by an infinite spirit."

The positivist does not mean to say that a sentence which is not analytic is cognitively meaningful only if it is *actually possible* to find out whether it is true or false. That there exists on Mars a rock exactly like the rock of Gibraltar is a factual proposition, he would admit, though it is at present *practically* impossible to verify it. All that the positivist requires of a man who utters a sentence in order to assert something is that he be able to describe the sort of observations, whether perceptual or introspective, which would confirm or disconfirm his statement *if* they were actually made. Take the physician's assertion, satirized by Molière, that opium tends to put those who consume it asleep because it has a sleep-inducing power. If the physician cannot specify what sort of observations would confirm or disconfirm his statement about the sleep-inducing power ("it is something hidden"), then, according to the positivist, he has not made a genuine assertion at all, he has just bluffed knowledge by means of pompous language. If, on the other hand, he replies that the empirical evidence for his assertion is that usually people fall asleep after consumption of opium, then *this* is what the statement about the sleep-inducing power really means, and it is absurd to bring it forth as an explanation of the observed fact.

This simple, and well-worn, illustration brings out that the verifiability theory of meaning in its original formulation consists really of two claims: that no factual (i.e., not analytic, not tautological) proposition is expressed by a sentence unless relevant empirical evidence which can be described; and that the empirical evidence which would make the sentence true *is* the meaning of the sentence, the factual proposition it expresses. Thus, devout Christians often speak of the ways in which God manifests Himself in human experience; they profess to feel certain indescribable emotions during worship which cannot but be manifestations of God. If only, they would say to a positivist, you will accept as "empirical evidence" modes of experience other than sense-perception, such as religious emotions, then undeniably there is empirical evidence for the existence of God. Here is the positivist's reply: I understand what "manifestation" means in such sentences as "smoke is a manifestation of fire," "ice is a manifestation of low temperature," "screams are manifestations of pain." For here that which is said to manifest itself is itself observable *apart from its manifestation*. But since, as you admit, God is not observable apart from His manifestations, it follows that in asserting His existence you assert nothing else than the existence of the "manifestations." Why not just report the psychological fact, then, that during worship you feel unique emotions; why produce obfuscation by a pseudo-explanation in terms of a transcendent spirit which is logically in the same boat as the explanation ridiculed by Molière.

The critics of logical positivism have fired back many arguments, some relevant, some irrelevant. The most important and serious of their counter-arguments are well presented by Ewing and Warnock (see Selections 64 and 65). The verifiability theory of meaning has proved most vulnerable in its second claim, the identification of the meaning of a statement with the evidence in terms of which it would be verified if it were true. Statements about past events beyond the reach of the speaker's and his contemporaries' memory can only be verified in terms of *present* evidence, like carefully preserved historical documents; but is a statement about the past then really a statement about the present? To this criticism some positivists reply by distinguishing between *direct* and *indirect* evidence. The meaning of a statement is to be identified only with the direct evidence for it. To assert that Caesar crossed the Rubicon at such and such a time is not to assert that it says so in such and such documents; it is to say that anyone alive at that time would have observed such and such if he had been suitably placed (cf. the discussion of phenomenalism, pp. 573 ff.!), for this alone would constitute direct evidence. This line of defense, however, seems to break down as we turn to statements about other minds, like "he sees blue," "she has warm feelings for me," "he feels a pain in his left foot," "he believes what he is saying now." Since such statements can be verified by their speakers only indirectly, by observing behavior (including speech behavior), facial expressions, states of the cerebro-neural system, etc., the identification of meaning and direct evidence seems to lead in this case to the preposterous conclusion that the speakers of such statements are not asserting anything at all. If, on the other hand, it is maintained that such statements are about observable behavior and physiological processes, that they must be rendered significant by a *behavioristic* interpretation, then a curious consequence seems to follow: when I say about you "you feel pain in your left foot" and you reply "yes, I feel pain in my left foot," we are not asserting the same fact at all; for surely you can truly say, with closed eyes, that you feel pain without having the faintest idea how you behave, what your face looks like, and what is happening in your brain.

Some have attempted to refute the verifiability theory of meaning by showing that it refutes itself (see Selection 64, pp. 770 ff.): if the theory were true, they argue, it would itself be meaningless. For it is not a tautology; and if it were an empirical proposition, then it would be conceivable that there are meaningful statements which are not empirically verifiable, just as it is conceivable that there should be crows which are not black. But this is just what the positivists deny. And if the theory is neither a tautology nor an empirical proposition, then it is either meaningless or else synthetic *a priori*. But it cannot be the latter on positivist principles, therefore it condemns itself as meaningless! What a formidable indictment of positivism! But perhaps one possibility has been overlooked: perhaps the verifiability theory of meaning is put forth as an *analysis* of an important sense of the word "meaningful." An analysis is not a tautology. In saying "a circle is a closed line all of whose points have the same distance from a given point enclosed by it," we are not giving an arbitrary definition of the word "circle" (if it were arbitrary, why not define a circle as a husband with an annual income of five thousand dollars?), nor are we just saying "a circle is a circle." And any positivist who is worth his salt would admit that some definitions are not arbitrary stipulations but analyses of more or less vague meanings.

The controversy about the justification of metaphysics in the light of criteria of cognitively significant language, i.e., language capable of expressing and communicating knowledge, which was belligerently started by the "Vienna Circle," has not ended yet. Howsoever the verifiability theory of meaning may have fared during the two decades of attack and counterattack after the publication of A. J. Ayer's manifesto of logical positivism, *Language, Truth, and Logic,* in 1936, one thing must be admitted by all advocates of *clear* philosophical writing and speaking: the positivist preoccupation with meaningful language has forced philosophers to be more self-critical about the language they use than they have ever been before, and quite apart from the intrinsic fascination of the problems of the philosophy of language, such criticism is good discipline. Nowhere is the temptation to talk nonsense parading as profundity as great as in philosophy. Further, in forcing philosophers' attention upon language, the positivists are continuing a tendency that is characteristic of the philosophy of Kant: to examine the tools of knowledge in order to discover the limits of possible knowledge. A wise fisherman will make sure that there are not too many holes in his net before he starts out fishing. A wise philosopher, said Kant, will inquire into the powers of human reason before exerting, perhaps wasting, his intellect to unfold the secrets of the universe. A wise philosopher, says the logical positivist, knows that only what can be expressed in meaningful statements deserves to be called "knowledge." Therefore he must try to discover the limits of meaningful language, to formulate a general criterion of significant statements.

A good many eminent contemporary philosophers join the critics of logical positivism in feeling that the formulation of a general criterion of distinction between sense and nonsense is a hopeless enterprise, or that at any rate the line of demarcation cannot be drawn in terms of the notion of empirical verification. Yet, these same philosophers are congenial to logical positivism, perhaps more so than they like to admit, in recognizing that analysis, or clarification of meanings, is the distinctive job of philosophers. Since our readings abound in original examples of specific analyses, it will not be necessary to give an abstract (probably obscure) definition of "analysis." What is the meaning of good, right, free will, mental, physical, necessity, certainty, truth, rational belief, cause, probability? In a sense we all know, but in a sense we don't. We know vaguely, not clearly. One of the tasks of philosophy is to produce a clearer understanding of such fundamental concepts. Whether this is *the* task of philosophy, or at least the only goal of philosophy that could not be better achieved by empirical science or formal logic, is a continuing dispute among professional philosophers—a more fundamental dispute than the one about the merits or demerits of the verifiability theory of meaning.

A. P.

62   Of the Origin of Ideas

David Hume

EVERYONE WILL READILY ALLOW THAT there is a considerable difference between the perceptions of the mind when a man feels the pain of excessive heat or the pleasure of moderate warmth, and when he afterwards recalls to his memory this sensation or anticipates it by his imagination. These faculties may mimic or copy the perceptions of the senses, but they never can entirely reach the force and vivacity of the original sentiment. The utmost we say of them, even when they operate with greatest vigor, is that they represent their object in so lively a manner that we could *almost* say we feel or see it. But, except the mind be disordered by disease or madness, they never can arrive at such a pitch of vivacity as to render these perceptions altogether undistinguishable. All the colors of poetry, however splendid, can never paint natural objects in such a manner as to make the description be taken for a real landscape. The most lively thought is still inferior to the dullest sensation.

We may observe a like distinction to run through all the other perceptions of the mind. A man in a fit of anger is actuated in a very different manner from one who only thinks of that emotion. If you tell me that any person is in love, I easily understand your meaning and form a just conception of his situation, but never can mistake that conception for the real disorders and agitations of the passion. When we reflect on our past sentiments and affections, our thought is a faithful mirror and copies its objects truly, but the colors which it employs are faint and dull in comparison of those in which our original perceptions were clothed. It requires no nice discernment or metaphysical head to mark the distinction between them.

Here, therefore, we may divide all the perceptions of the mind into two classes or species, which are distinguished by their different degrees of force and vivacity. The less forcible and lively are commonly denominated "thoughts" or "ideas." The other species want a name in our language, and

[This selection is Section II of Hume's *An Inquiry Concerning Human Understanding*, a book first published in 1748.]

in most others; I suppose, because it was not requisite for any but philosophical purposes to rank them under a general term or appellation. Let us, therefore, use a little freedom and call them "impressions," employing that word in a sense somewhat different from the usual. By the term "impression," then, I mean all our more lively perceptions, when we hear, or see, or feel, or love, or hate, or desire, or will. And impressions are distinguished from ideas, which are the less lively perceptions of which we are conscious when we reflect on any of those sensations or movements above mentioned.

Nothing, at first view, may seem more unbounded than the thought of man, which not only escapes all human power and authority, but is not even restrained within the limits of nature and reality. To form monsters and join incongruous shapes and appearances costs the imagination no more trouble than to conceive the most natural and familiar objects. And while the body is confined to one planet, along which it creeps with pain and difficulty, the thought can in an instant transport us into the most distant regions of the universe, or even beyond the universe into the unbounded chaos where nature is supposed to lie in total confusion. What never was seen or heard of, may yet be conceived, nor is anything beyond the power of thought except what implies an absolute contradiction.

But though our thought seems to possess this unbounded liberty, we shall find upon a nearer examination that it is really confined within very narrow limits, and that all this creative power of the mind amounts to no more than the faculty of compounding, transposing, augmenting, or diminishing the materials afforded us by the senses and experience. When we think of a golden mountain, we only join two consistent ideas, "gold" and "mountain," with which we were formerly acquainted. A virtuous horse we can conceive, because, from our own feeling, we can conceive virtue; and this we may unite to the figure and shape of a horse, which is an animal familiar to us. In short, all the materials of thinking are derived either from our outward or inward sentiment; the mixture and composition of these belongs alone to the mind and will, or, to express myself in philosophical language, all our ideas or more feeble perceptions are copies of our impressions or more lively ones.

To prove this, the two following arguments will, I hope, be sufficient. *First,* when we analyze our thoughts or ideas, however compounded or sublime, we always find that they resolve themselves into such simple ideas as were copied from a precedent feeling or sentiment. Even those ideas which at first view seem the most wide of this origin are found, upon a nearer scrutiny, to be derived from it. The idea of God, as meaning an infinitely intelligent, wise, and good Being, arises from reflecting on the operations of our own mind and augmenting, without limit, those qualities of goodness and wisdom. We may prosecute this inquiry to what length we please; where we shall always find that every idea which we examine is copied from a similar impression. Those who would assert that this position is not universally true, nor without exception, have only one, and that an easy, method of refuting it by producing that idea which, in their opinion, is not derived from this source. It will then be incumbent on us, if we would maintain our doctrine, to produce the impression or lively perception which corresponds to it.

Secondly, if it happen, from a defect of the organ, that a man is not susceptible of any species of sensation, we always find that he is as little susceptible of the correspondent idea. A blind man can form no notion of colors, a deaf man of sounds. Restore either of them that sense in which he is deficient by opening this new inlet for his sensations, you also open an inlet for the ideas, and he finds no difficulty in conceiving these objects. The case is the same if the object proper for exciting any sensation has never been applied to the organ. A Laplander or Negro has no notion of the relish of wine. And though there are few or no instances of a like deficiency in the mind where a person has never felt or is wholly incapable of a sentiment or passion that belongs to his species, yet we find the same observation to take place in a less degree. A man of mild manners can form no idea of inveterate revenge or cruelty, nor can a selfish heart easily conceive the heights of friendship and generosity. It is readily allowed that other beings may possess many senses of which we can have no conception, because the ideas of them have never been introduced to us in the only manner by which an idea can have access to the mind, to wit, by the actual feeling and sensation.

There is, however, one contradictory phenomenon which may prove that it is not absolutely impossible for ideas to arise independent of their correspondent impressions. I believe it will readily be allowed that the several distinct ideas of color, which enter by the eye, or those of sound, which are conveyed by the ear, are really different from each other, though at the same time resembling. Now, if this be true of different colors, it must be no less so of the different shades of the same color; and each shade produces a distinct idea, independent of the rest. For if this should be denied, it is possible, by the continual graduation of shades, to run a color insensibly into what is most remote from it; and if you will not allow any of the means to be different, you cannot, without absurdity, deny the extremes to be the same. Suppose, therefore, a person to have enjoyed his sight for thirty years and to have become perfectly acquainted with colors of all kinds, except one particular shade of blue, for instance, which it never has been his fortune to meet with; let all the different shades of that color, except that single one, be placed before him, descending gradually from the deepest to the lightest, it is plain that he will perceive a blank where that shade is wanting, and will be sensible that there is a greater distance in that place between the contiguous colors than in any other. Now I ask whether it be possible for him, from his own imagination, to supply this deficiency and raise up to himself the idea of that particular shade, though it had never been conveyed to him by his senses? I believe there are few but will be of opinion that he can; and this may serve as a proof that the simple ideas are not always, in every instance, derived from the correspondent impressions, though this instance is so singular that it is scarcely worth our observing, and does not merit that for it alone we should alter our general maxim.

Here, therefore, is a proposition which not only seems in itself simple and intelligible, but, if a proper use were made of it, might render every dispute equally intelligible, and banish all that jargon which has so long taken possession of metaphysical reasonings and drawn disgrace upon them. All ideas, especially abstract ones, are naturally faint and obscure. The mind has but a slender hold of them. They are apt to be confounded with other resembling ideas; and when we have often employed any term, though without a distinct meaning, we are apt to imagine it has a determinate idea annexed to it. On the contrary, all impressions, that is, all sensations either outward or inward, are strong and vivid. The limits between them are more exactly determined, nor is it easy to fall into any error or mistake with regard to them. When we entertain, therefore, any suspicion that a philosophical term is employed without any meaning or idea (as is but too frequent), we need but inquire, *from what impression is that supposed idea derived?* And if it be impossible to assign any, this will serve to confirm our suspicion. By bringing ideas in so clear a light, we may reasonably hope to remove all dispute which may arise concerning their nature and reality.

63   Demonstration of the
Impossibility of Metaphysics

A. J. Ayer

Foreword

THE VIEWS EXPRESSED IN THIS PAPER are not original. The work of Wittgenstein inspired it. The arguments which it contains are for the most part such as have been used by writers in *Erkenntnis,* notably by Moritz Schlick in his "Positivismus und Realismus" and Rudolf Carnap in his "Überwindung der Metaphysik durch logische Analyse der Sprache." But some may find my presentation of them the clearer. And I hope to convince others by whom the work of Wittgenstein and the Viennese school has so far been ignored or misunderstood.

Definition of Metaphysics

My purpose is to prove that any attempt to describe the nature or even to assert the existence of something lying beyond the reach of empirical observation must consist in the enunciation of pseudo-propositions, a pseudo-proposition being a series of words that may seem to have the structure of a sentence but is in fact meaningless. I call this a demonstra-

[This article originally appeared in *Mind,* 1934. It is here reprinted with the kind permission of the author and the editor of *Mind.* In fairness to Professor Ayer it should be mentioned that he later modified his views on certain of the topics he discussed in this early piece. He treated the same subject in Chapter I of *Language, Truth and Logic* (1936) and again in the preface to the second edition of the same work (1946). His most recent views on the subject may be found in his introduction to *Logical Positivism* (The Free Press, Glencoe, Illinois, 1959). *Logical Positivism* also contains English translations of the two papers mentioned in the first paragraph of this article.]

tion of the impossibility of metaphysics because I define a metaphysical enquiry as an enquiry into the nature of the reality underlying or transcending the phenomena which the special sciences are content to study. Accordingly if I succeeded in showing that even to ask whether there is a reality underlying the world of phenomena is to formulate a bogus question, so that any assertion about the existence or nature of such a reality is a piece of nonsense, I shall have demonstrated the impossibility of metaphysics in the sense in which I am using the term. If anyone considers this an arbitrary definition, let him refer to any work which he would call metaphysical, and consider how it differs from an enquiry in one of the special sciences. He will find, not that the authors are merely using different means to derive from the same empirical premises the same sort of knowledge, but that they are seeking totally different types of knowledge. The metaphysician is concerned with a reality transcending the phenomena about which the scientist makes his generalizations. The metaphysician rejects the methods of the scientist, not because he believes them to be unfruitful in the field in which the scientist operates, but because he believes that by his own metaphysical methods he will be able to obtain knowledge in his own metaphysical field. It will be shown in this paper not that the metaphysician ought to use scientific methods to attain his end, but that the end itself is vain. Whatever form of reasoning he employs, he succeeds in saying nothing.

Comparisons with Kant's Procedure

That the speculative reason falls into self-contradiction when it ventures out beyond the limits of experience is a proposition maintained by Kant. But by his formulation of the matter he is committed to a view different from that which will here be maintained. For he implies that there is a transcendent reality, but the constitution of our speculative reason is such that we cannot hope to gain knowledge of it: he should therefore find no absurdity in imagining that some other being, say a god, had knowledge of it, even though the existence of such a being could not be proved. Whereas on our view to say that there is or that there is not a transcendent reality is to utter a pseudo-proposition, a word-series empty of logical content: and no supposition about the knowledge of a higher reality possessed by a higher being is for us even a significant hypothesis. The difference between the two views is best expressed by saying that while the speculative reason was in virtue of its own nature incapable of solving, our aim is to show that these are not genuine problems.

No criticism of Kant's transcendental philosophy will be undertaken in this paper. But the method by which we demonstrate the impossibility of metaphysics, in the sense in which Kant too held it to be impossible, serves also to show that no knowledge is both synthetic and *a priori*. And this is enough to prove the impossibility of metaphysics, in the special sense which

Kant reserved for the term, though it in no way discredits the excellent pieces of philosophical analysis which the *Critique of Pure Reason* contains.

Formulation of a Criterion of Significance

The method of achieving these results lies in the provision of a criterion by which the genuineness of all *prima facie* propositions may be tested. Having laid down the conditions which must be fulfilled by whatever is to be a significant proposition, we shall find that the propositions of metaphysics fail to satisfy the conditions and are therefore meaningless.

What is it, then, that we are asking when we ask what is the meaning of a proposition? I say "ask the meaning of a proposition" rather than "ask the meaning of a concept," because questions about the meaning of concepts reduce themselves to questions about the meanings of propositions. To discover the meaning of a concept we form its corresponding primary proposition, *i.e.,* the simplest proposition in which it can significantly occur, and attempt to analyse this. I repeat "what is it that we are asking when we ask what is the meaning of a proposition?" There are various ways in which the correct answer can be formulated. One is to say that we are asking what are the propositions to which the proposition in question is reducible. For instance, if "being an amphisbæna" means "being a serpent with a head at both ends," then the proposition "X is an amphisbæna" is reducible to (or derivable from) the propositions "X is a serpent" and "X has a head at either end of its body." These propositions are in turn reducible to others until we reach the elementary propositions which are not descriptive at all but ostensive. When the analysis reaches its furthest point the meaning of the proposition can no longer be defined in terms of other propositions but only pointed to or shown. It is to this process that those philosophers refer who say that philosophy is an activity and not a doctrine.

Alternatively the procedure of definition may be described by saying that to give the meaning of a proposition is to give the conditions under which it would be true and those under which it would be false. I understand a proposition if I know what observations I must make in order to establish its truth or falsity. This may be more succinctly expressed by saying that I understand a proposition when I know what facts would verify it. To indicate the situation which verifies a proposition is to indicate what the proposition means.

Application of the Criterion

Let us assume that some one says of my cat that it is corylous. I fail to understand him and enquire what circumstances would make it true to say that the cat was corylous. He replies "its having blue eyes." I conclude that in the sense in which he uses the word corylous "X is corylous" means "X has blue eyes." If he says that, although the fact that my cat has blue eyes and no other fact makes it true to say that it is corylous, nevertheless he means by "corylous" something more than "blue-eyed," we may infer that the use of the word "corylous" has for him a certain emotional value which is absent when he merely says "blue-eyed." But so long as its having blue eyes is all that is necessary to establish the truth of the proposition that something is corylous, and its having eyes of another colour all that is necessary to establish its falsehood, then "having blue eyes" is all that "being corylous" means.

In the case when something is called corylous and no description or indication can be given of the situation which verifies the proposition, we must conclude that the assertion is meaningless. If the speaker protests that he does mean something, but nothing that mere observation can establish, we allow that he has certain feelings which are in some way connected with the emission of the sound "corylous": and it may be a matter of interest to us that he should express these feelings. But he does not thereby make any assertion about the world. He utters a succession of words, but they do not form a genuine proposition. His sentence may provide good evidence of his feelings. In itself it has no sense.

So in every case where we have a series of words which seems to be a good grammatical sentence, and we wish to discover whether it really makes sense—i.e., whether it expresses a genuine proposition—we must consider what are the circumstances in which the proposition apparently expressed would be called true or false: what difference in the world its truth or falsity would entail. And if those who have uttered it or profess to understand it are unable to describe what in the world would be different if it were true or false, or in any way to show how it could be verified, then we must conclude that nothing has been asserted. The series of words in question does not express a genuine proposition at all, but is as much a piece of nonsense as "the moon is the square root of three" or "Lenin or coffee how." The difference is merely that in some cases where a very slight transformation of the phrase, say the alteration of a single word, would turn it into a propositional sign, its senselessness is harder to detect.

Meaninglessness of Every Metaphysical Assertion

In this way it can quickly be shown that any metaphysical assertion is nonsensical. It is not necessary to take a list of metaphysical terms such as the Absolute, the Unconditioned, the Ego, and so forth, and prove each of them to be meaningless: for it follows from the task metaphysics sets itself that all its assertions must be nonsense. For it is the aim of metaphysics to describe a reality lying beyond experience, and therefore any proposition which would be verified by empirical observation is *ipso facto* not metaphysical. But what no observation could verify is not a proposition. The fundamental postulate of metaphysics "There is a super- (or hinter-) phenomenal reality" is itself not a proposition. For there is no observation or series of observations we could conceivably make by which its truth or falsehood would be determined. It may seem to be a proposition, having the sensible form of a proposition. But nothing is asserted by it.

An example may make this clearer. The old conflict between Idealism and Realism is a fine instance of an illusory problem. Let us assume that a picture is unearthed, and that the finder suggests that it was painted by Goya. There are definite means of settling this question. The critics examine the picture and consider what points of resemblance it has to other works of Goya. They see if there is any contemporary or subsequent reference to the existence of such a work—and so on. Suppose now that two of the experts have also read philosophy and raise a further point of dispute. One says that the picture is a collection of ideas (his own or God's): the other that its colours are objectively real. What possible means have they of settling the question? Can either of them indicate any circumstances in which to the question "are those colours a collection of ideas?" or to the question "are those colours objective sensibilia?" the answer "yes" or "no" could be given? If they cannot then no such questions arise. And plainly they cannot. If it is raining now outside my window my observations are different from what they would be if it were fine. I assert that it rains and my proposition is verifiable. I can indicate the situation by which its truth or falsity is established. But if I ask "is the rain real or ideal?" this is a question which no observations enable me to answer. It is accordingly not a genuine question at all.

It is advisable here to remove a possible source of misunderstanding. I am not maintaining that if we wish to discover whether in a *prima facie* proposition anything is really being asserted, we must consider whether what seems to be asserted is practically verifiable. As Professor Schlick has pointed out, it makes perfectly good sense to say "there is a mountain 10,000 feet high on the other side of the moon," although this is a proposition which through practical disabilities we are not and may never be in a position to verify. But it is in principle verifiable. We know what sort of observations would verify or falsify it. If we got to the other side of the moon we should know how to settle the question. But the assertions of metaphysics are in principle unverifiable. We may take up any position in space and time that our imagination allows us to occupy, no observation that we can make therefrom makes it even probable in the least degree that any answer to a metaphysical question is correct. And therefore we conclude that there are no such questions.

Metaphysical Assertions Not Hypotheses

So the conclusion is not that metaphysical assertions are uncertain or arbitrary or even false, but that they are nonsensical. They are not hypotheses, in the sense in which general propositions of law are hypotheses. It is true that assertions of such general propositions are not assertions of fact in the way that assertions of singular propositions are assertions of fact. To that extent they are in no better case than metaphysical assertions. But variable hypotheticals (general propositions of law) make sense in a way in which metaphysical assertions do not. For a hypothesis has grounds. A certain sequence of events occurs and a hypothesis is formulated to account for it—i.e., on the strength of the hypothesis, when we make one such observation, we assume that we shall be able to make the others. It is the essence of a hypothesis that it admits of being used. In fact, the meaning of such general propositions is defined by reference to the situations in which they serve as rules for prediction, just as their truth is defined by reference to the accuracy of the predictions to which believing them gives rise. A so-called hypothesis which is not relevant to any situation is not a hypothesis at all. As a general proposition it is senseless. Now there is no situation in which belief in a metaphysical proposition bridges past and potential observations, in the way in which my belief in the poisonousness of arsenic connects my observation of a man's swallowing it with my expectation that he will shortly die. Therefore metaphysical propositions are not hypotheses. For they account for nothing.

How Metaphysics Has Arisen. Defense against the Objection from Piety

There may be some who find no flaw in our reasoning and yet hesitate to accept the conclusion that all metaphysical assertions are nonsensical. For such hesitation there appear to remain three grounds. First, a failure to understand how, if they are unintentionally nonsensical, such assertions ever come to be made. Secondly, a doubt whether metaphysical assertions, if nonsensical, could be made so often. Thirdly, a reluctance to admit that so many men of great intellect could have made a number of what they considered to be true and important statements, which are in fact not statements at all. I proceed to answer these objections in the order in which they have been stated.

(1) The fact that sentences may appear grammatically on a level and yet have quite different logical forms makes it easy for philosophers to formulate bogus questions. For example, "he suffers from an imaginary illness" is grammatically on a par with "he suffers from a severe illness." And philosophers are in consequence misled into asking what sort of being imaginary objects have, on the ground that they must have some sort of being in order to be imaginary, since what has no being can have no property. But in fact, as a minority of distinguished philosophers have seen, being imaginary is not a property like being severe; and "his illness is imaginary" means "he is not ill although he thinks he is." When the proposition is so formulated, the bogus question "what is the ontological

status of an imaginary illness?" does not even seem to arise. The sentence "his illness is imaginary" is of a type calculated to lead philosophers astray; but it is translatable into a sentence wherein no such danger lies. The question "what type of object is an imaginary object?" and the answer sometimes given to it that "it is a subsistent entity" are both pieces of sheer nonsense.

The case of the word "subsist" illustrates how words which have meaning in a certain context are used by philosophers in a context where they are meaningless. The sentence "he subsists on a small income" makes perfectly good sense. "Subsists" here means "manages to exist," "keeps himself alive." Philosophers, falling into the trap mentioned above, wish to assert that imaginary and illusory objects have some sort of being. It seems a self-contradiction to say that they exist. But somehow or other they "manage to keep alive." Therefore it is said that they subsist. But in this usage the word "subsist" is nonsense. It is a mere symbol of confusion.

There is a further class of words which are coined as a direct outcome of logical mistakes and possess no meaning from the outset. Such is the word "being" used as a substantive. This error originated with the Greeks. Because where X is an incomplete symbol it makes sense in some cases to say "X exists" ($\dot{\epsilon}\sigma\tau\iota\nu$) and existence is wrongly assumed to be a property, it seems legitimate to talk about the being ($o\dot{\upsilon}\sigma\iota\alpha$) of X, just as one may talk about the cleverness of X where it makes sense to say that X is clever. Once it is seen that "X exists" means not that a something X has a certain property "being" but merely that something is X—is or is an X, the temptation to ask questions about "being" disappears.

(2) One reason for which men have persistently succumbed to the temptation to assert something metaphysical is that they are not content to make observations and generalisations and predictions but desire also to express their feelings about the world. Literature and the arts afford the most satisfactory medium for such expression. Metaphysics results when men attempt to extrapolate their emotions: they wish to present them not as feelings of their own, but somehow objectively as facts; therefore they express them in the form of argument and theory. But nothing is thereby asserted. All that has happened is that the form of a rational enquiry has been used for the expression of emotions which more commonly find their outlet in a work of literature or art.

Another motive for the construction of metaphysical systems arises from a man's desire to unify his knowledge. In the natural sciences one is not content with the discovery of some uniform sequence of events: one seeks also to explain it, that is, to show its occurrence to have been predictable from knowledge of some more general principle. The metaphysician feels this impulse. But, lacking either the patience or the ability to understand the propositions of natural science, being ignorant of the grounds on which the scientist's hypotheses are based and the uses which they serve, he postulates a new and superior kind of knowledge, obtainable by his own ready method of intellectual intuition. And succeeds in knowing nothing.

(3) We need not go to the length of saying that all the great men who have written books of metaphysics are poets who have chosen what seems to us an unsuitable medium of expression. For, in many cases, once the work has been made to shed its metaphysical coating, pieces of genuine philosophizing remain. For instance, Berkeley may be regarded not as one who denied the existence of matter, but as one who attempted to analyse the concept of a physical object. His merit is to have shown that when we make a proposition about a physical object we are giving some more complicated statement than the description of a single sense-datum. Similarly Locke, as Mr. Ryle has pointed out, deserves our gratitude for distinguishing our different types of inquiry, Leibniz for maintaining that what is meant by a body's having a certain position in space is that it lies in certain spatial relations to other bodies, and so forth. Whereby it appears that the discovery that all metaphysical assertions are nonsensical is consistent with piety towards the great philosophers of the past.

Justification of Our Procedure

In sum, as metaphysical propositions are by definition such as no possible experience could verify, and as the theoretical possibility of verification has been taken as our criterion of significance, there is no difficulty in concluding that metaphysical propositions are meaningless. There is no escape from this conclusion, provided that we can show that our criterion is correct. Can we do this?

If we assert that the meaning of a proposition consists in its method of verification, the proposition which this sentence would naturally be taken to assert would be a proposition about the meaning of the concept of meaning. So interpreted it would be an assertion about what was meant by the word "meaning" in one of its common uses; and as such a significant empirical proposition. Observation of the linguistic habits of the class of people whose use of the "meaning" the proposition was about would show it to be true or false: and whatever their linguistic habits were, they might logically have been otherwise. But this is not the proposition which formulating our criterion we intended to assert. In our criterion we have something that is presupposed in any enquiry into the meaning of meaning, or any other philosophical enquiry, and therefore cannot appear as the conclusion of such an enquiry. For the business of philosophy is to give definitions. And in setting out to define meaning or any other concept we must adopt some rule according to which we conduct our enquiry, and by reference to which we determine whether its conclusions are correct. In formulating our criterion we are attempting to show what this rule should be. We cannot do more.

It may be doubted by some whether we can even do as much. They would say that the *prima facie* proposition in which we formulated our criterion was itself nonsensical, and that it only seemed to be significant because we expressed it in sentences which, like the one given just above, would naturally be understood in a way other than we intended them to be. What we really mean was something that cannot be significantly said. To adopt this standpoint is to follow the example of Wittgenstein, who at the end of his *Tractatus Logico-Philosophicus* asserts that the propositions contained in it are nonsensical. They are a means for enabling the sympathetic reader to "see the world rightly." Having profited by them he must discard them. He must throw away the ladder after he has climbed up on it. But it is not a secure standpoint. Having said something which on your own showing no one can say, you attempt to save your face by pretending you really have not said it. But if you admit that your propositions are nonsensical, what ground have you given anybody for accepting the conclusions that you deduce from them? If we admit that the proposition in which we attempt to formulate our criterion of significance is nonsensical, does not our whole demonstration of the impossibility of metaphysics collapse? We may be able to *see* that metaphysical propositions are nonsensical and by making a special set of nonsensical utterances we may induce others to see it also: but for the rest we must do as Wittgenstein recommends: wait until some one says something metaphysical and then show him that he has used certain symbols to which no meaning can be attached; and this would only prove that one more attempt to assert a significant metaphysical proposition had been a failure, not that no attempt could ever be a success.

Fortunately we can assert all that we need without entering the realm of the unsayable. The proposition "the way to discover whether a *prima facie* proposition has meaning, and what its meaning is, is to consider what experience would verify it" is a significant empirical proposition. It asserts that certain discoveries, in fact those discoveries about the meaning of concepts which it is the business of philosophy to make, may be made and checked by using a certain criterion. We test the validity of the criterion by seeing if the results obtained by means of it are accurate. The difficulty is that in all doubtful cases, which means in very nearly all cases, we have recourse to the criterion to decide whether some suggested definition is correct. This procedure is obviously circular. What saves it from being wholly vicious is the possibility of determining psychologically in certain cases that a proposition is significant without it being necessary to apply the criterion. There are some *prima facie* propositions which by universal agreement are given as significant and some expressions which are agreed to be meaningless. Trusting our criterion if it accepts the former class and rejects the latter, we apply it to such doubtful cases as that of the propositions of metaphysics, and if they fail to satisfy it we pronounce them nonsensical. If we were to take as our criterion of significance the possibility of influencing action we should allow metaphysical propositions to be significant, but we should lose faith in our criterion when we found that it also admitted the significance of expressions which were universally agreed to be meaningless: since there is practically no limit to what can influence action.

If therefore a philosopher maintains that our criterion is too narrow and that metaphysical propositions are significant, it is for him to put forward a more liberal criterion: one that allows the significance of metaphysical propositions yet is not so liberal as to allow the significance of expressions such as "jealousy pronoun live" or "siffle hip brim" which are agreed by all parties to be meaningless. Until he can do this, he has no right to object to our procedure and no means of escaping our conclusions.

64   Meaninglessness

A. C. Ewing

IN THIS ARTICLE I INTEND TO EXAMINE
the conditions under which a sentence may be said to be meaningless. I
have been stimulated to do so by a belief that present-day thinkers are
often far too ready to dismiss a philosophical statement as meaningless,
and particularly by my opposition to the theory that the meaning of all
statements is to be analysed solely in terms of verification by sense-
experience. (Note that only sentences can be properly said to have meaning, not propositions. A proposition is what certain sorts of sentences
mean and cannot again itself have meaning except in a quite different
sense of the word, such as that in which the "meaning" of something is
equivalent to its implications. A meaningful sentence is a sentence which
expresses a proposition, a meaningless sentence is a sentence which expresses no proposition. "Statement," on the other hand, is used both to
stand for a proposition and for a sentence expressing a proposition. I
shall use it in the latter sense. I am not hereby intending to imply that
propositions are separate subsistent entities; this is not a theory which I
hold, but I have no time to discuss the question here). In this article
I shall use the term *positivist* for short to mean simply "upholder of any
of the verification theories which I shall consider." I shall use "meaning"
in the same sense in which it would be used, say, in the *Strand Magazine*.

The Verification Theory of Meaning Is Not Verifiable

I shall first take the extremer form of the theory, according to which
a statement is said to be verifiable, and therefore to have meaning, if and
only if its truth could be conclusively established by sense-experience.
"Sense-experience" is used to include (a) sense-perception, (b) intro-

[This article originally appeared in *Mind*, 1937. It is here reprinted, with omissions, by
the kind permission of the author and the editor of *Mind*.]

spection of images and emotions. Positivists would not usually admit that the occurrence of "mental acts" could be verified by experience, and would presumably have either to regard these as logical constructions out of sense-data and images, or deny their existence altogether. Still less would the term cover apprehension of "non-natural" properties or relations. Now I should have thought the first duty of any advocate of a verification theory of meaning would be to inquire how his theory itself was to be verified, and I propose to be a good positivist in this one case at least and put the question to myself. How could we verify the statement that all meaningful statements are verifiable?

The first difficulty is that it is a universal proposition and therefore can never be conclusively established merely by experience; but we shall relax the condition, as probably most positivists themselves would, so far as to allow of progressive and incomplete verification, and count the verification theory of meaning as verified for all practical purposes if an adequate number of samples of all the different kinds of meaningful statements we can think of are found on examination to be verifiable and we are unable to think of any which are not verifiable. I doubt the consistency of this but I will be as charitable as possible and let it pass. How could the theory then be verified in this sense? It would no doubt be verified if we could take examples of all the different kinds of statements which have ever been made, find by direct inspection what was meant by them, and then discover that they were all verifiable. But I do not think the positivist would or could admit that we can always detect the meanings of statements by direct inspection. If we always can, why all the difficulties about analysis? And it is not by any means sufficient for the purpose that we should *sometimes* be able to do so, for what has to be verified is a proposition about all, not about some, meaningful statements. I doubt in fact whether the positivist would even admit that meaning is the sort of thing that could ever be detected by direct inspection. Further, if we relied on the meaning that statements seem to have when we try to inspect their meaning directly, I do not see how we could ever become positivists. It is surely not by direct inspection of the propositions in question that a positivist learns that propositions about other people's toothache are really propositions about his own sense-data, or that so-called propositions about the past are merely rules for the prediction of those experiences in the future which would verify them. Surely they only come to such conclusions because they first assume the general principle that all meaningful statements are verifiable and then deduce that, since statements about other people can be verifiable only if they are analysed as statements about one's own sense-data, they must be thus analysed. No doubt they can find examples of meaningful statements which are directly verifiable. Perhaps even all meaningful statements on certain kinds of topics are thus verifiable, *e.g.,* all singular propositions about one's present sense-data; but to argue that, because this is true of all of one kind of proposition, it is true of other kinds is as dangerous as to argue that because cats always live on the land, and cats and whales are both mammals, whales must also live on the land. Finally, I do not see how the positivists could establish the truth of their view even in a single case merely by sense-experience. For how can we ever know by sense-experience that there is not a part of the meaning of a statement that we cannot verify? The fact that we do not have any sense-experience of such a part proves nothing, since the point at issue is whether there is something in what we mean beyond sense-experience; and how can we know by sense-experience that there is not?

It therefore seems impossible that the verification theory could be verified in the way suggested, and I cannot conceive what other way there could be of verifying it. For according to the fundamental principles of those who hold the theory it could not be established by any sort of *a priori* argument, and therefore it must presumably be established, if at all, by the empirical examination of particular cases. Now, not merely is it the case that it has not in fact been verified in that way; we have just seen that it is logically impossible that it could be so verified. The statement that all meaningful statements are verifiable is therefore not itself verifiable. It follows that if it is true it is meaningless. But a sentence cannot possibly be both true and meaningless. Therefore the sentence in question cannot be true, but must be either meaningless or false. According to my view it is the latter.

Perhaps it will be said that, although the verification theory is nonsense, it is important and useful nonsense, while the kind of nonsense I talk is unimportant and useless nonsense. But if the statement that it is important and useful nonsense is to be accepted this statement in turn ought to be verified by sense-experience, and how that could possibly be done puzzles me. It might be held that it is useful because it helps to solve philosophical problems; but how can we tell by sense-experience whether a philosophical problem is solved or not? The mere fact that we do not feel an emotion of puzzlement does not prove that we have reached a solution. Otherwise unlettered peasants would have solved all philosophical problems far better than philosophers, and persistent neglect to think would be the golden method for attaining success in philosophy. Also the method prescribed might easily remove the emotion of puzzlement in some men but not in others, and be useful for some philosophical problems but misleading for others.

The Verification Theory of Meaning
Is Not Susceptible of A Priori Proof

It might be suggested that the statement of the verification theory should be regarded as a tautology and therefore as meaningless only in the comparatively innocuous sense in which all correct *a priori* statements are meaningless according to the theory. But, if this line were taken, it would be necessary to show that some formal contradiction was committed by denying the theory; and this is not claimed. The only *a priori* propositions that the theory admits are analytic tautologies, if these indeed can be called propositions, but the statement of the theory itself is essentially synthetic. It gives new information, and information not capable of formal proof. The theory therefore cannot, if it is true, be known *a priori*. No *a priori* arguments for it are possible on its own showing since it is synthetic, and it therefore cannot be meaningful even in the modified sense in which a positivist might admit analytic *a priori* statements to be so. It can be meaningful only in the sense in which synthetic statements are supposed to be, i.e., in the sense of being verifiable by sense-experience, and this I claim to have shown it can never be. It is true that it might be deduced analytically from some definition of meaning, but the definition itself must, like all definitions, be synthetic. A proposition giving an analysis must be distinguished from an analytic proposition, or, to put the same thing in different language, a proposition true by definition is not the same as a definition. There can be no self-contradiction in denying a given analysis of the meaning of a term unless some definition is already presupposed, thus begging the question; for there certainly is no analytic logically necessary connection between a word and the analysis of its meaning, and this undoubtedly applies to the word, meaning, itself. That certain marks or noises express propositions and others do not is surely a synthetic proposition if any is. No doubt a positivist can decide to use "meaning" in any way he chooses, but then he will not be giving an analysis of the ordinary sense of "meaning," but inventing an arbitrary usage of his own. However, this can hardly be what he is doing, for he certainly claims that those who use meaning in a sense in which unverifiable statements are meaningful are committing an error, attributing to certain statements a property they do not possess.

The positivist is thus debarred from giving *a priori* reasons for his theory because it is synthetic, and also from giving empirical reasons because it cannot be based on an empirical inspection of meaning. His only refuge is to make his theory a purely arbitrary convention which therefore requires no justification. But, if this is allowed, a philosopher may assert anything whatever he pleases. The positivist is excused from having to prove his theory, but only at the expense of admitting that there is no more ground for accepting it than there is for accepting any theory whatever. Even such an argument as that it is simpler than other accounts or more useful for establishing deductive systems would be an appeal to a criterion conformity with which certainly cannot be discovered by sense-experience. And it remains true that his theory could mean nothing on its own showing, being neither an *a priori* analytic proposition nor one verifiable by sense-experience.

Now if a thory means nothing I really cannot be expected to refute it. Perhaps it is a very good lyrical expression of the positivist's emotions, but while not wishing to show any lack of sympathy towards his emotions I cannot see that this of itself could make it a useful contribution to philosophy. I add the autobiographical detail that I have never had any emotion myself of which it seemed to me at all a suitable expression. Or perhaps it is a command to treat only those propositions as meaningful which are verifiable; but with all due respect to the positivists I do not see why I should obey their commands unless they can show me that I (or the world) will gain by my doing so.

Is Experience Really Irrelevant to Metaphysical Statements?

Let us now turn to the milder form of the theory which was sponsored by Mr. Ayer in *Language, Truth and Logic*. According to this a statement is meaningful if and only if it is logically possible that observations might be made which would be relevant to its truth or falsehood, i.e., make its truth more or less probable (he does not use the word probable here, but since he thinks no conclusive verification of anything is possible this must be what he means). Now this formulation of the theory does not give Mr. Ayer nearly as much as he wants. For, with the possible exception of the ontological proof, which I do not wish to defend, it is doubtful whether any philosophers have ever asserted a proposition to the truth of which they did not think some experience or other was relevant. What I mean may be made clear by taking a few examples from among the most abstract of metaphysical arguments. The cosmological proof, for instance, starts with the premise that something or other exists, this being regarded as given in experience; the argument for an Absolute Mind including all human minds professes to start from the incomplete and incoherent character of our experience, which is held therefore to point to a more complete experience, and to be supported by citing the empirical facts of co-operation and love; the realist view of physical objects claims to be based on the experience of perception either as in itself a proof of their existence (the direct theory of perception) or as a premise from which causal inferences can be made showing that they probably exist. No doubt in some of the cases I have mentioned the metaphysician may be wrong in thinking that experience renders his conclusion probable, but we can only decide whether this is so after we have examined and refuted his argument. Since he claims that experience is relevant we cannot dismiss his theory as meaningless without examination, as the positivist would like to do, merely on the ground that its probability cannot be affected by any experience. Most metaphysical arguments may be hopelessly wrong, but I do not see how we can tell whether they are except by examining them separately on their own merits, to see whether they can really be supported by experience. We cannot nonsuit all of them *en masse* by the positivist criterion without begging the whole question.

The statement that the world of sense-experience is altogether unreal, which is taken by Mr. Ayer as a good example of a nonsensical utterance, is certainly a statement to the truth or falsity of which experience is relevant, and it should therefore by his criterion have a meaning. For it is contradicted by all our sense-experience and therefore ought to be rejected as false (not meaningless), unless the man who makes it is speaking in metaphors. And, even if he is speaking in metaphors and does not mean "altogether unreal," but, *e.g.,* "incoherent when taken by itself" or "relatively unimportant," his statement certainly claims to be based on the alleged self-contradictory or otherwise defective character of our sense-experience, and therefore the specific empirical character of our sense-experience is certainly relevant to it. Again take the statement that the whole universe was created by a morally perfect God. This would be held by Mr. Ayer to be meaningless, and would be generally admitted to be a metaphysical doctrine if anything is. Yet it is quite clear that empirical facts regarding the amount and distribution of suffering in the world will affect its probability. If we came to the conclusion that there was much more suffering in the world than we had thought and that there were hardly any empirical cases of suffering producing any good result, it would obviously make the truth of the belief in some degree less probable. Further, the truth of the belief would increase the probability of some propositions about the future being true. For it would certainly at least increase the probability of the proposition that I shall survive bodily death being true. Now the latter is a proposition which clearly could be verified and presumably will in fact be verified, if it is true. For if it is true I shall verify it by having experiences after bodily death. The metaphysical proposition about God is therefore one which is relevant to experiential propositions and to which experiential propositions are relevant.

Incidentally the question of survival seems to create a first-class puzzle for the positivists. That I shall survive bodily death is a proposition capable of future verification, if it is true, through my having experiences after death, but the contradictory proposition that I shall not survive bodily death could never by any possible chance be verified because I cannot experience myself as having no experiences. It seems then the positivist ought to conclude that the proposition that I shall survive death is logically necessary because the only alternative is meaningless. But that such a proposition should be logically necessary is obviously inconsistent with his theories; it is clearly synthetic. Therefore I fear he will not be as grateful to me as he ought to be for having shown that his theory has proved that we can never die.

Mr. Ayer has, therefore, not succeeded in giving a criterion which rules out metaphysics any more or less than the proposition he wishes to admit. Further, in its second, as in its first, form it remains highly doubtful whether the verification theory can itself be verified. For we could only verify it by examining all the different kinds of meaningful statements and seeing whether sense-experience was relevant to their truth, i.e., whether they could be proved or refuted by sense-experience or rendered more or less probable. But once a positivist has admitted, as Mr. Ayer has now done, that a statement may have meaning, even if it asserts something which cannot be directly experienced, provided only there could be experiences from which we might make legitimate inferences to the effect that its probability is increased or diminished, he is open to the objection that we cannot possibly learn from sense-experience alone whether an inference is legitimate or not. That B follows from A is not anything that can be sensed, and mere sense-experience cannot justify us even in thinking it probable that it will follow from A unless the sense-experience is accompanied by some principles of probable inference which are not themselves objects of the senses.

If I am right the verification theory is completely suicidal, because, if it succeeds, it shows itself to be meaningless, and therefore not true. But, even if you are not willing to go as far as this with me, you must remember that philosophers have no right to assert a theory without reasons, at least unless they seem to themselves to see quite clearly that it is self-evident; and this cannot be so in the present case, for the positivist would certainly reject self-evidence as a criterion of truth and therefore cannot use it in defense of his own doctrine. Further you must remember that, unless a theory is proved with complete certainty, part of its criterion lies in the consequences which can be deduced from it, and if these are very unplausible they will cast doubt on the theory itself. To refuse to reconsider a theory of yours because it leads to absurd consequences is, unless the theory has been proved with certainty, not to deserve praise for being logical but to deserve blame for being prejudiced. . . .

An Alternative Criterion of Meaninglessness

Having rejected the verification theory of meaning, it is perhaps incumbent on me to give some account of the conditions under which verbal expressions could be said to be meaningless. This I shall now proceed to do. It seems clear that the following classes of expressions, at least, are meaningless.

1. There are sentences which express exclamations, wishes, commands, exhortations. These do not assert propositions, and therefore there is a sense in which they have no meaning, though no doubt in another sense they have a meaning since they can certainly be understood (or misunderstood). It is possible that a philosopher might confuse such a sentence with a sentence expressing a proposition and so utter a

sentence which had no meaning, thinking it had a meaning, though I doubt whether this occurs at all frequently.

2. There are expressions such as "the table is beside" or "Cambridge is between York" which are meaningless because incomplete, i.e., the form of the expression is such as to require an additional term to give it meaning and the additional term is absent. In the first example there is a dyadic relation with only one term, in the second a triadic relation with only two terms. There are, I think, cases where philosophers have thought that probability was a quality, so that you could say A was probable significantly without either asserting or understanding any data to which the probability of A was relative, while probability is really a relative term (the statement, A is probable, made in ordinary conversation is not meaningless, because another term, i.e., one's present data, to which the probability is relative, is understood if not expressed).

3. An expression may be said to be meaningless if it includes some word or words which do not stand for anything. If the meaning of the word in question is complex, it might be said to be meaningless on the ground that it was self-contradictory, in which case it will come under a later heading; but apart from this we might conceivably have a sentence containing indefinable or undefined words which stood, not for something self-contradictory, but for absolutely nothing at all. I do not mean merely "for nothing existent" but for nothing of which we have any idea at all. I do not know any clear instances of sentences containing such words in any philosopher except Lewis Carroll, but it would no doubt be alleged by some philosophers that, *e.g.,* "subsist" as opposed to exist or "good" as used in *Principia Ethica* are examples.

4. An expression (we should hardly call it a sentence) might consist of words all of which had a meaning and yet be itself meaningless because the words were combined in a way contrary to the rules of syntax, *e.g.,* are of fond not dogs cats. The term "syntax" is used here in its strictly grammatical sense, not in the extended sense in which "grammar" is used by certain positivists. I do not know whether there are instances of such expressions in philosophical works excepting those due to momentary slips or misprints.

There no doubt are these four classes of meaningless expressions, but I come now to two other alleged classes of meaningless sentences, about which I feel a good deal of doubt. In fact I shall contend against most philosophers that they are not meaningless at all.

5. It is usually held that a sentence which ascribes to something a relatively determinate value of a determinable which does not qualify it is meaningless, whether the determinate value is asserted or denied of it. The most usual example of this cited lately at Cambridge is—Quadratic equations go to race-meeting, the example in my days at Oxford was— Virtue is a fire-shovel. It is generally held that such statements are not false but meaningless. It is further held that their contradictories,— Quadratic equations do not go to race-meetings—and Virtue is not a

fire-shovel,—are not true, but likewise meaningless. This, however, I am prepared to dispute. For after all—quadratic equations do not go to race-meetings—is entailed by—quadratic equations do not move in space, and entails—quadratic equations do not watch the Newmarket horse-races; but, if it is capable of entailing and being entailed, surely it must be a proposition and not a mere meaningless set of words. Again, surely you do really know that quadratic equations do not go to race-meetings? But how could you possibly know it if the words did not express a proposition, did not mean anything? There would be nothing to know.

No doubt if I frequently made assertions such as—Virtue is not a fireshovel—or—Quadratic equations do not go to race-meetings, I should be in danger of being consigned to an asylum, and it may be asked why I should be regarded as a lunatic because I say what is true. The answer is that to qualify as a lunatic it is not necessary to say what is false or meaningless; it is sufficient persistently to say what is true in an unsuitable context. The proposition—$2 + 2 = 4$—is impeccably and indisputably true, but if I frequently asserted this proposition in unsuitable contexts, *e.g.,* whenever anybody asked me a question about something totally different, I should soon be regarded as a lunatic. Now the proposition that quadratic equations do not go to race-meetings is a proposition of such a kind that there is hardly any context in which its assertion is suitable. It is, I hope, suitable in this article, but this is certainly the first occasion in my life on which I have found it suitable to assert it, and most people go through their whole lives without finding such an occasion at all. Consequently the assertion of it outside philosophical gatherings would generally be regarded as a mark of insanity. The reason why the context is never suitable is because the proposition is so obviously true that it can never enter into anybody's mind to think of questioning it, and because, unlike $2 + 2 = 4$, it also happens to be of such a kind that it can never, as far as I know, be used as a means of making inferences that are practically or theoretically useful.

The proposition that quadratic equations do not go to race-meetings belongs to a large class of propositions that may best be characterised as true but misleading. I shall give you another proposition that belongs to this class. The proposition is this—I did not commit more than six murders last week. This proposition, I assert, is true. I did not commit any murders last week, and therefore I did not commit more than six. But it is misleading because nobody would in fact ask whether I had committed more than six murders unless he assumed that I had probably committed some. Similarly, nobody would ask whether quadratic equations went to race-meetings unless he assumed that quadratic equations were at any rate the sort of things that could move in space. Other instances of true but misleading propositions are—I worked an hour yesterday (when I really worked eight), he has not stopped beating his wife (when he never started). No doubt there is an important difference between a proposition such as—Quadratic equations do not attend race-meetings—and the other examples I have mentioned in that it is logically impossible that quadratic equations should attend race-meetings while it is not logically impossible that, *e.g.,* I should have committed six murders last week. All I am suggesting is that the propositions are similar in being both true and misleading, not that they are similar in other respects. . . .*

* The sixth class of allegedly meaningless sentences, whose discussion is here omitted, consists of self-contradictory sentences. (Eds.)

65   Verification and the
Use of Language

G. J. Warnock

I N RECENT YEARS A GREAT DEAL OF attention has been devoted to the concepts of verification and verifiability. The notions of verifying, testing, and confirming have been compared and contrasted—often somewhat arbitrarily: "strong" and "weak" verification have been distinguished—often with misplaced attempts at complete precision. Verification no doubt deserves some such scrutiny on its own account; but it is clear that the main impulse to these inquiries has in fact derived from the belief that verification supplies the key to meaning, and that meaning is the peculiar concern of philosophers. In this article I propose to call in question this latter belief; and so I shall consider the relations between verification and meaning, rather than the notion of verification itself. This will involve the neglect of a good deal of detail; but I hope it will be seen that the neglected detail is inessential.

The position that I wish to establish is briefly this: that an account of meaning in terms of verification must be narrowly restricted, and may be seriously misleading; and that the acceptance of such an account tends to make philosophical arguments dogmatic, arid, and pointless.

(1) In an article called "Meaning and Verification," which appeared in *The Philosophical Review* in 1936, Schlick wrote: "The meaning of a proposition is the method of its verification."

This of course is a slogan, hardly more than a striking epigram. Schlick had other and better things than this to say about meaning. However, both he and others took this slogan more seriously than it deserves; it was brief, memorable, and constantly quoted. It is certainly a neat and convenient

[This is a slightly revised version of an article which originally appeared in *Revue Internationale de Philosophie*, 1951. It is reprinted with the kind permission of author and editor.]

text for discussion, and as such I propose to use it. By bringing out some of the numerous difficulties which it contains we shall, I think, find our way back to certain of Wittgenstein's ideas, which Schlick and others distorted while claiming to amplify them.

But first, it has to be remembered that most advocates of the so-called Verification Principle were by no means disinterested. They were not merely concerned to analyse and to clarify the concept of meaning, but also to "eliminate metaphysics." Conversely, their opponents were eager to keep a place for some such subject. Now it may be the case that, if we look closely into the concept of meaning, we shall find that on some definitions of "metaphysics" there can be no subject-matter to be so called. But there is no point in eliminating a subject arbitrarily characterised; and I do not know (I doubt whether anyone knows) how the term "metaphysics" really ought to be defined. I suspect indeed that it ought *not* to be defined —that it is useless to try to divide philosophy into compartments, and that we are better off without departmental titles. I suggest, then, that we should not concern ourselves either to disallow or to defend the use of the term "metaphysics"; and certainly we should not allow a discussion of meaning to be directed by the merely tactical aim of affixing the label "meaningless" to the work of certain philosophers. No doubt there are good and bad ways of doing philosophy; philosophers have made some wise and many foolish remarks; but there is no short way of separating the wheat from the chaff. The belief that some "principle" will do our work for us is, or may easily become, a lazy belief and an unhelpful prejudice.

(2) "The meaning of a *proposition* is the method of its verification." What then is a proposition? Here we meet at once a serious obscurity. Indeed, according to Schlick's own terminology his slogan must be wrongly stated. For he points out that we ask of a *sentence* what it means, and says that this is to ask what proposition the sentence "stands for" or expresses. (The proposition is "what the sentence means.") Now it would be absurd to speak of the meaning of the meaning of a sentence, or of the meaning of what a sentence "stands for." Presumably, then, we should make an amendment and read: "The meaning of a *sentence* is the method of its verification."

But this is not wholly clear either. Schlick describes a sentence as "a series of words," "a mere row of marks on paper," "a mere sequence of sounds." From these descriptions at least the risk of type-token ambiguity should be eliminated. If I say "It is raining," and you say "It is raining," have two sentences been uttered? Or has the same one sentence been uttered twice? It would be natural to say that, if I write down "It is raining" twice, I make two "rows of marks on paper;" but it is no less natural to say that I write down twice the same one sentence. It is, I believe, in this latter sense that Schlick wishes us to take the term "sentence," i.e. in the sense of "sentence-type." It seems clear, indeed, that we are not, except in very unusual circumstances, concerned with the meaning of a particular row of marks on paper. For I might point to such a row, ask for the meaning, and be told the meaning; and if someone then wrote down a second row of marks exactly like the first row, I would not ask again for the meaning of this second row. I would take it that, in making the second row of marks, he had written down the same sentence; and I have already been told the meaning of this sentence. (This assumption might sometimes be mistaken, but not usually.)

It is further obvious that not all rows of marks, series of words, or sequences of sounds, are sentence-tokens. They may instead be random scratches, lists of names, or tunes; and of such it would be a mistake to ask for the meaning. It would be difficult, perhaps impossible, to define sentence-tokens both usefully and exactly, but for present purposes this is not really necessary. It may be assumed that we can recognize sentence-tokens; and that we use the term "sentence" in such a way that any two or more sentence-tokens of the same type may be regarded as repetitions of the same sentence. I think it is certainly correct to say that it is in this sense that we ask what a sentence means.

(3) The next point is obvious enough, but has been so seldom noticed that it is almost surprising. Verification, however in the end we decide to define it, must certainly have some connection with truth and falsity. To verify p is to find out whether or not p is true (and perhaps, whether or not p is probably true, may be accepted or regarded as true). The notions of truth and falsity must, as etymology requires, come in somewhere. What, then, are we to do with all those meaningful sentences which have no concern whatever with truth and falsity?

Clearly there is an enormous number of such sentences. There are imperative sentences, used (mainly) to give orders; and interrogative sentences, used (mainly) to ask questions. There are sentences used as prayers; to make promises; to give verdicts; to express decisions; to pass moral judgments; or to make proposals. It is nonsensical to ask of a question, an order, a prayer, or a proposal, whether it is true or false. The judge who rules that the witness must answer the question cannot be told that what he says is untrue (and therefore it also cannot be said to be true); his ruling may be regarded as correct or improper, it may be disputed, accepted, upheld, or set aside; but it cannot be either verified or falsified. When the chairman says "I declare Mr. Jones elected," it would not be in place to question, or to affirm, the truth of what he says. It would be easy to multiply such instances as these. As soon as we think of the multifarious uses of language, it becomes glaringly obvious that there is a vast number of sentences in connection with which the question "Is it true or false?" is, in varying degrees, absurd or out of place. And to these sentences verification can have no possible application, however "weak" or "indirect." If it is nonsense and out of place to ask whether p is true or false, we cannot speak of a "method of verification" of p.

(4) There would seem to be two possible ways out of this predicament.

(a) We may continue to say that the meaning of a sentence is the method of its verification, and boldly assert that any sentence for which no such method exists is meaningless. But this bold policy is not really acceptable. For first, it would be fantastic to hold that all prayers, questions, orders, rulings, judgments, etc., are flatly meaningless; this is too patently untrue to be tolerable. And second, we should thus obliterate the vital distinction between, on the one hand, sentences which *pose* as being meaningful, which *purport* to make verifiable statements, and which are to be unmasked and condemned as impostors; and, on the other hand, sentences (*e.g.,* imperatives) which do not even *seem* to be verifiable, true or false, and which because they make no false pretensions ought not to be condemned. In desperation we may toy with the idea of distinguishing the latter as good nonsense from the former as bad; but I think we should be reluctant to do more than toy with this expedient. To adopt it would be rather like treating dummy cartridges as a good variety of bad ammunition.

(*b*) We may alternatively stipulate that our account of the meaning of sentences deals only with those about which it *can* be asked whether they are true or false, and about which we can ask for a "method of verification." Few advocates of the Verification Principle seem to have been aware of its limited range of application, and therefore few made, explicitly and deliberately, any such restrictive stipulation as this. (It was often assumed that, apart from the stating of facts, the only use of language was to express or to evoke emotion.) Carnap confines his attention to what he calls, rather vaguely, "cognitive" meaning; others spoke equally vaguely of "literal" meaning (but do not questions and the rest have literal meanings?); others undertook to discuss the meaning of "statements," or (more commonly) slipped uncomfortably back and forth between "sentence," "statement," and "proposition," as if it made little difference which term was used.

In view of the obvious absurdity of alternative (*a*) above, it may seem that this second path is the one we should follow. It is, however, by no means satisfactory. For, first, it requires us to abandon the idea of setting up a *general* criterion of meaningfulness; we must, it seems, restrict ourselves to part only of the field. Can we be sure, then, that our tactical aims will be achieved? Suppose metaphysics should lie quite outside the area in which we can operate with our restricted principle; in this case, metaphysics would escape unscathed. Second, and more seriously, such a restrictive stipulation as this has an uncomfortably arbitrary look about it. It may perhaps be true to say that sentences used to make true or false statements form, by certain standards and for certain purposes, a more important class than sentences used in other ways; and this might justify concentration on this sort of sentence. Nevertheless, it seems strange to offer an analysis of meaning which cannot possibly be applied to other sorts of sentences, since admittedly many other sorts of sentences are, even if less important, not less meaningful. It would naturally be expected that something at least could be said about meaning in general, not merely about the meaning of this or of that sort of sentence. This point will arise again later.

(5) Let us now take it, provisionally and with some disquiet, that we are to discuss the dictum "The meaning of a sentence is the method of its verification," accepting the idea that this is applicable, at best, only to sentences used, or purporting to be used, to make true or false statements. Even this, we shall find, is less clear and simple than it seems; some dilution of its apparent rigour is unavoidable.

(*a*) Suppose someone says to me "I have a pain in my ankle." It is natural to say that such an assertion may not be verifiable by me; for the assertion itself may be my only evidence for believing that the speaker has a pain in his ankle; certainly I cannot verify his assertion by feeling his pain. (I assume for the moment, what is in fact disputable, that he himself can properly be said to be able to verify his assertion.) Must I admit that, in a case of this sort, I do not and cannot know what the speaker means?

Advocates of the Verification Principle usually meet such difficulties as this by saying that, for a sentence to be verifiable and therefore meaningful, it need not be verifiable "by me," nor by any other particular person. So long as there is a method of verification available to *some* person—anyone at all—the sentence is to be regarded as verifiable.

(*b*) But all is not yet clear. Suppose that a historian were to say that on her twentieth birthday Cleopatra wore a red dress, and that when questioned he were to admit that there is not the slightest available evidence for or against this statement. Is this not to admit that the statement is not verifiable? And must it then be regarded as meaningless?

To meet this another qualification is required. We must say that for a sentence to be meaningful, to be understood *now,* it is not essential that any method of verifying it should *now* be available to anyone. So long as we can say how, *e.g.,* by a contemporary of Cleopatra's, our assertion about her dress *could* have been verified, that assertion is to be regarded as verifiable.

(*c*) But now suppose that we move into the regions of pre-history, and assert that, fifty thousand years before men appeared on the earth, rain fell at some particular place on some particular day. We do not know how to verify such a statement, and now we cannot even speak of the method of verification available to contemporary observers. There were no observers. Are we wrong, then, in thinking that we understand such assertions as this?

To meet this point one final manœuvre is required. It does not matter, we must say, that an assertion cannot be verified by anyone now, nor even that it could not in fact have been verified by anyone at any time. For it may still be said to be verifiable *in principle,* and if so it may also be accepted as meaningful. Schlick writes: "When we speak of verifiability we mean *logical* possibility of verification." So long as we can describe without contradiction some method of verifying an assertion, it does not matter if neither I nor anyone else, either now or at any time, can verify or could have verified that assertion.

Even this position is by no means impregnable, but let us pause here for a moment. For already the Principle has been seriously watered down. At first sight it seemed to be extremely definite, positive, and clear; as if we were to accept as meaningful only those sentences for which there *is,* available to ourselves, a method of verification. But it now appears that we are to accept also (1) those for which there is a method of verification available, perhaps, only to others; also (2) those for which there once was, but now is not, an available method of verification; and also (3) those for which there is not, and never was, an available method of verification, but for which we can describe a "logically possible" method. Now in any ordinary sense of the term "verifiable," assertions falling into the third, and I think also the second, of these groups would properly be said to be *not* verifiable. And this induces a certain feeling of discomfort. For if, to prevent our Principle from wreaking too much havoc, we have to allow that assertions which are not verifiable may nevertheless be verifiable "in principle," it is hard to resist the suspicion that verifiability is not really the notion we require. It will not fit the case without a great deal of stretching and manipulating; and although these operations are not always or necessarily objectionable, we should not resort to them unless there is a good case for doing so. Perhaps we may be able to find some notion, other than verifiability, which will fit the case properly, without so much pushing and pulling.

(6) I wish now to re-inforce the suggestion that verifiability is not the notion we require.

(*a*) The phrase "method of verification" is quite inappropriate. (Perhaps it is also inessential; but in any case let us get rid of it.) For what do we mean when we speak of *methods* of verification? In what sorts of cases do we use this expression? We might naturally say that an estimate of the National Income of Great Britain in 1926 can be verified by various methods; that there are various methods of verifying the statement that some given liquid is an acid; that there are different methods of verifying the claim that a certain picture was painted by Vermeer. In each of these cases, the methods in question would consist in the carrying out of certain definite, quite elaborate procedures—the handling of statistics, the performance of chemical experiments, the systematic scrutiny of style, paint, and canvas. The statistician, the chemist, and the expert on paintings are expected to have learned, to know of, and to be able to follow, certain methods appropriate to their subjects. But is there a *method* of verifying that grass is green and that the sky on a clear day is blue? What method of verification could I follow in assuring myself that I have a headache? If someone says "Here is a book," holding it out to me, do I resort to a *method* of verifying what he says? We *look at* the grass and the sky; I *feel* my headache; I *see* the book that is offered to me. Looking, feeling, and seeing are not *methods* of verification; no-one has to be taught how to see and to feel, and no-one claims to be an expert by reason of his mastery of these accomplishments. It is clear, then, that there are innumerable statements as to which what leads us to make them and to accept or reject them as being true or false, is by no means the following of a *method of verification*. This phrase is altogether too formal, over-elaborate; it is properly used of statements or hypotheses that fall within the purview of specialists —scientists, statisticians, historians, doctors, detectives. It is quite out of place in our ordinary daily conversation, which nevertheless we understand perfectly well.

(*b*) But there is a more fundamental difficulty than this. Suppose that we take a sentence, say "The curtains are blue," and ask how this sentence is to be verified. It is perfectly clear that we can say and do nothing at all, until we are told or discover *which* curtains are said to be blue. If the curtains now hanging in my room are those referred to, I can look at them and see that those curtains are indeed blue; if the curtains in the next room are meant, I can go there and see that they are actually not blue; if the sentence occurs in a historical narrative, attributed to a speaker in the seventeenth century, probably I can do nothing at all that will enable me to decide whether what was said is true or false. But in any case, merely by inspection of the *sentence* "The curtains are blue" it is quite impossible to decide what curtains are meant—not because the answer is hidden, but because it is not there. In order to discover what curtains are referred to, I must look, not at the sentence, but at the context in which it was uttered, written or spoken. Now some curtains are blue, others are not; we can ascertain the colour of some curtains, not of others; in some cases we can look at them, in others we must undertake historical research or examine witnesses. What then are we to say? Is the sentence "The curtains are blue" both true and false—true of some curtains, false of others? Is it both verifiable (in some cases) and unverifiable (in others)? Is its "method of verification" also different on different occasions? And if so, does the *meaning* of the sentence vary in Protean fashion from one occasion to another?

There is a way of freeing ourselves from these perplexities. Suppose that we distinguish between the *sentence* "The curtains are blue," and the *statements* which from time to time are made by its use. The statement that the curtains (in my room) are blue, is true: the statement that the curtains (in the next room) are blue, is false: the statement that the curtains (in some seventeenth-century room) were blue, is unverifiable. Here we have three statements, one true, one false, one undetermined; but each was made by the use of the very same sentence. It is not in these cases the *sentence* which is true or false; it is the *statements,* made on each occasion by the use of this sentence, which are true or false. The sentence itself, we may say, has no truth-value; it is nonsensical to ask for the truth-value of the sentence.

But if so it is nonsensical to speak of *verifying* the sentence, of finding out whether it is true or false. Even "in principle" the sentence is not verifiable—(nor, of course, does it *fail* to be verifiable.) Clearly, then, we shall have to re-write the Verification Principle.

(7) Suppose we try it in this way: "To know the meaning of a sentence is to know how to verify statements made by the use of it."

This, however, is rather vague and very peculiar. Must we know how to verify *every* statement made by the use of it? Plainly not. If I know, as I do, how to verify the statement that the curtains (in my room) are blue, how can it be of the least importance that I do *not* know how to verify the statement that some other curtains are blue? If I know how to verify at least some statements made by the use of this sentence, I at least understand the sentence whenever it is used; and it cannot be essential that I should also know, in every case, how to find out whether what is said in those words is true or false.

(In an odd way this has been recognized already in the retreat to the diluted "verifiability in principle"; but it is now clear that this is not, and need not have pretended to be, verifiability. In order to show that I know what is meant by a sentence, I may show that I know what must in fact be the case if the sentence is to be used to make a true statement; but there is no need to say I am thus indicating a "logically possible" method of verification. We could perhaps put the matter thus, by tormenting our language; but why should we?)

The case, then, is this: It is to *statements* that the grammatical predicates "true" and "false" are applicable; it is statements that can be verified or falsified. Whether or not the sentence (say) "The curtains are blue" is used in a particular context to make a *true* statement, depends on the question whether the particular curtains then referred to do or do not then have the character of being blue; and whether or not this statement is *verifiable* depends on the question whether it can or cannot be discovered what character is possessed by those particular curtains. But if this cannot be discovered (i.e. if the statement is not verifiable), what is said may nevertheless be understood; for the very same sentence, namely "The curtains are blue," may be used on very many other occasions, on at least some of which it will no doubt be possible to assure ourselves that what is stated is actually the case. It is known what *would* be the case, if any statement made in the words "The curtains are blue" were true; but this is not to say that any such statement (still less, the sentence) is "verifiable in principle"; it is to say only this—that it is known what *would* be the case, *if* it were true.

(8) Suppose we say, then, that to know the meaning of a sentence is to know in what *sort* of circumstances a statement made by its use would be true or false. We may call this "knowing how to use" the sentence—i.e. knowing how to use it to make statements. Now, surely, we can see how to extend our discussion to include quite other sorts of sentences.

It happens that to know the meaning of *some* sorts of sentences is to know how to use them in making true (or false) statements; but for the numerous sentences which are not used to make statements this is not an applicable criterion. But this is no longer of vital importance; for there are other criteria applicable to such cases, and *in general* to know the meaning of a sentence is to know how to use it, to know in what circumstances its use is correct or incorrect. We are no longer restricted to the case of statements. We know how to use sentences to make statements certainly, but also to ask questions, to give orders, to make offers and to utter threats. A sentence is meaningful if it *has* a use; we know its meaning if we *know* its use. To concentrate our attention on verification is to peer short-sightedly at one corner of the picture—rather as if we sought to define intelligence as the capacity for doing geometry.

(9) Strangely enough, Schlick made one or two remarks co-inciding very closely with the position we have now reached. "Whenever we ask about a sentence, 'What does it mean?' what we expect is instruction as to the circumstances in which the sentence is to be used." And similarly, "Stating the meaning of a sentence amounts to stating the rules according to which the sentence is to be used." In making these remarks, with which we are in substantial agreement, he very properly acknowledges a debt to the ideas of Wittgenstein. How then did he deviate into propounding his restrictive, vague, and defective slogan?

Without pretending to offer a complete diagnosis, I would suggest three reasons. (1) Schlick and his followers were mainly concerned to wage war against metaphysics on behalf of science. Now in both these fields there occur mainly indicative sentences which purport to make statements of fact; and there do not occur, except inessentially, exhortations, questions, prayers, orders, and so on. Thus, Schlick and his followers seem merely to have failed to notice any sort of discourse other than the statement of facts, and to have been quite unaware of the needless and severe restriction of their official analysis of meaning. (2) The findings and hypotheses of scientists are commonly expressed not in singular, but in general, sentences. And if a sentence has the form of a generalization, it is easy (though I think it is also incorrect) to assume that anyone who utters this sentence, in any context and at any time, makes the very same statement, which is either in every case true or in every case false. Here the distinction between a sentence and a statement does not catch the eye; it is not, as it is in the case of singular sentences, plainly essential. And finally (3) in speaking of the findings and hypotheses of scientists it is natural and proper to speak of "methods of verification." These three considerations together go a long way, I think, towards explaining the background and origins of Schlick's famous epigram; and they also serve to emphasise its unsuitability for more general employment.

(10) It is proposed, then, that in analysis of the concept of meaning the restrictive and inappropriate notion of verifiability should be replaced by the more appropriate and more generally applicable notion of "use." It is important, however, that too much should not be claimed for this manœuvre, and that it should not itself be allowed to breed confusion. It is plain, for a start, that the notions of meaning and of use are not simply identical: for many things, of many different kinds, can be said about what people say which, while in this sense or that throwing light on the use or uses of words, expressions, or sentences, would in no natural sense be said to throw light on their *meanings*. Thus it is desirable, and is a task awaiting

satisfactory execution, that those questions of "use" which might properly be taken as questions of meaning should be carefully distinguished and characterized *within* the wider and more various field of questions about the "use" of language in general. Otherwise confusion, if perhaps not worse confounded, is liable not to be greatly diminished. At the same time, it is desirable that philosophers should not unthinkingly swallow the assumption that *meaning* is their sole and proprietary concern. The wider extension— if you like, the greater vagueness—of the notion of use may be positively advantageous, if it serves to encourage philosophers not to ignore the many features and functions of linguistic expressions *other* than those traditionally taken to comprise their meanings.

Now one last comment should be made, on the notorious "anti-metaphysical" aspect of the Verification Principle. I do not say that this sort of hostility is necessarily to be deplored; for some kinds of philosophising may be actually dangerous, and not merely pretentious, misguided, or distasteful. But I think that, if we fully appreciate the complexity of the use of language, we shall be very cautious indeed in the application of the word "meaningless." The use of this word has been, I believe, philosophically disastrous, almost wholly a waste of time. It is clearly not the case that all so-called metaphysical pronouncements are meaningless, if by this we mean that they are utterly without any use or point. They are, of course, usually peculiar and paradoxical; they exhibit strange, and sometimes it may be mistaken, uses of language, but not the total absence of any use whatever. Philosophers often mislead and often speak strangely; they seldom, or at least less often, utter sheer rigmarole. When we are faced with some queer and paradoxical pronouncement, our task should be to discover how and why it came to be made—how and why deviation from plain modes of speech came about, and whether it came about for respectable reasons or from sheer confusion. Even if the reasons turn out to be respectable, genuinely revealing, we need not also speak strangely; we need not all be metaphysicians; but we may become aware of something—it may be only a pitfall—of which it is important for philosophy to take cognizance. The aim should be to become aware of the pitfalls, not to condemn or to ignore those who fall into them. It has been perhaps the most serious defect of the Verification Principle that it has seemed to sanction an easy, impatient dismissal of too many philosophical doctrines, conveying the impression that no good purpose can be served by asking why people say the strange things that they do. Indeed, if one took seriously the idea that the only questions that matter about any statement are the questions whether it is true, or false, or meaningless, one could hardly engage in philosophy at all. I do not say that all advocates of the Principle have in fact been guilty of this aridity of outlook; besides, for a short time aridity may be bracing and hygienic. But the Principle as it is stated tends inevitably to narrow and to cramp the field of philosophy, and it offers almost irresistible temptations to dogmatism. "Principles," perhaps, are always liable to induce dogmatic slumber, broken only by acrimonious controversy; and it is, perhaps, in this respect above all that the Verificationists have been unfaithful disciples of Wittgenstein. There are here and there, as we have found, certain echoes of Wittgenstein's voice in the writings of Schlick: but the echoes are faint, and the words seem to have succumbed to the pathetic fate of the sayings of Empedocles.

66   Unanswerable Questions?

Moritz Schlick

IT IS NATURAL THAT MANKIND SHOULD take great pride in the steady advance of its knowledge. The joy we feel in the contemplation of scientific progress is fully justified. One problem after another is solved by science; and the success of the past gives us ample reason for our hope that this process will go on, perhaps even at a quicker pace. But will it, can it, go on indefinitely? It seems a little ridiculous to suppose that a day might come when all imaginable problems would be solved, so that there would be no questions left for which the human mind would crave an answer. We feel sure that our curiosity will never be completely satisfied and that the progress of knowledge will not come to a stop when it has reached its last goal.

It is commonly assumed that there are other imperative reasons why scientific advance cannot go on for ever. Most people believe in the existence of barriers that cannot be scaled by human reason and by human experience. The final and perhaps the most important truths are thought to be permanently hidden from our eyes; the key to the Riddle of the Universe is believed to be buried in depths the access to which is barred to all mortals by the very nature of the Universe. According to this common belief, there are many questions which we can formulate, and whose meaning we can grasp completely, though it is definitely impossible to know their answer which is beyond the natural and necessary boundary of all knowledge. In

[This article was written by Schlick in English and published in *The Philosopher* (1935). It was subsequently reprinted in Schlick's *Gesammelte Aufsätze* (Vienna, 1938). It is reprinted here with the permission of Gerold and Co. of Vienna.]

regard to these questions a final ignorabimus is pronounced. Nature, it is said, does not wish her deepest secrets to be revealed; God has set a limit of knowledge which shall not be passed by his creatures, and beyond which faith must take the place of curiosity.

It is easy to understand how such a view originated, but it is not so clear why it should be considered to be a particularly pious or reverent attitude. Why should Nature seem more wonderful to us if she cannot be known completely? Surely she does not wish to conceal anything on purpose, for she has no secrets, nothing to be ashamed of. On the contrary, the more we know of the world the more we shall marvel at it: and if we should know its ultimate principles and its most general laws, our feeling of wonder and reverence would pass all bounds. Nothing is gained by picturing God as jealously hiding from his creatures the innermost structure of his creation, indeed a worthier conception of a Supreme Being should imply that no ultimate boundary should be set to the knowledge of beings to whom an infinite desire of knowledge has been given. The existence of an absolute ignorabimus would form an exceedingly vexing problem to a philosophical mind. It would be a great step forward in philosophy, if the burden of this bewildering problem could be thrown off.

This, one may argue, is evidently impossible, for without doubt there are unanswerable questions. It is very easy to ask questions the answers to which, we have the strongest reasons to believe, will never be known to any human being. What did Plato do at eight o'clock in the morning of his fiftieth birthday? How much did Homer weigh when he wrote the first line of the Iliad? Is there a piece of silver to be found on the other side of the moon, three inches long and shaped like a fish? Obviously, men will never know the answers to these questions, however hard they may try. But at the same time, we know that they would never try very hard. These problems, they will say, are of no importance, no philosopher would worry about them, and no historian or naturalist would care whether he knew the answers or not.

Here, then, we have certain questions whose insolubility does not trouble the philosopher; and evidently there are reasons why it need not trouble him. This is important. We must be content to have insoluble questions. But what if all of them could be shown to be of such a kind as not to cause any really serious concern to the philosopher? In that case he would be relieved. Although there would be many things he could not know, the real burden of the ignorabimus would be lifted from his shoulders. At first sight there seems to be little hope for this as some of the most important issues of philosophy are generally held to belong to the class of insoluble problems. Let us consider this point carefully.

What do we mean when we call a question important? When do we hold it to be of interest to the philosopher? Broadly speaking, when it is a question of principle; one that refers to a general feature of the world, not a detail; one that concerns the structure of the world, a valid law, not a single unique fact. This distinction may be described as the difference between the real nature of the Universe and the accidental form in which this nature manifests itself.

Correspondingly, the reasons why a given problem is insoluble may be of two entirely different kinds. In the first place, the impossibility of answering a given question may be an impossibility in principle or, as we shall call it, a logical impossibility. In the second place, it may be due to accidental circumstances which do not affect the general laws, and in this case we shall speak of an empirical impossibility.

In the simple instances given above, it is clear that the impossibility of answering these questions is of the empirical kind. It is merely a matter of chance that neither Plato nor any of his friends took exact notes of his doings on his fiftieth birthday (or that such notes were lost if any were taken); and a similar remark applies to the questions concerning the weight of Homer and things on the other side of the moon. It is practically or technically impossible for human beings to reach the moon and go around it, and most probably such an exploration of our earth's satellite will never take place.* But we cannot declare it impossible in principle. The moon happens to be very far off; it happens to turn always the same side towards the earth; it happens to possess no atmosphere in which human beings could breathe—but we can very easily imagine all these circumstances to be different. We are prevented from visiting the moon only by brute facts, by an unfortunate state of affairs, not by any principle by which certain things were deliberately withheld from our knowledge. Even if the impossibility of solving a certain question is due to a Law of Nature, we shall have to say that it is only empirical, not logical, provided we can indicate how the law would have to be changed in order to make the question answerable. After all, the existence of any Law of Nature must be considered as an empirical fact which might just as well be different. The scientist's whole interest is concentrated on the particular Laws of Nature; but the philosopher's general point of view must be independent of the validity of any particular one of them.

It is one of the most important contentions of the philosophy I am advocating that there are many questions which it is empirically impossible to answer, but not a single real question for which it would be logically impossible to find a solution. Since only the latter kind of impossibility would have that hopeless and fatal character which is implied by the ignorabimus and which could cause philosophers to speak of a "Riddle of the Universe" and to despair of such problems as the "cognition of things in themselves," and similar ones, it would seem that the acceptance of my opinion would bring the greatest relief to all those who have been unduly concerned about the essential incompetence of human knowledge in regard to the greatest issues. Nobody can reasonably complain about the empirical impossibility of knowing everything, for that would be equivalent to complaining that we cannot live at all times and be in all places simultaneously.

* It should be noted that this was written in 1935. (Ed.)

Nobody wants to know all the facts, and it is not important to know them: the really essential principles of the universe reveal themselves at any time and any place. I do not suggest, of course, that they lie open at first glance, but they can always be discovered by the careful and penetrating methods of science.

How can I prove my point? What assures us that the impossibility of answering questions never belongs to the question as such is never a matter of principle, but is always due to accidental empirical circumstances, which may some day change? There is no room here for a real proof;[1] but I can indicate in general how the result is obtained.

It is done by an analysis of the meaning of our questions. Evidently philosophical issues—and very often other problems too—are difficult to understand: we have to ask for an explanation of what is meant by them. How is such an explanation given? How do we indicate the meaning of a question?

A conscientious examination shows that all the various ways of explaining what is actually meant by a question are, ultimately, nothing but various descriptions of ways in which the answer to the question must be found. Every explanation or indication of the meaning of a question consists, in some way or other, of prescriptions for finding its answer. This principle has proved to be of fundamental importance for the method of science. For example, it led Einstein, as he himself admits, to the discovery of the Theory of Relativity. It may be empirically impossible to follow those prescriptions (like traveling around the moon), but it cannot be logically impossible. For what is logically impossible cannot even be described, i.e., it cannot be expressed by words or other means of communication.

The truth of this last statement is shown by an analysis of "description" and "expression" into which we cannot enter here. But taking it for granted, we see that no real question is in principle—i.e., logically—unanswerable. For the logical impossibility of solving a problem is equivalent to the impossibility of describing a method of finding its solution; and this, as we have stated, is equivalent to the impossibility of indicating the meaning of the problem. Thus a question which is unanswerable in principle can have no meaning, it can be no question at all: it is nothing but a nonsensical series of words with a question mark after them. As it is logically impossible to give an answer where there is no question, this cannot be a cause of wonder, dissatisfaction, or despair.

This conclusion can be made clearer by considering one or two examples. Our question as to the weight of Homer has meaning, of course,

---

1. For a more complete account of the matter I may refer the English reader to two lectures which appeared in the *Publications in Philosophy*, edited by the College of the Pacific in 1932, and more especially to an article on "Meaning and Verification" in a forthcoming issue of the *Philosophical Review*. [Schlick was killed before this article appeared in *The Philosophical Review* for 1936. It was subsequently reprinted in his *Gesammelte Aufsätze* and also in H. Feigl and W. Sellars, eds., *Readings in Philosophical Analysis* (New York: 1949—Ed.)]

because we can easily describe methods of weighing human bodies (even poets); in other words, the notion of weight is accurately defined. Probably Homer was never weighed, and it is empirically impossible to do it now, because his body no longer exists; but these accidental facts do not alter the sense of the question.

Or take the problem of survival after death. It is a meaningful question, because we can indicate ways in which it could be solved. One method of ascertaining one's own survival would simply consist in dying. It would also be possible to describe certain observations of scientific character that would lead us to accept a definite answer. That such observations could not be made thus far is an empirical fact which cannot entail a definite ignorabimus in regard to the problem.

Now consider the question: "What is the nature of time?" What does it mean? What do the words "the nature of" stand for? The scientist might, perhaps, invent some kind of explanation, he might suggest some statements which he would regard as possible answers to the question; but his explanation could be nothing but the description of a method of discovering which of the suggested answers is the true one. In other words, by giving a meaning to the question he has at the same time made it logically answerable, although he may not be able to make it empirically soluble. Without such an explanation, however, the words "What is the nature of time?" are no question at all. If a philosopher confronts us with a series of words like this and neglects to explain the meaning, he cannot wonder if no answer is forthcoming. It is as if he had asked us: "How much does philosophy weigh?" in which case it is immediately seen that this is not a question at all, but mere nonsense. Questions like "Can we know the Absolute?" and innumerable similar ones must be dealt with in the same way as the "problem" concerning the nature of time.

All great philosophical issues that have been discussed since the time of Parmenides to our present day are of one of two kinds; we can either give them a definite meaning by careful and accurate explanations and definitions, and then we are sure that they are soluble in principle, although they may give the scientist the greatest trouble and may even never be solved on account of unfavorable empirical circumstances, or we fail to give them any meaning, and then they are no questions at all. Neither case need cause uneasiness for the philosopher. His greatest troubles arose from a failure to distinguish between the two.

67   *Why?*

Paul Edwards

Lack of clarity about the uses of the word "why" is responsible for confusion on a number of philosophical fronts. In this article we shall confine ourselves to two groups of topics where greater attention to the proper and improper behavior of this word might well have avoided the adoption of misguided theories. There is, first, the contrast, or the alleged contrast, between the "how" and the "why" and the view, shared by writers of very different backgrounds, that science can deal only with how-questions. Second, there are certain "ultimate" or "cosmic" questions, such as "Why do we exist?" or, more radically, "Why does the world exist?" or "Why is there something rather than nothing?" Some, like Schopenhauer and Julian Huxley, regard these questions as unanswerable; others, like Leibniz and Gilson, believe that they can be answered; but whether these questions can be answered or not, it seems to be widely agreed that they are very "deep." These questions, in the words of the British astro-physicist A. C. B. Lovell, raise problems "which can tear the individual's mind asunder."[1] Speaking of the question "Why is there something rather than nothing?," Heidegger first remarks that it is "the fundamental question of metaphysics" and later adds that "with this question philosophy began and with this question it will end, provided that it ends in greatness and not in an impotent decline."[2]

[This selection is a slightly revised version of an article that first appeared in Volume 8 of the *Encyclopedia of Philosophy* (N.Y.: Macmillan and Free Press, 1967).]

1. *The Individual and the Universe*, New York, 1961, p. 125.
2. *An Introduction to Metaphysics*, Garden City, 1961, p. 20.

How and Why

The contrast between the how and the why has been insisted on for two rather different reasons. Some writers have done so in the interest of religion or metaphysics. Their position seems to be that while science and empirical research generally are competent to deal with how-questions, the very different and much deeper why-questions are properly the concern of religion or metaphysics or both. Thus, in a widely read book, the British psychiatrist David Stafford-Clark insists that the confusion between the how and the why is the "fundamental fallacy" behind "the whole idea that science and religion are really in conflict at all."[3] Freud in particular is accused of committing this fallacy in his antireligious writings. Stafford-Clark is not at all opposed to Freudian theory so long as it confines itself to the *how* of psychological phenomena. Psychoanalysis cannot, however, "begin by itself to answer a single question as to why man is so constructed that they should happen in this way."[4] Although he repeatedly expresses his own fervent belief in God, Stafford-Clark unfortunately does not tell us how religion answers the question *why* man is "constructed" the way he is. Perhaps he would answer it along the lines in which Newton answered a similar question about the sun. "Why is there one body in our system qualified to give light and heat to all the rest," Newton wrote in his first letter to Richard Bentley, "I know no reason, but because the author of the system thought it convenient."[5] I think it will be generally agreed that this is not a very illuminating answer.

Similar views are found in the writings of many professional philosophers. Thus, writing of Newton's work on gravitation, Whitehead observes that "he [Newton] made a magnificent beginning by isolating the stresses indicated by his law of gravitation." But Newton "left no hint, why in the nature of things there should be any stresses at all."[6] Similarly, discussing the limitations of science, Gilson declares that "scientists never ask themselves *why* things happen, but *how* they happen. . . . Why anything at all is, or exists, science knows not, precisely because it cannot even ask the question."[7] For Gilson the two topics mentioned at the beginning of this article appear to merge into one. The why of particular phenomena, he seems to argue, cannot be determined unless we answer the question "why this world, taken together with its laws . . . is or exists."[8]

Among those who have asserted that science can only deal with how-questions there are some who are not at all friendly to metaphysics or religion. These writers usually add to their remarks that science cannot

3. *Psychiatry Today,* Harmondsworth, 1952, p. 282.
4. *Ibid.,* p. 287.
5. *Opera,* London, 1779–1785, Vol. IV, pp. 429 ff.
6. *Modes of Thought,* New York and Cambridge, 1938, pp. 183–184.
7. *God and Philosophy,* New Haven, 1959, p. 140, Gilson's italics.
8. *Ibid.,* p. 72.

handle why-questions the comment that no other enterprise fares any better. This "agnostic positivism," as we may call it, goes at least as far back as Hume. We know, he writes, that milk and bread are proper nourishment for men and not for lions or tigers, but we cannot "give the ultimate reason why" this should be so.[9] Hume seems to imply that this unhappy state can never be remedied, regardless of the advances of physiology or any other science. Several writers in the second half of the nineteenth century advanced this position under the slogan "The task of science is to describe phenomena, not to explain them." Ernst Mach, Gustav Kirchhoff, and Joseph Petzoldt were among the best-known figures in central Europe who advocated this view. In England, Karl Pearson, its most influential exponent, conceded that there was no harm in speaking of "scientific explanations" so long as "explanation" is used "in the sense of the descriptive-how."[10] We can indeed "describe how a stone falls to the earth, but not why it does."[11] "No one knows why two ultimate particles influence each other's motion. Even if gravitation be analyzed and described by the motion of some simpler particle or ether-element, the whole will still be a description, and not an explanation, of motion. Science would still have to content itself with recording the how." No matter how far physics may progress, the why will "remain a mystery."[12]

Agnostic positivism is not as fashionable as it was seventy years ago, but it is far from dead. Thus, writing half a century after Pearson, W. T. Stace declares that

Scientific laws, properly formulated, never "explain" anything. They simply state, in an abbreviated and generalized form, what *happens*. No scientist, and in my opinion no philosopher, knows *why* anything happens, or can "explain" anything.[13]

Similarly, the English biologist, Joseph Needham, after dismissing vitalism as a mystical and scientifically fruitless theory, observes that "not only vitalists but all of us want to ask why living beings should exist and should act as they do." "About that," Needham continues, "the scientific method can tell us nothing." Living beings

are what they are because the properties of force and matter are what they

are, and at that point scientific thought has to hand the problem over to philosophical and religious thought.[14]

The American biologist, George Gaylord Simpson, who quotes this passage with approval, adds that when it comes to these "ultimate mysteries,"

9. *An Inquiry Concerning Human Understanding,* Sec. IV, Part I.
10. *The Grammar of Science,* London, 1937, p. 97, Pearson's italics. (*The Grammar of Science* was first published in 1892.)
11. *Ibid.,* p. 103.
12. *Ibid.,* p. 105.
13. *Man against Darkness,* Pittsburgh, 1967, p. 213, Stace's italics.
14. *Science, Religion and Reality,* New York, 1925, p. 245.

theology is no better off than science. It, too, is "powerless to pierce that ultimate veil."[15]

It is important to disentangle purely verbal from substantive issues in such declarations. Insofar as the various writers we have quoted merely wish to assert that causal statements and scientific laws in general are contingent and not logically necessary propositions, little exception could be taken to their remarks. However, they are, or at least they appear to be, saying a great deal more. They all seem to agree that there is a class of meaningful questions, naturally and properly introduced by the word "why" in one of its senses, which cannot be answered by the use of empirical methods. Writers belonging to the first group claim that the answers can be obtained elsewhere. The agnostic positivists maintain that human beings cannot obtain the answers at all.

It is this substantive issue which we shall discuss here, and it is necessary to point out that there are numerous confusions in all views of this kind. To begin with, although this is the least important observation, "how" and "why" do not always have contrasting functions but are in certain situations used to ask the very same questions. Thus, when we know or believe that a phenomenon, A, is the cause of another phenomenon, X, but at the same time are ignorant of the "mechanics" of A's causation of X, we indifferently use "how" and "why." We know, for example, that certain drugs cure certain diseases, but our knowledge is in a medical sense "purely empirical." Here we would be equally prepared to say that we do not know "why" the drug produces the cure and that we do not know "how" it does this. Or, to take a somewhat different case, it is widely believed that cigarette smoking is causally connected with lung cancer. It is also known that sometimes two people smoke the same amount and yet one of them develops lung cancer while the other one does not. In such a case the question naturally arises why cigarette smoking, if it is indeed the cause at all, leads to cancer in one case but not in the other. And we would be just as ready to express our ignorance or puzzlement by saying that we do not know how it is as by saying that we do not know why it is that smoking produced cancer in the first man but not in the second. In all such cases it is clear that science *is* in principle competent to deal with the "why" no less than with the "how," if only because they are used to ask the very same questions.

It is undeniable, however, that in certain contexts "how" and "why" are used to ask different questions. This contrast is most obvious when we deal with intentional, or more generally with "meaningful," human actions. What seems far from obvious, what in fact seems plainly false, is that empirical methods are not in principle adequate to determine the answers to why-questions in these contexts. Let us take as our example the recent theft of the Star of India sapphire and other gems from the Museum of Natural History in New York. We can here certainly distinguish the questions why the burglary was committed from the question how it was carried out. The

15. *This View of Life*, New York, 1963, p. 233.

latter question would concern itself with the details of the act—how the thieves got into the building, how they immobilized the alarm system, how they avoided the guards, and so on. The why-question, by contrast, would inquire into the aim or purpose of the theft—were the thieves just out to make a vast amount of money, or were there perhaps some other aims involved, such as proving to rival gangs how skillful they were or showing the incompetence of the police force? Now, the aim or purpose of a human being is surely not in principle undiscoverable, and frequently we know quite well what it is. The person himself usually, though not always, simply knows what his aim is. An orator, for example, who is advocating a certain policy, ostensibly because it is "for the good of the country," may at the same time know perfectly well that his real aim is personal advancement. It used to be said that in such situations a human being knows his own purpose by means of "introspection," where introspection was conceived of as a kind of "inner sense." This way of talking is not inappropriate to situations in which somebody is confused about his own motives, for then special attention to his own feelings, resembling in some ways the effort to discriminate the detailed features of a physical scene, may well be necessary in order to ascertain his "true" aims. Much more commonly, however, a human being simply knows what his aims are, and it would be much better to say that he knows this "without observation" than that he knows it by introspection. In order to find out the purpose of somebody else's action, it is in countless instances sufficient to ask the person a direct question about his aim. Where the agent's veracity is suspect or where a person is the victim of self-deception, it is necessary to resort to more elaborate investigations. In the former type of case one might ask the agent all kinds of other questions (that is, questions not directly about the purpose of his action), one might interview his friends and acquaintances and other witnesses of his conduct, one might tap his telephone and employ assorted bugging devices, and one might perhaps go so far as to question him after the administration of "truth" drugs. While the practical difficulties in the way of discovering the purpose of an action are no doubt insurmountable in many cases of both these types, empirical procedures are clearly in principle adequate to this task.

We also contrast how- and why-questions when the latter are not inquiries into the purpose of any agent. Here, however, "how" has a different meaning from any previously discussed. In all examples so far considered, how-questions were in one way or another *causal* questions—"How did the thieves carry out their plan of stealing the Star of India?" is a question about the means of achieving a certain goal, and "How is it that smoking produces cancer in one man but not in another?," although not a question about means, is nevertheless about the processes leading to a certain result. These causal "hows" should be distinguished from what one may call the "how" of "state" or "condition." "How cold does it get in New York in the winter?" "How does the decline in his powers manifest itself?" "How is his pain now —is it any better?" are examples of the "how" of state or condition, and it is how-questions of this kind which we contrast with non-teleological why-questions—"Why does it get so cold in New York in the winter?" "Why did his powers decline so early in life?" "Why is his pain not subsiding?"

It is sometimes maintained or implied, as in the remarks of Stafford-Clark quoted earlier, that why-questions are invariably inquiries about somebody's purpose or end—if not the purpose of a human being, then perhaps that of some supernatural intelligence. This is clearly not the case. There can be no doubt that "why" is often employed simply to ask questions about the cause of a phenomenon. Thus the question "Why are the winters in New York so much colder than in Genoa, although the two places are on the same geographical latitude?" would naturally be understood as a request for information about the cause of this climatic difference; and it is not necessary for the questioner to suppose that there is some kind of plan or purpose behind the climatic difference in order to be using the word "why" properly. In saying this, one is not begging any questions against the theory that natural phenomena like the cold of the winter in New York are the work of a supernatural being: one is merely calling attention to what is and what is not implied in the ordinary employment of "why" in these contexts.

Let us briefly summarize the results obtained so far: in some situations "how" and "why" are naturally employed to ask the very same questions; when we deal with intentional human actions, we naturally use "why" to inquire about the purpose or goal of the agent and "how" to learn about the means used to achieve that goal; finally, how-questions are frequently used to inquire about the state or condition of somebody or something, while why-questions inquire about the cause of that state or condition without necessarily implying that any purpose or plans are involved. In all these cases it appears to be in principle possible to answer why-questions no less than how-questions, and this without the aid of religion or metaphysics.

The Theological "Why"

Let us turn now to what we earlier called "cosmic" why-questions. Two such cosmic "whys" need to be distinguished, the first of which, for rather obvious reasons, will be referred to as the theological "why." Here the questioner would be satisfied with a theological answer if he found such an answer convincing. He may or may not accept it as true, but he would not regard it as irrelevant.

Gilson, whose remarks on the limitations of science were quoted earlier, immediately supplies the answer to the "supreme question" which science "cannot even ask." Why anything at all exists must be answered by saying:

(Each) and every particular existential energy, and each and every particular existing thing depends for its existence upon a pure Act of existence. In order to be the ultimate answer to all existential problems, this supreme cause has to be absolute existence. Being absolute, such a cause is self-sufficient; if it creates, its creative act must be free. Since it creates not only being but order, it must be something which at least eminently contains the only principle of order known to us in experience, namely, thought.[16]

There is no doubt that many people who ask such questions as "Why does the universe exist?" or "Why are we here?" would also, at least in certain moods, be satisfied with a theological answer, though they would not necessarily accept all the details of Gilson's Thomistic theology. It should be emphasized that one does not have to be a believer in God to be using "why" in this way. The American playwright Edward Albee, for example, recently remarked, "Why we are here is an impenetrable question." Everyone in the world, he went on, "hopes there is a God," and he later added, "I am neither pro-God nor anti-God."[17] Albee's question "Why are we here?" evidently amounts to asking whether there is a God and, if so, what divine purposes human beings are supposed to serve. He does not definitely accept the theological answer, presumably because he feels unsure of its truth, but he does regard it as very much to the point.

It should be observed in passing that people frequently use the word "why" to express a kind of cosmic complaint or bewilderment. In such cases they are not really asking for an answer, theological or otherwise. This use of "why" is in some respects similar to the theological "why" and may not inappropriately be referred to as the quasi-theological "why." A person who is and regards himself as a decent human being, but who is suffering a great deal, might easily exclaim "Why do I have to suffer so much, when so many scoundrels in the world, who never worked half as hard as I, are having such a lot of fun?" Such a question may well be asked by an unbeliever who is presumably expressing his regret that the workings of the universe are not in harmony with the moral demands of human beings. Even when believers ask questions of this kind, it may be doubted that they are invariably requesting information about the detailed workings of the Divine Mind. In the deeply moving first-act monologue of *Der Rosenkavalier,*[18] the Marschallin reflects on the inevitability of aging and death:

> I well remember a girl
> Who came fresh from the convent to be
>   forced into holy matrimony.
> Where is she now?
>
> . . . .
>
> How can it really be,
> That I was once the little Resi
> And that I will one day become the old
>   woman?

How, she exclaims, can something like this be? She is far from doubting the existence of God and proceeds to ask:

16. *God and Philosophy, op. cit.,* p. 140.
17. New York *Times,* January 21, 1965.
18. Opera by Richard Strauss with libretto by Hugo von Hofmannsthal.

Why does the dear Lord do it?

And worse, if he has to do it in this way:

Why does He let me watch it happen
With such clear senses? Why doesn't He
hide it from me?

The Marschallin obviously does not expect an answer to this question, not, or not merely, because she thinks that the world's metaphysicians and theologians are not quite up to it. She is not, strictly speaking, asking a question but expressing her regret and her feeling of complete helplessness.

However, let us return from the quasi-theological to the theological "why." The difficulties besetting an answer like Gilson's are notorious and need not be reviewed here at length. There are the difficulties, much stressed by recent writers, of saying anything intelligible about a disembodied mind, finite or infinite, and there are further difficulties of talking meaningfully about the creation of the universe. There are the rather different difficulties connected not with the intelligibility of the theological assertions but with the reasoning used to justify them. Schopenhauer referred to all such attempts to reach a final resting place in the series of causes as treating the causal principle like a "hired cab" which one dismisses when one has reached one's destination.[19] Bertrand Russell objects that such writers work with an obscure and objectionable notion of explanation: to explain something, we are not at all required to introduce a "self-sufficient" entity, whatever that may be.[20] Writing specifically in reply to Gilson, Nagel insists that it is perfectly legitimate to inquire into the reasons for the existence of the alleged absolute Being, the pure Act of existence. Those who reject such a question as illegitimate, he writes, are "dogmatically cutting short a discussion when the intellectual current runs against them."[21] Without wishing to minimize these difficulties, it is important to insist that there is a sense in which the theological why-questions *are* intelligible. The question can be answered for such a person if it can be shown that there is a God. If not, it cannot be answered. Albee and Gilson, for example, do not agree about the truth, or at any rate the logical standing, of the theological assertion, but they agree that it is relevant to *their* cosmic why-question. There is thus a sense in which the questioner here *knows what he is looking for.*

The Super-Ultimate "Why"

The theological "why" must be distinguished from what we are here going to call the super-ultimate "why." A person who is using "why" in the

19. *The Fourfold Root of the Principle of Sufficient Reason,* London, 1891, pp. 42–43.
20. See his debate on the existence of God with Father Copleston, Selection 41, pp. 477 ff. above.
21. *Sovereign Reason,* Glencoe, Ill., 1954, p. 30.

latter way would regard the theological answer as quite unsatisfactory, not (or not just) because it is meaningless or false but because it does not answer *his* question. It does not go far enough. For granting that there is a God and that human beings were created by God to serve certain of his purposes, our questioner would now ask "Why is there a God of this kind with these purposes and not another God with other purposes?" or, more radically, he would ask "Why was there at some time God rather than nothing?" The Biblical statement "In the beginning God created heaven and earth," Heidegger explicitly remarks, "is not an answer to . . . and cannot even be brought into relation with our question." The believer who stops with God is not pushing his questioning "to the very end."[22] (It is not certain how somebody pressing the super-ultimate why-question would react to the rejoinder of those theologians who maintain that God exists necessarily and that hence the question "Why was there at some time God rather than nothing?" is illegitimate. In all likelihood he would support the view, accepted by the majority of Western philosophers since Hume and Kant, that it makes no sense to talk about anything, natural or supernatural, as existing necessarily.)

There are times when most people would regard these super-ultimate why-questions as just absurd. Stafford-Clark himself speaks with impatience of the "rumination" and the tedious and interminable speculations of obsessional patients. " 'Why is the world?' was a question to which one patient could find no answer but from which he could find no relief."[23] Yet, at other times, most of us are ready to treat these why-questions as supremely profound, as riddles to which it would be wonderful to have the answer but which, because of our finite intellects, must forever remain unsolved. It is true that certain philosophers, like Schelling and Heidegger, who have frequently been denounced as obscurantists, have laid special emphasis on super-ultimate why-questions; but it would be a total misunderstanding of the situation to suppose that more empirical philosophers, or indeed ordinary people, are not given to asking them or to treating them with great seriousness. It is almost unavoidable that any reasonably intelligent and reflective person who starts wondering about the origin of the human race, of animal life, of the solar system, of our galaxy and other galaxies, or about the lack of justice in the world, the brevity of life, and the seemingly absolute finality of death, should sooner or later ask "Why this world and not another—why any world?" The scientist Julian Huxley is as far removed in temperament and philosophy from Heidegger as anybody could be. Yet he also speaks of the "basic and universal mystery—the mystery of existence in general . . . why does the world exist?" For Huxley it is science which "confronts us" with this mystery, but science cannot remove it. The only comment we can make is that "we do not know." We must accept the existence of the universe "and our own existence as the one

22. *An Introduction to Metaphysics*, pp. 6–7.
23. *Psychiatry Today*, p. 112.

basic mystery."[24] Ludwig Büchner was a materialist and an atheist. Yet he repeatedly spoke of the "inexplicability of the last ground of things." Nor are super-ultimate why-questions confined to those who do not believe in God or who have no metaphysical system. Schopenhauer was supremely confident that his was the true metaphysic, but he nevertheless remarks in the concluding chapter of his main work that his "philosophy does not pretend to explain the existence of the world in its ultimate grounds . . . After all my explanations," he adds, "one may still ask, for example, whence has sprung this will, the manifestation of which is the world. . . . A perfect understanding of the existence, nature, and origin of the world, extending to its ultimate ground and satisfying all demands, is impossible. So much as to the limits of my philosophy, and indeed of all philosophy."[25] Similarly, Voltaire, who was a firm and sincere believer in God and who never tired of denouncing atheists as blind and foolish, nevertheless asked, at the end of the article "Why?" in his *Philosophical Dictionary,* "Why is there anything?" without for a moment suggesting that an appeal to God's creation would be a solution.[26] William James, too, although he repeatedly defended supernaturalism, never claimed that it provided an answer to the question "How comes the world to be here at all instead of the non-entity which might be imagined in its place?" Philosophy, in James's opinion, whether it be naturalistic or supernaturalistic, "brings no reasoned solution" to this question, "for from nothing to being there is no logical bridge."[27] "The question of being," he observes later in the same discussion, is "the darkest in all philosophy. All of us are beggars here, and no school can speak disdainfully of another or give itself superior airs."[28]

Having pointed out how widespread is this tendency to ask and take seriously the super-ultimate why-question, it is necessary to explain why, in the opinion of a number of contemporary philosophers, it must nevertheless be condemned as meaningless. It is the mark of a meaningful question that not all answers can be ruled out *a priori;* but because of the way in which the super-ultimate why-question has been set up, it is *logically* impossible to obtain an answer. It is quite clear that the questioner will automatically reject any proposed answer as "not going back far enough"—as not answering *his* why. "All explanation," in the words of Peter Koestenbaum, an American disciple and expositor of Heidegger, "occurs within that which is to be explained . . . so the question applies to any possible answer as well,"[29] that is, there *cannot* be an answer. If, however, a question can be put at all, to quote Wittgenstein,

24. *Essays of a Humanist,* London, 1964, pp. 107–108.
25. *The World As Will and Idea,* 3 vols., translated by R. B. Haldane and J. Kemp, London, 1883, Ch. 50.
26. A six-volume English translation of the *Philosophical Dictionary* was published in London in 1824 by J. and H. L. Hunt. The passage quoted in the text is found in vol. 6, p. 358.
27. *Some Problems of Philosophy,* New York, 1911, pp. 38–40.
28. *Ibid.,* p. 46.
29. "The Sense of Subjectivity," *Review of Existential Psychology and Psychiatry,* 1962, p. 54.

then it *can* also be answered . . . doubt can only exist where there is a question; a question only where there is an answer, and this only where something *can* be *said*.[30]

"A question," wrote Friedrich Waismann,

is a request for a search. The question as it were introduces a movement of thought at the end of which there is the answer . . . If there is no answer, then the direction is missing which would give focus to the search; in that case the movement of thought does not exist and this means: *there is no question*.[31]

It must be emphasized that the super-ultimate "why" does *not* express ignorance about the "early" history of the universe. Büchner, for example, had no doubt that matter was eternal and that nothing which could be called "creation" had ever occurred; Voltaire similarly had no doubt that the physical universe was created by God and that God had always existed —yet both of them asked the super-ultimate "why" and regarded it as un-answerable. No doubt, some who have asked super-ultimate why-questions would, unlike Büchner and Voltaire, declare themselves ignorant of the remote history of the universe, but it is not this ignorance that they are expressing by means of the super-ultimate "why."

Those who insist that the super-ultimate why-question is meaningful do not usually deny that it very radically differs from *all* other meaningful why-questions. To mark the difference they occasionally refer to it by such labels as "mystery" or "miracle." Thus Koestenbaum remarks that "ques-tions of this sort do not lead to answers but to a state of mind that appre-ciates the miracle of existence," they call attention to "the greatest of all mysteries."[32] Heidegger writes that the question "is incommensurable with any other"[33] and subsequently observes that "not only what is asked after but also the asking itself is extraordinary."[34]

Calling the super-ultimate why-question a "mystery" or a "miracle" or "incommensurable" or "extraordinary" does not in any way remove the difficulty; it is just one way of acknowledging that there is one. If it is granted that in all other situations a question makes sense only if an answer to it is logically possible, one wonders why this principle or criterion is not to be applied in the present case. If the defender of the meaningfulness of the super-ultimate why-question admits that in the "ordinary" sense the question is meaningless but that in some other and perhaps deeper sense it is meaningful, one would like to be told what this other and deeper sense is.

30. *Tractatus Logico-Philosophicus*, 6.5 and 6.51, Wittgenstein's italics.
31. *Wittgenstein und der Wiener Kreis*, Oxford, 1967, Appendix B, p. 245. (See also page 227), Waismann's italics.
32. *Op. cit.*, pp. 54–55.
33. *Op. cit.*, p. 4.
34. *Ibid.*, p. 10.

Pascal's "Why"

The super-ultimate why is by no means the only unintelligible why-question people ask. The question we met earlier, why there is life, is another such case, if it is asked by an unbelieving scientist who implies that he would continue to ask it even if a complete scientific account of the origin of life were in our possession. Just what is such a questioner looking for? A further illustration is the question which most people ask at one time or another as to why they were born into a certain age and place when they might "just as well" have been born into any number of other ages and localities. Pascal expressed this bafflement in one of the most famous passages of his *Pensées* (Section 28):

> When I consider the short duration of my life, swallowed up in the eternity before and after, the small place which I fill, or even can see, engulfed in the infinite immensity of spaces of which I know nothing and which know nothing of me, I am frightened, and I am astonished at being here rather than there; for there is no reason why here rather than there, why now rather than then.

Similarly, Mr. Paul Roubiczek, a contemporary admirer of Pascal, in the course of listing the various unanswerable "fundamental" whys, comes to what he calls "the problem of birth with which the Existentialists are much occupied." This is the

> problem why I am born into this particular age, into a country and family which I could not choose, with a character and faculties which I must accept.[35]

The fact that I was born into this particular age into a certain country and family and not into another age and another country and into another family, along with the existence of matter, life and the fact that I was "born to die" are "inexplicable phenomena."[36]

Insofar as Pascal and Roubiczek are merely complaining about the brevity of life and the feebleness of human faculties, what they say is perfectly intelligible. What may be doubted is whether their "why" introduces an intelligible question and hence whether the "problem" of birth is a case of genuine ignorance. What are Pascal and Roubiczek looking for when they ask "why am I here and now rather than there and then?" Certainly not details about their family-trees. Pascal (and I am sure the same is true of Mr. Roubiczek) knew who his parents were and we may presume that he was familiar with the facts of biological reproduction. Furthermore, although both Pascal and Roubiczek believe in God, it is very doubtful that they are here asking questions about God's intentions. Certainly the question "why am I here and now and not there and then?" has often been raised by people who do not believe in any divine plan. But if the question

35. *Existentialism For and Against,* Cambridge, England, 1964. p. 161.
36. *Ibid.*

does not express a search, either for the details of the person's ancestry or the motives of the Divinity, what kind of a search do we have? Clearly one without direction, and hence the question has no sense. It should also be remarked that there is something spurious and perverse about Pascal's astonishment. Pascal was, in fact, born into seventeenth century France. Let us suppose that he expressed astonishment at not having been born into fourteenth century Italy or nineteenth century England. But what if he had been born into fourteenth century Italy or nineteenth century England? He now would (or could with just as much reason) express astonishment at not having been born into seventeenth century France. Pascal tells us of his astonishment at being here and now and not there and then, but it is clear that if he had been there and then, he would have expressed equal astonishment at not being here and now. If I express amazement over the occurrence of A in the place of B, but if I express equal amazement when, in otherwise similar circumstances, B does happen, I may not be guilty of a formal contradiction, but my behavior is clearly absurd and I commit what some writers refer to as a "pragmatic inconsistency."

Perhaps Pascal was astonished at having been born at all. This astonishment, however, would be no less perverse than astonishment at being here and now and not there and then. If one or both of Pascal's parents had suffered from a serious fertility-impediment, his retrospective astonishment at having been born would not be out of place; and if his delivery had been attended by serious difficulties, astonishment at having been born alive might well be appropriate. For all I know, Pascal's parents did have fertility problems and perhaps his birth was an exceptionally difficult one. But clearly this is not the sort of thing he had in mind. In so far as Pascal was astonished at the fact of having been born, it was an astonishment that he would regard as equally appropriate for all human beings, including those who had an easy birth and those whose parents were noted for their fertility. In the latter kind of case, however, retrospective astonishment would surely be absurd and the same is true of universal astonishment—astonishment at the birth of all human beings. This becomes particularly evident when we reflect that if the Pascalian astonishment were justified it would be equally appropriate in relation to the future birth of human beings. Yet what could be *less* astonishing than that if there are going to be human beings in the future, they too will reproduce! The moment one explores such "ultimate mysteries" in a critical spirit they dissolve into absurdity and emptiness.

Why Does the Universe Exist?

However, to return to our main topic. The conclusion that the super-ultimate why-question is meaningless can also be reached by attending to what has here happened to the word "why." A little reflection shows that in the super-ultimate question, "why" has lost any of its ordinary meanings without having been given a new one. Let us see how this works when the question is put in the form "Why does the universe exist?" and when the "universe" is taken to include everything that in fact exists. In *any* of its familiar senses, when we ask of anything, *x*, why it happens or why it is what it is—whether *x* is the collapse of an army, a case of lung cancer, the theft of a jewel, or the stalling of a car—we assume that there is something or some set of conditions, other than *x*, in terms of which it can be explained. We do not know what this other thing is that is suitably related to *x*, but unless it is in principle possible to go beyond *x* and find such another thing, the question does not make any sense. (This has to be slightly modified to be accurate. If we are interested in the "why" of a state of *x* at a certain time, then the answer can certainly refer to an earlier state of *x*. This does not affect the issue here discussed since, in the sense with which we are concerned, reference to an earlier state of *x* is going beyond *x*.) Now, if by "the universe" we mean the totality of things, then our *x* in "Why does the universe exist?" is so all-inclusive that it is *logically* impossible to find anything which could be suitably related to that whose explanations we appear to be seeking. "The sense of the world," wrote Wittgenstein, "must lie outside the world,"[37] but by definition nothing can be outside the world. Heidegger, who avoids the formulation "Why does the universe exist?" and who instead inquires into the why of *das seiende* (the official translation of this term is "the essent," but Koestenbaum and others quite properly translate it as "things"), nevertheless makes it clear that *das seiende* here "takes in everything, and this means not only everything that is present in the broadest sense but also everything that ever was or will be." "Our question," he writes a little later, presumably without seeing the implications of this admission, "reaches out so far that we can never go further."[38]

For anybody who is not clearly aware of what we may call the logical grammar of "why," it is very easy to move from meaningful why-questions about particular things to the meaningless why-question about the universe. This tendency is aided by the picture that many people have of "the universe" as a huge box which contains all the things "inside it." Voltaire's article "Why?" from which we quoted earlier, is a good example of such an illegitimate transition. Voltaire first asks a number of why-questions about specific phenomena, such as

> Why does one hardly ever do the tenth part good one might do? Why in half of Europe do girls pray to God in Latin, which they do not understand? Why in antiquity was there never a thelogical quarrel, and why were no people ever distinguished by the name of a sect?

He then gets more and more philosophical:

> Why, as we are so miserable, have we imagined that not to be is a great ill, when it is clear that it was not an ill not to be before we were born?

A little later we have what may well be a theological "why":

> Why do we exist?

37. *Tractatus Logico-Philosophicus,* 6.41.
38. Heidegger, *op. cit.,* p. 2.

Finally, as if there had been no shift in the meaning of "why," Voltaire asks:

Why is there anything?[39]

It should be noted that the argument we have just presented is not in any way based on an empiricist meaning criterion or on any question-begging assumptions in favor of naturalism. Anybody who uses the word "universe" in a more restricted sense, so that it is not antecedently impossible to get to an entity that might be the explanation of the universe, may be asking a meaningful question when *he* asks "Why does the universe exist?" Furthermore, even if "universe" is used in the all-inclusive sense, what we have said does not rule out the possibility that God or various divine beings are part of the universe in this sense. The point has simply been that the word "why" loses its meaning when it becomes logically impossible to go beyond what one is trying to explain. This is a matter on which there need not be any disagreement between atheists and theists or between rationalists and empiricists.

It will be well to bring together the main conclusions of this article:

(1) There is a sense in which "how" and "why" have roughly the same meaning. In this sense science is perfectly competent to deal with the "why."

(2) There are certain senses in which "how" and "why" serve to ask distinct questions, but here too both types of questions can in principle be answered by empirical procedures.

(3) One of the cosmic "whys"—what we have called the theological "why"—is used to ask meaningful questions, at least if certain semantic problems about theological utterances are disregarded. It was pointed out, however, that this does not imply that the theological answers are true or well supported.

(4) Some apparent questions introduced by "why" are really complaints and not questions, and for this reason unanswerable.

(5) The super-ultimate why-question, which has so widely been regarded as supremely profound, is meaningless.

39. *Op. cit.*, vol. 6, pp. 357–358.

Selected Bibliography

(ITEMS PROVIDED WITH ASTERISK ARE MORE ADVANCED)
(FOR KEY TO ABBREVIATIONS SEE PAGE XIX)

The history of the "Vienna Circle" and of its doctrines is covered in V. Kraft, *The Vienna Circle* (N.Y.: Philosophical Library, 1952) and in J. Joergensen, *The Development of Logical Empiricism* (Chicago: U. of Chicago

P., 1951). The following are systematic and sympathetic expositions of logical positivism: A. J. Ayer, *Language, Truth and Logic* (London: Gollancz, N.Y.: Dover, 2nd edition, 1946, p), R. Von Mises, *Positivism, A Study in Human Understanding* (Cambridge: Harvard U.P., 1951), and H. Reichenbach, *The Rise of Scientific Philosophy* (Berkeley and Los Angeles: U. of California P., 1951, p). R. Carnap, *Philosophy and Logical Syntax* (London: Kegan Paul, 1935), the whole of which is reprinted in W. P. Alston and G. Nakhnikian (eds.), *Twentieth Century Philosophy* (N.Y.: Free Press, 1963), is a concise and elementary exposition of the logical positivists' conception of philosophy as logical analysis of language and of their rejection of metaphysics. A. Pap, *Elements of Analytic Philosophy* (N.Y.: Macmillan, 1949), contains a sympathetic, but partly critical, exposition, with references to both the teachings of the Vienna Circle and those of the Cambridge analysts (Russell, Moore). Sympathetic discussions may also be found in J. Hospers, *An Introduction to Philosophical Analysis* (Englewood Cliffs: Prentice-Hall, 2nd ed., 1967), Ch. 4, and in K. Nielsen, *Reason and Practice* (N.Y.: Harper, 1971), Chs. 31–33. There is a very useful introductory exposition of the major tenets of logical positivism in H. Feigl's article, "Logical Empiricism," which is available in H. Feigl and W. Sellars (eds.), *Readings in Philosophical Analysis* (N.Y.: Appleton-Century-Crofts, 1949), and a more recent introductory exposition, together with critical commentary, in R. W. Ashby's contribution to D. J. O'Connor (ed.), *A Critical History of Western Philosophy* (N.Y.: Free Press, 1964). H. Feigl, "The Origin and Spirit of Logical Positivism," in P. Achinstein and S. F. Barker (eds.), *The Legacy of Logical Positivism* (Baltimore: Johns Hopkins Press, 1969) is a short account of the history of logical positivism. A. J. Ayer (ed.), *Logical Positivism* (N.Y.: Free Press, 1959, p) is a collection of papers by leading logical positivists. Most of these were originally published in German in *Erkenntnis*, the organ of the Vienna Circle, and are here available in English for the first time. There is a comprehensive discussion of the key doctrines of logical positivism in its early days in two articles by Ernest Nagel entitled "Impressions and Appraisals of Analytic Philosophy in Europe," *JP*, 1936, reprinted in E. Nagel, *Logic without Metaphysics* (N.Y.: Free Press, 1957). The entire movement is placed in its historical context in Ch. XVI of J. Passmore, *A Hundred Years of Philosophy* (Harmondsworth: Pelican Books, 2nd ed., 1968, p), Ch. IV of G. J. Warnock, *English Philosophy Since 1900* (London: Oxford U.P., 1958), and most fully in Part II of J. O. Urmson, *Philosophical Analysis: Its Development between the Two World Wars* (Oxford: Clarendon Press, 1956). Much of Urmson's book deals with the ideas contained in Ludwig Wittenstein's classic work, *Tractatus Logico-Philosophicus** (London: Kegan Paul, N.Y.: Harcourt Brace, 1922, new English translation by D. F. Pears and B. F. McGuinness, 1962), which greatly influenced the founders of the Vienna Circle. Critical discussions of logical positivism are to be found in W. F. H. Barnes, *The Philosophical Predicament* (London: A. & C. Black, 1950), C. E. M. Joad, *A Critique of Logical Positivism* (Chicago: U. of Chicago P., 1950), J. Weinberg, *A Critical Examination of Logical Positivism* (London: Kegan Paul, 1936), and F. C. Copleston, *Contemporary Philosophy* (London: Burns & Oates, 1956). The last-mentioned of these works is written from a Catholic standpoint. The most elaborate recent attack on logical positivism is contained in B. Blanshard, *Reason and Analysis* (London: Allen & Unwin, LaSalle, Illinois: Open Court, 1962). Ch. V of this work contains numerous arguments against the verifiability theory. A more recent and more concise critique of logical positivism is found in the same author's "In Defense of Metaphysics," in W. E. Kennick and M. Lazerowitz (eds.), *Metaphysics* (Englewood Cliffs: Prentice-Hall, 1966).

Charles Peirce's "How To Make Our Ideas Clear," in J. Buchler (ed.), *The Philosophy of Peirce* (N.Y.: Harcourt, Brace, 1940), is a classical statement of an empiricist theory of meaning by the founder of American pragmatism. W. P. Alston in "Pragmatism and the Verifiability Theory of Meaning," *PSt*, 1955, traces some of the connections between Peirce's theory and the later verifiability principle of the logical positivists. M. Schlick's "Meaning and Verification," *PR*, 1936, is a classic defense of the verifiability theory of meaning, against C. I. Lewis' "Experience and Meaning," *PR*, 1934. The essays by Schlick and C. I. Lewis are reprinted in Feigl and Sellars, *op. cit.* Schlick's is also available in Alston and Nakhnikian, *op. cit.* Another famous defense of the verifiability principle as well as of its destructive implication for traditional speculative philosophy is R. Carnap's "The Elimination of Metaphysics through Logical Analysis of Language," in A. J. Ayer (ed.), *Logical Positivism, op. cit.* The same author's "Testability and Meaning,"* *PS*, 1936–37, is a substantially revised and very precise formulation of the principle. It presupposes some knowledge of symbolic logic. The same is true of a recent exposition of the principle by W. Yourgrau and C. Works, "A New Formalized Version of the Verifiability Principle,"* *R*, 1968. "The Methodological Character of Theoretical Concepts,"* in H. Feigl and M. Scriven (eds.), *Minnesota Studies in Philosophy of Science*, Volume I (Minneapolis: U. of Minnesota P., 1956), contains Carnap's most recent full-length discussion of the problems in question, with special reference to "theoretical languages" like the language of theoretical physics. There are critical discussions of various aspects of Carnap's position by P. Frank, K. R. Popper, and P. Henle in P. A. Schilpp (ed.), *The Philosophy of Rudolf Carnap* (LaSalle, Illinois: Open Court, 1964), which also contains Carnap's account of the history of his views on the subject and replies to his critics. Although the Schilpp volume was not published until 1964, most of the contributions were written in the early or middle 1950's. A more recent criticism of Carnap is W. W. Rozeboom, "A Note on Carnap's Meaning Criterion," *PSt*, 1960. In "Problems and Changes in the Empiricist Criterion of Meaning," reprinted in A. J. Ayer (ed.), *Logical Positivism, op. cit.*, C. G. Hempel surveys the history of the principle and closes with a formulation that is closely patterned after Carnap's "Testability and Meaning." In "The Criterion of Cognitive Significance: A Reconsideration,"* in *Proc. of the American Academy of Arts and Sciences*, 1951, the same author doubts whether a sharp distinction between the cognitively meaningful and the cognitively meaningless can be drawn. Hempel has brought together highlights of both of these articles, with a number of revisions, in Ch. IV of his book, *Aspects of Explanation* (N.Y.: Free Press, 1965, p). An elaborate and critical discussion of the verifiability principle will also be found in Ch. IV of W. P. Alston, *Philosophy of Language* (Englewood Cliffs: Prentice-Hall, 1964, p). Two recent works on the philosophy of science —A. Pap, *An Introduction to the Philosophy of Science* (N.Y.: Free Press, 1962), and I. Scheffler, *The Anatomy of Inquiry* (N.Y.: Knopf, 1963)—contain detailed discussions of the verifiability principle, chiefly in connection with the problems raised by the use of disposition terms and the so-called theoretical terms in scientific discourse. There is a very clear account of the verifiability principle and of later developments in linguistic philosophy in the early chapters of F. Ferré, *Language, Logic and God* (N.Y.: Harper, 1961).

An early paper by Ayer, "The Genesis of Metaphysics," *A*, 1934, is available in M. MacDonald (ed.), *Philosophy and Analysis* (Oxford: Blackwell, 1954). His "The Principle of Verifiability," *M*, 1936, is a reply to criticisms in

W. T. Stace, "Metaphysics and Meaning," *M,* 1935. A later criticism of the verifiability theory of meaning by Stace is his "Positivism," *M,* 1944. Among other things Stace argues that the theory is not entailed by the principle of (concept) empiricism. Also critical of Ayer is M. Lazerowitz in a number of articles which have been reprinted in his *The Structure of Metaphysics* (London: Routledge, 1955). Ayer replied to several of his critics in the introduction to the second edition of *Language, Truth and Logic, op. cit.* This introduction, in turn, gave rise to several critical articles, including J. Wisdom, "Note on the New Edition of Professor Ayer's *Language, Truth and Logic,*" *M,* 1948, reprinted in his *Philosophy and Psycho-Analysis* (Oxford: Blackwell, 1953), and D. J. O'Connor, "Some Consequences of Professor Ayer's Verification Principle," *A,* 1950. O'Connor, in turn, is criticized by R. Brown and J. Watling, "Amending the Verification Principle," *M,* 1951. An important criticism of Ayer's later formulation is contained in Alonzo Church's review of the second edition of *Language, Truth and Logic* in the *Journal of Symbolic Logic,* 1949. There is a reply to Church by P. Nidditch in *M,* 1961. Ayer's most recent statement of his views, particularly concerning the status of the verifiability principle, is contained in his introduction to *Logical Positivism, op. cit.*

Gilbert Ryle, "Unverifiability-by-Me," *A,* 1936, discusses some of the difficulties in the notion of verifiability in principle. There are sympathetic discussions of the verifiability principle in C. H. Whiteley, "On Meaning and Verifiability," *A,* 1939, B. Kalish, "Meaning and Truth," in Volume 25 of the *University of California Publications in Philosophy* (Berkeley: U. of California P., 1950), A. Pap, "Other Minds and the Principle of Verifiability," *Revue Internationale de Philosophie,* 1951, D. Rynin, "Vindication of L*G*C*L*P*S*T*V*SM," *Proc. and Addresses of the American Philosophical Association,* 1957, and M. Zimmerman, "The Status of the Verifiability Principle," *PPR,* 1962. Critical in varying degrees are M. MacDonald, "Verification and Understanding," *Ar. Soc.,* 1933–34, L. S. Stebbing, "Communication and Verification," *Ar. Soc. Sup.,* 1934, C. J. Ducasse, "Verification, Verifiability and Meaningfulness," *JP,* 1936, A. D. Ritchie, "The Errors of Logical Positivism," *P,* 1937, I. Berlin, "Verification," *Ar. Soc.,* 1938–39, F. Waismann, "Verifiability,"* *Ar. Soc. Sup.,* 1945, reprinted in A. Flew (ed.), *Logic and Language,* First Series (Oxford: Blackwell, 1951), and also in Waismann's *How I See Philosophy* (London: Macmillan, 1968), Ch. 16 of the same author's posthumously published *The Principles of Linguistic Philosophy* (London: Macmillan, 1965), Bertrand Russell's "Logical Positivisim," *Polemic,* 1945, and his article by the same name written in 1950 and published in his book, *Logic and Knowledge* (London: Allen & Unwin, 1956), P. Marhenke, "The Criterion of Significance," *Proc. and Addresses of the American Philosophical Association,* 1950, which is reprinted in L. Linsky (ed.), *Semantics and the Philosophy of Language* (Urbana: U. of Illinois P., 1952), J. L. Evans, "On Meaning and Verification," *M,* 1953, W. P. Alston, "Are Positivists Metaphysicians?" *PR,* 1954, Ch. 5 of J. Passmore, *Philosophical Reasoning* (London: Duckworth, 1961), C. F. Presley, "Arguments About Meaninglessness,"* *BJPS,* 1961, Harry Ruja, "The Present Status of the Verifiability Criterion," *PPR,* 1961, G. Maxwell, "Criteria of Meaning and Demarcation," and W. C. Salmon, "Verifiability and Logic." The papers by Maxwell and Salmon are included in P. K. Feyerabend and G. Maxwell (eds.), *Mind, Matter and Method—Essays in Honor of Herbert Feigl* (Minneapolis: Minnesota U.P., 1967). The theologian E. L. Mascale attacks the verifiability principle in Ch. 1 of his *Words and Images* (London: Longmans, Green, 1957). The verifiability principle is also criticized in three recent articles by A. Ambrose—"Metamorphoses of the Principle of

Verifiability," in F. C. Dommeyer (ed.), *Current Philosophical Issues* (Springfield, Illinois: Thomas, 1966), "On Criteria of Literal Significance," *Critica* (Mexico), 1967, and in "Factual, Mathematical and Metaphysical Inventories," contained in her *Essays in Analysis* (London: Allen & Unwin, 1966). Ambrose, however, is not a champion of metaphysics. In the last-mentioned article she concludes that metaphysical theories give verbal information and do not tell anything "about what there is in the world." In *The Concept of Meaninglessness* (Baltimore: Johns Hopkins Press, 1970), E. Erwin argues against the possibility of developing a workable criterion of meaningfulness along verificationistic lines, maintaining that meaninglessness should be identified with "*a priori* falseness." In "Nonsense," *Me*, 1971, S. J. Odell argues that sense and nonsense are a matter of degree, that they constitute a continuum, not a dichotomy.

The article by G. J. Warnock, which is reprinted as Selection 65 in the present work, is fairly representative of the attitude of many Anglo-Saxon philosophers with a basically empiricistic outlook who, however, came to reject the logical positivist approach on some important questions. These writers maintain that the advocates of the verifiability principle, like other philosophers before them, have far too simple a view or model of the functions of language. While the challenge, "How could this sentence be verified?" may serve a useful purpose in certain contexts, it is in general more fruitful to ask for the *use* rather than for the meaning of a word or a sentence. This development is very clearly traced in Part III of Urmson, *Philosophical Analysis, op. cit.*, and several of its phases are discussed in Warnock, *English Philosophy Since 1900, op. cit.* Undoubtedly, the philosopher most responsible for this change in outlook was Wittgenstein, whose *Philosophical Investigations** (Oxford: Blackwell, 1953) was not published until two years after his death. He exercised his influence largely through the publications of those who attended his lectures at Cambridge in the 1930's and 1940's, especially two articles by J. Wisdom—"Philosophical Perplexity,"* *Ar. Soc.*, 1936–37, and "Metaphysics and Verification,"* *M*, 1938, both of which are reprinted in his *Philosophy and Psychoanalysis, op. cit.* Later essays defending or applying the new outlook are Gilbert Ryle's "Ordinary Language," *PR*, 1953, and "The Theory of Meaning," in C. A. Mace (ed.), *British Philosophy in the Mid-Century* (London: Allen & Unwin, N.Y.: Macmillan, 1957), and P. F. Strawson's "On Referring," *M*, 1950. The three papers just mentioned are available in C. E. Caton (ed.), *Philosophy and Ordinary Language* (Urbana: U. of Illinois P., 1963); Ryle's paper on "Ordinary Language" is also available in V. C. Chappell (ed.), *Ordinary Language: Essays in Philosophical Method* (Englewood Cliffs: Prentice-Hall, 1964, p). Questions about the relation between meaning and use and other related issues are discussed in Chs. 34–36 of K. Nielsen, *Reason and Practice, op. cit.*, O. P. Wood, "The Force of Linguistic Rules," *Ar. Soc.*, 1950–51, K. Baier, "The Ordinary Use of Words," *Ar. Soc.*, 1951–52, J. L. Evans, "On Meaning and Verification," *op. cit.*, which is criticized in R. Abelson, "Meaning, Use and Rules of Use," *PPR*, 1957 (there is an answer by Evans in *PPR*, 1961, with a rejoinder by Abelson in the same volume), R. W. Ashby, "Use and Verification," *Ar. Soc.*, 1955–56, M. Shorter, "Meaning and Grammar," *AJ*, 1956, M. Black, "Notes on the Meaning of 'Rule'," *T*, 1958, reprinted in his *Models and Metaphors* (Ithaca: Cornell U.P., 1962), P. Butchvarnov, "Meaning-as-Use and Meaning-as-Correspondence," *P*, 1960, G. Ryle and J. N. Findlay, "Use, Usage and Meaning," *Ar. Soc. Sup.*, 1961, J. R. Searle, "Meaning and Speech Acts," *PR*, 1962, R. Brown, "Meaning and Rules of Use," *M*, 1962, W. P. Alston, "Meaning and Use," *PQ*, 1963, the same author's "The Quest for Meanings," *M*, 1963, and "Linguistic Acts," *PQ*, 1964, and Bishop Anders

Nygren, "From Atomism to Context of Meaning in Philosophy," in *Philosophical Essays Dedicated to Gunnar Aspelin* (Lund, Sweden: Gleedup Bokförlag, 1963). In "Metamorphoses of the Verifiability Theory of Meaning," *M*, 1963, J. O. Wisdom (not to be confused with John Wisdom) argues first that the verifiability principle fails to "drive a wedge" between meaningful and meaningless utterances as intended by its advocates and then proceeds to examine the relation between the verifiability principle and what he calls "the principle of the 'use of'" employed by Ryle and other Oxford philosophers. He concludes that the principle of the "use of" either reduces to the verifiability principle or else does not succeed in "hitting" the philosophical theories that are to be ruled out by its application. The text of some of Wittgenstein's lectures during the 1930's has been published as *The Blue and Brown Books** (Oxford: Blackwell, 1958), and G. E. Moore, who attended some of them, published his recollections, together with critical observations, as a series of articles, "Wittgenstein's Lectures in 1930–1933," *M*, 1954 and 1955, reprinted in Moore's *Philosophical Papers* (London: Allen & Unwin, 1959, N.Y.: Collier Books, 1962, p). Those who can read German will find Wittgenstein's discussions of many philosophical questions, including problems about meaning, use and verification, in his *Philosophische Bemerkungen* (Oxford: Blackwell, 1964), *Philosophische Grammatik* (Oxford: Blackwell, 1969), and in F. Waismann, *Ludwig Wittgenstein und der Wiener Kreis* (Oxford: Blackwell, 1967). The last of these consists for the most part of notes Waismann took of conversations between Wittgenstein, Schlick, and himself in 1929–32. It also contains, as Appendix B, nine theses, formulated by Waismann in 1930, which constitute a kind of manifesto of logical positivism. The literature on Wittgenstein is immense. A good critical introduction to some of his leading ideas is found in Ch. 2 of A. Naess, *Four Modern Philosophers* (Chicago: U. of Chicago P., 1968). Ch. 1 of the same work gives an introduction to Carnap's philosophy. There are detailed discussions of the work of Wittgenstein, Carnap, and Schlick in W. Stegmüller, *Main Currents in Contemporary German, British and American Philosophy* (Bloomington: Indiana U.P., 1971).

With the decline in the popularity of the verifiability principle came a reluctance to condemn metaphysical utterances as simply "meaningless." It has been argued, especially by J. Wisdom, in "Metaphysics and Verification," *op. cit.*, and in his later paper, "Metaphysics," *Ar. Soc.*, 1950–51, which is reprinted in his *Other Minds* (Oxford: Blackwell, 1952), and by F. Waismann, in his "How I See Philosophy," in H. D. Lewis (ed.), *Contemporary British Philosophy, Third Series* (London: Allen & Unwin, N.Y.: Macmillan, 1956), reprinted in Waismann's *How I See Philosophy, op. cit.*, and in A. J. Ayer, *Logical Positivism, op. cit.*, that the paradoxical theses of metaphysicians may well embody some insights and call attention to facts that are commonly overlooked. Wisdom's most recent contribution to the discussion is "The Metamorphosis of Metaphysics," *Proc. of the British Academy*, 1963, reprinted in his *Paradox and Discovery* (Oxford: Blackwell, 1965). D. F. Pears (ed.), *The Nature of Metaphysics* (London: Macmillan, 1957), consists of BBC talks by a number of distinguished British philosophers on different aspects of metaphysics. While none of them endorses any of the traditional speculative systems or indeed advocates a revival of this kind of philosophizing, their verdict is in general more sympathetic and charitable than that of the philosophers of the Vienna Circle. Mention should also be made of two articles by J. W. N. Watkins— "Between Analytical and Empirical," *P*, 1957, and "Confirmable and Influential Metaphysics," *M*, 1958—in which he first criticizes the three-fold classification by the logical positivists of declarative sentences into empirical, analytic, and meaningless and then proceeds to give examples of what he calls "metaphysical" theories which are clearly meaningful and have served important uses in the progress of science but which are not open to any kind of empirical testing. The criticisms by Watkins are derived from certain of K. R. Popper's ideas on the subject which are stated most succinctly in Popper's papers "The Demarcation Between Science and Metaphysics" and "On the Status of Science and Metaphysics," both now available in Popper's book, *Conjectures and Refutations* (N.Y.: Harper, 1963). According to G. E. Myers in "Metaphysics and Extended Meaning," *AJ*, 1964, certain metaphysical utterances which at first seem baffling may turn out to be intelligible if we introduce the concept of "extended meaning." Indicative of the more moderate climate of recent empiricist writings on the subject is Y. Bar-Hillel, "A Prerequisite for Rational Philosophical Discussion," in *Logic and Language: Studies Dedicated to Professor Rudolf Carnap on the Occasion of His Seventieth Birthday* (Dordrecht-Holland: D. Reidel, 1962). Bar-Hillel is an Israeli philosopher who owes much more to Carnap than to Wittgenstein or the Oxford "ordinary language" philosophers, but rather than condemning his "speculative colleagues" as talking "nonsense," he attempts to lay down conditions for useful discussion between analytic philosophers and metaphysicians. A similar attitude is adopted in M. Thompson's critical survey-article, "Metaphysics," in R. M. Chisholm *et al., Philosophy—The Princeton Studies* (Englewood Cliffs: Prentice-Hall, 1964).

The question of the conditions that must be fulfilled in order for a question to be meaningful or genuine, which is discussed in our Selections 65 and 66, is also explored in sections 179 and 180 of R. Carnap, *The Logical Structure of the World* (Berkeley: U. of California P., 1967) and in Ch. 20 of F. Waismann, *The Principles of Linguistic Philosophy, op. cit.* The nature of questions is also discussed in the article on "Questions" by C. L. Hamblin in *The Encyclopedia of Philosophy* (7–49). Selection 67 contains numerous references to the writings of philosophers who concerned themselves with "ultimate" why-questions. The theological "why" is discussed in an essay by Leibniz, "On the Ultimate Origination of Things," which is included in most popular editions of Leibniz' works. There are some interesting remarks on the "quasi-theological" why in Ch. 14 of S. E. Toulmin, *The Place of Reason in Ethics* (Cambridge: Cambridge U.P., 1950). Heidegger is by no means the only German philosopher who regards the "super-ultimate" why-question as of tremendous importance. In an essay entitled "Von Wesen der Philosophie und der Moralischen Bedingung des philosophischen Erkennens," Max Scheler remarks that "he who has not, as it were, looked into the abyss of the absolute Nothing will completely overlook the eminently positive content of the realization that there is something rather than nothing" (*Gesammelte Werke*, Volume V, pages 93ff. Bern, Switzerland, 1954). In *The Mystery of Existence* (N.Y.: Appleton-Century-Crofts, 1965), M. K. Munitz argues, in opposition to the position presented in Selection 67, that the super-ultimate why-question is intelligible.

The following articles in the *Encyclopedia of Philosophy* deal with topics discussed in the present section: "Carnap, Rudolf" (N. M. Martin, 2–25), "Emotive Meaning" (W. P. Alston, 2–486), "Logical Positivism," (J. Passmore, 5–52), "Meaning" (W. P. Alston, 5–233), "Metaphor" (M. C. Beardsley, 5–284), "Metaphysics, History of" (R. Hancock, 5–289), "Metaphysics, Nature of" (W. H. Walsh, 5–300) "Nonsense" (A. C. Baier, 5–250), "Schlick, Moritz" (B. Juhos, 7–319), "Verifiability Principle" (R. W. Ashby, 8–240), and "Wittgenstein, Ludwig," (N. Malcolm, 8–327). Two recent paperback anthologies —A. and K. Lehrer (eds.), *Theory of Meaning* (Englewood Cliffs: Prentice-Hall, 1970) and G. H. R. Parkinson (ed.), *The Theory of Meaning* (London and N.Y.: Oxford U.P., 1968)—contain several papers dealing with questions treated in the present section.

There is a very full bibliography of writings by logical positivists (and their critics) as well as analytic philosophers, in a broad sense of that term, going up to 1958 in Ayer, *Logical Positivism, op. cit.* A less comprehensive but very useful bibliography will be found in R. Rorty (ed.), *The Linguistic Turn* (Chicago: U. of Chicago P., 1967). For bibliographical material on the question of the meaningfulness (or otherwise) of theological statements, see the Bibliography to Section 5, pages 561 ff. above.

Biographical Notes

ST. ANSELM (1033(?)–1109) was born in Aosta in Piedmont. After study-ing at Avranches in Burgundy and later at Bec he entered the Benedictine Order and became first Prior and subsequently Abbot of the Monastery of Bec which was, at that time, one of the greatest centers of learning in Europe. In 1093 he became Archbishop of Canterbury. Although Anselm himself did not make any sharp distinction between philosophy and theology, today we would classify most of his works as belonging primarily to theology. His chief philosophical writings are the *Monologion* (1076) and the *Proslogion* (1077–1078). The latter work contains the famous ontological argument, but the former is also of considerable interest. In it Anselm advances the proof from the degrees of perfection found in creatures as well as a form of the cosmologi-cal argument. In his exposition of the latter proof he has some trenchant re-marks about the meaning of "nothing," pointing out that it is equivalent to "not anything" and that it should not be regarded as the name of a shadowy, mysterious entity.

THOMAS AQUINAS (c. 1226–1274). St. Thomas is generally acknowledged as the greatest of the medieval philosophers. He produced an imposing intellec-tual system which was a synthesis of Christian theology and Aristotelian metaphysics. While many contemporary philosophers are not sympathetic either to his conclusions or his method, the sharpness and power of his mind are universally admired. The two main works of Aquinas are the *Summa Theolog-ica* and the *Summa contra Gentiles*. The latter of these is a philosophical de-fense of Christianity addressed to a reader who is assumed not to be already a Christian. In his attempts to refute anti-Christian doctrines, Aquinas took great care to state the opposing theories with full force and fairness—some-thing which is unfortunately not true of all great philosophers.

Aquinas was of noble descent. When quite young he joined the Dominican order which he selflessly served for the rest of his life. He was asked to fill numerous important posts in the Church, including that of Archbishop of Naples, but declined all such offers. In 1323 he was canonized by Pope John XXII. In 1879 Pope Leo XIII, in the Encyclical, *Aeterni Patris,* urged the Catholic clergy to make the teachings of Aquinas the basis of their theological outlook. Although his ideas became before long a conservative force, Aquinas was in his own day quite a bold innovator and on occasions he was de-nounced for his unorthodox positions.

A. J. AYER, born 1910, Wykeham Professor of Logic in the University of Oxford. Ayer is the leading exponent of logical positivism in Great Britain and his *Language, Truth and Logic* (1936) is regarded as a kind of textbook of this school. Few philosophical works in any age have been more widely discussed. His other works are *The Foundations of Empirical Knowledge* (1940), *Philosophical Essays* (1954), *The Problem of Knowledge* (1956), *The Concept of a Person and Other Essays* (1963), *The Origins of Pragmatism* (1968), *Metaphysics and Common Sense* (1969), *Russell and Moore: The Analytical Heritage* (1971), and *Probability and Evidence* (1972). He is also editor of *Logical Positivism* (1959). Ayer is a Fellow of the British Academy. He was knighted in 1970.

S. I. BENN, born in 1920, Senior Fellow in Philosophy at the Australian National University, Canberra. Before his present appointment, Mr. Benn was Lecturer in Political Theory at the University of Southampton. He has contributed articles, chiefly on political philosophy, to various periodicals and is co-author (with R. S. Peters) of *Social Principles and the Democratic State* (1959), (American edition, *The Principles of Political Thought* [1964]).

GEORGE BERKELEY (1685–1753). Born in Kilkenny County, Ireland, Berkeley studied at Trinity College, Dublin, and there became first a tutor and later a lecturer in Greek and Theology. Berkeley wrote his three most important works very early in life. These are *An Essay Towards a New Theory of Vision* (1709), *The Principles of Human Knowledge* (1710), and *Three Dialogues Between Hylas and Philonous* (1713). A projected volume on ethics was never published; Berkeley lost the manuscript while traveling in Italy and did not return to the subject. Like Locke and Hume, Berkeley was a critic of the abstractions dominant in scholastic philosophy, but he was equally critical of the mathematical abstractions, especially infinitesimals, that helped Newtonian physics to such spectacular success. His epistemological idealism (*esse est percipi*) was motivated partly by his dissatisfaction with Locke's theory of knowledge and partly by the desire to find a new justification for belief in God. He considerably influenced the German tradition of idealistic metaphysics, but his manner of philosophizing was much more akin to contemporary British analysis.

One of Berkeley's pet schemes was the foundation of a college in the Bermudas which would train missionaries and clergymen for the American colonies. This project brought him to America where he spent three years (1728–1731) at Newport, Rhode Island. The House of Commons, however, did not fulfill its promise of a substantial subsidy and the plan was never carried into practice. Berkeley, who was a model of theological orthodoxy, eventually became a Bishop in the Church of England (1734) and in his later years he was more occupied with his ecclesiastical duties than with philosophy.

MAX BLACK, born 1909, Susan Linn Sage Professor of Philosophy at Cornell University. Black studied at the Universities of Cambridge, Göttingen, and London where he received his Ph.D. He is a Fellow of the American Academy of Arts and Sciences. Black has been particularly interested in probability and induction and various problems in the philosophy of language. In addition to their many other virtues, Black's writings are distinguished for their great clarity and freedom from any kind of technical jargon. He is the author of *The Nature of Mathematics* (1933), *Critical Thinking* (1946), *Language and Philosophy* (1949), *Problems of Analysis* (1954), *Models and Metaphors* (1962), *A Companion to Wittgenstein's Tractatus* (1964), *The Labyrinth of Language* (1968), and *Margins of Precision* (1970). He is also the editor of two volumes of philosophical essays, *Philosophical Analysis* (1950) and *Philosophy in America* (1964), and a volume of essays on language, *The Importance of Language* (1962).

BRAND BLANSHARD, born 1892, Professor Emeritus at Yale. Blanshard is one of the most distinguished contemporary American philosophers. The fullest statement of his philosophical position is found in his *The Nature of Thought* (1939). A restatement of his epistemological and metaphysical theories, together with a detailed examination of the views of the logical positivists and other analytic philosophers, is contained in *Reason and Analysis* (1962). Blanshard's ethical theories are worked out in *Reason and Goodness* (1961). Usually classified as an "idealist," Blanshard himself prefers the label of "rationalist." Unlike other members of the idealist tradition, Blanshard is a master of lucid English prose. He is a past president of the American Philosophical Association and of the American Theological Society. Blanshard is a Fellow of the British Academy.

C. D. BROAD (1887–1971). Broad taught for many years at Cambridge University where he held the Knightsbridge Chair of Philosophy. He was one of the most influential British philosophers of recent years. He was particularly admired for the great thoroughness and lucidity of his treatment of the most diverse philosophical questions. His publications include *Perception, Physics and Reality* (1913), *Scientific Thought* (1923), *The Mind and Its Place in Nature* (1925), *Five Types of Ethical Theory* (1930), *An Examination of McTaggart's Philosophy* (1933 and 1938), *Ethics and the History of Philosophy* (1952), *Religion, Philosophy, and Psychical Research* (1953), *Lectures on Psychical Research* (1962), and *Induction, Probability and Causation* (1968). *The Philosophy of C. D. Broad* (1959, ed. P. A. Schilpp) contains an autobiographical sketch by Broad, a number of critical essays on different aspects of Broad's philosophy, as well as Broad's replies.

HENRY THOMAS BUCKLE (1821–1862) was the son of a prosperous businessman who left him sufficient money to devote his life to research and writing. Buckle never went to a University, but his natural talents and industry more than compensated for any lack of formal academic training. When quite young he decided to write a comprehensive history of civilization which would illustrate his theories about the causes of historical development. At the time of his death at the age of forty, only two volumes of the *History of Civilization in England* had appeared, and these were regarded by Buckle as no more than an introduction to the huge work he had planned. However, these volumes presented his chief philosophical convictions and they won the author great critical acclaim. According to Buckle, the fundamental agents of social development are not, as other writers had claimed, innate racial characteristics or "national spirits," but physical factors such as "Climate, Food, Soil and the General Aspect of Nature." Human rather than physical factors become causally effective in a civilization which does not suffer from overpopulation and in which the enjoyment of leisure has become possible. Buckle was, however, opposed to any kind of "great man" theory of history. Rulers of nations in his view are "creatures of the age, never its creators." Buckle was an unbeliever and on terms of personal friendship with some of the outstanding Victorian freethinkers, including Charles Darwin and John Stuart Mill.

C. A. CAMPBELL, born 1897, Professor Emeritus at the University of Glasgow. He is the author of *Scepticism and Construction* (1931), *Of Selfhood and Godhood* (1956), *In Defense of Free Will* (1967) and numerous articles in philosophical periodicals. Campbell has been acutely critical of many of the key doctrines of logical positivism. His own position may be described as a form of rationalistic idealism. He is a Fellow of the British Academy.

F. C. COPLESTON, S.J., born 1907, Professor of Metaphysics at the Pontifical Gregorian University, Rome, and of the History of Philosophy at Heythrop College, Oxford. Father Copleston has been a member of the Society of Jesus since 1930 and is widely considered the leading Catholic philosopher in the Anglo-Saxon world. His books include *Nietzsche* (1942), *Schopenhauer* (1946),

Medieval Philosophy (1952), *Aquinas* (1955), *Contemporary Philosophy* (1956), and the monumental *History of Philosophy* in 8 volumes. The last-mentioned work is widely admired for its painstaking scholarship and the fairness of its discussions.

CLARENCE DARROW (1857–1938). For nearly fifty years Darrow was one of the most colorful figures on the American scene. He appeared as counsel for the defense in many classic cases, especially in support of political radicals and pioneer union organizers. Believing that no human being is ever morally responsible for his actions, Darrow constantly worked for a more humane attitude towards criminals and was a leader in the movement to abolish capital punishment. In the sensational trial of the "Nietzschean" murderers, Loeb and Leopold, his moving plea saved the accused boys from an otherwise certain death sentence. Darrow was one of the very few men in American public life to speak out openly against religion and in 1925 he defended the biology teacher, John T. Scopes, in the notorious "monkey trial" in Dayton, Tennessee. His best-known books are *Resist Not Evil* (1904), *Farmington* (1905), *Crime, Its Cause and Treatment* (1925), *Infidels and Heretics* (1927, with Walter Rice), and *The Story of My Life* (1932). In recent years there has been a revival of interest in Darrow's ideas. His most famous pleas have been reprinted under the title of *Attorney for the Damned* (1957) and his occasional writings on philosophical, social, and literary topics under the title of *Verdicts Out of Court* (1963). The latter volume contains Darrow's defense of agnosticism, his views on immortality, and a statement of his pessimism.

RENÉ DESCARTES (1596–1650). Descartes is usually considered the founder of modern Western philosophy. In raising fundamental questions about the nature of the human mind and the extent to which our claims to knowledge can be trusted he was a forerunner of Kant's critique of dogmatic metaphysics. By his insistence that whatever we immediately know must be a content of our minds he greatly influenced the idealist movement. Although Descartes had much contempt for the scholastics he shared their view that the existence of God can be logically demonstrated. He endorsed some of the medieval arguments and to these he added one of his own. Descartes believed that animals were feelingless and unthinking automata all of whose actions could be completely explained in mechanical terms. By contrast, human beings possess both souls and bodies, and Descartes worked out a detailed theory of body-mind interaction. The automaton theory was extended by later philosophers to human beings and thus led to the materialism of the eighteenth and nineteenth centuries. Some of Descartes' immediate successors accepted his conception of the body and the mind as radically different substances, but could not see how interaction was possible between them. They became the founders of "parallelism."

Descartes was also intensely interested in science and mathematics. He invented analytic geometry and was one of the first to note the significance of the work of Galileo and Harvey. He did not dare to publish his great work *Le Monde* during his lifetime since it contained the heretical doctrines of the earth's rotation and the infinity of the universe. Lamettrie and other later unbelievers were convinced that Descartes was dissembling when he professed to be a champion of religion but most historians today agree that his professions of piety were sincere. His most important philosophical works are *The Discourse on Method* (1637), *The Meditations* (1641), *The Principles of Philosophy* (1644), and the *Passions of the Soul* (1650). Some of his most interesting observations are contained in his letters to Princess Elizabeth of Holland and in his answers to various critics.

FYODOR MIKHAILOVICH DOSTOEVSKY (1821–1881), was born in Moscow where his father was resident physician at a charity hospital. Dostoevsky's father was a disciplinarian and a conservative and saw to it that Fyodor was given a strict religious education. From an early age Dostoevsky showed a great interest in literature but his father decided that he was going to be an engineer. In 1837, shortly after his mother's death, he was sent to St. Petersburg to study at the Army Engineering College. At the same time Dostoevsky's father retired to his small estate near Moscow. Two years later he was murdered by his serfs whom he had treated with great brutality. Fyodor completed his studies in 1843 when he became attached to the Army Engineering Corps in St. Petersburg. Ever since his high school days he had devoted most of his time to reading and writing. In 1844 he resigned his commission and in 1845 he published his first novel, *Poor People,* which was an instant success. It was acclaimed by V. Belinsky, the most influential critic of the day, as a literary masterpiece that showed "a profound understanding and an artistic recreation of the tragic aspect of life." Dostoevsky always recalled Belinsky's praise as one of the great moments of his life. He became an intimate of the critic's circle of friends and a convert to their radical and atheistic ideas. Dostoevsky joined a group of utopian socialists which met on Friday evenings at the home of Mikhail Petrashevsky, a wealthy young liberal. At one of these meetings Dostoevsky made a long speech demanding freedom from censorship, the abolition of serfdom and reform of the law courts. In April 1849, along with other members of the group, Dostoevsky was arrested and imprisoned in the Petropavlovsk Fortress in St. Petersburg. At his interrogation he conducted himself with dignity and courage. He reaffirmed his liberal views and did his utmost to exonerate the other members of the Petrashevsky group. After eight months in prison, Dostoevsky and his associates were tried and sentenced to death. On the morning of December 22, 1849, the condemned men were led to the Semyonovsky Square to face a firing squad. The first three were bound to stakes and blindfolded. As the commanding officer was about to give the command of "Fire" an official came forward, stopped the execution and announced that the Emperor had mercifully commuted the sentences to eight years imprisonment in Siberia. Two days later Dostoevsky, with two of the other men, was put in chains and sent off to Siberia. Subsequently his sentence was reduced to four years. On being released from prison in 1854 he was forced to join the army. He was not allowed to return to St. Petersburg until the end of 1859.

Persecution makes some men into violent revolutionaries. On Dostoevsky it had the opposite effect. Already before his release from prison he had produced a number of fawning "Odes" addressed to members of the Royal family. From then until his death he became an increasingly fanatical defender of all the most reactionary tendencies in Russia. Although he continued to detest the nobility and never lost his sympathetic understanding of the sufferings of little people, Dostoevsky now became a believer in meek submission to the will of the authorities. In 1872 he accepted the editorship of the reactionary weekly "The Citizen" and four years later he started a monthly of his own, "The Diary of a Writer," in which he conducted violent campaigns against liberals and socialists. Dostoevsky grew ever more chauvinistic, declaring that it was the destiny of Russia to reconcile the "European contradictions" by uniting the nations of Europe under her leadership. Russia and the Orthodox Church were destined to lead Europe into the path of righteousness. Dostoevsky's hostility to those who opposed the autocratic regime of the Czar became so virulent that the great novelist Turgenev described him as the "most malignant Christian" he had ever met. Dostoevsky objected in particular to two notions held by liberals and socialists and all who adhered to the philosophy of the Enlightenment. The first was the notion that evil was not endemic to the human soul and that it could be eliminated by social reforms. "It is clear," Dostoevsky wrote, "that evil is buried more deeply in humanity than the cure-all socialists think, that evil cannot be avoided in any organization of society, . . . and that abnormality and sin arise from a man's soul." The second harmful mistake of Enlightenment ideology was the belief that there are all-inclusive laws governing human behavior which psychologists would gradually discover. Human beings are not rational and a great deal about them cannot be comprehended. They are also, contrary to the determinism of the Enlightenment philosophers, free agents. "One's own free and unfettered choice," Dostoevsky wrote, "one's own whims, however wild, one's own fancy, overwrought though it sometimes may be to the point of madness . . . is the most desirable good which . . . does not fit into any classification and against which all theories and systems are continually wrecked."

Dostoevsky's most famous novels and stories were written during the 20 years after his return to St. Petersburg in 1859. These include *The Insulted and the Injured* (1861), "Notes from the Underground" (1864), *Crime and Punishment* (1866), *The Idiot* (1869), *The Possessed* (1872), "The Dream of a Ridiculous Man" (1877), and *The Brothers Karamazov* (1879–80). Dostoevsky was a compulsive gambler. In spite of large earnings from his writings he was chronically in debt. To escape his creditors he spent many of his later years abroad. From 1871 on he was in constant ill-health. Since his student days Dostoevsky had suffered from epilepsy and during his last years he also suffered from emphysema. By the time he began work on *The Brothers Karamazov* he had become extremely emaciated. He died shortly after completing the book, on February 9, 1881, from a burst artery in his lungs which was aggravated by an epileptic attack.

One of the foremost authorities on Dostoevsky, David Magarshack, has pointed out a "curious dichotomy" in Dostoevsky's nature. In his journalistic works, Magarshack observes, Dostoevsky "expressed views and opinions which for sheer crudity and lack of vision can hardly be paralleled in the case of any other great writer, whereas in his creative works . . . he achieves a profundity of thought that surpasses anything written in his or, indeed, any other time." Dostoevsky never lost the ability to look at the world through the eyes of many different people; and this no doubt accounts for the fact that he could produce such convincing and even sympathetic portrayals of anarchists and unbelievers. Moreover, he remained torn by religious doubts and conflicts long after he had become a champion of orthodoxy. In 1870, in a letter to the poet Maikov, he remarks that the question to be dealt with in a new novel (which was never in fact written but whose basic ideas were later incorporated in *The Brothers Karamazov*) "will be the same as that which consciously and unconsciously tormented me all my life—the existence of God." In a letter fifteen years earlier, when he had already abandoned the radicalism of the Belinsky-period, he confessed that he was "a child of my age, a child of unbelief and doubt, and I remain to this very day . . . I shall remain so to my very grave." He went on to describe "the terrible torment" which his desire to believe causes him since "it grows all the stronger the more arguments I have against it." Ivan Karamazov, who refuses to believe in immortality or in a good God, is not just a character in a novel but clearly speaks for one of the conflicting forces in Dostoevsky's mind. Dostoevsky preferred Ivan's brother, Alyosha, who is an embodiment of Christian faith and love, but he never pretended that the believer has an answer to the problem of evil.

PAUL EDWARDS, born 1923, Professor of Philosophy at Brooklyn College and lecturer at The New School for Social Research. He is the author of *The Logic of Moral Discourse* (1955) and numerous articles in philosophical journals. He is also the editor-in-chief of the *Encyclopedia of Philosophy* (1967), co-editor (with Crane Brinton) of the Collier Classics and editor of Bertrand Russell's essays on religion, *Why I Am Not A Christian* (1957).

A. C. EWING, born 1899, Reader in Moral Science in the University of Cambridge. Ewing is one of the leading contemporary defenders of Rationalism. He has written numerous articles in philosophical journals including several which criticize the key doctrines of logical positivism. He is the author of *The Morality of Punishment* (1929), *Idealism: A Critical Survey* (1934), *The Individual, The State and World Government* (1947), *The Definition of Good* (1947), *The Fundamental Questions of Philosophy* (1951), *Second Thoughts on Moral Philosophy* (1959) and *Non-linguistic Philosophy* (1968). He is also the editor of *The Idealist Tradition—From Berkeley to Blanshard* (1957). Ewing is a Fellow of the British Academy.

EMIL L. FACKENHEIM, born 1916, Professor of Philosophy, University of Toronto. Fackenheim is one of the most influential Jewish theologians active at the present time. He is the author of *Paths to Jewish Belief* (1960), *Metaphysics and Historicity* (1961), *The Religious Dimension in Hegel's Thought* (1968), *Quest for Past and Future* (1968) and *God's Presence in History* (1970). He has contributed articles to *The Philosophical Quarterly, The Philosophical Review, The Review of Metaphysics,* and numerous other philosophical and theological journals.

ANTONY FLEW, born 1923, Professor of Philosophy in the University of Calgary, Alberta, Canada. He is the author of *A New Approach to Psychical Research* (1953), *Hume's Philosophy of Belief* (1961), *God and Philosophy* (1966), *Evolutionary Ethics* (1967), and *An Introduction to Western Philosophy* (1971). He is editor of *Logic and Language* (First Series, 1951, Second Series, 1953), *Essays in Conceptual Analysis* (1956), *Body, Mind and Death* (1964), *Malthus on Population* (1971), and co-editor (with Alasdair MacIntyre) of *New Essays in Philosophical Theology* (1955). Flew's best-known articles are criticisms of contemporary defenses of belief in God and immortality.

R. M. HARE, born 1919, White's Professor of Moral Philosophy at Oxford University and Fellow of Corpus Christi College. Hare is one of the most influential British philosophers of the postwar period and his book, *The Language of Morals* (1952), has been more widely discussed than any other book on ethics in recent years. His other publications include *Reason and Freedom* (1963), *Practical Inferences* (1971), *Essays on Philosophical Method* (1971), *Essays on the Moral Concepts* (1972), and *Applications of Moral Philosophy* (1972).

JOHN HICK, born 1922, H. G. Wood Professor of Theology at the University of Birmingham. Before starting his teaching career Hick served as the minister of a rural Presbyterian church in Northumberland, England. He is the author of *Faith and Knowledge* (1957), *Philosophy of Religion* (1963) and *Evil and the God of Love* (1966). He is editor of *Classical and Contemporary Readings in the Philosophy of Religion, The Existence of God, Faith and Philosophers* (all published in 1964) and co-editor (with A. C. McGill) of a volume of readings on the ontological argument, *The Many-Faced Argument* (1967).

JOHN HAYNES HOLMES (1879–1964) was for many years minister at the Community Church in New York. Dr. Holmes was a graduate of the Harvard Divinity School and held numerous honorary degrees. He was a very unorthodox minister for whom even the Unitarian Church was too conservative. He regarded Jesus as the greatest of spiritual teachers but he added that "neither with Moses nor with Jesus did God do any final business." In his social and political views he was strongly influenced by Gandhi and Clarence Darrow. He was among the founders of the American Civil Liberties Union and the National Association for the Advancement of Colored People. He also played an active part in many other liberal causes. He was a pacifist, a champion of birth control, and a leader in the movement to abolish capital punishment.

JOHN HOSPERS, born 1918, Director of the School of Philosophy, University of Southern California. Hospers is the author of *Meaning and Truth in the Arts* (1946), *Human Conduct* (1961), *Introduction to Philosophical Analysis* (sec. ed., 1967) and *Libertarianism* (1971). He is editor of *Readings in Introductory Philosophical Analysis* (1968), *Introductory Readings in Aesthetics* (1969) and co-editor (with W. Sellars) of *Readings in Ethical Theory* (sec. ed., 1970). Hospers has also published numerous articles, mainly in the field of aesthetics.

DAVID HUME (1711–1776). Hume is by general agreement one of the most important philosophers who ever lived. The two major elements in his philosophy are a scepticism concerning the justification of inferences beyond what has actually been experienced and an empiricist account of various troublesome concepts such as causation, the self, good and bad, universals, space and time, and freedom. According to Kant's own report. Hume wakened him out of his "dogmatic slumber" and stimulated the development of his "critical philosophy." The empiricist element in Hume's philosophy anticipates to a considerable extent the main doctrines of logical positivism. Hume's greatest philosophical work is the *Treatise of Human Nature* (1739). *An Inquiry Concerning Human Understanding* (1748) and *An Inquiry Concerning the Principles of Morals* (1751) are more popular restatements of many of the theories contained in the *Treatise*. These books are more polished, but less profound and thorough than the early work. In his own day and in the 19th century Hume was equally noted as a historian and his huge *History of England,* published in 1755 and succeeding years, is one of the classics of its kind.

Hume was very hostile to religion. He thought religious belief not only logically indefensible but also morally harmful. Several of his anti-religious writings such as the essays on immortality and suicide, and the *Dialogues Concerning Natural Religion* were published after his death. Hume was bitterly denounced for his lack of religious belief and could never attain an academic appointment. By his many friends, however, he was loved for his exquisite sense of humor and his great kindness. He was known as *le bon David* among the French encyclopedists. "I have always considered him," wrote Adam Smith, the economist, in a tribute to Hume's character, "both in his lifetime and since his death, as approaching as nearly to the ideal of a perfectly wise and virtuous man, as perhaps the nature of human frailty will permit."

T. H. HUXLEY (1825–1895). Huxley is probably best known as the man who fought the battle for the recognition of Darwin's theories against the attacks of certain ecclesiastical authorities and conservative scientists. He frequently called himself "Darwin's bulldog." Huxley was, however, a great biologist in his own right who made numerous important discoveries, especially in anatomy and physiology. He was secretary and president of the Royal Society. Huxley was also intensely interested in philosophy. He wrote a book on Hume and some important papers on the body-mind problem and other philosophical topics. It was Huxley who coined the term "agnosticism," though quite a number of people held this position in earlier times. His most important books are *Man's Place in Nature* (1863), the *Physical Basis of Life* (1868) and *Evolution and Ethics* (1893).

WILLIAM JAMES (1842–1910). James was one of the most original thinkers America has produced. He taught physiology and psychology for a number of years before becoming Professor of Philosophy at Harvard in 1880. His *Principles of Psychology,* which was published in two volumes in 1890, is a classic in the field. James had an intense interest in psychopathology and was one of the first to recognize the importance of Freud's theories. In philosophy his main ambition was to reconcile the fundamental tenets of religion with an empiricist theory of knowledge. He thought that the "pragmatic" theory of truth could be employed as a means to such a synthesis. James was always suspicious of stuffy traditions and, even when he supported conservative conclusions, the reasons he gave were novel and frequently quite shocking. His most important philosophical works are *The Will To Believe and Other Essays* (1897), *The Varieties of Religious Experience* (1902), *Pragmatism* (1907), *A Pluralistic Universe* (1909), and *The Meaning of Truth* (1909).

IMMANUEL KANT (1724–1804). Kant is one of the most important figures in the history of philosophy and his *Critique of Pure Reason* (1781) one of the most profound systematic books ever written by a philosopher. Kant believed that by his theory of knowledge he had effected a kind of "Copernican revolution." Just as Copernicus showed that the sun and not the earth is the central body of the planetary system, so Kant thought he had shown that a great deal of what we take to be features of objective reality—e.g., space and time and causality—are really in some sense manufactured by the human mind. In ethics Kant was an extreme rationalist, maintaining that moral principles are objectively valid commands of the *a priori* reason. An action, he argued, has moral worth only if it is done from a sense of duty—utilitarian considerations have no moral value. In religion and politics Kant was a liberal. He favored the American Revolution and also the French Revolution in its earlier, less violent stages, and he advocated international government as a means of preventing wars. He had some difficulties with the Prussian King over his lack of religious orthodoxy. In his early days Kant was preoccupied with physics and in his *A General Natural History and Theory of the Heavens* (1755) he anticipated the nebular hypothesis of the origin of planetary systems. Aside from the *Critique of Pure Reason,* his main works are *The Prolegomena to All Future Metaphysics* (1783), *The Foundations of the Metaphysics of Morals* (1785), *The Critique of Practical Reason* (1788), *The Critique of Judgment* (1790), *Religion Within the Limits of Pure Reason* (1793) and *Perpetual Peace* (1795).

SØREN AABYE KIERKEGAARD (1813–1855) was born in Copenhagen where he spent almost the whole of his life. Søren was the seventh and youngest child, born when his father was 56 and his mother 45. He was born with a hunched back and uneven legs. He was also exceptionally frail. "I was already an old man when I was born," Kierkegaard wrote in his *Journals,* "delicate, slender and weak, deprived of almost every condition for holding my own with other boys, or even for passing as a complete human being in comparison with others." His only defense against the world, he wrote, was an "eminently shrewd wit." His nickname within the family was "the Fork." As a child he was once rebuked for greedily devouring his food. He thereupon announced "I *am* a fork and I will stick you." Søren's father, Michael Kierkegaard, had moved from his native Jutland to Copenhagen where he became a highly successful wool merchant. At the age of 40 he retired to devote himself to religious meditation and the education of his large family. Michael Kierkegaard suffered from melancholia and believed that God's curse hung over him and his family. As a boy, while tending a herd of sheep on a Jutland heath, suffering from hunger, cold and loneliness, he had cursed God. From then on he believed that he was lost. Although it was part of his religion to think that God is love, this belief brought him no peace. Søren spent his childhood in the close company of his father who indoctrinated him with his own gloomy and anxiety-ridden version of Christianity. "I am in the deepest sense an unfortunate individual," Kierkegaard later wrote, "who has from earliest age been nailed fast to one suffering or another, to the very verge of insanity." He never ceased to recall his father's "frightful melancholy" and "the anxious dread" with which he filled Søren's mind.

In 1830 Kierkegaard entered the University of Copenhagen. He enrolled in the faculty of theology. However, he paid little attention to theology and studied instead philosophy, history and literature. For some years he was a skeptic, maintaining that philosophy and Christianity were incompatible. It was during this period that he was exposed to the Hegelian system which was then the fashionable philosophy throughout Germany and Scandinavia. Kierkegaard was at once repelled by its Rationalism and its pretentions to finality and completeness. Above all, the Hegelian philosophy could not give him what he most wanted—"a truth which is true *for me,* . . . the idea for which I can live and die." For some years Kierkegaard involved himself in the social life of the university, spending heavily on food, drink and clothes. In the spring of 1836 he was overcome by guilt over his cynical mode of life and contemplated suicide. He resolved to live on and lead what he called an "ethical" life. His religious faith also gradually returned and with this came new reflections about the curse that had been laid on his family. The idea of the curse appeared to be confirmed by a rapid succession of deaths in the family, leaving only the father, Søren and an older brother. In the course of his brooding Kierkegaard concocted an "infallible law of interpretation" from which it followed that the father would outlive both sons neither of whom would live beyond the age of 34. The law of interpretation, as it turned out, was not infallible. The father died in 1838 and Kierkegaard was genuinely surprised to be still living. He appropriately called his first book, published in the same year, *From the Papers of One Still Living.* In 1838 Kierkegaard also had a powerful religious experience which was accompanied by "indescribable joy." He returned to his theological studies and decided to become a pastor. In 1840 he passed his examinations and in 1841 he preached his first sermon. In the same year Kierkegaard became engaged to a seventeen-year-old girl by the name of Reine Olsen. Kierkegaard was at this time becoming gradually convinced that he had a special calling from God and that his unique vocation was incompatible with being a pastor. It was also incompatible with marriage. He therefore abandoned his pastorate and broke his engagement. He never ceased to feel acute guilt over his treatment of Regine who found his behavior utterly incomprehensible. Except for his involvement in two public controversies Kierkegaard from then on lived a totally withdrawn life as an author. The four years between 1843 and 1847 were the most productive period in his life. During these years he published *Either-Or, Fear and Trembling, Repetition* (all in 1843), *The Concept of Dread* and *Philosophical Fragments* (both in 1844), *Stages on Life's Way* (1845), *Concluding Unscientific Postscript* (1846) and *Edifying Discourses* (1847). Most of these books were published under such fanciful pseudonyms as Johannes de Silentio, Constantin Constantins, Johannes Climacus, Nicolaus Notabene, and Hilarius Bogbinder. Except for the *Edifying Discourses,* Christianity was presented in these works by means of what Kierkegaard called "indirect communication." The author of the book is speaking as an observer and not as an apologist. In the spring of 1848 Kierkegaard had a religious experience which impelled him to engage in what he called "direct communication." From now on he wrote as a totally committed adherent of the Christian faith and eventually he dropped the pseudonyms. During this later period Kierkegaard wrote *Ani-Climacus* and *Christian Discourses* (1848), *The Sickness Unto Death* and *Two Minor Ethico-Religious Treatises* (both in 1849), *On My Work as an Author* (1851) and three books—*Training in Christianity, For Self-Examination* and *Judge for Yourselves* (1850–1852)—in which he stated his version of undiluted Christianity. The essence of Christianity is to follow Christ in his lowliness which involves a life of suffering and sacrifice.

In 1845 Kierkegaard became embroiled in a painful controversy with the popular Copenhagen satirical paper, *Corsaren* ("The Corsair"). This paper mercilessly ridiculed public figures of every variety. Kierkegaard had been a notable exception since Meyer Goldschmidt, the editor, was a warm admirer of Kierkegaard's books. Kierkegaard on one occasion denounced the low moral standards of the paper and challenged Goldschmidt to extend *Corsaren's* scurrilous treatment to himself. Goldschmidt reluctantly accepted the challenge. Week after week, for an entire year, Kierkegaard's twisted back, his awkward gait and his uneven trouser legs were caricatured. Students at the university produced a skit with a ridiculus hero called Søren Kirk. Children taunted him in the street. The very name Søren became an abusive epithet and parents would admonish their children "Don't be a Søren!" Kierkegaard referred to his tormentors as "geese," but this did not make the experience less painful. "To let oneself be trampled by geese," he wrote in his *Journals,* "is a slow way of dying." Goldschmidt, it should be added, was so shaken by the episode that he closed down his paper.

Kierkegaard's last years were devoted to a frontal assault on the Lutheran Danish State Church. The leaders of the Church should admit, Kierkegaard demanded, that it was no longer a Christian institution. Luther had protested against the subordination of the Church to secular interests, but now it had become completely integrated with the state and it no longer even preached the need for asceticism and sacrifices. Between December 1854 and September 1855 Kierkegaard published 21 articles on this theme in the *Fatherland* and 9 pamphlets in a series known as *The Instant* (the former were subsequently collected as *The Attack on "Christendom"*). He satirized bishops and parsons and their sacramental ministrations. He violently assailed the new head of the Church, Hans Larsen Martensen, whom he remembered most unfavorably from his student days as a Hegelian metaphysician. In a "midnight cry" Kierkegaard urged people to refrain from public worship and he invited the Church to commit suicide—"Yes, truly, suicide, and yet an action well-pleasing to God." Kierkegaard did not anticipate any positive results from his attack but he did expect and probably hoped for his own imprisonment and death. He was not prosecuted and the Church officials decided to ignore him. However, the premonition of his impending death was correct. After completing the tenth installment of *The Instant* he suffered a fatal stroke. He refused to receive the sacrament from a pastor. "Pastors are royal officials," he said, "and royal officials have nothing to do with Christianity." He was serene during his last days and confident that he would soon sit astride a cloud and sing Alleluia. He received a religious burial. While the officiating Dean read the eulogy Kierkegaard's nephew interrupted to protest the Church's appropriation of its most outspoken opponent. For almost half a century Kierkegaard's writings were largely forgotten. Partly as a result of the efforts of two Danish scholars of world fame, Georg Brandes and Harald Høffding (both of them unbelievers), philosophers and theologians outside Denmark began to take an interest in Kierkegaard's works. His notion that faith involves a leap has become a major feature of contemporary Protestant thought. His analysis of guilt and dread and his discussions of the ways in which human beings seek to avoid taking ultimate decisions concerning their lives have strongly influenced the philosophies of Heidegger and Sartre.

GOTTFRIED WILHELM LEIBNIZ (1646–1716) was born in Leipzig, where his father was Professor of Moral Philosophy at the University. Leibniz was an extremely precocious child, studying Greek and scholastic philosophy when he was thirteen, and entering the University at the age of fifteen. In 1663 he went to Jena, where he studied mathematics, and then moved on to Altdorf, where he concentrated on jurisprudence and took a doctorate in Law in 1667. In 1673 he entered the service of the House of Hanover, with which he was associated for the rest of his life. Leibniz spent most of the years 1672–1676 in Paris, where he came to know Malebranche and Arnauld. During his last year in Paris, he invented the infinitesimal calculus. (He did not know of Newton's earlier unpublished writings on this subject, and an acrimonious dispute over the priority of this discovery lasted for many years.) On his way back to Germany, Leibniz paid a visit to Spinoza. They had numerous lengthy discussions and there is little doubt that Spinoza greatly influenced Leibniz, but chiefly because of Spinoza's reputation as an "atheist," Leibniz did his best to dissociate himself from Spinoza. According to Bertrand Russell, "there are two systems of philosophy which may be regarded as representing Leibniz: one, which he proclaimed, was optimistic, orthodox, fantastic, and shallow; the other, which has been slowly unearthed from his manuscripts by fairly recent editors, was profound, coherent, largely Spinozistic, and amazingly logical." This opinion is far from unanimous among Leibniz commentators, but Russell is unquestionably right in maintaining that much of the best work of Leibniz is found in manuscripts not published in his own lifetime. The complete edition of Leibniz's works was begun by the Prussian Academy of Sciences in 1923 and is as yet far from finished. During his own lifetime he published brief writings like the *New System of Nature and the Interaction of Substances, Principles of Nature and Grace,* and the *Monodology* (all in 1714), and the famous *Essays in Theodicy* (1710), which was a more substantial work. The latter, a reply to Bayle's views on the problem of evil, contains the doctrine that this is the best of all possible worlds, which Voltaire was to ridicule in *Candide.* The much more important *New Essays on Human Understanding* appeared posthumously in 1765. Russell and other students of Leibniz discovered in his unpublished manuscripts remarkable anticipations of some of the ideas of modern symbolic logic.

JOHN LOCKE (1632–1706). Locke's *Essay Concerning Human Understanding* (1690) is the first comprehensive treatise on the origin, analysis and extent of human knowledge. His view that the direct objects of knowledge are ideas and that we have only an indirect knowledge of physical objects (epistemological dualism) has been very influential in modern discussions of the problem of perception. In his criticism of the verbal abstractions which thrived in scholastic philosophy, Locke's work resembles that of contemporary analytic philosophers. Like most of the other major figures in British philosophy, Locke contributed both to the theory of knowledge and to social and political thought. His *Treatises on Government* (1685) present one of the first statements of the principles of democratic government. His *Letters on Toleration,* published in 1689 and succeeding years, advocated complete religious freedom for all groups except Roman Catholics and atheists. Locke's political ideas had an enormous influence on Jefferson and the other founding fathers of the American Republic and they also dominated the thought of the French encyclopedists.

H. D. LEWIS, born 1910, is Head of the Department of the History and Philosophy of Religion in the University of London and a Fellow of King's College, London. He is chairman of the Council of the Royal Institute of Philosophy and a past president of the Mind Association and the Aristotelian Society. He is the editor of the *Muirhead Library of Philosophy* and, since its inception in 1965, of *Religious Studies.* His own books include *Morals and Revelation* (1951), *Our Experience of God* (1959), *Freedom and History* (1962), and *The Elusive Mind* (1970). He is also the editor of *Clarity Is Not Enough* (1963).

JOHN MACKIE, born in Australia in 1917, is Professor of Philosophy at the University of York, in England. He previously taught at the Universities of Sydney and Otago. Mackie is the author of several widely discussed articles in ethics, philosophy of science, and philosophy of religion.

JOHN STUART MILL (1806–1873). Mill is an outstanding figure in the development of empiricism. Like Locke before him and Bertrand Russell after, he was actively engaged in practical affairs. In politics he carried on the radical reform ideas of Jeremy Bentham and his father James Mill. He was also one of the earliest advocates of birth control. For a short time Mill was a member of the House of Commons, where he set an almost unparalleled example for honesty and integrity. When Mill appeared at election meetings he made it a point to tell his voters, most of whom were pious believers, that he did not accept the Christian religion.

His most important philosophical work is the *System of Logic* (1843), which is really a comprehensive philosophy of science from the standpoint of empiricism. It is comparable in scope to Kant's *Critique of Pure Reason,* but immeasurably more lucid than Kant's great work. In the *System of Logic,* Mill presents his theories on many philosophical topics not usually discussed in books on logic. A fuller statement of his philosophical views is contained in *An Examination of Sir William Hamilton's Philosophy* (1865). His other important works include *The Principles of Political Economy* (1848), *On Liberty* (1859), *Utilitarianism* (1863), *Autobiography* (1873), and *Three Essays on Religion* (1874). It is not generally known that Mill was Bertrand Russell's godfather.

G. E. MOORE (1873–1958) was Professor of Philosophy at the University of Cambridge, 1925–1939, and editor of *Mind,* 1921–1947. Moore was one of the most influential philosophers of the twentieth century. He is renowned both for his work in moral philosophy and his defenses of "common sense" against "philosophical paradoxes." His most important works are *Principia Ethica* (1903), *Ethics* (1911), *Philosophical Studies* (1922), *Some Main Problems of Philosophy* (1953), and *Philosophical Papers* (1958). Moore's classical essay, "The Refutation of Idealism," is included in *Philosophical Studies;* the equally famous "A Defence of Common Sense" in *Philosophical Papers.* The valuable book *The Philosophy of G. E. Moore* (1942, edited by P. A. Schilpp) contains an autobiographical sketch by Moore, numerous critical articles, and Moore's rejoinder. Moore was a Fellow of the British Academy and a recipient of the Order of Merit.

ERNEST NAGEL, born 1901, University Professor of Philosophy at Columbia University. Nagel has been primarily interested in problems in the philosophy of science but he has also written provocatively on many other philosophical issues. Although he does not accept the Verifiability Principle, Nagel is opposed to any kind of speculative metaphysics. He describes his own standpoint as "contextualistic naturalism" and he considers himself, in a broad sense of the word, a materialist. His chief publications are *On the Logic of Measurement* (1930), *An Introduction to Logic and Scientific Method* (with M. R. Cohen, (1934), *Principles of the Theory of Probability* (1939), *Sovereign Reason* (1954), *Logic Without Metaphysics* (1956), *Gödel's Proof* (with J. R. Newman, 1958), and *The Structure of Science* (1961). Nagel is past president of the American Philosophical Association and the Association for Symbolic Logic.

WILLIAM PALEY (1743–1805). Before becoming a minister in the Church of England, Paley was a teacher of philosophy at Cambridge. He wrote an influential book on ethics, *The Principles of Moral and Political Philosophy* (1785), in which he advocated a kind of utilitarianism. Most of his other writings were in defense of Christian theology. Of these the most significant was his *Natural Theology, or Evidence of the Existence and Attributes of the Deity Collected from the Appearance of Nature* (1802). Paley was a liberal both in politics and in religion. He strenuously worked for the abolition of the slave trade. His liberal religious views prevented him from reaching the highest positions in the Church.

R. S. PETERS, born in 1919, is Professor of the Philosophy of Education at the University of London. He has written extensively on philosophical, psychological, and educational topics. He is the author of *Hobbes* (1956), *The Concept of Motivation* (1958), *Authority, Responsibility and Education* (1959), and he is co-author (with S. I. Benn) of *Social Principles and the Democratic State* (1959). Peters also revised and brought up to date Brett's well-known *History of Psychology* and he edited two volumes of Hobbes' works (*Body, Man and Citizen* and *The Leviathan,* both published in 1962).

PLATO (427–347 B.C.). Plato was an Athenian aristocrat who early in life came under the influence of Socrates. When Plato was twenty-eight Socrates was tried by the democratic rulers of Athens on the charge of undermining the morals of the young and sentenced to death. This event was decisive in Plato's life. He retired from Athens to Megara where he began to write his dialogues. The protagonist is always Socrates, though only the early dialogues, if even these, seem to be accounts of actual episodes in which Socrates participated. In general, Socrates functions simply as the transmitter of Plato's ideas. At the age of forty Plato returned to Athens, founding his Academy, which was in effect the first university in Europe. The subjects taught were philosophy, mathematics, and political science. At the same time he went on writing his dialogues. Plato's metaphysical theories—especially his theory of the "forms" and his dualism concerning body and mind—as well as his political ideas have been of tremendous influence on Western thought. His best-known writings are the *Apology, Crito, Protagoras, Meno, Gorgias, Symposium, Phaedo, Republic, Phaedrus, Theatetus, Parmenides, Sophist, Politicus, Philebus, Timaeus,* and the *Laws.* Plato was a consummate literary artist and even those who do not admire his theories usually find the dialogues delightful reading. Plato hoped to put some of his political theories into practice when he became adviser to Dionysius II of Syracuse. Through no fault of Plato's, the experiment did not turn out well and brought him nothing but grief.

PAUL RÉE (1849–1901). Rée was the son of a wealthy landowner. Already in his high-school days he developed a passionate interest in philosophy. However, on the urging of his parents, he enrolled as a law student at the University of Leipzig in 1868. His studies were interrupted by the Franco-Prussian war of 1870 in which Rée was wounded. On his return he abandoned his law studies and devoted himself wholly to philosophy. In 1875 he published *Psychologische Beobachtungen* ("Psychological Observations"), a slim volume of aphorisms. In 1877 he published the much more substantial *Ursprung der moralischen Empfindungen* ("The Origin of the Moral Sentiments"). On the strength of this book Rée was awarded a doctorate by the University of Halle. Strongly influenced by the British empiricists and the work of Darwin, Rée argued that there are no universal moral principles whose truth is given *a priori.* What is regarded as right or wrong in any given society reflects the needs and cultural conditions of that society. Nietzsche, who disagreed with many of the details of Rée's book but who shared his relativism and his interest in the evolution of moral ideas, commended Rée's work as a "decisive turning point in the history of moral philosophy." In 1885 Rée published two books on which he had been working for many years—*Die Illusion der Willensfreiheit* ("The Illusion of Free Will") and *Die Entstehung des Gewissens* ("The Origin of Conscience"). While working on the latter book Rée became appalled by his ignorance of the natural sciences. He proceeded to study science, especially biology, for a number of years and eventually, at the age of 37, decided to become a medical student. He obtained his M.D. from the University of Munich in 1890. He thereupon settled in Stibbe, the family manor in West Prussia. He practised medicine among the local population without ever charging a fee. When his own medical knowledge proved inadequate he sent the peasants and laborers who were his patients to hospitals in Breslau and Berlin, paying all of their expenses. Rée led a totally ascetic life during the ten years he spent at Stibbe and did not once leave this lonely part of the world. A good deal of his time was devoted to what he thought would become a major philosophical contribution. This work, which was not to be published in his lifetime, would contain the fruits of all his reflections. When it was finished, Rée told a friend, he would give up philosophy; but since he could not live without doing philosophy, the only thing for him to do was to die. This is more or less what in fact happened. In 1900, when Rée's book, to be called simply *Philosophie,* was nearly complete, his brother, who had been managing the family estate, decided to sell and move to Berlin. Rée could not bear city life. He took up residence in Celerina, a small town near St. Moritz, where he and Nietzsche had spent some happy hours 20 years earlier. He here again practised medicine without charging his patients. Rée was a passionate mountain-climber. At high noon on October 28, 1901, he fell to his death from a steep, icy ridge. *Philosophie* appeared in 1903 and was almost completely ignored. The book contains further reflections on the evolution of moral ideas, a defense of the regularity theory of causation, very acute criticisms of Kant, Schopenhauer and Leibniz, and a forthright defense of atheism. Metaphysical systems Rée dismisses as "fairy tales" and "lies." Religions, he concludes, "are true neither in the literal nor in an allegorical sense—they are untrue in every sense. Religion issues from a marriage of error and fear." There is no doubt that Rée was strongly influenced by Nietzsche who was five years older and with whom he was on terms of close friendship from 1873 till 1882. There is also good evidence that Nietzsche in turn was strongly influenced by Rée. This was denied by Nietzsche's sister in her biographical works about her brother, but the extensive correspondence between Nietzsche and Rée does not bear her out. Nietzsche was very fond of his sister but he also more than once called her a "vengeful anti-Semitic goose." Rée was Jewish and Nietzsche's sister, who eventually became a darling of the Nazis, always tried to play down the role of Jews in Nietzsche's life. In his last years Rée expressed a low opinion of Nietzsche's achievements. Granting that Nietzsche was often very clever and that he could write superbly, Rée dismissed Nietzsche's transvaluation of values as a "mixture of insanity and nonsense."

THOMAS REID (1710–1796), the founder of the Scottish "School of Common Sense," was the son of a minister and himself became a minister. He subsequently held a teaching position at King's College, Aberdeen, and eventually succeeded Adam Smith as professor of moral philosophy at Glasgow. His major works are *An Inquiry into the Human Mind on the Principles of Common Sense* (1764), *Essays on the Intellectual Powers of Man* (1785), and *Essays on the Active Powers of Man* (1788). The chief target of Reid's criticisms is what he calls the "theory of ideas"—the view, shared by Descartes, Locke, Berkeley, and Hume, that what is immediately given in perception are "ideas" rather than real objects. Hume alone of these philosophers brought into the open the paradoxical consequences logically implied by the theory of ideas. Hume, in Reid's words, showed that "there is neither matter nor mind in the universe; nothing but impressions and ideas. His system does not even leave him a *self* to claim the property of his impressions and ideas." We know, however, that matter and mind exist and that other of Hume's conclusions, such as his scepticism about induction, are false, and hence the theory of ideas must be false. The propositions asserting the existence of matter and mind and the assertion that "in the phenomena of nature what is to be will probably be like to what has been in similar circumstances" are among what Reid calls "principles of common sense." These are "original and natural judgments" which are "a part of that furniture which nature hath given to the human understanding. . . . They are a part of our constitution and all discoveries of our reason are grounded upon them . . . what is manifestly contrary to any of those first principles is what we call *absurd*." Other principles of common sense include our belief in memory—"those things did really happen which I distinctly remember," that our fellow men are not mere automata but possess intelligence and feeling, that we have some degree of power over our actions, and "that the natural faculties by which we distinguish truth from error are not fallacious." What marks a principle as one of common sense is not simply the fact that it is universally believed, but the further fact that it cannot, in practice, be seriously doubted by anybody. Even the sceptical philosopher has to accept these propositions when engaged in the activities of daily living. Common-sense propositions cannot strictly speaking be proven, but they are in no need of proof.

Reid's ideas were very influential in the first half of the nineteenth century.

Victor Cousin in France and Sir William Hamilton in Britain were among his disciples. In the second half of the nineteenth century his influence greatly declined, but in recent years G. E. Moore's defense of common sense stimulated a revival of interest in his work.

JOHN A. T. ROBINSON, born 1919, was educated at Marlborough and Cambridge. At the end of the Second World War he became a curate in Bristol, later a chaplain at Wells Theological College; he became Dean of Clare College, Cambridge, in 1951 and Bishop of Woolwich in 1959. Since 1969 he has been Dean of Trinity College, Cambridge. Bishop Robinson's booklet, *Honest to God* (1963), in which he attacked the belief in a God "out there," has been one of the most widely discussed theological works of the century. Bishop Robinson is also noted as a New Testament scholar. His other writings include *The Body* (1952), *Jesus and His Coming* (1957), *Twelve New Testament Studies* (1962), *Christian Morals Today* (1964), *The New Reformation?* (1965), *Explorations Into God* (1967), and *Christian Freedom in a Permissive Society* (1970).

BERTRAND RUSSELL (1872–1970) was one of the most influential thinkers of the twentieth century. Enormously productive, he made significant contributions to logic and the foundations of mathematics, the theory of knowledge, the philosophy of science, and almost every area of philosophy. He was also renowned for the graceful and witty style in which he expressed his ideas. His philosophical works include *An Essay on the Foundations of Geometry* (1897), *The Principles of Mathematics* (1903), *Philosophical Essays* (1910), *Principia Mathematica* (3 volumes, 1910–1913, with A. N. Whitehead), *The Problems of Philosophy* (1912), *Our Knowledge of the External World* (1914), *Mysticism and Logic* (1918), *Introduction to Mathematical Philosophy* (1919), *The Analysis of Mind* (1921), *The Analysis of Matter* (1927), *An Outline of Philosophy* (1927), *Religion and Science* (1935), *An Inquiry into Meaning and Truth* (1940), *A History of Western Philosophy* (1946), *Human Knowledge* (1948), *Human Society in Ethics and Politics* (1955), *Logic and Knowledge* (1956), *Why I Am Not a Christian and Other Essays* (1957), *My Philosophical Development* (1959), and *Wisdom of the West* (1959). *The Philosophy of Bertrand Russell* (1944, ed. P. A. Schilpp), is a valuable work containing an autobiographical sketch by Russell, numerous critical articles on his philosophy and Russell's reply to the critics.

Philosophy was not by any means the only interest in Russell's life. He was the author of important books on education, partly based on the experimental school he founded in 1927. His book *Marriage and Morals* (1929) created a great stir by its advocacy of a sexual moral code at variance with the code then officially sanctioned. For his radical views in politics and morals and his outspoken criticisms of religion, Russell was bitterly denounced and persecuted. During the First World War he was an ardent pacifist. He was dismissed from his position at Trinity College, Cambridge, and sentenced to six months in prison. In 1940 he was invited to become Professor of Philosophy at City College, New York. This appointment was judicially annulled on the ground that Russell was likely to undermine the "health and morals" of his students. Elsewhere, however, Russell's work received due recognition. He was a Fellow of the Royal Society and held numerous distinguished awards, including the Order of Merit and the Nobel Prize for Literature. During the last decade of his life Russell devoted most of his energy to a campaign for nuclear disarmament. Ever since 1920 Russell had been an outspoken and militant opponent of the Communist government in Russia. Among other things he had vigorously denounced the expansionistic designs of the Stalin regime. However, during his last years Russell came to regard American foreign policy as the worst menace to peace. In 1967 he organized an international tribunal, meeting in Stockholm with Jean-Paul Sartre as chairman, which tried and found the U.S. government guilty of war crimes in Vietnam. Between 1967 and 1969 Russell published the three volumes of his *Autobiography,* the first of which in particular was hailed as a literary masterpiece. A few weeks before his death he was interviewed about his views on religion. He contemptuously brushed aside the interviewer's suggestion that in view of his extremely advanced age he might have come to hope for an afterlife. Russell died, as he had wished to do, "while still at work . . . content in the thought that what was possible has been done." His papers and manuscripts are now kept at McMaster University in Hamilton, Ontario. McMaster University Press is publishing a quarterly called *Russell,* devoted to documents and other material relating to Russell's life and thought.

GILBERT RYLE, born 1900, Waynflete Professor of Metaphysical Philosophy (Emeritus) at Oxford University, editor of *Mind,* 1947–1971. Ryle is one of the most influential philosophers of the twentieth century and his most important book, *The Concept of Mind* (1949), has given rise to a vast amount of discussion. *The Concept of Mind* is a sustained attack on the traditional dualistic theory which conceives of man as a double entity—a publicly observable body and an "inner theatre," the mind. Ryle refers to this view as the "dogma of the Ghost in the Machine" and tries to show not only that it is mistaken but that it has led to a host of detailed mistakes concerning the nature of mental concepts. Against the "official theory" Ryle tries to establish that facts about bodily behavior are almost relevant to the truth or falsehood of statements "about the mind." A satisfactory account of mental phenomena can be given, he maintains, in terms of the manner of an individual's publicly observable performances and his disposition to perform in certain ways—without reference to any inner theatre. The statement that a person is intelligent, for example, is made true not by the existence of some private states inside the individual's mind but by his past performances and his ability to perform similarly in the present and future. There is a strong behaviorist flavor in many of Ryle's discussions, but he has denied that he is a behaviorist and most of his criticisms of the official theory are independent of a commitment to behaviorism. Even those who continue to support traditional dualism usually admit that Ryle's discussions of such topics as thinking, knowledge, emotion, sensation, will and intellect manage to expose all kinds of widepread confusions. In these discussions and in various of his other publications Ryle has introduced new concepts and distinctions which have become the common tools of analytic philosophers. From 1931 on Ryle had been in the forefront of philosophers who regard "analysis" as "the sole and whole function of philosophy" and in retrospect he described *The Concept of Mind* as "a sustained piece of analytical hatchet-work" directed on a "notorious and large-sized Gordian Knot." The task of philosophy, in his view, is, negatively, to free us from "conceptual traffic-jams" and, positively, to display the "logical geography" of our concepts—to show us what their roles are and how they are related to each other. Ryle has discussed the question of the function of philosophy in many places, including the influential early article "Systematically Misleading Expressions" (1931), in his Inaugural lecture, *Philosophical Arguments* (1945) and in *Dilemmas* (1954). Ryle's numerous essays and reviews have been brought together in two volumes of his *Collected Papers* (1971). The first volume contains several of Ryle's historical papers. Ryle has had a special interest in Plato.

He is the author of *Plato's Progress* (1966) and of the article on Plato in *The Encyclopedia of Philosophy*. All of Ryle's publications—books, articles, reviews, reminiscences—are informed by an idiosyncratic and extremely vivid style—terse, informal, epigrammatic and studded with fresh and illuminating metaphors.

VISCOUNT HERBERT SAMUEL (1870–1963), British politician and philosopher, was a Liberal member of the House of Commons from 1902 to 1918 and again from 1929 to 1935. He was Post-Master General 1910–1914 and Home Secretary in 1916 and again in 1931–32. He was the first Jew to attain Cabinet rank in England. Samuel was responsible for much humane and progressive legislation including the Children Act of 1908 which established juvenile courts and the probation system. In 1920 he was appointed the first High Commissioner for Palestine, a post he held with great distinction, improving Palestine's economy and fostering harmony among the different religious communities. In 1937 he was elevated to the House of Lords as Viscount Samuel of Mount Carmel. He was leader of the Liberty Party in the House of Lords from 1944 to 1955. All his life Samuel was intensely interested in philosophy. He wrote numerous articles and two books—*Practical Ethics* (1935) and *Belief and Action* (1937). Lord Samuel was president of the Royal Institute of Philosophy from 1931 to 1959.

MORITZ SCHLICK (1882–1936). Schlick was Professor of Philosophy at the University of Vienna until his death at the hands of a paranoid student. He was the founder of the Vienna Circle and one of the leading figures in the development of logical positivism. His books include *Space and Time in Modern Physics* (1920), *Allgemeine Erkenntnislehre* (1925), *The Problems of Ethics* (1931), and *Gesammelte Aufsätze* (1938). Schlick wrote with great ease in English and French as well as in German and several of the papers in the last-mentioned book are in English.

W. A. SINCLAIR (1905–1954), was, at the time of his death, Reader in Logic and Metaphysics at the University of Edinburgh. He was the author of *The Traditional Formal Logic* (1937), *An Introduction to Philosophy* (1944), and *The Conditions of Knowing* (1951). He also wrote two political books, *The Voice of the Nazi* (based on a series of war-time broadcasts, 1940) and *Socialism and the Individual* (1955, posthumously). Sinclair was a man of very wide interests. Among other things, he was politically active; he stood for Parliament as a Conservative in 1945, but joined the Labour Party before his death.

J. J. C. SMART, born 1920, Hughes Professor of Philosophy at the University of Adelaide, Australia. Smart is the author of *Outline of a System of Utilitarian Ethics* (1961), *Philosophy and Scientific Realism* (1963), *Between Science and Philosophy* (1968), and of numerous articles in philosophical periodicals, including the widely discussed essay, "The River of Time." He is also editor of *Problems of Space and Time* (1964). Smart is one of the leading and most outspoken contemporary defenders of materialism.

W. T. STACE (1886–1967). Stace was for many years Professor of Philosophy at Princeton University. Before coming to Princeton in 1932 he was a member of the Indian Civil Service. He was a District Judge in Ceylon and eventually became Mayor of Colombo. While still in the Civil Service he published *A Critical History of Greek Philosophy* (1920), *The Philosophy of Hegel* (1924), and *The Meaning of Beauty* (1930). His later works include *The Theory of Knowledge and Existence* (1932), *The Concept of Morals* (1936), *The Nature of the World* (1946), *Time and Eternity* (1952), *Mysticism and Philosophy* (1961), and *Man against Darkness* (1967). During the last years of his life Stace became a student and champion of mysticism and argued that acceptance of mysticism is not inconsistent with a thoroughgoing empiricism.

DAVID ELTON TRUEBLOOD, born 1900, Professor Emeritus at Earlham College. Trueblood, who has also taught at Harvard, Stanford and Haverford, is the author of 29 books, most of them expounding and defending theism and the Christian religion. These include *Studies in Quaker Pacifism* (1934), *The Knowledge of God* (1939), *The Logic of Belief* (1942), *The Predicament of Modern Man* (1944), *The Recovery of Family Life* (1953), and *General Philosophy* (1963). In 1952 Trueblood received the Churchman of the Year award.

JOHN TYNDALL (1820–1893), was Faraday's successor as Professor of Natural Philosophy at the Royal Institution. He did important research on diamagnetism, the absorption of radiant heat by gasses and vapors, and extended Pasteur's work on spontaneous generation. Tyndall was noted as a popular lecturer on scientific topics as well as for his interest in the philosophical implications of scientific results. He was an agnostic and a naturalist. In 1874 he delivered the Presidential Address to the British Association for the Advancement of Science, in which he expounded his philosophical position and criticized the theological outlook in no uncertain terms. This talk, which became known as the "Belfast Address," provoked numerous heated rejoinders on the part of religious apologists. Tyndall's philosophical writings, including the Belfast Address and the replies to his critics, are reprinted in the two-volume work, *Fragments of Science* (1881).

G. J. WARNOCK, born 1923, is Fellow and Tutor in Philosophy at Magdalen College, Oxford. Warnock has been prominently associated with the Oxford school of linguistic philosophy. He is the author of *Berkeley* (1953), *English Philosophy Since 1900* (1958), *Contemporary Moral Philosophy* (1967), and *The Object of Morality* (1971). He is also the editor of the late J. L. Austin's *Sense and Sensibilia* (1962) and (with J. O. Urmson) of Austin's *Philosophical Papers* (1961).

C. H. WHITELEY, born 1911, Reader in Philosophy in the University of Birmingham. Whiteley is the author of *An Introduction to Metaphysics* (1950) and (with Winifred Whiteley) of *The Permissive Morality* (1964). He is also a frequent contributor to British philosophical periodicals.

F. L. WILL, born 1909, Professor of Philosophy at the University of Illinois. Will is a distinguished representative of contemporary American analytic philosophy who has specialized in the problem of induction and probability.

BERNARD WILLIAMS, born 1929, Knightbridge Professor of Philosophy and Fellow of King's College, Cambridge University. Williams has also taught at Oxford University, the University College of Ghana, Princeton University, and the University of London. He is co-editor of *British Analytical Philosophy* (1966) and is the author of *Imagination and the Self* (the British Academy Lecture, 1966). Professor Williams has contributed numerous articles to philosophical journals and to *The Encyclopedia of Philosophy*.

Index
of
Names

INDEX OF NAMES

KEY: auth.—author; biog.—biographical sketch; fn.—footnote; ment.—mentioned; ref.—reference, bibliographical, in text or footnote. Where a subject is listed in connection with a name, it refers to a discussion or mention of the author's views *by another writer;* e.g., Locke; personal identity, 199 f. refers to a discussion of Locke's views on personal identity by Thomas Reid.

Aaron, R. I., ref., 285, 662
Abelson, R., ment., xi; ref., 103, 110, 364, 372, 554, 740, 814
Achinstein, P., ref., 168, 278, 744, 811
Acton, H. B., ref., 366, 660, 663
Adams, C. T. R., ment., xi
Adams, E. M., ref., 371, 661, 662
Adams, E. W., ref., 743
Adams, R. M., ref., 555, 556
Adler, M. J., ref., 99, 561
Adrian, E. D., quoted, 235
Agassi, J., ref., 167
Ahern, M. B., ref., 558
Aiken, H. D., ref., 368, 369, 559
Albee, E., ment., 802
Aldrich, V. C., ref., 280, 746
Alexander, A., ref., 113
Alexander, H. G., ref., 167, 745
Alexander, P., ref., 109, 277
Alexander, S., ref., 655, 657
Alger, W. R., ref., 283
Allen, A. H. B., ref., 277
Allen, R. E., ref., 554, 566
Allison, H. E., ref., 561, 565
Alston, W. P., ref., 110, 283, 285, 368, 370, 372, 548, 551, 554, 560, 566, 663, 811, 812, 813, 814, 816
Ambrose, A., ref., 101, 165, 169, 276, 365, 556, 743, 746, 813
Ames, V. M., ref., 104
Anderson, A. R., ment., 746; ref., 270
Anderson, J., ref., 550, 657
Anscombe, G. E. M., ref., 106, 114, 551
Anselm, auth., 403–407; biog., 819; ment., 376, 391; ref., 553
Anshen, R. N., ref., 367
Aquinas, auth., 408–410; biog., 819; ment., 375, 383, 411–418, 528; ref., 283, 551, 564; proof of God's existence, 377–385, 411–418

Arbini, R., ref., 746
Aristotle, ment., 97, 412, 490, 525, 551
Armstrong, D. M., ment., 660; ref., 280, 285, 654, 656, 659
Ashby, R. W., ment., 811; ref., 747, 814, 816
Atkins, R., ref., 104
Atkinson, R. F., ref., 371
Audi, R., ref., 110
Augustine, ref., 283
Aune, B., ment., xi; ref., 110, 112, 114, 165, 270, 275, 277, 278, 280, 286, 656, 659, 661 f., 741, 746
Austin, J. L., ref., 111, 276, 277, 662
Ayer, A. J., auth., 235–237, 329–337, 720–731, 760–769; biog., 819; ment., ix, xvi, 121, 238, 338, 535, 673f., 719 fn., 744, 755, 774 ff., 813; quoted, 175; ref., 90 fn., 100, 103, 106, 109, 112–113, 168, 232 fn., 274, 275, 276, 277, 280, 281, 329 fn., 368, 370, 549, 551, 561, 660, 662, 742 f., 811 f., 817
Ayers, M. R., ref., 106

Bacon, F., ment., 118, 165, 708
Baier, A. C., ref., 816
Baier, K., ref., 101, 105, 112, 279, 368, 372, 553, 556, 814
Baillie, J., ment., 394, 398; ref., 556, 557
Bain, A., ref., 99, 270, 742
Balguy, J., ref., 365
Bambrough, R., ref., 566
Barbour, I. G., ref., 563
Barclay, R., ment., 438; quoted, 437
Bar-Hillel, Y., 745
Barker, S. F., ref., 278, 742, 744, 747, 811
Barlow, N., ref., 550
Barnes, E. W., ref., 108
Barnes, W. F. H., ref., 367 f., 662, 811

Index
of
Subjects

INDEX OF SUBJECTS

Immortality, xi, 171–269, 250–260, 261–269, 470 ff., 513, 689; and eternal happiness, 491 f., 506–509; "proof" of (Kierkegaard), 514 ff.; *see also* Survival

Implication, 730 f; *see also* Necessity

Impressions, 686, 702, 706, 752, 757 ff.; and personal identity, 190 f., 198 f.

Indeterminism, 3, 45 f., 59 f., 480; and freedom, 3 f., 62 f.; and morality, 44 ff.; and responsibility, 65 f.; *see also* Heisenberg's principle of indeterminacy

Individual and the Universe, The (Lovell), 796 fn.

Induction, xiv, 115–164, 684, 698, 701 f., 707 f., 716 f.; and causality, 117–118; and experience, 157, 687, 722; inference from, 116 f., 120 f.; and logic, 117; and mathematics, 708, 730; and pragmatism, 161 ff.; principle of, 142, 119; and probability, 160 f.; and realism, 576; "by simple enumeration," 118; and verifiability, 771

Inference, 117, 130 f., 134 f., 139, 630, 734, 739; *a priori*, 735–740; and argument, 134 f.; and connection, 136 f.; and ethics, 318 f.; inductive, 119 ff.; from perceptions, 616 ff.; and realism, 573; and reality, 638 f., and the supernatural, 528; and tautologies, 729 ff.

Infinite good, *see* "Good,"

Infinite series, 378, 381 ff., 409, 415 f., 423 f.

Infinity, 706; *see also* Infinite series

Innate behavior patterns, 225 ff.

Innate ideas, 713

In Quest for Past and Future (Fackenheim), 523 fn.

Inquiry Concerning Human Understanding, An (Hume), 129 fn., 145, 756 fn., 798 fn.

Insensible particles, 569, 580

Intelligibility, 383 ff., 413, 438; *see also* Meaning

Intension, 725

Interactionism, 175 f., 182 f., 201–204, and conservation of energy, 205 f.

Introduction to Mathematics (Whitehead), 715 fn.

Introduction to Mathematical Philosophy (Russell), 730 fn.

Introduction to Metaphysics, An (Heidegger), 796 fn., 804 fn.

Introduction to Metaphysics, An (Whiteley), 637 fn.

Introduction to Philosophy, An (Sinclair), 647 fn.

Introspection, 752, 771, 800

Intuition, 5, 129, 135, 693, 702; and ethics, 318; and inference from, 137; and

Kantian concepts, 690 f., 728; and values, 308

Intuitionism, 292 f., 332

Irrational Man (Barrett), 505 f.

Irrationalism, 506 ff.

"I-Thou" relation (Buber), 531

Jesus and the Gospel of Love (Raven), 441 fn.

Journals of Kierkegaard, 506, 515

Judgments of regret, 25, 42 f.

Knowledge, 696, 706 f., 720 f., 725 f.; and analytic propositions, 725 f., *a posteriori* (*see A posteriori* knowledge); *a priori* (*see A priori* knowledge); and *a priori* propositions, 735–740; common-sense, 631 f.; empirical, 667, 686 f., 740; employment of, 687 f.; and ethics, 313; and experience, 666, 689 ff.; of general principles, 712–719; of God, 438 f., 498 f.; and induction, 143 f., 158; and logical principles, 712–719; and metaphysics, 766; of the past, 140; and perception, 625, 630 ff.; and personal identity, 194 f., 196; pure, 686 f.; and reason, 133; as recollection, 675–681; scientific, 696 f.; sources of, 137; types of, 761 f.; and values, 306

Language, conventions of, 672, 726; and empiricism, 773; and ethics, 330 ff.; and idealism, 576; and identity, 197 f.; and logic, 765 ff.; and mathematics, 708 f., 724; and matter, 157, 638; and meaning, 534, 539, 619, 632, 637 f. (*see also* Meaning); and personal identity, 191; and phenomenalism, 637; and redefinition, 517 f.; and religious experience, 438; *see also* Moral Language

Language of Morals, The (Hare), 352 fn.

Language, Truth and Logic (Ayer), 329 fn., 535 f., 720 fn., 755, 774

Law(s), 59 f., 67–71; of contradiction, 713, 719; descriptive vs. prescriptive, 60 ff., 67, 794; of excluded middle, 713; and fact, 142, 792 f.; formulation of, 618 f., 700 f.; of identity, 713; and induction, 143 f., 157; and morality, 47 ff.; of nature, 32, 131 f., 134, 155, 793; of thought, 713, 719; *see also* Necessity; Uniformity of Nature; Universality

Legal responsibility, 47 ff.

Leibniz-Selections (Wiener), 682

Libertarianism, 50, 72, 73, 79 ff.; *see also* Freedom; Indeterminism

Liberty, *see* Freedom

Linguistic philosophy, 529 f.